Learn
FileMaker® Pro 7

Jonathan Stars and Janice Child with Nonie Bernard

Wordware Publishing, Inc.

Library of Congress Cataloging-in-Publication Data

Stars, Jonathan.
    Learn FileMaker Pro 7 / by Jonathan Stars and Janice Child, with Nonie Bernard.
       p. cm.
    ISBN 1-55622-098-7 (paperback)
    1. FileMaker pro. 2. Database management. I. Child, Janice. II. Bernard,
Nonie. III. Title.

    QA76.9.D3S7245 2004
    005.75'65--dc22   2004006765

All inquiries for volume purchases of this book should be addressed to Wordware
Publishing, Inc., at the above address. Telephone inquiries may be made by calling:

(972) 423-0090

Contents

Part 2

Using FileMaker Pro

Part 3
Turning Your Data into Information

Part 4
Creating a Real Solution

Chapter 17   **Designing Your Printed Report Layouts. 292**

Part 5
Sharing Your Database

Chapter 18   **Personal Data Sharing 310**

Part 6

Protecting Your Information

Part 7
Beyond FileMaker

Preface

My Intent

This is meant to be a hands-on book. The idea is to have you do various exercises so that you become familiar with FileMaker Pro. The book doesn't have that much to do with theory, although you will learn some along the way. There are other books for theory, if that's something you care about.

The FileMaker Pro manual shows you features. What I want to do is take you through a group of exercises that use those features. That way, when you're done, you've actually created some databases that you can use, and you'll know what it feels like. I want you to learn how to drive by getting behind the wheel. You can read the manual for the rules of the road.

Writing and updating this book has been a combination of excitement and frustration. The excitement comes from discovering a new way of describing some feature of this program in a way that has the potential to really make it understandable. The frustration comes from knowing that someday there will be a better way. Let's face it: Indexes just aren't good enough, especially if you don't know the terminology. See if you recognize this: "How do I make the program do that thing I want it to do or that was called by another name in some other database I used to use?" Another frustration is that I'll give you an overview of an area, only to tell you there's more in another chapter. Somehow, I want to inject it into you all at once, like in a vaccination but with less pain!

There will come a day when you'll be able to just think about what you want to do, and it will be done. You probably won't even be near an object we now think of as a computer. You won't even have to know that what you want to do is accomplished with a database. That day can't possibly arrive soon enough for me! Until that day arrives . . .

I recommend that you work at your computer with this book. I don't recommend that you read this lying down. The thing that will keep you awake is getting your hands dirty working with the program.

Try to follow the steps exactly as given in the examples. You may have to do some of them over. There is so much detail that it may be hard to get the big picture the first time. Each chapter was designed to be completed in about one hour. But you can't put this book under your pillow for three nights and get it. You may be struggling with the details of a layout or a calculation or a script and miss the overall concept that I'm trying to present to you. If you're anything like me, hearing the definition of a new term once is not enough for the message to sink in. If you need to, go back and reread a chapter.

In the end, it may take you 40 or 50 or 100 hours. But that's a lot less time than it took me to stumble through multiple books and magazines trying to get what's all in this one book. Not to say that I've covered everything. Far from it. But I've tried very hard to include as many of the little things that you will absolutely need to get started.

If you've ever had difficulty finding the topic you needed from an index, you'll really enjoy the one in the back of this book. It has more than 3,000 listings, making it closer to a concordance than an index. It includes terms used in other database systems and previous versions of FileMaker (which have changed with version 7) to make it easier for users of those programs to find what they need faster.

There is even an area in the index called Problems, which lists nearly 100 areas for potential troubleshooting. Wish I'd had something like that when I started out!

I know everyone is not going to start out at the same level. You may already have some FileMaker experience. Although I want you to do the exercises, if you're further along, I don't want to force you to do the early exercises just to get the files ready for the chapter in which you want to work. So I've included a set of files in the downloadable files (www.wordware.com/files/fmpro7) that go along with each of the applicable book chapters starting with Chapter 4. You can take the files in the folder for the chapter where you want to begin doing the exercises and start following along with the text.

If I had written an introductory book on FileMaker about five or six years ago, it would have been much shorter. But, as is the case with most software, the programmers are constantly trying to give us users more powerful tools. That means just listing the tools takes longer. And showing you how to use the tools takes longer still.

This book assumes you already have access to a copy of the manual. However, I understand that companies that purchase site licenses for multiple copies of FileMaker Pro only get one copy of the manual. Honestly, you don't need the manual to get most of what you need from this book. It's just that there is not enough time to cover everything in a tutorial like this.

I know some people who find this type of reading exactly what they need to get over a bout with insomnia. I've come to understand that computers, and FileMaker Pro in particular, are just not for everybody. But if it's something you need to learn, I've done my absolute best to make it as easy as possible and keep it interesting.

And in the end, if you should happen to come to love FileMaker as I have, you'll understand why I say, "Data never knew how beautiful it could be until it was touched by FileMaker Pro."

About the Authors

An award-winning Las Vegas singer, songwriter, and comedian with 10 albums, **Jonathan Stars** began using the earliest version of FileMaker in 1986 to keep track of his entertainment business. People who saw his work began asking him to design databases for their businesses.

   Among his many projects, Jonathan has developed databases for State of Michigan governmental agencies, CRG Regional Telephone Directories, ICT Cable, various international associations, Marco Music Publishing in Nashville, Tennessee, and Yale University's NARCOMS database. He is a member of the FileMaker Solution Alliance and writes for *FileMaker Pro Advisor* magazine.

Janice Child is part of the marketing team — managing corporate communications and event planning — for a multi-line insurance company. Her working relationship with Jonathan Stars began when he developed a FileMaker solution for her event-planning responsibilities. "It changed the way we operate," she said, "and it made the process so much easier. I became a FileMaker fan right away." Since then, she has worked with him on numerous projects, developing manuals to accompany his FileMaker solutions for clients and articles on FileMaker solutions for a variety of publications. She is also an adjunct faculty member of the Department of Communications of Lansing Community College in Michigan, where she teaches business and technical writing.

Nonie Bernard is director of curriculum development for FMPtraining and an instructor with the Maricopa Community Colleges. She has developed train-the-trainer curricula and programs in higher education, and is responsible for ongoing enhancements to FMPtraining course materials. She has a degree in human resources, specializing in training and development, and more than 20 years of experience in training design and delivery, college teaching, and information management consulting and leadership. Nonie's ability to teach technical subjects to students with varying backgrounds, as well as her enthusiastic delivery, earn consistently high student evaluations. In a recent survey, her college students ranked her in the top 10% of all of their instructors. She lives in Phoenix, Arizona.

Acknowledgments

Thanks to Jeff Gagné from FileMaker, Inc. (now at Apple) for giving me the lead that got me started on this book.

To Randi Roger from MacMillan & Company who took it to the next step.

To Jeff Johnson and his business partner, Deborah, from Bake N' Cakes for letting me learn the relational details of FileMaker Pro 3.0 while building a set of files for Bake N' Cakes, their bakery in Lansing, Michigan. They made me a professional.

To writer Thom Cannell for convincing me I could write this book and keeping me going with each update by reminding me how it affects my career.

To Bill Harrison of Custom Photographic in Lansing, Michigan, for letting me try out the web stuff at his Internet Express office.

To Andy Frederick who showed me the basics of early FileMaker and kept me interested.

To Darren Terry of Pacific Data Management, Inc. (formerly the technical liaison for developer relations at FileMaker, Inc.) for solving a sticky problem I had with networking and another on the new FileMaker 7 relational model.

To Ken Black, Dave Folmsby, David Smith, Gene Burd, and the rest of the gang at Eubulus Computer Solutions who sent me out on so many jobs.

To Dave Riedle from Eubulus who filled me in on his experiences with the Palm OS.

To Corey Clemons from Eubulus for helping me test out all the finer points of web publishing in Windows 2000.

To Jason Hoss from Eubulus who helped me work out the networking issues with Windows XP and FileMaker Pro's Instant Web Publishing.

To Frank Holcomb from ACD.net for showing me detailed changes to the network control panels in Windows 2000.

To Dave Dowling who created the XML examples and helped me to understand what XML is all about.

To Kevin Mallon from FileMaker, Inc. who made sure I got all the latest versions of the software and answers to questions, and Claudia Rippert who kept me current with FileMaker Mobile.

To Andy LeCates from FileMaker, Inc. who answered my final set of questions on FileMaker Pro 7.

To Hudson Akridge from FileMaker, Inc. who answered all my in-depth technical questions on FileMaker Pro 6 to keep me on the straight and narrow. He also kept track of my bug reports so they were fixed in the updates.

To Brian Jaquet and Jennifer McMullen from Handspring, Inc. for their help with the Handspring Visor.

To Jim Hill at Wordware Publishing for agreeing to take the book to the final printed version, encouraging me throughout the process, and suggesting improvements and other opportunities along the way. I'm a little whiney and he's a good baby-sitter.

To Wes Beckwith, publisher at Wordware, who explained a lot of the details of the publishing business and worked very hard to get the book a better placement in bookstores and online publishing outfits.

To the rest of the crew at Wordware: editors Kellie Henderson (on the first two editions) and Beth Kohler; interior designer Martha McCuller; production specialist Denise McEvoy; and cover designer Alan McCuller. These people do way more than I ever imagined to make what I wrote sound and look professional and accurate. Many of them have special talents that I never knew existed.

To William Moss for being technical editor since the very first edition. He really made me look like I know what I'm talking about, and he submitted all his suggestions without making me feel foolish. I used many of his comments verbatim.

To Jerry Robin from FMPtraining who provided technical edits to some of the early chapters of the book and made many suggestions for improving the format. His encyclopedic knowledge of FileMaker is awesome.

To Alan Stirling of Alan Stirling Technology in England who helped me better understand the security issues of Instant Web Publishing.

To contributing author Nonie Bernard who added material to the book, making it more accessible to educators in a classroom environment.

To co-author Janice Child who came at the book with completely fresh eyes. She rewrote much of what you see from the perspective of a beginner — exactly what we needed with a software that has changed so dramatically with this version. She spent months being confused so that you won't have to.

Special thanks to Mom who actually did all the exercises in the first edition of the book and saved all of you much time and frustration by finding a number of major omissions. She also added immensely to the clarity of my approach in a number of areas of the book. If you find this book reasonably easy to understand, it is largely thanks to her. It was a tough job for her, but that's what moms do.

And finally, to the unknown guy at Kinko's in Salt Lake City, Utah, who showed me FileMaker for the first time.

Introduction

How It All Started

It was about 3:00 A.M. in Salt Lake City, Utah. The year was 1986, might have been spring. I had just finished performing a solo music and comedy show at a Fraternal Order of Eagles club. I needed to print out some promotional materials, so I headed over to the all-night Kinko's Copy Shop.

I was complaining to the guy behind the counter about how much trouble I had keeping track of all the clubs I was playing using a three-ring binder. He said, "Oh, you need a database."

I said, "What's that?" And he proceeded to show me FileMaker.

Well, I had just bought a Mac Plus computer so I could make MIDI music. It wasn't too much of a leap to buy the FileMaker software to experiment with.

Here's how running my entertainment business using FileMaker went: I'd sit down to make some calls to line up shows, and I'd think, "It would make more sense to move this field over there. Shouldn't I have a field for mileage? Hey, I'll bet I could print my contracts from here!" I'd look up and an hour had gone by. "Man, I'd better make some calls." It was fun, and I got a lot better at booking shows. I could make twice the number of calls in half the time because I was organized.

When I finished that tour, I joined a Mac user group back in my hometown of Lansing, Michigan. The group's president, Andy Frederick, happened to be pretty good at FileMaker and showed me a lot of things I didn't know existed, because I'd never read the manual. You know, Mac software is so easy, you don't have to read the manual, so I didn't. Good thing Andy was around.

Pretty soon, other members of the user group saw what I was doing and hired me to make databases for their businesses. I thought it was pretty neat to be doing that work, but I didn't think of it as a serious business. I was going to be a famous recording artist.

My first big relational job was for my wife, Deborah's, bakery. Her partner, Jeff Johnson, challenged me way beyond my knowledge and gave me nothing but encouragement to experiment.

A few years went by. As far as the entertaining business went, I was getting tired of all the driving, living out of a suitcase, setting up and tearing down equipment — and I wasn't getting famous! I mean, I was making a living, and I'd won some awards, but it seemed as if I was always begging for my next gig.

Meanwhile, my phone kept ringing to do FileMaker work. And I really enjoyed it, too. It was like getting paid to do puzzles. Well, after about two years of ignoring the obvious (you only have to hit me over the head with a sledgehammer three or four times), I decided to make it my primary business. Besides, it felt a whole lot better to have my phone ring than to beg.

When I wasn't doing work for clients, I was tinkering. Then I got an e-mail saying that *FileMaker Pro Advisor* magazine was looking for writers. So I submitted a couple of article proposals that came out of my tinkering, and they got accepted. One thing led to another until I was invited to write this book.

Conventions

- File, Open — Any menu title followed by a comma followed by another capitalized word indicates that a selection is being made from one of the menus. A second comma indicates a submenu. For example: View, Toolbars, Standard. To see the submenus, you have to pull down to the menu choice and the submenus will pop out.

- Screen — The whole computer screen. If I say look in the upper-left corner of your screen, on the Macintosh you will see the apple and on Windows computers you'll probably see the name of the program you're in.

- Active window — The frontmost working area on your computer. You can have many programs and files open at one time but only one is the frontmost active window.

- (Macintosh) — Refers to a command or menu choice for the Macintosh (or Mac) operating system.

- (Windows) — Refers to a command or menu choice for the Windows operating system.

- FileMaker Pro, FileMaker, and occasionally FMP and FMP7 are used interchangeably throughout this book.

- Key combinations are shown using a plus sign (+) between the keys. For example, Ctrl+N means hold down the Ctrl or Control key, and press the letter N. There are a few cases where other symbols are used in the combination. For example, Ctrl+– means hold down the Control key and press the minus (–) key. There may also be lengthy combinations such as Ctrl+Option+Shift+F.

- Unless otherwise noted, the Windows and Mac screens are interchangeable. There are slight differences such as the color and shading of the borders. But in general, you should not be confused by seeing one screen or the other. In the few cases where they differ significantly, I include screens for both platforms.

- With the update of the book to version 5.5, I started including a little "5.5" in superscript to indicate new features since version 5.0. I repeated that with 6.0. This version of FileMaker is so different, you'll need to convert your files before using them. Many, many features and ways of doing things are different this time around. I've added a superscript 7 to items that are completely new. That should help users of previous versions know they're looking at something completely new.

- Starting with the 6.0 edition, Jim Hill (the publisher of the first three versions of this book) and I brought in Nonie Bernard, a well-respected FileMaker trainer and writer of educational materials. She contributed to the structure of the additional text so it better fits an educational format. She has provided vocabulary lists at the beginning of the chapters and brought them all together at the end of the book. Then she added extra items to the chapter quizzes. You can test yourself open-book style. But, hey, try to get the answer before peeking in the back.

Updates

This version of FileMaker Pro is arguably the most dramatic upgrade in the history of the program. (I don't know who would do the arguing. I think it's revolutionary.) The most dramatic changes are the new relational model and the Accounts & Privileges security system. You can now build multiple tables in a single file (simplifying security design), and tables can now be linked via multiple unequal relationships and are represented graphically. The old users and groups security has been completely replaced by the Accounts & Privileges system, which is much more useful and intuitive. I also find it comforting that the files themselves are much better protected from the harm caused by a computer crash.

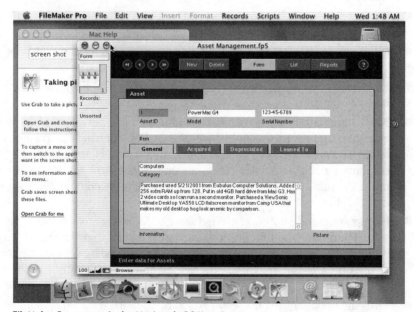

FileMaker Pro as seen in the Macintosh OS X environment.

Of course you'll find the changes listed throughout the book, but here are a few that don't seem to fit anywhere else:

If you're creating shared solutions, keep in mind that users who have an older version of the software won't be able to open FileMaker 7 files.

There have been quite a few keyboard command changes that deal specifically with moving, grouping, and locking objects in Layout mode. To get the lowdown, go to the Help menu, choose Content & Index, and choose the Index tab. Type in "keyboard commands." Then double-click "Layout mode keyboard commands..." for the OS you're using. Scroll down to "Object arrangement keyboard commands."

FileMaker 6 had changed how dates are handled to provide a more consistent conversion of two-digit years. For all the details, go to http://www.filemaker.com/legal/notice_y2k.html. I personally enter all dates using four digits for the year. That avoids any confusion. But imported data may need some special attention.

FileMaker has been certified for the Windows 2000 and XP (both Pro and Home editions) logos since version 6. It is accessible for the visually and hearing-impaired, and includes support for OnNow power management for laptops. It is also easier to provide software updates in large organizations.

Where there will be multiple users of FileMaker on the same Windows computer, each user can have a different user name and network protocol when they launch FileMaker for the first time. You can use Windows XP Fast User Switching between various user accounts without having to quit FileMaker.

FileMaker Pro began supporting Mac OS X starting with version 5.5. However, before you install and expect your solutions to work in OS X, you should be aware of some (hopefully temporary) limitations. OS X does not support the Dial Phone script step or AppleTalk (which is being abandoned in favor of faster, more reliable protocols). Any plug-ins you expect to use must be written specifically for OS X. OS X supports filenames up to 255 characters. But be aware of the problems long names might cause when moving solutions to other system software. While these limitations may cause some hesitation in adopting the Mac OS X platform, there is one big advantage. Since OS X features protected memory, when one program crashes, others remain untouched. Not only are FileMaker files safer in OS X, but they look great, too! FileMaker, Inc. is making a lot of headway to allow deployment outside the Mac and Windows platforms. For example, Chapter 23 in this book is about the update to FileMaker Mobile, which allows you to use and synchronize your files on the Palm platform, with certain limitations.

In March 2002 FileMaker, Inc. introduced FileMaker Mobile for i-mode (available in Japan only). This new product allows instant database publishing on the i-mode smart phones, used by more than 30 million people in Japan for mobile e-mail and Internet access. FMM for i-mode allows mobile users to instantly and dynamically browse, edit, add, delete, search, and sort records from i-mode phones. You can find out more at http://www.filemaker.com/products/mbl_home.html. There is already a version of FileMaker Server that runs on Linux. We'll be seeing a lot more changes like that in the near future, as FMP becomes available for Pocket PC and other platforms. FileMaker is on the move!

Also, FileMaker wants to know what you think. Let's say you're having problems with a function that just doesn't make sense. Or maybe there are features you'd like to suggest. If you're online, click the Help menu and select Send Feedback to FileMaker. That will bring up a web page where you'll need to click on Send Feedback to FileMaker again. There you can fill out a form that will help them understand exactly what you'd like to see in FileMaker. Obviously they can't add every feature that everyone comes up with. But who knows. Maybe your suggestion will have a profound effect on what happens next. It sure made a difference with this upgrade! After all, a million heads are better than one. FileMaker really is listening. That's what makes a great company, and I'm proud to be associated with them.

Companion Files

A variety of files are available to be downloaded from www.wordware.com/files/fmpro7. These are divided into the following folders:

- Chapter files—These files go along with the book, chapter by chapter, for readers to learn to work with FileMaker Pro.
- Developer files—Most of these solutions were provided by other FileMaker developers; some of these may require a fee to use beyond a trial period.
- J_Stars files—These include an explanation of what they're for. Simply click the question mark button on the main page of each file.
- Plugs-Ins—This little file points you to the web sites of plug-in companies I'm acquainted with. If you're connected to the web, just click the Go button and it will take you there. The link to the FileMaker, Inc. site takes you directly to their page that lists all registered plug-ins.

See the included Read Me file for more information.

Part 1

Learning the Basics

Chapter 1

Getting Acquainted with FileMaker Pro

Vocabulary

- Book (in the Status area)
- Clone
- Compacted copy
- Database
- Field

- File
- Layout
- Record
- Status area
- Table

Objectives

1. Define a database.
2. Open and quit the FileMaker Pro application.
3. Open and close a FileMaker database file.
4. Identify the components of a database system.
5. Create a new record.
6. Navigate within and between records.
7. Enter data into a record.
8. Understand how FileMaker saves your work.
9. Understand the three Save As file types.

Introduction

I'm assuming you've already installed FileMaker Pro and the template files on your computer. If you haven't, do that now, because when I am done with this first part, I want you to be able to get started right away.

The author of one of the first books I ever read on FileMaker Pro spent the first half of the book on database theory. Great reading if you need to fall asleep! I don't want to waste too much of your time before you get your hands on the program. I guarantee you'll be working with FileMaker in five minutes (unless you're a very slow reader), but I do want to get you excited about what is coming your way.

FileMaker Pro is the easiest relational database system to use on the face of the earth. I would argue that it is the best desktop database system as well. Pretty strong words, eh? Let's look at the facts.

Developers who create database systems in both FileMaker Pro and Microsoft Access say that when they prototype a system concept for a client in order to get a job, they do the work in FileMaker. Why? Because it takes half the time! That's significant because the developer often isn't being paid for his prototyping time. When the client is paying for the work and wants it in Access, of course the developers will do the work in Access. It takes twice as long and they make twice the money! The fact that you're reading this book means you won't be wasting your time and money either. You made the right choice in database applications.

FileMaker Pro is also the best-selling stand-alone database application in the world. There are more installed copies of Microsoft Access because for many years it was part of the Microsoft Office suite, but many owners don't use it. That means it's very possible that FileMaker is the most-used database system in the world. It is certainly the best-selling cross-platform database application. Access does not work on a Macintosh. Those who are serious about database systems research what's out there and they buy FileMaker Pro.

Its ease of use does not mean FileMaker is wimpy. It is just cleverly built to be easier — "user friendly" in the best sense of the phrase. The creators of FileMaker took a very different approach to their program from systems that came before. They were daring. And we reap the benefits. By the time you finish these 25 lessons, you'll be well on your way to understanding that power.

What Is a Database?

A *database* is simply a collection of information, or data. A *database system* is a set of procedures, devices, and rules for managing the information in a database. A database system can be as simple as a set of Rolodex™ cards used to keep track of your database of contact information. Because computer people love to shorten terms to the point of obscurity, they will often refer to computer-based database systems simply as databases. A single file with one or more tables, a group of related files, and the program that created the files (such as FileMaker Pro) are all sometimes referred to interchangeably as a database. Like most people, I'll be using the term loosely throughout the book. But I thought it'd be wise to point out the difference between the two terms while we're just starting out.

Database systems don't have to involve computers at all, but because computers are so good at storing, organizing, and retrieving data, a computer-based database system can be very powerful and flexible.

Sounds kind of boring. Put simply, a computer-based database system is the most glorious Rolodex ever built. Sorting those Rolodex cards by last name never worked very well for me because I can't remember names worth a rip. However, with a computer-based database system you can often find a person based on any piece of information in the file — sometimes even if you can't spell it!

For example, imagine you're trying to get in touch with a salesman about a product. You remember that his first name is George, but you can't recall his last name. In a database, you can do a search for George in the First Name field and just page through the few records that come up. Maybe you've forgotten his name completely, but you remember that he sells key chains and that you'd typed that information in the Notes field. Bingo! Try that with a Rolodex.

FileMaker Pro is a *relational* database system. That means you can create special rules for retrieving more information based on the information that you have already found. These connecting rules are called *relationships*. Going back to the Rolodex contact cards, imagine that on each person's card you wrote his or her favorite hobby. As you thumb through the cards one by one, you decide it would be handy to know who shares the same hobby. I see that Michael Cloud's favorite hobby is piano. Who else in my card database has piano as their favorite hobby? Doug Deal likes chess. Who else likes chess? To answer these questions, you'd have to compare the hobby on the current card with the hobby on every other card and see which ones match. This would take considerable effort with physical cards, but by using relationships you can have FileMaker provide the information quickly and automatically for each person in your database. Relationships are very powerful, but they can be a complex topic. We'll cover this in more depth in Chapters 2, 6, and 7.

You can use FileMaker Pro for something as simple as a mailing list, inventory system, convention registration, or scheduling, all the way up to purchase orders, billing, and accounting. You can share your files with other users on a network. And with some great tricks provided by the geniuses at FileMaker, Inc., you can share information with many other computer programs and even on the World Wide Web.

I promised you I wouldn't take more than five minutes. Are you fired up yet? Let's go!

Using FileMaker Pro

FileMaker Pro is the *application*, or program, in which you create files and tables and manipulate data. You have to get the program started before you can do anything else.

Opening FileMaker Pro

Start the FileMaker Pro application. If you're using a Macintosh computer, go into the Applications folder, open the FileMaker folder, and double-click on the FileMaker Pro icon. If you're on a Windows machine, find the Start menu, go to Programs, find FileMaker Pro 7 (they may not be in alphabetical order), and choose FileMaker Pro. If you chose to have a shortcut created on the desktop during the installation process, you can double-click the shortcut to start FileMaker Pro.

When FileMaker opens, you should see a window similar to the one in Figure 1-1. If you or somebody else has been using FileMaker already on this machine, this window may have been turned off in FileMaker's Application Preferences.

Figure 1-1
When you first open FileMaker Pro, you should see a window that looks like this.

➲ **NOTE** You can also open the FileMaker Pro application by double-clicking on the icon of any FileMaker Pro file. Of course, the file will also open. With some versions of OS X, you may find that it may not bring the FileMaker program to the front.

☒ **CAUTION** If you open one of the template files by double-clicking its icon, any changes you make to the file will become a permanent part of the template.

Opening a FileMaker Pro File

If you don't see the New Database window, go to the File menu in the upper-left corner of the screen, and choose New Database. (From now on, when I want you to choose an option from a menu I'll write it like this: File, New Database.)

Once you get going, you'll want to work with files that have your data in them. When you want to open a file you've already created, choose File, Open. To find the files you need, you will have to navigate your way through the

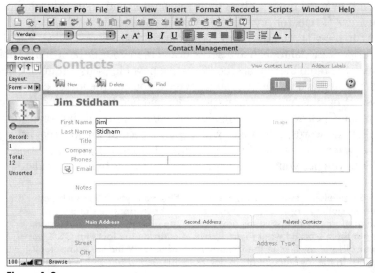

Figure 1-2
The FileMaker Pro screen. Notice the menu bar across the top and the Status area at the left.

directories on your computer. You can also open a file by double-clicking on the file's icon. That will also work with an alias of the file (Macintosh) or a shortcut (Windows).

The advantage of using the New Database window at this stage is that FileMaker knows where to find the templates, so you don't have to go searching through folders on your hard drive.

Database Concepts

I think it's easier to understand terminology if you're looking at the items I'm talking about as we go. So while we're in the middle of opening this file, I'll explain, continue working, and explain some more.

Files

A FileMaker *file* holds both your information and instructions on how you prefer to keep that information organized. This is similar to the way a word processor or spreadsheet stores its data. All of these applications keep track of the data you create in files on your hard disk.

To create a database system you'll need at least one FileMaker file, but your system can use many files if you prefer. Think back to the Rolodex. Our Rolodex was our database of contact information, but if we have both a business life and a personal life we could either keep everyone in the same system, or we could keep two separate systems. Similarly, we could keep everyone in the same FileMaker file, or split them into two files. Which is the "right" way? It depends on what we think is convenient and appropriate. Sometimes, only our experience will tell us.

Fortunately, FileMaker provides tools to allow separate files to communicate when they need to, as well as tools to partition and order the data into separate areas for clearer organization within a single file. With this in mind, don't get too hung up on how many files your database should have. FileMaker files are organizational tools like a set of drawers in your desk or filing cabinet.

Be sure the radio button labeled "Create a new file using a template" is selected. Scroll down the list on the right until you see the folder called Business - People & Assets. Open the folder and find the file called Contact Management. Click on it so it's highlighted and click the OK button or just double-click the words. FileMaker will display a second window that asks you where you want to save the file. (See Figures 1-3 and 1-4.) Pay attention to what folders you put your files in; you'll probably want to find them later.

⌘ **TIP**   If you develop a system to organize your files now, you'll be much better off later. After all, getting organized is what this is all about, right? If I'm on the Macintosh platform, I often save my new files to the desktop so I can find them later and put them where I want them. I have to override the fact that OS X wants to automatically put my files in the Documents folder. On Windows computers, I save new files in the My Documents folder. But you need to remember to go in there later to put things away. It's easy to forget and create quite a clutter.

Figure 1-3
The Macintosh window for creating a copy named Contact Management.

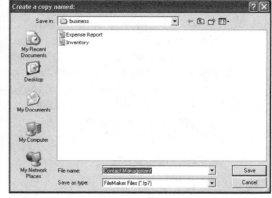

Figure 1-4
The window for creating a copy named Contact Management in Microsoft Windows.

The Contact Management file will probably open to a blank form. Regardless, click on the question mark in the upper right-hand corner of the screen. This will take you to an informational screen about FileMaker templates. Take a moment to read this screen.

Now click on the third tab to the left of the question mark. There's an arrow pointing to it in Figure 1-5. Notice how the screen appearance changes as you are returned to the blank form. This is a sample of a form. I'll teach you how to create your own buttons later. It's really easy to do and you'll love the power it gives you.

Figure 1-5
The Form tab in the Contact Management window.

Tables

Tables are collections of data concerning a specific subject, such as a list of customers or invoices. A FileMaker file can hold rules about just one type of table or many different types. For example, a file could have a table for customers and another table for invoices. In fact we'll be creating a file that contains those tables and more over the course of this book.

To help clarify a little, I have a database I use for groceries that only has a single table. You can have more tables in a file, but you certainly don't need to. It all depends upon the specific purpose you have in mind. You may be familiar with the grid-like appearance of tables in programs like Excel, and you can add tables to Microsoft Word documents. You can certainly choose to display your FileMaker table data in columns and rows. But FileMaker is much more flexible with its tables. You can display data so it looks like a form, or labels, or a report with summary information.

The idea that you can have multiple tables in a FileMaker file is a revolutionary concept for the program. We developers used to need a separate file to represent each table. The single-table-per-file arrangement sometimes required complex programming to move between the files to accomplish fairly simple tasks. This new system allows people who work with FileMaker to streamline their work considerably. And it allows newcomers to take advantage of some of FileMaker's more powerful features more quickly than ever before.

Records

Look over near the upper-left corner of the window. See the icon that looks like a three-ring binder? That's called the Book. It's a navigation tool that we'll get into later. But right now notice that there are 0 Records in this table. Oh? "What's a record?" you ask. It's like a card in our Rolodex. *Records* are what you add to a table as you are filling it up with your data. It's the information that you enter about a particular person, place, or thing. What's actually in a record depends on the rules that you've set up in the table.

Take your pointer and click in the white box to the right of the words First Name. Oops! No records, eh? Click the OK button to get rid of the dialog box. Choose Records, New Record. Notice in the menu that you can also make a new record by pressing the Command+N (Macintosh) or Ctrl+N (Windows) key combination. If you look over at the Book you should now have one record in your file — unless you were trying out the key combinations and now have two or three records. It's okay; try it out. You're not going to hurt anything. The worst that can happen is your computer will blow up, you'll lose a lot of important files, be fired from your job, and end up homeless. So go ahead — give it a shot. (Now isn't this a lot more fun than that sleep-inducing database theory book?)

Fields

You may notice that the cursor is blinking in the white box next to First Name and that most of the other white boxes have dotted lines around them. Those boxes are *fields*. That's where you put your information. A field is a little piece of information that's part of a record of your data. By itself it may not describe much, but when grouped with the other fields in the record it should give you a unique and useful description. While you're still in the First Name field, type your first name. Press the Tab key and the cursor moves to the Last Name field.

Type your last name. Tab three more times and enter your phone number. To the right of the Name, Company, and Phones fields is an unlabeled field about 2 inches square. You can store a picture (and some other cool things) in this Container field. Go ahead and click in it. Notice that the cursor doesn't blink when it's in a Container field. Look at the choices you have under the Insert menu. Yep, you can put a movie or a sound file in there if you want.

Look in the upper-left corner of the window. See that New button? Click it. You just created a new record without the key combination or the menu command. The flexibility is amazing.

Hey, your name disappeared! Relax; it's still in the file. It's just in a different record. Go to the Book and click on the left page, the one with the fake writing on it. Look at the record. There's your name. Now click on the right page of the Book to return to the blank record. Fill in the fields with information about someone you know.

Each record is like one of those Rolodex cards I told you about. Is the pattern starting to become clearer now? A record is just a collection of one or more fields, a table is just a collection of one or more records, a file is just a collection of one or more tables, and a database is just a collection of the data in one or more similar files. A database system is FileMaker itself and all of the rules that we put in our files for managing our information. And what is our information? Can you say database? I knew you could.

 SHORTCUT   Another way to navigate between records without using the Book is to hold down the Control key and press the up and down arrows — Control+ arrow (Macintosh) or Ctrl+arrow (Windows). It's not particularly intuitive. You click the down arrow to flip the right page of the book onto the next page. In contrast — and more in keeping with clicking the down arrow key — if you are viewing items in a list, you actually move down to the next record.

Layouts

Layouts are just different views of data and tables in your files. Look in the upper-right corner of this window to the left of the question mark. See those three tabs? Click the middle one. This brings you to the List View layout. You should see a list of the few records you have in the file. Some of them may be empty. Notice that this list does not have all the fields that were on the form. All the rest of the data is still in the file; it's just not visible on this layout. You can even have a layout with no fields on it at all. You could use a layout like that to make notes to yourself using the Text tool (more on that later) or to store some of your favorite icons that you would use on other layouts. Click on one of the items in the list to take you back to the form.

You could even have a layout containing nothing but buttons to act as a menu to other layouts or reports. That can be a great organizational tool and I often do just that for my clients. Think how cluttered the Form - Main Address layout would be if you had to cram every button for every function on there.

Click the Magnifying Glass icon (it's about two inches above the First Name field). You're in the same layout, just in Find mode.

The gray bar on the left side of the window that contains the Book is called the Status area. Notice that something new appeared there, about halfway down the window. Clicking the magnifying glass started running a script. Click the Cancel button below the

Figure 1-6
The Status area showing the Continue button.

word Script to go back to Browse mode (Figure 1-6). Now choose View, Layout Mode. Click the right page of the Book until the number 8 appears under the word Layout below the Book. If you click on the Layout list pop-up above the Book, you'll see that this layout is called Avery 5160. Before long you'll be able to create your own labels and even custom letters that combine data from your records into the text of your letters.

Choose View, Browse Mode. Unless you are looking at one of your blank data entry records, you should see someone's name on the label. Click on the right page of the Book. Do you see the label of the next person in your database? If you get a blank page instead, click on the Book again.

Saving a Copy of a FileMaker Pro File

As the psychiatrists say, "Our time is almost up," so we need to do a little housekeeping before we finish. FileMaker saves your work as you go. This is a little different from word processors, which often require that you save every few minutes to avoid losing your work. However, you will want to make various backups at the end of a session.

Choose File, Save a Copy As and click on "copy of current file" at the bottom of the window to look at your other choices. The Macintosh and Windows windows are somewhat different, so I've included both in Figures 1-7 and 1-8.

Notice that next to the filename, FileMaker knows to insert the word "Copy" at the end of the name. You can type over the name and call it anything you like. If you choose "clone (no records)" from the Type pop-up, FileMaker inserts the word "Clone" instead.

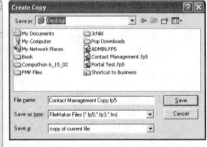

Figure 1-8
The window that appears when you choose Save a Copy As from the File menu in Microsoft Windows.

Figure 1-7
The Macintosh window that appears when you choose Save a Copy As from the File menu.

The three Save As file types and their purposes are:

■ Copy of current file — Makes a copy of the file.

■ Compacted copy (smaller) — FileMaker goes through the file and removes all unused space that may have built up over time. This is a good option for files that are fairly large and get a lot of use.

- Clone (no records) — This is used to make a template of a file. It is often used to make a safe backup in case the main file gets damaged.

For now, just save a copy of the current file.

 CAUTION   Save a Copy As in FMP is different from the Save As menu command you may be used to in other programs. In many programs when you choose Save As, the document you are working in immediately takes on the new document name. When you choose Save a Copy As in FileMaker, you remain in the document you were working in before you saved your copy.

Closing a FileMaker Pro File

There are a couple of ways to close your file. You can choose File, Close. On the Macintosh, you can click the red X button in the upper-left corner of the file window. On a Windows machine, click the X box in the upper right of the file window. (If you click the X in the upper-right corner of the whole screen, you'll exit the whole FileMaker program.)

 SHORTCUT   To close a window, use Command+W (Macintosh) or Ctrl+W (Windows).

Quitting FileMaker Pro

Quitting or exiting is done the same way as with any other program I can think of. Choose File, Quit (Macintosh) or File, Exit (Windows). In addition to the following keyboard shortcut, on a Windows machine, you can click the X box in the upper-right corner of the screen. You don't get a similar choice on the Mac.

SHORTCUT   To quit FileMaker Pro, use Command+Q (Macintosh). In Windows you can use either Ctrl+Q or Alt+F4.

Summary

This first chapter should have given you a certain comfort level with FileMaker Pro. You now know how to open and quit the FileMaker Pro application as well as how to open and close individual files. We've looked at fields and how any one field may or may not appear on various layouts. We've also seen that there are records in a table, one or more tables makes up a file, and one or more files make up a database. Many of the chapters to come still deal with basics. As you're learning these basics, you should start to get some of those "Ah-ha!" moments. That's when you'll recognize that FileMaker Pro can help you accomplish what you need to do in more ways than you'd dreamed. That's when you begin to control your destiny!

Are you having as much fun as I am? Check out the Q&A below, try the Workshop exercise, and answer the review questions. Then go get yourself some coffee, juice, or a soft drink. You deserve it. I'll see you in Chapter 2.

Q & A

Q How do I get my data back if I click the Delete button or choose Records, Delete Record, and then click the Delete button in the dialog box?

A You'd better hope that you have a copy of the record in a backup somewhere. Once a record is gone from the database, it's gone. That's why backing up regularly is so important. See Chapter 22 for more details.

Q What's that slotted gadget underneath the Book for?

A That's the Slider. You can use it to move between records by clicking and dragging it right and left. It can be quite helpful in tables with a large number of records for moving to the first or last record or somewhere between.

Workshop: Try it out on your own

Start FileMaker Pro and open a file from one of the templates folders. Try out some of the buttons. I don't mind if you even take a look at some of the other menus — it'll probably get your mind going with some questions. Create a new record or two and enter some data. In general, just rummage around. The worst you can do is... well, just try it out. Then see if you can save a copy of the file and quit or exit.

Review Questions

True-False

1. A database is a collection of information or data.
2. To open an existing FileMaker file, you choose File, Open.
3. You must choose the Save command to save your work in FileMaker.
4. The Save as Clone command makes a copy of the entire database file.
5. You must click into each field to enter data.

Short Answer

6. Name at least two ways you can open the FileMaker Pro application.
7. In a library card catalog database, what might each *record* represent?
8. Name two ways you can create a new record in a database table.
9. What item in the Status area can you use to navigate between records?
10. How do you enter data into all of the fields in a record?

Chapter 2

Menus and Modes

Vocabulary

- Lookup field
- Mode
- Related data
- Relationship

Objectives

1. Explore the Fields tab of the Define Database window.
2. Resize a window.
3. Explore the Relationships tab of the Define Database window.
4. Become familiar with lookups and related data.
5. Define the purpose of FileMaker's modes.
6. Navigate among the modes.
7. Identify FileMaker's layout types and their purposes.
8. Explore the Sort Records window.
9. Explore ScriptMaker's Define Scripts window.
10. Explore the Define Accounts & Privileges window.

Introduction

Welcome to the second chapter. This chapter continues to familiarize you with FileMaker Pro. First of all, I want to get into more detail about the various menus. Menus in FileMaker Pro, as well as most other modern computer programs, are the words that sit across the top of your screen and show you various commands of the program that you're working in. We're going to look at many of the specific FileMaker commands. You will find one of the most important commands under the File menu: Define. From here you can define your database by creating your tables, fields, and relationships; your value lists, which are options that frequently appear in fields (items such as Male and Female or a pop-up list of employees); your file references, which we will explore in Chapter 14; and accounts and privileges, which give or limit access to information. New to FileMaker 7 is the Define Database window, which contains three tabs.

Under the View menu you'll find FileMaker's four modes: Browse, Find, Layout, and Preview. These modes are where you do most of the work with data entry and define the way information appears. You might do a lot of your initial design with fields and scripts, but you and the people who share your data will work in these different modes.

Define Database New Approach!

Even though we'll go further into the details of table, field, and relationship definition in Chapter 3, "Creating Your First Database," I want to show you around the neighborhood so you'll be familiar with it when the time comes.

Open up the copy of the Contact Management file you created in the last chapter. If you deleted it or just can't find it, go back to Chapter 1 and follow the directions there to create a new copy.

Once the file is open, choose File, Define Database. You'll see a window that looks like the one in Figure 2-1. If not, click the Tables tab.

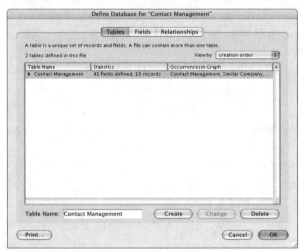

Figure 2-1
The Define Database Tables tab.

Tables Tab

Since FileMaker now allows multiple tables in a file, you need a place to create and name them. The Tables tab is that place. In the Contact Management file, there's currently only one table. When you first create a file, the first table is automatically given the same name as the file and the Define Database window's Fields tab is displayed. For every table you want to add to the file, you need to return to the Tables tab. No need for too much detail right now. I just want you to take a look around.

Go to the upper-right corner of the window and click on the pop-up list next to View by. Since there's only one table in this file, you really can't tell what effect making a selection would have. But "creation order" and "table name" are pretty obvious. Look at the little arrows to the left of the words Contact Management in the Table Name column. If there were other tables in this file, you'd be able to reorder them by clicking on the arrows and moving the table names up or down in the list. If you did move one of the table names, the View by pop-up would change to "custom order." You can also sort the list

Part 1

by table name by clicking the words Table Name at the top of the column. Clicking the other column heads has no effect on sorting the table names. Notice that you can tell how many fields and records are in a table by looking in the second column. The third column lists the Table Occurrences in the graph, which will appear under the Relationships tab. We'll take a look at that in a minute.

Fields Tab

Click the Fields tab. You should see a window that looks like the one in Figure 2-2. A field is the basic storage area of information in any database. When we were investigating the Contact Management records in the previous chapter, you typed information into some of the fields.

SHORTCUT To bring up the Define Database window, use Command+Shift+D (Macintosh) or Ctrl+Shift+D (Windows). You'll be returned to the tab you were on when you last left Define Database.

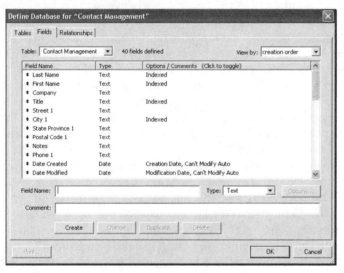

Figure 2-2
The Define Database Fields tab.

Next to the name of the table, Contact Management, in the Fields tab you'll notice that there are 40 fields in this table. The three column headings are Field Name, Type, and Options/Comments. The Type column matches the categories you'll find in the Type drop-down menu: Text, Number, Date, Time, Timestamp, Container, Calculation, and Summary. If you have a repeating field (which will be discussed in Chapter 4), you will see the number of field repetitions in this column as well. Options are determined in part by the field type and can be edited by selecting the field name and clicking the Options button.

The first field in your list is probably Address Type 1. Go to the upper-right corner of the window and click in the pop-up next to View by. The fields have been sorted by creation date. If you choose to sort by Field Name, the field names sort alphabetically. Try some of the other choices from the View by pop-up.

Now click on the words Field Name at the top of the first column. The field titles are once again sorted by name. Click it again and they sort in reverse alphabetical order. Notice that your last choice in the View by pop-up has now been replaced with "field name."

Click the Type column header. Click it again. I think you get the idea. Now click the Options/Comments column header. When you click this header, the column alternates between displaying options and comments. If the fields had any comments they would show up here. Click the column header again to redisplay the options.

NOTE Sometimes field names aren't long enough to be descriptive. You can use the Comment area to make whatever notes you like to indicate the purpose of the field. You enter this information in the Comment field in the lower portion of this screen. The Comment area will hold up to 30,000 characters per field. The only problem is that all your comments are on one line. Someday we may get a scrolling paragraph block. But for now a sentence or two should be enough.

When you place the cursor over the vertical line between the column headers, the cursor turns into a double-headed arrow pointing left and right. You can resize the columns by clicking and dragging on the line.

Use the scroll bar on the right to scroll down until you see a field with text in the Options column that extends off the window to the right. To view a little more of the text, you can expand the window by pulling on the knurled area in the lower-right corner of the window. When you leave the Define Fields window, FileMaker remembers the window size setting. The same applies to all the other resizable windows. Any changes are memorized globally, which means no matter what file you have open, each resizable window will be set the way you like it — even after closing and reopening the program. If you're using a Macintosh, you can use the left-right scroll bar to view more text. That is not an option on a Windows machine, but it's not a big issue when you can expand the window to fill your screen. If you click on the rows, you'll notice that the field name appears in the Field Name box and the Type pop-up changes to match the Type column. You can also double-click anywhere on one of the rows to see the Options field or to bring up the Specify Calculation window, or you can highlight a row and click the Options button. You might try that now, but be cautious not to permanently change anything in any of these windows. Feel free to make any changes you like and see what they'll do — as long as you make sure to click the Cancel button when leaving the Options area. That way none of your explorations will become permanent. Again, we'll deal more with field definitions in the next chapter.

After you're done exploring the Fields tab, click the Relationships tab.

Relationships Tab

The Relationships tab is where you build connections to other tables either in the same file or other files. If you're not already in the Relationships tab of the Define Database window, choose File, Define Database, and click the Relationships tab to open it. There are four Table Occurrences defined for this file already and three relationships between them. Your window may not be arranged exactly the same as the one in Figure 2-3, but it should have all the same elements.

I want to have you create a relationship so you can see just a little more about how it all works.

1. Click on the first icon under Tables/Relationships (there's an arrow point-ing to it in Figure 2-3) in the lower-left corner of the window. This opens the Specify Table window, from which you can add a table to the Relation-ships graph.

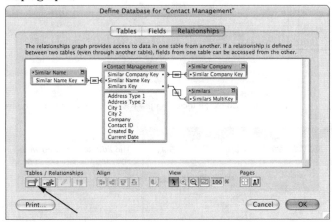

Figure 2-3
The Relationships tab showing the relationships in Contact Management.

2. In the Specify Table window (Figure 2-4), you can click on the **File** drop-down and choose **Add File Reference**.

3. Work your way back through the files on your machine until you find the Templates folder called Business - People & Assets and choose the **Asset Management** file. Highlight it and choose **Open**, or double-click it. You may still have to click **OK** to bring back up the Relationships tab, which should now look something like Figure 2-5 with the Asset Management table added.

4. To open the Edit Relationship window, click on the second icon under Table/Relationships, which lets you create a relationship. See Figure 2-6. The head of each column should say Table <unknown> at this point. Click on **<unknown>** on the left and choose **Contact Management**. On the right choose **Asset Management**. FileMaker automatically uses the names of the tables for the names of the Table Occurrences used in the relationship. If a second occurrence of the table is needed, you'll see a dia-log. But let's not go too far with this just yet. In fact, some of this next part may seem a little complex. For now, just follow along so you get a feel for the tools. Try to make it feel like play. Don't get bogged down in the details.

⌘ **TIP**   For a faster way to create relationships between tables, simply click on a field in one of the tables and drag to a field in the other table. The fields will move into the upper section of the table icons, and you'll see an equal sign on the line between the icons. You can double-click anywhere on the line between the icons to open the Edit Relationship window and make changes or just see the details.

Figure 2-4
The Specify Table window.

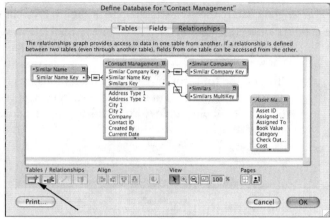

Figure 2-5
The Relationships tab including the Asset Management table reference.

Figure 2-6
The Edit Relationship window showing the two columns of the fields from both tables.

➲ **NOTE**   Normally, we'll be building relationships to other tables within the same file. But you need to know that you can also build relationships to other tables in other files.

⌘ **TIP**   You can build as many relationships to a table (or tables in other files) as you like and you don't have to use the name of the table. However, you are limited to using a different name for each Table Occurrence in the graph. Try to use names that will make sense to you in case you have to come back and work on it later. Also, some dialogs in FileMaker are not expandable, so it's a good idea to use the shortest names possible while still being descriptive.

The two lists are the names of fields in the two files. Choose First Name in the left column and try to choose Picture in the right column. You can't. Picture is grayed out because you cannot establish a relationship to it. The Picture field, a Container field, holds a different kind of data than most other fields and cannot be indexed. You can only establish relationships between the fields that appear in black.

⌘ **TIP**   When you place fields from a related table on a layout, four dots will appear before the field name. The four dots, or double colon, indicate that these are related fields from another table. FileMaker won't allow you to use a double colon in the name of a table reference.

Look at the check boxes near the bottom of the window. Deleting, creating, and sorting related records based on the relationship are all valuable options that are determined in this window. We'll get into the reasons for each in Chapter 6, "Working with Related Tables — Part 1."

Click Cancel twice to return to Browse mode in the file. Using relationships, you can either display the related data on your layouts or you can create Lookup fields that pull the data into your table. That way you can work with the data and even edit it without changing the original data in the source table.

Lookups

When you want to include information from another table (this could mean a table from another file) and have a copy of it brought into the current table, you would use a lookup. You might want to use a lookup in an ordering system where the price list might change, but where you want your current orders to reflect the prices at the time you made a quote to a customer. That way, no matter how the data changes in the Prices table, you'll always have a snapshot of what the price was at the time the invoice was created in the invoices table.

Lookups are created during the process of defining or editing a field by clicking the Options button and choosing the Auto-Enter tab. In order to have the data looked up from another table, you have to build a relationship to the other table. For that reason, FileMaker lets you define relationships while creating the field definition. See Figure 2-7.

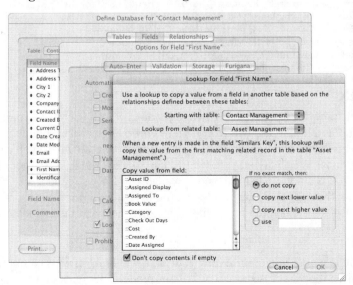

Figure 2-7
When creating a lookup from the Fields tab of the Define Database window, you can view, edit, and create relationships by clicking on the pop-up list in the upper-right corner of the window and selecting Define Relationships.

Related Data

The other way to use information from another table is to use related data. A field from another table can be placed on the layout of your current table. It can also be used in scripts and Calculation fields. Related data that is displayed on a layout can actually be edited from the current table, so you may need to take some precautions depending on what the information is and how it's being used. If the related goodies are line items of an invoice, it may be fine to be able to edit them. But you wouldn't want employees to accidentally change the prices in your products list. We'll discuss more on lookups and related data (and how to protect it) in Chapter 6.

Modes

Although I've spent all of this chapter up until now talking about various windows, most of the day-to-day work for the end user is done in the four modes. You can switch modes by choosing them from the View menu. You can also get to them from the Mode pop-up list near the lower-left corner of the window, as shown in Figure 2-8.

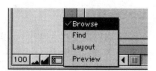

Figure 2-8
The Mode pop-up list in the lower-left corner is available in all four modes.

 SHORTCUT   Here are the keyboard equivalents for the four modes. I highly recommend that you memorize them. It takes about one second to press the keys and about five seconds to find the menus. Multiply that by the number of times you'll be using them each day and you'll be saving time. Your clicking muscles will thank you, too.

All except Preview are pretty intuitive. (The "P" is already used for the Print command.) I remember it by thinking "vUe."
- Browse mode — Command+B (Macintosh) or Ctrl+B (Windows)
- Find mode — Command+F (Macintosh) or Ctrl+F (Windows)
- Layout mode — Command+L (Macintosh) or Ctrl+L (Windows)
- Preview mode — Command+U (Macintosh) or Ctrl+U (Windows)

Browse Mode

In the last chapter, we learned that Browse mode is where you enter your name and phone number. It's where you view, enter, alter, and sort your data, where you can delete and hide records, and one of the places where you can format and choose which layout you want to use to view the data. Immediately above the Book is a pop-up list of layouts available in Browse mode. Depending on the user's access privileges, the user may or may not see a complete list of all the layouts in the file. Click on it now and take a look.

Layout Mode

Layout mode is where you choose how your data will look on your computer screen or when it prints. Choose View, Layout mode. Now, click on the Layout pop-up list above the Book. Layouts can be excluded from the pop-up that appears in all views except Layout mode — so in this file you have a longer list in Layout mode.

Notice that when you switch to Layout mode, the screen looks nearly the same except that there is no data. Using the pop-up list, go to the List layout. If you switch back to Browse mode, you'll see that Browse and Layout mode do not look the same for this layout. Also, take a look at the menus that appear under the headings across the top of the screen. Compare how they change when you switch between Layout and Browse.

➲ **NOTE** One of the hardest concepts to grasp has to do with the terminology used with layouts. I will often use the word "layout" to describe a particular view of the data. I might say, "When you're on this layout...." This gets confusing when I later refer to being in Layout mode where you can move objects around and control how the page looks. When I say, "Go to the List View layout," I mean choose List View from the Layout pop-up list above the Book. You could either be in Layout mode or Browse mode, depending on the context of the discussion. If you get this concept straight now, you'll be way ahead of the game.

When you look at the fields in Layout mode, you can see the field name. Switch back to the Form - Main Address layout and make sure you're in Layout mode. If you look at the field next to Phones, you'll see that the field name appears to be Phone1 instead of Phones. Double-click on that field to bring up the Specify Field window and you'll be able to see the field name there, too. Not only that, but you can actually change what field is in that position with the Specify Field window. Click Cancel to prevent accidentally changing the field.

Choose View, Show, Sample Data. Take a look at the fields now. When users see something that looks like real data when they're in Layout mode, it's easy to see how they might get confused and think they're in Browse mode. Choose View, Show, Sample Data to turn that option off before *you* get confused!

☒ **CAUTION** Before we move on, you had better acquaint yourself with the Undo command, which you can find directly under the Edit menu. If you move, change, duplicate, or delete a layout object accidentally, you can change it back with the Undo command, as long as you don't do anything else after making the mistake. Command+Z (Macintosh) or Ctrl+Z (Windows) will accomplish the same thing and is the convention for most other computer programs. If you really mess up a layout and haven't returned to Browse mode, go to the Layout menu and choose Revert Layout. All changes you've made will be discarded.

For an extra level of protection, you can make a change to FileMaker's Preferences. Windows users choose Edit, Preferences. Macintosh users click FileMaker Pro, Preferences. Now click the Layout tab. Uncheck the box next to "Save layout changes automatically (do not ask)." Now whenever you leave Layout mode you'll be asked if you want to save your changes. Although it can be a pain, the time will come when you thank the day you changed this setting. If you never goof, just go back into Preferences and check the box again.

Make sure you're still in Layout mode, then click on the First Name field label to the left of the First Name field. Notice that little squares appear on the corners of the label. These are the selection handles.

Selection handles refer to the small squares that appear at the corners or ends of layout objects. A line object only has two handles, while all other objects (even circles and ovals) have four. The color of the handles changes depending on the color of the background. If the color is solid, the object can be moved or reshaped. If the color is faded or speckled, the object is locked.

If you click and drag one of the handles on this or any other unlocked layout object, you can stretch or shrink the object. Since the handles are so small, positioning the tip of the selection arrow tool in just the right place may take a little getting used to. You can move an object simply by clicking on it and dragging. If the object is currently selected (the selection handles are showing), you can move it by clicking and dragging anywhere except the selection handles. Try to move one of the fields or the field labels now. Use Undo to put it back. Being able to make layouts look exactly the way you want is part of the power of FileMaker. I've seen some pretty amazing layouts from FileMaker users.

You can also copy and paste items, which is a valuable feature when adding a new field or heading to match the formatting of an object already on your layout. Just copy, paste, and change the text or field as needed. All the formatting is maintained.

☒ **CAUTION**   If a layout object is very large, its boundaries may extend off the screen and you may not see the handles. It is also possible to select and move multiple items when you don't intend to.

Layout Types

You may want to create some layouts from scratch, but it can be a tedious process. Fortunately, FileMaker has a number of preset layout types from which you can choose. FileMaker 5.0 introduced a Layout Assistant that simplifies the process even more. Although we'll get into how to use the Assistant in Chapter 9, "Creating New Layouts with the Layout Assistant," I want to acquaint you with the various layout types.

Choose Layouts, New Layout/Report to see a list of the layout types (see Figure 2-9). If you click on the name of each layout type on the left, over on the right you'll be able to see a miniature, grayscale version of what the layout looks like.

Click Cancel to exit the Assistant.

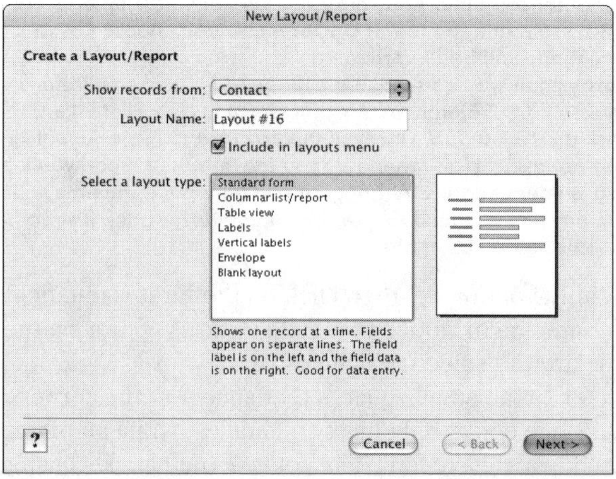

Figure 2-9
Choosing New Layout/Report under the Layouts menu brings up the first window of the Layout Assistant. The seven layout types are listed here.

Standard Form

In Standard form, items appear straight down the page — field title on the left and field on the right. While you're still in Layout mode, switch layouts and take a look at the Web Form layout. It is not a particularly easy or attractive way to enter data, but it's not a bad starting point.

Columnar List/Report

In this layout, field titles appear as column headings across the page. The data in a single record appears as a row, and all records appear in rows one after the other. One row can be as narrow as one field or as wide as the body in a layout.

You can look at any layout this way by choosing View, View as List. Go to the Form - Main Address layout and choose View as List. You may not be able to see the difference, but if you use the scroll bar on the right, you'll be able to scroll through the records. It's a little confusing so switch back to View as Form. Then go to the List layout for a more conventional example.

Table View

Table View is very similar in appearance and behavior to a spreadsheet. You can turn any layout into a Table View by choosing View, View as Table.

Labels

FileMaker has well over 100 predefined labels, and you can also make your own custom size label layouts. Switch to the Avery 5160 layout to look at an example.

Vertical Labels

Vertical labels are new for FileMaker 7. When you click to select them, the window says they're "adjusted to rotate Asian and Full-width characters so the labels can be used vertically." Once you make this choice, the windows that follow are the same as those for regular labels.

Envelope

Envelope layout is self-explanatory. You'll be making envelopes. There can be some issues formatting envelopes depending on the orientation of the envelope and the differences between various printers. But we'll talk about that briefly in Chapter 9, "Creating New Layouts with the Layout Assistant."

Blank Layout

You would use a Blank layout as a basis for building your own layout from scratch. This is the choice you would use to make a layout for buttons like on the Reports layout, to store icons, or for other special purposes.

Find Mode

This is the mode you use to ask FileMaker to search for records that contain specific data you're interested in. When you choose View, Find mode, you are presented with a blank record of whatever layout you are viewing so you can make your request. The blank form looks similar to a new blank record and is sometimes confusing to new users. Pay attention to the Find button in the Status area. That's the biggest clue that you're in Find mode. There is also a dashed border around data entry fields in Find mode that is slightly different from the dotted lines in Browse mode.

Preview Mode

Preview mode is a way to see what the page will look like when it's printed. Often your records will look the same in Preview mode as they do in Browse mode. However, sub-summaries that display summary data, variable data using special layout characters (like current date and page number), page margins, and column arrangements (like those used in mailing labels) will only appear on the printed page and in Preview mode. Conversely, some objects that appear in Browse mode can be made not to appear on a printout or in Preview mode.

Menu Commands

The fact that the menus change depending on what mode you're in certainly expands the possibilities of what you can do with FileMaker; it also makes it a lot more difficult to show you everything in this chapter. But there are a few more commands I'd like you to see now.

Sort Command

Choose Records, Sort Records. The Records menu only appears in Browse and Preview modes.

Notice the two columns. On the left is a list of fields in the current table. You can click on the pop-up at the top of the column to get a list of relationships to other tables. Choosing one of the relationships gives you a list of the fields in that table, so you can sort by that data, too. Not only that, but at the bottom of the pop-up is Define Database, which means you can make a new relationship right from here!

Double-clicking an item in the left column moves it to the Sort Order column on the right. Move a couple of the fields

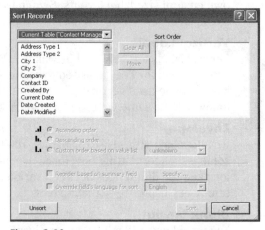

Figure 2-10
FileMaker's Sort Records window showing the field names in the left column and the list of sorting fields in the right column.

right now. To the left of the field names is a little double-pointed, vertical arrow. You can change the order of the fields by positioning the cursor over the arrow and using the old click-and-drag technique. Notice the radio buttons and other options at the bottom of this window. We'll spend more time on this in Chapter 8, "Finding and Sorting Your Data." Click the Cancel button to exit the window.

You also have the ability to access the Sort window by Control+clicking (Mac) or right-clicking (Windows) when in Browse mode. If you use these same keyboard/mouse shortcuts when clicking in a field, you'll see the context menu in Figure 2-11, which will allow you to sort by that specific field. This is a feature that will save developers a lot of time rather than having to create sort buttons at the top of columns in various list views. You can turn off this feature for selected users in the Passwords area by selecting Minimum in the Edit Privilege Set window. We will talk more about passwords in Chapter 21, "Keeping Your Data Secure."

Figure 2-11
FileMaker's Sort context menu.

🕐 **NOTE**   If you have a web site address stored in a field, you can also use these keyboard shortcuts to go directly to the web page. If you don't have a browser open, FileMaker will open it for you.

ScriptMaker

This is my very favorite part of FileMaker. You can make your files jump backward through hoops of fire with ScriptMaker! Choose Scripts, ScriptMaker to open the Define Scripts window. You'll see a list of scripts that were created in the template. You can change the order by dragging the double-pointed arrow. You can also make a script available under the Scripts menu by checking the box to the left of the script name or by highlighting the script name and checking the box labeled "Include in menu" above and to the right of the script name in the lower part of the window.

You can see the contents of a script by highlighting it and clicking the Edit button or by double-clicking on its name. Open the script called Go to Form Layout 1. (See Figure 2-12.)

The right column shows the programmed steps for the script. This script is not too hard and it even looks like English. Notice the list of available script steps in the left column. Use the scroll bar and take a look at what's available. Click Cancel to leave here without changing anything.

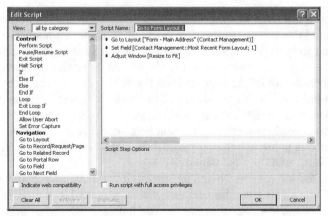

Figure 2-12
Script definition for the Go to Form Layout 1 script in the Contact Management template. Available script steps are in the left column and the actual script appears in the right column.

Double-click the Find script. There's a lot going on there! Don't worry; it won't be that bad once I show you around. We'll spend more time with ScriptMaker in Chapter 3, "Creating Your First Database," Chapter 8, "Finding and Sorting Your Data," and Chapter 14, "Automating Your Database with Scripts." As far as I'm concerned, ScriptMaker is the most powerful tool in FileMaker and it's a blast to work with. But then, I could be biased. Click Cancel twice to exit the script and ScriptMaker.

Accounts and Privileges

If nobody ever touches your computer, you're not on a network, and you don't use a cable modem, you should never have a need for access privileges and passwords. But as more and more of us sign up for always-on, fast Internet services, security is becoming an issue. You may not know it, but when you're online, depending on your other settings, you may be sharing your computer with the world! This is just a brief introduction; we'll really get into this in depth in Chapter 21, "Keeping Your Data Secure."

Choose File, Define, Accounts & Privileges. If you're working with the Contact Management file, you should see the window in Figure 2-13.

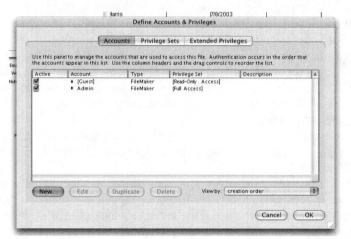

Figure 2-13
The Define Accounts & Privileges window showing the privilege check boxes.

To add access information for a new person, click on the New button in the lower-left portion of the screen. In the Edit Account window that appears (see Figure 2-14), you can type the person's name and password and select the privileges — full access, data entry, or read only — that he or she will have.

If you select other than full access, click on the Edit button to the right of the Privilege Set field. From this window, you can make a variety of decisions about what the user can do in the database. Feel free to investigate, but for now, delete any passwords you create. It might be disconcerting to lock yourself out of a file at this point. When you're finished, click the Cancel button, then the Discard button in the final window.

You may be asked for your name and password. If you have an account with full access, it will warn you if you haven't assigned a password. For now, just click Allow. If you've made any changes at all, you'll be asked for your account name and password. For now, if you haven't assigned a password for Admin, just enter Admin and click the OK button.

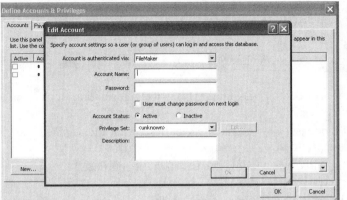

Part 1

Figure 2-14
The Edit Account window opens when you click the New button on the Define Accounts & Privileges window.

Summary

In this chapter I've continued your guided tour, giving you a chance to become familiar with various windows and menus as well as the four modes. We looked at the Define Database window's Fields and Relationships tabs, learned how to get around layouts, and found out about the various layout types. I also showed you the Sort, ScriptMaker, and Passwords windows. In Chapter 3, you'll actually start using what I've been showing you by creating a database from scratch. Don't worry, I'll be with you the whole way.

Q & A

Q When we were in Layout mode, I noticed the Status area had some new items. What are they?

A That is the Tool panel. These are the tools that control what you put on your layouts and how you change the appearance of layout objects. (The Tool panel is covered in Chapter 3.)

Q What are the little icons at the lower left of the window?

A Those are the Zoom and Status area controls. Click on them yourself and see if you can figure out what they do.

Workshop

In the Contact Management file, go to the Form - Main Address layout. Click the tabs for Mail Address, Second Address, and Related Contacts and notice that you actually change layouts and the fields that display in the lower third of that window. Go into Layout mode on each of the layouts and see what fields are there. Notice that the field names don't always match the labels that are near them.

Under Layouts, choose Duplicate layout. Above the Book, check to see that the new layout has the word "Copy" added to the end of it. Then, move various layout objects around to see how they're constructed. When you're done, choose Layouts, Delete Layout.

Review Questions

True-False

1. The only way you can view fields in the Define Fields window is by Field Name.

2. Lookups are good for maintaining historical information, such as price at the time of a sale.

3. Layout mode is a way to see, ahead of time, what the page will look like when it is printed.

4. In the Sort Records window, the fields on the left determine the order in which records will be sorted.

5. All of the menus on the menu bar stay the same, no matter what mode you are in.

Short Answer

6. How do you resize a window?

7. What is the purpose of the Relationships graph?

8. Name FileMaker's four modes.

9. What are the three ways in which you can switch from one mode to another?

10. Name the seven layout types.

11. From what other window can you access the Define Relationships window?

12. When you're in Form View in Browse mode and you switch to Layout mode, the screen looks very similar. Name at least two things that make Layout mode look different from Browse mode.

13. Name at least one way to sort the fields by field name when you're in the Define Fields window.

14. When you define a relationship, what table element do you use as the key to join the two tables?
    a) Body part
    b) Value list
    c) Field
    d) Layout
    e) Mode

Chapter 3

Creating Your First Database

Vocabulary

- Field borders
- Field options
- Size palette
- Specify Button window
- Tool panel
- T-squares

Objectives

1. Understand the database planning process.
2. Learn to create a new database file and define fields.
3. Become familiar with field options.
4. Work with the layout tools on the toolbars and in the layout Status area.
5. Understand placement of objects using object grids, T-squares, and arrow keys.
6. View and understand the Size palette.
7. Become familiar with ScriptMaker.
8. Learn to create a button to perform a script.
9. Become familiar with fields that have special requirements.
10. Learn the concept of breaking data into the smallest usable bits of information.

Introduction

Now that you have some idea of how to get around in FileMaker Pro, we can move to the next step: creating a database file from scratch. You'll find that it really isn't that difficult. And you'll learn some new tools and tricks along the way that will make creating a more complex system of interrelated tables a lot easier than you might imagine.

In this chapter, you'll learn about:

- Planning the database
- Creating and adding fields of various types
- Cleaning up your layouts with FileMaker's layout tools

■ Creating scripts

■ Attaching a script to a button

When you finish this chapter, you will have a fully functional, single-file database. You'll also have a pretty good idea about how to build a simple database of your own.

Planning the Database

There can be a lot of things to consider when planning a database. It all depends on what you intend to do with it, how many tables might be involved, how they'll interact, and who will be using it. Our planning in this chapter will be basic. We'll get into planning for a more complex system in Chapter 6, "Working with Related Tables — Part 1."

One of the great things about FileMaker Pro is that you can make changes to the structure of your files fairly easily. One of the worst things about FileMaker Pro is that the ease of change also makes it easy for users to skip the planning stage. If you learn to plan ahead now, you'll be ready when you work with more complex systems later on.

You can use the following questions as a checklist to work with every time you start a new database project. Although a more in-depth discussion will follow in Chapter 6, this list is the real deal.

1. What problem are you trying to solve?

2. If there is a current system (maybe even a paper system), what does it do well, and what could it do better?
   a. What new things would you add over the way the work has been done?
   b. If other people are involved, be sure to talk with them about the details of their job and why they do it the way they do. Also, ask them what they'd like to add.

3. What fields will you need to hold the necessary information?

4. Can the fields that are needed be divided into smaller sets? That will help determine what different tables you may need.

5. What will the relationships be between the tables? Are there other tables and files already in use from which you can draw information rather than creating new tables and files from scratch?

6. What do you want your screens (layouts) to look like? How many will you need and for what jobs?

7. If you will be sharing your data with other users:
   a. How will you need to adjust your layout for the way they'll be accessing it?
   b. How will you protect the data with FileMaker Pro security?

As you answer these questions, draw out a map of the files, tables, fields, and layouts and the connections between them.

Planning This Database

Since I'm going to lead you through the creation of this first database, we need it to be as simple as possible. For that reason, let's duplicate the functions of the old trusty Rolodex in the much easier-to-use form of a table in a FileMaker Pro file. We'll assume that no one else will be using the file. If we ask the seven planning questions listed above, we would answer them like this:

1. What problem are you trying to solve?
    A: I can't remember people's last names, so I can't find their cards when I need them.

2. If there is a current system (maybe even a paper system), what does it do well, and what could it do better?
    A: See answer to question #1.

    a. What new things would you add over the way the work has been done?
        A: I want to be able to make more notes about the person than I can get on a card. I might even want to type notes when I talk to people on the phone.

    b. If other people are involved, be sure to talk with them about the details of their job and why they do it the way they do. Also, ask them what they'd like to add.
        A: Not applicable.

3. What fields will you need to hold the necessary information?
    A: Name, address, four phone numbers, e-mail, web site, and notes.

4. Can the fields that are needed be divided into smaller sets? That will help determine what different tables you may need.
    A: It's really all one set.

5. What will the relationships be between the tables? Are there other tables or files already in use from which you can draw information rather than creating new tables and files from scratch?
    A: Not applicable. It's all on paper and will need to be entered by hand.

6. What do you want your screens (layouts) to look like? How many will you need and for what jobs?
    A: Just one screen. But, wait. I might want to send letters. That means envelopes and labels. And since my computer isn't always on, maybe I should print out a list (in alphabetical order) to keep by the phone. Well, maybe I should keep it simple for now. One screen.

7. If you will be sharing your data with other users:
    a. How will you need to adjust your layout for the way they'll be accessing it?
        A: Not applicable

    b. How will you protect the data with FileMaker Pro security?
        A: Not applicable

I made a drawing of what the screen might look like. It looks as if the screen space might be used a little more efficiently, but everything seems to be there. I think we're ready to give it a try.

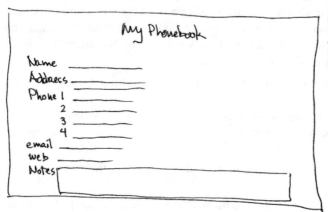

Figure 3-1
Hand drawing of what a phonebook file main layout might look like.

⊃ **NOTE**   I've made some choices in this design that will cause difficulties later on. We'll use FileMaker's easy change capabilities later in this chapter to adjust for them.

Creating the File

Open FileMaker Pro. When the New Database window appears, click the "Create a new empty file" radio button, then click OK. If the New Database window does not appear, choose File, New Database. The next window will prompt you for a filename and a place to save the file. Call the file My_Phonebook and save it in the My Documents folder or whatever other place you may decide to use to keep yourself organized.

☑ **BEST PRACTICES**   Notice that I used the underscore character in the filename. Using FileMaker Pro's Instant Web Publishing allows users to share files on intranets or the Internet. FileMaker also allows sharing by way of ODBC and JDBC. Browser and SQL languages don't take kindly to spaces. For the same reason, we will use similar methods for creating field names. Another option is to run words together using a capital letter at the beginning of each word (so-called "camel case"). An example of camel case would be ContactSerNum.

If you are absolutely positive you'll never use your files for these purposes, you don't need to worry about spaces. But once you start using FileMaker, you might be surprised what you'll end up doing with files you create! If you start using underscores or skipping the spaces altogether, you'll be way ahead of the game.

Adding Some Fields

1. When the Define Database window appears, choose the Fields tab if necessary and notice that the cursor is already blinking in the Field Name box and that Text appears in the Type drop-down list.

2. Type **Name** and click the **Create** button. Name is still highlighted in the Field Name box.

3. Now type **Address** and click the **Change** button. Drat! The Name field just became Address. It's better if you make this mistake now rather than later.

⌘ **TIP**   If a field name is highlighted in that lower part of the window, it can be overwritten. You don't need to do anything special except make sure you don't click the Change button unless you mean to change the name of the field.

4. While Address is still selected, type **Name** and click the **Create** button. It's okay, really. You do want to change it back this time.

5. Now type **Address** and click **Create**.

6. Now type **Phone1** (with no space) and click the Type drop-down list. Select **Number** and press the **Enter** or Return key this time instead of the Create button.

7. Type **Phone2** and press **Enter** or Return. FileMaker leaves the field type the same until you change it.

8. Go ahead and create the **Phone3** and **Phone4** fields.

9. Switch back to the **Text** field type and create the **Email**, **Web**, and **Notes** fields.

⌘ **TIP**   If you should accidentally click the Done button too early, you'll have to choose File, Define Database and go back to the Fields tab to finish creating your fields. When you're done, if the fields aren't on the layout, you'll have to use the Field tool to drag them there.

10. There are a couple more useful fields we haven't considered: a **CreationDate** field and a **SerialNumber** field. Add them now using **Date** and **Number** from the Type pop-up respectively.

11. Just for the sake of introducing it, add a **CreationTime** field and choose **Time** from the Type pop-up.

Adding Field Options

1. Click on the **CreationDate** field to highlight it, and then click the **Options** button.

2. Make sure the Auto-Enter tab is active and click the check box next to **Creation**. Also check that Date appears in the drop-down list next to Creation. That means that whenever you make a new record in this file, FileMaker will put the date in that field for you.

3. Click the **OK** button.

4. Click on the **CreationTime** field and do the same thing to it, except notice that Time already appears in the drop-down next to Creation. You can use that to keep track of changes made to individual records. Notice that there are other choices in the pop-up, even though you can't choose them.

5. Click **OK**.

(Just under the Creation check box is the Modification check box. If you were to create a field to keep track of when the record was last modified, you would check this box. Take a moment to look at the pop-up list beside Modification. You might find this field useful when you need to backtrack to find out when information was last entered.)

Another way to look at a field's options is to double-click the field name in the list. Try it. The Options window will open.

6. Select the **SerialNumber** field and click **Options**. Notice that you can use any of the choices from the pop-ups next to Creation and Modification this time, because a Number field does not have the specific limits that Date and Time fields have. But don't make any of those choices. Instead, click the check box next to **Serial Number**. FileMaker tells you that it will start by numbering the first record with a 1 and the serial number will increase by one for each new record. You can actually begin with any number you choose.

7. Click **OK**.

8. When you're done, the window should look something like Figure 3-2. Click **OK** to exit the Define Database window.

Figure 3-2
The Define Database window should look like this after you create the basic fields.

After the Define Database window closes, you will be returned to Browse mode and you'll see the results of your work. It doesn't look much like those colorful layouts in the template. That's one reason FileMaker, Inc., gives you the templates. It also gives you something to shoot for in your own designs. The Layout Assistant can help, too. For now, let's clean up our layout and see what we can make of it.

Cleaning Up the Layout

I like to see borders around fields on my layouts. To place borders around fields, follow these steps:

1. Choose **View, Layout mode**.

2. Click on the **Name** field (look for the selection handles) and choose **Format, Field Borders**.

3. When the Field Borders window appears, click the four borders: **Top**, **Bottom**, **Left**, and **Right**.

4. In the Format pop-up, make sure **Borders** is selected.

5. To the right of the word "format" are (from left to right) the color, pattern, and line width palettes. Click on the color palette and choose the black square.

6. Click on the pattern palette and choose the solid pattern (top icon of the second column from the left, which shows a solid black square overlapping a transparent square). Choose the **1 pt** line width from the third palette. You can see two of the palettes in Figures 3-3 and 3-4. Look in the Sample area at the right side of the window to see what the borders will look like. While you're at it, notice that the border tools are very similar to the line and fill tools in the Status area. Click **OK**. Then choose **View, Browse mode**.

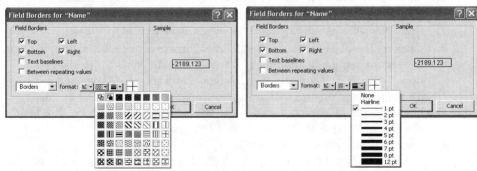

Figure 3-3
The Field Borders window showing the pattern palette pop-up.

Figure 3-4
The Field Borders window showing the line width palette pop-up.

One field down, 11 to go. This could get tiring. However, FileMaker provides you with a few shortcuts that will apply to this and many other layout chores.

7. Choose **View, Layout mode**. You can hold down the Shift key and click on each of the fields one after the other. But there's another, still faster way.

8. Click with your selection pointer outside of the group of fields, and drag diagonally until you have a dotted rectangle that surrounds all of the fields but not the field labels. See Figure 3-5. Now choose **Format, Field Borders** and give all 12 fields the same borders at one time. To see the results, click **OK**, then return to Browse mode.

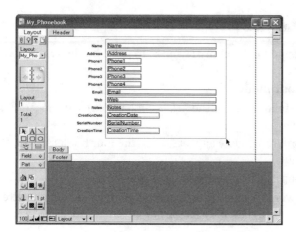

Figure 3-5
Using the Selection tool in Layout mode to surround a group of fields in order to format all of them at one time.

Format Painter

For an even faster method, try the Format Painter. With it you can copy the formatting of any FileMaker layout object and "paint" the format attributes onto any other layout object. It's a simple three-step process:

1. Go to Layout mode and click on an object that has the formatting you want to copy.

2. Go to the Standard toolbar (**View, Toolbars, Standard**) and click the **Paintbrush** icon. You can see it near the middle of the toolbar in Figure 3-7b. You can also access it by choosing Format, Format Painter.

3. Click on the object you want to change. You can also click and drag to form a selection rectangle around one or more objects you want to change.

As soon as you finish your selection, the tool is turned off. If you want to change a number of objects that are spread apart, you can lock the Format Painter by double-clicking the icon in the toolbar. Once you're done, you need to unlock it. In Windows, you select one of the buttons in the Status area. On a Mac, just double-click the icon again.

The Format Painter will not work on graphic objects you may have brought in from other applications. But it will work to change buttons, lines, and shaped object attributes, in addition to fields and text. You can also make it work across files. The only requirement is that both files be in Layout mode when you start. One of the files can even be hidden (minimized).

That all sounds great, but it won't pass on such attributes as value lists or number or date formats.

I would also advise exercising some caution against having more than one item selected when first clicking the brush. You don't know which attributes from which of the objects will be memorized by the brush.

You can move a color from a layout part (Header, Body, Footer, etc.) to a layout object, but not vice versa.

Duplicate

Another nice tool is the Duplicate command. Click on any layout object (or group of objects) to select it, then choose Edit, Duplicate to place an exact copy of your selection six pixels down and to the right of the original. This is very valuable when you want to copy a field that is formatted with numerous settings. If your selection was a single field, FileMaker presents you with the Specify Field window so you can even choose a different field if you like, which is usually exactly what you want to do.

Knowing that the new object's position is only off by six pixels means you can reposition it with six quick clicks on one of the arrow keys (see the upcoming "Arrow Keys" section). That puts it exactly vertical or horizontal of the original object, which is often just what you need.

A *layout object* is anything on a layout. That includes pretty much anything — fields, text, portals, lines, rectangles, ellipses, buttons, or images pasted into the layout.

 SHORTCUT   Using context menus, you can make a number of menu choices without having your mouse make the trip to the menu at the top of the screen. On the Macintosh, hold down the Control key while clicking on a layout object to access the menu. On the Windows platform, right-click on the layout object. See Figure 3-6. What's on the menu depends on the context of the mode and type of item on which you click.

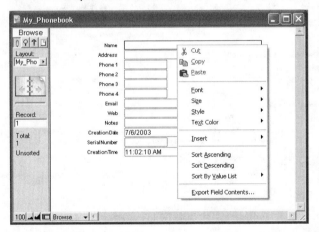

Figure 3-6
The contextual menu pop-up. Use this as a substitute for some menu choices at the top of the screen.

Now go back into Layout mode so I can show you some of the other layout tools.

Tool Panel

The Tool panel is the group of icons that appear in the Status area when you're in Layout mode. See Figures 3-7a through 3-7e for a word or two on each of the items. Notice that many of the items in the Tool panel are duplicated in the toolbars.

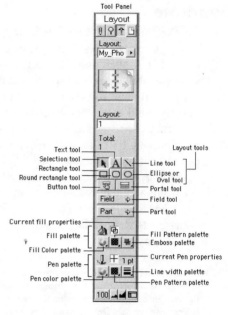

Figure 3-7a
Information about the Tool panel as seen in Layout mode.

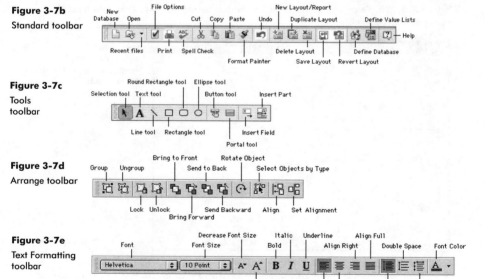

Figure 3-7b
Standard toolbar

Figure 3-7c
Tools toolbar

Figure 3-7d
Arrange toolbar

Figure 3-7e
Text Formatting toolbar

Layout Toolbars

By choosing View, Toolbars, you can decide whether or not any one of the toolbars appears across the top of the screen. The four toolbars in Layout mode are: Standard, Text Formatting, Arrange, and Tools. The Tools toolbar is duplicated in the Tool panel. All items in the other three toolbars except Select

Objects by Type (third from the right on the Arrange toolbar — see Figure 3-7d) are available from other menus and Tool panel icons.

⌘ **TIP**   The Allow Toolbars script lets you hide the toolbars and disable all the View Toolbars menu items. If you're working with an existing file and you can't get to the toolbars, they may have been turned off by a script. For more on scripts, see Chapter 14, "Automating Your Database with Scripts."

You can "tear off" the toolbars individually to position them anywhere on the screen that you like. If you move a toolbar near the side of the screen, it will reposition itself vertically. Once a toolbar is no longer docked near one of the edges of the screen, you can even resize it by pulling on the lower-right corner of its window. The only mode where all four toolbars are available is Layout mode.

Drawing Tools

Four of the six layout tools are known as drawing tools. They are the Line tool, Rectangle tool, Rounded Rectangle tool, and Ellipse or Oval tool. Click on each one in turn and draw shapes in the blank area on your layout. You can constrain how the objects are drawn (i.e., a square with the Rectangle tool or a circle with the Oval tool) by holding down Option (Macintosh) or Ctrl (Windows) while you draw.

With one or more of these objects selected, experiment with various items from the Pen palette and the Fill palette to see what effect they have. Switch to Browse mode to see what it really looks like. Return to Layout mode and delete what you've added while leaving the fields and field labels alone.

⌘ **TIP**   When you finish drawing an object, the Tool panel switches back to the Selection tool (the arrow). To lock a tool on, double-click it. When the tool is locked on Windows, the icon looks embossed on the toolbar. When it's locked on the Macintosh, the mark that represents the tool (a line, a rectangle, etc.) turns white on a gray background. This does not work for the Tools toolbar, just the Tool panel.

Whether a tool is locked or not, to switch between that tool and the Selection tool, press Enter (Macintosh) or Ctrl+Enter (Windows).

Object Grids

The Object Grids option is used to assist with consistent placement of layout objects. When you move objects on a layout with the Object Grids option turned on, they move in a jerky motion as they align to an invisible grid in six-pixel increments relative to where the object was when you started moving it. When you first create a file, the Object Grids option is turned on. You can turn the option on and off by choosing Arrange, Object Grids.

The word *pixel* is short for picture element. It's the smallest picture-forming unit on a computer screen. It's the size of the period at the end of a sentence or the dot on the lowercase letter "i."

NOTE   Both Mac OS X and Windows tout sub-pixel rendering, especially in antialiased text. Most of FileMaker deals with pixel-based rendering, except for antialiasing and hairline line widths. Hairline width lines on my screen look gray, but zoom to 400% magnification or print the layout and the line appears solid black but very thin.

SHORTCUT   You can turn the Object Grids option on and off by pressing Command+Y (Macintosh) or Ctrl+Y (Windows). You can temporarily override the effect of the grid by dragging objects while holding down Command (Macintosh) or Alt (Windows).

T-Squares

Another very handy layout tool is the T-Squares option found under the View menu. When it's turned on, a pair of intersecting lines appears on the layout, one horizontal and one vertical. This option is meant to imitate a tool used by drafters and architects for drawing perpendicular lines. The lines of the T-Squares option have a magnetic quality to them in that objects brought within six pixels of either line are pulled to it. Each line of the T-squares can be moved independently. This option can help greatly with positioning, resizing, and aligning layout objects.

Arrow Keys

When you don't want to haul out the T-squares and the object grids aren't giving you the results you want, you can get pixel-level control of layout object placement with the four arrow keys available on most keyboards. One press on an up, down, left, or right arrow key moves any selected object one pixel. Once I discovered the arrow keys shortcut, I find I use it more than any other object positioning option.

Size Palette

Choose View, Object Size to bring up the Size palette. Depending on your screen resolution, the Size palette is only about 1.5 by 2 inches, and it's free floating, so it's easy to miss. You may have to look around your screen to find it. Click on any layout object. The first four boxes in the Size palette tell you where the object is on the layout:

■ How far the left edge of the object is from the left border of the page. (This includes any fixed margins or the default paper size of the current printer.)

■ How far the top edge of the object is from the top of the layout (including margins).

■ How far the right edge of the object is from the left of the layout (including margins).

■ How far the bottom edge of the object is from the top of the layout (including margins).

The last two boxes show you how wide and how tall the object is, respectively.

You can change the unit of measurement from inches to centimeters to pixels by clicking on the two-letter abbreviation in the right column.

Here's how you can use the Size palette to resize fields:

1. Click on the **SerialNumber** field and copy the number in the width box of the Size palette (highlight the number in the box second from the bottom, then choose Edit, Copy).

2. Now click on the **CreationTime** field and notice the Size palette numbers reflect its size and position. Paste the SerialNumber field's width in the width box. (Highlight the number in the width box again, and choose **Edit, Paste** (Mac), **Paste Formatted Text** (Windows), or just use the keyboard shortcut, which is faster.)

3. Now click in any of the other size boxes, or press **Enter, Return,** or **Tab** instead.

Actually, you don't need to perform the copy-paste routine. You can simply type over any number in any box. It might seem a little tedious, but there are things you can accomplish with the Size palette that just can't be done any other way.

Another way to resize objects is with the selection handles. I discussed using them back in Chapter 2, but it's worth mentioning again here.

First, select a layout object, then click and drag one of the little black squares at the corner of the object to resize it. You can choose Edit, Undo Resize to change it back if necessary.

Alignment

1. Using the Selection tool, drag a rectangle around all the field labels to the left of the fields like we did for the fields themselves in Figure 3-5.

2. Make sure all of their selection handles are showing and select **Arrange, Set Alignment.** The Set Alignment window opens, as shown in Figure 3-8.

3. Click the different radio buttons (don't click on the OK button) and observe the changes in the Sample area in the lower-left corner of the window.

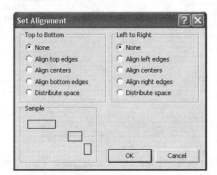

Figure 3-8
The Set Alignment window is used to align multiple layout objects.

4. Once you have some idea of what this does, choose **None** in the Top to Bottom column and **Align left edges** in the Left to Right column, and click **OK**. Notice how the left edges of the field labels now line up.

5. Choose **Arrange, Set Alignment** again, set the Left to Right column to **Align right edges**, and click **OK**. Notice that now the right edges of the field labels line up.

6. Go back into the dialog one more time, choose **Align top edges** in the Top to Bottom column and **None** in the Left to Right column, and click **OK**.

7. Since you would not want your objects to line up in this way, choose **Undo** from the Edit menu (or press the key combination).

This can be a very helpful tool for times when you've been moving a lot of layout objects around and need to clean it up quickly. Just don't get going so fast that you can't use Undo when you really need it. The alignment functionality only works on the selected set of objects and how they align with each other. It has nothing to do with where they will end up on the page.

Locking Objects

You may want to lock various layout objects to keep them in place while you're working with other objects, or to prevent other people from changing your layouts. Aside from preventing movement, locking prevents changes to an object's attributes (borders, fill, text style).

You can lock a selected object by choosing Arrange, Lock, or by pressing Ctrl+Alt+L. You can unlock an object by choosing Arrange, Unlock or by pressing Ctrl+Alt+Shift+L. This only locks the object in Layout mode and has no effect over data entry in Browse mode. Also, locking does not require passwords.

Using the tools I've just described, move the layout objects around until they look like the layout in Figure 3-9. Resize the CreationDate field with the arrow keys or the Size palette.

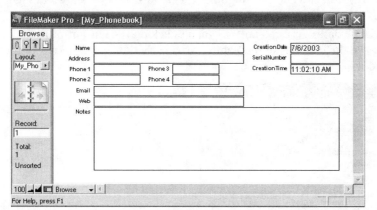

Figure 3-9
My_Phonebook in Browse mode after the layout has been redesigned to take better advantage of screen space.

We'll be looking at efficient layouts in Chapter 16, "Designing Your Screen Layouts." But examine this redesigned layout and start to think about why this makes better use of the screen space.

Part 1

Adding Some Data

Go back into Browse mode. Create a new record (Records, New Record) and enter the following information.

Name	Address	Phone1
Rich Bailey	123 Main St., Wilson, OH	333-4444
Bobby Joe Gentry	1919 Choctaw Ridge, Tallahassee, FL	333-1232
Richard Harris	500 MacArthur Park, Los Angeles, CA	121-9765

We'll do some experiments with this data in just a few minutes.

Adding a Script

In the last chapter, we looked at some scripts in the Contact Management template. You're going to create a couple of fairly easy scripts right now.

Simple New Record Script

To create a script that will make a new record, follow these steps:

1. Choose **Scripts**, **ScriptMaker**.
2. When the Define Scripts window appears, click on the **New** button.
3. In the Edit Script window, New Script will be highlighted in the Script Name box (see Figure 3-10). Type **New Record**.
4. Scroll down the left column until you see the Records heading and double-click **New Record/Request** (or highlight it and click the Move button).

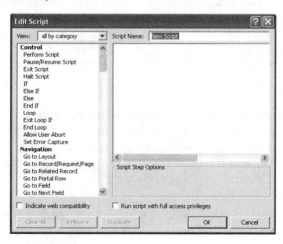

Figure 3-10
The Edit Script window.

⌘ **TIP** If you know the heading for the script step you want, choose it in the View pop-up at the top of the script steps column. Then you don't have to scroll up and down the list.

I've gotten so that I know where most script steps are by heart, so I can just click the right number of times on the gray bar just above the bottom arrow. That moves down the list one full screen at a time.

5. Click **OK**, then click **OK** again.
6. Click the Scripts menu and choose the **New Record** script. Voilà! A new blank record.

Notice that you can also access that script by pressing Command+1 (Macintosh) or Ctrl+1 (Windows). Of course, you can also create a new record by choosing Records, New Records or with the key combination. There are other reasons you might want to do this with a script. Just wait until you see what else you can do!

Simple Delete Record Script

To create a delete record script, follow these steps:

1. Choose **Scripts, ScriptMaker**. Click on **New**.
2. When the Edit Script window appears, type **Delete Record**.
3. Scroll down the left column until you see the Records heading. Double-click **Delete Record/Request**.
4. Click **OK**, then click **OK** again.
5. Click on the **Scripts** menu and choose **Delete Record**. Make sure you're not deleting one of the records with data in it. If you're not sure, choose **Cancel** and take a look first. Of course, you can delete a record by other methods. But, hey, we're learning something here.

Go back into ScriptMaker and double-click the Delete Record script. Notice the brackets at the end of the step? Click on the step. Just above the Duplicate button in the bottom center of the window is an Options area. Click in the check box next to "Perform without dialog" and notice that the brackets in the script step get filled in. That can be very handy for scripts that are supposed to run automatically for other purposes, but it can be dangerous if you're working with live data. Uncheck the box now, click OK, then click OK again. That way, whenever the button is clicked, any user will have the option to cancel before records disappear from the file.

Simple Find Script

To create a Find script, first locate the record for which you want to create the script. Enter Find mode, type Richard in the Name field, and click the Find button in the Status area (or press Enter or Return). Richard's record appears. Notice the new information in the Status area.

Do another find for Rich. Now you get two records.

We create the script as follows:

1. Choose **Scripts, ScriptMaker**. At the Define Scripts window, select **New**.
2. When the Edit Script window appears, type **Find Rich**.
3. Under Navigation, double-click **Enter Browse Mode** and **Go to Layout**.
4. Under Found Sets, double-click **Perform Find**. Click the **Specify** button (above the OK button) to open the Specify Find Requests window. Just click **OK** to verify the find criteria — My_Phonebook::Name:Rich — as seen in Figure 3-11.

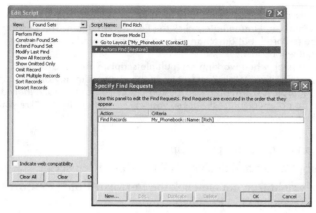

Figure 3-11
The Specify Find Requests window showing the details of the Perform Find script step.

5. When you return to the script you should see the word Restore has appeared in the brackets after Perform Find and a check mark next to Specify find requests. FileMaker remembers any Find you perform manually prior to adding the Perform Find script step, even if you don't click the Specify button. Of course, it won't perform that specific find unless the box is checked. But any time you click the Specify button later on, you can see what criteria were found manually and you can change them if you want to so you can include them in your script.

6. In the right column, click once on **Go to Layout**. Above the OK button next to the word Specify is a pop-up list of all the layouts in our file, as well as some other options for selecting layouts. (Currently there is only one layout.) Click on whatever appears there (probably "original layout") and choose **My_Phonebook**. When you're done, your window should look like the one in Figure 3-12.

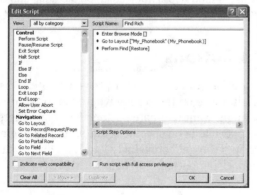

Figure 3-12
The Edit Script window showing the script Find Rich.

7. Click **OK**, then **OK** again.

8. Choose **Records**, **Show All Records** and notice the details in the Status area.

9. Click on the **Scripts** menu and choose **Find Rich**. The two records appear. What's great about this is that you can build a complex find request and ScriptMaker can memorize it.

⊃ **NOTE**   If you ever accidentally delete one or more steps when editing a script, click the Cancel button and immediately click the Edit button again. The previous set of steps will be restored, but any changes you may have made to the script since you opened it will be lost.

   If you really mess up when working on multiple scripts, you can click the Cancel button before exiting ScriptMaker and none of the changes in any of the scripts will be saved — regardless of whether you clicked OK as you exited each individual script. That could be potentially disastrous, so you will see one of those, "Are you sure..." dialogs first.

To change the find request for this script:

1.   Go into ScriptMaker and double-click the **Find Rich** script.

2.   In the upper right box, double-click the **Perform Find [Restore]** step to bring up the Specify Find Requests window.

3.   Click the single request to highlight and click the **Edit** button.

4.   Highlight the single find request in the upper part of the window.

5.   In the Criteria area, change Rich to **Richard** and click the **Change** button.

6.   Click **OK**, and **OK** again.

7.   Rename the script **Find Richard** and click **OK** and **OK** again to return to Browse mode.

8.   Choose **Records, Show All Records**, and run the script. Now we're talkin'! You could have separate scripts for Find Rich and Find Richard, not to mention Show All Records.

⊃ **NOTE**   For users of previous versions of FileMaker Pro, the Keep/Replace dialog does not appear anymore. Instead, you'll be working with details in the specific script steps. However you can simulate the old method by manually performing your find, sort, export, import, and/or print. Then go into the script or scripts you want to change. Double-click the desired step(s) from the list on the right, and click the Specify button to check your request. Delete the old step and move the new one into place.

Assigning Scripts to Buttons

You can place buttons on your layouts that run scripts you create. This puts the power of the scripts right there on the screen where you or your users can see them at a glance. You might want to create buttons for your scripts so that only certain features will be available on specific layouts. As you begin to use more scripts, the list of scripts can get confusingly long, and clarity should always be one of your goals. Using buttons can help with clarity.

1.   Enter Layout mode.

2.   Click on the **Button** icon in the Status area. It's the icon below the Rectangle tool, the one with the finger pointing at a button. As you move the mouse pointer over to your layout, it turns into a crosshair. Find a blank area on the layout and click and drag until you've drawn a rectangle about an inch square. The Specify Button window appears with Do Nothing highlighted in the left column.

3. Click on **Perform Script** in the left column. Then click on the **Specify** button in the Options area. When you do, you'll see a new window, Specify Script Options.

   Before we move on, I want you to notice the "Optional script parameter" box near the bottom of the Specify Script Options window. If you click the Edit button you'll see FileMaker's Specify Calculation window. This is a powerful new tool for FileMaker Pro 7 that allows a single script to work differently depending on choices you make here. We won't talk about it in detail until Chapter 14, but I wanted you to know where to find out more in case you were getting curious.

4. Select **Find Richard** and click **OK**. You are back on the Specify Button window. The box next to "Change to hand cursor over button" has been checked. This will make the cursor turn into a hand whenever it's over the button in Browse mode. Click **OK**.

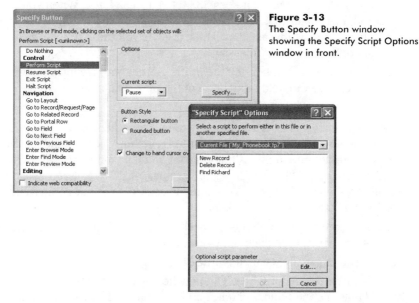

Figure 3-13
The Specify Button window showing the Specify Script Options window in front.

5. You should now be back in Layout mode with the cursor blinking in the button you just made. Type **Find Richard**. FileMaker expands the button to accommodate the words and the current font size. If you don't like the way it handles the text, you can resize the button or the font. Click somewhere off the button and resize it if you need to.

6. Go to Browse mode and try it out. **Choose Records, Show All Records** and try the button again.

7. Create another button and attach the New Record script to it. You get the idea.

⌘ **TIP**   If you need to edit the text on the button, click on the Text tool (the A icon), then click on the button. The text cursor will begin to flash in the button. Type away.

Special Situations

There may be situations in which the field type or the structure of a field does not accommodate your needs. For example, a field for phone numbers is set up as a Number field and does not allow you to search for a phone number prefix. Another example is a situation in which a field that contains customer names needs to broken into two fields to allow you to use the first name in a letter's salutation or sort the field by last name.

1. Do a find for 333 in the Phone1 field. This results in an error message.

2. Click **Cancel**.

    We know the numbers are definitely in the file, so what's wrong here?

    FileMaker looks at Number fields differently from the way it looks at Text fields. We found Richard even when we were only looking for Rich. But because Phone1 is formatted to be a Number field, FileMaker ignores the dash. That means it sees 333-4444 as 3,334,444. When you ask for 333, FileMaker looks in Phone1 and says, "I have numbers in the millions, but nothing as low as 333." Thus, it gives you the "No records match this set of find requests" message.

3. To find phone numbers by the prefix go back into Define Database, Fields and change the field type for all of the phone numbers to **Text**. Then try the find again.

Now look at the Name field. It's okay to have one field for the name, but there are some limitations. You might want to create form letters and include the person's first name in the salutation. But you'll be forced to use "Dear Rich Bailey" instead of "Dear Rich." Not very personal. Also, if you ever want to print out a phone list for times when you can't get to your computer, you'll probably want to sort by last name.

1. To create two name fields, go back into Define Fields and change Name to **NameFirst**, then click the **Change** button.

2. Create a new field called **NameLast**.

3. Go back to Layout mode. The new field may have appeared on the layout. If not, use the Field tool (click and drag on the Field icon) to place the NameLast field on the layout. You may have to change the formatting of the field so that it matches that of the other fields on the layout. Remember, you can use the Format Painter tool.

4. Now go back to Browse mode and go through the records, moving the last names into the NameLast field.

⌘ **TIP**   Break the data into the smallest *usable* bits of information that make sense. In addition to NameFirst and NameLast, when it comes to ways of dealing with names, you may see databases with fields for Salutation (Mr., Mrs., Ms., etc.), Title (Dr., Prof., etc.), NameMiddle or NameMI (for Middle Initial), and Nickname, as well as complex considerations for spouses with different last names and people living together.

☑ **BEST PRACTICES** The reason we're using NameFirst and NameLast is so the field names having to do with name will be grouped together when the field list is sorted by field name. This method is very useful when you use the Sort Order window and when importing and exporting records.

The same goes for address information: AddrStreet, AddrCity, AddrState, etc. Since the field labels on the layouts will be different, users may be a little lost the first time they need to work with the actual field names. But most users understand exactly why you name the fields this way the first time you show them.

Consider companies with multiple contact people in different departments. Do you list the company as the primary contact and create many fields to accommodate all the different people, mailing addresses, and phone numbers? Or do you make each person a separate contact with many records that have the same company name? (Answer: probably the latter.)

Look at the Address field again. There's sure a lot of information there that should be separated. Not to mention, where's the zip code? Once more, go back to the Fields tab of Define Database and add AddrCompany, AddrCity, AddrState, and AddrZip fields. And after our experience with the phone numbers, make the zip code into a Text field. What about the additional four numbers used in zip codes now? We should make a separate field for that as well, and call it AddrPlusFour. When you're done, use your newfound skills with the layout tools to move the fields around until your layout looks like the one in Figure 3-14. Remember to rename the field labels so they make sense. Then go back to Browse mode and break the address data into the right fields. It'll take a little while, but you'll be developing your skills.

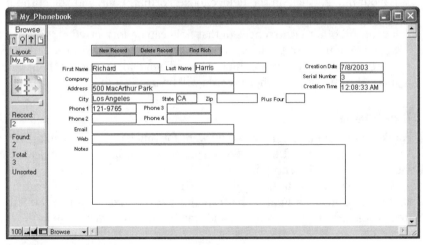

Figure 3-14
The updated layout with changes to accommodate new fields and the buttons.

Summary

We did a lot in this chapter. You've learned about planning a database, creating the fields, and moving fields around with the layout tools. You also created a few scripts and attached them to buttons. And you learned some important things about formatting fields. I'll bet you can feel the momentum building. Notice that as we got going, I didn't have to tell you every little move to make. I've gone from using the phrase "Go to the View menu and choose Layout mode" in the first chapter to "Go to Layout mode." And you knew what I was talking about and how to do it. You're gettin' good at this!

Q & A

Q What if I decide I want to change what a button does?

A Go to Layout mode and double-click the button. You'll see the Specify Button window again. You can assign the button to a different script or some other function in the list.

Q What if I want to change the text that's on a button?

A Use the Text tool. That's the icon with the letter "A" on it in the Status area. Then click on the button and type away.

Q What if I don't like the font that appears in a field?

A To permanently change the default font for the field in all records, go to Layout mode. Click on the field, choose Format, Font, and select the font you want. That will only affect the way that particular field appears on that layout. All other occurrences of that field can be formatted separately.

If you only want to change how a particular bit of text looks in a particular record in Browse mode, highlight it. Then choose Format, Font and make the change. All other records will be unaffected.

Workshop

Think of at least one field you would want for this file that I haven't given you. Add it using the correct field type and put it on your layout in a logical place with a field label to identify it.

Create a script with the single step Show All Records. Then create a button that uses it. Click Find Richard and look at the information in the Status area. Then click your new button and watch the numbers change in the Status area.

Review Questions

True-False

1. The best way to begin a new database is to create a new database file with all of the tables and fields you think you might need.
2. You can move and resize objects by using the various boxes in the Size palette.

3. You can move a layout object by clicking and dragging its handle.

4. A zip code field should be defined as a Number field.

5. You can define fields to automatically enter the date or time a field is created or modified.

Short Answer

6. Why would you not want to include spaces in your database filename?

7. Why might it be a good idea to have separate fields for first name and last name?

8. How do you access the ScriptMaker window?

9. How do you make a button perform a script?

10. Name the four toolbars that are available in Layout mode. Which of these are also available in Browse mode?

11. Aside from the button we made, name at least one other way to create a new record.

12. How would you go about drawing a square with a five-point black border that has the inside filled with red?

Using FileMaker Pro

Chapter 4

Creating a New Database

Vocabulary

- Calculation result type
- Field format
- Field type
- Open database structure
- Repeating field

Objectives

1. Understand field-naming rules, conventions, and considerations.
2. Become familiar with the eight field types.
3. Define a simple Calculation field.
4. Define a Summary field.
5. Understand the concept of Global fields.
6. Become familiar with the concept of Repeating fields.
7. Learn to format Date and Time fields.
8. Become familiar with text formatting options.

Introduction

In previous chapters, I showed you how to work with one of the template files and what to do when creating a database from scratch. In this chapter, I'll show you some things to consider when deciding which option to choose.

Then we'll dig deeper into the mysteries of fields — field-naming recommendations, details about the field types, what fields are used for, and how to format them in a layout. And, of course, we'll do all this while working in real files.

Considerations

In the last chapter, I gave you a questionnaire that you'll be able to use from now on to help you decide what elements you'll need in your database. Once you've done that, a good next step is to see if you have any files that already contain the elements you need.

Predefined Databases

Aside from the template files provided with your copy of FileMaker Pro, there are numerous commercial products already developed in FileMaker that may provide some or all of what you need. I've listed a number of resources for ready-made solutions in Appendix B and have also included a few in the downloadable files. Then the problem is how to find what you need, and how to know if it's any good.

Many companies have web sites that offer free downloads of limited versions of their products. You can get a copy, work with it for a while, and decide if it will work for your situation. An important consideration is whether the solution is open or not. An *open* database is one where the developers allow you to have full access to the files so you can add your own fields and scripts. That way you can make your own changes and integrate the commercial files with files you've created.

Freeware and shareware databases are available for download as well. Again, look in Appendix B and in the downloadable files.

Even if there is an existing solution, you may still have solid reasons to build something from the ground up. I had a client ask me recently what it would take to have me create an accounting system for them. Their needs were fairly simple, but it still cost more to build their bare-bones files than it would have to purchase a premade, full-featured system. However, with a custom system they have exactly what they want with the capability to change it anytime they choose. Cost is not the only consideration.

As you work more with FileMaker Pro, you will build up a library of your own files that you will be able to use as templates for new work.

Creating Your Own Database

If you followed along with all the steps in the last chapter and did the exercises at the end, you have a rough idea of what it takes to start a file from scratch. Of course, at this point, it's not exactly second nature. Remember how difficult driving a car was the first time — now you can pretty much do it without thinking. As you develop more skill, building databases in FileMaker will become not only more comfortable but also fun as well. It's like doing a jigsaw puzzle except that when you get all the pieces to fit, you'll have something that will be much more useful.

You can also start your files from the ground up and use layout elements from the templates. All the background layout objects can be cut and pasted for use with your fields. You can even copy the fields, but you'll have to redefine them in your new file. As you learn more about layout tools, you will find that there is a faster way than trying to create all those elements yourself.

And, of course, the Layout Assistant can be a great help. See Chapter 9, "Creating New Layouts with the Layout Assistant," for more on that topic.

A great feature of FileMaker Pro is the ability to import scripts. As much as I like creating scripts, there's no point in creating the same script over and over by hand. You can create a library of commonly used scripts and simply import them into your new files. This can be a big time-saver. We'll examine this in greater detail in Chapter 14, "Automating Your Database with Scripts."

What Are Fields?

A field is the area on a layout where the data goes. A field can also contain information that's calculated. In the My_Phonebook file that we created in the previous chapter, we tried to get the fields down to the most basic bits of information we might want to search for and sort on. On the other hand, with a field like the Notes field, you can store a lot of useful information that doesn't need to fit in a one- or two-word field. And don't forget that a Container field can store pictures, movies, OLE objects (Windows only), or sounds.

⊃ **NOTE** OLE objects allow you to use information from other applications right in FileMaker. OLE stands for Object Linking and Embedding. With it, you can place things like spreadsheets, images, and sounds in Container fields. While support for OLE objects is built into the Mac system, it is not supported for the Mac version of FileMaker Pro 7. In Windows applications, the OLE objects will automatically update from the originating application.

Creating a Field

Open up My_Phonebook, then choose File, Define Database, and click the Fields tab. To clarify the process I introduced in the last chapter, to create a field you:

1. Type a field name.
2. Choose a field type.
3. Click the Create button, or press Enter or Return.

Remember that after you have a field name and type, you can simply duplicate the field. Highlight the field you want to copy and click the Duplicate button. FileMaker automatically appends the word "Copy" to the end of the name and you can change it in almost any way you like.

About Field Names

There are some considerations to take into account when naming fields.

You cannot define fields with the same field name twice in the same table. That is not the same as having the same field appear on different layouts or even having multiple copies of the same field on the same layout.

When I gave you field names in the last chapter, I left out the spaces between words. I did that for the same reason I used the underscore character in My_Phonebook. If the file might ever be accessed using a browser, the HTML web language doesn't do well with spaces. Also Open Database Connectivity (ODBC) doesn't work properly with spaces in field names, and SQL keywords would also be a problem. See Chapter 20 for more information about FileMaker and ODBC.

Try to choose field names that will be short, yet descriptive. One of the reasons is that long field names in combination with relationship names can be difficult to read quickly in some of the windows. But keep clarity in mind. Remember that other people may have to fix something in your files when you're not around. You might even have to work on the file sometime in the future. Use names that make sense. Some of my old (and occasionally more recent) files are a little embarrassing to look at in that regard. I had shortened the field names using acronyms that meant something at the time but lost their meaning after a few months had passed.

When you name fields, tables, or files, you should avoid using any of the characters or items listed in any of the areas above the Formula box in the Specify Calculation window. Specific characters include & / " * ¶ - ( ) + = ≠ > < ≤ ≥ ^ . ; (semicolon) :: (two colons in a row) ' (apostrophe) , (comma). It's okay to use the colon symbol, but I try to avoid it since it is a special character and may cause confusion with the double colon. I often create Calculation fields that use the names of two other fields. For those, developers often use the " | " (pipe) character between the fields they're combining. For example, if I were to combine NameCompany and ID I might call it NameCompany|ID. That's because you can't use the & symbol or the word "and" in a field name if it might be used somewhere else in a calculation.

It probably sounds like a lot to worry about. But, in general, you won't be using symbols and function names in your field names if you're using good descriptive titles in the first place. FileMaker will warn you if you use illegal characters in a field name.

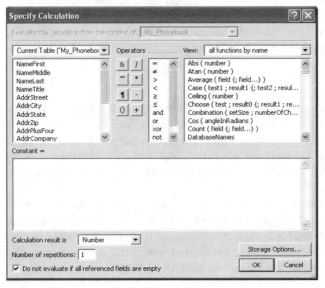

Figure 4-1
The Specify Calculation window showing operators and functions lists, and the mathematical and text operators buttons. Avoid using these symbols and functions when creating field, table, and file names.

The Eight Field Types

In the previous chapter, I had you add Text, Number, Date, and Time type fields to your file. FileMaker also provides Timestamp, Container, Calculation, and Summary field types. I want to give you the lowdown on all of them. In Chapter 10, "Keeping Your Data Clean and Neat," I'll discuss the Auto-Enter, Validation, and Storage field data entry options that can be accessed from the Fields tab.

Text Field

As we saw in the previous chapter, sometimes you will use a Text field for data you wouldn't expect, like phone numbers. You can also use it to store numbers that begin with one or more zeros. (If you were using a Number field, FileMaker would ignore leading zeros.) What I didn't tell you is that a Text field can hold up to one billion characters. You read that right! That's roughly equivalent to 500,000 pages of text. That's up quite a few pages from File-Maker's former six-page limit. I really can't imagine anyone ever needing that amount, but if you get too much text in there, you'll get the following warning: "Sorry, this operation could not be completed because you have reached text block limits." I'm betting your brain or your hard drive explodes first, though!

Number Field

You can store up to 255 characters in a Number field. FileMaker ignores any non-numeric characters, though it does recognize a period as a decimal point. It also interprets a leading dash or a leading open parenthesis to mean a negative number. You cannot use a return/carriage return in a Number field. FileMaker just plays the operating system beep sound when you try.

FileMaker Pro 7 has been updated to provide an amazing level of precision with numbers. It will handle up to 400 digits to the left and right of the decimal point with complete accuracy. That puts it on par with Mathematica.

Even though FileMaker may display numbers in scientific notation, you cannot type scientific notation directly into the field. For example, even though FileMaker might show 8,877,780,000 as $8.8878e+09$, it would interpret it as 88,879.

Date Field

A Date field accommodates dates only. When you enter a date in Browse mode, it all goes on one line (no returns allowed). Although you can format how the data displays, you must enter the date as numbers in the form: month, day, year. Actually, the year portion is optional. But with all the lessons we've learned about Y2K, you should get into the habit of entering the year in four-digit format.

Normally, people use the slash (/) or the dash (-) character to separate each item. But you can actually separate them with any non-numeric characters. You can get pretty wild here, but you must use the same character in place of the slash. If you try two different separators, you'll trigger a warning. Try a few experiments in the CreationDate field.

Time Field

Time fields hold time data only and it goes on one line, too. You have a lot of freedom in how you enter the time: hours, hours and minutes, or hours, minutes, and seconds. Again, use matching, non-numeric characters to separate the numbers. The standard is a colon (:). If you enter characters or times that are incorrect or too large, you get a warning. You might try putting some correct and incorrect times in the CreationTime field to see what happens. Oddly enough, you can put some numbers in the field that would seem wrong, but will still work. For example, try 32766 or 1:32766.

You can use 12- or 24- (often called military time) hour format. If you use the 12-hour format, you only need to add PM for times after noon. FileMaker assumes you mean AM if the number for the hour is 0 to 11.

Timestamp Field[7]

This is a new feature for FileMaker Pro 7. It combines the date and time into one field. It keeps track of the date and time in increments of one second starting from the date 1/1/0001. If you plan on performing calculations on the data in this field type, keep in mind that there are 86,400 seconds in a day.

⌘ **TIP** When you're working on a network, keep in mind that everyone's computer clocks are not likely to be synchronized. A record may be created on one person's machine at a real time of 1:00 PM and another might be created at real time 1:05 PM. Yet the database may show the 1:05 PM record being created at 12:58 because that's the time setting on that computer. To avoid any mix-ups of that kind, when you create a Time field, instead of using Auto-Enter Creation Time, check the box next to "Calculated value." When the Specify Calculation window appears, choose Get (CurrentHostTimestamp). When you click OK, check the box next to "Do not replace existing value for field (if any)." For you old-timers, this will work even for Server, which now has its own calculation engine and will pass the server time down to the user. (You can use Get (CurrentHostTimestamp) in scripts, too.)

Container Field

Container fields can hold sounds (i.e., music), pictures, movies, PDF files, and just about any other type of file you can think of — including other FileMaker files. This makes FileMaker a terrific document-tracking tool.

With my music background, I've had a lot of fun with Container fields. I store songwriting ideas in a Container field and then write a description of the idea or the lyrics in a Text field for easy searching. I've also stored scanned photographs with a description of where to find the film and negatives. If you are a Mac OS X user, starting with version 6.0 you can import a batch of photos directly from a digital camera into FMP fields. Take a look at the downloadable files for an example of everything except the OS X import.

1. Go into Define Fields and create a Container field called **Pic**.

2. Exit Define Fields and go to Layout mode.

3. If the new Pic field doesn't appear automatically, use the Field tool to place a copy somewhere on the layout.

4. Now switch to Preview mode and choose **Edit, Copy**.

5. Go back to Browse mode, click in the **Pic** field, and choose **Edit, Paste**. The result will depend on how the field is formatted as a graphic, but you can do some pretty impressive tricks by copying and pasting a page in Preview mode. And just wait until you start putting photos of people or QuickTime movies in a Container field!

Part 2

⌘ **TIP** The cursor doesn't flash when you click in a Container field, but once you've clicked on it, the field is active. Then you can paste items from the clipboard or choose Picture, QuickTime movie, or Sound from the Insert menu.

Calculation Field

A Calculation field uses data in each record or from related records to display a result. The calculation can also be or include constants or status functions as well as images. It sounds complicated, but FileMaker offers so many calculation options that it's hard to get a feel for it without a little more experience. You probably normally think of the result of a calculation as a number, but FileMaker goes way beyond that. You can also display the calculation as a Text, Date, Time, or Container result. The fact that you're able to display so many types of calculation results can be a great help.

Follow these steps to test this out:

1. Go into Define Fields and create a new field called **AddrCombo**, choosing the **Calculation** field type. The Specify Calculation window appears.

⌘ **TIP** You can type directly in the Specify Calculation window, or you can build the calculation by double-clicking on items in the field, function, and comparison operator lists and single-clicking on the comparison and logical operator buttons.

2. Enter the calculation exactly this way:

    NameFirst & " " & NameLast & "¶" &
    AddrStreet & "¶" &
    AddrCity & " " & AddrState & " " & AddrZip & "-" & AddrPlusFour

    When you see the quotation marks with nothing between them, be sure you actually press the Spacebar once there.

⌘ **TIP** You can put carriage returns between elements of a calculation without affecting the results of the calculation. This can be extremely valuable when trying to visualize what's going on when you work with longer calculations. You can even indent parameters of functions if that will make it easier to understand.

3. In the lower-left corner of the window you'll see the "Calculation result is" pop-up list. It always defaults to Number. Click the pop-up and choose **Text**.

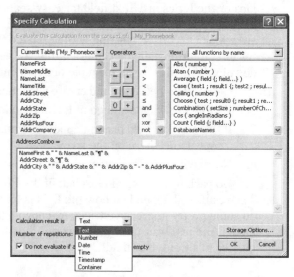

Figure 4-2
The Specify Calculation window for the AddrCombo field. Note the "Calculation result is" pop-up in the lower-left corner.

⊠ **CAUTION**   If you build a calculation and forget to choose the correct calculation result from the pop-up, you can get some pretty strange results. The data in the field can look completely foreign. The data might look just fine on the layout, but it might give incorrect summaries. It can also cause a lot of headaches if you use a calculation as part of a relationship to another table. You might have meant to link the tables by the same field type but actually chose two different type results.

4. Click **OK** and **OK** again to exit.

5. Go into Layout mode and place the new AddrCombo field on the layout if it's not already there. You'll want to grab one of the selection handles with the selection tool and open up the field to accommodate at least three lines of text.

6. Now go into Browse mode and take a look at the results. Notice that a dash appears regardless of whether or not there are Zip and PlusFour values. You can further refine the calculation using Case or If functions to prevent that. For now, just make up some zip codes. Notice that you can't type data directly into the Calculation field. Click through some of the other records in the file to see what they look like, too. If you want to experiment, go back and choose Date as the calculation result. Just don't forget to change it back.

Summary Field

Summary fields grab data from a single field across one or more records in the same (or related) tables. That might sound a little complicated, but think of a situation where you might want to see the grand total of all invoices written today. That would be a Summary field. (In contrast, Calculation fields work on one or more fields within a single record, such as Price x Quantity = Amount Due. There are exceptions, but this is a good general definition.) Summaries can calculate Total, Average, Count, Minimum, Maximum, Standard Deviation, and Fraction of a Total, as shown in Figure 4-3. Notice that some fields cannot be summarized. You can tell because they are gray in the field list in the center of the window.

The information that appears in a Summary field depends on where it is on a layout, what records are found, and how they are sorted. You also need to understand layout

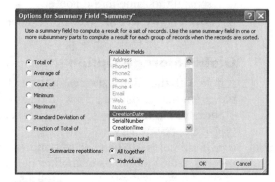

Figure 4-3
Window used to make choices for Summary fields.

parts so your reports properly reflect the results you're after. More on that in Chapter 15, "Making Sense of Your Information with Layouts."

When the Options for Summary Field window first appears, the "Total of" radio button is automatically selected. At the bottom of the field list is a "Running total" check box. That allows you to view running totals when a copy of

Part 2

the Summary field is placed in the Body part of the layout. Click down the radio buttons on the left and watch how the options change for the check box.

1. Define a Summary field called **CountSerial**.

2. When the Options for Summary Field window appears, choose the **Count of** radio button and the **SerialNumber** field, and check the **Running total** box. You select the SerialNumber field because it is an auto-enter field that cannot be modified.

3. Exit and go to Layout mode. Place a copy of CountSerial in the Body part of the layout. (See Figure 4-4.)

4. Then place a second copy in the Footer part.

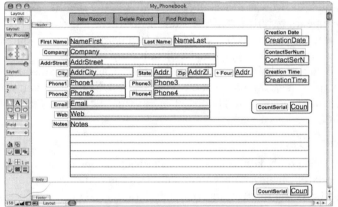

Figure 4-4
Layout mode showing the placement of two copies of the CountSerial Summary field enclosed in rounded rectangles.

5. Go into Browse mode and choose **Records, Show All Records**. Click through the records and notice how the numbers change in the Body but remain the same in the Footer.

6. Now choose **Records, Omit Record** and look at what happens to CountSerial in the Footer.

Global Storage Option

A field with the Global storage option selected contains one value or Container type item that is shared across all records in a table and can even be placed in other tables in the same file. You can specify Global storage for a field of any type except Summary.

Global fields can be used as temporary storage areas to move data between records, tables, or tables in another file. You can use them in conditional parts of scripts. For example, you can tell a script to start at the first record in a table and cycle through the records until it finds a company name that matches one stored in a Global field.

A Global field cannot be indexed. (I'll discuss indexing in Chapter 10.) When you enter Find mode, you can't get into a Global field. It wouldn't do any good anyway, since the search would just find all records. (Remember, it shares the same value across all records.) But values in Global fields can still be viewed in Find mode and passed to other fields in the find process using a script. You can also perform a find request in a Calculation field that uses a

Figure 4-5
A Global field begins as any other field.

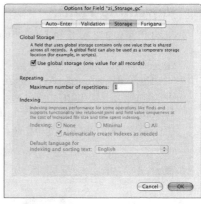

Figure 4-6
Selecting "Use global storage" in the Storage tab of the field options window is what makes a Global field.

Global field as part of its calculation. Basically, what I'm saying is that you can do a lot of neat tricks with Global fields.

For example, you could store a logo for a company in a Global field formatted as Container type and drop the field on various layouts. If the logo changes, you update one field and every occurrence of that logo changes throughout your tables. If you format it as Text type, you can do the same thing for an address.

When I first read about Global fields, I just couldn't figure out what I would use them for. But after a while I found them to be extremely valuable. We'll use them later in the book in some exercises so you'll get a better feel for how you might be able to use them.

✓ **BEST PRACTICES**   Notice the zc at the beginning of zc_SerNumMover_gn and gn at the end. When you have fields that are really not meant for regular data entry, putting a "z" at the beginning makes them appear at the bottom of the field list when the list is sorted by name. That way, developers (that's you!) can find all their utility fields together at the bottom of the list. The "c" stands for control, which is a general category for manipulating data. The "gn" means the field is formatting globally and that it's a Number field. For more information on naming conventions, review the information in the downloadable files.

Take a minute to create a Global field and pay attention to the windows you'll see. Choose the field name and type, and click the Create button. Then click on Options and, under the Storage tab, check the "Use global storage" box. Scripts and calculations won't work the way you expect if you're using a standard Text or Number field but think you're getting data from a Global field. I tell you this because I've done it more than once. Even more than twice. Okay, I've probably done it as many as thirty or forty times!

Repeating Field

A Repeating field is not a field type. It is a way of formatting any of the other field types except Summary. You can format a field with up to 32,000 repetitions.

Repeating fields were originally invented before FileMaker was a relational database. Back then, it was especially valuable for invoices. You could use one Repeating field, and each repetition would represent another line item on the invoice as shown in Figure 4-7.

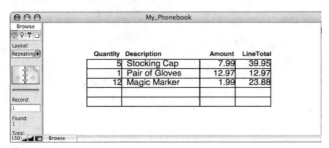

Figure 4-7
Number (Quantity and Amount), Text (Description), and Calculation (Line Total) fields formatted as Repeating fields.

You choose the number of repetitions in the Storage tab. (In a Calculation field, you'll find the number of repetitions in the bottom left of the Specify Calculation window.) Then you choose how many of those repetitions are visible as part of the formatting of the field on the layout (Format, Field Format).

Since FileMaker Pro became a relational database with version 3.0, Repeating fields are not used as often. You can do so much more in the way of reporting when line items are created as individual records in a related table. It probably sounds confusing at this point, but I think it will get clearer once we start working with our first relational tables. These days, the Repeating field format is most often used for storing multiple values in Global fields. That's interesting because Globals were introduced in version 3.0 — the same time FileMaker went relational.

Another use for Repeating fields was for phone numbers. To see how this worked, follow these steps:

1. Go back into Define Fields and double-click **Phone1**.

2. When you see the Options for Field "Phone1" window, click the **Storage** tab.

3. In the Repeating area, you can select the number of repetitions of this field that will appear on the layout. Type **10** after "Maximum number of repetitions:" and click **OK** and **OK** again.

4. Go into Layout mode and make a copy of the Phone1 field. Paste it in a blank area on your layout.

5. While the field is still selected, choose **Format**, **Field Format**.

6. In the middle of the Field Format window is the Repetitions area. As you can see, 10 repetitions are defined. You can show up to 10 repetitions on your layout. If you want to show only the first six, change the 10 to **6**.

7. Now select the orientation of those repetitions — whether they will appear horizontally or vertically — on your layout. Click **OK**.

8. Go to Browse mode. Notice that the number you typed in there earlier is still in the first repetition. Make up a number or two to fill in more repetitions.

Well, you get the idea. You might think this is the perfect solution. But even phone numbers are handled better using related records. One of the reasons is that there are script limitations on Repeating fields. We'll take a look at how to turn the phone numbers into related records in Chapter 6.

Formatting Your Fields in Japanese

With FileMaker 7, you can use software utilities that convert keystrokes into Japanese characters, and you can identify fields for which you would like a phonetic translation of that Japanese text. You can also format fields (Layout mode, Format, Field Behavior) to enter Japanese using additional software utilities.

Beyond that thin explanation, what I have to tell you here is really a cop-out. If you don't want to hear my sad excuses, just go to the Help files and do a find for "Formatting fields in Japanese" and "Furigana." In order to make use of these capabilities, there are some system requirements and extra software utilities I don't have. So my attempts to test these were futile. If you're determined, and you can get your machine set up correctly, I'm sure these are very useful functions.

Field Formats on Layouts

Once you have your fields defined, you need to decide how they'll appear on your layouts. FileMaker provides you with many very useful choices. Let's use My_Phonebook to continue our experiments.

Aside from borders and fonts, most fields won't need much formatting at all. But when you need special formatting, you must know where to go to do this. Keep in mind that you can format a number of fields of the same type at the same time, rather than one at a time. Just Shift+click on the fields you want to format and choose the appropriate menu to access the Format window. You can use the Format Painter to do the formatting.

Date Format

First, let's look at the DateCreate field.

1. Go into Layout mode, select the field, and choose **Format, Date**.

2. Click the **Format as** radio button and click on the pop-up list to see the list of common choices. See Figure 4-8. Pick any one of them and look in the Sample area near the bottom of the window to see what it will look like. If you switch to the Custom radio button, you can build your own date display including European format, which puts the day before the month. However, when you enter the date, you must still use the format month, day, year.

3. After you exit the field, it will display in the format you've chosen. Notice that by clicking the **Text Format** button in the lower-left corner of the window, you can even access the font, size, color, and style for customizing without going back to the program menus.

4. Click **OK** or **Cancel** to exit.

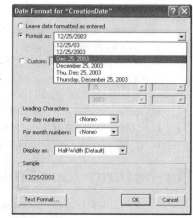

Figure 4-8
The Date Format window showing the choices in the Format as pop-up list.

Number Format

The only Number field in our file is the SerialNumber field. Right-click on it in Layout mode and choose Formatm Number. There just isn't enough space to explain every detail of this window, but as windows go, this one is pretty easy to understand. Notice that you can access the text formatting from here as well. Click OK or Cancel to exit.

If a number is longer than the field width, FileMaker will display a question mark — unless the field is formatted with the "General format" radio button.

General format was introduced in FileMaker Pro 5.0 and applies specifically to Number fields. If a Number field contains more than nine characters (and the field is wide enough to hold 10 characters), the number will be displayed in scientific notation. This may or may not be what you want, but the choice is there. If the width of the field is smaller than 10 characters, you'll see a question mark.

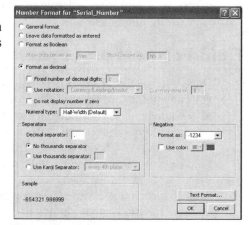

Figure 4-9
The Number Format window where you make choices about how a Number field will display on your layout.

Text Format

In Layout mode, click on the Notes field to select it. Then choose Format, Text. From this one window, you can access text formatting that would require stopping at many of the program menus at the top of the screen. If you click the Paragraph button in the lower-left corner, you can even format the fields for alignment, indentation, and line spacing. Clicking the Tabs button takes you one layer deeper to build a set of custom tabs. There is plenty of information in the FileMaker manual and the Help menu on these settings.

Time Format

In Layout mode, click on the CreationTime field and choose Format, Time. Click the radio button next to "Format as" and choose the format that suits you. Most of the time I prefer "hhmm." Then I usually click the button next to "12 hour notation."

Here's an interesting little item. If you have a Timestamp field, you'll notice there is no layout format for Timestamp. Instead, you choose Format, Date Format and make some choices there. Then you choose Format, Time Format and make some choices. If you select "Leave date formatted as entered" or "Leave time formatted as entered" in either of the windows, the entire timestamp remains unformatted. You might try creating a Timestamp field, creating a new record, and trying the layout format choices to see what happens.

⌘ **TIP** I find it helpful to format my Timestamp field with a dash between the date and time so it's easier to read. To do that, use the Custom button to format the date. In the fourth box on the right (after the year) type " - " (space, dash, space). After you click OK, choose your time format. When you're done, your Timestamp field should display something like 12/7/2004 - 2:11 PM.

Summary

In this chapter, we looked at the options available when creating a new database and what to consider when deciding whether to make one from scratch, from a template, or from a commercial product. Then we looked closely at the various field types and how to make them display on a layout. In the next chapter, we'll talk about what you'll be putting into those fields.

Q & A

Q With all these new fields we're creating, I'm starting to run out of room on the layout. What do I do?

A Go into Layout mode and notice the separators between layout parts. Near the Status area, you should see some tabs titled Header, Body, and Footer. Each has a dotted line running horizontally across the layout. If you click and drag on the Body tab, you can move it downward to expand your work area. You can also click on the dotted line, but it's a little harder to grab.

Q Some of the database tables I want to create are going to have more fields than will fit on one page. What then?

A Take a look at the Contact Management template again. By making use of the tabs (which are really buttons) in the middle of the page, you can switch to different layouts and group similar types of data that may not need to be seen on your main screen.

Part 2

Workshop

Go back to the Contact Management file. Take a look at the Define Database window and go to the Fields tab. Scan down the list of fields and see if you can tell what the fields are for without too much trouble. Would some of those fields suit a purpose you might have for a database? Take as much time as you can spare and look at the other template files, keeping in mind how you might be able to use them in your work.

Review Questions

True-False

1. A Text field can hold about six pages of type.
2. A Repeating field places the same data in every record in the database.
3. Data in a field with Global storage is available to every record in the database.
4. A Summary field can be used to add the values of two fields in a single record.
5. A birth date entered into a Date field as 4/9/75 is interpreted as April 9, 2075.

Short Answer

6. Why is it necessary to specify a calculation result type for a Calculation field?
7. Why should you consider *not* including word spaces in your field names?
8. If you wanted to create a Calculation field that displayed NameLast, a comma, a space, and NameFirst, what would the calculation formula look like?
9. If you defined a phone number field as Number type, how would FileMaker interpret the following entry: (800) 123-4567? In other words, what would be its numeric value?
10. How do you access the window to set indentation and line spacing for a Text field?
11. If you need to store a lot of information in a field, what field type would be the most likely choice?
12. When you look at the field names in Contact Management, some of them have spaces in them. Name at least one problem that spaces could cause.
13. Name at least three characters that would best be left out of field names.
14. Name at least four of the eight field types.
15. A Date field displays on a layout as 10/10/2004. How would you get it to appear as "Sunday, October 10, 2004"?

Chapter 5

Entering and Modifying Your Data

Vocabulary

- Drag-and-drop
- Find/Replace
- Replace Field Contents command
- Value list

Objectives

1. Understand selecting and exiting records and fields.
2. Become familiar with the Set Tab Order layout feature.
3. Learn and practice various ways to enter and modify data.
4. Add text formatting in Browse mode.
5. Learn to insert movies, pictures, and sounds in a Container field.
6. Create a simple value list.
7. Learn a variety of ways to select a record.
8. Practice using the spell checker.
9. Become familiar with Find/Replace.
10. Practice the Delete Record command.

Introduction

In this chapter, I want to show you more about creating new records and entering data in those records. Along the way I will give you a number of pointers that should make data entry much easier than having to type all the information into every single field.

We'll look at:

- Tab order
- Getting data from other records with duplicate information
- Deleting records
- Using value lists
- Getting movies, sounds, and pictures into Container fields

If you don't already have My_Phonebook open, go ahead and open it back up now. We'll use it sparingly at first, but then we'll pick up some steam.

Creating a New Record

It's not as if you don't know how to do this by now. In fact, we even created a button for it. As I mentioned before, I still prefer the key combination — Command+N (Macintosh) or Ctrl+N (Windows) — over the use of a button. I just don't like putting all those miles on my mouse muscles.

One method I didn't discuss is creating a record by choosing Records, Duplicate Record. If you're going to be creating a new record that will have much of the same data as the record you're already on, use the menu or press Command+D (Macintosh) or Ctrl+D (Windows). Then you only have to change the part of the data that is different for the newly duplicated record. This works very well for companies where you'll be using the same address and phone, but you want to have a different record for each person in the company. However, duplicating a record will not duplicate any items in a portal or a related table.

Of course, you can create scripts and attach them to buttons for any of these tasks (that is, if I can't talk you into learning the key combination). On the other hand, one advantage of creating a script is that you can have it run a subscript in another file. That way, you could perform some specific initialization task or duplicate related items if you needed to.

⌘ **TIP**   When you create a new record or duplicate an existing record, the record is added to the end of the table. However, if the records are sorted, the new record appears after the currently selected record, and the status changes to semi-sorted. This happens so that you can work on the new record while looking at the record you were working on, perhaps to copy and paste data. When the records are unsorted again, any new records will appear at the end of the table in creation order.

Selecting the Record

I already showed you how to get to a record in the found set by clicking pages of the Book in the Status area. There are a few other ways to move among records.

One such method also has to do with the Book. Notice the number circled under the word Record in Figure 5-1. In Browse mode, this is called the Current record number. If you click on it, the number will become highlighted, and you can type in a new number. When you press the Enter or Return key, FileMaker will go to that record. A second keep-your-hands-on-the-keyboard way to do the same thing is to press the Esc key to highlight the number. If you type a number larger than the current found set, FileMaker takes you to the last record.

Figure 5-1
Status area showing the Current record
number with a circle around it.

↪ **NOTE** In Preview mode, the number under the Book is called the "Current page number." In Find mode, it's the Current request number, and in Layout mode, it's the Current layout number.

A narrow vertical black line called the "Current record bar" located between the Status area and the record indicates the currently selected record. This is most obvious when you choose View as List or View as Table. To demonstrate how this works, look at our file, and choose View, View as List. Go to the first record using the technique I just described and click in the NameFirst field. Between the record itself and the Status area, you can see the Current record bar. It appears in Figure 5-2 surrounded with a rounded rectangle.

Figure 5-2
The Current record bar outlined with a rounded rectangle.

If you use the scroll bar on the right to move to the third record, you'll see the Current record bar is gone. If you click in any of the fields in that record, the bar appears on the left, showing it as the current record. This is important because you can be viewing a record that is not the current record. If you then press Tab, thinking you are editing the record you were viewing, the screen will snap to the true current record, and you'll end up editing the wrong record. You can always be sure you're editing the record you're viewing by clicking into it. To return our file to the way it was, choose View, View as Form.

Let's look at another example. Open up the Contact Management file. Add a few records to the table and click the List button tab. (It's the middle tab with gray horizontal lines in the upper-right corner.) Make sure you have more than one record showing. If not, choose Records, Show All Records. It's a lot easier to see the Current record bar here. If you click anywhere on the record except the little envelope with the arrow icon immediately to the left of the NameFirst field, FileMaker will take you back to the Form layout. Switching to

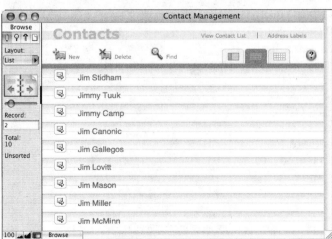

Figure 5-3
List View of a database showing a number of entries with the first name Jim. Clicking on the arrow icon switches to the Form layout where the details of Jim's record are available.

a list like that is a great technique for finding the record that you want to view in detail from a group. You might be working in a table that has thousands of entries and want to do a find for anyone with the name Jim. Scrolling through a list of records in the Form layout could take a long time. By switching to the List layout as in Figure 5-3, you can find the person you want much more quickly.

The final method to get to a specific record is to use a script.

1. Choose **Scripts**, **ScriptMaker** and create a script called **Go to Record**.

2. Double-click **Go to Record/Request/Page** from the Navigation heading.

3. Look at the choices available to you in the Specify pop-up in the Options area in Figure 5-4. Choose the **By Calculation** option. When the Specify Calculation window appears, as in Figure 5-5, type **0** (zero) in the empty box in the lower portion of the window.

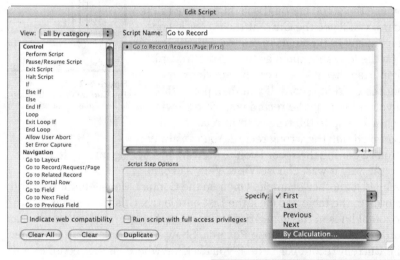

Figure 5-4
The Edit Script window showing the choices from the Specify pop-up for the Go to Record/ Request/Page script step.

4. Click **OK** three times to take you back to the screen in which you are viewing records as a list.

5. Choose the script from the Scripts menu. Type in the number of the record you want to go to, then click **OK** or press Enter or Return, and you're there. You can make a button for that if you want.

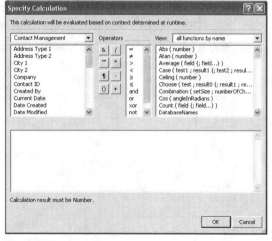

Figure 5-5
The Specify Calculation window.

Adding Data

Now that you've selected or created the record you want to work with, you need to get the data in there. You or the people you're making the file for need to get to the right field(s) and either enter new data or change what's already in there. Here we'll be talking about how to enter information directly into a FileMaker file. In Chapter 19, "Sharing Your Data on the Web," I'll show you how to enter data with a web browser.

Starting with FileMaker Pro 6.0, you can import a whole folder of files. This can be a great tool for people who want to store pictures from a digital camera. For more on this feature, see Chapter 20, "Sharing Your Data with Other Applications."

Selecting the Field

One important thing to know is that you may not be able to make entries into all fields. The following list gives a variety of situations in which a field is not accessible.

■ If you didn't set up the database, some fields may be locked through validation at the Define Database level (Define Database, Fields, Options, Validation tab) to prevent change.

■ They can also be locked at the Field Format level by having the "Allow entry into field" check box turned off. (This is different from locking the field in place on the layout.)

■ You cannot enter data into Calculation or Summary fields. And, although you can paste, import, or record into Container fields, you cannot type data in them. What you can do with a Global field depends on how it's been formatted as one of the other field types.

■ If you are looking at the database in Browse mode while in List View, fields that are in the Header, Footer, or Leading or Trailing Grand Summary parts of the layout will be unavailable for anything other than viewing. This even applies to fields that would otherwise be enterable. You can get to enterable fields in those areas by temporarily switching to View as Form.

■ A field can also be made into a button and removed from the tab order on the layout. Being able to turn a field (or any other layout object) into a button is a terrific tool in FileMaker. In this case, you could make it so that when users click on the field to enter it, that action triggers a script attached to the field. The script might be set to allow entry only under certain conditions, such as who the user is.

■ One final way that fields can be made inaccessible or read-only is through the use of access privileges. Individual fields can be restricted on a per-layout basis.

So you can see, there are plenty of paths to follow in troubleshooting why a field seems to be frustratingly unalterable. On the other hand, each of these limitations can be used as a tool for various purposes, including preventing accidental alteration of your data.

Part 2

Well, that takes care of why you may not be able to get into a field. Now let's talk about how you *can* get into a field. Yes, you can click on it, but let's look at the more conventional ways.

Using Tab Order

In the old days, the only way to get from field to field was to use the Tab and arrow keys. Then Douglas Engelbart invented the mouse. There are a lot of newcomers who think the only way to get around a screen is with the mouse. But that ends up being a pretty inefficient way to enter data. You don't want to take your hands off the keyboard every time you need to get to another field. That's where the tab order comes in.

Remember when we first looked at the Contact Management file? Tabbing through the record would be a little awkward if you went from First Name to Image to Last Name. It just wouldn't make sense. Open that file now.

1. Go to Layout mode, and choose **Layouts**, **Set Tab Order.** Tab arrows will appear on the layout, as shown in Figure 5-6. You'll also see the Set Tab Order dialog (shown in Figure 5-8) in the foreground, which you can move around if it covers up some of the fields.

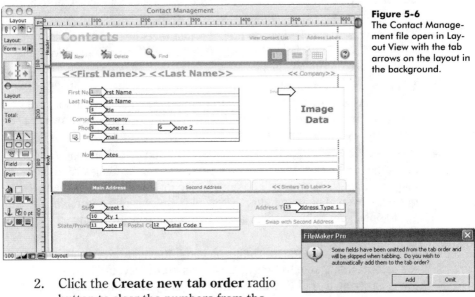

Figure 5-6
The Contact Management file open in Layout View with the tab arrows on the layout in the background.

Figure 5-7
The warning dialog box that appears when fields are excluded from the tab order.

2. Click the **Create new tab order** radio button to clear the numbers from the arrows.

3. Then simply click on the blank arrows in the order you choose. You can even leave out some fields. For example, you would want to leave out the Image field. When you're done, click **OK**. You'll be presented with the dialog box shown in Figure 5-7. Click the **Omit** button since we want Image left out of the tab order. (If you click Add, FileMaker will add the next unused number to the next unnumbered field and continue until all fields have a number.)

4. Now go to Browse mode and tab through the record. This tab order makes more sense, doesn't it? Notice that the tab order wraps around. When you get to the last field and press Tab again, you end up back in the first field. You can also go backward through the tab order by pressing Shift+Tab.

To edit an existing tab order:

1. Go back into Layout mode and bring up the Set Tab Order dialog box again.

2. This time leave the "Edit tab order" radio button as is. Now you can type directly in the arrows and change the order of just a few fields instead of starting over with all blank arrows. This can be a problem if you create a new field and want to add it high up in the tab order. Then you have to renumber every tab arrow that comes after it; the numbers don't just automatically shift forward.

If things get really messed up, you can just click the Revert To Default button and FileMaker reassigns the tab order. The default is to start numbering from the upper left and move through the fields from left to right and top to bottom — like reading a book in English.

If you don't want to make any changes, click Cancel.

⌘ **TIP**　If you have fields that are close together, the tab arrows may overlap so you can't get to them. Go to the lower-left corner of the window and click the Zoom In tool. (See Figure 5-8.) It allows you to magnify the layout until you can see enough detail to get to the arrows you need. When you're done, click the Zoom Out tool or click the number in the lower-left corner to revert to 100. The Zoom tools are available in all modes.

Occasionally fields will be too close to each other to work with even at 400% magnification. In that case, I will move a field up or down 10 clicks so I can see the arrows that overlap. After setting the tab order, I move the field back into place.

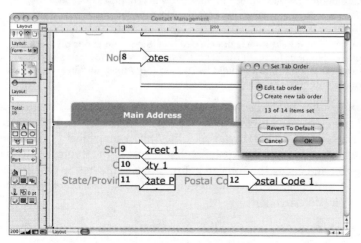

Figure 5-8
Layout mode showing how using the Zoom In tool gives better access to overlapping tab arrows.

Part 2

Data Entry Shortcuts

You already know how to enter data using your keyboard. But you need better, more accurate, and faster ways to fill up those fields. One great shortcut is not to have to enter any data at all in some fields. You do this by using predefined information and lookups as part of the field definition. I'll talk more about that in Chapter 10, "Keeping Your Data Clean and Neat."

Insert

Current Date — Go into My_Phonebook, be sure you're in Browse mode, and highlight the date in the CreationDate field. Now choose Insert, Current Date. Notice the key combination in case you might need to place today's date often. Use Command+– (Macintosh — that's Command and the minus sign) or Ctrl+– (Windows). Do the same with the CreationTime field except use the Current Time option from the menu.

Current User Name — Since we know that the Web field is empty, click on it and choose Insert, Current User Name. What pops in there will depend on your Preferences settings. If nothing appears, you should investigate further by choosing Edit, Preferences, Application and looking in the General tab under User Name.

↪ NOTE   Let's say that several people in a company have access to the program and can enter and change information. The program owners sometimes ask developers to provide ways to identify the person who adds or changes information. It's usually not intended as a way to place blame for incorrect information, but to determine if further training with the program is needed. Developers use the Current User Name field, which goes to the computer of the person making changes and fills in that person's name in the field. However, the Current User Name field cannot be relied on completely, because it collects the name each time the record is touched. If three people made changes to a record within minutes of each other, the name of the person who touched the record last would appear.

⌘ TIP   Triple-clicking in a field selects the current line. Since one line is all there is in a Time, Date, or Number field, you select the entire contents. You can select the current paragraph of a multi-line Text field by clicking four times. Clicking five times selects the entire contents of the field.

From Index — Click in the NameFirst field and choose Insert, From Index. FileMaker brings up a window with a list of all the values that are currently in any of the records in that field. If you click the "Show individual words" check box near the bottom, it does just that. To choose one of the items, double-click it, or highlight it and click OK. You can get to items in the list by typing one or more letters. You can also move among items in the list by using the up and down arrows on your keyboard.

↪ NOTE   FileMaker keeps indexes of the field contents of your files. By using Insert, From Index, you can see what the index of a specific field looks like. In some cases, indexing may be turned off for individual fields. The indexing system follows certain rules that may limit how many words or characters of a field are indexed. To find out more about using FileMaker's indexing system, see Chapter 10.

From Last Visited Record — If you're entering a lot of data, chances are you'll have a number of records in a row with information that will be the same from one record to the next. You can create a new record and type any information that is different in field after field. Then when you get to the field where the data was the same in the last record, use Insert, From Last Visited Record. To test this:

1. Go to the first record in the table.
2. Click in the **NameFirst** field.
3. Now go to the next record. If the cursor is not already there, move it into the NameFirst field.
4. Choose **Insert, From Last Visited Record**, or you can just press Command+' (Macintosh) or Ctrl+' (Windows). Memorize this key combination because it's another one you may use quite often.

Copy and Paste

If there's a lot of data in one field to transfer from one record to another or even from one application to another, you can use copy and paste. To do this:

1. Highlight the data you need, and choose **Edit, Copy** to place it on the clipboard.
2. Go to the field where you want the data to end up, and choose **Edit, Paste**. Don't forget these keyboard shortcuts for Copy (Command+C for Macintosh and Ctrl +C for Windows) and Paste (Command +V for Macintosh and Ctrl +V for Windows).

Remember that you have to work within the limits of the various field types. For instance, you can't paste "Rich" into a Date field, but you can copy a date into a Text field.

Drag-and-Drop

Another choice for moving data is to use the drag-and-drop feature. To turn that option on and use it:

1. Choose **Edit, Preferences, General**.
2. Click the check box for **Allow drag and drop text selection** and click **OK**.
3. In Browse mode, highlight some text.
4. Click and drag the text to another field.

If you want to use drag and drop to move between records, you have to use View as List. Even at that, it can be somewhat awkward. You can also effectively move data between two files (or two windows of tables in the same file) by positioning them next to each other on the screen so that the source field and the target field are both within view. Try using the drag-and-drop operation with two fields on the same layout.

You can also use the drag-and-drop feature between applications on both Macintosh and Windows. For example, if you have an e-mail from a client open and you can see a FileMaker field, you can just highlight the text in the e-mail window and drag it into the FileMaker field.

Part 2

On the Macintosh, you can also use clipping files. Clipping files are a big advantage if you need a temporary drop spot as you're moving data between records or applications. Just drag some data off to the desktop, and drag it back on when you find the right field. They also come in handy in Layout mode for moving fields and other layout objects around, either individually or as a group.

Getting items into Container fields will be discussed later in this chapter. Another great feature is the ability to import data from other files and applications, which I'll show you in Chapters 20 and 22.

Using Value Lists

Value lists are great tools for reducing the possibility of misspelled words and providing faster data entry. It will become obvious that this works best when you have a field that will use the same group of data over and over. There are four types of value lists provided by FileMaker:

- Pop-up list
- Pop-up menu
- Check boxes
- Radio buttons

FileMaker also gives you three ways to create a value list:

- In Layout mode by selecting a field and choosing Format, Field Format.
  - a.   Select one of the value list options.
  - b.   Click on the drop-down menu at "Display values from."
  - c.   Select Define Value List.
  - d.   At the Define Value List screen, click on New.
  - e.   At the Edit Value List screen, give your value list a meaningful name.
  - f.   Make sure that the radio button next to "Use custom values" is selected, and begin filling in the appropriate information in the box underneath.
  - g.   Click OK three times to get you back to your layout.
- In any mode, by choosing File, Define Value Lists. This takes you to the Define Value List window. See above for the process.
- In any mode, by choosing Define Database, selecting the field, and clicking on Options.
  - a.   At the field Validation tab (Define Database, Fields, Options, Validation), select the "Member of value list" check box when you're defining a field's options.
  - b.   Click on Define Value Lists and continue the process.

There are many subtleties and possibilities for value lists, and to cover them all would require more than one chapter. However, let me at least expose you to some of the possibilities by saying that value lists include the ability to create a list based on:

- A fixed list you type yourself when you create the value list
- A conditional value list that uses a relationship to generate the values

- A value list from another file
- Data that is already entered in a field
- Values that are not currently in the list but can be added as you go

Of the three ways FileMaker gives you to create a value list, the one I use the most is in Layout mode. Let's create one now:

1. Go into the My_Phonebook file and go to Layout mode.

2. Click on the **AddrState** field and choose **Format, Field Format**. You'll see the window in Figure 5-9.

3. Click the drop-down next to "Format field as" and choose **Pop-up List**. In the next window that appears, select **Define Value List** from the drop-down menu next to "Display values from."

4. When the next window, Define Value List for "My Phonebook," appears, click the **New** button.

5. You will see an Edit Value List window that looks something like Figure 5-10. In the area next to Value List Name, type **State**.

6. Make sure that **Use custom values** is selected, and begin entering abbreviations for a few states in the box below. (Look at the directions to the right of the custom values box.)

7. Click **OK** three times, and you are back at the layout in My_Phonebook.

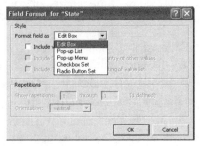

Figure 5-9
The Field Format window showing the pop-up list of the four types of value lists available.

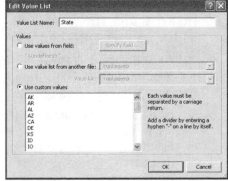

Figure 5-10
The Edit Value List window showing the value list called State.

Let's say that you forgot to add Vermont and you want to edit your list.

1. Go back into Layout mode, click on the **AddrState** field and choose **Format, Field Format**. Once again, you'll see the window in Figure 5-9.

2. This time, check the **Include 'Edit...' to allow editing of value list** box.

3. Get back to Browse mode. Click on **State**, and when the drop-down menu appears with your list of states, you'll see that the final option is Edit. When you click on **Edit**, you'll be taken to a screen called Edit Value List State.

4. Click in the box next to the final state you have listed, press **Enter** or **Return**, and add **VT** to your listing. Click **OK**.

For an easier way to build the list, read on.

1. Choose **File**, **Define Value Lists**, and double-click on the **State** value list.
2. Click the radio button next to **Use values from field**.
3. In the next window, Specify Fields for Value List, you must select the file from which to select your field, in this case, **My_Phonebook**. When you click on My_Phonebook, you see a list of all the fields available. Select **AddrState**. Click **OK** three times.
4. Click in the **State** field. FileMaker shows you a list that represents the states that are already in the file. Backspace over the state that's in the field and type **VT**. Click in the field again and you've changed the value list.

This way, the list builds as your file does. If an item isn't in the pop-up list, just type it in the field and it will be added to the list from now on.

Using Container Fields

Depending on what type of work you intend to do, Container fields can be the answer to some of your needs. For example, you can store employee or product photos, and build training files that include multimedia presentations.

Insert QuickTime

If you have a QuickTime movie, a PDF file, or just about any other type of file on your computer, you can pull it into a Container field.

1. In our My_Phonebook file, go to Browse mode and click on the **Pic** field.
2. Choose **Insert**, **QuickTime**. (You must have QuickTime installed.)
3. Find the file you want to place in the field by searching through your files and folders. It's best to keep the items in the same folder as the FileMaker file that will be using them. Once the movie is in your file, you will see the first frame.
4. Click on the picture to pop out the control bar, and use the controls to play the movie.

You can use the same controls to view a PDF file. The only difference is you don't want to click the play button since it will flip through the pages too quickly for reading. Instead, use the arrows to go forward and back one page at a time. You'll need to have Adobe Reader on your computer to read the PDFs. It's a free download.

Other file types cannot be viewed from within FileMaker and need to be exported first.

Insert Picture

Insert Picture works similarly to inserting a QuickTime movie, except the picture formats that are available are different on the Macintosh and Windows machines. See Figures 5-11 and 5-12. To keep the size of your FileMaker file down, you can click the check box next to "Store only a reference to the file." This is often the better choice since the size of your file expands when you actually store the images. However, if someone removes the file, it will no longer show in the field.

1. Go to Browse mode and click on the **Pic** field.
2. Choose **Insert**, **Picture**.
3. Find the file you want to place in the field by searching through your files and folders. As with movies, it's best to keep the items in the same folder as the FileMaker file that will be using them.
4. If your picture doesn't look right, go to Layout mode. Select the **Pic** field, then click **Format**, **Graphic** and either **Reduce** or **Enlarge**. Go back to Browse mode to see if it looks right. The field that holds the graphic must be formatted correctly. To learn more about formatting graphics, go to Chapter 16, "Designing Your Screen Layouts."

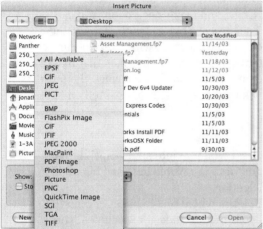

Figure 5-11
The Insert Picture window on the Macintosh showing the pop-up list of acceptable image file formats currently available.

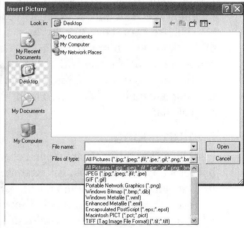

Figure 5-12
The Insert Picture window on a Windows computer showing the pop-up list of acceptable image file formats currently available. The "Store only a reference to the file" check box is not visible because it's under the pop-up list.

Insert Sound

There are three ways to get a sound into your computer: by copying and pasting it, using a script, or recording it directly into the field. The first way, opening a sound in another application, copying it to the clipboard, and pasting in into the container has one problem: It's not driven by the QuickTime application. That means that when you double-click on the Speaker icon to make it play, you can't stop it short of forcing FileMaker to quit or letting the sound play to the end.

My favorite way of adding a sound is to make a script with the following steps:

```
Go to Field ["Pic"]
Insert QuickTime[]
```

When you run the script, a window will open from which you can choose the file you want to import. The file needs to be an AIFF, WAV, or MP3 file.

Finally, you can record a sound directly into the field. Of course, you must be connected to a sound source such as a microphone and have the computer configured properly. To record a sound, choose Insert, Sound. In the next window, click the Record button. When you're done, click Stop. You can also choose to Pause during the recording. You can click the Play button to listen to the recording, then click Save or Cancel depending on how happy you are with the results. For more details, choose Help, FileMaker Pro Help.

Changing Data

There are various ways you might want to change your data. Of course, FileMaker provides a number of methods for making those changes.

Highlighting

I often want to call attention to information I have in a Text field. To do so, highlight the text, choose Format, Text Color, and make a selection. You can also choose Font, Font size, Style, etc. This process overrides the formatting of the field chosen in Layout mode. The new format stays with every occurrence of that field on any other layout, table, and even in other files that have a relationship to this one. This only works in a Text field. If you change the formatting of data in a Calculation field, any such formatting is not passed on to the calculation.

Spellchecking

FileMaker has a very helpful spell checker. I won't go into all its capabilities, but let's take a quick look. Enter some text into the Notes field and highlight it. Then choose Edit, Spelling, Check Selection.

You can also have the checker examine the whole record, a set of records, or all text on a layout when you're in Layout mode. On faster machines, you can have your spelling checked as you type. Choose Preferences, Document and click the Spelling tab.

Replace Command

The Replace command is a tool I use almost every day. Let's say you decided you would rather have the serial number for all the records start at 1000 instead of 1.

1. First choose **Records, Show All Records**.
2. Click in the **SerialNumber** field and choose **Records, Replace Field Contents**.
3. When the window shown in Figure 5-13 appears, click the radio button next to **Replace with serial numbers** and type **1000** in the "Initial value" box.

If you also choose the "Update serial number in Entry Options?" check box, FileMaker will make sure that new records you create will begin with the next available number. This check box will only be active if the field was defined for

Auto-Enter Serial numbers, as this one was. Using this check box is highly recommended for serial numbers.

Figure 5-13
The Replace window with the "Replace with serial numbers" radio button selected and the "Update serial number in Entry Options?" box checked.

☒ **CAUTION** Be careful with the Replace command when the field you're using it in is a key field. You could easily lose all references to any related data. See Chapter 6 for more on related data.

Another use for Replace would be if you found a number of records with the same word misspelled — let's say in the City field.

1. Perform a find for all occurrences of the misspelled word.

2. Click in the field and spell the word correctly.

3. Bring up the Replace window, leave the "Replace with" radio button selected, and click **Replace**.

It is worth mentioning the last radio button in the Replace window, even though this option won't make sense until we cover calculations later in the book. The "Replace with calculated result:" option allows you to perform extremely sophisticated replacements for data that might be in a field based on calculations. You can read more about it in FileMaker Pro's Help files and in the application manual. I am very enthusiastic about this choice, and it would be worth your time to investigate it further.

The Replace command can also be called by a script.

Find/Replace

Figure 5-14
FileMaker's Find/Replace window.

Take a look at Edit, Find/Replace, Find/Replace... The window that appears, shown in Figure 5-14, should be very familiar to people who work with word processing programs. It even provides the summary dialog seen in Figure 5-15 when the replace is finished. You can use this window to look for specific text and make the requested changes. But there are some subtleties you will be interested in:

■ You can make it work in all fields on the layout, including portal fields.

■ It works on Text, Number, Date, Time, and Timestamp fields, whether they are regular or formatted for Global storage. (You can also have it perform the find in Calculation and Summary fields, but it can't perform the replace.)

■ Replace will not be performed on fields formatted as radio buttons, pop-up menus, or check boxes. That's because those formats are used to restrict data entry. Bypassing that could cause problems.

■ It also works in Layout mode. That means you can change text on your layouts without having to go through the tedious process of first selecting the text everywhere it might appear. You will still need to go to each layout though.

■ It can work on one record or a found set of records.

■ If it is working on a found set of records, it only works on items in that found set, not on omitted items. Even though the function is called Find/Replace, you should not confuse it with FileMaker's Find mode. You can have Find/Replace perform its magic on whatever found set of records you want without messing up records you want to leave alone.

■ It is scriptable. The Open Find/Replace version of it is under the Open Menu Items category. It will open the window even if you have restricted the user's access privileges from reaching that menu.

■ The Perform Find/Replace script step is under the Editing category. The script creator will see the window in Figure 5-16. With this step you would be able to have users enter text into a Global field on a layout and control what happens next. (More on Scripting in Chapter 14, "Automating Your Database with Scripts.")

■ You should be cautious that the user is on a layout and in the table you want him or her on before allowing access to this potentially destructive tool. It might replace text you don't want touched. And it might do that in a bunch of fields! If you do script it, be sure you consider adding the Go to Layout script step before the window appears.

■ It is subject to record locking. That means that changes will not take place if a field is unavailable to the user because his or her password limits it or someone else is in a record in a shared file.

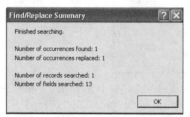

Figure 5-15
The Find/Replace Summary dialog that appears at the end of the process. This dialog will not appear when called by a script if you uncheck the "Perform without dialog" check box.

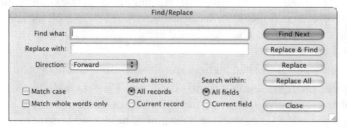

Figure 5-16
The Find/Replace window where you select various options when creating the Perform Find/Replace Script step.

☒ **CAUTION**   Don't change data that is used as a key field in a relationship to another table or file without careful consideration. The connection to any attached records will be lost and very difficult to retrieve. You can read more about key fields in Chapter 6.

Revert Command

A tool you should really know about once you start editing your data is the Revert command. If you've gone from field to field making changes here and there without exiting this specific record, you can revert to what it was before you started editing the record. Keep in mind that if you leave Browse mode or press the Enter key, you will exit the record. Give it a try.

1. Go to the **NameFirst** field and make the name bold.

2. Now tab to or click into the **NameLast** field and make that text red.

3. Choose **Records, Revert**.

Pretty smooth! Just remember, once you press Enter or click outside of the fields, you won't be able to revert.

A final technique to save time when changing data is with the Relookup command, also found under the Records menu. I'll talk more about that when we get to the "Looked-up Value" section of Chapter 10.

Deleting Data

You have a few options open to you when it comes to getting rid of data, depending on what you're trying to do. If you want to get rid of data in an unprotected field, other than a Calculation or Summary field, simply highlight the data and press the Backspace or Delete key.

To delete a single record (in our example, the target record will be a blank record):

1. Choose **Records, Show All Records**.

2. Click through the records until you find a blank one. If you don't have any blank records, create one using one of the techniques I taught you.

3. When you have a blank record in front of you, look over by the Book and note how many records are in this table.

4. Choose **Records, Delete Record**. FileMaker warns you that it's about to delete this record.

5. Click the **Delete** button. How many records are in the table now?

6. Find one of the records that has some data in it. Choose **Records, Duplicate Record**. Now you have two copies with the same information. You don't need that second record. Press **Command+E** (Macintosh) or **Ctrl+E** (Windows). You get the same delete warning. Go ahead and delete it.

To delete a group of records choose Records, Delete All Records. A warning dialog box appears that says, "Permanently delete All -- (dashes represent number in the currently found set) record(s)?" Now that's a warning to pay attention to! Click the Cancel button for now. But now you know what to do if you really wanted to get rid of a batch of records.

What if you had an invoicing system with 1,000 orders that had been carefully entered over six months and somebody chose that option and clicked the Delete button? You'd better have a recent backup somewhere!

☒ **CAUTION**   Always be very careful when deleting records. You cannot use Undo or Revert after you confirm that you want to delete one or more records. Unless you have a copy of the file somewhere else, you're out of luck.

I have seen someone accidentally choose Delete All Records in a large file. It takes a few minutes to complete the process, so when the person realized what he had done, he pulled the computer's power plug out of the wall. Then the company went through a lengthy process to recover the files afterward. This is not recommended because recovery may not be successful, and it definitely endangers the integrity of the file(s). But that was the only option at that point. They hadn't backed up in a couple of weeks. To revamp an old carpenter's saying, "Think twice, delete once."

Summary

In this chapter, I showed you more about creating records and ways to select a particular record. Then we looked at ways of getting into the fields, including how to create a tab order, and a number of shortcuts for inserting repetitive data into the fields. I showed you a little about placing movies, pictures, and sounds into Container fields. Finally, I covered ways to change data.

Q & A

Q What if I want to allow the user to select more than one of the choices given in a pop-up list?

A You should format the field with check boxes instead of a pop-up.

Q I was working with the tab order and missed a few of the fields. How do I correct it?

A If the Set Tab Order window is still on the screen, just click Cancel and the tab order will revert to what it was before you started. If you've already returned to Browse mode, you can go back into the Set Tab Order window and click the Revert To Default button. This won't return you to your previous tab order, but you don't have to start over from scratch either.

Workshop

Go into the Contact Management file to the Form - Main Address layout and enter Layout mode. Examine the light-colored tabs in the upper-right part of the window to the left of the question mark. Double-click them one at a time. (Hint: You need to click more toward the edge of the tabs. The lines and grid icons themselves really don't act as buttons.) Look at how the buttons are attached to scripts.

Go to Layout mode in My_Phonebook and select the State field. Use the Field Format window and see if you can format the field using the other types of value lists. (Hint: You may have to open up the field a little larger to show all the choices.) Make five copies of the field in a clear area of the layout, one for each value list type plus one formatted without a value list. Open up the unformatted field and make choices in the different value list fields to see how it affects the plain field.

Review Questions

True-False

1. A narrow, vertical black line is displayed to the left of the current record.
2. The tab order on a layout is always left to right, top to bottom.
3. A value list can speed data entry in a field that gets a limited variety of information from record to record.
4. The spell checker can check only field values in Browse mode.
5. FileMaker's Find/Replace function is similar to that used with word processing programs.

Short Answer

6. Name two ways to move data from field to field in the same or different records.
7. If you are on the first record of a database and you want to go to record 10, name two ways you can get there.
8. What types of data can be entered into fields via the Insert menu?
9. When creating a value list, what are the three different source choices for value list items?
10. What can you do if you accidentally delete all the records in your database via the Delete All Records command?
11. Name at least two types of value lists that can be displayed for a field on a layout.
12. Name at least one way to bring data from one record to another record.
13. Why do you need to be so careful when deleting records?

Part 2

Chapter 6

Working with Related Tables — Part 1

Vocabulary

- Child table
- Data normalization
- Flat file
- Key field (match field)
- Master table
- Parent table

- Portal
- Referential integrity
- Related field
- Related tables
- Table Occurrence

Objectives

1. Understand the concept of relational database design.
2. Define a database table.
3. Examine table relationships.
4. Understand the role of match (key) fields.
5. Define a key field.
6. Define relationships between tables.
7. Understand relationship options.
8. Create a portal to display related records.
9. Practice working with data in a portal.

Introduction

Now that you have some of the basics under your belt, let's move on to working with related tables. In this chapter, we'll:

- Create a file with related tables
- Look at the tools for working with relationships
- Look at how the tables are related to each other
- Examine a number of items to be aware of when working with multiple tables
- Create a portal and see how it works

One or Many Tables?

How do you know if it's time to work with more than one table? And how do you decide which items go in which tables? As you'll see, the answers are not cut and dried. However, the next two sections should go a long way in helping you know the answers.

One Table — Flat File Design

When there seems to be a logical connection between a group of fields, those fields should probably all be in the same table. For example, in a Customers table there is only one Customer number, one field for First Name, one for Last Name, one field for Company Name, etc. Your customer doesn't have two first names or three customer numbers. That means all these bits of data probably belong in the same table.

Many Tables — Relational Design

➲ **NOTE**   We began by creating the file My_Phonebook. At this time the file contains only the one table of records about people with whom you have contact. That will be changing, and we will be referring to the Contacts area as only one table within the file.

What's the difference between a file and a table, you may be asking.

In early versions of FileMaker Pro, a table and a file were the same thing. There was only one table per file; when you created fields, they were created in that single table. You could view the data in Table View, but you also had other options about how your data looked depending on what you decided to do with your layouts.

When you developed a solution that brought together the information in several files, you linked those files with relationships, and when your user opened the solution, the files opened as they were needed. The desire for convenience of having a solution open more quickly across a network and the simplification of the administration of accounts and passwords led FileMaker to develop multiple tables per file.

With FileMaker Pro 7, a file can have more than one table. Since each table is part of the same file, the entire solution opens as quickly as one file opens.

You start any database by creating a table and defining the fields for it. At this point, My_Phonebook is a file with one table in it. In this chapter, we're going to add tables to a file.

The first thing we want to do is to change the name of the file to Business, because the tables we'll be creating in this file need a name that more clearly suggests the scope of the tables that we'll be using.

➲ **NOTE**   I don't want you to get confused between a table and a view of a layout that looks like a table. They're not the same thing. A table is a collection of data — or fields — that relate to a subject. In the database file My_Phonebook, you collected information — name, address, and phone numbers — about people you know. If you selected Table View (View, View as Table) you would see the information you collected in a tabular format, like a spreadsheet. Each record takes up one row, and each field will be a column.

As we saw in our My_Phonebook file, customers may have more than one phone number. That situation required us to create four fields for phone numbers, and there could conceivably be more than that! Let's say someone with bad handwriting takes a message for you, and all you can read is the phone number. To find the record in your database you would have to search in four separate fields. This is when you should begin to think about creating another table.

Another reason you might want to work with a multiple-table system is for reporting. For example, in an invoicing table, you need to have a number of lines on the invoice so your customers can buy more than one item. You certainly don't want to make out a separate invoice for every single item in their shopping cart. You could create a separate field for every line on the invoice, but then it would be pretty difficult to find out how many widgets you sold in the month of May because you'd have to perform a find in each field. By moving the invoice lines to a separate table, you can get that report in short order. Every line will be a separate record that will either be part of your find or not.

You can see a pattern developing when you look at My_Phonebook and an invoicing system. Whenever you find yourself making a list of similar types of items in your database, you probably need another table. Let's create one.

Define Your Tables

Because our file will now be home to multiple tables, we need a name that will better encompass the purpose of the file. It's a good idea to think about these naming issues before you start a project.

1. Save a copy of the My_Phonebook file and name the copy **Business**. Pay attention to where you save it.

2. Close My_Phonebook and open Business.

3. Select **Define Database**, **Fields** and change the name of the SerialNumber field to **ContactSerNum_pk**.

⟫ **NOTE**   The pk stands for primary key. Shortly we'll use fk as a code to represent foreign key. The codes also operate as a reminder that these fields should not be deleted or tampered with for fear that our file structure may fail. They aren't required for building our relationships, but they are a common way developers comment the special purpose these fields serve. You can also use Field Comments in addition to or instead of these conventions. But you can't see the field comments when you're building relationships between tables.

When you rename a field, click on the field in the list, highlight the field name in the Field Name box, and begin typing the new name. If you highlight the field name and press Backspace or Delete, FileMaker assumes you want to create a new field. That means that after typing the changed name, the Save button will not be one of your choices.

Now start a new table called Phone in the Business file.

1. First, choose **File**, **Define Database** and select the **Tables** tab.

2. Click the name of the **My_Phonebook** table to highlight it in the list. Click on the text in the Table Name field and change it to **Contact** and click on the **Change** button.

3. To add another table, highlight the word **Contact** in the Table Name field. Type **Phone** and click on **Create**.

4. Add the following fields:

Field Name	Type	Options/Comments
ContactSerNum_fk	Number	Foreign key
Phone	Text	
Type	Text	
Notes	Text	

5. Your screen should look like Figure 6-1. When you're finished, click **OK**.

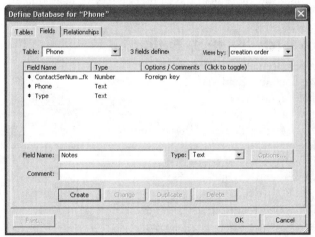

Figure 6-2
The Layout pop-up list showing the Contact layout selected.

Figure 6-1
The Define Database tab for the Phone table. Notice the "_fk" extension and the comment indicating the key field.

It doesn't matter what the layout looks like because you'll almost never be viewing the data from the Phone table.

Go to the layout pop-up (above the Book). See Figure 6-2. You have two layouts: Contact and Phone. Make sure that you have the Contact layout selected.

⌘ **TIP**   Aside from having multiple tables in a file, you can have many files open at one time. You can stack them one on top of the other, or you can have files open but hidden. To hide a file, make it the frontmost window, then choose Window, Hide Window. When you open a file to a layout that displays data from a related file, the related file opens hidden (if it's not already open).

You can also choose Window, Minimize (Windows) or click the minus sign in the upper-right corner of the window (Windows) or the yellow minus sign in the upper-left corner of the window (Macintosh). On Windows that has the effect of stacking a little rectangular representation of the window along the bottom of your screen. On a Mac, it will move the window to the Dock.

One of the major advantages of FMP7 is that you can now hide minimized windows that used to pile up at the bottom of the screen on Windows machines. On the other hand, FMP7 allows you to open a table in a new window. So it is easy to organize your screen display.

Normalize Your Information

Data normalization refers to the process of breaking down your information into separate tables, choosing the fields that will be in each of the tables, and creating the relationships between the tables.

What you hope to accomplish with normalization is the removal of duplicate or unnecessary data. (To be absolutely technically correct, I mean data that doesn't depend on the key.) For example, we could have included the name and address of our contact in our Phone table. But if we need to change a contact's address in the Contact table, we also have to find and change every occurrence of their address that appears in the Phone table. That could get very messy. By keeping the address in the Contact table, you can find all of what you need in one place. Normalization is for simplicity and clarity.

Determine Your Match, or Key, Fields

When you create a relationship between tables, you choose a field in each table that will compare data. These are the *match*, or *key*, fields. When there is a match in the data in the key field, FileMaker allows you to display information from any of the other fields in any records that also have a match. In Figure 6-3, you can see that more than one record in the Phone table has the same field, ContactSerNum_fk. We'll discuss how to get those records over into the Phone table in just a bit.

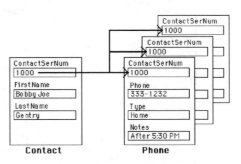

Figure 6-3
The Contact and Phone tables showing match, or key, fields. More than one record can have a match, which is the case with multiple phone numbers.

⊃ **NOTE**   I'd like to say a little about "match fields" and "key fields" here. In versions of FileMaker previous to 7, the only kind of relationship possible between tables was when values were an exact match. Starting in FMP7, you can now have unequal relationships. Using symbols like <, >, and ≠, you can tell FileMaker to show you items that are less than, greater than, or even completely unlike a value. It would seem then that the term "match field" would apply specifically to equal relationships. I think we'll see the term "key field" coming more to the forefront.

⊃ **NOTE**   I've been teaching you to give your key fields identical names in both tables. In my quest to show you good database technique, I may be causing some confusion. You can build relationships between tables using any two fields regardless of their names. You can even use fields that have incompatible types of data. The relationships may be invalid and unusable, but you can do it. I encourage you to experiment. There have been some very exciting discoveries made when developers tried things that "couldn't be done." However, you should know good technique so that when you make decisions to go against the standard, you'll know why.

Way back when we created My_Phonebook, we created a SerialNumber field, which we've now changed to ContactSerNum_pk.

⌘ **TIP**   Try to use the same basic* name for the key fields in both tables. For example, use InvoiceNum in both the Invoice and InvLI tables. That way, no matter which table you're in, it'll be easy to trace the relationship back.

(* I say "basic" name because I still want you to use development conventions to start and end the field names with other descriptive elements like _pk and _fk for the key type.)

You might think you could use a person's name or a product name as the key, and you can, but let me suggest that you save yourself a lot of trouble by not making that your primary key. To make critical relationships work, it's best if you use a unique key in one of the two tables. You want to use a field that does not contain active or volatile data. Instead, use a field that is somehow independent from the other information and something you won't be tempted to change.

For example, let's look at Business. What if you used a person's name as the key? If you had someone named John Smith in your table, as soon as you entered a second John Smith, the phone number of John number one would instantly appear in John number two's portal! (We'll get to portals in a minute.) And what if you had a woman who changed her name when she got married? As soon as you change her last name in her contact record, all phone numbers in the portal would disappear!

I'm speaking from the experience of many wasted hours when I tell you that you're much better off using unique numbers right from the start. A number is a good choice because it can be made unique. Use auto-entered serial numbers (without leading zeros), and protect them against modification. In fact, go into Define Database in the Contact table and double-click the ContactSerNum_pk field. Choose Options, and at the Auto-Enter tab, click the box next to "Prohibit modification of value" to check it. That doesn't mean that you can't create other relationships between tables based on information in other fields. It's just that your primary relationship should use that unique serial number as your key.

Making the Relationship

You should still be looking at the Contact table.

1. Choose **File, Define Database, Relationships**.
2. Click on the second icon from the left under Tables/Relationships. This will take you to the Edit Relationship window shown in Figure 6-4.
3. Select **Contact** from the Table pop-up list on the left and **Phone** from the Table pop-up list on the right.
4. Select **ContactSerNum_pk** from the list of fields on the left and **ContactSerNum_fk** on the right.
5. Make sure that the equal sign between the tables is selected.

Part 2

6. Click on the following boxes in the lower-right corner of the box: **Allow creation of records in this table via this relationship** and **Delete related records in this table when a record is deleted in the other table.**

7. Click **Add**, **OK**, and **OK**.

These will be the match, or key, fields between the tables. See Figure 6-5. Let's take a look at the other very important option check boxes in this window. (If you create files and tables regularly, please see "Notes to Developers about Naming Conventions" in Appendix A for information about naming fields and relationships.)

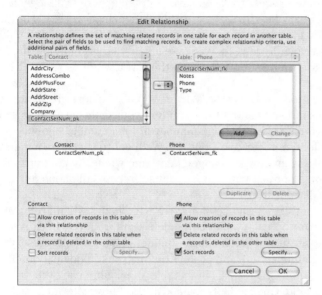

Figure 6-4
The Edit Relationship window showing the key fields.

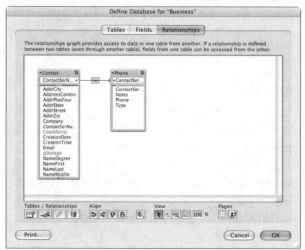

Figure 6-5
The Relationships tab showing the key fields between the Contact and Phone tables.

Relationship Tools[7]

Now that we actually have a relationship between tables in our file, I can tell you about the relationship tools in the Relationships graph. Take a look at Figures 6-6 and 6-7.

Each of these boxes represents one of the tables in this file. When in this window, I will refer to them as Table Occurrences or TOs. See my naming discussion under "Table Occurrence" in this section.

There is something that is not apparent from these figures: When you add a Table Occurrence from another file, the name of the table is italicized. It's just another visual aid to let you know what's going on with the relationships.

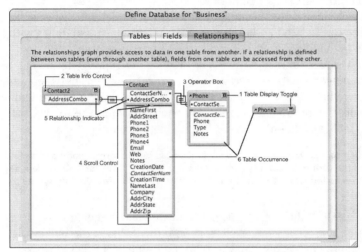

Figure 6-6
Functions of the Table Occurrences window.

Part 2

The numbered items are explained below.

1 Table Display Toggle — The table display toggle allows you to vary the appearance of the Table Occurrence between Full, Related fields only, and Table name only. The Contact and Phone tables are set to Full, Contact2 appears as Related Fields only, and Phone2 shows the Table Name only setting. You may notice there is a slight difference in the appearance of the little toggle icon depending on which appearance variation the TO is in.

2 Table Info Control — When you hover your mouse pointer over the table info control arrow, you can see the source table and the source file. This is helpful because these TOs can be named something other than their actual table name. And you can have tables from other files in this window. Yes, you can double-click the Table Occurrence icon to display that information, but you may find this faster and more to your way of working.

3 Operator Box — The operator box gives you some information about the type of relationship between the TOs. Starting with FileMaker Pro 7, you can build other than equal relationships between tables. That includes <, =, >, =, ≠, and x. If there is more than one criteria between the two TOs, it is considered a complex relationship and the symbol will appear as an "x."

4 Scroll Control — The scroll control triangle only appears if the Table Occurrence is in the Full display toggle setting and if all the fields are not visible. The fields appear in the list according to the View by pop-up in the Tables tab. If the first field in the list is the first field in the View by pop-up, the upper scroll triangle will disappear. As you scroll down and the last field appears at the bottom, the bottom scroll triangle will disappear.

5 Relationship Indicator — The relationship indicator square simply shows that there is a relationship to and from this field. You'll only see a relationship indicator if the field is in the top section of the TO. They will appear either on the left or right of the field name depending on whether there is a related TO on the left and/or right of it.

By the way, once a field becomes a key field in a relationship between TOs, it moves into the Related Fields area at the top and appears in italics with the other fields in the lower area, depending on the toggle status.

6 Table Occurrence — A Table Occurrence is a representation of a table. Table Occurrences are used to create and view relationships between tables. Notice that we have two occurrences of the Phone table: Phone and Phone2. They're really two occurrences of the same table. If you were to look at the data in the Table Occurrences, you'd see it is identical.

⊃ **NOTE** Much of this window was heavily influenced by the terminology of graph theory. Each little group of rectangles and lines is a "graph." The Table Occurrence boxes would be called "nodes," while the lines relating the nodes together would be called "paths."

You can resize the Table Occurrences by clicking and dragging either the sides, corners, top, or bottom. Well, sort of. If the TO is in the Full display setting, you can grab just about anywhere on the frame of the TO to resize it except the scroll control. In the other display modes, you can only grab one of the four sides to resize it.

You can also move and resize Table Occurrences with the arrow keys. Select one or more Table Occurrences. Press Control+right arrow to move the TOs. Press Control+Shift+right arrow to make the TOs wider. Try the other Control and Control+Shift+arrow combinations to see what they do. They all give you a little better control over moving and resizing than you can get by click+drag. Also, try using the arrow keys by themselves to move among the objects in the Relationships graph.

Now let's look at the tool icons in the bottom of the window.

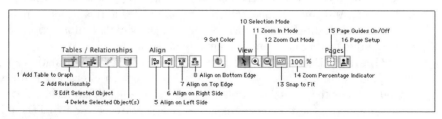

Figure 6-7
Relationships and Tables tools.

Tool Icons

1 Add Table Occurrence to Graph — This is where you go to add a Table Occurrence to the window. Clicking the icon brings up a Specify Table window. You can add Table Occurrences from the current file or from other files. When you click a table in the list its name appears in the Name of Table Occurrence area. FileMaker keeps track of the names of your TOs. If you already have one called Phone, it will add a number for you, calling it Phone 2. Since I suggest removing spaces, you'll want to rename it Phone2. But when you add the next occurrence of the Phone table, FileMaker will name it Phone 2 (Phone space 2) again. If you remove the space this time (thereby making it Phone2) you'll be warned that the name is already in use. Try Phone3. If you don't know how many occurrences there are, go ahead and let FileMaker name it. Then look around the Relationships window to locate the other occurrences, double-click the new occurrence, and give it the sequential name you want. It's a little awkward, but it will keep you consistent.

2 Add Relationship — Click this icon to bring up the Edit Relationship window seen in Figure 6-4. The Table pop-ups will bring up the current list of TOs available. If the table you need isn't there, click the Cancel button and create one with the Add Table button. After you choose the tables and define the relationship between them, if FileMaker needs another Table Occurrence of one of the tables it will tell you.

3 Edit Selected Object — The Edit Selected Object icon will be gray until you select a single TO or a relationship indicator. You cannot select more than one item. If you select a TO and click the pencil, you'll see the Specify Table window. If you select an operator box and click the pencil, you'll see the Edit Relationship window. I personally find it easier to double-click the items to bring up the window. The only time I've used the Edit Selected Object icon is to write this paragraph. Okay, so I didn't really write with the little pencil. But you know what I mean.

Originally I thought you would use the pencil to draw relationships between tables. Nope. But you can accomplish that by simply clicking on the name of the field you want to use as the key field in one TO and dragging to the second key field in the other TO.

4 Delete Selected Object(s) — What else would you use a trash can for? You can select multiple TOs (and the relationships between them) or single relationship indicators, then click the trash can. Yep, you could also just press your Backspace or Delete key — which is how I do it.

5 Align on Left Side — This allows you to align the left sides of the selected TOs to the left side of the selected TO furthest to the left. This and the next three icons are a lot like the Set Alignment tool in Layout mode. You might want to exercise some caution when using these tools because they can easily pile a bunch of Table Occurrences on top of one another. Keep your other hand poised over the Undo key combo.

6 Align on Right Side — Aligns the right sides of the selected TOs to the right side of the selected TO furthest to the right in the window.

7 Align on Top Edge — Aligns the top of the selected TOs to the top of the selected TO highest in the window.

Part 2

8 Align on Bottom Edge — Aligns the bottom of the selected Table Occurrences to the bottom of the selected TO lowest in the window.

9 Set Color — You can select one or more TOs and give them a color. This can be helpful especially when you start getting a fairly complicated system. You might choose to make all TOs of the same table the same color. Or you could make specific groupings the same color. Just keep in mind who will be using your color system. About seven percent of the population has some level of color blindness. And watch out! It is possible to turn the TO white, leaving only the text and a few of the control icons visible.

10 Selection Mode — This makes your mouse the selection tool so you can select TOs or relationship indicators. It's the setting you'll probably be using most.

11 Zoom In Mode — Turns the mouse pointer into a magnifying glass, allowing you to increase the magnification. If you're already at full magnification, the tool will be grayed out. If you're zoomed out and using the Zoom In Mode, once you get to full magnification the pointer switches to Selection mode and the icon turns gray. If the tool is active, you can use it to zoom out by holding down the Option key (Macintosh) or Alt key (Windows) and clicking with the tool.

12 Zoom Out Mode — Turns the mouse pointer into a magnifying glass, allowing you to decrease the magnification and get a better picture of the overall structure of your tables. You can go all the way out to 1% magnification. That's so small that with the four TOs shown in Figure 6-6 I couldn't even see a gray dot on the screen. I can't imagine that level of magnification would be of much use. If you're using the Zoom Out tool, once you get to 1% magnification the pointer switches to Selection mode and the icon turns gray. If the tool is active, you can use it to zoom in by holding down the Option key (Macintosh) or Alt key (Windows) and clicking with the tool.

13 Snap to Fit — If you can't see all your TOs, just click this button and the entire window will reset to the zoom level that shows them all. The window doesn't change size, just the zoom level. You can expand or contract the window manually using the knurled area in the lower-right corner. A change in the window size will affect what zoom level is needed to display all your TOs.

14 Zoom Percentage Indicator — This little box just shows you the zoom percentage. You can type a number directly in the box and then press the Tab or Return key. When I pressed the Enter key on the number pad, it was the same as if I'd clicked the OK button. I was kicked out of the window and back into Browse mode.

15 Page Guides On/Off — You click this icon to see where your pages will begin and end when printing your Relationships graph.

16 Page Setup — And this simply brings up the print window.

Allow Creation of Related Records

Each layout is set up to show records from one table. When you navigate a list of records with the Book, you won't ever swap into a different list. However, on your layouts, you can draw a portal to another table and see related records from that other table.

A *portal* is a data window from one table into another table (in the same or a different file). Depending on how the relationship is set up, the data in the fields in the portal can be viewed and even altered. But the field definitions and the actual data viewed through the portal can exist in the table that's related to (but different from) the table that's part of the current layout. (In a situation called a "self-join," tables can relate back to themselves. There will be a discussion of self-join relationships in the next chapter.)

Checking the box next to "Allow creation of records in the table via this relationship" allows you to click in a portal that uses an equal relationship and add new data that will end up in the other table. In some cases, you may only want related data displayed in a portal and not created. Of course, you would leave the check box empty in that case. Our situation calls for checking the box, so do that now.

One important note here: If you create a relationship between tables that is anything other than equal (using something other than the "=" sign) the check box for "Allow creation of records in this table via this relationship" turns gray and inactive. If you've created an equal relationship and check the box, and then go back and change the relationship to unequal, the box will become unchecked without warning. All relationships except equal are for display in a portal or for use with the Go to Related Record script step.

Parent and Child

In a typical relationship, a single record in one table will relate to several records in another table by way of the key field(s). The table that has the single record is known as the *master*, or *parent*, table. The table with potentially several related records is known as the *related*, or *child*, table.

In our Contact/Phone relationship, the child table is the Phone table, because a single contact record can relate to several phone number records. You can also think of the parent creating the children, which is pretty much what happens when new portal records are created. Not all relationships allow creation of related records. (Okay, in real life it takes two parents to create the children. But let's not get too literal here.)

In FMP7, since relationships to tables within the same file now go both ways, the determining factor of master/related or parent/child is whether a field on one side of the relationship has a unique value. (Having an auto-entered serial number provides implied uniqueness.) In our example, ContactSerNum_pk in the Contact table is unique. ContactSerNum_fk in the Phone table does not have to be unique. In fact, we want to be able to have more than one phone related back to each Contact record. That makes the Contact table the master or parent.

When you check the box next to "Allow creation of records in this table via this relationship" beneath one of the tables, you signal your intent to add records to that table through the portal (usually) and that this is the child table. When you look at the line or path that goes between the Table Occurrences for a parent/child relationship, you'll see a single line coming from the parent and a triple line or *crow's foot* attached to the child table as shown in Figure 6-6 between the Contact and Phone tables. Every set of crow's feet does not imply

Part 2

a parent/child relationship. The crow's foot means it's a one-to-many relationship. We'll be looking at that more in the next chapter.

Of course, there is nothing that would prevent you from creating a different relationship in the Phone table that named the Contact table as its related table, and there may be instances where you would want to do exactly that. (Probably not in the Phone table, however.) In this case, the Phone table would be the master table, and the Contact table would be the related table. If the master table is not going to be making records in the related table, it cannot be called the parent, since the parent creates offspring. In that case, it would be confusing (not to mention inaccurate) to call the Phone table the *parent* and the Contact table the *child* because the Phone table will not be creating contacts.

☒ **CAUTION**   It is possible to allow creation of related records in the table that would normally be considered the parent from the child table. I experimented with this by building a portal in the Phone table. I was able to create multiple records in the Contact table that had the identical serial number. I even went back and defined the ContactSerNum_pk in the Contact table to be unique. I was still able to create them by bypassing a warning dialog.

Creating parent records from the child table can really cause a mess because of identical serial numbers. When new phone numbers (or invoices or whatever) are created in a portal on the Contact layout, they appear in each of the Contact records that have that duplicate serial number. Let's just consider this a form of incest — something I'd highly advise against.

Allow Deletion of Related Records

If you lost track of someone in your Contact table and wanted to delete their record, you would probably want to get rid of the phone numbers, too. Checking the box next to "Delete related records in the table when a record is deleted in the other table" takes care of that for you.

If you had old phone numbers lying around in the Phone table, it probably wouldn't hurt anything. On the other hand, if you had an invoicing system where line items were left behind, that could be a different story. Let's say a report created in the InvLI table showed that 25 widgets had been purchased in May. But if 20 of those widgets were really orphaned records of a deleted invoice, your books could be off.

Protecting against orphaned records is part of a practice known as *referential integrity*. Good database design will make sure that if a record is deleted, any child records are either deleted or reassigned to another parent record. Another choice is to prevent deletion of the parent record if any child records exist.

Aside from using the "Delete related records in this table when a record is deleted in the other table" check box, complex methods for maintaining referential integrity with scripting and locking of menus exist. The details go beyond the scope of this book. But you need to know that such a concept exists and that FileMaker has provided a way to handle many situations without too much trouble.

⊠ **CAUTION** You should be cautious about turning on the option to allow deletion of related records when you're in a child table and creating a relationship back to the parent table. If you're working in an invoice and you delete an invoice line item, you will be unpleasantly surprised to find the whole invoice disappear before your eyes!

Sort Related Records

When you check the box next to "Sort records" in the Edit Relationship window (see Figure 6-4), FileMaker brings up the window shown in Figure 6-8. In this window, you can decide in what order items will appear in the portal. You can choose field values or a custom sort order based on a value list, and you can create the value list from here. You may want a portal to sort items by date, in alphabetical order, or by some other criteria, and you can sort by multiple items.

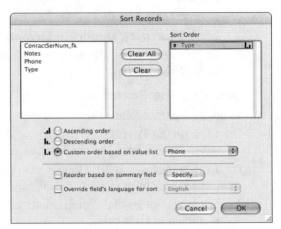

To demonstrate this option:

Figure 6-8
The Sort Records window where you choose how items will sort in a portal that uses the relationship.

1. Click the check box next to **Sort records** in the lower-right side of the Edit Relationship window.

2. In the next window, double-click **Type** to move it to the right column.

3. Highlight **Type** in the right column and click the radio button next to **Custom order based on value list**.

4. Click on the pop-up next to "Custom order based on value list" and choose **Define Value Lists**.

5. When the next window appears, click the **New** button and name this list **Phone**.

6. Now enter the following values in the box at the bottom of the screen, putting a Return between each item: **Home**, **Office**, **Cell**, **Car**, **eMail**, **Web**. Click **OK**, **OK**, **OK**, and **OK**.

Perhaps this is a little detailed for you, but please don't get discouraged. You can do some very sophisticated work and never have to go this far, but I do want you to know it's there if you want it.

⌘ **TIP** When you want to edit a value list, you must choose Define Value Lists. Then you can double-click the list you want to work with. It can be a little confusing because there is no option called Edit Value List.

➲ **NOTE** You can specify that any specific portal on a layout sorts independently from the sort you choose in the Define Relationships area. See the section titled "Sorting a Portal" later in this chapter.

Part 2

When we get done with the next section, you'll see how this value list affects the order in which items appear in the portal.

Making a Portal

So that nothing goes haywire, make a copy of the Contact layout by following these steps;

1. Above the Book, click the Layout list and select **Contact** if it's not already chosen.
2. Go into Layout mode.
3. Choose **Layouts, Duplicate Layout.**
4. On this new layout, delete all four phone fields as well as the eMail and Web fields and their labels.

Drawing the Portal

To create a portal, follow these steps:

1. Click on the **Portal** tool, which is next to the Button tool. (You can also select Insert, Portal or use the icon on the Tools toolbar.)
2. Draw a rectangle a little longer than the Company field in the newly cleared area of the layout and slightly taller than a field.
3. When you let go of the mouse button, you'll see the Portal Setup window as shown in Figure 6-9.

Figure 6-9
The Portal Setup window showing the settings to use for this particular portal.

4. Choose **Phone** from the pop-up.
5. Select **Allow deletion of portal records, 1** from the "Initial row" box, and **4** from the "Number of rows" box. Then choose **Show vertical scroll bar.**
6. Click **OK**.
7. At the next window, Add Fields to Portal, select **Type, Phone,** and **Notes**. Click **OK**.
8. If you can't see the scroll bar, it's possible that you have no line width selected for your portal or no solid line color. If this is the case, go back to "Cleaning Up the Layout" in Chapter 3.

You may have to resize the portal to match the one in Figure 6-10. When you select the portal, notice that the handles only appear in the first portal row. If your screen doesn't look exactly like this one, you may want to move the fields to make them line up. Pay particular attention to the fields within the portal. If a field is even one pixel beyond the border of the portal on any side, the information will not appear. Notice in Figure 6-10 that this layout has room to add another row of information in the portal.

Depending on the size of the rectangle you draw to represent the portal, you can get some strange results. See the section coming up shortly titled, "Portal Tool Behavior."

Placing the Fields in a Portal

With FileMaker Pro 7, when you create a portal, the fields appear in the portal in the order in which you selected them. You probably want to add field labels to the layout. To do that, follow these steps:

1. Double-click on the field.
2. At the bottom of the window, check the **Create field label** box.
3. Move the label where it will make the most sense on your layout, using Figure 6-10 as a guide.

Notice the double colon in front of the field name. That means this field will contain data from another Table Occurrence, in this case, the Phone table. (It is also possible to use data from the same table using a self-join relationship, discussed in Chapter 7. Even then, you will still see the double colon in the field name.) If the field font is too large or the wrong type, reformat it now.

> ☒ **CAUTION**　　It is very important that you choose the right fields for your portal. This will usually consist of fields from the same relationship that you used to set up your portal. If you choose fields from the parent table or some other relationship, your portal may behave unpredictably. Using the wrong fields can yield some pretty weird results. Sometimes FileMaker will display the words "<Unrelated Table>" in the field in Browse mode. Other times, your only clue that you have the wrong field is if you see the same values repeated in each portal record instead of separate values. For the specifics, see the "Portable Portals" section in Chapter 14.

> ☒ **CAUTION**　　Placement of the fields in a portal is also important. The top of the field can lay exactly on the outline of the portal, but if it goes one pixel higher, only the first portal row will show and you wouldn't be able to enter new data in the second row. Or if data already existed, you wouldn't be able to see beyond the first row. Pay attention to the left margin, too. If your field is one pixel over the border of the portal, you won't be able to key information into that field. When FileMaker places the fields within the portal, it provides a slight buffer between the fields and the top and bottom of the portal. In our example here, I've removed that buffer, making the layout more attractive. It took a little time to do this, but I think it's important to make your layouts look professional. Practice lining up and resizing your fields. As you become more skilled, you'll be very pleased with the results you achieve.

4. Resize the fields as necessary, then add the field labels as shown in Figure 6-10.

Notice that I didn't have you place the ContactSerNum_pk field in the portal. The key field only makes the connection between the tables and is not necessary in the layout. I've also left a little space to the right of the Notes field before the scroll bar. Make sure your layout has that little space. We will be adding a button there later. You may have to resize the portal again to make everything fit.

Part 2

Before we try it out, click on the Type field to select it, and choose Format, Field Format. In the pop-up menu next to "Format field as" select Pop-up list. Then choose Phone from the value list choices beside "Display values as." Click OK. Now go to Browse mode.

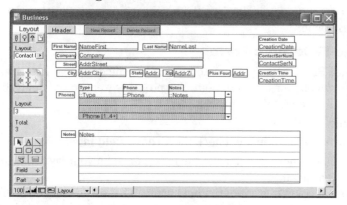

Figure 6-10
The Layout mode in the Contact table showing the placement of the Phone portal and the fields from the Phone table.

Adding Data to a Portal Field

To add data to a portal field, click in the Type field and choose Home from the pop-up list. Don't type the word Home. Use the pop-up list to make sure that the data is entered consistently. (To ensure that users do not override your pop-up list choices, format the field as a pop-up menu instead.) Then, make up a phone number and enter it in the Phone field. In the Notes field, you can add an extension number or the best time to reach the person, or just leave it empty. Notice that there is now a new line below the one you're working in because we checked the "Allow creation of related records" box in the Edit Relationship window. But if you try to click on the third line, you can't enter anything there. FileMaker creates a new record in the Phone table when you enter data, and then it gets ready for you to enter new data.

Notice that as you work, the portal is moving the records around — sorting them according to the sort order we defined as part of the relationship. If you don't make a choice from the pop-up list, blank items will sort to the bottom of the portal. Of course, you can turn that feature off by going back into Define Relationships.

⌘ **TIP**   When the entire portal row is selected, you can choose Records, Duplicate Record, and FileMaker will duplicate the portal record. This can be handy if the data in most of the fields in your portals will be the same. Just to be clear, it is not enough to have the cursor in a field in the portal. The whole portal row must be selected. You can tell if it's selected because the row will be highlighted.

To select a portal row, you must click somewhere on the row outside the fields. Because of the way I set up my portals, that can be a little tricky since I usually close up all available space between the fields. You could leave some space for that purpose. Or you could create a button in the portal with these script steps:

    Go to Portal Row [Select; No dialog; Get (PortalRowNumber)]
    Duplicate Record/Request
See Chapter 14 for more on scripts.

Portal Tool Behavior

When you draw the area you want for your portal, there are a number of things that happen depending on the size of the rectangle that represents where you want the portal to go.

If you draw a rectangle slightly taller than the currently selected font size, the rectangle will represent the size of the top portal row. The window will show the number of rows as 1. You can type over that number. When you click OK you move to the Add Fields to Portal window.

After you select your fields and click OK, the field size expands or contracts vertically to fill the portal row, allowing a buffer of one pixel above and two below in the first portal row. (Keep in mind that depending on your default settings, the portal itself may have one of the effects from the Emboss palette applied to it.) You will probably want to resize the field height. In some cases the field height will not be tall enough to see the bottoms of the letters in the fields. In other cases, the field height will be too tall and you'll need to change the field height to match the height of the font you've chosen. If you selected more than one field, the width will be squeezed or expanded horizontally to fit the portal row.

If you draw the rectangle slightly taller than the height of two (or more) fields of the currently selected font size (plus the three buffer pixels), the rectangle will represent two (or more) portal rows. The dialog will show the number of rows as 2 (or more). You can type over that number, too.

If you draw the rectangle smaller than the font height, the dialog shows the number of rows as 0. You must type a number larger than 0. Now this is where things get weird. When you type a number (let's say 3) and click OK, depending on the size of your layout, you may get a warning that "This operation will cause objects to extend off the layout." If you click the OK button, the portal rows draw quite tall based on some multiple of the rectangle you drew, and the layout gets expanded to accommodate all the portal rows. Then you move on to the Add Fields window. If you click the No button instead, you are moved to the Add Field to Portal window. When you finish adding your fields and you're returned to Layout mode, the portal borders are invisible! If you can find the edges of the portal (you'll probably need to move a field or two out of the way), you'll find it has line size and color attributes assigned to it. There is nothing you can do with any of the palettes to bring back the visibility of the portal! However, if you double-click the portal, the number of rows will have changed to accommodate the number that will fit the layout without expanding it. If you click OK, you go back to Layout mode and the portal now has visible borders and can be resized. Of course you'll need to resize the fields and the portal height. If the portal doesn't cause the layout to expand, the portal rows and the field height both draw quite tall based on some multiple of the rectangle you drew.

Part 2

❌ **CAUTION**   When duplicating or deleting portal rows, be sure that you have the row selected or you may inadvertently duplicate or delete a parent record. In the case of a deletion, FileMaker brings up a warning screen, "Permanently delete this one related record?" But people tend to ignore warnings after a while.

Continue to make up information until you've filled up four rows. To get to the fifth row, use the vertical scroll bar on the right of the portal. If you're in a field in the fourth row, you can also use the Tab key on the keyboard to move to the fifth row. Using a portal like this allows you to add as many phone numbers or other information as you want. Notice that using a portal this way can save space on your layout and you get more information. Before we put the portal here, we only listed the phones. Now, we not only have the phones, but we also have a Type and Notes field as well. And we can have unlimited numbers. When you look at your record in Browse mode, you will see the number of rows of data that you chose to display when you created the portal. If all rows are filled and you want to know if there is additional data in the portal, use the scroll bar. You could create a calculation to tell you if there are extra rows, but I'll leave that up to you to experiment with. (Hint: You'll need a self-referencing relationship and a field that counts matching data.)

Sorting a Portal

Before FileMaker 7, you had to make a separate relationship for every portal that required a different sort. It's true that portals will inherit any sort defined in the Relationships graph, but you can bypass that sort and add sorts specific to each portal if you prefer.

To "customize" the sort in a specific portal, go to Layout mode and double-click the portal to bring up the Portal Setup window. Click the Specify button next to "Sort portal records" to open the Sort Records window. You'll notice that the only fields available are the fields from the related table. How the heck do you include fields from other tables? What follows is not particularly intuitive, but it is the proper procedure and gives you all the power you need over the portal.

If you want to use fields from the portal table, double-click them to move them to the Sort Order area on the right, then click the OK button. If you don't want to use any of these fields, just click the Cancel button. Clicking either button will return you to the Portal Setup window. Notice the "show related records from" pop-up at the top of the window and memorize (or write down) the Table Occurrence that is associated with this portal. By choosing a different Table Occurrence from the pop-up, you can click the Specify button as many times as necessary to fill the Sort Order area with fields from any Table Occurrence you want. The most important thing to do as you finish making your field selections is to reselect the Table Occurrence you started with from the pop-up in the Portal Setup window before you click the final OK button.

Investigating the Related Table

Now that we have created our portal field, we can examine how related tables work. From this example, you will see that when we enter phone information for a person in the Contact table, the data is actually going into the Phone table.

To begin, switch to another record and make up some phone numbers there. Go to the Layout drop-down at the left of your screen and select Phone. Click through the records. To see all the records in a list, you can go into

Layout mode, shrink the Body part, and remove the Header and Footer altogether as shown in Figure 6-11 (or you could just choose View, View as Table). I'll explain about the FirstName and LastName fields later.

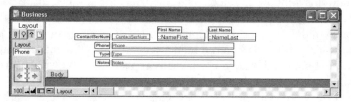

Figure 6-11
Layout mode in the Phone table showing Header and Footer parts removed and placement of related fields from the Contact table.

⌘ **TIP**   If you are looking for a table in another file, choose Window and select the name of the table. If you don't see it there, try Window, Show Window. Remember that the file must be open, because only open files appear in the Window menu. Hidden windows show in the Window, Show Window menu.

⌘ **TIP**   To remove a layout part (Header, Body, Footer, Summary, etc.) click on the part's name tab and press Backspace or Delete. If there are layout items in that part, you'll be warned and will have a chance to change your mind before the part is deleted.

You can also remove a layout part by clicking on the tab and dragging the part upward until it disappears into the window border (if it is the topmost part) or the part above it. If there are layout objects in that part, you won't be able to do that until you've deleted those objects.

Now go to Browse mode and choose View, View as List. Notice that the ContactSerNum_pk field has been entered without any effort from you. That happens because we checked the box for creation of related records when we made the relationship to the Phone table. FileMaker places the number from the key field in the parent table into the key field in the child table.

Notice that you can enter the ContactSerNum_pk field and change the number. That could cause trouble if other users access that field and change the data. You can choose to prohibit modification as part of the field definition, but that might pose a problem if you had to reassign the record to a different parent record to maintain referential integrity.

Here's another solution:

1. Go to Layout mode, select the **ContactSerNum_pk** field, and choose **Format, Field Behavior.**

2. To protect the information in the ContactSerNum_pk field so that it cannot be changed by mistake, make sure that the "In Browse mode" box is unchecked.

    If it turns out you need to get into the field regularly, you can check the box in the future or create a special layout that allows entry into a copy of the field. You could also create a special script for the purpose of entering the field. If you're beginning to wonder, the answer is: Yes, you can set up the same field with different properties on different layouts — or even on the same layout.

3. Click **OK,** then go back to Browse mode and notice that you can no longer enter the field.

FMP7 offers some new features. To allow access to this field only in Find mode, check the "In Find mode" box and uncheck the "In Browse mode" box. This will allow you to find records by clicking into that field to perform a Find.[7]

Look around this window. If you check the box beside "Select entire contents of field on entry," all text in the field is selected when you click into that field. If you need to delete the text, simply press the Backspace or Delete key. If you need to edit the text, click in the field a second time. The reason you might want all text selected is so you can easily replace the text without having to manually select it first.

If you use a software utility that converts keystrokes to Japanese characters, check the box next to "Set input method to." See Figure 6-12 for options. (See Chapter 4 for a brief explanation of the Furigana options you have when you define fields (File, Define Database, Fields tab, Options, Furigana).) The Help files will be much more valuable to you on this topic. One other note: The list in the pop-up on the Mac is much more limited than Windows.[7]

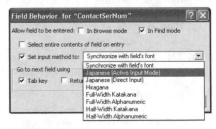

You can decide which key or keys are used to navigate to the next field. This is a very handy new feature that can prevent extra returns at the end of data fields. It's also useful for people who will use the number keypad for data entry.[7]

Figure 6-12
Field Behavior window showing Japanese character options.

Relating a Table Back to the Parent Table

(If you are not trying to create a relationship between files, you may want to skip this section.)

In older versions of FileMaker, you needed to create a relationship in the child file back to the parent file.

In version 7, with multiple tables within a single file, a relationship travels in both directions. So once we created the relationship between Contact to Phone, we automatically have the data from Contact available to the Phone table. However, if you find it necessary to use multiple files instead of multiple tables within one file, you will need to create a relationship back to the parent file.

⊃ **NOTE**   You may need to use a multiple file system in cases like the following:
■ If you converted a set of files from previous versions of FileMaker and there isn't time or budget to change all the files into multiple tables within one file.
■ If there is so much data in a single file that it would cause the file to approach FileMaker's 8 terabyte file-size limit, or the limits of the hard drive the file is on.
Here are some examples:
■ If you store images, rather than references to images
■ If you import large amounts of text into single fields
■ If you want to store data on separate servers
■ If there is a security problem raised by having a two-way relationship
A table of secret agents would need to set up a relationship into a table of world leaders to keep track of who is spying on whom. But if these tables were in the

same file, someone could follow the relationship from the other direction and get a list of which secret agents are spying on particular world leaders. By keeping the tables in separate files, it's possible to make the relationship flow in only one direction. Secret agents may be a silly example, but there are all sorts of new laws dealing with student grades, medical records, credit reporting, and even telemarketing phone numbers where privacy is legally required.

The instructions that follow assume that you have created a separate file called Phone and that you've made a relationship to it from the Contact table in the Business file. Since a file for phone numbers is not likely to become large enough to need this, we'll pretend it's a security feature to prevent someone from using a telephone number to look up a contact name. To create a relationship back to the parent file and table, in this case the Business file and the Contact table, follow these steps:

1. Open the Phone file.
2. Choose **File, Define Database, Relationships**.
3. The table for the Phone file appears. Click the **Add Table** tool, the first icon on the left under Tables/Relationships.
4. In the File pop-up in the Specify Table window, select the **Business** file.
5. You should see the Business file tables. Select **Contact** and click **OK**.
6. You should see table reference icons for both Phone and Contact. Click the **Add/Edit Relationship** tool, the second icon under Tables/Relationships.
7. At Edit Relationship, select **Phone** in the Table pop-up on the left and **Contact** in the Table pop-up on the right side of the window. Select **ContactSerNum_pk** under both tables. Click **Add**. Do not check any other boxes. Click **OK**.
8. At the Relationships window, you can see that the relationship exists. Click **OK**.
9. Now go back to the Contact table. Go to **File, Define Database, Relationships**. You won't see a relationship between your table named Phone and the Contact table unless you already created that relationship in the Business file.

When you are working with external files, you may need to create a relationship from the parent to the child and from the child to the parent to make data appear in both tables. (Don't get confused between the Phone table in the Business file and the Phone file outside the Business file.)

Performing a Find in a Portal

The reason we started this portal was to be able to perform a search in one place for multiple phone numbers. Click in one of the Phone fields with a number in it, select the whole number (Edit, Select All), and copy it.

 SHORTCUT   To select the entire contents of a field, place the cursor in the field and choose Command+A (Macintosh) or Ctrl+A (Windows).

Enter Find mode and paste the number in the Phone field in the first row of the portal. Click the Find button or press Enter or Return. The Status area should show one record found.

Performance Considerations

Finding data in a portal works just fine in a table with only a few records. But you need to know that the more records in the current table, the slower the portal search. You had a glimpse of the concordance FileMaker keeps for certain fields when you selected Insert, From Index while entering data in Chapter 5. This index is what makes FileMaker's searching so speedy when you perform a Find in the active table on a layout. But these indexes aren't much use to FileMaker when you're searching through a relationship in a portal or in a related field. Searching indexed fields becomes just as lethargic as searching unindexed fields when you access the same data through a relationship. I have a Contact table with over 3,000 records, and a Find is instantaneous — even across multiple fields. A Find in a Calculated field in a portal that has 100,000 child records is something else. In a case like that, it may be better to use scripts that structure the Find in the child table and bring you back to the related records in the parent table. If you'll be running a report like that once a month with an unshared file, speed may not be a big issue. But if this report will be a daily process with files shared on a network, you may want to reconsider.

⊠ **CAUTION**   Running complex finds and reports on a network with very actively shared files can cause severe slowdowns and crashes. When such reports are going to be run, it may be best to ask other users to quit the program. Another option is to run FileMaker Server, a separate, specialized program from FileMaker, Inc., to be used for just such a busy network.

➲ **NOTE**   When I say that records in a portal are treated as unindexed, I don't want to give you the impression that they are unindexed anywhere other than through relationships. If you go to the related table and perform a find in those very same fields, as long as the fields have been indexed, the find will run more quickly.

Another choice may be to create redundant lookup fields in the parent table for the purpose of such reporting. See Chapter 7 for more on lookup fields. Just remember, when you do that you reduce the level of normalization, which may create pockets of out-of-date data in your database. If you decide to use lookups to duplicate data, try to use fields that contain information that won't change.

Deleting a Record from a Portal

What if you find you no longer need one of the lines in the portal? Sure, you could just clear the fields, but then you have an empty line in the middle of the portal. This could be a big deal in an invoicing system where reports may turn up these empty records.

Remember that little space I had you leave in the portal just to the right of the Notes field? Click in it now. One line of the portal should become highlighted. If that's not what happens, go back into Layout mode, open the portal, and create the space as shown in Figure 6-10.

While that portal row is highlighted, choose Records, Delete Record. Notice that the dialog box in Figure 6-13 is different from the one that appears when you try to delete a parent record, because it mentions the "related record." If this is for one of those made-up phone numbers and you don't care about it, go ahead and click the Delete button. Just remember, there's no undo or revert for this.

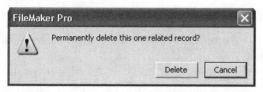

Figure 6-13
A warning dialog box that appears when you try to delete a related record.

Another alternative is to create a script that will delete a portal row and attach it to a button. Make the button small enough to fit on one line of the portal and drop it in the first portal row. The button will automatically be repeated for every row of information plus one empty row.

Dealing with "Portal Pop"

If you have more items in a portal than the number of rows can show, you can scroll down to take a look. But there has been a little annoyance since the beginning of portals in FileMaker. As soon as you entered any other fields on the layout, the portal would "pop" back to the top, and the lower records would once again be hidden from view. If your portals are doing that, and you want them to stay put, here's what you do:

1. Go to Layout mode and choose **Layouts, Layout Setup**.
2. On the **General** tab, uncheck the box next to **Show field frames when record is active**.
3. Click **OK**, go back to Browse mode, and notice that your portals will stay put as long as you are on that record.

Ah, but there is a price to pay. By unchecking the field frames box, you no longer see the field frames — those little dotted lines that appear around all fields in which you can enter data — while you enter data. If you really need your portals to stay in place, you may want to provide your data entry fields with borders so they're easier to spot.

Before We Go

Prior to creating the portal for phone numbers, we created a duplicate layout for Contact so that we could move fields around and add new features. Since this layout works so well, you'll probably want to delete the first Contact layout we developed.

1. Select the **Contact** layout.
2. Go to **Layouts, Delete Layout**.
3. At the "Permanently delete this layout?" prompt, select **Delete**.
4. Now go to **Contact, Copy Layout**. Select **Layouts, Layout Setup**. Under Layout Name, rename this layout **Contact** and click **OK**.

I also need to let you know that you can create relationships to tables in other files the same way we just created the relationship to the phone table. But there are a couple immediate advantages to working under the umbrella of a single file structure:

- Managing security in a single place
- Managing your schema in a single place

That's not to say there aren't reasons to work with multiple files. But you get immediate benefits with consolidation and it should be well considered when making plans for your database system.

In earlier versions of FileMaker, whenever you went to what was called the Define Relationships window from various other windows, you would see the currently selected relationship highlighted in a list of relationships. That is no longer the case now that we have the Relationships graph. Now you need to know what you're looking for. And as your solution gets more complicated, that will get more difficult. Sounds like another good reason for taking some time with color coding the Table Occurrences and organizing the window as you build relationships in it.

Summary

In this chapter, we learned when and why to use more than one table in our database. We built a two-table system complete with relationships, a portal, and related fields. We also looked at a number of potential problems in a multiple-table system and discussed ways of protecting against them.

Now we're gettin' into the good stuff! Are you starting to get the hang of it? You should probably find yourself being able to switch between the tables and modes, and moving fields around on the layouts pretty easily by now. In Chapter 7, we'll use our Contact table to build a real invoicing system using a total of five tables!

Q & A

Q All this, and it still doesn't look like the templates. How do I get that great, finished look?

A You can use the Layout tools to pull apart the templates, copy and paste any elements from there, and create whatever your heart desires. The more you practice, the better you'll get at it. We will deal more with layouts in Chapter 9, "Creating New Layouts with the Layout Assistant."

Q When we were in the Phone table and made a relationship back to Contact, who was the parent and who was the child?

A I believe that the names "parent" and "child" should be reserved specifically for relationships where creation of portal records takes place from the master side. "Master" and "related table" would probably be the more all-encompassing terminology to cover all relationships regardless of parenting capabilities. Whatever table is handing out its keys is the master table for that relationship. And whatever table is holding copies of those keys is the related table. That means that a table can be both a master and a related table to another table. It can also be master and related table to many other tables.

Workshop

Create a temporary relationship to one of the tables in the template files using anything that resembles a serial number. If there is no field like that, choose anything. In this case, check the box to allow creation of related records in the relationship. Put a portal on your layout and add some fields. Be sure to choose fields that are from the right relationship. Add a few records.

Now try changing the relationship by choosing a different key field from the template file. What happens to the records in the portal? What happens when you change the relationship back? When you are done, remove the new portal and fields from the layout, then delete the temporary relationship.

Review Questions

True-False

1. The purpose of a relational database is to allow you to store the same field data in several different tables.
2. A key field is one that is used to match data between related records.
3. A portal is a layout object that allows you to see many records from a related table.
4. Related key fields must have the same field name in both tables.
5. The purpose of a database table is to control the way information looks on the screen and when printed.

Short Answer

6. Name the three options that can be added to a relationship.
7. Why wouldn't a name field make a good key field?
8. When you add data to fields in a portal, where does the data get stored?
9. In Layout mode, how can you tell that a particular field is a related field?
10. In a relationship between automobile makes and automobile models, which would be the parent table and which would be the child table?
11. When you choose fields to be the primary key for relationship between tables, what type of field is the best choice?
12. When is it time to create a new table and build a relationship to it?
13. What is another term used to refer to the master table? The related table?
14. If you want to switch on the ability to create new items in a portal, what window do you need to be in?
15. Where do you determine the number of rows the portal will display?

Part 2

Chapter 7

Working with Related Tables — Part 2

Vocabulary

- Concatenate
- Entity
- ER diagram
- Foreign key
- Join (link) table
- Lookup field

- Many-to-many relationship
- Multiple-criteria relationship
- One-to-many relationship
- One-to-one relationship
- Primary key
- Self-join relationship

Objectives

1. Understand the importance of planning a database before building it.
2. Become familiar with the concept and features of the entity-relationship (ER) diagram.
3. Become familiar with the one-to-one, one-to-many, many-to-many, and self-join relationships.
4. Learn about primary and foreign key fields.
5. Learn how to resolve a many-to-many relationship.
6. Understand the purposes of join, or link, tables.
7. Learn how lookup fields can be useful in a relational database.
8. Add pop-up value lists and total fields.
9. Create a concatenated field.
10. Add a related field to a layout.

Introduction

In the last chapter, we created a fairly simple, two-table relational database. In this chapter, we'll build on what we learned there when we make a working invoicing system. As part of the project, we'll:

- Look at different types of relationships
- Learn how to diagram a multiple-table database

- Learn when to use related fields and when to use lookup fields
- Create the tables we diagram and enter some data

Along the way, I'll show you a number of potential stumbling blocks and ways to keep your footing among them.

Planning Your Database

Planning — I hate it! Some developers swear that 80 percent of your work should be gathering information, and that you shouldn't even turn on your computer until the last 20 percent of the job. This can be pretty hard to take if you're the type of person who likes to get your hands in the computer part of a project. The other side is that without good planning, you will probably end up wasting a lot of your time. If you intend to build FileMaker databases for other people as a profession, that can mean you'll end up working for free whenever you have to fix errors caused by bad planning. I've done it, and I've learned my lesson. Let me pass the lesson along to you.

The great thing about spreading out the data between more tables in a multi-table solution is that you have better possibilities for accurate reporting. At the same time, you increase the complexity and number of things to be careful about. All the more reason for good planning. You may have noticed that once we went from our single table, My_Phonebook, to the relational tables, Contact and Phone, there were quite a few extra steps and cautions to take into account.

Part of this planning can take place using the questionnaire I gave you in Chapter 3. Then you have to sit down and lay it all out on paper. Understanding the types of relationships and how to sketch them out will go a long way in the planning of your database.

Tricky Terms and Catchy Phrases

To get things started, you need to know that there is more than one type of relationship.

ER Diagram

An ER diagram is a way to represent how relationships work between files and tables. ER stands for entity-relationship. In database terminology, an *entity* generally refers to a file or a table. I don't know why they just don't call it a file- or table-relationship diagram — probably because the term came before FileMaker was invented. Figure 7-1 shows the basic ER diagram for our Business file. A more complete ER diagram would include fields, and the lines between the files would point to the key fields. Hmmm… Didn't we see something like that back in Chapter 6 when we looked at the Relationships tab in the Define Database window in the Contact Management file? That's right! Starting with FileMaker Pro 7, one form of an ER diagram is created automatically. Complete ER diagrams can show more detail about the types of relationships using little one-letter codes and icons. I won't go into that here. You might also want to know that you usually only want to show the main relationships between files at this stage of planning. Often, a number of utility relationships don't need to be indicated. If you get too many lines going, you won't be able to read the diagram.

Figure 7-1
Basic ER diagram for the Business file.

One-to-Many Relationship

When you created the Phone table and built the relationship to it from the Contact table, you made a one-to-many relationship. One contact can have many phone numbers.

⊃ **NOTE** Technically, this could be a many-to-many relationship since one phone number could belong to many people. Take, for example, the case of a small company where many people share a common phone number. But for now, let's keep it simple.

In Figure 7-1, you can see one line on the Contact side and three lines (crow's foot) on the Phone side. That means it's a one-to-many relationship. In an invoicing system, you can put many products on one invoice.

The inverse of this is the many-to-one relationship. When we created a relationship from the Contact table to the Phone table, a relationship was automatically created from the Phone table back to the Contact table. Using that, we can display the person's name in the Phone table. That is a many-to-one relationship. I've used it a lot. This inverse relationship is shown by only one set of lines on the diagram.

One-to-One Relationship

Putting everyone's last name in a child table instead of the parent table would be an example of a one-to-one relationship. It can be done, but why would you want to? (This assumes the use of a serial number as the primary key.) This relationship is sometimes used to keep confidential information (such as an employee's evaluation) away from prying eyes. But you could probably accomplish the same thing in a single file by using password protection to make the data in specific fields inaccessible (or grayed out).

There are some legitimate reasons to implement two files with a one-to-one relationship, so I don't want to leave you with the impression that it should never be done. For example:

■ If a file were reaching FileMaker's 8 terabyte limit, the developers might store some of the data in a separate file. You're more likely to run out of hard drive space first, which brings us to...

■ If a file were reaching the limits of the size of the hard drive.

And what if two complex files were developed separately in different departments and then brought together? It might be simpler to create a one-to-one relationship than to rebuild. I'm sure you can picture what a one-to-one ER diagram would look like — two boxes joined by one line.

In FileMaker's Relationships graph, a relationship will only appear to be one-to-one when both fields in a pair are defined as unique (validation) or expected to be unique (auto-enter serial number).

Oh, a terabyte? That's equal to 1024 gigabytes. And you can now have a file up to eight times that! That's a whole lot bigger than the previous file size limit of 2 gigabytes. Now that's power! But I sure don't have access to drives that big. The biggest hard drive I've ever owned is 250 gigabytes on my current computer.

Many-to-Many Relationship

In an invoicing system, one invoice could have many products on it, and one product from the Product table could appear on many invoices. This would be considered a many-to-many relationship. It's sort of a double-sided one-to-many.

There are uses for many-to-many relationships, but it's simply not allowed when it comes to making a relationship that allows creation of records in a portal.

Although rarely used in this context, one other option is to use a multi-valued field. You could have a number of Product IDs in a single Text field on one invoice. FileMaker is one of the few databases that supports multi-valued keys. This is a method that is difficult to support, so I won't go into any detail here.

Not only that, but you can't have a "many" side to the Invoice relationship if the invoice has a unique serial number. Unique denotes one, not many. So you would have to remove the unique feature. But what's the use of a bunch of invoices with the same number? Sound confusing? Just don't do it. Instead, use another table.

I do often use a many-to-many relationship to root out duplicate names and addresses in my files. Back in Chapter 4 in the section titled "Calculation Field" we created a field called AddressCombo. Using two Table Occurrences of the Contact table joined on both sides with AddressCombo, we can see when there are multiple copies of that specific name and address. You can see what this looks like in Figure 7-6 with the double crow's feet between the AddressCombo fields in the Contact and Contact2 TOs. A portal displaying this relationship would always show at least one item — the record itself. To really make this effective, you'd want to create a multi-criteria relationship (see the section coming up shortly) so that the portal only displayed other records with a matching name and address. Of course it wouldn't help you spot records where the data entry people used Bob one time and Robert the next, but it certainly will help you spot absolute duplicates.

In FileMaker's Relationships graph, a relationship will only appear to be many-to-many:

■ When both fields in a pair are neither unique (validation) nor expected to be unique (auto-enter serial number)

■ When the relationship uses the Cartesian "x" symbol between two fields

Part 2

⊃ **NOTE** Selecting the so-called Cartesian "x" symbol from the pop-up in the Edit Relationship dialog means that all records in one table are connected to all other records in the other table. It is especially useful for passing data into special fields formatted as global storage. It helps to eliminate the need for special constant calculation fields and relationships between those constant fields used by developers in earlier versions of FileMaker. It can also be useful for displaying all records from a special table that stores choices that you might want to display in a portal.

The Join, or Link, Table

The way to handle a many-to-many relationship is to create an in-between table called a join, or link, table. Each record in the join table would contain key fields (probably serial numbers) for both the invoice and the product. These are often called *foreign* keys because they refer to a specific record in another table. The fields in the join table don't need any auto-enter options turned on because they will be created from the other tables. For an invoicing system, this table would contain the invoice line items. We'll call it InvLI. Then you have a one-to-many relationship from Invoice to InvLI (one invoice shows many products) and a one-to-many relationship from the Product table to the InvLI table (one product can show up in many lines in the portal of the invoice).

Does this sound complicated? Don't worry. You'll understand it much better when you work through the example later in the chapter.

☑ **BEST PRACTICES** LI is an abbreviation often used to refer to line items. Accepted abbreviations like this make field names shorter, yet understandable.

If you find yourself drawing a many-to-many ER diagram when planning your files, just put another table between them as in Figure 7-2.

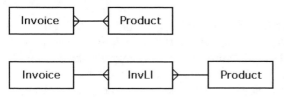

Figure 7-2
ER diagram showing a many-to-many relationship for an invoicing system and how it should be restructured using a third table. InvLI becomes the join table between Invoice and Product.

Whenever you see a table with two (or more) of the three-pronged crow's foot symbols attached to it, that table is a good candidate for *reporting*. The reason you do a report here is that it's more flexible than either of the other tables.

For example, let's say you have an invoice all nicely laid out in the Invoice table with a portal that shows 10 lines. A customer comes in and orders 12 items. Even though you can use the scroll bar and enter the data, only 10 lines will print out. You can expand the portal, but eventually some customer may order so many items that your portal extends down to another page. When you print invoices from now on, you'll have to print all those empty lines and a second page with your total at the bottom, even if other customers only order one item. This is tacky and unnecessary. Instead, print your invoice from the InvLI table and the "report" (invoice) can show just as many or as few items as your customer orders.

I've been involved in situations like this over and over again. My client swears, "We'll *never* need more than X repetitions." So I build a report, or a contract, or an invoice in the "one" side of the relationship. Eventually the system improves their business, and the "never" day comes. The temptation to build the report in only one table comes because, when you use data in a related table, you have to create one layout for day-to-day work and another for printing. And the amount of time you thought you'd have to spend on the work didn't include extra layouts and scripts. But experience dictates the need for both layouts.

Self-join Relationship

A self-join relationship is also called a self-referencing relationship. When you call up the Define Relationships graph or Edit Relationship window, you can create a relationship to the table you're in. You can create a self-join for any of the other types of relationships, although I use it most often with the one-to-many relationship. In our Contact table, we might have a number of people who work for the same company. You could create a self-join relationship by choosing CompanyName in both of the field lists. Then you make a portal on the layout that would show the names of anyone else who works at that company. To make this work, you will need to make sure the company name is spelled exactly the same in each record.

If you need to create a self-join relationship, you can choose the same table on both sides of the Edit Relationship window. But as soon as you select the fields and click OK, you'll find that FileMaker requires that you add another Table Occurrence to the graph. In our example, FileMaker would create a Table Occurrence called Contact 2 with all the same fields as Contact. If need be, you can create other self-joining relationships for the same table using multiple Table Occurrences. There are a couple of self-join relationships in Figure 7-6 between the various Contact Table Occurrences. The relationship between Contact2 and Contact3 is a multiple-criteria relationship, which we'll be discussing next.

⊃ **NOTE**   FileMaker will add a space and a number to each subsequent table reference. The next references would be Contact 3, Contact 4, and so on. Since fields can be placed on layouts using these Table Occurrence names, you should remove the space or replace it with an underscore or a similarly web-friendly character. (See Chapter 19.) This is in keeping with the requirements for web sharing and ODBC.

Multiple-Criteria Relationships[7]

FileMaker Pro 7 allows you to create multiple pairs of relationship criteria between the same pair of Table Occurrences. What advantage is there to this arrangement? Let's say you built a relationship between two TOs of the Contact table to show all the people in your file who work at the same company (Company = Company). A portal on the Contact layout using that relationship would also display the name of the contact person whose record you're looking at. There's not much value in that. Using the new multiple-criteria relationship tool, you can now edit the relationship and add a second criterion where

ContactSerNum_pk ? ContactSerNum_pk. Now no matter whose record you look at in that company, the only names to appear in the portal are the names of other employees.

There are a couple of multiple-criteria relationships in Figure 7-6 between Contact2 and Contact3 and Invoice and Invoice2. These also happen to be unequal relationships, which we'll be discussing next.

There are some limitations to this arrangement depending on the scheme with which you intend to work. Sometimes the field pairs you choose will prevent creation of records via the relationship. But that's not too hard to figure out since that choice is grayed out once you create your second pair of fields. But here's something that might not be so obvious: If you add a second pair of relationship criteria to a relationship that allows creation of related records, the check mark disappears without warning. Even if you immediately delete the second criteria set, if you click the OK button when leaving the Edit Relationship window, you may be surprised to find you can no longer create records in the portal.

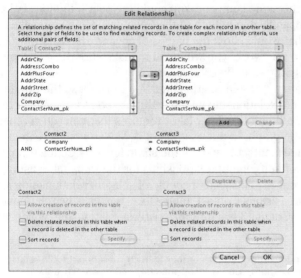

Figure 7-3
The Edit Relationship window showing a multiple-criteria relationship that includes an unequal relationship.

Unequal Relationships[7]

Previous versions of FileMaker only allowed equal relationships between fields. FMP7 lets you create various unequal relationships. This includes relationships based on field values being less than, greater than, and not equal to each other. For example, using the relationship symbols, you can build a portal to show all invoices created between two dates. The relationship would look something like this:

```
Invoice2::Date > zi_DateStart_gd and
Invoice2::Date < zi_DateEnd_gd
```

DateStart and DateEnd would be formatted as Global storage. You could put the fields on your layout and put any dates in them you want. Quick, easy, and flexible reporting! If your invoices included the name of the salesperson, you could add a Global field to filter for that, too. There's a lot of power here.

The most important part of this kind of report would be putting the portal on the right layout. If you put it on the Invoice layout, it will not filter the items in the portal by date as you might expect. You need to put it on a layout represented by the table occurrence with the dates — in this case Invoice2.

There are a couple of unequal relationships in Figure 7-6 between Contact2 and Contact3 and Invoice and Invoice2. You'll see the quick report I just talked about using the date fields in the upper right.

Also notice how the relationship lines (paths) next to zi_DateStart_gd and zi_DateEnd_gd have a little vertical line attached to them and don't quite touch the side of the Invoice2 Table Occurrence. That indicates that the fields next to them cannot be indexed. In this case it's because the fields are Global. A second interesting aspect of this particular relationship is that both of the Global date fields in Invoice2 terminate at a single Date field in Invoice.

○ **NOTE**   When you use one or more Global (or any other unindexed) fields on one side of a relationship, you can only find or display related records properly that "live" on the other side of the relationship. Even then, it only works if the key related field(s) are indexed and the portal (or related fields) are displayed on a lay-out that uses the appropriate Table Occurrence. Indexed records cannot find or display unindexed records. The only way to identify "related" records is if they're indexed. Relationships with one or more unindexed fields on each side of the rela-tionship will simply not work properly and should be considered invalid.

The Relationships Graph

FileMaker's Relationships graph can be very helpful in understanding your table relationships at a glance.

You may also be able to see if you have an invalid relationship. For exam-ple, if any relationship shows even one unindexed field on each end of the relationship, whatever function you intend to perform will fail.

I said you can learn a lot at a glance. But as your solutions become more complex, the graph can get so cluttered you may not be able to tell what's going on. Right now we only have a few connections (or paths) to ContactSerNum in our Business file. But it is conceivable that there could be dozens. Once more than one path connects to a field on the same side of the Table Occurrence, you may not be able to tell which is a one, many, or unindexed connection. You need to move the Table Occurrences around the graph and double-click the path symbol to view the details in the Edit Relation-ship window.

Other Notes

You don't need to tell FileMaker what type of relationship you're using, but knowing the relationship types is extremely helpful for good planning. That's how you recognize where data storage problems with a proposed system lie, and where you should do your user interface and reporting development.

Notice that the one-to-many (and its reverse, the many-to-one) relationships are the only ones that are regularly used. Your ER diagrams will probably also reflect that.

⊃ **NOTE** If you put enough thought into it, it's possible to complicate everything into a many-to-many relationship. This is especially true if you look at your data independent of time. For example, a person may only have one spouse at any given time, but looked at over a long time, a person could have many spouses. The goal isn't to make your database cover every situation; it's to make it descriptive of the information you need to gather and use. Make the entities and relationships in your database system as simple as possible, and no simpler.

Occasionally, you may see a dialog with the following warning: "This name is already in use. Please provide a unique name." The solution is simple: Just give the Table Occurrence a different name. You can make as many relationships to a table as you need. The only requirement is that each Table Occurrence has a different name.

Invoice System ER Diagram

Now that you know how to create and use an ER diagram, let me show you the ER diagram for the invoicing files we'll be building in this chapter. Figure 7-4 shows how the Contact and Phone files we've already made will be added to the invoicing system.

Some of the people in the Contact table will be customers. One customer will (hopefully) have many invoices with your store. The reason Contact and Product are tied together is that your suppliers can be in your Contact table as well as your customers. One contact (manufacturer or distributor) will supply you with many products.

Tying these together may not be practical in some cases where it would require too many specialized fields, but let's assume this for now.

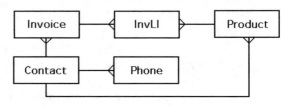

Figure 7-4
ER diagram for a basic invoicing system integrating the Contact table created earlier.

Connecting one contact to many products sounds good, but there is a potential problem. You may not order a given product from the same manufacturer every time. Prices change, and you'll want to take advantage of the best deal. Figure 7-5 shows how the ER diagram would change to accommodate that arrangement.

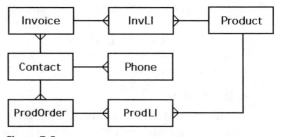

Figure 7-5
ER diagram for an invoicing system integrating two files for product orders.

Notice that ProdLI now has the double "many" symbol attached to it. That means the reporting will be done there. You might fill out the orders in ProdOrder, but you should print from ProdLI. Also notice that the "many" symbol that was attached to Product in Figure 7-4 has now turned around. Product is now "one" attached to many ProdLI records.

One more thing: remember that every time you create a relationship, you have to identify key, or match, fields. So, take this planning time as an opportunity to think through the fields that you'll need to create in each table, how each table will relate, and the kinds of reports you'll need.

If this is your first time working with a database, you're in for a real treat.

The more you work on your database solution, the more things you'll discover that you want your database solution to do. You'll discover just how powerful a tool FileMaker Pro is, and you'll wonder how you ever got along without it.

So, it's important to gather as much information as possible about the system you'll be building. It's also important to realize that every solution is not cut and dried.

I won't be demonstrating this modification to our basic invoicing system, but by the time you finish this book, you should have the knowledge you need to fill it out yourself.

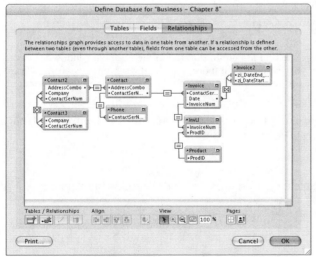

Figure 7-6
The Relationships graph in the Business table showing a variety of relationships.

Create the Tables

Looking back to Figure 7-4, you can see that we need to create three more tables: Invoice, InvLI, and Product. You already know how to create files and fields. So rather than tell you every little step, I want you to go ahead and do what you already know how to do. Even though the graph in Figure 7-6 has more elements than you'll have when you complete this exercise, it may give you some clues as to what the relationships will consist of.

Invoice Table

Start a new empty table called Invoice and add the following fields:

Field Name	Type	Options
InvoiceNum_pk	Number	Auto-enter Serial, Prohibit Modification
ContactSerNum_fk	Number	
Date	Date	Creation
InvoiceTotal	Number	

⊃ **NOTE** This table needs to be easy to work in on a day-to-day basis. It needs to be clear so the order taker knows what he or she is supposed to do to take the order. It doesn't need to be as pretty as the printouts from the InvLI table.

Invoice Line Items Table

Start a table called InvLI and add the following fields:

Field Name	Type	Options
InvoiceNum_pk	Number	
ProdID_fk	Text	
Description	Text	
Price	Number	
Quantity	Number	
LineTotal	Calculation	= Price * Quantity (result is Number)

⌘ **TIP** You do not need to add the equal sign (=) in the Formula window for this calculation. In fact, if you try to place it there, you'll get a warning when you click the OK button. This is just the way it shows up in the field list when you're done.

This table has to look good for printing reports. You'll probably want your company logo to appear here. One report could actually be the invoice itself, and customers will surely see that.

Product Table

Finally, create a table called Product and add the following fields:

Field Name	Type	Options
ProdID_pk	Text	Unique Value
Description	Text	
Price	Number	

Notice that ProdID_pk is a Text field. Many companies have their own product IDs that may incorporate numbers and letters. The ID is very ingrained in the way the entire company refers to the product line. A Text field will allow for such an arrangement, as long as the ID is unique. You can find the Unique Value option under the Validation tab.

⊃ **NOTE** The ProdID refers specifically to product numbers internal to the company. If the company is dealing with parts that come from other manufacturers, you will probably want a separate field for MfgProdID. In that case, you will want to allow duplicate values in that field, because different external manufacturers may have matching product ID numbers.

This is a utility table, so you don't have to worry about making it beautiful. But you should design it to be easy to work in for taking and printing inventory.

Other Possibilities

If you're really serious about this system, you'll probably also want to include the following fields in the Product table. I'll leave them out for the purpose of this demo. But I'm sure you can see their importance, and you may want to add them to your system.

Field Name	Type	Options
Cost	Number	
Quantity	Number	
MfgNumber	Text	
Picture	Container	
Taxable	Text	Yes/No
TaxRate	Number	Lookup from Global
zi_TaxRate_gn	Number	Global

Notice the Quantity field. In the process of taking orders, it would be possible to have items removed from inventory. You could easily generate a report to be run whenever you choose that will list the products whose quantities had fallen below the warning level.

Example Data

Add the following example data to the Product table:

ProdID	Description	Price
1001	Small Widget	9.99
1002	Medium Widget	14.99
1003	Large Widget	19.99

Create the Relationships

Now let's build the relationships between the tables.

Invoice and InvLI

1. Go to **File**, **Define Database**, **Relationships** (see Figure 7-7).
2. Click on the **Edit Relationships** icon, the second from the left under Tables/Relationships. You can use this icon not only to edit relationships, but to create them, as we demonstrated in Chapter 6.
3. At the Table pop-up on the left, select **Invoice**. At the pop-up on the right, select **InvLI**.
4. Select the key field **InvoiceNum** in both boxes. Make sure that you've selected an equal sign between those boxes.
5. Click **Add**.
6. As you can see in the box, InvoiceNum_pk in the Invoice table equals InvoiceNum_fk in the InvLI table.

7. At the bottom right under InvLI, click on the boxes next to **Allow creation of records in this table via this relationship** and **Delete related records in this table when a record is deleted in the other table**. By clicking on these boxes, you will be able to create new records in the InvLI table from the Invoice table and all InvLI items will be removed from that table when an invoice is deleted (see Figure 7-8).

☒ **CAUTION** Do not check the boxes in the lower left. Why? With the Delete option checked, any time you delete a line item from the invoice (customers do change their minds), the entire invoice will disappear! There is no point to having invoices created from the InvLI table. In some cases, you may choose to sort the portal. You don't need that here.

☒ **CAUTION** If you start moving your table reference icons around the Relationships graph, the appearance of the Edit Relationship window may change. For instance, if you drag the InvLI table to the left of the Invoice table (and it was initially on the right), the line between the tables will snap over to the left of Invoice. Double-clicking the equal sign will now show the columns have reversed with InvLI on the left and Invoice on the right. You don't need to be alarmed — only the appearance has changed. But if you're moving tables around and always expect to be clicking the Delete box on the right, you could be in for a rude awakening. Pay attention to *everything* in the Edit Relationship window whenever you make changes there.

8. Click **OK**. As you can see in the Relationships graph, you've created a one-to-many relationship between Invoice and InvLI. An equal sign is part of the link, and the field InvoiceNum is printed in italic in each table. Not only that, the upper block in each table in a relationship includes the key field name with the link from that key field to the corresponding key field in the other table in that relationship. If the equal sign is blue, you have it selected.

   ■ If you want to edit that relationship, double-click on the equal sign or anywhere on the line itself, and you will be taken to the Edit Relationship window.

   ■ If you want to cancel the relationship, select the equal sign and delete it. However, any table references created will remain unless you delete them.

Invoice and Contact

Create a relationship with Contact as the parent and Invoice as the child using ContactSerNum as the key field. In this case, you don't need to click any of the boxes under Contact or Invoice in the lower part of the Edit Relationship window.

InvLI and Product

Create a relationship between InvLI and Product with ProdID as the key field. You needn't click any of the boxes in the lower part of the window.

The first table we created in this Business file was Contact. From there, we created the Phone table. In the Contact table, you want to be able to have multiple phone numbers. When we created the relationship between these two tables, we selected "Allow the creation of records in this table via this relation-ship" in the Phone table.

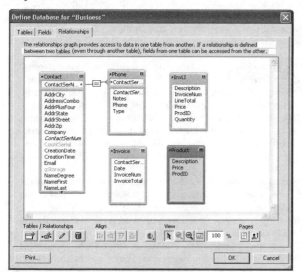

Figure 7-7
The Define Database Relation-ships tab showing various Table Occurrences.

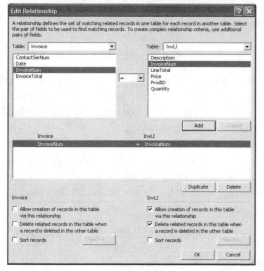

Figure 7-8
The Edit Relationship window showing the relationship between Invoice and InvLI as well as the check box selections.

Whenever your intent is to create new data in the child table from a portal on the parent table, you check the "Allow creation of records" box under the child table.

You might ask if the parent table — or the "one" table of the one-to-many relationship — must appear as the left table reference in the Edit Relationship window. The answer is no. As mentioned in the previous Caution, the columns may change whenever you move the table reference icons around the Rela-tionships tab.

☑ **BEST PRACTICES**　When you name a table (and the Table Occurrence icons), make sure that you don't separate words in the name. It could be a problem if your data is used for the web or ODBC. You can have multiple table references because of the equal and unequal relationships between tables. To rename a table, double-click on it. You'll see the Specify Table window. You can change the name near the bottom under Name of Table Occurrence.

☒ **CAUTION**　Once you begin building file references and relationships between files and adding scripts, don't change the names of the files. (You don't have to worry about that when dealing with tables within a single file.) It's usually best to keep related files in the same folder. Versions of FileMaker previous to 7 would search the entire network in an attempt to find a file. With the new File Reference dialog in version 7, once it has searched the places listed it will stop and present you with the File Not Found dialog. Even if you identify the file at that point, you really need to update the file reference in order to avoid seeing the File Not Found dialog in the future.

However, it's still a good idea to rename backup copies to prevent them from accidentally being opened. You might try putting an "X" or the date in front of the name of your backups. If you ever have to use the files again, just undo the changed name (and rename the ones you're taking out of service). If FileMaker finds an older version of a file or a file with the same name in some other database system, you may get some unpleasant surprises. FileMaker can now keep track of the network address of the machine of the file reference. That's just fine unless the server bites the dust and you put the files on a new server with a different machine number. Unless you assign the old machine number to the replacement server, all your file references will need to be reset. Better to reset the machine number!

Add the Lookups

When you enter information in an invoice, you'll want to do it as quickly as possible. After all, the customer is waiting. It would be great if we could just choose the ProdID and have the Description and Price appear automatically. We can do that by using FileMaker's lookup capabilities.

The reason we want to use lookup fields is that products and prices may change. We want any invoice, even the old ones, to reflect the products and prices as they were at the time the order was placed.

The fields we want to make into lookup fields are in the InvLI table.

1. Go to the InvLI layout.
2. Go into **Define Database, Fields.** You should be viewing the fields for the InvLI table.
3. Select the Description field and click on **Options**.
4. At the Auto-Enter tab, check the box beside **Look-up value**.
5. At the pop-up beside "Lookup from related table," select **Product** as the related table.
6. Select **Description** under "Copy value from field."
7. Click **OK** and **OK** again.

⊃ **NOTE**　The OK and Cancel buttons are reversed for Macintosh and Windows.

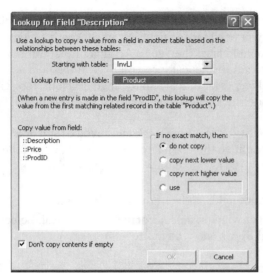

Figure 7-9
The Lookup window for the Description field in the InvLI table.

8. Now do the same for the Price field, except you want to copy the data from the Price field into InvLI table's Price field. Click **OK**, **OK**.

The Invoice Layout

Go back into the Invoice table in Layout mode, and move the fields around until they resemble Figure 7-10. I'll explain about the Customer field when we get to the section about adding pop-ups, so skip it for now. Add the InvLI portal and place the fields in the upper row of the portal, being very careful that they stay within the boundaries of the portal.

If your fields don't have borders in Browse mode, go back to Layout mode, select them, and right-click on one of them (Control+click (Macintosh)).

Select Field Borders. Make sure that you've specified borders at the top and bottom, left and right. Then go to the format section at the bottom of the window. Now make sure that you've selected black and a one-point line.

The X on the right of the portal is a button that will delete portal records.

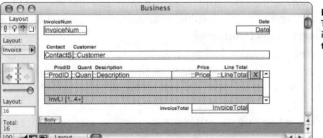

Figure 7-10
The Invoice layout showing example positions of the fields and the portal.

Notice that I shortened the field labels for ContactSerNum and Quantity. Whenever possible, I like to have the full name of the field on the label, but sometimes it's better to abbreviate to keep the layout from being too crowded. Unless your customers are ordering hundreds of thousands of items, you won't need a large space for the Quantity field, for example. Abbreviate the field labels to match the size you need for the field. As an alternative, you can rotate the field label. (Select the field label then go to Arrange, Rotate. It may take more than one rotation to get the appearance you like.) If the field names are long, though, this will take up a lot of real estate on your layout, too. The best alternative is to abbreviate the labels. I also removed the Header and the Footer layout parts.

The Product ID, Quantity, Price, LineTotal, and InvoiceTotal fields have their text aligned to the right so the number columns will line up. LineTotal and InvoiceTotal are formatted as numbers with two decimal places to represent price.

1. To do this, click on both fields. Select **Format, Number.**
2. At the Number Format window, select **Format as decimal.** Select **Fixed number of decimal digits** and type in the numeral **2.**
3. Click **OK.**

Adding Pop-ups to the Invoices

Some of the pop-ups we need to add to fields that appear on invoices will actually come from other tables. (If you intend to include value lists from other files, it's best to build them in the other files first.) When we click on the ProdID field, it would be very helpful to see both the ProdID and the Description because most people don't memorize the ID numbers of the products for their company.

Products Pop-up

What's the difference between a pop-up and a drop-down menu? There's no difference. We use the terms *pop-up* and *drop-down* interchangeably. Depending on where the field appears on a screen, it may either pop-up or drop-down, and in some cases it might pop out to one side or the other.

To create a pop-up menu for Products:

1. Choose **File, Define Value Lists.**
2. At the Define Value Lists window (see Figure 7-11), click on **New.**
3. The next window will be the Edit Value List window, but it is also the window from which you can create value lists. Name the Value List **Products,** and select **Use values from field.**
4. At the next window, Specify Fields for Value List for "Products," use the drop-down menu under "Use values from this field" to select **Product.** When you do, the three fields in the Product table will appear in the box below.
5. Select **ProdID.** When you do, other options that were previously grayed out will become available.
6. Select **Include all values.** Include all values gives you access to all information in that field in the pop-up. If you selected "Include only related values," you would see only information for which you had previously set up a relationship. (For example, let's say you were creating a pop-up for

customers, so you create a relationship back to the Contact table. There's no point in having family, friends, and other non-customer names appear in the pop-up. It would be better to create a check box field in Contact that identifies customers. Then you could have a Global field in Invoice that holds the word "customer," matching the word "customer" in the check box in Contact.)

7. If you want to display values from a second table or select a second field from the table you've already selected, click in the check box beside **Also display values from second field**. If you wanted to include information from a different table, you would do so at the drop-down menu. This is new for FileMaker 7. I'm not sure how you would use values from a different table. But I'm sure developers will come up with some interesting uses as they become more familiar with this feature.

8. Make sure that Product is the table selected, and when the fields appear, select **Description**.

9. Under Display Options, select **Sort by second field**. (The radio buttons for first field and second field do not refer to the first and second fields in either list. Rather, they refer to the field selected in the first column — the one on the left — and the field selected in the second column — the one on the right.) In our case, the first field would be ProdID, and the second, Description. When the items appear in the pop-up list, they'll be sorted alphabetically by the product name instead of the ID. In some companies, people will know the ID better than the product name. If you need to change it, this is the place to do it.

10. Click **OK**, **OK**, and **OK**.

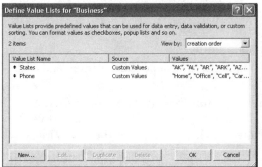

Figure 7-11
The Define Value Lists window.

Figure 7-12
The window to specify fields for the value list.

(If you were planning to use a value list from an external file, you might want to create a value list in that file first. Then you would come back to this file and create a file reference and define a value list that refers to that file reference and the value list in that external file.)

To try out your new pop-up, go to Layout mode, select the ProdID field in the portal, and format it with the Products pop-up list. Now go into Browse mode and try it out by adding a few items to the invoice.

Getting the Invoice Total

You may have noticed that InvoiceTotal is empty. We couldn't make the correct calculation until the relationships were in place. Go back into Define Database, Fields, and change InvoiceTotal into a Calculation field that reads: Sum(InvLI::LineTotal). Be sure that you choose "Calculation result as Number." Click OK and OK. Like magic, you'll see the total. Look again at the calculation. It's actually adding numbers based on the relationship. (If you have not followed along exactly, naming your relationships and fields as I have, you will not get the total. In fact, FileMaker won't let you leave the area where you create the calculation.)

Customers Pop-up

Wouldn't it be great to have a list of customers pop up like the products did? But what would you want to pop up as the second field — First Name, Last Name, or Company? You'd probably want a combination of fields. We can make a new field that concatenates (kon-KAT-e-nayt) all three of the other fields into one.

Concatenation is the process of combining character strings in a calculation. You can combine text from fields with other fields or any alphanumeric data you put in the calculation. The ampersand (&) is the concatenation symbol. In this case, you need to choose Text from the "Calculation result is" pop-up.

We did the same thing when we created the AddrCombo field in the "Calculation Field" section of Chapter 4, "Creating a New Database." We can build on that.

1. Go to **Define Database, Fields, Contact.**

2. Select the **AddrCombo** field, duplicate it, rename it **Customer**, and click **Create.**

3. Change the calculation so it reads: **NameFirst &** " " **& NameLast &** " - " **& Company**. (Since it might not show up very well in print here, I've added a space between the quotes and before and after the dash.) Make sure the calculation result is Text.

4. Click **OK** and **OK** again.

5. Now choose **Define Value Lists**. Create a value list called **Contacts**, and set it up like Figure 7-12 except choose **ContactSerNum** from the list on the left and the new **Customer** field on the right.

6. Click **OK, OK**, and **Done.**

7. Back in Layout mode, select the **ContactSerNum** field and format it with the Contacts pop-up list. Now go into Browse mode and try it out. You'll probably want to make up a few company names to go in the records in the Contact table.

☒ **CAUTION**   Here's a little glitch. There's a problem with having the customer pop-up sort by full name. If there are two people with the same name, FileMaker will only show you one! That's because FileMaker uses its indexing feature and only shows you unique values. If you have two John Smiths with no company name, you'll only see the first one. You can fix that by indexing on the unique ContactSerNum. Of course, then the list won't sort alphabetically. There are other solutions that require calculations, but that's beyond our cause today.

➲ **NOTE**   When using concatenated fields as a key, you need to be aware that FileMaker has a 100-character limit with regard to evaluating the uniqueness of any single word. (A "word" can consist of any combination of letters and numbers as long as there are no spaces in the string; however, I advise against using special characters such as #, %, *, etc. Stick with upper- and lowercase letters and numbers.) That means any field used as a key needs to determine uniqueness in fewer than 100 characters. I have sometimes found it necessary to insert spaces between the parts of a concatenation to make a calculated field work reliably as a key. If a single string concatenation without spaces doesn't seem to work for you, try inserting spaces before and after the dash character using the method described above. This has nothing to do with FileMaker's ability to find records; FileMaker indexes every word in an indexed field regardless of the field length.

Placing the Customer Field on the Layout

Now you'll want to put the Customer field on the layout.

1.   Go into Layout mode and use the **Field** tool.

2.   When the Specify Field window appears, choose the **Contact** relationship from the pop-up, and double-click the **Customer** field. Place it on the layout as shown in Figure 7-10.

3.   Go back into Browse mode and try it out by choosing a ContactSerNum. Notice that when you choose a different ContactSerNum from the pop-up, a different customer appears in the Customer box.

     Since Customer is a Calculated field, you can do a Find request in it, but the data cannot be altered accidentally.

⌘ **TIP**   Sometimes you'll need to protect data in a field, but that data will have to change in the future. That means selecting "Prohibit modification of value" is out of the question. And if you turn off "Allow entry into field," your users can't perform a Find request in that field.

In the "old" FileMaker, you would have to create a new Calculation field that is equal to the first field and place that on the common layout. Then make a separate, password-protected layout where the original field can be modified. Starting in FMP7 you can go to Layout mode and choose Format, Field Behavior and uncheck the box next to "Allow field to be entered In Browse mode." As long as the box is checked next to "In Find mode," your users can Find on the field, but not enter it in Browse mode. You could also protect specific fields from alteration by various users with accounts and privileges. For more on that, see Chapter 21, "Keeping Your Data Secure."

Other Considerations

For ease in data entry, you'll probably want to remove most of the fields from the tab order. The only fields you really need to tab into are ContactSerNum, ProdID, and Quantity.

When I was telling you about ER diagrams, I said that reporting would be done in the InvLI table. The question now is: How do you make the contact information appear and print in that table? One way to do this is to define new fields in the Invoice table that would look up the company name and full address from the Contact table using the Contact relationship. Each record created after the addition of those fields would have a copy of that information. Why not just show the related data from the Contact table? Well, what if the company changes its address? With invoices, it's important to have a copy of that information just the way it was when the invoice was created.

You'll have to update all records created before you added those fields. Go to the Invoice layout, and choose Records, Show All Records. Click in the ContactSerNum field, and choose Records, Relookup Field Content. When you click the OK button, all records will now have the current company and address information filled in. You can go back into the InvLI layout and make that same data show by dragging fields onto the layout and use the Invoice relationship from the pop-up list at the top of the Specify Field window.

⌘ **TIP**   Whenever you leave an area (Define Database, Specify Button, ScriptMaker) where you've just been looking around, unless you intended to make one or more changes, get in the habit of choosing the Cancel button. Many times I've watched users go to an area and make a change accidentally, only to have it become the new setting when they clicked OK. Of course, once it becomes a habit, you can just as easily forget to click OK when you really mean to make a change.

Summary

This has been some of the serious stuff. If you're following along with what we've been doing, you're well on your way to understanding the whole thing. Granted, there has been a lot of jumping around between tables. But if you're starting to catch on to why, that's what counts. If you find it's all getting a little confusing, take a break and then go back and review some of the earlier chapters. There's more on relationships in Chapter 14, "Automating Your Database with Scripts" in the section called "Portable Portals."

In this chapter, I showed you the three types of relationships and how and when to use a join table. That led directly to learning how to draw a diagram of the relationships between tables. Then you built the tables from the diagram, added lookups and pop-ups, and entered some data. Good job!

Q & A

Q It seems that there can be quite a bit of variation with how the same files can be put together. Isn't there one right way?

A No, because each situation will be different. That's why it's so important to gather as much information as you can before starting. Keep asking, "What if I (or some other users) do such and such?" and "How will I be able to show that report?" Then draw the ER diagram until it's clear.

Q After a while, I may have quite a few people in my Contact table. I won't want all of them showing up in the pop-up list. How do I limit it to real customers?

A You can add two more fields to Contact. One would be a Text field called CustList that you format with a radio button with values of "Yes" and "No." The second would be a Calculation field (call it CustListCalc) that would read as follows: If (CustList = "Yes", ContactSerNum, ""). This If statement says to show the serial number if the record is marked "Yes." Otherwise, show nothing (indicated by the two quotes with nothing between them — not even a space). If you use CustListCalc as the first field in your pop-up, any contact with "No" or where nothing is selected in the CustList field will not show up in the pop-up.

Workshop

Go into the Product table and change the Products value list so it sorts by the first field. Now go back into the invoice and notice how that affects the sort order of the ProdID pop-up.

Follow the directions in the section titled "Other Considerations" near the end of this chapter to place a lookup field for ContactSerNum. Then go back into Invoice and create a few line items. See if you can make the contact show up in the InvLI table.

Take a look at the Relationships tab. Does your ER diagram resemble the one created there by FileMaker?

Review Questions

True-False

1. Because FileMaker Pro is so user friendly, it is best to just start creating fields when you want to develop a new database.
2. It's a good idea to avoid creating a many-to-many relationship between tables.
3. To resolve a many-to-many relationship, you can create a join table.
4. When you create relational databases, you don't ever need to use lookup fields.
5. You can create Calculation fields to summarize data from another table through a relationship.

Short Answer

6. On an ER diagram, what does the three-pronged symbol at the end of a connector represent?
7. How is a foreign key used in a one-to-many relationship?
8. What is the purpose of a join (or link) table?
9. What is the ampersand (&) used for in a Calculation field?
10. When don't you need a portal to display information from a related table?
11. There are three types of relationships. Name at least two of them.
12. There's really only one relationship that gets used much. Which is it?
13. What is the purpose of using a lookup field?
14. How would you concatenate ZipCode and PlusFour zip fields?

Chapter 8

Finding and Sorting Your Data

Vocabulary

- AND find
- Find symbols
- Found set
- Omitted records
- OR find

Objectives

1. Practice finding records.
2. Become familiar with the Find symbols and the Omit check box.
3. Use the Modify Last Find command.
4. Learn to enhance Find requests by omitting records.
5. Learn to create AND and OR finds.
6. Become familiar with constraining and extending found sets.
7. Learn to store and retrieve Find and Sort criteria using scripts.
8. Practice sorting records, including sorting by Summary fields.

Introduction

Having all this data isn't much good unless you can find it when you need it. You need to organize it in a way that will make sense so you can make decisions — what products to order, what customers to give a price break to, what zip codes to send a mailing to, what payments you deducted from employees' paychecks, and what old records to delete from the file.

In this chapter, I'll show you how to:

- Find the records you need
- Omit any leftover records
- Sort the remaining records
- Do any repetitive versions of these jobs with the help of scripts

Finding Records

Remember when we were finding Rich and Richard back in Chapter 3? Then you have a pretty good idea of where we're going. When you choose View, Find mode, FileMaker presents you with a blank record. You then type the data you're looking for in any of the fields or related fields. When you click the Find button in the Status area or press Enter or Return on your keyboard, FileMaker shows you the records you requested. If no records are found, FileMaker displays a dialog box telling you "No records match this set of find requests."

If one or more records were found, the Status area shows how many. Then you can click through the found set of records, or do whatever else it is you need to do.

Any records that are not found are still in the file; they're just hidden or omitted from the current found set. To bring all records back, choose Records, Show All Records, or press Command+J (Macintosh) or Ctrl+J (Windows).

Methods

1. Go into the Contact layout and run the **Find Richard** script or click the button.

2. Now choose **Records, Modify Last Find**. FileMaker remembers the Find you just performed and allows you to make a change. This can be a great time-saver if you've just run a complex Find and need to make a change.

3. While you're still in Find mode and your cursor is in the First Name field, backspace until all you have left is **Rich**.

4. Finish the Find. You should have a different group of records. (I know, the First Name field is really NameFirst. But as far as the user is concerned — and that's you right now — the field is called First Name because that's what the field label says. When we're in Browse or Find mode that's what we'll call it. When we're defining the fields, working with scripts, import-ing, exporting, or sorting, we'll call it NameFirst.)

⌘ **TIP**   Modify Last Find is also referred to as Refind. The keyboard shortcut is Com-mand+R (Macintosh) or Ctrl+R (Windows).

5. Run Modify Last Find again. This time FileMaker remembers Rich.

6. Now put an = (equal) sign in front of Rich so it looks like =**Rich** and run the Find. This time, Richard is not in the found set. The equal sign is one of FileMaker's Find symbols. It stands for an exact match and means that you only want to find records that have that exact combination of letters in the field. Your search may result in records that contain other words or characters in the field, but they must be separated from the search string by spaces, returns, and certain Unicode characters. This may sound con-fusing the first time you hear it. Test it out using single words, as well as multiple words and spaces strung together, to get a better handle on it.

7. Duplicate the record so that you have two records with Rich.

8. In the second record, add the middle initial **A.** (include the period) in the First Name field.

9. Modify the last Find. (Modify Last Find allows you to make changes to a Find, although in this case, we are not going to make changes; we are just going to repeat it. Choose **Modify Last Find** to re-examine your last request, so that you can check the spelling or other criteria you may have entered. This is particularly useful for complex Finds, in which you don't want to retype everything.)

10. Complete the Find. You should show both records. The equal sign will also allow records with other information in the field to be found, as long as one of the words is an exact match.

11. Do a Refind (**Modify Last Find** or use the keyboard shortcut), add a second equal sign in front of Rich so it looks like **==Rich**, and perform the Find. You should only find the one record now. The double equal sign finds only records that have exactly the data that follows them and nothing else in the field. (That means that FileMaker will not find any records that contain any additional words or characters — including spaces or returns that you can't see — in that field. This contrasts with the single equal sign in that records *will* be found that contain other characters as long as they are separated by spaces or return characters. Results may vary if the field is indexed with Unicode.)

12. Do a Refind and add an **A** (without the period) in the First Name field. No records found. That's because you don't have a "Rich A" — you have a "Rich A." instead.

13. Try it again and include the period. Now try Refind and add an extra space between Rich and A. This Find symbol won't let you get away with anything! FileMaker Pro also has a set of features a bit different from Modify Last Find that allow you to extend or constrain your Find. For details on those features, look further in this chapter.

The Find Symbols

All the Find symbols are available in Find mode from a pop-up list in the Status area as shown in Figure 8-1. Click the triangle next to the word Symbols to make the list appear.

You may remember this and some of the other symbols in the upper area of the pop-up list from math class. Let's look at what the symbols mean.

Figure 8-1
The Find Symbols pop-up list.

Less Than (<)

The less than symbol is used to narrow your searches by eliminating values that are higher than or equal to your selected limit. As an example:

1. Select **Show All Records** and note the number in the ContactSerNum field in the last record.

2. Start a Find, and click in the **ContactSerNum** field.

3. Choose the less than sign (<), follow it with the serial number you just memorized, and finish the Find. You should have all records except the last one. You can also use the less than symbol to find dates, times, and even text.

4. Start a Find, type **<G** in the Last Name field, and finish the Find. You should find the Bailey records and any others you might have that begin with letters lower in the alphabet than G. It also works for partial or whole words. Do a find for "<Gump." This time FileMaker includes Gentry (at least in my file) because it's less than Gump.

⌘ **TIP**   You don't need to choose the Find symbols from the pop-up list; you can simply type the symbols right from your keyboard.

Less Than or Equal To (≤ or <= on Macintosh, <= on Windows)

This is much the same as less than, except it will also include the item typed in the results found. In the Find for ContactSerNum we tried above, you would have found all records.

Greater Than (>)

Just the opposite of less than. If you tried to find records greater than the last ContactSerNum, you wouldn't have found any.

Greater Than or Equal To (≥ or >= on Macintosh, >= on Windows)

Finds all records with a value greater than and including the item typed. In our example, you would have found the last record.

Exact Match (=)

We've already looked at this, but there's a twist. You can use this symbol to find fields that are empty or have unindexed values. Since many of the Notes fields are empty, do a Find in the Notes field and only put the equal sign in there. In essence, you're asking FileMaker to find all records that are equal to nothing in that field. Remember, though, that many keyboard characters are unindexed. For instance, if you only had a dash or an underscore character in the field, those records will turn up in your find as well. This can cause you some headaches when it comes to finding e-mail addresses, since all e-mail addresses include the @ symbol. Unless you have the field indexed as ASCII, you won't be able to find them. To learn how to index a field for ASCII, see the "Find Strategies" section later in this chapter.

Range (...)

This is used mostly for Date fields, but it works for numbers, times, and even text. To try it out, start by finding all records. Then go into the CreationDate field and put in a variety of dates. Perform a Find using one of the earlier dates and one of the later dates. Structure your Find like this: "5/22/2000...7/7/2001." The earlier date (meaning year, month, and day) should always go first. One little caution: If you try to use a date range in a Text field, you won't get the results you expect.

⊃ **NOTE** When you perform a Find using a date range in a Date field, FileMaker will reject invalid dates. For example, if your date range includes February 30, you will get a warning that the date is invalid.

Duplicates (!)

The Duplicates symbol can be handy for finding people with different names who live at the same address. Choose the field for which you want to find duplicates, and type the exclamation symbol. Of course, you might find people who live at the same address in different cities.

To take this to the extreme, you should be aware of a situation that could yield unexpected results. Let's say you had three records: John Smith who lives at 100 Elm Circle, John Smith who lives at 200 Main St., and Jalil Petroch who lives at 200 Main St. If you enter Find mode and put the exclamation symbol in the Name and Address fields, the Find will return the second John Smith. His name is a duplicate of another name and his address is a duplicate of another address, even though his record isn't a duplicate as a whole.

⌘ **TIP** A trick to finding duplicate entries in a database is to build a Calculation field that concatenates people's names and their street addresses. For example, DupCheck = NameFirst & NameLast & AddrStreet. Notice there are no spaces or dashes between the elements. That's because all we need is the data. Perform a find in this field, and you'll see all entries that are almost certainly duplicate records — barring data entry differences like William vs. Bill, or St. vs. Street. Then you can decide which ones you want to keep and which ones to delete. (If you have nothing but numbers in your field, make sure that the Field Calculation Result is Text.)

Using the multiple-criteria relationship discussed in Chapter 7, you can accomplish much the same thing without building this field. The relationship would be:

```
        Contact::NameFirst = Contact2::NameFirst
AND   Contact::NameLast = Contact2::NameLast
AND   Contact::AddrStreet = Contact2::AddrStreet
```

If any records are visible in the portal, there's a duplicate! (This assumes there is only one pre-existing Contact tables and you create the Contact2 table occurrence for the purpose of this relationship. I only mention that because I had already displayed some other Contact table occurrences in Figure 7-6 in the last chapter.)

Today's Date (//)

This only works in a Date or Timestamp field. FileMaker knows that when you put these two slash symbols in a Date field, you want to find items with today's date according to your computer's clock.

Invalid Date or Time (?)

FileMaker won't let you put an incorrect date or time in a field formatted as Date, Time, or Timestamp. For example, 7/44/2000 is an unacceptable date. However, incorrect data can be imported, entered by a script, or caused by converting some other type of file to FileMaker format. When data is incorrect in a Date or Time field, a question mark appears in that field. (You'll also see a question mark in a Number field if the number is too long to fit in the space allotted for it.) If you need to check Date or Time fields for improper data, do a Find using the question mark. Again, this won't work for a Number field.

Starting with version 6.0, FileMaker handles two-digit years in Date fields in a single, consistent manner. Look near the end of the FileMaker Pro 7 manual for the details. But once again, use four-digit years in a Date field to be safe. And be aware of potential problems when importing data from other sources.

One Character (@)

You can use the at symbol (@) as a substitute for one character of which you're unsure. For instance, if you're looking for someone named Smith in your file, but you're not sure if it's spelled Smyth, type Sm@th, and perform the Find. However, you have to be sure of the rest of the letters. In our file, if you type Bail@, no records will be found. The One Character Find only works in a Text field.

◯ **NOTE** If a field is formatted using ASCII and you want to find the @ symbol, put it in quotes. See the "Literal Text" and "Find Strategies" sections later in this chapter.

Zero or More Characters (*)

This Find symbol is more flexible than the @ symbol. In our previous example, if you instead type Bail*, you'd find Bailey and Bailor if we had them in the file. You can also use the symbol more than once in the text. For example, *i*y will work just fine and be helpful for people playing Wheel of Fortune. This symbol only works in Text fields.

Literal Text (" ")

The literal text quotes are used to locate something exactly as it appears between the quotes, including symbols, spaces, and punctuation. For example, use the quotes to find "meet @ 2:00". If the elements of the text appear in the field in any other order, for example "@ 2:00 meet", the record will not be found. This can be very handy for finding odd symbols in Text fields, too. The literal text search will also work with a Number field, but non-numeric characters cannot be found in a Number field.

Field Content Match (==)

We talked about this before. The double equal sign only finds records where the entire field contents match the data that follow the equal signs exactly. If there is an extra space in the field in a record, that record will not be among the found set. You can use the field content match when searching in Date, Time, and Number fields, but I can't think of a reason you would want to.

AND Finds

When you're in Find mode, you can put Find data in more than one field. That effectively performs an AND Find. For example, if you want to find all people named Smith who live in California, you'd type "Smith" (not including quotes) in the Last Name field and "CA" (not including quotes) in the State field. You are requesting "Smith" AND "CA."

OR Finds

I used FileMaker for three years before someone showed me that you can make more than one Find request at the same time. (I probably just didn't read the manual.) This is very handy. Here's how you do it:

■ While you're in Find mode and you've entered some data for which to search, choose Requests, Add New Request. You get another blank record to enter new find criteria. If you're on a layout in List View or Table View, you'll be able to see your multiple requests. Otherwise, look in the Status area just under the Book and you'll see the current number of requests.

■ Clicking the pages of the Book allows you to fine-tune the requests as you go. You can enter data in the same or different field(s) as the first Find request. Your Find could be for "Bailey OR Harris."

■ You can also combine the AND and the OR requests by putting data in more than one field in more than one request. This gives you tremendous flexibility.

Constrain and Extend Found Set

Both Constrain and Extend Found Set were introduced in FileMaker Pro 6.0. They perform variations of a function that I like to think of as a Find within a Find. They act in ways similar to Modify Last Find but with more flexibility and sometimes more simplicity.

Instead of starting your Find with the whole database of records, the Constrain and Extend Found Set commands start with just the currently found (or visible) records. If you've just run a Find command, you could simply use the Modify Last Find command to enter more options to get a smaller or bigger group of records. So why would you want to use the Constrain and Extend Found Set commands? Speed of searching is the biggest reason. If you have a large database, it's often much faster to Constrain or Extend the current found set than it is to redo the last Find on the whole database. This is especially true if your Find uses unindexed fields and if your Constrain or Extend does not involve the unindexed fields. If you do the first Find with only the indexed fields, and then Constrain (or Extend) the found set with the criteria in the unindexed fields, you'll get a faster result since FileMaker doesn't have to compute all the unindexed field values for every field in the database.

Additionally, there are situations where your found set wasn't created with the Find command, such as when you're using the Omit record commands or a Go to Related Records script step. The Constrain and Extend commands give you much more flexibility than you've ever had before. Let's take a look.

Constrain Found Set

1. Go to our Contact file and add someone named **Rick Cooper**.
2. Perform a Find using **Ri** in the First Name field. You should see four records: Rich, Rich A., Richard, and Rick.

3. Enter Find mode again, type **Rich** in the First Name field and choose **Requests, Constrain Found Set**. You're telling FileMaker, "Limit my last Find by showing me only people with Rich in the First Name field." Yes, you could have selected Modify Last Find and added the "ch." But Constrain/Extend become more valuable when your Finds are more complex and across multiple requests. Say you had just performed a complex Find, looked at the results, and needed to clean it up a little. Just enter Find mode again, make the change, and choose the Extend or Constrain function that suits the situation.

Extend Found Set

This works the same as Constrain Found Set except you use it to widen your Find. Although explaining and understanding the specifics of the Constrain Found Set and Extend Found Set functions turns out to be a bit complex, here are some points that may give you some ideas as to how they can be useful to you:

- You can perform an endless series of Extend and Constrain functions in any order on a set of records.
- You can perform a Modify Last Find and Constrain or Extend from there.
- You can manually omit records from a found set and continue to Constrain or Extend from there. The omitted records will not be included in your next move unless they are part of your new request.
- You can combine omitting records using the "Omit" check box (Find mode) with a request to Constrain or Extend Found Set.
- In effect, you can say things like, "Oops! I didn't mean to remove those people from the found set. Let me put them back in and try again."
- If you have been moving through a series of steps, extending and constraining a set of records, and you accidentally perform a regular Find (rather than selecting Requests, Extend/Constrain Found Set), your found set will be replaced with your last Find request. This point leads to one of the limitations of these functions which is…
- You cannot go backward through the steps of your Find.
- The functions are scriptable. (Use the Perform Find script step and make your choice from the Options Specify pop-up.) What happens in the script depends on whether the "Restore find requests" option is checked. If it is not checked, the script step will use the last manual or scripted find performed before this step runs.
- The functions allow you to perform an inclusive OR, an exclusive AND, or any combination of either. (This terminology may only be pertinent to mathematicians and statisticians.)

A couple of years ago I worked with a client to create a file that printed labels based on a complex Find in fields for counties, school grades, and buildings, each allowing multiple choices. It required some pretty tricky scripting, a set of special fields to mark records, using the Replace functions on a special layout, and an extra script to clear the marked records. Using Constrain Found

Set, we were able to shorten the scripts, the process became easier to understand, and we were able to get rid of the extra layout and the special marking fields.

For many Finds, I still prefer to see the full construction of the requests by creating a series of simultaneous requests or performing a Modify Last Find. Modify Last Find is especially handy when you've messed up your Find command and you want to make changes. With Constrain and Extend, you end up keeping much of your Find in your head. But you can look at the found set and fine-tune your Find without having to build a complex series of Find requests. To put it simply, you can operate more intuitively. And after all, that is one of the hallmarks of FileMaker Pro.

☒ CAUTION   ScriptMaker can only memorize one Find command with the Restore option checked. However, if you uncheck the Restore option, you can add any number of Find steps with Constrain and Extend options to a script.

Other Find Tricks

You can switch layouts while you're in Find mode, in case one of the fields you want to search for isn't on the layout you're currently viewing. To do this, open the Contact Management file and enter Find mode.

- ■ Click the tabs that switch to different layouts that include different fields: Main Address, Second Address, and Related Contacts. FileMaker stays in Find mode the whole time.

- ■ Now click on the Layout pop-up list above the Book. Choose one of the other layouts.

Of course, you can search in related fields just like we did in our Contact file when looking for phone numbers in the portal. That means you can do a Find that combines data from fields in the parent record and the child records in the portal.

➲ NOTE   This doesn't work when you're switching to layouts that use different tables. If you do switch tables, the Find will only be performed in the last table you were in. If you switch back to the first table, the found set will be the same records you found previously in that table. To keep everything straight, just be sure you stay with various layouts of the same table and you'll be fine.

Within Scripts

Back in Chapter 3, when we created the Find Richard script, you learned that scripts can memorize a set of Find criteria. FileMaker can remember more complex, multiple-request Finds as well.

Using scripts, you can have control over the way the requests are made. Go back to the Contact table and create a new script called Find Rich. Double-click script steps until you have the following;

```
Enter Browse Mode []
Go to Layout ["Contact" (Contact)]
Enter Find Mode [Pause]
Insert Text [Select]
Perform Find []
```

Be sure you select the Perform Find under the Found Sets heading. (Do not use the Perform Find/Replace step under the Editing heading.)

To clean up the script:

1. Click the **Enter Find Mode** step and uncheck the **Pause** box in the Options area.
2. Double-click the **Insert Text** step, then double-click the **NameFirst** field.
3. Click the lower **Specify** button and type **Rich**. Click **OK**.

When you're done, your script should look like this:

```
Enter Browse Mode []
Go to Layout ["Contact" (Contact)]
Enter Find Mode []
Insert Text [Select; Contact:: NameFirst;"Rich"]
Perform Find []
```

It might not look as if much has changed, but here's what we did: In the third step, we now remove any previously memorized Find so we get a blank Request form. It could really mess up what we're trying to do if any of the fields are already filled in. We also don't need the script to pause because we want it to move ahead and do the Find for us. In the fourth step, we tell the script to put Rich in the NameFirst field. Then in the fifth step, we again remove any previously memorized Find criteria so that FileMaker only performs this specific Find. The reason I had you leave the Go to Layout script step is because Insert Text can only be done on a layout that has a copy of the target field. Click OK and Done. Now try it out. Yes, it still finds Richard as well as Rich.

Go back into the script, select the Insert Text step, click the lower Specify button, and change it to include the equal sign (=) in front of Rich. Click OK, OK, and OK again. Try that out.

Although we will be spending more time with scripts in Chapter 14, "Automating Your Database with Scripts," this chapter is about finding, so let's dig a little deeper. To tell you the truth, the original Find Richard script could just as easily have been two steps:

```
Perform Find [Restore]
Go to Layout ["Layout #1"]
```

⌘ **TIP**   When you use the Perform Find [Restore] step, you don't need to worry about which layout you're on. It's not the same as Insert Text.

So why build the long script instead of the simple Find? First of all, you can see what the longer script does. On the other hand, you can show what the Find was in the short script by adding a Comment step, which can be found at the bottom of the steps list. Type whatever comment you want to remind yourself why you did something. Using comments is very, very helpful. There is nothing more confusing than coming back to one of your files a year later and trying to figure out what the heck you were thinking. Start developing this habit now.

I must admit, to my thinking, shorter scripting is better, but it's also helpful to know that there's more than one way to do things. Another instance in which you might want to use a longer set of steps is when you run the script under certain conditions. For instance, on a network, if the current user is one person, insert =Rich, and if it's anybody else, insert =Richard. (I would more likely have a script determine what layout a specific user would be switching to. But let's stay with our example for now.) To build on our previous example, it would look like this:

```
If ["Status(CurrentUserName) = "Jonathan Stars""]
     Insert Text [Select, "NameFirst", "=Rich"]
Else
     Insert Text [Select, "NameFirst", "=Richard"]
End If
Perform Find []
```

When you double-click the If step, you automatically get the End If step as well. You can move it up or down in the list as you please. Anything between the If and End If is indented except an Else step.

⌘ **TIP**   You will often see extra quote marks between the brackets in script steps. That's just the way they appear when you are in the Script Definition window. But it can be a little disconcerting trying to figure out exactly what you're supposed to enter in the Formula box. The best advice I can give you is to use quotes to enclose text constants. When you click OK, you'll be warned if there are too many quotes.

One other item I want to cover here is what happens if no matching records are found. The standard dialog box that pops up as seen in Figure 8-2 can be a little confusing, especially if it arrives when a user clicks a button and doesn't know anything about scripts or what the Find might have been.

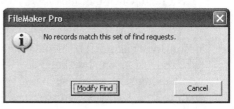

Figure 8-2
The dialog box that appears when a Find results in no records found.

FileMaker generates error messages when it runs scripts (and other processes), and you can use these messages to alter your scripts. Then you can substitute your own message screen, complete with buttons that let you control what happens next. Here's an example that continues the previous script:

```
Else
     Insert Text [Select, "NameFirst", "=Richard"]
End If
Set Error Capture [On]
Perform Find []
If ["Status(CurrentFoundCount) = 0"]
     Beep
     Show Message ["Sorry, none found. Want to try again?"]
```

```
    Comment [Button 1 = OK / Button 2 = Forget It]
    If ["Status(CurrentMessageChoice) = 1"]
        Modify Last Find
        Go to Field ["NameFirst"]
    Else
        Halt Script
    End If
End If
```

Notice that you can have the script recall the previous Find attempt, and even go to the field where the problem is. Okay, this is way beyond our original three- or even five-step script. But it covers most of the elements you could want in a Find script. If you study this one and get it, you're well on your way to advanced scripting. And guess what else — now you're programming!

Find Strategies

For a long time I thought you needed to find a person's whole name. Not so.

For example, in our Contact table, you can enter Find mode, type R in the First Name field, B in the Last Name field, and you'll find our dear Mr. Bailey. It's not that the special Find symbols wouldn't work; it's just a different technique.

Excluding data from a Find is also important — so important that there's a section on it called "Omitting Records" coming up.

You can change the way a Find works in a field by indexing it based on ASCII or a language other than English. You can go to Define Database, Fields, choose a field, and click the Options button. On the Storage tab there is an Indexing section with the pop-up list seen in Figure 8-3.

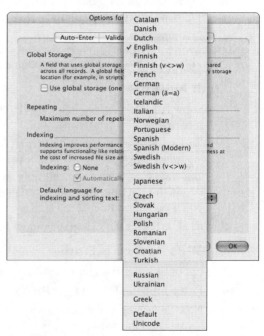

Figure 8-3
The Storage tab section of the Options for Field window showing the many language indexing choices.

Limitations

FileMaker can only memorize one Find [Restore] per script. However, you can use subscripts to accomplish various If and Else versions of a Find [Restore]. Of course, you can construct the script step by step as we did previously, which would avoid the need for a Restore.

⊠ **CAUTION**   More than once I've started entering data in what I thought was a new record, while I was actually in Find mode. When you go back to Browse mode, all that data is lost. FileMaker warns you after you've created ten Find Requests, but that could be a lot of data. If you're still in Find mode when you realize your error, you may want to scribble down what you've entered. Otherwise, when you return to Browse mode, it's gone.

Omitting Records

What to leave out is as important as what to find. When you find one or more records, the other records are omitted, and you can continue to omit records from the found set if they don't apply to your needs.

Methods

1. To give it a try, go into our Contact table, and do a manual Find (don't use the script) for Rich. That should turn up our records for Rich, Rich A., and Richard.
2. Click through the records until you find Richard.
3. Then choose **Records, Omit Record**.

 SHORTCUT   Omit Record is Command+T (Macintosh) or Ctrl+T (Windows); Omit Multiple is Command+Shift+T (Macintosh) or Ctrl+Shift+T (Windows).

Omit Multiple

1. Show All Records, and click until you're about halfway through the records.
2. Choose **Records, Omit Multiple**. You'll be presented with a window asking how many records you want to omit starting with the current record. You can type in whatever number you want. If you enter a number that is larger than the number of records left in the file and click the Omit button, you'll get a warning.
3. Click **OK** and the original window fills in the correct number.

Omit as Part of a Find

You can omit records as part of a Find request.

1. Enter Find mode, and type **Rich** in the First Name field.
2. Now look over in the Status area and click in the **Omit** check box just above the Find symbols.
3. Finish the Find and you'll have everybody except Rich and Richard.

You can even combine a regular Find with an Omit request.

1. Enter Find mode, and type **Rich** in the First Name field.
2. Choose **Requests, Add New Request**.
3. Type **Richard** in the First Name field.
4. Click the **Omit** box, and finish the Find.

Using that trick in a larger database, you can, for example, find everyone who lives in California except the people in Los Angeles.

Show Omitted

Sometimes it's easier to find what you don't want, and then find the opposite. Expanding on the last example, let's say you wanted to find everyone in all states in the U.S. except California, but you did want to include the people of Los Angeles. Perform the original Find, and then choose Records, Show Omitted. It's a bit deep, but with a little thought you can get just about anything you need.

Within Scripts

The same types of omits are available as script steps. You can find them under the Found Sets heading. Use the same omit methods mentioned previously, and combine them with what you learned in the previous "Within Scripts" section. With the Omit Multiple script step, you have the option to show the window asking for how many records to omit. You can also choose a preset number to be omitted, whether the window appears or not.

Strategies

Just as you can have multiple Find requests, you can have multiple Omit requests. You need to know how Omits are constructed to get the most out of your Find requests. When performing a Find, FileMaker starts with your first request and moves forward.

For example, if you construct a Find in the Contact table that places Richard in the first request and omits Rich in the second, FileMaker won't find any records. If you reverse the requests to omit Richard in the first request, but Find Rich in the second, all records will be found. For that reason, it's usually more logical to place your Omit requests after any Finds you want. You have to think it out, give it a try, and then fine-tune.

Limitations

You can also omit records from a portal as part of a Find. However, the individual portal record is not omitted from the portal. Instead, the parent record is omitted from the Find.

Sorting Records

I already introduced you to the Sort window under the Records menu back in Chapter 2. Sorting isn't really that complicated. We looked at how to sort portals in Chapter 6. Portals are sorted as part of the relationship definition. The windows are nearly the same, except when sorting records, you have the option to Unsort and to include Summary fields as a part of the sort.

Methods

1. Show All Records.
2. Create a new record and put the name **John Smith** in the appropriate fields.
3. Now create a record for **Sam Smith**.

4. Choose **Records**, **Sort Records**.

5. Now move **NameLast**, then **NameFirst** to the list on the right, and click the **Sort** button.

As I said in Chapter 2, you can also sort by related fields. The related fields can go anywhere in the sort order list. But if the field to be sorted is in a portal, and the portal itself is sorted as part of the relationship definition, the records will end up sorted by the data in the first portal row. Sorting by related fields works more reliably in a report constructed in a child table or file where the relationship is many-to-one.

You can sort by a custom order by creating a value list as we did when we sorted the portal in Chapter 6. The results are the same.

And finally, you can include a sort by a Summary field. Because of the complexity of this option, I'll cover this in a minute under the section titled "Strategies."

Within Scripts

Of course, FileMaker can memorize any of the most complex sorts you can dream up. While the sort is still in memory, create a script and add the Sort step by double-clicking it in the left column. When you choose the Sort script step, you have two choices in the Options area: "Perform without dialog" and "Specify sort order" — which allows you to create or modify a Sort order from right here in ScriptMaker.

■ If you just want the sort to be recreated as is and you don't want to be bothered with the window, leave both these boxes checked.

■ If you'd rather give yourself or your users the option to override the sort, uncheck "Perform without dialog." That way, you'll see what the default sort would be and have a chance to make a change. You may also want the window to appear temporarily as a method of debugging a script.

The only other Sort related script step is Unsort. It simply returns the found set to the order in which the records were entered into the file. There are no options available for Unsort.

Strategies

Sorting by a Summary field can get confusing, because there are so many different areas of FileMaker — some of which we haven't covered yet — that have to be in place to make it work. The idea is to get groups of records that already have sub-summaries to sort by a Summary field of your choice.

Sort By a Summary Field

To show this feature, I'm going to create a very simple file — one layout — and run the sorts, all without describing every little step. You may not have enough knowledge to make this work at this point. If you should need this capability at a later time, you should be able to come back here and put all the pieces together. There is more about layout parts in Chapter 17, "Designing Your Printed Report Layouts."

Create a database named Sub-sum_Test with the following fields:

Field Name	Type	Options
SalesPerson	Text	
Amount	Number	
SumAmount	Summary	=Total of Amount

The layout needs to be set up as shown in Figure 8-4. Use the Part tool in the Status area to drag the necessary layout parts onto the layout. Notice that the SumAmount field in the Sub-summary part is the same field as the Grand - SumAmount in the Trailing Grand Summary. It just has a different label.

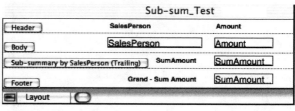

Figure 8-4
Layout showing position of fields and layout parts to demonstrate sorting by a Summary field.

⌘ **TIP** Sometimes you may need to move a layout part up or down, but get stopped by objects on the layout. You can make the part border move through layout objects by holding down the Shift key (Macintosh) or Alt key (Windows) while you drag the layout tab or dotted line.

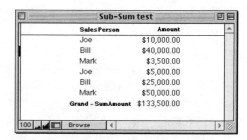

Figure 8-5
Enter this data in the Sub-sum_Test file.

Now, create the records shown in Figure 8-5. As you enter the data, the Grand - SumAmount amount increases, but none of the sub-summary amounts show. That's because you have to sort by SalesPerson and go to Preview mode to see those amounts.

Now run a sort by SalesPerson, and go to Preview mode. You should get the results shown in Figure 8-6.

Now run the sort as shown in Figure 8-7. To make the summary field, SumAmount, part of the sort, select SalesPerson and check the "Reorder based on summary field" box. In the next window, highlight SumAmount and click the OK button. The field SumAmount will still

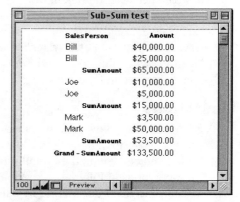

Figure 8-6
What the report looks like in Preview mode when sorted by SalesPerson.

be grayed out in the left column, but it will be included in the Sort. A Summary field must always appear at the end of any regular field sorts. Additionally, only one Summary field is allowed in a sort. You can move the Summary field to the Sort Order list at any time, but you must choose another field to sort by before you are allowed to perform the sort.

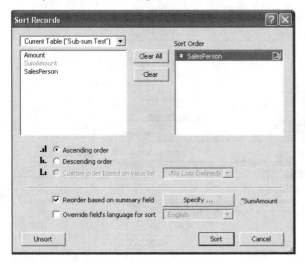

Figure 8-8
The Specify Field window that appears when you choose to reorder based on a Summary field.

Figure 8-7
The Sort window showing the SumAmount Summary field in the Sort Order list.

The result, shown in Figure 8-9, is that sorting by the Summary field overrides the sort by name. All the names are still together. But instead of Bill being listed first, based on an alphabetical sort, he's now last because he took in the most money. I put lines around each SalesPerson's grouped records so you can better visualize how they were shifted around from how they were in Figure 8-6.

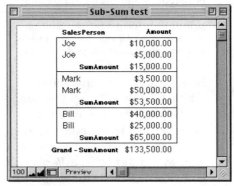

Figure 8-9
The final order using a Sort that includes a Summary field.

Limitations

FileMaker only allows one memorized Sort [Restore] step per script. But you can call subscripts that would allow other sorts. Use the same conditional concepts I showed you in the "Limitations" section for finding records.

In versions of FileMaker previous to 7, when you called for a sort (either by choosing Records, Sort, or by using the Sort Records script step), the currently selected record would be the first record in the found set. Starting with FMP7, the currently selected record will be the same record that was selected prior to the sort. If you have converted solutions with processes that depend on being on the first record as part of a script, you'll need to add the Go to Record/Request/Page [First] script step to make everything work properly. On the other hand, it will allow us developers to stop creating complex workarounds to get back to the record we began with.

Summary

In this chapter, we looked at finding and sorting records. You learned the ins and outs of Finds, including the Find symbols. You also saw how to omit records you don't need, how to sort what you have left, and how to attach even the most complex Finds and Sorts to a script.

This is the area where you make sense of sales figures and get lists ready for mailing labels. This is what keeps you organized. For me, being able to find a customer's record when I needed it is what got me started with FileMaker in the first place. Without Finds and Sorts, you might as well go back to the Rolodex.

Part 2

Q & A

Q This AND/OR Find terminology is a little confusing. If I wanted to find everyone who lives in Ohio and Florida, that seems like an AND Find to me.

A It does, doesn't it? However, you would need to use two requests to accomplish this. That's because you can't type two states in one field. You're not asking for individuals who live in both the state of Ohio AND the state of Florida at the same time. So for clarity, the way to phrase the Find is: "show me all the people in my file who live in either Ohio OR Florida."

Q Do I have to know all this complicated script stuff to be able to get through this?

A No. I used FileMaker for about five years before I discovered how to make scripts do more than change to a different layout. Learning scripting is really not that hard, though. The trick is to do something simple, then build on it. Scripting can't be beat for automating repetitive tasks.

Workshop

Build a complicated Find based on multiple fields in more than one record. Include an Omit as part of it. Then create a script for it. Now do a Refind (Modify Last Find), change the find criteria, and make a new script for that. Run one script after the other. Now sort the records and add the Sort to one of the scripts. Perform a different Sort and add that to the second script.

Review Questions

True-False

1. Clicking the Omit check box in a Find request instructs FileMaker to find all records except those that match the Find criteria specified.
2. If you perform a Find that returns ten records, then you omit three of them, and choose Show Omitted, your new found set includes just the three records you omitted.

3. To create an OR find, you need more than one Find request.

4. Extend Found Set allows you to find a greater number of records.

5. FileMaker does not allow you to sort records by a Summary field.

Short Answer

6. What is the keyboard shortcut to enter Find mode?

7. What happens when you choose the Modify Last Find command from the Records menu?

8. When might you want to find records with improper dates or times?

9. What would be the most efficient way to find records for people in every city except one?

10. When you create a new script that includes a Sort script step, how does it know how to sort the records?

11. When you find a group of records, how can you tell how many were found?

12. What happens to the records that are not in the found set after a Find is completed?

13. Name at least three of the Find symbols, show the symbol that goes with the name, and tell what it's for.

Chapter 9

Creating New Layouts with the Layout Assistant

Vocabulary

- Chevron
- Layout part
- Merge field
- Part label
- Part label control
- Sub-summary part

Objectives

1. Get acquainted with the Layout Assistant.
2. Create a Standard layout.
3. Modify a layout theme.
4. Set field defaults.
5. Create a Columnar list/report layout.
6. Create a Table View layout.
7. Define a Summary field from within the Layout Assistant.
8. Adjust layout objects.
9. Create a labels layout.
10. Create an envelope layout.

Introduction

Layout mode operates like most computer drawing programs (like MacDraw or CorelDRAW). But what sets FileMaker apart is that it's designed to also show data from the fields in the records of your database tables. You can create all sorts of layouts for use on screen or in printed reports. Remember though, no matter what beautiful or ugly way your layouts present your data, you aren't actually changing what's in the tables themselves (you can only do that in Browse mode).

The Layout Assistant gives users a terrific way to create layouts. Almost every window explains what it does in clear language. Because the Layout Assistant offers a number of choices at each point, resulting in millions of possibilities, I won't be able to show you every available combination. I'll only be able to get you started, but you'll do just fine.

We could use some other layouts in our invoicing system. So I'll have you build one of each of the layout types and show you the sights along the way.

Create a New Layout

First, let's create a new layout.

1. Go to the Business file.

2. To make a new layout, you first have to switch to Layout mode.

3. Choose **Layouts**, **New Layout/Report** or use the keyboard shortcut Command+N (Macintosh) or Ctrl+N (Windows). Notice it's the same shortcut as New Record in Browse mode. You should see the window shown in Figure 9-1.

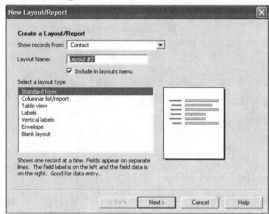

Figure 9-1
Choosing New Layout/Report under the Layouts menu brings up the first screen of the Layout Assistant.

Standard Form

4. Choose the **Contact** table from the "Show records from" pop-up list. We chose Contact because it's the table where the records we're interested in are stored. As you get more comfortable with making relationships, you may find that you'll choose the table that holds the primary keys for the relationship you're interested in. But when you're just starting out and things like keys and relations don't mean much to you, picking the table that's defined with most of the fields you want to show is a good rule of thumb.

5. Next, enter a name to identify your layout. You can give your layouts any name you like, even if it duplicates the name of another layout. FileMaker has other ways to keep track of the layouts, so the name here is strictly for us humans. For the sake of simplicity, call this layout **Standard**, and select **Standard form** in the layout type list.

6. Notice the check box for "Include in layouts menu." Leave it checked for now, but unchecking this box will hide the name from the Layout pop-up above the Book. All layout names will still show up in the pop-up when you're in Layout mode and the layout is still accessible by way of your

scripts and buttons. For a final level of protection, you can prevent users from getting to Layout mode by using passwords. We'll talk more about that later.

7. To move on, click the **Next** button.

Specify Fields

If there are any options concerning the layout dimensions you chose (such as when you choose labels or columnar lists), FileMaker will ask you some additional questions. In our case though, you'll see the Specify Fields screen in Figure 9-2. This would also be the second window if you had picked Table View. However, it would be the third window if you had chosen Columnar list/report; Choose Report Layout would have been second. In essence whatever fields you name in the right-hand list will be created on the layout for you (which can be a real time-saver).

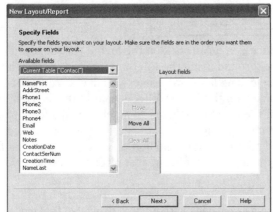

Figure 9-2
The Specify Fields screen of the New Layout/Report window in the Layout Assistant.

8. If you don't have too many fields, click the **Move All** button, then double-click any fields in the Layout fields list that you want to remove from this layout.

9. You can also remove fields from the list by clicking once on the field name to highlight it and clicking the Clear button. I think click-click is faster than click-move-the-mouse-click, but it's up to you. Remember, we're not using any of the phone numbers anymore.

10. Notice the "Available fields" pop-up on the left. You can choose fields from related files and tables, and you can even define relationships from here.

11. Now drag the fields up or down in the list until they're in the order you think you'll find most logical, and click the **Next** button.

Select a Theme

You'll also see the Select a Theme screen shown in Figure 9-3 when you choose the Columnar list/report and Table View layout types.

12. For now, choose **Blue and Gold Screen**, click the **Finish** button, and go to Browse mode.

Without too much effort, you've just created a pretty decent-looking layout. It's quite a bit better than the original black and white screen. The fields have some depth to them and stand out nicely from the background.

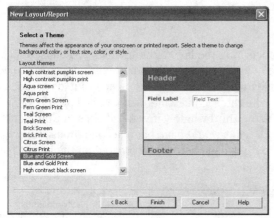

Figure 9-3
The Select a Theme screen is where you choose how the new layout will look.

If you go into Layout mode, you can click on the layout part tabs and change the color of the background using the Fill tools. You can also make any other changes and move fields and labels wherever you like. If you click on one of the fields and then click on the Object Effects palette (to the right of the Fill Pattern palette), you'll see that the fields have an engraved effect applied to them. The effect of this change might be quite subtle. The appearance depends on the theme you select and the field border width; be sure that field borders are turned on. If you left out any fields, just place them where you need them.

⌘ **TIP**   Want to place a field on a layout and match the style of another field that's already on the layout? Hold down the Command (Macintosh) or Ctrl (Windows) key and click on the field with the style you want to copy. All the attributes are instantly selected as the default. That includes the color of the field, the borders, and the font size, style, and color.

The defaults can also be set if you change an attribute with no object selected. For example, changing the fill color with nothing selected applies that fill color to any new objects you create. These defaults are also relevant here because the list of themes in the layout wizard includes Standard and Default, and in most cases they look quite similar. Standard is a black and white layout theme. Default uses whatever you have defined as a default attribute (field fill color, line widths, fonts, etc.).

⌘ **TIP**   You can create your own themes! On Windows look in FileMaker Pro 7\English Extras\Extensions\Themes. On Macintosh, look in the FileMaker Pro 7 folder and Control+click on the FileMaker Pro application icon. Choose Show Package Contents, then choose Contents\Resources\English.lproj\Themes. Open the folder, make a copy of one of the themes, rename it, and open it with a text editor. The text file is written in XML (Extensible Markup Language), which is similar to the web language HTML. XML is actually fairly easy to read. If you or someone you know is comfortable with HTML, you're on your way to creating quick, custom layouts. In fact, you may be able to figure it out on your own.

Columnar List/Report

There are quite a few steps and options to creating this layout type. But you wouldn't believe what it took to create the same report in older versions of FileMaker Pro. Since InvLI has two one-to-many relationships terminating on it, we should be doing some of our reporting there.

1. Go into Layout mode, and create a new layout/report.
2. Choose **InvLI** from the pop-up list at the top.
3. Call this layout **InvoicePrint**, select **Columnar list/report** as the layout type, and click the **Next** button.

Choose Report Layout

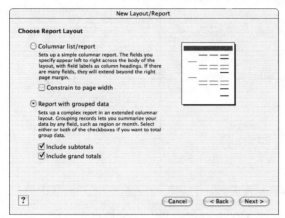

Figure 9-4
In the Choose Report Layout screen, you decide whether to display simple columns of data or a more complex report.

Part 2

4. Choose the **Report with grouped data** radio button, and check both the **Include subtotals** and **Include grand totals** boxes.
5. Click the **Next** button.
6. In the Specify Fields screen, click the **Move All** button, then click **Next**.

Organize Records by Category

As you can see in Figure 9-5, from the next screen you can choose more than one field to summarize, which you may want to do sometime in the future.

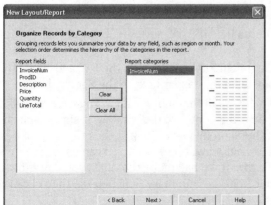

Figure 9-5
The Organize Records by Category screen lets you summarize data by field.

7. For now, just double-click **InvoiceNum** to move it to the Report categories list and click the **Next** button.

Sort Records

This screen ought to look familiar, as it is just like the Sort window. FileMaker's Layout Assistant assumes you want to reuse the last criteria you sorted with. So if you've been following along, Invoice number will be here. Otherwise just add it.

8. Click the **Next** button to move on.

Specify Subtotals

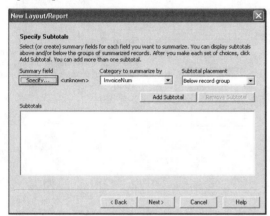

Figure 9-6
The Specify Subtotals screen is where you select or create Summary fields for the report.

The Specify Subtotals screen shown in Figure 9-6 offers quite a few choices. When we created our invoice layout in the Invoice table, we created a field to give us the invoice total, but we don't have that here.

9. Click on the **Specify** button under the Summary field header to bring up the Specify Field screen.

10. Click on **Current Table ("InvLI")** in the pop-up, scroll all the way to the bottom, and select **Define Database**.

11. Click the **Tables** tab and double-click **InvLI**. You'll actually be creating a new field here.

12. Call it **InvoiceTotal**, choose **Summary Type**, and click **Create**.

13. Highlight **LineTotal** in the field list. Be sure the **Total of** radio button is selected.

14. Click **OK, OK** again, highlight **InvoiceTotal** in the list, and click **OK** one more time. InvoiceTotal will now appear next to the Specify button.

15. To make InvoiceTotal show up in the Subtotals list, you have to click the **Add Subtotal** button near the center of the window. It should appear as InvLI::InvoiceTotal in the Subtotals box. Look at the other pop-ups just so you'll know what's there, but leave them as is. You can choose more than one subtotal in this window. If we had more subtotals, you'd first have to select the one you want from the Summary field pop-up, then click the

Add Subtotal button. Since we don't want any others right now, just click **Next**.

Specify Grand Totals

The term "grand totals" may not be familiar to you if you're not a statistics or accounting wizard. It's just a total of all the totals. Look around this screen to get familiar with it. It's not much different from the Specify Subtotals screen. Notice that you can decide where you want the total to appear on the report.

16. Specify the **InvoiceTotal** field.

17. Click the **Add Grand Total** button to move InvoiceTotal to the list and click **Next**.

18. You've already seen the Select a Theme screen, so these options will look familiar to you. If you don't want to print your invoices in color, select the **Standard** style, and click the **Next** button.

Header and Footer Information

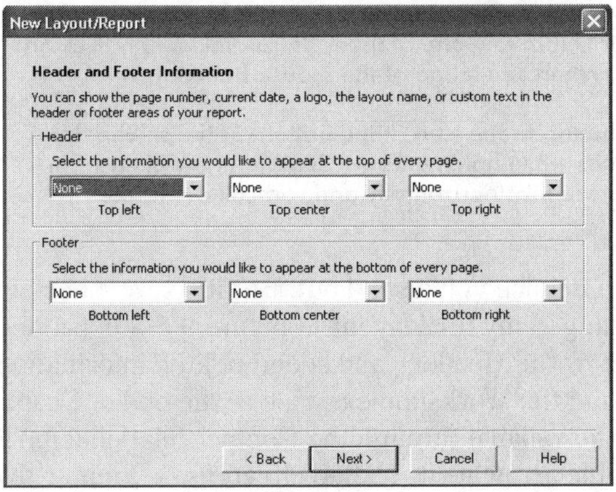

Figure 9-7
The Header and Footer Information screen lets you add a number of clarifying elements around the top and bottom margins of your report.

This screen, shown in Figure 9-7, tells you what it's for.

19. Under the Header section, click the "Top center" pop-up, choose **Large Custom Text**, and type what you like (I typed My Company, Inc.). Click **OK**.

20. In the "Top right" pop-up, choose **Current Date**.

21. For the "Bottom right" pop-up, choose **Page Number**. You get the idea.

22. Click **Next**.

Create a Script for This Report

Using this screen can save some time in the ScriptMaker department. If you don't like the default script, you can always delete it or edit it.

23. Go ahead and click the radio button next to **Create a script**, name it **InvoicePrint**, and click the **Next** button.

24. Whatever choice you make in the New Layout/Report window doesn't change much of anything. However, after I create a report, I like to go to Layout mode to do some cleanup. So, check the radio button that will take you to Layout mode and click **Finish**.

Cleaning Up

To make the report look nice, the first thing I'd do is shrink the InvoiceNum, ProdID, and Quantity fields. Then, I'd expand the Description field. Align the text in Price, Quantity, LineTotal, and both copies of InvoiceTotal to the right, and format all values but Quantity to contain dollar signs and two decimal places.

Switch back to Browse mode to make sure that you've left enough space for the numbers in Price, Quantity, Line Total, and Invoice Total and that your layout stays within the page margins.

⌘ **TIP**   The layout part tabs are tipped sideways. At the bottom of the window, to the left of the Mode pop-up (which should now read Layout), is a little icon called the Part label control, which will flip the tabs back to horizontal. But then, of course, they're in the way. To temporarily turn any one of them horizontal, simply click on the tab and hold for a second. When you let go of the mouse button, it will flip back out of the way.

If you don't want to make the trip to the icon at the bottom of the screen, try this: Click on one of the part tabs while holding down Command (Macintosh) or Ctrl (Windows). You can toggle the tabs horizontally and vertically with that shortcut.

Well, it's still not exactly an invoice you'd send out. But it's sure a heck of a start. You can see how I changed my final layout in Figure 9-8. I expanded the Leading Sub-summary (below the Header), and added related information about the customer. If you did the Workshop exercise at the end of Chapter 7, the customer data should be available through the Contact relationship. The left- and right-pointing double arrowheads (called chevrons — greater than and less than keys on your keyboard) in the illustration mean these are Merge fields. I'll show you how to create some Merge fields when we get to mailing labels later in this chapter.

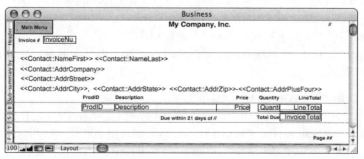

Figure 9-8
The Invoice report in InvLI table as created by the Layout Assistant with a few useful additions.

Sub-summary Part Definition

1. Double-click the **Trailing Sub-summary** tab (just below the Body tab) to access the Part Definition window.

2. Check the boxes next to **Page break after every 1 occurrence** and **Restart page numbers after each occurrence** to make each invoice appear on a separate page. There are other places to get to the Part Definition window, but I find this the most useful. Click **OK**.

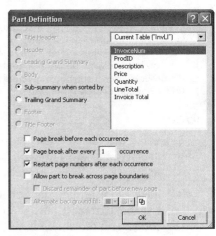

Figure 9-9
The Sub-summary Part Definition window showing page break options.

Table View

Let's use the Table View as a way to get a quick overview of our invoices.

1. Go to Layout mode, and start a new layout.

2. Choose **Invoice** from the "Show records from" pop-up list, and choose **Table View** from the type list. Call this layout **Table**, and click **Next**.

3. Click the **Move All** button, then click **Next**.

4. Choose a style you like, and click **Next**.

5. Click the **Finish** button.

That wasn't too hard.

Go to Layout mode. Notice that the layout looks more like the standard layout than a table. If you want, you could also have changed the view of the first layouts that were created to Table View.

6. Choose **Layouts**, **Layout Setup**, click the **Views** tab, and then click the **Properties** button. Take a look around this window to see what it has to offer. Many of these options are similar to spreadsheet options.

7. Now check the boxes next to **Sort data when selecting column** and **Include header part**. Click **OK**, and **OK** again.

8. While you're still in Layout mode, make a little button that goes to Invoice and put it in the Header part.

9. Go to Browse mode, and click the column title bars to see the invoices sort. Then click on one of the invoices in the list, and click the button in the header. It should take you to the invoice detail. This is no big deal with only a couple of invoices, but when the list gets long, you'll appreciate a quick way to move between the Table View and the invoice itself.

⌘ **TIP**   You can resize column widths in groups rather than one at a time in Table View. To select a contiguous group of columns, Shift+click on the column heads. To select discontinuous columns, use Command+click (Macintosh) or Control+click (Windows). Move your cursor to the divider on the right side of any one of the selected columns until you see the double-headed arrows. Click and drag to change the column size for all the columns.

If you can't see the double-headed arrows, go to Layout mode, choose Layouts, Layout Setup, and click the Views tab. Click the Properties button to bring up the Table View Properties window and check the box next to Resizable columns.

If you have a large number of fields on a layout and they don't all seem to show, it's probably because you've reached the 110-inch layout limit. By resizing the columns you can display more fields.

Labels

1. Go to the Contact file, get to Layout mode, and start a new layout.

2. Name the layout **Labels**, choose **Labels** from the type list, and click **Next**.

3. Take a look around the Labels window. The pop-up has a huge list of labels to choose from. (Check with your office supplier to see which labels you can buy off the shelf.) If nothing suits you, you can create your own custom labels. What more could you ask for? Use the default setting, and click the **Next** button.

4. Double-click on the field names to create your label until it looks like Figure 9-10. You can choose related fields as well, but what we need is right in this file. Notice the Merge characters (« », called chevrons) that set off these special fields. Feel free to type any text you want to appear on the label (commas, returns, even words) but don't add text between the chevrons since FileMaker needs that text to exactly match the name of a field.

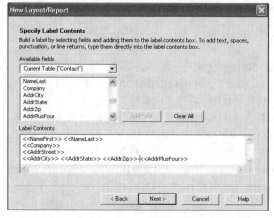

Figure 9-10
The Specify Label Contents window where you choose the Merge fields by clicking on the list.

5. Click **Next**, then click **Finish**. You'll be in Preview mode, and you should see the current found set as labels. To get rid of the dashes, see the Q & A at the end of this chapter.

⌘ **TIP**   If one or more of the labels seem to have incorrect information, you have to switch to one of the data entry layouts to make the corrections. The data in Merge fields cannot be edited; however, you can change which Merge fields appear on the layout. If you see labels with blank lines in them, you'll most likely find extra, invisible return characters in one of the fields. Sometimes people entering data press the Return key instead of the Tab key when trying to leave a field. Maybe you did it! To prevent that, see the "Validated By Calculation" section in Chapter 10.

⌘ **TIP**   To change a Merge field, you must be in Layout mode. Using the Text tool, double-click in the Merge text area so the cursor enters the text box. Delete the unwanted Merge field using normal text editing methods (backspace over it or highlight and delete). To add a different field, choose Insert, Merge field. Then choose the field from the field list. You can also enter the arrowheads and the field names directly.

⌘ **TIP**   One nifty thing to note about Merge fields is that the only part of the text that FileMaker looks at to get the style information is the first open angle bracket (<) for each of the Merge fields. If you format that bracket with the style you want (16-point Arial, for example), then you can highlight the rest of the text and make it a small size (like 6 or 8 point). That way it will take up less space on-screen. Sometimes in places where space is very constrained (like portals or buttons) this trick can help you fit "long" field names in the tight space. The downside is that it's harder to revise later on.

☒ **CAUTION**   If you intend to use Merge fields to keep people from editing the data, you need to know this: If someone chooses View, View as Table, Merge fields suddenly become active, editable fields! This was not the case in previous versions of FileMaker. You can keep users from having access to Table View on a layout-by-layout basis. Go to Layout mode and choose Layouts, Layout Setup, click the Views tab, and uncheck the box next to Table View. Problem solved.

Formatting dates, numbers, and times in Merge fields are a different story. For example, let's say you have two numbers that you want to format separately in a single block of text. If you want to format one with a dollar sign and the other with a percent sign, you're out of luck. You'd have to break them into separate blocks of text.

Envelope

This works exactly like the labels. Give it a try and see if you can do it without my help. When it comes to printing, that's another matter. Everything depends on the type of printer you're using and how you intend to feed the envelopes. With my printer, I finally gave up and just selected letter as the paper size instead of envelope. Maybe I gave up too soon, but it works just fine.

Blank Layout

Do you really need to ask? The only thing you need to do is decide on a name for it and decide if it should appear in the Layout pop-up. Then click Finish.

Summary

In this chapter, I showed you FileMaker Pro's Layout Assistant. We added one of each of the layout styles to the invoicing system to move it a little further along the way of making it a usable set of files. We also looked at quite a few of the Assistant's options along the way.

Q & A

Q When I looked at the labels, everyone who didn't have a plus four zip had a dash. What should I do about that?

A Create a Calculation field called PlusFourCalc that is figured as follows:
```
If(IsEmpty(PlusFour); ""; "-"&PlusFour)
```

For you real techies, a shorter version would be:
```
If(PlusFour; "-"; "") & PlusFour
```

Make sure you choose Text result. Then change the last line of the label so it reads:
```
<<City>> <<State>>  <<Zip>><<PlusFourCalc>>
```

⊠ **CAUTION**   I got the short version of PlusFourCalc to work reliably. But I could not repeat it for other calculations.

Workshop

In the Business file, I had you create a Table View of Invoice. Using the Invoice table, go back and make a Columnar list/report without the Summary information. When you're done, compare it with the Table View and see which you like better. Think about how you might use one or the other for various purposes.

Review Questions

True-False

1. When you create a new layout and choose the Standard form type, fields appear on separate lines, with the label to the left of the field.
2. Holding down the Command (Mac) or Ctrl (Windows) key and clicking on a field in Layout mode sets default attributes for any new fields you add to the layout.
3. To create a layout with sub-summaries, you must choose the Blank layout type.
4. You can define a Summary field from within the Layout Assistant.
5. A layout created via the Layout Assistant cannot be modified.

Short Answer

6. How do you change the background color of a layout part?
7. Name the seven different types of layouts you can create with the Layout Assistant.
8. What special kinds of fields are included on a newly created label or envelope layout?
9. Which layout type produces a layout that looks like a spreadsheet?
10. If you were going to create a form letter, which layout type would be the best to choose?
11. How do you edit the appearance of the data displayed with Merge fields?
12. How do you set it up so that you can make the columns sort in Table view? (I don't expect you to know this off the top of your head. Just go into FileMaker and see if you can get to the area where you make this choice.)

Part 3

Turning Your Data into Information

Chapter 10

Keeping Your Data Clean and Neat

Vocabulary

- Auto-enter options
- Storage options
- Unstored calculation
- Validation options

Objectives

1. Understand the value of adding field options.
2. Become familiar with the Options for Field window.
3. Learn about field auto-enter options.
4. Become familiar with the field-validation options.
5. Discover more about Repeating fields and their options.
6. Learn about field storage options and indexing.

Introduction

Incorrect data can cause problems. Zip codes with too many digits, the wrong price for a product on an invoice, or a check made out to the wrong person — all can cause problems that can bring a business to a screeching halt. We looked at some of the tools FileMaker offers when we used pop-up lists and lookups in our invoicing system. In this chapter, we'll explore data entry in depth, by looking at the details behind the:

- Auto-Enter tab
- Validation tab
- Storage tab
- Furigana tab

Not only do the options on these tabs keep your data correct, they often speed up your work. That spells savings.

Field Data Entry Options

The field type determines what lies behind the Options button of the Define Fields window. All field types except Summary have a Storage option. When you click the Options button for Text, Number, Date, Time, Timestamp, and Container fields, you are presented with the Options for Field window shown in Figure 10-1. In the case of a Container field, many of the options are not applicable, so they're grayed out. Although Calculation fields have storage options, they are not the same options pictured in Figure 10-1.

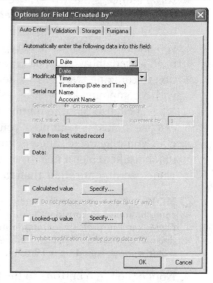

Figure 10-1
The Options for Field window showing the Creation/Modification pop-up list.

Auto-Enter Tab (Automatically Entering Values)

The choices behind the Auto-Enter tab allow you to set up a field so that data entry can be taken care of automatically. We've looked at a few of these choices already, so you should feel somewhat comfortable with them.

Creation

When you select the Creation check box, you can select the automatic entry of the Date, Time, Timestamp (which is date *and* time), Name, or Account Name for a field. If you're storing the data in a Text or a Number field, you can choose any of the items from the pop-up. Of course, a Number field can't index anything other than numbers. But surprisingly you can search for dates and times in a Number field. Text data (Creator Name) does show up in a Number field, but you can't perform a Find for it. If you're working with a Date or Time field, the pop-up displays inappropriate choices in gray.

Modification

The second check box, Modification, gives you the same five auto-entry options — Date, Time, Timestamp, Name, and Account Name. In a business with shared files, having a special field that keeps track of when a record was last modified and another for who did the modification can be very helpful. You can always check back with that person to get more details or just to check up on people's work.

Serial Number

We used the Auto-Enter Serial Number option in a number of our tables. One thing I didn't mention is that you can include text as part of what gets entered.

For example, having "MC-1" or "5-CR" in the Next Value field would create serial numbers like MC-1, MC-2, or 5-CR, 6-CR and so on. That could work well for a products file that needs such modifiers. Be careful whenever you put text in a Number field, though. Since you can't perform a Find for the letters, you should change the field type to Text. If your auto-entered value is being used for a database key, be careful. Better alternatives may be to use a calculation to combine two fields (a serial number and a code) or to use a relationship with a compound key.

Notice also that the numbers don't have to increase by a single digit. You can use almost any number you want in the Increment by box. To be more specific, you may use a range of integers from 1 to 32767. That rules out using a number like 0.5 or a negative number, in case you were trying to have the value decrement rather than increment.

◯ NOTE　Since you're talking about text in the auto-entered serial number, here's something else to consider. If you enter a decimal number in the Next Value field, FileMaker interprets everything to the left of the decimal as text rather than the decimal portion. So if you started with the next value 6.9, the next number that would appear would be 6.10 rather than 7.0 as you probably intended.

Notice the radio buttons to the right of Generate. Starting with FMP7, you can decide whether the serial number gets created when the record is created or once the user exits or commits the record. Sometimes users create records accidentally or get partway through and decide to stop. In cases like that, the serial numbers are no longer sequential, which bothers some people. The choices here can help prevent that. But it can also create a problem if the serial number will be a key field for records that will be created in a portal. The key field must receive a value before records can be created in the portal.

Value from Last Visited Record

If you're doing data entry for a large number of records, one after the other, that have the same data in one or more of the fields (for example, Company, Address, City, State), turn this feature on for the fields that need it. When you get to the next batch of records that are different, make the changes to the values in the affected fields. All records from then on will copy the new changes.

⌘ TIP　If you'll be turning a feature like this on temporarily for a number of fields, move the affected fields to the top of the field definition list. When you want to turn the feature off, they'll all be right there at the top of the list. The View by pop-up will display the words "Custom order." So don't set it back to "field name" or one of the other choices until you're done.

Data

If you check the box next to Data, you can type anything you like, up to 255 characters. You can have text or number data go into a Date or Time field, too, if you can find some reason for doing that. Should most of the people you enter in your Contact file live in the same city and state, you may want those fields set up to fill that in for you and just change them to accommodate the rare cases.

Calculated Value

This option is interesting! You can have a regular Text, Number, Date, Time, or Timestamp field that gets filled with a calculated value. But since it's a field that is otherwise modifiable, you can change it manually or with a script. Otherwise, it's protected from the kind of changes that happen to fields that use looked-up values. (See the next section on looked-up values.)

Here's why this is different: In a normal Calculation field, if you change the value in any of the fields to which it refers, the calculation result changes. Take our InvLI table for example, which contains LineTotal = Price * Quantity. If you change the Price or the Quantity, the LineTotal changes. With a field that enters data using a Calculated value, that wouldn't happen.

Also, in a regular field that's defined with the Lookup option, let's say you change the value over in the field that gets looked up. If you trigger a relookup, it overwrites the data in the lookup field. That doesn't happen with the Calculated value option turned on. The only time relookup will do anything with a field like this is if it's empty to start with (or if you uncheck the box next to "Do not replace existing value for field (if any)"). You can empty it first if you do want to trigger a relookup. If you empty the field and change one of the values that the calculation refers to, you'll get the calculation result.

The way I use this most often is if the value I need might come from more than one lookup table. For example, you might have a calculation refer to a regular price table and a sales price table (or a different field in the same table) if purchases are made during a specific date range. That is something you can't do with a regular lookup since a regular lookup must point at a single field.

If you intend to use this function, be sure to turn off the upper five check boxes in the Auto-Enter tab (Creation, Modification, Serial number, Value from last visited record, and Data). Otherwise, the value determined by the upper check box will go into the field first, and the calculation won't be triggered. By the way, you can make it act like a looked-up value by unchecking the box next to "Do not replace existing value for field (if any)." That gives the Calculated value more power than you can achieve with a regular looked-up value because the looked-up value is limited to grabbing data from a single table with a single relationship. But note that the values will only update if the fields that are being changed are in the current record in a layout that references the table the fields belong to. In other words, your calculation will not change reliably if a related field is part of the calculation and that related field gets changed.

⊠ CAUTION Don't think of this technique as the same as a lookup. If you change any of the values on which the calculated value is dependent, any value already calculated for this field will not change the way a lookup would. However, with the addition of the "Do not replace existing value for field (if any)" check box in FMP7, you can make it act exactly like a lookup — except with more power! Also be sure you choose the correct Table Occurrence from the pop-up next to "Evaluate this calculation from the context of" at the top of the Specify Calculation window. It is absolutely critical that you make the right choice when it comes to the context of the calculation.

Part 3

Looked-up Value

We used this feature in our InvLI table. Choose the ProductID from a pop-up, and the Description and Price come in automatically since they have been defined as lookup fields.

Zip code databases that include fields for city, state, and phone area code are available at very low cost or free. You can set up a file to look up the other fields based on the zip code as the match field. If you've ever purchased something over the phone, and the order-taker asked for your zip code and then verified your city and state, that's how they did it. Set up your databases to take advantage of this great time-saving feature. Those extra few seconds times how many data entry people taking how many orders every day can cost a lot of money to the company that doesn't take advantage of lookups like this.

You should know that you can relookup the values for fields that use a lookup. Once you've found one or a batch of records, click in the key field for the relationship and choose Records, Relookup Field Contents. You need to be somewhat cautious, though, since you cannot undo a relookup. Also, any other fields that use lookups based on the same key field will be affected.

Prohibit Modification

The last check box in this tab is "Prohibit modification of value during data entry." We used it to protect our InvSerNum field. I've seen this used in offices to protect a field that keeps track of the modifier name. That way no one can change a record and blame it on someone else — at least not while they're on their own machine! However, you'll also want to use passwords to protect user access to the Define Database window.

Validation Tab (Checking Data for Accuracy)

The check boxes on the Validation tab help you make sure data gets entered properly. You can check more than one box here to provide multiple validations and you can even send your own message to the user if the data isn't entered properly. Take a look at Figure 10-2.

Validate Data in This Field[7]

The upper section of the Validation tab is titled "Validate data in this field." Here you can select whether the data is validated only at data entry or if it is constantly monitored (including when importing data). This is a

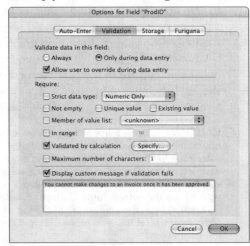

Figure 10-2
The selections under the Validation tab in the Options for Field window.

new feature for FileMaker Pro 7. It is most helpful when importing data. I can't tell you the number of times I've imported data that had incorrect date, time, and number formats. With the "Always" radio button selected for the fields targeted for import, you'll be notified that there were errors in the dialog in Figure 10-3 that appears at the end of the import procedure. Of course you'll have to go find the problem records. But it's a lot better than having useless data floating around inside your files.

You can also choose if the person doing the data entry can override the validation warnings. If the person doing the data entry is given authority to override the validation warning and enters information not within the requirements established for the field, he or she will see a message similar to the one in Figure 10-4a. Notice the No button.

On the other hand, if no such authority is given and he or she enters information outside the requirements for the field, a screen similar to the one in Figure 10-4b will pop up. In this case, the No button is missing. The dialog will continue to pop up until the data is entered correctly.

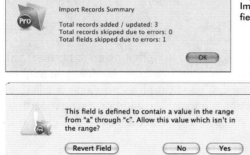

Figure 10-3
Import Records Summary dialog showing fields skipped due to errors in the data.

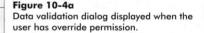

Figure 10-4a
Data validation dialog displayed when the user has override permission.

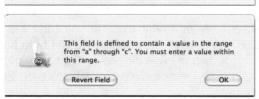

Figure 10-4b
Data validation dialog displayed when the user does not have override permission.

Strict Data Type

You only get three choices from the "Strict data type" pop-up: Numeric Only, 4-Digit Year Date, and Time of Day. With all the Y2K problems the computer industry had, you may want to use the 4-Digit Year Date selection to protect Date fields from future troubles. In fact, let me discourage you from allowing entry of dates with only two digits in the year, because FileMaker is going to fill in the first two digits for you and may guess wrong. Let's say that the field is Birthdate, and the person entering the data types in 03/14/32. FileMaker is going to guess that the intended year is 2032. FileMaker is always going to guess that the intended year is either within the next 30 years or the last 70.

> ⊠ **CAUTION** Whenever you click in the "Strict data type" pop-up, FileMaker auto-matically selects the check box next to Strict data type. You may unwittingly end up with requests to validate a field that doesn't require it. If that's not what you intend, be sure to uncheck that box.

Not Empty

For a retail ordering system, you could verify that there is a pickup date in every order. This option can be pretty handy if you find that users continually forget to fill in a specific piece of information. It can also be a pain if this option is used on fields that don't require a value. You just can't seem to escape the record. If you're sure you want to use this, also check the box next to Strict data type.

Unique Value

Remember when we talked about using a unique ProdID in the Products file? This is where you make that selection. Be sure to check the Strict data type check box. Otherwise, users will be able to override the warning box, and you'll have duplicate IDs. You can choose either the Unique Value or the Existing Value check box.

Existing Value

Using the Existing Value check box makes sure that users only select values that have already been entered in the file. (In a case like that, you might con-sider selecting "Member of value list" instead.) If a new value needs to be entered in the file, turn this option off, make the addition to the record, then turn it back on. Since this is the opposite of Unique, you cannot choose Unique at the same time.

Member of Value List

Checking this box urges the user to enter a value from the value list you choose before leaving the record. You can create a value list right from here if you want. You'll probably want to attach the specific pop-up list to any fields with this option turned on. Otherwise, users will have a heck of a time guess-ing what they're supposed to enter.

Currently on a Macintosh computer, you can't tab into a field that uses a pop-up menu even if you have full keyboard access turned on. However, if you format a field to use a pop-up list that allows tabbing, users can click in the field and type something that's not in the list. To prevent that, you could use this validation. Even at that, since this validation is based on FileMaker's indexing, it is not case sensitive. So you may still want to have users select from a pop-up menu.

In Range

Using this option, you can restrict data entry to a range of values. For instance, you could use a time range to make sure workers punch in and out within cer-tain hours. You can even enter a range of first initials or full words in the range boxes.

⊠ **CAUTION**   Avoid getting carried away with using a text range, because it can be tricky. For example, if you used a range from "a" to "bbb," entering something like "c" in the field would set off the warning. But an entry like "abcde" would not.

Validated By Calculation

This is the option with the most power. You can check for such errors as:

- A field that begins or ends with an extra space or contains or ends with a carriage return
- A State field that has more or less than two letters
- A Zip Code field that has anything other than five digits
- A Social Security Number field that is structured with anything other than three digits followed by a dash, two digits, dash, and four digits.
- A carriage return at the end of various parts of an address field. This usually happens when users hit the Return or Enter key instead of tabbing to the next field.

We'll be looking at calculations in Chapter 11, "Putting Your Data to Work for You."

Maximum Number of Characters

Checking this box lets you limit the number of characters users can enter in a Text, Number, Date, or Time field. You can do something similar with Validated by calculation, but it's a lot simpler here. Just type in a number and you're good to go.

⊠ **CAUTION**   Be careful about what other options you choose when deselecting the override option. When you uncheck the box next to "Allow user to override during data entry," and then check the box next to "Existing value," but the value has never been entered before, the only way to escape the looping dialog is to either revert the field or delete the record. You can't even quit or exit FileMaker. Since your users may not know that, they may panic and pull the plug on the machine. Test your work by using as many possible values as you can think of before inflicting it on other users.

Display Custom Message if Validation Fails

You can have a custom message displayed with or without the allow override option being selected. Use this to clarify what the user should do to correct his or her data entry if the FileMaker window isn't clear enough.

Try to be concise. You can type up to 255 characters in this box. That's 15 to 55 more characters than will actually fit in the dialog that appears if the validation fails. If you're not sure the text will fit, test it by returning to Browse mode and entering some incorrect data. In some cases you may find the standard error message can actually be more descriptive, especially for range errors. If you're developing for both Mac and Windows, be sure your message will fit in the dialog box on both platforms.

Storage Tab (Global Storage, Repeating, and Indexing)

The Storage tab, as seen in Figure 10-5, contains the choices for Global Storage, Repeating fields, and indexing.

Global Storage

This is the tab where you make the choice that turns a regular field into a Global field. Its features are mentioned elsewhere. Let me remind you again though, that for the sake of best practices, Global field names should start with zx_, where the x will be replaced with some other letter that represents the developer's purpose (Control, Interface, Keys, etc.) and end with _gx, where the x will represent the field type (Text, Number, Date, etc.).

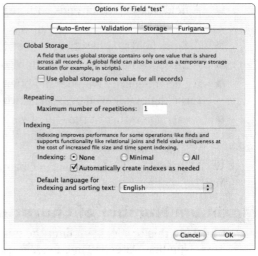

Figure 10-5
Storage tab of the Options for Field window showing Global Storage, Repeating fields, and indexing options.

Repeating Field Options

I covered the Repeating field option in Chapter 4. A Repeating field is just a way of formatting field types (except Summary) with multiple boxes for data entry. It was used quite a bit back in the days before FileMaker became a relational database. It's been maintained primarily so users who had developed databases back then can keep their files as is. However, many developers format Global fields as repeating to store multiple values and images for use throughout their files.

You can have up to 1,000 repetitions of a field. When you place a Repeating field on a layout using the field tool or by copying a single repetition version of the field from some other layout, there is no clue that the field repeats. You must choose Format, Field Format in Layout mode to access the area where you choose how it will appear on the layout. You can choose to display fewer repetitions (all the way down to 1) than appear in the Storage tab.

➲ **NOTE**   You can perform a Find for a value, and if it appears in any of the repetitions, the record will appear in the found set. For example, let's say you had a record with Dog in the first repetition and Cat in the second. A search for Cat in the first repetition or Dog in the second will find the record. If you have the field formatted with a single repetition, you won't be able to see the specified data even if you click in the single repetition. That would be a clue that it is defined as a Repeating field.

⊃ **NOTE**   There is a bug that rears its ugly head when you try to move data from one repetition of a Repeating field to a different repetition in another Repeating field. If you want to know more about it, you can read Tech Info Library Article #10426, "Some Functions Based on a Repeating Field Only Work in First Repeat," available at FileMaker.com. When you go beyond simple storage of values and images in Repeating fields, my advice is to look to relationships and portals for the answer to that job. There is just so much more you can do with them.

FileMaker's Indexing System

Imagine that you have an encyclopedia without an index. If you wanted to find every reference to Thomas Edison, you'd have to scan every page of every volume to find it. With an index, you're way ahead of the game.

Storage Options

FileMaker Pro has a similar index that keeps track of what data is in each field and what records contain those data. It does a fine job of taking care of everything behind the scenes, but because these indexes can get large, you have the option of turning them on and off on a per-field basis. It's like being able to decide that your encyclopedia will only list names and occupations. That makes for a nice slim index, and you'd be able to find Thomas Edison. But how are you going to find information about Cuba? With FileMaker, you can change your mind and add other fields to the index when you need them.

Remember that Number fields ignore any text that may be in them except for periods and dashes. That includes Calculation fields that are concatenated from Number and Text fields, but have a number result. If you look at the field, you'll see the text. But when you search for the text, you may feel as if you're dealing with a ghost. Knowing that is particularly important if you're using a special combination field as a key in a relationship. The relationship and the portal will act squirrelly. Of course the need for most of these calculated "combination" keys goes away for most people now that relationships allow compound keys.

⌘ **TIP**   If you have a relationship that is acting up and it's based on concatenated fields, check that the key fields on both sides of the relationship are the same field type. If they're both calculations, see that you have a match in the "Calculation result is" pop-up in the Specify Calculation window.

In indexed Text fields, all numbers and letters are indexed. Most other characters are not. However, you can search for them by putting quotes around the symbol you want. FileMaker can find it, but it takes a while in a large file. Remember, it has to look on every page.

⊃ **NOTE**   You can actually get FileMaker to index the special characters if you really need to. Go into Define Fields, choose the Storage tab, and select Unicode from the default language pop-up. Then why not just index every Text field as Unicode? Because it may give you headaches in other areas. For instance, when you perform a Find for Bob, it won't find bob. Upper- and lowercase Unicode characters are not considered the same character. Bummer!

Field Indexing Pros and Cons

Choosing whether to index fields is a balancing act. If every field is indexed in a big file, it takes longer to import records (they'll be indexing as they come in) and to perform lookups. The file also gets larger, since the index is stored as part of the file. That's not such a big issue with the new 8 terabyte file size limit and since larger hard drives keep getting cheaper almost daily.

On the other hand, if you turn indexing off for all fields, FileMaker will still perform a Find for you — it will just take longer. Turning indexing off also makes a field unusable as a key in a relationship from the foreign side (either table or file). Never uncheck "Automatically create indexes as needed" if the field will be used as a foreign key. (Using field naming conventions, you will, of course, note foreign keys by putting an _fk at the end, won't you? Now you're beginning to see why these naming conventions are so important.) Notice the indexing options in Figure 10-5. If you select the "None" radio button and uncheck the box next to "Automatically create indexes as needed," FileMaker will build a temporary index when needed. Unless you know that a field will be searched somewhere down the road, the simplest solution is to just ignore the whole thing and let FileMaker take care of it for you. If you need a more comprehensive explanation of these options, see the Help files.

Limitations

The results of a calculation cannot be stored if they use data in a field:

- Where the indexing is turned off
- That uses the GetSummary function
- That is Global
- That comes from a relationship

That's because the data can change across a set of records too easily. In previous versions of FileMaker, if you tried to create a relationship using an unstored key field in a child file or table, FileMaker would show you a warning. That is no longer the case. Starting with FMP7, you have to know the rules. You can go ahead and create the relationship, but nothing connected with it will work correctly.

☒ **CAUTION**   If you create a relationship and later change the key in the child table so it becomes unstored, you will not be notified that the relationship is now invalid. But be assured, if it works at all, it will not work properly. Pay attention to your key fields and treat them with care. This would be another good reason to identify your key fields with k_ or fk_ prefixes. (See "Notes to Developers about Naming Conventions" in Appendix A.)

Furigana Tab[7]

The Furigana tab is new for FileMaker Pro 7. It will only be of interest if you are working with Japanese text and looking for phonetic translation of that text. You'll define two fields. The first field will hold the Japanese text, and the second field will hold the phonetic translation. Choose the Furigana tab, check the box next to "Use Furigana Field," and select the first field you defined. Then go to the "Translate into" drop-down menu and choose the character set you want to use.

Summary

In this chapter, we looked at what you can do when defining fields to simplify data entry and avoid errors. These options appear behind the Auto-Enter, Validation, and Storage tabs. Good use of these tools makes for faster work and a more reliable database.

Q & A

Q If I choose to prohibit modification of a field, what's the point of allowing users into the field at all?

A If you intend to perform a Find on the field, you need to have a way to get into it. However, you can still construct a Find in a script that doesn't require entry into the field. Not only that, but you can also copy data from such a field.

Q Why shouldn't every validation message be set up as Strict? Why would I want users to override what I've set up?

A Until you know for sure that you have it set up correctly, you might want to leave yourself an out. You have to balance how serious the results will be: incorrect data entry against improperly closed files. You may also want the validation to be a very strong suggestion to the user, but not a requirement. For example, if an international order came into your database, you may want to complain that the zip code doesn't look right or is omitted. If there really were a strange or nonexistent zip code, then you'd probably want to allow the odd data but offer the validation as a "reminder" only.

Workshop

Go to the Contact table and experiment with items under the Validation tab on different types of fields. Try selecting "Numeric Only" on a Text field. If you get really daring, try selecting "Validation by calculation" on the AddrState field. See if you can make it check whether you have more or less than two letters in the field. Hint: Click Specify, and look at the text functions in the View pop-up list at the upper right.

Part 3

Review Questions

True-False

1. Auto-entered serial numbers must be defined as Number type.
2. Validation options help make sure that data gets entered properly.
3. If you define a field as a Repeating field, it automatically shows up on each layout with all of its repetitions.
4. Finding and sorting records can be faster with indexing turned on for the target field.
5. By defining a city field as an auto-entered lookup based on zip code, your users can avoid having to enter city names.

Short Answer

6. Name two benefits of using field options.
7. Name the four tabs in the Options for Field window.
8. Why might you not want to turn indexing on for every field in your database?
9. If you want to ensure that a particular field gets entered for each record, which option should you apply to that field?
10. How do you access the Options for Field window?
11. If you suspect that someone in an office has been changing data, what's one way you can find out who it might be?
12. Let's say you found that the boundaries of a city had been changed, absorbing a zip code that used to be in another city. Using information from this chapter, name one way you could update your Contact file.
13. What precaution should you take if you need to define an auto-enter serial number that requires a combination of letters and numbers, where users may later need to perform a Find?
14. Name at least one advantage to having any given field indexed.

Chapter 11

Putting Your Data to Work for You

Vocabulary

- Boolean
- Constant
- Function
- Operator

Objectives

1. Learn more about the Specify Calculation window.
2. Review and use mathematical operators.
3. Understand comparison operators.
4. Learn the logical operators.
5. Learn to use text operators.
6. Explore options in calculations.

Introduction

Buttons can do a lot of tricks for you by finding and sorting records, and moving between files and layouts. Lookups and other auto-enter fields do some of the data entry for you. Now let's put down those pocket calculators and let FMP Calculation fields do that work for you, too. You got your first taste of what can be done with Calculation fields in our InvLI table back in Chapter 7. We used them to provide line totals in the portal on the invoice, and the InvoiceTotal that gave us a grand total of all the line totals. We also used calculations to make a field that combined a customer's first and last names as well as company name.

In this chapter, we'll look at the four categories of operators you use in Calculation fields that:

- Perform the math
- Make comparisons
- Create complex comparisons
- Build calculations using text

Defining a Calculation Field

The Specify Calculation window should be familiar by now. Using it, you build a formula using FileMaker's functions and operators that combine data from various local fields, related fields, and constants.

A *constant* is a value right in the formula. The value of the constant doesn't change unless you redefine the formula. The constant can consist of text, date, number, or time information.

You can type the formula directly in the Formula box. But the more common method for entering a formula when you're getting started with FileMaker is to build it by clicking on items from the lists and buttons in the upper third of the window. You double-click everything except the Mathematical and Text Operators buttons, which only require a single click.

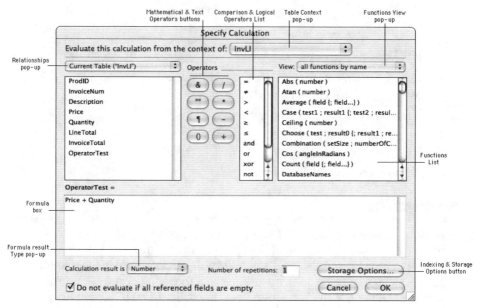

Figure 11-1
The Specify Calculation window.

There are so many functions that we won't be able to cover all of them. So Chapters 12 and 13 show some of the more useful functions in detail. It's also valuable to note that you can use scripts to place the results of these same calculations in appropriate field types in one or more records. Don't forget that the Replace window has a "Replace with Calculated Result" radio button that brings up the same Specify Calculation window. And now FileMaker Pro 7 allows you to specify a calculation when you define a button. It should be clear that developing some level of competency here will yield great dividends.

Operators

Operators are the symbols used to change the behavior of or provide different results from your data. Think of it this way: You have two Number fields. Each field has the number 2 in it. They just sit there. Then you create a Calculation field using the plus (+) operator between them. You get the idea.

Mathematical Operators

These are the operators you remember from math class. Even though I'm sure you know what to expect here, I want to set up a layout with a few fields where we can try out some examples. Maybe there will be a few surprises.

1. Go into our Business file, start a new layout/report using the InvLI table, and call it **Calcs**.
2. Choose the **Columnar list/report** type, click **Next**, and at the next window, Columnar list/report should already be selected, so click **Next** again.
3. At the Specify Fields screen, double-click **Price**, **Quantity**, and **LineTotal** for the Layout fields.
4. Then just keep clicking **Next** until you're in Preview mode.
5. Enter Browse mode and choose **Show All Records**. Hopefully, you created a few records when we were experimenting with the Invoice table. If you didn't, create a few records now, and make up some numbers for the Price and Quantity fields.
6. Now go into Define Database, choose the **InvLI** table, and make a new Calculation field called **OperatorTest**.

Addition (+)

If this operator doesn't look familiar to you, you're probably going to have a lot of trouble from here on.

1. Build the formula for OperatorTest by double-clicking the fields from the Field list and the + operator button until it looks like this:
    `Price + Quantity`
2. Click **OK**, **OK**, then go into Layout mode.
3. If your new field appeared on the layout, delete it and its label, then adjust the Body part. Copy one of the other fields and paste it to the right of the other fields to create a new column. Make sure it lines up horizontally with the other fields within the Body section. Double-click the field, and when the Specify Field window appears, double-click the new **OperatorTest** field in the list. When you're done, the layout should look something like the one in Figure 11-2.

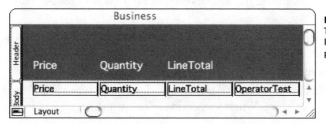

Figure 11-2
The Calcs layout in the InvLI table showing the position of the fields.

Part 3

4. Now go back to Browse mode and look at the results. When you add the first two columns, they should equal the new field in the fourth column.

5. Go back into Define Fields for the InvLI table and redefine the OperatorTest field so it reads like this:

    Price + Quantity + 15

    The number 15 is just an arbitrary figure to demonstrate how the constants work.

6. Click **OK** and **Done**, and go back to Browse mode. As you can see, you can string together any number of fields and constants.

⌘ **TIP**　You can use either a Number field or a Calculation field (with a number result) defined with global storage as a constant in another calculation. And starting in FMP7 you can redefine a field even while other users are sharing the file. But keep in mind that the value in the Global field on everyone else's machine will not change unless you are the host of the file. Even then, other users will receive the change only after they close and reopen the file.

An interesting characteristic in formulas that only use addition is that you can put the values in any order, and the calculation will still work.

Subtraction (–)

The minus symbol is used to subtract the second value from the first one. Here, the values have to be in a specific order. Reverse them and the results are not the same. That's not a FileMaker convention — it's a mathematical convention. In the following example, I want you to redefine the field by yourself. You should know how to get in and out of the Define Fields window by now, so just do it, and then go look at the results.

1. Go back and redefine OperatorTest so it reads:

    Price – Quantity – 15

2. Then change it to this:

    Quantity – Quantity – 15

What's the point, you might ask? Sometimes in your search for a solution, you can end up building very complex calculations with unnecessary elements. The last equation could be shortened to just –15.

Multiplication (*)

For an example of the multiplication function, look at the LineTotal field definition. Here again, you can reverse the order and you'll get the same results. Try this:

    Price * Quantity * .25

It gives you a reasonable markup, even though it doesn't round out evenly.

Division (/)

Using the divide symbol indicates that the result will divide the first value by the second value. Change OperatorTest so it reads:

    Price / Quantity

I do this at the grocery store all the time to figure out how much I'm paying per ounce for a product. When you divide, you turn the integers in the operation into decimal numbers, and any number divided by 100 is its percent equivalent.

Power of (^)

The power symbol is used to multiply a number by itself the number of times indicated by the value that appears after the sign.

Let's look at some large numbers:

```
Price ^ Quantity
```

Hey! What are all those symbols in the result? When a Number field is first placed on a layout, FileMaker uses the General format that I mentioned in Chapter 4.

1. To change it, go to Layout mode, select the field, and choose **Format, Number.**

2. Click the radio button next to **Leave data formatted as entered** and click **OK.** Now you'll have to make the field quite a bit longer — try three or four inches. When you go back to Browse mode, you'll see a question mark if the number is still too large. You can click in the field to see what it really is.

Granted, invoices are not the kind of situation where you'll use the power operator. In my 15 years working with FileMaker, I don't think I've ever used the power operator. It is pretty handy in statistics, probability, and calculating things like compound interest for an arbitrary number of months or the volume of an object.

Precedence ()

You use the precedence parentheses symbols to surround elements of the calculation that are supposed to occur first. Otherwise, the formula is figured from left to right, with multiplication and division results calculated before addition and subtraction.

1. Let's try a few:

```
Price + (Price * .25) * Quantity
```

Wait a minute. That number seems pretty low. I'm trying to mark up the price by 25%, and then multiply by the Quantity. However, FileMaker did the multiplication within the parentheses first. Doing the multiplication before the addition, it multiplied the result by the quantity. Then it added the first Price field last.

2. Rewrite it adding another precedence:

```
(Price + (Price * .25)) * Quantity
```

3. Now, to make all the numbers round out nicely, finish it off like this:

```
Round ((Price + (Price * .25)) * Quantity, 2)
```

I know I'm supposed to be saving functions for the next chapter, but the fields do look nice in Browse mode, don't they? Don't let the complexity of this calculation frighten you. I'll show you an easy way to add functions to a calculation without getting confused about all the precedence parentheses in the next chapter.

Part 3

Why, you might ask, would you do it this way instead of just formatting the field on the layout? Because your financial books will be off. The way numbers appear on a layout is independent of the way they are actually figured in calculations. How it appears is for your convenience. How it's figured is for your accountant, but you have to supply the correct figures.

➲ **NOTE** A common use of parentheses in mathematics is as a shortcut for multiplication. For example: 3 (2 + 4) = 18. You cannot use this shorthand in FileMaker. You must specify 3 * (2 + 4).

Comparison Operators

When you want to find out how similar two values are, you use comparison operators. The values can be fields, constants, or formulas. The calculation returns either True or False. The mathematical equivalent is a 1 or a 0. This type of True or False result is referred to as a Boolean value. Yes and No are also considered valid Boolean results. This concept also applies to the logical operators.

➲ **NOTE** The term Boolean is named after George Boole and honors his idea that a statement can only be true or false. It's a simple but powerful idea. Formatting a number to display in a Boolean format simply asks FileMaker to narrow down the contents of the field to one of two cases: no or false (0 or empty) or yes or true (1).

➲ **NOTE** (This note is a little technical, but I had to put it somewhere. If it helps you, great.)

Some computing environments offer a Boolean field type where you can only store a yes or no answer. FileMaker doesn't. You have to be careful because FileMaker can be a bit inconsistent about evaluating a null value. You would think that a field with a null value would be evaluated as false. But if the calculation has a check mark in the "Do not evaluate if all referenced fields are empty" box, the field may not result in either 0 or 1.

A couple of other details to be aware of: FileMaker will no longer evaluate Number fields beginning with T or Y as true. Also, if you enter both text and numbers in a Number field and you begin with either a T or an F, these fields will not evaluate as Boolean. Instead, they will evaluate as the numeric value in the field. "T111" is a legitimate entry and 111, not 1. "Fall333" evaluates as 333, not 0.

Equal to (=)

If the values on both sides of the equal symbol are the same, the value is 1.

1. Try the following:

    Price = Quantity

    You probably won't get any 1s in that batch.

2. Now try:

    Quantity = 2 * 5

    If you don't have a match, replace one of the numbers in the Quantity field with a 10.

3. Go into Layout mode, select the **OperatorTest** field, and choose **Format, Number.**

4. Click the radio button next to **Format as Boolean**. Leave Yes and No in the boxes just beneath the radio button.

5. Go back to Browse mode and check out the results.

6. Go back and reformat the field as a Number and type **Dah!** over the Yes and **Nyet** over the No.

7. Now try to perform a Find for Dah! — it doesn't work. Now try to Find for Nyet — failure! What's going on here? FileMaker simply displays what you tell it to when it evaluates a number as Boolean. But you can't perform a Find on what it displays. You can only perform your Find on that actual value in the field — the Boolean 0 or 1. But it's looking for a word to start with Y, and Dah! just doesn't cut it.

8. Before we move on, change the Dah! back to Yes, and Nyet back to No.

9. Try this as the calculation:
    ```
    2 * 5 = 10
    ```
    Each record shows a Dah! (unless you changed the format), because you're not referring to any fields, just the constants — all of which have a value.

10. Now select **Show All Records**.

○ **NOTE**   The equal sign can be a point of confusion for many novice FileMaker users, especially if they've used another programming language or even some spreadsheets. In many other languages, the equal sign assigns a value to the item on the left side of the equal sign. X = 5 + 7 would result in X having a value of 12. In FileMaker, the equal sign is an operator that will result in only one of two values: 0 or 1. So if you had "FieldX = 5 + 7" in a function, you would not be assigning 12 to FieldX. The function would simply return 1 if FieldX held a value of 12. Otherwise, it would return 0.

Not Equal to (<> or ≠)

If the values are different, this will yield a 1.

1. Try it for:
    ```
    Price <> Quantity
    ```

2. Change one of the prices to match the quantity in the same record so you have at least one dissenting value in OperatorTest.

⌘ **TIP**   On the Macintosh platform, you can use ≠ (Option+=) in place of <>. If the files are ever moved to a Windows machine, the <> will be automatically substituted in any calculations.

3. Try it with a constant:
    ```
    Quantity <> 10
    ```
    If all the results are the same, change one of the Quantity values to 10.

Greater Than (>)

If the value on the left is greater than the value on the right, this will show a 1.

1. Try this:
    ```
    Price > Quantity
    ```

2. Now try this:
    ```
    Quantity > Price
    ```

Depending on the numbers you have in your fields, you may not get the exact opposite results. That's because the opposite of Price > Quantity is Price <= Quantity. Read on.

Less Than (<)
If the value on the left is less than the value on the right, you'll get a 1. Run your own test.

Greater Than or Equal to (>= or ≥)
If the value on the left is greater than or equal to the value on the right, you'll get a 1.

Try the following, but make sure to have at least one Quantity field with 12 in it as well as larger and smaller amounts in other records:

```
Quantity >= 12
```

Less Than or Equal to (<= or ≤)
Be sure to have one record where Price and Quantity are the same. Watch that record change as you switch from the first to the second of the following calculations:

```
Price > Quantity
Price <= Quantity
```

These are the opposite of each other as are Price < Quantity and Price >= Quantity. Notice that if you flip either of them over you'll get the same result: Quantity > Price is the same as Price < Quantity. Price >= Quantity is the same as Quantity <= Price.

Logical Operators

Logical operators also return Boolean results (1 or 0). Understanding what they do is not that hard. But grasping an entire formula can be a little more difficult than simple comparison operators. That's because you're using these symbols to join two or more of the comparisons.

AND
The AND operator will produce a value of 1 or True if all comparisons in its string are true.

1. Change the OperatorTest field so it reads as follows:
    ```
    Description = "Large Widget" AND Price = 19.99
    ```

2. Go into Layout mode, shorten the field up to about one inch, and add the Description field to the list. If there are no Large Widgets with a price of 19.99 in the same record, make a couple.

⌘ **TIP**   FileMaker will recognize both "AND" and "and" as valid in the calculations. If you type AND, FileMaker converts it to lowercase anyway when you click OK. Nothing to be alarmed about.

3. Now try this:
    ```
    Description = "Large Widget" AND Price = 19.99 AND Quantity = 10
    ```

    You can go as deep as you want with this. While this might seem like a pointless exercise, you might find yourself in a situation in which someone asks you for specific information about two or more fields. You could scan through all the records, which would take a lot or time, or you could create a calculation that will help you find that information in seconds. Notice that you have to put quotes around the text constant (Large Widget), but you don't have to worry about numbers.

4. Now do one more test:
```
Description = "Large Widget" AND Price = Quantity AND Quantity = 10
```

If you are confused about these calculations, consider typing it with returns after the word AND, so it reads like this:
```
Description = "Large Widget" and
Price = Quantity and
Quantity = 10
```

In this one, the middle test compares the values in two fields as well as the two other constants. Of course, to test it in Browse mode, you'll need to make sure that all three conditions are met in at least one record.

OR
The OR operator will produce a value of 1 or True if any of the comparisons in its string are true. Just replace the ANDs from our last formula with ORs:
```
Description = "Large Widget" OR Price = Quantity OR Quantity = 10
```

AND and OR
Now look at combining both AND and OR in the same formula by changing either of the ORs back to an AND. For example:
```
Description = "Large Widget" AND Price = Quantity OR Quantity = 10
```

Change the numbers in some of the Quantity and Price fields to see how they affect the calculation. Is it what you expected?

XOR
Aside from wondering what XOR is, you might wonder where the spelling of XOR comes from. It's just short for X or Y, with the Y part left off. (It is also referred to as "Exclusive OR.") It's pronounced like the first part of "Zorro." You get a True result if either X or Y is true, but not both. If neither is true, you also get a Boolean false, no, or zero.

1. First try:
```
Description = "Large Widget" XOR Price = Quantity
```

2. You can combine this with AND and OR as well. So try:
```
Description = "Large Widget" XOR Price = Quantity AND Quantity = 10
```

This can be particularly confusing, because we are asking that the two parts of the Y portion match. In this case, the X part of the equation is Description = "Large Widget," and the Y is Price = Quantity AND Quantity =10.

■ If the Description is "Large Widget" and the Price and the Quantity are both 10, you will get a False result.

■ If the Description is "Medium Widget" and the Price and Quantity are both 10, you will get a True result.

■ If the Description is "Large Widget" and the Price and Quantity are not both 10, you will get a True result.

Part 3

It took me a long time to understand this concept. Let me give you a more concrete example of why somebody might want to use XOR.

Let's say I'm adding people to my database. I have two fields describing the person: BoughtMyBook and VisitedMyWebsite. The result of a BoughtMyBook XOR VisitedMyWebsite expression would give me a list of people who did at least one of the two but not both. This would be very handy for marketing to people who have shown interest in my work and getting them to look at other work of mine. That way I can leave out those people who haven't done either, as well as those people who've already done both and might not be receptive to more requests to view my work.

BoughtMyBook XOR VisitedMyWebsite is equivalent to:

(BoughtMyBook OR VisitedMyWebsite) AND (NOT (BoughtMyBook AND VisitedMyWebsite))

You can see that the XOR calculation is a handy shortcut, not to mention easier to understand — once you get the hang of it. Don't worry if you don't get it. I don't have to use this one very often, so I have to think it through carefully every time I work with it.

NOT

NOT is *not* used to combine other elements, although you can certainly use it in formulas that have two or more comparison elements. You have to combine NOT with parentheses that surround the value you're testing. Whatever is true in the parentheses returns a False result. Conversely, whatever is false in the parentheses returns a True (or a 1) result.

For example, if we use the calculation NOT (Quantity) = 10, and there is a 10 in the Quantity field, you'll get a 0. Why would you want to do that? Remember when we were working with Omit? Sometimes it's easier to find what is not true than what is true. For example, using the calculation NOT Left(Description, 5) = "Small", returns a 1 for any other kind of widget except Small. Notice that you can combine the NOT with other functions, operators, and constants.

One situation I often run into has to do with whether a field has a value in it. Let's say you need to make sure that every item in the invoice that has a Price also has a Description. In that case, you have to use something like NOT IsEmpty(Description). It sounds a little weird, but that's how you have to phrase it, because there is no function called IsFull(FieldName).

To see what it does, try NOT IsEmpty(Description). Then go into Browse mode and clear out whatever is in one of the Description fields. We'll look more closely at calculations in the next chapter.

➲ **NOTE**   Length(FieldName) also works. It returns 0 for an empty field and 1 for a field with text.

Text Operators

You use text operators to build calculations with a Text result. In a Calculation field built with text operators, you can't edit the field directly. But keep in mind that you can use a calculation as part of a script, Auto-Enter Calculation field option, or Replace function to fill a normal Text field that *can* be edited.

Concatenate (&)

We looked at concatenate in Chapter 7, when we combined the contact information as follows:

```
NameFirst & " " & NameLast & " - " & Company.
```

You're not limited to concatenating fields. You can combine various constants and fields in any combination you like. Be sure to choose a Text result, and try this on for size:

```
"The product is " & Description & " and it costs $" & Price
```

All those quotation marks bring us to...

Text Constant ("")

Any time you want to have specific text as a constant (appearing the same in every record), you have to place it between a set of quotation marks. Look at our preceding examples. If you forget to put quotes around text you intend to display as a constant, FileMaker will check to see if you are naming a function or if there is a field with the name as the text string. If not, you'll get the warning dialog shown in Figure 11-3.

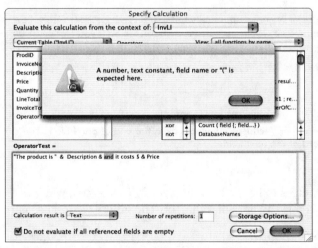

Figure 11-3
A warning dialog box that may appear when leaving a calculation that tells you that one or more of the elements is missing.

Part 3

FileMaker does a pretty good job of alerting you if a calculation is invalid. It's up to you to test the specific results. If you leave a required element out of a calculation, you won't be able to leave the Specify Calculation window until you correct it.

⌘ **TIP**   Let's say you've built a complex calculation but can't seem to get all the elements right. You'll lose all your work if you just click the Cancel button.
Instead, try this: Highlight all the text in your formula. Now press Command+C (Macintosh) or Ctrl+C (Windows) to get the formula onto the clipboard, then click the Cancel button. Exit Define Fields, and go into Layout mode. Find a nice empty place on one of the layouts, and press Command+V (Macintosh) or Ctrl+V (Windows). The whole formula will be right there when you need to copy and paste it back into the Formula box for another try.

➲ **NOTE** The Specify Calculation window can hold over 60,000 characters. There is no practical limit to text constants starting with FileMaker 7. Old-time FileMaker users may find this change a great relief. Text constants used to be limited to 235 characters. You could create longer constants, but you needed to break them into 235-character chunks and concatenate them. Those days are gone.

Return Marker (¶)

Enclose the Return marker operator in quotes to use carriage returns between items in the text calculation. Before FileMaker provided us with Merge fields, people often built address labels like this:

```
NameFirst & " " & NameLast & "¶" & Company & "¶" & AddrStreet & "¶" &
AddrCity & " " & AddrState & " " & AddrZip
```

There are other good uses for the Return marker in a calculation. The only hint I can give you at this point is that you can use it for a compound key in certain types of relationships.

⌘ **TIP** If you have Return markers as part of a calculation and the field is only one character tall, you won't be able to see the other lines of text unless you click in the field. You may want to enlarge the field in Layout mode to show more lines of text.

➲ **NOTE** Regular returns in quotes don't do what you'd expect. FileMaker treats a regular return the same as it would treat a space character. So if you typed:

```
NameFirst & NameLast &
Company &
City
```

you would get:

```
JonathanStarsData Design Pros, LLCLansing
```

Notice that leaving out the " " causes the words from the end of one field to run right into the first word of the next field.

Other Options

There are other choices to be made in the Specify Calculation window. Two of them were discussed in the previous chapter. The others we discuss here.

Storage Option

The Storage Options button (in the Specify Calculation window) brings up the window shown in Figure 11-4, which is a slightly shorter version of the one we looked at in the last chapter. It provides all the same choices minus the Repeating fields option (which you'll find in the lower portion of the Specify Calculation window). Otherwise, everything else applies. Notice, however, that

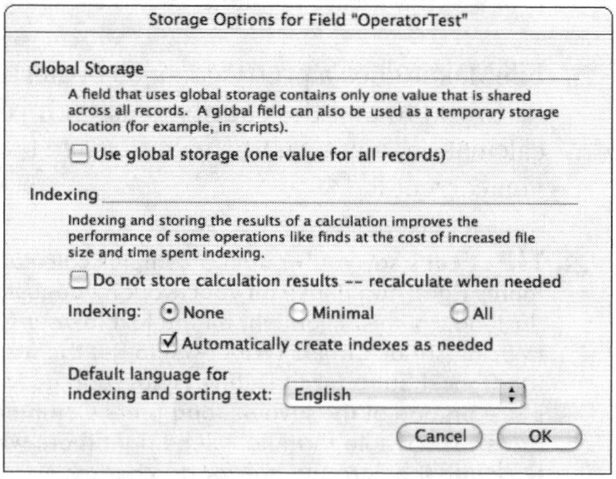

Figure 11-4
The abbreviated Storage Options window accessible from the Specify Calculation window.

if the calculation result is Number, the default language pop-up is grayed out. Numbers don't have much to do with any language except that of mathematics.

Repeating Field

The "Number of repetitions" check box is in the Specify Calculation window (see Figure 11-3) instead of behind the Storage Options button. The meaning is exactly the same as in the last chapter.

Do Not Evaluate

The "Do not evaluate if all referenced fields are empty" check box allows you to prevent FileMaker from placing a zero in the Calculated field until at least one of the fields involved in the calculation has data in it. That can also be a check against incomplete entries. A zero could be a valid result, whereas empty would not be.

Limitations

If the fields you're referencing are not of the type you think they are, your results will probably be off. For example, if you build a Calculation field with a Number result that gets data from another calculated field that has a Text result, the calculation will be wrong. It can happen, 'cause I've done it! If the data in a Calculation field looks wrong, this is one place to check. However, it's okay to have data from any other "Calculation result is" type appear in a Text result field.

To clarify this a bit further — the result type does not have to match the input types. For example, you could create a field that is the result of a Date field plus a Number field and choose to display the result as either a Date or a Number, or even use the GetAsText(date) function and display the result as Text. There are a lot of things you can do with the "Calculation result is" pop-up choices. You just need to make sure you choose the right one to get the results you're looking for.

⮑ **NOTE**   Speaking specifically about calculations and summaries that have number results, a Calculation field is not the same as a Summary field. Generally speaking, Calculation fields perform calculations on one or more Number fields (or other Calculation fields with number results) in the same record. Summary fields perform calculations on a single field in many records. There are a number of tricks you can use to go beyond this description, but these are the basics. You can use relationships and Global fields, as well as the aggregate and GetSummary functions, to push the limits, but I'll leave it at that for now.

Summary

In this chapter, we looked at how to get FileMaker to calculate fields with mathematical, comparison, complex comparison, and text results.

Q & A

Q How many logical operators can I use in a formula?

A The Formula box has a 64,000-character limit. Otherwise, you're only limited to being able to figure out what the darn thing means.

Q Can I use a Boolean result in another formula?

A Yes, but in FileMaker, the result is always seen as a 0 or a 1 regardless of how the calculation is formatted in the field definition or on the layout.

Workshop

Go to our Contact table and create a new Calculation field where the calculation result is Text. Experiment with some calculations combining various other Text, Number, and Date fields as well as some constant values or each type. Try using some of the Return markers (¶). Don't forget to open up the field so you can see all the lines.

Review Questions

True-False

1. The eight buttons at the top of the Specify Calculation window are used to add fields to a calculation.
2. The precedence, or order of operation, of numerical calculations can be controlled by using double quotes.
3. A calculation designed to return a True or False (or Yes or No, or 1 or 0) result is called a Boolean calculation.
4. To concatenate city, state, and zip_code fields into one field that displays city (comma space) state (space) zip_code, you need to insert text constants between the fields.
5. The "Calculation result is" type should always be the same as the fields in the Formula box.

Short Answer

6. Name two ways to add a field name to a calculation.
7. Which of the following are true: (a) 50 < 50, (b) 50 <= 50, (c) 50 > 50, (d) 50 >= 50, (e) 50 = 50, (f) 50 <> 50?
8. Name the four logical operators used in FileMaker Pro calculations.
9. If you wanted to create a Calculation field that had first_name on one line and phone_number on the second line, what would the calculation formula be?
10. What is the purpose of the "Do not evaluate if all referenced fields are empty" check box?
11. Name at least four of the mathematical operators.
12. In Boolean terminology, what does a 1 mean?
13. Using the OR logical operator, if both comparisons produce a true result, what it the Boolean result?
14. Using the XOR logical operator, if both comparisons produce a true result, what is the Boolean result?

Chapter 12

Real-World Calculations — Part 1

Vocabulary

- Function
- Nested function

- Parameter

Objectives

1. Begin using the FileMaker Pro Help files.
2. Learn the purpose and syntax of functions.
3. Use the View pop-up to see categories of functions.
4. Discover and use text, number, date, and time functions.
5. Practice using parameter templates.
6. Define a Calculation field with a nested function.
7. Create a Calculation field to format phone numbers.
8. Use the Case function.
9. Learn how to convert a Calculation field into a non-calculation field.
10. Create a simple time clock database.

Introduction

FileMaker Pro leaves a Rolodex in the dust once you get started using the operators and functions. This is where you turn your data into useful information. This is also where you check and correct data. You can take large amounts of data from other sources and whip it into shape, making all of it fit the proper format.

Rather than describing each of the functions, I'll show you some basic concrete examples and tell you about several hidden specifics. Then I'll show you tricks for combining functions into more complex calculations. That way you'll have a far better idea of how to make your own. The functions are listed in the manual and in the FileMaker Pro Help files.

FileMaker's Help Files

Starting with this chapter, knowing how to use the FileMaker Pro Help files will be extremely valuable. The Help files cover each function in detail and give you comprehensive alternative examples.

To use the Help files, you need to have installed them previously. If you did a full install of the FileMaker Pro application, the Help files should already be available. Choose Help, Contents and Index. (If that choice is not available, you'll need to get out your CD and follow the instructions for a custom install. Then install only the Help files.) When you choose the Index or Find tabs in the Help files, you can type directly in a text area to find more information on your topic. Otherwise, you can go to the Contents tab and click on the list. Each click takes you deeper, outline-style, until you find the topic for which you're searching.

The Help files have become increasingly useful in the past few years, providing better examples and some extremely useful solutions.

What Are Functions?

Put simply, a *function* is a formula that crunches data. You choose the function, give it the data to operate on, and it gives you the result. The functions are available from the list in the upper-right area of the Specify Calculation window, next to View or wherever you may find it. That includes:

- When you're defining a Calculation field
- When using the Replace menu choice
- When the "Validated by Calculation" check box is selected in Field Definitions
- From within the Set Field, Insert Calculated Result, and Replace script steps

Some of the functions are fairly easy to understand, and some are quite deep. Not only that, but you can combine even the easiest functions into complex expressions. You don't need to know them all in order to do well with FileMaker. But you should know which functions are available and where to find out how to make them work for you when the time comes.

The group of functions we'll discuss in this chapter operate on specific types of data: Text, Number, Date, and Time.

⊃ **NOTE** An expression in FileMaker is different from a phrase your grandmother used when she was annoyed with the paperboy. An expression is a value or a calculation that gives you a value. It can contain field values, functions, and constants.

⌘ **TIP** When you're working out the specifics of a calculation in a table that has a lot of records, it's often better to test it in a script rather than creating a field definition. When you exit Define Fields, it can take quite a while to recalculate every single record only to find that it's not quite right. Using the same calculation in a script can tell you whether it's working in much less time. You can have it drop the result into an empty field (maybe in one or more temporary test records) to test it out. Once you have it fine-tuned, copy and paste it into the field definition formula box.

⌘ **TIP**   Because FileMaker 7 allows you to work with multiple tables in a file, it is very important that you pay attention to the table in which you want to perform your work. At the top of the Specify Calculation window is the "Evaluate this calculation from the context of" drop-down menu. Make your table choice there.

Text Functions

Text functions operate on — you guessed it — text. You can use them to pull apart data and to build new groups of text. The calculations can include constants, data from other fields, the expressions we worked with in the last chapter, and even other functions. When we created the AddressCombo field in our Contact table, we were using text functions.

1. Go into the Contact table now, start a new Calculation field called **FunctionTest**, and click **Create**.

2. Click on the View pop-up in the upper-right corner, and pull down to Text functions.

3. Double-click on the first function, **Exact**.

When a function moves into the Formula box, the parameters or arguments you need to fill in are highlighted between the parentheses. This is called the parameter template. In the U.S. English version of FileMaker, semicolons separate the parameters that you need to replace. In other localized versions, other symbols may be used. Regardless, the functions in the list (and when double-clicked) will have the right types of separators in them.

⌘ **TIP**   Unless you know specifically what you want to replace the parameters with, it's usually best to click further down in the Formula box to deselect them. That gives you some time to find their replacements and work on them one by one.

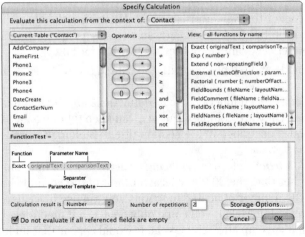

Figure 12-1
The Specify Calculation window showing a diagram of the Exact function.

Left

1. Highlight and delete the Exact function, then scroll down and double-click the **Left** function. The Left function looks like this:

    ```
    Left (text: numberOfCharacters)
    ```

Starting from the left, it plucks the number of characters from the "text" parameter that you choose with the "numberOfCharacters" parameter. You can put the number in directly, or have it come from a Number field, or it can even come from other functions.

2. Choose **Text** from the "Calculation result is" drop-down (lower-left corner of the Specify Calculation window) and try substituting this:
   ```
   Left(NameFirst; 4)
   ```
3. Click **OK** and **OK** again.
4. Go to Layout mode and place a copy of the field on the layout if one isn't already there.
5. Go to Browse mode and look at the results of the calculation in a few of the records.
6. Redefine the formula by putting quotes around NameFirst, which turns it into a constant. Click **OK** and **OK** again
7. Go back to Browse mode and take a look. Same result for each record!

A Calculation within a Calculation

This next section is a little trickier. We're going to use another function to replace one of the parameters.

1. Remove the quotes from around NameFirst.
2. Highlight the **4** and double-click the **Left** function in the function list. Your calculation should look like this:
   ```
   Left(NameFirst; Left(text; numberOfCharacters))
   ```
3. Now change the parameters so the formula reads like this:
   ```
   Left(NameFirst; Left(AddrStreet; 1))
   ```

   I'm asking FileMaker to grab letters from the NameFirst field based on the first character in the Address field (assuming it's a numeral). Granted, it's not a very practical example, but let's fly with it for now.
4. Go to Browse mode and try playing with the data in the Address field to see how FunctionTest recalculates.

This is an example of a nested function. Nested functions are the hallmark of complex calculations. They are complex, but you can keep them manageable by using the techniques described in the section titled "Building Complex Calculations" in this chapter.

The term *nested function* refers to replacing a parameter in a function with another function. Other than the 30,000-character limit of the Formula box, there is no limit to the number of nested functions you can use in a calculation. (In previous versions of FileMaker, you could only nest 125 If functions. I tested it this time and gave up after 250 levels. It would appear that limit is no longer in effect.)

LeftWords

The LeftWords function looks like this:
```
LeftWords (text; numberOfWords)
```

It works just like the Left function, except this does the counting based on spaces and other non-text characters (such as the underscore) between words. Choose "Calculation result is Text."

Remember back when we had our contact's whole name in a Name field? You would have been able to extract the first name from the field this way. It works great for entries with just a first and last name. But you would still have had to figure out what to do with entries that included middle names, initials, and various other combinations. (One way to handle this situation might be to use the Position function described below.)

Length

Length counts the number of characters in a field. It includes spaces, numbers, and special characters as well as text. The function looks like this:

```
Length (text)
```

Choose "Calculation result is Number" and substitute NameFirst for text:

```
Length (NameFirst)
```

By combining it with one of the logical functions, you can use Length to check that phone numbers, Social Security numbers, and credit card numbers are the correct length. This isn't exactly that test, but you might try it for fun:

```
If (Length(NameFirst) = 5; "Five"; "Not Five")
```

The If function can be found in the Logical functions. Sometimes I use a field like this that I've formatted to show large red letters on the layout when the validation fails, for example, if a needed field were left empty. (This type of "validation" is not to be confused with Validate by Calculation.) To use it that way, remove the word Five from the second parameter and let the quotes sit next to each other. Then nothing shows if the validation is okay. You could also use a calculation like this in the Validate by Calculation section of a field definition. You wouldn't get any large red letters that way, but once again it shows you how you can solve problems in FileMaker from different directions. Since Validate by Calculation uses Boolean logic, you could use the simpler calculation Length(NameFirst) = 5.

➡ **Note:** You may have noticed that sometimes there's a space between the name of the function and the left parenthesis for the parameter. In version 7, FileMaker automatically adds this space. Calculations in files converted from previous versions will work just the same; it's strictly a cosmetic issue.

Position

To use the Position function, choose "Calculation result is Number." It looks like this:

```
Position (text; searchString; start; occurrence)
```

This returns a number representing the number of characters from the start point (the third parameter), where the first character of the specified string begins. If the calculation returns a zero (0), it means that that particular occurrence of the "substring" wasn't found in the searched segment of text.

■　text is usually a field, but it can be an expression.

■　searchString is a Text field or expression. It is the specific text for which you're searching.

- start is a Number field or expression and it is determined by counting from the left.
- occurrence is a Number field or expression that specifies the repetition for which you're looking.
- Position is often used with other functions to extract data starting with the character found by the Position function.

Let's say you inherited a database with only one field for people's full name. You want to split the first name from the last name and create two fields: NameFirst and NameLast. You can use the position function Position (FullName; " "; 1; 1) to find out how many characters before the first space. With this calculation, FileMaker starts at the first character (start) in the FullName field and goes to the first space (occurrence), essentially splitting the field in two.

That's great, you say. Well, almost. What happens if some of the names in this field include a middle name or initial or a Junior, a designation, or a degree at the end? You'll need to keep using the Position function to keep splitting the information into fields that make more sense.

It sounds like work, but just think how much more work it would be without this function!

Building Complex Calculations

Trying to create complicated calculations to get the result you want can require so many nested functions that your eyes bug out. I've met a few people who can see these things in their heads, but I'm not one of them. So here's a technique I've developed that might work for you.

I've included the answers to the questions that apply to our example calculation. Then I describe the process, including techniques for making it go more smoothly. If you work along on your computer, you may be able to remember some of the methods when it comes time for you to figure out your own calculations.

This example is one I was asked to do for a client who had a number of phone directories stored in a word processing program. The street name needed to be extracted from the whole address string.

The Steps

1. Ask yourself what you want, and describe it in plain English.
   A: I want the street name without the number.
2. What will be the main function?
   A: The Right function
3. How can you single out what you want? What sets it apart (delimits it) from the rest of the data in the field in most records?
   A: There is a space in front of it. Not only that, but it's the first space in the field.
4. How do I define that delimiter? Should I use a constant or a function?
   A: Try the Position function.

5. Test the separate parts of the subfunction(s), and save each part that works.

6. Repeat steps 3 through 5 for each subfunction that will replace a parameter in the main function. Add other functions as you need them.
    A: I might need the Length function.

7. Then use the main function and drop the subfunction formulas into the parameter slots in the parameter template. Start over at step 2 if you find you picked the wrong main function.

Using the Process

1. Go to our FunctionTest field, highlight the existing formula, and delete it.

2. Because we'll be using the Position function as a subfunction, we need to solve that first. Choose the Text functions from the View pop-up, then find and double-click the **Position** function from the list. It will appear with the four parameters highlighted, as shown in Figure 12-2.

Position (text ; searchString ; start ; occurrence)

Figure 12-2
Immediately after you move any function into the Formula box, the parameter template is highlighted.

⌘ **TIP** Once you've added a function, click to the right end of it in the Formula box, press Return (carriage return) twice, then double-click the same function again. Once you start replacing the parameters, it's easy to forget which one you're working on. This way, you have the template sitting right in front of you.

⌘ **TIP** In the function parameter template, starting after the first parenthesis and then after each semicolon, add a Return (carriage return) to the first function until it looks like Figure 12-3. That way, each parameter is on a separate line. Even though semicolons separate each parameter, once you start replacing parameters with other functions (each with their own set of semicolons), you'll still be able to figure out where you are.

Position (
text ;
searchString ;
start ;
occurrence)

Position (text ; searchString ; start ; occurrence)

Figure 12-3
The Position function with returns inserted after the first parenthesis and after every semicolon.

Replacing the Parameter Template

3. Highlight the word "text" and replace it with **AddrStreet**, since that's the field we're searching in.

4. Highlight "searchString" and replace it with two quotes with a space between them (" "), because a space is the character that appears before the text for which we're looking.

5. Highlight "start" and replace it with a **1**, since you want to start counting from the first character from the left. Highlight "occurrence" and replace it with a **1**, since you want it to look for the first appearance of the space. When you're done, it should look like Figure 12-4.

```
Position (
AddrStreet ;
" " ;
1 ;
1 )

Position ( text ; searchString ; start ; occurrence )
```

Figure 12-4
The Position function once the parameter template has been replaced with specific data.

In order to test it out, you have to get rid of the second copy of the Position function. But you don't want to just erase it in case you need to rework the calculation.

⌘ **TIP**   Here's a trick for keeping the whole calculation (including the function templates) so you can work with it again. Put your cursor somewhere between the "real" calculation and the function template(s) in the Formula box and type "/*" (without the quotes). Now put your cursor to the right of the last function template and type "*/" (without the quotes). These characters tell FileMaker to ignore the text between them when performing the calculation. When you come back, everything will still be there waiting for you. For more details, see the section titled "Commenting Calculations" at the end of this chapter.

Testing the Results

6.   Count the number of characters after the space, and compare it with the number in FunctionTest. Uh, oh. That's not right. It's showing the position of the space, not the number of characters we need.

7.   Go back into the field definition, highlight the whole formula, and paste the full detail back in from the clipboard.

What went wrong? What we really want is the number of characters after that space. We still need the position of the space, but if we subtract it from the total number of characters in the field, we'll get the right number of characters.

⌘ **TIP**   If you have a calculation that almost works, but you're going to try something dramatic, make a duplicate of the field and add the word "Safety" to the end of it. Then, once everything works, delete the safety copy to prevent cluttering up your files. Also, starting with FileMaker Pro 7, you can add a Comment to the field definition to help you spot fields that are temporary. Click the Options/Comments header to view the comments for all the fields.

Making Adjustments

8.   Put a Return (carriage return) after the last function, then find and add the Length function. Now add a second copy at the top followed by a minus sign. When you get done, it should look like Figure 12-5.

```
Length (text) – Position (
AddrStreet ;
" " ;
1 ;
1 )

Position ( text ; searchString ; start ; occurrence )
Length (text)
```

Figure 12-5
The calculation after adding the Length function template.

9.   Replace "text" with **Address**. Now copy the whole formula to the clipboard, and delete the reference functions at the bottom. Click **OK** and

Done and go look at it. Aha! That's the number of characters we need. Now go back to the field definition, and get rid of the extra carriage returns until it looks like Figure 12-6.

Length (AddrStreet) – Position (AddrStreet ; " " ; 1 ; 1)

Figure 12-6
The calculation with all extra carriage returns and the other function templates removed.

Insert Subfunctions

Finally, we need to combine that number formula with the Right function.

10. Add two carriage returns after our calculation, and double-click the **Right** function. Copy the Length minus Position calculation, and paste it into the numberOfCharacters parameter. Replace the text parameter with the AddrStreet field. And finally, delete the original calculation. The formula should look like this:

    ```
    Right(AddrStreet; Length(AddrStreet) - Position(AddrStreet; ""; 1; 1))
    ```

11. Change the Calculation result is to **Text**, and go check it out. It works pretty well. This is exactly how I got the client the needed data.

Different Function, Same Result

Now here's a calculation that will scare you with its simplicity:

```
MiddleWords(AddrStreet; 2; 10)
```

Guess what? It gives you the same information as the longer calculation. The MiddleWords parameter template looks like this:

```
MiddleWords (text; startingWord; numberOfWords)
```

You can use "10" or some other suitably large number as the "number of words" even when there are not 10 words in the field. The function simply stops when it runs out of words to check. There are at least two other calculations that will give you the text we've requested. I didn't figure out this shorter version until later. How I got the answer didn't matter to my client. The main point is that understanding this process will put you on the road to finding solutions with your own complex calculations when you need them.

Make It Permanent

Here's how to turn a Calculation field into a permanent, editable, non-calculation field. After you've seen that the calculation works, go back into Define Fields. Highlight the Calculation field, and use the field type pop-up to choose the format you want (usually Text or Number). Click OK and then Save, and it will be permanently converted.

There are a few situations you need to be aware of to make this work:

■ After first creating the calculation or making any subsequent changes to the calculation, you must return to Browse mode. Then return to Define Fields and convert the calculation to a Text or Number field.

■ You cannot include Global or related fields anywhere in the formula. That's because they cannot be indexed. You can, however, use a related field by creating a temporary field and copying the data over using a script or a Replace by calculation. Then use the data in the temporary field in the calculation, convert the calculated field, and delete the temporary field afterward.

- ■ This one is probably obvious, but here goes anyway: Now that the field is no longer based on a calculation, it will no longer update when data changes in the fields that were originally referenced. It's just a plain old static field. As long as it's not locked down by one method or other, you can still change data in it. It just won't happen automatically.

Number Functions

Number functions will probably feel a little more familiar than the text functions. That's because they're more like math.

One of my clients wanted me to set up a table so phone numbers could be entered as straight numerals without dashes, and the dashes would appear automatically in the right places. What seemed to start out as a number function problem ended up using a lot of the text functions. But the trial and error and adjustment cycle in this real-life example is just too good to scrap simply because it's not all numbers.

The following example demonstrates one method that worked in FileMaker previous to version 7 and the lesson is still valid. For a method that works well in FMP7, read through to the section titled "A Calculation for FMP7."

The Process

To tackle the assignment, I answered the questions in the complex calculation questionnaire and then ran some experiments.

1. I want to put dashes between digits so it looks like a phone number.
2. Try the Left, Right, and Middle text functions.
3. There will be 10 digits. That should be pretty easy to break into smaller pieces.
4. Use a constant as a delimiter.
5. Test...
6. I don't think I'll need any other functions.

This shouldn't be too hard. Let's try it.

1. Go to the Phone table, and create a new Calculation field called **FormatPhone**. So you can follow along, create a new record and use this information in the Phone field:

   (613) 477-1234
   343-1235
   http://www.react.net/utopia1
   utopia@react.net

2. Use the Left, Middle, and Right functions, which start out like this:

   Left (text; numberOfCharacters)
   Middle (text; start; Number OfCharacters)
   Right (text; numberOfCharacters)

3. Put them together like this:

    ```
    Left(Phone; 3) & "-" & Middle(Phone; 4; 3) & "-" & Right(Phone; 4)
    ```

4. And here are the results! To get the same results I did, you'll need to go to Layout mode, select the **FormatPhone** field, choose **Format**, **Number**, and click the radio button next to **Leave data formatted as entered**.

    ```
    (61-3)-1234
    343--12-1235
    htt-p:/-pial
    uto-pia-.net
    ```

Yikes, maybe this isn't going to be so easy.

Make an Adjustment

Maybe I need to have the calculation ignore all the symbols in the Phone field. The GetAsNumber(text) function might work. Here's what I tried next:

```
Left(GetAsNumber(Phone); 3) & "-" & Middle(GetAsNumber (Phone); 4; 3) &
"-" & Right(GetAsNumber (Phone); 4)
```

And here's the result:

```
-61-347-1234
343-123-1235
.1--.1
```

It looks as if the conversion of Phone to a number is using the parentheses to indicate that the first phone number is a negative number. Now we're also confronting something I missed before. The second number doesn't include an area code because it's local. And, in the end, we do want the e-mail and web addresses to show up unaltered.

Modify Further

To make negative numbers appear as positive, let's try the Abs function:

```
Left(Abs (GetAsNumber (Phone)); 3) & "-" & Middle(Abs (GetAsNumber
(Phone)); 4, 3) & "-" & Right(Abs (GetAsNumber (Phone)); 4)
613-477-1234
343-123-1235
.1--.1
```

Well, that takes care of the first number, but what about the phone number with only seven digits? We have numbers with ten digits, some with seven, and anything that's left over should stay as text. This calls for either the If or the Case logical function. Either will allow for different results based on variations in input. If and Case work very similarly. I prefer the Case function because with longer nested functions, it uses fewer characters, so I just use it for everything.

Try, Try Again

Starting over with our first question, here's how we might make the statement in plain English: If the phone number has ten digits, format it as we already did. If it has seven digits, we only want the left three digits, then a dash, then the last four digits. Anything else should be left as entered in the Phone field to show as text.

Part 3

Case Function

Since the Phone field can have any number of characters in it, how do we get the calculation to recognize 10 characters? If it's converted to a number, the smallest 10-digit number is one billion. So we can say, "For any number over one billion, format it like a 10-digit phone number." The smallest seven-digit number is one million. So we can say, "For every number over one million, format it like a seven-digit phone number." For everything that's left over, leave it as is.

The Case function looks like this:

```
Case (test1; result1 {;test2; result2; …; defaultResult})
```

To break it up for easier visualization:

```
Case (
test1;
   result1;
test2;
   result2;
defaultResult)
```

Notice I added three spaces before each result. That's so your eyes can spot the differences between the test and the result. I also removed the brackets and the ellipsis near the end.

Plug It In

You can run as many tests as you like using the Case function. The only limit is 30,000 characters in the Formula box. (Warning to power users of earlier versions of FileMaker: The Formula box used to allow up to 64,000 characters.) Now, let's plug in the calculations. Be sure to choose "Calculation result is Text."

```
Case(
Abs(GetAsNumber (Phone)) > 1000000000;
   Left(Abs(GetAsNumber (Phone)); 3) & "-" & Middle(Abs(GetAsNumber
(Phone)); 4; 3) & "-" & Right(Abs(GetAsNumber (Phone)); 4);

Abs(GetAsNumber (Phone)) > 1000000;
   Left(Abs(GetAsNumber (Phone)); 3) & "-" & Right(Abs(GetAsNumber
(Phone)); 4);

Phone)
```

I also added extra carriage returns between each test and result set. It doesn't affect the formula, but it does make it easier to read, though it's still not very easy at that! Notice I've removed the Middle function from the second argument.

In the end, I found that I didn't need to use GetAsNumber. The Abs function converts the parameter within its parentheses into a number. (Abs will convert dates and times in ways you might not expect. It will even attempt to convert text.) In this case, it doesn't matter. It works both ways. The compulsive part of me believes that simpler is better, but where the client is concerned, faster and cheaper is better.

The Real Trick

We're not done yet! Even though users will enter a string of numbers when they're done, you want the delimited calculation to show. So here's how you pull that off. You have to stack the calculated field on top of the original Phone field. By that I mean both fields have to be exactly the same size (use the Size tool under the View menu), and you need to place them so that only one is visible. The Phone field is directly underneath the calculated field and completely obscured from view (use the Arrange menu). The upper field needs to be the calculated field with a solid fill color — white is a good choice. It also has to be formatted on the layout to prevent entry into the field. The Phone field must allow entry and can be included in the tab order. When you click on the upper field, since it's unenterable, FileMaker immediately transports you to the field below. You enter the data, and as soon as you exit the field, you see the properly formatted data in the calculated field.

A Calculation for FMP7

And now for an even easier method. FileMaker now has a check box for "Do not replace existing value of field (if any)" that can be unchecked, thereby allowing you to replace the value in a field with a Calculated value. You can use the "Calculated value" part of the Auto-Enter tab in the field definition and replace the phone number with a fully formatted version of itself. Assuming that the only data in the Phone field will either be a 10-digit phone number or a web or e-mail address, you can use the following Calculated value to format only items entered as phone numbers. The Phone field needs to be a Text field.

```
If(Length(Phone) = 10 and
PatternCount (Phone; "w") = 0 and
PatternCount (Phone; "@") = 0
Left(Phone; 3) & "-" &
Middle(Phone; 4; 3) & "-" &
Middle(Phone; 7; 4);
Phone)
```

As long as the Phone field has 10 digits in it and no "w" (which you would find in a web address — www) and no "@" symbol (which you would find in an e-mail address), it will automatically be replaced with the dashed format. Of course, this assumes the data entry people never make the mistake of missing a digit or entering extra digits. But they'll be able to see that there's a problem in an instant because the phone number won't pick up the dashed format.

Date and Time Functions

When you see a date in FileMaker, you're really seeing a formatting trick. Behind the scenes, FileMaker is keeping track of dates with a numbering system. Starting with 1/1/0001 as day 1, all dates get a serial number. It makes calculations for the program quite easy — all it has to do is use simple math.

The same simple math doesn't necessarily work so well for certain script steps that use dates. Since you can use functions in scripts, you need to know how to handle dates.

Part 3

- In the Set Field and Insert Calculated Result steps, if you're taking a date from a Date field or time from a Time field and placing it in a Text field, FileMaker will now format it so it is recognizable as a date or time (5:55:25 PM or 9/7/2004). If you want it unformatted strictly as the numbers FileMaker uses "behind the curtain," you need to use the GetAsNumber(text) function, which can be found under the Text functions.

- Conversely, if you're taking a date from a Text field and placing it in a Date field, you need to use the GetAsDate(text) function.

- Interestingly, if you click in a Text field and choose Records, Replace and select "Replace with Calculated result," you can use a Date field and get what looks like a date in the Text field. This won't work if you go the other way. You would have to use the GetAsDate(text) function.

Time Clock

Those things being said, let's look at an example that combines both date and time information into a simple time clock for keeping track of employee hours.

1. Start a new table called **TimeClock**, and create the following fields. For the Hours field, be sure to choose **Calculation result is Time**.

Field Name	Type	Options
Date	Date	Creation Date
TimeIn	Time	Creation Time
TimeOut	Time	
Hours	Calculation	TimeOut – TimeIn

2. Use the **Auto-Enter Creation Date** option for the Date field, and **Creation Time** for TimeIn.

3. Click **OK**. Go to TimeClock Browse mode, and choose **View, View as Table**.

4. Enter some appropriate times in the TimeOut field to see how the calculation does the math for you.

Third Shift

Now, what happens if the company goes to a second or third shift? Workers may get to work in the evening and leave after midnight.

1. Create a new record, and overwrite TimeIn with **9:00 P.M.**

2. Fill in TimeOut with **5:00 A.M.** Minus 16 hours?! This employee owes the company some money!
   What we need in a situation like this is a field that combines both the time and the date. Time to use FileMaker 7's new Timestamp field type.

3. Go back into Define Fields, change the name of the TimeIn field to **TimeStampIn**, and change the field type to **Timestamp**.

4. In the Auto-Enter tab, change the Creation drop-down to **Timestamp**.

5. Change TimeOut to **TimeStampOut** and change the field type to **Timestamp**. You won't even need the Date field any more.

Rebuild the Calculation

Before FileMaker Pro 7, you would have needed to create a second Date field called something like DateOut and add the TimeOut to it. Since this chapter is about calculations, I've decided to leave this section in because it will help you think about how hours are figured. There are situations where you may need the information about the number of seconds in a day. By the way, the old method still works. It's just that the new method is simpler. Here's the old way.

Now we need to rethink the Hours calculation. We need a combination of date and time data. Here's the trick: Time fields really keep track of the number of seconds since the beginning of a day. You can figure out the number of seconds in a day. There are 24 hours in a day, 60 minutes in each hour, and 60 seconds in each minute. That's 24 x 60 x 60 = 86,400 seconds in a day. The Hours calculation would be:

```
((DateOut * 86400) + TimeStampOut) - ((DateIn * 86400) + TimeStampIn)
```

After you exit Define Fields, you'll have to go to Layout mode and place the DateOut field on the layout (unless your preferences are set up to add new fields). When you return to Browse mode, the Hours field will be a mess because you don't have any of the DateOut fields filled in. Try a few combinations to check it out.

Another slightly shorter way to write the calculation would be:

```
((DateOut - DateIn) * 86400) + (TimeStampOut - TimeStampIn)
```

A Conditional Alert

Back to the new way of FMP7.

What if you want to be alerted when the employee has too many hours? Create a Calculation field ("Calculation result is Text") called OTProblem (OT for overtime) with the following calculation:

```
Case(Hours > 3600 * 12; "Check this out!"; "")
```

The value 3600 is the number of seconds in an hour. The reason I did it this way is that it isolates the number of hours so it's easy to change. You could substitute a field for the 12. That way, by creating a Global field formatted as a number, you'd be able to change the results of the calculation without redefining the field.

After you exit Define Fields, you'll have to go to Layout mode and place the OTProblem field on the layout. I recommend formatting this field with bold, red text. Return to Browse mode, and change the TimeOut field until you trigger the warning.

Commenting Calculations[7]

Some of the calculations we've looked at can be frightfully complex to build. Wouldn't it be nice to be able to add comments right in the calculation to remind you why you created it and what the various parts mean? Well, starting in FileMaker 7 you can. I'm just going to show you one method. It's good enough for everything I want to do. If you want other options, look in the Help files for "Adding comments to a formula."

Part 3

To add a comment to your calculation, simply start with the characters "/*" (without the quotes), type your comments, and end with "*/" (without the quotes).

If we were to add comments to our last calculation, it might look like this:

```
Case(Hours > 3600 * 12; /* If the employee  punched in for more than 12
hours (there are 3600 seconds in an hour)...  */
"Check this out!";  /* ...show me this text... */
"") /* ...otherwise, don't display anything. */
```

This works anyplace in FileMaker where you see the Calculation dialog — including scripts. Don't forget — in the define fields area you have a Comment box where you can remind yourself what the field is for. It's just much more convenient having it right there in the calculation, line by line.

Summary

In this chapter, we looked at some text, number, date, and time functions, and you learned how to put them together in complex calculations using some logical functions. You also learned that you can get most of the details that you need about specific functions from FileMaker Pro's Help files.

Q & A

Q When I start looking at all those functions with semicolons and parentheses, I just lose my place.

A Join the club! It helps if you try to see separate parts of a formula as groups or modules that can be plugged into one another. Many of the formulas in this chapter have sections that repeated. When I modified them, I could change whole sections by highlighting and replacing.

Using the returns between parameters can also help. Sometimes I'll copy a calculation and paste it into a word processing document so I can print it out. Then I'll draw lines around areas that represent the modules. You really don't have to understand the entire calculation at a glance. You can learn to grasp it in pieces. Think of it as a meal. You don't swallow everything on your plate in one gulp. But in the end, you're satisfied.

Workshop

Go back into the TimeClock table and create the Global field mentioned in that section. Change the number in the field and see if you can make it work with different trigger points. Now create two scripts: one that punches in and one that punches out. I'll leave it to you to see if you can figure that out. But I will give you one hint: Don't forget to add the Timestamp to the script. Then add a punch in and punch out button to the layout. The buttons won't show unless you choose View as Form or View as List.

Review Questions

True-False

1. The FileMaker Pro application includes on-line Help files that you can access on your computer.

2. The syntax of a function includes the function name followed by the parameters within parentheses.

3. In the Left function [Left (text; numberOfCharacters)], the number parameter refers to the number of words to be used.

4. To take a number and convert it to text within a calculation, use the GetAsText(data) function.

5. The Case function allows you to specify different results depending on the input.

Short Answer

6. How can you view only the date functions in the functions list in the Specify Calculation window?

7. How do you replace a function template parameter with an actual field name?

8. How do you replace a function template parameter with another function to create a nested function?

9. After you turn a Calculation field into a non-calculation field (i.e., Text, Number, Date, or Time), will the calculation still work?

10. What's the secret behind FileMaker Pro's ability to perform mathematical problems involving Date, Time, and Timestamp fields?

11. After a calculation works, how do you make it into an editable field?

12. What types of fields will not work when converting a calculation to an editable field?

13. How can you find out how many characters are in a field?

14. When making a time clock for a work situation with multiple shifts, what type of field do you need to include in the calculation?

15. In a large file with many records, what is another way to test a calculation?

Part 3

Chapter 13

Real-World Calculations — Part 2

Vocabulary

- Aggregate functions
- Custom functions
- Design functions
- External functions
- Financial functions
- Get functions
- Logical functions
- Plug-in
- Repeating functions
- Summary functions
- Text formatting functions
- Timestamp functions
- Trigonometric functions

Objectives

1. Learn about the aggregate functions.
2. Understand how Summary fields and the GetSummary function interact.
3. Use the GetRepetition function.
4. Explore the financial and trigonometric functions.
5. Examine and use the logical functions.
6. Discover the value of using Get functions.
7. Become familiar with the design functions.
8. Learn about external functions and plug-ins.

Introduction

This chapter continues our discussion about basic and complex calculations you might really use. Since I introduced you to a number of techniques for building complex calculations in the last chapter, I'll spend more time on specific uses in this chapter.

Aggregate Functions

Aggregate functions are meant to get information from a number of records, related records, or Repeating fields. That really makes sense when you look at the names of this group of functions:

Average
Count
Max (maximum)
Min (minimum)
Sum
StDev (standard deviation)
StDevP (standard deviation of population)
Variance (spread)
VarianceP (population spread)

Aggregate Examples

We already used one of the aggregate functions when we pulled the invoice total from the InvLI fields.

1. Go back to the Invoice table, go to Define Fields, and double-click on **InvoiceTotal** to review the field formula: Sum(InvLI::LineTotal).

2. While you're looking at the Specify Calculation window, choose **Aggregate functions** from the View pop-up.

3. Highlight the word **Sum** in the formula and type **Max**.

4. Now click **OK** and **Done**, then look at the amount in the InvoiceTotal field.

5. Click through a few records until you get the idea. Regardless of how many entries there are, the Max function finds the largest number.

6. Now go back into the definition, and replace Max with **Min**.

7. Exit the field definition and look at these new numbers.

8. Now try it with Count. Of course, the field is formatted with two decimal places, but the number in each record is correct. Now be sure you change the InvoiceTotal back so it reads:
   ```
   Sum(InvLI::LineTotal)
   ```

I used the following calculation for a phone number portal that shows five rows. I wanted to know how many rows were beyond the fifth row without scrolling.
```
Case(Count(Phone::Phone) > 5; Count(Phone::Phone) - 5; "")
```

The number only shows up next to the portal if there are hidden phone numbers that I need to scroll to see.

You may try the StDev, StDevP, Variance, and VarianceP functions if you like. They test for the amount of variation of values in a field. That can give you some idea of what would be considered a "normal" range.

Part 3

Summary Functions

Well, I guess the people at FileMaker, Inc., are preparing for future summary functions, because there's really only one right now. It's called GetSummary. This function was created because there are some limitations with regular Summary fields. You can only display summary data in Preview mode, and you cannot perform calculations on it. You're also limited to displaying Summary field results in special sections of the layout. The GetSummary function bypasses those limitations. Let's take a look.

GetSummary Example

To test various operators back in Chapter 11, we made a new layout called Calcs in the InvLI table. Go to the Calcs layout now.

1. Go into Define Database, create a new field called **SumLineTotal**, and choose **Summary** from the Type pop-up.

2. In the Options for Summary Field window, choose the **Total of** radio button and select **LineTotal** from the field list as shown in Figure 13-1.

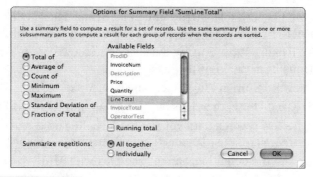

Figure 13-1
The Options for Summary Field window with selections for the SumLineTotal field in the InvLI table.

⌘ **TIP**   Even though the GetSummary parameter template should make it obvious that you need a Summary field, I've tried creating a GetSummary many times without one. It just doesn't work. Create your Summary field first. After all, you can't "get" a summary if there is no summary to get.

3. Now create a new field called **TotalByItem**, select **Calculation** from the Type pop-up, and press **Create**.

4. When the Specify Calculation window appears, choose **Summary functions** from the View pop-up list, then double-click the **GetSummary** function to move it into the Formula box. It should look like this:
    GetSummary (summaryField; breakField)

5. Replace the parameters with **SumLineTotal** and **Description**. Your final formula should look like this:
    GetSummary (SumLineTotal; Description)

6. Click **OK** and **OK**.

7. Go to Layout mode, double-click the **OperatorTest** field, and choose the new **TotalByItem** from the field list.

8. Go to Browse mode, and choose **Records, Show All Records**. (If that choice is not available, all records are probably already showing.) The new field is empty! And it should be. When we select a break field parameter, that means we're required to sort the records first. (If all you see is a 1, go back to Layout mode and reformat the TotalByItem so that it is not Boolean.)

⬥ **NOTE**   What is a break field parameter? According to the FMP7 glossary, "In a subsummary part, records are grouped (sorted) by values in another field, called the break field. Whenever the value of the break field changes, the report 'breaks' and FileMaker Pro inserts the subsummary part."

9. Choose **Records, Sort Records** and sort by **Description**.

Aha! So what's the big deal? Go into the new field in one of the records and copy the number. You'd never be able to do that in a subsummary part in Preview mode, and you can't see a subsummary field in Browse mode, let alone touch the fields.

So, why is this important? Once you start creating reports for people, they will ask to be able to grab pieces of data that you won't be able to get to, unless you use this GetSummary function.

You can get even more interesting results by adding other sorts to the mix. This time, sort by LineTotal on the first line and put Description in the second line of the sort. This is a result you simply cannot get using regular Summary field and subsummary parts.

Repeating Functions

Back in Chapter 4, I showed you Repeating fields. I also mentioned that there are some uses for them beyond the old method of invoicing and a short list of phone numbers. I'll show you one here. But first, look at Figure 13-2 to see the parameter templates of FileMaker's three repeating functions.

```
Extend ( non-repeatingField )
GetRepetition ( repeatingField ; number )
Last ( repeatingField )
```

Figure 13-2
FileMaker Pro's repeating functions.

GetRepetition Example

What I want you to see in this demonstration is how to highlight a field with a color based on a calculation. Sound interesting?

⬥ **BEST PRACTICES**   I used the "o" at the end of the upcoming Global field because it's a Container field. Since we're already using the "c" to identify Calculation Global fields, we instead we use the second letter in Container.

1. Go into the Invoice table and create a new field called **zi_Colors_go**. Select **Container** from the Type drop-down and click the **Create** button.

2. Click the **Options** button, select the **Storage** tab, and check the box to **Use global storage**. Click the check box next to **Repeating with a maximum number of 2 Repetitions**, and click **OK**.

3. Now make a new field called Color, click the **Calculation** type radio button, and click **Create**.

4. Click the View pop-up and choose **Repeating functions** from the list.

5. Double-click the **GetRepetition** function, then highlight the repeating-Field parameter and replace it by double-clicking the **zi_Colors_go** field from the field list in the upper left. Highlight the number parameter and type **1**. Your calculation should look like this:

   ```
   GetRepetition(zi_Colors_go; 1)
   ```

6. Finally, choose **Container** from the calculation result pop-up, and click **OK** and **OK**.

7. Go to Layout mode, and place a copy of the zi_Colors_go and Color fields side by side in an empty area of the layout near the InvoiceTotal field.

8. Select **zi_Colors_go**, and choose **Format**, **Field Format**. In the middle of the Field Format window, you'll find the message, "Show repetitions 1 through 1." (Both numbers can be altered, limited to the number of repetitions.) Enter **2** in the through Repetitions box, so it reads "Show repetitions 1 through 2" and click **OK**.

9. Using the Rectangle tool, draw a rectangle about 1 inch by 3 inches. Format it so it has no borders, and fill it with red. While it's still selected, choose **Edit**, **Copy**, and go to Browse mode.

10. Click in the first repetition of the zi_Colors_go field, and choose **Edit**, **Paste**. The red color should not only fill the zi_Colors_go field, but the Color field as well.

11. Go back to Layout mode and select the red rectangle and change it to some shade of blue. Choose **Edit**, **Cut**, and return to Browse mode.

12. Click the second repetition of the zi_Colors_go field and choose **Edit**, **Paste**.

13. Now go back to Define Fields and redefine the Colors calculation, replacing the 1 with a **2**.

14. Return to Browse mode to see that the Color field has turned blue. Now here comes the fun part. We can tie the color change to something other than a constant number.

15. Go back into the Color field definition and put a couple of carriage returns after the formula. Choose **Logical functions** from the View pop-up, and double-click the **If** function.

16. Click outside of the parameter template, add a couple more returns, and double-click the **If** function again so we have a copy to compare to the original.

17. Go back to the first If function, and put a carriage return following the first parenthesis and after the two semicolons so that the formula looks like this:

```
GetRepetition(zi_Colors_go; 2)
```

```
If (
test;
result one;
result two)
```

```
If (test; result one; result two)
```

18. Highlight **test** and replace it with **InvoiceTotal < 0.**
19. Copy the GetRepetition calculation and highlight and replace both **result one** and **result two** by pasting from the clipboard. Change the 2 in the first GetRepetition to **1**. Then delete all the other functions so the formula looks like this:

```
If (
InvoiceTotal < 0;
GetRepetition(zi_Colors_go; 1);
GetRepetition(zi_Colors_go; 2))
```

What we are saying here is that if our invoice is less than 0, please Mr. ColorField, grab the color — red — from the first repetition in the zi_Colors_go field. However, if the invoice is greater than 0, grab the second color — blue.

⊃ **NOTE**   I tend to write short calculations using If functions, because that's the way I express the question in my mind. But my technical editor, William Moss, sent me the following clever (and short) formula.

```
GetRepetition(zi_Colors_go; 1 + (InvoiceTotal >= 0))
```

Here, FileMaker is evaluating whether InvoiceTotal is greater than or equal to 0. The answer is a Boolean 1 or 0. So the result of 1 + 0 or 1 + 2 determines the color that will be displayed.

⌘ **TIP**   Be sure you set each test and its result apart with a semicolon. FileMaker will warn you if the function doesn't make sense. However, you might accidentally create a correct formula and still not get the data you're seeking. It is easy to miss a semicolon, especially if you've worked with earlier versions of the program where you needed to use commas.

1. Click **OK** and **Done**, and go back to Browse mode.
2. Since none of your invoices are likely to have a negative InvoiceTotal, enter **1** into the next empty Quantity field, and enter a negative number larger than the current InvoiceTotal in the Price field. You could also enter **Refund** in the Description field. When you're done, you should not only have a negative number in the InvoiceTotal field, but the Color field should have turned red.
3. Remove the negative number and the Color field should turn blue.

The color may not fill the field completely. I'll show you more about how to fix that in Chapter 16, "Designing Your Screen Layouts." You might want to use the trick I showed you in the last chapter (in the section titled "The Real Trick"): Send the Color field to the back and stack the InvoiceTotal field on top

Part 3

of it, then make InvoiceTotal transparent so the color shows through. If you don't want any color to show when InvoiceTotal is a positive number, click in the second repetition of the zi_Colors_go field and press Backspace or Delete. You might also want to choose a lighter shade of red so the black text is easier to read. You can delete the zi_Colors_go field from the layout and let the calculation take care of the rest.

There are some other clever uses for this type of calculation. You can store icons in a Repeating field, and use the same GetRepetition function so that the icons on buttons change based on data in some other field. The Repeating field doesn't always have to be formatted as a Container. The GetRepetition function will work just fine on Text, Number, Date, or Time fields as well. I used it recently to put different Text field labels at the top of a portal based on selections made from a pop-up list. That choice determined how the portal was to be used, so the labels needed to change accordingly.

Financial Functions

Look at Figure 13-3 for the four financial functions.

```
FV ( payment ; interestRate ; periods )
NPV ( payment ; interestRate )
PMT ( principal ; interestRate ; term )
PV ( payment ; interestRate ; periods )
```

Figure 13-3
FileMaker's four financial functions.

The most common of these is PMT because it can be used to figure interest rates on a mortgage, boat, or auto loan.

PMT Example

1. Rather than add more fields to our tables, let's just create a new empty database for this one. Call it **Mortgage** and create the following fields:

Field Name	Type	Options
Principal	Number	
InterestRate	Number	
Months	Number	
Payment	Calculation	PMT (Principal, InterestRate/ 12, Months)

You divide InterestRate by 12; otherwise the interest is figured annually. Most of us make monthly payments, so that's what most people are interested in.

2. Click **OK** and **Done**, and put in a few figures. For a home, try 90,000, .0725, and 360 (30 years times 12 months). I get:
613.958652050573

Whew! Maybe we'd better add some rounding to the formula.

3. Find the number functions and double-click the **Round** function:
Round (number; precision)

4. Now copy and paste our first calculation over the number parameter, and replace precision with **2**:

    Round (PMT(Principal; (InterestRate/12); Months); 2)

    During data entry, you'll have to put the InterestRate in as a decimal number so that .0725 represents 7.25%. If you want to simplify the data entry process, just change the formula to this:

    Round(PMT(Principal; (InterestRate/12) /100; Months); 2)

    On the other hand, you can enter the longer numbers and format the field to display the percent sign (%).

5. To do that, go to Layout mode, and choose **Format**, **Number**.

6. Click the **Format as decimal** radio button, check the box next to **Use notation**, and choose **Percent** from the pop-up list. You should understand that you can do one or the other but not both. Numbers entered as 7.25 with a field formatted as a percent will show up as 725%!

Another choice would be to build a calculated Text field that includes the percent sign, format it as unenterable on the layout, and stack it on top of the regular InterestRate field. I'll leave it up to your level of curiosity to handle that one.

Now before you get carried away and make plans to buy that new Ferrari, wait a second. Don't forget the down payment, taxes, insurance, and various and sundry upkeep costs. Oh, don't worry, the lender will turn you down if you can't afford it. Just don't sign away your house as collateral.

Trigonometric Functions

What is great about using trig functions is that you won't have to get out the old calculator; just plug the numbers into the fields.

See Figure 13-4 for the seven trigonometric functions.

Atan (number)
Cos (angleInRadians)
Degrees (angleInRadians)
Pi
Radians (angleInDegrees)
Sin (angleInRadians)
Tan (angleInRadians)

Figure 13-4
The seven trigonometric functions. Ln and Log have been moved to the Number functions.

Pi Example

For a quick example, let's use the Pi function to figure the area of a circle in a flash. Go back into the Mortgage file, and add two new fields:

Field Name	Type	Options
Radius	Number	
Area	Calculation	Pi * (Radius ^ 2)

Now drag the fields onto the layout, and put a number or two into the Radius field. This is another situation where you may want to round the results. After all, Pi goes on to infinity:

```
Round (Pi*(Radius^2); 2)
```

Logical Functions

I showed you an example of the Case logical function in the last chapter when we worked on automatically formatting a field to display a phone number complete with dashes. I want to spend a little more time with this group of functions, because I've found them so helpful. With version 7 of FileMaker, the number of logical functions has increased from five to thirteen! See the list in Figure 13-5.

```
Case ( test1 ; result1 {; test2 ; result2 ; ... ; defaultResult} )
Choose ( test ; result0 {; result1 ; result2...} )
Evaluate ( expression {; [field1 ; field2 ;...]} )
EvaluationError ( expression )
GetField ( fieldName )
If ( test ; resultOne ; resultTwo )
IsEmpty ( field )
IsValid ( field )
IsValidExpression ( expression )
Let ( {[} var1 = expression1 {; var2 = expression2...]} ; calculation )
Lookup ( sourceField {; failExpression} )
LookupNext ( sourceField ; lower/higherFlag )
Quote ( text )
```

Figure 13-5
The 13 logical functions.

The If and Case functions are very similar in that you can perform multiple tests and get multiple results. Choose is different because you run a single test that can have multiple results. Where the Case function is designed for multiple tests, the If function is really meant to perform a single test yielding one of two results. You can get the If function to perform like Case, but you have to nest successive If statements to get the same results.

The Case function is a more recent addition to FileMaker Pro. Users became very adept at building nested If statements prior to the introduction of Case. Not to belittle the If function, but many developers use it exclusively, even when the Case function will do a much better job. One thing is clear: When you start nesting If statements, it can be difficult to see where you're going.

If and Case

Look at the following two examples. The Case function requires 63 characters, while the If requires 73. Not only that, but some users find the group of parentheses at the end of the If a little confusing.

```
Case(Grade = 100; "A+"; Grade > 94; "A"; Grade > 87; "B"; Grade > 80;
"C"; "D")

If(Grade = 100; "A+"; If(Grade > 94; "A"; If(Grade > 87; "B";
If(Grade > 80; "C"; "D"))))
```

Of course, adding returns between groups of tests and results makes either formula much easier to read.

```
Case(
Grade > 100, "A+";
Grade > 94, "A";
Grade > 87, "B";
Grade > 80, "C";
"D")
```

➲ **NOTE**   There is a limit of 125 nested Ifs in the Formula box. The Case function has no such limit, but when you get beyond a dozen or so choices, it may be time to reconsider the arrangement. Whenever you need to update the values, you'll have to refigure the calculation. It may just be better to make the field into a lookup and create a special table listing the values. Such an arrangement is much easier to manage and update than a calculation.

The order in which the tests appear is important. You should use either mutually exclusive cases or continually greater than or less than subsets. Starting from the left, the calculation will display the result for the first test that fits.

➲ **NOTE**   In reference to the previous grades example, I used to think you had to use an AND operator so that it read ">93 AND <100." But it turns out that once the function has determined the value is not 100, it moves to the next test. So ">93" is all you need. The other test works; it's just unnecessarily long.

IsEmpty

I frequently work with the IsEmpty function. You use it to find out whether a field has any data in it. I use it most often in a script, but I want to show it to you here. The IsEmpty function is another one that gives the Boolean results of 1 (true, the field is empty) or 0 (false, the field is not empty). Then you can combine it with If or Case functions to give you all kinds of results.

1. Go into the InvLI table and open the Formula box of OperatorTest. Redefine it so that it reads:
    ```
    IsEmpty(Quantity)
    ```

2. Exit Define Fields and go to Layout mode to make sure there's a copy of the OperatorTest field still on the layout.

3. Go to Browse mode. Most of the values should appear as a 0, meaning that the Quantity fields are not empty.

4. Delete the number in one of the Quantity fields.

5. Check for the reverse of IsEmpty by putting **NOT** in front of it.

Evaluate[7]

There's a lot of excitement surrounding one of the logical functions that is new for FMP7 — the Evaluate function. The description of this function is that it evaluates an expression as a calculation. I'm going to give you an example by having you create a table that uses Evaluate. In it, we'll create some fields that would logically be multiplied together to yield a line total, but it will actually be a straight number field.

1. Create a table called NoCalcCalc and add these fields:

Field Name	Type	Options
Price	Number	
Quantity	Number	
Calc1	Text	Global
LineTotal	Number	

2. Double-click the **LineTotal** field, go to the Auto-Enter tab, and click the **Specify** button next to "Calculated value." Before you do anything else, be sure you choose **NoCalcCalc** from the pop-up next to "Evaluate this calculation from the context of" at the top of the window. I can't stress how important making the right choice is when it comes to choosing the context of the calculation. Enter this calculation:
   ```
   Evaluate (Calc1; [Price; Quantity])
   ```

3. Click **OK** and uncheck the box next to **Do not replace existing value of field (if any)**.

4. Click **OK** and **OK** again to bring you to Browse mode.

5. You should now be on the NoCalcCalc layout. If you're not, get there and choose **View, View as Table**. You'll probably want to make the Calc1 field a bit bigger.

6. Type this into the Calc1 field:
   ```
   Price * Quantity
   ```

7. Enter a Price and a Quantity. You get a LineTotal that is calculated without being a Calculation field! Change one of the numbers. The line total changes. That's because we unchecked that box back in the Fields tab and because we included the field name in brackets in the Evaluate function. If we had only put Quantity in the brackets, the LineTotal would only be recalculated when Quantity changed, not when Price changed. Every time you change one of the numbers, the LineTotal will be recalculated.

8. Create a new record and enter some different numbers for Price and Quantity.

9. Now change the Calc1 field so it reads like this:
   ```
   Case(Price * Quantity > 100, (Price * Quantity) – (.05 * (Price *
   Quantity)), Price * Quantity))
   ```

   Notice that none of the LineTotals have changed.

10. Create a new record and enter a Price and a Quantity so your LineTotal will be less than 100.

11. Create a new record and enter amounts that will equal more than 100. The calculation now says, in effect, "If the LineTotal will be more than $100, give them 5% off. Otherwise just calculate the LineTotal."

You could use something like this to calculate special prices during a sale and then return them to normal after the sale. The calculation could even be based on specific start and end dates.

Now, what if your Calc1 global field used a value list formatted as radio buttons that switched between different sets of formulas? You could add a script that recalculates LineTotal using the same Evaluate calculation and put a button on the layout so you don't have to change Price or Quantity to trigger the Auto-enter evaluation. I tried both the radio buttons and a Reevaluate button. Works great! I know someone who has built an industry-standard FileMaker solution for the printing industry. He's really looking forward to using the Evaluate function to replace nearly 1000 calculations he needs in his FMP6 files.

Let[7]

Another logical function I'm hearing a lot about is the Let function. It allows you to use variables in an expression for a specific calculation. The variables can come from fields on a layout, so it allows for a lot of flexibility in creating temporary calculations. Take a look at the Help files if you'd like to investigate further.

Get Functions[7]

The old status functions are now the Get functions. There are 71 Get functions that gather information about FileMaker Pro or the computer system you're using. I won't list them here, but there are quite a few very useful ones. I find them especially valuable in scripts. Take a look at this one:

Get(RecordNumber) Example

1. Go back to the InvLI table, and redefine OperatorTest so the formula reads like this:
   `Get(RecordNumber)`
2. Make sure Calculation result is **Number.**
3. Before you close the Specify Calculation window, click the **Storage Options** button and check the box next to **Do not store calculated results.**
4. Click **OK, OK,** and **OK** again.
5. Sort the records.
6. Now unsort them.
7. Choose one in the middle of the list and omit it. See what's happening?

⌘ **TIP**   Using Get(RecordNumber) in a calculation that uses data from related records can really slow a machine down, especially when scrolling through a long list. Instead, go to the layout, choose the Text tool, and click in the Body section with the Text insertion I-beam. Now choose Insert, Record Number Symbol. You can also just type "@@." Then return to Browse mode. These numbers will perform the same function as the calculation, but they'll operate more quickly.

Another of the Get functions I use quite a bit is Get(ActiveModifierKeys). I use it to determine how a script acts depending on what modifier key or keys the user is holding down. We'll look at this in greater detail in the next chapter.

Design Functions

You may never use FileMaker's design functions (or the external functions discussed in the next section) but you should know they're there if you need them. A few developers have used the design functions to create some excellent tools that analyze whole groups of files, listing everything from layouts and the fields on them to the details of relationships. In FileMaker 7 there are 20 design functions.

FieldNames and FieldStyle Examples

1. Go to the Contact table in the Business file and create a Calculation field called **Design** with a calculation result of **Text**.
2. When the Specify Calculation window appears, choose **Design functions** from the View pop-up in the upper-right corner.
3. Double-click the **FieldNames** function to move it to the Formula box. It should look like this:

    `FieldNames (fileName; layoutName)`
4. Substitute **"Business"** (include the quotes) for fileName and **"Contact"** for layoutName (if you have a layout with that name) so that it looks like this:

    `FieldNames ("Business"; "Contact")`

Of course, you need to use the name of your file. If you're working in Windows, you may find you need to enter Business.FP7 to make it work properly. (Don't get confused here. Contact is a table in the Business file. But it's also a layout — as long as you have followed along with our instructions.)

⌘ **TIP**   All parameters need to be put inside quotes when you use the design functions.

5. Click **OK**, **OK**, and go into Layout mode.
6. Make sure you're on the Contact layout, place a copy of the new Design field on your layout, and open it up so that it shows more than one line.
7. Now go to Browse mode, click in the new field, and use your up and down arrows to look at the names of the fields on the layout.
8. Now try changing the Design calculation to this:

    `FieldStyle("Business"; "Invoice"; "InvoiceTotal")`
9. Before you close the Specify Calculation window, click the **Storage Options** button and check the box next to **Do not store calculated results — recalculate when needed**.
10. Click **OK**, **OK**, and **OK**.

⌘ **TIP**   When using both the Get and design functions in a calculation, they work differently (and probably more the way you would expect) when the results are not stored. When indexing is turned on, FileMaker remembers the results from the last time it stored a change in the record. By turning indexing off, it continues to recalculate, and your results reflect the current status of the database.

My calculation shows Standard.

11. Go into Layout mode, go to the Invoice layout, and format InvoiceTotal as a pop-up list using the Contacts value list. Click **OK**.

12. Go back to Browse mode on the Contact layout and see what the Design field says.

13. Before you move on, go back to Layout mode on the Invoice layout and format the InvoiceTotal field back to **Exit Box**.

External Functions

The external functions deal specifically with getting information from FileMaker's plug-ins. *Plug-ins* are little programs that give specific extra functionality to FileMaker. Not all plug-ins make use of the external functions, but FileMaker's Auto Update plug-in does, and it should have been included when you installed FileMaker Pro.

If you're interested in plug-ins, you can go to FileMaker's web site for more information and for a list of developers who have written them. There are more than 150 registered plug-ins available and probably as many unregistered ones as well. Plug-ins add features not available from within FileMaker. If there is something you want FileMaker to do that is not among its current feature set, there is probably a plug-in that does it.

This demo simply reaches out to the Auto Update plug-in and tells you which version is installed on your machine. It lacks excitement, but it will familiarize you with the procedure.

1. Windows users choose **Edit, Preferences, Application**. Macintosh users choose **FileMaker Pro, Preferences**. Now choose the Plug-Ins tab. You should see Auto Update in the list. If there is no check mark next to it, click the box next to it so it gets one, then click **OK**.

2. Go to the Contact table. Choose **Scripts, ScriptMaker**, start a new script called **Auto Update Plug-in Script**, and click **Create**.

3. Under the Fields heading, double-click **Set field** to move it to your script window on the right.

4. Click the **Specify** button next to "Specify target field," and double-click **Notes** from the list.

5. Now click the **Specify** button next to "Calculated result," and choose **External Functions** from the View pop-up. If everything's okay, you should see the list shown in Figure 13-6.

```
FMSAUC_FindPlugIn (parameter)
FMSAUC_UpdatePlugin (parameter)
FMSAUC_Version (0)
```

Figure 13-6
The external functions available to FileMaker's Auto Update plug-in.

6. Double-click the third one: **FMSAUC_Version (0)**.

7. Click **OK, OK**, and **OK** one more time.

Part 3

8. Make sure you're on a layout with the Notes field on it, and choose **Script, Auto Update Plug-in Script**. The Notes field on the active record in my file reads, "FileMaker Auto Update PlugIn Version 7.0."

That's all there is to it. The other items listed for the Auto Update plug-in work with FileMaker Server to update plug-ins on client machines.

Text Formatting Functions[7]

New for FMP7 is a set of functions developers have been wanting for years. Using these functions, you can target specific text for a font, color, size, or style change. You can use the Position function and various other text functions to make a format change to a specific phrase, word, or character in a field as a calculation or part of a script.

1. Go to the Contact table and create a field called **PrettyType**. Make it a Calculation field with a Text result.

2. Select **TextColor** from the functions. It should read:
   ```
   TextColor (text: RGB(red;green;blue)).
   ```

3. Now make changes to the formula so that it reads:
   ```
   TextColor(Left(NameFirst;3); RGB(100;10;10)) &
   TextColor(Middle(NameFirst;4;10); RGB(10;100;150))
   ```

Put the field on the Contact layout and see what you think. Isn't that cool? Your first names will be in Technicolor. Since this is a Calculated field, you can't make changes to it unless you redefine the calculation or use Global fields to determine the position of the colors. But if you use a script to make changes to the text color in a normal text field, you can go back and change the colors of the text manually. You can do this with the font, size, and style, too.

Now what if we just used calculations to change the color of InvoiceTotal instead of stacking the highlight field like we did in the GetRepetition example earlier in this chapter? You could use a calculation (with a Number result) like this to color your text:

```
Case(
Sum(InvLI::LineTotal) > 0;
TextColor(Sum (InvLI::LineTotal); RGB(255;0;0));
TextColor(Sum (InvLI::LineTotal); RGB(0;0;255)))
```

Way cool!

Timestamp Functions

A little misleading to call this functions, since there's only one of them. There is nothing to explain here. Just go ahead and use it!

Custom Functions[7]

One other item in the View drop-down is the Custom Functions. That heading will probably leave you with an empty list because these functions are available only in the Developer edition of FileMaker Pro 7. These functions offer a lot of power in that the developer can create special formulas that need to be written only once and can be used over and over in fields and scripts throughout the file. If a change is needed, it can be made in one place. Once they're defined in the Developer edition, they can be used in the files run by the regular version of FileMaker Pro 7.

Summary

In this chapter, we looked at a few more of FileMaker Pro's growing number of functions. I demonstrated some of their uses and a few tricks to help make your work better.

Q & A

Q There are so many of these functions. How can I ever learn which is the one I'll need?

A Let the categories be your first clue as to which one you might need. You'll gradually learn new ones when you try to solve specific problems. Even when you search the list for the ones you need, you'll reject ones that don't sound right, which means you're becoming more familiar with them. Don't forget to use the Help files if you're not sure whether a particular function might work for you. That's where I go.

Q When I'm in the Specify Calculation window and I scan down the list of all functions, I don't see many of the Get functions. Where are they?

A Because there are so many of them, the people at FileMaker decided to show them all only when you select "Get functions" or "all by type" from the View pop-up. You'll also notice that only one generic external function, External (name, parameter), appears in the list. That's because the external functions will change depending on which plug-ins you have installed and active.

Workshop

Go to the InvLI table and rebuild the formula for OperatorTest using either the Case or If function to test this scenario: Price less than 19.99 and Quantity greater than 20. Make the results appear as some kind of text.

Review Questions

True-False

1. To get information about a group of records, you should use one of the aggregate functions.
2. To get data from a specific repetition in a Repeating field, you should use the Middle function.
3. For multiple tests, the syntax of the If function is easier to follow than the syntax of the Case function.

Part 3

4. The design functions return information about the database itself, rather than the data entered into it.

5. The external functions allow you to use plug-ins with your database.

Short Answer

6. What type of field must already be defined in order to use the GetSummary function?

7. Which financial function would you use to calculate payment based on principal amount, interest rate, and loan term?

8. Which Get function would you use to determine whether the database window was in Browse, Find, Layout, or Preview mode?

9. What operator could you place before the IsEmpty function to test that a field has data in it?

10. Which function would you use to determine the highest value in a field over a number of records?

11. How many summary functions are there?

12. Of the following, which is not an aggregate function?

    a) Average   b) PMT   c) Max   d) Min   e) Count

13. Name at least one difference between the If and Case functions.

14. When an If or Case function gets long or requires frequent changes to the formula, what is the recommended alternative?

Part 4

Creating a Real Solution

Chapter 14

Automating Your Database with Scripts

Vocabulary

- Loop
- Modular scripts
- Script

- Script parameter
- ScriptMaker

Objectives

1. Learn to use and control what appears in the Scripts menu.
2. Learn to plan a script before defining it and debug a script before deploying it.
3. Learn to use the Script Definition window to create scripts.
4. Understand script step options and how they appear in the list of script steps.
5. Understand the value of adding comments to scripts.
6. Become familiar with the If and Loop script steps.
7. Modularize scripts with the Perform Script script step.
8. Import a script from another file.
9. Learn about button options and startup and shutdown scripts.
10. Become familiar with the Show Custom Dialog script step.

Introduction

This chapter is all about scripts. If you don't remember my saying this earlier in the book, I love scripts! I could do a whole book on 'em. Now that that's out of the way....

We've built this group of tables, but nothing is set up to work very smoothly for you. We'll use scripting as the cure. In this chapter, we'll look at:

- What scripts are
- How to plan them
- How to debug them
- A quick overview of categories of script steps

■ How to import scripts from other files

We'll also create some scripts that will work in our tables using steps from many of the categories.

What Are Scripts?

We spent a little time with scripts in some of the earlier chapters, so this won't be foreign territory. In fact, you already have some buttons that perform simple Finds and Sorts. Scripts are similar to macros, which you may be familiar with from other applications. They're little program commands within FileMaker that perform one or more tasks. FileMaker's ScriptMaker uses what is called a high-level programming language. That means it's written in what looks like English instead of the strange-looking code you may have seen sometime in the past. That other weird code is actually going on behind the scenes, but you won't have to deal with it.

Most of the time you'll create permanent scripts that will be used again and again to perform repetitive tasks. There will also be times when you'll make a temporary script that you'll only use once to perform a specific job on a large group of records rather than do the job manually.

One Step at a Time

1. Open your Business file to the Invoice table in Layout mode.
2. Draw a button to bring up the Specify Button window. Scripts are often (but not always) attached to buttons. One thing that I mentioned before is that buttons can be attached to many of the individual script steps. That way, a button can perform a simple, one-step task when needed. When you want the button to provide a more complex task, you have to attach it to a script.
3. Click **Cancel** to exit here.

While I prefer to attach scripts to buttons, the other choice is to have them appear under the Scripts menu. If that's what you want and you're in ScriptMaker, simply check the box to the left of any script. The next time you click the Scripts menu, your script will be there, ready to use. One other cool thing is that the first 10 scripts will have a keyboard shortcut. If you want to have scripts to help users with data entry or with other frequent tasks, just make sure that the script is one of the first 10 "visible" in the Scripts menu. Be sure to pick carefully which scripts show up there, though. Some scripts are better left hidden, and once your users get used to the keyboard shortcut, don't change them!

⮕ **NOTE** On Mac OS X, the first 10 scripts are mapped to the Command+numerals 1-0 keys. Don't get these mixed up with the function keys.

4. Now choose **Scripts, ScriptMaker**.
5. At the Define Scripts window, click the **New** button.
6. At the Edit Script window, name this script **Test**. See Figure 14-1.

Part 4

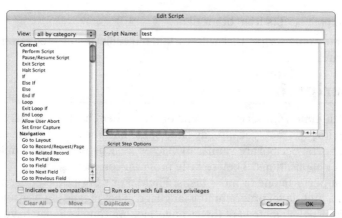

Figure 14-1
ScriptMaker's Edit Script window for the Test script.

➲ **NOTE**   What used to be called Page Setup on the Macintosh is now called Print Setup — same as on the Windows platform. You'll find that step under the Files heading.

When you first look at all the script steps available from the list on the left, it can be a little overwhelming. Fortunately, you build scripts one step at a time. You just have to know what you want, and run a set of trial-and-error experiments until you get it. That doesn't sound so bad, but keep in mind, scripts can be destructive. For example, you can construct a script that will show all records and delete all records without even showing the user a warning message!

☒ **CAUTION**   If you're experimenting with a script in a file with some valuable data, it's probably a good idea to save a copy of the file in a safe place first.

I'm not too worried about the current set of tables. Even if all the data is gone, the layouts and existing scripts will still be there. But if you've already entered real data for 100 customers or friends and relatives, you might want to make a backup first. I don't intend to show you any destructive scripts, but what if you goof up?! And let me just say, it's not only beginners who make that type of mistake (blush).

Script Options

7. Under the Navigation heading, find **Enter Browse Mode** and double-click it. You'll see that it has moved into the script area on the right. Notice the Options area in the lower third of the window now includes a Pause check box. Many of the script steps have options available. Some of the options are absolutely essential to the proper operation of your scripts.

8. Move a few other script steps into our test script by double-clicking them in the list on the left. Once they are in the list on the right, click each of these new script steps in turn to see which options are available for them. A script step needs to be highlighted in the steps list on the right in order to display its options. Some of the options are activated with check boxes, some with pop-up lists, some with radio buttons, and some with regular

buttons. This is an area I didn't pay much attention to for quite a few years. I missed out on a lot that way. I just want to suggest that you continue to check the Options area for each of your steps as you work with scripts.

Planning Your Script

Once you get beyond scripts that find and sort Rich and Richard, you'll have to do a little more planning. The easiest way to begin is to write on a sheet of paper in plain English what it is you want the script to do for you.

Of course, it helps if you understand what ScriptMaker can do in the first place. From the work we've already done, you've probably already figured out that you can make a script go to a different layout, perform a find or sort, and even print. But did you know you can have a script find a group of records, go through them one by one correcting specific errors, and then beep and show the message "All Done" after it hits the last record? Yep, and a whole bunch more!

First you have to imagine what you want. Usually that will consist of some chore you have to do over and over manually. Then you have to find a way to get ScriptMaker to do it for you. The better you know the set of steps from the list on the left, the more power you'll have.

When you double-click the Perform Script step under the Control category, this is what you get:

```
Perform Script [<unknown>]
```

Using this step, you can have this script perform other scripts. That includes scripts in other files. Perform Script offers tremendous power, but the flip side is that debugging (or figuring out why a script isn't working) gets more difficult.

Even if the script you're creating does all its work in the current file, there are some advantages to using subscripts rather than just writing one long script.

■ It's easier to debug shorter scripts.

■ With good planning, scripts can become modules you can use again in other scripts. One good example is various page and print setups you might use.

Some FileMaker professionals swear that a script should never be longer than the number of steps that can fit in the steps window (not including subscript steps). I wouldn't go that far, but it is easy to get confused when a script gets overly long.

The FileMaker Pro manual contains a marvelous list of considerations to take into account when planning your scripts. By all means read them, but you can start very simply by asking: Where am I now?, Where do I want to be when I finish?, and What do I want to do along the way? It's also a good idea to add one more question: What can go wrong along the way?

Part 4

Where Am I Now?

To begin any journey, you have to know where to start. Part of the next suggestion could also apply to the "What can go wrong" category. Users may have the file in some condition you didn't anticipate. For example, if the user is in Preview mode and chooses a script that goes to another layout without returning to Browse mode, none of the buttons on that layout will work. That's why Enter Browse Mode is often the first step in many scripts.

If the script will be attached to a button that only appears on specific layouts, you'll have a much better idea of where the users are when they start. On the other hand, if you allow the script to be run from the Scripts menu, you may need to do a little more planning.

When a script is called up, consider what mode, layout, file, and found set of records may be involved as the script starts. It is possible to have a script run tests to determine any of these various states. But most of the time it's just easier to force the setting to be what you need. For example, if you want the user to go to a summary layout in Browse mode, it would probably be easiest to change the layout and mode. If you're an old-time user, keep in mind that since FileMaker Pro 7 allows multiple tables per files, some scripts will work correctly only if the correct table is activated by selecting an associated layout from the Layout drop-down.

What Do I Want to Do?

This is usually where the thinking for most scripts begins. Finding the answer to this question actually requires several steps.

- Where do I need to go to accomplish what I want to do? If you have to enter data in certain fields, you may have to switch to a layout that has a copy of the field on it. In FileMaker 7, you need to be sure you're in the table on which you want the script to perform.

- What modes will I have to go through? Will I enter Find mode, run a Sort, display the results in Preview mode, and then return to Browse mode at the end?

- What other tables or files will be involved? You'll have to work out a way to get to any external files. Fortunately, the Perform Script step can run a script from another file.

Where Do I Want to Be When I Finish?

After the job has been run, the user should be back where he or she started or in some other familiar area in order to continue working.

In what file, in what table, on what layout, and in what mode do you want the user at the end?

What Can Go Wrong?

When you first start with ScriptMaker, there are all sorts of goofy things that can trip up your plans. But in the end, you'll be inventing your own scripts, some of which may have never been imagined before. Keep in mind that you'll need to learn to think ahead! That's something you'll get with experience. I'll try to give you some tips as we go along.

I already mentioned that being in the wrong mode at the beginning of a script can cause problems. Another common situation is that after performing a Find, occasionally no records may be found. You need to plan what you want your script to do when that happens. What if the script has a loop in it, and the Exit Loop If condition is never met?

Script Steps Overview

Look at the category list from the View pop-up in Figure 14-2.

One thing I can tell you is that in a few cases, the steps you're looking for may not be in the category where you expect to find them. Over time, you'll begin to get familiar with where they are. Don't forget FileMaker's Help files. They not only tell what the steps do, but they often give helpful examples.

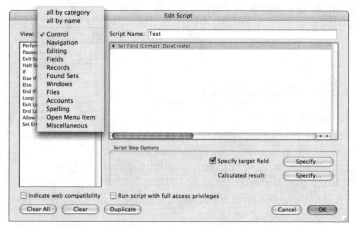

Figure 14-2
The View pop-up list of script categories.

Script Steps

What I want to do now is build some scripts that you will find useful in our Business file. These scripts will contain steps from various categories. Whenever I introduce a new step, I will put the category after it in parentheses, like this:

```
Enter Browse Mode [] (Navigation)
```

Items in the brackets are choices you make in the Options area. Empty brackets indicate that none of the options are in use. To keep things clear in your mind, I'll include the script names before every script, like this:

```
Script Name: Main Menu
Enter Browse Mode []
```

Control Category

You should still be in the Invoice table looking at your Test script. When you choose the Control category from the View pop-up, you should see the list in Figure 14-3.

I've added some dividing lines to the picture that you won't find in your Edit Script window. I've done this for clarity because the upper three groups of steps are related to one another and tend to be used together. In fact, when you double-click If, you'll always get an End If. They absolutely must be together, even though they may be spread apart by any number of other steps. The same goes for Loop and End Loop. If you leave one or the other out, you'll get a warning when you try to leave the window.

What might not be so obvious is that you do not need an Exit Script or Halt Script step for a script to finish. These are special steps you use to get a script to end early under certain circumstances. Otherwise, when a script ends, it just ends. Let's make a script that purposely uses the Halt Script step from the Control category.

Figure 14-3
The list of Control script steps from the View pop-up.

Main Menu Script Example

We'll start by creating a Main Menu layout in the Business file. No matter where you are in your database, you'll always be able to get back here and you'll be able to perform various tasks from here.

Use the skills you've already developed with the Layout Assistant to make a new Blank layout with no fields on it, and call it Main Menu. Even though it has no fields, it will be associated with one of the tables at the time you create it. In this case I used the Contact table.

Now create a script called "1 - Main Menu (Halt)" with the following steps:

```
Script Name: 1 - Main Menu (Halt)
Enter Browse Mode [] (Navigation)
Go to Layout ["Main Menu"(Contact)] (Navigation)
Adjust Window [Restore] (Windows)
Halt Script (Control)
```

The reason for the Halt Script step is that scripts from other files may come here. This way, no matter what other steps there might be in the other script, it will stop here at the Main Menu. Putting the word Halt in parentheses in the name of the script signals anyone calling it from any other scripts that everything will stop after that script has run. You also need the Adjust Window step in case the file happens to be minimized at the time the script is called.

⌘ **TIP** The Halt Script step stops everything. If the Halt Script step is in a script called by another script, that's the end of the line.

However, the Exit Script step only discontinues the current script that's running. If the script with the Exit Script step in it is being called by another script, the original script will continue any remaining steps and subscripts. If the exiting script wasn't originally called by another script, then it will end just like the Halt Script.

⌘ **TIP**   If you put a sequential number before each script name as you create it, you will simplify your ability to locate scripts in the scripts list tremendously. I use the numeral followed by space, dash, space. The details of this and other methods are in Appendix A under the heading "Notes to Developers about Naming Standards."

1. Exit ScriptMaker, and draw a button on the new Main Menu layout.
2. In the Specify Button window, choose **Go to Layout** from the list on the left.
3. From the Specify pop-up in the Options area of the screen, choose **Invoice**.
4. Click **OK**, and type **Invoice** on the face of the button.
5. Now go to the Invoice layout and make a new button.
6. Choose **Perform Script** from the Control heading, and choose **1 - Main Menu (Halt)** from the Specify pop-up in the Options area.
7. Click **OK** and **OK** again, and call this button **Main Menu**.
8. Copy the Main Menu button, go to the Contact layout, and paste the button there.
9. The standard place for this button would be in the upper-left corner of the layout. You may have to move some of your other buttons around to give you space up there.
10. Make it non-printing (see Note), and put a copy of it on all other layouts in your file.

➲ **NOTE**   To make anything on a layout non-printing, choose Format, Sliding Print-ing. In the lower-left corner of the Set Sliding/Printing window, check the box next to "Do not print the selected objects." We will discuss this more in the next chapter.

Going to Contact

We're also going to want to get to the Contact table from the Main Menu lay-out and other places in our database. So let's make one more script in our Business file that will tell any external files what they should do once they get here.

1. Create a new script and call it **2 - Land Here**.
2. Give it the following steps:
    ```
    Script Name: 2 - Land Here
    Enter Browse Mode [] (Navigation)
    Adjust Window [Restore] (Windows)
    Go to Layout ["Contact"] (Navigation)
    ```

⌘ **TIP**   If you rename your layout, FileMaker will automatically update any scripts that refer to that layout with the new name. Other database systems aren't so forgiving.

You might ask why I include the Enter Browse Mode step. In some cases, vari-ous functions you intend to have happen may fail if FileMaker is in some other mode. By adding this step to scripts that might be called from external files,

Part 4

you'll avoid that problem. That step is unnecessary when a script is simply going to another table within the same file. However, you can have similar problems if you choose to have multiple windows open in the same file — each window possibly open in a different mode.

3. Click **OK** and create a new script called **3 - Go to Contact**:

    Script Name: 3 - Go to Contact
    ```
    Go to Related Record [Show only related records; From table: "Contact";
    Using layout: "Contact" (Contact)] (Navigation)
    ```

    Well, it's only one script step, but there seems to be a lot to it. I'll actually suggest that we add some extra steps to this script in just a minute.

4. Click **OK**, and **OK** again.

Performing the Go to Related Record step may seem a little fancy when you could simply choose the Go to Layout step. But Go to Related Record is a quick and easy way to go right to the contact listed in the current record. That's not so important from the Main Menu layout, but it's really valuable when you want to look at more information about the specific contact when you're looking at their invoice.

Fail-safe

Earlier, I mentioned the importance of considering what can go wrong. This script is an example. If for some reason there are no records in the current found set in the Invoice table, or a contact has not been chosen yet, there will not be a valid relationship to the Contact table. You'll end up right where you started. I have to admit, I've only seen this happen a few times in many years, but lightning does strike. So here's the script rewritten to protect against those two possibilities:

```
Script Name: 3 - Go to Contact
Enter Browse Mode [] (Navigation)
If [Get(FoundCount) = 0] (Control)
    Show All Records (Found Sets)
End If (Control)
If [not IsValid(Contact::ContactSerNum)]
    Beep (Miscellaneous)
    Show Custom Dialog ["Sorry, there is no Contact chosen for this
record."] (Miscellaneous)
    # Button 1 = OK (Comment - Miscellaneous)
    Halt Script (Control)
End If
Go to Related Record [Show only related records; From table: "Contact";
Using layout: "Contact" (Contact)] (Navigation)
```

⤴ **NOTE**   The Comment step will actually appear in bold in your list of steps on the right. When you print scripts, comments will be italicized.

⌘ **TIP**   Adding comments to your scripts can save you time as your scripting gets more complex. Whenever you have a Find, Sort, Import, or Export, you can use a comment to remind yourself what you did. You can also use it during the development stage to remind yourself what you still need to do. (Starting with FileMaker 7, the name and file of external scripts show in the Perform Script step. That allows you to reduce some of the script comments that used to be required in previous versions of the program.)

You can also easily view (and modify) Sorts, Finds, Imports, and Exports by double-clicking the script step and clicking the Specify button. But you may find that you work faster having a Comment step with that information right in front of you without going into the specific Find or Sort step. I often add comments to show me what the buttons on my windows are. For example, Button 1 = OK / Button 2 = Cancel.

⌘ **TIP**   The only way to get to the Get functions is by choosing View, Get Functions. As I mentioned earlier, there are so many Get functions, it would make the "view by name" list prohibitively long.

Let's look at some of the parts of this script, starting with the first If step: If [Get(FoundCount) = 0).

1. When you click on the If script step in the Control category, the step will appear in the script block. Click on it twice, and you will be at the Specify Calculation screen.

2. In the View drop-down menu, look for the Get functions, and select **Get(FoundCount)**. (This particular Get function does not appear in the list of functions when listed alphabetically.)

3. Now look at the second If step: If [not IsValid(Contact::ContactSerNum)].

4. You won't find "not IsValid" in the list of functions, but you will find "IsValid." Select that and edit it by typing the word **not** and a space in front of it.

5. Finally, take a close look at the final step in this script: Go to Related Record [Show only related records; From table "Contact"; Using layout: "Contact".

6. You select **Go to Related Record** from the Navigation category, and when you double-click, you'll see the "Go to Related Record" Options window. Select the table and the layout, and check the **Show only related records** box (see Figure 14-4). Notice that you can even check a box to show the related records in a new window.

When you are in the Show Custom Dialog Options window for the Show Custom Dialog step, be sure to remove the word Cancel from the Button 2 caption box.

That's a lot of extra steps for a little protection, and you could probably get by without it. However, I've had some late-night phone calls that could have been avoided if I'd known to protect against these two problems.

The first few scripts you try may seem complicated, but don't worry. Pretty soon it will become second nature and you'll love this part of working with FileMaker as much as I do.

Part 4

Figure 14-4
The "Go to Related Record" Options window where you make selections for the records and layout.

7. Now add a little button on the actual invoice layout.

8. Put it right next to the contact's name, and attach the script to it. I usually type **<--Go** on these buttons. A user only needs to see how to use this button once. They never forget it.

Getting Back

After you get to the Contact table, you'll want to get right back to the invoice you came from. In the Contact table, create a button that goes to the Invoice layout and call it Back to Invoice. Keep in mind that the button could be a little confusing since your users might click it when viewing the contact under other circumstances. It will take you to the Invoice layout, but not necessarily to an invoice pertaining to the contact.

It's a little beyond the scope of these exercises, but let me at least explain how I handle this: I create a tab on the Contact layout that goes to a layout with a portal that lists of all the contact's invoices. The user can click a button in the portal to go to a specific invoice. Then the button on the Invoice layout takes the user to the layout with the invoices portal. A tab on the invoice portal layout takes the user back to the main Contact layout. You might try that if you think you've got the idea of portals and the buttons I've mentioned.

Testing

It's time to test the script. Go to Browse mode, and see if it takes you to the invoices. Go to a different invoice and see if the Go button will take you to that Contact record. Then come back. Try out the Main Menu layout buttons.

Access the Main Menu Layout from Other Files

Starting with FileMaker Pro 7, you are able to create multiple tables within a single file. This is a very efficient system and helps greatly in preventing a number of "gotchas" that can arise in a multi-file system. But there are still many situations in which you might need to create multiple-file solution scripts. (You may inherit a multiple-file solution converted from an earlier version of FileMaker and have to work with it without recreating all the tables and scripts in one main file.) Scripting in multiple-file solutions is a little more complicated, but I want to teach you about it for when that need arises.

Let's imagine an example where we have a different department in a warehouse that handles inventory. They want to be in control of their file —

changing layouts and adding fields when they need to — but the two departments need to be able to get back and forth between your files on your network. Let's create a new file called Inventory with the following fields:

ProdID   Text
Description   Text
Quantity   Number

Add the following example data to the Inventory table:

ProdID	Description	Quantity
1001	Small Widget	10
1002	Medium Widget	15
1003	Large Widget	20
1004	Terminal Pin	25

Now create a script to take you back to the Main Menu layout in the Business file:

```
File: Inventory
Script Name: 1 - Main Menu
Adjust Window [Hide] (Window)

Perform Script [<unknown>] (Control)
```

The reason I use the Adjust Window step is that opening a bunch of files can make the screen a mess.

Now you have to fix that Perform Script unknown step.

1. Click on the **Perform Script** step. Go to the Options area and click the **Specify** button.

2. Near the top of the Specify Script Options window, click on the words **Current File**. If the Business file were already in the list, you would choose it. Since it's not, scroll to the bottom and choose **Add File Reference** to create a connection to the Business file. This will take you back to the Specify External Script window.

3. Now all you need to do is choose the **1 - Main Menu (Halt)** script from the list. When you're done, your script should look like Figure 14-5.

```
✦ Adjust Window [Hide]
✦ Perform Script ["1 - Main Menu (Halt)" from file: "Business"]
```

Figure 14-5
Script steps for the Main Menu script in the Inventory file.

Add a button somewhere on the layout in the Inventory file, attach the Main Menu script to it, and call it Main Menu. But remember, if it's really someone else's file, get permission first.

Starting with FileMaker 7, you are able to create buttons that call scripts in other files without creating a script in the current file. That means that to get to the Main Menu layout from the Inventory file you could more easily have created a button right there in the Inventory file and attached it to the Main Menu (Halt) script that lives in the Business file. But since we want to hide the Inventory window, we need the Adjust Window [Hide] step.

Now create a button on the Main Menu to take you to the Inventory file. I think you can figure out how to do that. (Hint: You'll need to add a file reference.)

Go back to the Inventory file, and make a script called Go to Product with the following steps:

```
Script Name: 2 - Go to Product
Adjust Window [Hide]
Go to Related Record [From table: <unknown>; Using layout: <Current
Layout>]
```

1. Double-click the **Go to Related Record** step to bring up the Options window.

2. Click on **<unknown>** or **Inventory** and scroll down to **Define Database**. That's right, you can get to the Define Database window from right here.

3. Click the **Relationships** tab and click the **Add Table Reference** button in the lower-left corner.

4. When the Specify Table window appears, click on **Current File** and select **Add File Reference**.

5. Find and double-click the **Business** file.

6. When you get back to the Specify Table window, choose **Product** from the list and click **OK**.

7. Click on **ProdID** in the Inventory table reference and drag it over to the ProdID field in the Product table reference to quickly create an equal relationship between the tables.

8. Click **OK** again to return to the "Go to Related Record" Options window.

9. Choose **Product** from the "Get related record from" pop-up.

10. Check the boxes next to **Use external table's layouts** and **Show only related records**.

11. Click on **<Current Layout>** and choose **Product** from the pop-up.

12. When you're done, your script should look like this:
```
Adjust Window [Hide]
Go to Related Record [Show only related records; From table: "Product";
Using layout: "Product"]
```

The great thing about this script in FMP7 is that it does away with a number of issues in previous versions of FileMaker. First of all, you were required to create a script in the external file. (In our case, that would have been the Business file.) Secondly, you can tell the script what layout to display in the external file. And finally, regardless of what mode the external file is in, it will return to Browse mode to display the related records — that is, as long as there is a related record. If not, the script just stops.

Unfortunately, we're not done yet. What would happen if there are no related records in the Product table? How could that happen? Data entry errors from either department would be one possible reason. Another might be that one department knows about a new product that the other department hasn't been informed of. The answer to what would happen is — nothing. The user has no idea why he wasn't transported to the Product table. To protect against any confusion, you should probably polish off the script as follows:

```
If [IsValid (Product::ProdID)]
Adjust Window [Hide]
Go to Related Record [Show only related records; From table: "Product";
Using layout: "Product"  (Product)]
Else
Beep
Show Custom Dialog ["Sorry, there are no related records to this Product.
I'll take you to the Product table anyway."]
Perform Script ["Go to Product" from file: "Business"]
End If
```

What happened? When you got to the Perform Script step, did you discover that you needed a Go to Product script in the Business file? Did you create one? Whenever you are developing a solution, you may discover that in order to complete one script, you need to create another. Back in Chapter 7, I talked about planning your database. Most of what you need can be preplanned, but don't be hard on yourself if you discover that you need to take a step backward before you can move ahead.

You may decide that you don't want users to go to the Product file at this point. Maybe you want them to clear up the discrepancy. In that case you wouldn't include the Perform Script step.

Now add a button to the layout and attach this script to it.

To test it out, go to the Inventory file, look at the Small Widget, and click the button. Now come back and try it with the Terminal Pin. Aha! The terminal pin is not listed in the product table.

Using Layouts from Other Files[7]

This next exercise is a very exciting new feature of FileMaker Pro 7. It allows you to build layouts and use data from other files as if they were in the current file!

1. Start a new layout in your Business file and call it **Inventory**.
2. Click on whatever appears next to "Show records from" and select **Define Database**.
3. Click on the **Relationships** tab and click the **Add Table Reference** button in the lower-left corner of the window.
4. Click on the drop-down menu next to File and choose **Add File Reference**.
5. In the Open File window, double-click the **Inventory** file. That will take you back to the Specify Table window.
6. If there were more than one table in the file, you would select it here. Click **OK**.
7. Back at the Relationships tab you should see the table reference in the graph. Click **OK** to take you back to the New Layout/Report window.

8. Choose **Blank layout** as the layout type and click the **Finish** button.

9. Delete the Header and Footer from this layout, and open up the Body a little. Now comes the amazing part.

10. Under the Window menu go to the Inventory file (**Window, Show Window, Inventory**). Go to Layout mode, select the fields and their labels, and copy them.

11. Go back to the Business file in your new layout and paste the fields. Move them around until you're happy with their position on the layout.

12. Go back to Browse mode.

Amazing! Not only does the data show up immediately, but the table automatically displays all four records. In previous versions of FileMaker, you would have had to reconnect every field using the relationship just to display one record. Even at that, you would have only been able to see one record unless you were using a portal. This way, you are actually viewing and able to work with the data as if it were right here in this file — and indeed, it is!

You should be aware of a number of potential problems here:

■ The other file needs to be available through the network in order for the data to be available.

■ You can overwrite data here.

■ You can delete records on this layout.

That's right — if you delete a record in this table those records will disappear from the Inventory file, too! If the other department wants to be in charge of their own file and you have this much power over it right here in your file, you really need to take some precautions.

Portable Portals[7]

Here's another item new for FileMaker Pro 7. (Some of this is pretty deep, but many of us developers are quite excited about the new possibilities.) You can copy a portal from a layout within a file and move it to another layout within the same Table Occurrence Group (TOG). The data that displays in the copied portal will change based on the context of the new table. Before we run an exercise using invoices, let me give you an example that might make the concept more concrete.

Let's say you have a Company file with three tables: Company, Employee, and Appointment. On the Employee layout you have a portal into the Appointment table listing their appointments. If you copy the Appointment portal from the Employee table and drop it on the Company table, that portal will show all the appointments for all employees with that CompanyID.

Not only that, but you can do this from multiple tables (or even files) away, as long as they're connected on the graph. In previous versions of FileMaker, you often had to create special "pipeline" calculations in each of the tables between where the information came from and where you wanted to display it. You can also add fields to the portal from any of the tables along the Table Occurrence (TO) path — with mixed results. This is possible because in the

Relationships graph, every table in a Table Occurrence Group is related to every other table in that group — not just the ones directly connected to it. In the case of our Business file, there are really 20 relationships between the five connected tables rather than what appears to be four relationships. Keep in mind that every relationship acts as a filter of the data. Let's try an example.

1. Go to the Invoice layout, copy the portal there, and paste it onto your Contact layout.

2. Go to Browse mode. You should see all the items ever ordered by that contact in the portal.

   You'll probably need more data to get the full impact, so go over to the Invoice layout and create some more invoices. Be sure you create more than one invoice for your contacts and give them different creation dates.

3. Go back to Layout mode on the Contact layout and make the portal about three inches wider.

4. Add three more fields to the portal: **Invoice::Date**, **InvLI::InvoiceNum**, and **Product::Description**. Go to Browse mode.

Two of the fields we added come from tables other than InvLI. Okay, the Product::Description field information is redundant. However, it's really coming from a different table, and the data is accurate. That was impossible before FileMaker 7. Additionally, you can edit any of these extra fields as long as they're editable under normal circumstances (meaning they're not Calculation fields and you have edit privileges). Could this be the end of pipeline calculations?

Not exactly. Notice that the same Invoice Date is repeated all the way down the portal regardless of the dates on the invoices for this contact. What's going on? Here's the rule for adding a field to a portal from other tables along the path: Look at the graph. If the field you want to add comes from a TO between the layout TO and the portal TO, it probably won't work. Conversely, if the field you want to add comes from a TO further away from the layout TO than the portal TO, you're likely to get useful data. In short, context is king, and it may still be necessary to create "pipeline" calculations to display the data you want. Regardless of the limitations, this moving of portals is really powerful stuff and a big time-saver! (To pipeline the invoice date into the portal, you'd need to add a calculated field to the InvLI table equal to Invoice::Date.)

⌘ **TIP**   When you transport a portal to a layout represented by a different table, any sort order associated with the portal may act strangely because of the new context. However, you can change the sort order associated with any portal by simply redefining it in the Portal Setup dialog.

Print Invoices Example

For this next exercise, let's start by assuming that these are invoices you send out through the mail. This is a very common use for a database like this. We'll also assume that when payments come in, they'll be recorded by finding the original invoice and adding a Payment entry in the portal. Our goal is to find all invoices with an outstanding balance, charge 1.5% interest if they're more than 30 days old, and print them. Sketching that out as a rough pseudo-script, it might look like this:

```
Find invoices with outstanding positive balance.
Sort by Customer
Go to the first record in the found set.
Loop
    If the invoice is over 30 days old, add interest.
    Go to Next Record [exit after last]
End Loop
Go back to the first record in the set
Loop
    Go to the InvLI table to the InvLI_InvoicePrint layout and Print it
out.
    Go to Next Record [exit after last]
End Loop
```

This demo will not combine multiple invoices for one customer into a single statement. All invoices for the same customer will print one after the other.

Else If[7]

This section is almost a sidebar, taking us away from our current work. It's about the Else If step, which is new for FileMaker 7. Nothing that we're building will require it, but I think it is valuable enough to spend a little time explaining it. Previously, when you wanted to have a script evaluate a number of conditions, each would need to be accompanied by another If step followed by a final End If for each If. Not only that, but the steps would be indented another level. Depending on the complexity of the script, it was possible to have them appear out of the script box to the right. Here's a fairly mild example of how using multiple Ifs can get a bit complicated. Notice the string of End Ifs at the end.

```
If [Communication Choice = "USPS"]
    Go to Layout ["Letter"]
    If [Communication Choice = "Fax"
        Go to Layout ["Fax"]
        If [Communication Choice = "Email"]
            Go to Layout ["Email"]
        Else
            Perform Script[Dial Phone]
        End If
    End If
End If
```

I have a client who actually uses something very similar to this when they contact their members. It loops through the member records and either prints a letter, sends a fax, or sends an e-mail. In FileMaker Pro 7, the script can be constructed as follows, making it much easier to read, as well as shorter.

```
If [Communication Choice = "USPS"]
    Go to Layout ["Letter"]
```

```
Else If [Communication Choice = "Fax"
   Go to Layout ["Fax"]
Else If [Communication Choice = "Email"]
   Go to Layout ["Email"]
Else
   Perform Script[Dial Phone]
End If
```

The Else If step operates the same as an If step, except there must be an If step above it to start the sequence. Whenever an If or Else If step is evaluated as true, all other steps down to the next End If are ignored. That is not as complicated as it sounds. Look at the example script. If the Communication Choice were USPS, you really would want the script to go to the Letter layout and do its work there. You wouldn't want it to continue on and switch to the other layouts. By the way, scripts set up the old way will work just fine. If you find that easier, stay with it.

The Print Script

Let's set up the script that does the printing in InvLI. Go to that table, and sort the records by InvoiceNum. Then make a script called "4 - Print One Invoice" using the following steps:

```
Script Name: 4 - Print One Invoice
Go to Related Record [Show only related records; From table: "InvLI";
Using layout: "InvLI_InvoicePrint" (InvLI)] (Navigation)
Print Setup[Restore; No dialog] (File)
Print[Restore; No dialog] (Navigation)
```

Double-click the Print Setup step in the column on the right and make your settings there. If you had recently printed something, the settings will be just as they were when you last printed. Whether you like them as they are or make changes, as soon as you click OK, they'll be memorized in the script. Do the same with the Print step. You should be all set — unless somebody changes printers on you.

⊠ **CAUTION**   Different printers have different border requirements. Try to allow a little extra space around all four edges of your printing layouts to accommodate a wider range of printers.

The Invoices Scripts

Now go back to the Invoice layout, find all records with an InvoiceTotal greater than zero, and sort them by ContactSerNum. (It's not strictly necessary to perform the Find and Sort manually. You can make those choices within the script itself.) Create a script called "5 - Find Invoices with Balance Due" that has the following steps:

```
Script Name: 5 - Find Invoices with Balance Due
Go to Layout ["Invoice" (Invoice)](Navigation)
Perform Find [Restore] (Found Sets)
# InvoiceTotal > 0 (Comment – Miscellaneous)
Sort Records [Restore; No dialog] (Found Sets)
# Sort by ContactSerNum (Comment - Miscellaneous)
```

Part 4

Make sure you double-click the Perform Find step and click the OK button in the Specify Find Requests window to retain the Find you just performed manually. Do the same with the Sort step and uncheck the "Perform without dialog" box in the Script Step Options area.

Back in the Edit Script window, click OK, and start a script called " 6 - Add Interest Item." Notice that I've indented the script name by three spaces. That way it's easier to look in the scripts list and see that this is a script that's really meant to be called as a subscript.

```
Script Name:    6 - Add Interest Item
Go to Layout ["Invoice" (Invoice)]
Go to Field [InvLI::Description]
Go to Portal Row [Last] (Navigation)
Set Field [InvLI::Description, TextColor("Interest"; RGB(255; 51; 51))]
(Fields)
Set Field [InvLI::Quantity; 1]
Set Field [InvLI::Price, Round(Invoice::InvoiceTotal * .015; 2)]
```

⌘ **TIP** You'll only need a single set of quotes in the Formula box around the word Interest. Quotes always indicate text constants.

NOTE Here's how to get an RGB color you want: Go to Layout mode, click the paint bucket, and choose a color from the palette. Click the paint bucket again and choose Other Color. Click the sliders icon and pick RGB Sliders from the pop-up list. Now you have the RGB color you want, or you can make your own by moving the sliders.

NOTE When you call up either the Specify Find Requests or Edit Find Requests windows, you can create multiple criteria in each. Once a group of requests are in the window, you cannot move them up and down in the window. However, you can add, change, and remove items from the Edit Find Requests window. You can simulate being able to move items in the Specify Find Requests window by using the Duplicate and Delete buttons.

Notice the Set Field step. You'll find it in the Fields category. It's similar to Insert Text or Insert Calculated Result, except Set Field doesn't require the field to be on the currently chosen layout. It can even reach through a portal to a field that's not in the portal and add or change data in the remote record.

I'm afraid the use of the word "set" isn't really very descriptive of the power of this step. But I highly recommend you become familiar with it. I rely very heavily on Set Field. To help me visualize what it does, I used to imagine "setting" some dishes in the sink. Substitute the word "values" for dishes and "field" for sink, and you've got it. Maybe it would be easier for you to think of someone setting the time on a clock. Whatever works for you is fine. Just don't miss out on the power of this step because the terminology is unclear to you.

Notice that we're also using the TextColor[7] argument. This will cause the word Interest to appear in red type on the invoice — as long as you're printing invoices in color. It can alert the clients that if they pay their invoices within 30 days, they can avoid this charge. If you want to keep the text black, your step would look like this:

```
Set Field [InvLI::Description, "Interest"]
```

☒ **CAUTION**   If you have more than one portal on a layout, you need to name one of the fields in the portal, such as InvLI::Description, before using the Go to Portal Row script step. Otherwise, the step will attempt to work on the portal that was placed on the layout first, which may have unexpected results. When a field or a portal was placed on the layout is independent from whether you send a field to the back or bring it to the front of a layout. It is best to get into the habit of adding a field from the portal to the script as we have done here. Nothing will surprise you more than a script that doesn't work after you or someone else has made a change to a layout.

Along those same lines, because you can now build portals to display an initial row other than 1, you can place portals next to each other to more conveniently fit your layout purposes. However, this can present problems when scripting various functions, since a script can only identify the first copy of a portal displaying the same related data. If you have rows 1-8 on the left side of a window, and rows 9-16 on the right side, a script can only operate on rows 1-8. You can, however, leave a vertical scroll bar in the first portal so your script can work on the full set of related records when it needs to.

Figuring Interest

The Add Interest Item script will create an interest item in the portal. So now we need a script that will determine which invoices to add the interest to. Call this script "7 - Figure Interest on Found Set":

```
Script Name: 7 - Figure Interest on Found Set
Allow User Abort [Off] (Control)
Enter Browse Mode (Navigation)
Go to Layout ["Invoice"(Invoice)] (Navigation)
Perform Script ["5 - Find Invoices with Balance Due"] (Control)
Go to Record/Request/Page [First] (Navigation)
Loop (Control)
   If [Invoice::Date < Get(CurrentDate) - 30] (Control)
      Perform Script ["  6 - Add Interest Item"] (Control)
   End If (Control)
   Go to Record/Request/Page [Next; Exit after last] (Navigation)
   Exit Loop If [Get(ActiveModifierKeys) = 4] (Control)
End Loop
```

The first step is Allow User Abort [Off]. You don't want anybody stopping this script partway through. If it were started over at a later time, some customers might be charged interest twice. Then you would have to make excuses to irate customers.

Next you see Enter Browse Mode. The reason we add that step is you may choose to have the script run from the Scripts menu or in some cases from another file. In those cases, you could run into problems if the user were in some other mode. If the script will only run from a button on a specific layout in the same file, there is no need for that step. But it doesn't take much extra work to add the step.

You can see there is a set of If steps inside the Loop steps. You can "nest" as many of these as your brain can handle. Just remember, the more complicated it gets, the harder it will be to debug later. When you're tempted to make it complicated, it's usually better to find an easier answer, even if it takes more time.

Notice that the nested Go to Record step includes "Exit after last." Be sure you check this box in the Options area for this step. If you don't, the script will go into an endless loop. That's why I've included the Exit Loop If step.

⌘ **TIP**   When you're testing a script with a loop in it and Allow User Abort is Off, include the step Exit Loop If [Get(ActiveModifierKeys) = 4] just before the End Loop or just after the Loop step. Modifier key 4 is the Control or Ctrl key. If the script goes crazy, just hold down the Control key to regain "control." After the script has been tested, you can delete that step.

Printing One Invoice

Sometimes we'll need to print a single invoice from the invoice table without running the whole billing process. We can use the 4 - Print One Invoice script we already created. Simply add a button to the invoice layout and attach the 4 - Print One Invoice script to it. Keep in mind that this button will not create an interest item.

I didn't add any protection back in 4 - Print One Invoice, but it's possible for someone to try to print an invoice for a record that has no line items. You can use the set of If [not IsValid] steps, mentioned earlier in the "Fail-safe" section, as a template to safeguard against that if you like.

Monthly Billing Script

Finally, we string all of these pieces together with a script called "8 - Find & Print This Month's Invoices":

```
Script Name: 8 - Find & Print This Month's Invoices
Perform Script ["5 - Find Invoices with Balance Due"] (Control)
Perform Script ["7 - Figure Interest on Found Set"]
Go to Record/Request/Page [First]
Loop
    Perform Script ["4 - Print One Invoice"]
    Go to Record/Request/Page [Next; Exit after last]
    Exit Loop If [Get (ActiveModifierKeys) = 4]
End Loop
```

The nice thing about this modular scripts approach is you can also remove the second step if you prefer not to charge interest.

Testing Monthly Billing

1.   To test this properly, you should have about five invoices in your file. If you don't, create some now, choosing a Product ID and Quantity so you have InvoiceTotals with which to work.

2.   Set it up so that at least one of your invoices has an InvoiceTotal of 0 by clicking in the last empty line of the portal. Don't choose a ProductID. Make a Quantity of **1**, type **Payment** in the Description field, and make a negative Price equal to the InvoiceTotal.

3. Finally, click through the records to find at least one invoice that has an InvoiceTotal more than 0, and change the date so that it's older than 30 days.

4. Now add a button to your new Main Menu layout, and attach the Monthly Billing script to it.

5. Go to Browse mode and see if it works.

Thoughtful Additions

Since the script changes some of the records, you may want to add some extra steps that again take into account what can go wrong.

The very first steps could be to beep and show a message to check that the correct printer is selected and loaded with paper in the correct tray. Then allow users to cancel the script if everything isn't set properly.

You might also add a DateBilled field that could be filled in with the current date as each of the invoices is printed. That way, if there were a computer crash partway through the billing process, you'd be able to figure out where you left off. You could change the Find Invoices with Balance Due script so it only finds invoices that have not already been printed — invoices that have nothing in the DateBilled field.

Debugging Scripts

Now that you know how to make the scripts, you'll need to know how to fix them when they don't work properly.

I already gave you the most important debugging tool when I showed you how to exit the loop using the Control key.

Try your scripts under different conditions with different data. Notice the "special situations" data I gave you in the "Testing Monthly Billing" section earlier in this chapter. We have an invoice that's overdue and another with a zero balance, as well as normal invoices with a balance due. That way you have at least one of every combination of data to test for. Keep asking yourself, "What if the user does this…," and then try out those "what ifs" until the script works under all the conditions you can dream up. We never mentioned that an invoice might have a negative balance!

If those tests show there is a problem and you can't spot it, you need to break down the script to find out where it's failing. The way to do that is to run short sections of the script until you find the problem. Simply put a Halt Script step below the section you want to test. Once that section checks out, move the Halt Script step further down until you've worked out all the kinks.

In some cases, you'll need to preview some data that the script is entering, and then let it continue the rest of the steps. For those times, the Pause Script step is more appropriate.

And finally, there are times when you'll want to debug by bypassing a section of script entirely until later. For that, I use an If statement that can't be met, and place it around the steps I want to deactivate. For example:

```
If [1=2]
    [Steps I want to temporarily deactivate]
```

Part 4

```
        Find
        Print
    End If
```

Just don't forget to remove the extra Pause and Halt steps or deactivate the special If steps when you're done testing. That sounds like a given, but you'd be surprised. When you have a bunch of scripts linked together, it's easy to miss one.

⌘ **TIP**   If you want to view the details of your script without clicking every Find, Sort, and Print step, here's a great tip: When you print a script, FileMaker prints all the Find and Sort criteria. Choose Scripts, ScriptMaker, and select the script or scripts you want to print. Then click the Print button in the upper-right corner of the Define Scripts window. To select all the scripts for printing press Ctrl+A (Windows) or Command+A (Macintosh).

Important Hints

- The Commit Records/Requests step from the Records category should often be the last step in a script so that the cursor is out of all fields and any calculations can update. It just depends on what the script does. (This step used to be called Exit Record/Request.) This step has two options: Skip data entry validation and Perform without dialog. Since you can now have FileMaker ask users if they want to save the changes they've made to a record as they exit it, you would be able to use the "Perform without dialog" option.

- There is now a step called Open Record/Request under the Records category. You might think of it as making the record open for business. It actually locks the record from data entry by anybody else who might be sharing the file without requiring the user to put the cursor into a field. But you need to be careful with this step because it's possible to leave a record without releasing the lock by using the Window, New Window command or New Window script step. You would be well advised to follow it somewhere in the script with the Commit Records/Requests step. Now, is this something horrible? Not terribly so. Whenever someone is editing a record in a table, others users can't change that record (although they can view it and even enter the fields). It's just that starting with FMP7, any user can lock more than one record at a time. If someone locks one or more records and then goes to lunch… Well, I guess it depends on the situation, doesn't it? Users are notified if a record is locked and the dialog allows them to send a message to the person who has it locked. But again, if they're at lunch, it doesn't do much good.

- You can also lock all the child records in a portal by being in the parent record. Interestingly, if you go to the table where the child records live, you can make changes to any of the records there except any one of them which might be being edited (or locked with the Open Record/Request step) via the portal.

- Starting with FMP7, you can have multiple windows open. If you've made changes to a record and have a script that calls for a new window without using the Commit Records/Requests step, you could run into problems. If the new window uses the same table as the previous window, the data will not be updated. (The same would apply to a different table that might have a portal that uses records from the original table.) Not only that, but if you try to make changes to the same record as in the previous window, you'll find the record is locked. That could certainly be confusing for users. The answer is to use the Commit Records/Requests script step as part of your script.

↪ **NOTE** For users of versions of FileMaker previous to 7, the Set Field step also requires a Commit Records/Requests step — even though your cursor has not officially been active in any fields. Some developers also used the Go to Field step without declaring a field as a method of exiting or committing the record. That will no longer work either.

■ When using the steps from the Editing and Fields categories that have to do with entering data (which is nearly all of them), pay attention to the Options area. Choosing the Select option causes the new data to replace the existing data. Unchecking the box simply adds to the data that's already in the field.

■ A very common mistake is to have a script enter Find mode, enter some data into one or more request forms, and then forget to follow it up with the Perform Find step. I've done this myself in front of a client who was able to spot the problem immediately. Ouch! Even then, to make it work correctly, be sure you uncheck the box next to Restore.

■ And finally, sometimes unstored values such as calculations that use related data don't update properly on the screen to reflect the actual values. You may get the correct results by using Go to Layout mode, followed by Go to Browse mode as the last two steps in your script.

Import Scripts

Once you get going with FileMaker, you'll begin to realize that you use many of the same scripts over and over in many different files. Until version 5.0, when the Import Script feature was added, you had to recreate each new script by starting all over from scratch. This feature can be a real time-saver.

1. Open the Contact Management file, choose **ScriptMaker**, and click the **Import** button.
2. Find and double-click the **Business** file from the Files window.
3. In the Import Script window, click the check boxes to the left of the **4 - Print One Invoice** and **1 - Main Menu (Halt)** scripts, then click **OK**.
4. You will get a warning that errors were detected, but just click **OK**. Even when scripts import successfully, you need to check all steps that include variables such as subscripts, Finds, and Sorts. (For users pre-FMP7, the word "imported" is no longer appended to imported scripts.)
5. Double-click the **1 - Main Menu (Halt)** imported script. Because the script doesn't recognize the layouts in this file, this would be considered

an error, but it's certainly something that's easy to fix. Imagine importing a long, complicated script, and only having to fix one or two steps! Heavenly!

6. Click **Cancel**, and double-click the **4 - Print One Invoice** imported script. Before you'd make this a permanent addition to your file, you'd want to check all the variables like Sort and Page Setup (Macintosh) or Print Setup (Windows), but it sure beats creating all these steps manually.

7. Before you leave here, delete both of these scripts.

Version 5.0 of FileMaker was quite fussy about imported scripts. Starting with version 5.5, FileMaker no longer requires that the capitalization match in field or relationship names. Also regarding relationships, the key fields are not compared as long as the field names and types are the same. The main point is to make sure you have relationships and fields with matching names in both files. As always, there is more information in the Help files. Search the Index tab for "importing scripts."

Button Options (Pause, Halt, Exit, Resume)

Back in your Business file, go to the Invoice layout in Layout mode, and double-click the Main Menu button.

In the Options area, click on the pop-up (Figure 14-6) under the words Current Script. Your choices here determine what will happen to any other scripts that may be running when you click the button. Most of the time the Pause default will be just fine, but in certain circumstances, that may not be enough. For example, if some other script just brought a user to a special layout that puts him or her in Find mode and pauses, you'll probably want to use the Halt or Exit option for your Cancel button. If the Cancel button just takes users back to the data entry layout, they'll still be in Find mode. You may not need these button options often, but when you do, this is the only place to find them. You can also check the box next to "Change to hand cursor over button" to make the pointer turn into a hand whenever it's over the button in Browse and Find modes.

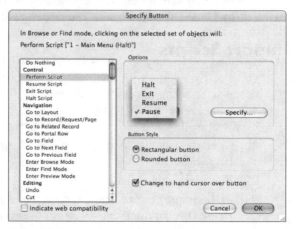

Figure 14-6
The Specify Button window showing the pop-up that determines what happens to the current script when clicking this button.

Startup/Shutdown Scripts

In Browse mode, choose File, File Options. There's just not enough space in this book to go into detail, but notice the two sections titled "When opening this file" and "When closing this file." You can have FileMaker perform a script (including any internal or external subscripts) during either of those operations. This just offers you another level of control over what happens with your files. I use it to warn myself if I don't have enough money in my checkbook (which, of course, I keep in FileMaker). I'll leave it up to you to figure out other situations in which you might use it.

A script set to run with document preferences will not run when a file opens hidden or minimized. To make sure that scripts do run in all related files of a solution, you'll have to add a script that runs when you open the main file. That script will run the external scripts you intended to run from the Preferences window when those files opened.

Show Custom Dialog Script Step

You can create your own dialog boxes and windows. Like the Comment step, Show Custom Dialog is also found under the Miscellaneous heading.

To show you one way to use this feature, I created a simple script called "9 - Custom Dialog - New Customer."

```
Script Name: 9 - Custom Dialog - New Customer
Go to Layout ["Contact" (Contact)] (Navigation)
New Record/Request (Records)
Show Custom Dialog ["New Customer"; "Please provide the name of the New
Customer"; Contact::NameFirst; Contact::NameLast]
If [Get(LastMessageChoice) = 2 ]
    Delete Record/Request[ No dialog ]
End If
```

Pay particular attention to the Show Custom Dialog step. There's a lot going on at this step that isn't obvious from the wording. You have to make several choices here.

1. At the "Show Custom Dialog" Options window, in the General tab, type **New Customer** in the Title box and the message **Please provide the name of the New Customer.** Since this is just text, you can type it directly into these boxes, and when you do, FileMaker will add quotation marks around your message. (You won't see the quotes until you switch to another area of the window or click OK. Or you can put them in yourself if you like.)

   If you need to include a calculation in the creation of the title or message or a field name, you could click on the Specify buttons, and you would be at the Specify Calculation window. This would allow you to set up a special one-record table and a layout with fields that contain the text of these dialogs. Then they could actually be edited in Browse mode without needing to edit the script. If you select a field name from a table or a calculation, FileMaker will not add the quotation marks.

2. In the lower portion of this screen are the boxes for the text that will appear on the buttons that show beneath your message in the message window. OK and Cancel are good choices for most uses.

> **NOTE** The text entry boxes for the buttons are bigger than the text that will fit on the buttons. The boxes look like they can fit about 20 characters, but you can really fit only about 12 characters on any button. The results will be different on the Mac than on Windows. So if you're creating a solution that will be used on both platforms, you should try it out before giving it to your users.

3. Now, click on the **Input Fields** tab at the top of the screen.

4. Put a check next to the **Show input field #1** box.

5. Click on **Specify** to the right of #1. This takes you to the Specify Field window. Select the **Contact** table in the drop-down menu at the top and then select **NameFirst**.

6. Type **First Name** in the box beside Label.

7. At Input field #2, select the **Contact** table, **NameLast**, and type **Last Name** in the box.

8. Notice the check mark beside "Use password character(•)" Don't check it now, but keep it in mind if you want to add a degree of security to this window — if you were to use it for some login system, for example.

9. Click **OK** to finish up the script step. But be sure to put a check mark next to "Run script with full access privileges" in the Script Step Options area. That will allow someone who doesn't have privileges to delete the newly created blank record if they back out of the process.

You can probably see pretty quickly how the choices I made in Figures 14-7 and 14-8 combine to create the custom dialog complete with text and fields in Figure 14-9.

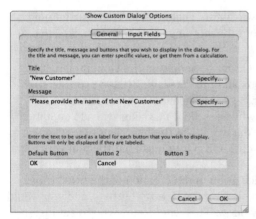

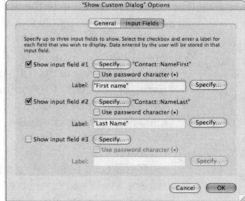

Figure 14-7
The "Show Custom Dialog" Options window's General tab.

Figure 14-8
The "Show Custom Dialog" Options window's Input Fields tab.

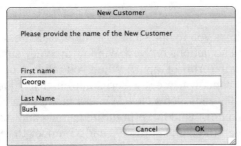

Figure 14-9
The custom dialog box the user sees.

There are a few things that might not be readily apparent about this script step:

- If the dialog appears when viewing an existing record, the data in the fields named in the Input Fields tab will only be displayed and changeable within the limits of the user's access privileges. That's why it's so important that you check the box next to "Run script with full access privileges" if you intend to have all users make the changes.

- If you intend to use fields in the dialog for data entry or change, data will only be affected when the user clicks the first button on the right. I often make the second button as the affirmative (OK or Do It) button so that users have to click it rather than simply hitting the Enter key. That is not an option with the custom dialog.

- If you intend to enter data from the dialog into a new record, you must create the record before displaying the custom dialog.

- The space allowed for the label name in the script step's dialog is a bit more generous than what will actually display when the dialog box appears to the user. It will only display about 50 characters.

- You can choose to display text that comes from a field for the window's title and message (Figure 14-7) and label names (Figure 14-8). To do so, you need to click the Specify button and use the Specify Calculation window to choose the fields that will provide the text. That means you can display different messages to different users based on text in various fields.

- The fields in the dialog bypass field validation and allow entry into fields not accessible on the layout in a manner similar to the Set Field script step.

- Because the Input Fields tab has the option to use the "•" password character, Show Custom Dialog can be used to create a custom login system. This will allow for a much simpler system than the various complex systems developers have had to create over the years. Yippee!

Other Features

There are a number of new script steps available with the introduction of FileMaker Pro 7. Even though we didn't use any of these next areas in any of our scripts, they are all very clever and powerful additions to the FileMaker arsenal.

Part 4

New Window[7]

The New Window script step allows you to open a new window on a file. Look at the window in Figure 14-10. (The options on New Window are very similar to those of Move/Resize Window in terms of input.) When you tell it to open a new window without selecting a window name, the script automatically just duplicates the current window. (There is also a New Window menu item below the Window menu that provides a new window without the naming and size options.) The new window is given the name of the file and a number to represent the new window. For example: Business becomes Business - 2. It also locates that window in the same position on the screen as the original, covering up the original. If you specify a name for the new window as part of your script, that name will appear at the top of the window regardless of the file name. If you also want to tell it to change to a specific layout or table, you would add the Go to Layout script step before the New Window step. That's important if the rest of your script will only operate on that specific table based on the fields, data, and relationships there.

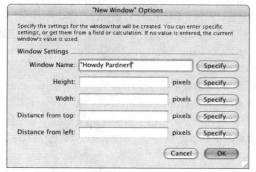

Figure 14-10
The "New Window" Options window.

Why would you want to use either the script step or the Window, New Window menu choice? How about these ideas:

- Perform a complicated Find for a set of records and check a different set of records without losing the first group.
- You can have different sorts of the same group of records.
- You can work in Layout mode in one window, Browse mode in another, and Preview mode in yet another.
- Have a List View of a found set of customers, click on a customer name, and have a new window open on the right side of the monitor where you can see the Detail View of the customer and either edit the record or make a call.
- Bring up a report in Preview mode where you cannot have any active buttons, and have a small, new window appear at the top or off to the side with active navigation buttons.
- Have a group of records in one window and a subset of that group in another without ever losing the first group.

You can create as many windows as you like, and you're not limited to sticking with the same table in the file either. For instance, you could call the Go to Related Record script step and follow it with New Window. One limitation I spotted was that if you try to view the records using the View As menu choices, each occurrence of the layout will change to your selection.

Let's look at some of the settings in the "New Window" Options window.

You can type the name for the new window directly in the Window Name field, or you can click the Specify button and use a calculation, which could include any number of If, Else, Then statements or values from various fields.

Then there are the four location fields, each with a Specify button of its own for precise positioning of the window on the monitor. The choices you have in New Window and Move/Resize Window can include field values as well as calculations. By the way, you can use any of the various Get(Window...) functions to set the current window size in a field for later reference from within the New Window script. It is now possible to position a window just about anywhere and any size you want. That includes an unusual option: By using negative values, you can make the window "appear" off the computer screen. I'm not sure why you might want to do that, but it can be done.

To test it out, I created a script that positioned the window offscreen and added the script step Adjust Window [Hide]. That baby was gone and untouchable. So then I added a script with these steps:

```
Select Window [Name: "offscreen"] (cause that's what I named it)
Adjust Window [Resize to Fit]
```

On a related note, it may also be difficult to place windows reliably across a computer that uses multiple monitors using these script steps.

Here's an interesting oddity: If your script calls for a new window with a specific name and you run it multiple times, all the new windows will have the same name. It will not append the window with any numbers. That can make it a bit difficult to select the right one from the Window list. Use some caution in that you can have more than one window open with the same name. When you use the Select Window script step and choose a specific window name, FileMaker will operate on the frontmost window with that name. Or if no name is selected, it will operate on the frontmost window regardless of its name.

The Select Window step simply brings the named window (or the file in which the script is running if the option is set to Current Window) to the front. Users of previous versions of FileMaker need to know that Select Window now replaces the Refresh Window [Bring to Front] step. It is critical in many applications because a script may depend on a specific table and window being frontmost.

All of the New Window functions are subject to the limitations of record locking. If you have not committed the record in a previous window that has a relationship to the new window, you will not be able to enter data in the new window. For the details, see the section titled "Important Hints" under "Debugging Scripts" earlier in this chapter.

Under the Window menu is a new item called Show Window. Even if a window is hidden, it appears in this list, unless the user's account prevents it.

Part 4

- You can call a window to the front and not have it show in the Window list.
- You can have many hidden windows, and if one is the active window, watch out! Scripting actions can be performed on the hidden, active window.
- You can have multiple windows with the same name. It's up to you to make sure you have the one you want to operate on.

Along with New Window, ScriptMaker now offers five other new steps in the Window category: Select Window, Adjust Window, Move/Resize Window, Close Window, and Arrange All Windows. Most of them are pretty intuitive. But it's Move/Resize Window that offers the same depth that New Window has.

Script Parameters[7]

Script parameters are also new for FileMaker Pro 7. Scripts now have a sort of temporary storage place. But I'd better back up just a little. What are parameters? One of the $2 definitions according to the *American Heritage Dictionary* is, "A constant in an equation that varies in other equations of the same general form." We looked at parameters back in Chapter 12, "Real-World Calculations — Part 1." You'll find parameters whenever you use the various functions in the upper right of the Specify Calculation window wherever you see it. Think of the function Length(text). Remember the word(s) you have to replace inside the parentheses? In this case it would be the word "text." The stuff you replace the words with are the parameters. In our example, Length(text), you would normally replace the word "text" with the name of some field, like Length(NameFirst). In this case, the parameter is NameFirst. I usually think of it as a value because parameters are often numbers. But as you see, somebody's name isn't really a number. So in the end, parameters can be text, numbers, or calculations.

Now that you know a little more about parameters, what are *script* parameters good for? As I said before, a script parameter is a temporary storage place. You can assign data or calculations to a script without the need to store it in a field. That's right, the entire Specify Calculation window is available to script parameters.

The big advantage is that now you can develop generic scripts and have them perform different tasks based on the parameters assigned to them. This is pretty new to us FileMaker developers, so I'll do the best I can to give you an example that might make sense. The Help files could fill out your knowledge a little bit beyond what I can do here, although the examples given don't really demonstrate the modularity I think we'll come to see over the next few years as developers create a variety of uses for this new tool.

There are only two places you can assign a parameter to a script: 1) in the window you see when you create a button and assign a script to it, and 2) in the "Specify Script Options" window you see when you add any subscripts to a script. That means the "parent" script can't have any parameters assigned to it — unless it was triggered by a button that has been assigned a parameter. And that makes sense since the purpose is to give scripts the ability to be more multi-purpose. Otherwise, if you intend to assign a permanent value to a script, just dump the value in a Global field and get the value from the field each time you need it. On the other hand, you can put Global fields on a layout and watch what happens as the script executes. Script parameters are hidden from view — unless you push them into a field somewhere. In that case, why not stick with a Global field to start with?

The best example of this modular approach I've heard so far was discussed at the 2003 FileMaker Developer Conference in Phoenix. This is based on a filtered portal trick some of us developers have been using for quite a while now. By putting a letter into a Global field and keying to the first letter of people's last names, you can filter the portal to only display last names that begin with a specific letter of the alphabet. Here's how:

1. In the Contact table create two fields:

FirstLetter	Calculation	= Left(NameLast; 1) [Be sure the calc result is Text!]
zi_Filter_gt	Text	Global

2. Create a relationship between two occurrences of the Contact table where zi_Filter_gt = FirstLetter.

3. Create a portal using the relationship and just put the NameFirst and NameLast fields in it.

4. Put the zi_Filter_gt field on the layout and type a letter in it. If you have anyone with a last name that starts with that letter in your file, you'll see their name in the list. Now try a different letter.

5. Then you put 26 buttons on the layout, one for every letter of the alphabet. Each button is attached to a script whose single step is Set Field[zi_Filter_gt; "A"] — or whatever letter you'll be using.

That, of course, requires 26 scripts, which is a lot of overhead. But now that we have script parameters, all 26 buttons can call one script. Each button has the script parameter that represents the letter on the button. So the A button's parameter would be "A," as in Figure 14-11, and the script would read:

> **Script Name: 10 - Filter Portal**
> Set Field[zi_Filter_gt; Get(ScriptParameter)]

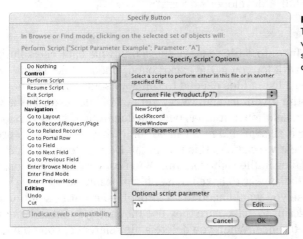

Figure 14-11
The "Specify Script" Options window seen from Specify Button showing the parameter defined as the letter A.

You still need to make 26 buttons, but you only need one script. Not bad!

The other half of this whole script parameter feature is the Get(ScriptParameter) script step. It really goes hand in hand with specifying a script parameter. If you just specify the parameter without doing anything with it, there really isn't much point, is there?

You can also specify a bunch of data as a parameter and parse it out as needed. I don't want to go into a full-fledged example with regard to a script parameter. But it's sitting out there if you're up to the task.

⊃ **NOTE**   *Parsing,* as far as developers use the term, is using a calculation to separate the specific data you need. A simple example would be if you inherited data
where people's first and last names were in one field. Using a calculation, you
would look for the space between the names as the delimiter to parse the data into
two separate fields.

Accounts Script Category[7]

The new Accounts script category allows for scripting user accounts without the need to use the Define Accounts & Privileges area. You could arrange it so that some users who normally wouldn't have access to that area could still work with setting up, enabling, and deleting accounts. Of course most of that won't mean much to you until you get to Chapter 21, "Keeping Your Data Secure." But since we're talking about scripts here, I feel I need to mention it.

The Accounts category includes:

- Add Account
- Delete Account
- Reset Account Password
- Change Password
- Re-Login

You can have your users place text in the dialogs these scripts generate or from fields. That also means you can combine it with the Show Custom Dialog script step, which will populate database fields with text from the Custom dialog, and then have a script perform the work of any of the other steps in this category. Very powerful! A developer's dream.

File References[7]

When you added the Inventory file to make this a multi-file database solution, FileMaker did some work for you in the background. Choose File, Define, File References. You'll see a list of files needed to run your solution. Right now it probably only shows the Inventory file. Every version of FileMaker has always kept track of files for a solution, but it has been hidden from view in versions previous to 7. Having it all available now can be somewhat confusing. In previous versions, the closest we came to this was in the Define Relationships window, which listed files in the right column. When converting solutions, you may see references that appear to have no use. It's probably best to just leave them alone. Otherwise you would need to go through your entire solution and double-check every script to make sure they use the table you intend them to before deleting the reference. When you delete a file reference, you do not get a warning that it may be used in a script. My attitude is, "If it ain't broke, don't fix it."

And Finally...

As a little last-minute cleanup you might want to remove the Invoice portal from the Contact layout.

Summary

In this chapter, we looked at what scripts are, and how to plan and debug them. We looked at the various categories of script steps and created some scripts using steps from many of the categories. And finally we looked at how to import scripts from other files, how to use the Show Custom Dialog script step, and how to use some script steps introduced in FMP7.

There are so many wonderful things you can do with scripts. It's discouraging that I can't show you more, but the fact is, you'll learn the most by getting in there and trying to make it do what you need to have done. Then you'll be ready for more advanced books on the subject.

Q & A

Q I'm getting lost going back and forth between the files. How can I make it clearer?

A You might draw some boxes on the paper where you do your planning to represent the files. Put numbers in the boxes to indicate the order in which you want the subscripts to perform. Then put the same numbers next to the plain language descriptions of what you want to have happen. You could even draw arrows between the boxes showing the direction of the scripts. Refer to the drawing as you work on your scripts.

Q Say I made a script that runs a script in another file. What if I want to change the remote script to a different remote script?

A Good question! When you're in the Script Definition window, select the perform script with the external script in it. Down by the OK button, you'll see the Specify button. When the "Specify Script" Options window appears, you can choose a different script. Not only that, but you can choose a script from an entirely different file by clicking on the File pop-up.

Workshop

Go to all the other files in this solution and add the Main Menu script. Then add Main Menu buttons to every layout. To keep them consistent, copy the first one you made so they'll all look the same. Just remember to attach it to the proper script once you take it to the new file.

In the section titled "Printing One Invoice," I talked about some extra protective steps that could be added to that script. Figure out what the external script should be, create it, and add the suggested steps.

Part 4

Review Questions

True-False

1. To make sure a script shows up in the Scripts menu, its name must begin with a number.

2. It's a good idea to plan a script before you begin to define it with ScriptMaker.

3. If you know why you included all of the steps in your script, you shouldn't add any comments.

4. The purpose of the Loop script step is to repeat one or more steps.

5. There is no way to move a script from one file to another.

Short Answer

6. Name two ways to add a script step to a script.

7. If you add a New Window script step, and specify the name as "My Special Window" and set the height at 300 pixels and the width as 600 pixels, how does the script step display?

8. Which script step facilitates modularizing your processes by breaking them into several small scripts?

9. How do you specify that a particular script gets performed each time a file is closed?

10. What is the purpose of the Show Custom Dialog script step?

11. If a script enters a field while it's working, what script step would leave all fields and allow any calculations to update?

12. There are at least four ways to exit a loop. Name one of them.

13. How can you know what Sort or Find will occur in a script just by looking at the steps?

14. When you're debugging a script, explain one way you can break it into small sections.

15. Which script step enables you to document within the script?

16. What script step can you add at the beginning of a script to make sure that it acts on the table you intend?

Chapter 15

Making Sense of Your Information with Layouts

Vocabulary

- Body part
- Footer part
- Grand Summary part
- Header part
- Sub-summary part
- Title Footer part
- Title Header part

Objectives

1. Understand the role that layouts play in a database.
2. Become familiar with the various layout types used for data entry and printing.
3. Use Sliding/Printing to control objects in Preview mode.
4. Become familiar with the eight layout parts.
5. Work with layout parts.

Introduction

How your information is organized on the screen is an extremely important element of how useful it is to you. Remember back in Chapter 5 when you saw how awkward it was to enter data when the tab order was not set up logically? Imagine what data entry would be like if the NameFirst field were in the upper left of the screen and the NameLast field were in the lower right. This is certainly an extreme example, but sometimes in our haste to get all the fields on a page, it's easy to forget how it will look to the end user. I had one client who hired me specifically to redesign their invoices and it took more than a couple hours to do it right.

In Chapter 16, "Designing Your Screen Layouts," we'll spend some time learning how to make layouts look good and flow logically for the user. In this chapter, I'll take you on an overview of layouts. We'll look at:

- Layout types, both for data entry and printing
- The various layout parts and their uses
- How to work with layout parts

What Is a Layout?

Having already placed fields and objects on a few layouts, you probably have a pretty good idea of what a layout is. The term *layout* is a carryover from the printing industry. Before a newspaper, magazine, or book went to press, the designers and editors would lay out all the picture and text elements on a flat surface, and move them around until they were satisfied with the appearance. Those tasks and the jargon have now moved over to the computer. When you think about it, it really makes sense to use the same term in FileMaker. We get to move all the elements of our file around until it looks just right, and in the end, we're often going to print the results.

The data in your file is actually separate from the field layout objects that display the data. For instance, in a price field, the number $9.99 is the same whether you choose to format the field in 48-point red type without the dollar sign, or 9-point black type with a dollar sign. Of course, if you don't place a field on the layout, you won't be able to see the data in it.

Layout Types

So far when dealing with layout appearance, we've spent most of the time looking at data entry. Data entry layouts will often look quite different from the layouts you create for printing purposes. When you run long reports and print invoices for customers, you don't want all those colored backgrounds. You can use up the ink pretty quickly trying to make it look pretty. If you're using black and white laser printers, all the colors just come out as shades of gray. On color laser printers, printing out a lot of colorful layouts can get very expensive. On the other hand, you need to provide adequate lines and shading to separate sections and make the report readable.

On-screen Layouts (Data Entry)

For data entry purposes, you want to use colors or shades of gray as well as graphic objects to help group similar items together. When users go to the layout to enter or find data, they shouldn't have to search too far. If you do your job well, you can help direct their eyes to the right data.

It's also important not to get too carried away with colors. Backgrounds and fields with extremely bright colors can make your eyes tired after a short time. You also need to be careful that there is reasonable contrast between the color of the font and the background color of the field. Black text on white or light-colored paper is considered the easiest to read, but some human interface studies compare reading black text on a white computer monitor to reading the words from the surface of a 75-watt bulb while it's turned on. You may want to temper your layouts away from black and white somewhat, but unless you're creating a database for a circus, take it easy with mixing in too many colors.

Look at the templates and the layouts created by the Layout Assistant for some hints. As time goes on, you'll notice other people's work and get ideas from that. A while ago I saw an amazing set of layouts designed for a database that's used by a number of companies in the fashion industry. It was strongly influenced by the *Babylon 5* TV series. The futuristic look made sense for trying to appeal to people in that forward-looking industry. Even at that, it was tastefully done, intuitive to negotiate, and easy to work in for hours on end.

Standard   We had a quick brush with the Standard layout in Chapter 9. Before the introduction of the Layout Assistant in 5.0, when you chose the Standard layout you got a copy of every field in the file. In a file with 100 or more fields, that was awkward, to say the least. Now you can choose the fields you want from the field list, and even include fields from related files. If you do want them all, you can get them with the click of a button — and that includes multiple copies of the same field. This is a much better arrangement. Let's take a look.

1. Go to Layout mode.

2. Choose **Layouts, New Layout/Report**.

3. Choose **Invoice** from the "Show records from" drop-down and **Standard form** from the Layout type, and click the **Next** button.

4. Notice the order of the fields in the list on the left. In my file, they appeared in the order given in Figure 15-1a.

InvoiceNum	AddCity
ContactSerNum	AddrCompany
Date	AddrPlusFour
InvoiceTotal	AddrState
AddrCompany	AddrStreet
AddrStreet	AddrZip
AddCity	Color
AddrState	ContactSerNum
AddrZip	Date
AddrPlusFour	InvoiceNum
zi_Colors_go	InvoiceTotal
Color	zi_Colors_go

Figures 15-1a and b
The list of fields in the Invoice table. The order in which they appear in the Layout Assistant is affected by the choices you make for field order in the Define Fields window.

5. Click the **Cancel** button and choose **Define Database, Fields**. In the upper-right corner, choose **View by Field Name** from the pop-up.

6. Click **OK**, and start a new layout, **Invoice_List**, until you get to the Specify Fields window again. The order of the fields has changed so it matches Figure 15-1b. In our file, that's really no big deal, but when you have a file with lots of fields, trying to move the ones you want into the Layout fields list on the right can be a mind bender. Depending on your situation, you may prefer to have them in creation order so the newer fields are at the bottom of the list. At other times, having them appear alphabetically is the best choice.

7. Of course, you can selectively move fields in and out of the Layout fields list, and even reorder them any way you like. While you're here, move the following fields into the list, and include the fields from the InvLI and Contact relationship. Maneuver them up and down in the order until your list looks like this:
InvoiceNum
Date

Part 4

ContactSerNum_fk
Contact:: AddrCompany
InvLI::InvTotal
InvLI::ProdID
InvLI::Description
InvLI::Price
InvLI::Quantity
InvLI::LineTotal

8. Then click the **Next** and **Finish** buttons. When you're done, your layout should look similar to the one in Figure 15-2.

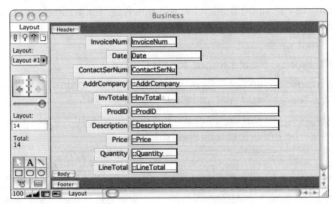

Figure 15-2
Layout mode showing the placement of specific fields when using the Standard layout from the Layout Assistant.

Notice that the ProdID field is as long as the Description field. That's because we chose to make that a Text field and FileMaker uses that as the default size for all Text fields. You can see that Number and Date fields have their own default sizes as well. You'll have to place the related fields in a portal to get them to display as they did on the layout we first created.

─────────────

⌘ **TIP**   When the fields are all crowded together in the area you want to work in, it can get a little claustrophobic. You may find it easier to grab the Body tab and expand it downward a few inches. Then choose Edit, Select All, and move the fields and their labels down the layout a few inches. Now you've got room to work.

Since this chapter is about layouts, take a few minutes to move items around on your layout until they look like Figure 15-3. Be sure to define the portal to allow deletion of portal records. Then format ContactSerNum_fk and ProdID with their appropriate pop-up value lists. The numbers are formatted to align to the right, and fields that represent money are formatted to include that detail, too. You'll also notice that I changed the size of the font for the field labels, removed the engraved look of the fields in the portal, and added a left border to them. At this point, the changes you make are up to your taste.

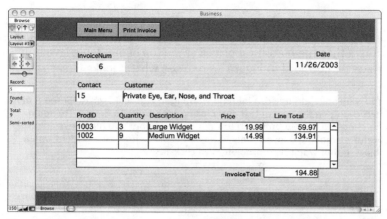

Figure 15-3
Browse mode showing the placement of the fields once they've been moved into more useful positions.

Columnar List/Report vs. Table View In Chapter 9, we created a Columnar List/Report in the InvLI table that will be the printed invoice. There are other reasons you might want to make a list. For example, using View as Table can be handy for many uses, but it has its limits, too.

1. Go to the Invoice table.
2. Get to Layout mode, and start a new layout. Name it **List View**.
3. Select **Columnar list/report**, and click **Next**. Click **Next** again.
4. In the Specify Fields window, choose the following fields:
   InvoiceNum
   Date
   ContactSerNum_fk
   Contact::Company
   InvoiceTotal
5. Click **Next** as many times as you need to until you see the Finish button, then click **Finish** as well. When you get back to Browse mode, the layout should look a lot like the Table View. The big difference is what you can do with the Body section of the layout.
6. Go to Layout mode, choose **Edit**, **Select All**, and move all the layout objects to the right so you have about an inch on the left.
7. Select the **Text** tool and type @@ close to the left edge of the layout. (@@ displays the record number.)
8. Now select the **Button** tool and make a small button between the @@ and the InvoiceNum field.
9. When the Specify Button window appears, choose **Go to Layout** under the Navigation heading. In the Options area, specify **Invoice** from the pop-up, and click **OK**.
10. When you're back in Layout mode, the cursor will be flashing on the new button. Type --> to make an arrow. If the font size is too large, choose a smaller one.

Part 4

11. Go to Browse mode. Now you can see the record numbers, and clicking on the arrow button will take you to the invoice detail. I think it's much more intuitive than the button we placed at the top of our Table layout in Invoice. Jump ahead to Figure 15-6 to see what it looks like.

⌘ **TIP**   You may have already run into the warning in Figure 15-4. You'll see it most often when changing the size of text and placing a portal on a layout. The main reason for choosing the No button in this dialog box is that you may have spent hours carefully tweaking a layout only to have it explode from an accident with a layout object. If that won't be a problem, just click Yes.

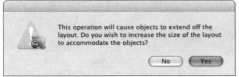

This operation will cause objects to extend off the layout. Do you wish to increase the size of the layout to accommodate the objects?

No   Yes

Figure 15-4
The warning dialog box that appears when the position of a layout object might cause the layout to change size.

12. If you're not on Invoice or Contact, go there now. Make a new button near the top of the layout that will take you to the Invoice_List layout, and type **List** on it. Now you can switch back and forth. You might add another button at the top of the List layout that will show all records. You could sort the records by the Contact::Company field, create a script that contains the sort, and make a button for that, too. Now you can see one of the advantages of Table View — you can sort the records just by clicking the column titles — as long as that feature is turned on. But then any buttons you placed in the Body area won't show up. Before you leave here, you will probably want to protect the fields from accidental entry.

If you really want to take advantage of the capabilities of both Table and List Views, try the following:

1. Make sure List View is set up to include a Header part (Layouts, Layout Setup, Views, Properties tab).
2. Then place a button in the Header section.
3. When the Specify Button window appears, choose **View As** under the Windows heading.
4. In the Options section, choose **Cycle** from the Specify pop-up, click **OK**, and name the button **View**. By clicking the button back in Browse mode, you should be able to switch to Table View to take advantage of sorting field labels, then go to List View to use the buttons in the Body.

You can set FMP to show a dialog when leaving a record where data was added or changed. (Leaving or "committing" a record consists of clicking out of all fields, hitting the Enter key, or changing layouts or modes. You do not leave a record when you change windows.) You can turn this feature on or off on a layout-by-layout basis. When you're in Layout mode, choose Layout Setup, click the General tab, and you'll see a check box next to "Save record changes automatically." If that is unchecked, it will bug you each time you change any data.

There is also a new feature in Layout Setup called "Show field frames when record is active." Field frames are the little dotted lines that appear around the fields that will accept data when the cursor is in one of the fields in a record. FMP has always done that. But now you can choose whether or not to display field frames. The frames are helpful if you have fields without borders, but I can imagine special layouts that might benefit from this feature. This is controllable on a layout-by-layout basis, too.

Printed Layouts

The other thing that sets data entry layouts apart from printed reports is the way data is displayed. As I mentioned in Chapter 2, some elements do not appear when you're in Browse mode. You can see what the printed page will look like by choosing View, Preview mode.

Sub-summaries and variable data will only appear on the printed page and in Preview mode. And even then, sub-summaries will only show when the layout is sorted correctly. To turn that around, you can make objects that appear in Browse mode disappear on a printout and in Preview mode.

Sliding/Printing   Let's assume you want a quick printout of your invoices. Go to the List View layout in the Invoice table if you're not already there. Make sure you're viewing it as a Table, then go to Preview mode. This looks like a pretty straightforward way to print the list, but if you have extra field labels or too much color, or if you made that View button, you won't want to print it as is.

Non-Printing Objects   Try this technique to keep items from printing:

1. Go into Layout mode, click the Header tab, and choose transparent (the two interlocking white squares) from the Fill pattern palette.

2. Do the same in the Body tab.

3. Now select all the field labels (Shift+click) and choose **Format**, **Sliding Printing**.

4. In the lower-left corner of the Set Sliding/Printing window, check the box next to **Do not print the selected objects**, and click **OK**.

5. Go to Preview mode and those field labels are gone! If you created that View button but didn't select it during this process, it's still on the page, but nothing happens when you click it in Preview mode.

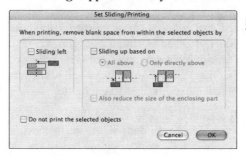

Figure 15-5
The Set Sliding/Printing window.

6. Go to Browse mode, choose **View as List** (or use your View button), and go to Preview mode. The field labels are gone. At this point you have to

decide which view you'll be printing. But now you have a technique to avoid printing selected items on layouts.

☒ **CAUTION** If you're designing layouts for other users, remember that buttons don't work in Preview mode. Since everyone who uses your file might not understand that, it's usually a good idea to take them to the preview by way of a script that includes a Pause step. That way the users can click the Continue button in the Status area (or press the Enter key), which will take them back to Browse mode where you can include Print and Cancel buttons. You want to make sure those buttons are non-printing so they won't show in Preview mode. There's nothing more frustrating for a user than to have buttons in front of them that don't work.

When you use the Layout Assistant, FileMaker colors the layout parts based on the theme. If you go to any of the template files and look at the form in Preview mode, some of the background colors will disappear. That's because the layout part colors have been left transparent, and the colors are provided by colored, non-printing rectangles. Layout part colors cannot be made non-printing. The only thing you can do is change the pattern to transparent.

Sliding Objects While we're at it, let's look at another feature of Sliding/Printing. One of the contacts in one of my invoices has a long company name. You can rearrange the layout to show the information, and use Sliding/Printing to make the printout look more professional. (If the names in that field are too short to make sense in this demo, go to the Contact record represented on one of these invoices and give it a long company name. Then come back and finish this exercise.)

1. Look at Figure 15-6. Drag the dotted line or the tab for the Body part down, and expand the Contact::AddrCompany field to show two lines.

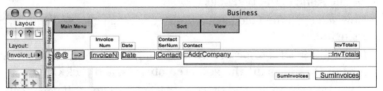

Figure 15-6
The Invoice_List layout in Layout mode showing the Contact::AddrCompany field opened up to accommodate a long name.

2. Choose **Format**, **Sliding Printing**, and check **Sliding up based on**. Leave the "All above" radio button as is, then check the box next to **Also reduce the size of the enclosing part**, and click **OK**. When you go to Preview mode, any long Contact::Company names will show on two lines, but all the shorter names will close up tight to each other.

☒ **CAUTION** Make sure that any expanded fields in the Body don't extend into the Trailing Grand Summary, Sub-summary, or Footer parts. If they do, the fields won't slide properly.

Using Sliding/Printing this way is something you may need to do on the Invoice layout in InvLI where a product name or description may be too long to fit on one line. There is a very good discussion of the finer points of Sliding/Printing in the FileMaker Pro manual and the Help files.

In Table View, you can simply expand the column to the right until it shows the whole company name. If you have a lot of fields, however, you may not be able to make all of them print on a page. In that case, the advantage goes to List View where you can use Sliding/Printing. You can also place fields one after the other in horizontal rows in List View. Remember, you'll never get sub-summaries in a printout of Table View. Table View is handy for viewing and printing quick and simple lists regardless of how complex the database, but it's just not meant for reports.

Layout Parts

FileMaker Pro has eight layout parts to choose from. So far, we've created all of our layouts using the Layout Assistant, where FileMaker took care of creating the layout parts for us. Now it's time to learn what they're all about.

Go to InvLI_Invoice layout, switch to Layout mode, and look at the Invoice layout we created in Chapter 9, shown here in Figure 15-7. Choose Layouts, Duplicate Layout so you can experiment without ruining the original.

Figure 15-7
The InvLI_Invoice layout showing six of the eight layout parts.

☒ **CAUTION**   Whenever you get ready to experiment with a layout you've worked hard to create, make a copy first.

The Part label control is the icon near the lower-left corner of the window to the left of the Mode pop-up (see Figure 15-8). Clicking on this icon toggles the layout part label tabs between displaying horizontally on the layout and flipping up vertically out of the way. When you use the Layout Assistant to create labels, envelopes, and reports, the tabs are turned sideways.

Figure 15-8
Clicking on the Part label control icon alternately shows and hides the layout part label tabs.

Double-clicking one of the tabs will bring up the Part Definition window shown in Figure 15-9. You can also call up this window by choosing Insert, Part from the menu bar. From here, you can change the current layout part to a different one. The radio buttons are only active for the specific parts that can go in that position on the layout. All others are dimmed. If you close the window and click on the other parts, you'll see that the available radio buttons will change. Let's look at the various parts and their uses.

Title Header

The Title Header only appears on the first page of a report no matter how many pages the report has.

Header

You'll find the Header at the top of every page unless the report has a Title Header. In that case, the Title Header replaces the Header on the first page.

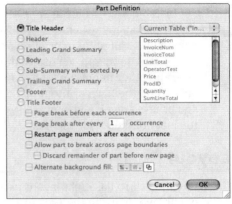

Figure 15-9
FileMaker's Part Definition window.

Body

The Body prints as many times as it will fit on a page when allowing for any other layout parts that also have to print. You can make the Body print in columns. That's how you're able to print multiple-column labels.

Leading and Trailing Sub-summaries

Sub-summaries print before or after a group of records, but only if the records are sorted by the field selected when creating the sub-summary. You can have as many of these on a layout as you can dream up, but the order in which they appear may seem somewhat unpredictable depending on how the records are sorted. When you look at all other layout parts, they print in the same order in which they appear on the page. But a Sub-summary part that is lower on the layout may actually appear above a different Sub-summary part if they are sorted in reverse order. In some cases, that may be exactly what you want. If the Sub-summary parts always appear in the same order as your sort, you'll have no surprises.

You have to create a Summary field for any numeric fields for which you want summaries. Placing that same Summary field in a Sub-summary part will display summary data for the subset of records based on the sort. All records with the same value in the sorted field will be summarized. That's what the InvoiceTotal field did for us in the InvLI table. We sorted by InvoiceNum, and regardless of how many line items came from an invoice, we could see the total of each invoice separately.

Now let's create a Summary field in the Invoice table called SumInvoices that will total the InvoiceTotal amounts. (You don't need to pay attention to the Summarize repetitions radio buttons in the lower left. Those are choices you'll only need to make when you are using repeating fields.) With this field, you'll be able to see how much each contact spent. Now, create a Trailing Grand Summary layout part, and place your SumInvoices field in that part. See Figure 15-10.

Don't get the idea that you need a Summary field to take advantage of a Sub-summary part. A common use of Sub-summary parts is to break a category by a "text" label. For example, in an Employee database, you could have a field for supervisor. If you wanted to print all of the employees grouped by supervisor, then you'd make a Sub-summary part, put the Supervisor field in that section, and sort by supervisor. No Summary field is needed to accomplish that.

Sub-summary objects and the data in the fields in these parts only show up in Preview mode or when printed, and only when the records are properly sorted. If a part doesn't show in your report, be sure to check the sort first.

☒ **CAUTION** If you have a Sub-summary that shows up in Preview mode but won't print, check your print window. Choosing the Current Record radio button from the FileMaker settings area in your print window will cause the sub-summaries not to print as you expect. If you're trying to get a look at one page of the report, choose "Print pages 1 to 1" in the print window instead.

My experience has been that simply reading about reports and doing a few exercises won't make you a master. You'll have to create some reports of your own based on what you've learned here and what you can get from the manual and the Help files. Then you need to experiment until you get them just the way you want. You know, practice makes perfect.

Leading and Trailing Grand Summaries

These parts only appear once on a report, but you can have one each of the Leading and Trailing Grand Summaries. Summary fields that are placed in these layout parts provide totals for all records in the found set.

We've removed the SumLineTotal Summary field from the Trailing Grand Summary part in InvLI. That's because when you print a group of invoices, you don't want that total going to the customer whose invoice prints last. You can avoid that by double-clicking the Trailing Grand Summary part tab, and checking the box next to "Page break before each occurrence." Of course, you'll also have to put the InvoiceTotal field back into that part. If getting the grand total isn't important, you could even delete that part from the layout.

Footer

The Footer appears at the bottom of every page unless there is a Title Footer part. In that case, the Title Footer takes the place of the Footer on the first page of the report.

Title Footer

The Title Footer only appears once in the report at the bottom of the first page.

Part 4

Working with Layout Parts

Be sure you're in Layout mode, and Choose Layouts, Part Setup. You should see the window shown in Figure 15-10. This is a great way to get an overview of the part structure of a layout. As you can see on your screen, some layout parts can be moved, while others are locked in place, indicated by the padlock icon.

Double-clicking on the listed part or single-clicking the Create button brings up the Part Definition window, which we've already seen.

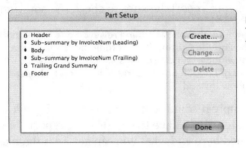

Figure 15-10
The Part Setup window showing the parts on the Invoice layout in the InvLI table.

Adding and Deleting Parts

If you want to add a part to the layout, you can use the Part tool and just drag parts onto the layout. You can also use Insert, Part from the menu bar. Or you can use the Create button in the Part Setup window. Only certain parts can be placed between specific other layout parts. You can also use the Part Setup window to delete a layout part. Alternatively, you can simply click on the part tab, and press Backspace or Delete. FileMaker will warn you if there are any layout objects within the boundaries of the part you're attempting to delete.

Modifying Parts

You can double-click the tab of an existing part and designate it to be something else, but you're limited to the parts that can go in that location on the layout.

⌘ **TIP**   Getting vertical lines for columns to show up across multiple parts was a nightmare until I learned the trick. A line will not print across three layout parts, but you can make a line appear to be continuous across multiple parts by placing one line across the upper and middle parts and overlapping it with another line that crosses the middle and lower parts.

If you followed along and created the duplicate Invoice layout, you may want to delete it now. Or you could give it another name, indicating that it's temporary, so you can experiment with it later.

Summary

In this chapter, we looked at how data entry layouts differ from layouts that will be used in printed reports. I showed you how to keep layout objects from printing but still appear on the screen.

Then we looked at the various layout parts, the differences between them, and how to add and delete them from the layouts.

Q & A

Q It looks as if you're saying we have to make two of every layout — one for viewing and one for printing.

A Not exactly. You won't even want to print some layouts, and some you'll print so rarely that it won't matter how they look. Reports for internal use and materials that customers will be seeing need different consideration. Some reports will never be printed either. Sometimes a user may just need a bit of information from a group of records in order to answer a question. If that's the case, there's no need to print it. But it should still be easy to find the data requested.

Q The details of these layout parts are confusing. How can I figure them out?

A Fortunately, the Layout Assistant takes a lot of the load off. Using it, you can create a complicated report, and then use the Part Definition and Part Setup windows to analyze it. Also read the FileMaker Pro manual and take a look at the Help files. Sometimes just seeing the same topic from another angle will make it click for you.

Workshop

Experiment with one of the layouts created with the Layout Assistant, and turn off the background colors. Then, substitute colored rectangles and make them non-printing. Once you create one on the layout, you'll have to choose Arrange, Send to Back so it doesn't cover up your other layout objects. Check it out in Preview mode. Using this technique, you can make data entry layouts that can still be printed without wasting ink.

Go back to Chapter 8 and find the section titled "Sort By a Summary Field." If you weren't able to do that exercise then, you should be able to now with what you learned in this chapter.

Review Questions

True-False

1. Layouts allow you to create different views of your databases.
2. A Title Footer appears at the bottom of the last page in Preview mode and the printed report.
3. Sliding is often applied to addresses to make them look professional when they're printed.

Part 4

4. A columnar list is better than a standard layout for viewing multiple records.

5. When you delete a part from a layout, all the objects within the part are also deleted.

Short Answer

6. Why might you use less color on a layout designed to be printed than one designed to be viewed on screen?

7. Which elements on a layout should be defined as non-printing so they don't confuse users in Preview mode?

8. Which layout parts can be defined as "leading" or "trailing"?

9. Name the three ways you can add a part to a layout.

10. Under what conditions does a Sub-summary part appear?

11. Name at least two advantages of a Columnar List/Report layout over a Table View.

12. What type of objects can you make non-printing?

13. Name at least one layout part that can be placed after the Body.

14. If the layout part label tabs are in the way on the layout, how can you move them?

Chapter 16

Designing Your Screen Layouts

Vocabulary

- Beta version
- Container field
- Grouping layout objects

- Locking layout objects
- Object effects

Objectives

1. Understand basic rules and best practices of layout design.
2. Learn to design effective screen layouts.
3. Learn to use group formatting techniques.
4. Use the items in the View menu.
5. Become familiar with the Arrange tools.
6. Learn about locking layout objects.
7. Learn to add and format graphical objects and movies.
8. Learn to use borders, fills, and object effects.

Introduction

You already know how to create layouts, and you know about layout parts and building reports. This chapter is about design and the specifics of the various FileMaker tools used to accomplish good design. In a way, it's a continuation of the last chapter where you put the right fields on the right layouts. Now you need to organize the fields with graphic elements, make it flow, and make it sing.

Computers are everywhere today. People see a lot of software and know what commercial products look like. With the proliferation of the Internet, we see web pages of all types. If you've done a little web surfing, you know that some web sites are easy to navigate, while others are total confusion. The reason for that is the design of the interface. You need to ask yourself what type of database you want to design — hopefully one that's clear, crisp, and easy to understand. How do you want users to feel while doing their work with what you've designed? I'll bet you thought you were just trying to keep track of data.

Because there are so many good interface designs out there, user expectations are high. You have to do a good job just to make it acceptable. I love it when my clients call to tell me a report that used to take them two days now only takes 15 minutes. They're using it, and it's saving them time. If you find that some areas aren't being used anymore or they're being neglected, it may be because of bad design.

Basic Design

One of the best ways to get started with design is to look at the FileMaker Pro templates. Use File, New Database, and choose the "Create a new file using a template" radio button. That way you can study these examples, tear them apart, and then delete the files from your computer afterward. Give the files names that will indicate they may be deleted later.

Each of the templates follows a modified Lavender screen theme of white, pale blue, and, yes, lavender. They show a simple set of navigation tools. Some text items along the top (which are really buttons) represent layouts that differ in the way information is presented, such as View Contact List and Address Labels. Below the text items are tabs with icons just beneath that for list and table. Some templates (Contact Management, for example) have more tabs partway down the Form screen that take you to other layouts that are nearly identical to the basic data entry layout but include a different subset of fields. The tabs and icons provide a fairly clear indication of what type of data can be found on those screens. This style of interface will be familiar to anyone who uses computers, and is quickly grasped by first-time users as well. I must admit, I was thrown by the text buttons just above the tabs at the upper right. I'm just not sure it's clear that clicking on the text in the gray bar near the top will do anything. The various text groupings in the gray bar are actually buttons. I would probably have used elements that look more like buttons.

A big design consideration should be finding out what the end users already use. Try to make your design something they will be familiar with. I often scan paper forms used in the offices, duplicate the forms in FileMaker layouts, and then try to improve on the design. This is really a good time to ask the staff what they would change about their forms. If your fields are in the same approximate position as the paper forms, the transition to your system will be that much easier.

Navigating through the database with buttons should mimic or be better than the current workflow. Remember, it doesn't have to be clear to you, it has to be clear to the user. There should always be a Home or Main Menu screen. Users should rarely have to go more than three clicks from the Main Menu to get to an area. Warning messages should make it clear what choices are expected from the user. That is why using FileMaker's custom messages in field validation and scripts can be so valuable to you as a developer.

After you've built a beta version, watch the end users work. See where they get lost, and rethink your work. The big software companies test their applications with video cameras watching both over the shoulders and on the faces of their testers, and you know how badly some of that software is designed! You can do better than they can if you pay attention. Don't explain too much; just listen. That doesn't mean all your solutions will be self-explanatory, but if most of the users get hung up at the same point, and it happens time after time, think again. Be humble. You might want to take a look at some user interface sites on the web like the Interface Hall of Shame at http://digilander.libero.it/chiediloapippo/Engineering/iarchitect/shame.htm, which provides examples of both the good and the bad.

Know What You Like

Look at more than one of the template files. Even though they use the same theme, each of the files offers a little different approach, especially the integrated files in the Product Catalog folder inside the Business - General folder. When you look at the Define Database, Tables tab, you'll see there are two tables in this file. For a real eye-opener, click the Relationships tab and look at the graph. Since the Table Occurrences have been named according to function, to find out which table they're associated with, hover your mouse pointer over the arrow in the upper-left corner of each TO.

The downloadable files include the Asset Management template FileMaker provided with earlier versions of the software. Look in Book Chapter files: Chapter 16 folder.

1. Ask yourself what you might do differently.

2. Duplicate one of the data entry layouts.

3. Start moving the layout parts around to see how the background is constructed. Some parts, like the black rectangle that provides the background in the Header, may be locked. Click to select them and choose Arrange, Unlock so you can move them around, too. Some layout objects are text blocks, while others are colored rectangles with transparent or "None" borders. A few items are actually buttons formatted with the Do Nothing script step. You can spot them because when you double-click them, the cursor goes immediately to the center and flashes, waiting for you to enter the button text.

Let's say that you like this layout, and you'd like to use it in your own solution. The only improvement you'd like to make is to change the colors to reflect your corporate logo colors. Let's do that now.

1. Go back to the original data entry layout in the template, and make another copy.

2. Delete all the fields and their labels, and change the colors to suit you.

3. Now choose **Edit, Select All**, then **Arrange, Group**, and copy the elements to the clipboard.

4. Open your Business file to the Invoice layout, and go to Layout mode.

5. Duplicate the layout, and paste the backgrounds onto your layout.

6. Before you do anything else, choose **Arrange, Send to Back**, and move them into place. You may have to work with the layout parts to get it to

Part 4

look right. Don't forget that the entire background is now grouped. You can select it and choose **Arrange, Ungroup** so you can work with individual elements again.

7. Remember that all your buttons will need to be reattached to the proper scripts (some not created as yet) and other Specify Button options. That means the tab buttons need to be attached to the proper layouts. When I do a transfer like this, I use the following trick to remind myself to fix them.

⌘ **TIP** After transferring a set of buttons from another file, they'll be attached to the wrong scripts. You should identify them as still needing work. Use the Text tool and type an X somewhere on the layout. Format the type as red, bold, and at least 18 points. Then make as many copies as you need to put one on each questionable button. As you fix the buttons, you can remove the Xs one at a time until the job is done. This allows you to work on other things and come back to finish this job at a later time. Regardless of how you make this look now, when you're doing work for other people, be sure you always think of your users.

Keep It Consistent

In most layouts in the templates, you'll notice the main buttons in exactly the same location. As much as possible, buttons that provide the same function should be in the same place on all the layouts. Don't try to provide all buttons for everything on every page. Too many buttons can be overwhelming. You may need to provide separate areas, sometimes in different files, where groups of functions will have matching buttons within that area only.

One thing you should always do is provide a Main Menu button on every layout. The upper-left corner is the position most often used by designers. That's not what FileMaker has done in these templates, but you'll want that in your more complex solutions.

Notice that when you arrive in an area, the button or tab that got you there changes color, but it's still on the page. You should also strive to let users know when they've changed layouts, but make it consistent enough that they understand how to go back to where they were.

Make the field labels conform to the same style and terminology from layout to layout. If you use Invoice No. on one layout, don't switch to Inv. # on another and InvNum on yet another. Using that same approach in the selection of short, descriptive file, table, layout, and script names will also help you to understand your own files when you have to come back to work on them later.

Group Formatting

Too many different fonts can add confusion to a layout. Use the same one or two fonts and font sizes as much as possible throughout your layouts. If you find you have too many font styles and sizes on one layout, you can reformat all of them at once. First, you need to select the group of items you want to change. You could be changing the fields themselves, their labels, or some other text on the layout. This technique will also work for other object types.

1. Select one of the items you want to change.
2. Press **Option+Command+A** (Macintosh) or **Ctrl+Shift+A** (Windows).

3. To deselect any items you don't want to change, hold down the **Shift** key and click on the object.

4. To reformat all selected items on the Macintosh, hold down the **Control** key and click on one of the selected objects in the group. On Windows machines, right-click on one of the selected objects.

5. Make the formatting changes.

Another way to select all of one type of object is to:

1. Click on the first object.

2. Click on the **Select Objects by Type** icon in the Arrange toolbar as seen in Figure 16-1.

3. If you think you might want to change them again later, choose **Arrange**, **Group**. Now you can get to all of them at one time. You can always ungroup them later should you need to move or otherwise work with them separately.

Select Objects by Type

Figure 16-1
By clicking on a layout item and using the Select Objects by Type icon from the Arrange toolbar, you can select all layout elements of the same type.

You can also reformat items by selecting just a couple of objects or text items. You don't have to select all items of one type on the layout.

Remember that you can use the Format Painter when changing the attributes of layout objects. For a complete discussion of the Format Painter, see Chapter 3, "Creating Your First Database."

☒ **CAUTION**   Be careful when choosing the Field Format window options on multiple fields. Any fields that have been formatted with value lists will either lose all their value lists or acquire the same value list as one of the other items — a major pain that you might not even discover for some time! That doesn't happen with the Format Painter tool.

⌘ **TIP**   Sometimes the default settings for fonts and graphics change mysteriously. If there is an object on the layout that has the formatting you want to make into the default, press Command (Macintosh) or Ctrl (Windows) while you click on the object. If you don't have a default you like, click in a blank space on the layout so that nothing is selected. Then make choices from the appropriate menus. Those will become the default settings. And finally, add graphic or text to the layout using any of the layout tools (pasting something onto the layout from the clipboard won't work). Now make changes to it before you deselect it. You guessed it — those are the new defaults.

Selecting Groups of Layout Objects

Here are some techniques you might find helpful when selecting a group of objects.

The first is by surrounding the objects. In Chapter 3, I described a method for selecting a group of objects by clicking and dragging with the Selection tool until you surrounded the objects. This method allows you to select a group of objects that are within or touching the selection rectangle.

Part 4

The second is by touching the objects.

1. In Layout mode, click outside of the group and drag until the selection rectangle is touching all the items you want to include.
2. Before releasing the mouse button, press the **Command** key (Macintosh) or **Ctrl** key (Windows), and then release the mouse button.

In Figure 16-2, I started in the upper-right corner above the NameFirst field label and dragged until I was partway into the City field. This selects all four fields and their labels. With the other method, I would have also had to surround the NameLast, State, and Zip fields and their labels as well, only to have to deselect them before proceeding. You can see the advantage! (On Macintosh computers you'll know you have it right because the whole area of the rectangle turns gray.)

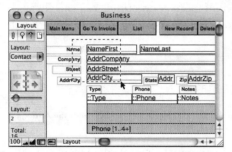

Figure 16-2
Selecting a group of objects without completely surrounding them.

Remember, you can always deselect any objects after they've been selected as part of a group.

Here's another helpful trick. To deselect an object underneath another:

1. Select both objects, then deselect the upper object by Shift+clicking on it. The bottom object is now the only item selected.
2. Choose **Arrange**, **Lock**. Now you can work with the upper object separately.

This is especially helpful when you then want to select and move a group of objects but include just that upper element.

How to Make It Pretty

Aside from using soft colors, the overriding rule to making layouts look nice is to keep it simple. It's not too early to discuss the final step in cleaning up your layouts. Stated simply: If you don't need it, take it out. Clutter is confusion. Your layout is not done when everything is there. It's done when you can't possibly take anything else out. Also note that something about the way our brains are organized seems to respond better if buttons, fields, and labels are aligned and uncluttered.

Arrange and View Menus

Use the tools in the Arrange and View menus to organize your layouts. I showed you a number of the tools available in the View menu in Chapter 3. Take a look at these valuable tools again in Figure 16-3. When you choose Show from this menu, there are some options we haven't seen before. Try them out on your own to see what they do. If there aren't any sliding or non-printing objects on your layout, select any object and format it with one of the two options. Then turn on the menu choice by choosing View, Show, Non-Printing Objects so you can see how it changes in appearance. (Once an item is selected, a check mark appears in front of it in the list. Of course, you can't see the check mark because the menu disappears. Selecting the menu item again turns if off.) I find Show, Text Boundaries especially helpful for aligning text items on the layout.

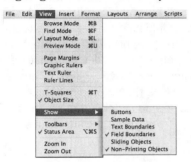

Figure 16-3
The list of tools and options under the View menu.

Rotate Layout Objects

You can also rotate any layout object (except a layout part or a portal) by selecting it and choosing Arrange, Rotate. Objects rotate in 90-degree clockwise increments. The keyboard shortcut is Command+Option+R (Macintosh) or Ctrl+Alt+R (Windows). In reports, if the field is short and the title is long, rotate it. You may still have to abbreviate it or break it into two lines to make it fit in a narrow Header part.

Icons

There has been a proliferation of icons in software in recent years. FileMaker Pro itself includes toolbars that are full of icons. The reason is that our brain can grasp an image more quickly than it can read words. After all, a picture is worth a thousand words. But you'll also notice that you can choose not to display the toolbars. Don't get carried away with too many icons in your files. If the same button is the same color and in the same place on the layout, users will know where to go automatically. Again, notice how simple the templates are.

⌘ **TIP** If you decide to provide icons on your buttons, don't fall in love with them. If your users don't understand one or more of them, it doesn't matter how much time you spent on them, the ones that don't work have to be taken out or redesigned.

The arrow icons (in the Asset Management template in the downloadable files) that indicate next, previous, first, and last record are simple and fairly universal in meaning. You see similar icons on cassette recorders, CD and DVD players, as well as VCRs. If you zoom in on the buttons in Layout mode, you'll find out they're made up of a series of very short lines created with

Part 4

FileMaker's Line tool. Graphics created with FileMaker's tools will usually draw faster on the screen, as long as the objects are not too complex.

⌘ **TIP**   When you do create icons, try to construct them with FileMaker's own graphics tools. Also, large graphics brought in from other sources can slow down screen redraws. In rare cases, they may contain a bit of information that causes a layout not to print properly.

If you simply must create graphics in other applications, use a 256-color setting rather than 32-bit. Storing a batch of 32-bit graphics will make the file large in a hurry. If you have the choice, it would be even better to use the web-safe 212-color palette, which is easy to share between Macintosh and Windows computers, not to mention the web. If you do decide to use external graphics, it is more efficient to use the same image over again whenever possible, rather than creating separate images. Once the graphic has loaded, FileMaker will redraw it from memory each time instead of returning to the disk or the server. If you have a layout that won't print, be suspicious of any imported graphics on the layout.

Locking Objects on a Layout

There are times when you may want to lock objects on your layouts. For instance, you may have a set of background objects right where you want them, but you want to move a few items in the foreground. If you try to click and drag to surround them, the background object(s) will move instead. In that case, lock the background elements by selecting them and choosing Arrange, Lock. Then you can easily work with the items in the foreground.

If other people will have access to Layout mode in the files, you may have to lock objects to prevent them from being moved. That can be especially problematic with portals and the fields in them. If a field extends even one pixel out of the portal, you may not be able to see or create anything beyond the first portal row. (You could also group the portal and the fields in it so that if they get moved, they'll at least move together.) Most users don't want to deal with Layout mode, but in situations where there are problems, you have the tool to handle it, at least until they discover the Unlock command!

I've also had to protect fields from myself. Occasionally, I've created scripts that performed a Copy, Paste, Replace, or Insert step. All of those commands require that the chosen field be on the current layout. And there is no warning if FileMaker can't find the field it needs on the layout. I spent 32 hours one weekend tracking down a bug in a long string of scripts. In the end I found I had deleted the field referred to in the script. Seems I thought I didn't need that field on that layout. Now I lock fields referred to by scripts that might not otherwise seem essential to a layout.

⊃ **NOTE**   Find/Replace script steps also require that any field they operate on be on the layout. So any script that uses the Find/Replace step should include a step to choose the layout where you want the user.

⌘ **TIP**   Here's a way to hide a script-essential field that might not otherwise need to be on a layout.
1. Move it to one of the corners of the visible screen (upper left is a good choice) and turn off all four borders.
2. Then choose a font and field background color that matches the layout background.
3. Remove the field from the tab order, and uncheck the box next to "Allow entry into field" in the Field Format window.
4. Now choose View, Object Size.
5. If cm or in appears to the left of the boxes, click until you see px (for pixels).
6. Type .014 in both of the bottom boxes, pressing the Tab key between entries.
7. With the up and down arrows, move it farther into the corner, send it to the back, and lock the field.

The point here is to keep the field accessible to the script but not to a human. A script doesn't care what size or color the text in the field is; it can find it as long as it's somewhere on the layout.

Adding Graphics and Movies to a Layout

You can place graphics directly in the layout or into a Container field using one of a number of methods. When you're in Layout mode, use drag-and-drop, copy and paste, or Insert, Picture. When in Browse mode, you have the same choices with one exception. In order to choose Insert, Picture, you first have to click in the Container field. Then your choices are Insert, Picture, QuickTime, and Sound. On the Windows platform, your choices also include Object. (See Chapter 20 for information about importing a folder of files.) When the graphic or movie goes into a field, you'll then want to format it as described in the next section.

Formatting Graphics on a Layout

Remember back in Chapter 13 where I showed you how to use GetRepetition in a calculation to highlight a negative invoice amount with a red rectangle? There was a little problem in that the color didn't completely fill up the calculated field. This is where I show you how to fill the rectangle to the edges.

1. Go back to the Invoice table. Since the Color field we want to work with is underneath Invoice Total, let me show you a technique to work with it.

⌘ **TIP**   When layout objects are stacked or very near each other, you may need to move some objects so you can work on others. Select the objects that are in the way, and move them by pressing the appropriate arrow key 10 times. When you're done working on the other field or layout element, you'll always know the other items have to go back into place exactly 10 clicks.

2. Select the InvoiceTotal field and move it 10 clicks downward.

3. Now highlight the Color field, and choose **Format, Graphic**. This will bring up the window shown in Figure 16-4.

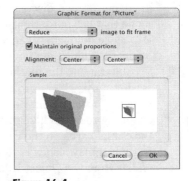

Figure 16-4
The Graphic Format window.

Part 4

Take a look at the choices in this window. As you make selections from the three pop-up lists, the Sample area gives you some idea of how they will affect your final image. With photographs and movies, you'll almost certainly want to choose the check box next to "Maintain original proportions." Otherwise, the images may appear unnaturally squashed or stretched. Since our purpose is for a simple patch of color, it may not be clear that these choices also apply to photos, movies, and objects placed in Container fields.

4. Choose **Enlarge** from the "Image to fit frame" pop-up.

5. Deselect the "Maintain original proportions" check box, and click **OK**.

6. Now select and move InvoiceTotal back up the layout — exactly 10 clicks.

7. Go to the record with the negative amount in it to see if it aligns the way you expect.

⊠ **CAUTION**   Be aware that images with lots of detail will cause the screen to redraw more slowly. If you have a fast machine, that may not be a problem. If the files are shared over a network, however, it could cause traffic to slow to a crawl. Most computer screens cannot display images with more than 72 dots per inch of detail anyway. If the images are absolutely necessary, it's better to use image-editing software to downsample the image before importing. You can also place the Container field that holds the image on a layout that will be referred to only when needed rather than one that comes into view constantly.

Customizing the Appearance of Objects on a Layout

As you develop your own style, you will want to make choices about how specific layout objects will look. Just remember, it takes time to do this work. If you're working on a project for yourself or a set of files that will be a commercial product, it's okay to labor over it. If someone else hired you, be sure they're willing to pay for some of the finer details. If you've quoted someone a price, you may end up absorbing the polish work yourself. Again, this is why the Layout Assistant is so valuable.

Adding Borders, Baselines, and Fills to Fields

Once you enter any of the fields in a form, you can see all the other fields outlined, but I find it disconcerting to look at an unentered screen in Browse mode that has borderless fields on it and not be able to tell where the fields are. Since field labels can logically be either to the side, above, or (less often) below the fields they identify, I prefer to make the borders visible.

You can use the method outlined in the section called "Group Formatting" earlier in this chapter to format one, a few, or all of the fields on your layout. Choose Format, Field Borders to open the Field Borders window. You can choose border and fill patterns in this window as well as add a text baseline. In the Sample area on the right, you can watch the effect of your choices. Afterward, you may also want to add Embossed, Engraved, and Drop Shadow effects from the Object Effects palette in the Status area. The Format Painter will work with all these attributes, including the object effects.

Adding Object Effects

Using the Object Effects palette (Figure 16-5) can really help give a finished look to your files. Of course, building your layouts with the Layout Assistant using themes will go a long way toward giving you a finished look with little effort.

As I mentioned before, some of the backgrounds in the template files are really buttons. However, they could just as easily be rectangles. In earlier versions of FileMaker Pro, you had to jump through hoops to get rectangles to have a 3D appearance, so buttons were often used instead. Now, providing depth to rectangles, ellipses, and fields is just a click away.

Embossed

To try out this effect:

1. Draw a button about 1 inch by 1 inch.
2. Now draw a rectangle with the same color and border width as the button, and use the Embossed effect. They should look identical.
3. While the rectangle is still selected, choose a wider border, say 3 point, just to see what it looks like.

Figure 16-5
FileMaker's Object Effects palette available in Layout mode.

Engraved

Using the Engraved effect gives the appearance that the layout object is etched into the surface. It's most effective against a background color other than white.

Select your rectangle, give it the Engraved effect, and then try some different point sizes for the border. Now try some different color combinations of border and fill.

Drop Shadow

Now choose Drop Shadow with a transparent border, but make the border 8 point. This gives you a nice floating rectangle effect. You don't get separate control over the color of the shadow. If you really need that much control, you can offset a stack of two rectangles like us old-timers used to do before FileMaker Pro 5.0! Then you can format each rectangle separately.

Changing Colors

We haven't talked much about the details of changing colors of layout objects. When you're in Layout mode and have an object selected, you've been selecting colors by using the Fill Color palette below the paint bucket in the Status area. Click the rainbow wheel below the bucket and scroll down to Other Color. On Windows, you can create your own custom color by clicking anywhere on the graduated color rectangle. You can also enter numbers directly in the Hue, Saturation, and Luminescence or Red, Green, and Blue fields. On Macintosh, you have five different tools for choosing colors. Three of the five

Part 4

tools have a number of additional options available from the pop-up list in each tool. If you're not happy with the standard color sets, this is where you make your own personal choices. Just remember, not everybody's computer will be able to display your favorite colors.

Summary

In this chapter, we talked about the overall appearance of files and the importance of simplicity and clarity of appearance and navigation. Then I showed you methods for working on individual and groups of layout objects so they can be formatted with a consistent appearance.

Q & A

Q What if I don't want to go beyond the layouts provided by the Layout Assistant?

A That shouldn't be a problem. Most of them look just fine, and anyone you work for will be happy that it takes you less time to do a job. However, some of the tools and shortcuts provided in this chapter can help you make requested changes very quickly once you've learned to use them.

Q What if I really want to go beyond the Layout Assistant? Where can I see more of what other people are doing?

A Look at other software programs first. See how they make navigation clear and understandable (or more confusing in many cases). Look at web pages that win awards for design and easy navigation. Go to the FileMaker web site and other sites listed at the back of this book, and download files created by other FileMaker professionals to see what work inspires you. If you develop a good eye, maybe you'll be the one to inspire other FileMaker users.

Workshop

Take the files we've been working on and try to find ways to tie them together with a similar appearance. Use the same fonts for field labels and in the fields themselves. Make the backgrounds the same color. If the layouts will print, make any backgrounds and buttons non-printing. Some developers strive to make a group of files feel as if they're one file. See if you can do that.

Review Questions

True-False

1. Buttons used on multiple screen layouts should be placed in the same location on each layout.
2. Variety in your layouts is good, because it will keep users awake.
3. Field labels can be rotated, but fields cannot be rotated.
4. Graphical objects can be placed directly on a layout in Layout mode or into a Container field in Browse mode.

5. On a screen layout, adding field borders and/or object effects can make it easier to see where the fields are.

Short Answer

6. How can you quickly select all of the field objects on a layout without selecting any other types of objects?

7. How can you quickly identify all of the objects on your layout that are set to slide or not print?

8. What effect does locking a field have on the ability to enter data into it in Browse mode?

9. How do you access the Graphic Format window?

10. Name the four effects available in the Object Effects palette.

11. Give at least one reason why you would want to lock objects on a layout.

12. If you're replacing an existing paper system, how can you determine what the data entry layouts should look like?

13. If you copy a group of background objects and buttons from one file for use in another file, what problem do you still have to deal with after everything is in place and sent to the back on the layout?

14. Name at least one way you can get a graphic into a Container field.

Part 4

Chapter 17

Designing Your Printed Report Layouts

Vocabulary

- Columnar report
- Detail information
- Extended columnar report
- Field behavior
- Find layout
- Summary information

Objectives

1. Understand what a report is.
2. Become familiar with what goes into a report in FileMaker Pro.
3. Learn to identify needs before designing a report.
4. Identify techniques to pull report data from other tables.
5. Explore report preparation layouts and processes.
6. Learn techniques to automate report processes.
7. Create a usable report.

Introduction

In earlier chapters, we created some basic reports. Now we'll do some real reporting. In this chapter, we'll look at:

- What a report is
- Two questions you need to answer before you start a report
- Two real-life reports we'll add to our file
- How to get to and from the reports with ease

What Is a Report?

Even though a single record can technically be a report, a report is usually thought of as a group of records and some summarized information about them. Whether the report is simply displayed on the screen or printed depends on how the data is to be used.

My concept of a report goes a bit further than how the data looks on the layout. It includes getting to and from the report in a way that makes it effortless to the user. If that process isn't well designed, the report will end up unused, and an unused report is not a report at all.

Creating a Useful and Attractive Report

You need to think about how the report will be organized so that users can find what they need without reading every single line. Summaries should be set apart visually, with lines, shading, or different type size or style, or all three. Section heads are just as important. When the reader finishes one area with a sub-summary, he or she should instantly know what the next section is about.

You can save time for your users by helping them get to the information they need more quickly. How many times have you looked for a piece of information in an advertisement or on a web page only to find it buried in some illogical place? Ask yourself: "What are the most important pieces of data?" and "How can I set them apart so they can be found quickly?"

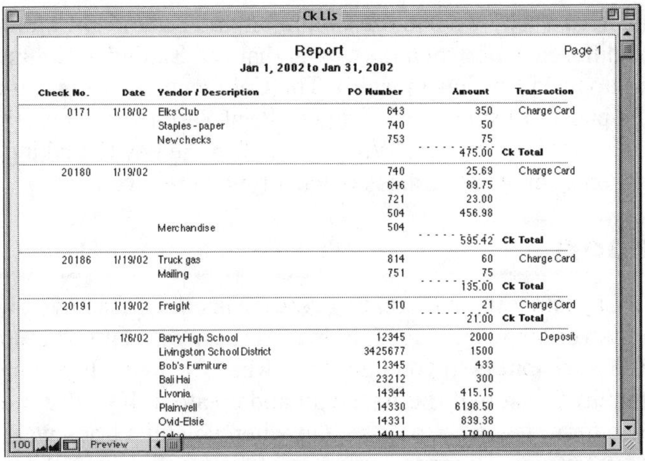

Figure 17-1
Rough draft of a checking account report. It's hard to tell where charge card entries end and deposits begin.

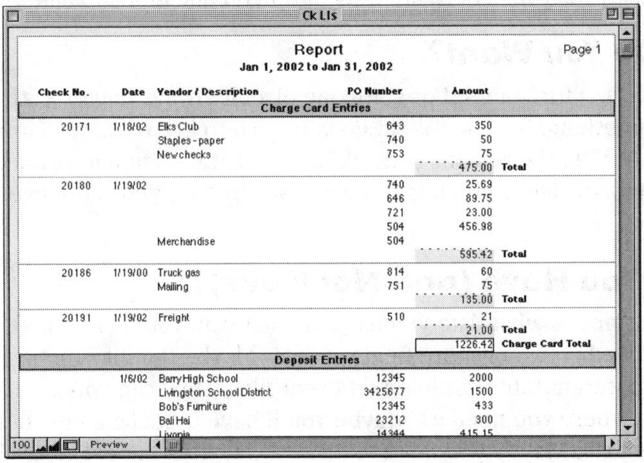

Figure 17-2
Finished checking account report with sections set apart for easier reading.

Part 4

Figures 17-1 and 17-2 show two versions of the same report. The first example is the rough draft. It's hard to read because you can't easily tell where charge card transactions leave off and deposits begin. By adding a Leading Sub-summaries part with shaded merged text as a divider, there's no longer any question where a new type of entry begins. In the second version, there is also a little shading around the totals, and there are borders around the section grand totals.

Report Types

A list of invoices or phone numbers can be a report. A printout of a customer's information layout can be a report. For that reason, the Standard Form or List View can be considered a report. At a school, someone may ask for a list of students whose grade point average has dropped to a D so they can meet for counseling. Putting together one of these reports is pretty straightforward. But even if that's all you'll be doing, in this chapter there are some techniques for getting to and from these reports that you will find very helpful.

Generally, reports include detail information along with some type of summary information. That's why we use the Columnar and Extended Columnar reports. The only difference between the two is that the Extended Columnar report can extend up to 111 inches in width. The Columnar report is confined to the width of the paper selected in the Page or Print Setup window at the time the report is created. Of course, "View as List" is the key to making multiple records show on a report regardless of what type of report it is.

Creating a Report

With FileMaker's Layout Assistant, creating reports is easier than ever, but you still need to answer some questions. In many cases, you can just stumble through and let the Assistant help you figure out what you need. If you find another field is required, just exit the Assistant and create it. If you're the type who just likes to go for it, feel free to do so, but when you hit a brick wall, I'll make recovery easy for you. There are only two main questions to ask.

What Results Do You Want?

Whether the report is for yourself or someone else, it always begins with a need to know something. So ask, "What do you need to know?" and "How do you want it to look?" Is there some precedent for what it should look like, such as a pre-existing form? Once you know the answer to that, you can move on to the next question.

What Data Do You Have (and Not Have)?

Yes, just as important as what data you have is what data you do not have. Often what you need is two or more fields of data. Maybe the information is available in two different tables or even different files. How can you get the data into one file where you need it? Maybe you'll have to make a new field and import some data. Maybe you need to make a Calculation field or a relationship to one or more tables or files.

Example Reports

The rest of this chapter will be spent creating two fairly typical reports. Many other reports can be made using the same concepts. The first one is necessarily lengthy, because it introduces all of the basic elements. The second report is less than half as long because we'll simply copy sections from the first. Understanding the copy and modify process is as important as creating the first report.

Customer Sales Report

Let's say we want to create a report to tell us how much each of our customers spends with us each year. That answers the question about what we want to know. We could pretty easily search our Invoice table using a date range, sort by ContactSerNum, and display a sub-summary, but let me save you the trouble. Since we're not using a true double-entry bookkeeping system, most of the invoices would show a balance of zero, because they'll be paid off.

So it appears that, once again, the report should be done in the "many" table of our one-to-many relationship; that means the InvLI table. The reason for this is that when we do our Find, we can omit any payment, discount, and interest item records. All that will be left is what the customer spent. That partly answers the question about what data we have, even though, as you'll see, we'll still need another field.

Setup — Making the Data Available

What's missing from the InvLI table is the customer data. At the end of Chapter 7, I said you needed the ContactSerNum in the InvLI table so you could use the contact information on the Invoice layout. Then I suggested you try it out in the Workshop. If you did that exercise and it worked, you should have a field called ContactSerNum that looks up from the Invoice. In that case, you may be interested in an alternative way of getting the information. If not, skip ahead to the next section. If you didn't do that Workshop, here's another way.

In the InvLI table, create a new Calculation field named ContactSerNum, with a numeric result:

```
ContactSerNum(Calculation) = Invoice::ContactSerNum
```

That's it! Now that we have the Contact data available, let's make the report.

Building the Report

1. Go to Layout mode, and choose **Layouts, New Layout/Report**.
2. Choose **InvLI** from the drop-down menu; name it **CustomerSalesReport**.
3. Choose **Columnar list/report** and click **Next**.
4. Click the radio button next to **Report with Grouped Data**.
5. Check both of the check boxes for **Include Sub Totals** and **Include Grand Totals**, and click **Next**.

6. Oddly enough, you really only need to choose one field at this point, so in the Specify Fields window, choose **Contact::Customer**. Be sure you use the Contact relationship to get the Customer field, then click Next.

7. In the Organize Records by Category window, double-click the **Contact::Customer** field to move it to the Report Categories list, and click **Next**.

8. Just click the **Next** button in the Sort Records window.

9. Click the **Specify** button under "Summary field" and choose **InvoiceTotal** from the Specify Field window. That's where we get the other piece of information we need. Click **OK**.

10. Then, from the Subtotal placement pop-up, choose **Above record group** and click the **Add Subtotal** button. When you're done, your screen should look like Figure 17-3. Click **Next**.

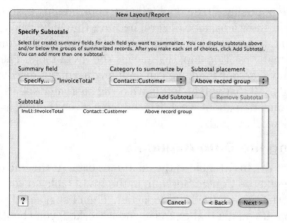

Figure 17-3
The Specify Subtotals window showing the settings in the pop-ups and InvoiceTotal in the Subtotals area.

11. At the Specify Grand Total screen, you could choose a Grand Total using the InvoiceTotal. It would tell you the total sales for all customers for the time period, but you don't need it. If you don't want it, just click the **Next** button.

12. Choose a theme you like, and click **Next**.

13. You are at the Header and Footer Information screen. From the "Top center" pop-up, choose **Large Custom Text**, type **Customer Sales Report**, and click **OK** and **Next**.

14. Choose the **Create a Script** radio button; if it's not filled in already, type **10 - Customer Sales Report**, and click **Next**.

15. At the You are finished! screen, select **View as Layout**.

16. Now click **Finish**.

17. Go into Layout mode, click on the Body label, and click **Delete**.

18. Now, go to Preview mode to look at your report.

Depending on the records that are in the current found set when you started building the report, the report may not look like the one in Figure 17-4. When I built it, it only had one record showing.

Touchup Work

Whenever I create a report this way I often get too much information. Don't let that worry you, though. It's considerably easier to remove information than it is to figure out what's missing. You'll find it's not too hard to make your reports look the way you want them to. You may want to change the fonts or some other part of the layout, but the information is usually all there. Figure 17-4 shows my final report. Don't worry about the dates shown in the Header part. I'll show you how to change that shortly.

Figure 17-4
Final version of Customer Sales Report listing just the customer and what they spent in the year.

How to Set Up a Find Layout

Now the report looks simple and clear, but how will we limit it to a specific date range? There's also a problem in that the amount shown reflects *all* transactions by each customer. That includes payments and various other such data with negative values. We only want to see their purchases, so we'll have to do a little more work here to omit the unwanted data.

1. Choose **Records, Show All Records**.
2. Choose the Customer Sales Report script to sort them properly.

You may have some customers showing zero or negative balances.

What I want to show you is a Find Setup layout I use for many of the reports for my clients. I use a pair of Global fields for start and end dates. That way, no matter what mode the users are in, they won't be touching any active data. Another advantage is that the script can take them to the layout in Browse mode and end without leaving the script paused. Paused scripts are too easy to unintentionally bypass while the user is still in Find mode, and there are a number of problems with that. Finally, if the search fails, you can bring the users back to the Find Setup layout. Their data request will still be in place so they can see what they asked for and make a minor edit if they need to. That's not so critical with a date range, but this system will also work should you decide to add other Global fields to filter the find for names, companies, and other specific data sets.

1. Create two Text fields (not Date fields) in the InvLI table called **zi_DateStart_gt** and **zi_DateEnd_gt**.
2. Go into the Options area under the Storage tab for each of the fields and check the **Use global storage** box. (Remember, the z will put these non-data fields at the end of the field list so they're easy to find when

Part 4

fields are sorted by name. The g indicates Global and the t stands for Text. You could also add a comment to remind yourself what the fields are for.)

3. Create a new blank layout using the Assistant, and call it **FindDateRange.**

4. Choose **InvLI** from the "Show records from" drop-down (although that's not strictly necessary). If you've been using a certain theme you may want to create a new standard form layout with the two Global fields on it. I usually delete the Header and Footer parts of the layout.

5. Add the text from Figure 17-5.

6. Drag the two new fields onto the layout.

7. Using the Invoice relationship, add **Invoice::Date** to the left side of the layout.

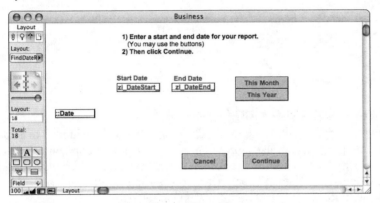

Figure 17-5
The FindDateRange layout showing the suggested position of text, buttons, and fields.

8. Now create the following scripts:
```
Script Name: 11 - Setup for Report
Enter Browse Mode [] (Navigation)
Go to Layout ["FindDateRange" (InvLI)] (Navigation)
Set Field [InvLI::zi_DateStart_gt; ""] (Fields)
Set Field [InvLI::zi_DateEnd_gt; ""]
Go to Field [InvLI::zi_DateStart_gt] (Navigation)
```

⊃ **Note** At the Set Field step, you'll first select the Specify target field button and then the calculated result Specify button. At the calculated result, type "" (two quotes right up against each other), which indicates that we will be emptying out the field. When you use quotation marks, you are indicating literal text or a text constant. In this case, we are indicating that there is no text.

Remember, when we give you script steps, we've identified the category in which you can find script steps in parentheses after the script step.
```
Script Name: 12 - Check for Complete Dates
If ["IsEmpty(InvLI::zi_DateStart_gt) or IsEmpty (InvLI::zi_DateEnd_gt)"]
(Control)
    Beep (Miscellaneous)
    Show Custom Dialog ["You must choose a Start AND End date."] (Control)
```

```
# Button 1 = OK (Comment  - Miscellaneous)
   Halt Script (Control)
End If
```

Script Name: 13 - If None Found
```
If ["Get(FoundCount) = 0"] (Control)
   Beep (Miscellaneous)
   Show Custom Dialog ["None Found. Want to try again?"] (Miscellaneous)
   # Button 1 = OK / Button 2 = Cancel (Comment  - Miscellaneous)
   If [ Get(LastMessageChoice) = 2]  (Control)
      Perform Script ["1 — Main Menu (Halt)"] (Control)
   Else
      Halt Script
   End If
End If
```

Now you can see why we placed a Halt Script step at the end of the Main Menu script back in Chapter 14. Without it, should the user choose button #2, he would end up right back here on the FindDateRange layout.

This next script uses a number of things we learned elsewhere in the book. It looks complex, and it is — if you look at it as a whole. But again, it can be broken down into simpler parts by asking these questions — "Where am I now?" and "Where do I want to be when I finish?" — and then writing it out in plain English. Some of the work is handled by subscripts.

The most complicated part is the Insert Calculated Result step. Make sure your step looks exactly like mine when you're in the Edit Script window — except yours won't spill down onto the next line. When you are creating this script step, make sure you select the Specify button next to Calculated result in the Script Step Options.

The second part that could be confusing is that after we complete the find for the items with the dates we want, we turn around and constrain the found set by omitting items we don't want. Looking at the script, you can't tell what those items are or even that they're items to be omitted without double-clicking the Constrain step.

And third, we have to use the If None Found subscript twice in this script because we essentially perform two different finds, each of which could result in records not being found. So let's give it a go.

Script Name: 14 - Continue Report
```
Perform Script ["12 — Check for Complete  Dates"] (Control)
Set Error Capture [On] (Control)
Enter Find Mode [] (Navigation)
Insert Calculated Result [Select; InvLI::zi_DateStart_gt & "..." &
InvLI::zi_DateEnd_gt]  (Fields)
Perform Find[] (Found Sets)
Perform Script ["13 — If None Found"] (Control)
Constrain Found Set [] (Found Sets)
Perform Script ["13 — If None Found"] (Control)
Go to Layout ["Customer Sales Report" (InvLI)] (Navigation)
# Sorted by Contact:: Customer (Comment — Miscellaneous)
```

```
Sort Records [Restore, No dialog] (Found Sets)
Enter Preview Mode [Pause] (Navigation)
Enter Browse Mode (Navigation)
```

The reason Set Error Capture is set to On is because FileMaker's default error messages can be confusing. We'll provide more meaningful error messages.

Now we need to touch it up a little.

9. Go back to the Constrain Found Set step and click the **Specify** button. If there are any Actions already in this window, click on them and delete them until the window is empty.

10. Click the **New** button.

11. In the Action drop-down, choose **Omit Records**.

12. In the "Omit records when" drop-down, be sure you are looking at fields from the InvLI table and choose the **Description** field.

13. In the Criteria area, type **==Payment** (see Figure 17-6).

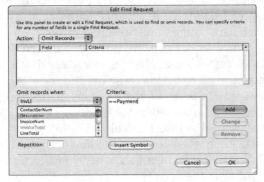

Figure 17-6
The Edit Find Request window.

14. Click the **Add** button and **OK**. Don't leave the Specify Find Requests window just yet.

15. Click the **Duplicate** button and the **Edit** button.

16. Highlight the Action listed there. That will allow you to change Payment to **Discount**.

17. Click the **Change** button and then **OK**.

18. Repeat steps 15 through 17 two more times, substituting the words **Refund** and **Interest** where Payment or Discount is.

19. When you're done, the window should look like Figure 17-7. Click **OK**.

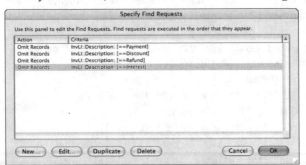

Figure 17-7
The details of the Specify Find Requests window showing the items to be omitted.

20. Now the Constrain Found Set should have "Restore" in brackets after it.

⊠ **CAUTION**   During data entry you'll have to make sure that the exact words for Payment, Discount, Refund, and Interest are used. A misspelling will cause the item to be included in the report. You may want to take care of that in the Invoice table by using a pop-up that includes those specific items. It will only be used when someone clicks in the Description field. It won't be disruptive to data entry since all product descriptions are entered by a lookup when the ProdID is chosen. You might even choose to create product codes for Payment, Discount, Refund, and Interest and prevent entry into the Description field altogether.

Did you notice the Comment step that told you what the sort should be? You have to select the Sort step and then click the Specify button to make sure you have the right sort.

I used the == in the Constrain step because it is possible that a product description field could contain one of the words we want to omit. By insisting that the field contents have the exact word and nothing but that word in each case, we avoid problems.

Whew! Imagine if all that were in one script — which you could do if you wanted. And remember, once you make these scripts, you'll be able to import them into other files in the future. This is a report I use for nearly all my clients, in one form or another, although not necessarily with the Constrain step.

⌘ **TIP**   If a report that contains sub-summaries doesn't look right, be suspicious of the sort. Check the Sub-summary layout part tab information against the actual sort that occurs after performing the script. If they don't match, you've found the culprit. To fix it, go into the script, double-click the Sort Records step, and click the Specify button. Set up the proper sort criteria, click OK to save the sort order, then OK to save the script.

A second possible problem could be the position of the Sub-summary field(s) in the layout part. If the top of the field is parallel to the part line, try moving it one click lower.

Notice the Set Error Capture step. That prevents FileMaker from displaying its own error message. Instead, the user will see the message we made in the If None Found script.

⊃ **NOTE**   Once you choose Set Error Capture [On], there are other possible errors that could occur during the execution of the script. I have had good luck with the script as it is, but if the possibility of other errors concerns you, add the following script steps:

```
If [Get(LastError)<>0 and Get(LastError)<>401]
    Beep
    Show Message ["An unknown error occurred"]
    Halt Script
End If
```

The Get(Last Error) step must appear immediately after the step that would generate the error. In the case of Script 14 - Continue Report, we already have a step that would do this for us. Notice that it comes right after the Perform Find step.

21. Now, to make data entry easier, add these date range scripts:

Part 4

Script Name: 15 - This Month
Set Field [InvLI::zi_DateStart_gt; Date(Month(Get(CurrentDate)), 1,
Year(Get(CurrentDate)))] (Fields)
Set Field [InvLI::zi_DateEnd_gt ; "Date(Month(Get(CurrentDate)) + 1; 1;
Year(Get(CurrentDate))) - 1]

Script Name: 16 - This Year
Set Field [InvLI::zi_DateStart_gt; Date(1; 1; Year(Get(CurrentDate)))]
Set Field [InvLI::zi_DateEnd_gt; Date(12; 31; Year(Get(CurrentDate)))]

22. Add the four buttons shown in Figure 17-5 to the layout, and attach them to the appropriate scripts. The Cancel button should be connected to the Main Menu script.

23. Finally, you need to protect the Invoice::Date field so nothing gets changed there accidentally. Remember, there's live data in that field.

   ■ Assuming you have a white background, format the field with white text, no borders, and no background. For any other color background, choose colors to match.

   ■ Use the Format Field Behavior window to turn off "Allow entry into field" in Browse mode. Leave the "In Find mode" box unchecked.

   ■ Remove the field from the tab order.

   ■ Lock it so it doesn't get removed from the layout accidentally. Refer back to Chapter 16 in the "Locking Objects on a Layout" section for how to make the field a 1 x 1 pixel square.

⌘ **TIP**   Interestingly, scripts can enter data into fields that are otherwise locked up tight from manual entry. That is not the case if the fields are locked from that user with passwords.

24. You may want to add a button to the Customer Sales Report layout to take you to the Main Menu since there's no navigation on that layout once you return to Browse mode. If you'll be printing this report, make a script for that with the settings you need and add a Print button.

25. Now go to the Main Menu layout and add a button to take you to the Customer Sales Report. See how this works?

26. One other thing I like to do is add the date range to the report just under the title like I did in Figure 17-4. I use Merge fields that pull the data from InvLI::zi_DateStart_gt and InvLI::zi_DateEnd_gt.

In reality, you may prefer to sort by Contact Last Name, but be cautious. The sort will place all people with the same last name in the same sub-summary! You'll be better off making a concatenated field. I'll leave it up to you to figure it out. Just remember you'll have to change your Sub-summary part(s) and the script to match.

Percent of Sales by Product Report

Let's look at another report where you want to know what percent of the total sales each item in the product line is earning. Using the information in this report, you can make decisions such as whether a product is overpriced, falling out of favor with your buyers, or just not being promoted properly.

Start by looking at what data we have and don't have. In the InvLI table, we have a ProdID, a Description, and a dollar amount as our LineTotal. What we don't have is the percentage of total sales. We can get sub-summaries of the LineTotal when sorting by ProdID, but we can't do a calculation from that. However, if we use the GetSummary function, we can use that in a calculation. To accomplish that, we'll need two new fields:

Field Name	Type	Options
GetSumProdAmount	Calculation	GetSummary(SumLineTotal,;ProdID)
PercentSalesAmount	Calculation	Round(GetSumProdAmount/SumLineTotal, 2)

Building the Report

1. Start a new layout called **Percent_Sales_by_ProdID**, use **InvLI** from the "Show records from" drop-down, choose **Columnar list/report**, and click **Next**.
2. Click the **Report with Grouped Data** radio button, check both the **Include Sub Totals** and **Include Grand Totals** boxes, and click **Next**.
3. Move the following fields to the Layout fields column on the right:
   ProdID
   Description
   PercentSalesAmount

   You don't need the SumLineTotal because we'll pick that up in the Sub-summary. Click **Next**.
4. Double-click the **ProdID** field to move it to the Report Categories list, and click **Next**.
5. In the Sort Records window just click the **Next** button.
6. Click the **Specify** button under Summary field and choose **SumLineTotal**.
7. Then from the Subtotal placement pop-up, choose **Below record group**.
8. Click the **Add Subtotal** button, and click **Next**.
9. You could choose a Grand Total using the SumLineTotal. It would tell you the total sales for the time period, but you don't need it. If you don't want it, just click the **Next** button.
10. Choose a theme that fits your overall plan, and click **Next**.
11. Choose **Large Custom Text** from the "Top center" pop-up, type **Percent Sales by Product ID**, and click **OK** and **Next**.
12. Choose the **Create a Script** radio button and, if you need to, enter **17 - Percent Sales by ProdID** but it should already be in there. Click **Next**.
13. Select **View in Layout Mode**.

Part 4

14. Finally, click **Finish**.

Touchup Work

15. Move both Description and PercentSalesAmount into the lower Sub-summary part.

16. Now delete the Body and upper Sub-summary parts.

17. When you go back to Preview mode, you should only see one line per ProdID. If you don't see those results, choose **Records**, **Show All Records**, **Sort by ProdID**, then go back to Preview mode. Your report won't look like mine. I did a lot of reformatting of my layout, and you won't have the date range that appears under the title in Figure 17-8. We'll be creating a script to do that shortly.

18. Take a look at Figure 17-8 and see how your report compares to mine. Another year like 2002 and we might consider dropping Small Widgets from our product line.

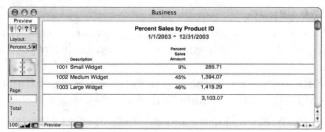

Figure 17-8
Percent Sales by ProdID report in Browse mode.

How to Set Up This Find Layout

We did most of the work to create this Find layout when we made the Customer Sales Report. All we have to do is duplicate some layouts and scripts, make a few changes, and attach everything to the right buttons. Let's go!

1. Go to the Find Date Range layout and duplicate it. Choose **Layouts**, **Layout Setup** and name it **Find_Products_Date_Range**.

2. Go to ScriptMaker, duplicate the 11 - Setup for Report script, pull it to the bottom of the Scripts list, and rename it **18 - Setup for Products Report**. The only script step you need to change is the one that tells which layout to go to. Select **Find_Product_Date_Range**.

3. Duplicate the 14 - Continue Report script, move it to the bottom of the Scripts list, and rename it **19 - Continue Product Report**. Near the end of the list of script steps you'll see the Go to Layout step. Reattach that to our Percent_Sales_by_ProdID layout, so it looks like this:

   `Go to Layout ["Percent_Sales_by_ProdID" (InvLI)]`

4. Change the Comment step so it reads:

   `# Sorted by ProdID (Comment  - Miscellaneous)`

5. Double-click the Sort Records step, clear the Sort Order and replace it with **ProdID**. Click **OK, OK**, and **OK**.

6. Add the following script step to the end of 19 - Continue Product Report:

   `Enter Browse Mode []`

7. Go to Layout mode on the Find_Products_Date_Range Report layout, and double-click the **Continue** button. Attach it to the 19 - Continue Product Report script.

8. Go back to the Main Menu, add a button (or copy one of the existing buttons to maintain the same formatting) and attach it to 18 - Setup for Products Report.

9. Finally, use Merge fields to add the date range to the report just under the title using zi_DateStart_gt and zi_DateEnd_gt.

Of course, you will probably want to put a Main Menu and a Print button on the report layout. However, be aware that once you're back in Browse mode, you won't be able to see the report (which only shows up in Preview mode). So, you'll have to instruct them that the Print button will work anyway.

Create a generic Print script and use it here.

Now run the report for various date ranges. Use the Main Menu to start the report over again. Yes, it was a lot of work, but somebody's gonna be very happy these reports are so fast and easy to run.

Other Common Reports

Other reports you might be interested in would be Sales by Salesperson and Overdue Invoices. Of course, we don't have salespeople in our file, but they could certainly be added fairly easily — probably in the Invoice table.

Avoiding the Today Function in Calculations

An Overdue Invoices report tells which invoices still have a balance due after 30, 60, and 90 days. A lot of people working with FileMaker Pro in the past have used the Today function in a Calculation field to build this report. Their file has a field that calculates Today and subtracts 30 (or 60 or 90) from it. In FileMaker 7 the Today function has been replaced with Get(CurrentDate), although files converted from previous versions will calculate correctly using the old Today function. Not only that, but you can still type in the word Today anyplace a function would appear and it will work, even though it is no longer in the list of functions in the upper-right corner of the Calculation window.

I'll do almost anything to keep from using the Today function in a Calculation field because every record must be recalculated whenever the file opens if the field indexing is stored. You can't trick the Today function by leaving the file open either. After midnight, any calculation using it won't update until the file is closed and reopened. In tables with lots of records, this can be agonizing, especially after a computer crash where the file has to go through a checking process first. Let me add that I have used the Today function in scripts quite often, since this has nothing to do with what happens when the file opens.

Using the Today function in a Calculation field is especially problematic with FileMaker Server, since the files are sometimes open continuously (on the server). That means the files have to be closed and opened at least once a day or the Today function won't get recalculated. If you only closed and backed up the files on your server once a week (on Sunday morning, for example), then your Today function would be updated only once a week, and then only if the files were closed, not just paused.

There are a number of strategies used by FileMaker professionals to avoid the Today function in a calculation. The one I prefer for this report is to base the calculation on a Global Date field. The disadvantage of using a field stored globally is that it cannot be indexed. That means that finds performed on the field will be slower, and the field can only be used on the "master" side in relationships. But it's still worth doing if the report will not be run on a daily basis. Regardless, it's nice to know that the Today function will soon be a thing of the past.

⮕ **NOTE**   The only way to identify "related" records is if they're indexed. The "master" record/table/field is the current record/table/field of context (i.e., where you are). The "related" field must be indexed in order to ensure expected behavior through the relationship.

1. Create the Date field in the Invoice table and call it **zi_Date_gd**. Click the Storage tab and check the box next to **Use global storage.**

2. Make a Calculation field called **Overdue** with a Text result:

    `Table: Invoice`
    `Field Name: Overdue`
    ```
    Case(Date < zi_Date_gd - 90, "Over 90",
    Date < zi_Date_gd - 60, "Over 60",
    Date < zi_Date_gd - 30, "Over 30", "")
    ```

    You can make a script that finds all invoices with a balance due and fills in the zi_Date_gd field with today's date.

3. Finally, sort the records by the Overdue field. Now you have a current report, and your file will open quickly.

There are two other common ways to bypass using the Today function in a calculation:

■ Use Get(CurrentDate) wherever you would use Today and leave the field unstored (Storage Options in the Field Definition area). This has the same problems as a Global Date field, but the advantage is that you don't have to make sure the Global Date field is populated with the right date value. FileMaker will take care of it.

■ Use a Date field (*not* specifying Global storage) on the layout, and run a Replace script step on it just before the field is needed so that it has the most recent date in it. This method is probably the worst in terms of making sure that the field has today's date in it, and you get a performance hit when running a script that needs it. However, it can be invaluable when you are dealing with a small found set or in a case where you absolutely must be able to index the field for finds or building relationships. (Remember, you will have a small found set if you first find all invoices with a balance due.)

Summary

Am I wrong, or is your file starting to look and act like something almost professional? In this chapter we looked at reports in detail, and created two reports in our file that can be used as is or as templates for other types of reports. We also went quite a bit further by adding buttons that create the reports automatically right from the Main Menu.

Q & A

Q When we made the scripts for the Find Date Range layout, why couldn't we use the Set Field step instead of Insert Calculation? Then we wouldn't need the Invoice::Date field on the layout and have to protect it.

A Try it. For some reason, Set Field doesn't work with date ranges. Instead, you have to be on a layout that has a copy of the field and use one of the script steps, like Insert or Paste, that actually touches the field.

Q You say that the Layout Assistant often gives you information you don't need. How am I going to know what to keep and what to throw away?

A Remember, you usually get too much information. When you start a report, you have a pretty good idea of what data you're looking for. Preview the report and remove what doesn't belong. Just be sure to perform a find on different sets of data to preview so you'll be able to test your expectations.

Workshop

Using the steps that you used to build your other reports (scripts, layouts, and any required fields) as a template, make a report for total quantity sales by ProdID. Hint: You'll need a Summary field.

Test your calculation skills. Copy the This Month and This Year scripts, and change them so they fill in the dates for last month and last year. This is really a troubleshooting exercise. I didn't figure these out on the first try. You just keep trying things that sound logical until you get it. If you give up, look at the following scripts:

Hey, you shouldn't give up so quickly!

Script Name: Last Month
```
Set Field [InvLI::zi_DateStart_gt; Date(Month(Get(CurrentDate)) -1; 1;
Year(Get(CurrentDate)))]
Set Field [InvLI::zi_DateEnd_gt; Date(Month(Get(CurrentDate)) ;1;
Year(Get(CurrentDate))) -1]
```

Script Name: Last Year
```
Set Field [InvLI::zi_DateStart_gt; Date(1; 1; Year(Get(CurrentDate)) -1)]
Set Field [InvLI::zi_DateEnd_gt; Date(12, 31, Year(Get(CurrentDate)) -1)]
```

Now add the buttons to the layout.

Part 4

Review Questions

True-False

1. A report generally represents a group of records and includes some summarized information about them.

2. Once you've created a report layout, you've done everything you can do to create a useful FileMaker report.

3. When you create a report in a file, you're limited to only the fields in that table.

4. The most useful FileMaker Pro reports involve scripts to direct the process for the user.

5. Choosing the Create a Script radio button when you use the Layout Assistant provides a basic script for the report, into which you can add other script steps to enhance the report process.

Short Answer

6. What are two important questions to answer before you create a new report in FileMaker?

7. Why might you want to include a Find layout as part of your report process?

8. How can the Beep and Show Message script steps aid the report running process for the user?

9. What's the purpose of the Set Error Capture [On] script step?

10. What does the Halt Script step do, and why is it important in a complex report script?

11. Is a printout of a customer's invoice a report?

12. If a report doesn't look right, name one thing you should check for.

Part 5

Sharing
Your
Database

Chapter 18

Personal Data Sharing

Vocabulary

- File sharing
- Firewall
- Guest
- Hidden file

- Host
- Network protocol
- Remote host
- TCP/IP

Objectives

1. Discover various ways to share FileMaker Pro databases.
2. Understand the Define File Reference option.
3. Learn the limits and special behaviors of shared files.
4. Learn about security concerns when sharing database files.
5. Discover tips for optimizing performance of shared databases.

Introduction

Databases become more valuable when you can share them over a network, especially in an office environment. Different users have access to the same information, and many people can be involved in data entry. FileMaker Pro allows both Macintosh and Windows users to transparently share the same database files on the same network at the same time. As more people are working away from the office, the fact that FileMaker can share files remotely by way of a modem and the Internet makes it all the more valuable.

The information in this chapter may not apply to everyone. It's mostly instructional and we won't be adding any functionality to our files. If your files will not be used on a network, this will only serve as a reference for when that day arrives.

In this chapter, we'll look at:

- How to share FileMaker files using built-in sharing capabilities
- The network requirements for sharing
- How to optimize sharing performance
- The capabilities and limitations of personal file sharing

What Is Personal Data Sharing?

There are a number of techniques for sharing data in FileMaker files:

- You can use a special product called FileMaker Server.
- You can share data from your files by way of an intranet or the Internet using a browser and FileMaker's Instant Web Publishing capabilities.
- You can just share the files on a network by turning on FileMaker's Sharing option.

We'll look at sharing data using a browser in Chapter 19, "Sharing Your Data on the Web." To share a large number of files with many users, you'll need FileMaker Server. For sharing files through a browser with more than a few users, you'll need FileMaker Server Advanced. However, the discussion in this chapter will deal specifically with the standard FileMaker Pro program.

Capabilities

FileMaker's sharing is independent from other types of file sharing. Of course, if the network is down, you won't be able to share FileMaker files. You do not need to see the icon of the network hard drive of the computer that contains the files you want to share on your desktop in order to use remote FileMaker files. Nor do you need to have file-level access to the files. No one has to set up any file sharing of any kind other than FileMaker's own Multi-User mode. If you are accessing the Internet through a modem, you can share files that are open on another machine connected to the Internet. You can even open shared files remotely through a dial-up modem by dialing directly to another computer. In order to make that work, you'll need to use a product like PCAnywhere, Timbuktu, or Apple Remote Desktop (all of which can be used much more efficiently via a fast Internet connection). FileMaker does not actually dial up the other computer. But once you've established the connection by other means, you can share your files. Otherwise, FileMaker is pretty flexible about communicating over whatever networks are available.

As long as you are on a network and your account privileges allow, as a host or a guest, you can:

- View, edit, sort, and print records
- Change modes, layouts, and views
- Import and export records
- Perform scripts
- Edit value lists

Network Requirements

Previous versions of FileMaker allowed file sharing using up to three different network protocols. Starting with FileMaker 7, all sharing is done via TCP/IP, the language of the Internet as well as many other networks. That simplifies sharing, because if two computers were set to different protocols, they couldn't see each other across the network.

○ **NOTE** The network protocols are simply the languages used by the computers to talk with each other.

You'll want to set up the machines so that the various copies of the FileMaker program on the network will be able to speak with each other. You do this by choosing Edit (Windows) or FileMaker Pro (Macintosh), then Sharing, FileMaker Network. Then simply click the radio button next to On. You have to do this for all machines that will be hosting files across the network. Just to be clear, it won't be necessary to do this with copies of FileMaker on machines that want to have access to the files being hosted on other machines — only on machines that want to say, "Hello, I have files to share with everyone."

In Figure 18-1 you can see a screen shot of the FileMaker Network Settings window.

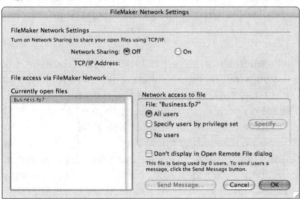

Figure 18-1
The FileMaker Network Settings window showing network sharing via TCP/IP currently turned off.

Using Personal File Sharing

Making your files available to other FileMaker users on your network is almost as easy as clicking a button. Of course, the network must be set up properly, FileMaker's own networking support software must be installed, and the files you want to share must be open. But all you need to do is choose Edit (Windows) or FileMaker Pro (Mac), then Sharing, FileMaker Network, select the files from the list of currently open files, and click the All users button. You can choose more details by selecting one file at a time and selecting "Specify users by privilege set." Figure 18-1 shows Business.fp7 to be the only currently open file.

Here are a few more items to be attentive to:

■ Files must be compatible with the FMP7 format. Files created in earlier versions of FileMaker must be converted first.

■ If you have a client outside your LAN firewall, the network administrator must remove blocking from TCP port 5003.

■ Windows users must be sure only one network adapter is installed for the protocol being used. If more than one network card is installed, FMP broadcasts only from the card with ID 0 (zero).

■ On a Mac, the FMP app must remain in the FMP folder and the TCP/IP OT Network file must be properly installed.

The check box next to "Don't display in Open Remote File dialog" is used for files that are not meant to be seen as hosted files. You can select multiple open files and check this box to affect them all at once.

Why would you want to have any files effectively invisible on the network?

If you create a solution that consists of a group of files, you may want one file to open and control when and how the other files open. Set up the control file without checking that box and set the other files as Don't display. All the hidden files will be called as needed by relationships, value lists, and scripts.

In a network environment with shared FileMaker files, you can be either a host of a file or a guest. The host is the first person to open a file. Anybody else who wants to use the file will be a guest. The details for how to do that are in the following section. Of course, you can still have files open on your computer that are not shared.

There is another situation in which a user can become a remote host. To become a remote host, you must have access to the files on the hard drive of another machine. Double-clicking on the icon of one of these files will bring up a warning that you are about to become the host of a file on another machine. Opening files this way works, but it can really slow down the network. See the section on optimizing performance later in this chapter. Remote hosting can also make recovery more precarious in the case of a crash. For all of these reasons, you should think of remote hosting as useful in temporary or emergency circumstances, but as a general practice, I would strongly discourage it.

Using Files as a Guest

Once files are open on a host machine, guests can access the files. Guests must be hooked up to the same network and be running FileMaker with network sharing set to on. Then, to become a guest:

1. Choose **File, Open**. (If you choose File, Open Remote you can skip to step 3.)

2. When the File window appears, click the **Remote** button.

3. After a few seconds, you'll be able to see a list of all the open (non-hidden), shared FileMaker files. Of course, you'll need to know the name of the file you're supposed to open.

4. Just open it as you would any other file. If you can't see any files and you've checked all

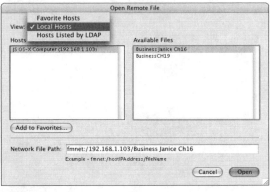

Figure 18-2
The Open Remote File window showing the available host(s) and files.

other settings, see the Tip in Chapter 19 in the section titled "If You Have an Internet Account."

With the exception of the limitations of shared files, working in the files is the same as working with a file on your own machine.

➲ **NOTE**   You can open a file using the Open File script step. Notice in Figure 18-3 that the Specify pop-up list includes choices to add and define file references. Figure 18-4 shows the Edit File Reference window. This window allows you to define multiple paths to a file in case one copy of the file is unavailable. Previous to FileMaker Pro 7, FileMaker would search the entire network for a file. This was time consuming, slowed down the network, and sometimes opened files with the same name that were not intended to be opened. Generally, you'll be looking for a specific file along one path in this window. You have access to this window from the Import Records, Open, Close, or Recover script steps as well as when you choose a relationship or a value list from another file.

You can still run into trouble if you have multiple files on the same volume with the same name. (See the Caution about renaming older versions of your files in the section titled "Create the Relationships" in Chapter 7.) Be aware that the reverse could also be a problem if a set of files is moved to a different server. The biggest advantage of the new Define File References area is that when FileMaker has finished searching the specific area, it stops, thereby speeding up the search and preventing accidents with unintended files.

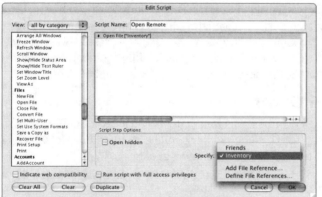

Figure 18-3
The Open File script step and the Specify pop-up list.

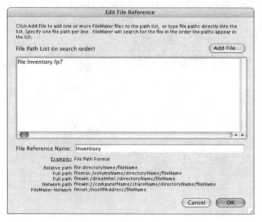

Figure 18-4
The Edit File Reference window showing a single path to the Inventory file.

Sharing Remotely by Way of Modem

You can also share files across the Internet. There are two ways to access files: by way of a modem or with another TCP Internet connection. If you have permission to open other files on the remote hard drive, and you know how to log on with a modem, you can mount the drive using TCP. Then, as long as no one else has the file open, you can simply double-click the icons that appear on your desktop.

The other way of sharing files is to use FileMaker's own sharing capabilities. For that to work, the host file has to be open with FileMaker network sharing set to on, on a computer connected to the Internet. Once you establish a connection to the Internet with your modem or other network, bring FileMaker to the front and choose Open Remote from the File menu, just as in the last section. You should see the window shown in Figure 18-2.

Unless you're on the same subnet, you have to know the IP address or the URL for the machine you're trying to connect to, but all you have to do is type it in. If you click the Add to Favorites button you'll be able to click on the name or number in the list under Hosts next time you want to go there. As soon as you click on a host in the list on the left, you'll see a list of all the open, shared files on that computer in the list on the right. Of course, you'll be limited by the speed of your modem and the phone or cable lines, but it works just fine. And when you think about it, it's pretty darn amazing!

File Sharing Caution

You should be aware that anyone else on the Internet who has the host name or IP address can open the files, too. That's why it's important to institute some sort of password protection when sharing files in that environment. Another choice is to have your network administrator put a firewall between your local machines and the outside world. As more home users are establishing permanent connections to the Internet via cable modem, this is becoming a critical issue. If that is your situation, you won't have a network administrator. That means it'll be up to you to protect your files. I'll talk more about that in Chapter 21, "Keeping Your Data Secure."

It might not seem like there'd be much of a chance of someone guessing one particular IP address. But I had only begun experimenting with this technique when I transposed the numbers of a friend's IP address. I found a database of student grades on a server at a school in New Hampshire. The file was not password protected, and I discovered I could actually change the grades! If someone a little more warped or mischievous than me (not to mention a disgruntled student) were to have gotten to those files... well, just make sure you protect any files that you share on the Internet.

This warning doesn't only apply to machines with a permanent connection to the Internet. If you don't have a permanent IP address, your provider assigns you a temporary address every time you dial up the Internet. That's so that when you make a request to view a web page, the other machine knows how to find you with the results of your request. Any FileMaker files you have open and shared on your computer are vulnerable during the time you're online. It's a little creepy when you think about it. You can always Quit or Exit

FileMaker before going online. But you can also password protect your files or just leave them set to "No users."

Now that I've sufficiently scared you, let me show you a script you can run before going online:

```
Script Name: Multi-User Off
Set Multi-User [Off] (Files catetory)
```

That script's not too hard, eh? It effectively turns FileMaker Network Sharing off. You can put that script in the files you use most often, and then create a single script in one of your favorite files that runs all the external scripts. Then you'll want to make another script for turning multi-user back on. Nevertheless, I really think that password protection is your best defense.

Limitations

Although personal file sharing is a valuable tool, there are some limitations. Two people cannot edit the same record, but one person can edit a record while another person views it. If a record is included in a report and someone edits it, the report won't reflect the change until the report is called up again. In versions of FileMaker prior to 7, while the files were being shared, neither the host nor the guest could define fields, change the order of layouts, or open the Access Privileges window. All that has changed with FMP7, increasing the power to developers a great deal. Guests of a file still cannot use the Save a Copy As command, but the host of the file can.

File and Guest Limits

There are some limits to FileMaker's standard, built-in file sharing. You may host up to five guests at the same time. If your needs are greater than that, it's time to get a copy of FileMaker Server, which is optimized for sharing large numbers of files with a limited group of workers, or FileMaker Server Advanced, which can share files with large groups of workers.

Global Fields and Shared Files

Here's a seemingly unrelated item that actually turns out to be pretty important. The values in fields formatted as Global are local. The values users see when they first open a file are those stored in fields formatted as Global on the server (keeping in mind that some opening scripts may alter those values). When I say that the values are local, it means that when a guest opens a file hosted on another machine, any changes that occur to values in Global fields do not travel back to the host file. I had quite a few surprises in my first major design using Global fields on a network, because I thought data was being saved in the host file when it was actually being dumped.

Even changes to Global fields in the host file do not travel out to the guests until they sign off and back on. As long as you understand that, there are some marvelous things you can do with Global fields that take advantage of this "limitation." You'll just have to work out some other arrangement for moving values to other machines on the network.

Optimizing Performance

There are a number of things you can do to get the best performance out of a network with shared FileMaker files. First, use the fastest machine possible to host the files (see the next section, "Hardware Considerations"). Next, make sure any other network software issues are resolved. If there are intermittent problems, check that all connectors are tightly seated between wires, computers, and hubs. Sometimes worn or poor quality wiring can be the cause of the trouble. I have a client who tried to save money by having a "friend" install some wiring for him. After his files crashed numerous times, he realized the $100 he saved on wiring had cost him nearly $1000 in data recovery.

As I mentioned before, if you have access to the files on the hard drives of other computers, you can open and host FileMaker files remotely. The problem with this arrangement is that when anyone else signs on as a guest, all the requests have to travel down the network through the remote host machine, back to the computer where the files are actually stored, back through the remote host machine, and back to the guest. This effectively doubles the network traffic, not to mention that it slows down the machine that is doing the remote hosting. Figure 18-5 illustrates the inefficiency of this arrangement. (More arrows means more traffic. More traffic means slower speeds.) Avoid remote hosting whenever possible. It's better to go to the computer with the stored files and open them so they can be hosted there.

Processing large reports can also slow down a network, especially if print jobs with complex graphics are traveling down the same lines. Try to work out such activities so they take place when there is low network traffic.

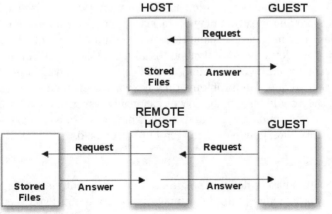

Figure 18-5
Diagram showing how remote hosting of files doubles the network traffic.

Hardware Considerations

The best way to share files, short of using FileMaker Server (see the next section), is to devote a machine to the FileMaker files. The computer should only be running FileMaker Pro, and no one should be running other programs on it. Additionally, the faster the machine, the better the response for all users. It can often be hard to convince the staff that the fastest computer should be

Part 5

devoted to FileMaker. Everyone wants the newest, fastest machine on his or her own desk. Almost every office I've been to that shares FileMaker files has relegated their oldest machine to be the server. Then they complain about how pokey FileMaker is, but it's not FileMaker's fault. A trip to the grocery store in a Model-T is pretty slow, too, even if the driver is an Indy 500 champion.

As a database, FileMaker Pro's functions are hard-drive intensive. Data is moved back and forth to the computer from the hard drive. That means that a faster hard drive will get better results, as long as the computer can use the information quickly enough. Simply installing a screamingly fast hard drive in an old clunker of a computer will not improve the operation of your databases.

⊠ **CAUTION**　Years ago I had dreams of speeding up FileMaker by putting files on a RAM disk. A RAM disk is a software trick that allows computer memory to act as if it were an extremely fast hard drive. Good idea! The only problem is, if you have a crash, all changes to the files are lost. It's much better to get the fastest hard drive you can afford.

The speed of the network can also influence the apparent speed of FileMaker. In its day, 10-base-T Ethernet was pretty quick, and many offices still operate fairly efficiently using that system. Most new machines, however, ship with 100-base-T cards installed. Whatever system is put to use, FileMaker can operate only as fast as the weakest link in the chain.

FileMaker Server

If you are working in an environment with many users accessing files, it is highly recommended that you consider the FileMaker Server product. You should experience a noticeable speed increase when using the files, because Server is optimized for this type of file sharing over a network. It is also a better way of organizing files that may otherwise be spread out over multiple machines, it has built-in backup capabilities, and it contains a set of administrative tools. However, don't even think about employing FileMaker Server unless you have a machine you're willing to dedicate to it. I have clients who haven't taken that advice. The problems they have are their own fault. I'll guarantee you they could have bought two reasonably fast machines for the amount they've spent on having me and another network professional come in to fix problems this "inexpensive" arrangement has caused.

Some Final Words

If you move a set of shared files to a single-user environment, depending on the settings on that machine, FileMaker may turn sharing off. If you then return the files to a multi-user environment, be sure to turn FileMaker Network Sharing back on for each file in the solution.

Closing Hosted Files

If you are the host, when you attempt to close a file, you will be presented with a dialog box listing any guests of the file. Clicking the Ask button will alert any users that you need to close the file. Users can delay the closing of the file by clicking Cancel on their end, but the dialog box will continue to present itself at irritatingly short intervals. If guests don't click either button (i.e., they're away from their desk), the file will close in 30 seconds. If all users click the Close Now button, the file closes immediately.

Slow Network Traffic

Because file sharing makes use of the network, there are times that other network traffic may affect the performance of your files. When network traffic causes a slowdown, your cursor will change to a double-pointed, zig-zagged arrow or a coffee cup. It's best just to be patient at times like these, but I have seen these icons stay on the screen when the network is completely locked up. My advice is to wait about five minutes. If the cursor hasn't returned to normal, quit or exit FileMaker. Worst case, you may find your machine locked up, and you'll have to reboot.

Summary

In this chapter, we looked at how to use FileMaker Pro's built-in sharing, how to set it up to work on a network, and the capabilities and limitations of the arrangement. We also saw how to optimize FileMaker's sharing and how to access files remotely with a modem.

Q & A

Q What if I need to change a field definition and I'm hosting a shared file?

A As long as no one else is a guest of the file, you can do any of the things you can do if the file were set up for single user. However, if guests are signed on, you'll have to ask them to close the file before you can work on it.

Workshop

If you're on a network with multiple copies of FileMaker on different machines, open one of the files and set network access to the file for all users. Go to one of the other computers, open a copy of FileMaker, make sure network sharing is on, and see if you can access the file remotely. Make sure both copies of FileMaker are set to the same network protocol.

Review Questions

True-False

1. FileMaker Pro does not need to be loaded on your computer if you are accessing files as a guest of another computer running FileMaker Pro.

2. The Edit File Reference window allows you to enter one or more paths to a file to ensure that FileMaker will look for the file where you have specified.

3. While a file is being shared via personal file sharing, only the host can define fields in the file.

4. If you share database files, it's a good idea to use some form of password protection to protect your data from unauthorized users.

Part 5

5. The best way to speed up sharing your FileMaker files is to put them on an old, unused computer.

Short Answer

6. Name four techniques for sharing data in FileMaker files.

7. When you have file sharing set to Multi-User for a database file, who has access to that file?

8. How can you avoid becoming the remote host of a database file on another computer?

9. What is the maximum number of users who can be guests of a file at the same time without using FileMaker Server or FileMaker Server Advanced?

10. What are the three network access to file choices in the FileMaker Network Settings window?

11. What do you have to do so that other FileMaker users can find a file that's open on your computer when they choose File, Open and click the Remote button?

12. If someone else has a shared FileMaker file open on the network, how can you open it on your computer?

13. When you're connected to the Internet, your files are vulnerable. Name one way you can protect them.

14. Only one of the following activities can be performed while a file is being shared. Which one is it?
    a) Change the order of the layouts
    b) Use the Save a Copy As command
    c) Change where fields are on a layout
    d) Open the Access Privileges window

Chapter 19

Sharing Your Data on the Web

Vocabulary

- Browser
- Instant Web Publishing

Objectives

1. Review the basics of preparing your computer to publish databases on the World Wide Web.
2. Learn how to set up FileMaker Pro to activate Instant Web Publishing.
3. Prepare database files to be shared via Instant Web Publishing.
4. Set up the styles and views through which your databases will interact with web browsers.
5. Understand basic security issues related to FileMaker web publishing.
6. Learn to test the web-based version of your database.

Introduction

FileMaker Pro 5.0 added an amazing built-in feature: If your computer is connected to the Internet or an intranet, you can make the data in your files available to other people through a browser. To protect your privacy, you can control who can access the information with the use of passwords or by limiting what machine IP addresses are allowed to connect to your files. For many people, this opens up a whole new world of possibilities.

In this chapter, you'll learn:

- How to set up your computer to take advantage of FileMaker's Instant Web Publishing
- How to set up FileMaker and your files to serve the data
- How to keep your data secure

Why Publish on the Web?

There are quite a few reasons why you might want to make some of your files available through a browser on an intranet or the Internet. Maybe you have a business or a hobby you would like to share with other people. Maybe you occasionally need to get to some of your data from a machine that doesn't have a copy of FileMaker Pro on it but does have an Internet browser. Perhaps other people in your office need to occasionally update information in your files. Maybe you want to start an Internet business where people will make purchases from your web site.

When I first heard about being able to publish on the web, I couldn't figure out what I'd do with it. About six months later, I had a lot of ideas. On my web site, potential clients can see screen shots of some of my databases. Before I built my web site, I used to print brochures and mail or hand them out. Now I can give someone my business card, and they can get a lot more information about what I do by checking out my web site than they could ever get from my printed materials. I've posted articles I've written about FileMaker, links to other FileMaker sites, and even some short stories I've written. Plus I can update my site quickly and easily. Maybe once you realize web publishing with FileMaker Pro is something you can do, you'll start to think of some uses of your own.

FileMaker and Instant Web Publishing (IWP)

Other databases can be set up to be available on the web, as long as they have all the right accessory software and all those programs are talking nicely to each other. FileMaker makes this easy, and you can do it without having to buy any extra software. With the click of a few buttons and some check boxes, you can literally make your databases instantly available on an intranet or the web. There are some considerations for protecting your data that require a little more than a couple of clicks, but you'll find you can handle that using the information in this and the next chapter. You'll also want to look at a file called FM 7 Instant Web Publishing.pdf, which you'll find inside the FileMaker Pro 7 folder, English Extras, Electronic Documentation on your hard drive. What FileMaker's software is actually doing here is turning your machine into a web server. If you have any other software that is doing web serving on the machine, we'll be turning it off as part of our setup.

Setting Up Your Computer

You'll need a static IP address and a machine that's connected to the network all the time. If you're on an intranet, you may already have an IP number assigned to your computer. However, I've seen some companies that routinely reassign IP numbers to their users. You need to find out how that is handled on your network and make sure the address stays the same. Then, of course, you'll need to tell other people how to find you. As you go through the steps for your machine, you may find it's already set up as described. If not, these instructions should get you there.

If You Have an Internet Account

☒ **CAUTION**   A little disclaimer before you get very far with this: There are a ton of system software versions. While the instructions that follow are correct for the versions of software I used to write this section (Mac OS X 10.2 and 10.3 and Windows 98, 2000, NT 4, and XP), it's completely possible that you might have an older version of Mac OS X. (FileMaker Pro 7 will not operate under Mac OS 9.) Potentially even more troublesome would be incompatible instructions for Windows users. Technical editor William Moss tells me that he had a great deal of difficulty trying to restore network settings in 98 and NT after making just a small change. (He has not tried 2000 or XP. I worked with XP and had no trouble.) He had to reinstall Windows because he could no longer see the network. Remember to check for software updates for your system, browser, and even FileMaker Pro. The reason the software is updated is that people report problems that need to be fixed.

The settings I talk about here are something that you should get from your Internet service provider. Otherwise, tread lightly with the awareness that things may go awry when making changes to your TCP/IP settings on the Windows platform. In other words, don't start this five minutes before an important deadline.

➲ **NOTE**   You can make Instant Web Publishing work through a router. The instructions that follow do not include the details of how to do that. The router will assign your machine a generic IP address. In order to serve through a router, you'll need the IP address assigned to the router by your Internet service provider. You probably have software on your computer that can look at the router and tell you what the IP address is. Then you may need to open up a port on the router so it can communicate with your FileMaker server. To avoid all this, you may just want to disconnect your router and temporarily connect directly to the cable (or other service-type) modem. Then you'll probably have to restart your machine. Don't get freaked out about all this at this point. If you're just looking at IWP and testing this out on your own machine, you don't need to concern yourself with such things.

To share regularly on the World Wide Web, you'll need a permanent connection to the Internet if you want people to be able to get to your data 24 hours a day. That can be accomplished with an ISDN, ADSL, cable modem, second phone line, or perhaps some arrangement with a satellite dish. However, when this becomes something you want to do all the time, you could also consider hiring the services of a provider who will keep your files on a web server for a monthly fee. On the other hand, assuming you don't have one of these services, you could specify certain times that your files will be available and only

This may seem like a silly example, and most of it won't make sense until after you've read the rest of the chapter, but here goes. I wanted to show my mother some pictures I had taken, and I needed her opinion quickly. I stuck the images in a Container field in a FileMaker file and turned on IWP. I was using a dial-up connection and only had one phone line. I called her and told her to check her e-mail in about five minutes. I dialed into my Internet provider. Then I went to TCP/IP on the Control Panel and copied down the IP address temporarily assigned to my machine. I sent Mom an e-mail giving her the URL including that machine number (http://192.168.0.2/) and telling her how to click on the file on the FileMaker IWP homepage. I left my connection open for 15 minutes. She went online with her browser and 20 minutes later we talked about the pictures she had seen. (This won't work if you're using a router between your computer and the Internet if it assigns generic machine addresses.)

leave your phone line open during those hours, but that really defeats the convenience of Instant Web Publishing.

Mac OS X 10.2.8 or Greater   To prepare a Macintosh computer so that you can use FileMaker for Instant Web Publishing, do the following:

1. In the System Preferences area, click the **Sharing** control panel and select the **Services** tab.

2. Make sure Personal Web Sharing is turned off because it will conflict with FileMaker's web sharing.

3. Go to the Network control panel. You'll need to be able to connect to some kind of network using either the built-in Ethernet or the internal modem. Double-click the one you want to work with.

4. Once it's open, click the **Assist me** button at the bottom of the window to make your settings.

   ■ When you're finished, if you're using the Built-in Ethernet option, you should see an IP address in the TCP/IP tab. Write that down so you can work with it later. If you don't see the numbers, restart your machine and return to the Network control panel; the new location should appear. You may have to reselect Built-in Ethernet in the Show pop-up to see the IP address. We tested on several machines and found it irritating that this process worked better on some machines than others.

   ■ If you're working with the internal modem, you won't be able to get the machine number until you dial in. That may be exactly what you want. But for testing Instant Web Publishing on the same machine as the browser, you can just go to the TCP/IP tab and choose **Manually** from the Configure pop-up. Then you can type in something like 192.168.0.2. Just make sure that the IP address on the other machine(s) you're connecting to is different. I set my system up so my second machine's IP number is 192.168.0.3, and so on sequentially.

5. Close the Network window. Now you can skip down to the section titled "Setting Up FileMaker Pro for IWP."

Windows 98   Windows 2000 and XP users, skip down to your section. Have your Windows 98 installation CD handy before you start this process.

1. Click the **Start** button in the lower-left corner of the window.

2. Choose **Settings, Control Panel**.

3. Double-click the **Network** icon.

4. Click the **Configuration** tab.

5. Select **Protocol** from the Select Network Component Type window, and click the **Add** button.

6. Choose **Microsoft** from the Manufacturers list on the left and **TCP/IP** from the Network Protocols list on the right, and click **OK**.

7. Now select **TCP/IP -> Diamond HomePNA & Ethernet Based Adapter** (or similar Ethernet network adapter) from the Configurations, and click the **Properties** button. (You will need to know what network card you're using. The first clue is that the name will probably sound like the name of a hardware card. I'm sorry, but that's the best I can do for you here.)

8. Click the **Specify an IP address** radio button and enter the number for your machine that has been provided by either your network administrator or your Internet service provider. You'll also want the subnet mask information.

9. Click **OK**, and **OK** again.

After a few seconds you may be asked to insert the CD. If so, go ahead and follow the instructions. Regardless, for the changes to take place, you'll have to restart your computer.

If you have your own home network, use a number like 192.168.0.2. Just make sure that the setting on the other machine you're connecting to is different. I set mine so my second machine's IP number is 192.168.0.3.

⌘ **TIP**   There is one other setting that may cause some problems on Windows 98 machines; if all the other settings are as described and you still can't see any shared files when you click the Hosts button, try the following:
1. Go to the Network control panel and select the **Configuration** tab. If you see TCP/IP ->Dial Up Adapter, you may have to remove it. CAUTION: You should write down all the settings on every tab in the adapter before removing it since this could affect your ability to connect to the Internet.
2. Go to the Control Panel and open **Add/Remove Programs**.
3. Click the **Windows Setup** tab, double-click **Communications**, and uncheck **Dial Up Networking**.
4. Click **OK**. You might have to insert the Windows CD, and of course you'll have to restart the computer.

Windows 2000   Have your Windows 2000 installation CD handy before you start this process. You probably won't need it, but you don't want to get stuck.

1. Click the **Start** button in the lower-left corner of the window.

2. Choose **Settings**, **Control Panel**, then **Network and Dial-up connections**.

3. Double-click the **Local Area Connection** icon. The Local Area Connection Properties window appears, displaying the network adapter in use and the network components used in this connection.

4. Click **Internet Protocol (TCP/IP)** and verify that the check box to the left of the entry is selected. (If you don't see the TCP/IP protocol, install it using the directions in the Windows Help files.)

5. Click the **Properties** button. The Internet Protocol (TCP/IP) Properties window appears.

6. Click the **Use the following IP address** radio button, and enter the number for your machine that has been provided by either your network

Part 5

administrator or your Internet service provider. You'll also want the subnet mask information.

7. Click **OK**, and **OK** again.

Windows XP Have your Windows XP installation CD available before you start this process. You probably won't need it, but it's better to have it handy.

1. Click the **Start** button in the lower-left corner of the window.

2. Choose **Control Panel**, then double-click **Network Connections**.

3. Double-click the **Local Area Connection** icon. You may be taken directly to the Local Area Connection Properties window. If not, when the Local Area Connection Status window appears, click the Properties button.

4. Click to highlight **Internet Protocol (TCP/IP)** and verify that the check box to the left of the entry is selected. (If you don't see the TCP/IP protocol, install it using the directions in the Windows Help files.)

5. Click the **Properties** button. The Internet Protocol (TCP/IP) Properties window appears.

6. (If you want to save this setting, click the Alternate Configuration tab — if it's available — before entering the IP address. If it's not available, write down the settings so you can re-enter it if needed.) Click the **Use the following IP address** radio button, and enter the number for your machine that has been provided by either your network administrator or your Internet service provider. You don't need to concern yourself with the subnet mask unless your network administrator has given it to you.

7. Click **OK**, and **OK** again, then **Close** (it may take up to one minute for the first window to close) and **Close** again.

Windows NT 4.0 I don't have access to a Windows NT 4.0 machine. My consultants told me that the platform is powerful but user hostile. In other words, you probably won't be trying IWP on an NT 4.0 machine unless you know what you're doing anyway. In that case, any instructions I give you would be trivial. Good enough cop-out? Not only that, but the system is getting a little long in the tooth. Time to upgrade, dude!

If You Don't Have an Internet Account

You may not have an Internet account or even be on a network, but you still might want to try this out. I worked with this technique quite a bit when I was developing my web site before I put it up on a server. You can experiment by tricking your computer into looking at itself as if it were a machine on the Internet. Just follow all the other directions for setting up TCP/IP, Instant Web Publishing, and FileMaker Pro in this chapter. When it comes time to put in the URL address, simply type http://localhost in the URL Address box. You could also use the number of the machine you used in the machine settings area — something like 192.168.0.3. Look at the Tip in the upcoming "Advanced Options" section for information on a special situation that may arise during this process. Of course, you must have the FileMaker files open and each file's web sharing option turned on in order to see them in the browser. That's what we'll be describing next.

Sometimes setting up Instant Web Publishing to serve files to yourself using a browser can act squirrelly. Recently I had FileMaker open before I set up TCP/IP. When it wouldn't work, I found I had to quit and restart FileMaker before I could activate IWP.

Setting up FileMaker Pro for IWP

FileMaker Pro 7 has greatly simplified the setup needed to activate Instant Web Publishing (IWP). But to say it is simplified doesn't mean that there isn't an amazing depth to what is possible here. In fact, all of FileMaker 7's accounts and privilege sets can be brought to bear in IWP.

There is now one main setup area in FileMaker Pro to activate Instant Web Publishing. Here are the three functions we'll be setting up:

■ FileMaker needs to use the TCP/IP network protocol and you must be connected to a network.

■ You'll have to allow Instant Web Publishing access to any files you want to share.

■ You'll select each individual file you want to share in the Instant Web Publishing window.

Instant Web Publishing Settings

Within each specific file, there are quite a few choices you can make, but you can keep it very simple if you prefer. You must be connected to a network for this to work; otherwise, you'll get a message that FileMaker cannot share any files.

1. With FileMaker as the frontmost application, open the files you want to share.

2. On Windows choose **Edit**, **Sharing**, **Instant Web Publishing**. On Macintosh choose **FileMaker Pro**, **Sharing**, **Instant Web Publishing**. You should see the window in Figure 19-1.

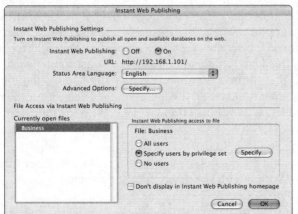

Figure 19-1
FileMaker's Instant Web Publishing window showing the feature turned on and the Business file as currently open.

3. Click the radio button next to **On**. On Windows you may see the hourglass for a few seconds. (On Macintosh it would be the spinning rainbow.) When you enable IWP on Mac OS X, you will see the Mac dialog asking for your

Part 5

user name and password. This is not a FileMaker dialog and actually requires the account information for the computer. Wait until your cursor turns back into the pointer.

4. Click on one of the files in the list in the Currently open files area.

5. Look over on the right and notice that you can choose to share with No users. Click the **Specify** button and take a look at how you can determine access by privilege sets. More on that in Chapter 21.

6. Click **Cancel**.

7. For now, click the **All users** radio button.

Advanced Options

1. Before you leave here, look at the middle of the window and click the **Specify** button next to Advanced Options. You should see the window shown in Figure 19-2.

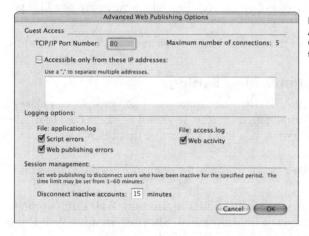

Figure 19-2
Advanced Web Publishing Options window showing the default settings.

2. Take a look around the Advanced Web Publishing Options window to get an idea of what other controls you can have over web access to your files. One important option is near the bottom where you choose how many minutes before you disconnect inactive accounts. You might feel generous and bump up the default time, but I'd advise against it. Some users will certainly quit their browsers without clicking the Log Out button. When that happens, they could tie up the file until the disconnect time runs out. For more on that, see the section titled "IWP Browser Interface" later in this chapter.

3. Click **OK** twice to leave here.
Even though we'll go into detail in Chapter 21, since you can control user access to IWP with FileMaker's Accounts & Privileges system, we need to preview it now.

4. Go to **File**, **Define**, **Accounts & Privileges**, choose the **Privilege Sets** tab, and double-click any one of the items in the list.

5. In the Edit Privilege Set window, look at the Extended Privileges area in the lower left. You can switch IWP access on and off for each account. This has the same effect as the check box in the IWP Sharing window.

6. Click **Cancel**.

7. Go to the Extended Privileges tab, and double-click **[fmiwp]**. Here again you can turn IWP on and off for any privilege set. The same check boxes are available in the Sharing, Instant Web Publishing, Specify users by privilege set area.

One setting that was particularly troubling to me a couple of years ago was the TCP/IP port number. Apparently, I had some other application that took over port 80. Port 80 is the default web server port. If you have two versions of FileMaker running (say, FMP6 and FMP7), they will both try to monopolize port 80, which will result in the error. Also, programs such as Lasso, Webstar, and Personal Web Sharing (Mac OS X) will try to use port 80. I never did figure out what program was causing the problem for me. If that happens to you, try using the information in the next Tip.

I wouldn't suggest making any changes here until you get more familiar with everything else. The default settings should work for you. You can find out more about the other settings in the manual, the electronic documentation, or the Help files.

8. Click **Cancel** and close the Instant Web Publishing window by clicking **OK**.

What we've done here is turn on Instant Web Publishing. Then we turned on access to each file we want to share. Think of it like this: In your home, you have light switches. To make each light work, you turn the switch on and off. If you turn off the master power switch, none of the lights work. Instant Web Publishing in the Sharing area is the master switch. The choices you make for each file are the individual light switches.

➲ **NOTE**   If you're in the FileMaker Network Settings window and you find you cannot turn on Instant Web Publishing, you may have TCP/IP turned off for the computer. After you turn it on, you'll have to restart FileMaker and reset FileMaker's Network Settings window.

⌘ **TIP**   If you cannot connect with your machine from a remote browser, try changing the port setting to 591. (This is probably more than you want to know, but port 591 is a UDP port, not a TCP port.) However, when you do, you'll have to change the address where users will find you by adding ":591" on the end. For example, if your machine number is 192.168.0.5, people will now have to use 192.168.0.5:591 instead. Likewise, if you're using a domain name, it will have to read something like http://JonathanStars.com:591 or http://localhost:591. (By the way, I don't have a web site called JonathanStars.com. You can find me at DataDesignPros.com.) You can actually use any port number you want that's not in use. This can be a nice tool to keep your info one step more secure. It's called "security by obscurity." Hackers can't simply find your FileMaker homepage by guessing the machine's IP number or domain name. Adding a port number is not foolproof, however. Hackers can still run a port scan.

By assigning FileMaker a port address, you can actually have two web servers on the same machine. But that's getting a bit beyond the scope here.

Part 5

Setting Up Your Database

There are a number of little things you might miss when getting everything ready to go. Here are some finer points of setting up the files:

- Web sharing is completely separate from FileMaker Network Sharing, so you do not need to set the network access to your files to All (or specific) users for web sharing to work. On the other hand, if you intend to share your files with other users who will be using their copy of the FileMaker application on an intranet or remotely through the web at the same time, you will need to have network access to those files turned on. In either case, you'll need to be attentive to password protecting your files. For more on that, see the "Web Security" section later in this chapter and Chapter 21, "Keeping Your Data Secure." Pay special attention to the section titled "A Word about Passwords" in Chapter 21.

- If you're familiar with Instant Web Publishing in earlier versions of FileMaker, you can no longer control access to the web version of files in the File Options window. You used to be able to check the box next to "Log in using" and select a password. Starting in version 7, that check box only controls how users enter the files using their version of the FileMaker Pro program. Instead, you activate the Guest account and have IWP turned on for the Guest account. Now all users have access to the file(s) without needing to see the Account Name and Password dialog.

- If the Guest account is enabled and has the IWP privilege set enabled, web users open the database without being prompted for an account name and password when they access the file. But keep in mind, if the Guest account has IWP turned off, each user will still be presented with the Account Name and Password dialog.

- To force users to log in when using a browser, the Guest account must be inactive or the Guest account must be turned off for fmiwp in the Extended Privilege area. For a user to be able to log-in, their account must be active, and they must have extended privileges turned on for Access via Instant Web Publishing. Any users set for auto log-in in the File Options area will not have any effect on IWP.

- In previous versions of FileMaker, you needed to make sure users had Export Records turned on. That is no longer necessary in order to make IWP work.

Browsers

Users who are looking at your database in a browser will see pages that look nearly identical to your layouts. Unfortunately, FileMaker Pro 7's IWP is only certified to be used with a limited set of browsers.

On Windows machines, you'll need Internet Explorer 6.0 or higher for:

- Windows 98
- Windows NT 4.0 (Service Pack 6a or higher)
- Windows 2000
- Windows XP

On the Macintosh you'll need one of the following:

■ Internet Explorer 5.1 or 5.2 on OS X 10.2.8

■ Safari 1.1 on OS X 10.3 (Safari will *not* work with 10.2.8)

■ Internet Explorer 5.2 on OS X 10.3

If you try to access the files using some other browser, you may not get anything at all. Or you may get the following message displayed on the database homepage just above the list of open files: "This site has been optimized for use with Internet Explorer 5.1 or later. Using another browser to access this site is not recommended." You will want to have your users stick with the browsers recommended by FileMaker.

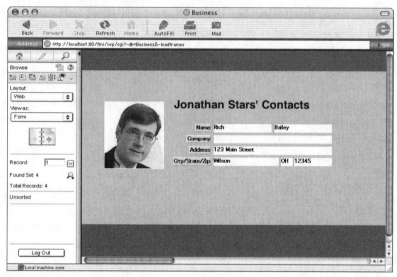

Figure 19-3
A layout optimized for web viewing.

Layouts

You can do some fancy design work to your FileMaker layouts so they look more like web pages. For the most consistent results, you should choose colors from the Web palette in FileMaker's Preferences. You won't get as much control as you would by having a custom-built web site, but this is for basic data viewing and/or entry, and it's free!

You'll probably want to make some special web layouts. There should be as few fields and graphics as possible on these layouts so they'll load more quickly in the browsers. Look at the simplified web layout I created in Figure 19-3 to get some idea of how few fields are arranged on the layout. The picture I used is a 72 dpi JPEG image resized to fit the field so it's web compatible and loads quickly. If none of your layouts seem appropriate, create a new layout, change access in Accounts & Privileges, and come back to choose it from the pop-up on the web page.

There are a few things you should be aware of when designing your layouts.

Part 5

■ Buttons you create on layouts will work in a browser, with some very specific limitations. The details are rather complex, but the results can give you a lot of control over what you can accomplish without having to build custom web pages.

■ Any buttons that appear on your layouts need to be attached to scripts that contain only web-compatible script steps.

There are now more than 70 script steps that can be run using a button on a web page. Since there are 129 script steps, that means not all steps can be run via buttons on the web. You need to check each script attached to each button on the layouts you'll be sharing on the web. When you're in the script editing window, if you check the box next to "Indicate web compatibility," any steps that won't run turn gray.

Here are a few other important considerations:

■ Some steps will depend on having the actual data sent back to the database from the web. You'll need to include a Commit Record/Request step where necessary.

■ When scripts run via the web interface, all scripts are run with Error Capture on. If you have any scripts that depend on Error Capture being off, you'll want to redesign.

■ The user account must be able to run the script.

■ Buttons will display only one line of text. If you're in the habit of creating buttons with two lines of text (as I am), you'll need to redesign that.

■ Round (circular or round-cornered) layout objects do not translate to IWP. They get converted to square or rectangular objects. This applies to buttons too.

So yes, you can put your files up on the Internet. And you can do it instantly. But it's not advisable to make it an everyday tool without consideration for your users and the security of your data.

Now we come to the issue of various users' privilege sets. Before you put the files out on the web, you should log in under each user account and test each button to see that they operate as you expect. All I can do for you here is scratch the surface. There is a more comprehensive, 32-page document titled FM7 Instant Web Publishing.pdf that discusses the finer points. You can find it by going to the FileMaker Pro 7 folder (with the other applications) and look inside English Extras\Electronic Documentation. The details include information about which script steps work and how they operate differently on the web. There is also information about extra steps that might be needed to ensure the results of the script.

Working with FileMaker Pro using a browser is not the same as working with your files using FileMaker. I say this because when IWP was first introduced a few years ago, some companies got the idea they could buy one copy of FileMaker and have everyone in the company work with the data using a browser. They were trying to avoid buying a site license for other copies of the FileMaker application. You simply do not get all of FileMaker's rich feature set via the web. I know of one company that spent over $50,000 having one of their people design a solution this way before they realized they couldn't get everything they wanted. Their site license would have cost far, far less. The IWP interface should be thought of as a convenience for rudimentary work with data. You can go further with custom web publishing in combination with products like Lasso. And working that way makes FileMaker a serious contender indeed. Just don't get the web interface confused with FileMaker's own capabilities.

Also, portals can appear on your page, and you can even edit data in the portals. So be sure you actually want the information in the portals to show. Even if the table from which the portal originates is protected from data entry, the data will show. If you don't want that information displayed, remove it from the layout or create a special web-only layout.

⌘ **TIP** Web sharing is where your layout names become critical. Name your layouts so you'll know what they are, but remove any spaces or non-web characters such as # @ % & *. Actually, spaces will work, but the URL inserts "%20" wherever spaces appear. If you really need a space, use the underscore character instead.

When you make decisions about which layouts to display on the web, choose layouts with as few fields and elements on the page as you can, so they'll draw faster. Even fast Internet connections can be frustratingly slow when your users have to wait between screen redraws.

IWP Browser Interface

In previous versions of Instant Web Publishing, users were very limited as to what they could see and do to FileMaker files using a browser. Much of the work developers (that's you) needed to do to ready files for the web has been transferred to the new web interface. Although you can override many of the following functions based on accounts and privileges (see Chapter 21), your users can otherwise basically:

■ Change modes

■ Change layouts

■ Change views (Form, List, or Table)

■ Change records

■ Create, edit, duplicate, and delete records

■ Perform finds

■ Omit records

■ Sort records

■ Print records

That's a lot of responsibility for the user. It means you may need to train anyone coming to your IWP pages so they'll be able to get around. Of course you can remove access to the Status area and have them use buttons you've created instead. That's more work for you.

○ **NOTE** Visitors of your web site who use the Find Mode icon (magnifying glass) have access to the Find symbols, which will appear beneath the Requests area under the Book.

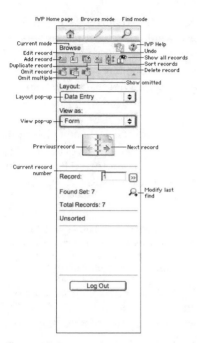

Figure 19-4
The Instant Web Publishing Browse mode
tools as seen in a browser.

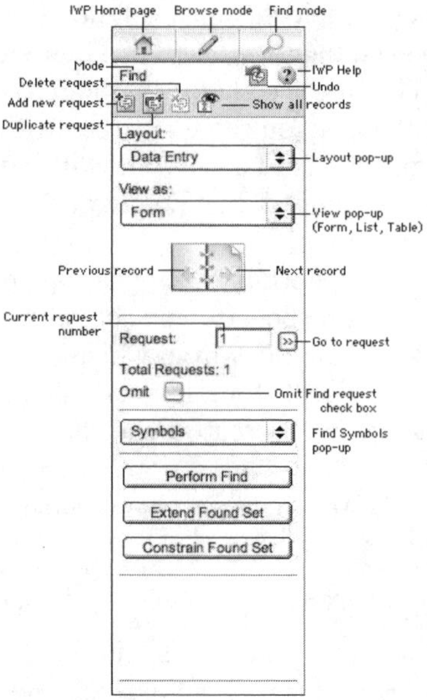

Figure 19-5
The Instant Web Publishing Find mode
tools as seen in a browser.

Look at Figures 19-4 and 19-5 for information about what the icons on the interface are for. There is a lot to this interface. You can click the ? button under the magnifying glass to bring up a complete set of instructions for your users. When you see what's there, you'll realize why I can't cover it all here.

Most important are the instructions regarding the log out. On each web page, there is a Log Out button near the bottom left. Users should log out when they're done. If they simply quit their browser, their connection to the FileMaker file stays active until it reaches the time-out limit. (To set the disconnect time, see the section titled "Setting Up FileMaker Pro for IWP" earlier in this chapter.) Other people could potentially access the files via the web. It also could prevent other users from accessing the files.

Here are some of the finer points to consider:

◼ I noticed that I had some problems when working with the files locally if I quit the browser without using the Log Out button. Sometimes the computer wouldn't let me quit FileMaker and continued to display a dialog saying the file was in use. At other times, after quitting FileMaker, I simply could not log back in through the browser without restarting the machine. I'm fairly certain that all users will not be clicking the Log Out button, so you need to be aware of where those problems might lie.

◼ If the user clicks the IWP Log Out button after their connection time has expired, they'll see a dialog that looks like Figure 19-6.

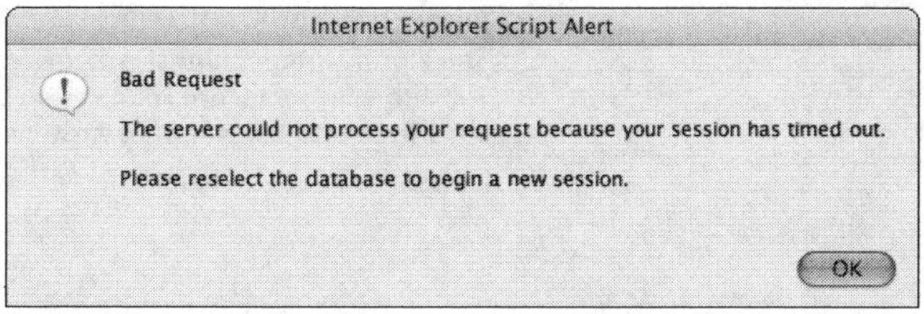

Figure 19-6
The Bad Request dialog that appears after a FileMaker web session has timed out.

⌘ **TIP** On my Windows XP laptop machine, the screen is so small that the Log Out button is not visible even when using the scroll bar on the right. I have to force the top of the browser window up beyond the edge of the display. If you have any users on laptops with this problem, see if you can get them to change the resolution of their screen to something higher than 800 x 600.

■ If you want a layout to appear on the web in a particular view (Form, List, or Table), you need to make that decision at the layout level in your file (View, Layout Mode, Layouts menu, Layout Setup, Views tab, and use the check boxes). In some cases, you may find it easier to use a specific layout for the web.

■ The List View of the web interface may be confusing down by the word Record because it is not the familiar FileMaker interface. Once you enter a specific record number in the box next to Record and click the > > button next to the box, the records previous to that record are no longer visible. Instead, your users will see that record and the next 19 of the current found set, if there are that many records available.

■ Sometimes the web page gets hopelessly scrambled — even after you click the Refresh button on the browser. To clear the browser's memory, I will often quit the browser and start it up again. That's probably the kind of thing you want to tell your users, but you might want to provide that information somewhere on the various pages they'll be accessing. And again, they should always click the Log Out button first.

■ My test showed that the browser allowed the user to click the "Edit current record" button, but there was no place to edit the record — no active fields. It even displayed Submit and Cancel buttons on the right side of the browser. I would have expected the browser to display an error telling the users that they are not allowed to edit any records (on this layout — or in this table) or better yet, the edit records button should be inactive.

■ Also, I logged in and logged out to test switching various accounts on and off. FileMaker seemed to remember that the Guest privilege account was still active. If I quit and restarted the browser, I would be presented with the window shown in Figure 19-7. Once I filled in the User ID and Password fields, the browser remembered the privileges until I quit and restarted the browser again.

■ You can create a button attached to a script using the Relogin script step. That way all users can come in easily on the Guest account and then users who need a higher level of access can get it as needed.

Part 5

Figure 19-7
The Connect to localhost window users will see when they are required to log in to the database via their browser.

- On one layout I had the Header part overlapping the first field in the browser. I changed it on the layout, then changed it back and it was okay. It just means you may see some inconsistencies.

- Remember the Delete buttons we added to the phone portal? For some reason my browser added a scroll bar at the bottom of the portal. When I scrolled the portal sideways with the arrow buttons, it scrolled and activated the Delete button at the same time. That changed the interface to verify a deletion, which is something I had not anticipated. Again, check your work, see what your users will see, and test what will happen when they use the web interface.

Web Security

Whether or not you've had to protect your FileMaker files with passwords in the past, you'll surely want to protect them before they go up on the web. When you're in a browser, that string of letters and numbers in the URL box (called Location or Address in various browsers) provides the information that tells the remote computer what to do. Starting with FileMaker 7, the whole request doesn't show in the Address area, but it does show in the lower-left corner of the browser momentarily. With FileMaker, that string can mean something like "Find and Sort certain records from that faraway computer and display them on my screen in a specific way." If you haven't taken security measures, hackers may be able to take that string and substitute another command for Find, which could adversely affect your data. That means it's a good idea to secure your master files somewhere and only put copies on the web.

Don't serve files that include sensitive data, even if you don't intend to display it. Why? Because it is possible for technically savvy users to remotely access your sensitive data. It's better to make a smaller file with just the essential data you want to share and leave out the sensitive fields. This means someone will have to go through the extra effort to keep the office and web files synchronized with each other. But the safety of your data is at stake here.

The first line of defense is to require users to log in with an account and password. Here's how:

1. Inactivate the Guest account. (Anytime the Guest account is active, the file(s) will be available without displaying the Account Name and Password dialog.)

2. Create an account for web users, deciding which layouts and data you want them to see.

A second protective measure is to restrict which IP addresses can get to your files. That certainly shrinks down the "World Wide" part of the web, though, doesn't it? Nevertheless, allowing a limited number of machines to connect may be all that you need.

1. To do that, go to **Edit** (Windows) or **FileMaker Pro** (Mac), **Sharing**, **Instant Web Publishing**, and click the **Specify** button next to Advanced Options.

2. Now you simply enter the list of IP addresses you want to have access to your web-shared data. Just remember, some networks (including Internet service providers) routinely reassign IP addresses to machines. You need to consider how often you'll need to re-enter those addresses. If your company or a company you want to serve data to has a range of IP addresses, you can serve to all of them. In the last position of the web address you simply substitute an asterisk (*) so the address looks something like 192.168.123.*. The only trouble with this shorthand is that you may want to serve only to addresses .10-.30. Your data would be available to any other companies who have the rest of the IP range. Of course they would need to know your data was there in the first place. And they would need to know your account names and passwords. You did protect your data with account names and passwords, didn't you?

You can also restrict which users can see which records by setting up record-level security in the Accounts & Privileges area of your files. See the section titled "Record-Level Security" in Chapter 21. There you'll learn how to protect your files with passwords using FileMaker's Accounts & Privileges system. You'll be able to individually control what your remote users can do with your files. You may decide that some users can only view certain data, while others will be able to add and delete records.

Try It Out

☒ **CAUTION**   Before you jump too far into this, make sure you're not working with files that have important data in them. Make some backup copies and experiment with those instead. The same applies to any files that might be called by these files.

To check out your work, you'll have to be connected to an intranet or the web. (On my Mac, I found all I needed to do was connect to a hub — even if there were no other computers connected to it. Machines that have wireless networking built in don't even need a hub. That would include computers equipped with infrared or AirPort networking. However, you must turn the wireless protocol on.)

Open a browser and type one of the following in the URL field:

- http://192.168.0.2/ (if you set up your machine the way we discussed earlier)

- http://localhost

- 127.0.0.1 (which is the absolute, cross-platform guaranteed "loopback" machine number)

If everything works correctly, you should be able to click to perform the various View, Search, Edit, Delete, and New Record functions. Then go to another machine that has access to the same network.

Part 5

1. Establish a connection to the network. Some browsers do this for you.
2. Open the browser if it's not already open.
3. Type in the IP address or URL. (If 80 doesn't work, try the :591 discussed earlier.)
4. You should see the Instant Web Publishing portal page similar to Figure 19-8. Click on the database name.
5. Enter a password if required.

See if you can perform the View, Search, Edit, Delete, and New Record functions. What functions you can perform will depend on what account you came in under. And remember, not all buttons may act as you expect since not all script steps are supported. If you see the layout with nothing in it, it might be that no records are selected. Click on the eye icon under Browse. This eye stands for Show All. Click on that now.

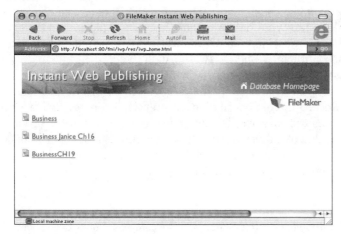

Figure 19-8
The Instant Web Publishing homepage.

If the files are vulnerable and you haven't been able to work out password protection yet, go back to the host machine, and turn off Instant Web Publishing or disconnect the machine from the network. If you had TCP/IP turned off for that machine before you started, you'll probably want to turn it back off.

Other Notes and Options

You can also create customized web sites that incorporate FileMaker data. Some of the other web page building programs now include the FileMaker tags. You should check out the details before buying any of those products since features change — sometimes on a daily basis. If you were heavily into Instant Web Publishing in the past, take note that CDML (Claris Dynamic Markup Language) is no longer supported. You will be able to convert your web pages created in CDML by replacing it with XSLT. Instructions will be included in a document that will be available with the FileMaker documentation. The name of that document is not available at press time.

Another big improvement this time around is that files can be served regardless of what the files are doing at the time. In previous versions, if any one of the FileMaker files you were trying to connect with was in anything except Browse mode or displayed the window for Define Fields, Define Relationships, or ScriptMaker, among others, it would prevent the browser from connecting with any of the files. Now even an error dialog on the host machine won't stop the browser from connecting.

Files can be anywhere on your machine, but FileMaker has to be running with the specific files open. One thing that wasn't clear to me when I started working with files on the web was that you do not need to put your FileMaker files in the Web folder inside the FileMaker folder. In fact, it's better if they're not in the Web folder. Because of the way Instant Web Publishing works, it actually makes the Web folder shared and vulnerable. Sneaky hackers can mess with data that's in the Web folder. That's another good reason to keep backups.

■ The regular version of FileMaker Pro will only allow web sharing using Instant Web Publishing with up to 10 files and up to five users at the same time. If you need better network speeds and the ability to serve to more simultaneous users than you can with regular FileMaker, you should get FileMaker Server Advanced, which allows much greater web sharing capacity, not to mention many other file sharing options. For users of previous versions of FileMaker's IWP, the FileMaker Pro Unlimited product has been eliminated in favor of the more powerful and flexible FileMaker Server Advanced version.

■ You can prevent users from seeing the area on the browser that looks like FileMaker's Status area. You do that by creating a script that runs whenever the file opens. Then you include Toggle Status Area [Lock;Hide] (the script category is Windows) early in the script. To make the script run at startup, choose File, File Options, and go to the Open/Close tab. In the "When opening this file" area, check the box next to Perform Script, and choose the script that should run on opening. But be sure this is your intent. Users will only be able to navigate your files with the button you provide for them. That could mean a lot of testing depending on how complex your solution is. If you choose not to display the Instant Web Publishing homepage (check box in Instant Web Publishing Settings window), you'll need to provide buttons to take your users through your web pages and consider what you want to use as the "home" page.

■ If you suspect trouble with hackers, you can check the access log file. You'll find it inside the FileMaker Pro 7 folder in a folder called Web logs. As long as you had the "Web activity" box checked in the Advanced Web Publishing Options window, you'll be able to see what machine numbers have made requests for information from your files. Don't expect to instantly know who the attack is from, though. Hackers often use other machines as aliases to keep their identities hidden. But if it's important enough, you can hire someone to trace it back and find out who's been messing with you.

Instant Web Publishing has a lot of power, but there are many finer points you need to be attentive to. If you go to the Help files, choose Index, and type "Instant Web Publishing," you'll be presented with a long list of topics. Also

Part 5

look inside FileMaker Pro\English Extras\Electronic Documentation for a file called FM 7 Instant Web Publishing.pdf. Once you get an idea of the scope of IWP, you'll see why I can't cover it all in just one chapter. It could easily take a whole book.

Making files available on the web can be costly unless you already have a full-time connection. The more important the application, the more you may want to consider having your FileMaker connected site hosted by companies that specialize in this service. For a partial list of such services, go to the FileMaker web site. Depending on your budget, you might consider purchasing a machine to provide FileMaker IWP right in your building where you can be in charge of the files. Or you could talk to your web provider about having them take your machine into their facility where they will likely have a number of safety features for automatically backing up your data, uninterruptible power supplies, and perhaps even generators.

Cool Web Sites Powered by FileMaker

More and more web sites are being powered by FileMaker all the time. Go to http://www.filemaker.com/ for a listing of sites powered by FileMaker. You may have to search for the specific page since the FileMaker site gets redesigned occasionally. Sites tend to jump around, but I will try to keep a list up on my site as well (www.DataDesignPros.com). Some of these sites are very interesting, and some have FileMaker files that you can download. Since this edition of the book is slated to hit the shelves shortly after the release of FileMaker Pro 7, I can't list any sites that are using the current version for IWP. But over time I expect to list some of them on my web site.

If you talk to someone about hosting your site and they don't want to bother with it, go to FileMaker, Inc.'s web site for a list of companies that provide FileMaker web hosting. Just don't let any web hosting company talk you out of using FileMaker. It's perfectly suited to those types of services. There are even some special high-end methods of serving busy web sites that consist of networking a series of inexpensive computers to handle the load.

Summary

In this chapter, we looked at how you can make the data in your FileMaker Pro files available to other people on an intranet or the Internet through a browser using Instant Web Publishing. You learned how to set up your computer, how to set up FileMaker Pro, and some basic considerations for keeping your shared data secure.

Q & A

Q I'd like to try this out, but it's not easy for me to get to another machine. Is there some other way I can see what the pages look like in my browser?

A If your machine is wired for Ethernet and you can get your hands on an inexpensive Ethernet hub, connect to it as if you were connecting to a network. Then follow the directions for the other settings. When it comes time to find your FileMaker files with the browser, use the same IP address you entered for the machine you're on. The browser will go out to the hub and come back to your own machine. I've also made this work on a laptop with an infrared network option instead of Ethernet. It didn't even require a hub.

Q This sounds pretty good, but some of my friends don't have Internet Explorer or Safari. I'm sure a lot of other people don't either. I want the pages to look the way I plan them.

A The IWP-certified browsers are both free downloads. To control the look of the page, you'll need to purchase specialized software for designing web pages. But be aware that it will take some time to develop your skills with any of these other programs. And don't forget, with all your planning, users have the ability to change the way things look in their browsers.

Workshop

Choose one of your files and set it up the way you want it to appear on the web. Set up the Guest account to display only a couple of the layouts. Then go to the browser and take a look at how the choices you made in the files affect what you see. Come back to the file and make a few more changes to the layouts and what is available to the Guest account. Then see what that looks like in the browser.

Click the Log Out button, inactivate the Guest account, and try signing in under various other accounts. Don't forget to log out of each one before trying to log in under another. (I had to quit and restart the browser each time I wanted to log in under a different account.)

Review Questions

True-False

1. To share your database files over the web, you must be connected to the Internet.
2. Setting up your computer to serve database files is the same no matter what system software you have.
3. You can password protect your web-based files by using FileMaker's Accounts & Privileges system.
4. Instant Web Publishing works so well that it's not necessary to test your web solution before publishing it on the World Wide Web.
5. You can view your web-enabled database files on your own computer by opening your browser and typing "http://localhost" in the URL field.
6. The Status area does not show on a database viewed via Instant Web Publishing.

Short Answer

7. After you have set up Instant Web Publishing, how do you make a database file web accessible?

Part 5

8. Which sharing option must you set in order to be able to publish FileMaker Pro databases on the web?

9. What must you remember about buttons on layouts when you serve your database via Instant Web Publishing?

10. What is the most obvious monetary advantage to using FileMaker Pro's Instant Web Publishing?

11. What network protocol must be selected in FileMaker in order to share files with Instant Web Publishing?

12. In ScriptMaker, how can you tell which script steps are web compatible?

13. Since you are sharing the data on the web or the intranet, does Network Sharing need to be turned on in the FileMaker Network Settings window?

Chapter 20

Sharing Your Data with Other Applications

Vocabulary

- Data source
- ODBC
- SQL

Objectives

1. Understand how to determine the best way to export to or import from other applications.
2. Become familiar with ODBC and SQL as they relate to data exchange with FileMaker Pro.
3. Understand how to make FileMaker data available to other applications.
4. Learn to get data from other applications into FileMaker Pro.
5. Become familiar with the Execute SQL script step.
6. Learn how to import a folder of files all at once.

Introduction

At some point, you may find a need to share FileMaker information with other programs, or maybe you'll need to get data from other applications for use in FileMaker Pro. Depending on the application and your needs, FileMaker provides the answer with the Import and Export Records commands, the ODBC control panel, and the ODBC/JDBC sharing window.

In this chapter, I'll explain:

- The use of imports and exports to share data between FileMaker and other applications
- How to use the ODBC control panel
- How to use the ODBC/JDBC Sharing window

Using FileMaker's Import and Export Commands

FileMaker has a nice array of file types it can import and export.

1. Open any FileMaker file, choose **File**, **Import Records**, and select **File**.

2. Now click the **Show** pop-up (Macintosh) or **Files of type** pop-up (Windows). To see the list of exportable file types, make sure you have at least one record in the current found set.

3. Then choose **File**, **Export Records** and click on the **Type** pop-up (Macintosh) or **Save as type** pop-up (Windows) to view that list.

By exporting and importing records in a common format, FileMaker is capable of communicating with applications such as Microsoft Office, Corel Office, WordPerfect, Quattro Pro, Lotus Smart Suite, and Word Pro, among others. You aren't going to see these applications listed in the Type pop-up list. The options that are given are common file formats. You need to check the manual of the application you're working with to find out what file formats it can read. For more on the basics of importing and exporting records, take a look at the sections titled "FileMaker Techniques" and "Import Data" in Chapter 22. Although not exhaustive, you should get a pretty good idea of the steps required. Later in this chapter I'll show you how to import a folder of files, a feature introduced in FileMaker Pro 6.

As important and valuable as importing and exporting are to FileMaker, these methods don't actually transmit and receive directly with the other programs in real time. For that, we need ODBC.

◑ **NOTE** At some point, XML (which was introduced with FileMaker 6) may become the new standard for sharing live data. But for now, ODBC is a more established method. Keep your eyes open. FileMaker is always on the forefront and is likely to be the leader here.

ODBC Sharing

Open Database Connectivity (ODBC) is an interface used to communicate between various computer programs in real time. The ODBC drivers provided on the FileMaker disk allow other applications to use FileMaker data via ODBC, and the ODBC Configure application (Mac OS X) and Data Sources control panel (Windows) tell FileMaker where to find data from the other applications.

You might think of the drivers and the control panel as translators. As long as the other programs you want to use support ODBC, and the plug-ins, drivers, or control panels for both applications are configured properly, you can get FileMaker to send and receive data. That includes being able to send Structured Query Language (SQL — pronounced *sequel*) requests back and forth.

Let's take the translators analogy a bit further. Imagine that you have a friend in another country. You want to call him or her for some information, but neither of you speaks the same language. Each of you has an acquaintance who speaks a second language, but it's not your friend's language. Fortunately, your interpreters speak each other's language, SQL. You speak FileMaker Pro, and your interpreter speaks FileMaker and SQL. Your friend speaks Excel, and his interpreter speaks Excel and SQL. Using these interpreters, you can ask a question, and your friend can answer. That's exactly how SQL works over ODBC. Think of SQL as the language and ODBC as the translator.

This capability allows you to share data with programs like Oracle, Microsoft Access, Excel, Microsoft SQL Server, and more than 50 others. The ODBC components for most applications are not normally installed unless you perform a custom install. Any of the ODBC drivers not available with your programs are available for purchase from third-party companies. Since ODBC is a Microsoft Windows standard (based on COM), drivers and ODBC-savvy applications are much more common on the Windows platform than on the Mac.

One terrific advantage of using ODBC is that it lets users work with the easy-to-learn FileMaker front end to access data in systems that are much harder to use. Even if you understand and can use such systems, your end users may not be able to. You can build solutions for them that they will find easy to use and modify. And it only takes about one-fourth of the time it would take to build something similar with other ODBC tools.

Maybe you work for a company where the IT people don't want to mess with FileMaker because they don't consider it a "serious" database. With ODBC sharing, FileMaker absolutely needs to be taken seriously!

Making FileMaker Data Available to Other Applications

To make your data available to other applications, you first have to set up your file correctly.

1. Choose **File**, **Define**, **Accounts & Privileges**.

2. Choose any of the existing accounts and click the **Edit** button. You need to choose the Guest account if you want everyone to have access to your data. If you want more control over who has access to the data, follow this procedure for each account that will have access.

3. Click the **Edit** button to the right of the Privilege Set pop-up. That will take you to the Edit Privilege Set window shown in Figure 20-1.

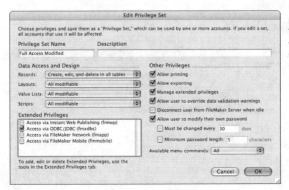

Figure 20-1
The Edit Privilege Set window with the Access via ODBC/JDBC box checked.

4. Check the box in the lower left next to **Access via ODBC/JDBC (fmxdbc).** When you click OK to leave here, you'll see the Account Name and Password dialog, which will require the information for an account

with All Access. When you convert or create a file, an Administration account is created automatically. You can read more about this in Chapter 21, "Keeping Your Data Secure." If you haven't already assigned a password, type **Admin** in the Account Name and leave the password blank. You can double-click the Admin account to look at it. If there are a number of bullets in the password area, a password has already been assigned. If you are having trouble with the passwords, read Chapter 21 first. You need to have Administration-level access (full access) to change the password. If someone else sets up the account and leaves the company without making a record of that password and letting you know where it's recorded, you'd be up the creek without a paddle. The password is not stored with the file. So be careful to keep records of all the passwords.

In our current set of files, the Admin account does not have a password.

5. You know enough to click **OK** as many times as needed to finish up from here, don't you?

6. If you see a blinking cursor at the Edit Account window, ignore it, and click **OK**.

7. If you see the Confirm Full Access Login dialog, type **Admin** for Full Access Account and no password.

Now you need to allow users to get to the data. Here's how.

1. On a Mac, choose **FileMaker Pro**, **Sharing**, **FileMaker Network**, **ODBC/JDBC**. On Windows, choose **Edit**, **Sharing**, **ODBC/JDBC**. That will bring up the ODBC/JDBC Sharing Settings window shown in Figure 20-2.

2. Click the **On** button next to ODBC/JDBC Sharing.

3. Select the file or files you want to share and click the radio buttons on the right to select the privilege sets. Notice that if you select more than one file you can only choose to share with All users or No users. The only way to choose Specify users by privilege set is by selecting one file at a time. Clearly you need to have the files you intend to share open at the time you work with this window.

4. Finish by clicking **OK**, etc.

This process is like the light switches I told you about when explaining web sharing: First you turn on the master switch, then you turn on the individual lights. The master switch here is the On button. The individual light switches are the specific files and the users allowed to connect.

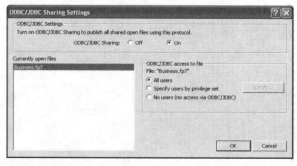

Figure 20-2
The ODBC/JDBC Sharing Settings window.

Once you've made these settings, any other program that talks ODBC can get information from the switched-on FileMaker files. The specifics of how to accomplish that in the other application is something you'll have to find out by looking in the manual for that program.

➲ **NOTE**   Keep in mind that sharing FileMaker data with other applications via ODBC is subject to any password restrictions placed on the individual files.

➲ **NOTE**   The database you want to share needs to be open to share its data.

Getting Data from Another Application

In this section, we'll actually be able to use ODBC to import some data. Because I can't know what programs you may have on your computer and/or network, the only example I can give you that I know you'll be able to work with uses one FileMaker file and a set of text files provided for this specific purpose. If you did the complete install, look inside the FileMaker Pro 7 folder, English Extras, Examples, ODBC Example for a file called Sales_Reports. You can go ahead and open the file now since we'll need it to perform a test import.

For all intents and purposes, the ODBC driver will look at a properly formatted text file the same way it will a table in Excel, for example. That brings us to one other important advantage: Even if another application is not ODBC compliant, if it can export data as text, you can create a link to the file using the ODBC control panel and build queries in FileMaker Pro. That gives you more power over how the data is handled than a simple import would provide.

This will be a simplified example. When you're running on a network, there are quite a few other settings to be considered. In most cases, someone else will be administering the other data sources. Hopefully, they'll know the settings from their side. Just be sure that you have a line open to the machine with the data you want to access. Of course, you'll get a message if something is set up improperly.

➲ **NOTE**   You do not need to activate the ODBC/JDBC sharing settings in order to import data from external data sources. They are only necessary when you want to make FileMaker data available to other applications.

At this point, Macintosh and Windows users will say "bye-bye" to each other. The screens and steps are similar but just different enough to be confusing if I jumble them all together. We'll meet up again at the section titled "Saving the Import as a Script." If you're a Windows user, skip ahead to the section titled "Setting Up the Data Source (Windows)."

Setting Up the Data Source (Macintosh OS X)

1. Go into the Applications, DataDirect ODBC folder and double-click **ODBC Configure**. Mine opens to the User DSN tab as shown in Figure 20-3. DSN stands for Data Source Name.

    If the DataDirect ODBC folder isn't in the Applications folder, go into the FileMaker Pro 7 folder and look for the ODBC Import Drivers folder. Inside you'll find the ODBC Import Drivers installer. Double-click it to install the drivers. That will provide the DataDirect folder.

Figure 20-3
The Configuration Manager window with the User DSN tab selected.

2. The next thing you have to do is tell FileMaker where to find the data you want. Click the **Add** button to bring you to the window shown in Figure 20-4 where you'll pick the driver for our example.

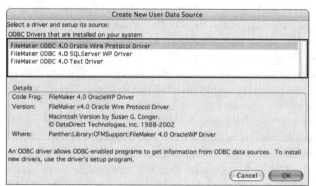

Figure 20-4
The Create New User Data Source window where you choose the driver for the type of data you'll be importing.

3. Choose **FileMaker ODBC 4.0 Text Driver** (or greater), and click the **OK** button.

4. In the Data Source Name box, type **Test**. In Description, type **Sales**.

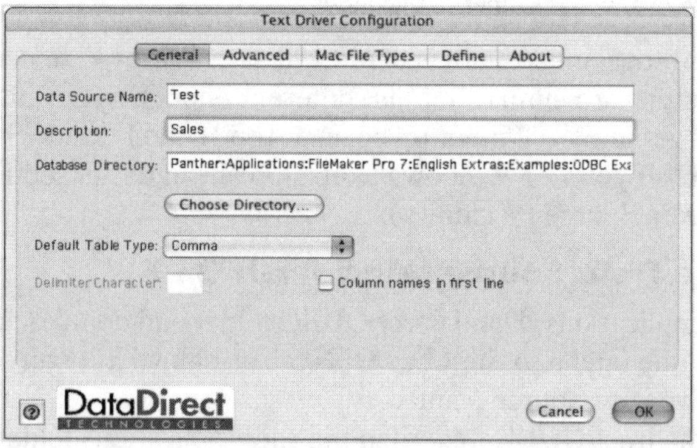

Figure 20-5
The General tab where you name the Data source and choose a directory.

5. Click the **Choose Directory** button.

6. Look inside FileMaker Pro 7\English Extras\Examples, and select the ODBC Example folder.

7. Don't bother trying to select any of the files inside the folder. Just select the ODBC Example folder itself like I have in Figure 20-6 and click the **Open** button. (Notice I have my Mac window set to display files and folders in columns, but the result is the same.) This will bring you back to the General tab.

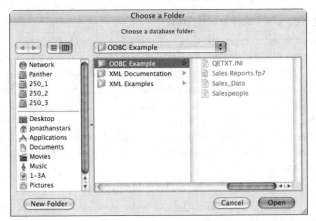

Figure 20-6
The window where you choose the folder that holds the data files.

8. Still in the General tab, click the **Column names in first line** box.

9. Now click the **Define** tab, which will bring you to the window in Figure 20-7. (The actual table and fields that appear in the window may be different than what is shown in the figure.)

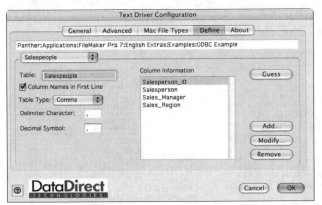

Figure 20-7
This is the window where you define the tables and columns to be used in your query in steps 10 and 11.

10. If it's not already selected, choose **Sales_Data** from the pop-up above Table. If the column names don't appear in the Column Information box, click the **Guess** button. Make sure there is an x in the "Column names in first line" box.

11. Then click the pop-up above Table again and choose **Salespeople**. If the column names don't appear, click the **Guess** button and be sure there's an x next to "Column names in first line."

12. The window should look like Figure 20-7. Click **OK**.

Part 5

13. Finally, click **OK** to close the Configuration Manager.

At any time in the future, you can come back and check your settings by opening the ODBC Configure application and double-clicking on the data source. If you have any trouble, you might check the Advanced tab to make sure that you chose Guess from the Action for Undefined Tables pop-up. You can also check the Mac File Types tab to see that the file type is TEXT. Normally, they should be selected automatically for this test.

Importing the Data (Macintosh)

Before you get carried away with this, let me warn you that at press time this would not work on OS X. By the time you read this there will likely be an update to FMP7 that will allow it. You can go to FileMaker's web site for the most current information. All the windows are in place, but not all the bugs had been worked out. FileMaker 7 can be used as an ODBC/JDBC client on OS X, but at press time not yet as a data source.

Now let's see if we can pull some data into a file using the ODBC data source we just set up. You should already have the Sales Reports file open. If you don't, open it now.

1. Choose **File**, **Import Records**, **ODBC Data Source**.

2. You should see the Select ODBC Data Source window shown in Figure 20-8. Select **Test** from the Data Source Name list and click **Continue**.

3. FileMaker will ask for a user name and password. Just click **OK**. Figure 20-9 shows the SQL Query Builder window.

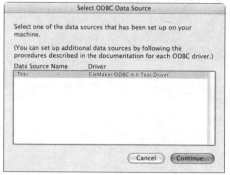

Figure 20-8
The Select ODBC Data Source window with the Test source created in the previous section.

Figure 20-9
The SQL Query Builder window where you construct the request for the specific data you want to find.

4. If there is any text in the SQL Query box in the lower part of this window, click the **Clear Query** button to empty it out. When you're asked if you're sure, click the **Clear** button.

If you know SQL, you can type right in the SQL Query box. However, FileMaker makes it easy to construct your own query without all that typing and without knowing the SQL syntax.

⊃ **NOTE** This is where some of the field-, table-, and file-naming guidelines we talked about earlier in the book come into play again. SQL (as well as HTML — the language of the Internet) cannot deal with periods, spaces, or special characters in the names of files or fields. Actually, you can work with spaces by using apostrophes around the field names. When FileMaker builds the query, it takes care of that for you.

5. Select **Sales_Data** from the Tables list and **Amount** from the Columns list, and click the **Insert into SQL Query** button. Notice that the proper SELECT and FROM headings are added and the fields and tables are placed in the query box.

     You don't have to click the Insert into SQL Query button. Once a table is selected, you can double-click on the column names. Continue by double-clicking on the other column names.

6. Select **Salespeople** from the Tables list, and double-click each of the column names from the Columns list except Salesperson_ID. It's okay if you do choose it; it's just that there won't be any field to match it up with in step 13. When you're done, your window should match the one in Figure 20-9.

7. Click the **WHERE** tab. This is where you create a relationship between the two text files, or a "join between tables" to use a SQL term.

8. Select **Sales_Data** from the Table.Column pop-up and **Salesperson_ID** from the pop-up to the right of that. Choose = as the Operator. Then choose **Salespeople** from the lower-left pop-up and **Salesperson_ID** from the lower-right pop-up. Make sure the **Column** radio button is selected. Look at Figure 20-10 to see what your screen should look like.

9. To move this part of the query into the SQL Query box, click the **Insert into SQL Query** button.

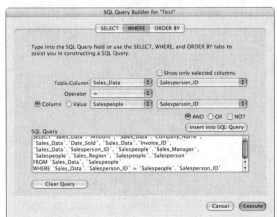

Figure 20-10
The WHERE tab of the SQL Query Builder window with the Test selections inserted into the query box.

10. Click the **ORDER BY** tab. This window is similar to FileMaker's Sort window. Double-click **Sales_Data.Amount** in the Columns list to move it to the Order By area.

11. Be sure it is selected in the right column, click the **Descending** radio button, and click the **Insert into SQL Query** button. When you're done, your screen should look like the one in Figure 20-11.

12. Click the **Execute** button.

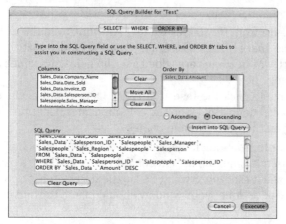

Figure 20-11
The ORDER BY tab of the SQL Query Builder window with the Sales_Data.Amount inserted into the Query box.

13. FileMaker will display the Import Field Mapping window shown in Figure 20-12. You'll see this window whenever you import data from other files. The specifics of this window are discussed in more detail in Chapter 22. To get you started, choose "matching names" from the Arrange by pop-up in the right middle of the window. Because most of the field names have underscores in them, only two fields will display the matching arrow. Click to match Company_Name with Company Name and so on down the list. The Arrange by pop-up will change to "custom import order."

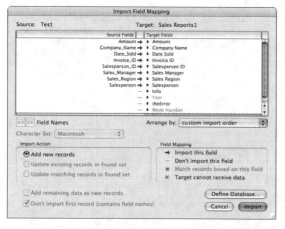

Figure 20-12
FileMaker's Import Field Mapping window.

14. Make sure the fields are lined up as they appear in Figure 20-12, including the arrows. Select the **Add new records** radio button, and click the **Import** button. After a few seconds, the screen will clear and you should have 250 new records in the file.

If you're a Macintosh user, skip forward to the section titled "Saving the Import as a Script."

Setting Up the Data Source (Windows)

The first thing you have to do is tell FileMaker where to find the data you want.

1. Click the **Start** menu, and choose **Settings, Control Panel, Administrative Tools**, and double-click **Data Sources (ODBC)**. If you can't find it, perhaps you didn't do the full install from the FileMaker CD-ROM. When the control panel opens, you'll see the window in Figure 20-13. DSN on the User DSN tab stands for Data Source Name.

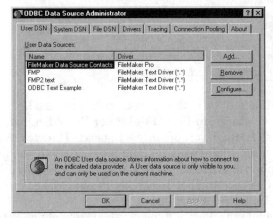

Figure 20-13
The ODBC Data Source Administrator window with the User DSN tab selected.

2. Click the **Add** button to bring up the dialog box shown in Figure 20-14 where you'll pick the driver for our example.

Figure 20-14
The Create New Data Source window where you choose the driver for the type of data you'll be importing.

3. Choose **FileMaker Text Driver (*.*)**, and click the **Finish** button. "Finish" is a misnomer, since you've barely begun, as you'll soon see.

4. In the Data Source Name box, type **Test**. In Description, type **Sales**. See Figure 20-15.

Part 5

Figure 20-15
The General tab where you name the data source and choose a directory.

5. You have to know the location of the file you want to access. If you trust your typing, enter **C:\Program Files\FileMaker Pro 7\English Extras\Examples\ODBC Example** in the Database Directory box. This, of course, assumes that you're working from the C drive. (If you have more than one version of FileMaker Pro on your machine, your directory may actually read C:\Program Files\FileMaker Pro\FileMaker Pro 7\English Extras\Examples\ODBC Example.)

   You could also find the folder in Explorer, then highlight and copy the address to the clipboard (Ctrl+C). Minimize Explorer to bring the control panel back to the front and paste (Ctrl+V) the address into the Database Directory box.

6. Check the box next to **Column Names in First Line**, then click the **Advanced** tab to bring up the window shown in Figure 20-16.

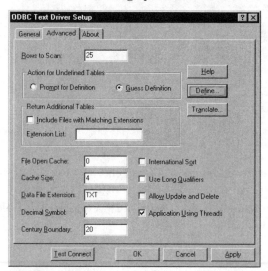

Figure 20-16
The Advanced tab of the ODBC Text Driver Setup window.

7. Click the **Define** button. In the next window, you'll need to find the ODBC Example file, which should be in the same directory you used in step 5. Choose **All Files** from the Files of type pop-up to display the items in Figure 20-17.

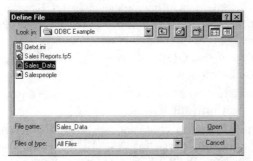

Figure 20-17
The Define File window where you choose the files that will be part of the data source.

8. Select **Sales_Data** and click the **Open** button. Figure 20-18 shows the Define Table window that appears.

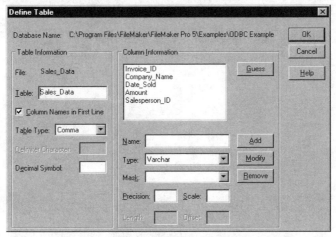

Figure 20-18
This is the window where you define the tables and columns to be used in your query.

9. If the column names don't appear in the Column Information box, click the **Guess** button. Make sure there is an x in the box next to **Column Names in First Line**, and click **OK**. (Windows XP users may need to type the table name, which should be the same as the file name above it. Then be sure to check the Column Names in First Line box before clicking the Guess button.) That will bring you back to the Define File window.

10. Go back to step 8 and repeat the steps for the Salespeople file.

11. When you finally return to the Define File window, click **Cancel**. I know that doesn't seem like the right choice, but it is. This will bring you back to the Advanced tab. Click the **OK** button, and click **OK** again to dismiss the ODBC Data Source Administrator window. This time you really are "finished."

At any time in the future, you can come back and check your settings by double-clicking on the data source. If you have any trouble, you might check the Advanced tab to make sure the file type is TXT and that you chose Guess

Definition from the Action for Undefined Tables area. Normally, they should be selected automatically for this test.

Importing the Data (Windows)

Now let's see if we can pull some data into a file using the ODBC data source we just set up. You should already have the Sales Reports file open. If you don't, open it now. You can find it in the ODBC Example folder.

1. Choose **File, Import Records, ODBC Source**. This will bring up the Select ODBC Data Source window.

2. Choose the **Test** that we just created. (Don't mix it up with any that might be called Text.) Click the **Continue** button.

3. You'll likely be prompted for a user name and password. If you haven't set up any for this file, use **Admin**, leave the password blank, and click **OK**. That should bring up the Specify ODBC SQL Query window.

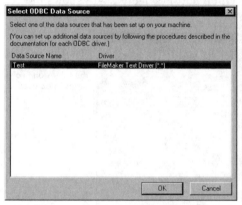

Figure 20-19
The Select ODBC Data Source window with the Test source created in the previous section.

Figure 20-20
The Specify ODBC SQL Query window where you construct the request for the specific data you want to find.

4. If there is any text in the SQL Query box in the lower part of this window, click the **Clear Query** button to empty it out. When you're asked if you're sure, click the **Clear** button.

   If you know SQL, you can type right in the SQL Query box. However, FileMaker makes it easy to construct your own query without all that typing and without knowing the SQL syntax.

⊃ **NOTE**   This is where some of the field-, table-, and file-naming guidelines we talked about earlier come into play again. SQL (as well as HTML — the language of the Internet) cannot deal with periods, spaces, or special characters in the names of files or fields. Actually, you can work with spaces by using apostrophes around the field names. When FileMaker builds the query, it takes care of that for you.

5. Select **Sales_Data** from the Tables list and **Amount** from the Columns list, and click the **Insert into SQL Query** button. Notice that the proper SELECT and FROM headings are added, and the fields and tables are placed in the query box.

6. You don't have to click the Insert into SQL Query button. Once a table is selected, you can double-click on the column names. Continue by double-clicking on the other column names.

7. Select **Salespeople** from the Table list, and double-click each of the column names from the Columns list except the Salesperson_ID. It's okay if you do choose it; it's just that there won't be any field to match it up with in step 11. When you're done, your window should match the one in Figure 20-21.

8. Click the **WHERE** tab. This is where you create a relationship between the two text files, or a "join between tables" to use a SQL term. Select **Sales_Data** from the Table.Column pop-up and **Salesperson_ID** from the pop-up to the right of that. Choose = as the Operator. Then select **Salespeople** from the lower-left pop-up and **Salesperson_ID** from the lower-right pop-up, and make sure the **Column** radio button is selected. Look at Figure 20-21 to see what your screen should look like. To move this part of the query into the SQL Query box, click the **Insert into SQL Query** button.

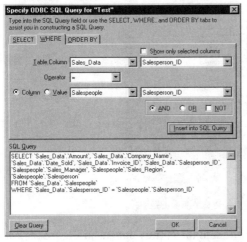

Figure 20-21
The WHERE tab of the Specify ODBC SQL Query window with the Test selections inserted into the query.

9. Click the **ORDER BY** tab. This window is similar to FileMaker's Sort window. Double-click **Sales_Data.Amount** in the Columns list to move it to the Order By area. Be sure Sales_DataAmount is selected in the box on the right, click the **Descending** radio button, and click the **Insert into SQL Query** button. When you're done, your screen should look like the one in Figure 20-22. Click **Execute** or **OK**, whichever appears on your button.

Part 5

Figure 20-22
The ORDER BY tab of the Specify ODBC SQL Query window with the Sales_Data.Amount inserted into the query.

10. FileMaker will display the Import Field Mapping window shown in Figure 20-23. You'll see this window whenever you import data from other files. The specifics of this window are discussed in more detail in Chapter 22. For now, choose "matching names" from the View by pop-up in the upper-right corner.

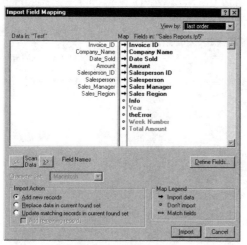

Figure 20-23
FileMaker's Import Field Mapping window.

11. Make sure the fields are lined up as they appear in Figure 20-23, including the arrows. Your fields may not be in the same order, but you should make sure the field names are lined up with matching names in the two columns. Select the **Add new records** radio button, and click the **Import** button. After a few seconds, the screen will clear and you should have 250 new records in the file.

Saving the Import as a Script

After you've created your ODBC import, if you expect to run it again, it would be very wise to create a script that will handle all the work automatically, especially while the details are still fresh in your mind. The process is slightly different from other imports described in this book. Here's how:

1. Choose **Scripts**, **ScriptMaker**, start a new script, and call it **Test ODBC Import**.

2. Find the **Import Records** step from the Records heading, and double-click it.

3. Click the **File** pop-up and choose **ODBC Data.** Then choose **Test** from the Select ODBC Data Source window, and click **OK** (on Macintosh) or **Continue** (on Windows).

4. The Enter Password window will show up next. Fill in the User name and Password boxes and click **OK**. (If your Guest account has been activated and it doesn't require a password, you can leave both boxes empty.)

5. In the Specify ODBC SQL Query window, make sure the query is the one you want, and click **OK**. This will return you to the Script Definition window. (In Windows XP, you may need to rebuild the query. I found a shortcut to that tedious process. I left the script and started the import process over with the query still in the box. I just copied it, backed out of the import, and went back to the script where I pasted it into the box.)

6. You'll also probably want to check the box next to **Perform without Dialog**. If you don't, users will be presented with the Data Source, Password, and Specify ODBC SQL Query windows before they actually import. That would only be an invitation to future errors.

7. When you're done, click **OK** and **OK** again.

Now try it out by running the script. This works fine with the sample text file, but if you're working with other applications, you'll need to turn on any plug-ins for that application before the data will actually import properly. Those plug-ins are what provide our "interpreter." If you're getting data from a remote computer, you'll also need to make sure the network is open and set to TCP/IP, and that you include the number of the machine you're trying to get data from.

Although some of this terminology may be new to you, stepping through these windows makes the complexities of ODBC queries considerably easier than learning standard ODBC query construction. If you are interested in SQL, you can find plenty of online tutorials by entering "SQL tutorial" in a search engine.

This has been a very simplified description of FileMaker's ODBC capabilities. Don't forget that this process works the other way around. In other words, you can access FileMaker data when you're working in other ODBC-compliant programs. You can get more information from the manual and the Help files. Look in the indexes under ODBC and SQL. Depending on the ODBC driver you work with, the windows may give you different options.

Part 5

Execute SQL Script Step

Starting back with version 5.5, FileMaker has been able to execute SQL statements with the Execute SQL script step. That means that not only can you get data into FileMaker from other SQL-savvy applications, but you can also manipulate and export data to them. This feature (along with the XML features introduced in FMP 6) expands FileMaker's value as a serious application in an enterprise setting.

In the previous section, "Saving the Import as a Script," that import is actually a static activity. With the Execute SQL step, you can run SQL statements based on data stored in fields (including Calculation and Global fields). The statements can operate dynamically for each record in the file if you want.

Working hand in hand with the Execute SQL step is the Get (LastODBC-Error) function. You'll want to have FileMaker check for any errors by placing this step immediately after any Execute SQL script step so you can plan a course of action in case it doesn't run properly (i.e., display an error message onscreen and/or halt the script). I would use it like this:

```
SetField [zi_ODBCError_gt; ""]
Execute SQL[]
SetField [Invoice::zi_ODBCError_gt; Get(LastODBCError)]
If [not IsEmpty(zi_ODBCError_gt)]
    Beep
    Show Message[There was an ODBC Error]
    Go to Layout [ODBC Error] (display the error in a field on this layout)
    Halt Script
End If
```

Getting the correctly matched set of drivers is critical and can cause a lot of frustration. Getting the right syntax for your query can be equally trying. Since a problem with either drivers or syntax will produce the same result — nothing — it's hard to know where to look. You may need to check out FileMaker, Inc.'s web site to find resources and get on a discussion list. But prepare yourself before asking your question. Find out the version numbers of each database (FMP and the other database — i.e., Oracle) and the ODBC drivers you're trying to use. Using FMP's window to help you construct the query (assuming you may not know the syntax) will go a long way in ruling out syntax as the problem.

I won't go into any more detail here. Maybe it's just the clients I work with, but in all my years as a FileMaker developer, none of them have asked me to implement any ODBC or SQL functions. That doesn't mean the functions aren't important, just that it's a little beyond the scope of this tutorial. There's a little more information in the Help files, but even they suggest you get a book on SQL if you want to go further. Good luck!

Converting and Importing Data from Microsoft Excel

You can send and receive data from Excel spreadsheets using ODBC. You can also convert an Excel spreadsheet into a FileMaker file. Then you can import the data when you need it, or build an ODBC connection to transfer data back and forth in real time.

FileMaker Pro 5.5 added functionality for importing named ranges from Excel. That becomes useful when there's more than one row of description in the Excel file, when there is more than one set of tabular data on the spreadsheet, or when data is labeled in the row above the data you want to import.

Assuming you have the Excel application and an Excel spreadsheet on your computer or accessible on a network:

1. Choose **File, Open** from within FileMaker.

2. Choose **Excel** from the pop-up list next to Show (Macintosh) or Files of type (Windows), select the file you want to convert, and click the **Open** button.

3. As shown in Figure 20-24, select a worksheet or named range and click **OK**.

4. The window in Figure 20-25 should appear. Choose the radio button for whether the first row or named range should be used as field names or data. This window will not appear if there are no named ranges.

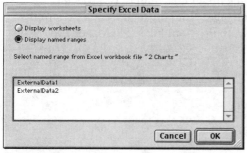

Figure 20-24
The Specify Excel Data window where you can select worksheets or named ranges to be converted.

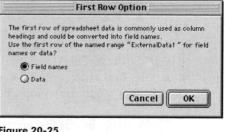

Figure 20-25
The First Row Option window.

5. Choose a name and location for your file, and click the **Save** button.

Depending on the size of the spreadsheet, this could take some time. Once your new file has been created, you can build an ODBC connection to it. If you only need to import information occasionally, you might choose to create a script to import from the spreadsheet. To do that, start a script and choose the Import Records step from the Records heading. Click the Specify File button, select the file, and run through the same windows as in steps 3 and 4.

To read more about this and other conversions and imports, see the FileMaker Help files. For more on field mapping when importing data, see the section titled "Importing Data" in Chapter 22.

Importing a Folder of Files in a Single Operation

I've been very happy with this feature, which was introduced in FileMaker Pro 6. It allows you to import a whole folder of files at one fell swoop. That includes importing graphics (GIF, JPEG, EPS, TIFF, PICT, BMP, and a bunch of other file types), PDFs and QuickTime movies into Container fields, as well as text files into Text, Number, Date, and Time fields. Along with the data, you can choose to import the file name and path and thumbnails of the images. This is a terrific time-saving organizational tool. Let me show you how I used it on a folder of pictures from my digital camera.

I first started taking photographs about 15 years ago. It wasn't long before I had trouble keeping track of where the pictures were, and I wasted a lot of time trying to find them and keep them organized. So I started to number the envelopes that came back from the developer and listing the shots in a FileMaker database. Before long I started scanning some of my favorites and keeping thumbnails in the file along with the text. A picture may be worth a thousand words, but it was sure a lot easier to find those photos using text than to look through that box of envelopes.

Scanning all those pictures was a very time-consuming process, and I soon found I wasn't keeping up with it. I was thrilled when I got my first digital camera and found I could simply hook it up to my computer and save the images to CD. But it was still pretty tricky trying to find them when I wanted them.

Enter FMP 6 and its feature for importing a file of folders! Just follow along with my first experience and see if this might be useful to you as well.

First I dragged the folder of new images from my digital camera onto the desktop of my computer. Then I went to Program Files, FileMaker Pro 7\English Extras\Templates\Home and opened the Photo Catalog.fp7 file. I chose File, Import Records, Folder. That brought me to the window in Figure 20-26.

Clicking the Specify button took me to the usual window for finding any folder or file. I hunted around on the desktop until I found the folder. It confused me when I double-clicked the folder to open it and found nothing inside. Backing out one level, I discovered you're just supposed to highlight the folder and click the Choose button. That took me back to the Options window and

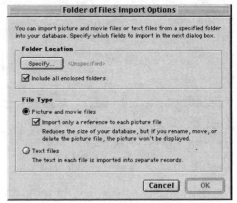

Figure 20-26
FileMaker's Folder of Files Import Options window.

the folder name appeared next to the Specify button. Since there were no enclosed folders, I simply unchecked that box.

Then I moved on to the File Type area and clicked the "Picture and movie files" radio button. I made sure to check the box next to "Import only a reference to each picture file." If you store the pictures right in the file, the file can get large pretty quickly. Think about it: My pictures come in at about 320 K. I had 167 pictures in this folder. The whole folder weighed in at 52.4 MB. Even though FileMaker files can now hold up to 8 terabytes of data, the size of your hard drive will more likely be the limiting factor. Storing a reference to the images keeps the file size down.

Next I clicked the OK button, which brought up FileMaker's Import Field Mapping window similar to the one in Figure 20-23. Of course, the fields are different from that figure. Since you may actually want to try this, I mapped the fields as follows (although your fields may be somewhat different):

Image	Image Data
File Name	Image File Name
File Path	Location
Image Thumbnail	Thumbnail Image Data

After clicking the radio button next to "Add new records" in the Import Action area, I clicked the Import button. In the Import Options window I checked the box next to "Perform auto-enter options" and clicked the OK or Import button.

It took a couple of minutes for all the pictures to come in. Sure enough, there were my pictures of the chili cook-off, my niece's graduation, my trip to Chicago for the FileMaker tech update, and my buddy Gene Burd's band at a jam session. I entered a little text about each of the important images.

This template has a List layout that shows the thumbnails seen in Figure 20-27. Clicking the thumbnail takes you to a larger version of the image. If I had taken advantage of FileMaker's Mac OS X import directly from the camera, I could have imported all the metadata about the shots as well. I do a lot of goofy things with aperture and exposure times, and it would be interesting to have that information come in auto-matically. You can't do that on Windows machines — yet.

Figure 20-27
FileMaker's Image Catalog template shows List View and fields for metadata from a digital camera.

In the old days, I would never have bothered to scan this many pictures. It would have taken way too long. This was a snap. I also like that I can choose to store the file path. I'll store the images on a CD-ROM as well; even if I delete them from the hard drive (or have a drive failure), I'll be able to find that folder on the CD. That's because I index all my CDs and store the index in, what else, FileMaker. The main trick is to make sure your camera is set up so the images are numbered sequentially and it doesn't reset to image number 1 when you insert a new memory card.

Just because I used this feature with my digital camera doesn't mean you have to stop there. You can also import a folder of text files. That means you can get all your text for many documents into one, easy-to-search place — FileMaker. The files must be straight .txt files. That means if the files are in Word or WordPerfect, you'll have to save them as text first, which means you'll likely lose some of the formatting. (FileMaker can now hold up to one billion characters in a Text field.)

Summary

In this chapter, we looked at using the Import and Export commands, as well as how to use the ODBC control panel and the ODBC/JDBC Sharing dialog to share data between FileMaker and other applications. Then we looked at the Folder of Files Import Options window, which allows us to import an entire folder at a time. In particular, the ODBC features place FileMaker in a whole new league regarding its place in large organizations.

Q & A

Q When we did the ODBC import, I noticed the "Update matching records in current found set" radio button. Does this mean FileMaker does file synchronization?

A Well, sort of. The main use of this function is to update files from a laptop to a desktop machine and vice versa. You pick a field that has a unique identifier (usually a serial number) in both files, perform a Find in each file for the specific records you want to update (or choose Show All Records), and choose which fields you want updated (or choose matching names). When you import, it will overwrite the selected data in the current file with the data from the file being imported from.

Some people mistakenly think this feature will provide file synchronization between multiple users and a master database in the home office. It would take some truly sophisticated scripting to avoid duplicating serial numbers for new entries. The same goes for making decisions about which entries will be considered the "master" when two records have changed since the last update. For more on this specific feature, see the manual or the Help files.

There are some subtleties to the "Update matching" that we haven't covered anywhere else. Only the current found set of records will be updated, and they'll only be updated from the data in the current found set in the other file. For that reason, if you intend to update all the records in the current file with the records in the other file, you would want to create a script that finds all records in both files before performing the update.

At the end of the update process, the number of records updated in the current file will become the found set. That caused me some grief recently when I was refining an import. I didn't realize my found set had continued to diminish each time I performed the update. Each attempt reduced the found set until finally no records at all were being updated. After my initial, "Huh?" I figured out what was happening. Now you'll know better. You are memorizing this entire book, aren't you?

Workshop

Delete the records from the Sales Reports file and try another import using different column combinations or maybe only one of the files. See what different numbers of records end up being imported.

Notice the button called Import Records in the Sales Reports file. Click it to take you to a layout with some buttons attached to scripts used in the ODBC demo in the FileMaker Pro 7 User's Guide. The two buttons on the right won't work properly yet. Follow the instructions for the example in the FileMaker Pro 7 User's Guide, which will give a different name to the Data Source, then try these buttons.

Review Questions

True-False

1. You can import data into FileMaker Pro only from other FileMaker databases.
2. The ODBC interface allows you to communicate between FileMaker Pro and other ODBC-compliant data sources in real time.
3. The ODBC Data Source Administrator window looks different on Macintosh and Windows, but it is designed to produce the same results: making data from a different source available to FileMaker Pro.
4. The Import Folder feature can be used only for importing graphics into FileMaker Pro.
5. You can use FileMaker as a real-time front end to a database written in Oracle.

Short Answer

6. What is the fundamental difference between ODBC and SQL?
7. Which driver must be installed in order to make FileMaker data available to programs on the same computer and on computers over a TCP/IP network?
8. Which ScriptMaker function should you use in conjunction with the Execute SQL script step to handle any errors that might occur?
9. After you convert an Excel spreadsheet into a FileMaker Pro database, how can you move data back and forth between the two in real time?
10. What is one danger of importing a folder of graphic files into a FileMaker Pro database, and how can you help avoid this danger?
11. What is an advantage of using ODBC to work with data as opposed to Import and Export?
12. Why is it so important to avoid using periods, spaces, and other special characters when naming fields and files?

Part 5

Protecting Your Information

Chapter 21

Keeping Your Data Secure

Vocabulary

- Password
- Privilege
- Privilege set
- Record-level security

Objectives

1. Learn to navigate the tabs on the Accounts & Privileges window.
2. Understand the difference between accounts and privilege sets, and how they interact.
3. Become familiar with script-based security methods.
4. Realize potential ramifications of using and maintaining FileMaker security.
5. Become familiar with record-level security.
6. Create accounts and assign privileges.
7. Understand the limitations of FileMaker security over the web.

Introduction

After all the work you've done to build your files, you'll want to protect the information you've collected either for yourself or for your employer.

In this chapter, we'll look at:

- How to set up FileMaker Pro's security
- How to protect data through scripts
- How to protect data through calculations

Why Protect Your Data?

There are three main reasons you'll need to protect FileMaker files: confidentiality, accidents, and vandalism. If you're storing information about customers, employees, finances, or medical records, it should be obvious that only certain people should be able to get to that data. Since the data is valuable (otherwise, why collect it?), you don't want it accidentally erased. Likewise, after all the time you've spent on the layouts, you'd hate to have someone go in and unintentionally rearrange or even delete your layouts. And let's not forget the

Internet hacker or disgruntled employee. All of these situations point to reasons to put a little extra time into making sure everything stays secure.

FileMaker Security

FileMaker Pro's security system has changed dramatically with version 7. Developers who have worked with the pre-release software are very pleased with the new model. The new approach is more logical than the old one and offers better protection. And after all, isn't that what security is all about?

Setting up FileMaker Pro's security consists of creating accounts, choosing passwords, and assigning privilege sets to the various records, layouts, and fields. That's right, you can even control whether specific users can enter or even see data in individual fields.

The two primary domains you control with FileMaker security are what users can do and what users can access. When you create a privilege set, you make decisions about what users can do, ranging from printing and going to Layout mode to viewing and deleting records. You decide what layouts they can go to and what fields they're allowed to see and enter data into.

Every account is assigned a privilege set and a password. Because a privilege set can easily be added and removed from an account, one or more accounts (and the individuals who go with them) can be temporarily assigned a privilege set for a particular project and removed when the job is done. The same applies to what records, layouts, and fields are available to a privilege set. Access to specific areas can be changed for an entire privilege set fairly quickly and easily.

Although FileMaker's built-in security scheme does not cover every combination of control functions you might be able to dream up, it's quite powerful and should take care of the majority of the user's needs. Let's take a look.

Accounts Tab[7]

Go to your Business file, and choose File, Define, Accounts & Privileges. You should be presented with a window similar to the one in Figure 21-1 except there will probably be fewer accounts in yours. Take a look at the View by pop-up in the lower right of this window. Just another way to help you organize. Since you see columns here, you might think that clicking the column headings might change the sort order. No such luck. Oh, well. You can, however, resize the columns by clicking and dragging the line between the column names. And if you're on a

Figure 21-1
The Accounts tab of the Define Accounts & Privileges window for the Business file showing five example accounts.

Macintosh, once you've selected an item in the View by pop-up, you can reverse the sort by clicking the triangle to the right of the Description column. Windows users don't get that choice. For both Mac and Windows users, if you do click the Account column heading after selecting one of the other choices in the pop-up, the View by will switch back to "account name."

Edit Account[7]

Guest Account[7]

Click the [Guest] account to highlight it. Notice the Duplicate and Delete buttons remain gray. There can only be one Guest account in a file. That's why you can't duplicate it. And at the same time there absolutely must be a Guest account in each file. That's why you can't delete it. Also notice that when a file is first created, the box under the Active column next to the Guest account is unchecked. FileMaker wants to make sure you decide for yourself whether that account should be active.

Click the Edit button to bring up the Edit Account window in Figure 21-2. (You can also double-click an account.) At this point you can rename the Guest account if you like, but you cannot assign it a password. By definition the Guest account (or whatever you decide to name it) does not require a password. That would seem to be a security risk, wouldn't it? But notice the Account Status radio buttons in the middle of the window. At any time you can choose to deactivate the Guest account.

Figure 21-2
The Edit Account window.

Notice also that the "Account is authenticated via" pop-up is disabled. Other accounts can be validated by an external server such as Apple OpenDirectory or Windows Domain. This is a long-requested feature that lets you use the server list instead of having to keep track of two sets of accounts, one for FileMaker and one for the server. All the rules for the external privilege set apply, such as:

- Too many attempts at entering a password and you're locked out.
- You can only log in during certain hours.
- Your password must change every 30 days.
- Your password must be a certain length.

The default privilege set for the Guest account is Read Only. But you can use the pop-up list to choose any privilege set you like, including the Full Access and Data Entry Only sets. You can type a description at the bottom of this window. Currently, I'm using this to remind myself about what the account is for and to store the password. I'm not sure that's the best place for passwords, but that's what I'm doing until I figure out something better. This text shows up in the Description column of the Accounts tab seen in Figure 21-1.

Click the Edit button to bring up the Edit Privilege Set window in Figure 21-3. We'll go into the details of this window later. But the reason I wanted you to see it now is that this is actually the very same window we've seen before. You're just accessing it from a different direction. You need to be aware that any changes you make here to a privilege set will affect all accounts with that privilege set. Don't assume that because you got here by way of a specific account that you're having an effect on that account alone.

Make sure your Guest account is still set to Data Entry Only, and you'll notice the only changes you can make here are the Extended Privileges in the lower-left corner. (There's more to this Extended Privileges thing than meets the eye. For more on that, read the section titled "Extended Privileges Tab" later in this chapter.) Click Cancel and Cancel again to take you back to the Accounts tab.

Admin Account[7]

Click the Admin account. Notice the Duplicate and Delete buttons are active. If you delete the account you'll just have to create it again before leaving the Accounts & Privileges area (unless you click the Cancel button).

⌘ **TIP**　At least one of the accounts must have the Full Access privilege set selected. This is a FileMaker requirement, so if you try to make some other arrangement, FileMaker will prevent you from making the change when you try to leave the Define Accounts & Privileges area.

By the way, you can experiment all you want in this window. If you click the Cancel button when you decide to leave Accounts & Privileges (regardless of which tab you're in), all your changes will be discarded.

Double-click the Admin account. You can make nearly any choices you want in the Edit Account window, including leaving Password empty. However, you are not allowed to have an account without a name. Also, every file must have one account with the Full Access privilege set. At this point in the file, since the Guest account has limited access, you may as well leave this set alone. Oh, you can choose some other set of privileges all right. But when you finally click the OK button to exit Define Accounts & Privileges, you'll get a dialog that tells you that at least one account must have Full Access. If you didn't intend to make any changes, click Cancel to restore your previous settings.

☒ **CAUTION**　You can click the Cancel button to discard all changes since you entered the Accounts & Privileges area. Just be sure that's what you want to do. It's possible to work here for hours only to discard everything at the click of a button!

You should still be looking at the Edit Account window for the Admin account. You can click the Edit button next to the Privilege Set pop-up to bring up the Edit Privilege Set window similar to Figure 21-3. The Full Access set is similar to the Data Entry Only set in that you can only make changes to the Extended Privileges area. Click Cancel and Cancel again.

New Account[7]

Click the New button to bring up the Edit Account window. Every account name must be unique. Of course, if you try to use the same name twice, you'll get a warning dialog. Even though account names must be unique, more than one account can have the same password. Name this account Sales and use Counter for the password. (See the Caution below.) Pay attention to the capitalization of the password. You'll need to retype it exactly. Account names aren't that fussy. Type PW: Counter in the Description field as a reminder. Notice the "User must change password on next login" check box in the middle of this window. If you want users to create their own passwords, you can create one here or leave it blank and let them change it next time they log in.

What problems might that cause? First of all, you have to give the user the first password you created before they can enter their own password. Of course that first password could be the same as the account name (or blank) to make your job easier. If they create a new password, the password you just typed into the Description area won't work any more. That could be a good thing. Since there is no way to know their password, passwords are truly personal. However, if they forget their password you have to come back in here and create a new one. (At least they're not locked out forever — as long as you remember the master password!) Regardless of the administrative problems this feature may cause, this version of FileMaker's security is tremendously more powerful than past versions. Now, you get a lot of additional choices.

By the way, you can create accounts without ever assigning any passwords. Of course that cuts your security level quite a bit. But if you're not too worried about people getting into the files, maybe one level of security is okay.

⊠ **CAUTION**   Never use the password "Master" in your files. A study was done recently that found that "Master" was used as a high-level password in an unbelievable number of corporate systems. If you want people to come in and mess with your work, I suppose that's a different thing. But otherwise, avoid the obvious.

A Word about Passwords

Choosing good passwords is a completely separate issue from keeping track of users' passwords. Even if you don't get too fancy, do keep in mind that passwords shouldn't be so easy that anyone can guess them or pick them up too easily by watching over someone's shoulder. Of course, if users are allowed to create their own passwords, a tutorial for them is in order. Maybe you'll decide that the security of your system is more important than your user's choices.

Be careful what you do with the passwords because there is no way to see them once you've created them. After you leave the window and return, whatever password you entered will be replaced with 22 dots, regardless of the length of the password you actually entered. So you won't even be able to guess based on counting the dot characters. You can assign a new password if you come in under an account with the All Access privilege set. I put the passwords in the Description area, but I'm not sure that's the best idea. This is a new animal and we developers haven't learned all about it yet.

Whatever you do, you should never use a password that consists of a word found in the dictionary. Hackers use software that tirelessly tries every word in the dictionary to break into files while they go to lunch. Use a combination of letters and numbers, and make it at least seven characters long.

Privilege Set[7]

Click the pop-up next to Privilege Set and choose New Privilege Set to bring up the Edit Privilege Set window in Figure 21-3. In the Privilege Set Name box type Sales. Notice that you can access all the check boxes and pop-ups now that you're no longer working with the Guest or Admin privilege sets. But also notice that the default settings have nearly everything turned off. That's so you don't accidentally give a new account any power without intending to.

In a minute we'll be coming back here via the Privilege Sets tab. What I'm saying is you can get to this window from more than one direction. Since you can access a privilege set when you're in an account, don't forget that any set you are editing may be attached to other accounts. Click OK and OK again to take you back to the Define Accounts & Privileges window.

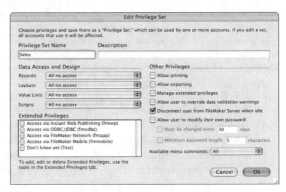

Figure 21-3
The Edit Privilege Set window.

Privilege Sets Tab[7]

Click the Privilege Sets tab to bring up the window shown in Figure 21-4. There are three default privilege sets created with every file: [Full Access], [Data Entry Only], and [Read-Only Access]. They're in brackets to tell you they can't be changed or deleted. If you click on the Full Access set, you'll notice that the Duplicate button is gray. The Full Access set is the only privilege set that has absolute power over the file. You can assign it to as many accounts as you like. But get this — you can create a privilege set where you manually make all the same choices that appear in the Full Access account, but it will not have the same power over the file.

Notice the Active accounts column shows you what accounts are assigned to the various sets. As the number of accounts in your file grows, it's likely the number of accounts assigned to a privilege set will grow as well.

The default privilege sets already have a description. We'll be able to add a description to our Sales set in a moment. By the way, neither the name nor the description of the default privilege sets can be changed.

When you click on the Data Entry Only and Read-Only Access accounts, notice that the Duplicate button becomes active. Both of these accounts are a good place to start when creating new sets for a file. You can add and delete various functions from a copy of either set.

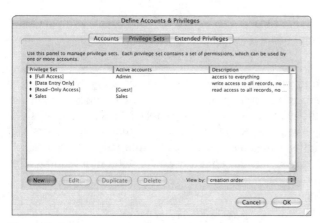

Figure 21-4
The Privilege Sets tab of the Define Accounts & Privileges window.

This window also has a View by pop-up list in the lower-right corner, and you can resize the columns. Here again on the Macintosh there's a triangle to the right of the Description column so you can reverse sort the Active accounts list based on the View by choice. Sorry, Windows users. Regardless of the order you select, if you click the Privilege Set column header, the sets will sort by Name and the View by will revert to "name." The View by pop-up in this window is different from the one in the Accounts window in that you can rearrange the sets manually. Click the two-headed arrow to the left of the set name and drag the set where you want it in the list. The View by will change to "custom order."

One more detail: If you try to delete a privilege set that is being used by one or more accounts, you'll get a message saying you can't do it. After you reassign different sets to the accounts, you can come back and delete the set.

(For info on how groups become privilege sets, see the section titled "Conversion Issues" at the end of the chapter.)

Edit Privilege Set[7]

Double-click the Full Access set. Say, we've seen this window before in Figure 21-3. As I already mentioned, you can also get to this window from the Accounts tab. Click the Cancel button. Now double-click the Sales set. In the Description field type "Cash register workers." In the Other Privileges area check the box next to Allow printing. Let's not check the box next to Allow exporting for now. I've had some of my clients concerned that departing employees might walk off with their customer list. When you think about it, that could be more of a concern for people in a managerial capacity. On the other hand, you may need to have various people export data to create text reports outside of FileMaker. Lots to decide, eh?

Data Access and Design

Look in the Data Access and Design area. There are four areas here; each influences the user's ability to work and view data in different ways.

Records   Click the pop-up to the right of Records in the Edit Privilege Set window. Figure 21-5 shows the default choices, which are pretty much self-explanatory. And then there is the Custom privileges option, which leads to an area that is deep indeed! Ready? Choose Custom privileges and let's go!

You should now see a window similar to the Custom Record Privileges window in Figure 21-6. Click the Contact table, and the Set Privileges area will probably more closely match the figure. You can start making choices from the pop-up lists, but notice you can't touch the Edit pop-up. Instead, click the Cancel button. Click the Records pop-up and choose "Create and edit in all tables." Click the pop-up again and select Custom privileges. Look at the difference when you click the Contact table. Now not only can you use the Edit pop-up, but all except the Delete pop-up have a higher level of privileges preset. You only need to disable the ones you want to protect. Interestingly, if you click OK at this point, Sales now shows Custom privileges although the privileges are the same as "Create and edit in all tables" privileges.

Figure 21-5
The Records pop-up under Data Access and Design.

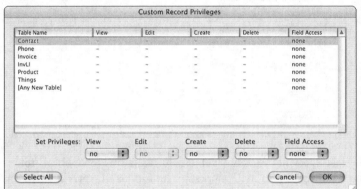

Figure 21-6
The Custom Record Privileges window.

You can edit multiple tables at one time by Shift-clicking them, or all tables with the Select All button (or the keyboard equivalent). That way you can make changes to, let's say, the Edit privileges, for all tables at once and still work on the Delete privileges separately for each table. That's smooth! In the old FileMaker, since every table was actually a different file, you had to do this separately for each file. You can see why I might be enthusiastic about this change. Let's dig a little deeper here before we move on to the other choices in the Data Access and Design area.

Now select a specific table and choose "limited" from the Field Access pop-up. That should bring up the Custom Field Privileges window seen in Figure 21-7. Here you can choose one or more fields and determine whether the user can modify, view, or have no access. When someone with the view only privilege is working in a field, they can actually click into the field and copy the data if necessary. They just can't make changes. If they have the no access privilege, they can't even see the data. The fields will still be on the layout, but the words <No Access> will appear where the data would be as in Figure 21-8. Click Cancel to return to the Custom Record Privileges window.

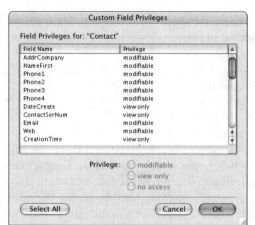

Figure 21-7
The Custom Field Privileges window.

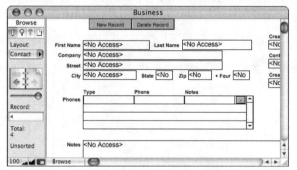

Figure 21-8
A FileMaker layout showing what fields look like when Custom Field Privileges are set to "no access."

Notice the last entry in the Table Name column, [Any New Table]. You can determine in advance what will happen in the file for this privilege set in any new tables as they are created. This is a particularly handy feature. I created a set of files for a client in a previous version of FileMaker that caused me some problems because this feature was not available. As I added new functions to their files, the new fields inherited the most restrictive characteristics of the other fields in that privilege. (They were called groups at the time.) Scripts were failing left and right, and it took me some time to figure out what had happened.

Look at the pop-up lists under the other Set privileges. You'll notice they're not all alike. Not only that, but the window you see when you select "limited" is different in some of the lists. We already saw the Limited window that appears when you choose Field Access. But in order to show you what happens when you choose Limited from some of the other Set Privileges pop-ups, we need to take a little side trip. This next part is where the records part of privilege sets can really get deep. I don't want to scare you with this; I've rarely needed to use this for my clients. But it is powerful, and you should know it's here. And honestly, it is pretty cool.

Record-Level Security   FileMaker allows you to set up security on a record-by-record level based on calculations. If you've been following along, you should already be at the Custom Record Privileges window in Figure 21-6. Look at the Set Privileges area in the lower part of the window. Notice the pop-up lists under View, Edit, and Delete. Select a table and choose "limited" from one of the pop-up lists. You will be presented with a Specify Calculation window. This requires a calculation with a Boolean result. (The calculations you would use here need to be done table by table. If you select more than one table, the "limited" option will appear in gray.)

For example, you could prevent salespeople from viewing or editing each other's records. If you had a Salesperson field where a name is entered when a new invoice is created, your calculation might look like this:

```
Salesperson = Get(UserName)
```

If the salesperson were to perform a Find for all invoices created this week, only his or her own records will turn up in the found set. If the salesperson chooses Records, Show All Records, invoices created by anyone else will appear with <No Access> in all the fields.

☒ **CAUTION**   Get(UserName) is determined in FileMaker Pro, Preferences (Macintosh) or Edit, Preferences (Windows) under the General tab. If a user changes the user name on his or her copy of the program, it can mess up your carefully crafted solution. In my solutions, I have users enter a login name and password in a special layout. Their login is compared to an Employees table. It then stores their name in a Global field, which is referred to in various script and password validations. It's complex and not for the faint of heart since it requires quite a few safeguards. Or you could just tell your users not to mess with the Preferences area. Unfortunately, you cannot lock users out of the Preferences area without a plug-in.

As powerful as this tool is, there are a number of things to consider when using it. If the View and Delete privileges don't match, users may be able to delete records they can't otherwise view. Here's another problem scenario: You could build a solution with a script that checks and replaces data in a field across a group of records when a file is first opened or when it's closed. That script would only update the records the user has access to, skipping the others. And it would do that without displaying a warning. Similar problems can occur when using lookups, relookups, Find and Replace, and Spell Check. And value lists that are drawn from data in fields where the records are not accessible to the user will simply not show the entire list.

I'm not saying you shouldn't use record-level security. On the contrary — developers have been asking for this feature for years. With it you can control access based on time, IP address, values in a Number field, and just about anything you can dream up. You should just thoroughly consider the effects and carefully test your solution before putting it to use.

Later in this chapter under the heading "Limiting Access through Field Calculations," I provide an example that could just as easily be handled with record-level security. The Help files also provide some examples and address the limitations and potential problems in more detail than I can here. In the Help files, search on "limiting access." Click and read the topic titled "Editing record access privileges." Record-level security is also available for databases published on the web.

A couple of notes before we leave Custom Record Privileges:

■ You can sort columns by clicking the column headers. For Windows users, clicking the column head a second time will reverse sort them. On the Macintosh you have to click the triangle in the upper right next to Field Access.

■ If you click the Cancel button, any changes you make to the Custom Record Privileges will disappear without warning. So be careful which button you click.

■ If you have the View option set to "no," it won't matter if you have Field Access set to "all." Users won't be able to get to the data.

■ If you have an account with Records set to any of the privileges above "All no access" but have the Layout pop-up set to "All no access," the user won't see any data.

■ In Custom Record Privileges you can make many of the settings apply to multiple tables by Shift-clicking the tables in the list. However, to make changes in the Limited window from the Field Access pop-up, you must select a single table at a time.

Don't make any changes here just yet. If you already did, click the Cancel button and come back in by choosing Custom privileges from the Records pop-up. (If you really got messed up, make sure you are customizing the "Create and edit in all tables" privilege set.) Let's make a couple of changes that we'll keep for the Sales crew.

1. Click the Product table and choose **no** under Create. We'll let the managers add new products.

2. Click the Contact table and select **limited** under Field Access.

3. Make sure all fields are modifiable. Then select **DateCreate**, **ContactSerNum_pk**, and **Creation Time**, and change them to **view only**.

Well, locking down ContactSerNum_pk for the Sales team isn't much of a challenge. We locked it down for everybody when we created the field. Isn't it interesting that there are so many places you can lock things down? Yeah, and it can be pretty confusing if you find something locked and need to figure out how to unlock it. Lots of places to look.

4. Click **OK** and **OK** again so these changes are memorized for the Sales privilege set.

5. Click **OK** one final time. If you have a full access account that has no password, you'll see a dialog now. It's okay to allow that. But you ought to make sure you know what accounts and passwords you've set up before leaving here. At the Confirm Full Access Login, you will be required to enter a name and password for a full access account. In this case, type **Admin** in the Full Access Account box, leave the Password box empty, and click **OK**.

6. Under the File menu, choose **File Options**. There should be a check next to "Log in using." Uncheck it now. That will force you (and other users) to log in when the file opens. Otherwise it opens with all privileges. Click the **OK** button.

7. Close the file and reopen it using the Sales account and Counter password, remembering to be attentive to case. Go to the Contact layout and try to change DateCreate or CreationTime. You don't need to test ContactSerNum. You wouldn't be able to change it anyway.

8. Close and reopen the file with all privileges. That will probably mean the Admin account and no password.

Layouts

1. Go back into the Business file, and choose **File, Define, Accounts & Privileges**.

2. Click the Privilege Sets tab and double-click the **Sales** privilege set.

3. Click the pop-up next to Layouts (Figure 21-9) and choose **All view only**.

4. Click on the pop-up again and choose **Custom privileges** to open the Custom Layout Privileges window in Figure 21-10.

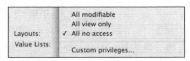

Figure 21-9
The Layouts (and Value Lists) pop-up under Data Access and Design.

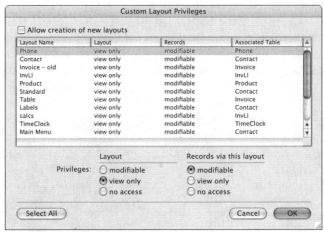

Figure 21-10
The Custom Layout Privileges window.

Here's where you decide what changes a privilege set can make to layouts. Clicking the column headers will sort them by that header. For Windows users, clicking the column head a second time will reverse sort them. On the Macintosh you have to click the triangle in the upper right next to Associated Table.

Regardless of how you sort the list, at the bottom is [Any New Layout]. This is just like the [Any New Table] options discussed previously. You get to decide in advance what will happen in the file for this privilege set in any new layouts as they are created.

Click on one or more of the tables to activate the radio buttons in the lower part of the window. If you choose the "no access" radio button under Layout, the buttons under "Records via this layout" turn gray. That makes sense. If you choose "view only" under Layout, you can also choose "no access" under

"Records via this layout." That provides you with a layout with no visible data. I don't know why you might want to do that, but it's there.

Here are some specifics to consider:

■ You can make a privilege set so all layouts are "no access," and [Any New Layout] is set to "modifiable." Then by selecting the radio button next to "view only," you can prevent the user from altering data in the very layout he or she created.

■ There's something rather interesting about the "Records via this layout" option. Even if you set up the file so users have full access to one of the tables in the file (say the Phone table), if you put a portal using data from that table on a different layout with "view only" or "no access," the user access will be limited accordingly. They won't have full access from that specific layout.

■ If you go to the Custom Layout Privileges window and select the "no access" radio button under "Records via this layout," even if you have the Custom Record Privileges window set up with Field Access set to All, the users will only see the words "<No Access>" in every field.

■ When you turn off access to layouts, the layout names will not even show up when those users click the Layout list above the Book. In fact, they won't show up in the List Layout mode even if the user is allowed access to other layouts in Layout mode. This brings control over specific layouts to specific users in both Browse and Layout modes. It's similar and yet subtly different from using the Layout Setup window in Layout mode and selecting whether layouts appear in the list for all users in Browse mode.

■ If the file opens automatically to a specific layout and the user doesn't have access to that layout, he'll see a screen that looks like Figure 21-11. That's something to be concerned about since the user won't be able to see or click on any buttons that might be on that layout. For the same reason, you should be cautious that any buttons on layouts users can access don't take them to layouts they can't get out of. That applies to the web interface as well.

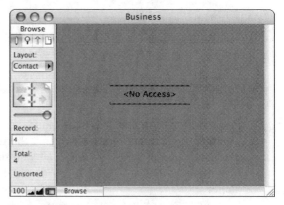

Figure 21-11
What a FileMaker layout looks like to an account where the Custom Layout Privileges are set to "no access."

■ There is a check box in the upper-left corner of the window that allows the account to create new layouts. That means you can prevent users from working in Layout mode throughout the file and still let them create their own letters and reports. Try that with earlier versions of FileMaker!

Don't make any changes here just yet. If you already did, click the Cancel button and come back in by choosing the Custom privileges from the Layout pop-up. (If you really got messed up, make sure you are customizing the "All modifiable" privilege set.) Let's make a couple changes that we'll keep for the Sales group.

1. Click the **Select All** button and set it to **view only** under Layout and **modifiable** under "Records via this layout."

2. Now select the **Phone** and **Product** layouts and set them to **no access**.

3. Select the **Contact** layout in the list and click the radio button to make it modifiable.

   Remember, your users will be able to see the Phone information in the portal on the Contact layout, and they'll be able to see the products in the pop-up list on the Invoice layout. They just won't be able to see those layouts in the Layout pop-up above the Book.

4. Click **OK** and **OK** again so these changes are memorized for the Sales privilege set.

5. Click **OK** one final time. Deal with any windows that appear.

6. Close the file and reopen it using the Sales account and Counter password.

7. Go to the Contact layout and click the pop-up list above the Book. You should no longer be able to see either the Phone or Product layouts.

8. Go to Layout mode and move something. No problemo. Use Undo to move it back. Now switch to the InvLI layout and try to move something. Aha! Foiled again!

9. Close and reopen the file with all privileges. That will probably mean the Admin account and no password.

Value Lists

1. Go back into the Business file, and choose **File, Define, Accounts & Privileges**.

2. Click the **Privilege Sets** tab and double-click the **Sales** privilege set.

3. Click the pop-up next to Value Lists (Figure 21-9) and choose **All view only**.

4. Click on the pop-up again and choose **Custom privileges** to bring up the Custom Value List Privileges window in Figure 21-12.

5. Here's where you decide what changes a privilege set can make to various value lists. Clicking the column headers will sort them by that header. For Windows users, clicking the column head a second time will reverse sort them. On the Macintosh you have to click the triangle in the upper right next to Privilege.

Regardless of how you sort the list, at the bottom is [Any New Value List]. This is just like the [Any New Table] and [Any New Layout] options. You get to decide in advance what will happen in the file for this privilege set in any new value lists as they are created.

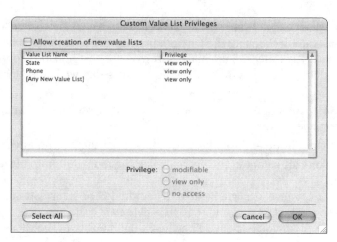

Figure 21-12
The Custom Value List Privileges window.

Here are some things to be aware of:

■ If you create a list to which a privilege set has no access, users won't even see the list. That means if you make a list using radio buttons, they won't even show on the layout!

■ If you create a pop-up list that uses values from a field and the privilege set can type in the field, users will be able to add the new value to the list. Doesn't sound much like it's "view only," does it?

■ If you're in Layout mode and you format the field by checking the box next to Include "Edit," the privilege set can change the value list even though the privilege would indicate that the user is view only.

■ In the upper-left corner of the window is a check box for "Allow creation of new value lists." That means you can prevent specific users from messing up your carefully created lists while letting them create lists they need for themselves. But you'll also have to select the [Any New Value List] and click the "modifiable" radio button to make it work.

■ If you allow a privilege set the right to create new value lists but prevent users from having access to all layouts, they won't be able to attach their value lists to any fields.

■ When a privilege set says "view only" and users go to the File menu, Define will be grayed out. So they can't even view the lists, let alone modify them.

My own little comment here is, although I think the idea is pretty good, the implementation of these particular privileges seem contradictory and not particularly useful. Maybe you'll find a better use for them than I've been able to.

Don't make any changes here just yet. If you already did, click the Cancel button and come back in by choosing "Custom privileges" from the Layout pop-up. (If you really got messed up, make sure you are customizing the "All modifiable" privilege set.) Let's make a couple of changes that we'll test on the Sales group.

1. Click the **Select All** button and set it to **view only**.

2. Now select **[Any New Value List]** and set it to **modifiable**, and check the box next to **Allow creation of new value lists**.

3. Select the **State** value list and click the radio button next to **no access**.

4. Remember, your users will be able to see the Phone information in the portal on the Contact layout, and they'll be able to see the products in the pop-up list on the Invoice layout. They just won't be able to see those layouts in the Layout pop-up above the Book.

5. Click **OK** and **OK** again so these changes are memorized for the Sales privilege set.

6. Click **OK** one final time. Deal with any dialogs that appear.

7. Close the file and reopen it using the Sales account and Counter password.

8. Go to the Contact layout and click the **State** field. You should no longer be able to see the pop-up list of states.

9. Go to **File**, **Define**, **Value Lists**. Double-click any of the lists and you should get a dialog saying your access privileges prevent editing.

10. Click the **New** button. You don't really need to create a new value list, do you? Click the **Cancel** button.

11. Close and reopen the file with all privileges. That will probably mean the Admin account and no password.

12. You'd better go back and give the Sales folks access to the State pop-up list. They might need it. You might also want to limit their ability to create new lists, too.

Scripts

1. Go back into the Business file, and choose **File, Define, Accounts & Privileges**.

2. Click the **Privilege Sets** tab and double-click the **Sales** privilege set.

3. Click the pop-up next to Scripts (Figure 21-13) and choose **All executable only**.

4. Click on the pop-up again and choose **Custom privileges** to open the window in Figure 21-14.

Figure 21-13
The Scripts pop-up under Data Access and Design.

5. Here's where you decide what changes a privilege set can make to various scripts — or if the script can be executed at all! Clicking the column headers will sort the scripts by that header. That means you can sort the script by name. That's something you can't even do in ScriptMaker! For Windows users, clicking the column head a second time will reverse sort them. On the Macintosh you have to click the triangle in the upper right next to Notes.

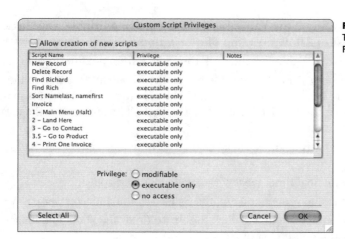

Figure 21-14
The Custom Script Privileges window.

Regardless of how you sort the list, at the bottom is [Any New Script]. You get to decide in advance what an account can do with each script.

This Custom Privilege window is the only one that includes a Notes column. The only note that currently shows here is if a script has the box checked next to "Run script with full access privileges."

Here are some things to be aware of:

■ In the upper-left corner of the window is an "Allow creation of new scripts" check box. With this option you can prevent specific users from messing up your carefully created scripts and still let them create scripts they need for themselves. But you'll also have to select [Any New Script] and click the "modifiable" radio button to make it work.

■ If the privilege set is allowed entry into ScriptMaker, any scripts that are tagged as no access to those users will not even be visible in the list.

■ That also means any numbering scheme you may be planning for the first 10 scripts could go out the window. If you're passing out a list of scripts that are supposed to be run with those key combinations, make sure you check the list while logging in under each account first. What will happen? The key combinations will shift down the list to the next available script, and you could be in for some unhappy surprises!

■ If a user can access ScriptMaker but only has executable access to a script, when they double-click that script, they'll get a message that their privileges don't allow modifying the script. However, scripts tagged as modifiable for that privilege set will open right up.

■ If you tag a script as no access for a privilege set and it runs as a part of another script the privilege set does have access to, it could mess up your plans.

■ If you tag a script as modifiable for a privilege set but you change the available menu commands to editing only, users won't be able to open ScriptMaker to edit the script.

■ If you set a script to no access but you leave the button on a layout accessible to the privilege set users, you would probably expect them to be somewhat frustrated and lose faith in the effect of any buttons.

Don't make any changes here just yet. If you already did, click the Cancel button and come back in by choosing "Custom privileges" from the Scripts pop-up. (If you really got messed up, make sure you are customizing the "All executable only" privilege set.) Let's make couple changes that we'll keep for the Sales group.

1. Click the **Select All** button and set it to **executable only.** That probably won't change a thing since that's the privilege set we began with.

2. Select the **Find Richard** script and set it to **modifiable.**

3. Select the **Delete Record** script and click the radio button to make it **no access.** Those salespeople shouldn't be deleting sales records anyway, right?

4. Click **OK** and **OK** again so these changes are memorized for the Sales privilege set.

5. Click **OK** one final time. Deal with any dialogs that appear.

6. Close the file and reopen it using the Sales account and Counter password.

7. Go to the Contact layout and click the **Delete Record** button. You should no longer be able to delete any records. But remember the confusion that might cause.

8. Go to **Scripts, ScriptMaker.** First notice that the Delete Record script is nowhere to be found!

9. Double-click the **New Record** script. Can't go there, eh?

10. Double-click **Find Richard.** We're in! Just don't make any changes and click **Cancel** and **Cancel** again.

Close and reopen the file with all privileges. That will probably mean the Admin account and no password.

Other Privileges[7]

Look under the Other Privileges heading on the right side of the Edit Privilege Set window. "Allow printing" and "Allow exporting" are pretty clear. "Manage extended privileges" generally refers to allowing access to items found on the Macintosh under FileMaker Pro, Sharing and on Windows under Edit, Sharing. These include the preset sharing items Instant Web Publishing, ODBC/JDBC, FileMaker Mobile, and FileMaker Network, as well as any additional extended privileges FileMaker and third-party companies may make available in the future. We'll look at that in a minute in the section titled "Extended Privileges Tab."

Next is the check box for "Allow user to override data validation warnings." I'm used to seeing that option at the field definition level under the Validation tab from previous versions of FileMaker. It's still there, although it's been moved near the top of that window. Placing this check box with the privilege set is something new. And in a way it does make sense that some users should have the ability to override those warnings. Leave the box unchecked in the Validation tab of the Options for Fields window and turn it on here to force specific users to stay within the data entry requirements. When users are allowed to override the value they'll see a dialog like this: "Price is defined to contain only specific values. You must enter a valid value." They'll see three buttons: Revert Record, No, and Yes. With the restriction placed by this check box, the dialog they see will read: "Price is defined to contain only specific values. Allow this value?" They'll only see two buttons: Revert Record and OK.

"Disconnect user from FileMaker Server when idle" can be set for each privilege set. The idle time length is set to the same variable number of minutes for all users in FileMaker Server.

The next three items are all new for FileMaker Pro 7 and add a great deal to the security of a solution while reducing administration.

Take a look at the pop-up next to "Available menu commands." The choices here provide some manner of control over menu access. The Editing Only choice shuts out access to ScriptMaker (users can still run scripts depending on their privileges), all of the Records menus, the ability to change modes or views, and most of the choices under the File menu. That means that you'd have to create buttons to provide any of those functions that you still wanted users to be able to access. The Minimum choice also removes all the choices under the Edit menu.

It would be nice to have more control over specific commands, but that's the way it is. However, there are some plug-ins created for just that purpose.

Extended Privileges[7]

And finally, in the lower-left corner as we work our way clockwise around the window, is the Extended Privileges area. As you can see, these include Instant Web Publishing, ODBC/JDBC, FileMaker Network, and FileMaker Mobile. Again, you can control which privilege sets have access to these various functions simply by using the check boxes here. Some of the check boxes are repeated in other windows. For instance in the Sharing, Instant Web Publishing window, when you click the Specify button you can choose which privilege sets have access to the file. Under the Sharing menu, you work with all privilege sets at once. In the Edit Privilege Set window, you work with one privilege set at a time, but all the Extended Privileges at once. That brings us to the details of the Extended Privileges tab.

Extended Privileges Tab[7]

The final tab of the Define Accounts & Privileges window is Extended Privileges, as seen in Figure 21-15. FileMaker, Inc. has provided add-on software products that work along with FileMaker. These add-on products are similar to plug-ins but often have wider capabilities. In fact, most of the current sets of Extended Privileges were former plug-ins. The Extended Privileges area is where you assign various accounts access to these accessories. As time goes on, we may see other such products from FileMaker and third-party software developers. At press time, the only Extended Privileges available are Instant Web Publishing, ODBC/JDBC, FileMaker Network, and FileMaker Mobile.

Click the Extended Privileges tab to examine the area. Clicking on the column heads does nothing. The four preset items we see here (the ones with brackets in the Keyword column) cannot be deleted.

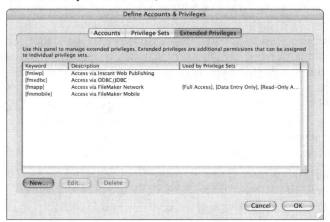

Figure 21-15
The Extended Privileges tab of the Define Accounts & Privileges window.

Part 6

Double-clicking Access via Instant Web Publishing brings up the Edit Extended Privilege window seen in Figure 21-16. Hey, we've seen this window before. Yep, there's one very similar in the Sharing, Instant Web Publishing area. There's also one each for Sharing, ODBC/JDBC and Sharing, FileMaker Network. By clicking the check box in the On column over on the left, you can toggle access to this extended privilege for each privilege set. When you're in this window, you cannot change the keyword or the description. About all you can do is check the check boxes and sort by privilege set. The advice in the FM 7 Security.pdf document is to avoid enabling extended privileges unless you need to. Uncheck all the boxes for each extended privilege set and only add them when users need the functions.

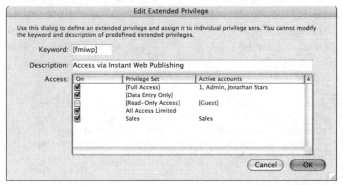

Figure 21-16
The Edit Extended Privilege window for Instant Web Publishing.

Click the Cancel button to take you back to the Extended Privileges tab. Notice the New button in the lower-left corner. There's really not any purpose to using this button unless you're installing a new extended privilege provided by FileMaker or a third-party vendor. In that case, you'd follow their directions for installing and naming the keyword. You could make up something for a new extended privilege, but it won't do anything.

Expand and/or Reduce Privileges

There is no dialog to expand or reduce privileges, but FileMaker's new Accounts & Privileges makes this capability a snap — and very powerful. One of the features of FMP7 is that it allows you to instantly add to or subtract privileges from any account on the fly. Now here comes the good part. That also means you can duplicate a complex privilege set, change as few or as many of the specific privileges as you need to, then assign it to the account for as long as needed.

To show you how powerful this can be, let's take a privilege set we've already created and duplicate it. Then we'll change it to temporarily expand the privileges to allow changes to all the layouts.

1. Click the **Privilege Sets** tab.
2. Highlight and duplicate the **Sales** account. Then double-click it to edit it. Under Privilege Set Name, change Sales Copy to **Sales + Layout Access**. In the Description area, type **Access to all layouts**.
3. In the Data Access and Design area, next to Layouts, select **Create and edit in all tables.** Click the **OK** button.
4. Click the **Accounts** tab and double-click the **Sales** account.
5. Click on the pop-up list next to Privilege Set and select **Sales + Layout Access**.
6. Click **OK**, **OK** again, and deal with any dialog that may be required as you leave Accounts & Privileges.
7. Close the file and open it using the Sales account and Counter password.
8. See if you can get to layout mode and see all the layouts.

Once you've created the modified privilege set, changing privileges this way is something you can do by simply accessing an account and making a different selection from the pop-up list. It couldn't be easier. With this feature you can expand or reduce anyone's privileges any way you want. The only challenge will be remembering to remove the extra privileges after the task is done. Speaking of that, you might want to go back and reset the Sales account to the Sales access privilege set.

➲ **NOTE**   For simplicity we've set this file up with only two additional accounts. Normally you would set up a file so that each user would have his or her own account and password. Each member of the sales team would be assigned to the Sales privilege set. That way a single person can be assigned the new privileges rather than a whole group of people.

➲ **NOTE**   Changing a password in one file of a multi-file solution can affect how groups of files open. When users first open a file in a multi-file solution, if subsequent files use the same account, FileMaker opens them without displaying the account and password window. If the account has been changed in the first file, FileMaker will display the window for *every* subsequent file that opens — a major pain. This used to be a big issue before FileMaker implemented multiple tables per file. But you may inherit a solution that uses the old format. And, as we've said before, there are reasons to build multi-file solutions even with the availability of the new multi-table structure.

That brings up another issue. Changing accounts in a group of files on a regular basis can be a big job. The DialogMagic plug-in from New Millennium Communications allows you to change accounts across a multi-file solution by entering information in one window. For more on plug-ins, see the files available at www.wordware.com/files/fmpro7 and the FileMaker, Inc. web site.

⌘ **TIP** FileMaker's password system is now case sensitive. That means variations of the same password can be assigned to different people. Counter, counter, CoUnTeR, COUNTer, and coUNTer are all considered different passwords starting with FMP7. That much variety is not required because different accounts are allowed to use the same password. However, account names must be unique, and are not case sensitive.

Editing and Deleting Accounts[7]

Making a change to an account's privileges couldn't be easier. Go to the Edit Account window, click on the Privilege Set pop-up, choose a different set of privileges, and click OK.

Editing

Any time you need to, you can come back to Define Accounts & Privileges and make changes by making selections that move you through the other windows. You can make any number of changes to a selected item without committing yourself. At any time you can click the Cancel button. However, if you click the OK button in any of the windows, those changes become final once you click the final OK button to leave Accounts & Privileges.

Cautions

You should test your solution very carefully before foisting it upon your end users. Try every combination of layouts and fields with each of the various accounts to be sure they perform the way you expect them to. I recently built a solution that was locked down pretty tight with various accounts. Then the client asked for some new features. I added new fields and didn't realize field access privileges were being assigned by FileMaker based on current restrictions. (Remember those items in brackets? Any New Table, Layout, Value List, and Script.) That meant accounts with lower-level privileges were not able to perform scripts that used fields to which they didn't have access. I had assumed all accounts would have access to the new fields unless I changed it — and I didn't test it. I found out pretty quickly that it doesn't work that way!

➲ **NOTE** If you want to test the results of changes to an account, you could set up a script to relogin. But if you're networked, you can also choose File, Open Remote to open a second copy of the file on the same machine you're working on. When the Open Remote File window appears, you will see a list of hosts. Just choose your machine and you'll see a list of files appear on the right. Select the file you want, click the Open button, and enter the account and password information. (If the Account window does not appear, you'll need to hold down the Shift key on Windows or the Option key on Macintosh when you click the Open button.) With both a high privilege set window and a restricted privilege set window open, you can click back and forth between them to run various tests without having to login over and over. You are limited to having two sessions open, and you must be networked. Of course, Network Sharing must be on and the network access to the file(s) must allow access to the account you want to test.

Keep careful records of your passwords, and keep them somewhere they won't be easily found, but make sure someone else knows where they are. Files that can't be updated can cause a lot of problems for an organization. A company with proper proof of ownership used to be able to get passwords from FileMaker, Inc., but this was a time-consuming process and a last resort for poor planning. Starting with version 7, the passwords will not be accessible to anyone — even at FileMaker, Inc. You've been warned!

If a button takes users to a layout that says Access Denied, they won't be able to see any buttons on the page to get them out of there. If you choose to have the Status area hidden, you should add appropriate script steps to prevent those groups from being able to go to those layouts. Your only other alternative is to provide a script to the Main Menu that will appear under the Scripts menu. Then you'll have to teach everyone in that group how to find it.

Many times you will be building a set of files that work together. If you use the same set of accounts and passwords for each of the files, the users will only have to enter their password once, and the other files will open without calling up the dialog. This is a great feature, but it can also cause problems. For example, if you want to change the access for a particular account, you may have to make the change in multiple files. Depending on the complexity of the files involved, you may want to make use of one of the other ways of limiting access discussed in the rest of this chapter.

If you intend to modify a solution offsite and then install it by importing the onsite data into your file(s), consider this: What if users have changed their passwords? What if administrators have changed privilege sets or created new accounts? None of those changes will be in the file you're installing.

One suggestion would be to use some of the Get functions to collect account names, extended privileges, and privilege set names. You would then write a looping script to create a new record for each account in a special table. The script would have to be set up ahead of time in the onsite file. Then you'd need a second looping script that would create the new accounts in the updated solution. It would require a lot of setup and it's beyond the scope of this book.

A second suggestion would involve using FileMaker Developer's Data Design Report to gather the information using XML. Once again, pretty complicated — but it may be necessary.

Even with these two possible workarounds, there would still be no way to harvest the passwords. You would need to set them back to blank or some other more generic word and have the users enter a password at next login. That could also cause some confusion if the update required setting passwords in multiple files — some of which might only open once a week.

The main point is you need to think about what could happen. It might just be easier to have everyone lock in their settings and passwords. Depending on the scope of the application, that may be just as difficult as creating the updating scripts.

Limiting Access through Scripting

One way of controlling where users go is with scripts. The best way is to have a script check what privilege set the user has to determine where they can go. The following script is an example.

Go to the Invoice table, and create a new script called "20 - Open" with the following steps:

```
Table: Invoice
Script Name: 20 - Open
If [Get(PrivilegeSetName) = "Sales"]
    Go to Layout ["Invoice" (Invoice)]
Else
    Go to Layout ["Main Menu" (Contact)]
End If
```

(You can do the same thing with account names using the Get(AccountName) function.) Click OK, uncheck the box in front of the script so it won't appear in the Scripts menu, and click Done. Now let's make this script run automatically when opening the file.

Startup Script

Choose File, File Options, Open/Close, and click the box next to "Perform script." Then click on the word <unknown>, and pull down to the 20 - Open script. Figure 21-17 shows what the window should look like when you're done. Click OK. What this will do is run the Open script when anyone opens the file. Of course, users will have to put in their account name and password when opening the file. The account name determines what privilege set they're in, and the Open script puts them on the appropriate layout.

To test it out, close the file, and reopen it using the Sales account and the Counter password. Notice which layout you're on. Close the file, and open it with one of the other passwords. It's magic!

This is only one example of such a script. I've seen some amazing solutions that control every move through the files, yet they appear completely transparent to the user. I used some of those ideas to create a solution for a bakery with areas for owners, managers, order takers, bakers, and decorators. Each worker only went to the areas they used, and often didn't even know that other areas of the files existed. New employees could learn how to take orders in half a day

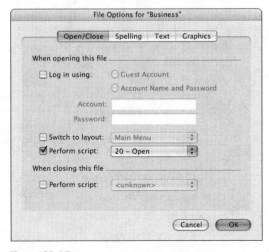

Figure 21-17
File Options window showing that the 20 - Open script will perform automatically when the file is opened.

using a point-and-click FileMaker system. Previously, the full training process using a paper system had taken six weeks.

Controlling Layout Access

Sending users to specific layouts isn't much help if they can just choose a different layout from the pop-up list above the Book. But the Layout pop-up can be set so users only see the current layout. Starting with FMP7, you can change the order of layouts even while other users are in the files. Go into Layout mode, and choose Layouts, Set Layout Order. By clicking the check box to the left of each layout name, you can hide or show specific layouts from the Layout pop-up.

Of course, anyone who has access privileges that allow them to view or modify all layouts will be able to see and select from the list when they're in Layout mode. Then you need to use privilege sets to prevent various users from having access to Layout mode or specific layouts. You'll have to follow that up by making sure users can get to the layouts they need with the buttons you provide for them. It requires a lot more work to set up files this way, but some situations will require that level of control.

Limiting Access through Field Calculations

Another method that is less often used (but is no less effective) is to limit access using field calculations. This method is used less often because it is more difficult to set up. One thing that can be done with this method that cannot be done with FileMaker's security in versions prior to 5.5 is that you can adjust who can see data based on the data in the records. For example, a group of marriage counselors needs to be able to get access to the same fields and layouts, but they shouldn't be able to see the troubles, sins, and confidential foibles of the patients of other counselors. Prior to version 5.5, FileMaker's password system was useless in this "record-level" security. The field calculation method (though much more difficult to establish) is more capable. I've seen about three different ways to limit access through calculations, but I'd like to offer my own version that uses validation by calculation. It won't make data invisible to other users, but it will prevent changes to specific records. Let me show you.

Let's assume that all invoices need to be approved by the manager or owner. Once they're approved, you don't want anyone except a manager or owner changing the invoice, for example, to prevent anyone from giving one of their buddies a price break so they can get a kickback. (This widget business is just full of corruption.)

1. Go to the Invoice table, and create a new Text field called **Approved**. Then click **OK**.

The Script

Now we need a script that only the owner or manager can use to approve an invoice. What the script will do is check to see what privilege set the user is from. If they're from the Owner or Manager group, clicking on the Approved field puts an X there. Since they may have to unapprove an invoice, it allows for that in the Else section of the script.

You could just as easily control this with field validation, but I think making a field into a button is a great technique.

2. Go to ScriptMaker and make a script called **21 - Approved** with the following steps:

    ```
    Table: Invoice
    Script Name: 21 - Approved
    If [Get(AccountName) = "Owner") or Get(AccountName) = "Manager")]
       If [IsEmpty(Invoice::Approved)]
          Set Field [Invoice::Approved ; "X"]
       Else
          Set Field [Invoice::Approved;""]
       End If
    End If
    ```

3. Click **OK**, uncheck the box in front of **Script Name**, and click **Done**. This, of course, assumes that you've created accounts for the Owner and Manager. If you haven't done that, make sure you do it now.

4. Now make the field into a button. Go to Layout mode, and put a copy of the Approved field in a logical place on the layout if one didn't appear automatically. Be sure the field is selected, and choose **Format**, **Button**. Choose **Perform Script** from the list on the left, select the new **21 - Approved** script from the pop-up on the right, and click **OK**.

5. You will also need to remove the Approved field from the tab order.

6. To test it out, click the field. Since these are new accounts, unless you've logged back in you shouldn't be able to change the field.

7. Close and reopen the file using one of the new accounts. Make sure this script only works if you have the right password. You don't want order takers approving invoices.

The Calculation

8. Now go to the InvLI table, go to **Define Fields**, and double-click the **ProdID** field. Click on the **Validation** tab, click the box next to **Validated by calculation**, and use the following:

    ```
    Invoice::Approved <> "X"
    ```

    If you don't have the Invoice relationship, create it now. Just connect InvoiceNum from this table to InvoiceNum in the Invoice table.

9. Check the box next to **Display custom message if validation fails**, type in the message in Figure 21-18, then click **OK** and **Done**.

10. Go to File, Define Accounts & Privileges, and select the **Accounts** tab. Double-click the **Sales** account and click the **Edit** button on the middle right. In the Other Privileges area on the right, make sure there is *not* a check mark in the box next to "Allow user to override data validation

warnings." (For users of previous versions of FileMaker, this check box used to be in the field definition Validation tab.)

11. Repeat step 10 for any other accounts you want to force to respond to the strict message.

12. Log in as one of the Sales team. Go back to Invoice, make sure there's an X in the Approved field, and try to change the ProdID. (If not, you'll have to log out and back in with higher privileges. Remember, Sales can't mark the Approved field.) As part of Sales, you should get the validation message, and you'll be forced to revert the field.

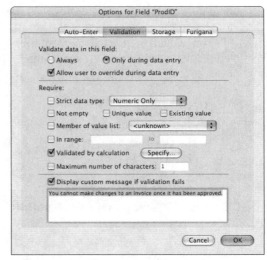

Figure 21-18
The Validation tab in the field definition for ProdID showing the text that will display when the validation fails.

13. Log in as the boss and uncheck the Approved box. Now log in under Sales and try to change ProdID now. Pretty cool, huh? To really make this complete, you'll need to use the same validation for the Description and Price fields.

Here's a slightly different approach. It would be much faster in tables where you need to prevent changes to all the fields at once. In this case, you can prevent specific privilege sets from making changes to any fields in records in the InvLI table once the Approved field has been checked by management in the related Invoice.

1. Go to Define Accounts & Privileges, Privilege Sets tab and double-click the **Sales** privilege set. In the Data Access and Design area, choose the pop-up next to Records and choose **Custom Privileges**.

2. Click **InvLI** table in the list. In the Set Privileges area at the bottom of the page, choose **limited** under the Edit column. That brings up the Specify Calculation window.

3. In the upper left, choose the **Invoice** table from the pop-up and double-click the **Approved** field from the list. Finish by making the calculation look like this:

```
Invoice::Approved ≠ "X"
```

Be sure to use the quotes.

Internet Considerations

If you'll be sharing a file on the web, you can turn off various privileges with the expected consequences.

FileMaker's Instant Web Publishing feature can now encrypt data using a Secure Socket Layout (SSL) when you use the FileMaker Server Advanced product.

Beyond that, you may need to purchase other software such as Blue World Communications' Lasso, which also provides SSL between FileMaker Pro and the outside world. Solutions like this are not for beginners, but if you need it, you'll have to start somewhere. For more information, see FileMaker's web site.

Conversion Issues

If you convert a solution created in a previous version of FileMaker, groups will be converted to privilege sets. In earlier versions of FileMaker, passwords could be associated with multiple groups. Since an FMP7 account can belong to only one privilege set, an account will inherit a privilege set named after all groups it was associated with. The privilege set will inherit the access privileges of the least restrictive group to which it belonged. If you'd rather not redesign very complex privilege sets after conversion, make sure that each password (that doesn't have full access to the file) is assigned to only one group in the old solution before converting.

Summary

In this chapter, we looked at protecting your data and layouts using FileMaker's built-in password security system. We also looked at controlling file use with scripts and calculations.

Q & A

Q I want the Owner to be able to have access to everything except the master password. How can I do that without taking away one of the other privileges?

A Simply uncheck the box next to "Access the entire file."

Q Most users just fit under one account and password. Isn't there some way to have the files open without having to type in the password?

A Yes. Choose File, File Options, check the box next to "Log in using," and enter the default account and password in the boxes. When you want to access the file with some other password, holding down the Option key (Macintosh) or Shift key (Windows) as you open the file will bring up the password window.

Workshop

If you didn't finish "locking down" the Description and Price fields in InvLI using validation by calculation, do it now and try it out. Make sure you try it with other passwords.

Create a special layout in Invoice to perform Finds. Make the Find button run scripts that take the user to a special layout where all fields are locked if the invoice has been approved and their privileges don't allow changing the data. If the user is the owner or manager, the script should take them to a layout where data can be edited.

Review Questions

True-False

1. The Define Accounts & Privileges window can be reached via the Window menu.

2. All security in FileMaker databases must be controlled via passwords.

3. When you modify the database structure, you should always test existing access privileges to make sure that users have appropriate access to any new features.

4. Record-level security allows you to set a validation that controls access to particular records in the database.

5. At least one account must have the All Access privilege set selected.

Short Answer

6. Which determines the layouts a user can see, password or privilege set?

7. How do you prevent users with a particular privilege set from deleting records in a table?

8. Where do you set up whether access is available through Instant Web Publishing?

9. How can you prevent users from seeing a layout name on the Layout pop-up in Browse mode?

10. If you select the Guest account in the Define Accounts & Privileges window, Accounts tab, why are the Duplicate and Delete buttons dimmed?

11. How can a script know what a user's password is?

Chapter 22

Backup and Recovery

Vocabulary

- Archive
- Clone
- Corruption
- Golden Clone
- Restoring

Objectives

1. Understand the importance of backing up files.
2. Learn to make backups from within FileMaker.
3. Become familiar with the advantages of FileMaker Server backup features.
4. Become familiar with commercial backup tools.
5. Understand the purpose and importance of saving clones.
6. Learn to develop and use backup routines.
7. Learn methods to restore damaged files.

Introduction

Perhaps more important than protecting your files with passwords is keeping good backups. Any number of things can happen to your files. Let's face it, without your data, your business is — well, out of business! This chapter is mostly a discussion, but I will have you save a clone and experiment with exporting and importing some records.

In this chapter, we'll look at:

- Why you need to do backups
- Commercial backup products
- Making a clone of a file
- Backups you can do with software you already have
- Good backup routines (schedule)
- Techniques from within FileMaker
- How to recover your data when the time comes

Why Back Up?

Power fluctuations or outages, hard drive mechanisms that go bad, and computer system conflicts can all spell trouble for your data, and let's not even mention fire, flood, and tornado. Stuff happens, and it can happen to your data.

In the old pre-computer days, people kept their records on paper. Remember those days? Business people did have to worry about fire and flood, and most companies didn't make a copy of every sheet of paper they generated. The loss of a company's records was devastating. Well, it still is today; it's just that all those records can now be concentrated on a hard drive. Because of the nature of digital information, making backups of a company's entire set of records is a simple procedure. Now you can make backups on media about one-quarter the size of a paperback book so they can easily be stored in multiple locations for added security. So what's the problem?

Sometimes people just forget. I try to back up every day, but when I started this chapter, I realized I'd forgotten to back up a couple of important files for about four days. Backing up is usually everybody's last thought when leaving the office after a long day.

Hardware cost is another issue. Many people strain their budget to get their computer. Then they go over budget to get some software. Now someone tells them they have to buy another machine to make backups. Forget it!

I know of a state agency that decided not to buy a backup system because it cost $2,000. (This was a few years ago.) Their computer tech kept warning them they were skating on thin ice. His favorite phrase was, "There are two kinds of hard drives: those that have lost data and those that will lose data." The day finally came when their only hard drive bit the dust and the data on it was unrecoverable. They lost the equivalent of eight people entering data, 40 hours a week for one year, or about $250,000 of employee pay and benefits. The little $2,000 backup device looked pretty cheap by comparison. That's why you need to make backups. Any questions?

FileMaker Server Backup Features

We haven't spent much time discussing FileMaker Server in this book because it is a separate product. However, it's worth mentioning Server's backup features, because they have much to offer the users of shared files that just aren't available when using standard FileMaker Pro sharing.

In a nutshell, FileMaker Server has the capability to automatically save copies of files while multiple users are sharing those files. You can save to different backup devices on any schedule you choose. This is an extremely convenient feature considering that from within the standard version of FileMaker Pro using peer-to-peer sharing, you need to have all users disconnect before you can make backups.

Using Commercial Backup Applications

There are some good products on the market for both Macintosh and Windows machines that will take care of scheduled backups for you. Retrospect for the Macintosh and PC Backup for Windows come to mind. You can also program

AppleScript to perform backups on the Macintosh. In Windows NT, you can use NT Scheduler.

You can perform any of these backups while your FileMaker files are up and running, and even while they're being shared by other users (see the following Caution). That's something you can't do from within FileMaker itself unless you're using the Server version.

☒ **CAUTION**   Although you can back up while FileMaker is running, it is not the recommended procedure. Even FileMaker Server pauses the database before performing its own backup. That gives it a chance to empty the cache for all users to the hard drive. Files that are backed up while they are active run the risk of corruption. The best solution is to close all files before running the backup (unless you're using FileMaker Server). It's a pain, but you'll feel a much greater pain if you can't use your files any more. Keep in mind that file corruption may not show up for quite some time after you begin using a backup.

I highly recommend that you back up to a removable medium or a portable hard drive. Don't forget to remove it from the mechanism after backing up. Non-removable backup hard drives are not a good choice because they are also subject to damage from power surges and lightning.

Problems with Tape

In the past year or so, I've had five different clients tell me they couldn't restore their data from tape backups. I suspect it's because they didn't replace the tapes in the required time. You should retire tapes after six to eight weeks of daily use or about 45 backups. Contrast that with CD-RW disks that can be rewritten 10,000 times. The problem with tape is that when it touches the heads, tiny amounts of the oxide material wear off. After many uses of an audiotape, you may begin to notice some high-frequency loss. This is not a big deal, but with digital data, if you lose a zero or a one, the backup software may not be able to reconstruct your files.

You shouldn't use the same tape 45 days in a row, anyway. The suggested backup routine discussed shortly recommends that any given media only be used once every two weeks. Besides, there are plenty of removable alternatives to tape, including Zip, CD-R, CD-RW, DVD, Jaz, Orb, Syquest, and removable media like USB drives.

☒ **CAUTION**   Don't count on any backup media forever. Even the durable CD only has an expected shelf life of 25 years. That is a good long time, but it's not forever, and that's as good as it gets. This means that every other media falls somewhere short of that.

➔ **NOTE** (to Windows 98 and 2000 users)   When a FileMaker file is written to a CD-ROM and you bring it back onto a Windows 98 or 2000 machine, the file becomes "read only." That means you'll be prevented from entering data in the files. You can make the files work, but you'll have to jump through a few hoops:
   1) Copy the normal FileMaker Pro file from the CD onto your hard drive.
   2) Using Windows Explorer, locate the file or files you want to return to read/write status.
   3) Right-click on the file(s) and choose Properties from the list.
   4) In the window, uncheck the box next to Read-only.
   5) Click the Apply button and then OK.

Now you can use the files in the normal way. (However, sometimes file names may have been truncated. You may need to find related files to rebuild relationships using the newly shortened file names.)

Whatever media you choose, date each backup and move it off the premises. You might try to get into the habit of taking the most recent backup home with you when you leave for the day. Don't do anything with it. Just take it and bring it back. It's also a good idea to keep a copy on-site, as well. When you have a failure, you don't want to have to run home after your only backup in order to get the business up and running again. And what about those days when you can't come into the office? If you were the only person to have a backup when it was needed, your co-workers would be stuck.

Another off-site backup method would be to use one of the Internet disks that are now available such as the iDisk portion of Apple's iTools. (To take a look at discussions about how this works, go to www.apple.com and click the Support tab. Type in iDisk and click the Search button.) This method of storage provides users with a low-cost, off-site, easily accessible, backed-up hard drive. Of course, using such a system would depend on how secure you feel about the possibility of your files being intercepted while traveling across the Internet or sitting on someone else's servers. You'll also want a fast Internet connection to take advantage of this option.

Database Corruption

Quite apart from the data, the database structure itself can be damaged beyond repair. That includes the field descriptions, relationships, scripts, and layouts. After all the time you've spent creating that structure, just getting back a list of customers and invoices probably wouldn't be very comforting. Even more worrisome is that this type of corruption can creep into a file over time and not be noticed for weeks or even months. To protect yourself against that event, you should work out a system of making clones of your files.

In versions of FileMaker previous to 7, your data was often spread across multiple files. Since FMP7 lets you create all your tables in a single file, this data corruption has the potential for even greater harmful consequences. I've heard developers tell stories about having to recreate single-table files from scratch after they had been damaged beyond repair. Imagine having to recreate a very complex multiple-table database from scratch.

As I write this, we developers have been doing our best for nearly a year to damage files in order to see what will happen. We've not been very successful, which goes to show how stable this product is. But just because FileMaker is stable doesn't mean hard drives can't slowly go bad. And even a small hard drive failure will corrupt your files. All it takes is one little area of the magnetic media to go bad and your database will have a lurking corruption that may not show up for months. Making a clone is so easy and the consequences for failing to perform this type of backup so dire, it just doesn't make sense to avoid learning the process. It could cost you weeks or months of your life trying to rebuild what you lost by not taking one minute out of every day of the development process.

What Is a Clone?

A *clone* of a FileMaker database is an empty copy of a file that includes all structure elements of the file: the tables, fields, relationships, scripts, and layouts.

Files usually get corrupted when they're closed improperly. That happens when FileMaker crashes or you have a power outage. Oh, I know, some of you have uninterruptable power supplies. But if the computer's power cord gets knocked out of the UPS, believe me, your work *will* be interrupted. The idea is to make a clone of each file, and then make copies of those clones in which to enter data, never again opening the original clone. When you want to make changes to the structure of a file, make a copy of the clone and work in that. If it turns out later that the data file has been corrupted, you can always go back to the untouched (or "golden") clone, make another copy, and pull the data into it. Figure 22-1 shows how the process works over a series of updates to a file.

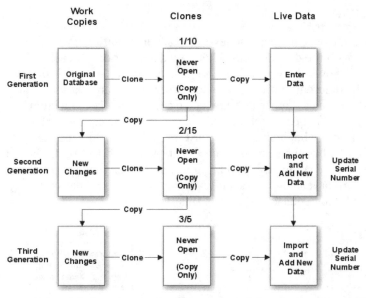

Figure 22-1
This diagram shows the recommended procedure for making clones of a file to reduce the likelihood of corruption over generations of changes to the file.

Date, label, and make backup copies of the clones of your files. This may seem like overkill, but there are more than a few horror stories of businesses nearly brought to their knees by data corruption. I won't even tell you about the terror experienced by the creators of those files. Needless to say, you don't want to be a member of that fraternity. And don't get the idea that this is just a FileMaker Pro problem. Every database on this planet experiences its share of corruption woes. When it comes to data recovery, FileMaker is among the best, but you need to help out, too.

Saving a Clone

Open your Business file. Choose File, Save a Copy As, which will bring up the window in Figure 22-2. The first time you open this window, the Type pop-up box will default to "copy of current file," and the word "Copy" appears after the name of the file you're currently in. Click and pull down to "clone (no records).'' As soon as you release the mouse button, the word "Clone" will replace "Copy" at the end of the filename. Click the Save button but pay attention to where the file is being saved.

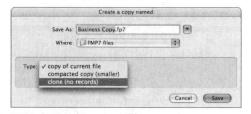

Before you open the file, make a copy of it from the Finder (Macintosh) or with Windows Explorer. Remember, you never

Figure 22-2
FileMaker's Save a Copy As window showing the pop-up list of types.

want to open the clone itself, only a copy of it. Now open the copy of the Business clone. You'll see a big empty file. Go into Define Database. Look familiar? If you look in ScriptMaker, you'll see the scripts you made. Keep this file handy. We'll pull some data into it later in this chapter.

Backup Routine

Aside from making clones of files whenever you add new features, you need to back up the files with the data in them. There are a number of approaches I've seen recommended over the years. The one I use seems to be a good compromise between the different methods I've seen described. I run a backup of all my files at least once a day for two weeks, using a new removable medium each day. Assuming a five-day workweek, I archive the copies at the end of days five and ten. At the beginning of the third week, I reuse the medium I used on the first day. I do the same until day 15 at the end of that week. Since I don't want to touch the archived copy, I bring in a new blank medium. I follow the same procedure of reusing media and archiving the last weekday copy. Look at Figure 22-3 for a quick overview of this technique.

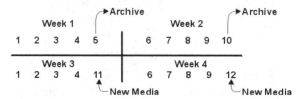

Figure 22-3
In this diagram, each number represents a backup medium. At the beginning of Week 3, begin to reuse the media.

After another month goes by, you can begin reusing your archived copies, but always keep at least one archive for each month. If you insist on using tape, put a mark on the label each time you use it. After 45 uses, discard it. With any other medium, put a date on it for the day it went into service. I'd start to question the reliability of media that gets to be five years old. Maybe I'm obsessive, but my computer can't read a lot of those floppies I relied on just a few years ago. When I take this approach, my blood pressure stays just fine. I've had Zip disks that went bad in less than a year, and hard drives that went bad in as little time.

Whatever your method, the worst thing in the world is to set up a backup schedule and not test out the backups until the day they're needed. It could be tragic to discover that you weren't backing up "properly" after a disaster had hit. Every so often you should try to reconstruct the files from the backups to see if they work. Be warned: Some backup software has settings that over-write the original file. Make sure you change that setting before you attempt the recovery test.

While You Work

Depending on how much data you can live without, you may want to run a backup more than once a day. I have some customers who back up their main data files every couple of hours. When I work on files, if I've put in three or four hours, I'll make a backup. I'm not anxious to do all that work over. And let me tell you, when you're developing a set of files, it's not too hard to cause a crash while you're trying out scripts and calculations on files containing a few thousand records. Backing up only takes a few seconds. Trying to recreate your work takes way longer.

Other Related Measures

Another way to reduce problems is to devote one machine to serving FileMaker files. Again, use the fastest machine you can spare. On this file server, run as few other programs as possible to prevent conflicts where the other programs may compete with FileMaker Pro for memory. That includes little accessories such as screen savers. If you're afraid of screen "burn in," just turn the screen off. FileMaker should be the frontmost application, and no one should be entering data on this machine.

Following are other maintenance procedures you should take to protect your data. Although only a couple of them are FileMaker related, a problem in any of these areas could threaten your data.

Daily

- Restart your computer. This takes care of any RAM fragmentation problems.

Weekly

- Run virus detecting software. Be sure to get the latest updates from the web.
- Run software to check the hard drive and system for errors.
- You should have an uninterruptible power supply (UPS) and test it weekly. Keeping the power line steady will go a long way in preventing crashes and data corruption.

Monthly

- Once a month, save a "compacted copy (smaller)" version of the files you use every day. The process is similar to saving a clone. You can see this option in the Type pop-up in Figure 22-2. This can take some time for larger files, since FileMaker copies the file one block at a time. In that case, you may want to perform this task overnight.
- Keep track of and install the most recent updates to FileMaker Pro. These updates include valuable bug fixes.
- Run disk optimization software.
- Defragment the hard drive once a month.

- On the Macintosh, rebuild the desktop.

Annually

- Completely back up and reformat the hard drive.
- Have the computer and keyboard cleaned out.

Put these events on a calendar and don't forget to copy each activity to the next year. I have a FileMaker reminder file (what else?) that I use for everything from my daily phone calls and birthdays to file and computer maintenance.

FileMaker Techniques

If you're the only user of a FileMaker file and you have the right account privileges, you can export records from within FileMaker Pro as a backup technique. Be sure to go to each table and choose Show All Records so that the current found set includes everything in all tables. Figure 22-4 shows the window that appears when you choose File, Export Records. By looking at this list, you can probably tell there are many other uses for an export besides backing up your data.

When you click the Save button, you'll be presented with the Specify Field Order for Export window in Figure 22-5. First you select the table from the pop-up in the upper left. Then you can select fields from the list on the left and move them to the list of fields that will be exported on the right, or just click the Move All button. Finally, you can reorder the fields to determine how they'll appear in the new file.

Once you've performed a particular export manually, you can create a script that will repeat the export for you in the future. One thing you need to be aware of is that all exports only export the current found set of records for the table selected in the Export window. Be sure to choose Show All Records or create a script to find a particular group of records before doing a backup export.

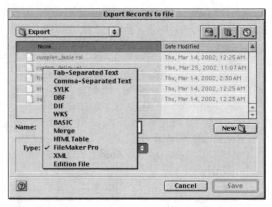

Figure 22-4
FileMaker's Export Records to File window showing the pop-up list of the various file export options.

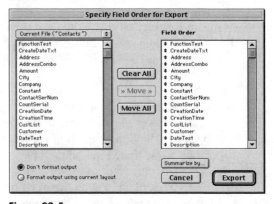

Figure 22-5
The Specify Field Order for Export window where you choose what fields will be exported in what order.

Another "gotcha" is that any export sends out the data based on the context of the currently selected layout and that layout's associated table. If you think you're exporting your contacts but the current table is Invoice, only the contacts who have ordered items from you will be exported! Every script that exports data now must add the Go to Layout [] (with the layout name filled in, of course) script step to make sure the correct data is exported.

To protect against that I would recommend a script similar to this:

```
Script Name: Export Contacts
Go to Layout ["Contact" (Contact)
Show All Records
Export Records [No dialog; "Contact.mer"; ASCII]
```

You would repeat that, making appropriate changes that refer to every table in your file.

The following is a list of steps to use in performing an export:

1. Go to the layout with the table you want to export
2. Find the records you want to export.
3. Choose **File**, **Export**.
4. Choose the file format you want to export and the final location of the file.
5. Choose the fields and the field order.
6. Click the **Save** button.
7. Create a script to do the next export automatically.

If you export all the data in all fields as tab-separated text or comma-separated text with the intention of pulling the data back into FileMaker, consider this: When you import a text file, you'll have to tell FileMaker which data you want to go into which fields. Depending on how many fields you have, this can be a tedious job. It's easier to go into Define Fields and reorder the fields by creation order before exporting the data. I've had very good luck exporting as a Merge file. Merge files maintain the field names so it's easy to match the fields back up using View by Matching Names.

If you want to save the font style or color formatting of your text, you'll need to export as a FileMaker Pro file. All other exports drop any such formatting, although they will maintain number and time formats based on the current layout *if* you click the radio button next to "Format output using current layout" on the Specify Field Order for Export window.

When you export as a FileMaker file, FileMaker creates a new file without any of the layouts or scripts. Any Calculation fields do not retain their formulas. Instead, they become the "Calculation result is" type chosen when you created the formula. If you have to pull the records back into the original file, matching field names is a lot easier.

Another interesting technique for running backups is to have a script run when your files either close or open. After you create the script, you tell it when to run in the General Document Preferences as demonstrated in Chapter 21. To make sure it only runs on the file server, use an If statement that uses Get (UserCount) = 1. A script like that can even target the removable disk to which you want to back up.

How far do you want to go with backups? One of my clients prints out a list of new orders and new customers at the end of every day as well as backing up to a removable hard drive. He does this because one time some data corruption got into his Invoices file, and he lost two weeks of orders. He did have backups, but each of them had been damaged and couldn't be recovered. Since his Customers file was okay, he looked at all customers at the end of the file that weren't attached to an invoice. His staff called the people and recreated their orders. He just had to wait for his repeat customers to come in to pick up their order, and do the best he could to satisfy them. It was a very uncomfortable time for the company, and he doesn't intend to go through that again.

More about Exporting

When you perform an export in FileMaker 7, you need to be aware of the context. The data you export depends on the table you're in and the found set in the active window — and that could lead to some surprises.

For instance, let's say you go to the Phone table and find all records with the intent of exporting all of them for backup. Now you go to the Invoice table and you see that only 10 of your 200 contact records are in the current found set. "No problem," you think. "It's the phone number I'm going export anyway." You choose File, Export Records or run a script with the Export Records step in it and choose the Phone table. When you look at the data that you exported, you're surprised to find only the phone numbers associated with the 10 contacts. In order to get the data you really want in this case, you need to switch to a layout that is connected to the table where your data lives.

Don't get me wrong. Sometimes you may want only the phones associated with a specific group of contacts. If that's what you want, stay right on the Contact layout and export the Phone table data.

In previous versions of FileMaker you were allowed only one Export script step per script. You could call any number of subscripts, each of which could have its own Export script step. Starting with FMP7 you can now include unlimited exports in one script. It's just that you would probably want to make sure each Export step was preceded by a Go to Layout step and perhaps a Find All Records step. Your script might look like this:

```
Go to Layout["Contact" (Contact)]
Show All Records
Export Records [No dialog; "Contact.tab"; Macintosh]
Go to Layout["Phone" (Phone)]
Show All Records
Export Records [No dialog; "Phone.tab"; Macintosh]
```

Oh, and you can export the same data (i.e., Contact) to multiple locations and in different formats in the same script step using the Specify Output file window. For instance you could export the contacts as both a tab-separated text file (.tab) and a Merge file (.mer) at the same time, sending one to the local hard drive and another copy to a computer on the other side of the world over the Internet! Now that's flexibility!

Part 6

One-Record Table

There is a trick used in the past by FileMaker developers in which they would create a one-record file that would hold special settings used in all the files in a solution via relationships. Included in such a file might be colors, logos, the corporate address, and advancing serial numbers (when not using FileMaker's auto-enter serial number feature).

Now that we have multiple tables in a file, storing those settings in a one-record table would seem a perfect opportunity to eliminate that external file and all those relationships. You could also create the layout, add the data you need, and delete the layout, thereby preventing anyone from accidentally changing that data. But what about exporting that data for backups and updating files?

Because you can only reliably export records from a table at the time you are on a layout associated with that table, if the layout is gone, how would you export the data? Here's how:

1. Go to the Define Database, Relationships tab and create a relationship between any field in the Settings table (my name for the one-record table) and ContactSerNum in the Contact table. Instead of using the equal sign between the tables, use the "x" from the pop-up.

Field Name	Type	Options
Constant	Calculation	=1

2. When it comes time to export the data from the Settings table, use the following script:

```
Go to Layout ["Contact" (Contact)]
Show All Records
Omit Record
Show Omitted Only
Export Records [No dialog; "Settings.mer"; ASCII]
```

Since a script can import to a table that has no layout associated with it, you don't have to make any special arrangements there. However, you must have a layout available associated with that table if you intend to import manually.

Nice trick! But it might just be easier to use FileMaker's Accounts & Privileges settings to remove the special Settings layout from the layout list of all users except those with the highest privilege sets. The only thing to keep in mind is that any account that has the Full Access privileges can create new records. So what? Well, if you're on the Settings layout with full access and create a new record, you no longer have a one-record table. I have a calendar file I created in FMP 4. It automatically opens with a password that prevents me from adding records to it and messing it up. I had to do that because more than once I added new records to the file when I pressed Command+N (Mac) accidentally when trying to hit Command+B or Command+J. With this new multi-table arrangement, you'd have to come in with access to everything except the ability to create new records in that table, or make getting to that layout darn difficult.

Using Your Backups

When things go wrong, and they eventually will, you'll need to know how to use the backups you've created to get up and running again. You'll know you're in trouble if you see one of the dialog boxes in Figure 22-6. Figure 22-7 shows one other message you'll see when a file is not closed properly. The message will stay onscreen while FileMaker goes through the file and corrects any errors it can find. I found it disconcerting the first few times I saw the warning, but the file usually turns out okay. It's only irritating and painful when it appears while opening large files. Keep in mind there could be unseen problems with the file after that. Fortunately, it looks as if FileMaker Pro 7 has a different way of handling these kinds of problems. I've been working with the program since early alpha versions of FMP7 and haven't seen any of these dialogs — even after what seemed like bad crashes. Hurray!

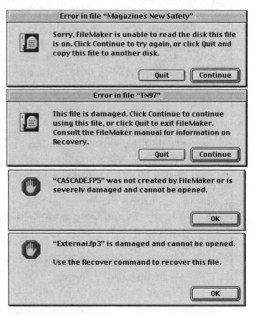

Figure 22-6
Any one of these four scary dialogs may appear at various times if a file is damaged.

> This file was not closed properly. FileMaker is now performing a consistency check.

Figure 22-7
The message FileMaker displays when a file is closed improperly.

Restoring

When you get a message that the file has been damaged, what you do next depends on a couple of issues. Depending on how much data has been entered since the last backup, it may be more economical to go to the last backup and recreate the new data.

The other choice is to open FileMaker Pro, choose File, Recover, find the damaged file wherever it lives on your hard drive, and open it. You will be prompted to name the file (see following Tip), and then FileMaker will run a 10-step process that attempts to recover your data and the file structure. This can take anywhere from a minute to several hours depending on the size of the file and the speed of your computer. Make sure you have enough room on your hard drive to create the new copy. It will take at least as much space as the original, and in some cases more. Again, you may just want to go to your last backup of the file. At the end of the process, you will see the dialog box in Figure 22-8.

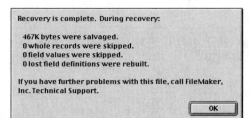

Figure 22-8
The dialog displayed at the end of file recovery.

Recovery is complete. During recovery:

467K bytes were salvaged.
0 whole records were skipped.
0 field values were skipped.
0 lost field definitions were rebuilt.

If you have further problems with this file, call FileMaker, Inc. Technical Support.

OK

⌘ **TIP**   FileMaker's method of helping you name a recovered file has caused many problems for my clients. The program suggests you leave the damaged file with the file's original name and name the repaired file by appending the word "Recovered" to the original file name. But here's what happens: When you next open your solution, any other files that need to refer to the new file through relationships will try to connect to the old damaged file (based on its unchanged file name), and FileMaker will tell you that "this file is damaged and needs to be recovered." Kind of confusing since you're positive you just recovered the file. I've gone to clients' offices where their solution folder was littered with half a dozen files named Invoice_Recovered1.FP7, Invoice_Recovered2.FP7, etc.

Instead, I recommend that when you have a damaged file, before you attempt recovery you name it something like Business_broke.FP7. Then when you use the Recover command and you're asked what to name the recovered file, give it the name the file has always had. That way all relationships, scripts, and field calculations will work immediately after you reopen the solution. Better yet, see if you have a fairly recent, undamaged backup you can use and skip the whole recovery process. You could still perform a recovery and just import the new records into your clean backup copy.

If any of the items in this dialog shows a number greater than zero (other than the number of bytes), you may have lost some of your data. In that case, you'll need to be vigilant to errors in any of your records. Sometimes the file is so severely damaged that the recovery process is unsuccessful. In that case, you have no alternative but to revert to your last saved copy.

My experience has been that more than 95 percent of the time the recovery is complete, and you can use the file as is. The problem is the other 5 percent of the time where there may still be some lurking damage to the file that could cause trouble days or even weeks later, leading to another crash. Rather than take any chances, I recommend exporting the data as a FileMaker Pro or Merge file and importing it into a copy of your most recent clone. Of course you'll lose any changes you've made to the structure of the files (new tables, fields, layouts, and scripts) since saving your last clone.

One other potential problem you should be attentive to at this point: Sometimes any custom formatting of the text itself in various fields can contribute to the corruption of the file. When you export as a FileMaker Pro file, text formatting is exported whether or not you chose "Don't format output" in the Specify Field Order window. A Merge file strips off any such formatting but retains the field names. That way, when you re-import the data, field mapping is a cinch.

Importing Data

Although our intent here is to get the data into an undamaged clone, most of what follows also applies to updating a file by bringing in a clone with new changes.

1. Open the copy of the clone.
2. Go to the layout associated with the table where you want the data to go.
3. Choose **File**, **Import**, and find the file you want to import from.
4. If it's a FileMaker file, choose the matching table from the data source file.
5. If the file is a FileMaker or Merge file, choose **Matching Names** from the Arrange by pop-up. See Figure 22-9. Otherwise, you'll have to match the data manually by moving the field names in the list on the right.

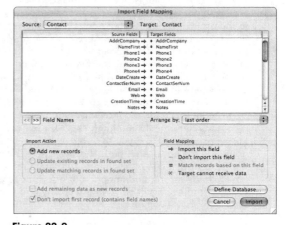

6. Select the **Add new records** radio button and click on **Import**.
7. Make selections from the Import Options window. Most of the time you will use the settings in Figure 22-10.

Figure 22-9
The Import Field Mapping window where you choose how the data will come into the current database.

8. Update any serial numbers (see the section titled "Tying Up the Loose Ends").

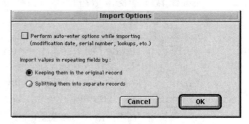

To try this out on the files we've been using, open the Business file, go to each table and choose Show All Records, and close it again. This

Figure 22-10
The Import Options window.

will be the data source, so imagine that it's the damaged file that's just been recovered. Now open the copy of the clone you created earlier in this chapter, and import the records from each of the tables in the Business file using the directions just listed. Before importing from a table, make sure you change to a layout that matches the table you'll be importing.

⊃ **NOTE**   You can only import data manually into a table if you are currently on a layout associated with the table into which you want the data to go. The window only shows the name of the current table in the upper-right corner. However, the window you use when importing records using a script is slightly different in that it allows you to choose the target table from a pop-up that appears in the upper-right corner.

That means whenever you want to update a file by importing data into a clone manually, you'll need to make sure you switch layouts before each import. If you create a script that runs a routine for you, you won't need to worry about which layout you're using as long as you select the target table from the pop-up.

⌘ **TIP**   If you perform the same import regularly, you might want to create a script that uses the Import Records script step. You can even have FileMaker match field names dynamically every time the script is run. To do that, begin your import. When the Import Field Mapping window appears, select "matching names" from the Arrange by pop-up. Finish the import and then define your script.

If you're trying to change an existing script, go back into the script, and click the Import Records script step. Be sure you have the right data source. Then click the Specify button and make sure the import is what you want. A second option would be to create a new script with the Import Records step and just click the Specify button. The import will already be memorized.

If you want to make sure the field mapping remains static, choose "Custom import order" as part of your import (Arrange by: custom import order), then save the script.

⌘ **TIP**   The Import Field Mapping window has a couple of other interesting features. Just above the Import Action area there are two arrowed buttons that let you preview the data before bringing it into your file. You can also click the Define Database button (if your access privileges permit) to create fields on the fly if there is incoming data you want to place into fields other than the ones previously created.

☒ **CAUTION**   If you are importing from a file that is open, there's something you need to check for. Remember that you can have multiple windows of the same file open with various found sets of the same table. Your import will include the found set of the frontmost window. If this will be a regular process, you'll probably want to create a simple script in the other file with the single step Show All Records as the first step in your routine.

More about Importing

Using the Import script step, you can import from multiple source files in multiple locations in the same step. For instance, you could import potential customers into the client table from a tab-separated text file (.tab) on your desktop and a Merge (.mer) file on a remote server in the same step. Simply select the Import Records script step in your script on the right, then click the check box next to "Specify data source" in the Script Step Options area. When you get to the Specify File window, click the Add File button and locate the file you'll be using. That's also where you can make additional file selections.

In previous versions of FileMaker you were allowed only one Import script step per script. You could call any number of subscripts, each of which could have its own Import script step. Starting with FMP7 you can now include unlimited imports in one script.

Tying Up the Loose Ends

To finish off this process, you'll need to perform a few other tasks. First, close all the files and make sure they have the right names. Remember what I told you a couple of Tips ago about the naming of recovered files.

Next, you should update any serial numbers in each table of the new clone. I can't tell you how important this is. If you have related records that use the serial number as the key and forget to update, here's what happens: Let's say you're working with the Invoice table, and just before a crash you were at InvoiceNum 1025. The last time you backed up or made a clone, that file was at InvoiceNum 1000. So you recover the file and import the data into the clone. When you create your next invoice record in the clone, the serial number will be 1001, but when you look at the portal, there will already be some data in it. Now you have two invoices with the number 1001 and each of them has a different customer. This is not good!

One way to handle this is to go into Define Fields in the Invoice table of the recovered file, and double-click the InvoiceNum field. Make sure you're on the Auto-Enter tab, and write down the number to the right of "next value." Exit Define Fields, and close the file. Now go back into the new clone file and put the number you just wrote down into the same field definition. You need to do that for every table that has an auto-enter serial number.

An even better way to handle the serial number issue is to use the Set Next Serial Value script step. With it, you can reach into a file (for example, a recovered file) for the number in the Next Value box (Define Database Fields tab, Auto-Enter tab) without having to enter the Define Fields area. First you would have to create a relationship to the file. Such a script has only one step:

```
File: Business Clone
Script Name: Update Next Serial Number
Go to Layout["Invoice" (Invoice)]
Set Next Serial Value [Invoice::InvoiceNum; GetNextSerialValue
("Business.FP7"; Invoice::InvoiceNum)] (Fields)
```

Set Next Serial Value is one of the design functions. Make sure you include the quotes around the database name — "Business.FP7" in this case. FileMaker will let you close the window without warning you there is a problem, and you'll get no other warning that it didn't work the way you expected.

Using the Set Next Serial Value and GetNextSerialValue in a single step like this will even grab serial number values that include text. Setting the next serial number using some other function would require a more complex calculation in order to incorporate text.

With versions of FileMaker Pro prior to 5.5 (and unless you use Set Next Serial Value), you won't be able to update the serial number while the files are being shared. However, if you've just recovered the files, you should perform this operation one way or another before making the files available to the other users anyway.

Prior to version 5.5, some developers had to create complex schemes whereby the serial number is created somewhere besides Define Fields, so that changes can be made while the files are being shared. It's beyond the scope of this book to explain them, but you should know there are some other options available for handling serial numbers.

Finally, file away the damaged and recovered files just in case there are still problems and you need to get to the data in them.

Summary

In this chapter, we looked at reasons to back up your files, how to make a clone of a file, a backup routine, some methods you can use to avoid database corruption, and how to recover from a problem using your backups and clones. You also learned about some commercial backup programs and some ways to back up from within FileMaker Pro.

Part 6

Q & A

Q Why not just make a clone of the most recent backup when a file turns out to be damaged instead of adding a cloning routine?

A You don't know when the corruption may have occurred to the file. You also don't know whether it was the data or the file structure that was damaged. Untouched clones are much more reliable because damage happens most often when files are closed improperly.

Workshop

Go to your other files and make clones of them. Make extra copies on some removable media and take a copy off-site. Export some data using the various formats. Then import it back into the original file, and notice the problems and advantages of each format. Remember to delete the extra data afterward or you'll have duplicate records.

Review Questions

True-False

1. The busier you are doing data entry, the more important it is to take time to back up your files.
2. One of the advantages of using FileMaker Server is its ability to save backups of files while they are being shared.
3. If your database contains records, it's not necessary to save clones of your files.
4. As long as you set up and follow a backup routine, you can "set it and forget it" until you need to recover data.
5. The Recover function runs a 10-step process that attempts to recover both the file structure and data.

Short Answer

6. Which is potentially more expensive — backup equipment, software, and planning; or labor and restoration services?
7. What are the three types of backups you can make from within FileMaker Pro's Create a copy As… window?
8. Name two commercial backup applications that can schedule and perform automatic backups of your databases.
9. How often should you save a clone of a database file?

10. Why is the Go to Layout script step important when you export records via a script?

11. What two things should you always do after importing records to a clone in order to make sure that your relationships work properly?

12. A backup tape should not be used more than how many times?

13. What is a clone?

14. How often should you back up a file?

Beyond FileMaker

Chapter 23

FileMaker Mobile 2.1

Vocabulary

- Palm operating system
- Personal digital assistant (PDA)
- Sync

Objectives

1. Become familiar with FileMaker Mobile (FMM).
2. Get an overview of the steps to install FMM.
3. Learn about properties specific to FMM.
4. Become familiar with the synchronization process (syncing).
5. Understand some of the similarities, differences, and limitations of FileMaker Mobile vs. FileMaker Pro.

Introduction

In November 2000, FileMaker, Inc., introduced FileMaker Mobile (FMM), a product that installs on personal digital assistants (PDAs) using the Palm operating system. With announcements made in May 2001 to deploy FileMaker on Linux, Pocket PC, and i-mode, it seemed clear that FileMaker Inc.'s intent was to make our FileMaker data available to us in as many convenient ways as possible. That should continue to widen the gap between FileMaker Pro and all the wannabes.

With that being said, let me add this: When the first version of FMM came out in November 2000 I was amazed. Amazed at how bad it was! It felt like going from living in a three-bedroom house to living in a bathroom. (Easy for me to say; I didn't have to do the programming. Here's the FileMaker company trying to offer us another way to use our data, and all I do is complain.) Despite my love for the desktop version of FMP, honestly I found FMM unusable and I just plain didn't like it.

But the people at FileMaker, Inc. do not sit still. They listened to users' comments and have done their homework.

I'm pleased to say FMM2.1 is actually a fine product. Does it do everything the desktop version of FMP does? Well, let me ask you this: Does the Palm Note Pad do everything Microsoft Word does? Of course not. But if I know the folks at FileMaker, Inc., as soon as the PDAs have the processing power to handle it, FMM will have that kind of power.

Not only is 2.1 a fine product, but this time around it adds support for Symbol bar code reading devices. Of course, you also need the appropriate Springboard or iPaq sleeve for iPaq and Visor devices. But it allows the import of the bar code data directly into fields. Click the field, scan, it's in there. The devices that have currently been tested are PPT2800, SPS3000, and CSM150. Unfortunately, 2.1 is not compatible with FileMaker Pro 7.

As we go to press, FileMaker Inc. announced the early summer 2004 release of FileMaker Mobile 7. This version will work with runtime versions of FileMaker. That means users won't need a copy of FileMaker as long as they have a copy of an application created with FileMaker Developer's runtime engine. FMM7 will be able to synchronize multiple FMM-carrying devices to databases on the desktop machine. As part of the synchronization process, users will be able to run scripts within FileMaker Pro before and after syncing. That means you'll be able to create scripts to "flatten" related data, sync, and reconstitute the flattened data back into related form — all as part of a one-step process.

In this chapter, I will outline the steps you'll need to get started with FMM. I'll also discuss how FMM is similar to and different from FileMaker Pro for the desktop PC. Of course you won't be able to make use of it until early summer. And some of the windows may look a little different. But the process is sure to be similar.

Installation Overview

You may still be thinking about whether to buy one of the PDA handheld computers. If so, this chapter may help you make that decision. I won't bother you with the step-by-step procedures of syncing a PDA with a PC or installing FMM on the PC and the PDA. There are complete instructions with the PDA and FMM. Rather, I'll give you an overview of the necessary installs and connections. Then I'll have you follow along with my first experience (which was on a Mac). Maybe it will help make the road a little smoother for you as well as give you an idea of what FMM does and doesn't do.

Here are the steps:

1. Connect the PDA cradle to your PC and place the PDA in it.
2. Install the Palm software on the computer following the instructions that came with your PDA.
3. Test that you can actually connect and sync.
4. Install the FMM application on the PC.
5. Using the PDA software on the PC, install (HotSync, Install Handheld files) the FileMaker Mobile.prc file. (The actual install will not take place until the next step.)

6. Pull the FMM application onto the PDA by performing a sync from the PDA. When the sync is complete, you should see the FileMaker icon on the PDA screen as in Figure 23-1.

7. Open at least one FileMaker file on the PC and set it up to be read by FMM by turning on the plug-in in FMP's preferences and in the file. You are allowed to sync with multi-user FMP files, but only on the host machine.

8. Run a normal sync from the PDA. The FMP files should transfer. When you click the FileMaker icon on the PDA, you should see a list of your files as shown in Figure 23-2.

Figure 23-1
The PDA screen with the FileMaker Mobile icon along with the other Palm OS programs.

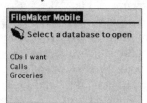

Figure 23-2
FileMaker Mobile's list of FileMaker files.

Setting Up Your Connections

I used a Handspring Visor Platinum and connected the cradle using the USB cable directly to the USB jack on the keyboard. Then I installed the Palm software onto my Mac. Connecting to the keyboard USB jack wouldn't allow me to sync, so I connected directly to an open USB port on the back of the computer.

And sure enough, that's what the instructions say to do. (Well, sort of. The instructions give you a short list of items you should not connect to. But the keyboard is not one of them.) Then I could run the HotSync by clicking the HotSync icon.

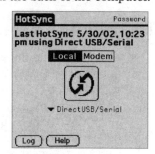

Figure 23-3
The Palm OS HotSync screen.

When I tried to install FileMaker Mobile.prc onto the Visor from the PDA software on my desktop machine according to the FMM instructions, I had difficulty finding the file. So I opened Sherlock (similar to Windows Explorer) to locate it. When I added FileMaker Mobile.prc to the install list, for some reason I could no longer use HotSync. I restarted the computer and still couldn't connect.

Not only that, but a dialog asked me to re-identify myself when I opened the Palm software. When I did, I entered my password but didn't capitalize it. Turns out, the Palm OS (like most other programs) is case sensitive regarding passwords.

Syncing

After another restart I was finally able to sync as shown in Figure 23-4. Be a little patient. It takes about five seconds for the sync process to begin. After you've seen it once or twice, you'll know what to expect. If you find yourself waiting 15 seconds, the sync is a dud. Even though the button says Cancel, clicking it does not stop the sync attempt. You just have to wait until it tells you it can't sync.

When I finally did connect, I found it interesting that you don't even need to have the Palm software open on the desktop machine to perform the sync. It happens automatically. Now that's the way software should work! With this second sync, FMM was finally passed to the PDA, and a little FileMaker icon appeared on the Visor in the application home area as in Figure 23-1. Great!

Figure 23-4
The screen you see when the Palm OS HotSync is in progress.

Part 7

Mobile Companion Plug-in

Back on my Mac, activating the Mobile Companion for Palm OS plug-in is similar to other FileMaker plug-ins. First, turn on the plug-in in FileMaker's Preferences. Then turn it on in each file you want to "mobilize." But when I tried to activate the plug-in in FileMaker's Preferences Plug-in tab, it wasn't there. I tried reinstalling FMM, but the installer said the files were already installed. So where are they? Well, the problem appeared to be that my version of FMM didn't like the Mac OS X version of FMP. I had to remove FMP 5.5 from the OS X disk so the FMM would install in the 5.5 Classic environment. It only took me an hour to work that out! You won't likely run into that much trouble. I did because I was working with a new computer, trying out the Visor, and installing FileMaker Mobile all at the same time.

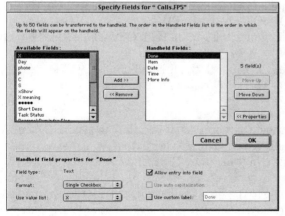

Figure 23-5
The Specify Fields window in FileMaker where you choose the fields and the properties they will have when they're sent out to the handheld computer.

Next, I opened one of my files and activated the plug-in there. The Specify Fields window in Figure 23-5 is odd because you can't move the field names up and down in the list using the familiar FileMaker method of grabbing a double arrow. There are no double arrows in this window. Instead, you have to select the field name and click a Move Up or Move Down button. What were they thinking? Will that be different in FMM7?

Properties

Just above the OK button is the Properties button. Click it and the Handheld field properties area opens as seen in the lower third of Figure 23-5. This is where some wonderful options are available. Once you move a field into the Handheld Fields list on the right, you determine how those fields will be handled in the Palm.

FMM recognizes Date and Time fields and you can choose to use the Palm OS Date and Time Picker when entering data. Or you can create your own value list.

Figure 23-6
A FileMaker Mobile Date field being edited with the Palm OS Date Picker.

One of the format choices for Text fields is Notes. A Notes field acts the same as a note in the Palm Date Book. You see the first line of text and everything after that appears as a little attachment. When you're entering data in a Note field, it opens to fill up the whole screen on the Palm rather than the little half-screen.

You don't have to stick with the same field names that you use in the desktop database. In the lower-right corner of the properties area you can provide a nice short name that will appear at the top of the column on the Palm.

You can also use value lists from your FMM files that come from your desktop files — within certain limits. You can't use lists that come from related files, for instance. I had to create a few lists specifically for my FMM files. No big deal. You just have to know you may have to do it.

You can investigate the other options in this area. I don't intend to explain everything here. Remember, we're just on a demo ride. But here are a few features on the Palm worth mentioning:

■ In the Preferences area is a check box that allows you to include your FMM field data in Global finds on the PDA.

■ You can insert phone numbers from the Palm OS Address Book directly into FMM2.1.

■ In spreadsheet style, you can lock the first column in List View so it will always be available as you scroll right and left.

Sync Me, Baby

After choosing the fields and their options, it was time to sync. Syncing with FileMaker happens automatically when you perform a regular sync on the Palm. Simply click the sync button on the PDA, and a window appears on the PC. I gotta tell ya, it's really cool watching it sync up as in Figure 23-4. Just remember, it will only sync to the files you have open with the Sharing plug-in activated at the time of the sync.

⊠ **CAUTION**   You can sync to multi-user files, but not while FileMaker Server is serving them. Also, when you perform a sync and forget to open files with which you intend to sync, everything acts the same whether the files update or not. There is no warning that files are closed. It's not like related files that open automatically in the background in FMP. That could be pretty scary if you're really depending on it for accuracy. So pay attention to what you're doing or you might think your data is current when it's not. If you realize your mistake, you can simply open the file(s) and perform another sync.

You do get a choice of how to handle conflicts, as shown in Figure 23-7, when records on both the PC and the PDA have changed since the last sync. That option is there to protect you from yourself — like when you come home and enter data in the desktop before syncing. In the plug-in, you decide which record, PC or PDA, gets overwritten when there is a conflict. Your other option is to create a new record in each file. But you'll have to develop a method for checking for those extra records — especially since they'll also duplicate any serial numbers.

Figure 23-7
The Mobile Settings window in FileMaker where you choose how records will be handled during synchronization with the PDA.

⌘ **TIP**   You can add a field to the list of fields you want to send to the Palm and it will go out on the next sync.

➲ **NOTE**   The syncing process wasn't too fussy about capitalization of words in data fields. I changed the case of one word both on the desktop and the Visor and it just updated to the Visor version. When I actually changed a word, I got the duplicate records I expected. Perhaps that will be more consistent in FMM7.

FMM2.1 allows you to rearrange the field order once the file is on the PDA. Simply click and drag the column header to the new location. Just make sure you hold down the pointing device once you click or you might find the column has sorted rather than moved. Be aware that if you change the order of the handheld fields on your desktop file, it will rearrange the field order in your FMM file on the Palm.

It was also delightful to find that with version 2 you can resize columns. Simply click and drag the line between column headers.

Going Mobile

Now that I had the software installed, I decided to test FMM using a list of CDs I'm looking for. I have just three fields in the CDs file: Item, Sort, and Got. Item can be an album name or an artist. Sort would be the album name or the artist with last name first. I mark the Got field with a "G" if I "got" it already or an "F" (for "Forget it!") if I bought it, hated it, and want to make sure I don't buy it again. That worked pretty well and replaced the dog-eared piece of paper I kept in my wallet.

FileMaker Appointments

Next, I brought over a file of appointments and calls I built in FMP some years ago. In FMM2.0 and later, clicking on a field in the list shown in Figure 23-8 brings up the text box in Figure 23-9. You can enter text in the box, the first line of which will appear back in List View, unless you turn off "Edit in list view" in the List View Options window (Figure 23-10). In that case, you'll be taken to Form View. More on that in a moment.

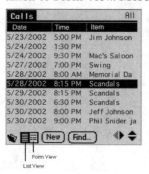

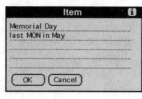

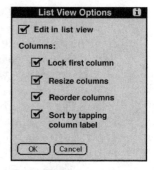

Figure 23-9
FMM's text edit screen in List View.

Figure 23-8
FileMaker Mobile's List View.

Figure 23-10
FMM's List View Options screen.

To get to the List View Options area (Figure 23-11), click the database name in the upper-left corner. Next click on Options and choose List View Options. You'll be presented with the List View Options screen in Figure 23-10. Unchecking the first box, Edit in list view, will lock all records so they can only be edited in Form View — unless you uncheck a similar box in the Form View Options screen (Figure 23-12). (To see the Form View Options screen, you must be in Form View.) It sounds a little complicated, but once you start to use it, you'll understand it in a very short time.

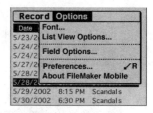

Figure 23-11
List View Options menu.

Figure 23-12
FMM's Form View Options screen.

⊃ **NOTE**   Some users simply want to carry data with them and avoid accidentally changing it. You can prevent data changes using List View Options and Form View Options. You can also prevent data changes on a field-by-field basis in the desktop version of FileMaker. Choose File, Sharing and click on the Mobile Companion plug-in. When you see the Specify Fields window, click the Handheld Fields Properties button (Figure 23-5). Uncheck the box next to "Allow entry into field." This could be important if you are an administrator sending out data you don't want changed. If the end users can just access anything, they might mess up your files when it comes time to sync again — unless you set the plug-in to overwrite the Palm at every sync.

If you chose not to allow data entry in List View back in the plug-in settings, clicking on a field takes you to the Form View in Figure 23-13. Since there is no Tab key, you have to click on a field to enter or change data.

There are so many choices regarding data entry settings that it can be a little confusing when the same action yields different results. For instance, if "Edit in list view" is unchecked, clicking on a record in List View will take you to Form View. But if that box is checked, it brings up an edit screen for text, date, or time, depending on the format of the field.

With editing allowed in List View, it took me a few minutes before I figured out how to get to Form View. I finally discovered the little Form View icon in the lower-left corner of the List View as shown in Figure 23-8. See the little file folder? The next icon to the right represents List View. It is reverse highlighted to indicate that it is the active view.

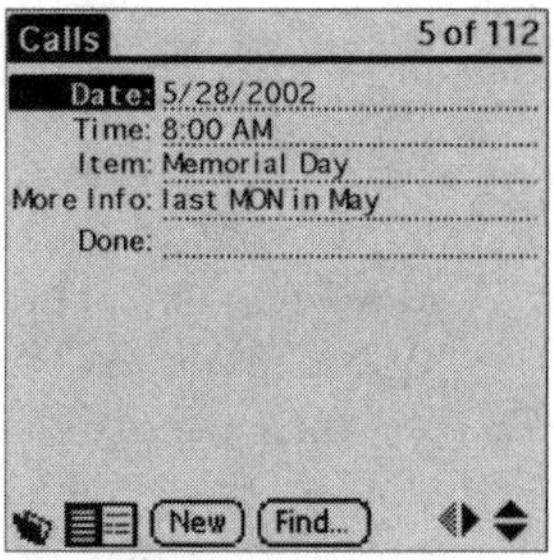

Figure 23-13
FMM's Form View.

PDA Calendar

I tried using the Palm OS Calendar since it looks pretty organized and professional. Following the directions in the Palm Desktop Help files, I exported my FMP appointment records as a tab-separated text file and imported the data into the calendar. It looks nice and the way it's organized makes sense, but I can't imagine trying to keep the FileMaker file updated to the one on the Palm, exporting and re-importing from one program to the other. For me, it's better to keep the data in the FileMaker and FMM appointments file where I can sync it more easily. I also like that I can change and script my FileMaker Pro files, which I can't do in the Palm calendar. But keep in mind, you can't script FMM either.

In FileMaker I often like to omit items from my current found set. That is not an option on the Palm platform. You can perform a find, but you don't have access to FileMaker's Find symbols. That means you can't find all empty fields like you'd normally do using the equal symbol.

Contacts

I also wanted to bring over my Contact file, but FMM doesn't deal with related records. I have the phone numbers set up in a portal the way I describe in Chapter 6. To access the phone numbers in FMM, you have to bring over the Phone file as well. Then when you want to look up a phone number, you find the contact person, copy their ContactSerNum, go to the Phone file, and find it there. Jeez! That's not too convenient.

To avoid all that, it would be possible to work out some type of lookup field(s) in the Contact file on the PC that would contain the phone numbers. Then you'd have to perform a relookup every time just before you sync. Sounds a bit tedious and potentially error prone, but it would work. Since FMM doesn't let you move Calculation fields, you can't trick it into calculating the phone number as the first record in the portal.

You could also create an in-between file to which you would export data from multiple sources. You would use relationships to match fields when importing the data into this file. Then you'd need a routine to send the data back to the source fields once it came back from the Palm. A bit complicated, but it could be done.

Grocery List

When I first tried using the PDA for my grocery list I didn't find it particularly convenient. I felt uncomfortable pushing that shopping cart with the wobbly wheel while holding the device in my hand. So I would memorize what I needed as I started down the aisle, put the PDA in my pocket, then drag it back out again at the next aisle.

I use it all the time now. I have a list of about 130 items, but only mark the few I need in a check box field. After grabbing the first few items I remove the check mark and do a Find for what's still left with a check mark, so the list keeps getting shorter. I have a column for which aisle the items are on, so I sort by that field as I get ready to shop and work my way through the store more efficiently.

FileMaker Mobile vs. FileMaker Pro

Finally, FileMaker Mobile is simply not FileMaker Pro. A good number of functions you come to expect with FileMaker Pro are just not available in FMM. Depending on your intended use for FMM, this could be a major issue.

Keep in mind that this chapter is about FMM 2.1. FileMaker, Inc. has continued to upgrade the product and has already announced FMM7 for FileMaker Pro 7. But the more features that get added to FMM, the less memory there will be for your data. On the other hand, the amount of memory in PDAs is really growing. There may be some exciting times ahead! The following list includes information available at press time regarding FMM7.

Similarities
Using FMM, you can:
- Find
- Sort
- Delete a record
- Delete all records
- Copy
- Paste
- Create new records
- Use Date, Time, and Number fields
- Use check boxes and pop-up lists (with limitations)
- Rearrange the field order like FMP Table View
- Enter data in List View
- Duplicate records
- Undo — There is an Undo menu command, but as in FMP, it won't undo any deleted records.
- Sync to run-time files
- Synchronize multiple handheld devices to a desktop database.
- Run scripts on the desktop database as part of the sync process.

Differences and Limitations
Following is a list of things you can't do in FMM.
- No relationships
- No field options — no data checking, lookups, auto-enter dates, or times
- No radio buttons
- No scripting in the Palm files
- Find on only one field at a time
- Sort on only one field at a time
- No FileMaker Find symbols
- No Calculation, Container, Summary, or Global fields
- No Layout mode
- No omit
- Only 50 fields per file
- 2,000-character limit per field

Summary

In this chapter, we looked at FileMaker Mobile for PDAs, a few ways it might be used, and how it is similar to and different from the FileMaker Pro program.

Q & A

Q If you can't sync related fields with FileMaker Mobile, how would you use a lookup field that could be sent over to the PDA?

A As I wrote in the chapter, it's not a simple thing to do. So I've included a set of files in the downloadable files that demo these lookup fields. Go to the J_Stars files folder, and look in the FMM_Phones folder. Then open FOR_FMM.FP7. You can study what I've done there and use it if you want.

Workshop

I'm not sure I can offer you a workshop unless you have FMM and a PDA. If you do have both of them, I wouldn't expect you to be waiting around for me to give you an assignment. But if I did, I'd say, have at it. Sync it up and bring over a couple FMP files and use them to see what FMM can and can't do.

Review Questions

True-False

1. Using FileMaker Mobile is a way to take your databases along with you via a PDA.
2. FMM allows you to format a Text field as a Notes field, so that it behaves similarly to other notes fields on your PDA.
3. Once you have the databases on your PDA, they're updated in real time with those on your PC.
4. You cannot delete records with FMM.

Short Answer

5. Where do you install the FileMaker Mobile application, on the PDA or on your PC?
6. How many fields can you specify for a sort in FMM?
7. Which types of fields can you not use with FMM?
8. What plug-in must be installed and activated in order to sync FMM files?
9. Which modes are not available in FMM on the PDA?
10. FileMaker Mobile is a program for what category of computers and what operating system is required?
11. Name at least three things you can do in both FMP and FMM.
12. Name at least four functions you cannot perform with FMM.

Part 7

Chapter 24

FileMaker and XML

Vocabulary

- HTML
- Style sheet
- XML
- XSL

Objectives

1. Understand the purpose of XML and XSL.
2. Discover ways XML can work with FileMaker Pro.
3. Learn to create a script to export records as XML type.
4. Discover resources for learning more about XML and XSL.

Introduction

Starting with FileMaker Pro 6.0, FileMaker, Inc. has chosen to embrace Extensible Markup Language (XML) technology wholeheartedly. FileMaker can now export, import, and open files using XML. XML is also the backbone of Instant Web Publishing. But what is this XML stuff all about? What can we who use FileMaker do with it? That's exactly what I wanted to know. So I started asking around.

In this chapter I want to tell you a little about what XML is and some ways I've seen it used. Then I'll take you through an exercise to create a document using an XML export from the files we've already created.

Unfortunately, I cannot provide you with a primer on XML in this book. All I can do is tell you a bit about what it is and why it is important based on the little research I've done. Whether or not it will be important to you with regard to your use of FileMaker is up to you and the requirements of your work. If you get excited about XML, there is a list of links at http://filemaker.com/xml/links.html where you can learn the basics. Also check out XML Central, found at: http://filemaker.com/xml/index.html.

What Is XML?

XML is a language standard for exchanging data in agreed-upon formats. Its primary purpose is similar to HTML: "mark up" some data in a way that enables it to be parsed and displayed in a specified fashion by the end user or an agent thereof (a browser, some other parser, style sheet, or whatever).

That's the textbook way of saying that when you and I send data back and forth, we're going to put it in a form we both can understand. And the form will not necessarily be FileMaker files. Groups can create their own languages for their own purposes. They just have to work within the XML standard.

XML is different from ODBC in that ODBC is sort of a pipeline for sending data between applications. XML actually translates the data into different forms. Using ODBC, you can pull data from a FileMaker file into an Excel spreadsheet. Using XML, you can export FileMaker data so that it ends up as an Excel spreadsheet. It will actually hit your desktop as a fully formatted spreadsheet complete with the little Excel icon ready for double-clickin'. (Note: You must be using Microsoft Excel 2002 (XP) for Windows or later to take advantage of XML format for spreadsheets.)

Just because I use the Excel example doesn't mean it stops there. What form do you need the data in? Word? You can do that. PageMaker? You can do that, too. And much, much more. You can transform data from *any* application format that supports XML. Wow! Currently onboard are applications such as QuickBooks, Microsoft Office, Lotus Notes, MySQL, Keynote, QuarkXPress, Adobe Acrobat, FedEx package tracking, SAP, Sieble, and PeopleSoft, to name a few. And there are over 450 vocabularies for various business and government applications rapidly replacing EDI as the primary means to exchange data.

And FileMaker can connect to SQL servers using XML without the need for ODBC drivers. This can be a great advantage since ODBC tends to be a bit slow. It can also be a pain for system administrators to keep up with the latest ODBC drivers for their systems. And let's not forget the licensing fees. XML may eventually do away with the licensing issue entirely.

Add in XSL

Extensible Stylesheet Language (XSL) is what tells your data how to look and act. Put XML with XSL and you get a document for a specific use. Using different style sheets, you can have the same data appear in a number of different forms. For example, you could have the data show as a list, and by simply clicking a link that calls a different style sheet, you could display the same data as a graph. There is actually a lot more to it than I'm telling you. But that pretty much covers the basics.

What Can I Use It For?

Starting with FileMaker 5.0, the people from FileMaker, Inc. have been using XML to provide us with the themes we choose when we create layouts. On Windows, look in FileMaker Pro 7\English Extras\Extensions\Themes. On Macintosh, look in the FileMaker Pro 7 folder and Control+click on the FileMaker Pro application icon and choose Show Package Contents. Choose Contents\Resources\English.lproj\Themes. In Chapter 9 I talked about how you can create your own themes by opening a copy and editing an existing theme in a word processing program. XML looks a lot like HTML, but don't get too scared. Since the folks at FileMaker want us to get going with this tool,

Part 7

they have an entire area of their web site devoted to XML style sheets for all types of uses.

XML is used to make the Web Companion work some of its magic in browsers that support cascading style sheets. Before XML, if you were using a dial-up modem, you would call for some data from a web site, watch the stuff start to load into your browser, and go get a cup of coffee. If you wanted to sort the data, you went for another cup because the browser would go get the data all over again along with all the information about what the page should look like. With XML, the browser says in effect, "Hey, I've already got the data. Why don't I just use XSL and display it in a different order?" There's no need to go back across the web and get the data all over again with a description of what the page should look like. This change in method speeds up the process a great deal, and it helps to keep from clogging up the network, too. Of course, now we want to have the Net deliver movies on demand and play networked games, but let's not go into that.

Ever have a client who doesn't use FileMaker and wants you to give them data in a Word file? Ever spent a lot of time formatting data for the accounting department? I have a client who puts out a booklet with all the company's vendors listed. They retype the booklet every year in PageMaker. We began discussing how the vendor list could come out of FileMaker with the PageMaker tags already attached so the headings were 16-point bold followed by a gray underline and double spaces between vendors. The process would take a couple of minutes rather than a week. I was going to create FileMaker fields to calculate all the tags. But I can use XSL to do that for me.

I saw a demonstration where the presenter clicked various clauses of a contract to build a custom document. When he exported it, it arrived on the desktop as a fully formatted Word document ready to be attached to e-mail for client approval. Using something like that could help more than one office I know do away with folders and folders of contract templates. Using XML they'd be able to build the contract on the fly.

You can export records from FileMaker and build a fully formatted web page. FileMaker has been able to export data as HTML since version 5.0. But the pages were quite generic — and boring. Using XSL, you can make it look as pretty as you please. And guess what. That's exactly what we'll be doing in this chapter.

How about using XML to encrypt data before sending it out and then unscramble it on the other end? You can take your data and build complex graphs to make it easier to understand. How about getting access to headlines on the web and pulling them into FileMaker, then turning them out as a custom newsletter? You can track packages from FedEx on the web. Or maybe you'd rather track your stock prices. Is this giving you any ideas?

Chris Trytten, director of product management for FileMaker, Inc., says that XML will allow for more focused results in search engines. How many times have you requested data in a search engine only to have 50 to 100 results? Most of them are not related at all to what you want to know. XML can do more than display the data — it can tell you what it means.

If you go to http://filemaker.com/xml/xslt_library.html, you'll find the FileMaker XML library describing a whole rack of uses and the files you can use for translating data back and forth from FileMaker.

Examples: Exporting XML as HTML

The following examples are something I dreamed up and Dave Dowling built. He's an FSA member and a very clever FileMaker developer who lives in Okemos, Michigan. He's been experimenting with XML for some time, so I asked him to help out by providing the example files for the downloadable. He has some other examples on his web site, which you'll find at www.davedowling.com.

What I/we will be showing you is how to take some data in the file we've been building in the chapters of this book and export it using XML and an XSL style sheet to create an HTML page you can open with a browser. Using the same export method, I'll also show you how to use the same data to build an HTML page using a style sheet that actually sits on my web site. Of course, you'll need to be online to access the second XSL document. I'm using this example because most people have a web browser on their machine, and I can't know what other applications you might have. If you haven't built the file, you can open the folder for Chapter 24 from the downloadable file and copy the folder onto your hard drive.

Using a Local XSL Style Sheet

If you are using your own files, there is a file you'll need from the downloadable. Look for Book Chapter files\Chapter 24\contact.xsl. Drag it into the same folder as your Business file.

1. Open your Business file, go to the Contact table, and choose **File, Export Records**.

2. Choose **XML** from the Type pop-up, and name the file **Contacts.htm**. You decide what directory you want it to go into. In this case, I prefer the folder where you keep the Business file because it will be easier to connect the XSL sheet. Click the **Save** button. You will see a window like Figure 24-1, but it won't be filled out yet.

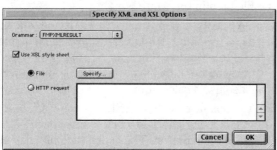

Figure 24-1
The Specify XML and XSL Options window.

3. Be sure the Grammar pop-up says FMPXMLRESULT, click the box next to "Use XSL style sheet" so a check mark appears there, then click the **File** radio button. (Notice that you could also type a web address in the HTTP request field.) You'll need to work your way through your directories until you find the contact.xsl file you got from the downloadable. When you find the file, select it and click the **Open** button. That will bring you back to the Specify XML and XSL Options window. Click **Continue**.

4. Make your field choices. I simply used NameFirst and NameLast. Then click the **Export** button.

5. You can hide or minimize FileMaker and open the Contacts.htm file with a browser to take a look at it. It's nothing fancy, but there it is! It's even got a little background color.

⮕ **NOTE** Once again, the field- and file-naming guidelines we discussed earlier come into play. XML cannot deal with periods, spaces, or special characters in the names of files or fields. You'll also want to avoid using numbers at the beginning of any field name.

Creating the Export XML Script

Follow the next set of directions carefully. The Specify Output File and Specify (XLS) File windows look almost identical, and it's easy to get confused when working your way through them.

1. Start a new script and call it **XML test**. (This is assuming you have followed the steps in the previous section so the export is still in FileMaker's memory.)

2. Under the Records heading, double-click the **Export Records** step.

3. While the step is highlighted, click the **Specify** button next to "Specify output file." In the Specify Output File window, click the **Add File** button, choose **XML** from the Type pop-up, and name the file **Contacts.htm**. (Be very careful not to give it a name that overwrites the XSL files in this folder.) You decide what directory you want it to go into. In this case, I prefer the folder where you keep the Contact file because it will be easier to connect the XSL sheet.

4. Click the **Save** button to return to the Specify Output File window. You should now see the file path in the white box.

5. Choose **XML** from the File Type pop-up and click **OK** and you will see a window like Figure 24-2. (Clicking that OK button when choosing XML is the only time you'll see this window. There is no other way to get here.) Notice that in the script you not only have the option to use a web address, but you can also use a calculation.

6. If there's a check in the box next to "Use XSL style sheet," click the **Specify** button. If the box is not checked, click it so a check mark appears there, then click the **File** radio button. The contact.xls file may already appear in the File Path window, but if not, you'll need to work your way through your directories until you find the contact.xsl file you got from the downloadable file. When you find the file, select it and click the **Open**

button. That will bring you back to the Specify XML and XSL Options window. Click **OK** and **OK** again.

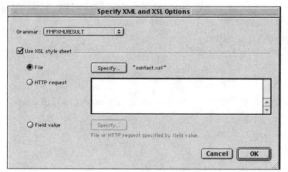

Figure 24-2
The Specify XML and XSL Options window found in the Export Records script step in ScriptMaker.

7. Now click the **Specify** button next to "Specify export order." NameFirst and NameLast should already be in the "Field export order" box in the lower right, but if they're not, add them now. If there's anything in the Group by box, clear it out, then click **OK**.

8. At this point, you can choose to click the "Perform without dialog" check box. It's up to you. If you're doing this for a group, you may want to check the box next to "Run script with full access privileges." Then click **OK**.

One other small detail: Export Records is not a web-compatible script step.

You can make a button on one of the layouts to perform the script automatically if you like. Each time you run the script, it will overwrite the previous file. That means you can choose a different set of records manually, click the button, and look at the file. I even went back and added the Open URL script step so it opens the file as soon as it exports the data. I'm not sure how this works in Windows, but on my Mac it looks like this:

file:///MacintoshHD/FileMaker%20Pfiles/Chapter%2024/Contacts.htm. The %20 is the web standard placeholder for a space.

You should be able to look at the style sheet by opening it with a text editor of any kind. But I found that opening and saving it in Word caused the file to break.

Using a Remote XSL Style Sheet

About the only thing you'll need to do differently for this exercise is make sure you have an open line to the web and change the XSL request in the Specify XML and XLS Options window. You'll be attaching a style sheet from my web site. When you see the window in Figure 24-2, click the button next to "HTTP request" and type in http://www.DataDesignPros.com/XSL/contactWeb.xsl. That's it. Everything else is the same.

If you make this into a script, you'll need to be connected to the web each time you run it. Not that this is such a great style sheet for that purpose. I only did this to give you a taste of the possibilities.

One way you might use this is to update reports for your clients by making changes to the style sheet. Instead of sending them new FMP files each time

they need a small change to a report (and going through the process of importing all their current data and updating serial numbers), build the reports as
XML exports. Then simply make the needed changes to the XSL style sheet
that lives on the web somewhere. Big time-saver!

My final script reads like this:

```
Script: XML Test Web
Beep
#1 = Yep! / 2 = No / 3 = Cancel
Show Custom Dialog ["WARNING"; "You should not perform this script unless
you are connected to the web. Are you connected?"]
If [Get (LastMessageChoice) = 2 or Get (LastMessageChoice) = 3]
    Halt Script
End If
Export Records [No dialog; "Contacts.htm"; "FMPXMLRESULT";
http://www.DataDesignPros.com/XSL/contactWeb.xsl; Unicode (UTF-8)]
Open URL [No dialog;
"filemac:/Panther/Users/jonathanstars/Desktop/FMP7files/Contacts.htm"]
```

Of course the paths to your files will be different from mine — all except the
path to the XSL style sheet on my web site.

Before you run the script to open the page, make sure you're still connected to the web. (In some of my trials I found the Contacts.htm page
wouldn't open automatically from FileMaker's Open URL script step. If that
happens to you, just double-click the file once it's created.) There are a couple
things about this page that are different from the earlier example that gathered
information from the Net. You are opening an HTML page that lives on your
machine, using a style sheet that lives on my web site, and displaying elements (my picture) that come from elsewhere on the web. Starting to get the
picture? Cool, eh?

And Beyond...

The HTML file we just built (Contacts.htm) uses a static export. If you open
the file in a word processor, you'll see the data embedded in the XML text. But
XML can operate on files that are shared on a network — whether that network is an intranet or the Internet. That means you can have a file on a server,
and, using XML and an XSL style sheet, you can build reports that draw from
the data as it is called for. You can also have different style sheets for various
ways you might want to display the same data. For a simple set of demo files
and different style sheets that demonstrate this capability, go to
http://filemaker.com/xml/xslt_library.html.

Profile of a FileMaker XML Web Request

Just so you know a little bit more about what happens with FMP and XML on
the web, here is how FileMaker uses XML and XSL to provide the final web
page with a browser that uses cascading style sheets (Microsoft Internet
Explorer or Apple's Safari):

1. The user fills out a form and/or clicks a button or link to make a request.
2. The browser sends the request to the server where the FMP files live.
3. The copy of FileMaker on the server sends the XML data back to the browser, but the data waits until...
4. The browser finds the required style sheet wherever it might live.
5. The browser takes the style sheet and formats the FileMaker XML data from step 3 into what will appear on the final page.

The value of this system over the old way of building a web request is that the FileMaker server is only required to send the data. Previously, the server was also required to format the data into the final web page and send the whole thing over the web channel. Using XML, the web browser on the user's machine builds the final page. That means less information needs to be sent down the pipeline to and from the server. The server can process more requests. And it means a big improvement in speed. It's even more efficient if the user then clicks a Sort button in their browser. The data and the style sheet are already on the user's machine. Only the order of the data needs to change — and very quickly at that.

Import XML

I'm not going to go into any detail regarding importing XML. If you choose File, Import Records, XML Source, you'll see the window in Figure 24-3. You can see the method is virtually the same as exporting from FMP using XML. The only difference is you'll have to map the incoming data to the proper fields in the FileMaker file.

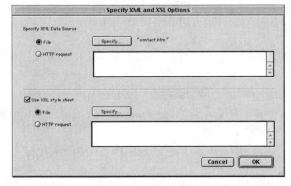

Figure 24-3
The Specify XML and XSL Options window that displays when importing and opening XML.

Open XML

Not to disappoint you, but I'm not going to go into any detail regarding opening XML either. If you choose File, Open, and choose XML Source from the Show pop-up, you'll see the same window as in Figure 24-3. Again, you can see the method is virtually the same as exporting and importing from FMP using XML. You can handle it.

Summary

In this chapter I introduced you to FileMaker's exciting Import, Export, and Open XML features. I gave you some reasons you might find XML a valuable tool and some links to pages on the FileMaker web site to get more information. Then we created a simple export example and made a script so we could run it again.

Q & A

Q How can I find out what other people are doing with XML and FileMaker?

A From the FileMaker XML Central home page (http://filemaker.com/xml/index.html), you can click the FileMaker XML Talk link to join a discussion group dedicated to the exchange of XML ideas among FileMaker users.

Q Can I use XML without having to use XSL, too?

A Yes. XSL just gives you more options, like sorting, different formats, etc. XML allows you to separate your data from formatting. Theoretically, XSL allows you to provide any other formatting to that data.

Workshop

Download one of the examples that interests you from http://filemaker.com/xml/xslt_library.html and work with it. See if you start to come up with more ways you might use XML for your company, clients, or yourself.

If you have a little XML knowledge, make some changes to a copy of the contact.xsl style sheet we used in the example in this chapter. Then run an export using that style sheet to see the results of your work.

Review Questions

True-False

1. XML is a language standard for universal data exchange.
2. XML translates data from different software tools into a language that can be understood by both tools.
3. With XML, FileMaker Pro can connect to SQL servers without using ODBC drivers.
4. XSL is used to create scripts to be passed to other applications.
5. In order to connect FileMaker to SQL servers using XML, you need to use ODBC drivers.

Short Answer

6. What does the acronym XML stand for?
7. What does the acronym XSL stand for?
8. What two links on the FileMaker web site can help you learn more about XML and XSL?

9. How can XML help you protect sensitive information while sending it over the Internet?

10. What must you specify in the Export Records step in order to script an export using XML?

11. How does XSL make XML more effective?

12. How might a mortgage company use FileMaker Pro and XML to speed the processing of mortgage documents?

13. What FileMaker feature/script step do you use to get data from a database file to be used by other applications?

Chapter 25

File Conversion Issues and Answers

Objectives

1. Become familiar with the file conversion process.
2. Identify some of the design elements that get changed through conversion.
3. Explore file references created in the conversion process.
4. Understand the need to clean up a converted solution.

Introduction

Because FileMaker Pro 7 is structurally quite different from previous versions, converting files from the FMP5 format (usable in FMP6) cannot be done without some attention to detail. This chapter will talk about the process of converting, some problems you might run up against, and what to do to make the transition as smooth as possible. There were rarely issues when upgrading between earlier versions. The fact that you have to pay any attention to the conversion process might make you wonder if the upgrade would be worth the trouble. But when I look at the new tools available, I definitely think it's worth it.

Documentation

This chapter will only be an overview. What you really need to do is look at a document that comes with the FileMaker Pro installation. Look in FileMaker Pro 7\English Extras\Electronic Documentation for a file called FM 7 Converting Databases.pdf. Why would I tell you to read that document instead of this chapter? Because it's a very comprehensive 82 pages. The longest chapter I have in this book is only 30-some pages long.

Don't get too scared by the length of their primer. There's a three-page table of contents, a three-page index, and a bunch of blank pages between sections, and quite a few items are repeated for clarity. You don't even get to the meat and potatoes until page 7. Much of what they cover has to do with complex solutions heavily laden with lots of scripting. That might have nothing to do with what you'll be converting. I converted a number of single-file solutions without incident. Be sure to look at the checklist on page 14.

What I'll do here is take you on a tour of a conversion while following the directions in that document. I'll actually write this chapter while performing my first multi-file solution conversion. Since I'm usually confused when dealing with installation, new software, and such, I think I can give you a pretty good idea of what you'll be up against. Let's just see what trouble I can get into.

Step By Step

There are different sets of instructions depending on whether your database consists of just a few files or if it's a more complex, multi-file solution. The conversion document has a great checklist where you can determine which items you need to pay attention to.

The solution I'll be converting is the one that went with the previous version of this book. By the time we hit Chapter 15, we had created eight files. It's not a terribly complex set of files. But it should work as a nice start.

A big part of what needs to be considered has to do with how the database is being used. Here are some pertinent questions:

1. Are the files being hosted with FileMaker Server or are they your own personal files?

2. Are the files being published on the web with Instant Web Publishing or Custom Web Publishing?
    Both these questions have a lot to do with FileMaker's new Accounts & Privileges model. If you're not using passwords in your files, many conversion issues will fall by the wayside, even though all new files will now have default accounts associated with them.

3. Are you using any plug-ins that need to be updated? (At least check with the vendor.)

4. Does anything in your files work with ActiveX, Apple events, or ODBC/JDBC? (May need updates there.)

5. Would it just be better to rebuild in 7 and import your data from the old files?

6. Are there any functions in your files that depend on undocumented behavior? (That functionality may disappear.)

It might be a really good idea to print the scripts, field definitions, and layouts in your current file before starting. If you use FMP Developer, it might be better to create a Database Design Report rather than a printed copy. I used two computers so I could see the difference file by file.

Part 7

The first thing to be aware of is that multi-file solutions will not be instantly converted to a single-file, multi-table solution. That might be a big disappointment. But the differences in file structure make that kind of conversion impossible.

As the file(s) convert, FileMaker creates a Conversion.log file in the same folder as the files. Look at the report to see what problems need to be solved. This should be one of your best tools.

After reading the conversion document it seems clear to me that if I mess up the first conversion, converting a second time wouldn't be that hard. So rather than checking everything out, I'm just going to convert and then take a look at the log file. I'll open both the old and new versions on computers next to each other and see how they look. (Converting files full of data could be time consuming, so that might not be the best solution for everybody. But that's what I'll be doing today. I can do a larger file later and clock it out — with consideration for the fact that I currently have the fastest personal computer on the planet!)

First I created a new folder on my hard drive called Chapter 25 convert from 6. I copied the files I'm converting from another folder and put them in this new folder. I added a folder at the same level called Chapter 25 converted to 7 so both folders showed up next to each other.

I started the FileMaker Pro 7 program. Then I dragged the folder with the files in it (Chapter 25 convert from 6) onto the FMP7 icon in my (Mac OS X) Dock and I got the window in Figure 25-1. Since I already created a folder where I want the files to go, I clicked the Specify button and found the folder. But you can see you're allowed to create a folder anywhere you want while you're in the middle of the process. Then I clicked the Open button.

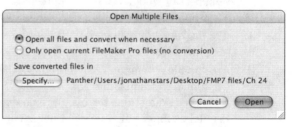

Figure 25-1
The Open Multiple Files window.

I got Mac OS X's "spinning rainbow candy of death" for about four seconds. This is a very fast computer and the files really are quite small. Very little data. Then I got a message that "FileMaker cannot share a file because FileMaker network sharing is turned off." Sounds logical. When I clicked OK to dismiss that dialog, all the files popped open.

I was then presented with the Account Name and Password window for the Invoice file. My name was already in the Account Name field. I figured I could use the Admin account, so I typed Admin where my name was and left Password empty. No dice! Uh, oh. I tried Admin, Admin. That didn't work. Finally I typed Master and Master. It worked! Remember that FileMaker 7 converts passwords to both account names and passwords and requires you to use the same name in both fields. Since FMP7 passwords are case sensitive, users who have not needed to pay attention to that in previous versions may be baffled when they can't get into the file using a password they've been using for years. So anyway, I'm in now.

As I moved files around so I could find the Contact file (remember, this is the old system where I have multiple files) I saw the Phones file displayed a <Field Missing> where FirstName should go. I looked at Define Database at the Relationships tab and saw that the Phones ContactSerNum field seemed to be connected to the Contacts Notes field. What's that about? I went back into the original FMP6 files and sure enough, that's what it looks like there. Not FMP7's fault.

Just for fun I chose File, Define, File References. I double-clicked the Contact file and got the following:

file:/Macintosh HD/Buttons/Part 3/All FlMkr/JSSA business files/FMP 5 book/Contact
file:/Contact

Apparently, FileMaker remembers some version of the files a couple of hard drives ago. The first one listed is a drive that committed suicide by self-immolation about two years ago. Kinda upset me to remember that sad time. I believe there was an incident involving an object flying through a window, the police, handcuffs…

We'll look at file references in more detail in a little bit.

Conversion Log

It's time to look at the conversion log. Wow! There are over four pages in the log with close to 200 items listed. It begins with the Contact file. One note says "Poor field name." Well! I think I should be the judge of that. The field was called Field::Name experiment. Right! I was experimenting with the problems a field would have with relationships, Instant Web Publishing, and ODBC if you used the double colon. Poor field name indeed! A field name should never have a double colon in it.

Some relationships converted. The Today function was replaced with a Today field and a startup script to update it. Interesting, since I dislike the Today function. Looked around but didn't see any field named Today. There is a Text field called DateTest. In field Validation I used the Today function, which has been converted to Get(CurrentDate). It was a field I was experimenting with in one of the earlier books but I never used it. Hey, maybe this will help me clean up the files!

Mostly it just says that fields, layouts, scripts, value lists, indexes, and records were converted just fine. In fact, as I scan down the list it appears that everything was converted correctly. No errors appear anywhere that I can see. Looking for errors at this point is actually very helpful, but since the list is so long, they can be hard to spot. Use a word processing program and search for the word "error."

Comparing Fields

Now I'm setting the two databases next to each other on two machines to see what differences appear in various places. I'll start with field definitions. The first difference I notice is that Phone1 shows the number 10 after the word

Text in the Type column. I like knowing at a glance how many repetitions there are to a repeating field.

Fields that were indexed before are indexed now, and fields that weren't indexed before are not indexed now. Makes sense. When I look behind the Storage tab, where indexing used to be On or Off, now the index is shown to be Minimal. When I look behind the Validation tab on State (AddrState) I see the window looks different with regard to the placement of "Allow user to override during data entry." In the FMP6 version this check box reads "Strict: Do not allow user to override data validation." Where that box used to be empty unless checked, the new one is checked until you uncheck it. No big deal, just different.

Oh, I also see that calculations are identified with specific tables. For example in FMP6, the AddrCombo field reads "NameFirst & " " & NameLast &..." In FMP7, it reads "from Contact, = NameFirst & " " & NameLast & ..." I suppose if I were to combine elements from other tables, I'd see those tables identified as well. A little test shows that the calculation is still associated with the specific table. The related field was tacked onto the end of the calculation. But when I switched back, removing the related field, the storage showed to be Unstored and I had to change it manually. Okay.

Global fields appear different according to the new model. Instead of the word Global in the Type column, it's now in the Options column as expected.

Everything else is simply a repetition of the things I already mentioned. I looked at a couple of the other files in the solution. More of the same. It's interesting that I now see how much I would gain by having this old, multi-file solution in a single file like we've built over the course of this book. Now let's see what happens with layouts.

Comparing Layouts

The first thing I noticed was that the buttons were colored slightly differently. Probably a difference in the displays I'm using and between Mac OS 9 and OS X. Next I found the converted file didn't remember the found set in my Contact file. That's not surprising.

The Status area is different from the previous version. The Book now works from left to right (more like a book) where it used to work up to down (like a Rolodex). The new mode buttons appear above the layout names, but that's about it. None of these are conversion issues.

Finally, the text aligns differently horizontally in the fields on my OS X machine than on my OS 9 Macintosh. The fonts also look ragged. That's because I turned off Font Smoothing, which makes my eyes feel as if I've got something smeared on my glasses. I don't like what I see either way, but it's a Mac problem, not FileMaker's.

Accounts & Privileges

In the Invoice file of my FMP6 files I had two passwords: Master and Sales. Master was defined with full privileges, so it took the place of the Admin account that it normally created when a file gets started. That explains my confusion when I couldn't get into the file with the Admin password.

Along with the Master account, I got an inactive Guest account with the Read-Only Access privilege set, and an active Sales account. When I click the Privilege Sets tab, I see the Data Entry Only privilege set and the Read-Only Access, neither of which is assigned to any accounts. Then there's a new Sales account faithfully based on the privileges assigned to the password in my old FMP6 file.

I clicked over to the Contact file, which was not protected with any passwords. There were only two accounts there: Admin and Guest. The Privilege Sets tab revealed the standard three sets: Full Access, Date Entry Only, and Read-Only Access. I looked at the File Options window. To prevent locking you out of a converted file that has no passwords, I see FileMaker sets the Admin account to log in automatically when opening the file. It's clear I'll want to change that if I intend to take advantage of all the new security tools available in FMP7. Looking back at the Invoice file, that check box is empty, forcing the user to log in when opening. Beyond that, there's nothing I can see here in Accounts & Privileges. It's all new.

Comparing Scripts

When I clicked the Main Menu button in my Contact file, it should have taken me to the Main Menu layout in the Invoice file. Instead it hid the Contact file and left me with a blank screen. Looking at the scripts I see that a final step has been added, Select Window [Name: "Invoice"]. Well, that didn't seem to help much. Windows now have three states: Active, Minimized, and Hidden. Many of my scripts on the Mac use the Toggle Window [Hidden] script step. Since Select Window can't find the Invoice window when it's hidden, it can't select it. I had to add an Adjust Window [Restore] step in the Main Menu script in the Invoice file to make it come to the front. Nothing tragic, but you will probably need to make adjustments to your files after conversion.

I have a script called Find All Records. It simply shows all records and sorts them. There's an extra step in the FMP7 version, Go to Record/Request/Page[First]. That's because after sorting, FileMaker now stays on the record that was selected when you started your sort. In order to act like the old FileMaker (which put you on the first record of the found set), you need this extra step. Some developers' solutions depend on this behavior. That's why the conversion adds the step.

Oh, here's an interesting one. I have a script called Function Test that looks at numbers in a Zip Code field. Since FMP7 recognized that the Zip field was a Number field (I don't recommend that, but…) it changed every reference to the Zip field to GetAsNumber(Contact::Zip). No problem.

Fields now have table names added to the front of them. The only other alteration I noticed was one of the export files I used for XML had "Unicode (UTF-8)" tacked onto the end of it.

Other scripts just seem to show changes to some script step and function names. But it sure is nice to double-click a find, sort, import, export, or print step and see the details stored and editable. These are the good new days!

Part 7

Comparing Relationships

Relationships have changed quite a bit. The old version showed three columns: Relationship Name, Relationship (the related fields), and the Related File. FMP6 showed two relationships in the list in my main file, Contact. Looking at the Relationships tab of Define Database in FMP7, I see the three Table Occurrences all strung together. One of the relationships is between a set of constant fields (calculation = 1). We used to need those constant fields to connect files to pass information back and forth between them. That's pretty much a thing of the past now. In the old version I needed to create calculations in the in-between file to pipeline data to the far ends of the relationships. Now you can pass it with no special calculations at all. That should reduce file and indexing overhead, not to mention a lot of extra work needed to figure out how to get information where you needed it. You may see Table Occurrences here that don't seem to make sense to your solution. I recommend you don't delete anything here. You may end up with layouts that end up unattached to the rest of your solution.

File References

After converting a FMP5 solution, you may see a large number of file references, many of which don't seem to make any sense at all and may have been valid years ago on different computers — both yours and those of your clients. In general, if things worked before, they'll continue to work. That's because, even with extra file references, there is usually a current valid one. Sometimes there are multiple pointers to the same file with different reference names.

You should be cautious about deleting these references. I left every file reference in the list, but I edited them by removing references to long-gone machines. When I'd finished, all that was left was the relative reference. For example, in the Contact file I edited the Invoice file reference so it now reads file:Invoice. That means these connected files will look inside the immediate solution folder for the file it needs. If you see file references named Invoice and Invoice 2, don't delete the second one just because it refers to the same file. That's where you'll get into trouble. You don't really need to clean them up at all as long as you have one valid item in the File Path List. For the set of files I had converted, only one reference had no valid item in the Path List. I simply added file:Contact so there would be no problems in case it were ever called from the solution.

FileMaker has always had an area where it kept track of file references; it was just hidden from the user. There's no harm in leaving this area alone except when you need to add new references. You can consolidate file references if it makes you crazy. But you shouldn't do it without checking every relationship, value list, and script to find out what files they expect to refer to, or you may be in for a few surprises. There are also some script steps that store their own file references apart from the Define File References window. Only three script steps refer to the files listed in the Define File References window. Any others keep track of their own references. If you have persistent calls for a file you know you're no longer using, you can delete it. Otherwise, my advice is to leave well enough alone.

New Millennium Communications makes a special tool called MetadataMagic. It can be a bit pricey depending on the number of files involved, but if you value your time and want to clean up the file references before you convert them to FMP7, it's a great tool and has a lot of other uses. Find them at www.newmillennium.com.

More on Accounts and Passwords

When files are converted from earlier versions of FileMaker, both the Account name and the Password are identical. If an eavesdropper who knew this little bit of information were to observe an administrator signing into an account shortly after a file conversion, all he or she would have to do is watch the account name the administrator typed. For that reason, FileMaker allows you to log in using just the password (which appears as bullets) when both the Account name and the Password are identical. Since the user name (set in FileMaker's Preferences area) fills the Account name field on login, all you have to do is empty it out, tab to the Password field, and type the secret word. The real advice is this: After file conversion, get to a private machine and change the passwords so they're not the same as the account names. Or, if you allow users to make up their own passwords, check the box next to "User must change password on next login" in the Edit Account dialog for each account.

Finishing Up

That's about all there is to it. I had it easy because the solution I converted was fairly uncomplicated and had so little data in each of the files. If you really want to talk about conversion that will take advantage of all the great new tools in FileMaker Pro 7, you'll need to recreate your database by building your tables into a single file. That's where you'll really begin to unleash the power of the new tools the software engineers at FileMaker, Inc. have been working on for more than three years.

There are programmers out there right now building tools that will help recreate the field definitions from one file into a new table in a multi-table file. Perhaps some will be available by the time you read this. That may be no big deal if your files have no more than 10 or 20 fields. But if you have 25 files, each with 150 fields in them, such a tool may be a necessity. You'll still have to recreate the layouts, but you'll be able to copy elements of your layouts from your converted multi-file solution. The big work will be scripting. Even then, you can import scripts and use what you need. This is the dawn of a new age of FileMaker. What developers invent in the next year should really get us all going. It's an exciting time!

Summary

In this chapter I showed you what it was like to convert a FileMaker 6 solution to FileMaker 7. I showed you some of the things I ran into as I examined the differences between how layouts, scripts, relationships, fields, accounts, and privileges looked in the two sets of files.

Q & A

Q We have a complicated solution that we want to convert over the weekend. What's the best way to approach a mission-critical conversion?

A Whoa, cowboy! Not so fast. Print and read the conversion document with a highlighter in hand. After you've carefully noted items that are important to your conversion, do a test run and put the solution on a machine where you can test it out in detail. Make notes about what doesn't work and how you corrected it so you'll be prepared when you make your final conversion. If you have both Mac and Windows users, be sure you test it on both platforms through a network. Then do the conversion at a time when the company isn't too rushed. You don't want your business to come to a screeching halt because you were in such a hurry.

Q Our company has a five-file solution. We just want to put everything into one file. How should we go about that?

A First convert to an FMP7 multi-file solution and see if everything works using the advice I gave in the answer to the previous question. Then decide which will be your main file and add a table to it, recreating the fields in your least complicated file. Import data into this table from the other file. Remember, you don't have to go live with it just yet. Duplicate your main layouts and see if you can make them work with the new table similar to the way everything worked with the other file. It may take some getting used to the new way of working from previous versions of FileMaker. Once you really have it working the way you want, make a backup of your files in their current state. Delete all the records from the new table and re-import the current set of live data from the other file. Replace the layouts with the work layouts. After that's been in use for a while, try another table.

Workshop

If you've used FileMaker before, convert one of your solutions and take a careful look at the Conversion.log file. Don't forget to watch for the word "error."

Review Questions

True-False

1. Once FileMaker does its conversion, you're ready to release the new version to users.

2. The conversion log can be helpful as you clean up your newly converted solution.

3. You must totally build accounts and privileges after you convert a solution.
4. Your newly converted solution may have more relationships than are necessary.
5. When you convert a multi-file solution, FileMaker creates one new database file, with a table representing each of the files in the old solution.

Short Answer

6. Why should you document your old solution as part of the conversion process?
7. What purpose does the conversion log serve?
8. Why does conversion add a Go to Record/Request/Page[First] step to a script that has a Sort step in it?
9. Where's a good place to find complete documentation on converting databases to FileMaker Pro 7?
10. Why should you double-check all the file references created in conversion?

Part 7

Leftover, but Important Stuff

There are just a few things that didn't seem to fit anywhere else in the book but I feel are important enough that I don't want to leave you without mentioning them.

Cleaning Up After Yourself

You may want to go back through your files and delete the unused fields. For example, in our Contact file, you still have fields Phone1 through Phone4, Web, and FunctionTest. In the Invoice file you still have the Design field. It's not absolutely necessary to delete these fields. In all likelihood, if you tested the speed of two copies of the file, one with the fields and one without them, even with sophisticated equipment you wouldn't be able to measure any difference. It just depends on how obsessive you are.

With more complex systems of files, it can be a problem to delete fields that haven't been carefully documented as being for experiment only. Get in the habit of documenting things you do to solve a problem, if you can train yourself. It'll make this cleanup work a whole lot easier.

Selecting Multiple Fields, Scripts, and Relationships

Deleting some of these fields gives me a chance to show you another feature you might need. You can choose multiple fields by selecting the first field, then holding down the Command key (Macintosh) or Ctrl key (Windows) and clicking on the other fields you want to select. Then you can delete or duplicate the fields all at once. This can be a big time-saver depending on what work you're doing. Holding down the Shift key will select all fields between your first and second selection.

You can do the same thing in the ScriptMaker window and in the Relationships tab of the Define Database window.

Circular File Opening

If you try to close a file but another window is open behind it that uses related data on the layout, the first file will open back up hidden (Macintosh) or minimized (Windows). If you try to close the second file, and then bring the first file to the foreground to close it but the first file has related data from the second file on the layout, the second file will reopen. This circular opening can be very frustrating!

There are a number of ways to handle this situation. One is to hide or minimize both windows and close them with Command+W (Macintosh) or Ctrl+W (Windows). Another way is to go to a layout that has none of the related data on it (including calculations that might use data from the file you want to close). You could also make scripts that take you to another layout (without any of the related fields) and close the offending file.

Network Error Message

You may get the messages in Figures A-1 and A-2. I see these when I change TCP/IP to go online but I'm not connected to the Internet. The messages come up when I first open the file, try to define fields, and under other circumstances. It can be very persistent and irritating. You may not realize that the messages pop up because you're not hooked up to a network, but that's all it is. Once you change your status, perhaps by connecting to an Ethernet hub, the messages will go away.

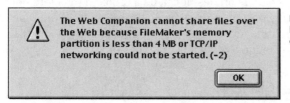

Figure A-1
FileMaker's "cannot share files"
error message.

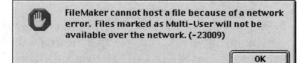

Figure A-2
FileMaker's "cannot host a file"
error message.

Preferences Including Dial Phone

I did not cover some of the other application and file Preference tabs. Most of them are not too difficult, although I don't think the Modem and Dialing Preferences are particularly intuitive. That's not FileMaker's fault. That's just the way it has to be because of the way modems operate.

Other than that, being able to make FileMaker dial phone numbers stored in your database at the click of a button is a terrific tool, especially if you do a lot of calling at your computer. I mean, once you've typed those numbers into the database, why should you have to retype them into the phone? I think I may be a touch dyslexic, so it sure makes my work easier.

After you work out the Modem and Dialing settings, make a script that uses the Dial Phone step near the bottom of the list. Remember, you can tell the script to use a number in a related field if you're using the Contact file. Then place a button in the portal row. Once you get used to it, you'll never want to go back. You can read more about these preferences in the manual and the Help files.

Script and Key Field Weirdness

Occasionally I make a script that will create a new record and enter some data in the first portal row. Sometimes it works and sometimes it doesn't. I seem to be able to make it work consistently by putting an Exit Record/Request script step before entering the portal. I'm guessing that by doing so, the data in the key field gets sent to the hard drive so the portal has the key it needs to create the new portal record. If that's really the case, I don't know why the script without the step would work some of the time. But if you run into this one, add the Exit Record/Request script step and see if it doesn't solve your problem.

Sending E-mail from FileMaker

In the past year, I've become enamored with using FileMaker as my e-mail program. I use a set of plug-ins, SMTPit to send the mail and POP3it to receive it. There is also a plug-in called MailIT, but I haven't investigated it. (You can find a complete list of registered plug-ins on the FileMaker web site at www.filemaker.com.)

FileMaker has a Send Mail script step. With it, you can build an e-mail message you can send to one of a few e-mail programs. Version 5.5 expanded the usable e-mail programs on the Macintosh platform. You can find out more about how to send messages in the Help files.

Personally, I like using the plug-ins better because I have control over both the sent and received messages. One thing that always frustrated me about e-mail programs was that I couldn't edit the messages. I always wanted to highlight part of the message someone sent to me, or add my own text between the lines. When my messages are sent and received in FileMaker, I can edit the text to my heart's content since the text is right there in an editable text field.

Another advantage is that I can search the text of my saved e-mails way faster than any of the e-mail programs I've used. I export all of them to an archive file that is attached to my Contact database. That way I can trace my exchanges with anyone through a portal. The e-mail programs I've used in the past kept my sent messages apart from the received ones in ways I found confusing. I can organize the messages any way I want in FileMaker. If you're interested, look at the e-mail plug-ins on FileMaker's web site.

Prevent Users from Creating Databases

You can choose to prevent users from creating databases when you install a copy of FileMaker Pro on a machine. Now why would you want to do that? This is really a tool for network administrators, and following are a couple of reasons why you might want to implement it.

FileMaker connects to related files based on file names. If workers are creating their own shared files with names that might accidentally match those in a solution somewhere else on the network, there is a danger that data could end up in the wrong files.

Secondly, creation of new files could potentially duplicate functions in files that might already be in use in other departments. This isn't dangerous, just a waste of time. Using this option, administrators can better control the data.

Notes to Developers about Naming Conventions

Naming of fields and relationships is particularly important to developers who create new and related files on a daily basis. Being able to quickly and easily come back and spot problem areas is critical to doing a good job — and keeping yourself sane. There are some naming conventions I became aware of since the first version of this book that I think are especially valuable.

Key fields — that is, fields that will be used to build relationships with other files — should begin with "k_" (lowercase letter k followed by an underscore). So a field called ContactSerNum would be k_ContactSerNum. If you are creating a field for use on the remote (child) side of the relationship, you should use "fk_" in front of the field name to represent foreign key. The value of these two conventions is that all key and foreign key field names will sort together when the field list is sorted by name. The second, and more important, reason is that you'll be reminded not to delete these fields without further consideration that they might really mess up the structure of the files.

Relationship names should contain both the name of the related file and the name of the related field. More often than I would like, something happens to a set of files that causes the relationship to get lost. You end up with the <field missing> text in various places throughout the files. By including the file *and* related field name, it's fairly easy to reestablish the relationship.

For example, in the Contact file used in this book, when creating the relationship to the Phone file, you would use Phone|fk_ContactSerNum. The vertical line between the file and field name is called the pipe symbol. You make it by typing Shift+backslash. (The backslash character is found in the upper right of your keyboard.) You'll also notice I used the foreign key abbreviation in front of the related field.

As I began to use these naming conventions for my clients, I solved a lot of problems fairly quickly. Prior to this I would have to find an archived copy of the file to figure out what the relationship should consist of. And I don't delete key fields anymore.

For a wonderfully comprehensive set of standards, see the downloadable files for a file titled Standards.pdf (in the Developer Files folder) prepared by CoreSolutions Development, Inc. or go to www.coresolutions.on.ca.

Here's something I bet you'll see become a standard in the next few years. It's a method I developed that has speeded up my debugging and development by about 50%. I number my scripts beginning with the first script in a file. Then I follow the number with a space, dash, space, and the name I choose for the script. A script might read "1 – Main Menu" or "12 – Check Current User Name." When I have 20 scripts in the file, I create a script with no steps in it called "20   20   20   20   20" as a divider so I can easily spot my position in the script list. I continue by adding dividers every 20 scripts using 40, 60, 80, and so on.

This speeds up debugging work tremendously. When you want to find out what a button does, simply double-click it in Layout mode. When you see the name of the script, memorize the number and head to ScriptMaker. The old standard required that you memorize the script name, which may or may not give you a clue as to where it lives in the list of possibly hundreds of scripts. If the name in the Specify Button dialog wasn't particularly helpful, sometimes you would have to click on the script name pop-up and locate the script position in the scripts list. Often, I'd find more than one script with a similar name and have to exit ScriptMaker and go back to the layout to the Specify Button dialog again. It can get pretty tedious.

Once the scripts are numbered this way, I rarely move one unless it just absolutely needs to be near another, related script. Then I renumber it.

Oh, and speaking of renumbering, watch out when duplicating scripts. You need to renumber the script immediately once it's copied to the bottom of the list. Also, when you want to point to scripts in other files, add a Comment script step and type in the number and name of the external script.

Debugging scripts that call other scripts is a cinch. You don't have to memorize or write down the names of the subscripts. Just write down their numbers and whisk yourself off to check 'em out.

This numbering system may cause some difficulties when trying to comply with the grouping standards set forth by CoreSolutions. There are probably a few ways to work with both standards. You can easily leave spaces between script numbers to leave room for future scripts under specific headings. And you can use some version of the Dewey Decimal System to insert a script between two other scripts with consecutive integers. Simply add a decimal point and one or more places to the right of the decimal.

Windows users have one possible inconvenience to be aware of. Any script you check to appear in the Scripts menu will be assigned a number that will appear before the number you give the script. A possible solution would be to leave off the number in your script name if you'll use it in that menu. Depending on where they are in the list, that can be okay or more complicated. Another solution would be to put a few spaces before the number in the script name.

All I can tell you is, I move like the wind under my new system. And I challenge anyone using any other system to beat me in a session that requires tracing your way back through a set of scripts that call sub-scripts.

This has worked so well that now I'm starting to number my layouts: "1 - Main Menu," "2 - List View," 3 - Letter - Thank You," and so on. Sure, FileMaker automatically numbers layouts. But it always puts the number at the end. I want these numbers to appear at the left. That way they show up as the first thing you read when moving from left to right in any dialog box. And it never gets chopped off if the layout (or script) name is longer than the dialog.

Try it. You'll like it. Trust me.

Getting More Help

Okay, you've read the book, you've done the exercises, but you're still having trouble. What do you do now?

Tech Support

You may have a complimentary call to tech support coming to you. When you buy FileMaker Pro, a card for that call comes in the box. If you're part of a company with a site license, you may have a support agreement with FileMaker, Inc. Ask your IT people about that.

To get the best out of any tech support services, prepare yourself. Make notes about what happened just before the problem started. Has it done this before? Under what conditions? What equipment are you using? What computer, printer, scanner, etc.? Yes, you're frustrated, but if you don't get your information together before making the call, you'll be even more frustrated once you get on the phone and can't describe the problem.

Keep in mind that the tech support people don't know your level of knowledge. They'll have to ask you some questions that may sound like they think you're an idiot, but let me tell you a short story to clarify their plight:

I was trying to help a new, non-computer-literate worker for one of my clients over the phone late one night after everyone else had gone home. She was trying to use a time clock I had built for them to punch in. I told her to take the mouse so that the cord was pointing away from her and move it toward the screen. I asked if the arrow on the screen moved. She said it hadn't moved at all. We tried moving the mouse left and right. After checking that the mouse was actually plugged in and the screen was on, I asked her where the mouse was. She said, "In front of the screen, about eight inches above the table in my hand."

Tech support is great, but you need to work with them and give them as much information about your situation as you can.

Hire a Consultant

After you use tech support, as a second choice, you could hire me. Yes, it is a shameless plug, but I do this for a living, and there's nothing wrong with a little advertising. I've built complete systems and trained employees for a number of clients. On other occasions, companies brought me in to provide answers for a specific problem. Their people already worked with FileMaker

Pro and took over from there to implement the changes.

A third situation is where I've been brought in to be the architect of a system so that a solution would be designed correctly before anybody started creating files. Then in-house people built the system. Sometimes another developer created a set of files but had since moved from the area. I've worked remotely. On some occasions I'll instruct an in-house person on the changes that need to be made as they make them at their computer. I've also worked using software that temporarily takes control of their computer through the phone lines.

Sometimes it's simply more cost effective to bring in a professional who can put the thing on course again. If you're a small company, your time might be better spent on other things. If you're part of a larger company, ask yourself: How many people's time is being wasted waiting for the answer I need?

That being said, let me point out that no consultant knows everything — not even me. There are times that clients request work that is beyond my areas of expertise. In cases like that, I'll consult with other developers I know who do have that expertise.

To find a consultant, go to the FileMaker, Inc. web site at http://www.filemaker.com/. On the main FileMaker tab, click Developers, then Find Developers at the top of the page; look for hypertext that reads "Find Consultants." You can search by Company, City, State, Zip Code, Phone Area Code, Country, and Keywords to find a list of developers in your area.

Just keep in mind, you don't have to hire the first person you talk to. Not everyone has the same amount of experience. You'll also want to choose someone whose personality will work with yours. If your project is so large that it requires a full-time FileMaker person, you may need to look for an employee to do the work. A full-time consultant could get expensive.

FileMaker's Web Site

FileMaker's web site is a fantastic source for FileMaker resources. Aside from consultants, the site has everything from trainers to plug-ins, books, magazines, templates, commercial solutions, and other sites powered by FileMaker. Once you head out to any of the other sites, you'll find each of them leads to other sites — each with resources of their own. The FileMaker community is large, active, and growing along with the great product they represent. Of course, the hard part is finding exactly what you need.

Companion Files

There is quite a variety of files available to be downloaded from www.wordware.com/files/fmpro7. These are divided into the following folders:

- Chapter files—These files go along with the book, chapter by chapter, for readers to learn to work with FileMaker Pro.
- Developer files—Most of these solutions were provided by other FileMaker developers; some of these may require a fee to use beyond a trial period.

■ J_Stars files—These include an explanation of what they're for. Simply click the question mark button on the main page of each file.

■ Plugs-Ins—This little file points you to the web sites of plug-in companies I'm acquainted with. If you're connected to the web, just click the Go button and it will take you there. The link to the FileMaker, Inc. site takes you directly to their page that lists all registered plug-ins.

See the included Read Me file for more information.

Appendixes

FileMaker Pro CD-ROM

The manual that came with your FileMaker Pro 7 installation CD-ROM is chock full of information. It lists solutions, partners, consultants, publications, and trainers, along with ads from many of the companies and some special price offers. If you are part of a large organization with a site license, ask your IT representative about materials that came with the company purchase.

Training Resources

There are companies that specialize in FileMaker Pro training. Some of them have sessions that move around the country and the world. You could even hire them to come to your site and train a group of workers.

It just so happens that I am an instructor for FMPTraining. It is "The world's best hands-on FileMaker Pro training." And it must be, because I'm doing it, right? Go to FMPtraining.com for the lowdown.

There are also sets of audio and video training tapes, workbooks, and CDs you can purchase, as well as online training. A fairly comprehensive list of these resources can be found on FileMaker's web site.

FileMaker Hosting

If there comes a time that you need to put information from your files up on the Internet, you may want to contact a company that specializes in web hosting. The value of working with one of these companies is that they can help you avoid some of the pitfalls you're likely to run into by doing it yourself. The more important the project is, the more you'll need an expert. You can find a list of companies that provide these services on the FileMaker site at http://www.filemaker.com/support/isp.html.

FileMaker Pro Advisor Magazine

The reason I wanted to write for *FileMaker Pro Advisor* magazine in the first place is that I thought it was such a great product. The editors include articles that appeal to every level of user. I find it most exciting when other developers demonstrate techniques they've created to solve their own problems, only to find that it solves my own. Additionally, the advertisements often put you in touch with other products and services you may need. The magazine is completely independent from FileMaker, Inc.

My Web Site

Of course, I have a web site. The URL is: http://www.DataDesignPros.com.

Among other things on my site, I have a list of sites that deal with FileMaker issues and some that have downloadable files. Many of those sites are listed in the Web_Sites database provided in the companion files.

I mentioned this earlier in the book, but it bears repeating. FileMaker 7 is so radically different I expect best practices and optimum procedures will continue to emerge over the next year. As I write this, developers are furiously discussing how to best use the new tools we've been given. I've done my best to test and explain everything I've learned about it over the past year and a half. But we'll really begin to understand what we're dealing with once we start building projects for our customers. That's why I'm adding an area to my web site where I'll post new information and clarifications to items in the book. Go to my home page at www.DataDesignPros.com and click the link near the bottom titled "FileMaker 7 book updates." If you make discoveries on your own that you think others might benefit from, e-mail me at Jstars@DataDesignPros.com and I'll try to include them.

Answers to Review Questions

Chapter 1

1. True.
2. True. You can also double-click the icon of the file.
3. False. FileMaker saves your work as you go.
4. False. Save as Clone creates a template of the file, which includes the database structure but no records.
5. False. You can tab from one field to the next.
6. On Windows, you can double-click on a FileMaker Pro shortcut, or find the Start menu, go to Programs, find FileMaker Pro 7, and choose FileMaker Pro. On Macintosh, you can go into the FileMaker folder and double-click on the FileMaker Pro icon, click on the FileMaker Pro button in Launcher, or double-click on a FileMaker Pro alias.
7. A book title, or an audio or video recording.
8. From the Records menu, choose New Record; or use the keyboard command (Command+N [Macintosh] or Ctrl+N [Windows]); or click a New Record button on the layout.
9. The Book.
10. Tab from field to field, and enter data as each field becomes active. You can click into specific fields as well. Keep in mind that some fields may not be on a specific layout, and some fields may not be enterable.

Chapter 2

1. False. You can click on the Field Name or Type column heads to sort by the contents of the column, or use the View by pull-down menu to view fields by creation order, field name, field type, or custom order. To toggle between showing field options or comments, click the Options/Comments column head.
2. True.
3. False. Layout mode is where you choose how your data will look on the screen or when it prints. Preview mode shows you what the page will look like when it is printed.

4. False. The fields on the left are all the fields that are available; the fields moved to the right side determine the sort order.

5. False. Several of the menus and menu items are different depending on the mode.

6. You can expand the window by pulling the knurled area in the lower-right corner. (If the window does not have knurls, it cannot be resized.)

7. The Relationships graph allows you to build and view connections between tables and files in your database.

8. Browse, Find, Layout, and Preview.

9. From the View menu, select a mode; or click the Mode pop-up menu at the bottom of the window; or use the keyboard command.

10. Standard Form, Columnar List/Report, Table View, Labels, Vertical Labels, Envelope, and Blank Layout.

11. From the Lookup window in Define Fields and from the Sort Records window (you can select Define Database, and then click the Relationships tab). It's also available from the Specify Field window when placing a field on a layout and from the Specify Field dialog for Value List window, but we haven't discussed those yet.

12. The menus change, and so does the Status area. The Mode pop-up in the lower-left section of the window changes to either Browse or Layout. In Layout mode, the fields normally display the actual field names. Although this hasn't been covered yet, the Book changes from switching between records in Browse mode to switching between layouts in Layout mode. Of course, you can move items around in Layout mode, but that does not constitute a different look.

13. Click on the Field Name heading or choose "field name" from the View by pop-up.

14. c) Field.

Chapter 3

1. False. You should plan the database before you create it.

2. True.

3. False. Dragging a handle resizes an object. You must click somewhere within the boundaries of an object in order to move it by dragging.

4. False. If you performed a zip code sort on a numerical zip code field, Zip+4 codes would all sort to the end. Zip codes should be defined as Text type so that they sort in order from left to right and the Zip+4 values will sort within the range of five-digit zip codes (e.g., 12345-6789 should sort between 12345 and 12346).

5. True.

6. Web browser and SQL languages can't handle filenames with spaces in them. Even if you don't plan to use your database this way, things may change, and it's a good habit to get into.

7. You might need to use part of the name in a letter, or you might want to sort by first name.

8. Click the Scripts menu, and choose ScriptMaker.

9. Creating a new button automatically opens the Specify Button window, in which you can click on Perform Script in the left column and choose the script to perform via the pop-up list next to Specify in the Options area. This assumes that you have already created the script you want to attach to the button.

10. The Standard and Text Formatting toolbars are available in both Browse and Layout modes. The Arrange and Tools toolbars are available only in Layout mode.

11. Records, New Record; Command+N (Macintosh) or Ctrl+N (Windows); or click the New Record icon on the Standard toolbar.

12. Go to Layout mode and use the Rectangle tool. Then press Option (Macintosh) or Ctrl (Windows) while you click and drag the crosshair on the layout. Using the Line tools, choose 5 pt, solid, and black. Then use the Fill tools to choose solid and red.

Chapter 4

1. False. A Text field can hold one billion characters, which is roughly equivalent to 500,000 pages!

2. False. A Repeating field allows you to store multiple values in a single field, in a single record.

3. True.

4. False. A Summary field is used to aggregate, or summarize, values across a group of records.

5. True. This is why you should enter years as four digits. Unless, of course, you are talking about someone born in the future.

6. Since a Calculation field can output data of Text, Number, Date, Time, or Container type, specifying an incorrect result type can produce unintended consequences.

7. Web, ODBC, SQL, and other non-FileMaker applications can misinterpret field names that contain word spaces. If you develop a habit of creating field names with no word spaces in them, your database fields will be ready to share with other applications.

8. NameLast & ", " & NameFirst. Note that there is a space after the comma.

9. Negative 8,001,234,567 (in a Number field where the first data character is an open parenthesis, FileMaker interprets the number as a negative, regardless of other non-numeric characters).

10. In Layout mode, choose Format, Text.

11. A Text field, which can hold up to a billion characters.

12. Problems with browsers, ODBC, and SQL keywords.

13. Avoid using any of the characters or items listed in any of the areas above the Formula box. Specific characters include & / " * ¶ - ( ) + = ≠ > < ≤ ≥ ^ . ; (semicolon) :: (two colons in a row) ' (apostrophe), (comma).

14. Text, Number, Date, Time, Timestamp, Container, Calculation, and Summary.

15. Go into Layout mode, select the field, and choose Format, Date. Then make the selection from the "Format as" pop-up list.

Chapter 5

1. True.

2. False. You can change the tab order in Layout mode by choosing Layouts, Set Tab Order.

3. True.

4. False. In Layout mode, it can also check all text on a layout.

5. True.

6. Copy and paste or drag-and-drop.

7. Click the current record indicator below the Book and enter 10; or press the Esc key and enter 10.

8. Picture, sound, movie, current date, current time, current user name, from index, or from last visited record.

9. Use values from field, use value list from another file, or use custom values.

10. Since you cannot Undo or Revert after you have confirmed a Delete Record or Delete All Records command, you will have to use your latest backup file to restore the data. You *do* have a recent backup, don't you?

11. Pop-up list, pop-up menu, check box set, and radio button set.

12. Copy and paste, drag-and-drop, Insert from last visited record, Replace, Relookup, value lists, and Paste from Index.

13. Because you can't undo or revert the Delete command. Once the records are gone, they're gone.

Chapter 6

1. False. Relational databases prevent redundancy and the need to store the same information in multiple tables or files.

2. True.

3. True.

4. False. Field names do not have to match, but it can be helpful in identifying them to give them the same or similar names.

5. False. A database table is a collection of fields that describe one entity, such as "people," or "invoices." It serves to keep information about a particular subject together.

Appendixes

6. Allow creation of records in this table via this relationship, delete related records in this table when a record is deleted in the other table, and sort records.

7. Names are not unique. Social security number would be better (but not recommended for legal reasons and because, believe it or not, the Social Security Administration does not guarantee they are unique), and an auto-entered serial number, protected against modification, would be better yet.

8. Data entered into a portal gets stored in the related table.

9. Related fields have two colons (::) preceding the field name.

10. Automobile makes would be the parent table, and automobile models would be the child table. (One automobile make may include several models, but any one automobile model belongs to a single automobile make.)

11. The primary key field should be set up as an auto-entered serial number. "Prohibit modification of value" should also be turned on. (The field can be defined as either a Number or Text data type, but remember that in order for a relationship to work consistently, the data type for both the primary key and foreign key should be the same, e.g., Number to Number or Text to Text.)

12. When you find yourself making a list of similar type items in your main file.

13. Master can be referred to as parent, and related can be referred to as child.

14. Define Relationships.

15. In the Portal Setup window accessed in Layout mode.

Chapter 7

1. False. You will avoid having to spend time fixing a database later if you spend some time planning before you begin to create files and define fields.

2. True.

3. True.

4. False. Lookup fields are good for bringing in "snapshot" data that should not change when the related data changes (e.g., a product price for an invoice should stay as it was at the time the invoice was created).

5. True.

6. The three-pronged symbol means that the file to which it is connected is on the "many" side of the relationship with the other file (in other words, potentially many records in this file can be related to a single record in the other file).

7. A foreign key is used on the many side of the relationship to relate to a single record on the one side of the relationship. (The key field on the "one" side is known as the primary key.)

8. A join table takes care of a many-to-many relationship by holding records that relate to both tables and relating the records back to each of the tables via foreign key fields in the join table.

9. The ampersand is used to concatenate two character strings.

10. You don't need to use a portal when only one record in the other table is related. (For example, when you're on the "many" side and want to see information from the "one" side of a one-to-many relationship. Also, when you are on the "one" side of the relationship and only want to see the first related record for one reason or another.)

11. One-to-one, one-to-many, many-to-many.

12. One-to-many.

13. The looked up data represent a "snapshot in time." It can also be used for faster finds and to build relationships to data in distant files.

14. ZipCode & "-" & PlusFour. The calculation result must be Text.

Chapter 8

1. True.

2. False. When you choose Show Omitted, FileMaker returns *all* of the records that are not in the current found set. You'd get the three records you omitted, plus all the rest of the database records not found through the original Find.

3. True.

4. True.

5. False. In order to see Summary fields in the Sort window, you must check the "Include summary fields" box.

6. Ctrl+F (Windows) or Command+F (Macintosh).

7. You are returned to Find mode, and the most recent Find requests are still there so that you may modify them without starting over.

8. After importing data with dates or times, it's a good idea to check for invalid dates or times, since FileMaker does not validate imported data.

9. In Find mode, enter the name of the city you don't want, click the Omit check box, then perform the Find.

10. FileMaker remembers and saves the most recently used Sort criteria into a new sort script step, or you may specify the Sort criteria from within ScriptMaker.

11. The number of found sets shows in the Status area.

12. They're hidden or omitted from the current found set. They're still in the file, though.

13. See "The Find Symbols" section in the chapter.

Chapter 9

1. True.

2. True.

3. False. Choose the Columnar list/report layout type to create a layout with Sub-summary parts.

4. True.

5. False. You can access any layout by entering Layout mode and selecting the layout you wish to modify, then you can modify it.

6. In Layout mode, click to select the part label, then choose a new color from the color palette.

7. Standard form, Columnar list/report, Table view, Labels, Vertical labels, Envelope, and Blank layout.

8. Merge fields.

9. Table view layout type.

10. The Blank layout type would give you a layout with nothing on it where you could add fields for the inside address and type the body of the letter.

11. Go into Layout mode, use the Text tool, and double-click where you want to make the change.

12. Go to Layout mode, choose Layouts, Layout Setup, then click the View tab. Click the Properties button, and check the box next to "Sort data when selecting columns."

Chapter 10

1. False. You can define a Text type field and create an auto-entered serial number that includes non-numeric characters.

2. True.

3. False. When you place a Repeating field on a layout, you must use the Repetitions options in Field Format if you want to show two or more repetitions.

4. True.

5. True.

6. Field options can help ensure correct data entry, and they can speed up data entry.

7. Auto-enter, Validation, Storage, and Furigana.

8. The file can get very large, and importing can take longer.

9. Not empty.

10. In the Define Fields window, with the field selected (highlighted), click the Options button.

11. Define a Text field and use Auto-Enter Modification Name or Account Name. Then set it to prohibit modification. It would also be a good idea to define either a Modification Timestamp field or both Modification Date and Modification Time fields, too, so you can pin down when it's happening.

12. Fix it in your zip code lookup table. Go into the Contact table, and perform a Find in the ZipCode field. Click in the field and choose Records, Relookup.

Alternative 1 (discussed in Chapter 5): Once the records are found, perform a Replace.

Alternative 2: Change the records manually, one at a time.

Alternative 3 (discussed in Chapter 14): Use a looping script that would paste or set the new value in each record of the found set.

13. Define it as a Text field. You should also check the "Prohibit modification of value during data entry" check box if the field will be used as a primary key.

14. Faster Finds, faster Sorts, and correct behavior when defined on the foreign side of a relationship.

Chapter 11

1. False. They are used to provide the operations between fields and functions.

2. False. Use the precedence parentheses symbols to surround elements of a calculation that are supposed to occur first.

3. True.

4. True.

5. False. You can combine many different field types in a Calculation field. For example, if you wanted to compare the value in one text field (say, residence_city) to the value in another text field (say, work_city) and return a Boolean result, the calculation result type must be Number, even though the fields compared are Text fields.

6. You can double-click on the field name in the field list to move it to the Formula box, or you can type the field name directly into the Formula box.

7. (b) 50 <= 50, (d) 50 >= 50, and (e) 50 = 50 are true.

8. AND, OR, XOR, NOT.

9. first_name & "¶" & phone_number

10. When checked, it prevents FileMaker Pro from calculating a result if all of the referenced fields are empty.

11. Add, subtract, multiply, divide, power of, precedence

12. True, yes, and, of course, 1

13. True, yes, or 1

14. False, no, or 0

Chapter 12

1. True.

2. True. In addition, multiple parameters for a function are separated by semicolons.

3. False. In the Left function, the number parameter refers to the number of characters.

4. False. To turn a number into text, use the NumToText function. Nope, we didn't discuss it, but now you know.

5. True.
6. Click the View pop-up list, and choose Date functions.
7. Highlight the parameter, then double-click the desired field name from the field list or type it directly.
8. Highlight the parameter, then double-click the desired function from the function list or type it directly.
9. No, because it's no longer a Calculation field.
10. FileMaker Pro converts date, time, and timestamp values into numbers to perform mathematical calculations, and then returns the result based on the result type specified in the Specify Calculation window.
11. Exit the field definition to Browse mode after the final version of the formula has been entered. Then go back and convert it to a Text, Number, Date, Time, or Timestamp field.
12. Related fields or Global fields (because they cannot be indexed).
13. Use the Length function.
14. A Timestamp field.
15. Use a script.

Chapter 13

1. True.
2. False. Use the GetRepetition function.
3. False. The Case function uses a series of parameters separated by semicolons, whereas the If function requires you to nest multiple If functions.
4. True.
5. True.
6. A Summary field.
7. The PMT function.
8. Get(WindowMode). Note: If the Get(Window Mode) function is used in a script, it will return the mode of the database window that is in the foreground. Did you have to look for that one in the functions list? Good! That's how you learn stuff.
9. NOT.
10. The Max (maximum) function.
11. One: GetSummary
12. b) PMT is a financial function.
13. The If function was designed for one test and two results, whereas Case can have many tests and many results. The If function is limited to 125 nested Ifs; Case has no limit. An If function that uses nested Ifs will be longer than a similar Case function.
14. Change the field to a standard data entry field rather than a Calculation. Then you can use it to look up values from another table.

Chapter 14

1. False. There must be a check mark to the left of a script for it to show up in the Scripts menu. The first 10 appear with a number next to them in the Scripts menu.
2. True.
3. False. Comments can be helpful later on after you've forgotten, and they can help others understand your scripts.
4. True.
5. False. You can import scripts into a file from another file.
6. Select the step from the script steps list, then click the Move button; or simply double-click the step in the script steps list.
7. New Window [Name: "My Special Window"; Height: 300; Width: 600]
8. Perform Script.
9. From Browse mode, choose Edit, Preferences, Document. Under "When closing...," click the check box next to "Perform script," and choose the script to perform from the pop-up. Then click OK.
10. The Show Custom Dialog script step allows you to create your own windows.
11. Exit Record/Request.
12. 1) Add a step that exits if a modifier key is pressed.
    2) Add some other Exit Loop If step.
    3) If the loop is going through a group of records, choose Exit After Last.
    4) Unless the developer has added an Allow User Abort [Off] step, the user can press Command+. (period) (Macintosh) or Escape (Windows).
    5) Force Quit FileMaker.
    6) Pull the plug on the computer.
    Neither of the last two are recommended.
13. You can't unless you added a Comment step that tells you. Otherwise, you have to highlight the script step and click the Specify button to view the details of the Sort or Find.
14. Add a Halt Script or Exit Script step, or enclose steps within an If statement that cannot be fulfilled. A Pause step can also be used. And finally, you can duplicate the script and delete steps so you can test small portions of the original.
15. Comment.
16. Go to Layout (specifying a layout that references the table you want).

Chapter 15

1. True.
2. False. A Title Footer appears only at the bottom of the first page in Preview mode and the printed report.

3. True.

4. True.

5. True.

6. Using too much color on a layout for printing could waste toner or ink.

7. Buttons are not available in Preview mode, so they should be defined as non-printing.

8. Sub-summaries and Grand Summaries.

9. Use the Part tool and drag a part onto the layout; choose Part from the Insert menu; or choose Part Setup from the Layouts menu and click the Create button.

10. Other than in Layout mode, Sub-summary parts appear only in Preview mode or when printed, and the records must be sorted by the field specified for that part.

11. 1) You can display buttons and other information in the Body part.

    2) You can preview and print Summaries and Sub-summaries.

    3) You can have more than one row of fields horizontally.

    4) Buttons can be right next to the items in the record they'll affect.

12. Any layout object except the background color of a layout part itself. A Sub-summary part and anything in it can also be made to not print by unsorting the records.

13. Trailing Sub-summary, Trailing Grand Summary, Footer, Title Footer.

14. You can drag them up and down, but the less destructive method is to click the Part Label Control icon in the lower-left part of the window frame.

Chapter 16

1. True.

2. False. Too much variety will confuse users. Keep your layouts consistent.

3. False. Any layout object can be rotated in 90-degree increments.

4. True.

5. True.

6. Select one field object; then either click the Select Objects by Type button on the Arrange toolbar, or press Option+Command+A (Macintosh) or Ctrl+Shift+A (Windows).

7. From the View menu, choose Show, Non-Printing Objects and Show, Sliding Objects. Each non-printing object will appear with a gray border, and each sliding object will appear with one or two arrows pointing in the direction(s) it can slide.

8. None. Locking a field prevents it from being changed in Layout mode only.

9. In Layout mode, choose Format, Graphic. Of course, if you want to be able to affect a specific object, you should select it first.

10. None, Embossed, Engraved, and Drop Shadow.

11. 1) To prevent users from moving or deleting them.

2) To prevent yourself from deleting them.

3) To keep portals and the portal fields in their proper places.

4) To keep background items in place when moving foreground objects or vice versa.

12. Ask for copies of all paper forms and letters that you'll be replacing.

13. The buttons will not be attached to the right scripts or other Specify Button choices.

14. 1) Copy and paste.

2) Drag-and-drop.

3) Insert, Picture.

4) Import a folder of files.

Chapter 17

1. True.

2. False. In FileMaker Pro, you can include preparation layouts and automated processes (scripts) to help the user produce the report.

3. False. You can use fields from related and unrelated tables, as well as from other files.

4. True.

5. True.

6. What results do you want? What data do you have (and not have)?

7. A Find layout can help the user isolate the records to be included in the report.

8. A beep can alert the user to read a message that explains a problem. (The script should then direct the user back to a place where the problem can be rectified.)

9. Set Error Capture [On] prevents FileMaker from displaying its default error messages. This lets you include a custom message that may be more meaningful and instructive to the user.

10. Halt Script stops any and all scripts that may be running or paused. Properly placed, it can help remove the user from an unknown place in a process.

11. Yes. Any information can be considered a report, including a message that says None Found!

12. Check to see if any Sub-summary parts require a Sort different from the one that appears in the Sort window. Check that the fields are positioned correctly on the layout, that no fields are overlapping part dividers, and Summary fields are in the Summary and Sub-summary layout parts.

Chapter 18

1. False. To use a FileMaker Pro database as a guest of another computer, you must also have FileMaker Pro installed on your (the guest) computer.

2. True.

3. False. Neither the host nor the guest can define fields in a file that is being shared via personal file sharing.

4. True.

5. False. The best way, short of using FileMaker Server, is to dedicate a fast computer to host the files.

6. Use FileMaker Server; use FileMaker Server Advanced; use FileMaker's Instant Web Publishing capabilities and share over the Internet; turn on FileMaker's sharing option.

7. Anyone who can find your computer on your local network or via the Internet. This assumes there are no password limitations.

8. Open the file first on the computer where it's stored so that it becomes the host, then return to your computer and open the file.

9. Five users.

10. All users, Specify users by privilege set, and No users.

11. Choose Edit (Windows) or FileMaker Pro Remote (Mac), then Sharing, FileMaker Network, and click the On radio button.

12. Choose File, Open and highlight the machine listed in the Hosts column on the left. When you see the list of files on the right, double-click the file you want to open.

13. 1) Set their FileMaker Network Sharing to Off.

    2) Use password protection to allow only authorized users access.

    3) Close the files.

    4) Get your network administrator to set up a firewall.

14. c) You can modify layouts while sharing files.

Chapter 19

1. True.

2. False. The behavior varies depending on system software. Although several are mentioned in this chapter, many more are not.

3. True.

4. False. Developers should never deploy solutions before thoroughly testing all aspects, and web publishing is no exception.

5. True. However, the machine must "believe" it is connected to a network. That can include infrared, AirPort, or connection to a hub.

6. False. Beginning in FileMaker Pro 7 IWP, the Status area is available via the browser.

7. First, make sure that all of the FileMaker files you want to share are open. Choose Edit (Windows) or FileMaker Pro (Mac), then Sharing, Instant Web Publishing. Click the radio button next to On. For each file in the Currently open files area, select it and specify how to share it.

8. You must set up the Instant Web Publishing sharing option.

9. Button labels can be only one line long. All buttons are rendered as rectangular. Scripts performed by buttons should include only web-compatible script steps.

10. It comes with the FileMaker Pro application; you do not need to buy additional software.

11. TCP/IP. (This is the only network protocol supported by FileMaker Pro 7.)

12. In the script editing window, check the box next to "Indicate web compatibility," and only the web-compatible steps will be available; the others will be grayed out.

13. No. Network Sharing is independent from the Web Publishing settings.

Chapter 20

1. False. You can import data into FileMaker Pro from several different file types, as well as through ODBC and XML (discussed in Chapter 24).

2. True.

3. True.

4. False. It can be used for importing text files as well.

5. True.

6. ODBC is an interface that allows various computers to communicate with each other; SQL is a language into which data is translated in order to be shared.

7. The ODBC driver.

8. Get(LastODBCError).

9. You can build an ODBC connection from the database to the spreadsheet.

10. Graphic files can be very large. Even though FileMaker Pro 7 has an 8 terabyte size limit, importing a lot of graphics could cause a file to grow too large for your hard drive well before it reaches the file size limit. However, if you import just a reference to the images, you will still be able to access the images (as long as you don't move them from the folder they're in).

11. You can work with live data. (Alternative answers could be: It's easier to use FileMaker as a front end to other, more complex data sources, or it's easier to construct SQL queries using FileMaker's query window.)

12. Because SQL queries (and HTML) can't deal with them.

Chapter 21

1. False. Go to File, Define, Accounts & Privileges.

2. False. Passwords are just a part of the array of FileMaker security options.

3. True.

4. True.

5. True.

6. Privilege set.

7. In the Define Accounts & Privileges window, Privilege Sets tab, select the privilege set you want to limit, then click Edit. When the Edit Privilege Set window opens, click the Records pop-up, then choose "Custom privileges." In the Custom Record Privileges window, select the table from which you don't want the user to delete records, then select "no" from the Delete pop-up.

8. In the Define Accounts & Privileges dialog, Extended Privileges tab.

9. In Layout mode, choose Layouts, Set Layout Order. If you deselect the check mark to the left of a layout name, it will appear only in Layout mode.

10. Because there can be only one Guest account in a file.

11. It can't. This is a trick question. It's still fair in light of the answer to question number 2. A script can only know the user's account or the privilege set assigned to the account. Then you use either Get(AccountName) or Get(PrivilegeSetName) to decide what the script will do next.

Chapter 22

1. True.

2. True.

3. False. If your database file becomes corrupted beyond repair, you can import data from the corrupted file into the clone.

4. False. You should run tests of the recovery process every so often to make sure that the backup will be useful when it's needed. Note: When you perform your tests, make sure you don't overwrite the current database files.

5. True.

6. The costs to recover data, in labor and restoration services, generally far outweigh the costs of planning ahead and providing the equipment and software necessary.

7. Copy of current file, compacted copy (smaller), and clone (no records).

8. Retrospect, PC Backup, AppleScript, NT Scheduler (and several others not mentioned in the chapter).

9. You should save a clone of a file each time you change its structure (define or edit fields, value lists, layouts, scripts, etc.).

10. The records that get exported depend on the table that is active at the time of the export. There is no "go to table" script step; but each layout is defined to show records from a particular table, and the Go to Layout step activates a layout that, in turn, "activates" its associated table.

11. Make sure the files have the right names, and update serial number options so you don't end up with two records with the same serial number.

12. 45.

13. It's a copy of a file with everything except the data.

14. That depends on how much data you can live without and how often you use it.

Chapter 23

1. True.
2. True.
3. False. Database files are synchronized only when you perform a sync on the Palm.
4. False. You can delete one record or all records.
5. FileMaker Mobile is installed on the Palm device. The Mobile Companion plug-in is installed in the FileMaker Extensions folder on the PC.
6. You can sort on only one field at a time.
7. Calculation, Summary, Container, or Global fields.
8. The Mobile Companion plug-in.
9. Layout and Preview modes.
10. Personal digital assistants (PDAs) running the Palm operating system.
11. See the list in the section titled "FileMaker Mobile vs. FileMaker Pro."
12. See the list in the section titled "FileMaker Mobile vs. FileMaker Pro."

Chapter 24

1. True.
2. True.
3. True.
4. False. XSL defines how data should look and act.
5. False. One of the advantages of XML is that it does not require additional drivers.
6. Extensible Markup Language.
7. Extensible Stylesheet Language.
8. http://filemaker.com/xml/links.html and http://filemaker.com/xml/index.html.
9. You can use XML to encrypt data and then unscramble it after it reaches its destination.
10. Click the Specify button, then choose XML from the Type pop-up.
11. XML makes the data available, and XSL defines various ways in which the data will be formatted, as well as how it will be sorted.
12. All the contracts and other documents could be created in MS Word, Excel, etc. Meanwhile, all of the information about the seller, buyer, property, purchase agreement, fees, etc., could be entered into a FileMaker Pro database. Then XML could be used to export the data and combine it with an XSL style sheet to create various other documents (MS Word, Excel, PageMaker, etc.) for effortless printing, faxing, signing, etc.
13. Export Records.

Chapter 25

1. False. You need to check several things before releasing the new version to users.

2. True.

3. False. You should *check* accounts and privileges to make sure they meet your needs and make any necessary changes.

4. True.

5. False. FileMaker creates a new file for each of the old files, and creates file references to link them.

6. Documentation of the old solution can help you understand the purpose of database design elements as you clean up the converted solution.

7. The conversion log points to design elements you should check out as you clean up the converted solution.

8. Unlike previous versions of FileMaker, where a Sort step automatically made the first record active, it now stays on the record that was active before the Sort step. The added step ensures that the script will behave as it would have in the old version.

9. In the FileMaker Pro 7\English Extras\Electronic Documentation folder, in a file called FM 7 Converting Databases.pdf.

10. FileMaker makes its best guess as it locates files needed to reference, but it may choose old (or otherwise incorrect) versions.

Glossary

account	An element of FileMaker security used to identify and authenticate a user who attempts to open a protected file. An account is identified by an account name and (usually but not always) a password. Each account is associated with a privilege set. (Chapter 21)
aggregate functions	Functions used to perform statistical analysis on several fields in a record, related fields, or Repeating fields. The aggregate functions are Average, Count, Max, Min, StDev, StDevP, Sum, Variance, and VarianceP. (Chapter 13)
AND find	A Find request that has criteria in more than one field. The AND find is meant to reduce the number of records found; an example would be to find records where the city is "New York" AND the name is "Smith." (Chapter 8)
archive	A historical copy of a database or the process of making a historical copy of a database. Archives are generally less accessible than recent backup copies but can prove to be extremely useful after a data loss. (Chapter 22)
auto-enter options	Field options that, when specified, cause FileMaker to automatically enter the creation or modification date, time, or timestamp; the creator name or modifier name; the creator account name or modifier account name; a serial number; the value entered in the last visited record; specified data; or a calculated or looked-up value; and/or to not allow a user to modify the value. Auto-enter options take place when a record is created (modification values are updated each time a record is modified). (Chapter 10)
beta version	A test version of a database, usually deployed for field-testing to a select few users, called "beta testers." Based on feedback from the beta testers, the designer can make improvements before deploying the final version. (Chapter 16)
Body part	Layout part that contains fields and other layout objects once for each record in the found set. Depending on the layout type and the view, you will see one or several records at a time. (Chapter 15)
Book	FileMaker's graphical navigation tool, which functions like a book with pages. In Browse mode, each page represents a record. In Find mode, each page represents a Find request. In Layout mode, each page represents a layout. In Preview mode, each page represents a printed page. (Chapter 1)
Boolean	A calculation or validation that results in either true or false; evaluated by FileMaker as either 1 (true) or 0 (false). (Chapter 11)
browser	An application program that allows you to read and interact with web pages (examples include Netscape Communicator, Internet Explorer, and Safari). (Chapter 19)

calculation result type	Must be assigned to a Calculation field so FileMaker will know how to interpret the results of the calculation. Calculation result types are Text, Number, Date, Time, Timestamp, and Container. (Chapter 4)
chevron	A left- or right-pointing double arrowhead, used to enclose a Merge field in a text block. Chevrons can be created by typing two less than (<<) or greater than (>>) symbols. (Chapter 9)
child table	In a relationship, a table that has potentially several records that relate to a single record in the other (*parent* or *master*) table. A child table is sometimes called a *related table*. (Chapter 6)
clone	One of the types of copies that can be created using the Save a Copy As… command, it duplicates the database structure (tables, fields, layouts, relationships, scripts, document preferences, value lists, etc.) but contains no records. You should always maintain clone copies of your database files in case they are needed to restore corrupted files. (Chapters 1 and 22)
columnar report	Layout type that displays records as a row in tabular format, with fields placed from left to right across the page and field names as column headings in the header part. Columnar reports most often contain sub-summaries, which summarize records based on a break (sort) field, and grand summaries, which summarize all of the records in the found set. Columnar reports can be limited to page width (based on page setup at the time the layout was created) or extended (unlimited width). (Chapter 17)
compacted copy	One of the types of copies that can be created using the Save a Copy As… command, it removes unused space in the file but leaves all the records intact. (Chapter 1)
concatenate	To combine text strings together in a calculation. Strings can consist of fields, text enclosed in quotes, and certain functions. The ampersand (&) operator is the concatenation symbol and must be placed between the strings in order to combine them. (Chapter 7)
constant	A character string that does not change. It can be used as a "literal string," placed within a calculation or field. In a lastname, firstname concatenation (lastname & ", " & firstname), the comma and space between the fields are referred to as constants, and they must be enclosed within quote marks. (The ampersands are operators, *not* constants.) The term also describes a field used as a key to relate to any or all records in a related table. (Chapter 11)
Container field	Field type designed to hold any file (graphic, movie, photo, bitmap, or sound file up to 4GB); multimedia file types supported by QuickTime 6; document file, including word processing, spreadsheet, PDF, and other types; or OLE object (Windows only). (Chapter 16)
conversion log	A document that is automatically created when you convert a FileMaker file from a previous version to .fp7. The conversion log contains conversion status messages and errors, which alert you to manual corrections you should make to your converted database before you use it. The conversion log can be opened with a text editor or FileMaker Pro. (Chapter 25)
convert	The process of taking a database file or multi-file solution that was created in an earlier version of FileMaker and opening it in FileMaker Pro 7. (Migrating, or moving, a complex database from an earlier version to FileMaker Pro 7 likely will involve some combination of converting and rebuilding.) (Chapter 25)

corruption	Damage that occurs to a database file when it crashes or is closed improperly. (Chapter 22)
custom functions	Functions that you create and save to use in calculations throughout your database. A custom function can include a combination of parameters, mathematical and text operators, and comparison and logical operators. When you define a Calculation field and include the function, you only need to enter the values for any parameters you have included in the custom function definition. Custom functions can be created only in FileMaker Developer. (Chapter 13)
data normalization	The process of breaking down tables into related tables to avoid redundancy (duplication of data). (Chapter 6)
data source	The application, computer, or document that contains data that is to be used by another application, computer, or document. (Examples include Excel files, mainframe data, and FileMaker Pro databases.) (Chapter 20)
database	A collection of information that can be organized in various ways. An electronic database, such as a FileMaker Pro database, contains records that can be quickly sorted, searched, displayed, printed, and/or shared. A database can consist of a single table, or it can be a relational database, containing several tables. (Chapter 1)
design functions	Functions that return information about the structure of a database. (Chapter 13)
detail information	In a report, the data listed for each record (as opposed to summary information). Fields for detail information must be placed in the Body part. (Chapter 17)
drag-and-drop	A method for moving data from field to field, file to file, and even between FileMaker Pro and other applications. Select the data you want to move, then click and drag it to a field or other location. (Chapter 5)
entity	An actual, or potential, database table, represented on an entity-relationship (ER) diagram. (Chapter 7)
ER diagram	Short for entity-relationship diagram. A visual representation of all of the entities (tables) in the database system and the main relationships between them. An ER diagram can be created in the planning stages to help design the database, or it can be created from an existing database to help document and/or troubleshoot it. (Chapter 7)
extended columnar report	A columnar report that is not constrained to the width of a page. Fields are placed side by side for as much horizontal space as it takes to display all the fields in the report. Not good for printing, extended columnar reports work better for browsing, when you want to see the maximum number of records per screen. (Chapter 17)
external functions	Functions that give FileMaker access to plug-ins. (Chapter 13)
field	A placeholder for a specific type of information about a record in a database. In FileMaker Pro, fields can hold text, numbers, dates, times, timestamps, or other files (pictures, sounds, movies, and OLE objects). Examples of fields are name, birthdate, and quantity. (Chapter 1)
field behavior	Defined in Layout mode, dictates whether a specific instance of a field on the layout can be entered in Browse and/or Find mode; whether to select the entire contents of the field when it is entered; and which keys (Tab, Return, and/or Enter) may be pressed to move to the next field. (Chapter 17)
field borders	Can be defined in Layout mode to display any combination of top, bottom, left, and right, as well as color, pattern, and pen width; these will show up in all modes. (To see field boundaries only in Layout mode, choose View, Show Field Boundaries.) (Chapter 3)

field format	Defined in Layout mode, determines how field values appear. Also used to apply value lists, and assign number of repeats and direction to display. (Chapter 4)
field options	Further define fields to automatically enter data, validate data entry, define repeating behavior, or index and store data. To see the Options for Field window, choose File, Define Database, Fields tab, select a field, and click the Options button. A variety of options are available under the Auto-Enter, Validation, and Storage tabs. (Chapter 3)
field type	Must be assigned to each field so FileMaker will know how to interpret data entry. Field types are Text, Number, Date, Time, Timestamp, Container, Calculation, and Summary. (Chapter 4)
file	In a database, a file consists of one or more tables, each of which contains records about one set of information, such as contacts or transactions. A file that contains multiple tables that work together is called a relational database. (Chapter 1)
file sharing	Allowing others to access one or more of your databases by turning on Network Sharing for open FileMaker files, and specifying in each file the extent to which network users will have access to it (all users, users by privilege set, or no users). (Chapter 18)
financial functions	Functions that perform financial calculations, such as future value, payment, etc. (Chapter 13)
Find layout	A layout created for the specific purpose of helping users through the Find process, often as part of a report process. When a user clicks on a button to run a report, a script is performed that enters Find mode and navigates to the Find layout, which includes only the necessary fields, along with instructions and buttons to either continue the report or cancel the process. When the user clicks Continue, the script performs the Find and navigates to the report layout. Find layouts are usually not in the Layout list in Browse mode because they are accessed only via scripts. (Chapter 17)
Find symbols	In Find mode, symbols available via the Symbols pop-up list in the Status area that act as operators or wild cards. (Chapter 8)
Find/Replace	Works similar to Find/Replace in word processing programs. You specify what you want to look for, where you want to find it, and what you want to replace it with. In Browse mode, you can choose to search across all records or the current record, and within all fields or the current field. (Chapter 5)
firewall	A system of hardware and/or software that is designed to prevent unauthorized external access into an organization's computer system. (Chapter 18)
flat file	A database file that contains only one table and does not relate dynamically to any other file. (Chapter 6)
Footer part	Layout part that appears at the bottom of every screen or page (except where superseded by a Title Footer). A non-summary field in the footer displays values from the last record on that page. (Chapter 15)
foreign key	A key field in a child table that is used to link records to a primary key field in a parent table. (Chapter 7)

found set	All of the records that are available to browse. Immediately after choosing Show All Records, the found set consists of all of the records in the current table. The number of records in the found set can be decreased by performing a Find or a Go to Related Records command, or by omitting records. If the found set consists of fewer than all of the records in the current table, the Status area will display both the total number of records in the table and the number of found records. (Chapter 8)
function	A predefined formula that performs an often-complex calculation and returns a specific value. Most functions include the function name and the parameters required by the function, which are enclosed in parentheses. (Chapters 11 and 12)
Get functions	Functions that provide information about your database and environment. There are more than 70 Get functions. Examples: Get(CurrentTimestamp) returns the system date and time of your computer to the nearest second, Get(FoundCount) returns the number of records in the current found set, Get(LastMessageChoice) returns a number that represents the button most recently clicked by the user in response to a custom dialog script step. (Chapter 13)
golden clone	A copy of the structure of your database that you keep protected, unused, and available if needed to replace a working database that has become corrupted or otherwise unusable. The process of putting a golden clone into active use requires creating another copy, so that a golden clone still remains available. (Chapter 22)
Grand Summary part	A layout part that displays summary information for all of the records in the found set. Can appear at the beginning (leading) or end (trailing) of all of the records. Any summary fields in a Grand Summary part will summarize all records in the found set. A non-summary field placed in a leading Grand Summary part displays the value in the first record in the found set. A non-summary field placed in a trailing Grand Summary part displays the value in the last record in the found set. (Chapter 15)
grouping layout objects	The process of selecting multiple objects and choosing the Group command, whereby any edit, arrange, and/or format commands affect all of the objects as if they were a single object. (Chapter 16)
guest	A user (or computer) that is using a database file located on another computer (the host computer) or is served via a file server. (Chapter 18)
Header part	Layout part that appears at the top of every screen or page (except where superseded by a Title Header). A non-summary field in the Header displays values from the first record on that page. (Chapter 15)
hidden file	A database file that is open but not visible. In Windows, the name of a hidden file is enclosed in parentheses. (Chapter 18)
host	The computer that is serving database files to guests. (Chapter 18)
HTML	Hypertext Markup Language; a standard markup language for preparing a file to be displayed on a web browser page. (Chapter 24)
Instant Web Publishing	A feature in FileMaker Pro that enables you to easily publish database files over the Internet. (Chapter 19)

join (link) table	A table used to resolve a many-to-many relationship between two other tables. The join table contains two foreign key fields, one from each of the parent tables. Each join table record holds detail information that relates to a single record in each parent table. An example is invoice line items, where each record pertains to one invoice and one product. The line item record contains a foreign key with invoice number, another foreign key with product number, as well as any number of other fields to further describe the line item (such as quantity, price, and extended price). (Chapter 7)
key field (match field)	A field used to define a relationship. In order for two records to relate, the value in the key field on one side of the relationship must match the value in the key field on the other side, based on the comparison operator(s) defined for the relationship. (Chapter 6)
layout	Determines the visual presentation of data for viewing or printing. A database file may contain several different layouts (such as a list, data entry form, report, and mailing labels) to make data available for different purposes. Each layout is associated with a specific Table Occurrence. (Chapter 1)
layout part	A section of a layout that affects how field values are treated and displayed in the other modes. Header and Footer parts display once on each page, the Body part appears once for each record, Title Headers and Title Footers appear only once, Sub-summary parts appear before or after groups of records and display summary information, and Grand Summary parts appear either before or after all of the found records and display summary information. In Layout mode, each layout part is designated by a dotted line and a part label. (Chapter 9)
locking layout objects	The process of selecting one or more objects and choosing the Lock command, thus preventing any movement or other change to be made to the object in Layout mode. (Chapter 16)
logical functions	Functions that test for a condition, evaluate parameters, allow you to set variables for an expression, work with lookup actions, or return text strings that include quotation marks. (Chapter 13)
lookup field	Copies data from a field in another table into a field in the current table. Data comes in through a relationship, but looked-up data remains static unless a relookup is performed. Lookups are useful for prices on an invoice, which you would want to remain unchanged even if the product price changes in the future. (Chapters 2 and 7)
loop	A script step that begins repeating a series of steps until some condition causes the loop to be exited. A Loop script step must have a corresponding End Loop step. (Chapter 14)
many-to-many relationship	A relationship where any one record in table A can relate to many records in table B, and any one record in table B can relate to many records in table A. With FileMaker Pro, you create a join (or link) table to resolve the many-to-many relationship into two separate one-to-many relationships. (Chapter 7)
master table	In a relationship, a table that has a single record that relates to potentially several records in the other (*related* or *child*) table. A master table is sometimes called a *parent* table. (Chapter 6)
Merge field	A placeholder for a field that expands or contracts as needed to fit the field's entire data contents in Browse or Preview mode, or when printed. In Layout mode, the field name is enclosed within chevrons. When browsed, previewed, or printed, the field value for the specific record appears in its place. (Chapter 9)

mode	Controls how you interact with the database. Browse mode is used primarily for data entry. Find mode allows you to enter search criteria and find records that match, at which time FileMaker switches back to Browse mode. Layout mode is where you set up different views of your database. Preview mode shows you how your printed data will look. (Chapter 2)
modular scripts	Small scripts that work together to perform a larger task. Using the Perform Script step, several subscripts, each of which performs a small chunk of the work, can be called from a single "master" script. Modular scripts can be called by any other script, so they can be used over and over. Common modular scripts perform sorts, print setups, layout changes, etc. (Chapter 14)
multiple-criteria relationship	A relationship in which two or more pairs of key (match) fields are compared. In order for the relationship to be valid, each of the pairs of key fields must relate based on its corresponding comparison operator. Another way to describe such a relationship is to call it an AND relationship. (Chapter 7)
nested function	Refers to replacing a parameter in a function with another function. It is a function within a function. (Chapter 12)
network protocol	A language used by computer networks to exchange information among computers attached to the network. (Chapter 18)
object effects	Formats that can be applied to an object to make it appear three-dimensional. For example, embossed, engraved, or drop shadow. To apply object effects, select an object, then choose an effect from the Object Effects palette on the Status area. (Chapter 16)
ODBC	Open Database Connectivity is an interface used to communicate between various computer programs in real time. (Chapter 20)
omitted records	Omitted records are all records that are not part of the found set. To view the omitted records, choose Records, Show Omitted. (Chapter 8)
one-to-many relationship	A relationship where any one record in table A can relate to many records in table B, and any one record in table B can relate to only one record in table A. This is the most common relationship seen in FileMaker databases. (Chapter 7)
one-to-one relationship	A relationship where any one record in table A can relate to only one record in table B, and any one record in table B can relate to only one record in table A. One-to-one relationships are rare; usually they are used to satisfy a particular business model. (Chapter 7)
open database structure	A database whose structure (fields, layouts, scripts, etc.) is completely available to be altered. (Chapter 4)
operator	A symbol used in a calculation to change the behavior or provide different results from your data. Operators are grouped into the following areas: mathematical ($+$, $-$, $*$, $/$, $(\ )$, $^\wedge$) comparison ($=$, $<>$ or $\neq$, $>$, $<$, $>=$ or $\geq$, $<=$ or $\leq$), logical (AND, OR, NOT, XOR), and text ($\&$, "", ¶). The Calculation window includes a group of mathematical and text operator buttons and a comparison and logical operators list. (Chapter 11)
OR find	A multiple-request find, where a single field can have any of several values to meet the find criteria; the OR find is meant to increase the number of records found. An example would be to find records where the city is "New York" OR "Los Angeles." (Chapter 8)
Palm operating system	The computer operating system used by certain handheld personal digital assistants (PDAs). (Chapter 23)

parameter	A value required by a function; it could be a text string (constant), field reference, mathematical expression, or another function. In a function with more than one parameter, parameters are separated by semicolons. (Chapter 12)
parent table	In a relationship, a table that has a single record that relates to potentially several records in the other (*child* or *related*) table. A parent table is sometimes called a *master* table. (Chapter 6)
Part label	In Layout mode, identifies each part by type. By clicking the part label control, labels can be positioned vertically to allow complete viewing of layout objects or horizontally to facilitate resizing layout parts. (Chapter 9)
part label control	In Layout mode, found at the bottom of the database window, between the toggle Status area control and the mode pop-up. By clicking the Part label control, labels can be positioned vertically to allow complete viewing of layout objects or horizontally to facilitate resizing layout parts. (Chapter 9)
password	An element of FileMaker security used to authenticate a user who attempts to open a protected file. A user enters an account name and password to gain access to the file; activities while in the file are controlled by the account's privilege set. (Chapter 21)
personal digital assistant (PDA)	A small, mobile, handheld computer. PDA makes and models include the Palm, the Handspring, and the famous, albeit short-lived, Newton. (Chapter 23)
plug-in	A separate piece of software that adds functionality to a program such as FileMaker Pro. The Auto Update plug-in is shipped with FileMaker Pro; other plug-ins are available from a number of sources. (Chapter 13)
portal	A layout object that is used to display several related records. You need to use a portal only when you are viewing child, or related, records. (If you're on a layout that represents the child table and wish to see the parent record, a portal is overkill — just a simple related field will do.) (Chapter 6)
primary key	A key field in a parent (master) table that is used to link a single record to a foreign key field in a child (related) table. The primary key should be unique and non-modifiable. (Chapter 7)
privilege	An element of FileMaker security at the file level, it describes a particular access item such as access to one or more layouts, menu items, tables, records, fields, etc. (Chapter 21)
privilege set	An element of FileMaker security, it is a defined group of privileges that serves as a level of access to a database file. A privilege set is assigned to a user via an account. (Chapter 21)
rebuild	The process of taking a database file or multi-file solution that was created in an earlier version of FileMaker and recreating it, from the ground up, in FileMaker Pro 7. (Migrating, or moving, a complex database from an earlier version to FileMaker Pro 7 likely will involve some combination of converting and rebuilding.) (Chapter 25)
record	All the information about one individual in a table. A single record comprises one each of the fields defined in the table, along with the values entered. (Chapter 1)
record-level security	A feature of FileMaker's Accounts & Privileges system that limits a user's access to view, edit, create, and delete data on a record-by-record basis, based on a Boolean calculation. Record-level security is a feature of the privilege set definition. (Chapter 21)

referential integrity	A principle of relational database design, whereby you prevent separating (orphaning) any child record from its parent record by inadvertently deleting the parent record or changing a value in a key field. (Chapter 6)
related data	Records that contain matching key-field values, as defined by a relationship. (Chapter 2)
related field	A field that is viewed or referenced through a relationship. In Layout mode or in a calculation formula, a related field is represented as the Table Occurrence name, followed by two colons (::) and then the field name. (Chapter 6)
related (child) table	In a relationship, a table that has potentially several records that relate to a single record in the other (*master* or *parent*) table. A related table is sometimes called a *child table*. (Chapter 6)
relationship	A user-defined link between two database tables (or a single table in the case of a self-join relationship). Key fields are identified, and records that have matching values in both key fields, based on the comparison operator(s), are said to be related. (Chapter 2)
remote host	The first user (or computer) to open a shared database on another computer via personal file sharing. Subsequent users become guests of the remote host, and all transactions will pass through the remote host computer. (Chapter 18)
Repeating field	A field formatted to hold more than one value (maximum 32,000 repetitions). (Chapter 4)
repeating functions	Functions that perform calculations on Repeating fields. (Chapter 13)
Replace field contents command	Replaces the contents of the current field in every record in the found set with a value, a calculation, or a serialized number. (Chapter 5)
restoring	The process of bringing a database back up after it has been corrupted. Choices for restoring a database include using a clone and importing backed-up data or using the Recover command. (Chapter 22)
script	A FileMaker utility that performs one or more tasks, similar to a macro. (Chapter 14)
script parameter	A constant or expression that is specified, within a button definition or in the Perform Script script step, for use as a variable in a script. (Chapter 14)
ScriptMaker	FileMaker's scripting tool, used to define, modify, and perform scripts. (Chapter 14)
self-join relationship	A relationship from a table back to the same table, either to the same field or to another field. Often used to display records that have some field value in common (such as department) in a portal. Can also be defined from a Global field to a non-Global field to enable utilizing the Go to Related Record command as a quick way to "find" records that match the value in the Global field without leaving Browse mode. (Chapter 7)
Size palette	In Layout mode, it allows you to view and edit the placement of the left and top edges of a selected object, and change the dimensions of the object. To view the Size palette, choose View, Object Size. By clicking the units indicator on any line, you can toggle between inches, centimeters, and pixels. (Chapter 3)
Specify Button window	Allows you to assign an action to a button. The Specify Button window opens automatically when you create a button using the Button tool, but you can turn any layout object into a button by selecting it, then choosing Format, Button. (Chapter 3)

SQL	Structured Query Language; a standard computer language for getting information from and adding information to a database. (Chapter 20)
Status area	The gray area at the left of the database window, it contains the Book and other information about the status of the database. It is used to access many of FileMaker Pro's tools and features. Individual elements in the Status area will vary depending on the current mode. (Chapter 1)
storage options	Field options used to specify a field as a Global or Repeating field, the indexing behavior of the field, and/or whether to store the results of a Calculation field. (Chapter 10)
style sheet	A language-based filter through which data is formatted for presentation as a document or web page. (Chapter 24)
Sub-summary part	Layout part that displays summary information for a group of records in the found set, as defined by a break (sort) field. A Sub-summary part can appear at the beginning (leading) or end (trailing) of each group. Any summary fields in a Sub-summary part will summarize all records in the group. A non-summary field placed in a leading Sub-summary part displays the value of the first record in the group. A non-summary field placed in a trailing Sub-summary part displays the value of the last record in the group. (Chapters 9 and 15)
summary functions	Functions that return summary or sub-summary values across several records. (Chapter 13)
summary information	In a report, the information that aggregates data across a group of records (as opposed to detail information). Summary fields (total, average, count, minimum, maximum, standard deviation, standard deviation across a population, and fraction of total), when placed in Sub-summary or Grand Summary parts, summarize according to the type of Summary field and the type of part into which each is placed. (Chapter 17)
sync	Short for synchronize, or hot-sync; the process of reconciling files between a personal computer and a personal digital assistant (PDA). The process compares the two versions and updates older data from the latest changes or as instructed by the user. Synchronizing also refers to the process of reconciling differences between two files, regardless of where they are stored. (Chapter 23)
table	In a database file, a table consists of records about one set of information, such as contacts or transactions. Individual tables work together in a relational database. (Chapter 1)
Table Occurrence	A Table Occurrence represents a table in the database and appears as an object on the Relationships graph. Each table can be represented by one or more Table Occurrences. The Table Occurrence name is used as the first part of any reference to a field that is not defined in the current table (the syntax is tableoccurrencename::fieldname). (Chapter 6)
TCP/IP	Transmission Control Protocol/Internet Protocol; the basic communication language of the Internet. (Chapter 18)
text formatting functions	Functions that are used to modify text color, font, or style. (Chapter 13)
timestamp functions	Functions that are used to mark the exact date and time of database events. (Chapter 13)
Title Footer part	Layout part that appears at the bottom of the first screen or page, it replaces a Footer part on the first page only. A field in the Title Footer displays data from the last record on the page. (Chapter 15)

Appendixes

Title Header part	Layout part that appears at the top of the first screen or page, it replaces a Header part on the first page only. A field in the Title Header displays data from the first record being browsed. (Chapter 15)
Tool panel	In Layout mode, the part of the Status area that displays the selection and object tools; fill color and pattern palettes; effects palette; current fill properties; line color, pattern, and width palettes; and current pen properties. (Chapter 3)
trigonometric functions	Functions that are used to calculate geometric data, such as angles, logarithms, and degrees. (Chapter 13)
T-squares	Movable horizontal and vertical lines to help you line up objects in Layout mode (they're not visible in any other mode). To access, choose View, T-Squares. (Chapter 3)
unstored calculation	A Calculation field with a result that is calculated only when the value is needed. You can choose to store or not to store the results of a calculation. However, any calculation that uses related (dynamic) data cannot be stored. (Chapter 10)
validation options	Field options that suggest or enforce that data entered meets the criteria specified. Options are strict data type (numeric only, four-digit year, or time of day); not empty, unique, or existing; a member of a specified value list; within a range (based on the field type); validated by a calculation; or limited to some number of characters. You can also specify whether the validation is always checked or only during data entry. Finally, you can specify a custom message to display if the validation fails. (Chapter 10)
value list	Assembles a list of values to promote ease and/or accuracy of data entry. Value lists can consist of custom values, values from a field, or the values in a list from another file. A value list can be displayed as a pop-up list, pop-up menu, check box set, or radio button set. (Chapter 5)
XML	Extensible Markup Language; a standard language that translates and allows computer programs to use data from other computer programs, without the need for special drivers. (Chapter 24)
XSL	Extensible Stylesheet Language; a standard language that translates and defines, using style sheets, how data transferred via XML will look and act. (Chapter 24)

Index

The world's best *hands-on*
FileMaker training!

Increase

your **FileMaker PRO***ficiency*

with ***hands-on*** *training*

from a select team of world-renowned FileMaker instructors, including:

- **Jerry Robin**, owner of FMPtraining.com and one of the highest-rated speakers at the annual FileMaker Developer Conferences
- **Darren Terry**, a top-rated Developer Conference speaker and former tech-support wizard for FileMaker, Inc.
- **Jonathan Stars** and **Nonie Bernard**, co-authors of *Learn FileMaker Pro 7*

All of our trainers are professional FileMaker consultants, and most have been speakers at the annual FileMaker Developer Conferences.

Visit our website for bios of all of our trainers, complete class descriptions, and testimonials from our students.

www.fmptraining.com
480.759.4844 *or **866.FMP.TRNG** (866.367.8764)*

Whether you're new to FileMaker Pro or a seasoned developer, FMPtraining has classes to help you enhance your skills as a FileMaker professional. From *Fundamentals of FileMaker Pro Development* to our intermediate and advanced curriculum, you're sure to find classes to fit your experience and needs.

- *Fundamentals of FileMaker Pro Development*
- *Relational Database Design*
- *Scriptology™ (FileMaker scripting demystified)*
- *The Art & Science of Calculations*
- *Database Administration & Networking*
- *Multi-User Database Design*
- *Custom & On-Site Classes…and more*

Based in Phoenix, Arizona, and offering classes in locations around the United States, FMPtraining has the most extensive selection of developer-level FileMaker training classes in the world!

Accelerate your learning with hands-on training

"Hands-on is definitely the best way to go. The training was entertaining, informative, and packed with tips, shortcuts and methods that make designing databases so much easier on the developer and more productive for the user."

Terri McCullough, Buckeye Local School District, Rayland, OH

This coupon is good for a $50 discount on any regularly scheduled hands-on workshop offered by FMPtraining.com. It may be combined with FMPtraining's published multi-class discounts. It may *not* be used in conjunction with multiple-student discounts, nor is it valid on custom or on-site classes. Limit one coupon per student per calendar year.

Original coupon must be submitted with class payment. Other restrictions may apply. Please call for details. Coupon must be redeemed by 12/31/2005.

Student Name _____

Class dates _____

Class title _____

LFMP7

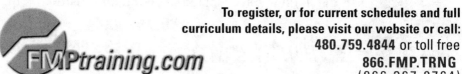

To register, or for current schedules and full curriculum details, please visit our website or call:
480.759.4844 or toll free
866.FMP.TRNG
(866.367.8764)

DOCUMENTING INDIVIDUAL IDENTITY

DOCUMENTING
INDIVIDUAL IDENTITY

THE DEVELOPMENT OF STATE
PRACTICES IN THE MODERN WORLD

Edited by Jane Caplan and John Torpey

PRINCETON UNIVERSITY PRESS   PRINCETON AND OXFORD

Library of Congress Cataloging-in-Publication Data

Documenting individual identity : the development of state practices
in the modern world / edited by Jane Caplan and John Torpey.
p. cm.
Includes bibliographical references and index.
ISBN 0-691-00911-2 (alk. paper)
ISBN 0-691-00912-0 (pbk : alk. paper)
1. Identification—History. 2. Passports—History.
3. Status (Law)—History. I. Caplan, Jane. II. Torpey, John C.
K3272.D63 2001
342′.082—dc21   2001036273

This book has been composed in Sabon

Printed on acid-free paper.∞

www.pup.princeton.edu

Printed in the United States of America

10 9 8 7 6 5 4 3 2 1

Contents

Acknowledgments _____

THIS BOOK is the product of a lengthy collaborative undertaking involving authors from North America and Europe and research undertaken on four different continents. We must therefore begin by thanking the inventors of the Internet for making so much faster and easier the scholarly exchanges required for producing a book of this kind.

The nucleus of this volume was a panel at the American Historical Association's Annual Meeting in January 1998, and we thank Anne Joseph, Alison Winter, and David Abraham for their participation in that event. Most of the authors of the essays collected in the book gathered together for a round of mutual criticism (and perhaps to escape from the cold at their home institutions) during a spectacular weekend in Laguna Beach, California in December 1998. We are grateful to them for their courage in venturing to the beaches of southern California in the dead of winter, and we thank all the contributors for their responsiveness to comments and their attention to deadlines as the book developed. Our discussions of the early drafts at this workshop were greatly enhanced by the trenchant criticisms of Michael Meranze and Ted Porter, who gave generously of their time and insights. We have also benefited from the thoughtful and constructive comments of the two reviewers who read the manuscript for Princeton University Press.

For their support in making it possible for the contributors to talk face to face and for help in defraying other expenses, we thank the provost of Bryn Mawr College, the Council for European Studies Workshop Support Program, the German-American Academic Council, the Program in Conference and Research Workshop Support of the University of California, Irvine, the Office of the Dean of the School of Social Sciences at UC Irvine, and the University of California's Humanities Research Institute. We are particularly grateful to the former director of the Humanities Research Institute, Pat O'Brien, for her enthusiasm about our project. We also thank Anna Canavan and Lorraine Kirschner of Bryn Mawr College for their help in decoding disks, retyping manuscripts, and handling correspondence, and Karoline Cook and Andrew Woolford for their assistance in compiling the bibliography.

Jane Caplan would like to thank Bryn Mawr College, the National Endowment for the Humanities, the Rockefeller Foundation's Bellagio Study and Conference Center, and the John Simon Guggenheim Foundation for sponsoring the research from which her contributions to this book are drawn. John Torpey thanks the National Endowment for the

Humanities, the German Marshall Fund, the European University Institute in Florence, Italy, and the University of California, Irvine for their support of his research on the topics addressed in the volume. Finally, our joint thanks to Brigitta van Rheinberg at Princeton University Press for her support of the book.

Michel Foucault cites Guillaume de la Perrière's definition of government in 1567 as "the right disposition of things, arranged so as to lead to a convenient end": we hope we have disposed of our collaborators' work not only to their convenience but also to the edification and enjoyment of readers of this book. Or as four musical collaborators once put it, "it's been a long time coming," but we hope it has been worth the wait.

Jane Caplan, Bryn Mawr College
John Torpey, University of British Columbia, Vancouver
September 2000

DOCUMENTING INDIVIDUAL IDENTITY

Introduction

JANE CAPLAN AND JOHN TORPEY

> To be governed is to be under surveillance, inspected, spied on, superintended, legislated, regulated, restrained, indoctrinated, preached at, controlled, appraised, assessed, censored, commanded. . . . To be governed is to be noted, registered, enumerated, accounted for, stamped, measured, classified, audited, patented, licensed, authorized, endorsed, reprimanded, prevented, reformed, rectified, and corrected, in every operation, every transaction, every movement.
> —PIERRE-JOSEPH PROUDHON, *"Idée générale de la révolution au XIX*^e *siècle"*

THE ESSAYS collected in this volume explore the history of one of the key methods by which modern governments have subjected their populations to the transactions catalogued by Proudhon: the documentation of individual identity. Establishing the identity of individual people—as workers, taxpayers, conscripts, travelers, criminal suspects—is increasingly recognized as fundamental to the multiple operations of the state. The creation of a "legible people," in James Scott's phrase[1]—a people open to the scrutiny of officialdom—has become a hallmark of modern statehood; conversely, the mechanisms by which this has been achieved on a universal scale, that is, the paraphernalia and personnel necessary to operate systems of standardized registration, have contributed in large part to the character of the modern bureaucratic state. And not only the state: private economic and commercial activities would also grind to a halt unless companies had the ability to identify and track individuals as property owners, employees, business partners, and customers.

This may now seem self-evident, but individual identification has not always been a prerequisite to the existence or efficacy of bureaucratic activities. Taxation and conscription can be imposed on a community as collective obligations, for example, and even judicial processes that may seem to depend crucially on identifying a particular individual have in the past been resolved by communal procedures such as compurgation (group oath) or collective fines. Scott's metaphor of "legibility" reminds us of the centrality of writing to modern forms of rule, so that universal systems

---

[1] Scott 1998: 65; see also Certeau 1984: ch. 3.

of individual identification are unthinkable without mass literacy and an
official culture of written records.[2] In one of the few existing studies of
identity documents as such, the French sociologist Claudine Dardy describes contemporary society as the "pays du tout en écritures"—the land
where everything is written down, where individual and social identities
are inscribed in the innumerable records that organize people's lives as
citizens, workers, taxpayers, drivers, mortgage-holders, pensioners, and
so on.[3] This returns us full circle to the genesis of writing itself, which
originated not as a means of recording speech but in order to facilitate
taxation, book-keeping, and property ownership.[4]

In Europe, the proximate origins of this culture of written records lie in
the early medieval transition from oral to written procedures, prompted
initially by royal interest in the reliable documentation of property ownership and legal processes. In fact, written records probably preceded and
stimulated the growth of literacy rather than vice versa, as Michael Clanchy has argued: people first had to develop confidence in the written document before it could supplant familiar oral and symbolic forms of record.[5]
The spread of documentation also created new, written forms of individual identification by name, including lists of estate inhabitants, or the
signatures of a copyist, party, or witness to a contract. These were the
foundations on which a proliferating apparatus for the verification of
identities began to be established. Thus in England, for example, "by the
second half of the thirteenth century it was imprudent for anybody to
wander far from his village without some form of identification in writing."[6] The need to identify and track those who had wandered or traveled
beyond the circle in which they were personally known was an original
and continuing stimulus to the development of the portable identity document in its modern form.

The evolution of procedures for individual identification was also tied
up with the more recent historical emergence of modern concepts of individuality and subjectivity, and with a public commitment to the moral
and philosophical significance of the human self. On the grandest scale,
this is a process that some would see as the autobiography of the modern
world, and hence not reducible to a few convenient phrases or markers.[7]
The philosophical origins and the history of theories of selfhood and identity underpin this book; so too the collective identities constructed on the
basis of religion, nationality, gender, or ethnicity, but these issues are also

[2] On this point, see Giddens 1987, and Goody 1986: ch. 3.
[3] Dardy 1998: 47.
[4] See Dudley 1991, Goody 1986, and Martin 1994: ch. 4.
[5] See Clanchy 1993.
[6] Ibid.: 33.
[7] See Taylor 1989.

individuality & subjectivity

beyond its scope. Our own horizons are perhaps more modest, but no less legitimate. The present volume can be epitomized as an exploration of the history of identification rather than of identities. Its logic is that, despite the fact that both these terms are intimately connected with the emergence of modern forms of public life, the issue of identification has been virtually ignored even in recent scholarship on the formation and meaning of identities.[8]

This book begins the work of repairing this striking omission. Our purpose is to discuss in detail the practices through which individual identity has been inscribed, codified, verified, and documented by official institutions in the modern world, especially the state. We look at the contexts within which these systems have been elaborated, and the purposes to which they have been put. In this our book differs significantly from numerous recent publications that have examined other aspects of what Foucault has called "governmentality," including the production of a modern sense of self, the construction and implementation of concepts of citizenship, and the emergence of the "quantifying spirit"—the elaboration of collective systems of registration and enumeration, including the census and related statistical projects.[9]

The relationships and tensions between identity and identification are closely interdependent, of course, like those between systems of collective and individual registration. The question "who is this person?" leaches constantly into the question "what kind of a person is this?" Identification as an individual is scarcely thinkable without categories of collective identity, and isolating one half of these pairs might therefore seem artificial. But by the same token one could justly complain that existing work has systematically neglected these connections, whereas the essays in this collection draw repeated attention to them. As the essays in Part III, "The Identification and Control of Movement," show, for example, the adoption of the passport regime in international travel is intimately tied to the development of citizenship rules, and Russian internal passports depended on and were deeply implicated in the revision of ethnic categorizations. By inverting the more familiar links between individual and collective, these essays disclose the extent to which the documentary apparatus of identification itself has driven the history of categories and collectivities.

[8] With a few notable exceptions, including Dardy 1998, Scheffler 1997, Scott 1998, Aly and Roth 2000, Heindl and Saurer 2000, and the previous publications of several contributors to this volume: Lyon 1994, Marx 1990, Noiriel 1991, Torpey 2000, and Geselle 2000.

[9] On quantification see, for example, Knight 1981, Daston 1988, Tort 1989, Frängsmyr et al. 1990, Wise 1995, Crosby 1997, Poovey 1998; on the modern sense of self, Heller et al. 1986, Nussbaum 1989, Taylor 1989, Giddens 1991; on statistics, governmentality, and citizenship, Glass 1973, Cullen 1975, Porter 1986, Stigler 1986, Hacking 1990, Brubaker 1992, Patriarca 1996, and Scott 1998.

The study of practices of identification in the contemporary world and of the political, social, and legal issues that these are now generating, is, for obvious reasons, a subject that has already received a good deal of public and critical attention, as the essays in Part IV of this collection indicate. But despite the ubiquity and significance of these practices in modern culture, their earlier history has received surprisingly little attention, and certainly has not yet achieved the secure place in contemporary debates that it deserves. Similarly, although historians have long used records of this kind as primary sources and subjected them to careful critical assessment, the records themselves are usually secondary to their objectives, and are much more rarely made the independent focus of research.

The present collection of essays is therefore intended as an initial contribution to mapping the contours of this field and indicating some directions for further inquiry. It explores the historical constitution and systematization of individual identity and its documentation as a legal and bureaucratic category, the emergence of precise protocols and apparatuses of documentary identification developed by government, police, and public institutions, and the intersection of individual and collective systems of registration and identification. The nineteen essays collected in the volume are the work of scholars from several disciplines, including history, sociology, history of science, and economics. This multidisciplinary authorship underscores the variety of paths that have historically led to the intensified documentation of individual identity: to corral it into the confines of a single discipline would do no justice to the scope of the subject. But the book makes no pretense to be "comprehensive," a claim that would be pointless at the current stage of research. The editors are well aware that, for example, the operations of state and police apparatuses claim a larger place in these essays than those of other institutions, including commercial enterprises, international bodies, or religious organizations; that the history of identifying practices has multiple origins and paths beyond the continents and cultures discussed here; and that more comparative work will be necessary to explain how and why national cultures of identification have differed in their origins, trajectories, and effects. Still, we believe that the scope of the book reflects the uneven and embryonic state of this emerging field, and we have aimed to bring a representative sample of the most interesting and suggestive current work to a wider audience. If some topics or areas are not as well covered as we might wish, we hope this will be seen less as a defect of this collection than as a commentary on the existing state of research. We will be well satisfied if this volume serves as a stimulus to further research into the specific historical, national, and supranational contexts within which regimes of documentary identity have been differently shaped.

One set of questions that seems especially challenging at this stage of research is the relationship between the emancipatory and the repressive aspects of identity documentation. Here the essays begin to chart some important but neglected tributaries to the mighty stream of what Max Weber called bureaucratic rationalization. For Weber, who saw himself and his contemporaries standing helpless before a great onrushing wave of impersonal administration, there was little doubt that the increasingly bureaucratic handling of everyday governmental concerns was inevitable. In his characteristically paradoxical and pessimistic fashion, Weber regarded the advance of mass democracy as unavoidably enhancing bureaucratization, precisely because both bureaucracy and democracy demand equal treatment for all. The demand for "equality before the law," in turn, resulted in the central state's "leveling of the governed," in contrast to corporate orders defined by their specific privileges. This leveling process tends to raise up persons and groups who had previously not been thought worthy of notice, yet it simultaneously reduces those subordinated to the state's governance to a status as subjects of direct administration and surveillance. The variable determining the degree of oppressiveness of bureaucratic processes that rely on documentation of individual identity is democracy itself, in its everyday as well as institutional forms—the extent to which the bureaucratic machinery can be restrained from "overtowering" society and all its members.[10] Released from such constraints, especially if combined with a regime that enjoys extensive popular loyalty or that rules through widespread fear, bureaucratic domination can lead to disaster.

Although the contributors to the present volume are alert to the danger that people may be lost in the flood of paper that has become essential to contemporary state administration, we also acknowledge the advantages that may flow from the practices of individual identification that this book explores. Here both Weber's pessimism and Proudhon's dyspeptic catalogue may stand in need of a corrective. Both suggest the culmination of specifically historical processes, yet they also convey only one side of the bureaucratic "identity equation." Proudhon's early hostility to the controlling eye of the state leaves out the ways in which individual identification, even in its most official forms, has been enabling as well as subordinating, and has created rights as well as police powers.

To be sure, bureaucratic processes of individual identification have been put to nightmarish uses, the most notorious example being the Nazis' use of population registers and identification documents to track Jewish and other "undesirable" populations.[11] Yet, as philosophers such as Charles

---

[10] Weber's discussion can be found in Gerth and Mills 1946: 224–32.
[11] See Luebke and Milton 1994; Aly and Roth 2000.

Taylor have eloquently demonstrated, identification and recognition are ineluctably conjoined in the modern world, and are the prerequisite for many individual and collective claims against the state and other authorities.[12] Registration and documentation of individual identity are essential if persons are to "count" in a world increasingly distant from the face-to-face encounters characteristic of less complex societies. Individual identification procedures register voters, refugees, schoolchildren, and welfare recipients as well as conscripts and taxpayers; they ease mobility and communication as well as controlling these activities; and they enhance public security at the same time as they expose everyone to the dispassionate eye of official surveillance. Voluntary means of identification have even preceded the adoption of "official" methods: striking examples include the regimental insignia that European soldiers chose to tattoo on their arms in the nineteenth century, or the improvised identification labels that American soldiers wore in the Civil War, before the official introduction of the "dog-tag."[13] These facilitative and, so to speak, *self*-reinforcing aspects of individual identification presumably underlie the dictum, asserted in Article 24 of the United Nations International Covenant on Civil and Political Rights (1966), that "every child shall be registered immediately after birth and shall have a name." Without such registration, the newborn may fail to gain recognition as a being with claims on the world and endowed with the power of creation that Hannah Arendt saw as the vital essence of human existence.[14]

Moreover, Proudhon's mere enumeration of identification-related constraints cannot capture the ways in which human ingenuity and recalcitrance have taken up the state's tools and turned them against themselves. This is not just a matter of forgeries and frauds, but of the creation of new identities and names, a parallel world of revised or resistant identities and relationships. As Claudine Dardy has suggested, echoing but inverting Proudhon's catalogue, "[Identity] papers are at one and the same time papers of constraint and control, including control by the state, but they are also purveyors of identity. For each and every one of us, our identity—at least a certain kind of identity—is enacted and reenacted, stamped, and affirmed in these papers."[15] Although bureaucracies organize this data with scant regard for personal needs, these records also furnish people with the means, together with private papers such as letters or diaries, to "write" themselves into life and history. In this they do not

---

[12] Taylor 1989.

[13] On tattoos, see Caplan 2000; thanks to Thomas Laqueur for information on Civil War soldiers.

[14] See Arendt 1958.

[15] Dardy 1998, 13; see also Scheffler 1997.

individual negotiations

just behave in accordance with the requirements of bureaucratic categories, but create themselves as "legible" subjects of their own lives.[16]

Moreover, to concede that the powers of states to classify, codify, and identify have grown enormously in the modern period is not to argue—*pace* some Foucauldians—that all human life now proceeds under the heel of an incessant and ill-intentioned surveillance. Human agency remains a decisive factor in the genealogy of identification practices, which tend automatically and immediately to generate strategies by individuals (and sometimes even by organized groups) to undermine their effectiveness.[17] The very multiplicity of these documents may, as Dardy argues, disrupt the state's ostensibly monolithic front. They open spaces in which administrators are driven to imperfect strategies of coordination and improvisation, while citizens can imagine and adopt new identities and relationships.[18] In short, states and their subjects/citizens routinely play cat-and-mouse with individual identification requirements. Yet even if, as these examples suggest, the game is never entirely decided in advance, it still seems realistic to concede that so far the cat has held the better cards.

✛ ✛ ✛ ✛

Readers familiar with the story of Martin Guerre—a sixteenth-century French peasant who was impersonated (for twelve years!) by an impostor until the real Guerre returned unexpectedly from his travels—will readily understand that criteria for the identification and authentication of persons have been in existence for a very long time. In order to set the stage for the examination of the modern era to which the book is principally addressed, Valentin Groebner's essay in Part I examines the origins of a conventionalized "art" of paper description and registration in the bureaucratizing states of northern Italy, France, and the Swiss and Rhine regions between the fifteenth and seventeenth centuries.

Yet it was the epoch of political development inaugurated by the French Revolution's creation of a specifically national citizenship that stimulated the spread of both the resources and the need to subject entire populations to large-scale documentary inventories, and hence the adoption of elaborate systems for tracking and verifying individual identities. Against the background of an increasingly mobile society in which older and more stable conventions of identification were dissolving, the "well-regulated

---

[16] Certeau 1984: 34ff., touches on this point but leaves it undeveloped in the absence of any adequate discussion of the "everyday practices" of bureaucratic writing.

[17] On the generation of these forms of resistance in everyday life, see Certeau 1984 and Scott 1990.

[18] Dardy 1998: 34, 55.

writing/reading body

police state" of late-eighteenth-century Europe generated a systematic interest in universal means of individual identification. The putatively universalist Enlightenment state gave up the selective outward identification of individuals and groups (e.g., marks on the body, sumptuary laws regulating dress) only by simultaneously asserting a newly comprehensive right of surveillance and identification that applied to *all* citizens.

From this flowed the nineteenth-century development of documentary practices through which every citizen, not just the delinquent or deviant, was to be made visible to the state: not by physical marks on the body, but by the indirect means of registrations, passes, censuses, and the like. Writing on the body gave way to reading off it. These emergent identification procedures drew on a repertoire of physical signs and measurements, but represented them in written and visual records, both individually portable and centrally filed. The elaboration of systematic regimes of representation disclosed a central tension in the project of identification, as opposed to mere classification. The identity document purports to be a record of uniqueness, but also has to be an element in a classifying series that reduces individuality to a unit in a series, and that is thus simultaneously deindividualizing. This discloses the fundamental instability of the concept of the "individual" as such, and helps to explain the uneasy sense that we never fully own or control our identity, that the identity document carries a threat of expropriation at the same time as it claims to represent who we "are."

As these systems were elaborated, much of the concern with documenting and tracking individual identity arose from the growing salience of nationalism as a legitimating ideology of states. The older regime of the police state underwent a transmutation into the "national" welfare state that offered various kinds of benefits to its own citizens, but *only* to them. Here, as in other contexts of "subjectification," identification conveyed a mixed message, at once of emancipation and of constraint. Creating categories of eligibility thus went hand in hand with establishing formal means for the identification and verification of those who fit them, as well as systems to store and retrieve this information. Gérard Noiriel's essay examines the founding project for the establishment and supervision of such criteria of civil status, which emerged in France after the Revolution. The other essays in Part I, by Jane Caplan, Charles Steinwedel, Marc Garcelon, and Jon Agar, explore further these historical antinomies of access and denial, discussing respectively the legal stabilization of the personal name in nineteenth-century Europe; the elaboration of identification documents into a complex network of political and social controls in nineteenth- and twentieth-century Russia and the Soviet Union; and the resistance to universal civil registration and identification in twentieth-century Britain. The scope of these essays demonstrates how deeply identification practices have been rooted in different traditions of political culture—from the republican nationalism of French administrative politics, to the centralizing and disciplinary pretensions of Russian autocracy and "partocracy," to the suspicious anti-statism of British official culture.

Police practices in the same period asserted a more specialized domain of authority over criminal identification and detection, which became a crucial site for further identificatory and supervisory developments that were then reappropriated into universal systems of civil identification. Policing in the narrow modern sense of the term—the prevention and detection of offenses against the law—was extracted in early-nineteenth-century Europe as a specialized subfield from the prior absolutist concept of policing as embracing the entire arena of public welfare and safety. The bureaucratization and professionalization of police forces is one of the central themes in the history of the nineteenth-century European state, and it is also integral to the history of identification practices. Both preventive policing and detection depended on the ability to identify, recognize, and track suspects or offenders across an expanding national and eventually international terrain. Policing was thus the source of repeated efforts to rationalize and standardize practices of identification and the systems for the storage and retrieval of the expanding documentation that this generated.

The essays in Part II are thus devoted to specific innovations in police identification procedures in the nineteenth century, including the development of the Bertillon system of anthropometry and its application to France's "nomad" populations (Martine Kaluszynski), the standardization of the police warrant in Germany (Peter Becker), and the practical emergence of systems of fingerprinting in Britain and Argentina that rivaled each other and that eventually eclipsed *bertillonage* and other forms of anthropometric description (Anne Joseph and Kristin Ruggiero). However, this is not a story of technical or professional determinism, for these innovations were by no means automatically or eagerly embraced. On the contrary, as several of these essays show, police forces were often resistant to or incapable of operating new methods, revealing the extent to which bureaucratization may be the enemy rather than the partner of rationalized efficiency. Conflicts of this kind extended to the international sphere too, as the rise of different national systems of police identification confronted the growing pressure for an internationally standardized criminal *fiche* that would ease the tracking of an increasingly mobile population of offenders.

The interlacing of national and international systems of registration and documentation is further explored in the four essays in Part III, which discuss issues of identification as these relate to mobility within and across national frontiers. They cover the period from the early nineteenth cen-

policing

tury (Andrea Geselle), through the supposed heyday of international mobility in the later nineteenth century (a supposition critically assessed by Andreas Fahrmeir and Leo Lucassen), to the solidification of a passport-based system of control and exclusion during and after World War I (John Torpey). Because of their preoccupation with according special rights to their own citizens with regard to movement and access to opportunities, nationalizing states have used such documentation to establish who has the authorization to enter, remain, and move about in the territories those states claimed to rule. Documentary controls over movement were sometimes part of a finely woven mesh of policing techniques that especially afflicted the lower orders, and could be marked with special symbols and information that enhanced the surveillance capacities of states. Gradually, however, "national" spaces in Western Europe and North America, at least, were opened to relatively untrammeled free movement during the course of the nineteenth century. While generally ratifying the notion of the relative advance of such freedom during the late nineteenth century, the essays in this section force us to qualify this conclusion, noting especially the disproportionate impact of documentary controls on the lower classes. We also learn here that passports and analogous documents may be used by states not to restrict but to facilitate departures, and thus to rid governments of undesirable elements. With respect to the question of the repressive or emancipatory consequences of individual identification documents, this is a paradox: while passports issued to smooth departures may ease rather than constrain human mobility, they may do so to serve the purposes of states as much as those of the individual.

Beginning with the First World War, strong controls over mobility within a country have resumed an air of illiberality, harking back as they do to slavery, serfdom, and absolutist power. The development of a system of mutually exclusive nation-states led to the consolidation in international law of the notion that people had an unambiguous right to enter only the country of which they were citizens. As a result, definitions of citizenship became strongly connected with the establishment of a person's eligibility to cross into and remain in particular places. The international passport system that was consolidated in the aftermath of World War I bore witness to the emergence of a system of controls over international movement that took as its baseline assumption "one country to a person." While the spread of passport controls points to the tremendous growth in states' capacities to regulate movement, the use of passports as proofs of citizenship also suggests the extent to which such identification documents can support claims to belonging to one country or another. Perhaps only those who have experienced the limbo of statelessness can adequately appreciate the value of that kind of belonging.

The final five essays, gathered together in Part IV, discuss contemporary issues in identification, relating these to the increasingly pervasive and sophisticated technologies of enumeration, categorization, and surveillance developed by both state and private institutions. Pamela Sankar's essay forms a bridge between this section and the earlier parts of the book by combining historical and contemporary perspectives; Sankar situates the most recent advances in DNA-typing in the context of the history of fingerprinting and highlights the behavioral as well as identificatory claims of both systems. David Lyon takes up the related issue of new biometric technologies that fix identity in or onto the body itself, a development that appears to herald the reversal of the earlier trend from "writing on" to "reading off" the body. Gary Marx explores pressures for and against the traditions of naming and anonymity in contemporary social and political relations. The two final essays present case studies in the operations of governmental registration. Dita Vogel discusses the documentation of foreign workers in contemporary Germany, relating these procedures to issues of immigration control in Germany and the United States. Timothy Longman rounds out the collection of essays with an exploration of the ultimately catastrophic results in postcolonial Rwanda of identity documentation initially introduced during the colonial era. Despite the widely attested contribution of these documents to the mass killing of Tutsis by Hutus in 1994, Longman shows that documents cannot unambiguously shape the identities of real, flesh-and-blood persons. Categories of eligibility and disqualification, of entrée and exclusion— and the procedures and mechanisms for identifying those who fall into each—have come powerfully to determine our lives, but the apparent finality of state-sponsored social categories is spurious.

As in the development of mechanisms for regulating human movement, the documentation of individual identity has become broadly implicated in states' strategies for keeping track of their populations, rendering them available to policing practices, and categorizing them according to ethnic and other criteria. These may have perfectly legitimate uses, to the extent that making distinctions between citizens and aliens has at least the sanction of international law, and tracking the well-being of particular subgroups of populations may be necessary to ameliorate discriminatory treatment. Indeed, techniques of individual identification may be valuable in establishing the innocence of alleged criminals, as suggested by recent public discussions of the use of DNA evidence to exonerate those wrongly accused.

Yet the remarkable scientific achievement of mapping the human genome and the proliferating genetic manipulation of biological organisms has heightened fears that an impure science may be put to nefarious uses, and that ordinary people are largely powerless to limit these applications.

It is also clear from the essays in this section that new practices are not necessarily limited by the purposes to which they were intended to be put by their initiators. For example, while DNA fingerprinting may have its ultimate sources in eugenic projects of the late nineteenth century, and the identity cards introduced by colonial overlords in Rwanda may have been intended to cement certain conceptions of identity, these aims were not necessarily achieved. Official objectives may be subverted or the applications of identification techniques may be ambiguous. Under these circumstances, the use of increasingly sophisticated techniques of individual identification by states and other entities has been subjected to intensified scrutiny, especially by those concerned with civil liberties.

This is because the consequences of individual identification can be catastrophic, as when the information encoded in documents makes possible the inclusion of individuals in groups marked out for doom. To be sure, people may for various reasons have an interest in being identified (and hence "recognized"), as such identification is the touchstone of eligibility for a host of activities to which access is restricted. Yet the drift toward techniques of identification anchored in the body itself, making them less readily circumvented, sharpens anxieties about how identification may be used if it falls into the wrong hands. After observing the role of identity cards in the Rwandan genocide of the mid-1990s, no one can afford to be too sanguine about the methods used for documenting individual identity.

✦ ✦ ✦ ✦

As the topics explored in these essays indicate, the history of identity documentation is integral to an understanding of the expansion of state and police practices that have constituted the modern bureaucratic welfare and security state, and that are becoming ever more elaborate. Individual identification also forms a crucial matrix for the cultural and political self-understanding of the subject and citizen. Yet this field has barely been studied, despite its pertinence to the emergence of the forms and practices of the modern state and the fact that it represents one of the principal sources of interaction and forms of communication between citizen and state. This volume offers an initial contribution to understanding these matters and a partial, provisional response to Aristide Zolberg's call for "a history of paperwork."[19] Our hope is that it will stimulate further research across the disciplines into a subject that will only grow in significance to us all, as scholars and as citizens.

[19] Cited by Leo Lucassen, p. 252, below. Zolberg was referring to paperwork associated with state regulation of migration, but we have pursued this question across a much wider range of activities.

Part One

CREATING APPARATUSES OF IDENTIFICATION

1

Describing the Person, Reading the Signs in Late Medieval and Renaissance Europe: Identity Papers, Vested Figures, and the Limits of Identification, 1400-1600

VALENTIN GROEBNER

WE ARE APT to describe the history of the premodern as a history of loss. We find ourselves representing life in the centuries of the Late Middle Ages and the Renaissance as brutal and unstable, yet at the same time more colorful, more intense, and somehow more authentic than the world we inhabit. In this we place ourselves consciously or unconsciously in the position of heirs to the romantics and nineteenth-century social scientists who, under the impact of industrialization, mass migration, and considerable social disintegration, constructed the Middle Ages as a utopian past in which everything was more socially integrated, more local, transparent, and "genuine" than in our own allegedly decadent, "uprooted," and alienated present. The Middle Ages and the Renaissance therefore present a special kind of paradox. On the one hand, they have been (and still are) used to provide a basis for alleged national cultural heritages, providing material for fabricating and presenting "roots" and "foundations." On the other hand, they are strange and alien to us—in their archaic character, their violence, their religiosity—and this again is what makes them appear so genuine. Under somewhat different auspices, both the Middle Ages and the Renaissance seem suited for grand narratives of genesis and origin, and for histories of loss, because they are distant enough from our own times, yet also tied to us by subterranean strands labeled "tradition," "origin," and "authenticity."[1]

At the same time the centuries between 1400 and 1600 stand for what we describe, with more or less enthusiasm, as the origin of the modern state system. In the cities and territories of Italy and Central and Western Europe, the growth of administration from the fourteenth century on ex-

---

[1] Freedman and Spiegel 1998. On different national traditions in constructing the Middle Ages, see von Moos 1994 and Oexle 1992.

tended the reach of the authorities over individuals, both native subjects and foreign visitors. Individuals' names were transposed from spoken to written language—a significant and radical change—and coded into registers. Be they native citizen or mobile stranger, taxpayer or receiver of alms, soldier or delinquent, individual persons were brought more and more sucessfully into direct contact with official systems of written registration.[2] This momentous process unfolded in regionally very diverse forms and at various rates of speed. Modern historians' conceptual conventions have sought to characterize it as the development of bureaucratization, as social control or state formation: the rise of the administrative state in the Renaissance and Baroque eras, with its civil servants, its archives, and its splendid, petty-minded, and pitiless systems of notation is perhaps *the* master narrative of social history in the past few decades. And there is a third equally romantic and powerful narrative of origin and ascent that assigns to this same epoch the "genesis" of modern individuality and subjectivity.[3]

Together, these narratives constitute the somewhat paradoxical background to the research project that I want to sketch out in the following. I am concerned not with stories of origin or loss, but with the prehistory of identification—something potentially rather different, as we shall see. For the history of bureaucracy in early modern Europe is the history of practices of authentification and identification. How were people described between the fourteenth and sixteenth centuries, in a world that was familiar with neither public officials nor addresses in the modern sense? How could individuals be described in order to be reidentified by others who had never seen them before in the centuries that predated the photograph, the fingerprint, the entire apparatus of administration and representation? While official certificates of identity such as letters of introduction were the privilege of specially accredited officeholders in the fifteenth century (and were available to ordinary travelers only at great expense), new documents of origin and identity came to be demanded as a matter of course from ever expanding groups of people in the sixteenth century. By the beginning of the eighteenth century, the failure to carry such an official document while traveling was already an offense that could attract considerable penalties. The growing importance of these papers seems to have been accompanied by their increasing illegal reproduction. Imposture merchants and false diplomats were only too well-known figures for Renaissance contemporaries, as were spies and secret agents, traveling first with "fraudulent signs" and then with forged papers. The prehistory of the wanted poster and the pass provides evidence

[2] Chittolini, Molho, and Schiera 1995.
[3] For a recent overview of the vast literature, see the bibliography in Martin 1997.

of signs and a semiotic system based on concepts of appearance, person, ethnicity, and sex that appear strange and unfamiliar to us. Yet at the same time we are still linked to this medieval and Renaissance repertoire of proto-images and proto-signs, linked by a number of notions, proverbs, plotlines we ourselves use in our games of significations: Who is Who?

The False Messenger

What does it mean, literally, to "identify" someone? Having spent the past several years working on gifts recorded in municipal registers between the fourteenth and sixteenth centuries, I realized how conspicuous among the recipients of these gifts were messengers and couriers, the bringers of information from afar.[4] The term *courier—Bote* in fifteenth-century German—covered men of varying rank, from poor craftsmen who delivered letters as a job on the side to councilors traveling on official political business. On handing over their information, they would be given a gift appropriate to their rank, the occasion, and the content of the message. Thus these couriers appear in virtually every official account book north of the Alps, not least because the volume of official written correspondence took off abruptly in the second half of the fifteenth century. The chancellery of the city of Bern, for example, averaged an output of fifty letters per night during the war against the Burgundian duke Charles the Bold (1474-77), a figure that only a generation earlier would not have been reached in a month. At the end of the fifteenth century, the system of fixed ambassadors with foreign residences and a regular diplomatic correspondence emerged: an institutionalized network of communications that produced enormous quantities of paper.[5]

While collecting information about the municipal messengers and the gifts they received, I noticed something else. The city records contained regular reports of couriers who had been attacked, robbed, or abducted. But equally frequent were the references to couriers of dubious provenance, such as the man who turned up before the city council of Solothurn in 1495 claiming that King Maximilian had just taken neighboring Basel and was about to set out to attack Solothurn; in return, he received a payment of 15 schillings and a good meal. During the 1489 trial of Hans Waldmann, the dismissed mayor of Zürich (according to a chronicler at the beginning of the sixteenth century), three messengers suddenly burst

---

[4] Groebner, forthcoming. See also Groebner 2000.

[5] On the rapid increase in written communications north of the Alps in the second half of the fifteenth century, see Sieber-Lehmann 1995 and Esch 1988; also the contributions in Bély 1997.

into the proceedings with the news that the emperor had crossed the Rhine with an army and was marching on the city in order to save Wald- mann—news that should have ensured his immediate execution.[6]

How could one be sure that a messenger was genuine? Official city couriers carried special insignia (badges) on their purse and clothing, and from the 1470s the couriers of Basel, Schlettstadt, and Strassburg wore special uniforms or uniform-like items of dress in the town colors. Tunics and badges of this kind were also worn by the Zürich messengers in the story we have just told, and the chronicler Brennwald added that before they entered the courtroom they had dampened their clothing in a foun- tain, "as if they were sweating."[7] The false messenger turns up as a stock figure in the literature of the fifteenth and sixteenth centuries. When Para- celsus writes in a tract on visibility in 1504, "For what other reason does a messenger wear a badge on his coat if not because from this alone can one tell that he is an ambassador," he also raises an enigmatic question about the clarity of the insignia. Is the messenger always on the road on behalf of whomever it is whose badge he is wearing? The Swiss courier who in June 1515 brought an urgent demand for troops from the Italian theater of war to the Confederation was to discover that, a day's journey before him, another messenger with official insignia was on the road, telling all and sundry that there was no need for more troops to go to Italy, and that the soldiers should make their way home again.[8]

Describing life in premodern Europe as being governed by "face-to- face" relationships therefore possibly misses the point—given that whose face one was looking at was evidently not always clear. How could the messenger be distinguished from his illicit double? How could anyone be "recognized" at all?

Insignia and Passes

The end of the fourteenth century saw the beginnings of an unprecedented expansion not only in the exchange of information but also in the use of written documents in administration, and this trend continued and accelerated in the course of the fifteenth century. The processes of identi- fication that underpinned these practices of registration have attracted comparatively little attention until now. The legal history of naming has been the subject of two intensive investigations in the past few years, and

---

[6] Morgenthaler 1919: 189; Brennwald 1910, vol. 2: 314.

[7] Brennwald 1910, vol. 2: 315. On couriers, see Heimann 1992 and Heimann 1993.

[8] Paracelsus cited in Lauffer 1954: 45; see also Usteri 1975: 195 and Sieber-Lehmann 1995: 356.

other studies have been devoted to the individuation of the signature.[9] Nevertheless, there has been no real history of premodern practices of the verification and control of identification. Between the fourteenth and seventeenth centuries, what was seen, recorded, and described as "individual?" From the perspective of the conditions of description, "identification" falls into two fundamental categories, involving different means of access, different types of sources, and different histories. In the first case, the individual concerned is absent: by what means can others recognize him? In the second case, he is present: who is he, and is he really who he claims to be?

"Identification" has therefore to be linked to larger bodies of medieval and Renaissance medical and juridical knowledge in which concepts of gender and race played a decisive role. Medical theories of the fifteenth and sixteenth centuries attributed a special capacity for pretense, disguise, and alteration of external appearance to women, because, in the Galenic view, their bodies were of a colder and damper consistency. Women were, according to the leading medical authorities of the day, more "fluid" and cold-blooded in the literal sense of the word, and therefore more pliant in the practices of simulation and dissimulation.[10] The medical tracts' concept of "complexion," which had long denoted the harmonious proportions desirable in the mixture of the Galenic humors (the *equatio complexionis*), became in the course of the early modern period an increasingly personalized feature, until it arrived at its present meaning of an individual physical quality. It is in this sense, with a special emphasis on skin color, that the word appears today in personal descriptions and passes in the English-speaking world. There seems to be a particular tension in the relationship among skin color, individual description, and identity documents. The earliest systematic references to invalid passes concern the "passports" and safe-conduct papers of gypsies in Europe, a group described by contemporary authors as especially dark-skinned, foreign, and "non-white." The German imperial *Reichspolizeiordnung* of 1551 and a long series of orders based on it instructed the authorities to confiscate and destroy any identity papers tendered by gypsies, on the grounds that they were bound to be forgeries: people of illegitimate status evidently could not, by definition, be in possession of legitimate documents.[11]

The history of compulsory identity documents in Europe remains largely unwritten—we still know very little about the conditions of their

[9] On the stabilization of personal names, see the comprehensive studies by Lefebvre-Taillard 1990 and Seutter 1996; on signatures, see Holzhauer 1973 and Fraenkel 1992.

[10] MacLean 1980; Cadden 1993: 170ff.

[11] Gronemeyer 1987: 89. For the imperial legislation on gypsies, see Schmauss and Senckenberg 1747, vol. 2: 609–32 (1551), §§81f.; and Härter 1993.

adoption and their usage. Daniel Nordman has shown how, between the second half of the fifteenth century and the end of the sixteenth, a form of *passaport* or official *laissez-passer* gradually evolved as a recognized travel document out of the safe-conducts handed out to diplomats, couriers, and especially merchants in the High and Late Middle Ages; these were issued at first for both goods and people, but later were intended exclusively for people. The pass and the obligation to carry it emerged on the frontier, from which it then migrated inland with some speed. The German traveler Hieronimus Münzer, en route to Spain in the fifteenth century, had to equip himself with a *litterae passus* in Amiens in order not to be harassed—*molestaremur*, as he succinctly put it—by soldiers posted at the frontier. In 1462, a royal decree in France required every furloughed soldier to carry a *cédule* issued by the military authorities, which contained details about his person and the reasons for his absence from his troop.[12] Similar *passaporti*, *pass brief*, or *Bassporten* were issued to men-at-arms in Italy and north of the Alps. From the second half of the fifteenth century on, the health passport (*billette de santé* or *bolleta di sanità*) also played an increasingly important role as a compulsory personal identity document. In 1470, the traveler Anselme Adorno needed no fewer than three separate safe-conducts in order to journey from Cologne to Aachen, whereas another pilgrim, Pierre Barbate, en route to Jerusalem, needed only a single *bolleta di sanità* inscribed with his name in order to go from Turin to Venice—and, as he proudly noted, he did not even have to pay a fee for it since clerics were exempt.[13]

In these cases, insignia played a particular role. Just as couriers were made known by their official insignia and letters, so were the numerous pilgrims on the road throughout the Late Middle Ages and into the sixteenth century obliged to wear their pilgrim badges in a conspicuous place. Like other groups—journeymen or beggars, for example—they were also increasingly expected to carry a letter with them issued by their local priest or bishop, which would contain information on who they were. Similarly, diplomats carried their patents of appointment and letters of recommendation—sometimes literally "upon them," attached to their hat or coat so that they were immediately visible. The poor laws of the sixteenth century, finally, not only often sought to register the needy by name, but also prescribed the wearing of various badges and the possession of written documents that gave information about their origin and status. Similar documents were rapidly extended to other groups of the

---

[12] Bertelsmann 1914; Valloton 1923; de Hartoy 1937; Delarue 1978; Société des Nations 1938; de Craecker-Dussart 1974; Nordman 1987; and on the royal decree of 1462, ibid.: 146. See also Nordman 1988.

[13] Schaufelberger 1952: 137f.; Heers 1978; Tucco-Chala und Pinzuti 1972: 93.

population: journeymen, servants, and travelers were all required to carry papers stating who they were.[14]

How could one really be sure that the name inscribed on these papers did in fact belong to the person who was in possession of them? The swindling merchant, the fraudulent messenger, the ambassador who was also an agent, and not least the figure of the spy, who first appears as the medieval era gave way to the early modern and who went on to have a remarkable career in Europe's collective imagination—all these were familiar figures in the early modern imaginary. The authorities were never entirely able to close up the threatening gap between appearance and description, between person and paper. Practitioners of simulation and dissimulation thus play a prominent role in the late medieval and early modern travel accounts. In the early modern period, travel offered the possibility that one could in fact appear as someone other than oneself—even if not every seventeenth-century traveler went as far as Augustin Günzer, a Calvinist journeyman from Colmar, who toured Italy pretending to be a Catholic and, in the role of a pious pauper, even had his feet washed by the bishop of Bologna in a Holy Week ceremony.[15]

In this context, "passes" cannot be sharply distinguished from "badges" (*Abzeichen*), and this was not simply because we cannot assume that all border guards, customs officers, and supervisory officials could read. Passes remained very closely connected with purely graphic signs and badges: a pass was genuine (and this remains true in the present day) to the extent that the authorities recognized their own signs in or on it. The validity of any pass is a combination of two contradictory dynamics. The individual, uninterchangeable person, genuine because he is "unique," is established as such by means of seals and signs that are authorized reproductions, which are thus genuine to the extent that they are plural elements in an endless series. Thus safe-conducts in the fifteenth and sixteenth centuries were rendered "genuine" by the seals with which the authorities authenticated them.

These seals were literally reproductions: they imprinted the arms or insignia of the sovereign power, a simplified coat of arms or a letter of the alphabet. As such, they strongly resembled the rudimentary badges of lead or tin that paupers also carried at this time—emblems of neediness that authorized the bearer to buy bread at a lower price in times of dearth, or which, pinned to their clothing, functioned as a license to beg and

---

[14] Favreau-Lilie 1994; on letters of accreditation for couriers and diplomats, see Queller 1967; on beggars and journeymen, see Geremek 1980, and for the German-speaking realm, Schubert 1995.

[15] See Sieber and Heiligensetzer 1999; Wilke 1994; Maczak and Teuteberg 1982; for further bibliographic references, Halm 1994: vol. 1 and Stagl 1995.

distinguished them from foreigners who did not enjoy this privilege. And they were reproductions also in another sense. Such badges were quickly copied and duplicated by handy paupers, with such skill that at the end of the sixteenth century the authorities in Cologne and Freiburg were obliged to call in these beggars' badges once a year and stamp them with a new date and serial number, so that the number of copies could at least be somewhat controlled. In the popular morality literature on beggars during the early decades of the sixteenth century, fraudulent beggars were represented in almost superhuman terms, equipped with the most impressive technical skills—the ability to change their sex by trickery, wear artificial breasts, make false copies of certificates, and, as a version of the *Liber Vagatorum* claimed in 1528, forge every kind of seal.[16]

Portraits and Faces

So we are left once again with the question of how a person can be "identified." If the idea of identification by signs seems strange (and somewhat naive) in comparison to our modern standards, what about the more familiar practice of identifying a person by his or her own face? The triumphal march of the portrait in the representational repertoire of the late medieval and early modern period has been well documented. Portraits played an important and complex role in court and city life from the fifteenth century on.[17] But the practices of identification were much less clearly focused on the pictorial reproduction of the face than we might at first sight expect. Images of sufficient quality to fulfill the conditions of authentification were very difficult to reproduce in any quantity between 1400 and 1700. Political images of individuals in Italian cities—either as positive political propaganda or as a means of identifying enemies and criminals, through the so-called *pitture infamante*—needed to be posted on publicly visible house or church walls in order to fulfill their informational function. Problems arose when portrait images of this kind had to be transported from one place to another, or, especially, from one social context to another: this is extensively documented by contemporary debates about the fidelity of portraits in general and the reliability of marriage portraits in particular.[18]

---

[16] Fischer 1980: 235; Lassota 1993: 234; Leitherer 1954; extracts from the *Liber Vagatorum* of 1528 with a preface by Martin Luther are reprinted in Sachsse and Tennstedt 1980: 50–53.

[17] For a survey of Renaissance portraits, see Körner 1993 and Courtine and Haroche 1988.

[18] Ortalli 1979.

The debates about portraits at the threshold of the early modern era were part of a powerful contemporary interest in bodily description and investigation—one's own as well as those of other people. The person and his or her face demanded to be read, through description as well as depiction. Work on the adoration of the face of Jesus in the fifteenth and sixteenth centuries has pointed to the enormous popularity and wide distribution of the so-called letter of Publius Lentulus, which contained a description of the (ideal) face of Jesus, stuffed with supporting references and analogies to physiognomical theory. The rediscovery, or rather reappropriation, of physiognomy after the thirteenth century gave new and influential life to a host of classical texts. Sometimes this occurred in surprising contexts—the standardized juridical Greek formula from antiquity for the description of people (the *eikonismos*) pops up in the Latin and then the vernacular literature on the history of Troy in the fourteenth century.

In mirrors of princes and in the famous *relazioni* of Italian diplomats from the end of the fifteenth century we find set pieces taken from the fourth-century *Physiognomicon* (ascribed to Aristotle), which included a description of how a person's specific characteristics could be recognized from both facial expressions and unalterable distinguishing features. Although physiognomy had never been entirely absent from the canon of European political science and was widely known through the pseudo-Aristotelian *Secretum Secretorum*, it underwent a process of intensive revaluation from the end of the fifteenth century.[19] Its adoption as a system of facial description had extensive consequences for the pictorial representations of these faces themselves. As Martin Warnke has shown, Lucas Cranach, for example, modified his various portraits of Luther according to complex political and physiognomic criteria, as needed. The image of an individual, his or her appearance, cannot easily be differentiated from how he or she is supposed to appear.[20]

The striving for portrait resemblance and facial research thus did not necessarily bring stability and accuracy to depictions of the person and his characteristics. Indeed, the opposite may be the case.[21] The merchant and accountant Matthäus Schwarz from Augsburg sought to depict, in

[19] On Christ's face and the Lentulus letter, see Wolf forthcoming and Körner 1993; on the tradition of the *eikonismos* formula, Dagron 1991; Getrevi 1991; Jacquart 1994; Degwitz 1988; Illgen 1921; Wurms 1970; Pseudo-Aristotle 1982; Eamon 1994.

[20] Warnke 1993.

[21] The famous *relazioni* of Italian ambassadors carefully combined physiognomic subtexts and hints with detailed descriptions of actual faces, like the Venetian Zaccaria Contarini in 1492 on Louis XII's eyes and lips. See di Frede 1982. See also Kartschoke 1992: vol. 1. By contrast, a Venetian ambassador in Rome in 1523 claimed to see in the "Laokoon" a portrait of one of his contemporaries, Franzoni: 321–22.

his "kleider büchlin" produced between 1521 and 1560, the history of
his life and city career by means of 137 portraits that paint the history of
his changing clothes. Obviously, he did not see the external form of his
self—"my *Gestalt*," as he put it—confined to his body and his face. In
the text attached to this fascinating autobiographical enterprise Schwarz
describes a coat whose color could be changed at will—green on the outside, red on the inside, or vice versa. This coat, as he noted with pride,
had facilitated a journey he made through rebellious Tyrol during the
Peasants' War in 1525, by deceiving his pursuers and allowing him to
appear as now one person, now another. Schwarz, obsessed with portraits, active as a buyer of paintings for his employers, the Augsburg Fug-
ger family, and so proud of presenting himself as a "juggler," as he wrote,
in changing his costumes, makes it quite clear that a person was not necessarily known or recognized by his face alone.[22]

Clothing, an expensive item among anyone's personal valuables, appears in this context of observation to be a part of the person, a "distinguishing characteristic" in the literal sense of the term. The ability to recognize people by their clothing is evidently an art in itself—in the medieval
sense of *ars*, meaning not "art" but an authorized canon of data and
categorization. I mentioned at the beginning of this essay that the arts of
identification always appear as two basic constructs: one in which the
person described is absent, and a second in which a person is present but
disguised (the incognito, a powerful literary tradition), in which case he
has to be identified as who he really is by means of written signs. Late
medieval and Renaissance courts liked to surround the ruler with identi-
cally clad favorites, dressed up as doubles, and to subject visitors to the
test of whether they could distinguish the genuine one. Baldassare Castiglione describes this as an amusing but rather risky game in his widely
read *Courtier* (1527), adding a warning that it could easily go wrong. But
despite this, or even because of it, similar games of disguise—perhaps
one should call them games of identification—are described in numerous
accounts of Italian, Burgundian, and French courts.[23]

As in any good game, what was at issue here is quite serious. The body
of the Burgundian duke Charles the Bold, killed on the battlefield at
Nancy in 1477, was discovered as a naked and frozen corpse only after
four days of arduous searching. The duke was finally identified by his
Italian page, his physician, his half brother, and the chronicler Oliver de
la Marche, by means of distinctive signs on his body: missing front teeth,
a scar on his neck, a sore on his stomach, and extremely long fingernails,

---

[22] See Groebner 1999; Schwarz's autobiography has been edited by Fink 1963.
[23] On the incognito in medieval literature, see Brandt 1993: 284–87; Castiglione 1564:
bk. 1, ch. 26.

all of which were detailed in a written protocol. Charles the Bold was evidently unrecognizable because he was naked: once he had been washed in water and wine, and was clothed, the rest of his court entourage was able to recognize him.[24] Or, in another example of the game "The Prince's Clothes," the Milanese duke Ludovico Moro, besieged in Novara without hope of relief in April 1500, was turned over by his Swiss mercenaries to his French enemies. However, Ludovico was disguised by remaining loyal followers and insinuated into the ranks of the Swiss soldiers, to whom a safe passage out of the city had been guaranteed. He almost succeeded in escaping by this ruse, remaining undiscovered despite an intensive search—only to be finally betrayed by the (genuine) Swiss soldier standing next to him. Taken out of the ranks, Ludovico's jerkin and cap were removed, and his long hair fell down—and at that moment everyone was able to recognize the prince.[25]

This is not to say that nobody in Renaissance Europe knew what the sovereign looked like. But contemporary observations indicate that he was not always and invariably known by his face, in spite of the numerous circulating copies—both Charles and Ludovico commissioned relatively large numbers of portraits of their outward appearances. It may not be pure coincidence that at the end of the fifteenth century Proteus, the god of polymorphous appearances, embarked on his remarkable career in Renaissance political literature through the writings of Pico de la Mirandola. Just as the face reveals itself as a potential site of deception, so too the rest of the body may convey equally untrustworthy information about a person. In the tales in Marguerite of Navarre's *Heptameron* and in Brantôme's *Les Dames galantes* husbands, wives, and lovers are repeatedly baffled in attempts to reliably identify a partner, including in circumstances that are described as very intimate. Like their cruder counterparts in the picaresque literature of the sixteenth and seventeenth centuries, all these stories play with great effect on the themes of disguise and confusion, the alias, and shifting identities.

Personal Description as Fiction

What did the posters and lists of "wanted" individuals look like in the late medieval and early modern epoch? We know at least that they were very sparing in their description of the face and the person in general. At the same time, they have a long history. From the beginning of the thir-

---

[24] The minutes of the duke's identification are printed in the document appendix of the Lenglet de Fresnoy, ed. 1747: 493ff. I owe this reference to Claudius Sieber.

[25] See the detailed accounts of witnesses published by Gagliardi 1919, vol. 1: 409–59.

teenth century, cities began to exchange lists of wanted criminals and out-
laws, but simply as lists of names. Only in the early fourteenth century
do we begin to find additional information about the appearance of the
wanted man or woman. A person's "appearance" specifically included his
or her clothing, or rather, made clothing a part of the persona. Fifteenth-
century legal sources yield many examples of such detailed descriptions—
the gray patched coats and black hats of two alleged Hussite arsonists,
the blue stockings of a card-trickster sought in Erfurt in 1412.[26] In 1475,
the Bern council, for example, described a fraudulent winemaker wanted
on an arrest warrant as "large fat Martin Walliser, and he has on him a
silk jerkin." The citizen who denounced the inciters of an alleged peasant
uprising to the authorities in the upper Rhine in 1517 gave no details
about the conspirators' faces, heights, or ages, but described them by their
clothing. According to his account, the notorious leader of the rebels, Jos
Fritz, was to be recognized by his black French overcoat, his brick-colored
coat, and his red, fashionably slashed stockings; the only permanent physical sign was a black mole on his left hand.[27]

By his mole, we might say, we too would have recognized the famous
rebel—were it not for the fact that precisely this mole on the left hand
already appears in the *Secretum Secretorum* as the mark of the traitor.
The rubric "permanent distinguishing mark" in our own identity documents and passports evidently has a long and rather complicated history
of its own. The categories in passports and search warrants, the signs on
faces and bodies seem to reveal less about a person's identity as such than
about the conditions and practices through which it is constituted, about
the flexible "arts" by means of which unambiguous certainty is produced.

I would thus propose a kind of archaeology of identification. From the
end of the Middle Ages on, an increasingly tightly knit network of control
posts was being extended across Europe—differentiating machines that
separated the "inner" from the "outer." When we ask what the boundaries of a person are and what is seen as his or her "permanent distinguishing mark," the limits and risks of ostensibly self-evident categories become visible, categories inherent to the principles of construction of these
differentiating machines. In early modern Europe, name and face were
coupled together by loose links that needed to be continually secured and
tightened.

I began this essay with a somewhat ironic outline of the three heroic
narratives that continue to shape the modern historian's work on the centuries between 1400 and 1600: the construction of lost origins, the emer-

---

[26] Nicklis 1992.
[27] For Bern in 1475, see Haller 1902, vol. 3: 110; the denunciation of 1517 is reprinted
in Rosenkranz 1927, vol. 2: 269–71.

gence of statehood, the genesis of the individual. Irony is usually an indicator of an author's restricted choice, an only too telling sign of a move of distancing himself from something he remains tied up with. Any future history of identification and its arts in the Renaissance is closely connected to these narratives—and perhaps inevitably so, given that our own historical category of the "premodern" is itself structured according to these teleological points of departure. The study of practices of identification and their contexts, however, turns out to be itself an ambiguous commentary on these stories of "loss," "origin," and "rise." The history of the identity document and the official production of certainty is necessarily a history of identification as fiction, of deception, pretense, and ambivalence. In grappling with impostors, twins, and Doppelgängers, Renaissance jurists and doctors shaped their paradigms of what constituted the likeness of a person with itself.[28] The fictional masters of deception celebrated in picaresque literature and the tales of error broadcast with such pleasure in the storytelling literature of the fifteenth to seventeenth centuries, in which people successfully pretend to be someone else in highly intimate situations, are, like the famous case of the man who usurped Martin Guerre's place in village and marriage bed, speculations about the bases of human judgment and a stylized literary form of erotic stimulation. Yet at the same time they are expeditions of reconnaissance into contemporary realities, exercises in "Möglichkeitswissenschaft," as Robert Musil so beautifully has put it—the "science of the possible," a context in which evidence of identity does not disclose itself spontaneously, but emerges in a forcefield of limits, norms, and imprinted signs that are literally ascribed to this or that individual. For what is "individuality" but the system of checking the definitions that others apply to us?

Fixed as their character may have been, all these identity papers, wanted posters, and passes thus remained—and in a sense remain for us still today—shadowed by a wild and disturbing potential for confusion and mix-up, for the stolen name and the double. The ambiguity of the links that tied together a person's name and physical description in the Middle Ages and the Renaissance offer good reasons why we should never fully trust the bureaucratic claims of our own official registers to know us to be ourselves alone, and no one else.

---

[28] See the comments on the historicization of the phenomenon of the confidence trickster by Davis 1997.

2

The Identification of the Citizen: The Birth of Republican Civil Status in France

GÉRARD NOIRIEL

Issues in the Decree of September 20, 1792

On September 20, 1792, the legislative assembly of France adopted a decree that regulated citizens' civil status. This decision followed directly from the Constitution of September 3, 1791, which stated that "[t]he legislative authority will establish for all inhabitants, without distinction, the manner in which births, marriages, and deaths will be certified; and it will designate the public officials who will receive and maintain these files" (Tit. II, art. 7). There was evidently a logical connection between this article and those that defined the criteria (of residence, parentage, age, status, etc.) that had to be fulfilled in order to qualify as a French citizen (Tit. II, art. 2) and as a full citizen (*citoyen actif*) (Tit. III, ch. 1, section II). For these decisions to become operative, it was obviously necessary to establish in advance some means of recognizing the civil identity of an individual.

It is true that for several centuries the parish registers of births, marriages, and deaths had already been used for this purpose. However, despite all these measures, civil status under the ancien régime was undermined by the contradiction implied in its dual nature, religious and civil. The royal power exercised its control on the maintenance of the civil registers only indirectly, through the church, and this explains the gap that loomed between the principles defined in the ordinances and the manner in which they were applied. As Louis Henry has remarked, "the seventeenth- and eighteenth-century registers identify an individual by his family and Christian names; age is often indicated but the date of birth is only rarely given; place of birth is irregularly mentioned and is not always exact. Residence and occupation are unevenly recorded." He adds that the patronymic "reveals variations of form due to pronunciation and or-

This essay is a shortened version of Gérard Noiriel, "L'identification des citoyens. Naissance de l'État civil républicain," *Genèses. Sciences sociales et histoire* 13 (1993): 3–28. Translated by Jane Caplan.

thography."[1] This heterogeneity is accentuated by the fact that for most priests, civil registration was no more than an accessory to religious ritual. In the region of Alençon, for example, "priests wrote down a host of facts that constituted a kind of summary account of local history, augmented by passages relevant to national history."[2] And because of the religious character of these documents, they referred only to Catholics: Jews had no civil status and Protestants were excluded from it until 1685. It was to remedy the problems caused by these exclusions that an edict of 1787 authorized non-Catholics to affirm their civil status to the local judge or priest. Even before the Revolution, the secularization of civil status was widely considered to be crucial to the order and welfare of society.

In this perspective, it was because the municipality was the natural site for the exercise of "citizenship"[3] that it should also be the place where the individual attained his civil status. In the same way, it was appropriate to choose the official charged with this task from among the elected municipal representatives because these men constituted the "permanent popular magistracy" in whom the citizens had placed their confidence.

In the course of the 1792 debate, several speakers demanded that the civic dimension of the project should be affirmed even more emphatically by the new law. For deputy Gohier, "slaves have no civil status. Only the free man has a city, a fatherland; only he is born, lives and dies a citizen. All the documents relevant to his birth, his marriage and his death should therefore declare this great character." To break with the "juridical formalism" reminiscent of the ancien régime, he argued, it was necessary to create "truly civic forms. . . . In all the communes of the realm a monument [should be raised], simple but worthy of the respect of all friends of liberty, . . . an altar to the fatherland in the form of a stone on which was engraved the Declaration of the Rights of Man. Before this altar . . . would take place all announcements and public acts relating to citizens' civil and political status."[4] This substitution of a civil for a religious ritual was intended to demonstrate that the individual, in declaring his civil

---

[1] Henry 1972. Research in demographic history provides rich material on the characteristics of civil status in the past, but the variations in the data of identification are usually seen as a "defect" and not as an object of research in themselves. This is the effect of a quantitative approach, which demands the homogenization of the data being entered into the computer.

[2] Bazille 1909.

[3] I place this term in inverted commas to indicate that contemporaries hardly ever used the word in this period (the same was true of "nationality," which is a nineteenth-century term). On the theoretical issues inherent in the use of terms unknown to actors at the time, see Koselleck 1990, esp. ch. 1: "Histoire des concepts et histoire sociale."

[4] A.P., vol. 45, June 19, 1792, 388–89. His proposal was sent on to the Committee of Public Instruction for further discussion.

status to the municipal official, became a member of the civil community, just as baptism marked entry into the community of Christians. Thus the proposed legislation provided for the newborn infant to be "presented" by his parents to the civic church represented by the "communal home."

These were the principles on which the question of individual identification in its proper sense was approached. To be sure, the decree took over most of the existing provisions aimed at preventing fraud and imposed heavy penalties on forgers; but most believed that it was above all the new civic ritual that would ensure the identification of citizens. For Gohier, if an altar in each commune was to be constructed, this was also because "it is essential to prevent the frauds which are usually the consequence of illegal opinions."[5] The declaration of civil status would serve as a "solemn and public act to ward off the threat of illegality," affirmed Muraire. Here the term *act* is tantamount to a synonym for *action* rather than *written document*, and the word *public* evokes a group of citizen-spectators who if necessary could bear witness to the validity of the act. In this perspective, it was only possible to identify people effectively by reducing the distance between the act as event and the act as document. This is why the argument for proximity was the leitmotiv of those who were insisting that civil status be transferred to the municipalities. If a person was known to the whole world, if the distance that had to be covered to make his declaration in person were minimized, how could his identity be dissembled?[6]

A number of deputies were highly critical of this project, however, on the grounds that the elected rural authorities were incompetent. This position was advanced most clearly by François de Neufchateau in his speech on March 17: "I ask you whether there are not entire departments in which the officials of the rural municipalities—so respected and worthy of the public's confidence as they are—are not even able to write. Those who have learned to form their letters have so little experience in writing that for the most part they are embarrassed to pen a simple missive; their ideas about this kind of work are so limited that they must fear to have misunderstood the rules that prescribe their duties; on the other hand, their own daily occupations leave them so little free time and their munici-

---

[5] A.P., vol. 45, June 26, 1792, 595.

[6] The decree gave parents twenty-four hours to declare the birth of a child, since it was assumed that "the proof was damaged [*dépérit*]" thereafter. There are many other examples of the role played by the "face-to-face" encounter in the definition of identity. Ministerial directives frequently instructed the prefects that decrees were to be "published and posted to the sound of a drumbeat." In July 1791, Andrieu opposed a major project for a population census on the grounds that "You know that in a town without a large population, no stranger could turn up without the whole town knowing it;" A.P., vol. 28, July 22, 1791, 200.

pal duties take up so much of it for other purposes that they perform most of their functions late or not at all, and always badly." The deputy added that the priests, despite repeated royal ordinances, despite their supervision by the bishops and public prosecutors, and despite the fact that they had studied and had been given appropriate specimens, "are unable to understand the purpose of these files or to complete them with accuracy."[7] These critics too appealed to the national interest as legitimation, privileging not a commitment to the virtues of civic registration but rather the idea that a society could not function unless its administrative tasks were correctly performed. For this reason, opponents argued that the documentation of civil status should be assigned to justices of the peace, notaries, and even to the teachers whose appointment was being planned. But the partisans of the project overturned all these suggestions, partly because they believed that they would deform the civic character of the registers, and partly because they undervalued "the maturity of the populace." To aid elected rural officials in the performance of their duties, it was planned to "send them simple instructions and clear specimens," such that these registrars of civil status "would have to do no more than set their signatures."

The troubles experienced in the country during the summer of 1792 (the flight of refractory clergy, which threw civil status into confusion; the insurrection of August 10, which marked the political emergence of the sans-culottes; the invasion by foreign troops) encouraged the deputies in the legislative assembly to accelerate their deliberations so that the law would be voted on before their recess; and both vote and recess took place on September 20.

The Construction of the Civil Order and Its Problems

1. A Profusion of Forgeries

In 1820, the Ministry of Justice ordered the public prosecutors to initiate inquiries into the state of the registers of civil status and submit written reports. These documents offer an excellent vantage-point for observing how the law of 1792 had been put into practice in its first thirty years.[8] Reading the reports, one is struck by the range of difficulties still entailed in applying the law. There was nowhere that the registers were being cor-

---

[7] A.P., vol. 40, March 17, 1792, 68–72.

[8] AN, BB1 212. The Civil Code repeated most of the provisions of this law, apart from two essential points. First, only the mayor (who was no longer elected, but designated by the prefect) or his assistant could certify civil status; second, the duplicate of the registers was now kept at the lower court and was no longer at the prefecture.

rectly maintained. The few statistics provided by the prosecutors are elo-
quent. In the district (*arrondissement*) of Bellay, for example, of 111 communes, only six had registers that conformed to the law; in the district of
Lyon, the proportion was nine out of 125. These lamentations only
echoed the numerous criticisms voiced by prefects on the subject since the
beginning of the century.[9] The infractions they describe can be grouped
into three general categories.

First, errors due to the incompetence of those in charge of the registers
were by far the most numerous, and affected the form of the files in particular. Prosecutors and prefects underlined the extremely frequent cases of
deletions, additions, or notations not authorized by the registrar. Similarly, they reported numerous registers that had not been concluded or
closed at the end of the year. The names of married persons were sometimes spelled differently in the published files recording marriage banns
and in the civil registers. Numerous registrations lacked the parties' signatures, and in some cases even the signature of the official himself was
missing. Many files were incomplete: in some cases, they lacked the time
at which the entry was made, in others information about the registrants
or the supporting documentation (birth certificate or consent of parents
for underage marriages) was missing. And then there were the practices
that the law forbade: in many places, for example, minors and in particular women were admitted as witnesses; in certain entries recording an
illegitimate birth the name of "the alleged father" is given, despite the fact
that the Civil Code expressly banned research into paternity in order to
maintain "family harmony."

Second, numerous files illustrated another type of offense—"arrangements" that obliged the parties. Registrars employed various methods to
give an appearance of legality to actions that were not in strict conformity
with the law, in particular with respect to the authentic date of an entry.
The public prosecutor in Amiens denounced "a very serious abuse which
the controllers cannot remedy. This is the practice of antedating an entry.
Circumstances arise far too often which lead to the insertion of an entry
at a date other than the correct one." Several clues allowed magistrates
to identify this kind of "fraud." There were frequent cases in which all
the entries in a register were signed by the same witness, a sure indication
that they had been docketed after the fact. Other registers were reported
to have "signatures placed in the middle of an entry, proving that the civil-
status officer had had them placed there before the entry was made." In
the district of Libourne, some mayors had made entries in a single register

---

[9] The present study is based on the analysis of several dozen boxes of files concerning
civil status held at the AN, especially AN F1a 50; F2 I 124–128; F2 I 379–428; F6 I 20; F19
11012; F20 105; F80 442; BB1 212; BB30 1164–1175; BB30 1606–1613.

alone, postponing the completion of a duplicate until a later date. If mayors or witnesses happened to disappear in the interim, their successors forged either false signatures or new registers with different names.

This example brings us to the third type of infraction, less frequent than the others but more serious: deliberate forgeries. The destruction of registers can be included in this category. In some departments the sites in which they were deposited were burned down (especially in Ariège, Vendée). In Corsica, thirty years after the law had been promulgated it was still not being applied by some mayors. According to the prefect, registers "were lacking in almost two-thirds of communes." An Interior Ministry circular of 1807 indicated that in many places "parents of newborns . . . neglect to declare the birth to the civil-status officer. Comparing the civil-status registers with the baptismal registers maintained by serving priests, we found a difference of more than a half in favor of the latter. In the same departments, declarations of deaths are made no more or less accurately than of births."[10] Official files were themselves sometimes falsified. In a report dating from Year XIII (1805), the chancellery wrote that in several French departments cases had been found where "boys' names [had been] changed into girls' . . . dates of birth and marriage falsified," and even marriages celebrated "between boys disguised by dress and by name." The prefect of Lozère estimated that in the 192 communes in his department, 96,000 individuals were affected. In the Ardèche, more than 1,500 entries had been falsified; thus some men found themselves married to women they had never seen, others to their aunts, and others to women of eighty or ninety.[11]

2. The Heterogeneity of French Society

All our sources show that for these thirty years it was the gulf between town and country that represented the first and major obstacle to the law's effective operation.[12] At the beginning of the 1820s, all the prosecutors-general met to agree with their colleague d'Agen that "in the towns, the registers are generally well maintained" and that it was above all "in the rural communes that omissions and contraventions of the law [are to be found]."[13] The optimistic and flattering discourse of "the people" that had animated the 1792 debate gave way in subsequent decades to incessant complaints denouncing the incompetence of rural mayors. Illiteracy

[10] AN F1a 50.
[11] On all this, see AN F2 I 380 and F2 I 382.
[12] On the scale of this gulf in the nineteenth century, see Weber 1976.
[13] These examples are taken from AN F2 I 379, F2 I 381, and BB1 212.

was a major bone of contention. "In almost all the rural communes," wrote the prosecutor-general in Caen in 1820, "the mayors and their assistants are small peasant proprietors, farmers or artisans who are unable to sign their name, do not know how to write, or can only write illegibly and with such mis-spellings that it is impossible to read their writing." In Mayenne, it was a similar story: the registers were declared to be "illegible and swarming with gross spelling and language errors." In the rural world, the legal formalities that the mayors were supposed to observe in order to conform to the law were far removed from their daily preoccupations. The prosecutor in Grenoble explained the unreliability of civil status by the fact that "most of these mayors, especially in the mountains, are men whose time is taken up by providing for their families"; this was why "a country mayor abandons his plough only reluctantly to take up these files." In Caen, similarly, the peasant mayors "are frequently absent visiting fairs and markets and working outside their commune; the maintenance of the files is put off until whenever the mayor or his assistant have returned, and then is simply neglected."

Elected officials in country areas had great difficulty in understanding the abstract principles that underlay bureaucratic logic, and this might make them follow recommendations to the letter. In the canton of the Aisne, there were complaints that the law did not specify the time at which civil status could be registered. They wished to know if they could do this "during the night," and if so "at what hour of the evening the night is considered to begin." A representative of the people of the town of Girod (in the Ain) wanted to know if he could celebrate a marriage involving a deaf and dumb woman, given that the law specified that the two parties had to declare their consent "out loud." The prefect of the Côtes du Nord, noting that the registers kept by the mayor of a small commune were never signed, wrote: "I am fully persuaded that this official believed that writing his name in the certification was equivalent to signing it." In another place, a mayor noted on a birth certificate that "the child's sex is legitimate." Sometimes it was the desire to do the job well that, paradoxically, led mayors to commit irregularities. In the Haut Rhin, mayors were "afraid of omitting some essential formality and when they were not used to their duties they received the information on scraps of paper and entered them or had them entered in the registers after the fact and without the parties being present." For this reason, "witnesses' names are often scratched out and replaced by the names of common witnesses who signed all the entries at the end of the year, including those which they had not personally witnessed."

Under these circumstances, the printed specimens and forms of words that were intended to resolve all problems did not have much effect. For one thing, they were not available everywhere but were distributed very unevenly, as a result of the repeated upheavals that disturbed the functioning of the administration: in Calvados in 1820, for example, mayors were still using printed forms that dated from 1792.[14] Moreover, the realities of everyday life produced a multitude of cases that the legislator had not initially foreseen and that complicated the mayors' work more and more. Thus twenty-two specimen procedures were transmitted to each municipality in Year XI to take account of the principal regulations of the Civil Code concerning illegitimate children, different means of recognition, and so on. Learning its lesson from previous failures, the Napoleonic administration insisted vehemently that mayors should not follow the model procedures down to the last letter.

A second type of difference that revealed the difficulties of establishing civil status was religious in origin. The transfer of parish registers to the civil power provoked lively resistance among the clergy in some places.[15] From Year V, an official report on the Ardèche emphasized that "defrocked priests have taken up their previous parishes again. There they perform their old functions: they baptize, marry and inter, they keep all the registers and give the people to understand that they do not need to address themselves to public officials." In numerous departments the influence of priests was identified as one of the principal reasons for the failure to declare civil status, but the Concordat of 1802 allowed a progressive reconciliation to develop between the civil and religious authorities, to such an extent that many priests became in effect the auxiliaries of the mayors, writing up entries that the latter then only had to sign.[16] More than the clergy themselves, it was religious tradition, still strongly rooted in the countryside, that constituted the most important obstacle. Peasants often did not declare a birth at the mayor's office because they believed that "the registers of baptisms maintained by clerics were adequate to attest to this." Elsewhere, families were observed to follow "the practice adopted in the church of admitting godmothers to baptisms and hence they [accepted] women as witnesses on birth certificates." Nevertheless, it is very important to emphasize that the legacy bequeathed by the Catholic Church was also a factor favorable to the acceptance of civil

[14] After the adoption of the decree of September 1792, specimen forms were sent to all municipalities. New versions were distributed in Year VIII, and again in Year XII to take account of revisions to the Civil Code.

[15] If the secularization of civil status had become urgent by 1792, this was because from 1791 defrocked priests were forbidding their parishioners to participate in the religious ceremonies held by the constitutional clergy. Many citizens thus found themselves without a civil status. On this question, see Sagnac 1898.

[16] In 1816, a draft law proposed to return civil status to the priesthood, and in the following years numerous petitions and resolutions of the departmental councils tended in the same direction. The Revolution of 1830 marked the end of these attempts.

status. It was thanks to the registers kept by the priests before the Revolution that the civil authorities were able to establish the status of persons born before 1792, and the republican legislation did no more than legalize a conception of the individual and the family that had been elaborated by the Church since the Middle Ages.

The issue was a good deal more complicated for citizens who were not Catholic. For Protestants born before 1792, the civil authorities in most cases had no registers of civil status. It was for this reason, according to the prefects, that in spite of the law most of them continued to escape any form of official registration. But the main problem presented itself in the case of Jews. In order for them to actually exercise the rights of citizenship that the Republic had recognized, they too had to possess a civil status. This was why the law of 1792 affected them as it did all citizens. But this legal formula was first and foremost an act of naming, by virtue of which the state assigned to each person a fixed and individual identity. The law of 11 Germinal, Year XI had imposed fixity of names on all citizens.[17] However, at the end of the eighteenth century a portion of the Jewish population, especially in the eastern regions of France, did not practice the patronymic system common among Christians.[18] By a decree of July 20, 1808, the public authorities aimed to force Jews born before 1792 to declare their civil identity in order that they should not escape the obligations (notably military obligations) that citizenship now entailed. For this reason, the decree not only prescribed the adoption of a fixed forename and surname by those who had not previously had these, but also required all Jews to declare their civil status to the mayor of their commune, so that he could inscribe them in a special register. The decree fixed a term of three months for this formality to be accomplished, on pain of expulsion. The fact that a special register of the Jewish population was initiated (since in theory the existing registers could have been used) shows clearly that this decree belongs among the discriminatory measures adopted at this time by Napoleon, in a context strongly marked by antisemitism, especially in Alsace-Lorraine. But at the same time this decision also constituted a decisive stage in the process of the integration of Jews into the national community, since, thanks to these registers, they could now participate fully in civil life.

[17] This law determined the list of authorized forenames and regulated the procedure for changes of patronym. From June 17, 1790, noble names were suppressed, and on Fructidor 6, Year II, the Convention forbade all individuals to use any name other than that recorded on their birth certificate; on all this, see Lefebvre-Taillard 1990.

[18] Of 40,000 Jews then living in France, an estimated 20,000 to 25,000 were living in Alsace-Lorraine. The rest, especially the "Portuguese" and "Provençal" Jews, had long since adopted the custom of fixed surnames and forenames. The fundamental study of the situation of the Jews at the beginning of the nineteenth century remains Anchel 1928.

Despite the intermediary work of the consistory authorities, who were charged with applying the law in the Jewish community, the establishment of civil status gave rise to numerous misunderstandings and provoked strong opposition. Thousands of individuals were confronted with a brutal logic of naming and identification that bore no relation to their own traditions. Among the popular classes of Alsace-Lorraine, some were illiterate and many spoke only a dialect. A study of the establishment of the register in Lunéville has shown that the Jews went to the mayoral office in groups of family members or trade workplace, the workers filing in behind their employers. On discovering their new name, many, especially the women, were unable to spell it or to sign it. Robert Anchel suggests that in Alsace the adoption of French usage was for many years no more than a concession to official demands, while in their daily lives and relationships the Jews preserved their traditional names.[19] The archives show that a not inconsiderable number of them regularized their situation only belatedly. This is further proof that at the beginning of the nineteenth century, the state reached all the individuals affected by its decisions only with difficulty. To justify their delay in responding, some people explained that they had been out of the country, on a trip, or in the army (many had been mobilized for the Spanish front). Others said they had still been children in 1808 and that no one had thought to make a declaration on their behalf; this was often the case with orphans. One young woman explained that she had been placed with a Catholic family and hence had "no further relation with her coreligionists." "Not being able to read or write," she knew nothing. Requests for regularizing of names were usually made at the time of marriage, it was noted, which is indicative of these people's minimal contact with civil life.[20]

A third important division revealed by the establishment of civil status was the regional structure. In general, the farther removed from the Parisian center, the more difficult the situation was. Language was the most serious problem. As the prosecutor in Metz pointed out in 1821, "the cantons in the Moselle department where the usual language is German are . . . those where the registers present the most numerous problems." His colleague in Colmar added that the numerous errors found in the compiling of the registers "must evidently be attributed solely to the fact

[19] Ibid., 433–61.

[20] These observations are especially relevant to the popular classes. In the better-off classes, changes of name were motivated mainly by the desire for gallicization or for differentiation from homonyms. Olry Hayem Worms (a banker and assistant to the mayor of the Vth arrondissement in Paris) asked to call himself Olry Romilly Worms in order not to be confused with numerous others who had the same occupation as his and were also called Worms, which was harming his business; cf. AN F19 11012.

that most mayors have little experience of writing the French language."[21]
The same problem repeated itself in the Pyrenees. If rural mayors were
unable to understand instructions, this was because "some of them do
not understand French. The registers in a commune in the district of Ba-
gnères were found to be written half in patois and half in French." And
the prosecutor referred to a recent assize court case in which "mayors
of the Basque region summoned as witnesses were unable to read their
depositions and . . . did not understand them: the documents had to be
translated into the Basque tongue so that they could be written down in
French and properly signed." In isolated regions, the establishment of
civil status came up against the power of local traditions. In Corsica, reports drawn up in 1820 by both the prefect and the prosecutor-general
reflected a state of total anarchy, attributed to "the partisan spirit which
divides most families." Thirty years after the law of 1792, not a single
commune possessed a regular and complete set of files on civil status. This
forced the public authorities to accept a whole series of claims based on
common knowledge, which rested solely on individuals' verbal statements. "There is a complete lack of reliable data, and fraud flourishes
with impunity in relation to an Administration which has no alternative
but to base its operations on these files."

3. Evasion of Conscription

To conclude this section, we shall look at the explanations for the extent
of the deliberate falsifications found in the recording of civil status
throughout this period. We have already pointed out that in the countryside many people saw no advantage in declaring their civil status. If they
did not see what rights were attached to civil status, citizens quickly understood, by contrast, the obligations that flowed from integration into
civil life. In fact, up to the Restoration, it was the problem of conscription
that constituted the central obstacle to the establishment of civil status.
The need to identify precisely all conscripts is an obsession that recurs
constantly in the official inquiries and reports. And it was in order to
escape this that a considerable number of male citizens committed fraudulent acts.

In 1820, the prefect of Corsica reported that of 1,699 young men involved in the military lottery, he counted 687 whose date of birth was not
registered. This explains the numerous "common-knowledge" depositions (actes de notoriété) that served in fact to "prove that someone had

---

[21] He added that in a large number of cases "an interpretation in the German language
[had to be] given to the parties," but that few mayors pointed this out.

passed the age [of military service] or not yet reached it." In the Ardèche, the government commissar with the Criminal Tribunal observed in his report of 26 Germinal, Year IX, that "a multitude of young people who do not want to serve in the army for dislike of it or for other reasons sought pretended marriages as a way of avoiding the military or labor conscription that threatened them." In 1807, in the same department, abuses of common-knowledge depositions were reported "in which deponents at will reduced or increased the age of birth of whoever was seeking this means of establishing his civil status." The southern part of the Hautes Alpes was reported to be "infested by false claims of marriage." Some erstwhile public officials, "in order to shield young people from conscription into the army or into labor, married them without formalities, often to persons they did not know," and let the duplicate records go missing.[22] Prefects also often reported failures to register deaths "because of declarations made to the authorities in relation to the financial rights of inheritance, which their heirs or beneficiaries hoped to evade by not registering the death of their deceased relations at the mayor's office."

Elements for a Social History of Identification

1. "Working from a Distance"

To understand the reason for all these difficulties, one must bear in mind the scale of the rupture represented by the decree of 1792. In order for the new republican citizenship to become effective, totally uniform procedures of individual identification had to be put in place throughout the entire country. The legislation on civil status had to reach every single individual in the territory of France, and to persuade each person to present himself at a new place, the mayoral office, to go through a formal procedure that was now utterly divorced from religious ritual. Given the logic inherent in the idea of municipal representation, the application of the law also depended on the collaboration of almost forty thousand civil-status officers who were for the most part scattered throughout the countryside. Max Weber emphasized the fact that "along with fiscal considerations, bureaucratic administration depends on conditions directly connected with the technology of communications. Its precision requires the railroad, the telegram, and the telephone, and it is inextricably linked to these."[23] But at the beginning of the nineteenth century this "communi-

---

[22] AN F2 I 382. The official investigations also uncovered the fact that Protestants used the excuse of the non-existence of registers before 1792 to protect young men from conscription.

[23] Weber 1971: 1, 230.

cational infrastructure" did not yet exist. Before the era of telephone and radio, writing was the only means of communication between one place and another. However, a considerable proportion of ordinary people had not yet mastered the elementary rules of written communication, and this, as we have seen, represented a major obstacle to the execution of the law in rural areas. In the same way, transport difficulties recur as a common theme in the prefectorial reports.

With the administrative disorganization resulting from the problems of the Revolution, printed materials, specimen forms, and instructions were often lacking, or were defective. "The paper provided up till now is in general of the very worst quality, gray in color, rough and heavy-grained," wrote the prefect of the Côte d'or in 1812, adding that "when one uses it, it will not take the impressions of the pen."

Currency was another essential means at the disposal of the state to "work from a distance." But here too the means were cruelly lacking at the start of the nineteenth century. The Treasury invariably had to deliver on credit the stamped paper needed for making up the registers. Repeated circulars were issued in a vain attempt to require the communes to pay their debts. Sometimes it was a lack of stamped paper that forced mayors to contravene the law by making their entries on unstamped paper. Corrections of civil status made by justices of the peace and the copies of decennial tables drawn up by clerks were often interrupted and always in arrears, because the administrative services were unable to face up to the costs.

Yet despite everything, the administrative system established itself under the empire little by little. At the end of the empire the management of civil status was, at least in some places, beginning to become routine.

2. Creating a Disciplined Administrative Personnel

The second major problem the government faced in putting into effect the legislation on civil status related to the fact that the corps of municipal officers charged with its application was not reliable. The report on falsifications of registers in the Ardèche cited above estimated that "perhaps 20,000 functionaries, public officials and citizens are at fault." Another inquiry stated that "the Administration does not dare to pay special attention to researching these offenses in order to bring them to court, because such research would compromise a very large number of individuals and would encumber the prisons with citizens and ex-municipal officers." Suppression was regarded as impossible because the functioning of the state would be jeopardized if such a large number of public servants were implicated. For this reason the investigations concluded that although it was necessary to rectify fraudulent acts, this should be done without reprimands and by adopting a method of "silence or forgetting." It was indeed the state's legitimacy that was at stake in these matters, since, in numerous places, the interests of the "local homeland" were coterminous with those of the national.

This situation was undoubtedly most serious in Corsica in the years following the fall of Napoleon. "I cannot explain," wrote the prefect in 1820, "the open effrontery with which people argue their case to the Council, in the conviction that the kind of case at issue is more honorable than criminal, because it involves a service to family or friends and deserves public acclaim."[24] The confidence and sense of proximity that the revolutionaries of 1792 hoped to inspire between the people and their elected representatives thus became a major obstacle to the construction of civil relations. In the Ardèche, not only were many mayors complicitous with frauds, but the judiciary itself was contaminated. The commissioner appointed to end these abuses in the region wrote that "there is an independent authority over which I have no power: the jurors. Some of those who are on the list of jurors have committed civil-status offenses to protect their son, nephew or other relation or their friend from conscription." As for those who were not party to frauds, they "listen to the voice of the public," and "believe that there is no need to punish an offense that has become so common." This social proximity also explains why a large number of mayors in the Ardèche felt "a well-founded fear of attracting the vengeance of a people who are the most quick-tempered and vindictive in the whole of France." And all this was aggravated by the fact that, without connections, the forgers were protected from arrest: "a penalty of two months' detention [did] not frighten them" because they lived in "almost inaccessible mountains [which] allow[ed] them to easily evade capture." Moreover, the central authorities were in no position to clamp down effectively on mayors who were still not really paid by the state. In Mayenne, the prefect opined that if "the authorities complain . . . against voluntary officials, an offer of resignation would soon be made." At Bordeaux, an excessively zealous prosecutor who had imposed sanctions on several mayors who had sent in their registers belatedly was entirely counterproductive since they all resigned. "As each of them was more or less the only person in the commune capable of carrying out the municipal duties for better or worse, the administration would find itself disorganized unless it took a philosophical attitude."

Learning the lesson from these difficulties, the Civil Code (1804) broke decisively with the logic that had prevailed in 1792, by defining the regis-

[24] AN F2 I 379.

tration of civil status not as a civic act but as a purely administrative formality. Only the mayors and their assistants were to be considered as civil-status officers and henceforth these were to be nominated by the central authorities rather than elected by the people. As well, the Civil Code transferred some of the prefect's competences to the judge, so that, as we have already seen, the duplicates of the registers were now deposited not at the prefecture but at the lower courts. The public prosecutor was now responsible for numbering and initialing the new registers, and also for henceforward authenticating the officer's signature. This transfer of authority was aimed primarily at the citizens.[25] Learning the lesson of the prefect's impotence vis-à-vis frauds, the drafters of the Civil Code abandoned the penalties for non-declaration imposed by the 1792 law, but imposed an obligation on individuals to petition the judge for any retrospective declaration later than the legally permissible three days. The new place given to the judge was intended above all to reinforce the control exercised over the mayors, who from now on were simultaneously dependent on the prefect and the prosecutor.

Other measures tended to the same end, especially the importance attached to the problem of signing official documents. While the mayors could delegate to their employees the power to receive and enter declarations, they were frequently reminded that "they alone must sign in person all the registers of entries that they submit." The increased use of printed materials and specimen forms, despite all the imperfections noted above, is also evidence of the efforts made by the central authorities to further integrate the lower levels of the administration. It was as if they hoped, by means of specimens written on paper, to "hold the hand" of the municipal officials from a distance. "In this way," wrote the public prosecutor in Dijon, "one ensures a more faithful execution of the prescribed formalities, because the printed form that the public official has to fill out in his writing reminds him by its very context of the conditions whose achievement is expressed in it. On the other hand, because the registration necessarily has to fit the space allowed on the form, the handwriting becomes less unclear, more legible and corrections can be made easily in the prescribed fashion."

All these arrangements, whether they were legal or administrative, were thus aimed at creating a corps of officials who would be neutral, objective, and in short detached from the surrounding society. But this act of administrative surgery demanded mayors who were provided with adequate tools. Hence the considerable efforts made by the drafters of the Civil

---

[25] This interference by the judiciary in questions of civil status provoked numerous conflicts between mayors and prosecutors, but also between the latter and the prefects, who were reluctant to see their prerogatives diminished; see, for example, AN F2 I 165.

legal v. medical discourses

Code to emancipate it, as a prefect wrote, from "equivocal and dangerous proofs such as testimonial proof, whose unreliability has always terrified the legislator." Article 1317 of the Code defined an "authentic act of registration" as "that which has been received by the public official who has the right to process it in the place in which the registration was made and with the required formalities."[26] In a parallel fashion, the Penal Code, breaking with the contours of earlier legislation, devoted an entire section to the question of fraud. A special procedure was created to deal with "written fraud." "Verbal fraud," a major preoccupation of earlier law, was henceforth relegated to another section of the Code, which covered "false witness." All these innovations are a perfect illustration of the place assigned to writing and administration in the processes of identification, even if the Code's provisions also showed that confidence continued to be placed in the visual as a means of confirming individual identity. Thus children still had to be presented to the mayor so that he could confirm their existence by his own eyes, and the presence of witnesses was regarded as essential for all acts of registration.[27]

In the following decades, the legal definition of true and false began to come in conflict with the other discourse whose authority was accepted in these matters, that of medicine. In 1829, the physician and statistician Louis-Réné Villermé submitted to the Interior Ministry a study of the higher infant mortality rate during the winter months, which he attributed to the custom of presenting newborns at the mayor's office.[28] Under the July Monarchy, physicians mobilized themselves against this practice. They reproached mayors for having interpreted the law too literally, given that they mostly did not verify the sex of the infant and were incapable of saying whether they were one, three, or eight days old. In addition, according to the physicians, the municipal officials were unable to determine the sex of a child in doubtful cases, for example, in the case of a hermaphrodite. Dr. Loir, the leading light of this modernizing trend, concluded his study of the subject by observing that "questions of identity, of substitution, are of the highest importance; they require guarantees that the current process of the registration of civil status cannot give."[29] If the public authorities remained deaf to the medical arguments for so long (the polemic lasted more than twenty years),[30] this was because they

[26] Bonnier 1888: 399, 462.

[27] As the bureaucratic techniques of identification improved, reliance on "material" witnesses for births was increasingly criticized as absurd, and was abandoned in 1924; see Lévy 1919.

[28] AN F2 I 380.

[29] Loir 1846.

[30] The presentation of newborns was abandoned under the Second Empire. From then on, births were certified by a declaration from the family doctor or from medical controllers

refused to allow the civil identification of individuals to be made dependent on an expert, even if he was a doctor. The Ministry of Justice believed that "to authorize a physician or any other mayoral delegate to record births would be to profoundly alter the rules that regulate civil status and to deprive it of a large part of its effectiveness." It was best to leave "civil status as an exclusive competence of the public officials to whom the law has wisely entrusted the maintenance of these records and the authentic investigation of the facts they contain." Physicians had no competence to determine "authenticity" because they had no connection with public functions.[31]

The law did not require mayors to declare the truth of an individual's "real" or "natural" identity (litigation on this point was referred to the judicial authorities); it was interested only in the registration of an individual's statement. It was not by chance that the Civil Code prescribed that the sex of an infant should be "stated" and not "verified," as the decree of 1792 had stipulated. In the preliminary discussions of the Code, the tribune Siméon invoked the abuses committed by the civil-status officers during the Revolution: "we saw them suspect the legitimacy that had been certified to them, deny or revoke as dubious marriages from which they were told that a child had been born, demanding proofs and treating as an inquisition simple functions that were limited to the acceptance of declarations." It was thus explicitly to protect individuals against arbitrary treatment and to ensure "family harmony" that the Civil Code defined civil identification as the certification of a statement and not research into the truth of an individual's identity.[32] Throughout the nineteenth century, physicians continued to try and challenge this liberal logic.[33] In relation to hermaphrodites, the chancellery suggested in 1816 that "it is up to the individuals concerned or to their parents to choose the sex that seems appropriate to them." At the end of the century, one of the founders of legal medicine, Alexandre Lacassagne, demanded the reverse of this—a reform of Article 57 of the Civil Code to impose a medical examination at puberty "that will determine the sex and inscribe a person as man, woman, or neuter in the registers of civil status."[34]

Herculine Barbin

---

appointed in large cities to identify newborns in their parents' home. In the twentieth century, obstetricians or midwives took on this task.

[31] Not being detached from the social body (unlike public servants), physicians might contribute to falsifications of civil status in order to oblige the families on whom their livelihood depended.

[32] See Locré 1805–8: 15. This also explains why all research into paternity was forbidden. On the general philosophy of the Civil Code, see Ewald 1989.

[33] The principles of the Civil Code in relation to civil status remain in existence to the present day, however; see Carbonnier 1955, vol. 1: 223–40.

[34] Lacassagne 1887: 91.

demanding rm for medical authority

3. The Issue of Forms

All the factors discussed above converged to make the written document a site and issue of decisive significance in the procedures of identification. The clash of opposing interests engaged in the specification of civil status affected the formal structure of the documents themselves. To get the legitimacy of their role recognized, the medical experts demanded that room be made in the documents for new kinds of information.[35] The conflicts between prefects and prosecutors turned on the question of who had the power to affix to the registers the official marks (signature, stamp) that conferred legality on them. But it was above all the constant struggle between forgers and protectors of "authenticity" that explains the endless labor devoted to forms.[36] As we have seen, techniques aimed at preventing forgery had basically been invented by the ancien régime; in the nineteenth and twentieth centuries it was simply a matter of perfecting them. Civil-status officers were required to follow more and more meticulous instructions. These concerned writing (from 1824, the impression of the stamp could not be covered by either writing or any alteration; nothing was to be written on the verso of the stamp; etc.), and page layout (no blank spaces were to be left between text and signature or at the bottom of the page, copies were to be separated from one another and signed individually not en masse; and so on.)[37] To identify all those involved in drawing up a document, all writing had to be perfectly legible. Thus "documents of civil-status must be written in French, which is the sole official language. The use of French regional dialects is therefore forbidden, and similarly in the annexed provinces of Nice and Savoy the Italian language may not legally be used."[38]

[35] "We readily believe that describing certain details of the ear in the registers of civil status, at the moment of birth, would be enough to render a substitution of persons impossible, even in adulthood," wrote Alphonse Bertillon, the "father" of anthropometric identification, at the end of the century; cited by Phéline 1985: 128.

[36] The public authorities also tried to ensure that the public did not confuse official documents and "lay" writings. A decree of July 11, 1791, motivated by a concern to "prevent all confusion between the pronouncements of magistrates and those of ordinary citizens," decided "to assign colored paper to all private advertisements and to reserve the use of white paper exclusively to the administrative and judicial authorities for their announcements"; AP, vol. 28, 508.

[37] Extract from the manual of Mersier 1892: 18, adding that "the practice is to set aside a quarter of the page width for the margin." Naturally, forgers were able to adapt to these innovations. In 1826, the minister of justice wrote that "the art of forgers has made such alarming progress in recent years that I believe we must approach the luminaries of the Academy of Sciences to find means to prevent the confusions that will be the inevitable consequence"; AN BB 1287.

[38] Mersier 1892: 16.

These demands also affected the signature that gave material form to the agreement between parties.[39] It was in the name of legibility that, in 1808, some officials wanted to forbid Jews to sign their names in Hebrew. The explanation given by the prosecutor in Colmar to justify this measure is a perfect illustration of the function now assigned to the signature in official documents: "Fear of counterfeiting may justify up to a certain point the use of highly peculiar signatures, but the signature must always fulfill its object, in the sense that the public official responsible for authenticating it and the witnesses who are present must be able to know with certainty that the more or less legible characters of which it consists do in fact represent the name of the signatory. But this certainty on the part of those involved does not exist when a signature is made in Hebrew characters, because civil-status officers in these two departments are generally unfamiliar with these, as also are all inhabitants who do not profess the Jewish faith."[40]

4. Identification and National Identity

The administrative formalities entailed by civil identification were in themselves a powerful factor in the process of national integration, not least because their "universality" extended only as far as the limits of the territory over which the state exercised its sovereignty. We have seen how the difficulties encountered in the course of the application of the laws on civil status derived in large part from the extreme heterogeneity of "French" society, notably in terms of language. The obligation imposed on mayors and citizens to register their civil status in French certainly contributed to the decline of regional dialects and patois, although more research is needed to support this argument. And with the decree of 1808 on the civil status of Jews, religious traditions too were undermined. In a circular of March 1810 addressed to all the Jewish communities in France, the *Consistoire Central*, which had been charged by Napoleon with implementing the new legislation, noted the persistence "in some temples [of] the custom of calling on a Jewish congregant to read a portion of the Law by his first name alone and that of his father, as in Jacob Bar Abraham. This former custom has now become improper, because at bottom it is contrary to the wishes of the law; it tends to perpetuate a usage which the law has proscribed and which cannot be countenanced without breaking the law." For this reason the *Consistoire Central* or-

[39] On the invention of the signature as a means of identification, see Fraenkel 1992.
[40] AN BB1 212.

dered that the cantor should "under penalty of deposition . . . in future call no coreligionist to the honor of reading a portion of the Law other than by the name given him at circumcision, followed by the family name he has adopted in conformity with the aforementioned decree."[41]

If the new identificatory logic played an especially important role in the construction of national identity, this was because it also and equally attacked individual identities. Here the whole question of the personal name was at issue, a problem that can only be briefly outlined here.[42] The law of 11 Germinal, Year XI, imposed fixed patronyms with the object of rendering individuals more easily identifiable, and established national regulations for the choice of forename and the transmission of the family name. Even today the rules about naming are very different from country to country, making the personal name an important element of the "sense of national belonging." Control of names thus represented a powerful factor of national integration. A study of the operation of civil status among the Jews of Lunéville in 1808 shows that the mayor automatically deformed their names by gallicizing the spelling (given that none of them had asked for a French name): thus the German *u* became the French *ou*, a *u* insinuated itself between the *g* and the *i*, and so on.[43] The same administrative logic explains the progressive disappearance of certain regional peculiarities of language. In Brittany, by very ancient custom, in names beginning with *Ker*, this syllable was replaced by a crossed-out *K*. But because this symbol was incomprehensible to mayoral officials in other regions of France, numerous patronyms were mutilated in the civil registers, especially those of emigrants—thus Kerandavelec became Kandavelec, and so on.[44] From the nineteenth century, the stigmatization of personal names became a central theme in xenophobic and antisemitic

---

[41] AN F19 11012. The collaboration of the *Consistoire Central* in the Napoleonic policy of assimilation was to provoke very serious and long-lived tensions in the Jewish community. Space is lacking here for a discussion of how the implementation of civil status in the French colonies obeyed the same logic of assimilation. In Algeria, after several failed attempts (in 1854 and 1873), the law of March 23, 1882, created an Algerian civil status. The administration began by establishing "family trees," and imposed fixed surnames and identity cards on every individual. The patronyms offered to the "natives" tried to respect "local customs." Religious names, terms attached to the Prophet, ethnic names, and even "surnames emphasizing character" (e.g., Seba = lion) were all authorized. Registers contained two columns, in French and in Arabic. On the first attempts at civil status in Algeria, see AN F80, 442; on the implementation of the law of 1882, Cornu 1889.

[42] This question is the subject of my current research.

[43] Job 1974: 44–52. At the beginning of the twentieth century, this gallicization still had racial connotations. The ban on marriages between whites and blacks that had disappeared during the Revolution reappeared under the Consulate; see AN F2 I 382.

[44] Cited by Lyon 1921: 51.

discourse.[45] It was in order to escape this that victims very often wished to gallicize their patronyms.[46]

Today, the formalities of civil status—the basis for the entire logic of modern identification practices—are part of administrative routine.[47] We all conform to them automatically, as if they are self-evident, and to such an extent that we find it hard to imagine that they might once have been contested. To study the genesis of these practices in which we are caught up allows us to grasp at the point of origin the social needs on which they rest. The progressive bureaucratization of civil status thrown into relief in this essay cannot be interpreted as a victory of "the state" over "the individual," as it is sometimes described.[48] In the sociohistorical perspective advanced here, the constant reinforcement of identificatory demands becomes explicable by the extension of the chains of interdependence that link humans together. We have seen that it was above all those sectors of society that were still poorly integrated into "civil life" that were opposed to the transformations of the Revolution. But the fact of not having a civil identity very quickly became one of the most extreme public misfortunes, especially in the cities. Louis Chevalier recalls that in the nineteenth century, uncertainty about civil status was an established fact among ordinary people who practiced exchange of children.[49] To put into relief, as we have done here, the misunderstandings, refusals, and sufferings entailed by the construction of the civil bond, is not the same as denouncing or questioning the need for it. As Max Weber has said, in reference to the bureaucracy, "our entire everyday life is held within its iron cage," yet at the same time without it "modern life would become impossible."[50]

[45] In France, it seems that it was "alien" names in particular that were stigmatized, including in antisemitic discourse; see Catane 1985: 339. For Germany, see Bering 1992; and for the special situation of women in this context, Hahn 1991.

[46] Since 1986, an estimated 7,500 surnames and first names annually have been gallicized by aliens admitted to French citizenship.

[47] From the July Monarchy on, protests on this subject became rarer; but it was not until the Third Republic (with the advent of railways and teachers) that the question was definitively regulated.

[48] This is the context in which Lefebvre-Taillard understands the history of the name; see Lefebvre-Taillard 1990.

[49] Chevalier 1978: 217.

[50] Weber 1971: 1, 299. In this sense, it is legitimate to claim that the state exercises a sort of "tyranny" (in the dictionary sense of "imperious coercion") over the individual, but this obviously is not the same as defending a political "concept" or denouncing a form of power.

3

"This or That Particular Person": Protocols of Identification in Nineteenth-Century Europe

JANE CAPLAN

THE TITLE of this essay is taken from J. G. Fichte's *Science of Rights* (1796), in a passage discussing a problem familiar to philosophers and police officers alike. How can they *reidentify* someone as the same person he once was known to be? And how can they *individuate* him from others like him? There is a philosophical tradition dating from Locke and Hume that has pondered the answer to these questions by means of puzzles isolating the difference between bodily persistence and memory (or "same consciousness") as criteria of personal identity.[1] In this passage of Fichte, however, the police officer stands to the fore with an apparently pragmatic response. To cite the passage at greater length: "The chief principle of a well-regulated police state is this: *That each citizen shall be at all times and places . . . recognized as this or that particular person.* No one must remain unknown to the police. This can be attained with certainty only in the following manner. Each one must always carry a pass with him, signed by his immediate government official, in which his person is accurately described. . . . No person should be received at any place who cannot thus make known by his pass his last place of residence and his name."[2] Particularity means identity, and identity is signaled perhaps

This is a preliminary report from ongoing research, and as will be seen it is heavily dependent on the work of other historians, to whom I acknowledge my debt. I am also grateful to my co-editor, John Torpey, for his comments on an earlier draft; and I thank the National Endowment for the Humanities, the John Simon Guggenheim Foundation, the Rockefeller Foundation's Bellagio Study and Conference Center, and Bryn Mawr College for their support of the research from which this essay is drawn.

[1] I am deliberately setting aside here the psychology and philosophy of identity as selfhood, along with related questions about the emergence and reproduction of modern concepts of individuality, individualism, autonomy, subjectivity, and interiority, which in different ways underlie the questions of identification with which I am concerned. Valuable introductions to this extensive literature include Nussbaum 1989, Taylor 1989, and Giddens 1991.

[2] Fichte 1796: 146; translation in Kroeger 1889: 378–79; this translation omits Fichte's final phrase, "and this without distinction of status." This is part of a discussion of two kinds of circulation, of people and of paper money: the pass was a paper that would identify

most publicly and self-evidently by a person's name.[3] This essay will concentrate on the personal name as a component in the apparatus of identification in nineteenth-century France, Germany, and England. By laying out some of the legal and procedural complexities entailed by this universal descriptive designation, I hope to expose some of the processes by which mechanisms of "identity" were made available for the purposes of "identification" in a particular historical context. As a preliminary, I offer some brief reflections on the problem of identification as such.

Identity and Recognition

"What *is* your name?" asks the captain in *Cards of Identity*, Nigel Dennis's 1955 satire on the experimental work of the "Identity Club"; "surely it is written on your ration-book and identity card?" To which the artless Mrs Chirk replies, "I've never thought to look, sir. What's come my way, I've eaten and been grateful for, with no thought to spare for the name that's brought it. Now, when I'd like to know, I can't find the dratted books."[4] As Dennis's enigmatic novel goes on to demonstrate, an effective system of identification depends on stabilizing personal identity, self-sameness, to an extent that is adequate to its operation as a unit in two systems of identification: the correspondence not only between a subjective claim (I am who I claim to be), but also between a person and a set of signs (this person corresponds to these signs).

A standardized system of identification and recognition such as Fichte recommends and Dennis satirizes is distinguished therefore both by the stability or replicability of its operations and by their relative invisibility, in contrast with older more public regimes that were sustained by the distinctively clothed or marked body and by individual face-to-face encounters.[5] And, as the same example shows, this new system of identity documents represented the addition of official authentication and verification to recognition alone. This was a crucial development in a society of increasing size, mobility, and anonymity, and it was also part of an older and much broader movement toward a culture of documentary

---

the traveler and authenticate his financial instruments. I am grateful to Isobel Hull for this reference.

[3] Research on personal identity in the contemporary United States has shown that "reference to one's own name was the single most frequent type of response" to the question "Who Are You?": Dion 1983: 246.

[4] Dennis 1955: 93. Lapierre 1995: 302, retells the anecdote of "the lunatic lost one winter's day in an isolated clinic building, who assured his finders that he was not cold, pointing as proof to his identity card that was sitting on the radiator."

[5] See Valentin Groebner's essay in this collection.

proofs in judicial and official transactions.[6] But in spite of every effort at standardization, the culture of identification was—is—essentially unruly, not only because of its vast scope and variety, but because even in its most controlling and technologized forms it is based on a concept that is itself difficult to stabilize and control. The term *identity*, as I have already suggested, incorporates the tension between "identity" as the *self-same*, in an individualizing, subjective sense, and "identity" as *sameness with another*, in a classifying, objective sense. Here the juridical identification of the individual actor meets the categorical identification of a type or class: in virtually any systematics of identification, everyone is not only "himself" but also potentially the embodiment of a type, and in an important respect the history of identification is a history not so much of individuality as of categories and their indicators. As Beatrice Fraenkel has pointed out in her imaginative history of the signature, "One ends by granting that identity is at the same time that which *distinguishes* an individual from others and that which *assimilates* him to others."[7] This dual meaning seems to give the term a peculiar internal incoherence, or at least to keep it constantly in motion against itself, even before one addresses any of the mechanical problems of operating an efficient system of identification in practice.

Jeremy Bentham formulated the fundamental question of identification as this: "Who are you, with whom I have to deal?"[8] In his study of anagnorisis, or the poetics of recognition, Terence Cave has observed that "the proof of [recognition] is not identity *per se* (that *would* be tautologous) but a sign which stands for the authentic object and that object only . . . in a relationship of contiguity. . . . The recognition sign is a synecdoche. Without this synecdochic *sêmeion*, difference cannot be resolved into identity; the token proclaims as unique an individual which *cannot on its own sufficiently make good its uniqueness*."[9] This, then, is the function of the identity document: it is the portable token of an originary act of bureaucratic recognition of the "authentic object"—an "accurate description" of the bearer recognized and signed by an accredited official, and available for repeated acts of probative ratification. The experience of self-sameness is thus never unmediated, either subjectively or objectively; it operates through a system of signs and recognitions that intrudes alterity into the heart of identity. This is the critical tension at the heart of a culture of identification. Indeed, according to Cave, although recognition

---

[6] For England, see the exemplary study by Clanchy 1993.

[7] Fraenkel 1992: 197; my emphasis. Cf. Elizabeth Eisenstein's observation that "diversity was . . . a concomitant of standardization," which has a suggestive power beyond its immediate application here to printing: Eisenstein 1993: 56.

[8] Bentham 1843: 557.

[9] Cave 1988: 245 (final emphasis is mine). I am grateful to Neil Kenny for this reference.

scenes may look like resolutions, they are actually what he calls "problem moments" that disclose an essential instability: "To tell a story which ends in recognition is to perform one of the most quintessential acts of fictional narration—the recognition scene is, as it were, the mark or signature of a fiction, so that even if something like it occurs as a fact, it still sounds like fiction and will probably be retold as such."[10]

This giddy spiral of tokens encompasses the relationship between fact and fiction, between the identity document and its bearer, and between the component signs or representations of identity and the document. How, then, does the "identity document" in fact document identity, in the sense of furnishing adequate proof of claims and correspondences for official purposes? Beatrice Fraenkel has suggested that although signs of identity are in one sense heterogeneous and disorderly, the elementary signs of modern identity have come to be conventionalized as the name, the portrait, and the fingerprint.[11] These correspond, by a logic that is surely not accidental, to C. S. Peirce's "second trichotomy of signs," namely, his differentiation among symbol, icon, and index according to the sign's own character. In the Peircian system of signs, the symbol (here the proper name) is the Saussurean signifier, that is, an arbitrary sign that has neither resemblance nor an existential relationship to its referent. The icon (the portrait) "represent[s] its object mainly by its similarity" to it: the relationship between signifier and signified is not arbitrary, but is one of resemblance or likeness. The index, finally, "refers to its object . . . because it is in dynamical . . . connection" with it: it does not resemble the object, but "has a real connection" with it—here the fingerprint (and more generally the trace, which Roland Barthes calls "a bit of information used to identify or pinpoint certain elements of time and space").[12]

If Fraenkel's analogy is correct, the imaginary or archetypal identity document thus triangulates the system of signification that underpins the field of modern semiology as such. Its appropriate history is not simply the history of the emergence and use of any particular document—the passport, the police *fiche*, the register—but also the practical history of the signs that have come to comprise documentary identification as such. In a brilliant analysis, Fraenkel demonstrates how only an examination of the intricate history of the signature is able to disclose its combined

---

[10] Cave 1988: 489, 4. The entanglement of fact and fiction in the nineteenth-century regime of recognition will be self-evident to any fan of the detective story, just as the insufficiency of the self to authorize its own identity is frequently experienced at the moment of proffering a passport.

[11] Fraenkel 1992: 200.

[12] Peirce in Buchler 1955: 102–9; Peirce's own examples of the index were not confined to "traces" in the above sense, but included clothing that would identify a man's occupation, or the sundial or clock that signifies time; and Barthes 1967: Part II.

"trace" as privileged sign of identity

character as symbol, icon, and trace, even though in its modern form it conserves only its character as trace. Arguably, the trace is in fact the privileged sign of modern identity, with the fingerprint having become the unofficial emblem of modern identity culture: for all practical purposes qualitatively unique, yet capable of being enrolled in a numerical series for the purposes of classification, retrieval, and communication.[13] The fingerprint also symbolizes the police and criminological procedures that often threaten to occupy the entire field of identification as a theme of historical research. However, it is important also to yield space to civil and legal practices beyond the limits of the criminal law alone, since they also throw up problems of recognition and verification that only sometimes fall under the purview of criminal law strictly speaking.[14] For as the elements of identity come to be objectified and situated in a legal matrix, so issues of stabilization, property, and alienability are thrown up. How are the "elementary signs of identity" stabilized as legal and practical objects? How do they come to have a recognized official status? Conversely, by what legal means, if any, can persons be said to "own" or have rights over the signs and mechanisms of their identity: their name, image, handwriting, or indeed their physical body? How might we trace the historical dialectic between the claim to an identity, the disguise of the person, and the forgery of a document? All these issues were matters of legal as well as forensic discussion in nineteenth-century Europe, and constitute the matrix in which the contemporary discourse of identification was shaped.[15]

In the remainder of this essay I concentrate on the personal name as a component of the apparatus of identification. I begin by very briefly outlining the main themes in the history of the stabilization of personal names in Western Europe, and then look at the process by which the name was

[13] Since I will not be discussing fingerprints further in this essay, I will not cite the voluminous literature since Herschel, Henry, and Galton, but I want to acknowledge here the author who started me thinking about traces of identity, Ginzburg 1980b; see also Joseph and Winter 1996; and the essays in Part II of the present volume.

[14] This is parallel to the points made about surveillance above. It is interesting in this connection that the *Encyclopaedia of the Social Sciences* registered a significant shift in approaches to the subject between the 1932 and 1967 editions. The author of the entry on "Identification" in the 1932 edition contested the assumption that identification was solely the province of criminal law, arguing instead that "In the modern state . . . with its intricate network of social relationships, governed by a multitude of rules which define the legal rights and responsibilities of the citizen, identification has become an increasingly important means of safeguarding civil rights" (Seligman and Johnson 1932, vol. 7: 573). The 1967 edition replaces the entry on "Identification" with one on "Identity" as a social concept.

[15] For an extraordinarily rich and wide-ranging discussion of the relationship between "original" and "copy," see Schwartz 1996, and for a similarly imaginative treatment of mimesis, Taussig 1993.

forced into contention as a legal object in nineteenth-century France, Germany, and England.

Stabilizing the Name

According to the author of a contemporary German legal text, "The name, as the most important distinguishing feature among people, plays . . . a decisive role wherever people are registered in books or files or take part in various legal procedures. The task of the name is to guarantee, at least approximately, an exact identification of the person: this renders it the object of legal regulation, especially of the law of public order (*Ordnungsrecht*), and thus also makes it into a legal instrument."[16] This is a modern legal view of the matter, and its perspective is, from the point of view of the historian, somewhat one-sided. It is not simply the identificatory precision of the name that makes it into a legal object, but also the law itself that demands and imposes this precision, and to that extent creates the name as a means of identification. The legal seizure of the personal name in Europe is a recent and highly uneven development that followed centuries of stabilization by usage and custom alone.[17]

A brief and inadequate conspectus of the emergence in Western Europe of the contemporary conventional form of the personal name (i.e., forename plus inherited surname) would note that the single name became the universal practice after the dissolution of the western Roman Empire (and the Roman *tria nomina* or three-part name), and that as Christianity advanced this was most commonly the baptismal name. From about the eleventh century, a second name or surname began to be added, as a kind of adjective modifying and extending the limited stock of baptismal names.[18] Surnames are normally distinguished by genealogists and historians into four or five categories according to type, that is, filiation (patronymic), place of origin (locative), object (toponymic), occupation, and

[16] Enste 1983: 2. A similarly robust view of the legal purpose of the name is taken by the latest German contributor to this literature: "In der Rechtswissenschaft wird der Name in erster Linie als Identifikationsmittel definiert, *das einer effizienten Verwaltung dienen soll*" (my emphasis): Seutter 1996: 2.

[17] Contrast with the legal references in the previous footnote the observations of a French historian: "Institution sociale avant que d'être juridique, le nom a pendant longtemps été laissé en effet à l'usage, notion dont la souplesse paraît le mieux adaptée à la double fonction du nom, à savoir d'identifier un être humain, de l'individualiser, mais aussi de le situer socialement en le rattachant à un groupe social" (Lefebvre-Taillard 1990: 7). For an excellent recent history of naming practices in Europe that discusses the issues summarized below, see Wilson 1998.

[18] The metaphor is from Rogers 1995: 145.

sobriquet; but the process and pace by which surnames became heritable and hence more stable as family names is not always easy to reconstruct. It clearly differed radically among regions and classes, in response to the varieties of demographic growth, the elaboration of economic and property relations, and the expansion of written records.[19] Precise pathways here were far from straightforward: among the early medieval landholding class in England, for example, place-names that may look like surnames were often descriptive of a current property and status only—new estates brought new names, to the landholder, to his sons on dividing an inheritance or marrying an heiress.[20] Thus even after heritable patronymic surnames begin to become more generally visible (roughly in the thirteenth/fourteenth centuries), their diffusion was slow and uneven by region and class, and was subject to countervailing social and economic influences. In sixteenth-century France, the easiest way to achieve ennoblement was to purchase a noble estate and assume its name (Molière satirized this in his 1662 play *École des femmes*, where a peasant buys a field, digs a muddy ditch round it, and calls himself "Monsieur de l'Isle"). Similarly, in eighteenth-century England, changes of surname certified by act of Parliament were (allegedly) common in order to comply with the terms of wills.[21]

These relatively fluid naming regimes reflected a system of distinction rather than identification, and in a culture of landed property and status the title or honorific took precedence over the personal name for the upper classes. Moreover, the customary, adjectival origin of the family name reminds us that it was the baptismal, or sacramental, name that was a person's more important name, her or his "real" name, both in canon law and in popular usage, until well into the seventeenth century. Nevertheless, factors favoring the changeability of surnames were unable to impede an inexorable process toward their stabilization as heritable family names. This process was entangled in a combination of social pressures and changes (for example, the crystallization of a concept of the family that privileged genealogical identity, or the growing significance of movable over immovable property), and of legal and state enactments.

[19] The influence of the church on regimes of naming was also visible, for example, in moves to require the use of biblical and saints' names at baptism, or to institute parish registration of baptisms in the interest of enforcing the rules on consanguineous marriages (Lapierre 1995: 30–35; Tate 1969: 43ff., who points out that Cardinal Ximenes' motive for the late-fifteenth-century register campaign was to stem the tide of divorces on spurious grounds of affinity.)

[20] Fox-Davies and Carlyon-Britten 1906: 15ff.

[21] Lapierre 1995: 35; Linell 1938: 28–29; for a similar case in Germany, see von der Planitz 1841: 348.

France: Legal Stabilization

Absolutist France can stand as the paradigmatic case for the transition from the customary stabilization to the legal immutability of names, in the course of the centralization of royal power between the sixteenth and eighteenth centuries. The stabilization of the patronymic, as the historian Lefebvre-Taillard reminds us, was primarily a social process tied to the power of the family in medieval society; its use had been enforced by repetition and custom, and this preceded any significant enactments by the state.[22] The first moves to enforce registration of baptisms were then ecclesiastical—the institution of parish registers in the early sixteenth century—and royal authority advanced initially through its assertion of control over the church. Thus the Crown's first intervention was to prescribe the maintenance of these registers in order to have firm evidence of the age (i.e., majority) of its nominees for ecclesiastical benefices.[23] Although the Crown rejected the authority of the Council of Trent (1545–63) to reform the French Catholic Church where this conflicted with the Crown's own absolutist claims, it endorsed the spirit of the council's own works by instituting parish registration of marriages and deaths in 1579 (significantly, in order to substitute written records for the uncertainties of witness testimonial).[24] By 1667, the registers had become the normal legal means for proving an identity. Signposts along this route were also laid by new provisions for signing legal documents: thus in 1554 notaries had to ratify documents with autograph signatures of their name, while the code Michau in 1629 required all signatories to use their family, not their seigneurial (i.e., fief) names.[25]

---

[22] Lefebvre-Taillard 1990: 31–32. In conformity with medieval concepts of property, it was the principle of long and undisputed *usage* that "seised" a person of his name, or as we would now say, conferred a right to it (pp. 43–48). (This principle still holds for the English law of names, as will be discusssed below.)

[23] Ordinance of Villers-Cotterêts, 1539, art. 51. The state's right of nomination was secured by the 1516 Concordat of Boulogne; details in Lefebvre-Taillard 1990: 91ff.

[24] The replacement of orality by written records in law and government is a crucial step in the emergence of a culture of documentary proof; cf. the studies already cited above by Fraenkel (signature) and Clanchy (English written records). The nineteenth-century police science of handwriting expertise can be traced back in France, where it was especially highly developed, at least to this sixteenth/seventeenth-century advancement of written records; see Bonzon 1899.

[25] Fraenkel 1992: 98; Salveton 1887: 247. Fraenkel discusses in detail the process by which the autograph signature superseded the combination of seal and subscription plus paraph or *ruche* as the documentary authentication of identity. She is correct in saying that the name had to be sufficiently stabilized to support this ordinance of 1554, but one must also recognize the law's effect of itself reinforcing this process. On signatures, see Guigue

The climax of this solidification of names was the revolutionary transition from stabilization to full legal immutability, first enacted by the law of August 23, 1794 (6 Fructidor, An II), which forbade citizens to bear any names other than those registered at birth. This legislation must be read in the context of both the attack on aristocratic titles and the chaos of renaming unleashed by the Revolution.[26] This restrictive regime was confirmed by the law of April 1, 1803 (11 Germinal, An XI), which remained the basis of French name law until 1993.[27] It forbade the adoption or use (whether by substitution or addition) of any fore- or surname other than those registered at birth, required the resumption of original names where these had been changed since the Revolution, and prescribed that all valid legal and public documents must refer to individuals by their full registered name only. The 1803 law also limited the choice of forenames to calendrical and historical names, and set out a complex and highly restrictive procedure for applications for change of name. The procedure took up to three years, and required a combination of public declaration, police and administrative review, opinion by the Conseil d'état, decision by the chancellery, and enactment by decree. Fewer than a hundred changes were authorized between 1803 and 1814; under the Third Republic, an average of fifty changes were decreed annually; most were additions or changes of a name to perpetuate a family name threatened with extinction, or to distinguish between family branches. After 1945, with less restrictive standards applied, about five hundred changes were authorized annually. Not until 1993 was the *loi de Germinal* repealed, and new regulations introduced entitling anyone with "a legitimate interest" to petition for a change of name and simplifying the procedure somewhat.[28]

1863; Tessier 1962: chs. 1, 2, 12; Clanchy 1993: 304–8; Holzhauer 1973; also Harris 1995: ch. 11.

[26] This situation was briefly sanctioned by the short-lived law of November 14/16, 1793, which recognized the citizen's right to change his name at will; as Salveton commented, "To leave free passage to anyone who might fancy changing all or part of his name would be tantamount to making it impossible to confirm the identity of anyone who might have made use of this latitude" (Salveton 1887: 261). Full civil registration had been introduced in September 1792: for this and other aspects of the history of registration in France, see the essay by Noiriel in this volume.

[27] See Lefebvre-Taillard 1990: 113–34, who argues that the "primary, in fact the sole aim of the law was to ban the naming of a child with the name of an 'existing' family name," and that the prescriptive method chosen for this was merely a matter of convenience (p. 128)—a modestly limited origin for a regulation that had much farther-reaching consequences for French practice; and see also Lapierre 1995: 20–29; Salveton 1887: 261–63.

[28] Regulations of January 8, 1993, in force as of February 1, 1994. A separate question was the gallicization of foreign names on naturalization: this was debated intermittently in the interwar period, but resolved only by legislation in 1945 and 1950.

Like all previous attempts to enforce a single standard, the restrictive regime of 1794/1803 was undoubtedly slow to penetrate the provinces, where it met resistance both from burdened local officials and from male citizens keen to evade conscription. Inevitably too, the official insistence on French name-forms as well as on immutability conjured a complex dual regime of civil and social names, the former stabilized by the state, the latter subject to all manner of local usages, such as the custom of changing forenames at major life stages or of using different names in different social circles. As one male inhabitant of a village in the Châtillon-nais told an investigating anthropologist in the 1970s, "Pour mes enfants, je mets un prénom à la mairie, j'en mets plusieurs à l'église"; from another informant came the statement "dans la famille, il y'avait le Louis, dit Georges, et la Marguerite elle s'appelait en vérité Jeanne"; and the tomb-stone that read "le vingt novembre est decédé Emile, Lucien, Albert, Fréd-éric, dit Jean Camuset" showed that custom was impervious even to death.[29]

This brief summary serves to record only in barest outline the emergence of a regime of extreme stabilization by a rationalizing, centralizing state. While the adoption of fixed names can scarcely be reduced to the effect of administrative enactment, the official character of the French system makes the close yet ambiguous relationship among naming, citizenship, and control unusually visible. The officially recognized name, as Nicole Lapierre points out, yields combinations of control and protection that varied from population to population. Thus in France, as in other Euro-pean countries, the emancipation of the Jews was accompanied by regula-tions requiring them to register fixed surnames, under rules that aimed to assimilate these names to those of the "general" population (e.g., no place-names or names drawn from the Old Testament).[30] The Crémieux decree of 1870 allowed assimilated Algerian Jews to gallicize names taken directly from the Hebrew or Arabic; and in the later nineteenth century requests for permission to gallicize foreign-sounding names became more numerous. These processes were the forerunner of political debates about galliciza-tion in the 1920s/1930s, which pointed up the antinomy between the as-similationism fostered by existing practice and a nationalist resistance to the effacement of difference through the disguise of "real," alien identity. (I omit discussion of the changing situation after 1945.) On the other hand, when the French government required Algerian heads of household to adopt patronymic surnames in 1882 (and imposed names on anyone who refused this edict) it also introduced a regime of identity cards for the first time in French law. Thus the colonized Algerians were given official iden-

---

[29] Zonabend 1977: 266–67.
[30] For Gemany, see Bering 1992.

tity without citizenship. The disjunction between the two civil statuses (official identity; citizenship) was underlined by subsequent regulations, including the introduction of anthropometric passes for "nomads" in 1912 and of identity cards for foreigners in 1917. The latter rule gave rise to the sardonic phrase that circulated among Eastern European Jewish immigrants in France in the 1920s: "Liberté, égalité, identité"[31]—a neat enough epigram for the character of French name law.

Germany: The Contest of Public and Private

From the legal point of view, the name is both a private and a public matter, and German nineteenth-century theory and practice can be seen largely as a contest between these two arms of the law as they evolved through the century. Who has rights vis-à-vis a person's name? German positive law had been generally silent on the matter of names until this time. The prevailing view among seventeenth- and eighteenth-century German jurists was that German practice was ruled by Roman law (the constitutions of Diocletian and Maximian), with, it seems, an admixture of common law. Accordingly, the state was understood to have no interest in a person's name, but viewed it as a natural right that was left to his own discretion to choose and to public consensus to underwrite. In Christian Germany, once the two-part name convention came to be established in medieval times, both men and women received their family name by inheritance, and their forename by parental conferral, normally through baptism (much later, women would adopt their husband's family name on marriage). Thereafter, so the jurists argued, free men, and to some extent women, were entitled to change, modify, acquire, or discard both baptismal and family names as they wished: hence, for example, the snobbish Latinization of so many academics' and lawyers' names in early modern Germany. The only restrictions they acknowledged were that no third party could be injured; that anyone who assumed a name for dishonest purposes could be prosecuted as a "Falsarius"; and that indecent, sacrilegious, or treasonable names were unacceptable.

This principle was interestingly updated in a transitional text published in 1800 by Tileman Dothias Wiarda, who set out the principle that "Everyone [he means every free person] is entitled to be master and creator of his name; thus the name is his property, over which he has free dominion according to the concept of property."[32] Much of the rest of Wiarda's text

---

[31] Information here summarized from Lapierre 1995: 39–53, 93–105.

[32] Wiarda 1800: 193. The same concept of the name as a form of property was advanced in nineteenth-century France: see Salveton 1887: ch. III.

is in fact a demonstration of the difficulty of upholding this notion of name as property, particularly the difficulty of precisely defining the circumstances under which the adoption of someone else's name constituted a tort. Not surprisingly for a text concerned mainly with issues of property, the main example here is a person who adopts someone else's name with the intent to insinuate an advantageous connection with that individual's family.

Within a few years in any case this position was being undermined both in practice and in theory. With the introduction of Napoleonic law into Germany, the left bank of the Rhine and a few other regions began to follow French legal practice, which as we have seen embodied an explicit principle of state interest in personal names. This principle, already signaled in some scattered earlier governmental decisions, now began to be urged as appropriate in Germany too.[33] But this was not simply, I would suggest, the result of French influence, but also because in the balance between the private and public status of the name, the weight was swinging increasingly toward the public, a sphere that was being constituted as well as enlarged through a growing number of relationships and transactions in which documented identity was requisite. Thus the major regulations concerning the acquisition of fixed names by Jews had followed their state-sanctioned emancipation in the early decades of the nineteenth century.[34] Wiarda had already conceded in 1800 that a man was not entitled to change his name in order to elude "the eye of the state," and it was this principle that was expanded in the course of the century. Prussia, for example, forbade the use of a name other than one's own in 1816, on grounds of public order, and in 1822 forbade changes of name without the sovereign's permission.[35] Thus by 1841 a commentator in Saxony could write:

> Insofar as in an orderly political community [*Staatsverband*] the purely personal and the civic [*staatsbürgerlich*] situation of an individual stand in the closest and most direct mutual relationship, name-bearing [*Namensführung*] by the citizen and member of a political community also appears to be of quite decisive importance for that community. This is because the name in and of itself must be seen as the necessary and distinctive designation of the person or family, without which their existence within the totality of political community [*Staatsgesellschaft*] is hardly conceivable. It cannot be contested therefore that the state has a well-founded claim that each of its members should make use of this

[33] See Enste 1983: 46ff.
[34] See Bering 1992.
[35] Enste 1983: 47.

distinguishing designation of his person in his public life [*Verhältnissen zum Gemeinwesen*] . . . [and that his name should be] a permanent one, not subject to change at his own discretion.[36]

By the 1860s it was possible to compile a long list of the public purposes and contexts that had by then accumulated where the state had a clear interest in the stability and recognizability of names: for example, voting, legal processes, taxation, military conscription, the security and welfare police, and so on.[37] At the same time as the state's interest was declared, the individual was also argued to have his own interest in seeking state authorization for any change of name, since only the state had the power to guarantee the public recognition that was the point of a person's name as such (a stark contrast to English legal principles, as we shall see).

The public-law status of the personal name thus began to be clarified, in piecemeal fashion, as German states in the non-French law regions issued new laws and ordinances on the subject in the mid-century. New regulations were restrictive both of the choice of baptismal names and of the right to change one's name, which increasingly was made the object of administrative regulation. A watershed was reached following the adoption of the new Reich law on registration and marriage (the *Personenstandsgesetz*) in February 1875. This secularizing law, part of Bismarck's struggle with the Catholic Church, or *Kirchenkampf*, enforced civil registration for the first time, and provided for the establishment of a network of registration districts and offices (*Standesämter*) throughout Germany. After its adoption, each state issued its own regulations for the admissibility of forenames and on the alterability of the personal name in general. Thus a number of states (Hessen, Reuss älterer Linie) restricted the choice of forename to those that were "customary": for example "Jesus" was unacceptable, also Bebeline and Lassalline (although precise standards varied from state to state).[38] Other states (Sachsen-Weimar, Sachsen-Meiningen) tried to ensure that the registered name of a newborn should not be identical to that of any other local inhabitant (which would often rule out local customs of giving a child the same forenames as its father or another relative). States also enforced new regulations on the

---

[36] Von der Planitz 1841: 350. Compare Enste 1983: 90–91: "In order to guarantee a reliable system of identification, it is essential that every individual citizen use a consistent name. . . . The name can fulfil its regulative function in the context of the social community only if it is not subject to individual disposition, but can be changed only by official process according to specified legal rules which judge the grounds on which a change of name is sought according to objective considerations."

[37] Hermann 1862: 264.

[38] Ramdohr 1899: 30.

procedure for changes of name, which now were generally declared to need administrative or court authorization.[39]

By 1895, Otto Gierke, the great authority on German law, could declare that "a change of family name may be granted by authority of the state. It is not permissible without state authorization."[40] The same principle was enunciated at greater length some years later: "The great interest that the public administration has in the reliable designation of every individual and in his differentiation from others . . . entails that the regulation of name matters [*Namenswesen*] proceeds according to public-law principles and by means of fixed rules. The right to choose or change one's family name is therefore no longer a matter of individual discretion, and while the forename may be freely chosen, the individual is not empowered to change it at will."[41] By the end of the nineteenth century, then, the citizen no longer possessed any residual rights to change his name at will, and was under a legal obligation, by the terms of the Penal Code, to use his correct name in all transactions with the state (Strafgesetzbuch §360).

The parallel question of the civil-law status of the personal name also became an object of growing legal interest toward the end of the century as the commercial demands of copyright, trademark, libel law, stage names and other pseudonyms, and the like became more complex. I cannot go into these commercial questions here, but it is important to note that civil protection against unauthorized use of a personal name was embodied for the first time in the new Civil Code of 1896 (BGB §12). The *right* to a name was commonly understood to belong to the evolving sphere of the *Persönlichkeitsrechte*, the general right of human personality or dignity. Indeed, this section of the BGB was the first statutory recognition of this emerging area of law.[42] As Gierke put it, these were the state-protected rights "that are specifically intended to guarantee to the individual in his existence as such [*Fürsichsein*] a private sphere of the self," for example, the right to life and to integrity of the physical body, to personal freedom and honor.[43] The name as such was a "subjective private right," a rather different legal matter. Indeed, the BGB recognized this by protecting not the name itself, but only its unauthorized use (*Gebrauch*)—although here legal opinion differed on whether an actual damage had to be demonstrated. In Germany, the right to change one's name

---

[39] Von Sicherer 1890: 158–61.

[40] Gierke 1895: 719.

[41] Adler 1921: 2–3.

[42] Wieacker 1995: 310, 417. This is related to but not identical with the concept of fundamental human rights; perhaps it could be described as transitional between this and an older concept of legally defensible personal "honor?"

[43] Gierke 1895: 705.

thus became the object of legal regulation and restriction by the state in the course of the nineteenth century, but at the same time the right of legal remedy for the unauthorized use of one's name was clarified.

England: Common Law

The ambiguities and silences of English name law offer a striking contrast to the French and German states' claims to a primary interest in their citizens' names. Suffice it to say that the English state has had no effective control over or stake in the stabilization of the personal name, which has long been regarded as a matter of common law. As an English contemporary of Gierke put it in 1878, "The law of surnames may be concisely stated: there is none at all."[44]

Historically, in England as elsewhere in medieval Europe, the first and more significant name was the forename, which was acquired by baptism. The statutory authority conferred on the Prayer Book in the sixteenth century gave statutory force to the baptismal name as recorded in the parish register, which was thereafter unchangeable (except by Act of Parliament). But first names acquired by methods other than baptism in the Church of England have no other force than what they can acquire by repute; and repute is the sole foundation on which the force of a non-baptismal forename in England rests. Thus the civil registration of births, first adopted in England in 1836 and expanded and improved in 1874 (and 1938, 1960, etc.), does not confer a name, but merely commences a repute. The surname (initially acquired by inheritance)[45] was even more a matter of custom. From Herle C.J.'s statement in 1334 ("Homme peut a divers temps aver divers nosmes") to that of his successors Tindal C.J. in 1835 ("A man may, if he pleases, and it is not for any fraudulent purpose, take a name and work his way in the world with his new name as well as he can") and Stirling J. in 1890 ("there is no law to prevent a man assuming any name he likes"), the majority legal view has been that surnames are a matter of repute or "notoriety" alone, and can be changed at pleasure.[46] The various procedures available—Act of Parliament, royal

---

[44] Amphlett 1878: 499.

[45] As one nineteenth-century antiquarian put it, "The Christian name may be regarded as held only upon a leasehold tenure, for a term of life, whereas a surname is a very old property with an hereditary bondage." Anon. 1862: 82–99.

[46] Linell 1938: ch. 4. The current edition of Halsbury's *Laws of England* (1994: 767–73) states that "The law concerns itself only with the question whether [a man] has in fact assumed and has come to be known by a name different from that by which he was originally known . . . [and] prescribes no rules limiting a person's liberty to change his name," as long as it is not for false pretenses (e.g., impersonation). See also Mead 1995.

license, or deed poll—are to be understood as authenticating rather than conferring the name.

Deed polls (i.e., a deed or document to which there is only one party, registered in the central office of the Supreme Court) became the method of choice from the mid-nineteenth century. This followed a celebrated case in the 1860s, which raised doubts whether the assumption of a new name also founded a right to require it to be used and recognized by all third parties.[47] "Repute," after all, requires a long time and persistent usage to become established, and as one legal commentator observed, "It is too much to say, that the initiatory act does, per se, entitle the initiator to require others to treat him as a person who has actually acquired the new name. . . . A declaration by Smith, that he has taken the name of Brown, operates as a *request* that . . . the parties may be addressed, and may be spoken and written of by the latter name."[48] But another contributor to the same debate inveighed in populist tone against the suggestion that only a royal license could authorize a change of name: "Are labourers not to have the names of distinguished families . . . or are country esquires to be forbidden to assume the names of labourers or tradesmen? Are offensive names . . . not to be got rid of without great cost or expense? Is Mr Bridecake not to change his name to Brideoake; or is Mr Shufflebottom to be content with the unrelenting ridicule which his name suggests; is Mr Hogflesh not to become Mr Hofleish; and is Mr Bug or Mr Humbug, with fortune, influence, and talent, to be laughed off the hustings?"[49]

The silence of English law on the matter of names is consonant with a governmental system in which registration and identity cards have not normally been part of the apparatus of administration. At the end of the eighteenth century, Jeremy Bentham deplored what he called "the nominal confusion" that prevailed in England. "It is to be regretted," he wrote, "that the proper names of individuals are on so irregular a footing [that they] only imperfectly accomplish their object in a great nation." He suggested the utility of "a new nomenclature . . . so arranged, that, in a whole nation, every individual should have a proper name which should belong

[47] This was the case of Jones/Herbert of Clytha, which turned essentially on a complaint that the Lord Lieutenant of Monmouthshire had refused to recognize a voluntary change of name, on the grounds that no formalities had been executed; see Fox-Davies and Carlyon-Britton 1906: 68–73; Phillimore 1905: 19–23; *Hansard* 1863, vol. 169: 1573–84; Falconer 1862.

[48] Manning 1863: 759 (my emphasis).

[49] Falconer 1862: p. 37. The petition alluded to here by "Joshua Bug" to change his name to "Norfolk Howard" appears to have been inserted in the *Times* in June 1862 by a practical joker; see Anon. 1863: 22. For a similarly humorous treatment of the name *Bug*, see the review of J. Finlayson's *Surnames and Sirenames* (Anon. 1863: 608); arguably humor was the primary genre in which issues of naming were publicly discussed in this period.

Bentham-name tattoos

to him alone." This rationalized system of legal nomenclature would include family name, a single baptismal or forename, and place and date of
birth. Bentham then went on to propose the universal adoption of what
he describes as "a common custom among English sailors, of printing
their family and christian names upon their wrists, in well-formed and
indelible characters." He was suggesting, in other words, that everyone
should have their name *tattooed* on their wrist—a policy, he says, that
"would be a new spring for morality, a new source of power for the laws,
an almost infallible precaution against a multitude of offences."

The vision of the tattoo as "a spring for morality" will appear startling
to a culture that has come to see tattoos as degrading and vicious, or more
recently as a form of transgressive ornamentation.[50] And to an Anglo-
American audience, Bentham's proposal for a rationalized system of national nomenclature will seem scarcely less bizarre. Bentham himself dismissed it as a fantasy for his own time, and it never came to prevail in
English law. Even during the period in which the National Register was
in force, between 1939 and 1952, a British citizen could (in theory)
change his or her name by declaration to the General Register Office and
receive a new identity card and ration book. Freedom to change a name
was, however, forbidden for enemy aliens in 1916 and for all aliens in
1919, and these provisions, which allowed exemptions only by permission of the Home Secretary, were not repealed until 1971.[51]

non/citizen provisions
for name change

Conclusion

I am aware that the rather esoteric legal career of the name that I have
sketched here only scratches the surface of this topic, which itself is part
of the larger social, cultural, and linguistic history of names. The stabilization of names in any particular historical context depended on much more
than just legislative enactment or official procedures. It was affected, for
example, not only by the changes in the nature and extent of private property and the expansion of legal transactions, but by processes such as the
growth of literacy and the stabilization of orthography. The subjective
relationship between individuals and their names has also been subtly
modified as names came to be uttered not just in a small circle of family
and friends, but in the wider world of official and paper transactions,
where the written or signed name might appear either as alienation or
threat, or as a confirmation of identity. The linking of names to number,
or the outright substitution of one for the other—school number, con-

[50] See Caplan 1997: 107–42.
[51] For registration in Britain, see the essay by Jon Agar in this volume.

scription or matriculation number, prison number—may open a further
existential gap in the sense of self. This at least is reflected in the stern
warning issued by the captain to his servant Mrs Chirk in Dennis's *Cards
of Identity*—a warning that positions the state as the benign guardian of
its citizens' failing sense of self:

> You must try and understand that the old days are over—the days when you
> could take your identity for granted. Nowadays, all the old means of self-recog-
> nition have been swept away, leaving even the best people in a state of personal
> dubiety. . . . Very wisely, governments all over the world have sought to stop
> this rot before the entire human population has been reduced to anonymous
> grains. They give you cards, on which they inscribe in capital letters the name
> which your fading memory supplies before it is too late. It is their hope that by
> continually reading and re-reading your *name*, you will be able to keep your
> hold on a past that no longer exists, and thus bring an illusion of self into the
> present. . . . What I want to emphasize is: don't lose your name again, Mrs
> Chirk. Don't, at least, lose the cards on which that name is written.[52]

On the largest and most profound scale, finally, we need to look to
structural processes in the history of state formation and law to account
for the national differences outlined in this essay. Thus in France the drive
toward centralization began under early modern absolutism even before
it was pushed forward with such energy by the revolutionary and republican regimes after 1789. Germany's history of particularism, Prussianism,
and the reception of Roman law produced a complex mix of state practices that was further disturbed by the late-nineteenth-century processes
of central state formation and legal codification. In England local and
parliamentary government placed limits on the reach of the bureaucratic
state and the elaboration of governmental science, with the result that
experiments in these fields were displaced to more tractable colonial territories, notably Ireland and British India. But these grand political narratives of territorial sovereignty and the formation of the nation-state not
only depended upon the technical capacity to establish and administer
systems of identification and control, but *are* in certain respects the history of these apparatuses as such: "the state" as an institution constituted
itself in the fragmented and multifarious processes of its administrative
activities.

[52] Dennis 1955: 94–95.

4

Making Social Groups, One Person at a Time: The Identification of Individuals by Estate, Religious Confession, and Ethnicity in Late Imperial Russia

CHARLES STEINWEDEL

> To live as our fathers and grandfathers lived will not do. The village resident more and more feels that his life is connected by thousands of invisible threads not only with his fellow villagers, with the nearest rural township, but this connection goes much farther. He dimly perceives that he is a subject of a vast state, and that events taking place far from his place of birth can have a much greater influence on his life than some event in his village.[1]
>
> —PETR KOROPACHINSKII, Ufa Provincial Zemstvo Chairman, 1906

WHEN Koropachinskii wrote these words, he viewed the "invisible threads" connecting the villager with the state as a new political consciousness gained primarily through the political mobilization of the 1905 revolution. Salient features of this mobilization, such as political parties, their programs, and a freer press, drew the attention of political actors at the time and, subsequently, of historians of late imperial Russia. We might consider these connections from another perspective, however: that of the state and the "invisible threads" it used to connect with its subjects. Furthermore, many of these connections were not so much invisible threads as paper trails—written documents found in the files of bureaucracies staffed by officials who sought to extend the regime's knowledge about

I would like to thank the editors, the members of the Workshop on "Documenting Individual Identity," and Yanni Kotsonis for their helpful comments on earlier versions of this essay, and the American Council of Teachers of Russian, the International Research and Exchanges Board, and the Harriman Institute for their support of my research.

[1] Petr Koropachinskii, "O nashei gazete," *Ufimskaia zemskaia gazeta*, no. 1 (March 1, 1906): 7.

and, ideally, its grasp of the tsar's subjects.[2] Written documents such as excerpts from metrical books—parish registers in which births, marriages, and deaths were recorded—and internal passports that governed residence and movement within the empire linked the individual subject with the regime. This essay addresses the tsarist regime's attempts to identify the population it governed in the regime's last century. I focus on metrical books and internal passports as techniques through which the autocracy aimed to fix the population according to estate and religious confession.[3] These attempts varied according to the regime's changing designs for the civic order. Metrical books kept by religious leaders and passports identifying their holders by estate status and religious confession remained fundamental documents of identification until 1917. However, in an attempt to achieve greater civic inclusion and to connect with individuals rather than with collective institutions, the tsarist regime began to erode legal differences among religious confessions and estate status groups, especially after 1905. Alexis de Tocqueville, Max Weber, and Charles Tilly have described, in various contexts and in different ways, this "leveling of the governed" and their more direct relationship with centralizing authority as distinguishing characteristics of modern states.[4] In Russia, this process made estate status and religious confession less useful as means of structuring the empire's civic order. After 1905, when identity documentation became most widespread, those categories decreased in power. The state's more frequent identification of subjects by ethnicity or nationality, expressed as *narodnost'* or *natsional'nost'* in Russian, was one sign of this change.[5] In particular contexts, ethnicity supplemented estate status and religious confession, and sometimes replaced the latter.

[2] For a discussion of modern states and their attempts to "grasp" their populations, see Torpey 1997.

[3] Passports have received surprisingly little attention from historians of late imperial Russia. Mervyn Matthews' (1993) description of the pre-revolutionary passport system is a notable exception. Jeffrey Burds (1991) discusses the issuance of passports in his study of the social control of peasant labor. The use of metrical books under the tsarist regime has received virtually no attention.

[4] Alexis de Tocqueville (1955) described the emergence of a strong central authority governing an increasingly homogeneous population as a trend in Old Regime France that the Revolution of 1789 furthered. Max Weber (1978: 983–85) described "the leveling of the governed in face of the governing and bureaucratically articulated group" as a decisive aspect of modern states. Charles Tilly (1990: 103–17) asserts the centrality of the shift from indirect to direct rule in European state formation. On civic equalization, universal inclusion, and the movement from large collectives to individuals as objects of government focus in the Russian context, see Kotsonis 1998.

[5] For a discussion of concepts of ethnicity and nationality and their use in the classification of people in late imperial Russia, see Steinwedel 2000.

Metrical Books

The registration of births, marriages, and deaths entered Russian state life during the reign of Peter I (1682–1725).[6] Continually hungry for recruits and taxes to support his military campaigns and state-building projects, Peter sought a means of registering individuals instead of households as the Muscovite state had done in the seventeenth century. In 1724, the Holy Synod instructed Orthodox priests to record all births and deaths in their parishes, and to forward this information to church officials.[7] Until the reign of Alexander I (1801–25) and the formation of ministerial government, improvements in the compilation of the metrical books came slowly. By the reign of Nicholas I (1825–55), the purpose of the metrical books had become clearer. The state took steps to standardize the books' form in 1831.[8] Priests were supposed to record the dates of birth and baptism of all Orthodox children, as well as the names, estate statuses, and religious confessions of their parents. Priests also registered marriages and deaths. Metrical books had many flaws that limited their reliability, however. The transfer of information from a priest to the parish church to the provincial church consistory often resulted in the loss or corruption of metrical information. The law established no specific punishments for mishandling metrical books, which caused one commentator to call them "one of the weaker sides of our legal system."[9]

Despite their flaws, metrical books served as the fundamental register of identity in imperial Russia. They provided the basis for civil status— for the protection of a person's property and inheritance rights, for the official recognition of marriages and children, and for claiming the privileges commensurate with one's estate status. From 1831 to 1834, the presentation of metrical information became mandatory for those entering state service, for those who sought to be ennobled, and for noblemen who desired to prove that they had attained the age of majority. Metrical information also helped determine a male's eligibility for conscription.[10]

[6] In Europe, registration of baptisms took place in monasteries as early as the third century, and such registrations had become questions of state importance by the sixteenth century. See Ianovskii 1896: 201.

[7] Ibid.

[8] In an 1843 law, those born before 1831 who sought to be entered into the noble register were allowed to substitute other information. *PSZRI*, series II, vol. 20, no. 19,185 (1843).

[9] Ianovskii 1896: 204.

[10] *PSZRI*, series II, vol. 6, no. 4,313 (January 1, 1831): 116; no. 4,989 (December 6, 1831): 250. Inspections (*revizii*) were made intermittently to establish tax rolls and conscription lists. When inspections were not performed frequently enough, the list of those eligible for conscription was drawn from metrical books. *PSZRI*, series II, vol. 6, no. 4,677 (June 28, 1831): 504.

To present such information as required, a person requested that the church consistory provide him or her with the relevant excerpt from the metrical book, which could then be supplied to whomever insisted on proof of identity.

The use of metrical books was an innovation in the Russian Empire. Previously, the tsarist regime had only periodically counted taxpayers, potential recruits, or households by means of inspections (*revizii*). State officials intended metrical books to provide a continuous and more thorough registration of all the tsar's subjects. The issuance of metrical information on demand made this an individual identification, a piece of paper that a subject possessed and that established that he or she belonged to a particular social status group and religious confession. Metrical books connected subjects most firmly to a particular religious confession. Since the parish priest kept track of all metrical records, a person was literally written into the church at the beginning of his or her life. One's civil status depended upon one's connection with the church and its records, giving civil status a strong religious content.

Registration through the state church presented complications in an empire composed of many religious groups. Not all of the tsar's subjects were Orthodox. What to do about the rest? As Gérard Noiriel has pointed out, the Old Regime in France had faced a similar problem. Registration by Catholic priests left many Jews and Protestants without civil status. In 1792, the revolutionary Republic addressed this situation by secularizing registration and requiring municipal authorities to register all French citizens.[11] This option held little attraction for the Russian state, where an autocrat ruled an empire organized by legal estates. Tsar Nicholas I had no interest in creating citizens. As protector of the Orthodox Church, Nicholas I did not desire to eliminate religious registration, either.[12]

Nonetheless, Nicholas I and his officials did seek to identify the tsar's subjects and to include them in the civic order. The tsarist regime attempted to achieve the civic inclusion of the non-Orthodox by insisting that they register with their own religious institutions. Between 1826 and 1837, the tsar decreed that Catholic priests, Muslim imams, Lutheran pastors, and Jewish rabbis must keep metrical registers.[13] These laws did not extend civil status to all religious groups. Religious dissenters known

---

[11] Noiriel 1996: xviii and his essay in this volume.

[12] Napoleon introduced civil registration when he conquered Russian Poland in 1807, but this move was annulled with the issuance of a new civil law code in 1826. Ianovskii 1896: 204.

[13] The decrees are found in *PSZRI*, series II, vol. 3, no. 2,296 (September 21, 1828): 837–39; *PSZRI*, series II, vol. 7, no. 5,870 (December 28, 1832): 980; *PSZRI*, series II, vol. 7, no. 5,770 (November 24, 1832): 859–60; *PSZRI*, series II, vol. 10, no. 8,054 (April 13, 1835): 320; *PSZRI*, series II, vol. 12, no. 9,991 (March 3, 1837): 132–35.

as Old Believers, numbering as much as 10 percent of the empire's population, and animist peoples were notable exceptions.[14] The Orthodox Church claimed Old Believers as part of its flock, but the dissenters had rejected seventeenth-century reforms in the liturgy and generally wanted nothing to do with the Orthodox clergy. Furthermore, the expansion of metrical registration came at the expense of uniformity. Muslim imams did not report estate status. Religious leaders who did not know Russian could maintain the books in their native languages—the imams could use Tatar, for instance.[15] Nonetheless, the expansion of metrical books in the 1820s and 1830s represented a major step toward the inclusion of the empire's non-Orthodox residents into legally recognized subjecthood.

The Great Reform era brought a new governing ethos to the empire, one that changed the role of metrical registration. Reform-minded bureaucrats sought to increase the population's participation in the administration of the empire and to reduce the importance of estate distinctions. The state emancipated the peasantry, introduced a new court system, and allowed elected units of self-administration (*zemstvos*) a limited role in local affairs. The military service reform of 1874 marked a shift toward the equalization of male subjects in law. Before 1874, military service was an obligation for those of lower status. The military reform of 1874 made males of all estates liable for military service. A universal military obligation, with reduced burdens based on educational achievement, replaced an estate-based system. After the Great Reforms, the autocracy took the first, halting steps toward a more inclusive, less particularistic civic order.

The reformist vision of a new civic order produced pressure to incorporate previously excluded groups such as the Old Believers into the metrical system in 1874. The regime's means of doing so, however, differed from previous practice. The government decided to make the Old Believers the first religious group to register with civil authorities. The tsar decreed that Old Believers report their births, marriages, and deaths to local police administrations, which would record them in metrical books and issue metrical information just as church consistories did.[16] For the Old Believers, civil status had become a secular matter not connected to any religious authorities. The increased intervention of civil authorities in metrical matters provided a precedent. In 1879, the Baptists, a Protestant denomination deeply distrusted by the state, were instructed to register their metri-

---

[14] Robson 1995: 20–21.

[15] By allowing such variations in metrical registration, the empire demonstrated greater flexibility than Old Regime France had. Over time, the Russian state did aspire to greater uniformity, however. As of 1891, for instance, the law required that Lutheran metrical books be kept in Russian. *PSZRI*, series III, vol. 11, no. 7,798 (June 3, 1891): 357.

[16] *PSZRI*, series II, vol. 49, no. 53,391 (April 19, 1874): 652–56; *PSZRI*, series II, vol. 49, no. 53,886 (September 18, 1874): 234, and prilozhenie to no. 53,886: 420.

cal information with the police as well.[17] For members of these periodically harassed or persecuted groups, contact with the police was probably little more attractive than collaboration with Orthodox clergy. The degree of compliance with the decrees is unclear. Yet civil registration marked a break with the past emphasis on religious registration, and one in keeping with the civic order envisioned by those who drafted the Great Reforms.

Around 1900, economic change and political unrest revived debate on the nature of the empire's civic life in a manner not seen since Alexander II's assassination in 1881 had brought an end to Great Reform initiatives. Even some leading statesmen who had shown little interest in reform, such as Sergei Witte, minister of finance (1892–1903) and chairman of the Council of Ministers (1903–05), discussed reforms that would make administrative institutions more rational and promote a "proper civil life for all members of society" under the direction of the autocrat.[18] Civil status in a reformed state would retain a religious component, however. Even to a bureaucrat such as Witte, religion was the "chief foundation of morality."[19] Drawing all the tsar's subjects into the civic order demanded that all be able to practice their religion freely. All would then partake of religion, and thus participate in civic life. Somewhat later, in 1912, Witte identified religious toleration as a key component in the creation of a "national [natsional'nogo] state" of a certain type, since, in Witte's opinion, toleration established "relations of the government to all citizens [grazhdanam] and of them amongst themselves on the basis of firm and identical laws for all."[20] Individuals would be written into the civic order through religious institutions.

On April 17, 1905, the tsar issued a decree on religious toleration. For the first time in Russian history, the tsar's Orthodox subjects had a legally recognized ability to leave the Church. Dissident communities such as Old Believers received the right to organize and to construct houses of worship.[21] In developing legislation on toleration, the Committee of Ministers under Witte's direction stressed that the civic order required religious toleration and cited the importance of metrical registration. According to the Committee of Ministers, efforts to convert people of non-Orthodox religions to Orthodoxy had over time produced substantial

---

[17] *PSZRI*, series II, vol. 54, no. 59,452 (March 27, 1879): 277.

[18] Wcislo 1990: 80–81.

[19] *Zhurnaly Komiteta Ministrov* 1905: 160.

[20] Witte offered Otto von Bismarck as an example of someone who had created a national government that featured "religious toleration with respect to non-predominant confessions, even non-Christian [ones]," and the "equality of all citizens independent of religious confession and origin [proiskhozhdeniia]." Witte 1912: 4.

[21] *PSZRI*, series III, vol. 25, no. 26,126 (April 17, 1905): 258–59.

groups unyielding in their resistance to or apostasy from Orthodoxy. Such persons were Orthodox "only in name." They could not openly practice their real religions, and law forbade non-Orthodox clergy from ministering to their needs. Yet they refused to practice Orthodoxy and have Orthodox clergy minister to them. As a result, such people were "left completely without religion." Beyond the "moral suffering" experienced by people left without "spiritual comfort" at difficult moments in life, the Committee of Ministers focused on the fact that such people were "deprived of essential civil rights [*grazhdanskikh prav*]." Since their births, marriages, and deaths were typically not entered into metrical books, they did not have legally recognized families and therefore lacked firm property rights.[22] The committee resolved that persons who practiced a faith other than Orthodoxy be allowed to join officially the sect or religion that they actually practiced. Then they could be registered in metrical books and enter civic life on terms more or less equal with the Orthodox.

Religious toleration proved to have an uncertain future in the last years of the empire. Legislative projects that would have elaborated toleration's impact on a wide variety of institutions failed to win approval in the State Duma. A successor of Witte, Peter Stolypin, eventually gave up on these projects in 1909. As a result of the 1905 Manifesto on Toleration, however, non-Orthodox religious communities formed and grew rapidly in number. Old Believer communities in particular benefited from the new rules. The maintenance of metrical books, now called "books of civil status of sectarians," was specifically entrusted to these communities.[23] Laws on toleration did not equalize all religious groups — significant differences remained. But when nearly all the tsar's subjects could belong to an officially recognized religious faith, the Orthodox Church lost some of its particular importance. Toleration allowed most people, although not all, to register metrical information and thus acquire elementary civil status through their religious confession.

Passports

As the 1894 law on certifications of residence—internal passports—indicated, the documents served two functions: "as a certificate of identity [*udostovereniem lichnosti*]" and to establish "equally the right of absence

---

[22] *Zhurnaly Komiteta Ministrov* 1905: 157–58.

[23] Registration with civil authorities became a last recourse in cases in which a sectarian community did not recognize any member of its community as an authority and no one could be held responsible for the metrical books. *PSZRI*, series III, vol. 26, no. 28,424 (October 17, 1906): 914.

from the place of permanent residence in those cases when this right must be certified."[24] Passports identified an individual in a more thorough manner than metrical registers did. Metrical registers did not indicate current information about holders such as their residence, signature, or identifying marks. Passports did. Passports also regulated movement. They fixed a person's residence to a particular place and regulated travel to other places in the empire. The passport system in Russia originated at roughly the same time as metrical books. In 1719, Peter I decreed, "No one can be absent from his place of residence without legal permit or passport."[25] Travel documents became standardized, and their use obligatory.[26] Passports became a means of preventing the evasion of the new head tax and conscription.

Control of movement in Russia had much longer roots, however. The registration of peasants' places of residence had originated at least as early as the seventeenth century in order to support the division of society into privileged noble serfowners and non-privileged serf laborers who could move only with their owner's permission. In the course of the eighteenth and nineteenth centuries, passport rules were elaborated to reflect the empire's complex social distinctions.[27] Passport laws did not apply equally to all the tsar's subjects. Members of privileged estates—nobles, state servitors, honored citizens, and merchants—could choose as their official places of residence wherever they had established homes in conjunction with state service, employment, or the ownership of real estate. By contrast, members of lower orders had no such ability to choose. Those who belonged to lower urban and artisan groups (*meshchane* and *remeslenniki*) registered with particular estate administrative institutions and rural residents registered with particular rural societies. Registration reinforced the notion that each person belonged to one particular social group and belonged in a particular place.[28] The two groups also differed greatly in what sorts of passports they could receive. Those in higher orders received from the police a passport booklet that did not expire, allowing them to move about freely and without requesting special permission. Members of lower orders received passport booklets valid for five years, after which they had to renew their documents. Since lower orders were held responsible for the collective burden of taxes levied on their social group, they received their passports only with the approval of their urban estate administration in the case of townspeople (the *meshchanskaia* or *remeslen-*

---

[24] *PSZRI*, series III, vol. 14, no. 10,709 (June 3, 1894): 349.
[25] *Svod zakonov Rossiiskoi imperii* 1857: 3.
[26] Matthews 1993: 2; Beketov 1897: 923.
[27] Chulkov 1889: 81.
[28] *PSZRI*, series III, vol. 4, no. 10,709 (June 3, 1894): 349.

naia uprava) and only with the approval of their rural township administration (*volostnoi starshina*) if they were rural residents.[29] The lower orders also had to pay a yearly fee for the use of the passport as a sort of
tax on their movement. For members of lower orders, permission to be
absent from their residence could extend for up to one year, but again
only with the permission of their estate administrative institution. Other
groups faced additional restrictions on movement. Jews could only reside
within the "pale of settlement," which included the empire's seventeen
westernmost provinces. They could travel outside the pale only in certain
limited circumstances.[30] Women of all status groups could receive their
own passports only with their husbands' or fathers' permission. Otherwise, their husbands' or fathers' passports listed them. The law denied
completely the rights of some persons to have passports.[31] Despite great
political and legal transformations between 1857 and 1894, passport
rules changed little.[32] Rural township administrations simply assumed the
responsibility for regulating peasant movement that serfowners relin-
quished after the emancipation of the peasantry in 1861.

Passports recorded slightly different information depending upon
whether members of privileged estate groups or the non-privileged held
them. Passports for both groups stated the holder's full name, estate status,[33] date of birth or age, religious confession, marital status, and
whether the holder was subject to military service obligations. Not all
passports included a physical description of the passport's holder. Literate
passport holders, who were more likely to be from privileged estate
groups, signed their passport booklet. Passport holders who were illiterate had their height, hair color, and "special marks [*osobyia primety*]"
recorded. The information recorded in the passport differed in one other
respect. Point 5 in the passports of privileged persons recorded their
"place of permanent residence," but the "type of occupation" of those

[29] Ibid.: 354. Strategies for allowing or denying passports varied by rural administration.
See Burds 1991.

[30] Szeftel 1976: 248; Stanislawski 1983: 36–37.

[31] People deprived of their rights through legal proceedings, those under police surveillance, handicapped people unable to provide for themselves, and gypsies could not receive
passports at all. Volkov 1910: 322.

[32] In 1894, urban dwellers were no longer required to hold a certificate of residence in
their place of permanent residence, people could travel within their home county and up to
about thirty-five miles outside it, and people could take agricultural work outside their home
areas without a passport. *PSZRI*, series III, vol. 14, no. 10,709 (June 3, 1894): 350; Matthews 1993: 11.

[33] The word used on the passports was *zvanie*. Gregory Freeze (1986: 31) writes that
zvanie could indicate either occupation or social estate. Since passports for the lower orders
also had a category "type of occupation," *zvanie* here would seem to indicate something
broader than occupation.

less privileged.[34] In sum, a person's estate status determined who issued his or her passport, whether a person could choose his or her place of residence, the type of passport he or she received, and what information the document contained.

As in the case of metrical books, the events of 1905 produced a fundamental change in passport regulations. When Peter Stolypin became chairman of the Council of Ministers in 1906, he, like Sergei Witte before him, sought to reconstruct the empire's civil life by drawing more of the population into a direct and equal relationship with the state and eroding the estate basis of social and political institutions. The tsar issued a decree to this end on October 5, 1906.[35] Among other measures, the law applied to the peasants and petty urban strata the same residence requirements and passport laws that had applied to the nobility and other higher-status groups. People belonging to non-privileged estates could choose their official places of permanent residence on the basis of either where they were employed or where they owned property.[36] They received permanent passports that did not expire. If they remained in the place to which they had been ascribed, they would receive passports from their estate administrative institutions. If not, they received their passports from the police administration. The lower orders were now essentially equal to their superiors with respect to movement and residence.[37]

After 1906 passports no longer fixed higher or lower orders to one place of residence, but still served as identification and helped regulate movement. Most of the tsar's subjects could now choose their place of permanent residence, but they were still expected to have a passport which specified that place. Data on passports for rural residents indicates that passport issuance continued to increase after 1906. Between 1906 and 1910, nearly one in eight peasants in provinces of European Russia received passports.[38] Furthermore, the new, more liberal passport laws did not apply everywhere. The rule that "no one is obligated to have a

[34] *PSZRI*, series III, vol. 14, no. 10,709 (June 3, 1894): supplement to no. 10,709: 286, 289. The Jews were an exception to this rule. All had to have their "special marks" recorded whether or not they were literate. Since passport restrictions on Jews were much more severe, state officials presumably perceived that Jews had an increased incentive to try to circumvent the rules and sought to reduce this possibility.

[35] The October 5, 1906 decree elaborated on the article of the empire's Fundamental Laws issued April 23, 1906, which specified that "[e]very Russian subject has the right to choose freely his place of residence . . . and to travel freely beyond the limits of the state." Szeftel 1976: 98.

[36] *PSZRI*, series III, vol. 26, no. 28,392 (October 5, 1906): 891–93.

[37] Ibid.: 892. The passport booklet remained essentially the same, however.

[38] The average percentage of village population issued passports in the forty-three provinces of European Russia increased from 2.9 percent in 1861–70 to 12 percent in 1906–10, or by about four times. See Burds 1991: 56–57.

residence permit in the place of permanent residence" did not apply to St. Petersburg and Moscow. Similarly, passport regulations were suspended in regions surrounding factories and mines. The state still sought to control who could live in the capitals and around factories. The verification of identification—passport checks—was more common in these areas.[39] Law still forbade most Jews to live outside the pale of settlement, and married women could receive separate passports only with the permission of their husbands.[40]

Emergency security regulations designed to increase state security indicated a tendency contrary to that of the liberal reforms of 1906. The regulations greatly increased the state's ability to control movement and residence. Introduced following Tsar Alexander II's assassination in 1881, the emergency laws were originally conceived as a temporary measure. Succeeding governments continued to renew the laws, however, and they remained an option for the regime until 1917.[41] Under each type of emergency regulation, passport laws did not apply. Provincial governors could deny individuals the right to reside in areas under their charge, and they could banish from their provinces people they considered undesirable.[42]

The revolution of 1905 greatly increased the application of emergency security measures. In the last months of 1905, tsarist authority nearly collapsed throughout the empire. The restoration of authority under Peter Stolypin entailed political reform, but featured an unprecedented application of police power as well. By March 1906, the state had applied some sort of emergency law to thirty of the empire's seventy-eight provinces, and officials with such powers governed sizable portions of another thirty provinces.[43] As late as 1913, much of the empire remained under reinforced or extraordinary security, including the capitals, thirteen provinces in their entirety and substantial portions of many more, several major cities, and predominantly non-Russian areas such as Poland and Central Asia.[44] As the state reduced estate institutions' control over the movement

[39] Rogovin 1913: 1.

[40] Szeftel 1976: 250. Only in August 1915, during the First World War, did the state allow most Jews to live outside the pale of settlement. So many Jews had been forced to flee military front zones or had been deported to the empire's interior that the minister of internal affairs officially permitted Jews to live in cities outside the pale. Ibid.: 148. Regarding women, see Rogovin 1913: 9–10.

[41] The regulations allowed three levels of special measures: reinforced security, extraordinary security, and martial law—which allowed local officials to disregard legal procedures in various ways and to various extents. See Daly 1995: 602–29; Pipes 1974: 305–9; and Ascher 1988: 110.

[42] Daly 1995: 613, 616; *PSZRI*, series III, vol. 1, no. 350 (August 14, 1881): 263–66.

[43] Ascher 1988: 111.

[44] Rogovin 1913: 273–75.

of non-privileged orders, the state increased its own direct power over movement through the application of emergency security regulations.

Nationality

Metrical registers and internal passports remained the most widely used techniques of identification, and religious confession and estate status remained the most important ascribed categories until the end of the Old Regime. Before 1917, however, the changing nature of the civic order and resulting new political practices caused these categories to be perceived as less than fully reliable means of identifying a subject's political loyalty, economic potential, and place in that civic order. When nearly all religious establishments could provide a path to civil status, the importance of distinctions among religious confessions decreased. When movement restrictions and passports no longer distinguished privileged from non-privileged estates, the legal importance of one's estate status declined. As state policy began to erode the power of estate status and religious confession to situate people in the civic order, ethnicity or nationality became an important supplement to such traditional categories. Even officials within the regime came to define the population by nationality.

Migration was one such practice associated with identification by ethnicity. Pressure on land in central Russian provinces prompted many to move east or south in search of land. For example, by 1897, recent migrants made up about one-tenth of the population of Ufa province, on the eastern edge of European Russia. Around 1896, the regime began to promote migration as a solution to rural impoverishment in central Russia, and resettlement increased.[45] In the post–Great Reform period, local administrations perceived as their mission the incorporation of subjects into a civic order that would foster a productive population. Newcomers who "lived outside the law" could not be managed effectively to provide taxes and recruits.[46] Migrants had left far behind the network of religious institutions, estate organizations, and police administration that fixed them in the civic order and ascertained their reliability and economic potential.

Migrants were not all alike, either. Many came from nearby provinces, but some came from other regions entirely. Their different agricultural practices were often perceived as better developed than those of the native residents of newly colonized areas. Officials associated various ethnic groups with different levels of agricultural development. Such differences would not be reflected in the categories of estate status and religious con-

[45] Usmanov 1981: 72–73.
[46] Ibid.

fession. As early as the 1860s, local officials in Ufa began to encourage the in-migration of the "Russian element" to increase agricultural productivity on the empire's borderlands.[47]

To obtain more knowledge of migrants, the regime had a form printed specifically to identify groups of migrants as they sought to resettle. One example dating from 1895 contains a list of questions to be asked each family of settlers. The questions included the full name, place of origin, nationality (*natsional'nost'*), and estate status of the settlers. Officials also questioned settlers extensively regarding their economic means and previous agricultural practices.[48] Significantly, the form did not even ask for the settlers' religious confession. In June 1904, major legislation that reduced the power of estate institutions to control the migration of members of lower orders further reflected state officials' interest in the nationality of those who migrated. The legislation specified that "only persons of native Russian origin [*korennogo russkogo proiskhozhdeniia*] and the Orthodox confession" were allowed to migrate to Central Asia and the Caucasus.[49]

The 1905 revolution and the State Duma, created in 1906, provided another context in which state officials expressed interest in the nationality of individuals. People of all estate statuses and religious confessions participated in oppositional politics in 1905, making these categories seem less effective as means of organizing the civic order. The revolution and elections to the State Duma mobilized religious groups in new ways, making what many officials perceived as secular political threats, often interpreted as national ones, out of older religious rivalries.[50] Officials began to use nationality as a means of identifying groups within the population with particular interests that required representation in political institutions or with interests that the state sought to exclude from politics.

Elections to the State Duma catalyzed classification by nationality at the individual level. Elections to the first two convocations of the Duma in 1906 and in early 1907 took place through a complex system of curiae that represented a mix of estate and property criteria. This electoral system yielded Dumas with which the tsar and his prime minister, Stolypin, could not work. The tsar closed the Duma on June 3, 1907, and cited the substantial participation of non-Russian delegates as a primary cause for his disappointment with the institution. Nicholas II decided that non-Russian groups should be represented in future Dumas, but that

[47] *Vsepoddaneishii raport* 1899: 2; Usmanov 1981: 61–62.

[48] Central State Historical Archive of the Republic of Bashkortostan (hereafter TsGIA RB), f. I-11, op. 1, ed. khr. 1272, ll. 171-171aob.

[49] *PSZRI*, series III, vol. 24, no. 24,701 (June 6, 1904): 604.

[50] For a discussion of this process in one region, see Steinwedel 1999: ch. 4.

non-Russians should not have decisive voices in "purely Russian" questions.[51] The electoral system for the third and fourth convocations of the Duma reduced representation from the countryside and from non-Russian regions.

Signifying the regime's sensitivity to the national composition of the Duma, the new electoral law specified that preliminary electoral meetings could be segregated by estate and nationality (*natsional'nost'*) where appropriate.[52] As a result, when local units of self-administration compiled lists of eligible voters, they included the category of nationality as well as estate status, place of residence, and the voters' landholdings. The lists indicate both the importance attached to nationality and the difficulty that even educated Russians working in local self-administration had in categorizing people by nationality. By the time elections to the fourth Duma in Ufa province took place in 1912, ethnic classifications were still not consistent among its six counties. People with Muslim surnames were listed as Muslim in Belebei county, as Bashkirs in Birsk county, and as Tatars in Menzelinsk county. The nationalities of some were not specified.[53] The tsar had declared nationality to be of great importance to the functioning of the Duma, but what exactly it meant was not yet clear.

Education was another field in which identification by nationality became common after 1905. As late as 1906, the educational administration on the eastern border of European Russia identified students only by their estate and religion in its annual report.[54] By 1911, the Ministry of Education routinely collected information on the nationality of the student population based primarily on a student's native language.[55] A form to be completed by school inspectors in 1912 asked for information on the nationality (*natsional'nost'*) and religious confession of students but did not request their estate status.[56]

The identification of students' native language became the subject of special attention in 1912. The decree on religious toleration of April 17, 1905, had specified that the tsar's subjects were permitted to have religious instruction in state schools in their native language. The parents of a student were supposed to register the native language of their son or daughter. However, experience had convinced the educational administration that in areas where the population was illiterate or had "a weakly expressed national self-consciousness," parents were unable to do so. Es-

---

[51] *PSZRI*, series III, vol. 27, no. 29,240 (June 3, 1907): 320.

[52] Ibid.: 324.

[53] *Ufimskie Gubernskie Vedomosti*, prilozhenie to no. 60 (August 1, 1912); prilozhenie to no. 61 (August 4, 1912).

[54] TsGIA RB, f. I-109, op. 1, d. 167, l. 55l.

[55] Ryzhkov 1915: 207.

[56] "S formoi vedomosti" 1912: 513–14.

pecially in western regions of the empire, Catholic clergy had taken advantage of this policy to have Belorussian and Lithuanian speakers declare Polish as their native language. To avoid such a situation, on October 27, 1912, the Ministry of Education declared that the heads of primary schools must address the parents of students orally or in writing in order to determine their native language so that non-Orthodox clergy would not have an opportunity to influence the process.[57] The educators sought to identify native language directly from individuals and without the participation of religious institutions.

Conclusion

Throughout the nineteenth century, metrical books and passports showed the regime's desire to organize a civic order based on religious confession and estate status. Metrical books connected the tsar's subjects directly with religious institutions, and religious toleration expanded this link to more of the population. Distinctions between passports of privileged and non-privileged orders supported the estate hierarchy, as did the issuance of passports for the lower orders only with the permission of estate institutions.

In the time of crisis, 1905–06, tsarist officials aimed to establish more direct relations between the state and a greater proportion of the tsar's subjects. Policy regarding metrical registers and passports reflected this goal, although the strategy pursued in each case differed. The tsar's manifesto on toleration reinforced the connection of civil status and religious institutions. By expanding civil status through religion to nearly all groups, however, civil status ceased to depend upon membership in a few approved faiths and became nearly universal. Shortly thereafter, the state reduced the role of estate institutions in the control of mobility and increased its direct control of residence and movement through expanded application of emergency laws. Thus, as the state expanded identification by estate status and religious confession to more of the population, it undermined particularistic institutions. As expanded metrical registration and passport issuance increased the regime's power to identify individuals by estate status and religious confession, the power of these categories to order civic life decreased. Policy regarding metrical registration and passports reflected the tsarist state's efforts to "level" the tsar's subjects before its centralizing authority in the manner de Tocqueville and Weber had identified.

[57] "O iazyke prepodavaniia" 1913: 17–18.

At the same time, the tsar's officials began to employ nationality more frequently as a means of identifying a person's economic potential and political loyalty. The ascription of nationality held advantages for the regime that estate status and religious confession lacked. Nationality was not racial in the Russian Empire, but it was perceived to be more durable than estate or religion. One might be able to gain status through service or good fortune, and one could convert to a different religion. One's language, culture, and descent seemed harder to shed. Nationality, although not universalistic, did not fix a person to concrete, local church and estate institutions. The state's ascription of nationality connected a subject to a broader "imagined" national community and the politics, cultural practices, and even agricultural techniques that went with it. However, the tsarist regime's basic techniques for identifying its subjects, metrical registers and passports, never included nationality. Therefore, after 1906, when the regime identified its subjects by estate status and religious confession in identity documentation, it did so in ways that no longer fully reflected the categories even the regime itself considered important. In its last years, the tsarist regime eroded its traditional basis of rule, a hierarchy of estates and religious confessions, but it did not and perhaps could not embrace an alternative and identify its subjects accordingly.

5

Colonizing the Subject: The Genealogy and Legacy of the Soviet Internal Passport

MARC GARCELON

INSTITUTIONAL practices leave traces that echo in the social world long after their institutional architecture disintegrates. Take the case of relations between Soviet practices of classifying, monitoring, and controlling the place of residence, career trajectory, and officially designated nationality of Soviet citizens, on the one hand, and the economic, social, and political problems faced by the successor states of the Soviet Union in the 1990s, on the other. The "surveillance order" erected by a Party-state intent on fashioning a mechanism for flexibly deploying and redistributing entire populations through an apparatus of centralized administrative command has shaped the developmental history of problems in the post-Soviet states as diverse as land reform, housing shortages, the status of refugee populations, and nationality conflicts.[1] A centralized system of internal passports formed the administrative fulcrum of this surveillance order, for the residential housing permits (*propiski*) needed to secure a legal domicile and the work books (*trudovye knizhki*) required to secure employment were issued only with the presentation and registration of a valid passport at a local police office. For these reasons, the genealogy of the Soviet internal passport is inseparable from that of the Soviet system itself.

An internal passport, as distinct from an external or international passport, is a form of pass document by means of which the mobility of bearers may be restricted within the jurisdiction of a single state. External or international passports serve both to facilitate the rights of an issuer state's citizens abroad, and to secure state control of movement across international boundaries. In contrast, internal passports "may be a state's principal means for discriminating among its subjects in terms of rights and privileges . . . [and] may be used to regulate the movements of certain groups of subjects, to restrict their entry into certain areas, and to deny them the freedom to depart their places of residence."[2] The Soviet pass-

---

[1] The concept of a "surveillance order" is loosely adapted from Foucault 1977.
[2] Torpey 1998a: 254.

port served precisely as such a mechanism of administrative domination of the Soviet population, and thus should be sharply distinguished from the international passport familiar to Westerners. To travel abroad, for instance, a Soviet citizen first had to obtain both a second, external passport and an "exit visa" (*vyezdnaia viza*). Institutionally speaking, the Soviet internal passport was therefore much closer to the notorious pass documents used by the apartheid regime in South Africa to dominate the African population than it was to the international passports familiar to travelers in contemporary Western societies. Moreover, as in the South African case, the genealogy of the Soviet internal passport maps a distinctively Soviet pattern of "internal colonialism."

All modern states are to a significant extent marked by a history of internal colonialism, "the political incorporation of culturally distinct groups by the [dominant] core."[3] This follows directly from the origin of all modern states in expansive conquest, the subjugation of alien populations, and the eventual incorporation of these subject populations into larger territorial entities.[4] On the basis of this "universal history" of state origination, Michael Hechter proposed the concept of internal colonialism as an alternative to what he called the "modernization" or "diffusion" model of national development.[5] In this view, internal colonialism represents the first phase of state-building.

Internal colonialism generates a "frontier-colonizer" mentality within the dominant group, and a consciousness of oppression and resistance among peripheral, colonized groups. This dynamic stems from the center's attempt to militarily annex a territory and then transform frontier areas into its own image, all the while reducing outsider populations or classes to subaltern roles in the new order. Colonial Brazil, Ireland under English rule, and the nineteenth-century United States stand as classic examples of such frontier societies.[6] Above all, internal colonialism entails "*administrative differentiation* such that there are both citizens and subjects, as dictated by the colonial analogy."[7]

Alvin Gouldner argued over twenty years ago that the concept of internal colonialism served as a particularly apt description of the relation between the Party *apparat* and the nominal citizen in the Soviet Union, the archetypal Party-state of the twentieth century.[8] After all, the cadres of the Bolshevik Party in effect colonized the groups that fell under their domination by forcibly mobilizing such groups into the project of "build-

[3] Hechter 1975: 32.
[4] Elias 1982.
[5] Hechter 1975: 3–43.
[6] Gouldner 1977.
[7] Hechter 1975: 33.
[8] Gouldner 1977.

ing socialism," along the way subjecting them to the administrative fiat, organizational principles, and ideological norms of Soviet power. In so doing, the Party leadership sought to cultivate a distinctively Soviet mentality befitting the "new man" of socialism. This strategy entailed marginalizing and co-opting prior identities in favor of Soviet ideological norms, a project that paralleled the subordination of the indigenous cultures of colonized groups to the dominant culture of the colonizing center in the building of Western nation-states.[9] As we shall see in what follows, the Soviet internal passport gradually evolved into a crucial instrumentality of these sweeping political and social aims.

Economic and Disciplinary Aspects of the Soviet Passport Regime

The building of the Party-state did not occur in a historical vacuum, as Soviet internal colonialism developed on the ruins of a prior imperialist project—namely, the expansionist autocracy of tsarism. Indeed, during the heyday of "building socialism," the autocratic modus operandi of the Stalinist leadership mirrored the Party-state's drive to subordinate producers to the new planning regime of socialism, much as tsarist methods mirrored the imperial autocracy's drive to subordinate the population to patrimonial institutions. The Weberian ideal type of patrimonial domination emphasizes the autocratic proclivity to organize society as an extension of the autocrat's private household.[10] Where tsarist patrimonialism organized the Russian Empire as an extension of the tsar's personal dominion,[11] Soviet socialism organized the Soviet Empire as an extension of centralized Party dominion. At the center of this dominion stood the "partocracy" (*partokratiia*), the upper stratum of Party officials who formed the nucleus of the *nomenklatura*—that is, the senior administrative *apparat* of managerial positions in state, economic, and social organizations. *Nomenklaturshchiki* were appointed directly by the Central Committee of the Communist Party of the Soviet Union (CPSU) in line with a centralized list—the "nomenclature"—of potential candidates for positions designated as strategic by CPSU leaders.[12] The Soviet Party-state

[9] For the complex relation among Soviet nationality policies, regionally specific ethnic identities, and the communist project of fashioning a generic Soviet identity complementing the administrative designation of Soviet citizenship, see Abrahamian 1998 and Suny 1993.

[10] "*Patrimonialism* . . . tend[s] to arise whenever traditional domination develops an administration and a military force which are purely personal instruments of the master" (Weber 1978: 231).

[11] For a seminal treatment of tsarist patrimonialism, see Pipes 1992.

[12] In the post-Stalin period, *partokratiia* and *nomenklatura* functioned in everyday Russian speech as synonyms for the ruling strata of Party and state officials; see Garcelon 1997.

can thus be characterized as a distinctive variant of patrimonialism, "*partocratic patrimonialism*," in which the whole range of social life outside the domestic sphere of friends and family was subordinated to the personalistic *diktat* of the "partocrats" and their plenipotentiaries.

Like the state nobility of tsarist patrimonialism, the partocracy and *nomenklatura* formed an archetypal stratum of rent-seekers, appropriators of wealth produced by dependent subjects. "It does not demand great intellectual effort to perceive the connection between the Petrine Table of Ranks and the Soviet [*nomenklatura*] system."[13] Rent-based elites strive to monopolize economic opportunities in order to preserve and expand their control over producers,[14] and this "structural imperative" predisposed both Russian imperial and Soviet leaders to centralized, administrative approaches to economic organization. Much as patrimonial domination under the tsars entailed the subordination of market relations to the imperatives of the economic tribute on which the autocratic regime depended, the economic design of Stalinist socialism aimed at abolishing market relationships in favor of the centralized planning of physical inputs—including labor—and the administrative redistribution of productive outputs. In the Soviet Union, internal colonialism and document-based control of the population developed symbiotically as elements of the emergent Soviet command economy of "*industrial patrimonialism*"—the economic *Doppelgänger* of the personalistic political domination of the partocrats—which subordinated the agrarian "periphery" to the urban-*apparat* "core" through the process of forced collectivization.[15] In a manner reminiscent of tsarist-era serfdom, forced collectivization bound peasants to the land in order to extract surplus product from the countryside on terms wholly unfavorable to agricultural labor, condemning peasants to political subjection. The internal passport stood as a principal instrument of controlling the agrarian population under both tsarist and Soviet domination.

Historically, internal passports arose under absolutist regimes from France to Russia as an instrument for monitoring the movement of peasants.[16] The Soviet system of internal passports revived this autocratic practice and took it in new directions. From their introduction at the height of "the building of socialism" in the early 1930s through the demise of the

---

[13] Fehér et al. 1983: 38.

[14] Weber 1978: 1090–99.

[15] For a systematic treatment of the command economy as an institutional model, see Grossman 1970. For a fuller treatment of the concepts of partocratic and industrial patrimonialism, see Garcelon 1997. For an overview of convergences between traditional forms of personalistic domination and *nomenklatura* rule in the post-Stalin Soviet Union, see Jowitt 1992.

[16] Torpey 1997.

Soviet Union, internal passports functioned as the principal disciplinary mechanism by which the *apparat* consolidated its dominant position and inculcated the cultural standards of "new Soviet man" among the peoples living beneath the edifice of the Party-state. Those who ran afoul of Soviet domination, from educated urban dissidents to "punished peoples"—entire ethnic groups like the Chechens singled out by Stalin as "enemies of the people" in the wake of the Second World War[17]—discovered that the *pasportnyi rezhim* effectively condemned them to the marginal ranks of physical laborers, internal exiles, and labor camp inmates. On the other hand, much of the population quickly learned that an enthusiastic embrace of the socialist project in the form of shows of ritual obeisance to Soviet authority was the usual precondition of access to the benefits doled out through the passport system, such as apartments and jobs in "closed cities" (*rezhimnye goroda*) established under the passport regime.

What were the closed cities? A closed city under Soviet communism required a residence permit (*propiska*) in order to legally receive a housing assignment from the state. And the issuance of a *propiska* in turn depended on the certification of one's legal status under the passport regime, either by a city official or, most commonly, by a local enterprise. In this way, the Party-state linked access to residences in closed cities to the labor needs of enterprises in these same cities, a linkage administered through the passport system. And access to many consumer products and ration coupons in turn depended on the official registration in the internal passport of one's place of residence and employment. Birth was the only way of gaining residency in such a city outside the *pasportnyi rezhim*. Even travel to and from closed cities was tightly controlled through the system of internal passports and residence permits.[18] By restricting residence and employment opportunities in major cities and strategically crucial "company towns" like Magnitogorsk, the giant steel complex built under Stalin on a desolate steppe on the Ural River,[19] the Party-state effectively stratified territories in line with the pyramidal engineering of occupational groups under industrial patrimonialism. This "stratification of places" thus excluded "strategically secondary" and exploited groups like the peasantry from access to work and life in the most dynamic urban areas of Soviet society.[20]

The archipelago of closed cities created by "passportization" (*pasportizatziia*) formed a pivot of *nomenklatura* control over the allocation of

---

[17] For a history of such stigmatized ethnic groups under Stalinism, see Helsinki Watch 1991 and Nekrich 1978.

[18] For an extended analysis of closed cities in the Soviet period, see Zaslavsky 1982.

[19] For a history of this exemplary "socialist city," see Kotkin 1995.

[20] For the concept of "the stratification of places," see Logan 1978.

labor, privilege, and internal movement under "actually existing social-ism." For instance, the state construction industry often supplemented tight labor supplies in closed cities by "importing" temporary laborers to complete a specific project. Such "internal migrant laborers" (*limitchiki*) were denied *propiski* and were often forced to reside in temporary bar-racks near the construction site, thus creating a subaltern stratum of sec-ond-class workers at the margins of closed cities.[21] Indeed, the concentra-tion in the hands of local *apparatchiki* of discretionary control over the distribution to underlings in the workforce of a sweeping array of goods, services, and petty privileges functioned as a powerful tool of personalistic domination, ideological monitoring, and hierarchization in the command economy.

While the Soviet internal passport system indeed formed "the heart of police power in the USSR,"[22] the enmeshing of the *pasportnyi rezhim* with a comprehensive system of material rewards tied to the ideological evalua-tion of behavior rendered it a "disciplinary apparatus" in Michel Fou-cault's sense. For Foucault, a "disciplinary apparatus" constructed sub-jects like "prisoners" through an array of practices on the levels both of organizational routine and of specialized discourses linked to these routines.[23] As an array of disciplinary practices, the passport regime linked rewards and punishments to degrees of public conformity to stan-dardized ideological discourses. Over time, the institutionalization of such rituals of conformity inscribed the Soviet "order of things" in the bodies and everyday speech of its subjects.

The disciplinary function of the Soviet passport system underscores the purely administrative character of citizenship in the Soviet Union, for So-viet citizens lacked recourse to any effective mechanism of rights enforce-ment, and instead were forced into cultivating personalistic ties to admin-istrative superiors as the only effective means of establishing some level of security in daily life. In effect, legality (*zakonnost'*) was subordinated to "Party-spiritedness" (*partiinost'*) as an organizing principle in everyday life, patrimonializing access to needs and stripping the concept of citizen-ship in the Soviet order of any substantive relation to the Western under-standing of citizenship as a right of participation in a political commu-nity.[24] The privileges associated with placement in a closed city under Soviet communism thus should only with great caution be compared to

---

[21] Zaslavsky 1982: 144–46.

[22] Shelley 1996: xv.

[23] Foucault 1977. In his later work, Foucault broadened his earlier focus on disciplinary apparatuses into an analysis of modern "governmentality," "which bears essentially on pop-ulation and . . . [corresponds] to a type of society controlled by apparatuses of security" (Foucault 1991: 104).

[24] For the distinction between *partiinost'* and *zakonnost'*, see Sharlett 1977.

the privileges associated with citizenship in medieval and early modern towns in the Occident, as placement in a closed city in no way entailed enjoyment of any specific *political rights* under Soviet communism. To the extent that one can speak of citizenship in the political sense of the term at all in the Soviet context, one is speaking by and large of the partocracy and some segments of the broader *nomenklatura*. However, even at fairly senior levels, politics resembled more the personalistic "court politics" of traditional autocracies, rather than the participatory politics of effective citizenries in Western towns and cities.

Archival materials indicate the extent to which Soviet leaders explicitly intended the internal passport to function as a comprehensive disciplinary apparatus. Especially telling is a top-secret speech delivered on April 16, 1935, by Genrikh Yagoda, the People's Commissar of Internal Affairs. Yagoda spoke to a special Conference on Chiefs of the Regional Directorates of the Workers' and Peasants' Police convened by the People's Commissariat of Internal Affairs (NKVD) to emphasize the implementation of the passport laws:

> You need to ensure that every precinct inspector has his own so-called "household" [*podvornyi*] and village network, that is, in each residential apartment building and in each residential village he must have two or three people able to inform him regarding suspicious persons, those persons without a passport or a *propiska* [residence permit], those huddling in attics or sheds or involved with hooliganism, theft or anything else. In every apartment and village there are people who know who these people are. . . . All information of a political character discovered in this way must be sent to the Directorate of State Security for processing and the taking of appropriate measures. . . . The passport is a powerful means for the purging of our cities, workers' settlements, industrial enterprises and construction sites not only of criminal, but also of anti-Soviet, counter-revolutionary elements. In order to realize this, it is necessary to make it unthinkable that a person can live in an apartment or a barracks without a passport or a propiska. . . . *We need to create an atmosphere such that each citizen feels that without a passport he will be unable to travel anywhere, that the single document confirming his identity is the passport.* The first question you must ask a detained citizen is—show me your passport.[25]

As in all effective disciplinary systems, however, coercion was only one side of the story. The paternalistic "concern" of the *apparat* for "the people" formed the flip side of obedience to cadres and conformity to the new identity embodied in the Soviet passport. Thus, the Party-state organized various competitions, award ceremonies, and letter-writing campaigns so-

---

[25] GA RF, f. 9401, op. 12, d. 135, l. 119; my emphasis. My thanks to Paul Hagenloh for directing me to Yagoda's speech in the archives.

liciting "comradely" criticism from below alongside the passport regime's sweeping surveillance order and its draconian enforcement mechanisms. Thus *apparat* domination came "cooked in the rhetoric of 'caring about' the people," underscoring the common paternalistic thread between tsarist and partocratic patrimonialism.[26]

The Origins and Development of the Soviet Internal Passport

The Soviet system of internal passports was introduced at the end of 1932 as part of a comprehensive package of administrative mechanisms designed to mobilize and discipline labor inputs during the industrialization drive embarked upon by the Soviet leadership under Stalin. Above all, the internal passport tied access to foodstuffs, housing, and employment to a police-regulated document system coordinated with the management of industrial enterprises and collective farms. The denial to collective farmers (*kolkhozniki*) of the right to an internal passport formed the cornerstone of the *pasportnyi rezhim* by confining them to the collective farms (*kolkhozy*). *Kolkhozniki* thus could not travel legally or obtain food supplies or housing beyond the boundaries of the *kolkhoz* without first obtaining special passes from the officialdom.[27] By stratifying the population spatially, the internal passport created a device by which closed cities could be designated, "anti-Soviet elements cleared out" (*razgruzka antisovetskikh elementov*), and the mass migrations from countryside to city engendered by forced collectivization and industrialization regulated in line with the labor requirements of the Five-Year Plans and the Party-state's urban planning objectives.

The introduction of the Soviet internal passport in 1932 at first glance seemed to mark a return to tsarist practices. After all, the Russian Empire from the time of Peter the Great used internal passports as a means of monitoring political opponents, and especially as an instrument for binding serfs physically to the landed gentry to which they were subordinated by custom, tradition, and law. Devised to segregate the population into free and unfree social categories and to keep the latter firmly under the thumb of the former, tsarist-era passports—like their Soviet successors—were used to register their holders through the assignment of *propiski*

---

[26] Siegelbaum 1998: 127. Siegelbaum's study of Soviet paternalism in rural areas in the mid-1930s reveals the dynamic of carrot and stick in the construction of Soviet identity, and especially of the Soviet state as a "wise, stern, but also beneficent father."

[27] For more on the collective farms as a "second serfdom," see Zaslavsky 1982 and Fitzpatrick 1995.

(residence permits) indicating their "social status" (*sotsial'noe sostaia-nie*), social origin (e.g., "peasant"), and place of residence.[28]

One of the first acts of Lenin's new government upon coming to power was the abolition of the *propiska*, a detested symbol of tsarist oppression, still in force among peasants and urban workers in 1917. Yet shortly thereafter—as the civil war spread, various "black marketeers" in goods proliferated, and workers began to abandon the factories in search of food and to avoid Bolshevik pressings into the Red Army—the infant Soviet regime reverted back toward a system of de facto internal passes. The implementation of work books (*trudovye knizhki*) signaled a Bolshevik turn toward an autocratic command system of labor allocation. Work books were introduced in two stages by decrees of the Council of People's Commissars (*Soviet narodnykh komissarov* or SNK).[29] The introduction of work books was occasioned by the collapse of the urban food supply and the Bolsheviks' mid-1918 decision to roll back the brief flowering of workers' control of management, and thus served first and foremost as a means of controlling "parasitical elements" and compelling workers to remain on the shop floor under adverse conditions.[30]

Both SNK decrees make clear that work books functioned as pass documents: bearers were required to register every month in the local soviet where the work book was issued, and enterprise and housing officials were to assign jobs and places of residence only to those holding valid work books. When combined with the reintroduction of internal passports as "a form of identification that each citizen of the Republic is required to possess" just six months after the Bolshevik victory in the civil war, these decrees signaled a consolidation of a new regime of internal controls on movement.[31] A fateful pattern had been established: when faced with a choice between compromising revolutionary ideals or the extent of administrative surveillance of populations in the territories it militarily occupied, the Bolshevik regime consistently opted for the former.

In the early 1920s, however, the Bolshevik power relaxed the incipient system of document-based control over internal movement in line with Lenin's New Economic Policy (NEP). The NEP backed away from the

---

[28] For overviews of the history of internal passports under tsarism, see Liubarskii 1994 and Matthews 1993.

[29] The SNK directives establishing work books were issued on October 5, 1918, and June 25,1919, respectively. The text of both decrees is reproduced in Khobotov and Zheludkova 1990:9–10 and 12–15.

[30] For the rapid demise of workers' control of industry in 1918, see Avrich 1963. For the rapid decline in the size of the urban proletariat in 1918, see Smith 1983: 243.

[31] For the text of the February 23, 1922 "Law on Passports," see Khobotov and Zheludkova 1990: 24–29.

regime's civil war practice of relying on forcible grain requisitions to maintain urban food supplies, establishing in their stead market principles as the chief basis for the exchange of agricultural and industrial goods. These measures aimed to blunt the growing hostility of the peasantry toward the regime in Moscow and Petrograd, a regime that only four years before had rallied the rural poor behind the slogan "Land, Bread, and Peace." "Not regarding the peasantry as a reliable political ally, but scarcely having a proletariat of its own to 'lead' (especially after its decimation and exhaustion following the Civil War), the CPSU was radically isolated. . . . What had been brought into being was an urban-centered power elite that had set out to dominate a largely rural society to which they related as an alien colonial power; it was an internal colonialism mobilizing its state power against colonial tributaries in rural territories."[32]

Lenin's push for a relative relaxation of central economic controls under the NEP was thus designed to buy time on the part of a weak "core" dealing with a rural "periphery" ravaged by war, starvation, and the disastrous economic policies of war communism.[33] Lenin made perfectly clear the tactical character of this easing of centralized autocratic control by simultaneously and successfully pushing the Party leadership to adopt the notorious ban on factions at the 10th Congress of the Communist Party in 1922 and intensifying repression of political opponents.[34] The NEP in effect legalized a restricted market economy under the monopolistic regulation of the embattled Bolshevik dictatorship in the cities. As part of this shift back toward market arrangements, the regime passed a law establishing "freedom of movement for each citizen of the Russian Federation." This law was adopted in January 1922—just one month prior to the adoption of the stillborn February 1922 internal passport law—as part of the Bolsheviks' retreat from the use of work books and internal pass documents.

By relaxing control of movement in the countryside and allowing peasants to market grain, the regime hoped to spur agricultural production in rural areas. This trend culminated in the abolition of internal passports and work books, effective January 1, 1924, by a decree of the SNK issued on June 20, 1923, in line with the requisites of reviving a labor market under the NEP.[35] According to this decree, any written form of personal

---

[32] Gouldner 1977: 13.

[33] Total grain production dropped almost 50 percent between the last prewar harvest in 1913 and the last year of the civil war in 1921; see Atkinson 1983: 226. Historians generally agree on a figure of seven million deaths from starvation during the civil war. For a comparison of the economics of War Communism and the NEP, see Nove 1982: 46–118.

[34] Schapiro 1977: 314–42.

[35] Khobotov and Zheludkova 1990: 52–56; Liubarskii 1994: 17.

identification registered by the police in a person's place of residence would now be accepted as valid.

The relative freedom of movement of the NEP began to erode once more, however, with the drift toward forced industrialization and collectivization in the late 1920s. In the middle and late 1920s, the problem of how to find the capital needed for industrialization preoccupied various factions in the Bolshevik leadership.[36] Stalin consolidated a personal dictatorship in the Communist Party in part by rallying the more radical rank and file behind his new "revolution from above" against the so-called Right Opposition of Nikolai Bukharin and other Bolshevik leaders hostile to Stalin's emerging program. Stalin's "left offensive" sought to finish with the forces of "NEP capitalism" by collectivizing the grain harvest and thereby maximizing the surplus extracted from agriculture that was necessary to finance industrialization and feed the cities. Stalin's strategy tacitly converged with that of the later "Trotskyist" oppositionist Evgenii Preobrazhensky, who first proposed "alienating the surplus of the peasantry" as the solution to this problem of "socialist accumulation" in 1924.[37] Although Stalin forbade the use of Preobrazhensky's terminology to describe forced collectivization, the reasoning behind the "revolution from above" was identical to that of Preobrazhensky.[38] Above all, forced collectivization aimed to overcome the "scissors crisis" of the late 1920s, the widening gap between high prices for manufactured goods and low prices for agricultural products.

By 1927, the persistent and glaring price imbalance between low agricultural prices and high prices for finished industrial goods in the countryside—"the scissors"—was functioning as a disincentive steering peasants away from state grain buyers, as sale on the private market, whether legal or black, brought a better price. And where a better price couldn't be found, the storing of grain for personal consumption began to make more and more economic sense to peasants. After all, the Party-state coveted peasant grain and labor as the primary source for capitalizing rapid industrialization, and its leaders displayed a marked ideological hostility toward "the petty-bourgeois mentality" of small farmers. The scissors of relatively high industrial and relatively low agricultural prices, although engineered by the state itself as part of its NEP-era strategy for extracting surpluses from the countryside in order to finance industrial investment, had cumulatively starved the state of the agricultural goods needed to feed workers and amass capital for the all-important goal of rapid indus-

[36] Lewin 1975: 132–71.

[37] Preobrazhensky 1987.

[38] For a full treatment of the factional conflicts over agricultural and industrial policies in the Party leadership in the 1920s, see Cohen 1971.

trialization. Although by 1927 agricultural production had recovered to 92 percent of its 1913 level, the regime's arbitrary and inconsistent pricing policies foreshadowed a coming crisis with the peasantry over industrialization and exactions from the countryside.[39] Stalin justified the "left turn" of the late 1920s by arguing that the Party had to subject the peasantry irreversibly to centralized state control. This was to be realized by designating small farmers able to hold their own in the market as "rich peasants"—so-called kulaks—in order to extract the necessary amount of grain foreseen in the new Five-Year Plan. Kulaks, of course, were quickly branded "class enemies."[40] Stalin thus contrived an ideological cover for abolishing the NEP and waging what amounted to a civil war against the peasantry as part of his larger aim of destroying private holdings of whatever size in Soviet agriculture.[41]

The social upheaval that resulted from the forced industrialization and collectivization drive between 1928 and 1932 created enormous problems for the new Stalinist leadership. On December 27, 1932, the Politburo decreed mandatory passportization (*pasportizatsiia*) of key urban areas as a means of stemming mass migration from the countryside to the cities, expelling rural refugees from urban settlements, and thus bureaucratically consigning peasants to agricultural areas. Passportization signaled the ascent of repression as the principal means of containing the civil war conditions fostered by the regime's policies in many rural localities. In one stroke, the Stalinist core opted for a strategy of "total" administrative control over the movement of the population as a means of compelling a recalcitrant labor force—especially peasants, a group utterly peripheral to the Stalinist vision of industrial socialism—into compliance with the dictates of the Five-Year Plan.[42] This strategy realized the worst fears of the principal opponent of Stalin's "revolution from above" in the Soviet leadership, Nikolai Bukharin, who warned in 1928 that Stalin's "left turn" would culminate in "the military-feudal exploitation of the peasantry."[43]

By any measure, collectivization was an unmitigated disaster for peasants under Soviet domination. Nominal agricultural incomes did not recover until the mid-1950s, and in many areas, particularly Ukraine, widespread starvation ensued. Most scholars now consider 10 million deaths from starvation—the vast majority of them in the countryside—the price

---

[39] The many zigs and zags of agricultural pricing policies—which culminated in the so-called procurement crisis of 1928 and Stalin's subsequent consolidation of autocratic power—are detailed in Lewin 1975: 172–293.

[40] The hiring of a single agricultural hand at some point during the year was sufficient to brand a peasant a kulak under Stalin's draconian criteria; see Lewin 1975: 490–91.

[41] Kuromiya 1988: 4–11.

[42] Schwarz 1952: 106–7.

[43] Cohen 1971: 307.

paid for collectivization.[44] But from the point of view of the Stalinist center, collectivization succeeded in its primary goal of subjecting agricultural labor to the tributary imperatives of the command economy: whereas in 1927, 98.3 percent of peasants remained private economic actors, by 1936, 89.6 percent of peasants had been collectivized.[45]

The denial of internal passports to the overwhelming majority of peasants, thus tying them to the few square kilometers around their assigned collective farms, was the linchpin of the new order. The administrative design of the new system emerges clearly from the 1932 decree and the list of appended "Passport Regulations." The decree called for the complete passportization of seven key cities, as well as the passportization of transport workers and key "workers' settlements" and construction sites such as the Magnitogorsk metal-factory complex east of the Urals. "Anti-Soviet" and "anti-social" elements—from "oppositionists" and "kulaks" to "criminals," "vagabonds," and "parasites"—not explicitly assigned work in official organizations and enterprises were to be "cleared out" (razgruzka), that is, expelled or arrested. The introduction of passports effectively abolished all other forms of identification; in those areas not yet "passportized," new temporary identification documents were to be issued by local soviet organs when a citizen needed to travel or wished to get married, acquire housing or another job, and so on.[46]

The decree emphasized that the "registration of persons in areas where the passport system has been established is absolutely mandatory" and that residents moving into "closed" (i.e., "passportized") areas "present their passports for purposes of registration to the organs of the police, through the proper housing bureau, no later than twenty-four hours after their arrival." Persons required to have a passport but found without one were "subject to administrative measures." A second violation of passport regulations could trigger prosecution as a "criminal." All citizens in designated areas above the age of sixteen were to be "passportized." Thus *control over movement* formed the alpha and omega of the new system,

---

[44] Note that this figure excludes deaths from repressions. Chirot 1986: 147–54, provides a telling synopsis of scholarship on the scale of human suffering in the Soviet Union in the 1930s and 1940s.

[45] Nove 1982: 106 and 174.

[46] The decree establishing the Soviet internal passport system was entitled "On the Establishment of a Unitary Passport System in the USSR and the Mandatory Registration of Passports" and was issued jointly by the Central Executive Committee and the Council of People's Ministers of the USSR on December 27, 1932; Kalinin and Enukidze signed for the Central Executive Committee, and Molotov for the Council of Ministers. All citations of this decree and the "Passport Regulations" issued with it are from copies in a file of "Orders and Decrees of the OGPU-NKVD USSR on Passports and Passportization" held in the State Archives of the Russian Federation (*Gosudarstennyi arkhiv Rossiiskoi Federatsii*), GA RF f. 9401, op. 12, d. 135, ll. 36–38.

with the rural populace consigned by lack of documents to the enclosed space of the *kolkhoz*.

Soviet internal passports would also be used as a handy compendium of biographical information on their holders available for on-the-spot inspection by Party-state administrators and local police officials. Beyond "class background" as a "worker," "bourgeois," "landlord," "peasant," or "intellectual," one of over a hundred official nationality designations was to be entered in each passport. Designation of social status and nationality were permanent and irrevocable; in the case of nationality, only children of mixed marriages had a choice, between the nationality of either parent, and only once in life—at the age of sixteen. Additional information to be placed in passports included past military service, criminal record, place of work, persons on whose authority the passport was issued, and permanent place of residence.

At the end of the Soviet period, the nationality designation in the internal passports would prove to have momentous unintended consequences. The indication of the bearer's nationality was originally intended as an administrative tool facilitating bureaucratic control of the population and the management of potential ethnic tensions. On the one hand, official recognition of titular nationalities formally fulfilled earlier Bolshevik pledges of "liberation" to non-Russian minorities.[47] On the other hand, the substantive consequence of this designation as an instrument of official nationality policy was to engineer local "compradors," core-dependent, ethnically homogeneous non-Russian elites in localities and regions across the Soviet Union. Ironically, the nationality principle enforced via passportization backfired spectacularly on the center in the Gorbachev period. In the end, regional ethnic elites engineered in this fashion proved perfectly capable of leading insurgencies against the center, an outcome entirely unanticipated by Soviet leaders.[48]

The close connection between access to housing and the possession of a valid passport merits reiteration here. The passport system directly determined access to housing via the *propiska*, issued only with the registration of a valid passport at the local police headquarters. An integral component of the Soviet internal passport, the *propiska* in effect functioned as a supplementary document by means of which labor supply and access to goods could be tightly subordinated to the "one man rule" (*edinonachalie*) of local cadres.[49] The mandatory inclusion of photographs in each

---

[47] Abrahamian 1998.

[48] For more on the unintended nation-building consequences of the nationality designation in Soviet passports, see Brubaker 1994 and Slezkine 1994.

[49] Kotkin 1995: 56–57. The principle of *edinonachalie* in management and administration was established in the early 1930s during the industrialization drive.

passport in 1937, at the height of the Great Terror, further strengthened internal passports as the principal administrative element of control over internal movement under Soviet socialism.[50]

Soviet leaders expanded the passport regime relentlessly throughout the Soviet period, regardless of the stated objectives of numerous surface-level administrative reforms of the passport system. By the late 1960s, dozens of closed cities had been designated and passportization extended throughout the country. Only in 1979 were collective farmers ceded the right to a passport, although in practice this reform was all but ignored until the last days of perestroika.[51] To this day, although the post-Soviet Russian government has abolished much of the passport regime on paper, many of its elements continue to function as a key component of political power at the local and regional levels. In the fall of 1995, for instance, the mayor of Moscow, Yuri Luzhkov, ordered the local police to clear the city of unregistered persons from the Caucasus and Central Asia on the basis of passport designations, a practice resumed in response to the renewed flaring-up of hostilities between the Russian army and Islamist forces in Dagestan and Chechnya in late 1999. Luzhkov has also obstinately continued to enforce the *propiska* as a means of deterring migration to the city and maintaining mayoral control over the city's housing stock, despite the abolition of the *propiska* by federal legislation.

Of course, the history of decrees and regulations is often distinct from the history of their implementation. In the case of the Soviet internal passport and *propiska*, however, repressive decrees and orders were widely and systematically implemented. Internal memos of the Ministry of Internal Affairs state that in 1952 alone, for instance,

> [A]s a result of the observance of regulations for issuing passports and *propiski* in accordance with passport regulations, 9,423 criminals were discovered and detained . . . 25,036 unauthorized persons in restricted localities were identified and removed . . . along with 74,839 homeless persons [*bez opredelennogo mesto zhitel'stva i zaniatii*] . . . 12,934 persons without proper papers were discovered traveling in forbidden areas . . . 441,823 persons who in the past had committed crimes were uncovered and brought to account . . . 107,220 persons were investigated through the address bureaus . . . 12,825 persons were brought to trial for criminal violations of passport regulations . . . and 849,886 persons were subject to administrative penalties for passport violations.

The total number of violators of the *pasportnyi rezhim* listed in the archives of the Ministry of Internal Affairs for 1955 and 1956 were, re-

---

[50] GA RF f. 9401, op. 12, d. 135, l. 197.
[51] Liubarskii 1994.

spectively, 1,192,500 and 1,667,018.[52] Such figures indicate the scale of repressive control established by the system of internal passports over the Soviet population, which in 1952 officially numbered 188 million persons.[53] In effect, citizenship had been transformed into an administrative mechanism for putting a colonized populace under surveillance.

Conclusion

The ubiquity of the *pasportnyi rezhim* as a disciplinary apparatus in Soviet life, and the extent of the "second serfdom" suffered by peasants under Soviet domination, stand out from the brief overview presented above. The passport system shaped the social history of Soviet society profoundly, as it steered patterns of social, ethnic, and geographic stratification that continue to exert centrifugal pressure on the Russian Federation in the postcommunist period. Indeed, the war in Chechnya in the mid-1990s was waged on the Chechen side by the sons and daughters of the 957,000-odd Chechens deported en masse to Central Asia and beyond by Stalin in the 1940s, a group branded "enemies of the people" by the Chechen nationality designation in their passports. Although these measures were officially rescinded under Khrushchev and survivors of the deportation were allowed to return to Chechnya in 1957, roughly a quarter of the deportees had perished as a direct result of the forced dislocations, fueling the bitter hatred of Russian authorities among Chechens that erupted in the 1990s.[54]

With the aid of the internal passport, the Soviet Union during and after Stalin sought, with considerable success, to restrict the access of the Soviet population to the goods and opportunities available in closed cities and to reduce the possibility of unconstrained rural-urban migration. Members of collective farms were subjected, at least until the late 1970s, to restrictions on their movement that bore remarkable similarities to those of tsarist-era serfdom. The political economy of the post-Stalin Soviet Union, built on the mechanism of allocating labor through the *pasportnyi*

[52] Figures for 1952 are from GA RF f. 9415, op. 3c, d. 1443, ll. 4–5. Figures for 1955 and 1956 are from GA RF f. 9415, op. 3c, d. 1447, l. 2. Both files are stamped "Secret." These fragments of Ministry of Internal Affairs archives are among a small number available in the State Archives of the Russian Federation; most such archives remain in the former Ministry's own archive, which to my knowledge has still not been made available to Western scholars.

[53] Zaleski 1980: 633.

[54] For details of the Chechen deportation, see Nekrich 1978: 42–60; and Helsinki Watch 1991: 6 and 21–25.

rezhim, engendered a stratification of economic sectors and geographic spaces. This sectoral and spatial pattern of stratification mirrored, and resonated with, the inequalities in Soviet life that flowed from the Communist Party's patrimonialization of collective resources.[55]

In the Brezhnev era, the spatial, sectoral, and ethnic patterns of stratification mapped out in the passport regime ossified into the social order described above as industrial patrimonialism, a hierarchical ordering of closed estates, status groups, and ethno-territorial social configurations reminiscent of a traditional agrarian order but incorporating industrial organization and techniques and anchored in the economic dependence of citizens on local *apparat* notables of the Party-state.[56] The remnants of industrial patrimonialism—from ethnic-based local elites to giant company towns based on single industries to the continuing use of residence permits to exclude migrants from big cities—bequeathed a legacy that profoundly shapes the most intractable social problems of the post-Soviet states.

Indeed, the internal passport replicated particular national identities at the expense of the internationalist ideology of "new Soviet man," rather than gradually dissolving them into a generic Soviet identity as Soviet leaders had hoped. Although the geographical binding of agricultural labor to collective farms remained the primary purpose of passportization under Stalin, the auxiliary use of national identity as designated in passports to engineer loyal "comprador" elites in non-Russian areas backfired in the long run. Indeed, the *pasportnyi rezhim*'s construction of local-elite identity on the dual basis of "Sovietness" and "nationality" created an alternative basis of power for local elites once perestroika relaxed the "total" grip of the center. Under the changed circumstances of the late 1980s, such local elites often opted to challenge the dominion of imperial partocrats in Moscow on the basis of their "national" identifications and power-bases. Ironically, Mikhail Gorbachev augmented these dynamics by conducting a sweeping purge of regional partocrats opposed to perestroika, thus creating a power vacuum that "national" *nomenklaturshchiki* and intellectuals would eventually fill.[57] The persistence of national identities in part reproduced through the passport system thus played a

[55] See Pierre Bourdieu's definition of "political capital under state socialism" in Bourdieu 1991.

[56] "Commercial classes arise in a market-oriented economy, but status groups arise within the framework of organizations which satisfy their wants through monopolistic liturgies, or in feudal or in *ständisch*-patrimonial fashion. Depending on the prevailing mode of stratification, we shall speak of a 'status society' or a 'class society' " (Weber 1978: 306). In Weber's terms, then, I am classifying Soviet society as such a status society.

[57] For the purge of regional *obkom* party secretaries carried out in the 1980s, see Helf 1994.

prominent role in the disintegration of the Soviet Union. In retrospect, the disciplinary project of deploying a comprehensive apparatus of document-based control over movement, labor, and housing as a means of engineering an ideologically prescribed identity foundered on its own contradictory practice of abetting the reproduction of the very "national" identities it aimed to displace.

6

Modern Horrors: British Identity and Identity Cards

JON AGAR

"Do you have an identity card?"
"It is in my car, officer."
"Your car?"
"My car is outside. My bag, I brought in."
"I see. May I ask you other ladies and gentlemen for your cards of identity?"
They look confused. "Well," says the policeman, "ration-books, licenses—anything like that."
They fumble in their robes, but nothing comes out except the stub of a ticket for the Old Vic dated April 15, 1934.
"I can identify my *car*, officer," says the doctor.[1]

IN RECENT YEARS there have been several calls for the British to be issued identity cards in order to combat perceived threats to social order—most recently, football hooliganism, underage drinking, and benefit fraud. In the debates that follow such calls, the pros and cons of identity card systems found in continental Europe are discussed. It is rarely noted that ID cards have been introduced twice in Britain, during the First and Second World Wars, but dismantled both times soon after for interesting reasons. Outside this period their appearance was quickly forgotten, and the question "do you have an identity card?" would be met with confusion—as in Nigel Dennis's 1950s farce quoted above. In this essay I examine the arguments that sustained the introduction, and led to the breakdown, of British identity cards.

A continuing theme in debates about identity cards has been the distinctiveness of a British "character," opposed to various European mod-

I wish to thank the editors, participants in the "Documenting Individual Identity" workshop, and members of CHSTM, Manchester University, for helpful criticisms of earlier drafts of this essay.
[1] Dennis 1955: 369.

parasitic vitality

els, from anxieties over "Prussification" in the early period of National Registration to the European Community in the past few decades. While the emphasis of arguments against identity cards in recent years has been on surveillance aspects, this is not the focus of my essay. Instead, I attempt to answer two questions. First, how have conceptions of national identity, particularly within the relevant government departments and the national press, been mobilized in discussions of identity cards? In particular, does "Britishness" explain the rejection of such schemes? Second, how have forms of official identity been creatively used by subjects? Stressing the interpretative flexibility of official identity provides a means of undermining simplistic surveillance stories. Cases of wartime fraud or impersonation through forgery of (official) identity—a twentieth-century return of Martin Guerre—as well as modern horrors and media panics, about bigamy in particular, will illustrate these responses.

bigamy

The emphasis put on bigamy by commentators on British identity cards was a great surprise to me at the beginning of my research. Surprise turned to insight. Bigamy was the prism through which were refracted many public fears—of duplicity, of the growth of state power, and of disruption to social order in a century of unprecedented conflict. Its history demonstrated a generalization: that bureaucratic attempts to pin unitary identities on individuals were never a matter of simple top-down imposition. Instead, such efforts brought to light the popular use of a multitude of identities. It is even fair to say that the availability of state-approved single identities was a powerful new resource for the creation of further multiples, as evidence of a range of new crimes will testify. In matters of surveillance, power never flows merely one-way.

Faced with the practical difficulties of attaching identity cards to individuals, civil servants improvised a range of techniques to meet their objectives. The details of these innovations were specific to the case study, but again generalizations can be drawn. Abandoning the direct approach, the identification of persons was hitched to wider systems. In a felicitous phrase, identity cards were described as gaining "parasitic vitality" from attachment to other systems, for example, food rationing. This push to interlink created the opportunities for "data creep" as systematized knowledge of individuals circulated between government departments. Finally, the phenomenon of parasitic vitality helps us understand why a Briton was—and is—more likely to be identified by a car than by a card. While the system of drivers' licenses was not universal, car use was embedded in everyday private life. The introduction of universal identity card systems has only been politically achievable in Britain in times of universal mobilization for war. In peacetime, partial systems gave the appearance of liberty—and therefore distance from continental models.

Identity, Cards, and the Great War

"National identity" is a slippery term: while often a motley collection of representations, clichés, stereotypes, institutions, and imagined ways of life, it is both undeniably powerful as a cultural resource and therefore fascinating to the historian (particularly recently as a means of reviving national political history), but also for the same reason dangerous: essentialism, for example, lurks not far away.[2] National identity meant different things at different times to different people—although some loose overlap at any one time was often crucial to its working. Before the First World War, British national identity was particularly vague, an amalgam of imperial roles and anti-Catholicism (a negative construction, strengthened by the reactions to Irish nationalism). "Britishness" was often interchangeable with "Englishness"—hardly a reflection of a context in which national identity was strongly contested (at least by the English)! However as J. M. Winter has recently argued, the Great War threw some aspects of "Britishness" into sharp relief. In particular he points to a celebration of the "character" of the British soldier (first the private Tommy and only later the officer—middle-class, patriotic, unemotional, unintellectual, and masculine), but also a process of differentiation: what was "English" was defined in opposition to what was taken to be German: decency versus bullying, fair play versus atrocities, amateurism versus militarism.[3]

Such national differentiation was work done across many cultural registers: from the popular press (thundering against atrocities) to classical music (Elgar rather than Wagner). Most important for this essay, the upper echelons of civil servants—those who might advise government ministers, for example—were also involved: the aspect of Germany that they chose to contrast was bureaucratic, especially "Prussian" bureaucracy, portrayed in popular culture as on the one hand frighteningly efficient, and on the other a labyrinth of paperwork and a trial by petty officialdom. "Prussification" encapsulated undue interference by government in everyday life. However, a war that demanded mobilization of nearly all industry and population inevitably led to an expansion of the state in Britain: political actions that would have been unthinkable before 1914 now became necessities. There was a remarkable tension between the construction of national identity and national administrative policies, of which I take the introduction of identity cards as a rich example.

[2] For an introduction to the literature on British national identity, see Samuel 1989.
[3] Winter 1996: 261–77.

tension btwn nat'l identity &
nat'l admin policies

A system of identity cards needs a bureaucratic mirror: a register held centrally, or a collection of local lists. Registers accompanying certificates already existed in Britain. Births, deaths, and later stillbirths had to be registered at local offices from the mid-nineteenth century, and a central repository of certified copies of certificates was kept in London (there were 160 million in vaults by 1931). More and more information on the population began to be acquired by government in the early decades of the twentieth century.[4] Registers actively maintained in 1914 included ones of marriages, voters, TB sufferers, the mentally deficient, pupils at school, and contributors to National Insurance. However, none of these lists aimed at both universality *and* contained an up-to-date address: everyone had a birth certificate but it did not pinpoint the current location of the holder. To know a population in this individualized way, a new system was needed.

The prompt for a National Register (NR)—a listing of the names and addresses of the population—was to furnish "information as to the numbers of persons available for (a) industrial purposes and (b) military and naval purposes," although the use of the Register was soon sucked into arguments over conscription.[5] Despite attempts to reinforce voluntarism as the principle of recruitment, the scale of the hostilities soon led to its abandonment. An act rushed through Parliament in the summer of 1915 provided that for the duration of the war a "Register shall be formed of all persons male and female, between the ages of fifteen and sixty-five," with the only exceptions being members of the armed forces, or "any prisoner in a prison, certified lunatic or defective, or inmate of any poor law institution hospital or other prescribed institution, or to a prisoner of war or a person who is interned." The significance of the NR lay in its comprehensiveness: those excepted by the act were already listed on specialized registers, but now *all* the population, except some of the young and old, would have an individual place in the official records. Unlike any census the British people would be known not in aggregate but by unit.

Having completed a form at a "local registration authority" (in practice a local government office), a person was given a certificate that he or she signed, and, by the National Registration Act, was obliged to preserve. This document was the first general identity card issued in Britain. No provision was made for the signature to be witnessed by the issuing authority—indeed many certificates were never signed. The bearer was meant to inform the local registration authority if she or he moved, or if

---

[4] Vincent 1998: 141.
[5] Public Record Office (hereafter PRO) RG 28/1. "Memorandum on the National Register, 1915–1919," May 31, 1919.

the card was lost (if so, a free new card was issued). The question of legal enforcement caused unease within Whitehall:

> The most radical fallacy of the whole system is the assumption that the individual members of the population can be brought to perform even the simplest operation by being subjected to a legal obligation to do so. It is in the first place more difficult than anyone outside the Insurance Department would believe to convey effectively any sort of instructions or information to individual members of the masses on matters of this kind. Millions of leaflets have been issued by the Department, with little or no apparent effect. The knowledge of their duties and rights in connection with State Insurance, so far as it now exists, has come by a slow process of gradual education. But no system of legal obligation and penalties, even if the individual were aware of them, will induce or compel the general population to take steps which from their point of view are difficult and complicated, and the point and importance of which they cannot realize. This is not due to any lack of patriotism or of respect for the law, but has its cause deep down in the genius of the nation, the freedom of its private life from bureaucratic incursions, its unfamiliarity with and distaste for formalities or procedure and "red tape". Such a system could only be successful when enforced, as in Germany, by a rigorous and ubiquitous police system upon a nation accustomed to be regulated in all minor matters of life. Any system of registration which is intended to operate successfully in this country must be based on different principles.[6]

This attitude was not speculative: the system of National Insurance introduced before the war had nearly broken down because the problems of internal migration had been underestimated. Just within London 600,000 notices of "removals" (when a person changed place of residence or job) had paralyzed the accounting system covering an insured population of 1,450,000. With the NR the population had an even weaker sense of personal benefit than with National Insurance, and therefore legal penalties were arguably necessary. However, throughout the discussions differences between Germany and Britain were emphasized. Would the public "tolerate a system of universal registration, which involves the continual reporting of removals etc and a considerable amount of interference with individuals," a system described as a "Prussianizing" institution?[7] Likewise a scheme for "national book-keeping"—a sort of moral NR—proposed by Noel Pemberton Billing (a far-right Member of Parliament, pioneer aviator, and would-be scourge of the 47,000 "Privy Councillors, wives of Cabinet Ministers, even Cabinet Ministers themselves,

---

[6] PRO RG 28/1. "Memorandum on the NR scheme," by SPV (Vivian), July 1, 1915.
[7] PRO RG 28/7. Sir H. Munro to Hayes Fisher and President of Local Government Board, September 22, 1916.

diplomats, poets, bankers, editors, newspaper proprietors, and members of His Majesty's Household" who he claimed were losing the war through decadence) was rejected, not primarily because of Billing's politics, but because

> although the experience of the war may have prepared the average Englishman for a fuller registration system than he knew before, it is difficult to imagine that he would tolerate such a system as this, with its never-ceasing entries and its almost daily handling of the registration record by employers, schoolmasters and workmen alike.[8]

I suggest two processes were at work here. First, civil servants were undoubtedly preparing the ground for explaining the failure of National Registration, which they saw as having being hijacked in the conscription arguments in the Cabinet. Second, they were participating in cultural work on the home front: the cultural differentiation of defining Englishness against German stereotypes. However, the fact that many of the civil servants regarded a properly organized National Register as an invaluable tool of government shows that the first process could outweigh the second: the anti-German rhetoric evaporated when they sought to persuade their superiors of the benefits of a permanent peacetime Register and identity card system.

The Second National Registration

The British identity card of the First World War had a quiet death, and a nearly forgotten grave. The movement of people and the loss of cards led to numerous applications for new cards from the citizenry, but new cards were often not matched to old cards. The rapid growth in number of records in the National Register caused by this process of "inflation" led to the system becoming first unwieldy and later useless. By July 1919, the *Manchester Guardian* could remark: "Apparently, National Registration had survived merely in order to be forgotten, and the news that the Government no longer desires that it shall be kept up to date sounds rather like reading the funeral service over a mummy."[9]

Yet civil servants remained keen that some form of individual documentation should continue. Reflecting on the experience of the wartime NR, the General Register Office's detailed inquest concluded that "it would appear that the present register, with all its defects, has proved itself to be

---

[8] PRO RG 29/110. Phillips to Hayes Fisher, January 11, 1918. For more on Pemberton Billing's scheme, see Agar forthcoming. For more on Billing's 47,000, see Hoare 1997.

[9] *Manchester Guardian*, July 17, 1919.

invaluable for the existing recruiting system; it has only been less valuable in other directions because its potentialities have not been exploited, and if put on a permanent basis it would [suitably modified] . . . undoubtedly justify itself as an addition to our national institutions."[10] Elsewhere, the Middlesex County Council Association argued that a new NR would help "having regard to the necessity of tracing aliens of enemy nationality," although the official experience was that inclusion of aliens had been confusing and "unnecessary."[11] During the interwar years the pressure for a new National Register came from the military. The Committee of Imperial Defence (CID) pressed through the 1920s for a new NR: "in a Great War (as in the last) the nation would be compelled to call up its last man and comb and re-comb the classes previously passed over or disregarded. . . . A sound system [of NR] was most important." As part of plans for "national service in a future war," the CID proposed that in the meantime "the electoral registration system, the census organisation, and the births, marriages and deaths registration system should be amalgamated so as to provide a uniform system of registration for all purposes."[12] A peacetime NR was deemed "impracticable," the main problem being the extreme difficulty of attaching official identity to individuals:

> If it [NR] cannot be given enough real peace value of its own it must be given a borrowed and artificial peace value; i.e. its use and production and the quoting or recording of the number upon it must be made obligatory in regard to as many as possible of the organised activities in close touch with the life of the people. If it has not sufficient vitality of its own, it must derive a *parasitic vitality from* established national institutions and social organisations.[13]

Such problems—the slippage between official reference and referent—ruled out a peacetime NR in Britain. However, plans for immediate implementation on the outbreak of war were formed: the War Book—the administrative handbook for organizing future war—spelled out the details. The civil servants' problem was how to make an identity card valuable to the public, so that this crucial instrument of wartime administration would function, and not collapse, under inflation. The key, decided Registrar-General Sylvanus Vivian, was food:

> Any system of NR, as being an instrument of conscription, would obviously be received by the public with some reserve and suspicion, and in its actual administrative working, when established, would be exposed to a hostile bias

[10] PRO RG 28/1. "Memorandum on the National Register, 1915–1919," May 31, 1919.
[11] *Sunday Times*, April 6, 1919. PRO RG 28/1. "Memorandum," May 31, 1919.
[12] PRO RG 28/25. "Subject matter of Sub-Committees on National Service," February–March 1923.
[13] Ibid.; my italics.

on the part of the individual members of the public. By linking that system with the equally necessary system of registration for food rationing purposes . . . motives would be interlocked. . . . In the case of machinery serving both purposes these risks would cancel out and the interlocking motives would make for far greater effectiveness in both respects.[14]

The public had to eat; therefore, the public could be made to carry official identity cards. Rationing was both a cause and an effect: the fair distribution of food could only be secured with some form of universal identity card, but this necessity also ensured that the card was there for other bureaucratic purposes.

British identity cards and National Registration were introduced for the second time swiftly in 1939. The Ministry of Health assumed overall responsibility, with local registers under the registrar-general, and an innovation, a Central National Registration Office opened at Southport, north of Liverpool. Introducing the bill to Parliament, the minister of health stressed the social benefits, arguing that "the stale statistics" of the 1931 census should be updated,

> in order that we may make the best possible use of man-power and woman-power available for our national activities, and also to facilitate other measures such, for instance, as the distribution of food, food supplies, and the preservation of contact between members of families which have been dispersed for example under the evacuation scheme.[15]

The emphasis was therefore on dissipating the effects of war: identity cards would allow food shortages to be eased, or the East End parent to be in touch with a child evacuated to rural Wales. However, the register was also, of course, an instrument of war, as suggested by the euphemism "national activities": a means of facilitating call-up for compulsory service. The registration was taken on September 29, 1939, within a month of the invasion of Poland, and buff-colored identity cards bearing name and address were issued.

At Southport, seven thousand transcript books contained the details of 40 million registrations. While the personal card was kept simple, at the Central Register a mass of extra information could be stored: sex, marital status, whether the individual had been called up for national service, or if the person was wanted, for example, for desertion. The Register could also link up with other databases: people receiving family allowances, or the electoral register. Police, and those guarding secure sites, could demand to see an identity card, and although the police had no explicit

---

[14] PRO RG 28/28. Vivian to Foley, February 14, 1934.
[15] PRO RG 28/261. Report on CNRO, by John W. Foster, December 1947.

simple card but more info in register

power to detain anyone who did not produce a card, a combination of sweeping Defence Regulations gave them this power in practice.[16]

But the card was also useful to the card-holder for official purposes: for application for a passport, to open an account or withdraw money from a post office savings bank, to collect parcels from the post office, and especially for claiming ration books—a person had to present his or her card periodically to obtain them. Since the card was useful—essential, indeed, for many—people cooperated with the system, and the Central Register was well maintained. Local food and national registration offices were combined in 1943, when all cards were reissued, to knit the operations even closer. This reissue was also designed to catch deserters and other evaders of national service. The paucity of information on the card (name, number, and address), compared to that on the Central Register, was key: a deserter with a forged or stolen card would have to guess a date of birth, which could then be cross-checked. For this reason a card with a photographic portrait (i.e., more information) was rejected, except for use within Whitehall and sensitive military areas where the "Green" identity card was introduced following fears of fifth-columnists. (The suggestion to use photographs on the Green card came to the registrar-general from his brother, Valentine Vivian, head of counterespionage at the Secret Intelligence Service, more commonly known as MI6. This filial link between public and secret state bodies is intriguing but nearly impossible to reconstruct using available documents.) It was the combination of a surprisingly simple card and a scrupulously maintained centralized listing that gave NR "so great a range of power."[17] An accurate Central Register meant that it was a reliable source of statistics: providing the General Register Office with up-to-date information on movements of the population, mobilization, and demobilization. Finally, the card was important for the often difficult task of identifying the dead and the bureaucratic process of informing relatives.

Opposition to identity cards and National Registration increased with the end of the war in 1945. Food rationing continued for a few years, but could not remain the means of securing the public's cooperation. The new prompt was welfare: the bureaucracy of the National Health Service, launched under Attlee's postwar administration, needed some form of registration to keep track of patients' files. A universal registration scheme could therefore continue to be justified, now under the auspices of health.

---

[16] PRO CAB 103/396. "History of National Registration: Comments by GRO," May 1950.

[17] PRO CAB 103/396. Vivian to Acheson, December 12, 1948. Vivian thought this feature such a novelty as to justify (successfully, even now) keeping the detailed history of the NR secret.

Combined medical, insurance, and NR cards were planned. Indeed, the NR was used to compile the first National Health Service Central Register in 1948.[18] However, when National Registration collapsed in February 1952 following the *Willcock v. Muckle* decision, British identity cards also ended, much to the frustration of Whitehall.

Young Liberal Clarence Willcock had refused to show his identity card when stopped in his car by a police officer. Willcock argued that identity cards were invalid, since the National Registration Act ended with the onset of peace. In December 1950, Middlesex magistrates concluded that the act was still in force, and therefore Willcock was guilty, but they also gave him an absolute discharge. The case went to appeal at the King's Bench Divisional Court in January 1951, and attracted much press interest. During the First World War, some newspaper articles or editorials had supported identity cards. While the Northcliffe press had clamored for National Registration, political magazines such as *The Nation*—which was also against national service—asked, "by what right will [NR officials] ask, under penalty, such questions as whether a woman is married or has children," by what right were they the "proper recipients of the private secrets of their neighbours?"[19] During the Second World War reaction against identity cards was muted, even when, after 1941, police officers routinely asked for cards in ordinary driving incidents. After 1945 the widespread attitude of editorials was that identity cards were a wartime necessity but not acceptable in peacetime Britain. The *Daily Express*, for example, remonstrated: "Except as a wartime measure the system is intolerable. It is un-British. . . . It turns every village policeman into a Gestapo agent" (before adding with a snobbish shudder, "It can put the law-abiding citizen in the same row of filing cabinets as the common thief with a record").[20] This anti-card argument echoed from heavyweight papers such as the *Manchester Guardian* or the *Scotsman*, to the mass-circulation *News of the World*, to smaller papers, such as the *Hendon and Finchley Times and Guardian*, which supported local hero Clarence Willcock: "Identity cards have put another weapon into the hands of many minor officials to badger the innocent public. They have outlived their usefulness. Let's be done with them. Give us back this little bit of our traditional freedom."[21]

On June 26, 1951, the Court rejected Willcock's appeal, but expressed its "emphatic approval of the way the Justices [in Middlesex] dealt with

---

[18] Flaherty 1979.

[19] "A London Diary," *The Nation*, July 3, 1915.

[20] "Identity," *Daily Express*, March 12, 1945.

[21] *Hendon and Finchley Times and Guardian*, June 15, 1951. Willcock was in fact a Yorkshireman, but the case was first heard at the Middlesex Magistrates' Court, which had the local jurisdiction.

[handwritten margin note, left: women]

[handwritten note, bottom: ＊ minor officials]

the case by granting an absolute discharge."[22] The press cheered the concluding remarks of Lord Goddard, the presiding judge of seven and Lord
Chief Justice:

> To demand registration cards of all and sundry—from a lady leaving her car
> outside a shop longer than she should for instance—is wholly unreasonable. . . .
> We have always prided ourselves on the good feeling between the police and
> public, but this tends to make people resent the acts of the police, to obstruct
> instead of assist them.

National registration was holed beneath the water line, and despite pleas
within Whitehall that "we *must* attempt to carry on," NR and British
identity cards sank within the year.[23]

The identity card returned to its position in the interwar years, existing
only as part of the plans of the War Book. The Defence Committee in
March 1953 decided that a national registration based on house-to-house
enumeration would still be needed in time of war. Their plan called for
eighty thousand trained enumerators to issue cards within six weeks, sort
and check returns after twelve weeks, and establish a new central register
after a further sixteen weeks. However, by the mid-1950s a strategic shift,
brought on by the devastating power of the hydrogen bomb—a more
radical leap in destructive technology than that between conventional and
fission warheads—led to a rethink. With only one day's warning, and the
probability of widespread damage, dislocation of communications and
transport, and large numbers of unidentifiable dead, a new enumeration
would be impossible. Food would still need to be rationed, so the plans
that were laid in 1956 were for an identity card issued against the existing
National Health Service card. The Central War Plans Secretariat expressed hope that the Ministry of Health would "examine the possibilities
of improving in peace-time the value of the NHS medical card as an emergency document for personal identification."[24] Again the official strategy
was to secure public cooperation with identity cards by securing their
parasitic vitality.

Flexible Friends: Creative Uses of Cards

The attitudes of the public toward identity cards are harder to uncover,
but more interesting, than the machinations of the civil servants. Direct

[22] PRO RG 28/95. Court transcript "Clarence Henry Willcock v. Harold Muckle," June
26, 1951.

[23] PRO RG 28/95. Internal note, June 23, 1951.

[24] PRO RG 28/308. "National registration and food rationing in war," March 1956.

evidence of attitudes is scarce, but some analysis can be made from three sources: maintenance problems, the evidence of new "crimes," and the reaction of the press to the NR's demise. We have already seen that the day-to-day problems of maintaining the Register, in particular failure to notify removals, suggest that the identity cards were not cared for. Cards were lost, or left in jacket pockets. The *Daily Chronicle* in 1919 remarked about the "forgotten National Register" that "nobody troubles now to notify a change of address or to preserve the original card," while the *Sunday Pictorial* noted that "great numbers of officers back from Germany have no documents and have never heard of them."[25] There is some evidence of reception sensitive to class; certainly it was the opinion of the *Westminster Gazette* that "the Register was never popular with the working classes," naturally since they were the prime objects of conscription.[26] A residuum, or underclass, category was especially troublesome: the Ministry of National Service was well aware that it was "men living in caravans, in common lodging houses, in hotels, and on board ships" who were hardest to trace, but also that these were the "class of man not likely to furnish any considerable number of useful recruits."[27] In "round ups" at railway stations "the absence of a registration certificate was the badge of outlawry."[28]

If everyday attitudes toward the identity card ranged from docility to hostility, evidence of new crimes made possible by the introduction of the certificate shows that a small segment of the population could treat ID productively and creatively. Indeed the possibilities were apparent in official circles early on: "there will be an enormously enlarged field of 'crime' opened and a corresponding necessity for official surveillance. The former result will be unfortunate, the latter both irritating and expensive."[29]

What was regarded as criminal, in particular fraudulent, within Whitehall can also be seen as creative appropriation of official identities, a useful resource during harsh times. The evidence available for an underworld that played with official identity is refracted through bureaucratic categories, and does not reveal what the fraud meant to the perpetrators. Nor does the evidence indicate the exact scale of the phenomenon—except the crude indication that since civil servants regarded it as a serious problem for National Registration then the numbers could not have been negligible. Wartime investigations *using* the Register threw up diverse stories

[25] *Daily Chronicle*, May 28, 1919. *Sunday Pictorial*, February 9, 1919.

[26] *Westminster Gazette*, May 27, 1919.

[27] PRO RG 28/1. "Issue of NR certificates to men with no fixed address," paper for Registration Advisory Board, Ministry of National Service, May 1918.

[28] *Manchester Guardian*, July 17, 1919.

[29] PRO RG 28/7. Sir H. Munro to Hayes Fisher and President of Local Government Board, September 22, 1916.

involving suspect cards: married women avoiding employment bars, underage boys seeking to join the Royal Air Force, as well as bigamists, deserters, and perpetrators of ration book fraud.

Of course successful impersonators could not be counted. But they could be categorized: drawing on the Ministry of Food's First World War experience, frauds were divided into two groups. The first was named "frauds of the lost or stolen Registration Certificate": the perpetrator presented someone else's card in order to gain extra ration books.[30] A quick check of the card's number against a blacklist revealed the fraud. A variant was more tricky, since it was difficult pinning an identity on someone returning from war: "a person, having already a Registration Certificate, and having sold it or made use of it himself for his own purposes, alleges that he has never had a Registration Certificate, etc, owing to his recently [having] (a) come into the country from Overseas or (b) been discharged from the Forces." Official identity could easily be thus denied. The second group was classed as "the frauds of the double life and the imaginary person." Frauds of the double life arose "through one person or a family obtaining two distinct sets of ration papers or cards under double personality, i.e., under different names." No complete remedy could be suggested against such a proliferation of identities. The hardest fraud to counter, however, was the "fraud of the imaginary person": a "householder, in making an application, simply overstating the number in his household," the simplest version being "to claim a child or children who has never existed or had died."

The creation of new official identities therefore allowed new crimes of deception: either pretending to be someone else, pretending to be more than one person, or pretending that someone else existed. All of these ploys of course predate identity cards, but the perpetrators now had an extra, and powerful, resource: appropriating the authority of the state to support their claims. The state's answer was technical: better methods of sorting cards, and other cross-checks—and therefore the appearance of such frauds constituted a pressure toward greater surveillance. However, it would be a mistake to write such history purely as a growth of such techniques: National Registration was not merely an extension of the state's ability to identify and track individuals, it also created a power that was not available before and that could be creatively appropriated.

The related area of using the central register of identity card numbers for state purposes, such as welfare administration or criminal investigations, illustrates the extent of the increased surveillance possibilities. Although many of the documents relating to communication of information from the National Register remain closed, the policy that guided Second

[30] PRO RG 28/27. Draft report of subcommittee, undated (late 1938).

World War practice can be reconstructed. Theoretically, disclosure was confined to communication of information relating to serious crime or national security. In practice, requests from other government departments, or ones with government backing, were granted, except in debt cases when they were declined (unless the police "forgot" to mention what offense was being investigated). For example, wartime social surveys were built from National Register data, whereas school geography projects were rejected. Likewise, requests for addresses to trace missing tuberculosis cases were accepted once they had been routed via the Ministry of Health. No address was disclosed in inquiries from individuals about individuals, such as wives trying to locate husbands, although an offer to forward a letter was made if it was of "benefit to the person inquired after."[31] By far the most publicized investigation was that of the murder of the three-year-old June Anne Devaney in Blackburn in 1948—although the press championed the heroic fingerprint search more than the use of the National Register.[32] The use of National Registration information illustrates the phenomenon known now as "data creep": the 1939 act provided for three administrative applications (national service, security, and food rationing), but eleven years later thirty-nine government agencies made use of the records.[33]

The reaction of the press to the abandonment of a National Register and identity card system was remarkably similar in 1919 and the early 1950s. The case for keeping identity cards contained a stable set of arguments. The *Sunday Times* op-ed piece by trade unionist W. L. George was typical. First, the nation would have a better knowledge of itself—"a continuous picture of the condition of the people." However, such administrative boons were not the most important. For, second, identity cards made life more convenient for carriers. A card provided "an excellent evidence of identity. . . . There are many circumstances such as the receipt of registered letters, recovery of luggage, elections, disturbances,

---

[31] PRO RG 28/119. Application from probation officer for present address of woman under her Supervision who has failed to report, from "Note on applications for information from NR," February 12, 1947.

[32] Fingerprints were found on a "Winchester Quart" bottle near where the child had been snatched from the hospital. Police first worked with the electoral register arranged in street order and took the fingerprint, name, address, and NR number in a house-to-house check. Fingerprints were taken to the Local Food Office and checked off with the alphabetically arranged records (food offices were integrated with the NR). This check revealed one hundred persons whose names were not on the electoral roll and had not been fingerprinted. The subsequent visits led to the arrest of Peter Griffiths, the 46,253rd person to have been fingerprinted in the investigation. PRO RG 28/123. C. G. Looms (Chief Constable, Blackburn Police) to J. M. Ross (GRO), November 9, 1948.

[33] PRO HO45/25015. "Report of the Committee on National Registration," 1950.

where evidence of identity saves the public much annoyance."[34] Indeed, George went further and presented a vision more akin to Pemberton Billing's national book-keeping of morals:

> I should like to see this idea of citizen identity carried much further, and to have the registration card incorporated into a system of personal history, rather akin to the medical history of each recruit that now stands on the War Office file. Registration would enable us to set up an *état-civil* of each individual, showing where and when he was born and married, whether convicted, sent to an asylum or home for inebriates, and what is very important, *whether and how he had been treated for infectious diseases.*[35]

Such an inquisitorial system was justified by a simple appeal that recurs in almost every argument for an identity card system: "we must fasten to this: have nothing to hide and you need hide nothing." Only the guilty need be afraid; indeed, for George, "Secrecy is hateful; it breeds evils, and I would that all houses might be made of glass."

Bigamy: Double Identities and the Social Order

The crime on which George and many others fixed was bigamy: "a growing evil in this country . . . you may obtain a marriage licence with no greater difficulty than a dog licence; indeed if you are married by certificate it costs six-pence less to acquire a wife than to acquire a dog." Likewise, a pro-card piece by the "Man O'The People"—the *People* was a large-circulation tabloid—thundered against bigamy in the early 1950s: "far from wishing to abolish Identity Cards, I should like to see them made more detailed and complete—to the benefit of decent citizens and the undoing of rogues, vagabonds, spies, deserters, bigamists and all 'the lunatic fringe' which scums the rim of our community pool," adding the clichéd homily that "possession of this card is a privilege to law-abiding folk and the non-possession of it a handicap to wasters and crooks." "If this NR system were rigidly enforced, we could round up half our deserters, keep an eye on more than half our spies and 'fellow travellers', reduce the shocking rate of bigamy in Britain—and cause no trouble at all to ordinary folk."[36]

[34] W. L. George, "National Registration. Why it should be maintained," *Sunday Times*, April 6, 1919.

[35] George's emphasis.

[36] Man O'The People, "Let's give him a big hand and hope he loses!" *The People*, June 17, 1951.

bigamy

The spies were a fad—the Harwell atom spy Klaus Fuchs had been unmasked the year before, and Guy Burgess and Donald Maclean had just fled to the Soviet Union (ironically, leaving Valentine Vivian's protégé Kim Philby as yet undiscovered)—but we must look for a more structural explanation to account for the fixation on bigamy in the popular media. Officials were somewhat embarrassed by the emphasis. Sylvanus Percival Vivian, registrar-general and proponent of universal registration, noted in 1938 that the crime could "almost wholly be prevented. . . .The prevalence of bigamy has, however, never been sufficient to justify the erection of a scheme."[37] In 1929 he had even rejected a similar suggestion on the grounds that "many people disguise their ages on getting married . . . the proposed change might be unpopular." When the *News of the World* argued in 1950 against the use of identity cards to counter bigamy and for an "inalienable right to privacy," an aide forwarded the article to Vivian with the note "you may be pleased to see that somebody is on our side." So encouragement from government will not explain the recurrence of bigamy as a topic.

Part of the explanation resides in a real increase in the crime. The increased mobility and dislocations during war put a massive strain on family structures in general, and monogamy in particular: "Men separated for long years from their wives, unhappy and lonely, were taking an illegal short cut to a fresh start for happiness."[38] Relations were difficult to reestablish, and pamphlets competed to offer advice to wives: be patient and understanding.[39] Nevertheless, divorce cases rocketed, and bigamy convictions increased from 262 in 1940 to 902 in 1942, although still negligible in absolute terms.[40] Bigamy, more villainous than the everyday tragedies of divorce and more public when cases came to trial, was a useful media target for those seeking to shore up the family. Furthermore, bigamy starkly highlighted the extent to which social institutions depended on individuals living under one, and only one, identity.

The 1940s campaign to stop bigamy through bureaucracy was led by two figures: a Manchester solicitor, H. Mottershead, who suggested using birth certificates, and Lord Mottistone of Mottistone Manor, Isle of Wight, who favored the identity card. The latter promoted his solution in 1944 in the House of Lords, attracting considerable interest among newspaper editors and clergy. The Public Morality Council, a body in-

[37] PRO RG 28/27. "Note by the Registrar-General," 1938.

[38] John Hilton, "The people who want to be alone: dangers of disclosing addresses," *News of the World*, May 14, 1950.

[39] Haste 1992.

[40] Gillis 1985: 209, 236 and Outhwaite 1981: 8, for a critical view.

name + number

cluding nine bishops, noted with satisfaction the outcome of Mottistone's pressure, a warning against the offense of bigamy printed on forms at the Register Office, perhaps not least because it left church services unchanged.[41] The episode illustrates the dilemma posed by identity cards and national identity. Previous sensational bigamy cases, such as a rash of them in the 1860s, were made to do cultural work of national differentiation. For example, in the novelization of a lurid case in which the Protestant villain Captain William Charles Yelverton married Catholic Englishwoman Theresa Longworth, the religions of the protagonists were reversed: as Linda Colley has shown for a slightly earlier period, anti-Catholicism was a backbone structuring British national identity.[42] The dilemma therefore was whether to use a foreign technique—"something alien to the English way of life," as a minister of health described identity cards—to stop bigamy. In France, noted a local registrar in 1941, "bigamy is practically non-existent . . . because each person, male or female, has a special record card issued by the local Maire."[43] The national histories of bigamy are complex: Britain unlike France, Germany, or Czechoslovakia at the end of the First World War, or Nazi Germany, or the United States after the American Civil War, was not home to a campaign to legalize bigamy.[44] If bigamy was regarded as a foreign practice, then the noisy pronouncements of the pro-card press can be seen as part of a cultural program of differentiation—despite the fact that the chosen tool had once been seen as "Prussian." However, the way bigamy was conceived was more telling than national facts: the low statistics trumped by a monstrous unknown, imagined as a massive threat to social order.

Conclusion

In 1939, William Morris, the chairman—and possibly sole employee—of British Monomarks Ltd., attempted to interest government officials in his grand scheme: "that the State should issue to each individual an absolutely unduplicated mark of identity, to be considered as his or her 'NATIONAL NUMBER' and used as an appendage to the name for all purposes—State or private."[45] "William Thomas Smith" thus would

[41] PRO RG 48/1695. George Tomlinson to registrar-general, December 19, 1944.

[42] Colley 1992. For Yelverton, see Fahnestock 1981: 47–71; many novels were influenced by the Yelverton case, most lavishly, according to Fahnestock, Cyrus Redding's *A Wife and Not a Wife* (1867).

[43] PRO RG 48/1690. Mellor to registrar-general, February 22, 1941.

[44] Cairncross 1974: 210–12.

[45] PRO RG 28/117. William Morris, "National numbers," June 1939.

tattooing

✗

permanently add the letters "XOX4P" to his name, and this unambiguous monomark would thread together all the documents of Smith's life: birth certificate, school and university records, employment and national insurance files, driving licenses, passports, legal documents, and, finally, his gravestone and death certificate. (Monomarks would also, of course, end bigamy.) Morris's scheme was not rejected out-of-hand; indeed, his objectives were met with "a great deal of sympathy."[46] What the civil servants knew well was the immense work that was needed to attach an unambiguous identity to an individual. A number, the registrar-general sadly noted, was "far from inseparable from the individual; and it is, indeed, very hard in practice to make it adhere to him with sufficient permanence to render it of any value at all." Indeed as the statistician and administrator Lord Stamp joked to Vivian: "if you would only face up to branding each one of us on the left arm at the time of vaccination."[47]

Jeremy Bentham, whom Vivian admired as "a very thorough and exhaustive analyst of administrative requirements," had noted in *Principles of Penal Law* that only the extreme state measure of tattooing the population would solve the moral and political question, "who are you?"[48] It was not an option available to Vivian. While perhaps the most general point I want to make in this essay is to stress the sheer effort that is needed to pinpoint, affix, and maintain unitary identities—especially official identities—I also want to draw out some conclusions specific to the case study. As the two cases of identity cards in Britain show, the experience and use of cards were shaped by the context of their introduction. In both periods (1915–19 and 1939–52), warfare prompted, excused, and gave meaning to the identity card. Only under the cover of war could the "sheer regimentation" needed to attach a universal number to a British subject be defended.[49] Likewise, only with an identity card could efficient food rationing, or conscription, be planned. This martial context raised uncomfortable problems of national differentiation: did they make Britain more, or less, like its enemies? In 1915 the project of National Registration, and accompanying identity cards, was seen as uncomfortably Prussian and, by opposition, not British. By the time of the Somme, the extension of the state achieved by listing all men and women, a trespass on personal liberty to some (like vaccination),[50] had been accepted as a neces-

[46] PRO RG 28/117. Vivian to Lord Stamp, January 13, 1939.

[47] PRO RG 28/117. Stamp to Vivian, January 16, 1939.

[48] PRO HO 45/25014. Ross to Vivian, October 7, 1942, and Vivian to Ross, October 9, 1942. Ross refers to "Principles of the Penal Code," rather than to the correct title.

[49] The phrase is Vivian's on the monomark, but he was drawing attention to the difficulties of all schemes, including national registration.

[50] Porter and Porter 1988: 231–52; MacLeod 1967; Lambert 1967: 1–18.

sary but temporary evil. When war ended so did the identity card. Many authors have written of the powerful role played by the experience of the First World War in shaping national remembrance and forgetting.[51] Ironically, while England began to submerge division and recrimination by remembering the unknown soldier, the apparatus that made soldiers known was forgotten.[52]

Yet "the National Register was a big enough Pharaoh in its day . . . its taking went far to overshadow more combatant aspects of war, and August 15th, 1915, was as big a day for contemporary vision as September 25th and the opening of the luckless Loos offensive." As this remarkable passage from the *Manchester Guardian* in July 1919 suggests, there was an uneasy paradox at the heart of British identity cards: what on the one hand was symbolic of monumental government—indeed with undertones of otherness and death—was on the other an instrument of modernity. For some civil servants the National Register was not as inscrutable as the Sphinx; instead, identity cards combined with a universal register were the hallmarks of efficient, modern bureaucracy, and not an emergency measure. It was "not only possible but probable that a National Registration system . . . would have quite considerable advantages as a permanent peacetime institution," wrote Vivian in 1938. Permanent NR promised a continuous statistical picture of the nation, coordination and cross-referencing of existing smaller registers enabling government departments to work seamlessly together. He was to be disappointed when, after over twelve years of operation, British identity cards collapsed for a second time in 1952. By experience, cards were only kept when they were given a vampyric "parasitic vitality" through attachment to something valued by the public, in particular food supply. An attempt to attach the dying National Register to the National Health Service card failed (although it was used to construct the NHS Central Register and remained in the War Book). As far as I can tell it was never suggested that the British identity card be integrally linked to the payment of taxation (as with the French *carnet d'identité*), or made essential for travel (as with the old Russian internal passport).

Yet this vision of modern bureaucracy was difficult to impose. Bodies moved in different directions: "each organization works under its own special conditions and has special objects to secure; and to induce or force all such organizations, whether state, public utility or private, to adopt a single series of 'national numbers' is a very different proposition from the simple conception that when a number has been allotted to each individ-

---

[51] Fussell 1975; Evans and Lunn 1997.

[52] For a fine discussion of the invention of remembrance, see Bushaway 1992: 136–67, and for a remarkable account of "dis-memberment" see Bourke 1996, esp. 210–52.

ual the thing is done."[53] Not only did complexity undermine simple identification, it also provided a resource for the creative underworld. Like Dr.
Jekyll and Mr. Hyde, the flip-side of identity cards held modern horrors:
frauds of the double life and the imaginary person. The most "modern"
aspect of the National Register was its assumption of a social order based
on a unitary identity. Bigamy, which struck at the foundations of this
order, was the recurrent—and imaginary—opponent.

[53] PRO RG 28/117. Vivian to Lord Stamp, January 13, 1939.

Part Two

IDENTIFICATION PRACTICES AND POLICING

7

Republican Identity: Bertillonage as Government Technique

MARTINE KALUSZYNSKI

BY THE END of the nineteenth century in France, industrial growth and urbanization had radically transformed the way of life and destabilized the existence of a significant proportion of the population. The response of the Third Republic was to extol the virtues of order, stability, and work, and it did all in its power to enforce respect for these values. This was the context in which police anthropometry emerged. Invented by Alphonse Bertillon (1853–1914), anthropometry was not simply a new weapon in the armory of repression, but a revolutionary technique: it placed identity and identification at the heart of government policy, introducing a spirit and set of principles that still exist today. By tracing the evolution, consequences, and implications of this system, we shall see how it enabled first the maintenance of order and repression, and then the establishment of a technique and a politics of republican government based on the concept of identity. It was in the context of criminal policy, confronted by the struggle against crime and by galloping rates of recidivism, that this politics of identity was to emerge.

The Problem of Recidivism

In the complex and turbulent circumstances of the late nineteenth century, French society was plagued by a mounting crisis of recidivism, despite persistent efforts to curb it.[1] A series of legislative initiatives were adopted in the attempt to attack the problem, notably the laws of May 27, 1885 (on transportation and restrictions on the rights of settlement)[2] and of March 26, 1891 (on suspended sentences). These and other laws were based on the principle of dividing offenders into two categories, first offenders and recidivists. First offenders were to be rehabilitated through

[1] Schnapper 1991.
[2] Kaluszynski 1999.

generous policies that would encourage personal reformation and social reintegration. By contrast, recidivists faced the threat of severe punishment, and the incorrigible were to be segregated from the rest of society.[3] In order to implement these laws, the authorities needed to investigate techniques for the reliable identification of those arrested for criminal violations. By this time it was no longer possible to brand or crop the ears of an offender in order to be able to recognize him subsequently. Branding by hot iron had been abolished by law in 1832, and with it all possibility of such a comprehensively effective system. Thus identification of the individual as such became the key to an effective system of crime control.

It was from this perspective that the police administration experimented with a number of different methods for the identification of recidivists, although on the whole they turned out to be rudimentary and ineffectual. Already in 1819, Huvet, a clerk in the prison bureau, had suggested that the police establish a rogues' gallery of portraits obtained by the mechanism of the "physionotrace," a contraption that allowed the body's shadow to be projected onto paper in silhouette when the subject was placed between the mechanism and a light source. Huvet's proposal was not adopted, but the idea of recording physical particulars by means of an image came into its own with the invention of photography.[4] Photography was in use in sections of the police prefecture in Paris as early as 1872. The photographic department had been established unofficially for the purposes of political research, and together with the printing department comprised the criminal investigation department of the police prefecture. From this time on, all suspects were photographed, but very unsystematically—from various angles and with varying degrees of expertise—and the prints accumulated in disorderly piles. They were catalogued by name alone, which meant that they were useless for identifying any malefactor who simply changed his name. Thus the problem was how to match the sixty thousand photographs assembled by the criminal investigation service with any of the hundred individuals arrested in the city every day. The techniques developed by the police were far from rigorous and very inadequate. A suspect could easily disguise his identity by claiming that he had been born abroad or in the IVth arrondissement in Paris, whose town hall had been burned down during the Commune. He could also choose a common name, which would add to the difficulty of investigating him in alphabetical files, and blithely claim to be an orphan without any living relatives or else insist that he did not know where his family lived. There were no mechanisms for exposing these lies.

[3] Kaluszynski 1988.
[4] *Liaisons*, 243 (September–October 1943).

Confronted both by ineffective means of identification and by the growing problem of recidivism, anthropometry emerged in the 1880s as a solution that was founded on the systematic scientific verification of identity. Alphonse Bertillon, a police clerk whose job was to record criminal descriptions on index cards, was the originator of this much more rigorous system of criminal anthropometry.[5] Bertillon was not exactly an ordinary police clerk, and his method was the product of a series of far from accidental influences. Even if it was professional chance that provided him with the context and opportunity to stand out, his own family origins were largely responsible for his angle of approach. He was the "difficult child" of a family that had multiple connections with the worlds of science, medicine, and anthropology.[6] The young Bertillon had difficulty in committing himself to a career: he had not distinguished himself in his mathematical studies; he took up and abandoned several jobs, joined the army, and spent some time in medical school, where he studied and measured the skeleton with enthusiasm, but left after passing the first exam. His father had to use all his influence to find him a post in the police prefecture, which he took up on March 15, 1879.[7] By the end of that winter, he had set himself to discover an objective and infallible means of identifying recidivists. His family background, his own unfinished training as a physician, and his admiration for Italian criminal anthropologists, who used osteometric observations to support their theories, had a cumulative influence on his own research.

Bertillon's system was based on the measurement of certain dimensions of the body—including head, arms, and legs—and in this respect echoed the kind of observations he had made during his medical studies. His method proceeded in two stages, description (*signalement*) and classification. To establish the descriptive data, Bertillon started from the observations that the human bone structure was more or less absolutely fixed by the age of twenty, and that the skeleton varied tremendously in its dimensions between one person and another. On the basis of these observations, it was possible to establish descriptive data that derived from specific bone measurements. Anthropometry was premised on a proven principle: all human measurements, of whatever kind, obeyed a natural

---

[5] Bertillon 1941. Mention should also be made of the excellent catalogue of the exhibition at the Centre national de la photographie, *Identité. De Disdéri au Photomaton* (Paris, 1985).

[6] His grandfather, Achille Guillard, an enthusiast for statistics, coined the term *demography*; his father, the physician Louis Adolphe Bertillon, was a co-founder of the École d'anthropologie; and his elder brother, Jacques Bertillon, also a physician, was the well-known author of several publications on statistics and director of statistics for the city of Paris.

[7] Archives Préfecture de police, BA 960, Dossier Bertillon.

law of statistical distribution. The choice of features to be measured had to be based on their non-correlation as well as on their fixity and clarity. This represented a noteworthy bid to move away from a model confined to generalizations: here it was the detail, the particular, that mattered.[8]

Bertillon presented a memorandum on his system to the prefect of police, Louis Andrieu, on October 15, 1879, but Andrieu thought Bertillon was crazy and rejected it out of hand. However, Andrieu's successor, Camescasse, showed more interest in Bertillon's ideas and allowed him to conduct some trials of his methods for the first time. On December 15, 1882, Bertillon began to measure all arrested persons brought into headquarters: the results were much better than expected, but certain problems were revealed, notably the inapplicability of the system to women and children, since their measurements did not conform to the statistical norms. As well, errors in taking the measurements were always possible. The system was in fact only a means of negative identification that enabled probable but not absolute identifications—the most flagrant case of identical measurements would be in the case of truly identical twins.

Thus Bertillon's system was far from achieving the desired degree of infallibility. However, having made anthropometry the basis of his system of identification, he needed some means of giving it absolute authority in the eyes of magistrates and validating it as a formal means of judicial proof. The identification of recidivists had to be made unquestionable, and for this the support of complementary procedures was indispensable. Anthropometry was a method of elimination that could prove *non*-identity, but a series of additional descriptive techniques was devised in order to allow the establishment of positive identity: the *portrait parlé*, or verbal portrait, which allowed the identification of escaped delinquents; the tabulation of distinctive marks, which alone could ensure forensic certainty; and the addition of photographs, which personalized the anthropometric measurements. Forensic photography then developed in two further directions as a method of criminal investigation: descriptive photography (*photographie signalétique*) for people, and sectional photography for crime scenes.[9] These techniques were gradually developed

[8] See Carlo Ginzburg's highly original discussion of the significance attached to clues and traces at the end of the nineteenth century, which was part of the emergence of a new scientific paradigm of individual identity: Ginzburg 1980a.

[9] Descriptive photography was incorporated in the anthropometric conception of description from the start. Seen as an objective and impartial document—not a "portrait" in the artistic or usual sense of the term—the photograph was intended to be a perfectly consistent medium of representation whose precise and accurate record of physical traits would serve for all subsequent comparisons. Hence the descriptive photograph was taken in rigorously prescribed conditions, including size (one-seventh reduction) and position (full-face,

by Bertillon in order to meet his goal of ensuring effective implementation of the criminal law, but their systematic elaboration proceeded with some difficulty, and it was not until 1893 that the Criminal Identification Department (*Service d'identité judiciare*) was established.

It was evidently the arrest of the anarchist Ravachol and his identification by Bertillon in 1892 that gave definitive sanction to the anthropometric system, which thenceforth revealed itself as not just interesting but essential. By then, this system of identification had already taken a decade to establish itself. In 1882 there had been nothing more than an identity bureau attached to the security service. On the initiative of Louis Herbette, director of criminal administration in the Interior Ministry, the system of anthropometrical identification was extended throughout France by circulars issued on August 28 and November 13, 1885. From 1887, all penal establishments were under orders to apply the Bertillon method to their inmates, and to file a duplicate of each set of measurements with the prefecture, where it would be classified. Prison warders were provided with a newly written set of instructions.[10] Sometime before 1888, the prefect of police in conjunction with Herbette began to plan the creation of a special office dedicated to anthropometric services, and on February 1, 1888, the office of criminal identification was established under the eaves of the Palais de Justice in Paris. Administrative problems and delays had thus not spared Bertillon, but he had been able to lean on the support of crucial friends, including as well as Camescasse and Herbette the police prefect Lépine.[11] From now on the Criminal Identification Department finally had a budget and an apparatus commensurate with its tasks. It embraced the services of anthropometry, photography, and detective expertise, and thus constituted a functional unity for the first time.

Bertillon's work now developed in two principal directions: description and identification on the one hand, and forensic photography and the use of clues on the other. In rapid succession he directed his research into detectable clues to the crime sites themselves, and in this sense the use of clues, forensic photography, and anthropometry together contributed to the crystallization of what came to be called "criminal science" (*criminalistique*), that is, the sum of procedures for the material investigation of a crime in order to determine the different factors contributing to it.

---

profile), and with improved equipment; see Bertillon 1890. Sectional or geometric photography was useful for reconstructing the state of a crime scene exactly as it was at the moment of the first investigation of a crime or theft. The survey and the photograph are the prime means of fixing the memory of a place, and the sectional photograph combined these two operations into one: all the perspectival data was recorded and measured by geometrical coordinates; see Bertillon 1913.

[10] Bertillon 1893.

[11] For Lépine's role, see Berlière 1996.

Thus the Criminal Identification Department had expanded its services to a considerable extent. Anthropometry, the fundamental technique on which it was based, was adopted by police services all over the world. By 1888, the system was in use in prisons in the United States; in the following years, England, Germany, Switzerland, Belgium, Russia, British India, Rumania, the South American republics, and Denmark all began to exploit the technique, and showed their respect for its originator by showering Bertillon with honors and even titles of nobility.

A Compromised Success

Anthropometry was both the motive force behind the radical transformation of the traditional detective police and an effective contribution to the system of criminal justice, and it enabled the development of systems for maintaining public order against the menace of criminality. Yet at the last moment before it seemed likely to dominate the future, anthropometry was to undergo a rude shock. Its success had barely been established and savored when its supremacy began to falter in the face of a new and infallible technique: dactyloscopy, or fingerprinting. This technique, of ancient origin but only recently applied to criminal identification, was to deal a fatal blow to anthropometry, by delivering a degree of accuracy that the latter was quite unable to achieve.[12]

The fingerprint is a physical sign that cannot be falsified or disguised, and the mathematical likelihood of two individuals having identical fingerprints is infinitely small. Unlike many other physical traits of the face or the body, which change over the course of time, the pattern of the papillary lines appears before birth, as soon as the dermis is formed. It is resistant to all kinds of accidents that affect the epidermis, such as burns, and survives death. In 1902, Bertillon was among the first detectives in the world to identify a suspect by fingerprints alone: an unknown and unsuspected murderer was identified solely by comparing fingerprints left on a broken window with those collected from other individuals. In the same year, fingerprints became accepted as an adequate means of forensic proof: a suspect could be convicted on the evidence of fingerprints alone. The problem of identification that had exercised so many nineteenth-century policemen and politicians had thus been fully and finally solved, but it was not anthropometry that was the solution. Despite its earlier significance in revolutionizing police practice, its decline was to be as rapid as its growth. But the genius of this technique turned out to be its capacity for adaptation and redeployment: having emerged as a weapon in the

---

[12] See also the essay by Anne Joseph in this volume.

struggle against recidivism, anthropometry now found a new life as a means of securing the social, political, and ideological order in France.

From Security to Ideology: The "Nomad" Law of 1912[13]

As a simple and methodical system, anthropometry was to win a central place in the organization of the French Republic's mixed system of "security and repression." The efficacy of this system was to be secured with the support of severe and often unjustified measures of surveillance and control, the victims of which would be "gypsies" and "nomads." These groups were guilty of an excessive mobility and liberty, not only in geographical terms but spiritually and socially as well. Theirs is a history of eternal rejection. In the nineteenth century, public opinion, the press, and the authorities were united against these marginals, and demanded repressive measures against them. A campaign was launched, public opinion roared its disapproval, and the government attempted to respond. Confinement rather than exclusion emerged as the dominant political response in France, and the nineteenth century was at the axis of this new trend.[14]

A policy of detention had always existed in France, but up to this time it had not been the dominant approach. There were many reasons for the turnaround in policy, for the alternative of exclusion had many disadvantages. Transportation was not a "good investment" in economic terms, because the judicial pursuit of people cost human and material resources. There were mass arrests of gypsies in the nineteenth century with the aim of deportation or condemnation to forced labor; but ultimately the attack on gypsies "took the form of detention, understood as a means of authoritarian and generally violent integration of the gypsies in the surrounding society. . . . Instead of the geographical disappearance envisaged by a transportation that was synonymous with distance, disappearance would become social, through the detention and internal rupturing of a group that would then be made to conform to the rest of the population."[15]

The non-gypsy population in France found gypsies more and more difficult to accept. This was evidence of a dynamic that fed on itself and that had several origins. The most absurd rumors circulated concerning the gypsies' alleged barbarities. They were not only regarded as thieves, liars,

---

[13] See Delclitte 1995: 23–31.

[14] "In most [European] states, policies of exclusion were declining in force in the course of the nineteenth century, and were replaced by attempts at confinement which emerged at the beginning of the twentieth century and lasted until about 1950": Liégeois 1994: 142.

[15] Ibid., loc. cit.

and poachers, but were now accused of abducting children. "Public opinion" began to express its anxiety on the subject of these "undocumented" strangers. France's defeat in the Franco-Prussian war hardened this suspicion of strangers after 1871. France was in a nationalist mood, and gypsies were not welcome in a society where there were still few aliens in residence. An offensive launched by politicians was taken up by the press, which now began its own campaign against the "undocumented." The press circulated what little information was available on them, and opened its columns to the politicians for their own grandstanding. Politicians used this opportunity to plant racist ideas and to create a stereotype of the gypsy: "Throughout these articles, the 'romanies' were described as 'rodents', as 'impertinent parasites', as a people characterized by 'bestiality' and ferocity."[16]

At the same time, the reputation of traveling showmen (*forains*) and aliens underwent a certain rehabilitation, suggesting that the ostracism suffered by the gypsies was not simply a response to their vagrant way of life.[17] This rehabilitation was visible by the beginning of the twentieth century: "The time is past—fortunately—when itinerants, stigmatized by public prejudice, were forcibly isolated from social life."[18] The showmen themselves contributed to this campaign by founding their own organizations and publications. But although the kind of vagrancy common in earlier centuries was decreasing at this time, the public sense of insecurity was reinforced by the presence of more and more numerous groups of gypsies. "Romanies" from Hungary and Eastern Europe were arriving during the Second Empire, and a new wave of immigration followed the abolition of slavery in Moldavia and Wallachia in 1856 (also Balkan gypsies, who were mainly not circus people but performing bear masters). After the defeat at Sedan in 1870, when Alsace-Lorraine became German, gypsies were among those who left these provinces in order to remain French citizens. Thus the climate was favorable for the introduction of new legislation or regulations, for nomads were under surveillance yet poorly identified. It was in this context that two projects took shape that foreshadowed the severe measures to come.

First, in a ministerial circular of March 12–13, 1895, instructions were issued for a general census of nomads and gypsies. To analyze the results of this national inquiry, an extraparliamentary commission was established in 1897, at the initiative of Interior Minister Louis Barthou, and

[16] Delclitte 1995: 25.

[17] See, for example, the editorial in *Le Petit Parisien*, August 3, 1907: "The gypsy or romany, who one must be careful not to confuse with the travelling showman, whose virtuous labors I will one day recount"; cited in Delclitte 1995: 27.

[18] *Le Petit Journal*, April 29, 1900.

was charged with the task of "investigating the procedures appropriate to ensure closer supervision of vagrants and people who are not vouched for, in order to facilitate the detection of those responsible for crimes and offenses." This investigation intensified the already serious anxieties of the authorities, for its report of March 29, 1898, counted a total of 400,000 vagabonds, of whom 25,000 were "bands of nomads, traveling in caravans."[19] This number appears to be an exaggeration, and numerous anomalies can be identified: gypsies were counted several times in different places, individuals who were not "romanies" were assigned to this category, which thus included journeymen, agricultural workers, miscellaneous itinerants, vagrants, traveling workers, and traveling entertainers. It is even possible to find people included in the census who had declared a sedentary occupation: café or hotel waiter, saddler, carpenter, mason, building worker, domestic servant, baker, gardener, tailor, bookbinder. The commission recommended at least two solutions to the problems created by vagabondage. To begin with, it demanded the introduction of a special identity card, which would "oblige nomads to keep in their possession a means of identification—passport, card, or passbook [livret]—issued by the prefect in every department, of uniform design, and available for inspection where vagrancy is suspected."[20] Subsequently, intensified police controls were demanded.[21]

Another step was taken in a circular issued on April 4, 1907, which permitted the preventive registration of nomads. At the suggestion of Georges Clémenceau, this was legally established as the duty of new mobile police squads, whose "exclusive function [was to] support the judicial authorities in the repression of crimes and offenses against common law."[22] The squads were required to photograph and identify "at any time when this is legally possible vagrant nomads and romanies traveling individually or in groups, and to submit to the supervisory authorities photographs and descriptive identifications, taken according to the anthropometric method." Here "for the first time files were established based on categories attached to 'racial characteristics'."[23] Itinerance itself became

---

[19] Asséo 1994: 88.

[20] The commission was also inspired by an earlier project of Louis XV, who in 1724 decreed "the establishment of an identity passport"; see Liégeois 1977: 1.

[21] These proposals were intended to urge that "it is not too rash to suppose that all these regulations, which are hardly compatible with bohemian and romany life, will have the effect of removing them from our French territory, which will be seen as too inhospitable, and of persuading them to cease coming here to practice their menacing mendicity"; cited in Charlemagne 1972: 94, and in Liégeois 1977: 1.

[22] Proposal published in the Journal Officiel, cited by Delclitte 1995.

[23] Ibid.: 25.

a "pre-offense," as witness a 1905 investigation that categorized gypsies according to whether they were sedentary or nomadic.

Thus the idea of creating special identity papers for gypsies was already familiar well before the law of 1912. By this date several laws had been proposed, all tending in the same direction, but without success.[24] It was not until 1912 that these ideas were concretized in a law that also solidified the principles of anthropometry by introducing the "anthropometric nomad passbook" (carnet anthropométrique des nomades). By then parliament, under pressure from a good part of the electorate, had turned its attention to restricting free movement where it seemed liable to endanger public order. Politicians from all parties and from all over France were unanimous in calling for effective measures against nomads, and were vehement and energetic in pushing for a solution.

A draft of this law was laid before the National Assembly early in 1911; it was subjected to its first debate in the senate on March 11, presented by Senator Pierre-Etienne Flandrin. Here one can find expressed the essentials of what has already been written about the social representation of the gypsy in this period:

> Among individuals traveling through France and exercizing or claiming to exercize itinerant occupations, one must distinguish nomads in the true sense of the word, caravan-dwellers without domicile, residence, or homeland, mostly vagabonds of an ethnic type, romanies, bohemians, gypsies. Their miserable caravans are certain to contain a numerous tribe. The head of the family always represents himself as exercizing the trade of basket-maker, chair-mender, or tinker, but in reality the tribe lives from begging, practiced by a long retinue of children of all ages, and even more from petty theft along with poaching of game and fish. These nomads live off our land like a tribe of conquerors, with no interest in the rules of hygiene or the prescriptions of our civil law, professing an equal contempt for our penal and our fiscal laws. They seem to have the right to all privileges among us. These caravans and flying camps of bohemians and romanies are the terror of our countryside, where they carry out their depredations with impunity. . . . The nomads over whom we intend to exercize an indispensable supervision are dubious caravan-dwellers who, with their suspect claims of occupation, carry their idleness and instincts of thievery the length of the roads. While we wait for the international agreement that will allow us to deport them to their country of origin, it is essential that we enact security measures against them. It is not far-fetched to think that close supervision, in-

---

[24] In 1903, Georges Berry proposed a law that was rejected; the marquis de Pommereu did the same in 1907. In the same year, another deputy, Jean Cruppi, "proposed a series of measures intended to prevent and repress mendicity"; in 1908, further such proposals were made by Pierre-Etienne Flandrin and Albert Lebrun; see Liégeois 1977: 2.

compatible as it is with the way of life of bohemians and romanies, will have the effect of removing them from our territory.[25]

The law adopted on July 16, 1912, bore the title "Law on the exercize of itinerant professions and the regulation of the mobility of nomads." Its first three articles were devoted to definitions of the populations to be subjected to the law, which together demonstrate effectively the attempt to make the gypsies a people apart.[26] It is noticeable that the group categorizations in these articles are structured by the concepts of resident/non-resident, French national/alien, and worker/non-worker. The three articles gather in themselves the contradictions of a law that sought to injure a group that it had great difficulty defining. For how could one distinguish legally between gypsies and other nomads? This distinction was even more difficult given that France was a country of positive law, which made it impossible to introduce a law based on ethnicity.

A first solution was found in the creation of a new concept of law, the concept of residence. This was the first categorization in the law, distinguishing between those who did and did not have a fixed abode. But difficulties began with the second of these groups, which simultaneously included traveling showmen and gypsies. This amalgamation was not to the taste of the former. "Before the Senate pronounces on the project of the law concerning the mobility of nomads, the showmen, compelled to produce proofs of identity, protest in the name of universal equality against regulations that tend to assimilate them to a criminal population, and refuse to accept a 'bertillonage' which means establishing a law of exception."[27] To this end, they tried to distinguish themselves from this group of "potential criminals" by various means: they invoked their patriotic sentiments; they exploited to their own advantage the hostility against gypsies; and they were finally successful. The senatorial committee became anxious in its turn about the merger of the two groups, on the grounds that the law might be "abusively extended to citizens who were not its object." For this reason the senate adopted a fundamental modification of the initial draft of the law, establishing a notion of nationality in order to distinguish between the two groups. Traveling showmen were now treated as French citizens, which was not the case for gypsies.[28] But even the senators had problems in making a clear distinction, because the definition of "nomad" in article 3 of the law remained fluid, namely, "all

[25] *Journal Officiel*, Senat, March 10, 1911.

[26] Charlemagne and Pigault 1988: 15.

[27] Delclitte 1995: 27.

[28] "Gypsies in France had certain historic rights to claim this citizenship, fulfilled the obligations linked to citizenship (some of them had done their military service), and some had French nationality." Delclittle 1995:28.

individuals traveling in France without domicile or fixed abode, and not covered by any of the categories below." The definition was established by default. In any case, the criterion of nationality remained an illusion. In effect, this article of the law covered foreign nomads, itinerants traveling on their own, and "romanies." A distinction of this kind allowed the creation of legal procedures that were geometrically variable according to the group concerned.

The text of the new law established drastic obligations, especially in the case of gypsies, and the first of these was the creation of new identity papers. For those who had a fixed place of residence, there was no other duty than to make a declaration that "will include the names, first names, occupations, domiciles, residences, and places of birth of the persons making the statement. A receipt will be issued on proof of identity alone."[29] These people were issued a documentary receipt that did not amount to an identity document as such, but could be presented for police checks of persons who were not commercially active in a fixed place. By this means the state could conduct checks in order to avoid certain abuses. A second provision regulated the obligations of persons without a fixed abode who were exercising "the profession of traveling salesmen or tradesmen." These had to have a kind of occupational identity card printed. One might imagine that this regulation would not especially penalize traveling tradesmen, even though it was unusual to have an identity card at this time. In fact, one finds a lesser degree of tolerance of this group when one looks at the penalties to which they were subject for violations of the law. The levels of fines were higher for them than for traveling tradesmen who had a fixed abode, and the same was true for the length of jail sentences. Even though they were on their way to becoming rehabilitated at the beginning of the century, they did suffer from a certain discrimination. Despite their urgings during the drafting of the law, they were not regarded on the same plane of equality as sedentary workers.

The "Carnet anthropométrique"

The new law reveals its truly discriminatory side article 3 and in those that follow. The essential part of article 3 reads as follows:

> The administration will be under no obligation to issue an anthropometric pass. The pass will affect neither the enforcement of the provisions of the law of December 3, 1840, concerning temporary residence by foreigners in France, nor the exercize of the rights enjoyed by mayors on the territory of their

---

[29] Charlemagne and Pigault 1988: 15.

commune by the laws and regulations concerning temporary halts by nomads. All nomads staying temporarily in a commune are, on arrival and departure, obliged to present their passes to be visaed, either to the police superintendent if there is one in the commune, or else to the commander of the rural police, or if there is no local police presence, to the mayor. The anthropometric identity pass is to be presented by its holder on request to the criminal investigation police or to any agents of the police or public authority. All infractions of the regulations of this article will be punished by the penalties provided for vagrancy.

This anthropometric pass, a new form of identity document, was introduced by the 1912 law, although only its outlines were described in the text itself.[30] A full description was issued in a decree of February 16, 1913. The pass consisted of a hundred or so pages, divided into two sections. The first section consisted of pages of squared paper on which visas could be stamped. The second was something more than just an identity card, since it was a collective record that recounted the physical characteristics of each member of the group. It listed body height, size of chest and armspan, length and breadth of head, length of right ear, length of the middle and little fingers of the left hand, of the left arm extended, and the left foot, and data on pigmentation such as eye color. The fingerprints were also recorded, along with two photographs, one full-face and the other in profile. Children under thirteen were exempted, because up to this age facial structure and body dimensions were still developing. But children between the ages of two and thirteen had to have all ten fingerprints recorded on the collective pass.

In the end, it is difficult to characterize this pass. It was simultaneously a family passbook (which recorded details of marriages and births), a military identity card (all male French citizens had to include details of their military service), and a kind of minutely detailed identity card. On top of this it was a precocious health certificate, in that the 1912 law specified that there should be "a special public regulation," drawn up in consultation with the Commission for Public Health in France, to determine what preventive measures (such as periodic vaccinations) were to be imposed on itinerant showmen and nomads. This was, therefore, a

---

[30] Article 4: "The collective identity pass includes all family members. The information to be recorded on these passes will be determined by administrative regulations under article 10 of the present law. They will include in particular: civil status and description of all persons traveling with the head of the family, as also the legal or kin relations connecting each of these persons. Secondly they will record, insofar as these pertain, the official data on birth, marriage, divorce, and death of the persons previously recorded. For each of these circumstances the pass will be shown to the civil-status officers in order that they may enter the said items"; ibid.: 17.

document quite different in kind from the documentary receipt or the itinerant worker's papers: it was, rather, an instrument of intensive control that could justify an endless process of administrative harassment. In sum, then, the anthropometric pass was extremely constraining. It had to be conscientiously filled out, on pain of heavy fines. And this process, however iniquitous and discriminatory, might have been more tolerable to the gypsies if it had not also been followed by a succession of increasingly burdensome regulations.

The law put great emphasis on the repression of any behavior that contravened its provisions. The fines levied for defects in the completion of the anthropometric pass were prohibitive by any standards. In cases of falsification and the use of forged papers the penalties were also very severe, and this was again the case for the use of an alias.[31] The law was especially notable for establishing a system of constant and constraining supervision of gypsies. One only has to recall the demands of the parliamentary deputies that the whereabouts of these roving bands should be permanently known. Article 3 satisfied their demands completely: a quick check of the pass could show the exact route of travel taken by any gypsy. And to these daily visas was added the unpredictable right of control exercised by the public authorities. Gypsies were treated as equivalent to convicts, who one might think were subject to somewhat less stringent controls at this time.[32] This juridical power of ostracism was accentuated by the granting to mayors of plenary powers over local legislation on temporary sojourn. In practice, this provision left the mayors the absolute right to authorize or forbid gypsies to camp within the territory of their commune. Placards sprang up at the entrance to towns and villages announcing the decision of the municipal council on this point, and it goes without saying that numerous communes were declared off-limits to nomads by this means. And one final discriminatory element in the 1912 law remains to be mentioned: article 7, which is almost never cited. This article provided for the seizure of a gypsy's possessions for all infractions, including those that did not come under the framework of the 1912 law.[33]

---

[31] See article 5, which imposed a penalty of two to five years' imprisonment and a fine of 100 to 1,000 francs for the manufacture or use of falsified or altered passes; and article 6, which imposed terms of two to six months' imprisonment, and a fine of 50 to 500 francs for the use of an alias; ibid.: 17.

[32] "The anthropometric pass had to be carried by habitual criminals banned from residence: the parallel with the unwanted gypsies is flagrant. But the regime was not identical: it was much less severe for the habitual criminals banned from residence, whose obligations in carrying the pass were already less constraining at the start and were lightened considerably by a law of June 1, 1955"; Liégeois 1977: 6.

[33] Article 7: "In case of violations of the present law, or of police laws and regulations, the vehicles and animals of the nomads may be temporarily seized, in lieu of an adequate bond. The costs of foddering will be paid by the delinquent or offender; in case of non-

Even though this law announced a somber future for the gypsies, the politicians congratulated themselves on having finally produced a law that regulated the "romany" problem. Their law had two major results. First, some gypsies did renounce their itinerant way of life, once the constraints attached to it became too heavy.[34] For those who remained on the road, their mobility was perversely accentuated, and in this sense the political will that generated the 1912 law experienced a defeat. Where the aim had been to restrain mobility, the result was actually to increase the pace of migration between communes. These everyday problems were actually enhanced by police instructions: "The perfect policeman should interrogate all individuals who appear to be vagrants, suspect characters, peddlers, street entertainers, open-air traders." The *Handbook of Practical Exercizes* for the national police specified in relation to the 1912 law that it should "reduce the number of nomads and especially of foreign nomads by forbidding them access to French territory, by requiring them either to take up a permanent abode or to leave France. It would thus be contrary to the spirit of the law to aid them in the exercize of an itinerant occupation. . . . The provisions of the law can only be fully effective if all individuals practising an itinerant trade, profession, or industry are made the objects of constant control and continual supervision."[35] Thus the application of the law was difficult and the constraints that resulted from it were extremely troublesome.

Conclusion

The 1912 law implicitly took "racial indicators" into account. The nomad was regarded as an element in the population who was distinguished by his allegedly criminal otherness, and was not regarded as worthy of citizenship.[36] It signaled the birth of a repressive system that was to last almost twenty-five years after the Second World War (until 1969). It was xenophobic and biased, and used anthropometry for disciplinary and discriminatory purposes. It constituted a remarkable precedent, when one thinks of the treatment inflicted on gypsies and bohemians by the Nazi government, which led to an attempt at systematic extermination.

---

payment, the sentence of conviction will order a sale under the conditions specified in article 617 of the Civil Code." This provision was iniquitous because the article applied only to gypsies, and distraints could take place on petty grounds.

[34] Henriette Asséo describes it thus: "These measures disturbed the rhythm of an economic mobility determined by the constraints of fairs, harvests, the *vendange* etc., and the fines encumbered a budget that was by its nature fluctuating. The result was that traveling was abandoned by families that had been on the move for over a century"; Asséo 1994: 89.

[35] Charlemagne 1972: 260.

[36] Braconnier 1996.

The legislation adopted at the beginning of the century provided the legal framework for the internment of gypsies in France during the Second World War.[37] The Vichy regime was hardly a propitious moment for the modification of the law, even if France did not ship its "romanies" off to the death camps (unlike other countries such as Yugoslavia). But by a decree of April 6, 1940, the government organized the mass internment of nomads, and these camps were scattered across the entire nation.[38] The law retained its repressive arsenal intact after the war's end. It constituted a kind of historical-legal capital that ruled an ensemble of social relations between sedentary and gypsy populations that always remained ambiguous. Even today, gypsies remain the bearers of special documents and passes that control their mobility.

Thus the anthropometric pass initiated the officially documented stigmatization of a group of individuals according to the indicators of race and nationality. Although originally intended for recidivists, police anthropometry revealed itself as a technique of republican government addressed to society at large, containing the issue of access to citizenship at its heart.

[37] Peschanski 1994.
[38] Hubert 1995.

8

The Standardized Gaze:
The Standardization of the Search Warrant
in Nineteenth-Century Germany

PETER BECKER

> Instead of undressing prisoners upon their arrival in order to record all
> their distinguishing marks, some officials still leave this task to their clerks
> and ushers who do not know on what this task mainly depends.[1]

THESE CRITICAL remarks about the incompetence and negligence of officials were published in 1841 by an official with practical experience in
the field of policing. His voice was not the only one to reprimand his
fellow-officials for their habitual carelessness and indifference. Ambitious
practitioners[2] in the field of "crime control" saw themselves exposed to
the rapidly expanding threat of an organized criminal subculture, against
which only the combined efforts of all public officials seemed likely to
offer any hope.

From this perspective, professional property criminals (*Gauner*) and
their tightly knit network of support were particularly damaging to society. The successful thefts and frauds carried out by these professionals
exacted a heavy toll from the people. By exploiting the new forms of
commerce for their fraudulent schemes, they even seemed to evoke anxieties about the mechanisms of the marketplace itself. The fight against
Gauner was therefore regarded as a crucial task, and it was exactly this
task to which the anonymous author was referring in his remarks. To
accomplish it, police experts tried to elaborate strategies aimed at de-
feating the *Gauner*'s expertise in disguise and deceit. For the *Gauner* was
skilled in obtaining realistic false documents; he tended to disguise himself
more in the actual carrying out of criminal acts rather than in fleeing

---

[1] Anon. 1841: 108.

[2] This heading brings together a rather dispersed group of people, who shared a work
experience in crime control agencies, that is, police, criminal courts, prisons, and work-
houses, and who showed interest in exchanging ideas about the best possible ways to organize their fight against crime and deviance.

from the authorities, and he made use of a functioning infrastructure that provided him with a hiding place, alibis, and clothes. Thus police experts reminded their colleagues over and over again that they had to employ more elaborate tools and schemes for catching the *Gauner* than for pursuing escaped servants, deserters, and itinerant traders.

Many of these projects aimed at improving the police practitioners' gaze at suspects. To combat the cleverness and experience of the *Gauner*, a specialized and differentiated knowledge had to be deployed in their observation and description. As the anonymous author indicated, this kind of knowledge was only fully available to officials, and not to their clerks and assistants. Clerks or office workers regarded it as sufficient to record the personal details of dress, physical size, hair and eye color, and the shape of the nose and mouth. Trained officials, on the other hand, studied the whole body of the prisoner, above all in order to detect "unusual characteristics." Among these, the author included "scars, warts, burn marks, deformities, tattoos, etc."[3]

Nineteenth-century practitioners regarded the disguises of the *Gauner* as requiring special attention to bodily characteristics, especially to "unusual characteristics," which could not be manipulated easily. This strategy made use of the circumstantial paradigm, as described by Carlo Ginzburg. The relevance of Ginzburg's observations for the description of criminological techniques of the identification of persons is indisputable, but it tells only one part of the story. In order to capture the other part of the story, we have to look at the mind-set of police experts in the first half of the nineteenth century. Their obsessive concern with deceit and their fear of a well-organized, but also well-disguised criminal class provided the framework for the implementation of identification strategies based on the circumstantial paradigm.

Police experts were, however, not only concerned with the choice of proper characteristics for the description and identification of criminals. As we see from the quotation above, they worried equally about the procedures to be adopted for the recording of these characteristics. They were well aware that negligence and indifference in the recording of personal descriptions posed a real threat to the efforts of the *res publica criminalistica* to combat professional crime. This anxiety will be the main focus of

---

[3] For a discussion of the need to record particular characteristics as part of personal descriptions, see Pfister 1820: 624f. He directed the gaze of police experts on the imprints of corporal punishment on the body of suspects. A systematic, but rather awkward classification of particular characteristics was suggested by the criminalist Rademacher. He lumped together physical and psychological anomalies in the same categories. Under category I (corporal), A (visible), a (natural), 1 (stable), Greek Delta (lack of organs, senses, and body parts), Greek Beta-Beta (complete lack) should be classified: deaf-mute and one-armed by birth: Rademacher 1837: 238.

my essay. It was part of the debate about the possibilities of representing reality by means of language, that is, in the written records of the court and the police. Among police experts this discussion was not on a highly theoretical but rather on a practical level. They blamed subordinate officials' lack of discipline, experience, and knowledge for misrepresentations of reality in writing. They were as much concerned about the use of improper phrases as about the inadequate structure of personal descriptions.

To contain these threats, experts recommended two strategies: first, the standardization of descriptions and descriptors by the introduction of forms; second, the substitution of mechanized forms of recording and documentation for language. My discussion of these two strategies is influenced by Lorraine Daston, whose work on "communitarian" and "mechanical" objectivity provides the conceptual framework for understanding the discussions of police experts in the nineteenth century. Communitarian objectivity aimed at establishing a common language and system of classification, while mechanical objectivity wanted to abandon language as a means of representation altogether.[4]

In this essay, I use Daston's analytical framework in order to gain new insights into the representational strategies of bureaucrats. First, I concentrate on the standardization of language, that is, "communitarian objectivity" as described by Daston. Second, I discuss some of the projects in which police experts tried to abandon language as a tool for personal description. I argue that language could never be completely abandoned in their representations. Even photographs as a method for the apparently mechanical representation of physiognomic characteristics had to rely on linguistic classifications of the data to provide efficient access to a suspect's identity.

Analytical Approaches to Physiognomies and Bodies

The standardization of personal descriptions required a shared semiotic strategy based on two elements: an analytical approach to physiognomy and body, and a commonly available set of descriptors. At the beginning of the nineteenth century, the analytical deconstruction was based on experience, that is, the "practical gaze" of police experts. During the second half of the nineteenth century it was more and more structured by the reception of physiological and anatomical knowledge.[5] This reception furnished the "practical gaze" with a set of normative expectations, which

---

[4] Daston 2001.

[5] This reception was facilitated by the fact that the "practical gaze" of police experts was structured similarly to the medical gaze. Both were based on the conjectural paradigm described by Ginzburg 1988.

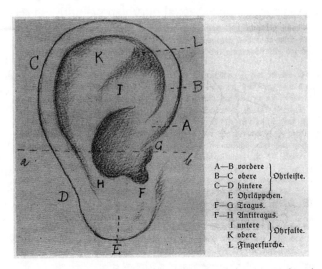

Illustration 1: Criminalistic description of the ear (Dehmal
1933: 278)

were instrumental both for the identification of individual persons and
for the disclosure of a hidden criminal identity through a differentiated
look at the body. Already in the first half of the century, the police experts'
look at the body was in many respects comparable to the medical gaze.
Both used specialized knowledge to direct their attention to those parts
of the body that provided them with the most significant information
regarding the identity of a person and the nature of his or her disease.

Ginzburg's circumstantial paradigm stresses the primary importance of
the apparently most insignificant parts of the body, such as the lobe of the
ear, but these were not likely to be noted by the inexperienced onlooker.
To achieve an analytical approach of this kind, police experts required
trained observation, which attempted, first, to decompose a particular appearance into meaningful elements and, second, to reconstitute it in a new
way on the basis of theoretical and practical experience. Accordingly, each
discursive practice had its own way of reading this evidence: the ear was
also studied outside criminology and practitioners, but was looked at by
criminologists and criminalists in a specific way. (See Illustration 1.)

The semiotics of police experts used the "dividing practices" described
by Michel Foucault.[6] Individuals who became subjects in the discourses
and practices of science and administration were exposed to an analytical
approach to their bodies and life histories. The results of this analysis

[6] Foucault 1982: 208.

were stored in systematically linked records of public authorities. As we learn from the opening quotation, the implementation of standardized analytical practices in police departments and prisons brought some difficulties. As the main problem, experts identified an inevitable hierarchy of reason, which seemed to coincide with the official's position within office hierarchy. This meant, in other words, that a sufficient analytical capability was expected only from well-trained officials and not from less proficient subordinates: "clerks and ushers" just did not "know on what the task mainly depends."

Further evidence for this concern with the hierarchy of reason can be found in the writings of the police expert Gustav Zimmermann from Hanover. He embedded the hierarchical difference of analytical capabilities in the framework of a division of labor within police departments. His concept of observation was based on the assumption that hierarchical and cognitive differences concurred. Even if subordinates made exact observations, they could only "remark" (*bemerken*)—an activity that Zimmermann (with explicit reference to the "great Kant") carefully distinguished from observing (*beobachten*).[7] For more subtle observations authorities had to rely on the service of better-trained officials, "who made conclusive observations."[8] These officials could employ their "practical gaze" as an interpretative approach to the social world. Their observations were built on their "general knowledge about human nature," on local knowledge, and on an interpretation of facial expressions. This enabled them to reconstruct hidden causalities and to recognize the true identity of persons.[9]

In order to adapt this concept of cognitive differences to the realities of policing, Zimmermann and other police experts in the first half of the nineteenth century assumed that perceptions (*Wahrnehmungen*) of the rank-and-file policemen were neutral representations of the social and physical reality. If gendarmes, police sergeants, and patrolmen were trained in attentive surveillance, they could fulfill one of the requisites of observation, that is, "exact perception and attentive listening, in order to recognize the facts as they really are."[10] This relieved the higher-ranking officials from spending their time on the tiring task of personally making observations in the streets. Instead, they could apply their superior analytical abilities to the reports of their subordinates. Therefore, they were able to observe without ever leaving their offices. In Zimmermann's view, observation only became an "art" when all perceptions had been system-

[7] Zimmermann 1845–49: 421.
[8] Zimmermann 1852: 48.
[9] See Zimmermann 1845–49, vol. 2: 413.
[10] Zimmermann 1845–49, vol. 3: 1126.

atically processed within the police headquarters, where the reports of rank-and-file officers were classified, gathered together, and enriched by the superior reason of the chief officers.[11]

Zimmermann's theory of observation was thus built on two main ideas: first, the hierarchy of reason, and, second, quite elaborate concepts for the institutional processing of information. According to the organizational principles of the nineteenth century, subordinate officers communicated their perceptions through the chain of command. Before these were stored in specialized databases or personal dossiers, they were enriched by an interpretative reading of the chief officers. After having been stored, these observations were incorporated into a national and—in most cases—even a transnational information network.[12]

This concept of observation is of primary importance for our understanding of the efforts made by the police to standardize the format of personal descriptions. The cognitive hierarchy engendered a suspicion of the validity of the perceptions reported by the policemen on the beat, and this called for a systematic training of their perceptive abilities. Moreover, the need to feed their reports into a comprehensive information system required a highly standardized system of description. The two incentives for standardization reinforced each other. The existence of an information network required well-defined schemata for reports; the use of these schemata directed the gaze of policemen to particular points of reference and thereby contributed to a further standardizing of their "practical gaze." These schemata thus taught the practitioners a new way of looking at, and also a new representation of, physiognomies.[13] They "should act as memory triggers for the officials making the descriptions, so that they do not forget anything essential," as Robert Heindl still argued at the beginning of the twentieth century.[14]

Evidence for this argument is provided by a circular rescript (decree) issued by the Prussian minister for internal affairs and the police on January 13, 1828. In this decree, all Prussian governments, as well as the Berlin police headquarters, were instructed to use a particular form to record personal descriptions (see Table 1). The measure was justified by reference to the increasing problems experienced by gendarmes in working with a highly diverse set of personal descriptions of wanted subjects: as the minister argued, the lack of standardization in the description of individuals

[11] See Zimmermann 1852: 40.

[12] For a description of Zimmermann's concept of observation as the main criminalistic procedure of the police, see Becker 1992: 115f.

[13] There is a rather long tradition of this approach to physiognomies, which can be traced back to Renaissance painters. See Zeller 1994: 376f.

[14] Heindl 1927: 543.

had "made the proper control of the work of the gendarmes in these matters extremely difficult."[15]

This form introduced in 1828 will be discussed in greater detail in the following section. At this point, I would only like to point out that the standardization of categories for personal descriptions and their compulsory character were a significant improvement. It is true that it was not the first form employed for personal descriptions. Similar forms had been in use since the beginning of the eighteenth century,[16] and the 1828 form did not introduce new standards in terms of what information was required. A look at the excellent collection of personal descriptions from many countries of the German Empire, issued between the seventeenth and eighteenth centuries and now in the *Landesarchiv* in Graz, shows a far-reaching compatibility between the personal descriptions of the early modern times and their later counterparts in the pre-revolutionary period. But the most significant difference from norms and practices of the earlier periods was that for the first time the 1828 form made a standardized description scheme compulsory for all Prussian police departments.

Standardizing Personal Descriptions

The 1828 decree provides the starting point for my reconstruction of the traces of "communitarian objectivity" within criminalistic discourse and practice. As further items of evidence, I examine Alphonse Bertillon's project of a modern scheme for personal descriptions and Robert Heindl's proposal for the introduction of a new form to be used for the same purpose. These three schemata represent important steps in the ongoing process of standardization. Bertillon was a key figure within this process; he was famous for his innovations in the field of criminalistics, especially for his introduction of anthropometry and for the standardization of police photographs.[17] Heindl was the criminalistic celebrity in Germany at the beginning of the twentieth century; he pioneered the introduction of fingerprinting in Germany.

All three models contributed both to a standardization of personal descriptions and to a further training of the "practical gaze." Through them a paradox of human perception was to be overcome: today's experimental psychology has discovered that people have the ability to distinguish

---

[15] Circular-Rescript des Königl. Ministeriums des Innern und der Polizei an sämmtliche Königl. Regierungen und an das Polizei-Präsidium zu Berlin, die Mittheilung der Steckbriefe an die Gendarmerie betreffend (13.1.1828).

[16] See Schubert 1983: 321.

[17] See the essay by Martine Kaluszynksi in this volume.

TABLE 1
Schemes for Personal Descriptions

Personal description form 1828	Personal description form by Heindl	Portrait parlé by Bertillon
Age	Age (0)	Age (25)
Height	Height (1)	Height (26)
Hair	Hair (2)	Hair, Head, and Beard (17)
Forehead		Forehead (1)
Eyebrows	Eyebrows (4)	Eyebrows (9)
Eyes	Eyes (5)	Eyelids (10)
		Eyeball (11)
		Eye socket (12)
		Interocular distance (13)
		Color of the eye (16)
Nose	Nose (6)	Nose (2)
	Ears, right and left (7)	Ears, six characteristics (3)
Mouth	Mouth (8)	Mouth (5)
		Lips (4)
Teeth	Teeth (9)	
Beard	Beard (3)	
Chin	Chin (10)	Chin (6)
Complexion		Complexion (15)
Features	Head, three characteristics (11)	Shape of the head (7)
		Enface-Contour (8)
		Wrinkles (14)
	Neck (12)	

TABLE 1
Schemes for Personal Descriptions (*cont'd*)

Personal description form 1828	Personal description form by Heindl	Portrait parlé by Bertillon
Figure	Arms and hands (13)	Corpulence (18)
	Legs and feet (14)	Posture (19)
	Figure (18)	Body movement (20)
	Posture (19)	
Speech	Speech (21)	Speech (22)
	Race and Type (20)	
Distinguishing marks	Scars (15)	Distinguishing marks (27)
	Visible signs of diseases (16)	
	Tattoos (17)	
	Distinguishing habits (22)	Distinguishing habits (21)
Dress	Dress (23)	Dress (23)
Coat		
Jacket		
Waistcoat		
Pants		
Boots		
Shoes		
Hat		
Cap		
	Jewelry (24)	
Particular circumstances		
	Handwriting sample (25)	

Source: Circular-Reskript 1828; Heindl 1927: 504ff. (description of Bertillon's *portrait parlé*) and 543ff. (Heindl's own proposal).

among thousands of faces, and also to recognize them later, but without being able to provide conclusive evidence for their recognition. This explains the difficulties experienced by police experts in providing a framework for the communication of physiognomies that would enable officers to identify even individuals unknown to them.[18]

A personal description form, like that prescribed in 1828, could not definitively solve this problem. It still left to officials the discretion to choose the descriptors for the completion of the form. Given the lack of a commonly shared language for a differentiated description of physiognomies, this discretion still undermined the efforts of standardization. A first systematic attempt to solve this problem was made by Bertillon, who provided a list of descriptors for most of the fields. His *portrait parlé*, as he called the formalized personal description, was intended to allow for the unambiguous identification of already documented persons. For this purpose anthropometrical measures were accompanied by a standardized description of physiognomic and bodily details.[19]

The *portrait parlé* was the most comprehensive physiognomic description among the models discussed here. One of its most striking peculiarities is the absence of any kind of social information, by contrast with the five such categories in the personal description of 1828: namely, birthplace, country of origin, place of residence, religion, status (*Stand*), and profession (for reasons of space, these are not reproduced in Table 1). If one also counts the information about clothing in the 1828 form as social information, it is clear that criminalistic observation focused on the subject as social individual until the end of the nineteenth century. Bertillon, by contrast, emphasized anatomical characteristics of the physiognomy, such as the ear and the eye. In doing so, he deprived his subjects almost completely of their social context, isolated them, and subjected them to a physiologically and anatomically based dividing observation. (See Illustration 2.)

The ear represented one of the most important physiognomic characteristics for the police experts of the late nineteenth and the twentieth centuries, since it did not change in the course of a life and could be described in formal terms.[20] A second main characteristic, which had been of significance as a means of identification for a long time, was the eye. It was considered to be the privileged means of access to the soul, but was robbed of its metaphysical content by Bertillon. This can be shown most clearly by a comparison between Johann Christian August Heinroth's and Bertil-

[18] See Bruyer 1987: 7f. and 87. This argument concurs with the critical attitude of many police experts toward the reliability and usefulness of personal descriptions: see Dennstedt and von Wolffsburg 1855–56: 625ff.; Wennmohs 1823, vol. 1: 181.

[19] See Ginzburg 1988: 111; Kaluszynski 1987: 10f.

[20] Cf. Heilmann 1994: 42–43.

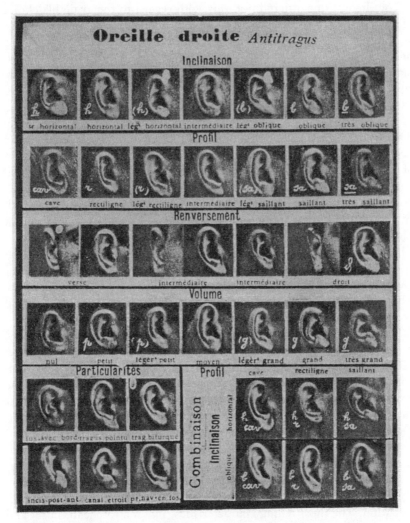

Illustration 2: Bertillon's descriptor for some parts of the ear (Heindl 1927: 516)

lon's descriptions. As a psychiatrist of the romantics, Heinroth spoke about a blank, weak, lively, piercing, or soulless look;[21] Bertillon, however, directed his attention to anatomical peculiarities like the opening, position, and particularity of the eyelids, the projection of the eyeballs, and the nature of the eye sockets.

[21] In his account of the signs to discover insanity, Heinroth considered the subjects' gaze as access to their soul to be of main importance; Heinroth 1825: 287.

The three forms differed not only with regard to the available choice of descriptors. They also provided different models for an analytical gaze at physiognomies, as we can learn from the differences in the organization of information in the registration form. Table 1 presents the order of information in a comparative way. All columns follow the organizational principle of the form of 1828. To make the differences visible, ranking numbers are given to the characteristics for the two other personal description forms. In 1828, police experts saw themselves confronted with a model that required them (after providing information about social characteristics, which are not reproduced in the table) to start with the age and height of suspects. Then their gaze was directed to the details of the physiognomy, starting with the hair, moving on to the forehead, and proceeding down the facial features to the chin. Only after this analysis did the quasi-synthetic information about the shape of the face, color, and build follow. The gaze of the police expert traveled along the contours of the face, which provided the only "natural" structural principle for a physiognomic description.[22] Because of its orientation to the "natural order," this physiognomic narrative was comparable to the reports of magistrates, who had to represent their subject in a chronological order as the "natural order of things" in the social and physical world.[23]

Bertillon's practitioner had to train his observation technique anew, since his gaze could no longer follow the "natural order" of the face. Bertillon classified the physiognomic characteristics on two levels: systematically and according to their relevance. The systematic grouping can be shown in the handling of hair and beard. Personal descriptions of the first half of the century recorded these two characteristics at the beginning and at the end respectively, that is, how they appeared in the natural facial order. Bertillon, by contrast, grouped them together and recorded them next to each other, because they belonged to the same group of characteristics. Another important feature of Bertillon's model was the introduction of a hierarchical order, defined by the degree of significance for individuation. The most telling characteristics, like the forehead, nose, and ears, were recorded first; the less significant ones later. The degree of reliability was assessed by the standards of the specialized gaze of police experts, who gained most information from details that were virtually

---

[22] The personal description form of 1828 is more or less identical with a scheme suggested by the Berlin police expert Carl Falkenberg in 1818: Falkenberg 1818, vol. 2: 118ff. The main difference can be found in the description of the beard, which followed in Falkenberg's scheme immediately after the description of the hair. This organization of personal description forms did not follow the "natural order" of the physiognomy and was not followed by the Ministry.

[23] Cf. Jagemann 1838: 431.

hidden to the untrained eye.[24] Clothing and other clues to a person's social and local identity, on which laymen focused for the purpose of identification, were either omitted or placed at the very end of Bertillon's scheme. This does not mean, however, that Bertillon did not care about this aspect of a suspect's identity. In fact, in his scheme, too, social identity remained an important element among the information to be reconstructed, but the type of reconstruction was different from what it had been previously.[25] By relying on anatomical characteristics that could not easily be willfully changed, Bertillon and his colleagues were applying an evidential paradigm in order to ascertain the personal and social identity of their subjects.

Bertillon's system was not a successful practical solution, however, because taken as a whole it was too complex; even the descriptors for the single fields were not clearly distinguished from each other. This was especially true for the recording of a person's height, for which a scale of 7 degrees was given, arranged according to Quetelet's rule of statistical distribution: very small, small, medium small, medium, medium large, large, very large. As Heindl pointed out, these 7 degrees lacked clear delimitations, and he urged the use of unambiguous data for the description of height, such as the physical height in centimeters, accompanied by an indication of the relative height through the broad categories of large and small.[26] Yet Heindl did not really overcome the imminent problems of Bertillon's description, as his proposal of these two broad categories proves. Instead of using the rather clumsy scale of 7 degrees, he wanted to register deviations from a norm which was not, however, specified in a satisfactory way.[27]

Nevertheless, according to Heindl, Bertillon's *portrait parlé* performed an important service for the police: "It taught the policemen to see. The *portrait parlé* is an excellent means to get policemen used to exact observation. Lessons in *portrait parlé* should therefore not be omitted in any police school."[28] The value of the *portrait parlé* was that it entailed both

---

[24] In a memorandum for the preparation of the pre-conference for the German Police Conference, Heindl refers to an experiment in which he tested the reliability of personal descriptions with "ordinary people." According to him, age and height were among the characteristics that "lay" people could observe best: Robert Heindl, "Der Nachrichtendienst der Kriminalpolizei. Denkschrift im Auftrage der Vorkonferenz zum 1. deutschen Polizeikongress," Archiv der Hansestadt Lübeck, Polizeiamt 10, Akten betreffend Polizeikonferenzen 1912–30, 9.

[25] Cf. Becker 1992: 121ff.

[26] In 1852, the Hessian magistrate Dael called for a standardization of the statement of the height in personal descriptions on the basis of the metric system: Dael 1852: 7–8.

[27] Cf. Heindl 1927: 543ff. For discussion of Quetelet's influence on Bertillon, see Dehmal 1933: 275.

[28] Heindl 1927: 536. The curriculum of the institute of criminalistics of the police department in Vienna proves that Bertillon's *portrait parlé* was taught in German-speaking police

a new, analytical look at the face, and a list of standardized descriptors. Familiarity with this terminology would improve the quality of both the description and the analytical observation. To illustrate this argument, Heindl listed the characteristics of the peculiarities of the helix of the ear as follows (see also Illustration 2):

> Darwin lumps; Darwin enlargement; Darwin projection; Darwin bumps; "creased" rear ear; melted rear ear; acute-angle upper ear; sharp corner between fore and upper ear; sharp corner between upper and rear ear; right corner between fore and upper ear; right corner between upper and rear ear; right corner between fore, upper, and rear ear; sharp and blunt corner between fore, upper, and rear ear.[29]

Bertillon's efforts to standardize the descriptive language clearly followed the model of "communitarian objectivity," but produced a result that was unsuitable for the daily routines of the police. Above all, it was inappropriate for its immediate task, the identification of fugitive criminals on the street by police officers, who carried with them a pocket lexicon with personal descriptions classified by physical characteristics. Heindl's response to this inadequacy was his recommendation for a new personal description form, which was presented to the preliminary meeting for the German Police Conference of 1912,[30] and can be read as a compromise between standardization and flexibility. It combined the logic of the traditional personal description form with elements from Bertillon's *portrait parlé* and included a less elaborate list of descriptors.

As Table 1 shows, Heindl followed the "practical gaze" of the police experts of the first half of the nineteenth century, in that his form once again was organized according to the "natural order" of the face. The only exception was the absence of an entry for the forehead, which he treated as part of the description of the head. Improvements in dentistry now allowed a fuller description of the person, not only through detectable missing teeth, but also by indicating the presence of fillings or of an artificial bite. In the 1935 model personal description by the Austrian police expert Arnold Lichem, the description of teeth was further formalized: in his form, there was an illustration of the upper and lower jaw—similar to the treatment protocol of dentists—in which the police official had to enter the particulars of the bite.[31]

---

schools. (Curriculum 1926, in archive of Austrian sociology, Ernst Seelig's papers). Therefore, I cannot concur with Darmon's argument that the knowledge of the *portrait parlé* was restricted to a small group of initiated people: Darmon 1987: 47f.

[29] Heindl 1927: 512f.

[30] A copy of the first draft of Heindl's proposal, which deviates somewhat from the published version, can be found in Archiv der Hansestadt Lübeck, Polizeiamt, 10: Akten betreffend Polizeikonferenzen 1912–30.

[31] Lichem 1935: 99.

Heindl's model demanded a highly differentiated description of the habitus and of particular characteristics. He urged in particular an exact recording of tattoos according to place, length, width, color, and thematic subject. Here Heindl was reviving a long tradition of the usage of tattoos for the purpose of identification; police journals such as the *Merkerschen Mitteilungen* had offered their readers registers of tattoos and of other particular characteristics in the first half of the nineteenth century.

The standardization of the "practical gaze" through the provision of forms and lists of descriptors could not remove the biased focus of the policemen's observation of a specific group of people, nor was this its aim. The higher degree of objectivity intended by these measures concerned only the procedure but not the material principles of police work. A brief look at the descriptors for the categories of "race and type" and "particular habits" (present only in Heindl's model) will illustrate this point. They enable us to understand that even the most standardized mode of representation could express and reproduce a prejudicial mindset. In the first category, the national and racial enemies were categorized in the following way: "Negro, Mulatto, Chinese, Japanese, Jew, Gypsy."[32]

The descriptors for the category "particular customs" described the lifestyle of the "anti-citizen," his sexuality, and his consumption and leisure habits. They emphasized and reproduced the idea of a systematic, "total" difference between the criminal and the decent, self-controlled citizen: "Alcoholism, morphinism, heavy smoking . . . tobacco chewing, tobacco snorting, chewing of finger nails, passion for gambling, homosexuality, patronage of cafés, bars, race-courses, criminal pubs, relations with prostitutes, passion for certain animals, etc."[33]

The "practical gaze," in its most standardized form, also remained directed at objects of observation that were defined socially and politically. Observation was increasingly supported by the "memory aids" of the list of descriptors, which aimed at removing the individual observer's discretionary power. The forms thus furnished guidelines for the policeman's perceptions, but in a rather different way from that suggested in Heindl's commentary to the *portrait parlé*.

Objectivity of Portrait and Photography

The standardization of personal descriptions and the inclusion of lists of descriptors together represented the first of two attempts to objectify police representations. A second strategy to deal with the increasing insecu-

---

[32] Heindl 1927: 546.
[33] Heindl 1927: 546f.

rity in the recording of subjects of interest aimed at the elimination of language altogether. Practitioners and criminologists identified a need for standardized, mechanical pictorial representations even before the introduction of photography. This anticipation can be read as another indicator of the concurrence between scientific and administrative concerns about language as a means of reproduction. Lorraine Daston and Peter Galison argue that photography played an important role within the scientific discussion about mechanical objectivity, but that its use neither caused this discussion nor ended it.[34] The production of illustrations for scientific atlases, which are the empirical reference point for Daston and Galison, has this in common with the illustration of physiognomic information for criminalistic purposes: both arose not only with the invention of photography, but already from uneasiness about existing techniques of linguistic, as well as artistic, forms of representation.[35]

An anticipation of photographs as a mechanical means of representation can be found in proposals made by police experts during the first half of the nineteenth century, including one by the magistrate Rademacher, who wanted to have portraits drawn of the most dangerous individuals. This would have made their features accessible in pictorial rather than linguistic form. According to Rademacher, the advantage of the portrait was that it could provide the basis for an unambiguous identification of wanted persons, and rule out any confusion of identities. It was easier, moreover, to compare the external appearance of a person with a picture, by means of a "direct and complete sensory contemplation," than with a written personal description, which was also often negligently drawn up. And finally, the portrait produced a much deeper, longer-lasting imprint on the memory of practitioners than the dry letters of a personal description.[36] It was impossible to expose criminals everywhere to a large group of police officials in person: this could happen only in the larger police departments, in Berlin or Paris, where professional thieves and other dangerous criminals were paraded before police officials at regular sessions. The Berlin police expert Carl Falkenberg argued that this procedure made identification in subsequent offenses considerably easier.[37] Rademacher's proposal to establish a portrait gallery of the most dangerous felons can be regarded as an attempt to provide a similar service to colleagues from the provinces. On the basis of his experience with decentralized cooperation among small authorities, it made perfect sense for him to recommend the publication of half-length portraits in police journals.

[34] Daston and Galison 1992: 98.
[35] Daston 2001.
[36] Rademacher 1837: 8.
[37] Falkenberg 1818: 46ff. and 59.

Rademacher's proposal was futuristic and visionary for his time, however. This is clearly shown if one compares it to other contemporary proposals. In 1819, the administration in Cleve was still recommending the recording of brands to trace criminals disguised behind the mask of a false social identity. Even though an ordinance of 1799 in theory still allowed this kind of stigmatization, to meet the increasing incidence of theft,[38] branding was no longer acceptable at the beginning of the nineteenth century. The Prussian Ministry of Internal Affairs and the police therefore rejected the Cleve authorities' suggestion that brands should be reintroduced as a means of solving the problem of vagrancy.[39] In the nineteenth century, the stigma was no longer directly inscribed on the body of the perpetrator,[40] but was rather administered in collections of data by the police: here pictures offered a new means of documentation and of access to personal files.[41]

Rademacher's proposals had already been anticipated in France, where portraits of criminals had been collected since 1819 in the "redaction du bureau des prisons."[42] In the German-speaking world, his proposals found ready audience in Friedrich Eberhardt, the editor of the *Allgemeine Polizei-Anzeiger*. In the same volume as the one in which he presented Rademacher's ideas, Eberhardt picked up the idea of "the highly esteemed magistrate Rademacher," and slightly modified it. For Eberhardt, the portrayal was not mechanical enough, and was therefore too dependent on

---

[38] Decree of February 26, §25: regarding the punishment of larceny and similar crimes, quoted from Mannkopff 1836: 643. A similar proposal can be found in Schwencken 1822: 74.

[39] The rescript of the Prussian Ministry of Interior Affairs and the Police of January 16, 1820, replied to the report of the Prussian administration in Cleve of November 16, 1819. In this report, the administration in Cleve suggested two strategies to finally solve the problem of vagrancy: (1) every person who is labeled as vagrant by a legal court or by the administration should lose any protection of the law; (2) "all vagrants should be tattooed, so that a permanent sign be applied on their bodies, from which every police authority will be able to recognize them easily." Both proposals were commented on negatively by the Ministry: the protection of the law cannot easily be taken from individuals; vagrants should instead be subjected to legal norms, which provide sufficient means to ban them from the Prussian lands. In response to the second proposal, the Ministry argued that even previously branding was only applied in the most serious crimes and that it did not belong to acceptable punishments. "Even if the administration in Cleve does not want to accept this fact, the degradation of this measure is obvious and it would be a cruelty of the highest degree, to imprint tattoos as an indelible reminder on the body of vagrants" (quoted from Rönne and Simon 1840: 527).

[40] The decree of the court chancellery of May 12, 1848, and his majesty's resolution of May 22, 1848, finally abandoned branding in the Habsburg monarchy too as an aggravated form of punishment. See for this legislation Ogris 1975, vol. 2: 564–65.

[41] For an account of the similar discussion in France, where photographs were explicitly characterized as the new form of branding, see Phéline 1985: 17.

[42] Kaluszynski 1987: 271–72.

Illustration 3: Silhouette of Johann Conrad
Volcker (Eberhardt 1837: 4)

the presence of a "very practiced and gifted artist." From his perspective,
silhouettes (see Illustration 3) had the advantage that their preparation
"is a more mechanical business, which can easily be made by someone
who is used to working with care and detail."[43]

If one compares the proposals of Eberhardt and Rademacher, it is obvious that the only advantage of silhouettes was their more mechanical production. They had, however, serious disadvantages: they barely showed
any characteristics by which a successful identification could be made,
and thus were completely unsuitable for the purpose of police identifications. They tended to replace visualization by abstraction, but not by an
abstraction that was based on the analytical view of the practitioners. Yet
portraits were not a realistic serious alternative. They required skilled
artists to be present in the police departments, and artistic representations
were subject to the same kind of critique as linguistic ones. Already by
the mid-ninteenth century, practitioners were therefore beginning to look

---

[43] Eberhardt 1837: 228. In his argument, Friedrich Eberhard followed the Swiss priest
Johann Caspar Lavater, one of the most outspoken promoters of physiognomy at the end
of the eighteenth century, who recommended the drawing of silhouettes as a means of improving the observation skills of non-artistically gifted people. For a reconstruction of this
argument, see Stadler 1996: 88.

for alternatives that would allow both mechanical and comprehensive representations of physiognomies; and this was finally found in photographs, as an anonyomous author writing in a German police gazette in 1852 pointed out:[44]

> Thieves, fraudsters, and crooks of all classes flee and often thwart the efforts of the security authorities with their refinements. . . . To remove all these obstacles is a very difficult task . . . the invention of daguerreotype must also be used for police security purposes. The preparation of pictures of dangerous inmates and the duplication of the originals by lithography has proven itself in many different cases.[45]

This quotation is quite revealing. The author considers the photograph a more efficient means of stigmatizing those criminals who pursued their evil trade under fake identities. The Swiss State Council was among the first to put this idea into practice on a large scale. In its decision of October 22, 1852, the State Council ordered the systematic photographing of homeless people and vagabonds, in order to mark them through the means of photography ("durch das Mittel der Daguerotypie zu kennzeichnen").[46] The phrasing of this decision of the Swiss authorities is telling, as it expressly identified the daguerreotype as the modern functional equivalent to branding.

The use of photographs was a helpful, if not infallible, aid in the search for people. Here the search for suspicious persons must be understood in the widest sense. In the nineteenth century, it was not uncommon for persons to be arrested and for their identity to remain hidden. Professional criminals had every reason to conceal their identity from the authorities. If the police and legal authorities could not reconstruct their biographies against their silent or verbose resistance, they usually got away with a lenient punishment, if they had not been caught red-handed. Police gazettes of the mid-century are full of requests for assistance in the identification of a suspicious person who had been jailed and whose pretended biography had turned out to be fictitious. The widespread use of photographs as one means for revealing the true identity of detainees

---

[44] Between 1850 and 1855, when Swiss authorities started a systematic photographing of vagrants and German police gazettes used lithographed photographs as part of personal descriptions for the first time, the future usage of photographs as privileged means of representation in several disciplines was decided: Phéline 1985: 23.

[45] Anon. 1852: 127–28. These first attempts to introduce photographs systematically into criminalistic practice fell into oblivion again. This can be learned from a brief remark of Heindl 1927: 553, where he argues that the earliest publication to use photographs for personal identification can be traced back to 1854.

[46] Quoted from Bult 1990: 37. On the Swiss efforts to establish a catalogue of homeless and vagabonds, see Meier and Wolfensberger 1998: 9–23.

Illustration 4: Photograph of Hermann Krause
(*Hannoversches Polizeiblatt* 1855: 276)

can already be found in the 1850s. These pictures for the first time realized
Rademacher's dream of a comprehensive collection of visual images of
the most dangerous criminals. Their publication aimed to simplify the
"task of comparison" by offering the means for direct, visual perception
of distinguishing characteristics.

The police journal of Hanover, for example, increasingly used lithographed photographs to support urgent investigations, as an example in
1855 will show.[47] Hermann Krause, a detainee held on charges of fraudulent acts, was described as "a highly mischievous and dangerous individual," who "for some reason avoids his residence, and in order not to be
sent back there, attempts to deceive the authorities as to his personal and
residence circumstances."[48] For this reason, other authorities were asked
for assistance, and in order to revive their memory about the suspect in
question, lithographed photographs were reproduced, together with the
personal description (Illustration 4). Hermann Krause appears here in a
full-face, half-length picture, which was rather unusual for the time. Most
photographs published in police journals were three-quarter pictures

[47] The use of photographs for the identification of fugitives was not limited to the prosecution of well-known political "criminals," as Siemann argues: Siemann 1985: 264.
[48] Entry number 22111, *Hannoversches Polizeiblatt* 9 (1855), 276–77.

showing parts of the profile, like the ear, which offered additional reference points for identification. The photographs were not yet reduced to the representation of the physiognomy alone but showed part of the clothing too, thereby permitting conclusions about a suspect's social status. The success of this strategy was limited, as one can glean from the repeated calls for help in the determination of the identity of the pictured persons.

As soon as the individual authorities had a greater number of portraits of criminals at their disposal, a "portrait gallery" of especially dangerous criminals emerged.[49] This confronted officials with the problem of classifying and organizing their collections in a way that would best serve the purposes of police identification. The first attempts to meet this challenge produced quite undifferentiated collections, in which all available photographs were assembled into an album of criminals.[50] At first, many of these albums were bound into books, as in the case of the collected photographs of Swiss homeless people. Very soon, the number of documented criminals grew too large to be contained in a single album. The Berlin criminal album, begun in 1876, contained the photographs of 32,533 persons by 1909.[51] The same enormous quantities of visual information could also be found in other German police authorities. The photography department of the Hamburg police authority produced a total of 900,000 pictures between 1889 and 1912, including 120,000 photographs of persons, 1,300 of crime scenes, and 2,000 of handwriting samples.[52]

This mass of information demanded the development of an adequate system of access that could respond to the complex character of this information. A first attempt at classification sorted the pictures of professional criminals, notably the pictures of property offenders and anarchists, according to their specialization. Soon this classification was no longer feasible, and further subdivisions were introduced according to height, age, and physiognomic details—information that also played an essential role in the recording of personal descriptions.

Conclusion

The analytical approach to physiognomy made possible the amendment of the personal description form according to new methods of reading the

[49] Rademacher 1837: 8.

[50] In 1860, police departments started the first criminal albums. See for this aspect Regener 1992: 70ff.

[51] See Funk 1986: 246ff.; from 1914 on, the Berlin police department was capable of reproducing photographs in larger numbers; see Gadebusch Bondio 1995: 93.

[52] See Roscher 1912: 64ff.

face. An essential element in this analysis was the reevaluation of physiognomic details that remained rather in the background in the everyday consideration of a face. With this, criminologists were relying on an evidential identification paradigm, as described by Ginzburg. The process of identification was closely related to the anatomical and physiological discourse about identity.[53] On account of the increasing use of police photographs around the end of the nineteenth century, the physiological details gained new relevance as a means of accessing the vast amount of visual information stored in albums full of photographs.

Portraits and photographs made the "task of comparison" easier, as long as their numbers allowed for their storage in the memory of police officials, from which they could be flexibly recalled. But as soon as the numbers became excessive, as happened in the larger European police authorities in the late nineteenth century, practitioners needed to rely on numerical or linguistic categories to access them in an efficient way. A modern answer to this problem was the use of anthropometrical measurements, or of numerical classifications of fingerprints to improve the access to the identity of suspects. Before physiognomic details could be used as an efficient means of accessing photographs, the analytical view of physiognomy had to be broadly standardized. The standardized gaze at physiognomic characteristics helped to introduce an organization of information that structurally resembled a relational database system. Registers of particular characteristics, which were already employed as a method to track down fugitive criminals before the introduction of photographs,[54] provided clues for accessing a suspect's identity and biography. Bodily characteristics could be used in many ways as classification criteria for accessing the fast growing quantity of personal data within police departments. In this sense, Bertillon's analytical approach to physiognomies had lasting importance for identification procedures.[55] The personal description register and the criminal album in Dresden are cases in point. Here, so-called riders, indicating specific physiognomic details, were used with the record cards, in order to speed up the search process[56] (Illustration 5).

Around the turn of the century, the Dresden police department introduced a new register to determine the identity of persons who were particularly urgently sought. This register was used for those suspects who had been brought to police headquarters and whose names could not be deter-

[53] Cf. Ginzburg 1988.

[54] See Rademacher 1837: 237ff.

[55] The Austrian police expert Heinrich Dehmal emphasized the relevance of this analytical approach to physiognomies for the organization of writing samples of suspects: Dehmal 1933: 337.

[56] See for the organization of records outside police departments Leroi-Gourhan 1984: 329.

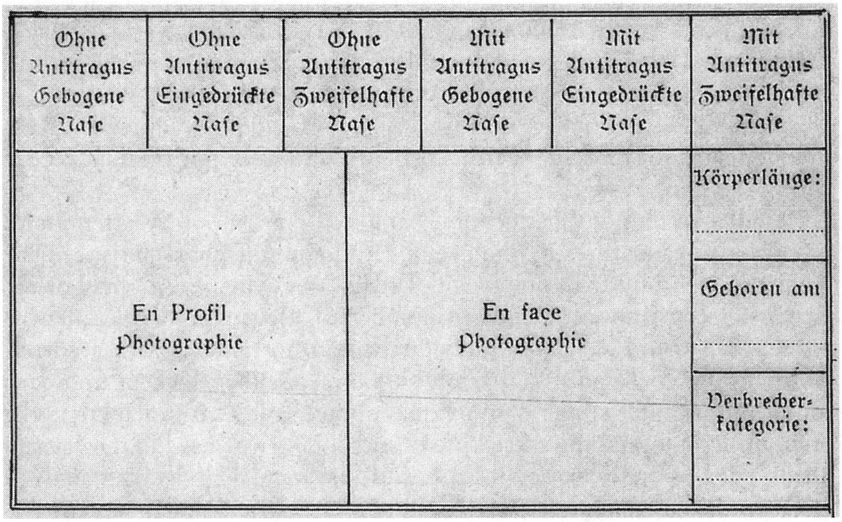

Ohne Antitragus Gebogene Nase	Ohne Antitragus Eingedrückte Nase	Ohne Antitragus Zweifelhafte Nase	Mit Antitragus Gebogene Nase	Mit Antitragus Eingedrückte Nase	Mit Antitragus Zweifelhafte Nase
					Körperlänge: ....
En Profil Photographie		En face Photographie			Geboren am ....
					Verbrecher= kategorie: ....

Illustration 5: Register card from Dresden (Robert Heindl, "Der Nachrichten-dienst der Kriminalpolizei. Denkschrift im Autrag der Vorkonferenz zum 1. Deutschen Polizeikongress in Dresden vom 28.-29.9.1912": 12 (Archiv der Hansestadt Lübeck, Polizeiamt 10, Akten betreffend Polizeikonferenzen, 1912–1930))

mined after fingerprinting. The register contained records with photographs that were either taken out of the Berlin daily report, or from the records of other police stations. Illustration 5 shows schematically one of these cards, which were sorted according to two physiognomic characteristics—the form of the nose and ear. Through removable flaps, a card could be classified only with those riders that corresponded to the physiognomy of the fugitive. The approach to registered persons was thereby considerably simplified.

According to Heindl, the network of "pictures," through which German police authorities were linked together, had to be based on modern techniques of information processing. Only then were the police considered to have access to and control over those social groups that were regarded as especially threatening to security.[57] This meant that the collective memory of police departments, which was in most cases extended by the influx of information to the editors of police journals, could be made widely accessible. Thereby, the network of control was pulled tighter, and the room for deviations from the standards of normal citizen behavior

[57] John Tagg has already traced the links between an increasing number of "images" in the archives of police departments and the bureaucratic control over the people with evidence from British police authorities: Tagg 1987: 300ff.

reduced.[58] An essential aim of this strategy was the improved control of itinerant professional criminals in the whole German Reich and its neighboring states. This made great demands on the capacities of police authorities. Heindl's classification system, fingerprints, and anthropometry were all attempts to satisfy these demands. They offered possibilities of access to the identity of those dangerous persons who were not (yet) on record within the filing systems.

Heindl's system of classification exploited contemporary attempts to reveal hidden identities by the use of physiognomic characteristics. The renaissance of physiognomy was linked to a new analytical view of the face. Focusing only on a limited number of physiognomic details, the practitioner could use every individual photo in tandem with a corresponding analytical gaze at the physiognomy in the "task of comparison."[59] In the comparison of individual photographs with each other, the practitioner adopted the same kind of method as was used in the classification of physiognomic details in Heindl's system. The detailed analysis of ears with a magnifying glass aimed at an analytical description of this organ: in Heindl's register of urgently sought criminals this analytical look at photographs was at the core of the classification procedure, which helped to organize the register by physiognomic characteristics. Heindl thus incorporated the analytical gaze at physiognomy into a bureaucratic procedure, and thereby took account of the division of labor that was characteristic of large police authorities.

A classification of physiognomies as differentiated as possible was necessary for the organization of information within large data sets. It could only be achieved by a systematic collaboration of several people, whose approach had to be widely standardized in order to be compatible. This process of standardization, which also affected the personal description form, can be seen as a general trend of nineteenth-century administration. The development of forms and the use of differentiated methods of indexing and registration was, in the end, also an opportunity to settle the assumed differences between the higher officials and their employees with regard to their intellectual capacities and specialized knowledge. The opportunity to use "memory aids," and systematic instruction in the differentiated gaze at physiognomies, was expected to improve and to stan-

---

[58] The availability of these registers tightened control over the vagrant population. At the same time, new means of communication dramatically sped up the transmission of information. Police experts in the mid-nineteenth century considered the use of telegraphs as a way to overcome the threat of the increasing mobility of criminals. While railways helped professional thieves to escape with their loot, the telegraphed message could arrive even before they did: Anon. 1847: 191–92. The use of telegraphs required a systematic standardization of messages to be transmitted.

[59] See Weingart 1904: 18.

dardize subordinate officials' abilities in observation, so that they could be used as "mechanical agents" or as "telescopes" with which the police "wandered through and oversaw [their] entire area."[60]

This success story of an ever-increasing formalization and standardization of personal descriptions certainly contributed to the implementation of formalized bureaucratic methods for the classification and identification of individuals. This rationalization remained, however, restricted to the procedures and did not challenge the strong bias of the policeman's "practical gaze" at the homeless, vagrants, foreigners, workers, and members of political opposition movements. Moreover, photographs, which helped to objectify the representation of physiognomies, always served a dual purpose for practitioners. First, they provided access to the personal identity of suspects; second, they seemed to contain direct evidence about their criminal identity. Toward the end of the nineteenth century, criminologists like Cesare Lombroso used photographs as main proof for the existence of *criminal man*. This is well known, but less familiar are the attempts of practitioners in the first half of the century to engage in comparable projects. Rademacher, whom we met earlier, described a picture gallery of offenders as a kind of trophy collection for practitioners.[61] The most rationalized means of representation thus led practitioners and criminologists alike on the first steps toward a new totalization of evil.

[60] Zimmermann 1845–49, vol. 2: 404.
[61] Rademacher 1837: 8, footnote.

9

Anthropometry, the Police Expert, and the Deptford Murders: The Contested Introduction of Fingerprinting for the Identification of Criminals in Late Victorian and Edwardian Britain

ANNE M. JOSEPH

> With dramatic suddenness he struck a match and by its light exposed a stain of blood upon the whitewashed wall. As he held the match nearer I saw that it was more than a stain. It was the well-marked print of a thumb.
> "Look at that with your magnifying glass, Mr. Holmes."
> "Yes, I am doing so."
> "You are aware that no two thumb marks are alike?"
> "I have heard something of the kind."
> "Well, then, will you please compare that print with this wax impression of young McFarlane's right thumb, taken by my orders this morning?"
> As he held the waxen print close to the blood-stain it did not take a magnifying glass to see that the two were undoubtedly from the same thumb. It was evident to me that our unfortunate client was lost.
> —SIR ARTHUR CONAN DOYLE, *"The Adventure of the Norwood Builder"*[1]

THE IDENTIFICATION of individuals in a society is necessary for governing and attempting to maintain social order. In the late nineteenth century, conflict arose in elite administrative forums as to how best to identify and, hence, control criminals in England.[2] As late Victorian cities expanded in population and space, crime rates grew but at a slower rate than urban population. With rising attention being given to crime and to allegedly

I would like to thank Henry Atmore, Abraham Goldstein, John Langbein, Douglas Lichtman, Michael Meranze, James Secord, and Alison Winter for helpful discussions on this essay. An earlier version was presented at the Annual Meetings of the American Historical Association, January 1998.
  [1] Doyle 1993: 146–47.
  [2] Ginzburg 1990: 119.

deterministic elements of criminality, the ability to track and restrain criminals, particularly repeat offenders, increased in importance.[3] I am interested in the competition between various systems designed for criminal identification and how the tracking of criminals was resolved during the closing decade of the nineteenth century and the first decade of the twentieth century in Britain. This story occurs in different spaces—government committees, the courtroom, serial novels in newspapers—and places practical concerns about the implementation and operation of identification systems in the wider context of what constitutes criminal identification.

The problem of identification preoccupied late Victorian bureaucracy. In October 1893, Home Secretary Asquith established a committee to investigate the best method available for identifying habitual criminals. Under Chairman Charles Troup, the committee examined current systems of identification: anthropometry as used by Alphonse Bertillon, the chief of the Department of Judicial Identity of the Paris Police Préfecture; and fingerprinting as being developed by Sir Francis Galton in England.[4] In deciding which system or combination of systems to adopt, the Troup Committee established the following criteria:

1. The descriptions, measurements or marks, which are the basis of the system, must be such as can be taken readily with sufficient accuracy by prison warders or police officers of ordinary intelligence.

2. The classification of the descriptions must be such that on the arrest of an old offender who gives a false name his record may be found readily and with certainty.

3. When the case has been found among the classified descriptions, it is desirable that convincing evidence of identity should be afforded.[5]

These conditions demonstrate the concern about ease of recording and classifying marks of identity as well as the level of proof of identity in the late-nineteenth-century administrative state.

The transition from photographs, line-ups, and route forms[6] to fingerprints for the identification of criminals was neither automatic nor uncon-

---

[3] Read 1979: ix, 255; Wiener 1990: 12, 14–15, 148–49, 338, 342. With the decline of transportation (i.e., the deportation of criminals), more criminals remained in England. Luke 1980: 39–40.

[4] The following were named to the Committee: Charles Edward Troup, Esq. (Home Office), Major Arthur Griffiths (Inspector of Prisons), and Melville Leslie Macnaghten, Esq. (Chief Constable in the Metropolitan Police Force). Harry Butler, Esq. (Home Office) was named as the Secretary.

[5] Troup Committee 1894: 29.

[6] Route forms contained a description of an arrested person and typically a photograph. The form was "routed" to all police offices where it was suspected that someone might recognize the person and be able to provide information about previous convictions. It was for "*tracing*, never for the purpose of *proving* identity (original emphasis)." Ibid.: 11–12.

tested. Carlo Ginzburg has argued that fingerprinting was the best system on offer in the last decade of the nineteenth century because it provided a method to prove, positively, the identity of individuals. He rejects photographs as lacking precision and dismisses Bertillon's anthropometric measurements as purely negative, positing that such measurements only distinguished among individuals.[7] The adoption of fingerprinting signals for Ginzburg an epistemological shift from the Galilean model of quantification, with numbers representing body part lengths, to a qualitative model of the conjectural sciences, with images of fingerprints. But Ginzburg's intellectual history of identification systems, which evaluates techniques on whether they could establish positive proof of identity, does not engage with how these techniques were practiced.

The shift in identification practices involved more than a transition in epistemology. Methods of identification also depend on the techniques used to produce, classify, and search the requisite information. Simon Schaffer's work on the "personal equation" in astronomical measurement (a term attributed by "astronomers after Bessel to the differences in measured transit times recorded by observers in the same situation") provides a complementary explanatory structure for changes in identification systems based on training practices and the social negotiation of what constitutes a valid measurement.[8] Using Schaffer's theory, a history of identification practices would focus on the difficulty in training police officers and other workers to record individual characteristics, whether anthropometric measurements or fingerprints. The transition from anthropometric measurements to fingerprinting reflects to a considerable degree the eventual dominance of the latter in the *production* of identification.

A comprehensive account of the eventual "success" of the fingerprint system in Britain at the turn of the century should therefore draw from both Ginzburg's intellectual history of the conjectural sciences and Schaffer's theories of training and measurement. Stories of police authority, the administrative state, and the courtroom also shape my narrative of the conflict over identification practices and its resolution. This narrative is primarily one of changing conceptions of expertise. Fingerprinting transformed the practices of the police, establishing layers of authority from obtaining to classifying prints; simultaneously and somewhat paradoxically, it also fueled the imaginations of the public.

The Troup Committee in 1894 concluded that a combination of anthropometric measurements and fingerprints should be adopted for the tracking of criminals. In 1900, the Belper Committee, which was established to review these methods for the identification of criminals, advo-

[7] Ginzburg 1990: 120.
[8] Schaffer 1988: 115.

cated the adoption of a system based entirely on fingerprinting.[9] I examine these two committees and the issues they raised in advance of the 1905 Deptford murders trial, in which a thumbprint contributed to the hanging of two brothers who had no other direct physical link to the crime scene. The trial provides an interesting opportunity to pull apart issues of expertise, clues, and the popular culture surrounding identification, issues that have been left unexamined in other more cursory renditions of the case. Instead of focusing on the achieved consensus in criminal policy around the turn of the century, I concentrate on the dissension.[10]

Bureaucratic Reporting: Committees and the Tracking of Individuals

It [the anthropometric method] permitted the elimination of those whose details on examination did not match up, but it could not prove that two sets of identical details referred to the same person. The elusive quality of individuality could not be shut out: chased out through the door by quantification, it came back through the window.... In a very short time the new method [fingerprinting] was introduced in England, and thence gradually to the rest of the world (one of the last countries to give in to it was France). Thus every human being ... acquired an identity.

—CARLO GINZBURG, "Morelli, Freud, and Sherlock Holmes: Clues and Scientific Method"[11]

When the Troup Committee was deliberating in 1893–94 and the Belper Committee was grappling with evidence in 1900 over what system of identification to propose, proof of identity was but one condition. The Troup Committee articulated objectives—not only the need to positively identify habitual criminals, but also the desire to avoid misidentifications and to economize on the amount of needed labor—that indicate social and political concerns about authority and efficiency.[12] The Troup Committee wanted a system of identification that was practical and effective; it did not explicitly prioritize these goals. Prior to fingerprinting and anthropometry, the police had relied on photographs, distinctive marks

[9] The following were named to the Committee: Lord Henry Belper, Frederick Albert Bosanquet, Esq., Q.C. (Common Sergeant), Albert de Rutzen, Esq., C.B. (Magistrate of the Police Courts of the Metropolis), Charles Stewart Murdoch, Esq. (Assistant Under Secretary of State for the Home Department), and Charles Edward Troup, Esq. (Home Office). Cecil Lubbock, Esq. was named as the Secretary.

[10] Wiener 1990: 342–44.

[11] Ginzburg 1980b: 25, 27.

[12] Troup Committee 1894: 13–18.

(e.g., tattoos and scars), and detailed records.[13] Earlier still, officials relied on personal recollection to identify criminals.[14] These previous methods of photographs, route forms, distinctive marks, and line-ups were labor-intensive. The inspection of unconvicted prisoners at Holloway required thirty police officers in attendance three days a week (yielding about four identifications weekly by police) and the classification of photographs consisted only in the sporadic compilation of books in chronological order.[15] A new identification system may have promised to be more effective, but the police were wary of an increased workload.

In 1894, primarily due to operational advantages, the anthropometric system won out over fingerprinting as the main system of identification. In his 1893 *Instructions Signalétiques*, Bertillon advocated the following measurements to identify people: length of head, width of head, length of left foot, length of left middle finger, length of left forearm, height, span of arms, height of trunk (sitting height), length of right ear, width of right ear, and length of left little finger. The first five measurements were considered to be the most important and made up the primary classification system.[16] For confirmation and additional differentiation, Bertillon also recorded eye color and a short physical description including distinctive marks and attached a photograph; later he added fingerprints to the anthropometric card. The Troup Committee traveled to Paris to observe the Bertillon system of anthropometric measurements in operation and consulted Dr. John Garson, vice president of the Anthropological Institute, and Arthur Thompson, professor of human anatomy at Oxford University, on the system.

The Troup Committee believed that Bertillon had taken all necessary precautions against filing cards incorrectly and not identifying a previously measured criminal, and the members found that the system met the committee's own criteria for criminal identification.[17] Although the committee was even convinced that anthropometric measurements could make positive matches of identification (allowing a small variation of less than 2 millimeters in the primary measurements), anthropometry's strongest selling point lay not in the proof of identity, but rather in its simple and effective system of classification, which Galton's system of fingerprinting lacked in 1893. The Troup Committee believed that fingerprinting satisfied its first and third conditions (i.e., the ability of police officers to take the fingerprints of suspected criminals "with sufficient

---

[13] Ibid.: 7; Forbes 1985: 218.
[14] Ibid.
[15] Troup Committee 1894: 18.
[16] Ibid.: 20–21.
[17] Ibid.: 19–20, 22–24.

accuracy" and the use of such evidence to make positive identifications), but since fingerprinting did not have a working classification procedure, it was not selected as the primary system.

Although the Troup Committee proposed anthropometry as the primary system of identification and classification of criminals, and fingerprinting for secondary classification and verification, it grilled witnesses about the training required for taking useful anthropometric measurements. Anthropometry supporters promoted the system as an "objective" and numerical demarcation of individuals into statistical groups, but, ironically, such classification relied on human observation and complicated instruments. The individual body was not allowed to change in size, which made anthropometry unworkable for juvenile criminals. J. P. Manning, the governor of Pentonville Prison, argued in front of the Troup Committee for the selection of fingerprinting over Bertillon's system because of the difficulty in obtaining reliable measurements. Under questioning, he acknowledged that his men had not been properly trained in the anthropometric system. Training and discipline were seen as necessary to keep variations in line. Garson, who had studied medicine at the University of Edinburgh, advocated the adoption of Bertillon's system, which he used when he was one of the vice presidents of the Anthropological Institute, and emphasized that any reasonably dexterous person could be trained to take measurements in front of the Troup Committee. He also suggested that training should be given by an "experienced teacher who has had a scientific training," and he immediately offered his services to the committee.[18] Consequently, Garson was named scientific adviser for the new Anthropometric Registry that was established upon the acceptance of the Troup Committee's recommendations.

Some lingering doubts about anthropometric measurements remained. Although training could potentially ameliorate many problems in taking and recording measurements, some witnesses questioned whether such measurements could provide positive proof of identity. Galton, in his testimony before the Troup Committee, indicated that certain measurements were correlated (e.g., a person with a long left forearm might also have a long left middle finger), undermining the purported independence of each element, and consequently, the individuality of the combined data.[19]

After its adoption by the Troup Committee, the anthropometric system of identification increasingly came under attack, not because of Galton's theoretical concerns but due to variations in the measurements of the same criminal taken by different people. At the 1899 annual meeting of the British Association for the Advancement of Science in Dover, Garson

[18] Ibid.: 52–53.
[19] Ibid.: 59.

presented a paper on the "personal equation" and anthropometry.[20] Garson believed that solid training could minimize measurement error so as not to damage the efficacy of the Bertillon system. Such an emphasis on training, however, implicitly assumed that the underlying system needed no social interpretation. In contrast, Schaffer argues that the foundation of any measurement system requires explanation:

> Measurement is given its meaning when situated in specific contexts of styles of work and institutions. Disciplines give meanings to values, and often resist attempts by others to redefine these meanings or to gain authority over measurement. Quantification is not a self-evident nor inevitable process in science's history, but possesses a remarkable cultural history of its own.[21]

For the identification of criminals, discipline over measurement had to be established throughout the prison system. Adopting the French procedure for anthropometric measurements, the British even used instruments in the metric system. Police wardens were taught how to read off the numbers but not about the measurement system itself. Not only did bodies change in size, but the measurements were also taken on a foreign (French) metric, undermining the consistency and efficacy of the anthropometric system in England. On the level of practice, the anthropometric system was increasingly construed as unreliable.

Several historians construct the downfall of Bertillon's system in Britain as a failure to provide positive identification.[22] The use of the anthropometric system, however, was already declining in Britain before the case of the two "Will Wests" in Leavenworth, Kansas, in 1903, who were distinguished only by their fingerprints. Although the Troup Committee selected anthropometric measurements as the primary identification system, the Home Office's first memo to police in March 1897 suggested that officers should refrain from commonly using the system so as not to "prejudice the working of the entire system." As the Belper Committee reported, the recommendations of the Troup Committee were not pushed vigorously in practice.[23] This lack of enthusiasm for the anthropometric system stemmed, to a large degree, from the difficulty in taking and recording the requisite measurements. Henry, as commissioner of the Criminal Investigation Department at New Scotland Yard, listed the following disadvantages of anthropometry for the identification of criminals: costly instrumentation that required calibration, training on the decimal scale,

---

[20] *Report of the British Association for the Advancement of Science 1899* : 868. Garson's paper is not reproduced in the report; papers by Galton and Henry are included.
[21] Schaffer 1988: 115.
[22] Moenssens 1971: 19.
[23] Belper Committee 1901: 7.

error in transcribing measurements, the time to take measurements (each one was done three times), the "personal equation" factor, and a complicated procedure for searching through records.[24] A solution to this problem of measurement would involve, according to Schaffer, "the integration of instrumentation and training."[25] As an alternative to the anthropometric system, Henry stressed the material and labor advantages of fingerprinting, which required only inexpensive equipment and minimal training.

On top of these operational concerns, I would suggest that, crucially, a fingerprinting system controlled suspected criminals and operators of the system with much tighter discipline than the Bertillon system could. Suspected criminals could not change their fingerprints, but they could curve their body to change their height (vaulting) or control their abdominal muscles (trickery) in attempts to fool people taking their anthropometric measurements.[26] Moreover, a fingerprinting system reinforced the differentiation in skill between local prisons and centralized bureaus, requiring minimal training in the taking of prints and delegating their interpretation to those specially trained in classifying prints. The prison warder was likely to make far fewer mistakes in placing fingerprints on the requisite form than in taking a series of complicated measurements on a foreign metric, and a higher level of technical experts could interpret and classify the prints. By recording genuinely permanent traces of identity, officials could attempt to maintain control over criminals as well as those who took the fingerprints. In addition to internal bureaucratic control, fingerprints offered assistance to the police detective at a crime scene, spurring the public imagination: criminals might leave their fingerprints at the scene of a crime, but never dropped lists of their anthropometric measurements.[27]

With the anthropometric system under fire in Britain, and the adoption of fingerprinting as the primary method to identify criminals in Argentina in 1896 (using Vucetich's classification system) and in India in 1897 (using Henry's classification system),[28] Home Secretary Ridley appointed Lord Henry Belper to head a committee to inquire into the method of identification of criminals by measurements and fingerprints in 1900. The Belper Committee Report declined to delineate criteria like those of the Troup Committee; it did, however, consider all of the conditions of the Troup Committee Report—the feasibility of taking and classifying prints or measurements and the ability to positively identify individuals. The Belper

[24] Henry 1913: 72–74.
[25] Schaffer 1995: 159.
[26] Chapel 1941: 15–16.
[27] *Judy*, July 1, 1891: 3.
[28] Bridges 1942: 156–61; Moenssens 1971: 13–15; Kristin Ruggiero's essay in this volume; Pamela Sankar's essay in this volume.

Committee Report listed the advantages of fingerprinting alone over the combined system adopted after the Troup Committee Report: low cost and simplicity of instruments, the simplicity of the process, the permanence of the prints throughout life, and the inclusion of young persons. After listing these practical advantages, the report suggested that the "advantage of finger prints as a means of *proving* identity is no longer open to discussion."[29]

The Belper Committee Report hinged its selection of a criminal identification system on the practicality of obtaining and classifying information by emphasizing two questions:

1. Is there any substantial difficulty in getting legible prints?
2. Assuming that the prints are legible, could a collection of one hundred thousand sets or more be classified with sufficient precision?[30]

Garson, highlighting his medical background, testified again in front of the Belper Committee against the adoption of fingerprinting as the sole system for the identification of criminals. In response to the first question, he suggested that criminals would mutilate their finger marks. However, other witnesses testified to the permanence of the impressions and to the fact that any attempted mutilation would leave visible scars.

The conflict over the adoption of fingerprinting was not simply between medical practitioners and police personnel. In fact, the physician Garson and the Paris Chief of Judicial Identity Bertillon both supported anthropometry; whereas, the scientist Galton and the Inspector General of Police in Bengal (and later Commissioner of the Criminal Investigation Department at New Scotland Yard) Henry favored fingerprinting. The divisive battle was over which system would control the boundaries of identification and record-keeping. Anthropometry relied on a numerical list of measurements; fingerprinting focused on permanent images and patterns.

Fingerprinting's production of visual images paradoxically coincided with increasing dependence on the explanatory power of statistical results.[31] Fingerprinting obviously relied on "prints"; yet, the interpretation of these images employed the numbering of similarities and the attachment of statistical "certainty" to matching prints. In Henry's classification system, a set of ten fingerprints was first divided into whorls and loops. Assigning point values for each whorl in given pairings (e.g., a whorl in the first pair of the right thumb and right index finger counted for 16 points), an algorithm produced a final number that gave the primary class.[32] Ridges were then counted and traced. To determine identity, dis-

---

[29] Belper Committee 1901: 9 (original emphasis).
[30] Ibid.: 10.
[31] Hacking 1990.
[32] Henry 1900: 870.

tinctive characteristics (e.g., an island in a print) were also compared. Fingerprinting combined both sides of an inherent tension—the visual (and often messy) character of the prints with the quantification of patterns and "statistical" odds of matching prints.

The second question of classification was in a sense postponed by the Belper Committee, which had information on Henry's classification system but was unable to observe the system in operation. Fingerprints had been used as verification of the anthropometric system and increasingly on their own in Britain before the Belper Committee deliberations. The framework for a database had thus been established, easing the transition to a different system of identification. The Belper Committee recommended a trial of fingerprinting as the primary means for the identification of criminals, and in July 1901, the police forces of England and Wales adopted the fingerprint system.[33]

Statistically, the fingerprint system was successful, as judged by counts of searches and identifications. In the first decade of the twentieth century, the use of anthropometric measurements declined while the use of fingerprints burgeoned. In 1900, there were 462 identifications by the Bertillon method in England. In 1901, there were 410 such identifications and 93 identifications by fingerprints. In 1902, there were 1,032 identifications by fingerprints out of 5,032 searches by the Metropolitan Police and 690 identifications by fingerprints out of 1,794 searches by provincial police. In each subsequent year, the number of fingerprint searches and resulting identifications increased.[34]

The adoption of fingerprinting as the primary system for the identification of criminals in Britain raised concerns over who should implement and oversee it. The combination system of anthropometric measurements and fingerprinting, advocated and established by the Troup Committee, had been assigned to a branch of the Habitual Criminals Registry located at New Scotland Yard, the domain of the Metropolitan Police. The Belper Committee did not find this arrangement to be satisfactory: "We have come to the conclusion that the system requires skilled control distinct from the ordinary police administration."[35] For the fingerprinting system, the Belper Committee recommended the establishment of one central office, the Criminal Registry "under the direct control of the Home Office" to hold all English, Irish and Scottish records, which the police would be encouraged to use.[36] In 1901, a new fingerprint department was established, however, at New Scotland Yard, a decision signaling the links

---

[33] Habitual Criminals' Registry, New Scotland Yard 1909: 17.
[34] Ibid.: 19–20.
[35] Belper Committee 1901: 12.
[36] Ibid.

among criminal detection, criminal identification, and the police. Henry was appointed to be the new assistant commissioner of the Metropolitan Police in charge of the Criminal Investigation Department, under which the new fingerprint bureau was established.[37] Henry brought Detective Sergeant Collins, Detective Inspector Steadman, and Detective Constable Hunt, all from the Anthropometric Department, to work in his branch; he did not ask Garson to join them.

Identity Evidence in the Courtroom: Conflict over Fingerprints in the Deptford Murders Trial

"I made these pantagraph copies [of fingerprints] last night, and will so swear when I go upon the witness stand." . . .

He passed a powerful magnifying-glass to the foreman. . . .

Wilson said to the foreman:

"Please turn that cardboard face down, and take this one, and compare it searchingly, by the magnifier, with the fatal signature upon the knife-handle, and report your finding to the court."

Again the jury made minute examination, and again reported:

"We find them to be exactly identical, your honour."

—MARK TWAIN, *Pudd'nhead Wilson*[38]

After government officials debated and eventually confirmed the merits of a fingerprinting system to *identify* criminals, police detectives had to fight for its acceptance in the courtroom to *convict* criminals.[39] In these governmental committee deliberations, some participants stressed their desire to adopt a criminal identification system that could provide comprehensible and convincing proof of identity to a court. The Troup Committee Report briefly mentioned the use of fingerprinting in a court by dismissing the objection that such identification would be too complicated or unacceptable to juries.[40] Galton testified in front of the Troup Committee that copies of fingerprints could be enlarged and explained to a jury.[41] The Belper Committee, which included Albert de Rutzen, a magistrate of the Police Courts in London, placed more emphasis on the use of identification in judicial forums by concluding with a discussion of the use of fingerprints as potential legal evidence.[42] Committee members wanted consistent and powerful evidence of identity. Older identification

---

[37] Browne and Brock 1953: 48.
[38] Twain 1986: 220.
[39] Wilton 1938: 151–59.
[40] Troup Committee 1894: 28.
[41] Ibid.: 57.
[42] Belper Committee 1901: 14.

techniques were not performing well; personal recollection had resulted in troubling misidentifications. In late Victorian Britain, a police officer who had seen an arrested person ten years previously would have been called to testify if he thought he could "determine" a defendant's identity. In contrast to such testimony, fingerprints appeared to be more reliable.[43]

Not only did the Belper Committee contemplate the persuasiveness of identification methods, it also raised questions about how such evidence should be presented in court. In particular, the committee suggested the officer who "took" a defendant's prints would not ordinarily testify; instead, an expert should explain the similarity in prints to a court and "his evidence should be admissible in the same way as that of an expert in handwriting."[44] The Belper Committee also cited an 1899 act that had been passed in India to allow fingerprint testimony as relevant evidence in the courts.[45] These arguments generally played out well in practice. After the adoption of fingerprinting for criminal identification, more arrested persons were being not only identified but also convicted as habitual offenders.[46]

The transition from identifying habitual criminals to tracing and proving the identity of perpetrators from marks left at a crime scene was, however, neither certain nor simple. Fingerprint evidence was first presented in the Central Criminal Court during the September 1902 trial of a June burglary of billiard balls at Denmark Hill. According to *The Times* and the court transcript, one of the burglars had left his fingerprints on a recently painted windowsill. The parlor maid, Rose Guilder, testified at the trial that she discovered the billiard room had been broken into the previous night: "I also observed a thumb mark on the sash of one of the windows that had been painted—it was not there the night before, and I called the attention of the police to it when they came."[47] Harry Jackson was arrested several months later in August 1902 after being caught with burglary tools and was fingerprinted (he had also been fingerprinted in July 1901 on another charge). The June billiard room prints and the August arrest prints appeared to match.

Because fingerprinting evidence was not routinely accepted in the courts, Criminal Investigation Department Commissioner Henry arranged for barrister Richard Muir to prosecute the case after being instructed in the fingerprint system by Detective Sergeant Collins, who testified at length during the trial.[48] After outlining his background and the

[43] Troup Committee 1894: 13–15.
[44] Belper Committee 1901: 15.
[45] Moenssens 1971: 13–14.
[46] Browne and Brock 1953: 52; Wiener 1990: 304, 342.
[47] Jackson 1902: 976, 977.
[48] Browne and Brock 1953: 53.

fingerprint system of identification, Collins compared the print on the windowsill and the prisoner's left thumbprint and pointed out similar characteristics. He concluded, "[I]n my opinion it is impossible for any two persons to have any one of the peculiarities I have selected and described."[49] Detective Inspector Steadman also testified to corroborate Collins's conclusions. According to *The Times* on September 15, 1902, "The photographs [of the fingerprints] were produced in Court, and were examined with much interest by the jury."[50] Jackson, the accused, asked only about the permanence of the ridges. Although Jackson claimed that he received the stolen material from a friend who had asked him to sell it, the jury found Jackson guilty, and the common sergeant sentenced him to seven years of penal servitude. The proof of identity was not inherent in the two prints alone. A top counsel, who would not have ordinarily taken such a case, skillfully questioned Collins and Steadman, two fingerprint experts, and elicited the claim that the probability of a false match was basically zero.

It was not until 1905 that fingerprint evidence was contested in a capital case. On Monday, March 27, 1905, Thomas Farrow was found murdered and his wife was found unconscious (she died several days later) in the oil and color shop that they managed on High Street in Deptford. The money from a cash box that Mr. Farrow usually gave to George Chapman, the owner, on Mondays was gone. But the box remained with a bloody thumbprint.[51] The print did not drive the investigation because no matching print in the archives of habitual criminals could be found. After witnesses recounted seeing the two Stratton brothers near the shop on the morning of the murders, the police arrested and fingerprinted the two men in early April 1905. The thumbprint of Alfred Stratton seemed to match the thumbprint on the cash box.

The trial for the murder of Thomas Farrow opened on May 5, 1905, with Justice Channell presiding. Muir, aided by Bodkin and Fitzgerald, served again as counsel, and he called thirty-five witnesses to build up a highly circumstantial case against the Stratton brothers. Alhough Chief Inspector Frederick Fox of New Scotland Yard mentioned the thumbprint early in the trial, all but the last of the prosecution witnesses testified about other matters—about either the crime scene or highly circumstantial sightings of the two Stratton brothers before or after the murders. The two closest witnesses to the crime were Henry Jennings, a milkman, and his young assistant, Edward Russell, who both saw two men leaving the oil and color shop around 7:15 A.M. on the day of the murders. Muir

---

[49] Jackson 1902: 978.
[50] "Central Criminal Court," *The Times*, September 15, 1902: 12.
[51] "The Deptford Murder Trial," *The Times*, May 6, 1905: 19.

called the two men to testify near the end, but before the fingerprinting experts, as the milkman and his assistant could not positively identify whether the Stratton brothers were the two men they observed.

The last three witnesses for the prosecution were fingerprinting experts: Detective Inspector Collins of New Scotland Yard; Detective Inspector Steadman of New Scotland Yard, in charge of the Finger Print Department; and Police Sergeant Alden, who took the prints that were reproduced into the courtroom. Collins provided the most detailed testimony, outlining eleven characteristics that agreed in the prints. Under cross-examination, he had to justify the purported matching items:

> I cannot see any practical difference whatever—these vertical lines are scratches which were on the cash box—you can see them on it now—one point I depend upon is the little island between points 3 and 5—there is a difference in size and shape between it and the one in the lower print, but that is accounted for in my experience by pressure.[52]

Collins was forced to explain and account for discrepancies, and he even took the impressions of a juryman's thumb to illustrate the effect of pressure on fingerprints.[53]

The defense did not leave Collins's testimony unanswered. Garson, who had testified in front of both the Troup and Belper Committees in opposition to the adoption of fingerprinting for criminal identification and who had lost a job when the anthropometric system was abandoned, was the defense's star witness. Garson's testimony relied on his medical training and experience measuring corpses at the Anthropological Institute. He articulated points of dissimilarity in the prints, usually indicating differences in the length of various ridges. He argued against the island as a characteristic similar in both prints:

> [P]oints 3 and 5 really mark what is called the "lake"—I do not agree that the lake in the upper print agrees with the lake in the lower print—it is very obvious, on looking at the prints, that in the upper print it is much longer and proportionately narrower than in the lower print—I have measured the lengths and I find that the length of the lake in the upper print is thirteen millimeters, while in the lower it is eleven millimeters—that is a difference of 11.8 per cent.[54]

While Collins spoke of spatial patterns within the fingerprints, Garson in the tradition of the anthropometric system instead emphasized numerical measurements.

[52] Stratton and Stratton 1905: 978, 1003.
[53] Ibid.: 1003–4.
[54] Ibid.: 1006.

Under cross-examination, Garson seemed to explode at suggestions that he was not a credible witness:

> I agree to a certain extent that two persons measuring the same part of the same body get different results—very fine measurements were required, only a difference of a millimeter being allowed in the principal measurements—when the system of measurement was abandoned in October, 1901, my services were dispensed with, and I have not had any connection with the Finger Print Department since that date. . . . I saw that Inspector Collins had spoken, according to the papers, a great deal of nonsense about finger prints . . . about the number of cases you would require before you found the same finger print occurring twice, a mathematical calculation of the chances.... I, as a *scientific man*, came to the conclusion that it was nonsense.[55]

However, instead of having his attack on the dissimilarities between the fingerprints taken seriously, Garson was humiliated in front of the court. Before the trial, he had apparently written two letters to offer his services, one to the prosecution and one to the defense. When these were read aloud to the court, Garson exclaimed, "I am an independent witness."[56] The reply of Justice Channell did not appear in the trial transcripts but was printed in *The Times* on May 8, 1905: "An absolutely untrustworthy one, I should think, after writing two such letters."[57]

Neither this humiliation of Garson nor the trio of Scotland Yard experts was the pinnacle of the prosecution's case. The strongest piece of evidence was Albert Stratton's comment to William Gittings, the assistant jailer at Tower Bridge Police Court, on April 18, 1905. Albert Stratton apparently asked what his chances were and stated that his brother "had led me into this."[58] This comment was tantamount to a confession; it was not some trace left at a crime scene or a tentative identification near the shop. The judge instructed the jury members not to let Albert Stratton's comments prejudice their decision against his brother, Alfred. The judge also cautioned the jury about relying too heavily on the fingerprint evidence; he did not think the jury should base its decision on it alone. The Stratton brothers had not been positively identified by the milkman and his assistant, who were the only two people who had seen the murderers leave the shop. In less than two hours, the jury returned a guilty verdict and the Stratton brothers were sentenced to death.[59] Despite the existence of circumstantial evidence and a near confession, the prosecution's success in

[55] Ibid.: 1008–9 (my emphasis).
[56] Ibid.: 1009.
[57] "The Deptford Murder Trial," *The Times*, May 8, 1905: 4.
[58] Stratton and Stratton 1905: 985.
[59] "The Deptford Murder Trial," *The Times*, May 8, 1905: 4.

obtaining a guilty verdict was portrayed as a success for the fingerprinting system of identification.

Because murder was a media sensation for the late Victorian and Edwardian press,[60] the Deptford murders trial played out not only in the courtroom but in the newspaper too.[61] Several witnesses from Deptford who testified at the trial of the Stratton brothers mentioned the descriptions of the suspects and the details of the crime that they had read in the *Morning Leader*, which was started in 1892 as a companion to the evening *Star*. In this less conventional and liberal half-penny paper, which one of its own lead writers described as "cheap, popular and sometimes vulgar,"[62] the Deptford murders were prominent news. After the trial, the sensation of this new evidence did not subside. On July 20, 1905, two months after the convictions of the Stratton brothers, *The Daily Express* launched a "novel and interesting competition" worth £100 accompanying a two-month serial novel entitled *Finger-Prints of Fate*:

> This absorbing story centres on the mysterious death of an old country solicitor and the endeavours of his daughter to trace the hand at which his death was received. Two tumblers are discovered, one bearing the imprints of the old man's fingers, the other a stranger's finger prints. Both these prints are given for the reader's inspection. As the heroine collects the finger prints of various characters in the story, these also are reproduced, and by carefully reading the story and comparing the finger prints the reader will be enabled to discover by whose hand the solicitor met his death. *A prize of One Hundred Pounds will be paid by the Editor of the "Express" for the best solution of the mystery.*[63]

The serial story threw in several New Scotland Yard fingerprint experts, a dramatic courtroom scene, and even some romance. The contest highlights the tension between the expertise needed for interpretation in the courtroom and the popular image that jurors or readers could determine whether particular prints were identical.

Ironically, an article, "How to Read Finger Prints," by Garson prepared the reader for this contest.[64] The biographical note before his article described Garson as "one of the most eminent among British authorities on the metric system of the identification of criminals." Included in the recitation of his anthropometric and medical training was information about his introduction of particular powders for making finger marks

---

[60] Wiener 1990: 16.

[61] There was no real outcry (except from criminals) about individual liberty and incrimination from fingerprinting. Browne and Brock 1953: 49–50.

[62] H. N. Brailsford, in Koss 1981: 426–27.

[63] "£100 Prize for Readers," *The Daily Express*, July 20, 1905: 7.

[64] Garson, "How to Read Finger Prints," *The Daily Express*, July 20, 1905: 7 (original emphasis).

visible.[65] After being humiliated in the Deptford murders trial, Garson had tried to bolster his reputation by attempting to locate fingerprint expertise in the discipline of medicine. In May 1905, an unsigned article appeared in the *Lancet* claiming that the variation between prints found at a crime scene and the full set of prints taken of a prisoner in custody could be interpreted only by a person who "possess[ed] thorough and practical knowledge as well as trained mental powers of discrimination." It continued: "to intrust the duty to partially skilled persons is in the highest degree dangerous from a public point of view."[66]

Police detectives quickly fought back against this maneuver. G. A. Anson, the chief constable of Staffordshire, wrote in a letter to the *Daily Express*:

> [D]octors are not by any means the only people who possess "trained mental powers of discrimination" [quoting Garson], and though a doctor may be as good as any other person for the purpose in question, many another man may be at least equally as good as the doctor. To talk of the highly-trained and experienced staff at Scotland-yard as "partially skilled persons" is as ridiculous as it is incorrect.[67]

During the Deptford murders trial, the evidentiary relevance of fingerprints and who had the expertise to interpret and comment on such evidence were both questioned.[68] Having lost the administrative and court battles, Garson did not want the police detective to control the new identification system. Yet he seemed to be losing this fight as well.

The conviction of the Stratton brothers did not guarantee the acceptance of fingerprints in future cases. Albert Stratton's confession to the assistant jailer at the Tower Bridge Police Court likely played a role in the verdict, along with the string of witnesses who saw the two brothers around the oil and color shop run by the Farrows near the time of the murders. The conviction did, however, help to increase confidence in the fingerprinting system. The Convict Supervision Office of the Metropolitan Police drew attention to "several cases" that had been solved and

---

[65] Ibid.

[66] "Identification by Finger Prints," *The Lancet*, May 13, 1905: 1280–81. This article was written by Garson.

[67] Anson, "Finger-Prints as Clues," *The Daily Express*, July 28, 1905: 4.

[68] Several historians view the testimony of Dr. Garson and the presence of Dr. Henry Faulds for the defense of the Stratton brothers as part of a conspiracy narrative; these historians see the battle as an *internal* struggle for credibility, with police detectives edging out medical experts. Their accounts cite Faulds' 1880 letter to *Nature* indicating the possible use of finger marks for criminal identification, the subsequent battle for priority with Herschel, and the exclusion of Faulds from the identification disputes as providing motivation for Faulds to attack work done by Galton, Henry, and others. See Browne and Brock 1953: 57–58; Faulds 1912; Wilton 1951.

prosecuted with fingerprint evidence in a 1904 *Memorandum on the Working of the Finger Print System of Identification*. In 1909, New Scotland Yard released the memorandum again with an important change to "many cases" where "finger print evidence has been given in court, admitted by the judges, and accepted by the jury."[69]

The testimony of designated fingerprint experts, who relied on the successful implementation of the new identification system, was of crucial importance. In the 1902 trial of Jackson and the 1905 trial of the Stratton brothers, Detective Collins testified to the size of the fingerprint collection and claimed that he had never found two identical prints from separate people. This practical testimony by Collins and others was necessary to buttress the theoretical claims that each individual has unique fingerprints.

Collins was the primary expert witness for fingerprints in Britain. Unlike other witnesses in a court of law, an expert (once proving his background and experience in a particular field) could offer an opinion on admitted evidence.[70] In Britain, the use of expert evidence increased considerably during the nineteenth century.[71] Legal treatises in the early nineteenth century contained only cursory references to expert opinion testimony, but by the middle of the nineteenth century, as Stephan Landsman argues, there was "full appreciation of the potentially adversarial quality of expert evidence and concern about the possibility of its abuse."[72] Operating under a paradox of partisanship, experts confronted increasing demands for certainty in their testimony from advocates and judges as well as negative reaction to any perceived partisan advocacy of a particular outcome.[73] Like Collins and Steadman in the Deptford murders case, many expert witnesses in murder cases appeared at the end of the prosecution's line-up of witnesses.[74] Forbes argues that an expert had an elevated role in the courtroom: "In the eyes of the law he occupies a special position, for he possesses knowledge and skill not shared by all."[75] Yet the judge determined whether a witness had such status to offer an opinion, and it was up to the jury how to weigh the evidence in its deliberations.

Fingerprinting expertise around the turn of the century combined concerns about science, policing, and administration. Its advocates in the courtroom, including Collins and Steadman, were police officers and detectives involved in the practical culture of apprehending and identifying

---

[69] Habitual Criminals' Registry, New Scotland Yard, 1909: 20; Metropolitan Police, Convict Supervision Office, New Scotland Yard 1904.

[70] Cowger 1983: 207–8; Landsman 1998: 445.

[71] Smith 1981: 77.

[72] Landsman 1998: 492–94.

[73] Ibid.: 450, 456, 461.

[74] Ibid.: 453.

[75] Forbes 1985: 26.

criminals. Its advocates before the Troup and Belper Committees were police officers and men of science, including Galton and Henry. The shared spaces among science, criminal enforcement, and the courts allow us to enter the entangled disputes that were not limited to a particular discipline. Science, the police, and the courts were not isolated from late Victorian and Edwardian society. Each institution's criteria for what constituted sufficient method and proof of identification drew upon changing notions of identity, detection of criminals, and the authority of various disciplines.

Conclusion

> Toward future—that was divination proper; toward past, present and future—that was the medical science of symptoms, with its double character, diagnostic, explaining past and present, and prognostic, suggesting the likely future; and toward past—that was jurisprudence, or legal knowledge. But lurking behind this symptomatic or divinatory model one glimpses the gesture which is the oldest, perhaps, of the intellectual history of the human race: the hunter crouched in the mud, examining a quarry's tracks.
>
> —CARLO GINZBURG, *"Morelli, Freud, and Sherlock Holmes: Clues and the Scientific Method"*[76]

Ginzburg argues that there was a shift in epistemological paradigms at the end of the nineteenth century, from a Galilean model based on quantification to a conjectural sciences model based on traces and the individual. The transition from photographs, anthropometric measurements, and other methods to fingerprints, in this framework, was a movement from numbers to images. The police detective of the late Victorian era was a practitioner of the conjectural sciences, tracking and finding criminals from the clues they deposited at crime scenes and wore on their bodies.[77] Although integral to a history of identification practices, Ginzburg's account of such a paradigm shift neglects critical concerns over the training, equipment, and operation of identification systems. Like the observatory in Schaffer's analysis, New Scotland Yard and police forces "became a factory"; police officers "were relegated to the base of a hierarchy of management and vigilance," with another level of detectives inspecting and interpreting the prints that the local police officers collected.[78]

[76] Ginzburg 1980b: 14.
[77] Caprettini 1983: 140.
[78] Schaffer 1988: 119.

Fingerprinting—dependent on a roller, ink, and paper for the taking of prints and trained observation skills for the classification of prints—produces images that simultaneously define, with interpretation, an individual and to some extent wrest control from the accused to the state and the courts. Its adoption in late Victorian Britain signaled a changing conception of identity—from a frozen image in a photograph and a string of measurements of body parts to an image of patterned lines and ridges; from a construction that construed identity as emanating from the whole to a formulation of permanent identification from a part. It also signaled a changing conception of expertise—at the crime scene, in the police station, and in the courtroom. This new system of identification for criminals was established through conflict but depended on an eventual consensus that cut across police work, science, and government. The Troup and Belper Committees and the Deptford murders trial not only negotiated the means of identifying criminals in late Victorian and Edwardian Britain, but they also suggested narratives for what constituted the larger issue of identity itself and the expertise required to determine it.

10

Fingerprinting and the Argentine Plan for Universal Identification in the Late Nineteenth and Early Twentieth Centuries

KRISTIN RUGGIERO

OPENING THIS ESSAY with a transatlantic criminal investigation will help provide the particular context for the development of identification techniques in Argentina. When the famous murder case of Farbos-Tremblié occurred in Buenos Aires in 1894, the city's police force employed all the latest techniques available to investigate the crime, except one: fingerprinting. Raul Tremblié had slit the throat of his fellow countryman, Frenchman Francisco Farbos, quartered the body, bagged the parts separately, and deposited the sacks in different parts of Buenos Aires, making clever use of the many construction sites in the growing city; he left for France a few days later.[1] It was unfortunate that fingerprinting was not used in the investigation, because it would have been helpful in identifying the victim and the assassin.

Tremblié was one of those products of European immigration—"degenerates and criminals"—that the Buenos Aires police and other Argentines lamented; they called them "Europe's dregs," who brought with them disorder and crime. Buenos Aires' crime statistics, including the large number of repeat offenders, indicated to many observers that the city was a unique center of delinquency, fed by "Europe which sends Argentina armies of professional" criminals.[2] Some criminologists held that the Latin "race," which was so predominant in Argentina, was biologi-

I would like to thank the staff of the Museo de Policía in La Plata, Argentina, for their generosity and kindness during my research visit to the museum that houses the Juan Vucetich material. I would also like to thank the editors of this volume, Jane Caplan and John Torpey, for their valuable comments on this essay.

[1] I have been unable to find the actual transcript of this case in the National Archives in Buenos Aires, but it is included as one of Argentina's most famous cases in secondary works. Flores 1975: 65–75; Bataille 1897: 198–204. The case was also cited by jurists and criminologists as an example of perversity, in that Tremblié reportedly did not feel anything even though he committed an atrociously savage act. Olivera 1900: 363.

[2] Quesada 1901: 121.

cally more apt to be responsible for bloody crimes like Tremblié's than other "races," and although by no means wholly accepted, this view was generally diffused throughout the Western world.[3] Murderers such as Tremblié probably appeared to justify for some people the extremist proposals for the castration and elimination of criminals. Not too long after the entire body was found, the Buenos Aires police had gathered sufficient evidence against Tremblié for a local judge to form a case against him and telegraph the French police, who arrested him when he disembarked in Dunkirk. To facilitate Tremblié's trial, the French judges requested that the principal professionals and witnesses involved in the case be brought over to France from Buenos Aires to testify, at a substantial cost to the French court.[4]

During the trial of Tremblié, who eventually received the death penalty and later a pardon from the president of France, the French court complimented the Buenos Aires police and judicial system on their thorough investigation. The praise was unique in light of the suspicion held by most Europeans of Latin American science and civilization. But Argentina would prove to be in the vanguard in identification techniques and philosophy.

The Reception of Anthropometry in Buenos Aires

Argentina's trajectory of scientific identification was directed by, as in the above case, its immigration and rapid urbanization. For Argentine police and criminologists, it was not just a matter of keeping up with European innovations, but rather that Buenos Aires was in a sense under assault from an alluvial immigration movement, especially from Latin countries, which had left Buenos Aires with as much as 60 percent of its population foreign-born and unidentified in any systematic way. The Anthropometric Office of Buenos Aires, using Bertillon's system, performed well in the Farbos-Tremblié case, measuring, weighing, modeling, and photographing the victim. The office had been established in 1889 at the initiative of Alberto Capdevila, chief of police, and Agustin Drago, who became the office's first director, to address the problem of the city's growing population and increasing crime rate. Drago, when he was in Paris in 1887, had been commissioned by the police department to study Bertillon's system of anthropometry in order to be able to establish the system in Buenos Aires.[5] Up to this point, police and magistrates had relied

[3] Solari 1902: 388.
[4] Bataille 1897: 201–2.
[5] Quesada 1901: 97; Revista de Policía 1897: 93.

mainly on registers of people under suspicion, on trial, or convicted as criminals, so that the creation of an anthropometric office marked a very progressive step.[6] Not only was the Buenos Aires office the first anthropometric office in all of Latin America, it also predated this innovation in much of the "civilized" world. Only France, England, and the United States had already established offices, in 1885.[7]

While Capdevila and Drago were enthusiastic about the office, many people were skeptical about the way in which the office was established and employed in Buenos Aires; its integration into the police department and judicial system; who had jurisdiction over it; and the efficacy of the system itself. The way in which the office was created, by a police "order of the day," started the office out on a weak footing in the view of Ernesto Quesada, who was one of the period's more important magistrates and who not surprisingly favored transferring the anthropometric office to the judiciary. A law, an executive decree, or a ministerial resolution, he argued, would have given the office a firmer base. The police order itself that created the anthropometric office was unclear about when and to whom its methods could be applied. The issue was whether the anthropometric office was an internal part of police administration, an independent department, or an auxiliary office of the courts under judges' jurisdiction. According to the order, police precincts were obligated to send the day's detainees and prisoners to the office for measuring and photographing. At the same time, however, the office supposedly could not proceed to identify these people without a judge's authorization; that is, although the office was under police jurisdiction, the judges and courts also had their own jurisdiction over it. The order further blurred the picture when it permitted the application of anthropometric techniques only on conviction, and stipulated that the records of measurements taken in cases of acquittal, even if the acquittal was merely for lack of proof, were allowed to be destroyed, if the convicted person requested it and the judge ordered it. To clear up the confusion and establish its right to jurisdiction, the Buenos Aires police department requested the Court of Appeals in September 1889 to obligate judges to cooperate with the office's full program of measuring detainees and prisoners, but the court held that "bertillonage [involved] the mistreatment of people being prosecuted and that judges should not authorize it," because of the view that measuring and photographing were intrusive and were like calumny and slander, and damaged reputation. Thus, the office's efficiency was problematic from its inception.

[6] Romay 1975: 40.
[7] Rodríguez 1981: 161.

The undermining of the office at this high level, along with steady challenges and non-compliance, led to a reduction in the office's importance, even within the police department itself. The police department was, however, self-critical. In articles in the department's journal, the *Revista de Policía*, the police berated their own department for allowing the office to fall behind as a leader in the application of anthropometric techniques, when it had once been a model laboratory in the Americas. By police order, the office was restricted to the identification of those criminals involved in acts against property; in serious crimes against persons if the accused was not a recidivist and as long as the victim had not suffered injury; and in cases of the falsification of money. For any other detainees, the chief of police had to authorize the use of identification. The refusal to apply bertillonage to *all* delinquents "spelled inefficiency and gave people reason to call the office arbitrary, illegal, and depressing." As Quesada observed, this order "effectively nullified the service of identification, since [it allowed] only three types of delinquents to be measured." With such restrictions, he argued, how could the police possibly identify recidivists; and, not knowing if a person was a recidivist, argued Police Chief Beazley, how could Argentine judges apply the "aggravation of penalties" section of the Penal Code?[8] Recidivism was a growing problem, especially in Buenos Aires, and it seemed to people like Quesada that the justice system had no credible method to fight it. There were two scandalous cases in 1900 that proved that even recidivists were not being measured and photographed by the police.[9] Moreover, when records *were* kept by the police and the anthropometric office, they contradicted each other about people's antecedents, age, nationality, and the like, so frequently that they were unreliable.[10]

Because the very concept of identification lacked general acceptance, detainees and even prisoners were successful in their refusals to be measured, which made the office an "almost useless wheel of penal justice," an office without authorization. The office's weak foundation made people's "natural" suspicions about measuring and photographing grow even more resolute. While the resistance of people to being identified occurred in other countries too, there it was a "passing thing," wrote Quesada, while in Argentina it still persisted even after ten years. Bertillon, when faced with this problem, had maintained that once identification became obligatory, delinquents submitted to it "with pleasure," being convinced that it was their last time. Quesada speculated that this remark was typical

[8] *Revista de Policía* 1897: 94.
[9] *Revista de Policía* 1900.
[10] Quesada 1901: 127.

destruction of identifying info

of Bertillon's "exaggerated optimism," and did not foresee this happening in Argentina, where he saw more resistance to identification techniques.[11]

So strong was the resistance to anthropometry that the measurements and other personal data were regularly destroyed, not only of accused persons who were later absolved, but also of criminals who had completed their sentences, thus completely undermining the identification of recidivists. A judge in 1897, for example, ordered the destruction of identifying information on an indicted person and a "notorious recidivist," after the man had fulfilled his sentence. In 1900, a judge gave a man convicted of homicide the "favor" (*gracia*) of exempting him from anthropometric measurement.[12]

Popularizing identification techniques was proving to be difficult. The logic that measurements and so on were scientific "advances" was rejected because people saw their implications for honor. All the arguments that these advances secured a person's innocence; that measurements were just a perfection or extension of other information, such as name, age, and height; that "identification" by anthropometric means was simply a person's police "civil state" and was the same as his inscription in other kinds of registers, like registers of birth and marriage, did not convince the public, nor even all officials.[13] "The Argentine courts are the only ones, among all the other nations which have adopted bertillonage," complained the Buenos Aires police chief Beazley, "that have given in to the demands that anthropometric information be destroyed and that do not recognize this faculty of the police."[14]

The Argentine Debate over Vucetich's Dactyloscopy versus Bertillon's Anthropometry

Certainly among the reasons for the lack of application of bertillonage were the limitations of the system itself. In the view of Juan Vucetich, the La Plata policeman who was to become internationally known for his classification system of fingerprints, dactyloscopy was preferable to anthropometry because it had a lower percentage of error; was less expensive; needed fewer personnel and less preparation; and could be used on non-adults and women. Moreover, prints were often left at the scene of the crime and could be taken after death. Bertillonage, on the other hand, according to Vucetich, required expensive instruments, training to use them, time to take the measurements and to search the files to make the

[11] Ibid.: 102–3.
[12] Ibid.: 113 and 119.
[13] Ibid.: 113.
[14] *Revista de Policía* 1897: 94.

correct identification, and it was limited to people who had reached their full growth. Human error also had to be taken into account, as Vucetich found when he visited the laboratory of Drago, who had even studied with Bertillon in France, and found Drago in the midst of measuring the left foot of a subject without removing the man's socks and shoes.[15]

Most important from the point of view of penal justice, bertillonage could not actually confirm identity; it could only describe and classify. Since measurements were only approximate, they could only eliminate suspects, that is, they could only show the *non*-identity of a person, whereas fingerprinting provided exact and positive identification.[16] After several years of unsatisfactory experience with anthropometry in La Plata, Vucetich concluded that the system was "annoying . . . and full of complications" and argued that Bertillon himself had recognized this. In fact, Bertillon had been forced to introduce a "table of tolerance" to compensate for the inexactness of his "verbal portrait," which had converted his system, critics charged, into a "disordered mixture" of science and spiritism.[17]

Argentine scientists had been in on the debate over bertillonage, in use in France since 1882, from the beginning. Samuel Gache, an Argentine delegate to the Penitentiary Congress of Rome in 1886, was an early skeptic and took on Bertillon face to face. At the congress, Bertillon put on a demonstration of his instruments for osteometry and showed photos of delinquents whom he had measured. After Bertillon's talk, Gache asked Bertillon to take his (Gache's) measurements, "assuring the nice maestro that I [Gache] was a recalcitrant recidivist of moral crimes. He smiled at my pretensions, but agreed. I hoped that he would at least declare me a psychopath, but he told me that I was healthy in body and mind. So I consoled myself by thinking that half of humanity suffers from my illness—of moral crime—and that my crimes do not figure among those punished by the penal codes of modern societies, since they are crimes that are more perversions of conscience. Fifty percent of men are psychopaths, or suffer from neurosis." Gache's mockery of Bertillon's system was motivated, a fellow conference participant explained, by Gache's suspicion of the positive school, whereas bertillonage was strictly a mechanical system that had nothing to do with the positive school. The same participant objected to Gache's challenges to Bertillon, saying that Bertillon was not so foolish as to immediately declare someone a criminal on the basis of his physiology. Rather, a great deal of information went into such a judgment.[18]

[15] Reyna Almandos 1909: 20.

[16] Ibid.: 66.

[17] Ibid.: 71–75; interview with Juan Vucetich in *El Argentino* (September 1, 1924) no pages; Quesada 1901: 145.

[18] Gache 1886: 1028–36, and Brusa 1886: 1051–74.

Finally, the philosophy of identification was undergoing some significant changes at the time. An important condition of new modes of identification of the late nineteenth century was that they should be non-stigmatizing. Special clothing, brands, mutilations, and tattoos were now seen as intolerably defamatory. Although prisons experimented with less offensive marks than branding in the early twentieth century, such as the implantation of a bit of glycerine under the skin of prisoners, most penologists were attempting to find other ways of identification that were less prejudicial. Underlying these attempts was the public's sensitization to the concept of "honor," explained by a lawyer as "the highest symbol of the human personality," or as is meant, "identity." Someone who made the "personality," that is, the "identity," of a person "disappear" was not just guilty of an outrage; rather he was also guilty of a crime. This is much as we have experienced in our own time in terms of the violations of a person's civil rights. A strike on identity was a crime against the person, a stain that could never be erased. Argentine law safeguarded this highest symbol of the human personality, namely, honor.[19] Protecting one's honor was thus a legitimate, laudable, and even necessary act, even when it involved a crime, such as infanticide or homicide. Sensitive to honor and dishonor, the public objected to measurements and other "advances" as stigmatizing and prejudicial.[20] Taking measurements, for example, necessitated that the subject disrobe, which was offensive to the modesty of women, and, because of honor, also objectionable to men.[21] Photographs of criminals, which were posted in police stations, also fell into this category. The reference to honor is implicit, for example, in a public prosecutor's argument in 1896 that the police expression of "sending a suspect to be photographed" was considered to be in the legal sense a "serious injury, which sounded like the crack of a whip to the reputation of an innocent person."[22]

Given the limitations of anthropometry, what would have greatly aided in criminal investigations like that involving Farbos and Tremblié was the fingerprinting system that Juan Vucetich was using in La Plata, just fifty miles south of Buenos Aires, at exactly the moment of the case. Fingerprints had the advantage of being permanent and were there before birth and after death. Fingerprints did not change over time, and even if the fingertips were burned or mutilated, they would usually grow back with the same print. Fingerprints were also of infinite variety and thus totally

---

[19] Archivo General de la Nación (Buenos Aires, Argentina), Tribunal Criminal, 2nd series, A,58,1904, case against Agustin Acre for the homicide of his wife, Cristina Malagrini; quoting defense lawyer to appeals court.

[20] Reyna Almandos 1909: 71–75; Rodríguez 1981: 162.

[21] Ibid.: 23–24; Quesada 1901: 159.

[22] Quesada 1901: 106–7.

individual. Vucetich's contribution to the history of fingerprinting, already developed by Francis Galton and others, was his classification system. In contrast to Galton's three-type classification, Vucetich created a new system formed with four fundamental types of papillary lines: the arch; the loop with internal inclination; the loop with external inclination; and the whorl. Each of these had five subtypes, and the patterns were further subdivided by counting the ridges. He further developed an apparatus that represented a dactyloscopic card with the ten digital impressions, within whose ten gyrating hidden discs were the "four types," which instantly showed all the possible dactyloscopic combinations or formulas, that is, a total of 1,048,576.[23]

Introduced to Galton's work on fingerprinting in a journal article given to him by his police chief in 1890, Vucetich subjected the conclusions to his own experiments, taking prints of the arrestees who were brought to his office and examining the prints of cadavers at the morgue and of the Egyptian mummies at the La Plata museum. Having worked out his own classification system by July 1891, he registered it on September 1 of that year.[24] Vucetich put his system officially in use in La Plata in 1891, using it along with the anthropometric system of Bertillon, in spite of his doubts about anthropometry, because he was required to by the police department. His solution of the infanticide case against Francisca Rojas in 1892 using fingerprints left at the scene of the crime represented a real breakthrough for dactyloscopy. This was the first time a murder case had been solved this way. In spite of this success, the police chief ordered him to return to using anthropometry in 1893, a ban that was rescinded by the new police chief in 1894.[25] In 1895, the La Plata police officially adopted dactyloscopy as a complement to bertillonage, and in 1896 they abandoned anthropometry altogether and adopted dactyloscopy. The La Plata police department's move marked another major breakthrough in that it was the first time in the world that a police force had decided to use *only* fingerprinting for making identifications.[26]

The rest of the country slowly began to adopt dactyloscopy, with the Buenos Aires police officially adopting it in 1905, and the 1906 Code of Penal Procedures incorporating fingerprinting in several of its articles: for detainees and the condemned; to verify a person's antecedents; and to identify cadavers. In 1909, the provincial government gave Vucetich the title of *perito identificador,* "expert identifier," meaning that only he could testify in court regarding fingerprints.[27] Vucetich's system began to be im-

[23] Rodríguez 1942: 12.
[24] Thorwald 1965: 51–52, and Reyna Almandos 1925: 2.
[25] Cole 1998: 228, and Thorwald 1965: 53–55.
[26] Rodríguez 1942: 12, and Thorwald 1965: 56.
[27] Reyna Almandos 1909: 80–81, 144.

plemented for immigrants in 1912 when the Direction of Immigration established a Register of Identification of Immigrants. Fingerprinting also began to be used for illiterate municipal employees, so that they could get paid, as well as for the identification of police agents, prostitutes, the residents of neighborhoods, voters, domestics, mendicants, bank employees, and conscripts.[28] But Vucetich and his colleague, Luis Reyna Almandos, had a grander scheme for fingerprints.

The Universal "Right of Identification"

In the plans of Vucetich and Reyna Almandos, fingerprints were to become the basis for nothing less than, to use a modern term, a new world order. Believing that selective and sporadic identification was what the public objected to, Vucetich proposed to combat their resistance by instituting nothing less than a universal system of identification, one applied without distinctions. Unlike brands, for example, fingerprinting left no permanent mark, and unlike measurements, the taking of prints was done inoffensively. Dactyloscopy was proposed to be universally applied, that is, to honest people and delinquents; this was every person's right. Vucetich's grandiose plan to establish three intercontinental laboratories of identification that would function on the La Plata model was introduced and debated at the Second Latin American Scientific Congress held in Montevideo, Uruguay, in 1901. Vucetich, of course, had been using dactyloscopy for at least ten years, but for other conference participants, this system was still just a laboratory method. For them, Vucetich's plan landed "like a bomb." Bertillonage, after all, still dominated in police departments around the world and the bertillonage bloc at the conference made sure that Vucetich's plan was voted down, although the congress in the end voted Vucetich's system a "useful complement for the identification of persons and very good for the identification of cadavers."[29] Then in 1902 came a real coup when the Paris police began teaching Vucetich's dactyloscopy to its agents, and even Bertillon adopted Vucetich's dactyloscopic identity card as a complement to his own system in 1903, although he did not cite Vucetich as its creator.[30] Vucetich's book, *Dactiloscopia comparada*, published in 1904, received worldwide attention. In 1905, an International Police Convention was approved at the Scientific Congress of Rio de Janeiro in Brazil, among the police of La Plata, Buenos Aires, Rio de Janeiro, Montevideo, and Santiago de Chile, which estab-

[28] Ibid.: 214–22.
[29] Ibid.: 90, and Rodríguez 1942: 13.
[30] Vucetich 1924.

lished not only an identity card based on dactyloscopy for delinquents, but also, for the first time, an identity card for "honest" citizens based on Vucetich's model, which he had been issuing in La Plata since 1899. The convention also approved the plan to create the three proposed intercontinental laboratories.[31] Two major figures in French criminal science, Alexandre Lacassagne and Edmond Locard, paid tribute to Vucetich, Lacassagne by renaming the system *vucetichismo*, and Locard, by declaring it a "perfect" system.[32] But the idea of identifying an entire population was still viewed with suspicion in Argentina. In 1916, the provincial legislature of Buenos Aires sanctioned a law creating a general register of identification, which would have been the first regional register in the world based on dactyloscopic identification. Nine months later, however, the plan was declared unconstitutional by the national intervenor for the province, and all the personal data that had been collected was destroyed. Vucetich, who likened this travesty to the destruction of the library of Alexandria, was not deterred from pursuing, along with Reyna Almandos, the broader applications of fingerprinting.

To Vucetich, fingerprints were as sublime as something like moral "truth." Just as Gabriel Tarde had argued that in the *moral* world each person had his own interior mark, his unalterable trait, his own essence that was permanent from birth to death, a "first element" that had "stored powers," so too had Vucetich identified special marks in a person's *physical* world. Fingerprints, Vucetich argued, were the "perfect expression of the physical ego," and contained "more distinctive traits than the face and perhaps more distinctive traits than the whole exterior body."[33] Like a moral code that controls through prevention, so too was Vucetich's system in a sense a preventative system, with a panoptical vision. If a person knew, Vucetich argued, that he could be tracked throughout the world by means of his fingerprints, it was possible that he would "try not to commit transgressions and would respect the law of others." The implications for the promotion of "civilization" in the world were important, especially to the Argentine elite who had been working through the dichotomy of "civilization and barbarism" since the mid-century. Not only would social relations improve within nations with national programs of fingerprinting, but so too would international identification systems contribute to harmony between nations.[34]

By creating a symbol for all persons that would prove their identity, their "self," argued Vucetich, individuals could be assured of having a

international crime fighting

[31] Reyna Almandos 1909: 56–57.
[32] Ibid.: 55–58.
[33] Vucetich 1924 and Reyna Almandos 1909: xlv.
[34] Vucetich 1929: 97.

well-defined personality, what he called a "legal or juridical personality."
Thus, personality/identity would include in his system the "history of civil
individuality," that is, the origin and civil evolution of each person, that
is, birth, marriage, death, judicial sentencing, divorce, nullification of
marriage, description including scars and defects, and change of name.
He envisioned that each person's identification card would contain the
number and series of the act of registration, and place and date of issuance; personal data, including visible individual signs or defects of formation; the print of the right thumb; photo of the right profile; signature;
and signature of the director or head of the Civil Register. Of course, the
general register would also include more specialized lists, of people who
were only marginally "innocent," that is, potential criminals, prostitutes,
the insane, and delinquents.[35] Identification was a guarantee for the "honest" individual against confusion of name and antecedents with "dishonest" people.[36] It was protection against "simulation," a major concern
in this period, especially within the context of "honor." Concerns about
simulation and honor may have actually aided the campaign to encourage
people to accept identification as their "right" and as a means of their
protection.

Vucetich's friend and successor, Reyna Almandos, writing in the 1930s,
carried the idea of identification as a natural right further, arguing that
this right was even a new juridical concept. Evidence that this reflected a
changing view can be found in the 1932 edition of the *Encyclopedia of
the Social Sciences*, which explained the change from the idea that identification was only for criminals, to the view that it had become an increasingly important means of safeguarding civil rights.[37] The question was
what sign to use. It had to be something that was precise, permanent, not
confuseable, and peculiar to each human being; and something that
would serve as a link between the individual and the exterior world.
Brands and other marks were out. Photographs too were out as it was
possible to end up with substantially different photos of the same person.[38] Anthropometry did not achieve sufficient differentiation and had
other limitations. Birthmarks and other natural signs on the body were
too nebulous to be used. Names did not constitute a link because they
were not "in the body" of man. Nor were signatures in the body of man.
And even though signatures were considered to be the closest thing to the
perfect identifying sign, according to Reyna Almandos, they were still not
a true system of identification. Fingerprints, although they could abso-

---

[35] Ibid.: 101–2.
[36] Ibid.: 99.
[37] Seligman and Johnson 1932.
[38] Reyna Almandos 1936: 13–14.

lutely identify a person, could not be used to maintain a register of individuals, because formulas were arranged first by group and only then by individual and because the dactyloscopic number had too many digits.[39]

Reyna Almandos' contribution, then, was to use Vucetich's dactyloscopic system as the basis for, in his words, a "personal number" that could be used to build a national and even international "book of personality." It was a mathematical expression, just like fingerprints. To indicate the universal symbol of identity, he chose the symbol Y, which he took from the word *yu* meaning "law or judicial tie" in the language of the Brahmans. A possible number for John Doe then would be Y1,597,000. This number was exclusive, successive, untransferable, perpetual, individual, and social. It even had a moral character as a register of a person's rights, actions, and property and because in Reyna Almandos' scheme, personality/identity was the same as honor. Identity was an individual's property, just as honor was. The personal number corresponded to one individual only and was based on the dactyloscopic system. "Every number," explained Reyna Almandos, "would be the individual himself; it would be the 'civil person' of every man. By it, a person would be known, given rights, and held responsible for his actions."[40] This is still a panoptical vision of the world.

The personal number was to be the basis of a new social organization within the state—a national register that would be a summary of the nation, a civil biography of all inhabitants. At the same time, it would be a coordinated conjunction of all individual biographies within the juridical concept of personality. The resulting "national book of personality" would owe its existence to two factors: the dactyloscopic formula and the personal number. Only with this combination, Reyna Almandos argued, could a society organize the colossal files of individuals. The national book of personality for Argentina, for example, would have 24,000 volumes of 500 pages each, equaling the country's total population at that time of 12 million inhabitants. Although Reyna Almandos recognized that this was a grandiose project, he maintained that it was quite in line with other colossal projects such as the eighteenth-century Chinese collection of classical authors. Its considerable cost would be well worth it, he said, because, among other things, it would act as a permanent national census that would save Argentina money and time.[41]

In an interview in 1924, shortly before his death, Vucetich commented that the role of fingerprinting had finally been expanded to the "vast field of social progress." It was a means of organizing the "permanent defense

[39] Ibid.: 6–7.
[40] Ibid.: 8.
[41] Ibid.: 11–13.

of life and affairs, individual rights, and the collective well-being," and had become a "factor of social evolution." His desire had been to perfect man and improve society, and he felt he had found the "infallible instrument of prophylaxis of the moral life of man," thus serving justice and social order.[42]

Reyna Almandos expanded these ideas, also emphasizing the "civilizing" advantage of his identification system. In his pamphlet "The Personal Number and the National Book of Personality," originally published in Spanish in a Brazilian journal in 1934 and then in English in a Spanish-language journal in 1936, he included the following dedication: "To the promoters of civilization in Brazil, Chile and Mexico: my respects." In this article, he argues that the personal number was a "civilizing undertaking" that would "guarantee the defense of Order and Law." Grandiose as it might seem, he also argued that the personal number would stabilize international relations, bring about a universal order and justice, perfect relationships, eliminate warfare, and strengthen the family.[43]

A final caveat about Reyna Almandos' enthusiastic claims makes an appropriate conclusion to this essay. He was so enthusiastic about his proposed system that he actually advised that "remembering or carrying one's number should become, in the process of time, a habit of healthy foresight—tattooing the personal number [on people's bodies], for example."[44] Thus, he had moved from a condemnation of branding bodies, to a condemnation of measuring bodies, to a revision of Vucetich's fingerprinting system, and finally, back to branding bodies with a tattoo! That tattooing the personal number onto people's bodies would have found acceptance and been welcomed in a period that was sensitive to dishonor is doubtful, but it is interesting that Reyna Almandos took this as "civilizing." This is part of the background perhaps for what was to come later in the 1930s, when the "end" of social progress, justice, and social order warranted any "means." Reyna Almandos had gone full circle from rejecting visible signs known to all, such as brands and special clothing, to visible signs known to experts, such as head measurements and fingerprints, to assigning this complex of traits a number that would appear in a register and be known only to experts, to making it known to the public by tattooing it on the body, but in this case, for the person's own use and well-being as well as for society's.

[42] Vucetich 1924.
[43] Reyna Almandos 1936: 19–20.
[44] Ibid.: 18.

Part Three

IDENTIFICATION AND CONTROL OF MOVEMENT

11

Domenica Saba Takes to the Road: Origins and Development of a Modern Passport System in Lombardy-Veneto

ANDREA GESELLE

The humble undersigned Domenica Saba, resident in San Gerolamo in the diocese of San Marziale, has an opportunity to take up a position as a servant-girl in the house of the merchant firm of Isach Tedesco and Sons in Verona; she thus beseeches you to have issued to her a passport in order that she might be able to take up this position and by her work and effort to take advantage of this opportunity for an optimal post with a good family. She makes this request with great urgency and submits humbly to your good favor.[1]

THIS PASSPORT request of the unmarried thirty-year-old Venetian servant-girl Domenica Saba was received at the police headquarters of the Veneto (*I.R. Direzione Generale di Polizia*) on December 7, 1822. At the time, Venice was not only the capital of the Austrian *Kronland* (crown territory) of Veneto, but also, like Verona, one of the eight provincial capitals of that *Kronland* which, together with the *Kronland* of Lombardy, had since 1816 comprised the Kingdom of Lombardy-Veneto, one of the principal components of the Austrian Empire. Although Domenica Saba wished to leave neither the territory of Austria nor that of her own *Kronland*, she needed a passport for her trip from Venice to Verona. In the first half of the nineteenth century, the inhabitants of Veneto were required to equip themselves with internal passports simply to leave their province of origin, as well as to travel to another Austrian *Kronland*.

This essay presents portions of a larger work generated in the context of a research project on "Borders and Border Crossings: The Meaning of the Border for the Political and Social Development of the Habsburg Empire from the Mid-Eighteenth to the Mid-Nineteenth Century," under the direction of Professors Edith Saurer and Waltraud Heindl, Vienna (cf. Geselle 2000). The project was funded by the research project "Austria Unbound" (*Grenzenloses Österreich*) of the Austrian Ministry of Science and Transport. Translated by John Torpey.
  [1] Passport application of Domenica Saba, December 1822, Archivio di Stato, Venezia (hereafter: ASV), Polizia (1822) tit. VI, box 24.

As a resident of Venice, Domenica Saba could have taken her passport request directly to the police headquarters, but she would have had to traverse half the city to get from her dwelling at the extreme end of the neighborhood of Cannaregio to the imposing complex of buildings at San Severo in the district of Castello, in which were housed both the police headquarters and the Venice prison. The young woman chose instead to go to the small police station in Cannaregio, where she could plead her case before the police commissioner, whom she knew personally. Whereas passports for domestic or foreign travel were only issued to married women upon presentation of written permission from their husbands, as a single adult woman Domenica Saba—like women who were widowed or legally separated from their husbands—was eligible to act with complete independence in all passport matters. She was required to present to the police commissioner a written declaration from her new employer, along with a document called a *carta d'iscrizione*, which confirmed that she was entered in the local residential register (*ruolo generale di popolazione*). Because she was not seeking to leave Austrian territory, she did not need the attestations vouchsafing her good name and declaring her assets that would otherwise be demanded as a way of guaranteeing her return. The police commissioner of Cannaregio drew up a written passport application for her and, along with a police evaluation, sent it on to police headquarters at San Severo.

This evaluation was of paramount importance for the outcome of the passport application, and it would have been demanded even if Domenica Saba had submitted her application directly to police headquarters. The procedure was similar in the other provincial capitals, where the residents of the city could submit their requests for both domestic and foreign passports directly to the provincial authorities (*I.R. Delegazione Provinciale*). In these cases, too, the evaluation of the local chief of police (*commissario superiore*) was necessary in order to initiate the application procedure. In the other cities and in the countryside, the inhabitants were required to present their passport requests to the commissioners of their administrative districts. For the most part, these officials were authorized to issue internal passports themselves; passports for foreign travel, however, had to be forwarded along with the evaluation to the provincial authorities, from which they would be sent on to the governor's office in Venice or Milan. In order to process applications for foreign travel, the governor also required the evaluation of the territorial police headquarters, but as a rule passports were not issued without a positive assessment from the city and district police chiefs (*commissari superiori e distrittuali*).[2]

---

[2] Cf. Fontana 1846: 144.

The police chiefs, who knew the applicant and his or her social milieu personally, thus constituted an important level of decision-making and control with respect to both internal and external passports. It was their task to check the accuracy of all information given by the passport applicant, to give the next administrative level insight into his or her circumstances, and to anticipate possible untoward consequences of issuing a passport. Because Domenica Saba had, according to the police chief in Cannaregio, a spotless record, she was able to go to San Severo within a few days to pick up her passport. There a personal description of the young woman was entered into her passport and, insofar as she was capable of writing, she had to sign the document in the presence of the issuing official.

As a rule, internal passports were issued upon presentation of the *carta d'iscrizione* along with an explanation of the reasons for travel. Internal passports could be restricted to a particular locality or to a short period of validity, or they might authorize numerous unscheduled trips within the specified area for an entire year. Itinerant workers, artisans, and businesspeople were often issued passports valid for a year for the entire Kingdom of Lombardy-Veneto, or for one or more other principalities.

While the passport application procedure was the same for everybody, the fees differed according to each applicant's assets and income. As a servant without means in Lombardy-Veneto, Domenica Saba had a right to a passport *gratis*. It is true that, beginning in 1814, all documents for domestic travel were issued without a fee, while external passports cost 2 lire each. Still, internal passports remained subject to a stamp fee of 50 centesimi for both domestic and foreign passports.[3] This fee was charged not only for the passport, but for each supporting document as well. Only the passport application itself was free of charge. As a holder of a passport issued *gratis*, Domenica Saba was exempted from any kind of fees.[4]

Once the police had affixed to her passport a visa for Padua, the next provincial capital, she was at liberty to take possession of her no-cost travel document and embark upon her journey to Verona. As soon as she left the province of Venice, irrespective of her mode of travel she was required to remain on the main roads, which perforce would take her to

---

[3] In the period between 1815 and 1848 (the so-called *Vormärz*), a Milanese mason earned, on average, 170 gulden (= 510 lire) annually, and an agricultural worker in the Veneto received an annual wage of 60 to 170 gulden (= 180 to 510 lire). Cf. De Maddalena 1974: 419–20, and Berengo 1973: 219.

[4] This changed in 1840, when class-specific stamp fees were introduced as part of a new stamp law. The normal fee for a stamp was raised to 1.50 lire, but all servants, apprentices, artisans, and manual workers who did not earn more than an average wage had to pay a fee of 30 centesimi for their travel documents and other certificates requiring a stamp. Cf. the stamp ordinance of January 27, 1840, in Guazzo 1853: 438.

Padua and Vicenza. At the gates of each of these cities, the financial officer on duty would compel her to hand over her passport. This functionary would register the document and send it on to the passport office in the city, where it would then be visaed for travel to the next provincial capital and sent back to the appropriate city gate. Depending on the amount of traffic at the gates, this process could take as long as two hours. On leaving the city, Domenica Saba would once again have to have her passport inspected at the gate from which she departed and entered into a register kept there for that purpose. In addition, once outside Venice, her province of origin, she was required to have her passport stamped by the police in any place where she remained for longer than twenty-four hours. Once she had reached Verona, her passport would be taken from her at the city gate; armed with the "receipt" she would be given at that time, she was required to appear at the city's passport office within twenty-four hours of her arrival. There she would receive a temporary residence permit (*carta di permanenza*) that would allow her to move about freely in the City and Province of Verona.[5]

The case of Domenica Saba illustrates the workings of a fine-meshed passport system designed to regulate and control all personal movement in the Kingdom of Lombardy-Veneto, and which was apparently familiar to and accepted by even the humblest levels of society as early as the 1820s. Such a thoroughgoing passport system, concentrating the regulation of mobility exclusively in the hands of the state, could only be developed in a modern state with a far-flung, decentralized administrative apparatus able to assert the state's sovereignty throughout its entire territory. The passport system was not just an epiphenomenal aspect of the emergence of modern state and administrative apparatuses, however. It was rather an instrument with which modern states, defined by their territories and their linear borders, bounded themselves toward the outside and implemented a territory-wide domination internally—an instrument with which a new, purely "territorial relationship"[6] could be constructed between the state and its subjects or citizens and with which each individual could be "laid hold of" (*erfasst*) and firmly integrated into the body of the state.

In Lombardy and Veneto, a tightly woven passport system aimed at meeting the demands of this territorial state had emerged in barely a decade. The development of this system ran parallel to the consolidation into a unitary, modern territorial state of those previously independent territories not annexed by France after the Napoleonic wars. The im-

---

[5] In the *Kronland* of Veneto, this residence permit was called the *carta di permanenza*, whereas in the *Kronland* of Lombardy it was called the *carta di sicurezza*.

[6] Raffestin, "L'immagine della frontiera," *Volontà* 4 (1992): 48.

portant contribution made by the passport system to the formation of modern territorial states is nowhere clearer than in the states created in northern Italy under French domination in the late eighteenth and early nineteenth centuries.

The Origins of the Passport System in Lombardy-Veneto

The Josephine Emigration Edict of 1784, which for the first time codified the various passport and travel restrictions in force in the Austrian states,[7] had never been implemented in the Duchy of Milan, which was under Austrian domination until 1796. Passports were issued there only for departure from and entry into Austrian Lombardy. The same practice was in force in the area of the former Republic of Venice, which fell into Austrian hands after 1798 as a result of the Peace of Campoformio. According to the entry regulations for Venice laid down in an edict of January 14, 1799, foreigners were only permitted to enter this territory with a passport from the Austrian authorities. While subjects of the emperor from the Austrian dynastic lands could apply for this passport from the officials of their government, all other foreigners had to go to the chancellery in Vienna, the General Command of the imperial army, or the government of Veneto.[8] While these passports were all issued by state authorities, there were no fixed criteria for the form they should take and the authorities were free to devise them as they wished. This state of affairs changed after the Peace of Lunéville of 1801. In anticipation of an increased flow of both foreign travelers and trade, and as a result of the growing nervousness about revolutionary unrest, new regulations were issued for all foreigners entering the Austrian states.[9] These regulations laid down a number of essential elements for passports that all issuing authorities were thenceforth required to include in any such documents they issued. In addition to the name, address, route to be traveled, and the period of validity, all passports for foreigners traveling in the Austrian states now had to include a description of the passport-holder as well as his or her signature—requirements that had been in force in France since 1792 and introduced in the Napoleonic *Repubblica Cisalpina*, which bordered on the Austrian Veneto. The stipulation of binding criteria was not intended simply to standardize state-issued passports. With the inclusion of a personal description and the signature of the bearer, the passport acquired a

---

[7] Cf. Komlosy 1995: 64.

[8] Cf. Editti Regj Imperiali pubblicati in Venezia dall'arrivo delle truppe di Sua Maestà I.R.A. Francesco II. nel Veneto Stato, vol. 1: 227.

[9] Editti Regj Imperiali, vol. 4 (12/1): 39.

completely new character. Henceforth the passport played the role of an identification document in which the unambiguous identity of the bearer was to be established. Thus not only was misuse of the document to be prevented, but also better control of every foreign traveler in the country was to be facilitated. This objective was also to be achieved through the introduction of a "security card" (*carta di sicurezza*), which was issued to all foreign travelers who wished to deviate from the route indicated in their passports. The explicit aim of the passport regulations of 1801 was to facilitate the influx of foreign businesspeople and other unsuspicious travelers, and to prevent "shady" and "work-shy" foreigners from entering or remaining.

The inhabitants of Veneto needed passports only for departure from its territory. Irrespective of whether they intended to travel to another territory of the Austrian monarchy or outside those lands, they were required to apply for a passport from the Veneto government, giving their reasons for travel and the expected duration of their absence.[10] The temporary wartime travel restrictions within the provinces of Veneto were lifted in October 1801, as a result of which the inhabitants of the *Kronland* were once again free to move about internally without restriction. The only exception was that those who wished to enter the city of Venice and who were not personally known to the soldiers at the guard posts around the lagoon were required to show a notarized certificate that "identified them as that which they are."[11]

Thus in both Lombardy and Veneto the state-imposed passport system was oriented above all toward constraining the departure of the inhabitants and the entry of foreigners. Within the territory itself, the movements of foreigners were to be kept under surveillance—a control that in Veneto was especially strict because of the fear of revolutionary activity. Control over the domestic population, by contrast, was limited to those moments when one of the inhabitants sought to leave the territory of the state. Internally, the mobility of the indigenous population was free of state control. But that situation would be fundamentally transformed with the absorption of Lombardy and Veneto into the newly founded states of northern Italy under French domination. In these states, a passport system was developed that placed the internal movements of the population under strict surveillance and thus facilitated access of the state to each and every one of its citizens.

---

[10] Cf. Directive of the Venice Police Headquarters, May 29, 1801, Editti Regj Imperiali, vol. IV (12/1): 50.

[11] Directive of the Venice Police Headquarters, October 5, 1801, Editti Regj Imperiali, vol. IV (12/1): 109.

The ancien régime in France operated a strict passport regime for both external and internal travel. In the course of the Revolution, this system was regarded as an intolerable infringement on personal freedom and individual rights and thus in need of elimination. Accordingly, the first paragraph of the constitution of September 3, 1791, announced the complete abolition of any passport obligations.[12] Yet the city administration of Paris soon complained of the uncontrolled arrival of beggars, and the communes of the countryside found themselves exposed to the depredations not only of roving bands of robbers, but of active counter-revolutionary elements as well. That is why the debate over passports was reopened in the National Assembly, culminating in the reintroduction of passport obligations in February 1792. With the law of February 1–March 28, 1792, "external" and internal passports were fully rehabilitated; in addition, the officials authorized to issue passports and the features of the passport itself came to be defined precisely. Along with name, age, and occupation, a valid passport also had to include the bearer's place of residence, nationality, and physical description.[13]

In the *Repubblica Cisalpina*, which in 1797 had brought together the areas of northern Italy not annexed by France, the indigenous population initially needed passports only to traverse the external borders, while foreigners who wished to establish themselves in the territory for any length of time were required to have a "security card." With the constitution of the *Repubblica Italiana*[14] of January 26, 1802, however, the earlier liberal mood of the Revolution began to wane in these regions.[15] Limitations of personal rights affecting individual mobility adumbrated in the constitution found expression in the Police Ordinance of March 27, 1802, which first codified a comprehensive law concerning passports and foreigners in northern Italy. In order to enter the territory, foreigners would henceforth be required to have in their possession a passport issued either by the authorities of the Republic or by their own government. Once within the territory, they needed an official authorization for stopping more than twenty-four hours in any given place; this document was to be affixed to their passports. Foreigners were allowed to take up permanent residence in the country only with the permission of the Interior Ministry and upon demonstration of their moral rectitude, good conduct, and ability to support themselves. Indigenous citizens were permitted to travel abroad only

---

[12] Zironda 1906: 725.

[13] Cf. Sée 1907: 43–44; for an extended discussion, see also Torpey 2000: ch. 2.

[14] After the Peace of Lunéville, the *Repubblica Cisalpina* was renamed the *Repubblica Italiana* in 1802.

[15] Cf. Roberti 1946: 364.

with passports signed by the same Ministry. In order to travel within the country, they henceforth needed a "security card" issued by the authorities in their place of domicile, and stamped by the prefect of the relevant district administration.[16]

Although the security card had hitherto been used simply as an identification document for foreigners temporarily in the territory, it now became obligatory for all citizens wishing to depart from their place of residence. The new passport legislation instituted a systematic social control of the population, for henceforth the police and other state organs were empowered to detain the inhabitants of the country in areas where they were not personally known to the authorities and to demand that they produce a security card. Moreover, the prefect's stamp could simply be denied to any person whose movements the authorities regarded as undesirable; residents of the country without a stamped security card could only move about within the area in which they were personally known to the authorities. As soon as they traversed the "virtual" boundaries of that area, they became "illegal migrants" liable to be arrested or otherwise hindered in their movements.

The assertion of control became even clearer when, alongside the passport restrictions, the state sought to create general registers of the population overtly intended to facilitate the collection of personal taxes.[17] The underlying purpose, however, as early as 1802, was the creation of continuously updated registers of residents, which were to become the foundation of the modern administrative bureaucracy. These new residential registers were to serve as an efficient instrument of conscription and to lodge control over population fluctuations in the hands of the state.[18] Yet the realization of this project encountered serious difficulties, not least of a financial nature. It was only in 1811, after repeated demands from the higher authorities, that all the communal administrations of the *Regno d'Italia*[19]—to which Veneto had belonged since its cession by Austria to France in 1806—instituted the new continuous population registers (*ruolo generale di popolazione*).[20]

Napoleon's occupation of northern Italy resulted not only in the emergence of a new kind of state, but also in a new region over which domination had to be consolidated. This aim was achieved not merely through the sharp separation of "internal" and "external" and the creation of

[16] Police ordinance of March 27, 1802, *Bollettino delle leggi*, 1802, nr. 115: 41–46.

[17] Cf. Faron 1997: 34.

[18] The registration of births, marriages, and deaths remained the task of the individual parishes, however. See Caccialupi 1863: 188.

[19] In 1805, Napoleon had himself crowned king of Italy, and thus the Republic of Italy was transformed into a kingdom.

[20] Cf. Faron 1997: 38.

a distinction between aliens and nationals that became constitutionally anchored with the definition of Italian citizenship in 1806.[21] With the aid of travel documents for internal movement and the new population registers, the entire territory was subjected to a capillary form of domination thanks to this spatial structuring and organization.[22] Foucault speaks in this connection of the emergence of a "disciplinary space."[23] "Its aim was to establish presences and absences, to know where and how to locate individuals."[24] Out of the territory of a state there thus emerged an "analytical space."

The establishment of comprehensive, accurate, continuous population registers was a long-term process, however, which developed further under Austrian domination, but was still not complete in 1848. The residential registers included entries for all persons, regardless of age or sex, who had their legal residence in the municipality. The "place of residence" thus became the administrative basis for locating and controlling the population, as well as the fundamental administrative category within the state. Each individual was ascribed to a residence, which thus became an essential element of his or her identity—an identity that was bureaucratically stabilized and therefore easily "graspable" by the state. John Torpey has seen in this process of bureaucratic identity-formation a fundamental characteristic of all modern states, which are concerned "to establish and maintain control over particular territories by constructing enduring identities that permit them to 'lay hold of' their subjects/citizens."[25]

For the population of the *Regno d'Italia*, the introduction of the modern administrative category of "place of residence" signified a further constraint on their freedom of movement. This already became clear with the new general passport law, which went into effect in 1812;[26] the law could only be formulated on the basis of the previous structuring of the territorial space and an identification of the country's inhabitants on the basis of their place of residence. The increasingly precise spatial ordering of

[21] The criteria for the acquisition and loss of nationality (*cittadinanza*) in the *Regno d'Italia* were laid down in its Civil Code, which was a translation of the French *Code civil* and had taken effect in the *Regno d'Italia* on March 30, 1806. See *Collezione completa dei moderni Codici Civili degli Stati d'Italia* 1845: 1ff.

[22] The implementation of this modern, territorial sovereignty was also furthered by the administrative reorganization of the territory, which helped to undermine traditional dynastic spatial divisions. With the annexation of Veneto, as of 1806 the *Regno d'Italia* came to be composed of twenty-four *départements*. The borders of these new administrative districts were drawn according to the waterways, and each *département* bore the name of its most important river border. Cf. Antonielli 1983.

[23] Foucault 1979: 143.

[24] Ibid.

[25] Torpey 1997: 838.

[26] Passport law of June 11, 1811, *Bollettino delle leggi* (1811) no. 136: 570–85.

the state's territory and its individual elements promoted a systematic "thickening" of the space of domination. As a result of its enmeshment with the newly introduced population registers, the passport law constituted the culmination of a fine-gauged system of control.

Whereas the inhabitants of the *Regno d'Italia* had so far been able to move about freely in the entire territory with only a security card stamped by the prefect, they now had to obtain from the mayor or police commissioner of the municipality a certificate attesting that they had been entered into the local population registry. This certificate of residential registration included all personal data, a physical description, and the signature of the bearer, and as a result assumed the function of an official identity document.[27] Bearers of this so-called *carta d'iscrizione* were free to move about within the administrative district to which they belonged by virtue of their places of residence. The *carta d'iscrizione* was thus both an identification document and a travel document, and was valid for one year. It could be renewed regularly, however, upon payment of a fee of 25 centesimi. This document was no longer sufficient, however, if the inhabitants of the *Regno d'Italia* wanted to leave the boundaries of their administrative district—which would happen if, for example, a Milanese wanted to travel from his city, which lay in the administrative district of Olona, to Como, some forty kilometers away, which was in the administrative district of Lario. For such trips within the kingdom, the inhabitants needed an internal passport costing one lira plus a stamp fee and issued by the prefect of their administrative district or the vice prefect of the county upon presentation of a *carta d'iscrizione*, with a maximum validity of one year. The new passport law also modified the competencies of officials empowered to issue passports. Thenceforth the prefects of the administrative districts were authorized to issue passports for travel abroad, but only with the assent of the municipality in which the applicant had his or her legal residence. Passports for travel abroad were issued to both nationals and foreigners who had their official residence in the country, but only for a particular trip and at a cost of 2 lira plus stamp fee.

Foreigners who wished to cross the border and to transit through the *Regno d'Italia* now needed to have a regular passport issued by the authorities in their own state and visaed by a French ambassador or consulate. Foreigners wishing to travel within the *Regno d'Italia* had their passports taken from them at the border and replaced with a pass-card (*carta*

---

[27] In his treatise on the personal identity card and the passport, Nicola Corvino lists the *carta d'iscrizione* as a predecessor of the identity card; he states incorrectly, however, that it was first introduced in 1836 under the name of the *carta di sicurezza*. See Corvino 1993: 17.

di passo) that had to be deposited with the local prefect whenever the bearer remained in a place for more than three days. If the traveler's stay lasted more than ten days, he or she was issued a security card. Like internal passports, pass-cards and security cards cost one lira plus stamp fee.

The new passport law regulating the entire realm of passport controls and the attendant treatment of foreigners, which came into effect in the *Regno d'Italia* in 1812, above all had the effect of sharply and permanently reducing the freedom of movement of the kingdom's inhabitants. It was not just that legal movement had become expensive; in addition, such movement was now possible only under the condition that the inhabitants accepted and reproduced the identity ascribed to them by the state. The creation of decentralized offices authorized to issue passports across the entire territory of the country made it clear, however, that the state took into account its subjects' legitimate need to move about and thus sought to facilitate their access to regular travel documents at all times. The state strove to control all the movements of its subjects, in order to hinder those movements regarded as damaging to the state.

The new passport law that completed the development of the fine-tuned system of passport controls reveals also the ambivalent nature of the modern state, which expresses itself in its claim to both protect and dominate its citizens and subjects.[28] On the one hand, the bearer of a valid travel document was guaranteed untrammeled movement under the protection of the state and, when abroad, assistance from its diplomatic representatives. At the same time, the fine-spun regulation of mobility offered comprehensive possibilities of control that went far beyond the restraint of illegal emigration and the flight of capital, labor power, and those owing military obligations.

The passport law of 1812 was not just crucial to the relationship between the state and its subjects, however, but also set a new tone for the relation between the state and other states, and for its embedding in a system of states. The passport law clearly restricted the sovereignty of the state to the territory of the state and to those living within it. Regular passports were henceforth issued only to inhabitants of the country itself. In the case of passports for travel abroad, the state assumed a binding guarantee vis-à-vis other states. Foreigners within the country were thus kept under surveillance by documents issued by the state itself, but they were only permitted to enter the state with regular passports issued by their own governments. As non-nationals, they were subject to another sovereign that had to legitimate and vouch for them.

[28] See Torpey 1998b: 241.

The Development of the Passport System in the Kingdom of Lombardy-Veneto

After the Austrian reconquest of northern Italy in May 1814, Lombardy and Veneto became two independent *Kronländer*, each with its own capital and government. Together the two new *Kronländer* formed the Kingdom of Lombardy-Veneto and thus stood in a close administrative relationship. The fourteen administrative districts into which the Lombard and Veneto regions of the *Regno d'Italia* had formerly been sectioned were now divided into nine Lombard and eight Veneto provinces, each with its own provincial capital.[29] The role of the prefects that had governed the individual administrative districts in the *Regno d'Italia* was transferred to the "provincial delegates," who were entrusted with the administration of the districts. Thus despite the new division of the territory, the Napoleonic administrative apparatus remained essentially intact, and the Kingdom of Lombardy-Veneto became the best-structured region of the entire Austrian monarchy in administrative terms. Nonetheless, the capillary bureaucratic penetration of the state's territory by the administrative apparatus could not be completely maintained in the face of the attendant costs.

Still, the comprehensive institution of the population registers introduced under Napoleon continued under Austrian rule, and with the same objective.[30] With the population registers, the "place of residence" remained in Lombardy-Veneto the modern spatial category of organization, which differed decisively from the more statist principle that prevailed in the Austrian dynastic lands. In those areas, the spatial ascription of individuals depended above all on their place of birth.

For the inhabitants of the Kingdom of Lombardy-Veneto, the *carta d'iscrizione* remained the precondition for legal movement. During the transitional period between the dissolution of the old government and the emergence of the new, the range of validity of these documents in Lombardy was silently extended to the entire *Kronland*. Thus under Austrian rule, an inhabitant of Lombardy with a *carta d'iscrizione* could travel across the entire principality, while the inhabitants of Veneto who wished to travel across provincial boundaries within their principality still needed a regular internal passport.

Leaving aside the liberalization of travel within the *Kronland* of Lombardy, the Napoleonic law of June 11, 1811, initially remained the fundamental legal basis for passports and matters concerning foreigners, to

---

[29] See Meriggi 1987: 33–34.

[30] The problematic development of the population registry in the city of Venice under Austrian domination during the years 1815–48 is documented in Barizza 1982: 172–75.

which the police headquarters in Milan and Venice constantly appealed in carrying out their duties. Numerous Austrian ordinances and decrees were placed alongside the Napoleonic passport law, however. On the one hand, the Lombard-Veneto passport system was to have been assimilated to the Austrian passport laws. On the other hand, these ordinances reflect Francis I's chronic anxiety about the Italian Freemasons and secret societies, as well as his efforts to erase any vestiges of the Revolution exported to the newly conquered northern Italian provinces by Napoleon's troops.[31] Rigorous political control of the new Italian subjects was to be implemented with the help of the passport regime. This control was to be attained above all through the redistribution of the authorities empowered to issue passports—a process that not only thoroughly confused the lower-level officials, but also seriously undermined the efficiency of the existing passport system.

In December 1813, the prefects of Veneto were forbidden to issue passports for the Austrian hereditary lands or for travel abroad. Applications for passports of this kind were henceforth to be forwarded to the governor of Veneto.[32] The prefects and police headquarters thus entirely lost their earlier power to issue passports for travel abroad, and the authority of the Venetian government in such matters was much restricted. Without the consent of the court in Vienna, passports for travel abroad were to be issued only if they did not exceed a period of validity of three months and if they had been requested on the basis of urgent business or family concerns.[33]

After the constitution of the Kingdom of Lombardy-Veneto on January 1, 1816, and after repeated inquiries of the governors of Lombardy and Veneto, the kingdom received the status of "internal territory" vis-à-vis the Austrian Empire with respect to passport matters. The provincial delegates and police headquarters in Milan and Venice were thus granted the authority to issue passports for all the other *Kronländer* of the monarchy on the forms normally used for internal passports. Only Vienna was excluded from these new competencies of the delegates, an exception that remained in force until 1825.

Yet this new regulation was unable to keep pace with the lively traffic across the borders of the provinces and the other *Kronländer,* or with the travel habits of the population of the Kingdom of Lombardy-Veneto more generally. The delegates of the provinces repeatedly complained to the

[31] See Meriggi 1987: 23.

[32] See the circular of December 29, 1813, *Collezione di Leggi e Regolamenti del Governo (1813–1814)* vol. 1, part 1, no. 14: 54.

[33] From Count Ugarte (*Hofkammer* in Vienna) to the governor of Veneto, Prince Reuss von Plauen, August 4, 1814, ASV, Presidio di Governo (1814), box 22, no. 1033.

police chief of Veneto that the urgent need for internal passports concerned above all those of the poorer classes, who were forced to make their living on the basis of temporary labor migrations. The loss of time and the costs of a journey to the provincial capital, which was often some distance away, could impose a severe burden on these groups.[34] The delegates thus urged that the new district commissioners who were distributed around the provinces should receive the same competencies as the former vice prefects. In March 1816, the new governor, Count Goëss, thus decided—in contravention of the orders from Vienna—to transfer to the district commissioners the responsibility for issuing internal passports valid up to three months for all provinces of the Kingdom of Lombardy-Veneto.[35] Within the same year, the district commissioners also received the authority to issue internal passports—at least to the working people of the country—for the other Austrian *Kronländer*. Internal passports were henceforth delivered to the district commissioners as blank forms already signed and stamped by the provincial delegations. Similar procedures were adopted in the *Kronland* of Lombardy.

While the competencies of the former vice prefects of the *Regno d'Italia* with respect to internal passports had thus been almost completely restored by 1816, the issue of passports for travel abroad was still governed by such rigid and hierarchical criteria that the entire system was in danger of collapsing. A handwritten directive of the emperor from April 23, 1815, regarding external passports dictated completely new regulations in this area, which were to be valid not only for the Kingdom of Lombardy-Veneto, but for all provinces of the Austrian monarchy.[36] With this imperial order, the competencies of the governors of Lombardy and Veneto were once again reduced; passports for travel abroad were henceforth to be issued by the governments of the two *Kronländer* only to businesspeople "for their occupational affairs" and to persons who could demonstrate urgent family reasons for traveling and who wished to be away for less than six weeks.[37] In all other cases, external passports were to be requested from the appropriate office in the imperial court, which in turn was required to submit the request—after gaining the permission of the imperial chancellery—to the "most high decision of his majesty." As a practical matter, however, this centralization of the decision-making authority had the consequence that Austrian subjects from the Italian prov-

[34] From the Belluno provincial delegate to the governor's office, February 10, 1816, ASV, Presidio di Governo (1815–19), box 49.

[35] See ibid., the circular of the governor of Veneto to all provincial delegates and to the police headquarters, March 5, 1816.

[36] See ibid., from Baron Franz von Haager (*Polizeihofstelle* in Vienna) to the governor of Veneto Count Goëss, April 27, 1815.

[37] Ibid.

inces were increasingly encountered abroad either without any passport whatsoever, or with passports issued by foreign authorities.

In fact, the once-so-efficient Napoleonic administrative apparatus, upon which the successful operation of the passport system was based, had been extensively undermined, for the functionaries in the Italian provinces now had a much more limited range of action and decision-making.[38] However, to the differentiated society of the Kingdom of Lombardy-Veneto—a society that had already left feudalism behind and had already had the experience of an efficiently organized, needs-oriented administrative apparatus—such an organization could not do justice.

From the point of view of the prefects in the provinces of Lombardy-Veneto, the considerable time required for processing passport requests, their brief term of validity, and the need for voluminous documentation of reasons for travel led to insurmountable complications in the administration of the passport regulations. The victims of the convoluted procedures for issuing passports were above all the businesspeople who counted on a timely processing of their requests, and destitute workers who were compelled to leave the country in search of work and who were not in a position to bear the costs of a regular passport and the attendant documentation. For the prefects and, later, the delegates, there was only one way to put an end to a flow of travelers that had gotten out of control and to the corresponding stream of complaints: the restoration of the authority of the prefects, so that the future delegates and their subordinates could issue all of the many varieties of travel documents.

When the prefects' findings were communicated to Vienna they did not yield any change in the official competencies regarding the issuance of passports in the *Kronland* of Veneto, but in May the governors of Lombardy and Veneto were given the authority to issue external passports with a validity of up to one year, as long as they furnished quarterly inventories of the passports they had distributed. The emperor nonetheless retained the authority to grant all passport requests for non-urgent travel on the part of state officials and nobles, for "luxury trips," for passports with a validity of more than one year, and finally for passports concerning the issue of which the governor and the chief of the police headquarters had had divergent views.[39]

The distinction that was thus drawn between necessary and unnecessary travel, and the clear aim of "facilitating" the former did not mollify the ill temper of the populace of Lombardy-Veneto with regard to the

---

[38] See Meriggi 1987: 85. On the inefficiency in all branches of the government of the Habsburg monarchy, see also Beidtel 1968: 61–65 and 349–52.

[39] See Franz von Haager to Goëss, August 17, 1816, ASV, Presidio di Governo (1815–19), box 49.

passport regulations, however. Traveling in the Italian provinces, even Prince von Metternich could not ignore the "bad impression" caused by the passport restrictions, which seemed to him ill-suited to the extravagant sociability of the Venetians and their pronounced disposition toward pleasure excursions. As the result of his desire to take greater account "of the national customs and habits of the Italian provinces,"[40] the Lombard and Venetian governors were also conceded the authority to issue all passports for non-imperial Italy, including to nobles and state officials.

Until the end of the 1820s, the governors of the Kingdom of Lombardy-Veneto were inclined to maintain the passport system that had developed in these areas, even in contravention of the directives from Vienna, in order not to inhibit the well-developed flows of traders and travelers. Later attempts to make the passport system conform to the norms outlined in Vienna remained without effect during the entire *Vormärz*, because they collided head-on with the need for free circulation generated by the economy and by the populace itself. The complete abolition of the peculiarities of the Lombardy-Veneto passport system would not take place until after the bourgeois revolution of 1848, in the course of the thorough, neo-absolutist reorganization of the state administration. This process expressed itself in the rationalization of the administrative apparatus and introduced into the Austrian imperial state structures that increasingly approximated those of a modern state. During the last decade of its existence, the Kingdom of Lombardy-Veneto was integrated into the state structure of the empire as never before,[41] and a number of enduring effects of this process of integration on the everyday life of the populace can be seen in the development of the passport system.

The Reform of the Passport System

The Austrian reconquest of Lombardy-Veneto was completed with the takeover of Venice on August 22, 1849. In contrast to the governments in the other *Kronländer*, those in the southern provinces now were accountable not only to the Interior Ministry in Vienna, but also to a military and civil-general government under the direction of Field Marshall Radetzky in Verona. In addition, in the aftermath of the military reconquest, a state of emergency had been declared throughout the entire kingdom. For reasons of state security, until the abolition of the state of emergency in 1854, the passport system as well as other important elements of the administration were placed under the control of the military

---

[40] Ibid., Franz von Haager to Goëss, July 2, 1817.
[41] See Mazohl-Wallnig 1981: 14.

governors newly installed in each of the *Kronländer*. This situation initially hindered the full integration of the southern provinces into the larger process of unifying the passport regulations—a process that had had its start with the introduction of the *Heimatschein* (a municipal document that certifies membership in a municipality) throughout the empire. The *Heimatschein* had been introduced in the other *Kronländer* as a result of the provisional law on municipalities (*Gemeindegesetz*) of 1849. The document was to be issued by the magistrates of the municipality or the municipal authorities, and corresponded in its function as a document establishing the identity and municipal membership of its bearer, to the *carta d'iscrizione* of Lombardy-Veneto, which henceforth was referred to in all German-language texts as the *Heimatschein*.[42] With an April 1850 circular from the Interior Ministry, the *carta d'iscrizione* was accorded the status of a document valid for domestic travel,[43] and thus it was taken over throughout the monarchy as the fundamental document for purposes of identification and travel. The *Heimatschein*, however, was granted a period and range of validity that at first was denied to the *carta d'iscrizione* because of the state of emergency in Lombardy-Veneto, and which also was not widened after that state of emergency came to an end. The *Heimatschein* gave its bearer the right to travel in the territory of an entire *Kronland* and could be used throughout the territory of the monarchy, assuming it had been properly stamped by the political authorities. The range of validity of the *carta d'iscrizione* of Lombardy-Veneto was restricted, however, to the individual *Kronland* itself, and from the point of view of Lombardy this represented no advance at all.

The truly revolutionary aspect of this travel document, now instituted throughout the monarchy—namely, the potential elimination of internal borders with respect to personal travel, at least at the administrative level—thus had no impact whatsoever in Lombardy-Veneto. Yet in view of the steady increase and acceleration of long-distance travel, even the complete elimination of provincial borders for purposes of personal travel constituted an important (and, indeed, urgently needed) advance in the

[42] The law on municipalities never took effect in the Kingdom of Lombardy-Veneto. While in Lombardy-Veneto the place of residence (*Wohnsitz*) remained the fundamental principle of spatial order that determined an individual's place of membership, in the other Austrian principalities the law on municipalities inaugurated the *Heimatrecht* (the right to be a member of a municipality) as the fundamental category of spatial order. Persons had the *Heimatrecht* in a particular municipality either on the basis of their birth—that is, because their parents already had that right; in virtue of at least forty years of uninterrupted residence; or on the basis of an official act of the municipality. See Goldemund et al. 1969: 587–91.

[43] See Radetzky to the governor of Veneto, May 3, 1850, ASV, I.R. Presidenza della Luogotenenza (1849–51) box 15, I12/2–4909.

Kingdom of Lombardy-Veneto. This becomes especially clear when one considers that, during the first six months of its operation, some 140,000 people rode on the inaugural stretch of the Lombardy-Veneto railway, which opened between Marghera and Padua in December 1842.[44] The further extension of the railroad quickly reached the borders of the *Kronland* of Veneto, and thus the *carta d'iscrizione* ran up against the limits of its range of validity. This state of affairs first developed in 1851 with the opening of the rail connection between the city of Verona in Veneto and the Lombard city of Mantua. In order to ensure smooth passage along this stretch, the range of validity of the Venetian *carta d'iscrizione* was extended to include the city of Mantua, and that of Mantua was now valid for the entire *Kronland* of Veneto. Yet even the police authorities understood clearly that this arrangement could not comprise a long-term solution to the problem, and they therefore urged the government to extend the range of validity of the *carta d'iscrizione* at least to the entire Kingdom of Lombardy-Veneto. The time-consuming procedures for inspecting and affixing visas to passports were already far out of step with the precisely calculated train schedules and the rapid movement of people now made possible by trains and steamboats, and this led to increasingly severe hindrances for travelers.

As in the other countries of Europe, the technological miracle of rail travel impelled a "fundamental engagement with the problem of physical mobility" in the Austrian empire,[45] from which the passport system could hardly be excluded. In July 1855, the Supreme Police Authority in Vienna informed the governors of Lombardy-Veneto that a thoroughgoing reform of domestic travel regulations was being undertaken, with the aim of limiting the police controls on travel documents to the moment of entry and exit at the "external" border, along with a stricter implementation of the population registration systems (*Meldewesen*). For this purpose, there already existed old regulations that not only obliged travelers to report their temporary stay in a particular place to the local police authorities, but also required the residents to report the presence of their out-of-town guests—requirements of which the residents were to be reminded via circulars and advertisements. Beyond these regulations, there also now existed in Lombardy-Veneto the instrument of the continuous residential register. Even to the police officials of Lombardy-Veneto, these tools of population registration seemed adequate to the challenge of controlling those traveling in the country.

[44] See Bernardello 1996: 392.
[45] Pankoke 1970: 23.

In keeping with the passport ordinance of February 15, 1857, and the parallel ordinance on population registration,[46] the *Legitimationskarte* was instituted as a new travel and identification document. It was valid for a year and gave all inhabitants of the Austrian Empire the right to travel without police control throughout the territory of the empire. This reform of the passport system represented not only a consolidation of the imperial state that could be experienced by each and every inhabitant. In addition, the former subjects, who had hitherto been regarded as potential opponents of the state, were now recognized as responsible, independent citizens who were also co-participants in securing the state from dangers. If Domenica Saba had decided to take her trip to Verona—or indeed to any place within the monarchy—thirty-five years later, all she would have had to do was board the train and go.

[46] "Verordnung der Ministerien des Äusseren, des Innern und des Handels, der obersten Polizeibehörde und des Armee-Ober-Commando," February 15, 1857, pursuant to which new passport regulations were promulgated; *Bollettino ufficiale delle leggi e degli atti ufficiali per il Veneto* (1857) Abteilung 1, Stück II: 45–51; and, on population registration, "Verordnung des Ministeriums des Innern und der Obersten Polizeibehörde," February 15, 1857, ibid.: 51–55.

12

Governments and Forgers: Passports in Nineteenth-Century Europe

ANDREAS FAHRMEIR

WHEN A PERSON comes in contact with others who do not recognize him, he may have to establish his identity. The most obvious way of doing so is simply to state his name, together with additional information, such as occupation, age, or place of residence, which distinguishes him from others also called, say, "John Smith." However, because there are many circumstances in which individuals wish to hide their true identity, evidence to back up their assertions is usually required. What is considered conclusive evidence of identity is indicative of the way in which societies are organized, how they define individual identity, and to which institutions they entrust the business of certifying it. In most parts of the world today, individuals are expected to produce official identity documents issued by a government agency. Even in countries where citizens are not required to possess official ID, government-issued documents—passports—must be presented upon entering the country.

The fact that passports are issued by governments, not least in order to document their bearers' nationality, indicates the immense importance of citizenship in a world of nation-states. In medieval and early modern Europe, by contrast, national borders were of less significance than today, whereas the importance of social rank—of membership in one of the various orders (*Stände*) of society—was greater. Corporations of various sorts, rather than powerful centralized states, were responsible for establishing the identity of their members, in a domestic context as well as abroad. Journeymen received passes (known as *Kundschaften* in the German-speaking world) from the guilds of which they were members, and localities certified that individuals were freemen, burgesses, or residents. People could also identify themselves by displaying specialized knowledge which proved their initiation into the "mysteries" of a trade or profession, or which demonstrated their membership in a community. In the case of Arnaud du Thil, who assumed the identity of one Martin Guerre in the French village of Artigat in 1556, living there with Guerre's wife for several years before being discovered, tried, and executed, there is no reference to forged identity papers that du Thil presented to a local constable. It was accepted that he was Martin Guerre because he knew stories that only Guerre himself could be expected to know.[1]

Of course, documents called "passports" existed in early modern Europe, but relatively few people used them.[2] The modern compulsory identity documents for all (international) travelers with which we are familiar are intimately connected to the concept of distinct nation-states inhabited by subjects or citizens equal before the law and distinguished only by wealth, not rank, which developed in the more radical eighteenth-century absolutist states. This idea achieved its first breakthrough in revolutionary France, where the first modern passport regulations, which obliged all travelers to carry state-issued official identity documents with them at all times, were introduced in 1792. The motives for this were mainly political. Identity papers and restrictions on travel were supposed to prevent the assembly of discontented persons at strategic locations and the infiltration of the country by the agents of hostile foreign governments, as well as to help suppress vagrancy, banditry, and crime.[3] Compulsory passports and identity cards for travelers were introduced for similar reasons in other European states during the revolutionary and Napoleonic wars.[4] While passports were retained in continental Europe after the return of peace so that governments could continue their surveillance of migrants (not least in order to prevent the immigration of unemployed foreign laborers), the requirement to have a passport to enter or travel in Britain, where immigration restrictions had remained controversial ever since their introduction in 1793, was abolished in 1826.[5]

On the Continent, passports and identity cards fulfilled several functions after 1815. First, they were certificates of identity. As the 1817 Prussian *Passinstruktion* put it, they were "to provide the blameless and honest traveler, who is unknown in the area to which he comes, with a simple [. . .] means of providing the legally required proof that he is who he pretends to be."[6]

---

[1] On *Kundschaften* and journeymen's rituals, see Ehmer 1997: 172–99, esp. 188–94; Davis 1983: 42ff.

[2] Sée 1907: 18; Faron 1997: 60.

[3] Torpey 1997: 844–47; Noiriel 1991a: 35f.

[4] For the case of the northern Italian states of the Habsburg Empire during this period, see Geselle in this volume.

[5] For general histories of passports, see Bertelsmann 1914 and Sée 1907; John Torpey's recent contributions listed in the bibliography, Noiriel 1998, and Fahrmeir 2000: ch. 3.

[6] "Pässe sollen [. . .] dem unbescholtenen und redlichen, aber in der Gegend, wohin er kommt, unbekannten Reisenden ein einfaches Mittel gewähren, den ihm gesetzlich obliegenden Nachweis, dass er derjenige, wofür er sich ausgibt, sei, auf die kürzeste [. . .] Art zu führen," *Gesetz-Sammlung für die Königlich Preussischen Staaten* (1817), printed in Rauer

Second, they allowed state officials to distinguish citizens from foreigners at a glance and therefore facilitated the imposition of legislation specifically directed at aliens.

Third, passports were a means of controlling travel, and for taxing it through the imposition of fees for passports and some types of visas. Until the 1850s or 1860s, depending on the country, travelers had to obtain visas to cross international frontiers, and most states obliged travelers to present passports or identity cards to the police at regular intervals, or at the very least to enter passport details into a residence book at every inn. This allowed the police to monitor the movements of travelers closely, and to assign particular routes to them if necessary.

Fourth, passports could be used for clandestine communication between police officials; coded entries on passports could convey information about travelers' political views.

In order for passports to fulfill these different purposes, they had to be reliable. The information that was initially entered in them had to be correct; once they were issued, they had to be linked to their bearer in such a way as to prevent others from using them; and it had to be difficult to counterfeit or manipulate them.

Yet the format of these modern travel documents evolved only slowly from the early modern "passports" that had preceded them, which had had different purposes. Early modern passports were semi-formalized letters of recommendation used mainly by three groups of travelers: persons on official business; travelers from the upper ranks of society, who wished to receive preferential treatment; and paupers who needed protection against arrest and punishment as vagrants.

These documents had not required many security features, particularly when used within comparatively small networks of diplomats, officials, or professionals. They did not usually contain a description of their bearer. To be sure, a passport issued to the Venetian adventurer Giacomo Casanova in 1758 by the Dutch ambassador in Paris asked all "admirals, generals, governors, [and] commanders" to allow Casanova to pass freely to the Netherlands by land or by sea for fifteen days, thus merely permitting entry into a country during wartime, not conferring special status; but this was the exception rather than the rule. Casanova's account of travel in eighteenth-century Europe is mainly concerned with such documents because they "made people respect you" (*faisaient respecter*), not because they were necessary to cross borders.[7] Travelers were required to have passports only in times of political crisis or epidemics.

1844: 1, which is a useful summary of the passport regulations of Prussia and other states from which much of the information in the following paragraphs is derived.

[7] Casanova de Seingalt 1993: vol. 2, appendix (passport), 67 (*faisaient respecter*), and *passim.*

Even though they changed their function in the decades around 1800, passports at first retained a formula in which the issuer recommends the bearer to foreign authorities, sometimes personally rather than in his official capacity. (In many countries, for example, the Netherlands, Ukraine, the United Kingdom, and the United States, a similar formula is still inserted into travel documents today, even though it is sometimes all but hidden on the inside front or back cover.) An 1853 British passport read as follows:

> We, George William Frederick Earl of Clarendon, Baron Hyde of Hindon, a Peer of the United Kingdom of Great Britain and Ireland, a Member of Her Britannic Majesty's Most Honourable Privy Council, Knight of the Most Noble Order of the Garter, and Knight Grand Cross of the Most Honourable Order of the Bath, Her Majesty's Principal Secretary of State for Foreign Affairs & c. &c. &c. Request and require in the Name of Her Majesty, all those whom it may concern, to allow [N. N., a British subject/naturalized British subject] to pass freely without let or hindrance, and to afford [N. N.] every assistance and protection of which [N. N.] may stand in need.[8]

The name of the foreign secretary is no longer mentioned in present-day British passports, and even in the nineteenth century it was among the more unusual features of British travel documents that they mirrored every change of government. Other states' passports were issued in the name of the reigning monarch, referred to by title, and requested assistance for the bearer with somewhat less confidence. In a passport issued in 1853 "In the Name of His Royal Highness the Grand Duke of Hesse and by Rhine &c. &c.," the grand-ducal *Kreisamt* merely requested assistance for the traveler "under the promise of complete reciprocity."[9] The formula of recommendation was abandoned altogether when the North German Federation began to issue passports in 1866, and has not to my knowledge ever reappeared in German passports.[10]

But contrary to what the passports' texts suggested, identity documents were issued by officials who had most likely never met the persons they were recommending. Hence the first problem in the passport-issuing process was: how could one be sure that the applicant for a passport was who he or she claimed to be? Travelers were usually required to possess passports (or other identity documents) only if they left the vicinity of their permanent place of residence. The short period of validity—one

---

[8] Public Record Office London (henceforth: PRO) HO 45/6225/1.

[9] "unter dem Versprechen vollkommener Erwiederung": Hesse-Darmstadt passport issued by Kreisamt Schotten, Hessisches Staatsarchiv Darmstadt (henceforth: StADa) G 15 Schotten Q 146.

[10] StADa G 15 Alsfeld G 92, blank Hesse-Darmstadt passport, printed between 1867 and 1870.

officials verifying identities

journey or a maximum of one year—as well as the relatively high cost of travel documents for people who were not granted exemption from fees[11] probably saw to it that many, if not most, applications for passports were for new documents, not for renewals. It would perhaps have been best to assign the duty of issuing passports to local officials, because they would have been able to verify the applicants' identities most easily, particularly in smaller villages where they knew many of the inhabitants personally. However, several considerations made this appear inadvisable. Members of the higher ranks of the bureaucracy were skeptical as to the abilities of their subordinates. Around 1800, French occupation forces in western Germany had considered the incompetence of local officials one of the factors that made it so difficult to wipe out banditry. Moreover, distributing blank passport forms to many local administrative offices would have increased the likelihood of theft. Therefore, in German states only officials from the district (*Kreis*) level upwards were allowed to issue such documents from the beginning of the nineteenth century on.[12]

conduct

But local officials were responsible for identifying applicants, to whom they issued a provisional document allowing its bearer to travel to the issuing office to apply for a passport there. In 1820s Hesse-Darmstadt, for instance, such *Erlaubnis-Scheine*, valid for two days, stated that the bearer had conducted himself or herself in an orderly fashion and could therefore be granted a passport to his or her destination. This document was printed on normal paper without a coat of arms, and had to be signed and sealed by the issuing officer. On the lefthand side, it contained space for the so-called *signalement*, a physical description of the applicant which, in the absence of fingerprints or photographs, was intended to make it impossible for him or her to pass the provisional document, or indeed the passport, on to someone else. The applicant's signature, which was required on the passport, was not included in the application form, not even in 1866, when surely most Hesse-Darmstadt citizens were literate (see Illustration 1). This is all the more surprising, as asking persons to reproduce the signature on their passport was apparently one of the most reliable methods available to the police for establishing whether the passports they presented actually belonged to them.[13]

In addition to information on name, "estate" (*Stand*), place of birth, place of residence and age, the *signalement* described height, "hair color, brow, color of the eyebrows, of the eyes, nose, mouth, beard, shape of

---

[11] Rauer 1844: esp. 133; Sée 1907: 85; memorandum dated May 16, 1831, PRO FO 612/3.

[12] Gebhardt 1992: 153; Wirsing 1991: 52; Küther 1987: 134.

[13] *Erlaubnis-Schein*, StADa G 15 Alsfeld Q 92. A *Passbericht*-form printed in the 1850s, but still in use in 1866, which was quite similar, can be found in StADa G 15 Schotten Q 70; Stärkle 1921: 69.

physical description

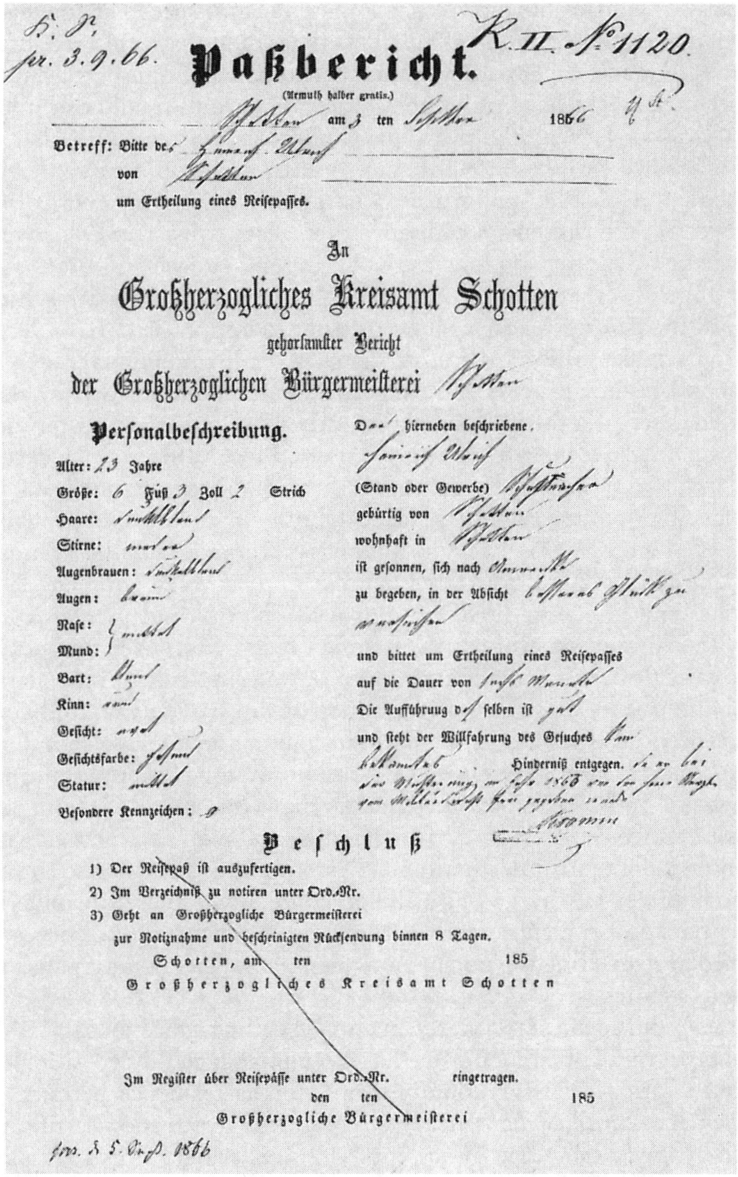

pr. 3.9.66. **Paßbericht.** K. II. № 1120.

(Armuth halber gratis.)

am 3 ten 1866

Betreff: Bitte des

von

um Ertheilung eines Reisepasses.

An

Großherzogliches Kreisamt Schotten

gehorsamster Bericht

der Großherzoglichen Bürgermeisterei

Personalbeschreibung.

Alter: 23 Jahre

Größe: 6 Fuß 3 Zoll 2 Strich

Haare:

Stirne:

Augenbrauen:

Augen:

Nase:

Mund:

Bart:

Kinn:

Gesicht:

Gesichtsfarbe:

Statur:

Besondere Kennzeichen:

Der hierneben beschriebene

(Stand oder Gewerbe)

gebürtig von

wohnhaft in

ist gesonnen, sich nach

zu begeben, in der Absicht

und bittet um Ertheilung eines Reisepasses

auf die Dauer von

Die Aufführung desselben ist gut

und steht der Willfahrung des Gesuches

Hinderniß entgegen.

Beschluß

1) Der Reisepaß ist auszufertigen.

2) Im Verzeichniß zu notiren unter Ord.-Nr.

3) Geht an Großherzogliche Bürgermeisterei zur Notiznahme und bescheinigten Rücksendung binnen 8 Tagen.

Schotten, am ten 185

Großherzogliches Kreisamt Schotten

Im Register über Reisepässe unter Ord.-Nr. eingetragen.

den ten 185

Großherzogliche Bürgermeisterei

Illustration 1: Hesse-Darmstadt passport application (*Passbericht*), 1866 (Hessisches Staatsarchiv Darmstadt, G 15 Schotten Q 146)

the chin, shape of the face, skin complexion, and special characteristics."
Such descriptions contained few facts that could not be altered, or which
meant the same thing to all persons. One officer's "round" face and "normal" nose might be another one's normal face and small nose, and what
exactly was a "healthy" or a "pale" complexion anyway? What would
have seemed healthy enough for a professional would surely have been
described as deathly pallor if encountered in a rural laborer. Moreover,
hair color, the presence or absence of a beard, and skin color were not
permanent features. As long as the height and age were not too far off, a
determined forger stood a reasonable chance of adapting himself or herself to the description in a found or stolen passport.

Some police officers therefore considered this preliminary step of the
passport-issuing process as the most vulnerable to forgery. They also suggested that blank forms were relatively easy to come by, at least in German
states, either by theft from poorly guarded local offices or by deception.
All that had to be done once a blank form had been obtained was to add
a plausible-looking signature and seal, both of which would probably not
be examined very closely by the busy passport sections of the *Kreisämter*.[14]

A number of factors reduced the importance of this problem. Theft of
forms could be prevented by improved security and greater attention
to the seal and signature at the issuing offices. Moreover, passports that
had already been filled out and were lost by or stolen from travelers were
of limited value to others, even if they fit the *signalement* and could, if
necessary, produce a convincing imitation of the owner's signature, for
two reasons. First, passports were valid only for a limited time, and re-
newing a "false" passport involved a renewed risk of detection. Second,
passports were visaed at certain intervals, and might well contain a mention of the intended destination. They were thus only of use to persons
who intended to travel along a similar route. It was therefore understandable that governments' main efforts to prevent fraud and forgery were
aimed at protecting the documents themselves against manipulation and
counterfeiting.

When European states readjusted to peacetime conditions in 1815, several types of identity documents had been introduced. There were various
identity cards used for domestic travel or as residence permits, called
cartes de securité, *Sicherheitskarten*, or aliens' registration certificates (issued by the British Alien Office until 1826). Special identity cards, known
as *Aufenthaltskarten*, were required in some Prussian towns as proof of
legal entry and residence, and similar cards were compulsory in Frank-
furt-on-Main for the duration of the local trade fair from 1834. All these

---

[14] Pfeiffer 1828: 21f.; Pfister 1812: 203f.; Innenministerium circular, December 14, 1832,
StADa G 15 Alsfeld Q 92.

[handwritten margin note: limited value of stolen passport]

anti-forgery updates

documents were relatively unpretentious. *Sicherheitskarten* issued by the Duchy of Nassau, for instance, were smallish (about 21 cm x 15 cm) documents with a simple design, containing only the printed text, manuscript entries, and a plain frame around the document.[15] Passports, which could be used for domestic or international travel, were considerably larger (about 30 cm x 21 cm). Their design depended to some extent on the issuing office, which could be a district office, the Foreign or Interior Ministry, or any department in between. *Wanderbücher* or *livrets d'ouvrier* were passports for traveling journeymen or laborers. As their names indicate, they were small booklets, roughly the size of a modern passport, into which the routes and employment record of journeymen were entered by the authorities and the bearers' employers.[16] German states also issued so-called *Heimatscheine*, which were certificates of nationality and residence rights analogous to settlement certificates issued under the British poor law. While such *Heimatscheine* could be used as identity documents for domestic travel, for international travel they usually had to be supplemented by a proper passport.[17]

Government efforts to prevent fraud in the nineteenth century concentrated on the design of passport forms, thus starting a technological race between forgers and governments that continues unabated to the present day. In the first decades of the nineteenth century, the Duchy of Nassau's passports, for instance, had been printed in plain text on normal paper and surrounded by a simple black border (see Illustration 2).[18] They look as though they could have been reproduced by any typesetter using a standard printing press. After 1815, an engraved coat of arms was added at the top center of the page and the black border was replaced with a more intricate pattern, thus requiring the cooperation of an engraver for possible counterfeiting.[19] While the graphic design of the passports, particularly the engravings, became slightly more sophisticated in the 1830s and 1840s, the next major step forward occurred in the 1850s, when many countries began to experiment with "security paper."[20]

Security paper was designed to meet two objectives. First, it was to help prevent the reprinting of passport forms by using sophisticated printing

[15] Rauer 1844: 118–21; *Protokolle der deutschen Bundesversammlung* (1834): 266; *Sicherheitskarte* in HStAWi 229/556; 33 Geo. III, c. 4; 35 Geo. III, c. 24; 36 Geo. III, c. 109 (descriptions of registration tickets).

[16] Bekers 1975: 27–64 and illustrations; Grandjonc 1975: 43f.; *Wanderbuch* in HStAWi 229/556.

[17] See, e.g., *Archiv der Grossherzoglich Hessischen Gesetze und Verordnungen* 1834–39: vol. I: 272f., 280f., 387.

[18] See HStAWi 210/774 and HStAWi 229/556.

[19] HStAWi 229/556.

[20] Avé-Lallement 1858–62: 235.

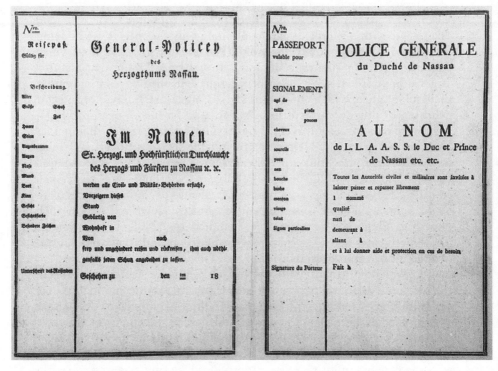

Illustration 2: Duchy of Nassau passport, c. 1810 (Hessisches Hauptstaatsarchiv Wiebaden, Abt. 210, Nr. 774)

techniques. The background of the forms was now covered by some intricate pattern in light colors. In Prussian passports, for instance, the words *Königreich Preussen* appeared throughout the background; Austrian passports used a pattern of light blue lines that produced the appearance of a three-dimensional Austrian coat of arms (see Illustration 3).[21] While these documents can be reproduced by photography or the most advanced xerox machines, their security features still baffle standard photocopiers today. This method of making documents forger-proof was not improved upon in principle until the recent introduction of holograms; the first machines that seriously challenged it, laser color copiers, have appeared on the market only in the past few years. Second, to prevent the manipulation of passports, special types of ink were used that changed color if attempts were made to erase the text. In this respect, nineteenth-century experiments appear to have been far less successful. The first type of Prussian

[21] HStAWi 317/934; Knaack 1960: appendix.

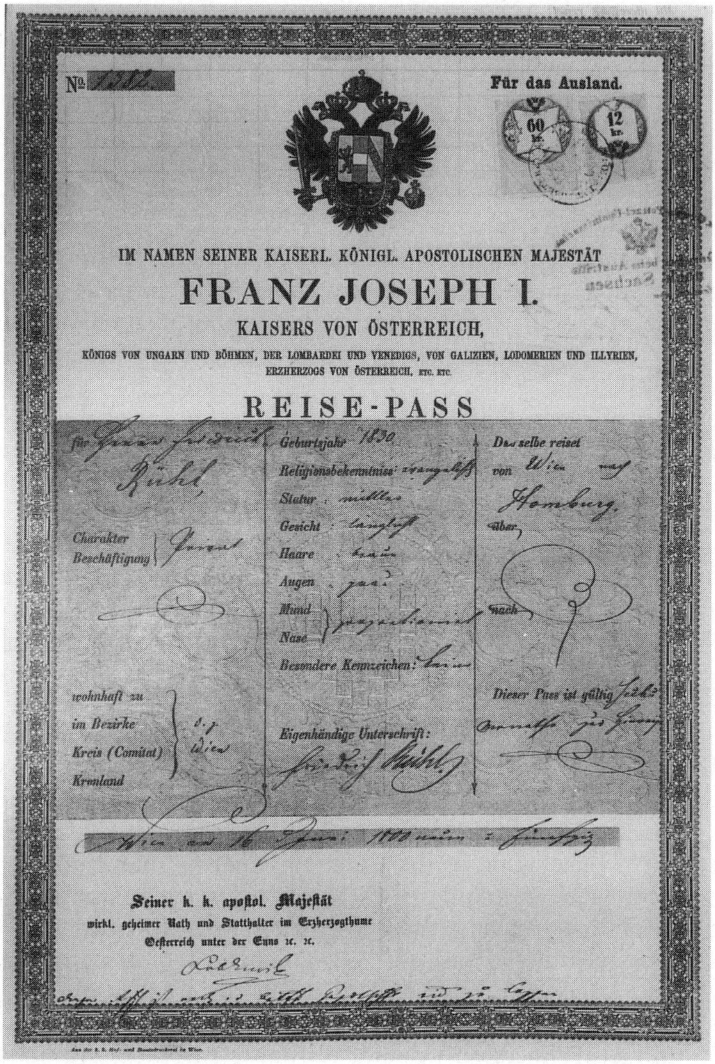
Für das Ausland.

IM NAMEN SEINER KAISERL. KÖNIGL. APOSTOLISCHEN MAJESTÄT

FRANZ JOSEPH I.

KAISERS VON ÖSTERREICH,

KÖNIGS VON UNGARN UND BÖHMEN, DER LOMBARDEI UND VENEDIGS, VON GALIZIEN, LODOMERIEN UND ILLYRIEN, ERZHERZOGS VON ÖSTERREICH, ETC. ETC.

REISE-PASS

für

Charakter
Beschäftigung

wohnhaft zu
im Bezirke
Kreis (Comitat)
Kronland

Geburtsjahr 1830
Religionsbekenntniss:
Statur:
Gesicht:
Haare:
Augen:
Mund
Nase
Besondere Kennzeichen:

Eigenhändige Unterschrift:

Dasselbe reiset
von
über
nach

Dieser Pass ist gültig

Seiner k. k. apostol. Majestät
wirkl. geheimer Rath und Statthalter im Erzherzogthume
Oesterreich unter der Enns ꝛc. ꝛc.

Illustration 3: Austrian passport on security paper, issued 1859
(Hessisches Hauptstaatsarchiv Wiesbaden, Abt. 317, Nr. 934)

security paper was so sturdy that the text written on the forms in manu-script could be removed with bleach without altering the background, so that every passport was a potential blank passport form.[22]

The usefulness of seals was controversial. While a well-made three-dimensional seal could provide additional security (just as holograms do today), whatever is attached to a form can also be removed from one and placed on another. If the replacement is done skillfully, there is only a slight difference between original and forgery, so that the presence of such security features can produce a misleading impression of authenticity. In 1836, the government of the Electorate of Hesse-Kassel thus or-dered its officials to use stamps, not seals.[23] Later in the century, the police officer Friedrich Christian Benedict Avé-Lallement countered that stamps had problems as well. Frequently made from poor material and applied carelessly, their impression was so unclear that it could be counterfeited with ease.[24]

However, all the technical improvements did not resolve an inherent problem of the nineteenth-century passport system: its explicit or implicit focus on social status, which was not always compatible with protection against forgery. Passports sometimes stated the position of their bearers in society explicitly by naming their occupations, and always implicitly by the form of the document itself. Nineteenth-century officials were very concerned not to infringe upon the dignity of middle- and upper-class travelers by obliging them to be described in a *signalement*, because *sig-nalements* were considered offensive. As foreign secretary, Viscount Palm-erston headed the most exclusive passport-issuing agency in the nine-teenth century, the British Foreign Office's Passport Office, for much of the period discussed here: until 1858, British Foreign Office passports were only issued to the friends and acquaintances of the foreign secretary, or to persons recommended by a London banker.[25] In 1852, Palmerston made it clear once again in the Commons that he found unacceptable "those picturesque descriptions which some foreign passports contain, being a definition of the particular features which the individual who bears the passport may boast of."[26] His adamant refusal to countenance *signalements* on British passports had already led to great difficulties for British travelers with Foreign Office passports at the Belgian frontier in 1835.[27] In fact, Palmerston's valiant resistance was more symbolic than

---

[22] See Beck and Schmidt 1993: 504, 628.

[23] *Sammlung von Gesetzen, Verordnungen, Ausschreiben und sonstigen allgemeinen Ver-fügungen für die kurhessischen Staaten* 1836: 77f.

[24] Avé-Lallement 1858–62: 135.

[25] PRO 612/1ff., *passim* (Passport Office files), Passport Office regulations.

[26] *Hansard* 1852: col. 514.

[27] Ridley 1970: 362.

effective: most countries added a *signalement* to the visas they issued to British travelers, and passports issued by British ambassadors actually contained a *signalement*.[28] However, even Prussia exempted travelers of the "higher orders" (*aus den höheren Ständen*) from the obligation to have the size of their noses classified by subordinate officials. Prussian passports for "reliable" members of the upper classes were issued without a *signalement*, and this automatically exempted their bearers from visa requirements in Prussia.[29] If such a passport was lost or stolen, it was of course much more useful than a "normal" passport: it contained no physical description of its bearer and no indication of the past or future route. The officials in charge of the passport system may have assumed that the criminals or "revolutionaries" whose travel they wished to supervise would not be able to pass themselves off as respectable citizens, but this was surely questionable.

Social distinctions made themselves felt in other ways as well. Until 1866, when the North-German Federation's passports were issued as booklets, only *Wanderbücher* for journeymen and laborers contained pre-numbered sheets bound together, while passports were issued as single sheets. Visas were usually stamped on the back. If the passport was full, either the bearer or an official had to add additional blank pages. Orders to quit a country or to adhere to a certain route or timetable could thus be made to disappear with relative ease, provided they were not written on the back of the passport itself. In the case of British passports, the paper used was so fragile that it was customary to have it mounted on some more durable material and bound together with a number of blank pages for visas. London travel agencies offered passport-procuring and -binding services. As most British travelers did not travel on British passports, but preferred to obtain cheaper passports from consulates or vice consulates of foreign states, primarily France, which could be exchanged free of charge for British passports at British consulates or embassies abroad, this demonstrates that the practice was common in other countries as well.[30]

The bearers' autonomy in determining the final shape of the travel documents issued to them presented them with opportunities to hide manipulations. In the late 1850s, when security paper was not yet in use everywhere, officers were advised to check passports for unauthorized erasures by holding them up to the light, because the paper was thinner where writing had

---

[28] PRO FO 612/4.

[29] Rauer 1844: 6, 9, 11, 118.

[30] Advertisement from Bradshaw's Continental Guide Office, May 1855, PRO FO 612/11. On the use of foreign passports by British travelers, see chief clerk's report on passports issued, May 17, 1837, PRO FO 612/3; [Murray] 1843: xixf.; [Murray] 1850: xixf.; [Murray] 1854: xviii.

easier to fraudulently use passport of a "respectable" citizen

been removed and replaced. If the forger had pasted a thin piece of paper over the spot in order to conceal it, this could be discovered by moistening the passport and dissolving the glue.[31] But pasting the passport as a whole on cloth or cardboard effectively hid this sort of manipulation.

The control exercised over their documents by persons who obtained regular passports, rather than *livrets d'ouvrier* or *Wanderbücher*, could therefore increase the possibilities for fraud. The nineteenth-century passport system thus made fraud and manipulation, if not outright counterfeiting, much easier if it involved documents issued to "respectable" citizens rather than those used by travelers from the lower classes. Passports for the "respectable" had no *signalement*, did not contain as detailed a record of the bearers' journey as "lower-class" passports did, and exempted their bearers from the frequent contact with police officers that the visa regulations of many states prescribed, at least in theory. It would be interesting to explore whether this fact contributed to the prominence of impostors in the nineteenth century. In his recent book on the German underworld, Richard J. Evans has selected one of them, a certain Franz Ernst, as a representative of one of the half-dozen types of criminal behavior and state sanctions he deals with.[32] Whether Evans' choice of Ernst the impostor accurately reflects the importance of the phenomenon in nineteenth-century Germany or Europe remains to be seen (although Thomas Mann's *Felix Krull* suggests he would have agreed), but one can speculate as to why this might have been the case. By introducing official identity documents, which also contained information on the bearers' social position, state governments turned themselves into guardians of individual personal and social identity. Passports and other identity documents became a proof of identity that would not usually be questioned, but which determined people could manipulate with relative ease.

It was in this sense that passports, as the Frankfurt *Polizeiassessor* George Wilhelm Pfeiffer wrote as early as 1828, "are burdens for honest men, but means of security for scoundrels."[33] From the late 1850s on, the vulnerability of the passport system to abuse may have increased. Even though passports became increasingly difficult to reproduce, the extension of their validity, combined with the likelihood that the bearer's physical appearance would change with time, made the link between passport and bearer even more tenuous, as long as the bearer could produce a reasonably convincing copy of the signature on the passport—or had the increasingly exceptional good luck to come across a passport issued to an illiterate person. While the passport system was reasonably effective in

[31] Avé-Lallement 1858–62: 232–35.
[32] Evans 1998: 136–65.
[33] "dass ein Pass für den rechtlichen Mann eine Plage, für den Spitzbuben aber ein Sicherheitsmittel ist," Pfeiffer 1828: 21.

controlling migratory movements as a whole and in tracing illegal immigrants when this was desired by all levels of a state's administration,[34] it was much less so when it came to documenting individual identity in specific cases. Whether the introduction of photographs at a later date did much to change this is an open question, because photographs on passports were probably not much more difficult to replace than seals.

How easy it was in practice to exploit the various weaknesses of the passport system, and whether forgeries and manipulations of one sort or another were really widespread, is of course impossible to tell with any degree of precision. Most information about forgeries is contained in police records. The police obviously only knew about cases that were discovered, and thus only made the acquaintance of unsuccessful forgers and possibly underestimated the incidence of counterfeiting. Moreover, there are constraints on police reporting. Individual officials who had unintentionally aided forgers in some way—by leaving blank passport forms lying about in their offices or by visaing false passports, for instance—were probably not keen to advertise the fact to their superiors. Warnings about false passports in circulation or instructions on how to detect forgeries could aid would-be forgers in improving their products.

Nonetheless, a few things can be deduced from the available evidence. Examples from German states suggest that some persons who went to the trouble to reprint or manipulate passports were almost incredibly careless, stupid, or reckless. In 1851, police were informed that counterfeit Hesse-Darmstadt *Wanderbücher* were in circulation, easily recognizable by the number of misprints in the text.[35] In a copy of a seal of the Bavarian district of Lower Franconia, the arrangement of text and coat of arms was different from the original; someone had copied the seal of the Hanau police without noticing that it used the archaic spelling *Policei* rather than the modern *Polizei*.[36] To be sure, in a number of other cases the difference between original and forgery was due to recent changes in stamps or forms of which forgers could not have been aware, for example, when the official name of the Waldeck capital changed from Arholzen to Arolsen in 1835.[37]

However, the existence of such documents almost begging to be discovered suggests that at least some members of the "underworld" of passport forgers believed that documents would not be subjected to close examina-

[34] On the effectiveness of the passport system as a means of migration control, cf. Fahrmeir 2000: ch. 3.

[35] Regierung Fulda circular, June 17, 1851, StAMa, 100/5466.

[36] Regierung Fulda circular, May 14, 1851, StAMa, 100/5466; Landesregierung circular, January 30, 1821, HStAWi, 211/16210, fol. 90.

[37] Regierung Fulda circular, April 15, 1835, StAMa, 100/5466. Cf. also Werner 1981: 205; Mergen 1973: 65.

standardizing passports internationally

tion, so that any vaguely-official looking document would be acceptable. This assumption was probably not entirely incorrect. German-speaking Central Europe alone was divided into some forty states. Each of these had several passport-issuing offices, which used different forms. Even though there was some attempt at standardization, this often remained half-hearted or incomplete—not least because a uniform format would have reduced the difference between the passports for "respectable" travelers, most likely issued by a Ministry, and the district-level documents carried by ordinary travelers. When Hanover introduced a standard passport form in 1838, this was not used by military officials, consulates, or embassies.[38] As mentioned above, British passports changed with each administration. It would thus have been all but impossible for police officers to recognize all passports presented to them. If what they saw looked like a passport, they probably assumed that it was genuine. Even those printers who manufactured *Wanderbücher* with spelling mistakes could have pointed to cases of illiterate police officers as a justification for their scant attention to detail.[39]

In these circumstances, schemes that had been developed in various states—with particular intensity, of course, in "police states" such as Austria—for surreptitiously indicating on passports which travelers were considered suspicious were all but doomed to failure. Subtleties such as underlined visa numbers, double-crossed t's and double-dotted i's, which were supposed to make the passports of suspect persons stand out, were almost certainly overlooked most of the time.[40] What was most important, therefore, was the general impression made by the passport. As soon as one left one linguistic area, the text, usually only in the national language of the issuing country, became indecipherable to most passport officials anyway. The more important a travel document looked, the more important it was considered. But features that made travel documents look "important" were not necessarily ones that increased protection against forgery or manipulation. For instance, despite their drawbacks from the point of view of security, wax seals were treated with considerable awe throughout the nineteenth century. Fancy lettering and a long list of titles that stressed the importance of the issuing officials were additional assets. An official in the British Treasury noted in 1850 that the passports which came closest to this ideal were actually issued by the "Civic Chief" of Edinburgh.[41] As the *Illustrated London News* put it:

[38] Landesregierung circular, January 6, 1840, HStAWi, 211/15593, fol. 40; Siemann 1985: 207.

[39] Wirsing 1991: 133; Förster 1887: 151.

[40] Siemann 1985: 197; Hughes 1994: 67.

[41] Correspondence between W. Gibson Craig of the Treasury and G. Lenox Conyngham of the Passport Office, 1850/51, PRO FO 612/15.

It seems that the municipal head of "Auld Reekie" rejoices in a vast multiplicity of obsolete titles—"Lord High Admiral of the Firth of Forth" is one of the smallest, but all of which are stated at most imposing length in the passport, the effect being to inspire all manners of frontier officials with a deep and pervading awe for this dreadful potentate, and a corresponding degree of civility towards the lucky personages armed with his most imperial mandate. Add to these characteristics a number of vast seals of antique and venerable aspect, and nearly as big as saucers, and the charm is complete.[42]

The theoretically much more important passports from the secretary of state did not usually have wax seals, a defect aggravated by the fact that passports issued while the blank forms for a new foreign secretary were being engraved did have such seals.[43]

Of course, some passport counterfeiters were much more careful. In 1851, a number of flawless reproductions of seals and stamps from various police and consular authorities were found in a meadow near Bayreuth.[44] Nevertheless, the introduction of more advanced printing techniques appears to have rendered the difference between originals and copies apparent even to a casual observer.

It was therefore a fortunate coincidence for governments that the introduction of security paper occurred at a time when the function of passports was undergoing considerable change. Faced with a rising number of international travelers and the various problems of the passport system, European states abandoned visa requirements and passport controls at the frontiers from the late 1850s on. This meant that passports could no longer be used to reconstruct a route and thus became easier to exchange. However, as travel guides never ceased to point out (particularly to British tourists, who were not used to carrying identity papers at home), in those countries where registration requirements existed some official means of identification was still required, quite apart from the fact that such documents were also useful in post offices, banks, and occasionally even museums.[45] Even though they were no longer absolutely necessary for travel, passports and similar documents had become a feature of everyday life as official identity documents, whereas their role as travel and residence permits was taken over by other types of "papers." For foreign laborers, for example, the *livret d'ouvrier* was replaced by or supplemented with residence and work permits issued in the form of cards in different colors

---

[42] *Illustrated London News*, September 6, 1851.

[43] Foreign office memorandum, June 27, 1853, PRO FO 612/9, arising from a correspondence with the Sardinian minister in London, who wished to be informed about the different classes of Foreign Office passports.

[44] Regierung Fulda circular, May 7, 1851, StAMa 100/5466.

[45] Printed notice in PRO FO 612/41. [Murray] 1867: xvi–xviii, 213.

on the eve of the First World War.[46] On the other end of the social scale, it could still be necessary to supplement passports with additional proof of respectability, and certificates made of traditional materials appear to have remained the best way of doing this for some time. A history of the London Livery Companies published in the 1930s claimed that the City's freedom certificates, all but worthless in practice, could be used to make foreign officials believe their bearer occupied some exalted social station because they were made from parchment and had "an impressive seal in a neat little case."[47]

In the long run, however, governments' attempts to win the technological race against forgers led to the sacrifice of almost all aesthetic considerations. Much like banknotes, passports and identity cards have become smaller, less designed to "impress," and equipped with ever more security features. Perhaps global information networks will ultimately turn identity cards into nothing more than a means of calling up information—such as voice, face, or hand profiles—stored in a database elsewhere. But what is perhaps most striking is the apparent lack of any serious and sustained attempt to clearly distinguish government-issued identity documents from others. Such diverse documents as driver's licenses, company security cards, credit cards with photographs, airport access cards, the photograph pages on passports, and identity cards now all look much the same: small plastic cards with a photograph, some text, and symbols. Platinum-colored credit or frequent-flyer cards issued by private companies have replaced wax seals imprinted by officials as tokens of exalted status. This may be a sign of the strength of the modern allegiance to states: it may no longer be necessary to distinguish the official proof of identity from other, less certain ones; the demands of security, similar for all types of ID, can become paramount for the design of documents. But it could also mean that we are returning to competition between states and other agencies for the monopoly on the certification of identity: government-issued documents could once again become just one proof of identity among others.

---

[46] Schäfer 1982: 202f.
[47] Blackham 1931: 78f.

13

A Many-Headed Monster: The Evolution of the Passport System in the Netherlands and Germany in the Long Nineteenth Century

LEO LUCASSEN

ACCORDING TO the distinguished Canadian historian Michael Marrus, "throughout the nineteenth century there were no serious administrative impediments to the movement of persons between states."[1] This rather sweeping statement will not strike many students of the nineteenth century as particularly bold or controversial. Most scholars of migration and state formation regard the First World War as the end of the freedom of movement in the Western world and the beginning of the passport regime—a regime that contrasts sharply with the supposed laissez-faire of the long nineteenth century.[2] To a certain extent this is correct. Before the Great War, in most European states as well as in the Americas, people could indeed normally travel without passports. When one looks closer at the history of passport controls, however—a task that has scarcely been undertaken[3]—it soon becomes clear that this impression needs to be qualified. At least four reservations should be registered:[4]

I thank Corrie van Eijl, Cees Groenendijk, and Jan Lucassen for their critical remarks on an earlier version of this essay.

  [1] Marrus 1985: 92.

  [2] See, for example, Kern 1983: 195; Erler 1984; Marrus 1985; Dummett and Nicol 1990; Zolberg 1990; Noiriel 1991a; Moch 1992; Skran 1995: 14; Lucassen 1998.

  [3] Exceptions are Noiriel on France, Matthews and Kolchin on Russia, and Torpey on Europe and the United States.

  [4] These reservations follow from an analysis of the Dutch passport regulations and the information that Dutch archives contain about other countries. In researching this essay, I gathered all Dutch acts, regulations, and circulars from 1792 on. Most of these were published in the *Staatsblad* (Law Gazette), the Bijlagen tot het Staatsblad (Appendix to the Law Gazette, abbreviated *BSB*), the Nederlandsche Staatscourant (*NSC*), and the Algemeen Politieblad (General Police Journal). Furthermore, I examined a number of files in the Algemeen Rijksarchief (Dutch Central State Archive, abbreviated *ARA*), which offer insight into the preparation of legislative acts and the correspondence between central and local authorities. This preliminary research amounted to some 1,100 documents. Most correspondence was carried on between the Ministries of Foreign Affairs (MFA), Justice (MJ), and the Interior (MI).

1. Before the middle of the nineteenth century, passport regulations were manifold for those traveling within and across state boundaries. The era of free international migration only began around 1860, and even then state controls on movement did not vanish entirely.

2. Moreover, not everybody was able to take advantage of the liberal wind. Some categories of aliens suffered discrimination, such as the Chinese in the United States and the Poles in Germany, while traveling groups (often indiscriminately referred to as "gypsies") and the migrant poor in general were regarded with suspicion, increasingly hindered in their movements, and often expelled.[5]

3. The new regime did not encompass all states, as the strict passport regulations in the Russian Empire (later continued by the Soviet Union) and Turkey indicate.[6]

4. Finally, migration was not only controlled by passports. For a full understanding of the relationship between migrants and the state, other documents used for checking a person's identity and origin must be analyzed as well.

Freedom of movement in the nineteenth century was therefore restricted in time, in place, and by class.[7] This leads to the question of how we should understand these variations.

Before going into the evolution of the passport system, at least from the Napoleonic era on,[8] we have to distinguish among various kinds of passport documents:[9] foreign passports for aliens; foreign passports for citizens and alien residents; and internal passports for citizens and alien residents. All three categories were closely linked, but at the same time served different functions. Elaborating on the ideas of Groenendijk (1986), I distinguish between the functions of these documents for the holder and for the state, respectively (see Table 1).

---

[5] Zolberg 1997; Dohse 1981: 81; Lucassen, Willems, and Cottaar 1998; Lucassen 1997b.

[6] Matthews 1993.

[7] During the Middle Ages and the early modern period, the restriction and control of movement was quite common, especially in countries in which the freedom of labor was curtailed by servitude or forms of indenture (widespread in both Europe and the American colonies; see, for example, Steinfeld 1991). To identify and control persons, work books and other documents were used instead of passports (see also Noiriel 1991a: 157, footnote 1).

[8] The restriction to the nineteenth and twentieth centuries is not justified by the absence of passports in earlier periods, but by the fact that national states became much more prominent after the Napoleonic wars. For earlier regulations on passports, see, for example, Vallotton 1923: 18–22; Nitschke 1990: 134–44; Schwartz 1988: 194; MacStay-Adams 1990: 257; Torpey 1997 and 1998a; and Lucassen 1999.

[9] There were even more kinds of passports, like the "sea-letters" or "Turkish passports," in which a captain declared what kind of freight his ship carried. Here we will limit ourselves to the three most important types.

TABLE 1
Functions of Passports

A: Functions for the holder	B: Functions for the state
— the right to move freely — a proof of one's nationality — a proof of one's identity — right to assistance by embassy and consulate — protection against expulsion	1: Preventing the departure of its own citizens — to enforce military service — to collect taxes and settle debts — to apprehend wanted criminals — to protect the national economy[a]
	2: To stimulate the departure of its own citizens — to decrease perceived overpopulation — to get rid of unwanted segments of the population (poor, unemployed, criminals)
	3: To control the entrance and movement of aliens — preventing unwanted aliens from entering the country — expelling unwanted aliens — guaranteeing that aliens leave when deemed necessary
	4: To monitor the population — to monitor the movements of citizens (by internal passports) — the possibility of tracking down aliens (by special alien registration procedures)

[a] The best examples are from mercantilist states in the eighteenth and early nineteenth centuries that regarded their population as one of the most valuable assets. Modern examples are attempts to prevent important members of the workforce from leaving, as in the case of Dutch metalworkers during World War I (Lucassen 1998).

In this essay, I first analyze the passport as a means for the state to control and monitor migrants moving about within and crossing their borders (see Table 1, B3 and B4). Next, I deal with the reverse side of the coin: the attempts of the state, especially after 1860, to facilitate the export of its own citizens, again by providing them with passports or other certificates that proved their nationality (Table 1, B2). In both cases, the perspective of the state will be linked to that of the migrant, by showing the sheltering functions of passports for the holder (A). These considerations have led me to formulate the following principal questions:

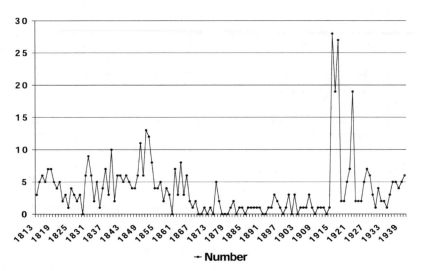

Number of acts and regulations concerning passports and declarations of nationality in the Netherlands, 1813–1920.
Source: See footnote 4. Selection: all acts and regulations issued by authorities at
the central level (Ministries).

    1. How did the passport system in the Netherlands evolve during
the long nineteenth century?
    2. What were the main motives for the state to control and monitor
migrants?
    3. To what extent could migrants use passports and other means
of identification as a weapon?
    4. To what extent did passport regulations restrict migration?

Passports as a Means of Controlling and Monitoring Migrants

Before going into the specific history of passports, let us first look at what
one might call the "business cycle" of passport legislation in the Netherlands. To get a sense of the extent of the Dutch authorities' involvement
with passport matters, I put the number of acts and regulations relating
to the three kinds of passport mentioned above in the graph at the top of
this page.
    Of course, the graph itself does not explain the fluctuations. As we will
see, however, the ups and downs reflect to a great extent the long-term
history of the passport in the Netherlands, and in most Western European
countries as well: the upsurge of passport regulations after the defeat of

Napoleon, the separation of Belgium in 1830, the abolishment of passport requirements around 1860 heralding the advent of the (alleged) period of free movement, and finally the return of the passport regime with the start of World War I. To clarify the significance of this graph, I first discuss the content of these regulations in the Netherlands.

The French Revolution and the Birth of the Dutch Passport Regime, 1790–1813

The discussion among French revolutionaries on the issue of passports in the early 1790s reveals the limits of the pursuit of liberty. Many revolution-aries associated passports with the despised ancien régime, and critics warned in the journal Le Moniteur that the use of passports for restricting individual mobility could lead to a tyrannical police state. The irony of fate decreed that when Louis XVI tried to flee his kingdom in June 1791 car-rying a false passport, this was a sign for the regime to make passports obligatory for all French citizens who wanted to leave the country. Borders were monitored in order to stop the emigration of nobles and other oppo-nents of the revolutionary regime. Whereas the 1791 act soon fell into disuse, in March 1792 an act with a more enduring influence—it has been described as the beginning of the modern French passport legislation[10]—made passports obligatory both for French persons who wanted to travel inside their own country and for anyone who wanted to cross the border.

The French example deeply influenced the legislation on passports in the Netherlands, especially when, after a "velvet revolution," democratic forces in January 1795 founded the Batavian Republic, which replaced the loose federal Union of the old Dutch Republic.[11] Only a few months later the National Constituency was elected, and alongside the emancipa-tion of the Jews and the separation of church and state, a decree laid down that nobody was to leave the Republic without a passport.[12] Ten years later, when Louis Napoleon became king of Holland, the influence of French regulations became much stronger. Finally, with the incorporation of the Kingdom of Holland in the French Empire in 1810, the Netherlands felt the full weight of French legislation, including that concerning pass-ports. Although French rule only lasted until the Battle of Leipzig (the so-called Völkerschlacht) in October 1813, its legal legacy was considerable. This became clear when the new Dutch king, William I, was installed in

---

[10] Hartoy 1937: 39–52. Although the act of March 28, 1792, was temporarily abolished in September 1792, it was reinstated soon thereafter (February 1793) (idem: 62).

[11] For a concise history, see Tilly 1993: ch. 3.

[12] ARA, 2.09.01, 4788.

December of the same year. Only twelve days into his regency, he issued a royal decree that made passports obligatory for Dutch citizens who wanted to go abroad, and for foreigners wishing to visit the Netherlands.[13]

The French Legacy in the Dutch Kingdom, 1813–1830

In July 1814, the Treaty of London established the union of the former Dutch Republic with the southern Netherlands (now Belgium). This was part of the grand scheme to keep France in check by surrounding it with strong states. As France, which thus became a direct neighbor, was considered a potential center of dangerous revolutionary ideas, its citizens were looked upon with suspicion by Dutch authorities. The general obligation requiring aliens entering the Netherlands to carry passports was therefore mainly aimed at the French. Notwithstanding the return of the old regime headed by the conservative king Louis XVIII, France was still regarded as an unstable country—and not without reason, as the turmoil before and after the assassination of the duke de Berry (cousin of the king) in the summer of 1820 showed. The Dutch government immediately issued extra measures instructing local authorities to treat French travelers even more severely than before.[14] On the other hand, English travelers, who in most cases did not have passports because the English state was believed to oppose this kind of state interference with individual freedom,[15] were treated much more leniently.[16]

Dutch citizens as well as foreign residents who wanted to leave the country also needed passports, because many states demanded them. The Dutch government therefore strongly recommended that its citizens provide themselves with passports for foreign travel. It would be misleading to regard these documents solely as a service of the state to its citizens, however. As far as the Ministry of Foreign Affairs was concerned, the issuance of a passport was a favor that was only granted under certain conditions. The most important criteria of eligibility were that the applicant (implicitly assumed to be male) had to have fulfilled his obligations toward the state, especially that of military service (also introduced in

---

[13] Sovereign Decision, December 12, 1813, published in the *NSC* of January 5, 1814, no. 42. This decision still constitutes the legal basis for the issuance of Dutch visas.

[14] Circular of the MJ, July 13, 1820, no. 24 (*ARA*, 2.09.01, 4788).

[15] Matthews 1993; Dummett and Nicol 1990: 40. The Dutch MFA wrote on July 3, 1840, that the government of Great Britain "has the overconfident idea that its citizens will be admitted in foreign countries without a passport" (*ARA*, 2.05.01, 3209).

[16] See, for example, the Royal Decision of March 29, 1815 (article 3) (*NSC*, April 1, 1815, no. 78), and the letter of the attorney-general in South Holland to the chief of police in Rotterdam, October 8, 1821, no. 13 (*ARA*, 2.09.01, 4788).

the French period), and that he was not wanted for any crimes.[17] These conditions applied to both Dutch citizens and foreign residents, because the latter were held to profit in similar fashion from the benefits afforded by residence in the country. Here we touch upon an interesting aspect of early-nineteenth-century thinking about nationality and citizenship: although the issuance of passports to Dutch citizens was a way to demarcate nationals from aliens, citizenship was not yet firmly linked to nationality, but rather to residence or birth.

The use of internal passports—again for both Dutch nationals and non-Dutch residents—was much more restricted during this period. The very first passport regulation of the Dutch kingdom, dated December 12, 1813, explicitly laid down that the state "would avoid everything that could be associated with the spirit of harassment and inquisition that has characterized the occupation of the past few years." All inhabitants of the Netherlands were therefore granted freedom of movement within the realm. The chief exception to this policy, adopted at a time when Napoleon had still not been defeated, was that internal passports were obligatory in the direct vicinity of enemy or allied armies (at that time) and close to the southern borders. Obviously the authorities were concerned about spies and wanted to be able to ascertain the identity of suspicious persons.[18] As soon as the political situation stabilized and the military threat diminished, the call to abolish internal passports was raised. The government, represented mainly by the Ministries of Justice and Foreign Affairs, was reluctant to heed these demands. Internal policy documents from around 1825 indicate that, especially in the southern provinces (now Belgium), the authorities wanted internal passport requirements to remain in force because they expected great difficulties in distinguishing between their French-speaking (Walloon) citizens and French immigrants. Nevertheless, the mood was clearly in favor of abolishing internal passports in most parts of the Netherlands, and they probably fell into disuse during the second half of the 1820s.

The Belgian Uprising and Its Aftermath, 1830–1848

This liberal interlude did not last long, however. When the southern provinces of the Dutch kingdom revolted and in October 1830 a provisional

[17] These aims are very clearly stated in a letter from the MFA to the provincial governor of Overijssel, June 5, 1839, no. 11 (*ARA*, 2.05.01, 1774).

[18] In contrast to foreign passports, which were issued by the Ministry of Foreign Affairs (a task delegated, however, to the provincial governors), internal passports were issued by local authorities.

government was proclaimed in Brussels, the Dutch government immediately reacted by issuing a new set of regulations concerning aliens. The most important of these was a decision requiring owners of boarding houses and hotels, as well as private persons, who lodged someone from another municipality not only to keep a register of all guests, but also to report these visitors to the police within six hours of their arrival.[19] Furthermore, they were constrained to instruct their guests to appear before the police, who would provide them with a special safety-card (*veiligheidskaart*). In exchange for this identity card, the holder had to deposit his passport with the local police. The safety-card was initially valid for fourteen days, after which it could be renewed.[20] Because local authorities could not always distinguish aliens from indigenous travelers, many Dutch citizens and residents who wanted to travel inside the kingdom requested internal passports in order to avoid unnecessary difficulties. Thus the government used internal and foreign passports to set up a surveillance system, mainly for political reasons, that affected their own citizens as well as aliens. Internal passports were furthermore needed for the transport of goods, especially near the southern border of the country. The use of internal passports, which were free of charge, therefore increased during the 1830s. When the Netherlands finally acknowledged Belgium as a separate state in 1839, the situation was normalized and most of these regulations were withdrawn. The most fundamental one, which compelled travelers to carry safety-cards,[21] remained in force, but in practice its application was reserved exclusively for aliens.

The end of the Belgian troubles did not mean that internal passports passed into oblivion again, however. Many Dutch citizens, especially those in border areas, had had the experience that authorities in both Belgium and Prussia often accepted internal passports as a legitimate means of identification.[22] The advantage for the holder was obvious: whereas foreign passports cost a considerable sum and were only granted under certain conditions, internal passports were free of charge and could not be refused. Another reason to request an internal passport was that, again mainly in the border regions, authorities often had trouble distin-

[19] Royal Decision, October 9, 1830 (*Staatsblad* 1830, no. 66).

[20] The system of safety-cards was used for the first time in March 1815, probably as a reaction to the landing of Napoleon in France after his stay at Elba on March 1 (see the Royal Decision of March 24, 1815, no. 21, published in the *BSB*, 1848, no. 111). It probably soon fell into disuse after the situation in France stabilized. As we will see, however, these requirements were revived in 1830 and 1848.

[21] The Royal Decision of October 9, 1830.

[22] MFA to MJ, dd. September 17, 1839 (*ARA*, 2.05.01, 3209) and letter of the attorney general of North Brabant to MJ, dd. March 6, 1840 (*ARA*, 2.09.01, 4788).

guishing between Dutch nationals and aliens,[23] so that an internal passport could protect the owner inside his own country against harassment by the police and the gendarmerie. The government was not pleased about this abuse of internal passports, the more so because there was no uniform model and some printers even sold these documents directly to the public.

The use of passports for international travel by foreigners in the Netherlands did not diminish in the 1830s and 1840s. After the July Revolution of 1830, the new French king Louis Philippe made bargains with the Republicans, but agitation and insurrectionary movements remained widespread, especially in the first half of the 1830s.[24] As Palmer and Colton have put it, "The July monarchy was a platform of boards built on a volcano."[25] Fearing that the populace might be susceptible to infection by the revolutionary contagion, the Dutch central authorities in March 1833 ordered French travelers not only to carry passports, but also to have a visa (written permission to enter the Netherlands, issued by a Dutch diplomatic representative)—a requirement that was only abolished six years later.[26]

Tracking the vicissitudes of politics reveals only one side of the coin, however. During the 1840s, socioeconomic arguments slowly gained importance and became a steady undercurrent as the "social question" assumed increasing importance on the European stage. The main fear among government officials throughout the nineteenth century,[27] as remains the case in present-day welfare states, was that the would-be settler would become a "public charge" and thus burden the system of poor relief.[28] To prevent this from happening, potentially destitute aliens had to be kept out. The problem, however, was how to determine who be-

[23] Letter of the mayor of Zevenaar to the public prosecutor in Arnhem, September 17, 1844 (*ARA*, 2.09.01, 4788) and MJ to the provincial governor of North Brabant, January 11, 1850 (*ARA*, 2.09.01, 4789).

[24] Stearns 1974: 25, and Tilly, Tilly, and Tilly 1975: 41–43.

[25] Palmer and Colton 1978: 463.

[26] Circular of the governor of North Brabant, March 22, 1833 to the mayors (*BSB*, 1833, no. 66) and the letter of the MFA to the MJ, October 7, 1839 (*ARA*, 2.09.01, 4788).

[27] Before the nineteenth century, these concerns manifested themselves mainly on the local level (see Leeuwen 1994).

[28] Law on Poor Relief, November 28, 1818: admitted aliens who resided for six years in a Dutch municipality are entitled to poor relief (article 6) (*Staatsblad* 1818, no. 40). The relation between restrictive legislation toward aliens and poor relief has been noted by many scholars, especially those working in the field of poor relief. Their studies show that until the breakthrough of the national state in the nineteenth century, the "foreigner" was not linked to state-citizenship, but was defined as somebody without a permanent residence in a certain city or municipality. Only after 1815 did the term *foreigner* gradually acquire a more national status, when states became responsible for poor relief. See in this respect Brubaker 1992 and Lucassen 1996a.

longed in this category, apart from outright beggars and tramps. Furthermore, the police apparatus was not at all equipped to carry out such a task. This made it all the more important that immigrants be able to identify themselves satisfactorily. Provided that they could do so, the police would at least know to which country to return them when it appeared that they could not earn their own bread. Moreover, the Dutch state had some guarantee that the state where an indigent alien belonged would be prepared to readmit such a person. As the bulk of immigrants who came to the Netherlands in this period, as well as before and after,[29] came from German states (especially Prussia), the regulations and circulars issued by the government mainly had to do with them.[30]

Concern in other countries about potential poor relief burdens touched Dutch citizens who wanted to settle or work abroad as well. Austria and Russia adopted especially strict policies to avoid such burdens. In 1833, the Austrian government took measures to stop the unlimited immigration of foreign artisans, whereas the Russian Empire in 1847 explicitly prohibited foreign laborers and artisans from entering the country—with the exception of British citizens, because the latter were regarded as superior craftsmen.[31] More relevant for Dutch citizens, however, were the regulations issued by Belgium and the German states. The new neighbor to the south more than once made clear that it would refuse entry to Dutch citizens deemed likely to become public charges. Especially those who got their passports for free ran a considerable risk of being sent back. Here we touch an important clash of interests within the passport regime. Whereas the Dutch state purposely did not charge its poor citizens who wanted a passport in order thus to alleviate its own poor relief obligations, receiving states—at least those that could distinguish between passports distributed *gratis* and normal passports—tried to keep out the holders of such passports.[32] To get rid of poor immigrants, not only passports were demanded, though. In the 1840s, both Prussia and Hanover required foreign laborers or servants to produce certificates of good behavior as well as guarantees from their "sending" municipality that it would take back its inhabitant in the event that he or she became a public charge.

[29] Lucassen and Penninx 1997.

[30] See the circulars of the MJ, March 19, 1844 (*BSB*, 1844, no. 91), and December 8, 1845 (*BSB*, 1845, no. 342).

[31] Letter of the Dutch MFA, August 19, 1833, no. 3b to the MJ and the circular of the MFA to the provincial governors, November 24, 1847, no. 2a (*ARA*, 2.05.01, 3209). For pass regulations both for aliens and citizens in Austria, see Gebhardt 1992: 176–80.

[32] Circular from the MFA to the provincial governors, February 18, 1840, no. 2 (*ARA*, 2.05.01, 3209) and the letter of the same Ministry to the MJ, November 28, 1848, no. 28 (*ARA*, 2.09.01, 4789).

Finally, just in case these measures did not suffice, Hanover also demanded a bond of some 500 Dutch guilders.[33]

On the other hand, passport regulations were not to interfere with the labor market. Accordingly, the Dutch local police were instructed to turn a blind eye to seasonal foreign workers (mainly from Germany) who had no passports.[34] In the case of foreign laborers, work books were regarded as a sufficient form of personal identification and even workers without any paperwork were normally admitted.[35]

The Revolutions of 1848 and the Vanishing of the Passport Regime, 1848–1914

It will come as no surprise that after the uprising in Paris in February 1848 and the subsequent abdication of King Louis Philippe, the Dutch government immediately strengthened its surveillance of foreign travelers, especially the French, and reminded local authorities that the system of safety-cards was still in force.[36] How strongly these measures were prompted by the revolutionary climate of the moment is illustrated by the letter of the Dutch Ministry of Foreign Affairs to the ambassador of Prussia in October 1848: "The present political circumstances make it necessary to regulate as strictly as possible the admission of aliens. This means that all aliens must have a passport with a visa. If not, they will be expelled, in the same manner as vagrants and beggars."[37]

After the revolutionary mood in Europe ebbed away in the 1850s, a more liberal climate began to prevail with respect to the movement of people across international borders. Especially after the Crimean war, the idea that freedom of movement had to be stimulated in peacetime became widely accepted. Between 1857 and 1863 most countries, with the excep-

[33] It is not very likely that this demand was put into practice, however, because this was a very high sum (about twice the average annual wage of a laborer at that time). The Prussian and Hanoverian policies are mentioned in a letter of the Dutch MFA, October 2, 1843, no. 171 to the MJ (*ARA*, 2.09.01, 4788). On the relation between identity control and poor relief in German states, see also Brubaker 1992: 63; Lüdtke 1982; and Lucassen 1996a: 118–22.

[34] Letter on behalf of the king, March 31, 1816, no. 144/63 to the MJ (*ARA*, 2.09.01, 4788).

[35] In an undated document (c. 1825), the admission of German, Danish, and Austrian workers was also authorized when they were in the possession of a *livret*, provided it had a visa from a Dutch consul (*ARA*, 2.09.01, 4788).

[36] See the letter of the MJ to the provincial governor of Gelderland, in which the MJ makes clear that the local authorities were expected to apply the earlier instructions about surveillance and safety-cards issued in 1815 and 1830 (*ARA*, 2.09.01, 4788).

[37] Letter dated October 17, 1848, no. 34 (*ARA*, 2.05.01, 3470).

tion of Russia, Romania, Turkey, and the Papal States, decided to abolish the obligation for foreigners to carry passports, or at least no longer demand visas from Dutch citizens.

This new passportless regime, which coincides with the economic liberalization in most European countries, lasted until World War I, with brief exceptions in times of war (mainly the Franco-Prussian war of 1870). It did not, however, imply that states suddenly abandoned their concerns about aliens. A good illustration of this point is the first Dutch Aliens Act, which became effective in August 1849. This very liberal act stipulated that all aliens were welcome in the Netherlands, except political trouble-makers and vagrants. The liberal aspect is well articulated in an elucidation of the act published two weeks later: "The aim of the Act is surely not to harass aliens. It only gives the government a means to expel dangerous and poor immigrants. [. . .] The task of the police is to avoid everything that can cause trouble or delay to an alien."[38] Trustworthy and industrious immigrants were not to be hindered, even when they did not have a passport or if they had no means of identification at all. Only dangerous and (above all) poor aliens had to be kept out or expelled. The crucial question was whether a given alien had the means to support himself or could be expected to find work.

Notwithstanding the liberal tone of the Dutch Aliens Act and the abolishment of passport requirements after 1860, most foreign migrants still carried passports or some other form of identification. This becomes clear when we look at the alien registers, which were kept in all major Dutch cities from about 1850 on (Table 2).[39] Although not all foreigners who visited these cities were registered by the police,[40] this source provides some idea of the sort of personal documentation that aliens took with them.

First of all we see from this table that although the significance of passports dwindled after 1860, they did not disappear entirely. More interesting, however, is that the identification function was taken over by documents issued by local authorities in the municipality where the foreign migrants originally came from: certificates verifying the registration or departure of an inhabitant. Only very few people traveled without any

[38] Circular dated August 18, 1849, no. 80 of the MJ to the local police and mayors (*BSB*, 1849, no. 166).

[39] In The Hague, such registration can be documented from 1875 on, but it may have started earlier (Cottaar 1998). On the registration of aliens in the Netherlands in general, see Lucassen and van der Harst 1998.

[40] Especially after 1860, the number of aliens who were recorded declined dramatically (in Amsterdam from about six thousand in the 1850s to some seven hundred in the 1870s). It is still unclear what the new criteria for registration were that led to this decline.

TABLE 2
Documents Used for Identification by Aliens in Amsterdam, 1850-1905
(in percentages)

	1850	1875	1886	1895	1905
Travel-documents [a]	66	33	18	15	16
Work-documents [b]	26	22	24	20	1
Certificates of Nationality [c]	1	18	16	7	8
Identification documents [d]	4	13	3	5	4
Population registration documents [e]	—	2	26	43	59
Military passports	3	10	10	9	8
Miscellaneous	—	2	1	1	2
No identification	—	—	2	—	2
Total	100	100	100	100	100
N=	800	708	284	303	238

Source: Municipal Archive Amsterdam, Police archive (5225), registers of travel and residence passes, inv. nos 873, 911, 917, 919, and 925.

[a] Mostly passports.
[b] Such as booklets used by artisans and servants (like the German *Wanderbuch*, *Arbeits-buch*, and *Dienstbuch* and the Belgian and French *livrets*), containing their personal information, travel route, and remarks by their successive employers).
[c] Documents that gave proof of a person's nationality, such as the German *Heimatschein*.
[d] Such as declarations issued by local authorities in the place of birth or residence.
[e] Such as certificates of registration in (or removal from) a municipality, as well as birth and marriage certificates.

means of identification at all. We may not (yet) know how representative these alien registrations are, but it does not seem too far-fetched to assume that at least most labor migrants had some sort of document. Seen from the perspective of the migrants, the main reason seems to be that possession of such documents made them less vulnerable to attempts by the state to frustrate their geographical mobility. Certificates that captured their identity served as an insurance policy against official harassment. In the first place, the documents ensured the Dutch authorities that a migrant could be expelled in case he were to become destitute. Not only did the authorities know to which state to send someone, but possession of such documents also greatly increased the chance that the authorities of that state would accept such a person. Non-wealthy looking migrants without any means of identification posed a threat to the authorities, because they could burden the poor relief system.

A second reason for migrants to carry papers, at least within the Netherlands, was that these were necessary to obtain a so-called travel and residence pass (TRP). This pass was introduced as part of the Aliens Act of 1849 and was valid for three months, after which it could be extended.[41] Only aliens who were given such a pass could be considered to have been legally admitted. Precisely because of the legal protection it offered, the police were instructed to be cautious in issuing such a permit. The more aliens without such a pass in their possession, the greater the discretionary power of the police to act (and expel) as they deemed necessary. The Ministry of Justice therefore explicitly directed the local police not to give a TRP to aliens of whom it could be expected that they might become a public charge. Musicians, peddlers, showmen, and other people with itinerant occupations were to be excluded as a general rule.[42] Although the issuance of TRPs soon diminished in most municipalities, it did not disappear entirely. Especially aliens who ran the risk of being expelled tried to get a TRP anyway, and often succeeded—to the frustration of the Ministry of Justice.[43] A good example of this phenomenon are the members of itinerant groups, who were increasingly labeled as gypsies after 1870. For them, passports were even more important. From about 1870 on, several circulars were issued by the Ministry of Justice, urging local authorities not to admit gypsies and to expel them if possible. In reaction many Hungarian, Russian, and Austrian "gypsies" made sure they had valid passports. Being so equipped helped reduce the risk of being expelled and gave them the possibility of claiming support from their country's embassy in the Netherlands, often with success.[44] This strategy of the less fortunate in a way turned passports and other documents into a Trojan horse. Although these papers were meant to control migration and to prevent the immigration of certain categories, migrants could use passports in their favor and achieve exactly the opposite result.

[41] *Reis- en verblijfpas* in Dutch.

[42] Lucassen 1990: 31–33.

[43] A good example are groups that were labeled as gypsies. Although considered to be unwanted aliens *optima forma*, many of them nevertheless were successful in getting TRPs (Lucassen 1990).

[44] From the 1860s on, authorities indiscriminately labeled all people who traveled in family groups and who slept in tents or caravans as "gypsies" (*zigeuners* in Dutch) (Lucassen 1990; Lucassen et al. 1998). A similar reaction is documented for Germany (Lucassen 1996a).

Passports as a Means of Facilitating Emigration
Dutch Workers in Germany, 1860–1914

In April 1862, the attorney general in the Dutch province of Limburg wrote to the provincial governor that the poor were increasingly demanding passports, mainly because they were not admitted into Belgium and Prussia without such a document.[45] He further informed the governor that Prussia was notorious for maintaining strict surveillance on the identity papers of workers who settled there. Even foreign residents who had lived there for years had to make sure that their papers were in order. If not, they ran a considerable risk of being expelled.[46]

This letter is another indication that the liberalization of the passport regime after 1860 did not put an end to documenting the identity of aliens in the Netherlands, nor in its neighboring countries. Moreover, it reveals the other side of the passport-coin: the use of passports by sending states to ensure the emigration of their citizens. In this section I illustrate this reverse function by looking briefly at the Dutch and German situation.[47]

This policy, which was also applied in a number of German states (Hanover, Württemberg, and Saxony, among others), was based on special acts which stipulated that aliens embarked on a search for (menial) work or who practiced itinerant trades were exempted from the new passportless regime.[48] Throughout this period Dutch (and other alien) workers who wanted to find a job abroad had to prove not only who they were, but also which state and municipality was responsible for them in case they needed poor relief. The stipulation applied most of all to the thousands of Dutch workers who went to look for a job in the fast-developing industrial area of the Ruhr valley from about 1870 on. They could only be hired if they showed a declaration of nationality.[49] Such a declaration, issued by the provincial governors in the Netherlands, was more or less

---

[45] Letter dated April 30, 1862, no. 184 (*ARA*, 2.05.01, 3209).

[46] In the Netherlands an alien had a right to poor relief when he or she had resided for six years in a Dutch municipality (article 6 of the Act on poor relief, November 28, 1818, *Staatsblad* 1818, no. 40, renewed in the act on Poor Relief of June 28, 1854, article 30, *Staatsblad* 1854, no. 100).

[47] Future research will have to include other European countries as well. For the moment it seems that Prussia (and after 1870 most German states) was most severe with respect to documenting identity, whereas Great Britain finds itself at the other end of the spectrum. For a discussion of the 1901 Italian passport law, which was mainly intended to facilitate the entry of Italians into their destinations in the Americas, see Torpey in this volume.

[48] Circular of the MFA, December 13, 1865, no. 121, published in the *BSB* (1865, no. 323, based on the *Gesetz-Sammlung für das Königreich Hannover*, 1865, Heft 37, no. 75).

[49] In Dutch *nationaliteitsbewijs*.

equivalent to the German *Heimatschein*,[50] and became important after 1870, as Graph 1 shows. Apparently a declaration of nationality was considered more reliable by the German authorities than a regular Dutch passport, perhaps because it explicitly stated that the person would be readmitted into the country if he or she were to become a public charge.[51] After the signing of the Treaty of Establishment[52] between the Netherlands and Germany in 1904, which allowed citizens of the two countries to settle in either and stipulated under what conditions they could be sent back, things became more liberal, but some sort of proof of one's identity remained obligatory.[53] In 1909, finally, the German government decided to introduce special passes for all foreign laborers, the so-called *Arbeiterlegitimationskarte* (worker's identification card).[54]

Monitoring Internal Migration Through Registration

The increasing insistence of states on personal identification during the passportless era did not affect foreigners only. In the Netherlands, as well as in Belgium and Italy, from 1850 on a system of population registration began to function, which enabled local authorities to keep track of all residential changes. These registers listed name, place and date of birth, last residence, occupation, and composition of the bearer's household. In Prussia, where the bureaucratic surveillance of all travelers emerged already in the beginning of the nineteenth century,[55] a similar system was

---

[50] When Prussian citizens changed residence within the German confederation, they needed a *Staasangehörigkeitsausweis*; those who went abroad were given a *Heimatschein* (*Handwörterbuch der Preusischen Verwaltung*, Leipzig 1906, volume I, under *Heimatscheine*: (8). Both had the function of assuring the receiving municipality or state that the person would be taken back if he or she were to become indigent. Although *Heimatscheine* officially did not exist in the Netherlands, mayors issued similar documents anyway for residents who wanted to work in Germany. After 1875, Dutch authorities stopped issuing *Heimatscheine* and replaced these with declarations of nationality (circular by the provincial governor of Limburg, dd. 27-1-1876, in *BSB* 1876, no. 24). See for the function of the *Heimatschein* and in Germany also Lucassen 1996a: 118–22 and Lucassen 1997b: 243–46. On the *Heimatrecht* (Home Law), see Walker 1971: 347–53.

[51] See the model prescribed in 1886 by the MI (*BSB* 1886, no. 39).

[52] In Dutch *Vestigingsverdrag*. It was signed on December 17, 1904, and became effective on January 19, 1907 (*Staatsblad* 1906, no. 279).

[53] This treaty was signed in 1904, but became effective only in 1907 (*Staatsblad* 1906, no. 279). From 1907 on, German authorities also accepted internal passports, birth certificates, and even extracts from the population registers (circular of the MI, April 12, 1911, no. 1485, published in the *BSB* of 1911, no. 191).

[54] Herbert 1990: 34–36; and Del Fabbro 1996: 109–11. This card was obligatory for the greatest part of Germany (Bavaria and some other southern states exempted).

[55] Hochstadt 1999: 58–59. See especially footnote 8 on p. 58.

applied more systematically after the restructuring of the system of poor relief in 1842; from then on, citizens had to report every change in residence to the police.[56] Apart from this general *Meldepflicht*, a number of regulations obliged especially the laboring classes to carry some sort of identification. People who wanted to change residence needed a declaration of nationality;[57] from 1832 on, travelers who remained more than three days in a particular place had to ask for a residence permit, whereas a year earlier a journeyman's book (*Wanderbuch*) for workers and artisans was made compulsory.[58] As Beck has demonstrated, the liberal legislation concerning poor relief and the freedom to choose one's residence of 1842 paradoxically led to a greater degree of control by the police. The authorities feared the consequences of this increasing lower-class mobility.[59] Thus in 1846 identity papers were introduced for both farmhands and railroad workers, and the activities of the police increasingly focused on the issuance and oversight of all this paperwork.[60] Elaine Spencer has offered a good illustration of the bureaucratic implications: in 1857 in the city of Barmen (with approximately 40,000 inhabitants in 1850), the police issued 1,448 travel passes and other forms of identification, validated 3,404 passes for visitors, and issued 5,138 permits for temporary and permanent residence.[61]

When the unification of Germany at the end of the 1860s was completed, the liberal maxim of "freedom of establishment" (*Freizügigkeit*) became the standard throughout the new empire (with the exception of Bavaria and Württemberg). This posture was intended to stimulate economic activities, trade, and freedom of movement. The latter was elaborated in the Passport Act of October 12, 1867, which abolished all passports and thus facilitated internal migration, which had increased dramatically since about 1850.[62] Again, however, as in the 1840s, the elimination of passport requirements did not end the supervision of migrants. Apart from the general obligation to register noted earlier, certain

[56] In contrast to the Netherlands, Belgium, and Italy (where the registration of the population was carried out by civil authorities), the local police forces in Germany did not exchange this information in an extensive way with previous or subsequent places of residence (Jackson 1997: 353). See also Beck 1995: 150–68, and Steinmetz 1993: 113–15 on the 1842 legislation.

[57] See footnote 47.

[58] Lüdtke 1982: 174–75; Jackson 1997: 351; Schildt 1986: 297.

[59] Beck 1995: 164–67.

[60] Lüdtke 1982: 175; Beck 1995: 23; Wehler 1987: 169.

[61] Spencer 1992: 45. On October 21, 1850, in Dresden, a passport-treaty (*Passkartenvertrag*) was signed by all German states and Austria, introducing a uniform internal passport (Vallotton 1923: 29).

[62] Hochstadt 1999; Jackson 1997: 298. The *Reichspassgesetz* was valid for the entire empire, with the exception of Alsace-Lorraine.

groups were especially subject to surveillance by the police. At least for the Ruhr area it has been established that highly mobile occupational groups (factory workers, apprentices, and domestic servants) were expected to carry their registration papers with them in order to prove that they had a legal right to work.[63] Finally, an even more mobile group— including itinerant craftsmen, showmen, and peddlers, as well as their families, who were often referred to simply as "gypsies"—confronted a very suspicious police force and could be fined if they were unable to identify themselves. They also needed special permits (*Wandergewerbescheine*) in order to perform their trades.[64]

Conclusion

This essay is a provisional exploration of what the American migration scholar Aristide Zolberg, referring to the need for investigation of the bureaucratic implications of migration control, once called "the history of paperwork."[65] Our overview of passport regulations in the Netherlands (the *first question*) has demonstrated that the long nineteenth century was far from a paradise of free movement for migrants. As we have seen, until the 1860s passports and visa requirements were more the rule than the exception in most European states. This fact is mainly explained by the political turmoil that dominated the European scene from the French Revolution on. The turbulent political climate that resulted from that great upheaval led many states to set up systems to monitor the movements of alien (and also internal) migrants, in which passports played a crucial role. With the exception of the Belgian crisis in the 1830s, which added a specific Dutch ingredient to the paranoiac atmosphere, the ups and downs in the Dutch passport regime mirrored to a great extent the larger European picture.

But we have also shown that, contrary to widespread opinion, the abolishment of passport requirements in most European states during the 1860s did not herald the dawning of an era in which papers for proving one's identity had become irrelevant. The lack of need for papers may have been true for well-off travelers from elite and bourgeois circles, but

---

[63] Jackson 1997: 353 and personal communication with the author.

[64] Lucassen 1996a: 170. After 1870 local authorities were urged not to issue *Wandergewerbescheine* to gypsies and other suspect itinerants, but this policy was only partly carried out. The procedure is well explained in the *Handwörterbuch der Preussischen Verwaltung* 1906, vol. I: 715, 728, under the headings "Gewerbescheine" and "Gewerbebetrieb im Umherziehen."

[65] Remark made at a workshop at the NIAS in Wassenaar on September 23, 1993 (the proceedings of this meeting have been published in Lucassen and Lucassen 1997).

the experiences of most migrants were quite different. As the German historian Hans-Ulrich Wehler once remarked, liberalism always stops at the gates of the lower classes,[66] who were also the most migration-prone. When they wanted to cross international borders—and, in states such as Prussia, internal administrative borders as well—until 1867 many of them continued to carry passports or similar documents such as declarations of nationality because these certificates offered protection against potential harassment by the police and other authorities, who wanted to check their identity and sometimes tried to frustrate their geographical mobility. The most vulnerable groups in this respect, itinerants and gypsies, tried to obtain passports throughout the nineteenth century. Both the Dutch and the German cases show that, although passports may have been officially abolished in the 1860s, large categories of the population were still expected to prove their identity when they migrated and for this reason carried residence registration papers. As Torpey has suggested, this was to a great extent stimulated precisely by the fact that passports were abolished, as becomes copiously clear in the debates in the Reichstag over the 1867 law.[67]

This analysis reveals two main motives behind states' adoption of acts and regulations concerning passports and other forms of identification, which brings us to the *second question* raised in the introduction. Roughly speaking, in the first half of the nineteenth century authorities used passports and visas mainly for the purpose of monitoring aliens they considered to be political troublemakers. Surveillance systems were used not so much to curb immigration, but to detect (politically) unwanted aliens. From the moment that the political situation in Europe stabilized (after 1860), this motive vanished, together with the passport requirements. Socioeconomic motives, particularly concern about influxes of poor and destitute immigrants, were not absent, but remained clearly subordinate during this period. Only when the central state's responsibility for poor relief increased did this motive become more important. Here we find an interesting difference between Germany and the Netherlands. Especially after 1870, the German authorities began to worry about undocumented poor labor migrants from abroad, and therefore began to demand documents (often in the form of declarations of nationality) indicating to which country potentially destitute migrants could be returned. In contrast, these concerns troubled the authorities in the Netherlands much less. The explanation probably lies in the fact that the German state assumed responsibility for poor relief much earlier than the Dutch.

[66] Wehler 1987: 169.
[67] Torpey 2000: 81–88.

A third and final motive underlying the evolution of the passport regime is linked to the general process of state formation. In the course of the nineteenth century many states began to monitor the geographical mobility of their inhabitants (both citizens and aliens) by registering their populations, thus making them "legible," to use the vocabulary of James Scott.[68] Especially from the middle of the nineteenth century, states increasingly tried to keep tabs on their inhabitants in order to promote their own interests. This important transition phase in state formation was, as Charles Tilly has demonstrated, primarily motivated by the need for strong armies, for which efficient taxation and general conscription were necessary.[69] Later the state gradually took on other, more socioeconomic as well as ideological functions (such as stimulating national identity). One of the results of this process was a growing "administrative power," defined by Giddens as control over the timing and spacing of human activities.[70] All the ways to establish individual identity, including passports, identification documents, and population registers, fit well in this larger picture. Deducing from the liberalization of the passport regime in the 1860s that states (both sending and receiving) were not interested in migrants anymore thus amounts to turning a blind eye to the socioeconomic motives (poor relief, taxation, criminality) for monitoring and controlling them. Measures aimed at documenting the movements and identity of people existed throughout the nineteenth century (and before, albeit in the ancien régime more at the local than on the national level), but became increasingly important as states became more powerful and intrusive.[71]

Monitoring and the need to carry personal identification cannot simply be equated with restricting the freedom of movement, however, nor were passports and other forms of identification only instruments in the interest of the state, which brings us to the *third and fourth questions*. As we have seen, passports and other documents could also turn into "weapons of the weak"[72]—in our case, of migrants—because these documents could protect them against the arbitrary power of local authorities. Furthermore, the increasing monitoring and the need for large segments of the migrants who crossed national borders to carry some sort of identification enlarged states' knowledge about the movements of people, but it did not immediately lead to extensive interference with international migration. Stopping people at the border or expelling them was restricted to short periods following specific political upheavals, mainly revolutions, and to

---

[68] Scott 1998: ch. 2.
[69] Tilly 1990.
[70] Giddens 1987: 47, 147.
[71] For a general discussion of these processes, see Torpey 1998b and Scott 1998: ch. 2.
[72] Scott 1985.

specific groups, such as people labeled as gypsies, vagrants, or political agitators. The bulk of the migrants were left in peace. The explanation for this relatively liberal attitude is simple. Until the First World War most states had no great inclination to interfere in the economic domain and were therefore not interested in excluding non-citizens from the labor market.[73] States' interest in immigrants was limited to concerns about taxation and public safety,[74] for which purposes simple monitoring was sufficient. Only when the question of poor relief became a major concern for national states—a development that coincided with the growth of labor movements—did states become more attentive to calls to protect the national labor market.[75] When these structural shifts coincided with the outbreak of World War I (and the revolutionary aftermath in Russia, the Netherlands, and Germany), passports and visa requirements were reintroduced, and permanently so. Yet since that time passports have principally been used as an instrument to regulate the entrance of aliens into national labor markets, and much less for the purpose of tracking revolutionaries and spies.

[73] A good illustration is offered by Del Fabbro (1996: 110), who counted only 5,646 expulsions from the German Empire in the years 1903–12, most of which arose from accusations of breaches of labor contracts.

[74] See also Jackson 1997: 17.

[75] Lucassen 1998.

14

The Great War and the Birth of the Modern Passport System

JOHN TORPEY

ON THE VERY eve of the First World War, Werner Bertelsmann, a German student of passport controls, wrote that "because in recent times the position of foreigners has grown much different from before . . . most modern states have, with but a few exceptions, abolished their passport laws or at least neutralized them through non-enforcement. . . . [Foreigners] are no longer viewed by states with suspicion and mistrust but rather, in recognition of the tremendous value that can be derived from trade and exchange, welcomed with open arms and, for this reason, hindrances are removed from their path to the greatest extent possible."[1] These remarks suggest the enormous influence that economic liberalism still held in the minds of many Europeans. It was this set of ideas that had undergirded an unprecedented trend toward the relaxation of passport controls on movement in late-nineteenth-century Western Europe, a period that has been called "the closest approximation to an open world in modern times."[2] A counter-trend had been afoot for some time, however, and the Great War would definitively reverse that state of affairs, ushering in what would prove to be a rigorous and extremely effective system of documentary controls on human movement.

Despite its usefulness to states in restricting unwanted movements, the international passport to which we have grown accustomed since World War I is a document of considerable ambiguity. As the documentary expression of modern states' efforts to monopolize the "legitimate means of movement," the passport concentrates in itself the enormous increase in

I am grateful to the participants in the workshop on "Documenting Individual Identity" held in Laguna Beach, California, in December 1998, and especially to Leo Lucassen and my co-editor, Jane Caplan, for their helpful comments on an earlier version. This essay draws on some of the material previously published in John Torpey, *The Invention of the Passport: Surveillance, Citizenship, and the State* (Cambridge University Press, 2000).

[1] Bertelsmann 1914: 18–19. In his survey of the international legal opinion available in his time (pp. 13–17), Bertelsmann was unable to muster any consensus for the view that states had an unequivocal right to bar foreigners from entry into their territory.

[2] Dowty 1987: 54.

modern states' control over individual existence that has evolved since the nineteenth century.[3] At the same time, in a world in which documentary attestation of identity is generally required for the legal traversal of state boundaries, passports facilitate people's movements. In addition, passports ensure that their bearers may avail themselves of the protections that states may provide in an uncertain and potentially hostile world. Modern international passports thus join together diplomatic functions with mechanisms of state control. Their spread and more vigorous enforcement during and after World War I—as nationalist fervor reached its height, opportunities for mass travel expanded, and nation-states sought to consolidate their control over territories and populations—indicate that the control function predominates, and that aspect will receive the bulk of the attention here.

World War I and the "Temporary" Reimposition of Passport Controls

The booming of the guns of August 1914 brought to a sudden close the era during which governments viewed foreigners without "suspicion and mistrust" and allowed them to traverse borders relatively unmolested— a situation that Bertelsmann had considerably overstated in any case. As was typical of wartime, the conflagration generated hostility toward those who might bear the *patrie* ill-will and a renewed preoccupation with controlling their movements. Mobilization for war stiffens the backs of states and, like the threat of a hanging, concentrates their minds; administration becomes focused on one single and overriding aim. The achievement of that aim during the First World War led to the consolidation of views about foreigners and methods for restricting their movements that would prove to be an enduring part of our world. It was not only foreigners that were affected, however, even if they bore the brunt of the new restrictions; the nationals of the various countries involved in the conflagration were subjected to intensified documentary surveillance during the Great War as well.

In pursuit of the objective of greater control over the movements of the national and the alien alike, passport controls that had been eliminated or had fallen into desuetude were reintroduced across the Continent. At first, reflecting the persistence of the view that such controls were acceptable only during time of war, the newly reinstituted passport requirements were typically said to be provisional measures, responses to a state of emergency. That the war would ultimately have the effect of bringing an

[3] On this process, see Torpey 1998b.

end to the laissez-faire era in international migration would not have been predicted by many contemporaries.[4]

Thus, for example, French passport restrictions from the revolutionary period that had been "allowed to lapse" were restored in the face of the crisis.[5] In addition, French lawmakers used the crisis to enhance the documentary demarcation between Frenchman and foreigner. Despite official protests from the French trade union confederation Confédération générale du travail (CGT) that some of the newly adopted fingerprinted identification cards treated the citizen like "a convict," war-inspired xenophobia allowed the government to strengthen the documentary identification requirements for foreigners. In consequence of two decrees promulgated in April 1917, identification cards became mandatory for all foreigners above the age of fifteen living in France. These decrees realized the aim of a 1915 bill requiring all foreigners to carry identification cards after the end of the war. The cards were to include the bearer's nationality, civil status, occupation, photograph, and signature, and special color codes were employed to mark out wage earners in agriculture and industry.[6] Foreigners, and especially "immigrant workers," were becoming more and more intelligible by the documents they carried.

In Britain, the Aliens Restriction Act of 1914 sharply enhanced the power of the government, "when a state of war exists," to prohibit or impose restrictions on the landing or embarkation of aliens in the United Kingdom. The law made no explicit mention of passport requirements, for these had already been rejuvenated in 1905 in response to the perceived threat of a large-scale influx of East European Jews. That departure from Britain's earlier laissez-faire attitude toward immigration came about only after long years of opposition to an Aliens bill by the stalwartly Manchesterian Liberals. The 1905 law was adopted against a background in which the term *immigrants* had become synonymous with Jews, "a group so undesirable that they were compared unfavorably with the despised Irish and ... categorized [in the popular mind] as close to the Chinese."[7] The Aliens Restriction Act sharpened the earlier requirements by putting the onus of proving that a person is not an alien on that person and thus making documentary evidence of one's nationality largely unavoidable, particularly if one did not look or sound "British," whatever that meant. It also provided for the possibility of requiring aliens to live, or of prohibiting them from living, in certain areas, and of registering with the authorities their place of domicile, change of abode, or move-

---

[4] See Lucassen 1997a: 2.
[5] Plender 1988: 90 n.132; see also Burguière and Revel 1989: 67.
[6] Noiriel 1996: 61, 273–74.
[7] Zolberg 1997: 312–13.

ment within the United Kingdom. Finally, the act made provision for the appointment of immigration officers to carry out the order, an expansion of immigration bureaucracy that helped strengthen the momentum for keeping passport controls in place after the war.[8]

The German government, too, adopted new passport controls under the emergency clauses of its liberal 1867 passport law, which had abolished passport requirements for all persons entering, leaving, or circulating within the territory of the North German Confederation and then the empire. Already on July 31, 1914, Germany implemented "temporary" passport restrictions on anyone entering the empire from abroad. In the interest of permitting the return of eager or otherwise mobilized soldiers, the requirement was relaxed for those who could produce papers demonstrating that they were German subjects, stateless former Germans, or permanent residents of the *Reich* who had only been abroad temporarily. This provision was implemented for the good reason that these people might very well not have had passports when they originally left Germany. Meanwhile, in order to avoid the flight of unwilling cannon fodder, those owing military service were to be eligible for passports for exit from Germany only with the approval of their commanding officers. At the same time, foreigners in any area of the empire declared to be in a state of war were required to have a passport giving a proper account of their person. In the absence of a passport, other satisfactory documents were to be accepted, presumably because the new regulations might have caught them with their papers down.[9]

Before the year was out, Germany strengthened these regulations further. Now, anyone who wished to enter *or leave* the territory of the empire (excluding Alsace-Lorraine) was to be in possession of a passport. Foreigners *anywhere* in that territory, not just in war zones, also were required to have a passport or other acceptable document. All such passports, moreover, had to include a personal description, photograph, and signature of the bearer, along with an official certification that the "bearer is actually the person represented in the photograph." Finally, foreign passports for purposes of entry into the empire had to have a visa from German diplomatic or consular authorities. At least during this early phase of the war, the Germans were nearly as concerned about controlling

---

[8] 4 & 5 Geo. 5, c. 12, 5th August 1914, *The Public and General Acts*, 1914: 26–28. In a pattern that would recur in British history after World War II, the nearly simultaneous British Nationality and Status of Aliens Act of 1914 (7th August 1914, 4 & 5 Geo. 5 c. 17), further described as an "Act to consolidate and amend the Enactments relating to British Nationality and the Status of Aliens," was promulgated at the same time in order to determine who exactly was an alien for purposes of alien restriction.

[9] "Verordnung, betreffend die vorübergehende Einführung der Passpflicht," July 31, 1914, *Reichsgesetzblatt* 1914: 264–65.

the movements of German nationals—in part, no doubt, in order to keep the soldiery fresh with recruits—as they were about keeping an eye on those of foreigners.[10]

The next step in securing the territory of the *patrie* at war, taken in mid-1916, added to the passport requirements that a visa (*Sichtvermerk*) from German authorities in the country of origin was to be required from everyone, German or foreign, entering or leaving the territory of the empire as well as of certain occupied areas.[11] Such requirements both complicated the task of departing from German territory and fortified the ability of the German military and consular bureaucracy to restrict the movements of those wishing to enter from abroad. After the war, such systems of "remote control"[12] would become a critical feature of more effective immigration management rooted in documentary controls.

An accompanying order detailed, with stereotypically German precision, by and to whom German passports could be issued, the information they were to include, a standard passport form, the acceptable form of a *foreign* passport (which was supposed to conform to all the criteria of a German passport, including photograph, etc.), the form of a personal identity document (*Personalausweis*) acceptable in place of a passport, and the terms and conditions for the issuance of visas, depending on whether these were for exit from, entry into, or transit through German territory. The order reaffirmed the late-nineteenth-century stricture that German passports could be issued only to German nationals, a status that was to be appropriately recorded. Notably, if the passport bearer had previously been stateless or of non-German nationality, such prior nationality or lack thereof and the date of naturalization to German citizenship were to be duly indicated in the passport.[13] Clearly, the German authorities thought it was best to be aware of the possibility that someone might have divided loyalties, even despite having undergone the rigors of naturalization.

The Italians' first step concerning documentary controls on movement after the outbreak of hostilities was not to issue new passports, but rather to recall those already in circulation among their citizens. By a decree of August 6, 1914, the government suspended the right of emigration of those obliged to do military service, annulling all passports in their possession. Like the German passport regulations, this order indicated the close

---

[10] "Verordnung, betreffend anderweite Regelung der Passpflicht," December 16, 1914, *Reichsgesetzblatt* 1914: 521–22.

[11] "Verordnung, betreffend anderweite Regelung der Passpflicht," June 21, 1916, *Reichsgesetzblatt* 1916: 599–601.

[12] The term is Aristide Zolberg's; see Zolberg 1997: 311.

[13] "Bekanntmachung, betreffend Ausführungsvorschriften zu der Passverordnung," June 24, 1916, *Reichsgesetzblatt* 1916: 601–9.

connection between passport controls and efforts to ensure that military recruits for the defense of the *patrie* would not be wanting, even though at this point Italy remained neutral in the conflict.[14] The Italian government followed these measures with a veritable flood of legislation intended mainly to keep Italians from leaving, rather than to keep outsiders from entering.

In an effort to forestall any untoward departures, the government tightened the passport requirements for Italians going abroad to work in May 1915. These new restrictions came immediately on the heels of the Treaty of London (April 26) which brought Italy into the war on the Allied side. Now, those bound *anywhere*, and not just those crossing the Atlantic, as the passport law of 1901 had mandated, had to have a passport in order to leave. In order to get the necessary documents, Italians were required to present a work contract to the officials of the Royal Commissariat of Emigration. This, too, was intended as a "transitory" restriction, and unlike other ostensibly temporary measures was abandoned once peace returned and Italy resumed its then-familiar position as labor supplier to the more developed world.[15]

On the same day, the Italian government imposed passport requirements on foreigners wishing to enter the kingdom, reversing many years of an open-door policy. They made up for lost time, however, by immediately requiring not just passports but visas issued by Italian diplomatic or consular authorities in the place of departure as well. The severe law went on to require foreigners to present themselves to public security officials within twenty-four hours of their arrival to explain the circumstances of their sojourn in Italy, as well as any military obligations that they might owe to the state of which they were nationals. A copy of this written declaration was to be sent to district officials responsible for public security; the declarants received a certificate attesting that they had fulfilled the requirements of the law. The papers necessary for moving around within Italy as a foreigner began to multiply. In addition, the law made residents of Italy part of the apparatus for surveilling foreigners. Anyone, citizen or foreigner, sheltering a foreigner had to submit to police officials a list of such persons within five days of their arrival, and within twenty-

---

[14] "R. decreto del 6 agosto 1914, n. 803, che sospende la facoltá di emigrare ai militari del R. esercito e della R. Marina," *Raccolta Ufficiale delle Leggi e dei Decreti del Regno d'Italia*, 1914, vol. 3 (Rome: Stamperia Reale): 2804–5.

[15] "R. decreto 2 maggio 1915, n. 635, concernente l'espatrio per ragioni di lavoro," *Raccolta Ufficiale*, 1915, vol. 2: 1723–27 and "Decreto Luogotenenziale 23 dicembre 1915, n. 1825, che proroga sino alla fine della guerra il termine di validita' stabilito nell'art. 12 del R. decreto 2 maggio 1915, n. 635, circa l'espatrio per ragioni di lavoro," *Raccolta Ufficiale*, 1915, vol. 5: 4623–24. I am grateful to Jane Caplan for helping to clarify the context in which these decisions were taken.

four hours had to inform those officials of their departure and "the direction they have taken." In an indication of the growing reliance on modern technology to control movement, the Italians, like the Germans, demanded that such passports include a photograph and a signature authenticated by the issuing authority.[16] Yet the fact that the various governments felt the need to state such requirements also reflected the incoherence of the passport system of the time and the uncertain status of these documents in international law. One country's insistence that the passports of those entering its territory conform to its standards could not make them do so.

The year 1916 intensified the Italian government's concern with documentary controls on movement, yet all three of the regulations issued concerned Italians rather than foreigners. A decree of March 16 temporarily suspended the issuance of passports for travel abroad, whether for work or any other purpose.[17] Three months later, another required a passport of every Italian citizen entering or leaving the kingdom. While this decree again made passports available for going abroad, such passports had to include a visa from the district public security office. Visas from an Italian embassy or legation were also necessary for entering the kingdom, and these had to indicate both the length of the visa's validity and the precise location at which the person would enter Italian territory. Subjects of Austria-Hungary who were Italian nationals were required to have a special passport described in the decree.[18] Finally, an order of August 27 revived internal passports, a document last addressed in statute in the public security law of 1889. In order to be valid, these passes, too, had to have photographs and had to conform to the new model attached to the decree.[19]

What is striking about the wartime Italian laws is that, despite having reversed a long-standing policy of undocumented entry to foreigners, most of the restrictive legislation actually concerned Italians wishing to leave the country. Italy's traditional experience as a country of emigration suggests that, when the exigencies of war demanded stepped-up military recruitment, retaining Italians who might have sought to shirk their soldierly obligations in favor of seeking work abroad was a larger problem for the government than keeping out foreigners. Given the over-represen-

[16] "Decreto-legge del 2 maggio 1915 [n. 634], concernente il soggiorno degli stranieri in Italia," *Raccolta Ufficiale*, 1915, vol. 2: 1708–22.

[17] "Decreto Luogotenenziale 16 marzo 1916, n. 339, che sospende temporaneamente il rilascio dei passaporti per l'estero," *Raccolta Ufficiale*, 1916, vol. 1: 643–44.

[18] "Decreto Luogotenenziale 23 luglio 1916, n. 895, che approva le norme relative all'entrata e all'uscita di persone dal Regno," *Raccolta Ufficiale*, 1916, vol. 2: 1896–1918.

[19] "Decreto Luogotenenziale 27 agosto 1916, riguardante la concessione dei passaporti per l'interno," *Raccolta Ufficiale*, 1916, vol. 3: 2369–71.

tation in the poorly paid and worse-fed infantry of southern Italians with only a weak sense of national loyalties, it was hardly surprising that the Italian government might expect conscripts to abscond if given the chance. The anxieties of the Italian political elite in this regard were not misplaced: some 290,000 soldiers—about 6 percent of the total—faced courts-martial in Italy between May 1915 and September 1919, usually for desertion.[20]

The generalized anxiety about borders that existed during the war did not subside with its end. Instead, the "temporary" measures implemented to control access to and departure from the territories of European states persisted into the shallow, fragile peace that was the interwar period. An order of June 1919 reiterated and rendered permanent the wartime requirement that anyone crossing the borders of the German *Reich* in either direction be in possession of a passport with visa, and reaffirmed the paragraph insisting that all foreigners in the territory of the empire carry a passport.[21] In Britain, similarly, the wartime restrictions on aliens won greater permanence with the Aliens Order of 1920, which extended the validity of previous restrictions beyond the war's end. These restrictions, according to the order, "should continue in force . . . not only in the [wartime] circumstances aforesaid, but at any time." Henceforward, *anyone* entering or leaving the United Kingdom was required to have "either a valid passport furnished with a photograph of himself or some other document satisfactorily establishing his national status and identity." The passport became the backbone of the system of documentary substantiation of identity used to register and keep track of the movements of aliens in the United Kingdom. As in Italy during the war, foreigners in the United Kingdom were now subject to extensive reporting and documentary requirements, and keepers of inns in which aliens might happen to stay were drawn into the apparatus of surveillance over foreigners. The order also mandated the maintenance of a "central register of aliens" under the direction of the secretary of state.[22]

The Italians remained the anomaly in that their restrictions focused principally on emigration, not immigration. A decree of May 1919 reaffirmed the wartime requirement that emigrants have a passport in order to leave, whatever their destination.[23] According to a study of emigration

[20] See Clark 1984: 186–88.

[21] "Verordnung, über die Abänderung der Verordnung vom 21. Juni 1916, betreffend anderweite Regelung der Passpflicht," June 10, 1919, *Reichsgesetzblatt*, 1919: 516–17.

[22] Aliens Order, 1920, March 25, 1920, *Statutory Rules and Orders and Statutory Instruments Revised to December 31, 1948*, 1850, vol. 2: 1–48.

[23] "Decreto-legge Luogotenenziale 18 maggio 1919, n. 1093, che stabilisce l'obbligo del passaporto per I cittadini che sono considerati o si presumono emigranti, fissando altresí norme per il suo rilascio e le penalitá da infliggersi ai contravventori," *Raccolta Ufficiale*, 1919, vol. 3: 2381–84.

restrictions by the International Labor Office, moreover, Italians intending to depart for work in countries that required passports had to
show a work contract before receiving their travel documents.[24] Again,
however, what might have appeared to be—and, when necessary, could
be transformed into—restrictions are better understood from the point of
view of Italy's continued interest in exporting workers. As passport controls remained in force across Europe and in the United States after the
war, the obligation that Italian emigrants have a passport and, where required, a work contract in order to get it comprised efforts to *facilitate*
rather than limit emigration. The passport obligations for foreigners entering Italy during the war years were never abolished, but this matter
was of considerably less import to the Italian government than that of
ensuring that would-be emigrant workers be in a position to enter their
destination countries, at least until the early 1920s, when the new fascist
government sought to limit departures once again in the interest of bol-
stering Italy's armed forces.

The United States and the End of the
Laissez-Faire Era in Migration

The U.S. government first responded to the renewal of European restrictions on movement with an executive order on December 15, 1915, requiring all persons leaving the United States for a foreign country to have
a passport visaed by American officials before departure—a prudent
enough measure in view of the fact that such documents had once again
come to be required in many destination countries.[25] Then, in early 1917,
the U.S. Congress adopted a law—over repeated vetoes by President Wilson—that excluded adult immigrants unable to pass a simple literacy test
in their native language, which had the effect of excluding large numbers
of people from areas of Europe that offered their inhabitants little school-
ing. In addition, the law prohibited entry by those from a "barred zone"
in the Pacific. With Chinese, Japanese, and Korean immigration largely
forbidden already before the war, the main targets of this legislation were
Asian Indians who were technically "Aryans" or "Caucasians," and who
were thus excluded on geographical rather than ethnoracial grounds.[26]

Finally, on May 22, 1918—with the war nearly at an end—Congress
adopted "An Act to prevent in time of war departure from or entry

[24] International Labour Office 1928: 85.
[25] Executive Order No. 2285, December 15, 1915.
[26] See Higham 1988: 203–4, and Chan 1990: 63; the text of the law can be found at 39
stat. 874 (1917). For some of the legal complications of American racial classifications during this period, see Haney-Lopez 1996.

into the United States contrary to the public safety," which authorized the American president to impose specific restrictions on aliens wishing to enter or leave the country. The act gave statutory foundation to the passport requirements adopted by executive order in December 1915. On August 8, 1918, President Wilson gave the law teeth with an executive order mandating that "hostile aliens must obtain permits for all departures from, and entries into, the United States."[27] Soon enough, however, the war would be over and the preoccupation with "hostile aliens" would target not military enemies but simply certain groups of foreigners as such.

The erection of paper barriers to movement contributed substantially to bringing "the laissez-faire era in international labor migration ... to a close."[28] Because the United States was the destination country for so many migrants in the North Atlantic world, its policies and postures were an important cause of this caesura. For it, too, allowed initially temporary, wartime passport restrictions on aliens to persist into the postwar period. Immediately after the war came to a close, immigration to the country picked up, rising from 24,627 in 1919 to 246, 295 the following year and 652,364 in 1921. Yet when the United States extended the range of national groups who were denied the right to immigrate from long-excluded Asian groups to a variety of Europeans, the numbers began to decline very quickly and documentary controls played an important role in enforcing the new restrictions.[29]

At the end of 1919, Congress passed a revised version of the 1918 law that addressed only the issue of entry into the United States and dropped any mention of the proviso that the country find itself "in time of war."[30] As a result of these laws, the putatively "temporary" measures designed to ferret out "hostile aliens" were transmuted into weapons in the fight against "the undesirable, the enemy of law and order, the breeder of revolution, and the advocate of anarchy." Passport controls came to play an important role at this point; one indication of this fact is that the various regional sections of the 1918 report of the commissioner general of immigration included only one separate discussion of "passport matters," whereas by 1919 all of the regions did so.[31] With Asians from the "barred zone" almost entirely excluded, literacy tests required, and documentary

[27] U.S. *Statutes at Large*, vol. 40, part I: 559; Executive Order No. 2932, August 8, 1918.

[28] Dowty 1987: 83.

[29] Zolberg 1999: 80.

[30] Public Law #79, "An Act To regulate further the entry of aliens into the United States," November 10, 1919, U.S. *Statutes at Large*, vol. 41, part I: 353.

[31] The quotation is from Commissioner General of Immigration Anthony Caminetti in U.S. Department of Labor 1919: 67–68.

restrictions in place, the stage was set for more thoroughgoing exclusionary measures.

In 1921, the United States adopted the first "national origins" quotas, restricting immigration to a small percentage of the targeted nationalities represented in the U.S. population in the 1910 census. Realizing subsequently that large numbers of Southern and Eastern Europeans had entered the country by that time, the defenders of white America returned to the ramparts three years later to pass another law that took as a baseline the 1890 census, when the "Nordic" stock of the country was more predominant.[32] But restriction of incoming persons along these lines was easier said than done. Because the 1921 law had mandated a quota system without adequate provision for its implementation, hundreds of excess visas were issued abroad to steamship passengers making their way to the United States. As a result, steamer captains would seek "to bring their passengers into the United States at the earliest possible moment after the opening of the new quota month. Midnight ship racing into New York Harbor in order to cross the entrance line before quotas were exhausted became a monthly event, and much distress and many deportations usually followed."[33] This arrangement simply would not do.

The Immigration Act of 1924 thus provided that American consuls abroad be charged with the task of administering the quotas themselves, and distributing immigration visas accordingly. In the process, various other prerequisites for admission—including police checks, medical fitness, financial responsibility determinations, and political interviews—could be established long before the intending immigrant reached the United States. As many who have taken the tour of Ellis Island National Park will know, the stated purpose of this approach was to avoid situations in which eager but impecunious emigrants might sell off all their worldly possessions in order to purchase a steamship ticket, only to be told upon arrival that they were inadmissible for any number of reasons. In contrast to this interpretation, Aristide Zolberg has characterized this set of procedures as a form of "remote border control," a major innovation in immigration policy implementation that "proved remarkably effective from the time of [its] institutionalization in the 1920s until well into [the] 1970s . . . [and] which by any reasonable standard must be reckoned as a remarkable administrative achievement."[34]

While both interpretations of the new requirement may be correct without contradiction, for our purposes it is essential to see that the system

[32] See Higham 1988: ch. 11. Canadians and Latin Americans were exempted from the quota limitations.

[33] U.S. Department of Labor 1934, Lecture No. 9: 2.

[34] Zolberg 1997: 308–9; see also Higham 1988: 324, and Fitzgerald 1996: 132. For details on the workings of the system, see U.S. Department of Labor 1934: 2ff.

could work only on the basis of documentary requirements that power-fully supported the claims of states to monopolize the legitimate means of movement. The passport requirements for foreigners left intact after World War I provided the essential administrative basis for the implemen-tation of the restrictionary immigration laws of the 1920s. Using the pass-port as a document attesting identity, the consular officer charged with determining eligibility for entry into the United States simply added a visa indicating the conditions of a person's stay on American soil, or denied entry altogether.

Yet in one region that comprised a significant source of immigrant flows, namely Mexico, restrictionism failed to carry the day, although not for lack of official attention. It should be recalled here that U.S. involve-ment in World War I had been sparked to a considerable extent by the "Zimmermann telegram," which was published in the American press on March 1, 1917. It instructed the German minister in Mexico City to offer his country's support to Mexican efforts to recover Texas, New Mexico, and Arizona in the event of war between Germany and the United States.[35] With fears of enemy alien infiltration from the south on the rise, beginning in 1917 border control measures along the Mexican frontier grew fever-ish. In February 1918, however, the assiduous supervising inspector of the Immigration Bureau responsible for the border, Frank Berkshire, in-formed his boss that his resources were inadequate to patrol the border effectively, and that the cooperation of other government agencies and the military, while willing, was too uncoordinated to be of use. Berkshire thus proposed the creation of a separate, permanent organization, "simi-lar perhaps to the Northwest Mounted Police of Canada," numbering two thousand to three thousand men and charged specifically and exclu-sively with the task of controlling movements across the border.[36]

Apparently Berkshire failed to receive the immediate help he had re-quested, for he soon felt compelled to inform his superiors that the efforts of his subordinates to control the border had been largely unavailing. Indeed, to the extent that they accomplished anything at all, they had exercised control over the wrong people. In the 1918 report of the com-missioner general of immigration, Berkshire wrote in the section of his summary concerning "Passport Matters" that the number of agents de-tailed to monitor the border was simply insufficient to be effective. Berk-shire noted that passport controls, however meticulously carried out, could be undertaken only at the "regular immigration ports of entry,"

---

[35] See Paxton 1975: 95.

[36] Letter of F. W. Berkshire, supervising inspector, Mexican Border District, El Paso, Texas, to commissioner-general of immigration, February 5, 1918, U.S. Department of Labor, Immigration Service File No. 54261/276.

which left many miles of "remote and unfrequented points," easy targets for the movements of enemy operatives. Accordingly, Berkshire concluded, "It is logical to assume that the most dangerous of the enemy's agents have sought, and will continue to seek, these points to avoid attracting attention. In the main, therefore, the passport regulations as now enforced discommode thousands of loyal, or in any event, not unfriendly persons whose legitimate business or innocent pleasures naturally take them through the regular channels, while the frontier elsewhere is inadequately guarded."[37]

In essence, Berkshire was pointing to the much greater difficulty of using documents to control a land border than to restrict the entry of passengers on steamships (or, later, airplanes). A few years later, as the futility of paper barriers in the face of so much open country came to be recognized, his pleas for more manpower to control the lengthy Mexican frontier would be answered with the creation of the Border Patrol in 1924. Despite its preoccupation nowadays with managing the movements of Mexican nationals, the Border Patrol initially focused on restricting the entry of Europeans and Asians whose immigration had been circumscribed by the various acts of the preceding years. With the late-nineteenth-century exclusion of cheap immigrant labor from across the Pacific and the growing restrictions on European immigrants, Mexico had come to serve as a critical source of low-wage labor in Southwestern agriculture and industry—a function it continues to serve to the present day. The new Border Patrol, gradually retooled to focus its attention on the influx of relatively poor workers from south of the border, would ultimately come to play an important if ambiguous role in regulating the flow of Mexican labor into the United States. In doing so, it would have to navigate gingerly between the conflicting pressures of labor-hungry agricultural interests, on the one hand, and domestic political groups bent on restriction, on the other.[38]

The creation of the Border Patrol, which took place in the context of a much broader restrictionist thrust on the part of the American government, rounded out the development of immigration bureaucracies that could, if they wished, effectively seal off entry into the United States from abroad. It is always easier to control people in containers of some sort than pedestrians, however, so the use of documentary controls such as passports and visas played a central role in the restriction of immigration coming from overseas during the 1920s. After the imposition of the 1921 quota law, immigration from Europe fell sharply, and was cut again with

---

[37] See United States, Department of Labor, Bureau of Immigration 1918: 321.

[38] See Calavita 1992. I am grateful to Professor Calavita for a personal communication (August 12, 1998) concerning the origins of the Border Patrol.

the adoption of the more restrictive law of 1924. The era of easy immigration was indeed over. The major exception to this generalization in Western Europe during the 1920s was France, which despite its wartime moves to demarcate sharply between French and foreigner remained relatively receptive to newcomers. Out of concern for its demographic decline, France admitted some 1.5 million—a substantial proportion of whom were refugees—over the course of the decade.[39]

Conclusion

The newly permanent passport controls that persisted after World War I generally applied not just to foreigners, but to both citizens and aliens. This was a necessary outcome of the desire to control borders against unwanted entrants, however, and aliens had increasingly come to be seen as lacking any prima facie claim to access to the territory of a state other than their own. In the absence of telltale markers such as language or skin color—which are themselves inconclusive as indicators of one's national identity, of course, but which nonetheless frequently have been taken as such—a person's nationality simply cannot be determined without recourse to documents. As an ascribed status, it cannot be read off a person's appearance.

The (re-)imposition of passport controls by numerous West European countries and the United States during the First World War and their persistence after the war was an essential aspect of that "identification revolution"[40] that vastly enhanced the ability of governments to identify their citizens, to distinguish them from non-citizens, and thus to construct themselves as "nation-states." With the general rise of the "protectionist state" out of the fires of World War I, the countries of the North Atlantic world became caught up in a trend toward nationalist self-defense against foreigners, itself part of a larger process of what has aptly been called the "naturalization of nativism."[41] Documents such as passports and identification cards that help determine "who is in" and "who is out" of the nation here took center stage, and thus became an enduring and omnipresent part of our world.

These documents were an essential element of that burgeoning "infrastructural" power to "grasp" individuals that distinguished modern states from their predecessors.[42] Specific historical forces such as nationalist ide-

---

[39] Zolberg et al. 1989: 18.

[40] See Noiriel 1991a and 1996: ch. 2.

[41] Zolberg 1997: 315. On the "protectionist state," see Strikwerda 1997: 51–70.

[42] On the concept of "infrastructural power" and its importance for understanding the novelty of European states since the nineteenth century, see Mann 1993: 59–61. For a dis-

ology, the development of welfare states, and the rise of labor movements seeking to control access to jobs and social benefits played their part in promoting immigration controls and sharpening states' capacities to distinguish between "them" and "us."[43] In states understood as "nation-states," the advantages of membership came to be reserved to citizens only, and thus the issue of who actually comprised the people took on greater importance. To the extent that they facilitated sharper distinctions between nationals and non-nationals and toward the exclusion of the latter from the benefits dispensed by protectionist states, passports became an essential prop to the bureaucratic administration of modern mass migration, just as identity cards have become something like the "currency" of domestic administration, marking out eligibles from ineligibles in the areas of voting, social services, and much more besides.

In 1926, B. Traven, the German-speaking radical best known as the author of the *Treasure of the Sierra Madre*, penned a novel-length screed against passports and other documentary requirements for ordinary travelers, which he regarded as one of the chief outcomes of World War I. In his story of adventure on the high seas entitled *The Death Ship*, Traven wrote: "It seems to me the sailor's card, and not the sun, is the center of the universe. I am positive that the great war was fought, not for democracy and justice, but for no other reason than that a cop, or an immigration officer, may have the legal right to ask you, and be well paid for asking you, to show him your sailor's card, or what have you. Before the war nobody asked you for a passport."[44] Traven's remarks concerning the official preoccupation with identity documents designed to regulate human movement bore witness to the culmination of an era that had seen an extraordinary expansion of the capacity of states to control the migration of populations using documentary means. The growth of this capacity was, in fact, one of the central features of their development *as* states.

---

cussion of the importance of identification documents in facilitating states' "grasp" of their citizens/subjects, see Torpey 1998b.

[43] See Lucassen 1998b.

[44] Traven 1926; I quote from the translation in Traven 1991: 40–41.

Part Four

CONTEMPORARY ISSUES IN IDENTIFICATION

15

DNA-Typing: Galton's Eugenic Dream Realized?

PAMELA SANKAR

IN LATE 1998 the U.S. federal government announced the start of its long-awaited Combined DNA Index System (CODIS), a national forensic DNA database.[1] The *New York Times* awarded the news a front-page, above-the-fold slot, and network news shows enlisted enthusiastic experts for comment. Hailed as a "superior crime-fighting weapon," CODIS will act as a clearing-house, linking forensic DNA-typing collections from all fifty states and the federal government. In theory, now, a stray hair left at a crime scene in Hawaii can identify an assailant who moves his operations to Maine. CODIS's power inheres not just in the material it uses, DNA, but in its national, centralized organization.

Ten years in development, CODIS is the first new national criminal identification database in the United States since the federal fingerprint collection began nearly one hundred years ago. CODIS and the national fingerprint collection resemble each other not just in their national scope and remarkable long-distance identification capacity. They also share a relationship to genetic research. Just as DNA-typing is a product of the "new genetics,"[2] fingerprinting was invented in the course of Francis Galton's then-new eugenic research in England in the 1880s.

Subsequent research proved Galton's hypothesized relationship between fingerprints and heredity scientifically wrong; nonetheless the interests driving the research remain vital. Galton's eugenics and the criminal application of fingerprinting advance the same simple scheme for social control. Locate the bad actor—an individual or some heritable flaw—sequester, eliminate, or overwhelm it, and safeguard society from ne'er-do-wells or bad blood lines.

The new genetics and DNA-typing are motivated by similar goals, although the main focus of new genetics is more narrowly medical. New genetics attacks disease by seeking the responsible genes, and then tries to modify or eliminate their ill-effects through new gene therapies (although these have yet to work) or through controlled reproduction. DNA-typing

[1] Wade 1998: A1.
[2] Buchanan 1996: 18–46.

works in much the same way as fingerprinting, matching one unique trace to another, although its genetic basis gives it the potential to move beyond simple proofs of individual identity.

Eugenics, fingerprinting, new genetics, and DNA-typing all advance strategies which embody the belief that social threats are located within free-standing individuals. Poverty and violence, which foster criminal behavior, or poor diet, inadequate health care, and polluted environments, which typically contribute more to ill health than genetic predispositions, are set aside. These individually focused technologies are embraced despite their narrow practical efficacy in part because they offer solutions, sometimes dramatic ones, to serious social problems without subjecting those problems to serious debate. They are also popular because they rely on gee-whiz science, sophisticated in its era and strongly associated with certainty and progress. This popularity allowed officials to rapidly extend fingerprinting beyond its narrow province of tracking down fugitive felons, and seems also to be supporting a similar elaboration of DNA-typing.

Eugenics and the Invention of Fingerprinting

In the mid- to late nineteenth century in Europe, intellectuals and government leaders worried over the paradox of progress: industrial growth and colonial expansion accompanied by rising crime rates, poverty, and other social problems. They feared deeply that the ranks of habitual criminals, alcoholics, prostitutes, and street urchins would overwhelm the good forces of society. Explanations for the concentration of social problems among the poor often overlooked the psychological and physical effects of extreme impoverishment and looked instead to biological factors. Analysts posed a "putative biological force of degeneration" as the cause of these trends.[3]

In the spirit of these concerns, Francis Galton, eminent biostatistician and theorist of heredity, began to investigate different strategies to reverse the alleged degeneration of the English population. Galton postulated that a large variety of traits were genetic, including obesity, piety, beauty, genius, idiocy, industry, and indolence. By encouraging or discouraging reproduction of these traits, Galton hoped he could rid society of obese and indolent folk. He sought to encourage marriages between people with good traits, which he hoped would result in intelligent, beautiful, productive, and law-abiding citizens. His hope was that this superior group would come to outnumber and then overwhelm the bad stock.

[3] Pick 1996: 21.

Galton also saw criminality as inherited. As he wrote in 1890:

It is well ascertained that many persons are born with such natures that they
are almost certain to become criminals. The instincts of most children are those
of primeval man; in many respects thoroughly savage, and such as would deliver
an adult very quickly into the hands of the law. The natural criminal retains
those same characteristics in his adult life.[4]

To address the transmission of serious criminality or extreme expressions of other undesirable traits, Galton embraced a more aggressive strategy. Instead of relying on good breeders to simply outnumber the undesir-
ables, Galton suggested that some matches be prevented. While giving a
speech advocating compulsory marriages between people with good traits
that would produce in turn more good breeders, Galton described an
alternative strategy to eliminate serious negative traits, such as criminality: "I think that stern compulsion ought to be exerted to prevent the free
propagation of the stock of those who are seriously afflicted by lunacy,
feeble-mindedness, habitual criminality, and pauperism."[5]

When he encountered fingerprints, Galton hoped that he had found the
outward sign of inward character that would allow him to easily distinguish who ought and who ought not be breeding, and with whom. Galton
encountered his first fingerprint collection in the 1880s while he was reviewing the utility of criminal identification based on anthropometry for
the London police.[6] With his overriding interest in inheritance, Galton did
not focus on fingerprints as an alternative identification system. Instead
he proposed that these odd papillary ridges might be useful for studying
inheritance. Perhaps, he ventured, he had found an external marker of
heredity: the "undeniable evidence" carried "visibly about [a person's]
body" of his or her "parentage and near kinships."[7] Galton quickly
learned, however, that fingerprints did not track the groups that interested
him:

I have examined large numbers of persons of different races to our own [white],
as Jews, Basques, Red Indians, East Indians of various origins, Negroes, and a
fair number of Chinese. Also persons of very different characters and tempera-
ments, as students of science, students of art, Quakers, notabilities of various
kinds, and a considerable number of idiots . . . without finding any pattern that
was characteristic of any of them.[8]

[4] Galton 1890: 75–76.
[5] Galton 1908: 311.
[6] Galton 1888: 173–77, 201–2.
[7] Ibid.: 202.
[8] Galton 1908: 252.

Fingerprints, then, could not provide to Galton his long-sought external marker of internal character. Galton attributed this finding to "panmixia"—the indiscriminate mixing of races and types that had occurred over the millennia. He hoped, still, that fingerprints could serve his social improvement agenda.[9]

If the features that made up the patterns of fingerprints did not vary according to some discernible pattern, and thus could reveal nothing about human types, perhaps, instead, they were demonstrably unique and would be useful for personal identification. Galton proved this hypothesis correct—that indeed fingerprints were unique and permanent—and quickly began a campaign advocating widespread use of fingerprints as a means of identification. From casting fingerprints as an external sign of heredity that could provide the underpinning for a program to cleanse the gene pool of bad stock, to viewing them as identifiers that would assure a place in jail for habitual criminals, was a small step for Galton. The notion of prevention and social control underlying both uses was the same: identify, sequester, control. For the next ten years Galton dedicated considerable energy to promoting fingerprinting, writing twenty-four articles between 1888 and 1896 on fingerprinting's benefits for the control of colonial populations and the prevention of crime.[10]

Seeing fingerprinting as a useful tool in the fight against crime, large urban police departments in the United States and Europe were adopting fingerprinting by the turn of the century. At the same time, fingerprinting became a regular topic of conversation at meetings of the International Association of Chiefs of Police (IACP), a professional organization that drew members from Canada and the United States. At the 1911 IACP convention, a speaker addressing both fingerprinting and criminal identification through anthropometric measurements emphasized how these technologies could address the problem of habitual criminals. He complained that these repeat offenders could not be put to death outright:

> Only permanent elimination, therefore, of these individuals [habitual criminals] from that society with which they are constantly at war can result in permanent relief. Permanent elimination of these criminals from society, however, is too much to hope for at this time when the tendency is all in the other direction.[11]

In the breach, however, at least police departments have these new identification technologies that allow "putting dangerous men away for long periods and keeping them there."[12]

---

[9] Pearson 1930: 169.
[10] Galton 1908: appendix III.
[11] *International Association of Chiefs of Police* 1911: 158–59.
[12] Ibid.: 158–59.

The Spread of Fingerprinting

The New York City Police Department was first in the United States to adopt the new technology in 1904. Several other large urban police departments soon followed suit. Although the federal government was slow to embrace fingerprinting at first, by the late 1930s, the federal collections (the Department of Justice collection was by far the largest) numbered in the tens of millions. Twenty years later these collections had increased tenfold, and had gone from a strictly criminal collection to one that incorporated nearly as many law-abiding citizens.

State, local, and federal governments increased the size of the fingerprint collections by expanding them along two legal criteria: type of offense (felony or misdemeanor) and status of charge (under suspicion, arrested, arraigned, or convicted). Combining these two criteria, the narrowest category for criminal fingerprinting is convicted felons. The broadest category lowers the threshold to include misdemeanants, and widens its reach to include people in all phases of the arrest and conviction process, starting with those being detained by police for questioning.

One of the first legal actions protesting fingerprinting concerned a man accused of a felony, but who had not yet been arraigned (*Gow v. Bingham*). The state lost this 1907 case to Gow, the accused felon, and the judge declared that fingerprinting before trial constituted an "indignity," and a "startling invasion of personal liberty" that contravened the citizen's "natural right" to "complete immunity" and "to be let alone." [13] Subsequently, however, state courts moved in the opposite direction and became increasingly supportive of fingerprinting felons upon arrest, and misdemeanants. In the 1931 case *State v. Kelly*,[14] the Supreme Court handed down its first judgment on fingerprinting. Considering a case in which a misdemeanant had been arrested, but not yet tried, the justices found that fingerprinting "as a physical invasion . . . amounts to almost nothing" and is "no more humiliating than any other means of identification." The *State v. Kelly* decision also referred to fingerprinting as "a sanctioned police power," which legitimated fingerprinting in a wide variety of situations, even absent an authorizing statute. In only a short time, the courts had moved a considerable distance—from contesting the fingerprinting of felons who had been arraigned but not tried, to approving it for *any suspect* upon arrest.

As police and criminal justice officials pushed to increase the number of criminals to be fingerprinted, state, local, and (especially) the federal

[13] *Gow v. Bingham* (107 NY Supp 1011): 1015, 1014.
[14] *U.S. v. Kelly* (55 F. [2d] 67): 126–27.

TABLE 1
Function Creep: Fingerprinting

Original Function	Additional Functions	Example
Monitor resident population due to fear of treason or subversion during W.W.I	Criminal checks	German-American Aliens, 1918-21[a]
Identify military deserters trying to reenlist; identify dead and wounded	Criminal checks and labor and anti-government activist checks	Military, early 1930s and onwards, intermittently[b]
One-time security check in war-related industries for subversives	Criminal checks	Employees in communications industry, 1943[c]
Identification cards, background checks	Criminal checks	New Deal participants (CCC, Welfare recipients, etc.)[d]

[a] U. S. Congress, House. 1917. Committee on Immigration and Naturalization: 21.

[b] U. S. Congress, House. 1932. Committee on Naval Affairs.

[c] Lowenthal 1950: 384–85.

[d] U. S. Congress, House. 1940. Committee on Appropriations: 108, 111; ibid. 1941: 129, 123–24.

governments, spurred on by FBI director J. Edgar Hoover, expanded the uses for fingerprinting. Table 1 describes instances when the government brought prints into its collections for one purpose, or function, and then used them later for others. The government rarely mentioned when it was adding new functions to established collections. In only two instances— the expanded use of military prints for criminal checks and the inclusion of fingerprints from the communications industry—did this expansion come to public attention.

The military fingerprint collection originated in 1906, when the Army began fingerprinting enlistees to detect deserters who tried to reenlist, and to determine whether new recruits had criminal records.[15] The Navy and Marine Corps soon followed suit. In the 1930s, when Hoover began to build the FBI's fingerprint system, he also began to pester the Armed Forces to use his Identification Division to run criminal checks on military fingerprints, which he promised then to return afterwards.[16] Later, he

[15] U.S. War Department, General Order #68, April 7, 1906 (National Archives: General Correspondence—Bureau of Navigation, File 5397–1, RG 24.2.1).

[16] U.S. Congress, House. Committee on Appropriations. 1937: 63; ibid. 1938: 141; ibid. 1939: 109–10; ibid. 1940: 127–28.

wanted to keep military prints permanently at the FBI, to which the Army agreed in the mid-1930s.[17] The Navy and the Marine Corps staunchly resisted, stating that they did not want to stigmatize their personnel by inclusion in the FBI's database, known only as a collection for criminals. Eventually, national security fears of World War II made continued opposition too costly and all branches capitulated.[18] In a similar move, also in the mid-1930s, the FBI incorporated nearly 250,000 prints that it had been given by the Federal Communication Commission for criminal checks. The FBI fought for and won the right to keep these prints in its own collection.[19]

What was once a small federal collection limited to fingerprints of convicted felons became, by the 1940s, a vast storehouse of tens of millions of prints taken not only from anyone who had ever had a brush with the law, but also from many people who had not. The additional fingerprints came from military enlistees, communication workers, members of the New Deal's Civilian Conservation Corps, and hundreds of thousands of citizens who responded independently to vague FBI statements that having prints on file was a useful precaution for anyone.[20] By incorporating millions of prints collected typically as a condition of employment, the FBI dramatically improved its ability to identify criminal suspects by increasing the number of prints against which it could compare new, unidentified prints. In so doing, it also altered the function of these prints from fulfilling a one-time work-eligibility requirement into providing an enduring identity record with which officials could monitor the legal (typically political) conduct of law-abiding U.S. residents.

DNA-typing for criminal identification is now tightly controlled and narrowly applied. DNA-typing's similar fit with established crime prevention mandates and its technological simplicity, however, suggest its functions might expand through means similar to those evident in the expansion of fingerprinting. Furthermore, DNA-typing's genetic basis introduces the potential for identification practices that move beyond a simple matching of one pattern with another.

New Genetics

DNA-typing developed within the context of "new genetics." Recent accounts of genetic research attach "new" to "genetics" in the hope that this prefix will distinguish it from past negative associations with Nazi

[17] U.S. Congress, House. Committee on Naval Affairs. 1932.
[18] U. S. Congress, House. Committee on Appropriations. 1946: 241–42.
[19] Lowenthal 1950: 384–85.
[20] *School and Society* 1937.

eugenics of the Second World War.[21] The label also invokes the numerous new projects associated with the Human Genome Project (HGP), the recently successful effort to map the entire human genome. This massive effort has produced numerous theoretical and technological advances in genetics, allowing the discovery of thousands of disease genes, including the genes for breast and colon cancer, Huntington's Disease, and cystic fibrosis.

New genetics and eugenics are similar in at least one goal: eliminating "inferior" genes. New geneticists seek to do this by locating mutated or altered genes associated with particular diseases or conditions. They then seek to eliminate the gene or mitigate its effects through various reproductive technologies or gene therapy. Most genetic diseases discussed as candidates for elimination are serious single-gene disorders, such as Huntington's Disease—the end of which few people would protest. But the goal of disease elimination or control is shared also by scientists researching behavioral conditions.

Behavioral geneticists study the genetic contributions to human behaviors as diverse as musical ability and schizophrenia. Some of this research looks at certain socially unacceptable behaviors such as criminality, alcoholism, aggression, violence, over-eating, and even poor social skills.[22] Efforts to reduce or control these behaviors through genetic solutions are ill-founded, if for no other reason than they lack sufficient conceptual stability for scientific examination. Definitions of well-described, long-recognized diseases, such as breast cancer, remain subject to periodic scientific debate.[23] Phenomena like crime, obesity, or alcoholism (the boundaries of which shift continually across cultures and throughout history in relation to social beliefs about conformity and deviance), are far more contingent and nullify any attempt at enduring and shared definitions. Precisely what scientists would be eliminating if they eliminated genetic contributions to crime is unclear.

However, the difficulty of defining central research concepts, such as crime or aggression,[24] does not stop some researchers from pursuing this course. And their long-term goals are the same as those of the medical geneticist: locate the genes and try to attenuate their effects, or eliminate them altogether through reproductive interventions or gene therapies.

Reproductive interventions include choosing not to procreate, undergoing genetic testing and aborting a possibly unhealthy fetus, or undergoing

[21] Buchanan 1996:18.
[22] Horgan 1993: 124; *Chicago Tribune*, June 12, 1997: 8; Hellmich 1995: A1; Kotulak 1998: C17; Skuse et al. 1997: 705–8; Moffit et al. 1997: 231–49; Clement et al. 1995: 352–54.
[23] Page and Dupont 1998: 1048–50.
[24] Horgan 1993: 121.

preimplantation diagnosis to select and implant a blastomere (an embryo at the eight-cell stage of development) that lacks the mutation in question.[25] In the future, scientists may also be able to correct mutations through gene therapy, although so far the technique has failed.[26] If any of these strategies were widely pursued, near eradication of the mutation might result.[27]

Thus far, parents confronting the fact that they may pass on a serious genetic condition to their offspring have been left to make their own choices about how to proceed. In an action reminiscent of early-twentieth-century eugenics, however, the British government recently embraced the promise of the new genetics to locate and eliminate genetic mutations. In 1996, the British government tried to institute a routine prenatal program screening women for Fragile X. Fragile X is a mutation associated with mental retardation. In some cases, those with Fragile X might only be distinctive for mildly disruptive behavior, in others they may be prone to violence, or incapable of independent living. The screening program would have allowed women to choose an abortion, if the fetus tested positive for the syndrome. A scientist involved in the effort commented, "There could be a case for screening everyone and offering termination of pregnancy to affected mothers."[28]

The program became controversial and the government withdrew its support. Still, it highlights a troublesome attitude. The deficits of Fragile X children vary considerably, as recent research has shown.[29] The reasons for or patterns of that variation are unknown. The program seems to have been embraced as an easy response to concerns about unruly, demanding children, ill-suited for standard education or care. The British program was not the first attempt to reduce the Fragile X population. A school-based testing program in Denver in the mid-1990s also sought to eliminate the gene by eliminating its carriers, this time through the more indirect approach of relying on better sex education for teen carriers of the mutation.[30] Both of these programs were terminated in response to public criticism; however, support for genetic solutions to anti-social behavior continues. Its evidence can often be found in publications from extensive, well-funded research projects,[31] or in news accounts describing a project's findings or reflecting on its implications, as in this 1995 newspaper article:

[25] Baron and Rainer 1988: 741–53; Bowman 1996: 491–517; Schulman et al. 1996: 57–58.

[26] Hanania et al. 1995: 537–52; Kay et al. 2000: 257–61.

[27] Caskey 1992: 112–35.

[28] Rogers 1996: Home News.

[29] Heldermann van den Enden 1999: 253–57.

[30] Staney et al. 1995: 33–37; Hagerman et al. 1994: 474–81.

[31] Mellins et al. 1996.

Modern science opens up new and different possibilities. If there are genes conferring on certain people a genetic predisposition to crime, could they and their carriers be identified, perhaps as early as the womb? What should happen to those embryos? If someone is born with a criminal mind, what should be done with them?[32]

Posing the question, "what should be done?" implies that something could be done, although the article leaves unspecified what that might be. It presents reliance on genetics to prevent crime as a real possibility. As this passage and the Fragile X programs and related accounts highlight, there exists a degree of ready—if naive—public support for such options.[33] The willingness to turn to genetics for solutions to social problems is replicated in the increasing acceptance of forensic DNA-typing systems.

DNA-Typing

Deoxyribonucleic acid (DNA) consists of four amino acids, joined in a limited set of pairs, that provide the chemical instructions by which the human organism develops and lives. Humans share most of their DNA, but not all. Those parts that are distinct account for physical and mental differences among human beings. Based on these small, but individually important distinctions, each human being's DNA is unique. DNA is present in every human cell and—barring exceptional events like radiation or successful genetic therapy—remains stable over time. Every cell within a given person contains the same DNA. This DNA can be extracted easily from blood, saliva, semen, and sometimes stray hairs or skin flakes. Anyone who stays in one place for a time or is involved in intense physical activity will almost certainly leave behind some trace of DNA. Current technology allows scientists to extract DNA from even a single cell.[34]

DNA's stability, pervasiveness, permanence, ease of retrieval, and uniqueness combine to make it a highly appealing individual identifier. Although some of DNA's qualities have long been known, only recently have scientists devised relatively easy and inexpensive methods to demonstrate consistently DNA's uniqueness in a way that allows for reliable comparisons between samples from different individuals.

Alec Jeffreys, a geneticist working in England on blood anomalies in the early 1980s, invented DNA-typing, a process analysts use to form

[32] Connor 1995: B8.
[33] Lindee and Nelkin 1995.
[34] Wade 1997: F1.

DNA into designs that can be easily analyzed for uniqueness. He used a chemical process to force the long DNA strands to separate into shorter bits at predictable but variable points. These bits then can be arranged by size to create a set of horizontal bars resembling a bar code. The bar code can be replicated and printed. Other DNA samples subjected to similar processing also produce this bar code arrangement, similar in its overall form, but highly variable in its detail. Bar codes from two different samples can be compared at specific sites and will either match one another, or not, and show whether the samples came from the same person. Jeffreys brought the common knowledge of DNA's uniqueness into an analysis and printing method which made that uniqueness accessible as evidence.

Jeffreys developed DNA-typing while devising new research techniques for his own genetics work, rather than as a result of specifically seeking a mechanism for personal identification.[35] Regardless of his intent at the moment, however, Jeffreys quickly recognized the implications of his findings and sought through Cellmark Diagnostics Corporation to patent his technique. In 1984, he quietly offered the Leicester police his technique to solve a particularly vicious rape and murder that had occurred in a small town near his lab. In a second rape-murder case in 1987, the investigation of which came to include deception, false accusations, and a collection of 5,500 blood and saliva samples from local townspeople, Jeffreys' method finally prevailed. In 1987, DNA-typing identified the perpetrator, Colin Pitchfork. Although the technique had by then been used in a handful of other cases, it was the Pitchfork case that brought DNA-typing to national and international prominence.[36] Early press accounts called DNA-typing "the biggest advance in the science of crime detection in a century" and attributed to it a capacity to distinguish one individual from among trillions.[37] Although that turned out to be an overstatement, DNA-typing had been proven effective and is now used routinely by state, local, and federal governments.[38]

CODIS

CODIS functions primarily as a federal clearing house for state-based DNA samples, rather than possessing its own samples. At the center of the CODIS system is a computer (housed in a secret location) that contains thousands of 13-digit codes. Using a process similar to Jeffreys', these

[35] Gill, Jeffreys, and Werrett 1985: 577–79.
[36] Marshall 1987: 6.
[37] Lohr 1987: A9.
[38] Certain problems continue to plague DNA evidence: Lander 1992.

codes are derived from analysis of short tandem repeats (STRs) found in
a person's DNA. A set of computer commands allows authorized state
personnel to submit one of these 13-digit codes and have it checked
against all the other codes currently in the database. In this way, each
state has access to the information produced from samples contributed
by all the other states. If the computer finds a match, it alerts the submit-
ting state and indicates which other states should be contacted to get more
information about the sample. Such information might include its owner's name, and perhaps an address, or at least the police circumstances
under which the earlier samples were collected.

An oft-told story in the promotion of CODIS is one involving Rosie
Gordon, an eleven-year-old abducted from her front lawn, raped, murdered, and dumped five miles away. Over the previous two years, in the
same area, someone had abducted four other young girls under similar
circumstances, although none had been murdered. Eventually a man
named Randall Beers was convicted for one of those abductions. John
Hicks, associate director of the FBI's effort to establish a national DNA
forensic database, asserts that had a DNA sample been on file, along with
a description of the crimes, Beers might have been caught due to the first
molestation's similarity to the second, third, or fourth. Beers might have
been jailed and, thus, never gone on to murder Rosie Gordon. Hicks con-
cludes the tale, "One can only speculate on the outcome of the Rosie
Gordon case . . . if technology and the CODIS system had been available
at that time [of her abduction]. . . . [A] coordinated effort might have . . .
prevented her death."[39]

Hicks' story is effective in part because its tragedy makes the reader
wish CODIS were up and running, everywhere, and soon. The story also
illustrates well the standard logic of crime prevention.[40] The multiple attacks in Rosie Gordon's neighborhood provided multiple chances for police to catch, convict, eliminate the wrongdoer (*maybe* the right one) and,
thus, prevent his future crimes. But because CODIS was not operative at
the time, the police perceived the multiple attacks as separate events and
failed to apply information gleaned from one event to the next. Had
CODIS been operative, Hicks implies, police would have submitted
DNA-evidence from each crime. A CODIS check would have revealed
that only one perpetrator, later proven to be Beers, was responsible. This
information would have sped the perpetrator's identification as Beers and
resulted in his capture before Rosie Gordon's tragic mishap.

The story mentions only in passing that Beers was never tried for Rosie
Gordon's murder, and that her murderer may remain at large today. Nor

[39] Hicks 1998.
[40] Ibid.; *New York Times*, October 12, 1998: 10A.

does it address the fact that the system is ineffective in catching new or careful attackers, or in reducing the number of such people created in our society in the first place. The simplicity and logic of Hicks' story and of similar anecdotes have helped build support for DNA-typing. This support is also helped along by DNA-typing's capacity to free prisoners wrongfully convicted. Officials in Texas and New York City have become so enthusiastic about DNA-typing that they recently proposed typing all children at birth.

Privacy advocates complain that these systems threaten the confidentiality of people whose samples are stored in the databases. According to the government, however, STRs allow experts to confirm whether or not two samples came from the same person, but gives investigators no information about the sample owner's health, appearance, or behavior. CODIS may rely on highly personal genetic material, but it cannot derive personal information from it. On this basis, the federal government claims to address the privacy concerns generated by its apparent access to genetic information about hundreds of thousands—and, eventually, perhaps millions—of its citizens.

Indeed, a data bank full of these 13-digit codes does provide less information than other DNA databases, such as the medical databases that are created to locate and study disease genes. Medical databases often store information by subject name, among other variables, although this practice is coming under criticism.[41] By looking through these data banks, one can easily learn private information, such as statements about a subject's BRCA1/2 status—which indicates whether a person tests positive for a breast cancer gene, or a person's Fragile X status. CODIS, in contrast, contains no such information. It consists only of codes and, most important, does not store the blood or tissue samples from which these codes were derived.

Furthermore, advocates of DNA-typing point out, typing uses only "junk DNA." DNA is labeled "junk" when it apparently does not code for any function currently known to affect human development. At least some of it is believed to be "left over" from past evolutionary innovations. As left-overs, junk DNA supposedly cannot reveal anything personal or sensitive about an individual, and this feature reassures privacy advocates concerned about using genetic material for identification purposes. This reassurance may rest on shaky grounds, however. First, functions for junk DNA may yet be found, and analyses based on it may reveal more than a simple match of one person's pattern to another's.[42] Second, working within the competitive genetics field, researchers are always seeking new

---

[41] Merz and Sankar 1998.
[42] McEwen 1998.

and better methods. Rejecting junk DNA, analysts in the early 1990s used the "DQ-alpha locus," which "resides within a gene that controls a range of immunological processes and is associated with disease."[43] Events surrounding this change are unclear, but its occurrence is notable. Presumably DQ-Alpha was useful for some reason—its variability perhaps—and this utility won out over what seemed to be very minor privacy concerns.

The example of straying away from junk DNA to other sites suggests a willingness to demote privacy concerns for technical advantage. Next time, the "better" site might be one with highly personal information that codes for physical appearance or, putatively, for anti-social behavior. Indeed, although current DNA-typing techniques (including STRs) turn up little of interest beyond confirming or disconfirming a match, government-funded research already underway in Great Britain suggests that this could change.[44] The Forensic Science Service has already conducted two studies, one seeking "genetic markers for skin, hair and eye colour" and the other to find "genetic markers for race." They claim success already for red hair and, implausibly, for the rather diverse group of people labeled in the West as Asian.[45]

Great Britain is more enthusiastic about DNA-collecting than is the United States. British police are already allowed to collect DNA samples from any suspect they choose, and a campaign to establish a universal DNA collection of all the inhabitants of Britain has been discussed. Similar trends characterized the U.S. history of fingerprinting, and may be in DNA-typing's future here as well. In the face of serious social concern about crime in the United States, the integration of "appearance" information into forensic DNA-typing practices might conceivably occur.

Combining behavioral or medical genetic information with DNA-typing might be the next step in creating a state-identification system of remarkable power. Such a system could reveal not only that a sample taken in one setting matched a second taken elsewhere, but that the sample's source possessed the putative genetic markers for various targeted and perhaps highly stigmatized behaviors or diseases. Such a database may seem an implausible development given the current regulations governing CODIS and contributing state systems. The history of fingerprinting, however, demonstrates that criminal identification databases are powerful resources subject to political maneuvers that can quickly push them beyond

---

[43] Ibid.: 318.

[44] The Forensic Science Service in Great Britain is a quasi-governmental forensic services agency that conducts various kinds of scientific analyses of evidence. The British government requires that the evidence services fund themselves, but the government pays for all research efforts.

[45] New Scientist (London), May 23, 1998: 18; Marshall 1998.

their original mandates. During this era, the well-established and growing interest in behavioral genetics may contribute to these maneuverings.

Extending DNA-Typing

DNA-typing was introduced a decade ago for those criminals thought most likely to leave behind easily retrieved tissue samples, including blood, semen, saliva, and hair. These criminals included violent felons and sex offenders.[46] By 1997, thirty states had established DNA-typing databases and were collecting for these categories, and soon several states began adding more categories. Virginia now collects samples from all felons after conviction, while South Dakota has gone ahead and expanded its collection to include all persons *merely arrested* for particular crimes.[47] Arizona collects DNA samples from those convicted of sodomy and sexual misconduct.[48] Other states have proposed even more extreme applications, such as requiring DNA donation from those found guilty of issuing "abortional [sic] articles," or of using "profane, obscene or impure language or slanderous statements [in] a sporting event."[49] None of these proposals has passed, but their very existence indicates an interest in extending DNA-typing well beyond the group of criminals for which it was originally intended.

Function creep in DNA-typing—when the government finds a new use for DNA collected for a different purpose—has begun in a slightly different fashion than it did with fingerprinting. CODIS is less the brain-child of one person (as the national fingerprint collection was for Hoover), and more a brokered solution among often contentious parties. Its development is closely watched by the public, the government, legal scholars, and ethicists.[50] So far, there has been no official push to expand the uses for CODIS information. This conservative course, however, has not been followed in all of the government-run DNA-typing databases. Officials in charge of other federal, state, and local databases have indeed already collected DNA samples for one purpose and used them for another.

When the military introduced mandatory DNA donation by soldiers, its use of the samples was restricted to identification of dead or injured soldiers. In June 1995, Victor Weedn, program manager of the Department of Defense Armed Forces DNA Registry, emphatically declared that

[46] *New York Times: Sunday Magazine* December 11, 1988.
[47] McEwen and Reilly 1994.
[48] Arizona Revised Statutes 1995.
[49] McEwen and Reilly 1994: 945.
[50] Wade 1998: A1; Sachs 1999: B21.

DNA samples used for typing by the Armed Forces Registry would not be used for other purposes, such as law enforcement.[51]

A set of "policy refinements" from the registry announced a year later (April 2, 1996), however, contradicted Weedn's statements and outlined the four conditions under which samples could be used for legal proceedings.[52] Nearly simultaneous (March 29, 1996) with these "refinements," an Army task force issued recommendations to the U.S. Army surgeon general concerning genetics and the military.[53] The "Final Report of the Process Action Team for a Consolidated Military Genetics/DNA Program" addressed the place of genetics in the Army more generally, including, for example, recommendations about the use of genetics in clinical health settings, and in research concerning reactions to environmental toxins. While recognizing that the Armed Forces DNA Registry was developed for identification purposes only, the Process Action Team Report emphasized the economic utility of using the registry for research:

> Although the direct costs of a duplicate repository may be reasonable, there would also be indirect costs, such as lost training time involved in collecting separate samples. These additional resources might be better spent on research and readiness, rather than preserving the existing repository's sole usage for post-mortem identification.[54]

These recommendations have not yet been adopted. Their existence, however, effectively illustrates how function creep begins.

Table 2 describes three instances where DNA has been collected for one reason and analyzed for another.

The "Blue Dress" test refers to the test conducted on Monica Lewinsky's dress to see whether the DNA in the semen stain matched President Clinton's. The tissue sample that the testers used for matching was one that Clinton had previously provided during a routine medical visit to Walter Reed Hospital. The Alabama State Code is the only state code that permits DNA samples collected for criminal purposes to be used for medical research, with identifiers removed. The Armed Forces DNA collection, discussed above, has moved already from restricted use for post-

---

[51] Weedn 1995. During this speech, Weedn declared that the military's DNA-typing system "will not be used for law enforcement purposes." Victor Weedn was then the program manager of the Department of Defense DNA Registry at the Armed Forces Institute of Pathology.

[52] S. C. Joseph, to the Secretary of the Army, Washington, D.C., April 2, 1996, Policy Refinements for the Armed Forces Repository of Specimen Samples for the Identification of Remains, memorandum.

[53] Process Action Team 1996.

[54] Ibid.: 20–21.

TABLE 2
Function Creep: DNA-Typing

Original Use	Additional Functions	Example
Medical	Criminal identity	The Blue Dress (and other instances)[a]
Criminal identity	Medical research	Alabama State Code[b]
Identify injured and dead soldiers	Legal proceedings proposed for medical research	Armed Forces DNA Registry[c]

[a] Babcock 1998: A22.
[b] Alabama Code 1994.
[c] See Footnotes 51, 52, and 53.

mortem recognition to legal proceedings, and may, based on the Policy Action Team Report, move on to medical research.

These examples are few but noteworthy. Once DNA samples exist, it is difficult to restrict their use. If analysis of a sample can solve a serious dispute—from the Clinton–Lewinsky affair to concerns about hereditary disease or paternity—privacy advocates may find themselves outvoted.

Conclusion

As fingerprinting's history has illustrated, policies ushering in a new technology evolve along with the technology in response to changes in the way people perceive the technology's potential, and adjust or refine its procedures. Depending on the prevailing political climate, there is nothing to stop officials from amending statutes to allow state forensic DNA collections to be analyzed for research. The federal government could also change CODIS regulations and begin to link its career criminal data with information supplied by behavioral genetics, despite the conceptual ambiguities of this work.

Promises to limit the functions of forensic DNA-typing collections—such as Weedn's commitment to restrict Armed Forces DNA Repository samples to identification of soldiers injured or killed—are vulnerable to modification because DNA-based technologies seem so attractive. As the basis of possible social control procedures aimed at individuals as sources of disease and crime, DNA is popular for both its association with sophisticated science and the ease with which it can be used. More importantly, it also holds out the possibility of moving state identification practices well beyond a simple matching of bar codes with names, addresses, and social security numbers. As genetic material, it provides the opportunity to incorporate statements about character, intelligence, and disposition. Exploiting DNA in this way will both draw on eugenic, racist theories popular during in the early to mid-twentieth century, and will provide them with a new legitimation.

16

Under My Skin: From Identification
Papers to Body Surveillance

DAVID LYON

A RUSSIAN PROVERB says that humans may be thought of as "body, soul, and passport" and a few years ago I suggested this be updated to "body, soul, and credit card."[1] The point, of course, is that documenting individual identity underwent a shift in the twentieth century, from predominantly print-based information required by the state, to the proliferation of electronically stored data required by commercial businesses. In this essay, however, I want to consider what might be thought of as a return to the "body and soul" definition, although the latter has little or no significant role either. This is not a contraction of demands for identification so much as the co-opting of the body itself as a means of identification. Those intricate lines that form a fingerprint, the geometry of hands, thumbs, or fingers, and the patterns of cones and rods on the retina are the most common candidates for what might be termed "body surveillance." To these may be added voice modulations and images of the face, and genetic clues that may be gleaned from body fluids. Such identification relies on electronic databases, and still relates in part to the state, but its implications take us well beyond the world of passports and credit cards.

In the last part of the twentieth century, a subtle shift began to take place. The body became, once again, a source as well as a site of surveillance. I say "once again," because there is nothing intrinsically new about the body being used in this way. Over a hundred years ago, criminal anthropometry claimed that body shapes, especially the head, could spontaneously reveal the unlawful proclivities of the person. Today, the development of new biometric technologies means that the body itself can be directly scrutinized and interrogated as a provider of surveillance data. Information for identification may now be extracted from the body that can override the person's own claims to a particular identity. And data originating in the body is used for the same kinds of purposes as more

[1] Lyon 1994: 3.

conventional modes of surveillance, to sort and classify, to determine eligibility, to qualify and to disqualify, to include and to exclude. The body need no longer merely be watched to track its behavior or its whereabouts. Surveillance now goes under the skin to monitor, check, and test in order to identify and to classify. The subtle shift is one of technological sophistication in body surveillance, and its broadened use from potentially criminal to general populations of citizens and consumers.

From the birth of modernity, the body achieved new prominence as a site of surveillance. Bodies could be rationally ordered through classification in order to socialize them within the emerging new nation-state. Bodies tended to be distrusted as sensual, irrational, and thus in need of taming, of disciplinary shaping to new purposes.[2] By associating a name or, later, a number with the body, each person could be distinguished from the next. Thus if, for example, a name appears on a voters' list, and if an embodied person shows up to record a vote, then the citizen can be recorded as having voted, after which that person may not vote again. Similarly, citizens of modern nation-states are required to carry all manner of personal identifiers that ensure their smooth passage through benefits offices or customs and immigration departments. Papers and cards are part of the essential personal paraphernalia of modern life.[3]

In these cases, however, the means of identification is external to the body. Indeed, the volatile and unpredictable body is put in its place by the cognitive focus on the name or the number. This situation still obtained during the period of large-scale bureaucratic computerization from the 1960s on. Although at some point it might be necessary to ask the person to identify herself verbally, the trend set in train with computerization was toward the automated cross-checking of identity. Trustworthy third-party sources could be enlisted to ensure that the individuated person was indeed eligible for benefits or qualified to drive a car. Thus a web of first documentary, and then digital identification systems could locate and distinguish individuals when required. It was often almost incidental that a body was also associated with the person whose identity was being checked. The number and name were what really mattered.

But computerization was to bring other issues in its train, especially as communication and information technologies (CITs) make possible the almost instantaneous transfer of documents and and financial, medical, or other sensitive information. The ease with which these can be intercepted by third parties has generated what the U.S. Public Interest Research Group calls "identity theft," said to be the "fastest growing crime

body is incidental

[2] Mellor and Shilling 1997: 147.
[3] See Lyon 1994: 3–21.

☒ the body as an identity document

in the nation."[4] It occurs in various ways, including at automated bank machines, through e-mail that uses others' addresses, by sending false messages on the Internet, or by breaking into computer systems to gain access to personal data. Various forms of encryption that provide digital signatures or pseudonyms have proliferated as means of combatting such "identity theft." They are often referred to collectively as "Privacy Enchancing Technologies," or PETs.

The quest for accuracy and precision continues, however, and now other new technologies are enlisted as adjuncts to the computer. These techniques are known generically as "biometrics" because they refer to measuring or monitoring parts of the body. In 1998, for instance, the Nationwide Building Society in the United Kingdom tested iris-scanning equipment at some of their automated bank machines.[5] The concentrated wealth of features in the iris makes it an ideal candidate for automated identification. But the human fingerprint also remains popular as a means of identification, especially since the capacity of digitized print images has grown greater, and costs have fallen. Its uses range from a traffic control system in Shaanxi Province of Central China, where smart cards holding drivers' records are verified by stored fingerprints,[6] to a "BioMouse" that uses fingerprints as passwords into laptops or computer systems.[7] Hand scanners serve similar purposes, for example, allowing only authorized users to work out in the University of Montreal's athletic complex.[8]

Several significant issues are raised by this. I begin by charting the background to body surveillance, in various kinds of documentary and digital identification. This social-historical account serves to show how the new biometric technologies are given their chance. Although enabled by computerization, body surveillance represents a merging of techniques not previously thought of as "information" technologies. Despite their relative novelty, however, these new techniques are appearing in all surveillance sectors. They are seen in government administration, and in policing, but also in the workplace and consumer spheres. In each sector, moreover, it is important to examine the implications of body surveillance for reconfigured relations of time and space, for the boundaries between the public and the private, and for the interactions between technology and society. Lastly, I return to the central issue of the body as a "document" for identification, and what this means for surveillance in a world of identity politics and risk management.

[4] U.S. Public Interest Research Group 1996: 14, cited in Cavoukian 1997.
[5] Pearsall 1998: 11.
[6] Kirbyson 1996: 6.
[7] Guly 1997: 23.
[8] Beiser 1997: 40.

Identity, Identification, and Modernity

Recognizing a person's separate identity depends on three things; a body, a memory, and rights and responsibilities. Erving Goffman, in his classic work on *The Presentation of Self in Everyday Life*,[9] stressed the importance of the face and the body for recognition and everyday encounters. A person is an ineluctably social being; individuals are "embodied social agents."[10] We require the recognition of others to be identified as individuals. But the body does not suffice on its own. We must also give an account of ourselves that confirms our identity, and must also be committed to that story. This authorizes our past as truly ours. Beyond this, a person's identity is also bound up with social expectation; agents are responsible for their actions. A growing emphasis of the modern world, paralleling the focus on responsibility, has been to attribute rights to individuals, to which they or others may appeal in law.

In early modernity, as Nicholas Abercrombie and others point out, the long, drawn-out discovery of the individual had contradictory consequences. "As individuals become more separate and different, they are more recognizably unique. In turn, uniqueness and identity are closely connected and the identification of individuals makes their control that much easier."[11] How did this happen? The coming of modernity meant that individuals were granted an increasing range of rights, starting with civil rights before the law, and moving to political rights of citizens, and social rights to welfare. But to obtain these rights, bureaucratic structures required careful scrutiny of the grounds of entitlement according to consistent rules. So people had to be registered, and their personal details filed, which of course paradoxically facilitated their increased surveillance. Freedom from one set of constraints—those of feudal societies— gave opportunities for new forms of surveillance and control.

By the last quarter of the twentieth century, extensive systems of mass surveillance had been established throughout all liberal capitalist societies, each of which depended on the documentary identification of individuals. In the late 1970s, for example, James Rule and others examined the uses of six of the most widely held personal documents in the United States: birth certificates, driver's licenses, social security cards, passports, bank books, and credit cards.[12] These documents provided vital links between the individuals holding them and the organizations issuing them. Just how document-dependent individuals become is dramatized when

[9] Goffman 1956.
[10] Abercrombie, Hill, and Turner 1986: 33.
[11] Ibid.: 189.
[12] Rule, McAdam, Stearns, and Uglow 1983.

something goes wrong. We all know how awkward and inconvenient it is when one of them is lost or destroyed. From the organizational viewpoint, certainty is given grounds, when dealing with large numbers of otherwise anonymous individuals. Which motorist can renew a license, and which is wanted for violations? Which welfare claimant is a genuine case, and which is double-dipping? Which consumer can purchase this appliance, and which is liable for outstanding debt? The documents will tell.

Rule and his associates noted a trend occurring in the 1970s: the move from self-identification to direct checking. Birth certificates, the production of which is a routine requirement for other documents, are easily obtained by fraudulent means. Yet they still retain some aura of credibility despite their lack of solid warrant. Where credibility is felt to be lacking, however, organizations could increasingly resort to direct checking. Rule found that independent outside sources such as credit bureaus would be used for credit card applications, police records and driver registries for driver's licenses, or immigration databases to check passport presentation at borders. Rule and associates concluded that "[t]he perfection of direct checking within and among organizations is the wave of the future in mass surveillance,"[13] and so it turned out. Increased computerization made direct checking easier and more efficient, even though individual agents are often still warned at some stage that they should not provide false information.

By the 1990s it became clear that so-called information societies were from another point of view surveillance societies, such was the pervasive degree of routine monitoring of almost all aspects of daily life. Surveillance—as focused attention to life details—influences populations in all such societies, although the strength of influence differs according to social factors. The black single mother in the American inner city will find her life much more closely and punitively scrutinized than her counterpart who is an affluent divorcee in the suburbs. The computer-assisted aspect of this, which Roger Clarke calls "dataveillance," had become a taken-for-granted aspect of modern life as new configurations of computing with telecommunications capacities became available.[14] Cross-checking is made simpler through dispersed and networked computer systems. With a range of personal data systems, remote from each other but connected electronically, and a consistent mode of identification, dataveillance can flourish, "feeding on itself," as Rule would say.

However, dataveillance did not proliferate just because new technologies became available. As Colin Bennett notes, these practices were "especially eagerly embraced by governments with neo-conservative

aura of credibility in spite of forgery possibilities

[13] Ibid.: 233.
[14] Clarke 1988.

agendas."[15] Arguably, it is just such choices, emerging from the new political economy of the 1990s, that lay behind the development of the technologies, including their much hyped "convergence."[16] While Manuel Castells' shorthand "information age" may sum up neatly some key characteristics of contemporary societies, it is, as he insists, the implication of new technologies within the current restructuring of capitalism that gives that age its unique dynamic.[17] They permit a new level of networking, particularly of financial flows, and they also make possible the globalization of capitalism. But the same restructuring also demands greater attention to detail, as competition, and awareness of risk, grows. Such details include knowledge of production processes and of consumption, which are gleaned through surveillance.

A key aspect of this restructuring is risk management, a mode of operation that finds echoes in several surveillance sectors. Generalizing from police work, for example, Richard Ericson and Kevin Haggerty claim that "institutionalized risk communication systems form the foundation of contemporary society and provide the governing basis of social life."[18] Within neo-liberal market societies, they suggest, police form just one agency that collects and classifies personal data on behalf of other institutions. But while the knowledge sought may in a sense be personal, it is really only individual, and relates to risk at that. That is, the knowledge is inevitably abstracted from the flesh-and-blood person who relates to others.[19] And in order more exactly to determine the nature and extent of risk, more and more precise knowledge is sought. To decide questions of eligibility, or even of guilt, the risk profile becomes crucially important. And in order to work properly, for most purposes it must also be attached to an accurate identity.

It is thus risk management practices within restructuring capitalist societies that generate the quest for more foolproof, and fraudproof, methods of establishing identity. And this is how the body is brought back in. Once it was merely the existence of unique bodies that was part of the rationale for individuation, and for stabilizing difference. But now, for example, through fingerprinting, other signs of bodily distinctiveness are appealed to. Direct checking from the 1970s on became a matter of verification by a third-party organization. This was done digitally by methods such as data matching once dataveillance regimes were electronically established in the 1980s. But from the 1990s, it became clear that direct checking

---

[15] Bennett 1996: 237.

[16] This is argued in a related context in Lyon 1988: ch. 2. See also Winseck 1998.

[17] Castells 1996.

[18] Ericson and Haggerty 1997: 426–27.

[19] This distinction between persons and individuals is similar to that appearing in the work of James 1996: xii, 170–71.

would take on yet another meaning: access to tissues, fluids, images, and patterns available from the body itself. Just as direct checking across agencies avoided confrontation with the embodied agent, so direct checking of data produced from within bodies also requires no access to the speech or the memory of the person. It is, once again, abstracted from the person.

Body Surveillance Technologies

To gain entry to a secure or sensitive place one conventionally has to use a password to prove identity and eligibility. Some coded message, memorized by the intending entrant, is repeated at the threshold, before entry is permitted. In the later twentieth century, magnetic stripes and barcoded cards were commonly used for such purposes, whether to enter the laboratory, the prison, or the bank vault. The emergence of body surveillance technologies, however, dispenses with cryptic words and numeric codes. Some part of the physical body—eye, hand, finger, face, voice—is presented to the verification machine. Another level of coding, beyond words and numbers, and relying neither on memory nor on the need to produce a card, turns the body into a password.[20] Apart from the ways in which this may (re)constitute the body as a text, it is a reminder of how access and inclusion, and the distribution of entitlements or powers, may now depend on the display of some body feature.

The machine that confirms identities is usually some form of computerized scanner, which checks the biological feature against the digital file that contains exactly the same characteristics. Thus inmates in Cook County, Illinois, submit to retinal scanning every time they go from jail to court and back; welfare recipients in Connecticut and Pennsylvania have their identities matched to their records by finger imaging; and frequent travelers from Montana to Canada may use an automated voice verification system run by the U.S. Immigration and Naturalization Service to cross the border. According to Davis, in 1997 there were already over ten thousand locations in the United States, from bank vaults to blood banks, where one had to present a body part to go through a door or gain access to a file.[21] Although commercial sources exaggerate the significance of each new product, biometric measures are not merely science fiction. Enough evidence exists to indicate that these modes of identification are becoming increasingly important.

Of course, the use of body parts or processes for identification and surveillance purposes is not new. Fingerprinting has been carried out rou-

[20] See Davis 1997.
[21] Ibid.: 132.

body surveillance *behavior prevention*

tinely for many decades, as has the use of polygraphs or "lie detectors," which were first used in the United States in the 1930s. As Steven Nock argues, such techniques come in a long tradition of "ordeals" that are meted out to establish or maintain reputations.[22] However, these body surveillance technologies are very limited in scope and they are not always acceptable, for instance, in a court of law.[23] They are used, typically, in cases where suspicion about activities or doubt about identity already exists. They relate to a concept of justice that relies on testimony and evidence to determine individual guilt, not one that routinely places whole populations under "categorical suspicion."[24] Body surveillance is consistent with the emergence of a behavioral approach that cares more about prevention than causes of certain behaviors or social conditions that may help give rise to them.[25]

A consistent feature of contemporary body surveillance technologies is their computer-dependence. In the United States, for example, the FBI began in 1990 to convert its 40 million fingerprint cards and crime history records into digitized records, as part of its ongoing computerization program.[26] As computer power grows, so more applications, previously beyond the reach of automation, become possible. It makes sense, from the point of view of surveillance studies at least, to consider certain biotechnologies as information technologies.[27] This is partly because computerization provides a common digital language for generating, storing, retrieving, processing, and transmitting data from different technological fields, especially in this case, from biotechnology. But more profoundly, when it comes to genetic information, the connections come even closer. Decoding, manipulation, and reprogramming are central to genetic sciences. The Human Genome Project, to take the most significant example, is committed to nothing less than the creation of a vast genetic database that determines the location and chemical sequence of all genes. It has huge surveillance implications.

For instance, some "genomics" companies see their task as using genetic information to increase the production of certain drugs. Others, however, such as Incyte Pharmaceuticals in Palo Alto, California, or Cel-

[22] Nock 1993: 76.

[23] The polygraph is not admissible in Canadian courts, although police may use it to sort out suspicions of criminality. See Ericson and Haggerty 1997: 247. The polygraph is also unacceptable to the American Psychological Association because it turns up "an unacceptable number of false positives"; cited by Marx 1988: 229.

[24] The term is Gary Marx's. See Marx 1988: 219.

[25] Crang 1996.

[26] *New York Times* 1998.

[27] Castells 1996: 30 considers biological and genetic sciences within the "information revolution."

era, in Rockville, Maryland, sell only data that others use to identify potential drug targets—persons, in other words—depending for their predictions on massive computer power. Along with other agencies that have become more concerned with anticipation and preemption, enabled by new surveillance technologies, the emergent health care paradigm moves steadily from detect-and-treat to predict-and-prevent, with specific therapies aimed at the causes of disease.[28]

Through mapping human genes, detailed information may be obtained about biologically determined features of individuals.[29] The biosurveillance made possible by this relates to the likely course of physical and psychological development of individuals. Such scientific foreknowledge of potential life courses is thus of great interest, especially to employers and insurance companies, who wish to use such data as a means of discrimination between candidates or clients, based on genetic testing and screening. As we shall see, the combination of rising employer health insurance costs and the increasing reliability of genetic testing is likely to encourage the development of such biosurveillance on the large scale. Once again, the body becomes the password, with which (genetic) code entry or exclusion may have very serious social as well as personal consequences.

The drive for perfect knowledge, which includes information about future developments and not merely about past histories, is fostered by risk management discourses, which are in turn the stuff of which insurance companies are made. Restructuring capitalism, and the technological facilitation of fusion among different kinds of information, permits surveillance to move beyond paper files and digitized documents and to infiltrate the body itself. The body, in turn, is treated like a text. It becomes a pass-*word*, providing a document for decoding. But texts are best understood in contexts. To illustrate this, we will examine body surveillance as it appears across the whole range of surveillance sectors.

Body Surveillance in Different Sectors

Body surveillance may be found in all social sectors. Two things should be noted about this. The first is that the very notion of sectors sounds rather watertight, when in fact they are increasingly porous. Deregulation and networking means that surveillance data leaks with greater ease from one sector to another, making it less discrete. Nonetheless, the sectors may still be considered to be existing at different points along a spectrum

[28] See *The Sunday (Straits) Times* 1999: 42–43.
[29] Regan 1995: 170.

"control society"

from more to less coercive power. Categorical suspicion may classify subjects at the sharp end of, say, policing, while categorical seduction is more likely to operate at the other, corporate, end. The second point is that by examining the ways in which biometrics are actually used in each sector, some dangers of technological determinism may be avoided. The tendency of studies that focus on the technological is to accept the hype produced by designers and manufacturers, which exaggerates both the use and the usefulness of novel techniques. The fact that some companies are testing biometrics that use body odor today[30] does not mean that we will be passing through smell scanners tomorrow. A survey of the current surveillance uses of biometrics shows that the humble fingerprint, now digitally scanned and stored, is still the technique of choice, although in the workplace genetic screening and testing is gaining ground.

During 1997, the Canadian province of Ontario started to follow the lead of states south of the border in easing the way for increased government use of biometric technologies. The Social Assistance Act was reformed to allow municipalities and the province to identify welfare recipients using biometric data. The aim was to ensure that applicants are only registered once, that when they claim, their identity can be authenticated, and also to permit applicants, recipients, spouses, and adult dependents to gain access to their records.[31] It was estimated at the time that Metropolitan Toronto could save $4.5 million a year in reduced welfare caseloads, and a further $2.7 million in reduced check processing and other administrative expenses.[32] Of course, a neo-conservative agenda is also visible here, one that desires to demonstrate that it has no time for the feckless or the fraudulent. The provincial premier, Mike Harris, expressed his hope that schemes would be established to consolidate health cards, driver's licenses, and other government identification on one card, based on finger-scanning technology.

Such scanners, rather like supermarket checkouts, have glass plates on which the finger is placed. A high-resolution optical image is caught by a camera, and is then converted into a template containing a mathematical equation. For user verification or identification, the system takes a live scan of the fingerprint, comparing it with the stored template. As long as the finger scan is encrypted in different ways for different uses—say, drivers' records and health records—the same scan may be used for different purposes, without the danger of records being shared between agencies. Such reassurances do not always satisfy those closest to welfare recipients, who argue that fingerprinting of any sort is too reminiscent of the

[30] See Davis 1997.
[31] Gage 1997: 32.
[32] Ross 1997: A1, A7.

way that criminals are treated. A further concern is that if biometric methods become universally popular, then the only way of ensuring that they are carried at all times will be to install a chip under the skin of the individual.[33] Because of the already proven use of fingerprinting for law enforcement, and because of the high cost and potential inaccuracies still experienced with some other methods—such as retinal scans or face-recognition—fingerprinting is likely to be seen as one of the best biometric options available.

It cannot be denied that many if not most biosurveillance methods develop from policing and security sectors, which is why when government administration or commercial organizations such as Mastercard propose the use of fingerprint scanning, they have to deal with the question of stigma. The FBI spent $640 million on its "Afis" (automated fingerprint identification system), which was completed in 1999, with 43 million records.[34] But some countries are quicker to adopt biometrics than others, and some techniques catch on in one country but not another. Higher levels of concern about security, and greater fear of crime, may help to account for the faster take-up rate of digitized fingerprinting in the United States than, say, in Canada.[35] Equally, the more intensive use of video surveillance via closed circuit TV in the United Kingdom may explain why face-recognition technologies are being developed more rapidly there than in some other countries.

So while banks such as Citicorp may test face-recognition technologies,[36] their development is more likely to take place in law enforcement contexts. Britain, where photographic technologies have been added to the more familiar convergence between computing and telecommunications, is the world leader in this field. The British Home Office, Police Foundation, and Marks and Spencer's have joined forces to produce reliable automatic visual recognition of suspects.[37] Limited systems are already in use, such as the "Football Intelligence System" in Greater Manchester. Information and photographic records of suspects and offenders associated with soccer violence is collated such that pictures of "likely suspects" can be drawn from the database. The equivalent National Criminal Intelligence Service database used photophones to transmit digitized photographs of suspected hooligans to participating football grounds in the 1996 European championship. Similar systems are being developed for use at Sydney International Airport in Australia.[38]

[33] Clarke 1997.
[34] Cottrill 1997: 11.
[35] Keenan, cited in Gage 1997: 32.
[36] Davis 1997.
[37] Norris et al. 1996: 265.
[38] Ibid.: 267.

Other techniques that cross the border from policing and law enforcement to the economic private sector include genetic testing. The use of DNA samples from suspected rapists and murderers is well known, and has led to a number of convictions and retrials. Evidence of criminal activity or involvement may be obtained from DNA samples in plucked hair, blood, and saliva that match each unique individual. The American CODIS ("Combined DNA Index System") is a national DNA identification system. Fifteen or more states are now using collected samples to add to the CODIS databank. In Canada and the United Kingdom, too, such samples may be collected without consent, as DNA profiling becomes routine.[39] Whatever might be said about the diminution of due process in such cases, the fact remains that DNA testing by police is relatively uncontroversial. The same may not be said for genetic tests and screens in the workplace.

Employers, wishing to minimize risk, may use genetic screening to determine susceptibility to disease, such as breast, ovarian, colon, thyroid, eye, kidney, and skin cancers, or Huntington's Disease, among employees, or to check levels of damage from exposure to hazardous materials at work. But genetic discrimination could result on the basis of such tests. At the same time, fear of such discrimination could discourage some people from undergoing tests from which they might benefit. This points up, once more, the all-too-frequently forgotten fact that surveillance has two faces. The same genetic test, in this case, may be the means of personal benefit, say, enabling the person to seek treatment for a medical condition before it is too advanced, and of personal discrimination, blocking the path to promotion or retention.

It should be remembered that the desire to control the workforce is far from new, and that concerns with aspects of the body and its condition are not new either. But during the twentieth century technical and bureaucratic types of control became less effective, which is one reason for the turn toward "personal control." An additional reason is the perceived failure of socializing institutions such as family and school. What is new is to see the workplace as the locus for social control over personality and health, via pre-hire screening, drug testing, polygraph testing, stress management, wellness programs, AIDS testing, and programs for alcoholism, weight reduction, and gambling addiction.[40] This is the background to the use of DNA evidence in workplace body tests, and also represents a blurring of the boundary between state-sponsored and private forms of social control. In many cases, such as urinalysis for drug testing, part of the purpose is indeed to produce the "perfect worker," but another part

[39] Ericson and Haggerty 1997: 248. See also Pamela Sankar's essay in the present volume.
[40] Wagner 1987: 540–41.

is to make a symbolic moral gesture to the public as to where true standards are to be found.[41]

Controversy breaks out when genetic testing starts to be used as a condition of employment, and it is against such discrimination that legal protection has been sought in the United States and elsewhere. In the late 1990s Lawrence Berkeley National Laboratory in California was successfully sued by seven employees who learned that blood and urine obtained during preemployment medical examinations had been tested for syphilis, sickle cell anemia (black applicants), and pregnancy (female applicants). The appeals court ruled that such tests required the consent of the employee, or that they have a direct bearing on one's ability to do the job.[42] Further controversy surrounds the accuracy of genetic testing. After all, genes alone do not determine an individual's future health. Diet, exercise, psychosocial factors, and economic class may affect an individual's health almost as much as genetics.[43]

If in the workplace the capitalist corporation intensifies its body surveillance in an attempt to perfect the worker, in the marketplace the consumer is increasingly subject to biometrics, a process that is stimulated particularly by the projected growth of electronic commerce. While the potential for electronic commerce has been clear for some time, the relative lack of security—especially of identification—has proved a major deterrent for some. But not only burgeoning electronic commerce is behind the quest for biometric identifiers. Risk management in general lies behind many attempts to ensure biometrically that identification of clients and customers is as accurate and as efficient as possible.

While fingerprint-based biometrics are, understandably, still prevalent in government administration and policing, the situation is much more volatile in the private sector. Here, fingerprint biometrics are not unknown—MasterCard is moving to such a system to combat credit card fraud[44]—but other methods are more widespread. While genetic profiling and screening is perhaps the fastest growing—and the most controversial—form of body surveillance in the workplace, in its present state of development it is unlikely to become popular in the marketplace. In the commercial, consumer sector, a range of biometrics is vying for preeminence, and none is yet a clear winner. Indeed, competition will probably ensure that this situation will continue for some time, at least until some

---

[41] Boyes-Watson 1997. See also Hartwell, Steele, French, and Rodman 1996, who argue that it is drug abuse rather than the larger employment problem, alcohol abuse, for which employees are more frequently tested (two times as much, in fact) in the United States. Alcohol use is not in itself illegal or against company policies.

[42] Mineham 1998: 208.

[43] Smith 1998: 38.

[44] Surtees 1996: B4.

standards have been established. The first commercial biometric, a hand scanner used in a Wall Street firm to monitor employee attendance, was introduced in 1974,[45] but it was only in the 1990s that the techniques improved and the prices fell sufficiently to make them commercially viable. Lotus employees pass through a hand scanner to pick up their children from day care, and Coca Cola uses them to ensure that only identified employees punch their time cards.[46]

The most widely used commercial biometric is the handkey,[47] which is in use for frequent travelers in New York and Toronto airports, at immigration desks, and was the means of controlling access of 65,000 atheletes and their teams to the Olympic Village in Atlanta in 1996. Despite some negative responses to them, biometrics based on fingerprints are also in use commercially, including the so-called biomouse, used for securing access to computers. Single fingers, or all fingers and thumbs, can be scanned in, scrambled, reduced, and stored, ready for use each time the authorized person wishes to use the machine. Systems such as this are likely to prove popular because they can also be used for remote log-in, ID card validation, electronic signature, and financial transaction authorization.[48]

The eye is another key body part suitable for biometrics. Although retinal scans are the most accurate identifiers, because of their expense and their slightly awkward use they tend to be favored mainly by governments. The CIA, for instance, uses retinal scanners, along with voiceprints, in its top security computer vault in Langley, Virginia. The person has to lean over and place his or her face on a bar close to the machine, which passes a red light beam across the eye. Iris scans, on the other hand, are favored for automated bank machines, partly because they dispense with positioning devices and beams. As the customer approaches, video cameras zoom in to identify the form as a person, then to fix the person's coordinates. From a meter away, an eye image is taken, to be matched—in two or three seconds—with the digitally encoded iris image on file.[49] OKI Electric Industry, Japan, and NCR Knowledge Lab in London, United Kingdom, are among those testing iris scanning devices.

Body Surveillance: Movement, Action, and Risk

The body has become not only a site of surveillance, but a source of surveillance data. The practice of locating, tracking, and controlling bodies

[45] Beiser 1997: 40.
[46] Davis 1997: 132.
[47] Beiser 1997: 40.
[48] Guly 1997: 23.
[49] Powell 1997: E1, E11.

is as old as history, although it was routinized and intensified by the disciplines of modernity. The idea of checking identities by reference to unique features, above all faces, is equally ancient, although only in modern times have distinguishing characteristics such as fingerprints become important for verifying identity. Today, both aspects of body surveillance are becoming increasingly significant at the same time, which suggests that they may be related. Looking at movement, action, and risk shows how.

First, modern societies are marked by mobility, which means that bodies are on the move. Today's transportation enables people to travel, by transit systems across the city and by airline systems around the world. People travel for work and for pleasure, in the tourist delights of the rich and in the tragic displacements of refugees. Mobility means different things to people in different social groups. Travel is experienced differently by the urban commuter in his air-conditioned car on the freeway than by the low-wage earner who waits in the rain for a crowded bus to get to work. Such mobility also means that we tend to interact more and more with strangers, people with whom we have no real relationship, who do not know who we are or if they can trust us. So symbols of the stable self, such as driver's licenses, credit cards, passports, or identity papers, have to be presented to prove ourselves. The society of strangers requires tokens of trust.[50]

wm

Each token of trust, however, now connects with others in a web of identification and credential surveillance systems. Such systems serve to keep tabs on those moving bodies and to ensure that only authorized bodies enter certain rooms, cross certain borders, claim certain benefits, or travel on certain highways or airlines. They are a means of social control, social orchestration, and social influence. But actual moving bodies are not the only things to be caught in the electronic eye. An increasing proportion of significant interaction today is bodyless, mediated above all by electronic means. And this is how the two kinds of body surveillance come to be connected.

The more other means of mediating social relationships appear, the more the signs of surveillance appear with them as well. What worked to coordinate and control bodies in conventional time and space can be transposed into the virtual world of cyberspace. This newer sphere of transactions, and thus of flows of information and power, is now a further site of surveillance. As Paul Virilio says, here "people can't be separated by physical obstacles or by temporal distances. With the interfacing of computer terminals and video-monitors, distinctions of *here* and *there* no longer mean anything."[51] But it is precisely in those channels that carry

[50] Giddens 1990.
[51] Virilio 1991: 13.

eliminating contextualization by reading the body

the flows of information that precision is increasingly required. They are too porous for cyberspace to be secure, hence the quest of PETs and of body surveillance to keep identities intact.

Second, consider the category of action. By this, I refer back to my introductory comments on personal identity as being a matter of recognizing a unique body, of gaining access to memory, and of according responsibilities and rights to the person. Body surveillance reduces identity questions to what can be found in the text of the body itself. It bypasses the acting subject, who may wish to explain herself, or to put things in a longer historical context, by appealing only to the speechless "truth" that DNA samples or handscans can provide. It is data from the object of the body rather than speech from the acting subject that is to be relied on in the last analysis. Good reasons for using body surveillance may be produced, showing that criminals may more easily be apprehended or that fraud may be reduced in commerce, but body surveillance should also be viewed as part of wider social trends.

Ontario's information and privacy commissioner, Ann Cavoukian, is an advocate of biometric encryption for secure identification, for instance, in health information networks. She points to the paradox that biometrics is a sinister surveillance threat if it is identifiable, but when encrypted becomes a "protector of privacy."[52] Thus the interests of both individuals and organizations are served. Individuals can keep their privacy through the anonymity of encryption, and organizations can be assured of the authenticity of individuals they conduct business with. Few would wish to quarrel with this argument. It does not mean, however, that organizations are any less distrustful of individuals they deal with, or that such individuals are any less concerned to guard their privacy. It is, after all, because of the quest for privacy within the society of strangers that tokens of trust are required in the first place.

The choice to take surveillance through the threshold of the skin and inside the physical body may raise privacy questions—are our truly private parts now within the body rather than on its surface?—but it also has to be seen in the context of a new behaviorism that treats the body as authoritative text. In the quest for more knowledge to combat risk, body surveillance appears as a worthy source. It promises to offer not only detail of what has happened in the past—how many times previously this person has entered this building or has made that transaction—but also of what will happen in the future. Risk discourses are especially concerned with knowledge of the future. As Ulrich Beck says, the "centre of risk consciousness lies not in the present but in the future."[53] Thus body

[52] Cavoukian 1999: 117.
[53] Beck 1992: 34.

surveillance, above all that which uses DNA, appears as the natural next wave. This is not merely the perfect match, sought so assiduously by those obsessed with identification, but the dynamic match, that holds histories and simulated futures for comparison and checking.

The result is that body surveillance takes its place as part of a more general transformation of the ways social activities and human agency are understood. In the workplace, it is no longer merely one's qualifications, aptitude for the job, or personal bearing at interview that counts. A fifty-three-year-old man being interviewed for a job with an insurance company revealed that he has hemochromatosis but was asymptomatic. At the second interview he was told he might be hired, but with no insurance plan. He agreed to this but at the third interview was told that he could not be hired because of his genetic condition.[54] One's potential future health condition is now grounds for job discrimination, segregation, and classification. In policing, too, the future is in focus. As Ericson shows, "Risk communication systems turn the moral discourse of deviance into a utilitarian morality of probability calculus. . . . Gutted of moral wrongdoing, deviance is treated as a normal accident . . . a contingency for which there are risk technologies to spread the loss and to prevent recurrence."[55] Body surveillance, bound up with identities and identification provided by police, signals another moment in the shift toward actuarial justice.

Risk and security may appear to be highly important to social well-being. This is especially so in societies that tend to minimize the significance of the past, and are prepared to rely on imagined futures, simulations, to guide practices and policy in the present. If the primary documentary identification is the human body itself, then this is bound to sit uneasily with views of identity that go beyond what can be learned from a bodily ordeal or the testing of tissue and fluid. Autobiography and the social web of identities are diminished if not discounted in such body surveillance identification regimes. Beyond this, too, one must ask what is the likely next stage. And one may ask this, not as another exercise in social science fiction, but as a way of following current technologics. If it becomes common to have to present a chip—in a smart card—bearing a biometric identifier, then the requirement to carry this chip at all times will become strong. The only way to guarantee this would be, as Roger Clarke says, to "mount it in the carrier," that is, "to install it in the person's body."[56]

Third, such a scenario raises further questions. These are not just questions of moving bodies and bodyless transactions, coordinated in time and space, or of the paradoxes of the private and of human action, when

[54] National Genome Project Research Institute 1998: 3.
[55] Ericson and Haggerty 1997: 448.
[56] Clarke 1997: 2.

identification is reduced to direct access to the body. The further questions concern relations between technology and society in general. For surveillance attempts constantly to upgrade the knowledge it obtains for risk management, in the belief that the more advanced the technoscience instrument, the more accurate the knowledge. In the case of body surveillance and identification, precision is the aim. But what do the "advances" entail? On the one hand, as I have shown, a new mode of justice emerges to keep in step with the focus on the future and on risk. On the other, the possibility is mooted of body modification in the interests of infallible identification. Are these the prices that must be paid for "advance"?

One obvious question concerns the reliability of the new body surveillance technologies. As noted above, the most reliable identifiers are also the most expensive. Digital fingerprinting, which builds on older technologies, tends to be used for administration purposes, particularly welfare. But fingerprinting can exclude otherwise eligible persons who may have skin diseases. A case in point is Kenneth Payne, a Los Angeles man who qualified as a teacher in his forties. He cannot obtain employment because he suffers from atopic dermatitis, which makes his skin blister and peel, thus spoiling his fingerprint. For security reasons California requires all teachers to pass a fingerprint test. No print, no job.[57] The much more accurate retinal scan is restricted due to its price. Understandably, people also feel protective of their eyes and are concerned about light beams passing across them. Voiceprints and facial scanning have yet to find widespread use, and there are questions about accuracy. Faces may change considerably at different times of the day, and a voice may alter when someone has a cold.[58]

Similarly with the use of DNA, accuracy is not guaranteed by any means. Moreover, employers may use genetic information in different ways, depending on the situation. When testing applicants for jobs, it may be assumed that the genetic predisposition alone is enough to disqualify someone—this despite what is known about other factors, such as environment, that will affect an individual's susceptibility to disease. If, on the other hand, screening for the effects of toxic materials is in question, employers have been known to bring the "other factors" into play. "They tend to give the benefit of the doubt to the chemicals" and to "hold the outside environment or people's lifestyle choices responsible for worker disease."[59] And as with biometrics, it must be acknowledged that the body itself may be incapable of yielding the secrets for which it is infiltrated. None of us has perfect genes.

[57] Reed 1998.
[58] Gage 1997: 32.
[59] Draper 1997: 11.

televangelism against biometrics

Huge potential dangers are raised of biometric data circulating among databases and being traded among companies. These hazards lie behind the pressure for encryption and for one-to-one—smart card—matching systems. When identification is required, the biometric reader would simply match the particular body part with the data on the card.[60] The person holding the card would retain control, or at least that is the theory. It is particularly when the next step, chip implants, is proposed, that other surveillance specters raise their heads. Civil libertarians balk at this, and in so doing find themselves in the unfamiliar company of religious fundamentalists. In 1995, for instance, American televangelist Pat Robertson hosted a segment called "Biometrics: Chipping Away Your Rights." He declared that "The Bible says that the time is going to come that you cannot buy or sell except with a mark placed on your hand or on your forehead."[61] The so-called mark of the beast appears to have arrived with biometrics and genetic IDs.

It is interesting that this implant has such negative connotations among civil libertarians and fundamentalists. This is the other side of the coin, it seems, from the cyborg as a liberator, that allows for playful transgressions of old boundaries and the political potential to revise categories such as gender.[62] Sadie Plant, for instance, examines ways, not of altering the body, but of transcending it technologically so that bodies can be represented more flexibly.[63] But such flexible representation stands in rather stark contrast with the desire directly to tap into the body to obtain information untainted by the subject. This latter cyborg, it seems, is stripped of consciousness and the capacity to answer for herself, all in the paradoxical interests of accurate identification. In order to work, the old disciplinary technologies that attempted to direct the body still relied on ideas such as reflexivity, self-consciousness, even conscience. Newer regimes of risk, surveillance, and security require less and less that the subject be—literally—response-able.

Body Surveillance, Identification, and Identity

To connect the biblical book of Revelation directly with biometrics is a typically literalistic ploy of fundamentalism. It tends to produce cynically dismissive responses, which could, ironically, fuel the very complacency that the more apocalyptic doomwatchers wish to combat. A non-literalist

[60] Davis 1997: 6.
[61] Cited in ibid.: 4.
[62] See, for example, Haraway 1997.
[63] Plant 1995.

reading of the same text, however, is salutory. This ancient book, which warns of things to come and promises hope for the faithful, is surprisingly appropriate in its assessments of power and knowledge. The beast whose mark is inscribed in the bodies of would-be buyers and sellers is a "beast from the earth,"[64] the symbol of a kind of false faith or, as Michael Wilcock suggests, an ideology.[65]

By this interpretation neither the technology nor the social entity need be identified precisely. But the relevance of the idea of the beast's mark to any kind of identifiers, including biometrics, becomes both more plain and more plausible. Simulated surveillance, which attempts to bring imagined futures to bear on the practices of the present, depends upon a dream of perfect knowledge.[66] This dream has ideological power to breathe life into the polycentric webs of the contemporary network society. The mystical mark confirms those in the thrall of the system. But the dream is a deceit, no less than was Jeremy Bentham's when he first projected the Panopticon as secular omniscience.[67]

In the steady shift from identification papers to body surveillance, reliance on data images rather than persons-with-distinctive-identities is further strengthened. Risk management, obsessed with accurate information, now sends its surveillance probes under the skin. New technologies are rapidly being developed, harnessed, and—importantly—recombined, to pursue these ends. Whether or not implants become a widespread reality,[68] the resulting involuntary cyborg will be increasingly dependent on technologically encoded body data for access and eligibility to the mundane functions of everyday life. Given this reality, urgent questions are raised about the means, political, educational, and, yes, technological— such as encrypted biometrics—of limiting the potential damage that such deepened dependence on the data image could cause.

[64] Revelation 13: 16–17.

[65] Wilcock 1975: 127.

[66] This is a key theme of Bogard 1996. One need not accept all aspects of his "social science fiction" to see that this present point is well made by him.

[67] Lyon 1991: 98.

[68] Kevin Warwick at Reading University, United Kingdom, voluntarily implanted a chip under his skin in August 1998, in order more fully to control his surrounding environment. Needless to say the same kind of chip has the potential to be used in ways that monitor and influence the person in which body the chip is mounted.

17

Identity and Anonymity: Some Conceptual Distinctions and Issues for Research

GARY T. MARX

> "You ought to have some papers to show who you are." The police officer advised me.
> "I do not need any paper. I know who I am," I said.
> "Maybe so. Other people are also interested in knowing who you are."
> —B. TRAVEN, *The Death Ship*

THE DOCUMENTATION of individual identity, whether by the state, private organizations, or individuals, can be located within a broader set of questions concerning identity and anonymity.[1] This topic involves the sociology of personal information and of information more generally. These in turn nestle within the wider field of the sociology of knowledge. Current developments in the area of personal identification are a small part of broader changes in contemporary means of information collection, processing, and communication.

My interest in the topic grows out of research on the "new surveillance," which includes technologies such as computer matching and profiling, video cameras, electronic location monitoring, and biometric devices, which have the potential to identify individuals, independent of their will and even knowledge.[2] Developments in biometric identification and smart card technology and debates over national ID cards and privacy are also elements of this.

The extractive power of the new surveillance leads to value and policy questions such as "under what conditions is it right or wrong to collect various kinds of personal information with and without consent?" and "when should individuals be compelled to reveal and when should they have a right to conceal?" While these are normative questions, answers

---

[1] This essay draws from a book tentatively entitled *Windows Into the Soul: Surveillance and Society in an Age of High Technology* based on the American Sociological Association–Duke University Jensen Lectures.

[2] See, for example, Rule 1973; Foucault 1977; Laudon 1986; Marx 1988; Clarke 1988: 29–45; Gandy 1993; Lyon 1994; Lyon and Zureik 1996; Curry 1998; and Staples 1997.

to them are improved with a firm empirical grounding with respect to questions such as "what are the major types of identity knowledge?", "how are requests for the collection of personal information socially patterned?", "how does this differ across countries and cultures?", and, as we move into a (in some ways) more fragmented and global world in which traditional borders are weakened, "how are identification processes changing and how do individuals respond?"

In this essay I lay out some of the conceptual landscape and research issues. The emphasis is on the cultural level, on normative expectations and justifications, more than on describing actual behavior. I deal with individuals rather than group or organizational identities (of course, these may be linked as with infiltrators using pseudonyms working for false front intelligence agencies). To ask about conditions and processes of identification also involves asking (if sometimes implicitly) about non-identification. Identifiability at one extreme can be contrasted with anonymity at the other. Describing a variety of kinds of identity knowledge and approaching these as distinct continua brings us closer to the messiness of the empirical world and suggests variations to be explained.

I identify seven types of identity knowledge (or ignorance). The requirement or at least possibility of identification must be considered alongside the requirement or possibility of non-identification. I specify social settings where the opposing values of anonymity or identity are required by law, policy, or social expectations. The final section of the essay argues that the forms, uses, and meaning of identity appear to be undergoing profound changes, and identifies issues for research.

Seven Types of Identity Knowledge

Identity knowledge has multiple components and there are degrees of identifiability. Among seven broad types of identity knowledge are: (1) legal name; (2) locatability; (3) pseudonyms that can be linked to legal name and/or locatability—literally a form of pseudo-anonymity; (4) pseudonyms that cannot be linked to other forms of identity knowledge—the equivalent of "real" anonymity (except that the name chosen may hint at some aspects of "real" identity, as with undercover agents encouraged to take names close to their own); (5) pattern knowledge; (6) social categorization; and (7) symbols of eligibility/non-eligibility.

1. Identification may involve a person's legal name. Even though names such as John Smith may be widely shared, the assumption is made that there is only one John Smith born to particular parents at a given time and place. Even identical twins have different first names and birth

times. Name usually involves connection to a biological or social lineage and can be a key to a vast amount of other information. It tends to convey a literal meaning (e.g., the child of Joseph and Mary). This aspect of identification is usually the answer given to the question "who are you?"

The use of first names only, as was said to traditionally be the case for both providers and clients in houses of ill-repute, can offer partial anonymity. The question of whether full, last, first, or no name is expected in social settings may appear to be a trivial issue that only a sociologist could love. But it is in fact the kind of little detail in which big social meanings may reside.

2. Identification can refer to a person's address. This involves location and "reachability," whether in actual space or in cyberspace (telephone number, mail or e-mail address, an account number). This need not involve knowing the actual legal/birth identity or even a pseudonym. But it does involve the ability to locate and take various forms of action, such as blocking, granting access, delivering or picking up, charging, penalizing, rewarding, or apprehending. It answers a "where" rather than a "who" question. The "where" question need not be linked with the "who" question. Thus the identity of fugitives is known but not how they can be reached. Even with both known they may be unreachable, as when there is no extradition treaty or they are otherwise protected. For example, the U.S. authorities knew that Robert Vesco was in Cuba but they were unable to arrest him there. Address need not be unique and can be complicated by multiple users of the same address.

3. Identification may involve unique alphabetic, numerical, or other symbols such as a social security number or biometric patterns or pseudonyms that can be linked back to a person or an address under restricted conditions. A trusted intermediary and confidentiality are often involved here. These in effect create a buffer and are a compromise solution in which some protection is given to literal identity or location, while meeting the need for some degree of identification. As with name, the symbol is intended to refer to only one individual. (But unlike a given name, which can be shared, letters and numbers are sufficient as unique identifiers. By contrast, when there is more than one John Smith in question, unique identity requires matching to other aspects of identity such as birth date and parents or address.) Examples include the number given persons calling tip hot-lines for a reward, anonymous bank accounts, on-line services that permit the use of pseudonyms in chat rooms and on bulletin boards, and representations of biometric patterns. These may be linked back to a legal/birth identity.

4. Identification may involve symbols, names, or pseudonyms that cannot in the normal course of events be linked back to a person or an address

by intermediaries. This may be because of a protective policy against collecting the information. For example, in some states those tested for AIDS are given a number and receive results by calling in their number without ever giving their name or address. Or it may be because a duped audience does not know that the person they are dealing with is using fraudulent identification—for example, spies, undercover operatives, and con-artists.

5. Identification may be made by reference to distinctive appearance or behavior patterns of persons (apart from whether actual identity or locatability is known). They may be unknown because of the impersonal conditions of urban life or secrecy. Being unnamed is not necessarily the same as being unknown. Some information is always evident in face-to-face interaction because we are all ambulatory autobiographies continuously and unavoidably emitting data for others' senses and machines. The uncontrollable leakage of some information is a condition of physical and social existence. This has been greatly expanded by new technologies.

A distinction Erving Goffman makes between knowing a person in the sense of being acquainted with them and knowing *of* them applies here. The patterned conditions of urban life mean that we identify many persons we don't "know" (that is, we know neither their names, nor do we know them personally). Instead we know some form of their social signature—whether it is face, a voice heard over mass media or on the phone, or some distinctive element of style. In everyday encounters (say riding the subway each day at 8 A.M.) we may come to "know" other riders in the sense of recognizing them.

Style issues fit here. Skilled graffiti writers may become well known by their "tags" (signed nicknames) or just their distinctive style, even as their real identity is unknown to most persons.[3] Persons making anonymous postings to a computer bulletin board may come to be "known" by others because of the content, tone, or style of their communications. Similarly, detectives may attribute reoccurring crimes to a given individual even though they don't know the person's name (e.g., the Unabomber, the Son of Sam, the Red Light Bandit, Jack the Ripper). There are also pro-social examples, such as anonymous donors with a history of giving in predictable ways which makes them "known" to charities. They are anonymous in the sense that their name and location is not known, but they are different from the anonymous donor who gives only once and leaves few tracks.

6. Identification may involve social categorization. Many sources of identity are social and do not differentiate the individual from others sharing them (e.g., gender, ethnicity, religion, age, class, education, region,

[3] Ferrell 1996.

sexual orientation, linguistic patterns, organizational memberships and classifications, health status, employment, leisure activities, friendship patterns). Simply being at certain places at particular times or associating with particular kinds of people (note the folk wisdom that "birds of a feather flock together" or "you are known by the company you keep") can also be a key to presumed identity.

Of particular interest is the expansion of the abstract categorizations noted by Foucault and associated with the people-processing of the modern state. These involve technical measurements and locating the individual relative to others. Such profiled identities (credit risk, IQ, SAT scores, lifestyle categorization for mass marketing, etc.) often involve predictions about future behavior. They may or may not be known to individuals, and if known may be at variance with how persons see themselves. The issue of the "fit" between the identity imputations of others and how one sees oneself is a nice research question. The gap is likely to be greatest for negative risk assessments, for example, by banks, insurance companies, and potential employers.

7. Identification may involve certification in which the possession of knowledge (secret passwords, codes), artifacts (tickets, badges, tattoos, uniforms), or skills (performances such as the ability to swim) labels one as a particular kind of person to be treated in a given way. This is categorical and identifies their possessor as an eligible or ineligible person, with no necessary reference to anything more (although the codes and symbols can be highly differentiated with respect to categories of person and levels of eligibility). This may be linked back to a unique person/place identity, but need not be. This is vital to contemporary discussions because it offers a way of balancing control of personal information with legitimate needs, such as for reimbursement of expenses (e.g., for tolls, phones, photocopy machines, subways), and of excluding system abusers. Smart card technologies with encryption and segmentation make this form of increased importance.

Socially Sanctioned Contexts of Concealment and Revelation

What is the ecology or field of identity revelation and concealment? How are these distributed in social space and time? What structures and processes can be identified? When and why does society require or expect (whether by laws, policies, or manners) that various aspects of identity will not be revealed? Under what conditions does the opposite apply— that is, when is the revelation of the various aspects of identity expected by law, policy, or custom? The lists that follow, while not exhaustive,

hopefully cover the most common contexts in which anonymity and identifiability are viewed as socially desirable. I have classified these by their
major justifications.[4]

1. Rationales in Support of (Full or Partial) Anonymity

a. To facilitate the flow of information and communication on public issues (this is the "if you kill the messenger you won't hear the bad
news" rationale): for example, hot lines for reporting problems and
violations; news media sources; various communication channels for
whistleblowers; unsigned or pseudonymous political communications;
the use of pen names and the nom-de-plume (e.g., George Sand or the
black-listed Hollywood writers).

b. To obtain personal information for research in which persons are
assumed not to want to give publicly attributable answers or data: for
example, studies of sexual and criminal behavior and other social research; informational audits; medical research.

c. To encourage attention to the content of a message or behavior
rather than to the nominal characteristics of the messenger which may
detract from that: for example, persons with a well-known public reputation writing in a different area may want to avoid being "type cast";
for dramatic reasons to fit cultural images of what a stage name should
be or to enhance presumed marketability, as with film stars changing
ethnic minority names to short Anglicized names.

d. To encourage reporting, information seeking, communicating,
sharing, and self-help for conditions that are stigmatizing or that can
put the person at a strategic disadvantage or are simply very personal:
for example, self-help requests and discussion and support groups for
alcohol, drug, and family abuse, sexual identity, mental and physical
illness; tests for AIDS and other socially transmitted sexual diseases, or
for pregnancy; communicating about personal problems and issues
with technologically distanced (and presumably safer) strangers.[5]

---

[4] I make these observations as a social observer and not as a moralist or empiricist (in
the sense of subjecting claims to some kind of empirical standard). I argue neither that these
justifications are necessarily good, nor that the claimed empirical consequences (and no
unintended or other consequences) necessarily follow. To have a pony in those races requires
analysis beyond the scope of this essay. Here I simply take claimed justifications at face
value and report them. This is a first step to empirically testing such claims. Three additional
tasks involve (a) trying to find a pattern in the attachment of moral evaluations to the various forms of behavior, (b) systematically relating the types of identity knowledge listed on
pp. 312–14 to the two sets of rationales listed on pp. 316–19 and 319–21, and (c) as a
citizen taking a moral position on what it is that the society has normatively offered up
regarding identity knowledge.

[5] See, for example, the discussion in Virnoche 1997.

e. To obtain a resource or encourage a condition using means that involve illegality or are morally impugnable, but in which the goal sought is seen as the lesser evil: for example, amnesty programs for the return of contraband (guns, stolen goods) "no questions asked"; needle exchange programs.

f. To protect donors of a resource or those taking action seen as necessary but unpopular from subsequent obligations, demands, labeling, entanglements, or retribution: for example, anonymous gift-giving to charitable organizations in which donors are protected from additional demands or advertising their wealth; sperm and egg donors, birth parents giving a child up for adoption; hiding the identity of judges of competitions and in courts to protect them from inappropriate influence; hangmen in England wearing hoods, in part to protect them from retaliation but perhaps also to enhance the drama; identification numbers rather than names worn by police.

g. To protect strategic economic interests, whether as a buyer or a seller: for example, a developer may be quietly purchasing small parcels of land under an assumed name or names, in preparation for a coming development.

h. To protect one's time, space, and person from unwanted intrusions: for example, unlisted phone numbers; opposition to caller-ID unless there is a blocking option; women using a neutral or male name or an initial rather than a first name in phone books and other directories; women wearing a veil or clothes that conceal feminine distinctiveness; post office box addresses identified only by number; mail forwarding services; providing only minimal information on warranty cards; giving a fake name, or refusing to give one's name when seeking commercial information; celebrities who at the times they don't want to be recognized, use assumed names and the cliché of wearing dark glasses.

i. To increase the likelihood that judgments will be carried out according to designated standards and not personal characteristics deemed to be irrelevant: for example, having musicians competing for orchestra positions perform behind a screen so that judges cannot see them (where the proof is in the consumption, as with listening to music or in a pie-eating or wine-tasting contest, this may be a good idea; for many complicated personnel decisions where reputation is a central factor beyond some immediate demonstration of dexterity, it is impossible); the blind reviewing of articles for scholarly journals or grading student exams; reviewing college applications with names and gender deleted.

j. To protect reputation and assets. The "theft of identity" and sending of inauthentic messages has emerged as a significant by-product of the expansion of electronically mediated (as against face-to-face) interactions.[6]

k. To avoid persecution.

l. To enhance rituals, games, play, and celebrations. Letting go, pretending, and playing new roles are seen as factors in mental and social health. Part of the fun and suspense of the game is not knowing who: for example, Halloween masks, masked balls, costume parties, role reversal rituals in traditional societies; the preparations around surprise parties and some of the actual guests (although in this case there may be a move from anonymity or a deceptive identity to actual identification at the gathering); some board and computer games involve lack of clarity as to identity (either or both the real identity of the players and hidden identity in the game); on-line role-playing and fantasy in which service providers offer a limited number of pseudonyms.

m. To encourage experimentation and risk taking without facing large consequences, risk of failure, or embarrassment since one's identity is protected. This is a kind of cost-free test drive of alternative identities, behavior, and reading material (the "anti-chill" justification): for example, pretending to be of a different gender, ethnicity, sexual preference, political persuasion, and so on in on-line communication.

n. To protect personhood, or "it's none of your business." What is central here is not some instrumental goal, as with most of the above, but simply the autonomy of the person. This can be an aspect of manners and involves an expectation of anonymity as part of respect for the dignity of the person and recognition of the fact that the revelation of personal information is tied to intimacy.[7]

o. Traditional expectations. This is a bit different from the above, because the custom that is honored does not appear to have emerged from a reasoned policy decision, but rather is an artifact of the way a technology developed or the way group life evolved. This then becomes associated with expectations about what is normal or natural, and hence expected and preferred. The telephone is a good example. When caller-ID was announced there was significant public resistance because people were accustomed to being able to make a phone call without having to reveal their phone number (and all that could be associated with it). However, that was not the case historically where all calls had to go through an operator.

---

[6] Marx 1990 and Cavoukian 1996.
[7] Marx 1994.

Mention may also be made of some related contexts in which anonymity is present simply because the conditions of complex urban life
permit it. For example (absent the new technologies), not being easily
identified by name or having to identify oneself when in public is the
default condition—whether sitting on a park bench, walking on a
crowded street, or cheering in a stadium.

Another environment where there is a degree of de facto anonymity
is when one is away from home, whether as a tourist, traveler, or expa-
triate. Not only is one less likely to be personally known, but many of
the symbols (accent, dress, body language) that present clues to identity
will go uninterpreted or simply serve to put one in the broad class of
foreigner. Since the stranger may be seeking this anonymity, locals may
have an economic or political interest in granting it. It would be interesting to study isolated areas and frontier towns in this regard. One
may note places such as the small western town where the fugitive in
the novel *The Falcon and the Snowman* [8] was living when he was captured, in which there is a tradition of not asking who people were, or
where they came from.

2. Rationales in Support of Identifiability

A consideration of contexts and rationales where anonymity is permitted or required must be balanced by a consideration of the opposite.
When is identifiability required, expected, or permitted? The rationales
here seem simpler, clearer, and less disputed. While there are buffers
and degrees of identification, the majority of interactions of any significance or duration tilt toward identification of at least some form. As
David Hume argued, human sentiments and social needs favor it: it is
more difficult to do ill to others when we know who they are and must
face the possibility of confronting them. Mutual revelation is a sign of
good faith that makes it easier to trust (not unlike the handshake,
whose origin reportedly was to show that one was not carrying a
weapon). It is a kind of free sampling of one's inner worth or an early
showing of part of one's hand. It also makes possible reciprocity, perhaps the most significant of social processes.

Thinking of society without personal identities is like imagining a
modern building without a foundation. The number of contexts where
it is expected and even required far exceeds those where its opposite is
required or expected. Indeed, failure to identify one's self often leads
to suspicion rather than the reverse. As with the Lone Ranger, we ask
"who was that masked man?" Just try the simple experiment of wearing a hood or Halloween mask throughout the day and note how it

[8] Lindsey 1985.

will bring to the surface the usually tacit norms regarding identification and a variety of control responses.

Central to many of the contexts where some form of identifiability is required or at least expected we find the following conditions or expectations.

a. To aid in accountability. Saints and those with strongly internalized moral codes respect the rules regardless of whether or not they are watched (or are potentially locatable). But for others who can resist anything but temptation, especially if under cover of anonymity, this is less likely. Because individuals generally want to avoid negative sanctions and for others to think well of them, normative behavior is more likely when people are identifiable. One extreme form is the anti-mask laws of some states (adopted as an anti-KKK strategy). The numbers on police badges are intended to hold police accountable while creating a buffer in their personal life from irate citizens. In contrast are the names worn by airline clerks and on the legitimacy-confirming badges of door-to-door solicitors. The current emphasis on identifying and tracking absent fathers with children supported by welfare is another example of accountability.

b. To judge reputation. In contrast to the small homogeneous group without strangers, mass impersonal societies rely on name, and the records and recommendations it can be associated with, to determine personal qualities. In small communities where membership itself is a form of vouching, these are taken for granted.

c. To pay dues or receive just deserts. Reciprocity is among the most fundamental of social forms and it requires being able to locate those we interact with. An identity peg makes it possible to have guarantees (such as collateral for a loan), to extract payments (of whatever sort), and to distribute justice and rewards, although this need not always involve literal identity.

d. To aid efficiency and improve service. The modern ethos and competitive environments view knowledge as power and generate seemingly insatiable organizational appetites for personal information to serve organizational ends and, in their words, "to better serve the customer."

e. To determine bureaucratic eligibility—to vote, drive a car, fix the sink, cut hair, do surgery, work with children, collect benefits, enter or exit (whether national borders, bars, or adult cinemas). Administrative needs in a complex division of labor require differentiation and complex norm enforcement, which in turn may depend on personal characteristics linked to name and place. A characteristic of modern society is ever-increased differentiation and the proliferation of fine-grained categories for treating persons, and of requirements for being able to perform various roles. This is believed to involve both efficiency and justice. These require unique identities, although not necessarily actual name. But the latter is seen to enhance validity, beyond its being an organizational marker (or in some cases skewer). Compare, for example, the evolution of the contemporary wallet with its space for multiple cards, with the paucity of identification documents required in the nineteenth century and earlier, simpler carrying devices.

f. To guarantee interactions that are distanced or mediated by time and space. This is the case with ordering by credit card or paying with a check rather than cash (of course, various types of impersonal vouchers such as a postal mail order offer alternatives). However, even in the latter case an address is frequently needed to deliver goods or to handle complaints and disputes. It used to be that one could simply call and make a restaurant reservation (often using as a *nom-de-guerre* the name of a famous scholar or author); then restaurants began asking for phone numbers and now some even require a credit card number to hold the place. Such identity becomes an alternative to the generalized trust more characteristic of small communities.

g. To aid research. Research may benefit from links to other types of personal data. Longitudinal research may require tracking unique individuals, although identity can be masked with statistical techniques.

h. To protect health and consumers. These protections may require identifying individuals with particular predispositions or experiences, such as exposure to a substance discovered to be toxic, or purchasers of a product later found to have a safety defect. Concern over genetic predispositions to illness may be one reason why records are kept (if often confidential) of sperm and egg donors or birth parents giving a child up for adoption. The need to identify persons in death (as with the DNA samples required of those in the military which are to be used only for that purpose), or to obtain personal information helpful in a medical emergency are other examples.

i. To aid in relationship building. The currency of friendship and intimacy is a reciprocal, gradual revealing of personal information that starts with name and location. Here information is a resource like a down payment, followed perhaps by a series of balloon payments over time, but it also has a symbolic meaning beyond its specific content.

j. To aid in social orientation. It used to be said at baseball stadiums, "You can't tell the players without a program" (although we have seen a move from numbers to names on jerseys). More broadly, social orientation to strangers and social regulation are aided by the clues about other aspects of identity presumed to be revealed by name and location (e.g., ethnicity, religion, lifestyle).

Some Trends and Questions for Future Research

Suggesting types of identification and the justifications and related types of social setting in which personal information must be presented, or is protected, is a first step toward a more systematic theory and its empirical assessment. We are clearly in the midst of major changes in identification that may prove to be every bit as profound as those associated with the rise of bureaucracy and the nation-state. Our current situation is quite dynamic and rapidly changing. This works against sweeping generalizations or gaining perspective. Yet the observing classes still need to observe. Based on my research on undercover police and new information technologies, let me note some empirical trends that suggest issues for research.[9] I state these in the form of hypotheses.

1. The kinds of information (biometric, behavioral) available to determine unique, "embodied" identities (as Goffman puts it)[10] has greatly expanded with respect to the following situations. First, the correspondence or fit between presumed indicators of identity and a unique person (e.g., matching DNA information found at different places or times to determine if it is from the same individual or handprint geometry, retinal patterns, facial, voice, and writing recognition systems). This answers the question, "is this the same person?" The indelible and inherent quality of DNA can also inform questions about paternity and maternity. Second, the ability to link indicators of unique identity to a particular person "known" (or believed) to be a given individual as defined by a legal name and biological descent. This requires either a database against which the indicators can be compared to discover who they "belong" to, or the presence of a person or his or her data that can be compared. With apologies to Sesame Street, this answers the question "who is it?" While one must be very wary of any single determinism, this is a nice example of how a technical development can drive a social development. Note the emergence of law enforcement, military, and other DNA databases (and forms such as voice prints) with explicit links to the "who" question. For effective use the unidentified DNA (and other) data "requires" organizational databases tied to known individuals.

2. The validity of the above forms of identification is in general very strong compared to the crude links (and frequent miscarriages of justice, whether convicting the innocent or freeing the guilty) found with nineteenth-century Lombrosian and related forms of categorical or group identification.

[9] Some of these ideas are developed at greater length in Marx 1989, 1994, and 1997 a,b.
[10] Goffman 1961.

3. The nineteenth-century ways of classifying individuals that Foucault associated with the development of institutions have continued to expand. The validity of these abstractly constructed, indirect, profiled indicators is in general lower than with the simple determination of legal name and biological identity noted above.

4. There has been a major expansion of laws, policies, and procedures mandating that individuals provide personal information. This has not been matched by equivalent protections for personal information, although these have increased as well. The former involves an increase in the kinds of information that must be presented and the conditions under which it must be presented. Anyone trying to check into a major hotel, fly on an airplane, and (increasingly) even make a credit card purchase— "But sir, we need your phone number in case there is a mistake or the product is called back"—has learned that. At a more abstract level the need to provide identification to enter gated communities, to access a building, and to use an elevator also fits here. In many ways the reins are tightening. Partly this involves "surveillance creep"—for example, note the demand for a social security number in so many contexts unrelated to its original purpose. There are many reasons for this, but the ability to know more (and the assumption that more knowledge is better), coupled with perceptions of increased risk associated with the ironic vulnerabilities of a technologically interdependent society (e.g., nuclear power plants, electrical power and communication grids, air travel, financial transactions, contagious diseases), are central. The interactions with strangers across vast distances brought by credit card and cyberspace dealings also requires substitutes for the identification that came from face-to-face interactions with a "known" person. This opens up vast markets, and entrepreneurs have played a major role in the commodification of personal information.

5. Some aspects of identity and, more broadly, of an individual's past have a greater presence than ever before. With contemporary forms of data collection, storage, and retrieval, elements of the past that tended to be forgotten are now preserved. For both better and worse elements of the individual's past cease to be past and instead are passed on. Compare, for example, the potential reach and durability of e-mail and posting on electronic bulletin boards with postcards, or taking a note down from a physical bulletin board in a fixed location. This goes beyond technology. The expanding 1960s and Watergate ethos of openness has broad impacts. Consider, for example, the increased availability of information about birth parents to those who were adopted. Consider also increases in the police practice known as "field investigations," in which police interrogate persons who appear not to "belong" to a given place, road

blocks to check for alcohol, and recent congressional legislation that sought (unsuccessfully this time) to make it possibile to unseal juvenile arrest records.

6. Parallel or shadow selves or identities have emerged alongside those we are aware of and may have a degree of control over (or at least control over whether or not we share them with others). With the rise of ever more varied organizational means of classification, we are increasingly subjected to imputed identities of which we are unaware. At one level these are generic, such as in the dividing of the United States by zip codes into clusters for mass marketing[11] or participation in a social or commercial network. But they are also individualized, such as scores for assessing credit or health risks (I recently learned my credit score, but I have no idea what that "means," since it is relative to other rankings and its "meaning" will vary depending on the standards of the organization using it; nor can I effectively lobby that my real number is something else). Organizations that comb and combine public and private records and repackage this information for sale to mass marketers, insurers, employers, and others are another example. Even where individuals are aware and sought classification, as with SAT scores, the classification rests with a third party rather than with the individual. Such organizational classifications play a major (and often unduly sub-rosa) role in affecting life chances.

7. Individuals have an expanding variety of identities to adopt. Some identities that historically tended to be largely inherited, such as social status or religion, are less so now. Even seemingly permanent physical attributes such as gender, height, body shape, or facial appearance can be altered, whether by hormones or surgery. This partly represents increased social mobility and twentieth-century expansions of civil liberties and civil rights. It also represents technologies that make it possible to alter the body, the forming of cyberspace communities, and the ease of presenting fraudulent cyberspace identities divorced from the traditional constraints of place and time. America On-Line offers subscribers up to five aliases and fantasy chat rooms. Individuals in some ways are freer to make or remake themselves than ever before. This ties back to the emergence of the self as a commodity and an object to be worked on, just as one would work on a plot of land or carve a block of wood. And this relates in turn to the ethos of American optimism, pragmatism, and self-help.

8. In a dialectical process, the use of false or misleading identification by subjects is increasing in self-defense and because of new opportunities.

---

[11] See the discussion in Larson 1992.

For example, in one large case in 1998, the Immigration and Naturalization Service seized 2 million fake government ID cards, including resident alien cards, immigration forms, driver's licenses, social security cards, credit cards, traveler's checks, and printing equipment. The use of false identification in many settings is not dependent on such counterfeit documents. There is a wonderful example in the film *The Big Lebowski*, when a police officer asks Lebowski for his identification and he has only his Ralph's Supermarket card to offer (we don't see what name is actually on it). My local supermarket card identifies me as Georg Simmel; I also get junk mail for Emile Durkheim and of course Karl Marx. Research on the accuracy of information provided to websites as a condition for entry suggests a high rate of falsification.

9. A variety of new forms of identification intended to mask or mediate between the individual's name and location are appearing and will continue to appear. Combining elements of anonymity and general or specific identifiability, these may certify the individual as being a certain kind of person and therefore eligible or ineligible to be treated in a particular way, or they may permit interactions with the unique individual in question, but not permit knowing the individual's legal identity or physical "meat space" location. As more and more actions are remotely tracked in cyberspace (phone communication, highway travel, consumer transactions) the pseudonym equivalent will become an increasingly common and accepted form of presenting the self for particular purposes (whether as a unique individual or as a member of a particular category). Certainly in many contexts what matters is continuity of personhood and the validity of the claims the individual makes (whether of the ability to pay for something, access to relevant resources, or expertise and experience) and their legitimacy to perform a particular role. Legal name may be irrelevant but verification is not. The crucial issue then becomes authentication of the pseudonymity. Smart cards and new crypto protocols make this easier.

Modern technology offers a variety of ways of uncoupling verification from unique identity. Validity, authenticity, and eligibility can be determined without having to know a person's name or location. Public policy debates will increasingly focus on when verification with anonymity is or is not appropriate, and on various intermediary mechanisms that offer pseudonymous buffers but not full identification. Since the cognitive appetite is difficult to sate, organizations will push for more rather than less information on individuals, although they will not necessarily want to share information with each other.

10. The state's reasons for collecting and using identification have broadened. In the twentieth century its traditional claimed needs to identify for reasons of internal security, the draft, to protect borders, and for

taxation, were supplemented by regulatory needs and the desire to do good (as defined by those with power) via the welfare state. The private sector, whether for employment or commercial reasons, has greatly expanded its use of personal data. Unlike the state's use of personal data, this is barely controlled by law.

11. The importance of physical place, localism, and national borders for identity is lessening in some ways, with ironic consequences. More inclusive units such as the European Union involve a lessening of border controls and ID checks between countries, but this may also mean an intensification of surveillance within countries and at the wider parameters of the new unit.

12. Identities are becoming relatively less unitary, homogeneous, fixed, and enduring, as the modernist idea of being able to choose who we are continues to expand, along with globalization processes and increased integration. Sex change operations are at one extreme—there may be uncertainty for persons who knew the individual before the operation. But more common are the new identities created through the increased intermarriage of ethnically, racially, religiously, and nationally distinct groups. Increases in children of mixed marriages, in those holding dual citizenships, and in immigration, tourism, and communities in cyberspace all illustrate this. New categories for marginal, hybrid, and anomalous groups will appear. As just one example, take the millions of Americans who, as products of a mixed marriage, consider themselves *both* Christian and Jewish, white and black, or Asian and Hispanic.

13. The lines between the public and private sectors with respect to identification are more blurred than ever before. Consider new public/private places such as shopping malls, industrial parks, and university campuses, the privatization of many traditional state functions, and the rise of private database companies drawing on public record data. The blurring of lines between work and home, as an increasing number of persons work at home and workplaces provide recreational, day-care, and health facilities, is another example.

Considered together, some of the above changes may appear ironic, paradoxical, or contradictory. I take this as a sign of both reality's ability to overflow our either/or categories and our lack of empirical research.

As the competing rationales discussed above suggest, there are value conflicts and conflicting needs and consequences that make it difficult to take a broad and consistent position in favor of, or against, expanding or restricting various kinds of identification and the conditions that govern them. To mention only some of these conflicts, there are the contradictions of liberty and order; accountability and privacy; community and individualism; freedom of expression and the right not to be defamed or harassed; honesty in communications and civility/diplomacy; creativity and experimentation versus exploitation and irresponsible behavior; encouragement of whistle-blowing and due process; the right to know and the right to control personal information; the universalistic treatment due to citizens and the efficiency of fine-honed personal differentiations; the desire to be noticed and the need to be left alone.

Whatever action is taken, there are likely costs and gains. At best we can hope to find a compass rather than a map and a moving equilibrium rather than a fixed point. Continued empirical research and policy and ethical analysis are central to this. The process of continual intellectual engagement with the issues is as important as the content of the solutions.

18

Identifying Unauthorized Foreign Workers in the German Labor Market

DITA VOGEL

MANY INDUSTRIAL countries regard unauthorized employment of foreign nationals as a major problem. Reducing the job magnet is seen as an important way to reduce undocumented immigration. In an effort to achieve this goal, Germany, like most European countries and the United States, uses employer sanctions—that is, threats of punishment for employers using unauthorized workers—as a means of dampening the "pull" of employment opportunities.[1]

This arrangement raises the question of how the unauthorized status of a worker can be determined by the authorities who are responsible for enforcing the law or by the employer, who is thus made to fulfill an immigration gatekeeper function in the labor market. Secure identification systems have been recognized as a vital factor in the success of employer sanctions.[2] Such systems function very differently in different countries.

This point can be illustrated by some comparative observations on the situation in the United States and Germany, respectively. Many American experts argue that employers in the United States need better means for identifying unauthorized workers in the hiring context. For example, a German-American working group states that the effectiveness of employer sanctions "has been hampered greatly by the availability of fraudulent documents." These analysts argue for the introduction of a "single, counterfeit-resistant employment identifier," and reassure those who fear violations of civil liberties by pointing to the relative lack of such problems in the German experience with employer sanctions.[3]

Similarly, the U.S. Commission on Immigration Reform concluded that the "single most important step that could be taken to reduce unlawful migration is the development of a more effective system for verifying work authorisation" to aid the "large majority of employers" who "will not

[1] United Nations 1998: 223.
[2] Freeman 1994: 25.
[3] Hailbronner et al. 1998: 218.

knowingly hire illegal aliens."[4] Pilot programs have been introduced in which voluntarily participating employers can receive employment verification on-line or with touchtone phones, using the social security number as the identifier.

In Germany, by contrast, the issue of identification requirements in the hiring situation scarcely arises. It is generally assumed that unauthorized workers are employed in the irregular underground economy, defined here as that part of the economy in which payroll taxes are evaded. Payroll taxes and supplementary benefits such as mandatory paid vacations are very costly in Germany. A publication by the Ministry of Labor notes that unauthorized work is nearly always combined with the evasion of taxes and social security contributions.[5] Consequently, state efforts to detect unauthorized workers in the underground economy have been increased. In the German context, however, fraudulent documents are discussed in terms of efforts to deceive labor market inspectors on raids, not as efforts to deceive inadvertent employers.

As other contributions in the present volume suggest, the existence or lack of secure documents and of residential registration requirements clearly distinguish national identification capacities and practices from one another. Surely, the existence of a national ID card and strict residential registration requirements have an impact on labor market control in Germany. Yet this essay argues that it is not so much residential registration requirements as it is cooperation requirements and data-sharing capacities of different German administrative authorities that form the core of the German regime for controlling unauthorized access to the labor market. These requirements and capacities largely explain why the inadvertent employment of unauthorized foreigners is only a minor problem in Germany as compared to in the United States, as well as why the process of European integration is perceived as a major challenge to the control regime.

To support this view, I take the reader on a journey into the dense jungle of German documentation, registration, and data management practices by following the paths of two hypothetical unauthorized immigrants as they attempt to negotiate their way in the German labor market. In the course of these hypothetical bureaucratic gauntlets, I focus not only on the persons and the way they are identified, but also on the personal data they submit and the identification practices related to this data. Although the problems of matching a person to a document or register will remain central to all identification practices in the modern world, computerization increases the importance of data management practices for the

---

[4] U.S. Commission on Immigration Reform 1997: 113–14.
[5] Bundesministerium für Arbeit und Sozialordnung 1998: 32.

overall identification regimes. The data-sharing and verification practices in the German labor market can be interpreted as one response to this challenge.

Because identification practices rest on legal rules, I also examine the legal background to the identification procedures discussed.[6] Nonetheless, this essay does not focus on legal structures but aims to describe those identification procedures that are of special empirical relevance. In order to assess more effectively which of these procedures are of greater practical importance, I have looked at administrative reports[7] and essays written by government officials,[8] and I have conducted qualitative interviews with practitioners in labor market control and migrant counseling.[9] Furthermore, the migrants' perspective on control structures has been taken into account wherever possible.[10] I have also drawn on newspaper coverage of police raids and of identification practices whenever these were available.

Identification of Unauthorized Immigrant Workers in the Labor Market

Choice of Examples

In this section, we follow the experience of two hypothetical young migrants without work permits as they attempt to make their way into the labor market, and thus examine how registration and identification practices limit their opportunities.

Imagine a young man from Poland—let us call him Carol. He comes to Germany because he wants to work and save money there. He entered the country completely legally at a regular land border port of entry, as Poles can enter Germany as tourists visa-free. He is very unlikely to be stopped as a potential illegal worker unless he is wearing dirty work

---

[6] Cremer 1998 gives an overview of the legal situation concerning internal controls and actual removal of deportable aliens.

[7] Especially Bundesregierung 1992 and 1996.

[8] Lüpke 1997, Severin 1997, Griesbeck 1997, Hellenthal 1995, and Wecker 1995.

[9] Interviews were conducted in the course of a study on migration control in Germany and the United States, financed by the German Marshall Fund of the United States and supported by the Centre for Social Policy Research, University of Bremen. See Vogel 1998a and 1998b.

[10] Literature on this subject is very limited in Germany, especially compared to that of the United States. I have relied on several studies by Cyrus 1995 and 1998 on Polish migrants, a book edited by Marburger 1994, and a study conducted with Brazilians in Berlin and London (see Jordan and Vogel 1997 and Estrella et al. 1997). A more comprehensive study

clothes and is carrying a bag of tools with him.[11] He is legally in the country, and even if he stays for years he could still claim to have entered only a few days before, as his date of arrival is nowhere registered or stamped into his passport. If the authorities can demonstrate that he is working, however, he is subject to expulsion because he is not allowed to work.

As a second example, imagine a young woman from Zaire—let's call her Maria—who has applied for political asylum in Germany. She has probably entered the country illegally.[12] Her chances of recognition as an asylee are low. At present, she is waiting for a decision on her asylum application, living in a public shelter for asylum-seekers where she receives food and a small amount of spending money. She would like to work and save some money to send to her family in Zaire.

The examples of Carol and Maria have been chosen in order to demonstrate the workings of internal controls in the labor market. The two have already overcome external migration controls with more (Maria) or less (Carol) difficulty, but have no legal right to work. It is assumed that they do not revert to criminal activities (such as theft or robbery) as a means to sustain themselves, but neither do they shy away from illegal activities that do not harm anyone (at least directly), such as staying illegally, possessing false documents, or working without paying taxes. In contrast to David Martin, whose discussion of the American system for removing unauthorized immigrants inspired this method of presentation, I do not assume a rational, well-informed "homo oeconomicus,"[13] but rather take two stylized but typical examples and vary their circumstances in order to demonstrate the role that identification practices play in labor market control.

wm

Access to the Regular Economy

Would Carol and Maria have the chance to find a regular, full-time job in a production line? This is almost impossible to imagine, but describing the improbable helps to show why this is not likely to be the case. The

---

focusing on the eastern part of Germany (Alt 1999) only appeared after this contribution was completed.

[11] In 1995, 9,945 persons were refused admittance at the border because of suspicions that they were planning to work illegally (Bundesministerium des Innern 1996:13). According to border police officials, clear indications of work intent as described above were mainly responsible for these refusals.

[12] Otherwise she would have been refused entry at the border, subjected to an abbreviated airport asylum determination procedure and sent back to a transit country, or treated as somebody with a manifestly unfounded asylum claim; the latter can be deported relatively easily.

[13] See Martin 1998.

employer is required to ask them for their social security cards and their tax cards and to register the job with each employee's health insurance provider. Carol and Maria have neither of these. The tax card serves to keep track of wages for tax purposes, and it would be difficult for either of our unauthorized workers to get a real tax card. Tax cards are handed out by the local residential registration offices (*Einwohnermeldebehör-den*), where all residents—Germans and foreign nationals alike—must register their place of domicile. Maria is registered, but the residential registration offices should and probably would want to check her work permit before issuing the tax card.

Could Carol and Maria get work permits? Definitely not in Carol's case.[14] The employer could apply for a work permit for Maria if she had been in Germany for a certain period of time.[15] The employer would then have to wait four weeks, during which time the local bureau of the Federal Labor Office (*Arbeitsamt*) could send the employer suitable unemployed persons whom she or he cannot decline to employ without good reason. Only after this waiting period had expired would the employer be able to employ Maria legally. If a work permit were to be issued, the local bureau would send this information to a central database where all work permits can be identified by the recipient's social security number, as well as inform the local aliens' authorities (*Ausländerbehörde*). Thus, getting a work permit is difficult, and we further assume that Maria did not get a work permit for this job.

It would be possible for both Carol and Maria to get a real social security card. The employer could apply for the card, and the social security administration would send it out automatically without checking the applicant's immigration status or informing the local aliens' authorities. The employer would then be able to pay social security taxes on behalf of these workers. But if the employer had had previous experience with employing foreign nationals, he or she would either expect them to have a social security number or ask them to cooperate in order to get a work permit.

Carol and Maria could try to get false documents to present to their employers. The tax card is a simple, easily falsifiable form, and although it is harder to produce a social security card that an expert would find convincing, it may well be possible to produce one that an employer

[14] There are legal work opportunities for Poles as border-crossers, seasonal workers, and contract workers. Legal employment in these statuses often blends with illegal employment, as employers get a work permit for their workers but break the conditions of the contract. These complicated evasion issues are not discussed in this essay, as they are important more in connection with the upholding of labor standards than in connection with identification issues.

[15] The minimum length of stay required for receiving a work permit has varied considerably between zero and five years since it was first introduced in the early 1980s.

would accept as genuine. Let's imagine that false papers had convinced their employers, Carol and Maria had started work, and the employers had registered them with the statutory health insurance providers mainly used by their respective companies.[16] The health insurance provider would run a computer program to check for invented or misspelled social security numbers. This verification procedure is made possible by the fact that the last two numbers of any social security number are calculated from the other numbers. If Carol and Maria had simply invented social security numbers, their employers would soon get a letter asking for verification of the numbers.

If Carol and Maria have not invented the numbers but instead have "borrowed" them from somebody else's papers, the fraud would not be discovered at this stage. Then the health insurance provider would send the employment notice to a central employment register where several programs are run to detect fraud.[17] Does the person with this social security number receive unemployment benefits? Does he or she work in another job below the contribution exemption limit, and thus become liable for social security taxes as a result of this additional employment? Does the number belong to a foreign national who has no work permit for this job?

If the answer to any of these questions is "yes," the local branch of the Federal Labor Office will be notified. The Federal Labor Office has several public labor market functions, mainly those of administering unemployment insurance and serving as an employment agency, and plays a major role in fighting illegal employment by Germans and foreign nationals. The local office will investigate the case on the basis of its local files and ask the employer for clarification of the situation, as late or missing data may have led to the questions. Then the office decides whether to impose a fine on employee and/or employer.[18]

As I understand the process, using someone else's social security number does not lead to problems as long as the other person is neither receiving benefits nor is engaged in employment below the contribution limit.

[16] Most probably this would be the AOK, which is the name of the only health insurance provider that had to accept everybody before the system was changed in 1996. AOK also controlled the collection of all social security taxes on behalf of the statutory insurances and has now finished the process of handing over this task to the statutory pension scheme. (In Germany the term *social insurance* refers to all statutory insurances, that is, sickness, long-term care, unemployment, and pension insurance.)

[17] Lüpke 1997.

[18] As these paperwork violations are included in Federal Labor Office statistics on unauthorized work, they partly explain the low average level of fines. Additionally, at least in some regions (definitely Bremen), cases of unauthorized work were in the past not counted if the foreign nationals involved were also illegally resident and facing deportation after detection. These and some other peculiarities of the German statistics on unauthorized work

Assuming the identity of another person is the most reliable method for an undocumented worker to secure a legitimate job. But the potential for such fraud is limited by the number of persons who are able and willing to lend their papers. As births and deaths are recorded in local residential registers, moreover, it is not easy to assume the identity of a person who has died.

If our hypothetical unauthorized workers are to get themselves real social security numbers or to use the number of another foreign national without a work permit, the illegality of their employment will be discovered. The detection of their unauthorized status may well take a while, as the labor office compares work permit data with employment data only quarterly. Short-term employment stints may already have come under the statute of limitation by the time they are discovered.

These procedures will be known neither to Carol and Maria nor to their employers, and even many people in control functions outside the Federal Labor Office do not know about them. The employers, however, will be familiar with their registration obligations and may well suspect that there is a much more efficient system of data cross-checking than the one that actually exists.

Indeed, data cross-checking filters out many attempts by unauthorized workers to secure work in a legitimate job. These procedures will not normally lead to the detection of undocumented immigrants or to anything more than a warning letter to an employer, but as a general rule they will prevent the inadvertent hiring of undocumented immigrants into jobs in the regular economy.

Considering these tax-related registration practices, easier personal identification in the hiring situation plays only a secondary role in the control regime. Employers are nonetheless advised to check the passports of foreign nationals in order to prevent hiring unauthorized foreign nationals. In contrast to the situation in the United States, discriminatory identification procedures are perfectly legal. Although employers do not require white persons with a good command of the German language to show their passports, they may ask Carol to do so because of his poor German-language abilities, and they may ask this of Maria because she is black. But Germans generally would not find it an undue burden to be asked to show their passports or identity cards if asked to do so by the authorities or by their employers.

On the other hand, as the main verification task is fulfilled within the public sector, employers run hardly any risk of sanctions if they hire foreign-looking or -sounding persons in possession of a social security card

---

make them a highly problematic database for analysis, and more so for international comparisons (as in Snowden 1998).

and a tax card and register them with the sickness insurance. Therefore, employers' desires to avoid sanctions do not lead them to hire workers on a discriminatory basis. Foreign-looking or -sounding Germans or permanent residents may have to face discriminatory identification checks by the authorities, but no discriminatory hiring practices associated with labor market control.[19] In contrast, the American practice of strictly forbidding discriminatory identification practices by employers—demanding documents from some workers that one does not demand from others—increases the probability that employers will engage in discriminatory hiring practices, because the employer can always escape censure for such discrimination by claiming that other reasons motivated a particular job applicant's rejection.

Controls on Work in the Underground Economy

As Carol and Maria have little prospect of being hired inadvertently for a legitimate job by a gullible employer, they would probably not even try this avenue. Other immigrants would probably have advised them that they would be unable to secure a legitimate job, but that they would instead have to look for work in the underground economy.

In the underground economy, employers do not necessarily know that their employee has no work permit, but they certainly know that they should be taking out payroll taxes for all of their employees. Payroll taxes are very high in Germany—about a third of labor costs (gross wages plus employer contributions) have to be deducted as social security taxes. Social security taxation starts at incomes below subsistence level, and total tax rates including income taxation may well exceed 50 percent for middle-class taxpayers.[20]

Once they start looking for off-the-books employment, Carol and Maria are more likely to find such jobs in the tertiary than in the secondary sector, in small rather than in large companies, in private households rather than in companies, for limited periods rather than for permanent

[19] Of course there may also be other reasons for discrimination.

[20] Contribution rates are calculated from gross wages without employer contributions. They add up to 21 percent in 1998 for the employee, and the employer has to pay the same amount. Income taxation starts at a rate of 26 percent, but leaves tax-free a certain portion of income that is determined by family circumstances. Jobs paying wages below the tax exemption limit of the social insurance were liable to a flat rate income tax of 20 percent. In 1999, this flat rate income tax was replaced by a partial inclusion in social security contributions, a change that weighs heavily on holders of second jobs but is less important in this connection as the jobs already had to be registered under the social security number before the recent changes.

employment, and for unskilled rather than for skilled work.[21] The illegality of their employment can only be detected if they are identified on the job, as they do not appear in any books or employment registers.

Working without the necessary permit is a regulatory offense for the employee. For the employer, it is also only a regulatory offense, unless he or she is proven to have profited for a long time, or repeatedly, or to have paid exceptionally low wages. Evading payroll taxes will often be the more serious and criminal offense which will be prosecuted.

Let us first consider Carol's case. Carol may well find a job in the construction sector. He may have heard about the street markets for day laborers that exist in some large German cities; or he may have heard in Poland about a company that functions as a subcontractor to a large construction firm and hires only a small part of its employees regularly on its official books; or he may know a fellow national doing construction or renovation work in private households who needs some help.

The construction sector is a very unusual sector for several reasons. Some of these have to do with the nature of the work: high visibility on the one hand, and projects of limited duration and changing worksites on the other. In Germany, construction has traditionally been a male-dominated sector with strong union representation, high wages, and generous supplementary social benefits. Workers in the construction sector have something to lose.

One of the unusual benefits enjoyed by workers in construction is the sectoral holiday fund (*Urlaubskasse*), which is obligatory for the employee but administered by employer associations and unions in the industry. This holiday fund is the most comprehensive obligatory social scheme in any industrial sector. Even those employees that are tax- and contribution-free in Germany because they work under an international contract-worker arrangement must be registered with this fund. The fund has added additional staff to enhance cooperation with labor market control agencies. Labor office inspectors may ask holiday fund staff via telephone whether a specific person is registered with the fund, a negative response being an indication that a closer check for illegal employment may be in order.

This development exemplifies the general attitude toward cooperation between the authorities responsible for controlling unauthorized work and semi-state agencies such as the holiday fund: cooperation is the norm, and non-cooperation results not from principled opposition but from bureaucratic deficiencies and personnel shortages. This point is reinforced by the way I heard about this procedure: I was allowed to attend a bimonthly informal information meeting of agencies involved in labor

---

[21] Bundesregierung 1996: 52.

work site raids for documentation

market control in the city-state of Bremen, where a construction workers' union representative described the procedure to the control agents in attendance.

We now turn to the hypothetical situation of Maria, the Zairean asylum-seeker. She may have taken a job washing dishes in a restaurant kitchen or a cleaning job in a private household. She may have found her job in the classified section of a local newspaper, but more probably someone recommended her for the job.[22] In contrast to Carol's job, Maria's would probably be permanent but part-time. Her work is thus likely to be located in a female-dominated, low-wage environment where unions are not important and employer-employee relations often have a substantial personal component.

Both Carol's and Maria's underground employment can only be detected if the authorities check them while they are working. Enforcement units of the Federal Labor Office and of the customs authorities are responsible for this kind of inspection.[23] Their worksite raids serve not only to detect the employment of unauthorized foreign nationals, but also to ferret out social security tax evasion and unemployment benefit fraud by Germans and authorized foreign nationals. Staff for these enforcement units has been beefed up since the 1980s. Today, at least 3,500 inspectors check the identity papers of more than 600,000 persons annually during such raids.[24]

Enforcement staff have almost complete discretion in their choice of worksites, but they mostly act on tips from competitors, neighbors, and other authorities, and concentrate on the construction sector. Therefore, Carol has a much higher risk of being checked in one of these raids than Maria. Her work is considerably less visible, and thus it is less likely that a neighbor or competitor would accidentally observe her working and inform the authorities. In the construction sector, there are also more authorities checking the workplace regularly for one reason or another, and in some places the union encourages informers.

Once the enforcement units enter the workplace, they try to make sure that nobody leaves. They demand to see everyone's identification. Foreign nationals are also asked to produce work authorization. As during the hiring process, discriminatory identification practices are the rule. It is up to the inspectors whether they rely on the testimony of co-workers,

[22] Our interviews with Brazilians indicated that it is difficult to find a job without a recommendation. See Estrella et al. 1997.

[23] With the implementation of the Single European Market, some customs officers became superfluous. Customs authorities got additional responsibilities in labor market control that were formerly only fulfilled by labor inspectors from the Federal Labor Office.

[24] My calculation is based on limited data, partly based on a three-year average. Data from Bundesregierung 1996: 54, and Lüpke 1997: 31.

photocopies of work authorizations, social security cards, or passports for identification purposes. Inspectors openly admitted to me that they used the accents and looks of a person as a criterion for insisting on passports for identification. Both Carol and Maria would be candidates for closer inspection.

Carol and his employer are more likely to be prepared to show some type of document to the enforcement units. Carol may have a false work permit or social security card, hoping he can get away with it. He may also have been instructed to say that he is only on the worksite by coincidence, or that he is just helping out for the day. He will probably not be able or willing to name his employer, and it will be difficult to prove an employment relation to a specific employer without this information. Therefore, joint liability on the part of general contractors and subcontractors has been discussed by labor market enforcement officials and legislators as one way to improve the effectiveness of these controls, especially in the construction sector.[25] If Maria is controlled in a restaurant or private household, of course, it is much more obvious who is her employer, even without any information from her.

It is a curiosity of the labor market control regime that inspectors from the Federal Labor Office lack the authority to apprehend suspected violators of immigration laws, whereas customs officers who basically do the same job have such power. If labor inspectors suspect false papers or illegal residence before starting a raid, they ask the police to cooperate in the raid. If their suspicion only arises during the course of the raid itself, the labor inspectors inform the police. They would not be allowed to detain anyone at the site just because of uncertainty concerning someone's identity, so workers who run away will probably not be stopped and will escape. But Carol may not know which authorities can stop him and which cannot, so he may stick around to await apprehension by the police.

What happens afterwards depends upon discretionary decisions of the police, public attorneys, and aliens' authorities. These officials are supposed to interpret the law in a uniform way, but their decisions are also influenced by the availability of resources such as police manpower, officials of the aliens' authorities, and the detention and transport facilities.[26]

Carol may be released to return to Poland on his own, in the process of which he will be required to hand over to the border police a border-crossing certificate (*Grenzübertrittsbescheinigung*) as he leaves Germany.

[25] Martin 1998: 32.

[26] Authorities may be inclined to deny this, as it is not the way they are supposed to use their discretionary power. An official government publication recognizes this problem (Bundesregierung 1996: 55).

IDENTIFYING UNAUTHORIZED WORKERS   339

If he fails to produce such a certificate at the border within the given time limit (e.g., two weeks), this will be taken as a sign that he is still in the country and he will get a "wanted person" notation in the Central Aliens Register.[27] Or he may be detained and deported to Poland, which will also be noted in the Central Aliens Register.

Maria does not have her passport with her because the Federal Office for the Recognition of Foreign Refugees (*Bundesamt für die Anerkennung ausländischer Flüchtlinge*) will have kept it when she applied for asylum. This practice has been adopted to ensure that rejected asylum-seekers can be deported, because a lost or destroyed passport may delay or prevent deportation. In place of her passport, Maria has been issued a document recognizing her status as an asylum-seeker (*Aufenthaltsgestattung*) that includes her photograph.

If she can be identified clearly by showing her substitute photo ID, the officers will let her go home. Later, officials of the Federal Labor Office may send her a warning or a fine for her regulatory offense, and they will also fine her employer. Both will also face investigations because of tax evasion and benefit fraud.

Let us imagine that Maria forgot her ID and that she does not understand the question about her name and address. Under these circumstances, the customs or labor inspectors have no easy way to find out who she is. They cannot ring the residents' registration office and ask whether a "Maria X" is registered under a certain address. The police would have to investigate further in order to establish her identity. They could do so with the help of an interpreter, or by taking her fingerprints and comparing them with police registers and the register of the fingerprints of all asylum-seekers. Here the police would find her name and, eventually, with the help of other databases on asylum-seekers, her address.

Imagine that Maria wants to submerge after her asylum application has been rejected—whether simply because she wants to make some money before returning to her home country, or because she is terrified to return for some reason which is not believed or recognized as a legitimate reason for asylum or suspension of deportation. A well-falsified passport of another EU member state would pose the biggest problem for the authorities. If she had a French passport, spoke some French, and had an address, there would be no reason to suspect a false identity. Maria could even register and get a residence status, but that would mean that she would have had to present herself to the registration and aliens' authorities and thus expose herself to the risk of detection and apprehension by the police. Authorities are supposed to call the police if they discover undocumented residence in the course of their work.

[27] For a description of the Central Aliens Register, see Streit 1996.

Even if she had not registered her residence, this would be only a minor offense for a citizen of a member-country of the European Union. If the labor inspectors suspected falsified papers, there would be no quick and easy way to clarify this because as an apparent EU citizen there would be no reason for her to appear in any German registers. Only if the inspectors rightly suspected her to be an asylum-seeker could they learn her real identity in the register of asylum-seekers' fingerprints. If she had not even applied for asylum but had gone underground immediately, even this would not be possible. Only careful document analysis or information from French authorities could reveal the fraud. Consequently, labor inspectors have characterized falsified EU passports as a major difficulty for their identification tasks.

The difficulty of detecting labor market fraud of this kind helps explain why German authorities have been the driving force behind the efforts to develop registers embracing all of the countries of the European Union. The first register of this type is the Schengen Information System (SIS), which is basically a European-wide "wanted persons" list. The Schengen states decide independently about which data from national databases they wish to feed into the European system. Germany transmits a large proportion of the data entered into the system, but only the data that is fed in from other states enhances the identification capacities of the German authorities. There are also efforts to build up a European fingerprint identification system, which would improve German capacities to send asylum-seekers back to the place where they were first registered.

Registers and Identification Documents in the German Labor Market: A Summary

Having mentioned a number of control agencies, registers, and documents in the German labor market, this section sums up the basic features of the most important ones.

Identification procedures in the German labor market are characterized by organizational decentralization and fragmentation, on the one hand, and cooperation and central databases, on the other. Decentralization and fragmentation are characteristics of the German model of federalism. Nearly all public functions are fulfilled exclusively by the *Länder* (states) and, within the *Länder*, by the local communities. The federal level exercises its power mainly by legislatively restricting the discretion of lower levels of government. For example, the investigation of *all* criminal matters is the task of the *Länder* police, although some limited tasks are reserved for the federal border police (*Bundesgrenzschutz*).

The term *fragmentation* is used to characterize an organizational structure in which important public competences are delegated to intermediary

paper files
Germans
online data
immigrants

organizations (functional federalism, functional decentralization). The social security system is largely organized in statutory compulsory social insurance systems that also participate in the collection of contributions and in labor market control. The Federal Labor Office, which is mainly responsible for unemployment insurance and employment services, is the key actor in labor market control. Its local offices cooperate with local branches of the customs authorities, which are organizationally independent authorities within the state administration.

On the other hand, strictly public authorities and quasi-public intermediaries in Germany are generally supposed to cooperate closely with each other, and they must do so if the state wishes successfully to prevent unauthorized work. Labor market inspectors detect unauthorized workers, police arrest those without residence status or of doubtful identity, and aliens' authorities are responsible for making decisions on identity, nationality, toleration, removal, and the like, whereas actual deportations are organized by the state police in cooperation with the federal border police. With so many organizations involved in the control regime, information-sharing is of central importance for its proper functioning.

Several national databases have been developed to compensate for the decentralized and fragmented organizational structure. These databases form an important feature of the German labor market control regime. Some of them serve general control functions such as residence registration, whereas others are specially designed to regulate the labor market (employment registers) or to track foreign nationals (Central Aliens Register). Table 1 gives an overview of the most important databases in this connection.

Whereas Germans are only registered in decentralized residential registers that often still use only paper files rather than computerized databases, foreign nationals are registered in a national database with quick or even on-line access. There is even a fingerprint register for asylum-seekers, primarily to prevent abuse through multiple applications under different identities.

The Central Employment Register in connection with the Central Work Permit Register is used to prevent unauthorized work in regular tax-paying jobs. These registers use the social security number as the identifier, and there is only limited cooperation with the other registration authorities—namely, information-sharing on work permits between the local branch of the Federal Labor Office and the local aliens' authority.

Conclusion

In this essay, I have presented evidence that extensive registration requirements and cooperation among different government agencies, especially

TABLE 1
Labor Market and Immigration Registers in Germany

Register	Local Residents' Registers	Central Aliens Register	Fingerprint Identification System for Asylum-Seekers (AFIS)	Central Employment Register	Central Work Permit Register
Corresponding documents	German passport, national identity card, tax card	Residence permit (usually stamped in passport)	Substitute identification paper for asylum seekers (Aufenthalts-gestat-tung)	Social Security Card	Work permit
Authority responsible for entry, change, and invalidation	Local residential registration offices	Local aliens authorities, Federal Agency for the Recognition of Foreign Refugees, Police	Federal Agency for the Recognition of Foreign Refugees	Sickness insurances (collection) and pension insurances	Local employment offices
Main identifier	Name, address	Name, address	Fingerprints	Social security number	Social security number
Right to make inquiries on individuals	Name, address: everybody, e.g., by phone	Alien authorities, police, embassies, etc., partly on-line	Federal Agency for the Recognition of Foreign Refugees, police; on-line	n/a	Federal Labor Office, written inquiry
Standardized information-sharing procedures	Case-by-case information to alien authorities		Comparison with criminal registers and wanted persons lists on registration	Data cross-checking to detect multiple minor jobs, benefit fraud, and unauthorized work	Quarterly cross-checking with Central Employment Register, information of alien authorities

Note: The table does not give a complete description in the legal sense, but emphasizes the main features of each register. Laws and ordinances regulate in detail which authorities may change, request, and receive which information.

In Germany, docs are less important than registers

in the form of data-sharing, form the core of the German labor market control regime for preventing unauthorized work by non-Germans. A second element is the largely undebated practice of discriminatory identification by employers and control agents—that is, that employers and officials involved in enforcing the relevant laws may and do ask to see more or other documents from foreign-looking or -sounding persons than they request of Germans (or those who seem to be German).

Cooperation practices vary widely among the different *Länder* and sectors of the economy, and not all of these variations could be accounted for in this essay. But cooperation among the agencies concerned seems to be the norm, and non-cooperation between different authorities arises more from bureaucratic problems or lack of personnel than as a conscious policy option for independent agencies.

These practices largely explain why the employment of undocumented immigrants in the regular tax-paying economy receives little attention in Germany. To be sure, high payroll taxes make the regular employment of undocumented immigrants less atttractive in Germany than in other countries in the first place. Thus, increased efforts to combat the employment of unauthorized workers have focused primarily on the underground economy. The numbers of workplace inspectors who check the documents of individual workers and examine employers' personnel records have increased rapidly since the 1980s.

This extensive reliance on cooperation and data exchange also explains why German officials perceive the process of European integration as a major challenge for the control regime. Data exchange is much more difficult across national borders, and not only for practical reasons but also because other countries have different cultures of cooperation. When it comes to people who present passports from other European Union countries, control agents have to rely on those identification measures that have been discussed in a number of the other contributions in this volume: the analysis of documents and the matching of persons to documents.

In the German context, the role of documents in establishing individual identity—especially the national identity card—is easily overestimated. Checking identity documents can often be substituted for or supplemented by checking the registers to which they are related, and this kind of procedure is facilitated by computerization and data exchange requirements among different authorities. For the same reason, employer document-verification duties are not as burdensome in Germany as they are, for example, in the United States. Employers are not document experts. But if they fulfill their registration duties and the authorities check the data and find unauthorized employment, employers usually will not face sanctions.

In a situation in which the information entered in registers plays a major role in identifying individuals and individual data, documents not only serve the aim of the authorities to control individuals, but also protect the individual against the authorities. As with all databases, mistakes occur, and a document carried by the individual may serve him or her as insurance against such mistakes—the consequences of which may be quite serious in a world in which individual identity has come to play such a powerful role in determining eligibility for so many desirable things.

19

Identity Cards, Ethnic Self-Perception, and Genocide in Rwanda

TIMOTHY LONGMAN

"CLAUDETTE"[1] grew up in the hills of southern Rwanda believing that she knew her ethnic identity. Like her parents and siblings, Claudette carried an identity card that classified her as a member of the Hutu ethnic group, the group that comprised nearly 85 percent of Rwanda's population. As a Hutu, Claudette lived free from the discrimination that plagued her Tutsi neighbors. She gained easy entrance to secondary school, while her Tutsi friends had to compete for a limited number of available spots. Like other southern Hutu, she was critical of the government for being dominated by northerners, but she did not live in fear of ethnic violence like her Tutsi neighbors, whose families had suffered attacks in the 1960s and who were distressed by the anti-Tutsi rhetoric that had been spreading through the country since 1990.

In April 1994, Claudette's world suddenly collapsed around her. When President Juvénal Habyarimana was killed in a mysterious plane crash, his supporters launched a campaign of mass violence against their perceived enemies, initially targeting political opponents regardless of ethnicity, but then, as the violence spread from the capital, focusing almost exclusively on Tutsi. Throughout the country, soldiers and civilian militia drove Tutsi out of their homes, gathered them in supposed sanctuaries—churches, schools, and government offices—and systematically slaughtered them. In every community, "civil defense" patrols were organized to search for Tutsi who had evaded extermination, including not only those in hiding, but also those who might be attempting to pass for Hutu. Rumors began to spread in Claudette's community that her family might not truly be Hutu. Since they had only moved into the area during her father's childhood, a delegation was dispatched to their community of origin to investigate, and, indeed, word came back that Claudette's grandfather, her father's father, had been known as a Tutsi before he moved. Somehow, when

---

[1] This story was gathered through extensive interviews with the subject during March and April 1996. Her name has been changed to protect her identity.

he had settled in a new community, he had received a new identity card that stated his ethnicity as Hutu, and he had passed this new ethnic identity down through patrilineal succession to Claudette and her siblings.

Overnight, Claudette's family found themselves transformed into targets of murder. Her grandfather refused to leave his home and was slaughtered there. Her father fled, and because he had a Hutu identity card, he was able to find safety in another community, but eventually people from his home community found him and killed him. Claudette's younger sister was saved from death only because she was young and beautiful; a soldier took her as his concubine and offered her protection in exchange for sex. When he fled to Zaire in July, he took her along. A third sister, who had lived in Kigali, was never suspected of being Tutsi and instead lived as a Hutu and fled into Zaire with other Hutu in July. Claudette, who had been home from secondary school on Easter break when the genocide began, took refuge with a group of Catholic nuns who sheltered her for two months until the Tutsi rebel group, the Rwandan Patriotic Front (RPF), arrived and ended the genocide.

In the aftermath of the 1994 genocide, Claudette has been struggling to understand who she is and how she fits into society. The RPF now rules Rwanda, and Tutsi enjoy extensive benefits, holding government offices, school positions, and other opportunities far out of proportion to their percentage of the population. The majority Hutu now must live in fear of being accused of involvement in the genocide and facing imprisonment. Claudette and her family, like other Tutsi, suffered during the genocide for their ethnic origins, yet Claudette's position as a Tutsi is suspect, since before the genocide her family had enjoyed the benefits of being Hutu. Claudette has moved to Kigali, where she presents herself as Tutsi, but in private conversation, she tells me, "I do not really know what I am. I do not know what it means to be Tutsi."

Claudette's story demonstrates the problematic relationship between official documentation and identity in Rwanda, as in much of Africa. Political authorities in both colonial and postcolonial Africa have used official documentation as a means of attempting to fix group identities, and this documentation has clearly had an impact on how individuals themselves perceive their identities. In Rwanda, the Belgians "instituted a system of rigid ethnic classification, involving such 'modern scientific' methods as the measurement of nose and skull sizes, and the attribution of obligatory identity papers stating one's ethnicity."[2] Students of Rwandan history commonly trace the roots of the 1994 genocide to official colonial policies that fixed group identities, arranged groups in a hierarchy, and

colonial policies

[2] Uvin 1997: 95.

Flexibility of identity can't be prevented by documents

instilled in the Rwandan groups a hatred and distrust of one another. As Gérard Prunier writes, "The time-bomb had been set and it was now only a question of when it would go off."[3] Postcolonial policies maintained the official registration of ethnic identities and reinforced group divisions.

While the official policies that divided Hutu and Tutsi clearly created an environment where genocide became possible, the experience of Claudette's family cautions against overestimating the degree to which official documents are capable of fixing individual identities. Even in as volatile an environment as Rwanda, identity retains a flexibility that official documents cannot prevent. Individuals may actually use documentation as a tool in their efforts to mold their identity, contravening the intentions of those who established the systems of documentation. During the genocide, the realization that official documents could be forged created an uncertainty about individual identities. This suggests that in Rwanda today ethnic identity is understood as an essential characteristic of individuals, not an official designation. Thus, ironically, while official documents were not a reliable determinant of individual identity, their usage by colonial and postcolonial governments nevertheless helped to transform the manner in which Rwandans regard identity. In part because of the issuance of identity cards, most Rwandans today, unlike in precolonial times, believe that ethnicity is a fixed trait of individuals.

Pass Laws and Identity Documentation in Colonial Africa

The implementation of forms of identity documentation was common practice for colonial governments in Africa, usually as part of efforts to regulate the supply of labor. The first laws requiring Africans to carry identity passes were adopted in the Cape Colony (in what is today South Africa) in the 1700s to maintain control over slave labor on the farms of Dutch settlers.[4] After taking possession of the Cape Colony in 1806, Britain maintained pass laws for Africans, eventually expanding them in the 1870s as part of an effort to force Africans into the labor market. As the Dutch-speaking Afrikaner population trekked inland in the 1800s to avoid British rule, they once again implemented pass laws for Africans living in territories under their control as they sought to secure cheap farm labor.[5] After the discovery of diamonds and gold in the Afrikaner republics, the mining industry pushed for a significant strengthening of pass laws. As Shula Marks explains:

[3] Prunier 1995: 39.
[4] Marks 1985b: 422–92.
[5] Marks 1985a: 359–421.

At the insistence of the Chamber of Mines, under law 31 of 1896 the [South African] Republic's *Volksraad* (the legislature) provided that Africans entering the mining areas had to have passes authorising them to seek employment for three days. Once employed, the worker handed his pass to his employer until he was discharged, and was provided with an "employers" pass in exchange: failure to produce a pass on demand rendered an African liable to a £3 fine or three weeks' hard labour for a first offence, and a rising scale of penalties for any offence thereafter.[6]

After conquering the South African Republic in the Boer War of 1899-1902, the British, as they had done in the Cape, maintained most of the legal structure of the Afrikaner state, including pass laws.[7]

Pass laws were subsequently adopted in several other British settler colonies of eastern and southern Africa, where hindering the free movement of Africans helped guarantee cheap labor for the mines and plantations. As British settlers moved into Rhodesia and Nyasaland (the modern states of Zambia, Zimbabwe, and Malawi), the British administration implemented pass laws together with laws punishing Africans for breach of contract, hence making it difficult for blacks to leave white employment once engaged. As Teresa Barnes explains, "A fully developed pass control system minimized workers' freedom and maximized the control that capital and the state could exercise over their physical movements and economic options." Pass violations were the largest category of criminal prosecution for African men in colonial Rhodesia.[8] The colonial administration of Kenya similarly adopted regulations in 1920 requiring all adult men to carry a registration certificate, while similar laws were considered and rejected in the Gold Coast.[9]

While pass laws in British Africa were not initially intended to structure group membership and individual identity, they were easily adapted to this purpose. Passes such as those implemented in South Africa and Rhodesia "set out identity details (such as a man's name, date of birth, home area, chief's name), employment details (name and location of last employer, previous wages and whether the worker had the employer's consent to leave the job and comments on his character or work record) and tax payment."[10] From their inception, passes in southern Africa identified race, since they were issued only to non-whites, and gender, since they were required only of men.[11] Among the principles central to the apartheid

---

[6] Marks 1985b: 466.
[7] Ibid. 486.
[8] Barnes 1997: 59–81; McCracken 1986: 602–48.
[9] Roberts 1986: 649–701; Dorward 1986: 399–459.
[10] Barnes 1997: 59–60.
[11] Ibid. 60–62.

system set up by the National Party government after it came to power in South Africa in 1948 was that blacks were not citizens of the Republic of South Africa but of various African "homelands," territories carved out of South Africa and designated as "native reserves," African states theoretically moving toward complete autonomy. The homeland system required identifying the membership of each African in a specific ethnic group, in whose homeland their citizenship would reside, and the pass books, which already contained information on place of origin, served that purpose.[12]

The intention of the white government in establishing the homelands was to divide the African population and discourage the formation of a common sense of South African nationality by encouraging identification with subnational identities. These efforts had only partial success. Limited economic opportunities in the homelands required most adult men to seek employment in areas officially reserved for whites (the vast majority of the national territory), and since the pass laws played a major role in constraining mobility, they became an important focus of protest for blacks in South Africa, including the one that ended in the massacre at Sharpeville in 1960. Even the leaders of the homelands, those whom the white government had hoped to co-opt, spoke out against the homeland system after the June 1976 revolt in Soweto. Nevertheless, the requirements of pass books and other official documents forced black South Africans to maintain some contact with the homelands, and the violence between supporters of the Zulu nationalist Inkatha Freedom Party and supporters of the African National Congress in the waning days of apartheid demonstrated the potential power of these officially sponsored ethnic identities.[13]

While pass books were the most onerous form of official documentation, since they greatly limited the mobility of Africans, other forms of identity documentation may have had a more profound impact on group and individual identity formation. The British and Belgians ruled most of their territories through a system known as "indirect rule," in which indigenous leaders were left in place and used to administer colonial policies. Indirect rule, however, required both clearly defined ethnic groups and clearly defined indigenous leaders, conditions that were frequently not in place. Hence, the colonial governments set about carefully defining regional boundaries and categorizing Africans by ethnicity, and where necessary they created both groups and "traditional" leaders. Africans' relations to the colonial state were structured through these groups and leaders, requiring individuals to accept the officially designated identities

[12] Price and Rosberg 1980; Thompson 1990.
[13] Price and Rosberg 1980.

at least for official purposes—paying taxes, seeking formal employment, receiving education, health, and other services, and legal action. The lasting impact of the official organization of ethnic identities has been well documented, as ethnic identities have remained important principles for political mobilization in postcolonial Africa. Many of the groups created for purely administrative purposes have continued to exist as distinct groups, and the descendants of those Africans placed in these groups maintain a strong ethnic identification. While Africa's other main colonial powers, the French and Portuguese, did not use indirect rule, they nevertheless also sought to categorize Africans into distinct ethnic groups, and various official documents they used, ranging from birth records to identity cards, specified ethnic membership.[14] The Rwandan case effectively demonstrates the degree to which such official documentation could affect how individuals perceived their own identity—and the limitations on documentation's impact on the individual.

Identity Cards in Colonial Ruanda-Urundi

The categories *Hutu*, *Tutsi*, and *Twa* existed in Rwanda and Burundi prior to the establishment of colonial rule, but their exact meaning in precolonial society remains widely contested among students of the region. Some scholars have contended that they referred to occupational categories—the Hutu living primarily as farmers, the Tutsi as herders, and the Twa as hunter-gathers and potters.[15] Others have argued that they referred more to status distinctions, with Tutsi dominating most political positions and serving as overlords in a feudal system based on cattle. According to this view, as the monarchy in Rwanda expanded its control from a small, central domain to other regions, it extended the usage of the terms as a means of tying people to the state. Prior to the extension of central state control, according to this view, other identities such as clan and region were more important.[16] Scholars are almost unanimous, however, in agreeing that these identities were relatively flexible. Intermarriage was common, and identities could change. A family that gained

[14] Cf. Horowitz 1985: 141–228; Vail 1989; Young 1976. The higher levels of ethnic conflict in former Belgian and British colonies as opposed to former French colonies suggests the degree to which colonial practices of ethnic identification have had a lasting impact on group identities.

[15] Cf. Chrétien 1993: 313–41; Chrétien 1997.

[16] For this argument, see Newbury 1988. See also Des Forges 1999: 31–34; Reyntjens 1994; Newbury 1998.

Hutu/Tutsi status could change over a couple generations

wealth or status would come to be viewed as Tutsi within a few generations, while one that lost position would eventually be regarded as Hutu.[17]

When Europeans arrived in Rwanda and Burundi in the last decades of the 1800s, their encounter with the local population was shaped by contemporary ideas about race that assumed that all the people of the world fit into distinct and clearly defined groups, and that these groups could be ranked hierarchically in terms of their capacities. The complex and centralized political structures and highly cultured ruling caste that early colonial administrators and missionaries found in Rwanda and Burundi challenged the accepted idea that Africans could not govern themselves effectively and lacked civilization. Rather than changing their theories, however, the Europeans changed their perceptions of the local residents. The Europeans found in Tutsis' physical appearance—features such as their narrow noses and tall stature—evidence that Tutsi were more closely related to Europeans than other Africans. A theory emerged that Tutsi were in fact neither a Bantu people, like the Hutu, nor a Pygmoid people, like the Twa, but a Hamitic tribe, descendants of Noah's son Ham, who had migrated into Africa from the Middle East. Given their supposed closer evolutionary link to Europeans, the Tutsi were considered naturally superior to the other groups and destined to rule them.[18]

The royal courts of Rwanda and Burundi, which had been seeking to centralize and consolidate their rule even before the arrival of the Europeans, recognized a clear opportunity and sought to reinforce the mistaken European interpretations of Rwandan society. Rwandan intellectuals worked with Catholic missionaries to develop a history that would conform to European racial expectation. According to this history, supposedly based on oral tradition within the royal courts, the Twa, the original inhabitants of Rwanda, were conquered by Bantu people migrating from the west over a millennium ago. Several hundred years later, Tutsi herders from Somalia or Ethiopia migrated into the region and, due to their natural superiority, conquered the Hutu and Twa despite being grossly outnumbered.[19]

Although the myth of Tutsi migration and conquest is contradicted by historical and anthropological evidence, the Europeans embraced it as accurate history and made it a basis for their colonial policies. They assumed that Tutsi, Hutu, and Twa were completely distinct and antagonistic groups, and they developed a physical stereotype for each racial group. According to these ideas, Tutsi were tall, thin, and light-skinned with nar-

[17] Lemarchand 1994; Gravel 1968.
[18] On the Hamitic hypothesis, see Sanders 1969.
[19] On the myths of Rwandan history, see Prunier 1995: 1–40; Des Forges 1995a.

row noses and fingers, Hutu were shorter, heavier, and darker with broader features, while Twa were diminutive, very dark, with very broad features. While the actual complexities of migration into the region, rates of intermarriage, and the flexibility of the categories in precolonial Rwanda and Burundi meant that few Hutu, Tutsi, and Twa fit their racial stereotypes, an assumed physical difference nevertheless became key to group identities in both Rwanda and Burundi. After the Belgians assumed control of the territory of Ruanda-Urundi from Germany in 1916, they implemented a system of indirect rule based on the principles of racial hierarchy. Administrative reforms centralized power in the two kingdoms, eliminating much of the complexity of the precolonial political systems and replacing a number of Hutu chiefs with Tutsi. As a result of these reforms, Hutu found their political power significantly diminished, while the power of the central government was substantially increased.

Because of the significant role identity cards played in singling out Tutsi as targets for the 1994 genocide in Rwanda, many analysts have referred to the origins of identity cards in Rwanda's colonial past, but surprisingly little research has been done on the actual implementation of official identity documentation. According to a widely believed interpretation, the Belgian administration first issued identity cards as part of the effort to implement indirect rule. If they were to regard all Hutu as subjects and all Tutsi as chiefs or potential chiefs, then they needed to know just who was Hutu and who was Tutsi. Hence, the administration went through the country, labeled every family, and issued them identity cards.[20] One oft-repeated myth claims that, because ethnic identities were actually flexible and not all people were sure how to categorize themselves, the administrators counted the number of cattle they owned to determine their category.

In fact, the meager available evidence regarding the origins of the policy of official identity registration suggests that identity cards were issued not with the intention of fixing ethnic membership but for more mundane administrative purposes. As early as 1914, a colonial administrator in Belgian Congo suggested fingerprinting as a means of fixing the identities of subjects, because of the unreliability of names as a means of identifying individuals.[21] The perceived need to fix identities was not, however, unique to the Belgian colonies. The issuance of identity cards in Ruanda-Urundi in the 1930s seems to have been an extension of a policy of issuing identity papers implemented in Belgium during the interwar years. Since ethnic identity was relevant to the administration of Ruanda-Urundi, ethnic membership was included on identity cards there, but it does not ap-

[20] Cf. Uvin 1997; DesForges 1999: 37–38.
[21] Borgerhoff 1914.

pear that the cards were issued for the express purpose of registering ethnic identities. Rather, registering ethnicity was merely one component of
a broader program to increase the regulation of Belgian subjects.[22]

Regardless of their intentions, the impact of identity cards on ethnic
identities in Rwanda was profound. Whereas group membership had previously been flexible, documenting each person's group identity eliminated the possibility of changing identities through traditional means, although in practice people found new ways to circumvent official attempts
at fixing identity. According to regulations adopted by the administration,
supposedly reflecting "traditional" practice, children would automatically and necessarily adopt the ethnic identity of their fathers. At the same
time, discriminatory colonial policies drastically increased the significance
of ethnicity, elevating it over regional, clan, and other identities. To be
Hutu in Belgian Ruanda-Urundi meant to be denied opportunities for
education and employment, to completely lack political power, to pay
heavy taxes, and to be kept in an economically marginalized position. As
Alison Des Forges writes, "These administrative measures made it almost
impossible for Hutu to become Tutsi just at a time when being Tutsi
brought all the advantages."[23]

Colonial policies, therefore, transformed Hutu, Tutsi, and Twa into relatively rigid ethnic categories of great political significance. Regardless of
their historical meanings, the ethnic categories, because of colonial policies, largely determined people's life opportunities. Since schools,
churches, and the government all promoted the idea of ethnic differentiation and since the actual experience of individuals demonstrated the importance of the categories, most Rwandans themselves came to believe
the history of Rwanda as developed by the missionaries and Tutsi elite,
and in the clear division of the population into ethnic groups. The Hutu
ethnonationalist movement that arose in the 1950s did not challenge the
established interpretation of Rwandan society but rather denounced the
injustice of the subordination of the majority population. When a 1959
revolt brought Hutu to power in Rwanda, the new Hutu leaders used the
claim that Tutsi had dominated them for centuries to justify the exclusion
of Tutsi from all governmental positions.

At the same time, official efforts to fix identity were not entirely successful. During the colonial period, Hutu who wanted to gain opportunities
could attempt to have themselves reclassified as Tutsi, generally through
illicit means. Following the Hutu assumption of political power, some
Tutsi who feared suffering discrimination or violence for their identities

[22] This according to conversations with Alison Des Forges and Filip Reyntjens. See also
Des Forges 1999: 37–38.
[23] Des Forges 1995b: 2.

managed to have themselves redefined as Hutu. With their official group label changed, individuals could then assume a new group identity, provided their neighbors were unclear about their original identity. (This was clearly most possible for those relocating in a new area.) Official documentation was, thus, not a perfect means of fixing identity, but the idea that every individual could be clearly categorized and labeled nevertheless shaped the way in which individuals understood the nature of identity.

Identity Cards and the Rwandan Genocide

The first decade of Rwanda's independence was marked by repeated anti-Tutsi violence in Rwanda. Thousands of Tutsi fled the country for exile in Uganda, Burundi, and Congo, and attempts by bands of armed Tutsi refugees to retake power by force elicited massacres of Tutsi remaining in Rwanda. In Burundi, the fear of similar violence and loss of power led the Tutsi government to increase its repression of the Hutu majority, including a massacre of some two hundred thousand Hutu in Burundi in 1972 that inspired a wave of anti-Tutsi attacks in Rwanda. To be Tutsi in Rwanda was transformed from being a member of a naturally superior racial group with privileged access to education and employment to being a member of marginalized minority with limited opportunities and a serious danger of facing violence at the hands of the majority.[24]

In 1973, when the head of the army, Juvénal Habyarimana, took power in a coup, he promised to eliminate ethnic conflict, which he did fairly effectively until his own regime was challenged in the early 1990s. Habyarimana then sought to rebuild his popular support by resurrecting Hutu ethnonationalist arguments. He claimed that he was the defender of Hutu interests, while his opposition wanted to restore the Tutsi dominance that had exploited the Hutu for centuries. With a group of Tutsi refugees, the Rwandan Patriotic Front (RPF), attacking the borders of the country and seeking the right for Tutsi to return to Rwanda, Habyarimana's claims gained credence. Habyarimana's supporters controlled the media and used it to create fear of the RPF and distrust of Tutsi in general. They also organized militia groups that harassed both Hutu and Tutsi opponents of the president and received military training to defend against the "Tutsi menace."

By the time President Habyarimana was killed on April 6, 1994, plans were already in place for a massive slaughter of Tutsi and moderate Hutu, and within hours after Habyarimana's death, probably at the hands of

[24] On the late colonial and early independence period, see Lemarchand 1970.

his own presidential guard, the plans for genocide were put into action. The presidential guards and other elite troops spread out into the capital with lists of moderate Hutu and Tutsi to kill—opposition politicians, human rights activists, progressive priests. In subsequent days, the violence spread into the countryside. While some moderate Hutu continued to be killed, the violence focused increasingly on Tutsi and developed into a pogrom to exterminate all Tutsi from the country. Most Tutsi were killed in mass slaughters carried out in public buildings, but following these massacres, community leaders organized patrols to seek out hiding Tutsi and set up barricades on all roads and paths in order to prevent Tutsi from escaping the country.[25]

Identity cards became an important tool during the genocide, because they were an easy way to identify Tutsi. Since every Rwandan was required to carry an identity card, people who guarded barricades demanded that everyone show their cards before being allowed to pass. Those with "Tutsi" marked on their cards were generally killed on the spot. Those without cards were usually suspected of being Tutsi trying to escape and killed. The cards, however, were not always a reliable indicator of ethnic identity. Because of the discrimination and violence against Tutsi following independence, many Tutsi had sought to become officially Hutu by using official connections, bribes, or other means to receive new identity cards that marked them as Hutu. Such a transformation was difficult for people who lived in a local community where their identity was well-known, but for those who moved to other areas, particularly urban areas, such a transformation was possible, at least up to a point. Because of the possibility that identity cards had been changed, those checking identity cards during the genocide did not necessarily trust the label "Hutu." Instead, they tried to research the past of people they suspected of having Tutsi origins, as in the case of Claudette's family. Two of my close friends who were officially "Hutu" were similarly killed during the genocide because others who knew their past revealed that their parents had been Tutsi. In other cases, death squads at barricades killed people they did not know who *looked* Tutsi, who fit the stereotypical phenotype, even if they carried Hutu identity cards. As one friend told me, "There were many people killed for their *morphology* [physical appearance]."

Implications of the Rwandan Case

Rwanda is certainly not the only African country where the ethnicity of individuals is officially documented. Identity cards are used in most other

[25] For details on the genocide, see Des Forges 1999; Prunier 1995.

African countries, and in some cases they state people's ethnic origins. In other cases, registration for school, census records, tax rolls, or other official documents specify ethnic affiliation. The use of identity cards in Rwanda demonstrates both the potential and the limitations of official documentation in defining individual identity on the continent. There were many people in Rwanda like Claudette whose belief in their ethnic identity was reinforced by the official designation of their ethnicity. But her case also shows how this system could be subverted. Claudette's grandfather, like many Tutsi, sought to change his identity by changing the documentation. Yet in his case, as in the case of many other Rwandans, this effort ultimately failed. Because those participating in the genocide knew that identity cards could be altered, what made someone Tutsi, Hutu, or Twa was ultimately not their official ethnic designation but rather a "Hutuness" or "Tutsiness" revealed by their lineage, physical appearance, and other factors; the official documentation was not enough in and of itself to create a Hutu or Tutsi.

Nevertheless, the official registration of group membership did have a profound impact on how Rwandans viewed ethnic identity. According to Claudette, when she asked her grandfather why he had become Hutu, he told her, "Well, I was not rich, I had no power, so why should I be called Tutsi?" In precolonial Rwanda a Tutsi family without wealth and status would have come to be considered Hutu within a few generations, but with the implementation of identity cards, Hutu, Tutsi, and Twa were transformed into rigid ethnic categories. While Rwandans did not necessarily trust identity cards to accurately reveal individual identities, Rwandans nevertheless came to accept the principle behind the cards: that identities were fixed and unchanging, that everyone in the country could be clearly classified into one of three categories based on their parentage. It is this ethnicization of Rwandan society that ultimately made genocide possible.

In the aftermath of the genocide, the people of Rwanda are reassessing the meaning of identity. Identity cards no longer carry an ethnic label, but after the massacres of 1994, most people have an intense sense of their group membership. Some, however, like Claudette, are struggling to understand who they are and where they fit in. Are they Tutsi because their grandparents were, or are they Hutu because they grew up with that identity? One person I know, "George," had a Hutu father, and so his identity card called him Hutu, but his mother was Tutsi, and he looked stereotypically Tutsi—tall, thin, and light-skinned. As a result of his appearance, he suffered during the war and had to flee for his life. He is now a soldier in the RPF and is reconstructing an identity for himself as a Tutsi, conforming his self-identity to the identity people attribute to him based on his appearance. The stories of Claudette and George are merely two of thousands of such stories that can be heard not only in Rwanda but throughout Africa as individuals attempt to negotiate the difficulties of reconciling the flexible nature of group identities with the rigidity of official documentation in their efforts to construct their personal identities.

Bibliography

Archival Sources

Algemeen Rijksarchief (ARA), Netherlands.

Archiv der Hansestadt Lübeck, Polizeiamt.

Archives nationales (AN), Paris.

Archives Parlamentaires (A.P.), Paris.

Archives de la Préfecture de Police (Paris), BA 960, Dossier Bertillon.

Archivo General de la Nación (Buenos Aires, Argentina), Tribunal Criminal.

Gosudarstvennyi arkhiv Rossiiskoi Federatsii (State Archives of the Russian Federation), R.F.

Kantseliariia Popechitelia Orenburgskogo Uchebnogo Okruga (Chancellery of the Curator of the Orenburg Educational District).

Kantseliariia Ufimskogo Grazhdanskogo Gubernatora (Chancellery of the Ufa Civilian Governor) f. I-109.

National Archives, Washington, D.C., U.S. War Department.

Public Record Office (P.R.O.) London, Cabinet Office (CAB), Home Office (HO) Registrar-General (RG).

Tsentral'nyi Gosudarstvennyi Istoricheskii Arkhiv Respubliki Bashkortostan (Central State Archive of the Republic of Bashkortostan, Ufa), f. I-11 (TsGIA).

Printed and Secondary Sources

Abercrombie, Nicholas, Stephen Hill, and Bryan Turner. 1986. *Sovereign Individuals of Capitalism*. London: Allen and Unwin.

Abrahamian, Levon Hm. 1998. "Mother Tongue: Linguistic Nationalism and the Cult of Translation in Postcommunist Armenia." *Berkeley Program in Soviet and Post-Soviet Studies Working Paper Series*. Berkeley: Berkeley Program in Soviet and Post-Soviet Studies, University of California, Berkeley.

Adler, Emanuel. 1921. *Der Name im deutschen und österreichischen Recht*. Berlin: Franz Vahlen.

Afanas'ev, Mikhail N. 1997. *Klientelism i rossiiskaia gosudarstvennost'*. Moscow: Moskovskii.

Agar, Jon. Forthcoming. *The Government Machine*. Cambridge, Massachusetts: MIT Press.

Alabama Code 1994. Title 36 @ 18–27 Cumulative Supplement ed.

Algemeen Politieblad.

Alt, Jörg. 1999. *Illegal in Deutschland: Forschungsprojekt zur Lebenssituation "illegaler" Migranten in Leipzig*. Edited by Jesuit Refugee Service Europe. Karlsruhe: Loeper.

Aly, Götz, and Karl-Heinz Roth. 2000. *Die restlose Erfassung: Volkszählen, Identifizieren, Aussondern im Nationalsozialismus*. Rev. ed. Frankfurt am Main: Fischer.

Amphlett, John. 1878. "The Law of Surnames." *The Gentleman's Magazine* 243, October, pp. 499–504.

Anchel, R. 1928. *Napoléon et les juifs: Essai sur les rapports de l'État français et du culte israélite de 1806 à 1815*. Paris: PUF.

Andrieu, Louis. 1885. *Souvenirs d'un préfet de police*. Paris: Jules Rouff.

Anon. 1841. "Ueber die Unvollständigkeit der Signalements." *Allgemeiner Polizei-Anzeiger* 12, p. 108.

Anon. 1847. "Ueber Benutzung der electro-magnetischen Telegraphen an den Eisenbahnen zur Verfolgung flüchtiger Verbrecher etc." *Allgemeiner Polizei-Anzeiger* 25, pp. 191–92.

Anon. 1852. "Das Daguerrotypiren der Portraits gefährlicher Gauner als bewährtes Mittel zur Entlarvung des Fortkommens derselben etc." *Allgemeiner Polizei-Anzeiger* 34, pp. 127–28.

Anon. 1862. "Surnames and Arms." *Cornhill Magazine* 6, July, pp. 82–99.

Anon. 1863. "Change of Name Proprio Motu." In *The Herald and Genealogist*, vol. 1, edited by J. Gough Nicholls, pp. 11–35. London: J. B. Nicholls.

Anon. 1863. Review of *Surnames and Sirenames* by J. Finlayson. *The Athenaeum* 1880, November 7, p. 608.

Anson, G. A. 1905. "Finger-Prints as Clues." *The Daily Express*, July 28, p. 4.

Antonielli, Livio. 1983. *I prefetti dell'Italia napoleonica*. Bologna: il Mulino.

Archiv der Grossherzoglich Hessischen Gesetze und Verordnungen. 1834–39. 7 vols. Darmstadt.

Arendt, Hannah. 1958. *The Human Condition*. Chicago: University of Chicago Press.

Arizona Revised Statutes. 1995. Annotated title 13@ 1411.

Ascher, Abraham. 1988. *The Revolution of 1905: Russia in Disarray*. Stanford: Stanford University Press.

Asséo, Henriette. 1994. *Les Tsiganes, une destinée européenne*. Paris: Gallimard, Collection Découverte.

Atkinson, Dorothy. 1983. *The End of the Russian Land Commune 1905–1930*. Stanford: Stanford University Press.

Avé-Lallement, Friedrich Christian Benedict. n.d. [1858–62]. *Das deutsche Gaunertum in seiner sozialpolitischen, literarischen und linguistischen Ausbildung zu seinem heutigen Bestande*. Reprint ed. Wiesbaden: Schier.

Avrich, Paul H. 1963. "The Bolshevik Revolution and Workers' Control in Russian Industry." *Slavic Review* 22, no. 1, pp. 47–63.

Babcock, Charles R. 1998. "The DNA Test." *The Washington Post*, September 22, p. A22.

Badinter, Robert. 1992. *La prison républicaine*. Paris: Fayard.

Barizza, Sergio. 1982. *Il Comune di Venezia 1806–1946: L'istituzione - il territorio. Guida inventario dell'Archivio municipale*. Venezia: Comune di Venezia.

Barnes, Teresa. 1997. " 'Am I a Man?': Gender and the Pass Laws in Urban Colonial Zimbabwe, 1930–80." *African Studies Review* 40, April, pp. 59–81.

Baron, Miron, and John D. Rainer. 1988. "Molecular Genetics and Human Disease: Implications for Modern Psychiatric Research and Practice." *British Journal of Psychiatry* 152, pp. 741–53.

Barthes, Roland. 1967. *Elements of Semiology*. London: Jonathan Cape.

Bataille, Albert. 1897. "Proceso Tremblié." *Revista de Policía* 1, no. 13, pp. 198–204.

Bazille, M. 1909. "Étude sur les registres paroissiaux antérieurs à l'établissement des registres de l'état civil." *Bulletin Historique et Philologique.*

Beck, Friedrich, and Walter Schmidt, eds. 1993. *Die Polizeikonferenzen deutscher Staaten 1851–1866: Präliminardokumente, Protokolle und Anlagen.* Vienna: Böhlau.

Beck, Hermann. 1995. *The Origins of the Authoritarian Welfare State in Prussia: Conservatives, Bureaucrats and the Social Question, 1815–1870.* Ann Arbor: University of Michigan Press.

Beck, Ulrich. 1992. *Risk Society: Towards a New Modernity.* London: Sage.

Becker, Peter. 1992. "Vom 'Haltlosen' zur 'Bestie': Das polizeiliche Bild des 'Verbrechers' im 19. Jahrhundert." In *"Sicherheit" und "Gemeinwohl": Polizei, Gesellschaft und Herrschaft im 19. und 20. Jahrhundert,* edited by Alf Lüdtke, pp. 97–132. Frankfurt am Main: Suhrkamp.

Beidtel, Ignaz. 1968 [1896/98]. *Geschichte der österreichischen Staatsverwaltung 1740–1848.* Frankfurt am Main: Sauer and Auvermann.

Beiser, Vince. 1997. "The Keyless Society." *McLean's.* August 25, p. 34.

Bekers, J. 1975. "Elaboration des lois, 19ᵉ–20ᵉ siècle: la loi du 10 juillet [1883] concernant les livrets d'ouvrier." In *La décision politique et judiciaire dans le passé et dans le présent: Exposition 15 avril–17 mai 1975 à l'occasion du colloque "Sources de l'histoire des Institutions de la Belgique."* Brussels: Archives générales du royaume.

Beketov, A. N. 1897. "Pasport." In *Entsiklopedicheskii slovar',* vol. 44, edited by F. A. Brokgauz and I. A. Efron, pp. 923–25. Leipzig/St. Petersburg: Brokgauz and Efron.

Belper Committee. 1901. *Method of Identification of Criminals by Measurements and Finger Prints.* London: Printed for Her Majesty's Stationary Office by Wyman and Sons, Ltd.

Bély, Lucien, ed. 1997. *L'invention de la diplomatie: Moyen Age - Temps Modernes.* Paris: PUF.

Bennett, C. J. 1997. "Pick a Card: Surveillance, Smart Identification and the Structure of Advanced Industrial States." Paper presented at the 1997 Canadian Political Science Association Annual Meetings, St. John's, Newfoundland.

Bennett, Colin. 1996. "The Public Surveillance of Personal Data: A Cross-National Analysis." In *Computers, Surveillance, and Privacy,* edited by David Lyon and Elia Zureik. Minneapolis: University of Minnesota Press.

Bentham, Jeremy. 1843. "Principles of Penal Law." In *The Works of Jeremy Bentham,* vol. 1, edited by John Bowring. Edinburgh: William Tait.

Berengo, Marino. 1973. *L'agricoltura veneta dalla caduta della Repubblica all'Unità.* Milan: Capriolo and Massimino.

Bering, Dietz. 1992. *The Stigma of Names: Antisemitism in German Daily Life, 1812–1933.* Oxford: Polity.

Berlière, Jean-Marc. 1993. *Le préfet Lépine: Vers la naissance de la police moderne.* Paris: Denoël.

Berlière, Jean-Marc. 1996. *Le monde des polices en France.* Paris: édit. Complexe.

Bernardello, Adolfo. 1996. *La prima ferrovia tra Venezia e Milano: Storia della Imperial-Regia Privilegiata Strada Ferrata Fernandea Lombardo-Veneta 1835–1852*. Venice: Istituto.

Bertelsmann, Werner. 1914. *Das Passwesen: Eine völkerrechtliche Studie*. Strassburg: Heitz.

Bertillon, Alphonse. 1881. "Une application pratique de l'anthropométrie sur un procédé d'identification permettant de retrouver le nom du récidiviste au moyen de son seul signalement." *Annales de Démographie internationale*, vol. 8.

Bertillon, Alphonse. 1883. "L'identité des récidivistes et la loi de relégation." *Annales de Démographie internationale*, vol. 8.

Bertillon, Alphonse. 1887. "Description, forme du nez avec gravures." *Revue d'Anthropologie* (March).

Bertillon, Alphonse. 1890. *La photographie judiciaire: Avec un appendice sur la classification et l'identification anthropométriques*. Paris: Gauthier-Villars.

Bertillon, Alphonse. 1893. *Identification anthropométrique: Instructions signalétiques*. Paris: Impr. Administrative.

Bertillon, Alphonse. 1913. *Photographie métrique: Archéologie. Identification judiciaire. Anthropologie*. Paris: Lacour Betethel.

Bertillon, Suzanne. 1941. *Vie d'Alphonse Bertillon, inventeur de l'anthropométrie*. Paris: NRF/Gallimard.

Bijlagen tot het Staatsblad (BSB).

Blackham, Robert J. 1931. *The Soul of the City: London's Livery Companies: Their Storied Past, Their Living Present*. London: Sampson Low and Co.

Bogard, William. 1996. *The Simulation of Surveillance*. New York: Cambridge University Press.

Bok, Sissela. 1978. *Lying: Moral Choice in Public and Private Life*. New York: Pantheon.

Bonnier, Édouard Louis Joseph. 1888. *Traité théorique et pratique des preuves en droit civil et en droit criminal*. Paris: Plon-Maresq.

Bonzon, Jacques. 1899. *La corporation des maîtres écrivains et l'expertise en écritures sous l'ancien régime*. Paris: V. Giard et E. Brière.

Borgerhoff, L. 1914. "Project d'identification, par la dactyloscopie, des indigènes du Congo Belge." *Revue de Droit Pénal et de Criminologie*, July, pp. 571–84.

Bourdieu, Pierre. 1991. "Politisches Kapital als Differenzierungsprinzip im Staatssozialismus." In *Die Intellektuellen und die Macht*, edited by Irene Dölling. Hamburg: VSA-Verlag.

Bourke, Joanna. 1996. *Dismembering the Male: Men's Bodies, Britain and the Great War*. London: Reaktion.

Bowles, Paul. 1978. *The Sheltering Sky*. New York: Ecco.

Bowman, James E. 1996. "The Road to Eugenics." The University of Chicago Law School Round Table, *Symposium on Genetics and the Law: On the Ethical, Legal, and Social Implications of Genetic Technology and Biomedical Ethics* 3, pp. 491–517.

Boyes-Watson, Carolyn. 1997. "Corporations as Drug Warriors: The Symbolic Significance of Employee Drug Testing." *Studies in Law, Politics, and Society* 17, pp. 185–223.

Braconnier, Karine. 1996. *La législation française concernant les Tsiganes en République: Du rejet à l'intégration: Approche historique de la politique française vis-à-vis des SDF entre 1945 et 1989.* 2 vols. Mémoire DEA-IEP de Grenoble. Grenoble: Mémoire.

Brandt, Rüdiger. 1993. *Enklaven-Exklaven. Zur literarischen Darstellung von Öffentlichkeit und Nichtöffentlichkeit im Mittelalter.* München: Fink.

Brennwald, Heinrich. 1910. *Schweizerchronik.* Edited by Rudolf Luginbühl. 2 vols. Basel: Quellen zur Schweizergeschichte, N.F. Chroniken 1. Vol. 2.

Bridges, Burtis C. 1942. *Practical Fingerprinting.* New York/London: Funk and Wagnalls.

Browne, Douglas C., and Alan Brock. 1953. *Fingerprints: Fifty Years of Scientific Crime Detection.* London: George C. Harrap.

Brubaker, Rogers. 1992. *Citizenship and Nationhood in France and Germany.* Cambridge, Massachusetts: Harvard University Press.

Brubaker, Rogers. 1994. "Nationhood and the National Question in the Soviet Union and Post-Soviet Eurasia: An Institutional Account." *Theory and Society* 23, no. 1, pp. 47–78.

Brusa, Emilio. 1886. "Derecho penal: El tercer congreso internacional penitenciario y El antropológico-criminal." *Revista de Jurídica* 3, pp. 1051–74.

Bruyer, Raymond. 1987. *Les mécanismes de reconnaissance des visages. Un bilan des modèles théoriques.* Grenoble: Presses Universitaires de Grenoble.

Buchanan, A. 1996. "Choosing Who Will Be Disabled: Genetic Intervention and the Morality of Inclusion." *Social Philosophy and Policy* 13, no. 2, pp. 18–46.

Buchler, J., ed. 1955. *Philosophical Writings of Peirce.* New York: Dover.

Bult, Christiane. 1990. *Schattenbilder im Lichte der Polizei: Ueber das "Album der frühern Schweizerischen Heimathlosen und Vaganten, eine jetzt beseitigte Calamität" (um 1856).* MA thesis, Basel.

Bundesministerium des Innern. 1996. *Tätigkeitsbericht des Bundesgrenzschutzes 1995.* Bonn: Referat Presse- und Öffentlichkeitsarbeit.

Bundesministerium für Arbeit und Sozialordnung. 1998. *Illegale Beschäftigung und Schwarzarbeit schaden uns allen.* Bonn: Referat Presse- und Öffentlichkeitsarbeit.

Bundesregierung. 1992. *Siebter Bericht der Bundesregierung über Erfahrungen bei der Anwendung des Arbeitnehmerüberlassungsgesetzes - AÜG - sowie über die Auswirkungen des Gesetzes zur Bekämpfung der illegalen Beschäftigung.* Bundestagsdrucksache, 12/3180, August 21.

Bundesregierung. 1996. *Achter Bericht der Bundesregierung über Erfahrungen bei der Anwendung des Arbeitnehmerüberlassungsgesetzes - AÜG - sowie über die Auswirkungen des Gesetzes zur Bekämpfung der illegalen Beschäftigung.* Bundestagsdrucksache, 13/5498, September 6.

Burds, Jeffrey. 1991. "The Social Control of Peasant Labor in Russia: The Response of Village Communities to Labor Migration in the Central Industrial Region, 1861–1905." In *Peasant Economy, Culture, and Politics of European Russia, 1800–1921,* edited by Esther Kingston-Mann and Timothy Mixter, pp. 52–100. Princeton: Princeton University Press.

Burguière André, and Jacques Revel, eds. 1989. *Histoire de la France: L'Espace français.* Vol. 1. Paris: Editions Seuil.

Bushaway, Bob. 1992. "Name upon Name: The Great War and Remembrance."
In *Myths of the English*, edited by Roy Porter, pp. 136–67. Cambridge: Polity.

Caccialupi, Giovanni. 1863. *Della naturalità lombarda ne' rapporti politici ana-
grafici ed in genere dello Stato e movimento della popolazione*. Milan: Pirola.

Cadden, Joan. 1993. *Meanings of Sex Differences in the Middle Ages: Medicine,
Science and Culture*. Cambridge: Cambridge University Press.

Cairncross, John. 1974. *After Polygamy Was Made a Sin: The Social History of
Christian Polygamy*. London: Routledge and Kegan Paul.

Calavita, Kitty. 1992. *Inside the State: The Bracero Program, Immigration, and
the I.N.S.* New York: Routledge.

Caplan, Jane. 1997. " 'Speaking Scars': The Tattoo in Popular Practice and Med-
ico-Legal Debate in Nineteenth-Century Europe." *History Workshop Journal*
44, pp. 107–42.

Caplan, Jane. 2000. " 'National Tattooing': Traditions of Tattooing in Nine-
teenth-Century Europe." In *Written on the Body: The Tattoo in European and
American History*, edited by Jane Caplan, pp. 156–73. London: Reaktion
Books/Princeton: Princeton University Press.

Caprettini, Gian Paolo. 1983. "Peirce, Holmes, Popper." In *The Sign of Three*,
edited by Umberto Eco and Thomas A. Sebeok, pp. 135–53. Bloomington: Indiana University Press.

Carbonnier, Jean. 1955. *Droit Civil*. Paris: PUF.

Casanova de Seingalt, Jacques. 1993. *Histoire de ma vie suivie des textes inédits*.
3 vols. Paris: Robert Laffont.

Caskey, C. Thomas. 1992. "DNA-Based Medicine: Prevention and Therapy." In
The Code of Codes: Social Issues in the Human Genome Project, edited by
Daniel J. Kevles and Leroy Hood, pp. 191–210. Cambridge, Massachusetts:
Harvard University Press.

Castells, Manuel. 1996. *The Rise of the Network Society*. Oxford/New York:
Blackwell.

Castiglione, Baldassare. 1564. *Il Cortegiano*. Vinegia: Apresso Gabriel Giolito
de'Ferrari.

Catane, M. 1985. "L'élément français dans l'onomastique juive." *Revue d'Études
Juives* 44, no. 4, p. 339.

Cave, Terence. 1988. *Recognitions: A Study in Poetics*. Oxford: Clarendon.

Cavoukian, Ann. 1996. *The Theft of Identity*. Office of Privacy Commissioner,
Ontario, Canada.

Cavoukian, Ann. 1999. "The Promise of Privacy-Enhancing Technologies: Applications in Health Information Networks." In *Visions of Privacy: Policy Choices
for the Digital Age*, edited by Colin Bennett and Rebecca Grant. Toronto: University of Toronto Press.

Cavoukian, Anna. 1997. *Identity Theft: Who's Using Your Name?*. Toronto: IPC.

Certeau, Michel de. 1984. *The Practice of Everyday Life*. Berkeley: University of
California Press.

Chan, Sucheng. 1990. "European and Asian Immigration into the United States
in Comparative Perspective, 1820s to 1920s." In *Immigration Reconsidered:
History, Sociology, Politics*, edited by Virginia Yans-Mclaughlin. New York:
Oxford University Press.

Chapel, Charles Edward. 1941. *Fingerprinting: A Manual of Identification*. New York: Coward McCann, Inc.

Charlemagne, Jacqueline. 1972. *Criminalité et inadaptation chez les Tsiganes*. Paris: Université de Paris-II.

Charlemagne, Jacqueline. 1986. "Tsiganes et législation: minorité spécifique ou catégorie défavorisée?" *Études tsiganes* 1, pp. 7–12.

Charlemagne, Jacqueline, and Gérard Pigault. 1988. *Répertoire des textes législatifs et réglementaires concernant les personnes Sans Domicile Fixe*. Paris: UNISAT.

Chevalier, Louis. 1978. *Classes laborieuses, classes dangereuses*. Paris: Hachette-Pluriel.

Chicago Tribune. 1997. "Study Suggests Why Girls Outdo Boys, are Less Vulnerable to Autism: Some Social Skills are Linked to Gene," June 12, p. 8.

Chirot, Daniel. 1986. *Social Change in the Modern Era*. New York: Harcourt Brace Jovanovich.

Chittolini, Giorgio, Anthony Molho, and Pierangelo Schiera, eds. 1995. *The Origins of the State in Italy 1300–1600. Journal of Modern History* supplement.

Chrétien, Jean-Pierre. 1993. *Burundi, L'histoire retrouvée: 25 ans de métier d'historien en Afrique*. Paris: Karthala.

Chrétien, Jean-Pierre. 1997. *Le défi de l'ethnisme: Rwanda et Burundi 1990–1996*. Paris: Karthala.

Chulkov, Ivan, comp. 1889. *Sistematicheskii sbornik uzakonenii (2500 statei) dlia chinov gorodskoi politsii sostavlennyi iz piatnadtsati tomov sv. zak. po izdaniiu i prodolzheniiam 1857–1887*. Moscow: L. and A. Snegdrevyi.

Clanchy, Michael. 1993. *From Memory to Written Record: England 1066–1307*. Oxford: Blackwell.

Clark, Martin. 1984. *Modern Italy, 1871–1982*. New York: Longman.

Clarke, Roger. 1988. "Information Technology and Dataveillance." *Communications of the ACM* 31, no. 5, pp. 498–512.

Clarke, Roger. 1997. "Five Most Vital Privacy Issues." July 31, <*http://www. anu.edu.au/people/Roger.Clarke/DV/VitalPriv.html*>.

Clement, Karine, Christian Vaise, Brian St. J. Manning, Arnaud Basdevant, Bernard Guy-Grand, Juan Ruiz, Kristi D. Silver, Alan R. Shuldiner, Phillippe Froguel, and A. Donny Strosberg. 1995. "Genetic Variation in the (Beta)(Sub 3)-Adrenergic Receptor and an Increased Capacity to Gain Weight in Patients with Morbid Obesity." *New England Journal of Medicine* 333, pp. 352–54.

Cohen, Stephen F. 1971. *Bukharin and the Bolshevik Revolution: A Political Biography, 1888–1938*. New York: Oxford University Press.

Cole, Simon Ablon. 1998. "Manufacturing Identity: A History of Criminal Identification Techniques from Photography through Fingerprinting." Ph.D. thesis, Cornell University.

Colley, Linda. 1992. *Britons: Forging the Nation, 1707–1837*. London: Yale University Press.

Collezione completa dei moderni codici civili degli Stati d'Italia. 1845. Turin.

Connor, Steve. 1995. "Is Killer Instinct Genetic? Jury Is Still Out." *Toronto Star*, March 4, p. B8.

Cornu, E. 1889. *Guide pratique pour la constitution de l'état civil des indigènes.* Algiers: Librairie Adolphe Jourdan.

Corvino, Nicola. 1993. *La carta d'identità e il passaporto.* Rimini: Maggioli Editore.

Cottaar, Annemarie. 1998. *Ik had een neef in Den Haag: Nieuwkomers in de twintigste eeuw.* Zwolle: Waanders.

Cottrill, Ken. 1997. "Reading Between the Lines," *The Guardian*, November 6.

Courtine, Jean-Jacques, and Claudine Haroche. 1988. *Histoire du visage: exprimer et taire ses émotions.* Paris: Gallimard.

Cowger, James E. 1983. *Friction Ridge Skin: Comparison and Identification of Fingerprints.* New York: Elsevier Science.

Craecker-Dussart, Claude de. 1974. "L'evolution du sauf-conduit dans les principautés de la Basse-Lotharingie du VIIIe au XIVe siècle." *Moyen Age* 80, pp. 185–243.

Crang, M. 1996. "Watching the City: Video, Surveillance, and Resistance." *Environment and Planning A*, vol. 28, pp. 99–104.

Cremer, Hans-Joachim. 1998. "Internal Controls and Actual Removal of Deportable Aliens: The Current Legal Situation in the Federal Republic of Germany." In *Immigration Controls: The Search for Workable Policies in Germany and the United States*, edited by Kay Hailbronner, David Martin, and Hiroshi Motomura, pp. 45–116. Providence/Oxford: Berghahn.

Crosby, Alfred. 1997. *The Measure of Reality: Quantification and Western Society 1250–1600.* Cambridge: Cambridge University Press.

Cullen, Michael. 1975. *The Statistical Movement in Early Victorian Britain. The Foundations of Empirical Research.* New York: Barnes and Noble.

Curry, Michael. 1998. *Digital Places: Living with Geographic Information Technologies.* London: Routledge.

Cyrus, Norbert. 1995. *Polnische Pendler/innen in Berlin: Bestandsaufnahme der rechtlichen und sozialen Lagen polnischer Staatsangehöriger mit unsicherem, befristetem oder ohne Aufenthaltsstatus.* Berlin: Bericht für die Ausländerbeauftragte des Senats von Berlin.

Cyrus, Norbert. 1998. "Grenzkultur und Stigmamanagement: Nachfolgende Ethnographie und Situationsanalyse eines irregulär beschäftigten polnischen Wanderarbeiters." *Kea* 10, pp. 83–104.

Dael. 1852. "Ueber Grössen-Angaben in den Signalements." *Allgemeiner Polizei-Anzeiger* 35, pp. 7–8.

The Daily Express. 1905. "£100 Prize for Readers," July 20, p. 7.

The Daily Express. 1945. "Identity," March 12.

Dagron, Gilbert. 1991. "Holy Images and Likeness." *Dumbarton Oaks Papers* 45, pp. 23–33.

Daly, Jonathan W. 1995. "On the Significance of Emergency Legislation in Late Imperial Russia." *Slavic Review* 54, no. 3, Fall, pp. 602–29.

Dardy, Claudine. 1998. *Identités de papiers.* Paris: L'Harmattan.

Darmon, Pierre. 1987. "Bertillon: Le Fondateur de la Police Scientifique." *L'Histoire* 105, pp. 42–48.

Daston, Lorraine. 2001. "Scientific Objectivity With and Without Words." In *Little Tools of Knowledge*, edited by Peter Becker and William Clark. Ann Arbor: University of Michigan Press.

Daston, Lorraine. 1988. *Classical Probability in the Enlightenment*. Princeton: Princeton University Press.

Daston, Lorraine, and Peter Galison. 1992. "The Image of Objectivity." *Representations* 40, pp. 81–128.

Davies, S. 1995. *A Case of Mistaken Identity: An International Study of Identity Cards*. Toronto: Information and Privacy Commissioner of Ontario.

Davis, Ann. 1997. "The Body as Password." *Wired*, 5, no. 7, July, pp. 132–40.

Davis, Mike. 1990. *City of Quartz*. London: Verso.

Davis, Natalie Zemon. 1983. *The Return of Martin Guerre*. Cambridge, Massachusetts: Harvard University Press.

Davis, Natalie Zemon. 1997. "From Prodigious to Heinous: Simon Goulart and the Reframing of Imposture." In *L'Histoire Grande Ouverte: Hommages à Emmanuel Le Roy-Ladurie*, edited by André Burguière, Joseph Goy, and Marie-Jeanne Tits-Dieuaide, pp. 274–83. Paris: Gallimard.

Degwitz, Andreas. 1988. *Die pseudo-aristotelischen Physiognomica*. Phil.Diss., Freiburg.

Dehmal, Heinrich. 1933. "Die Hilfsmittel der modernen Kriminalpolizei." In *Der österreichische Bundes-Kriminalbeamte: Gedenkwerk anlässlich des 80-jährigen Bestehens des Kriminalbeamtenkorps Österreichs*, edited by Oskar Daranyi, pp. 253–354. Vienna: Verlag für polizeiliche Fachliteratur.

Del Fabbro, Rene. 1996. *Transalpini: Italienische Arbeitswanderung nach Süddeutschland im Kaiserreich 1870–1918*. Osnabrück: Rasch.

Delarue, Jacques. 1978. "Les origines de la carte d'identité." *Histoire*, September, pp. 95–9.

Delclitte, Christophe. 1995. "La catégorie 'normale' dans la loi de 1912." *Hommes et migration* 1188/1189, pp. 23–30.

Dennis, Nigel. 1955. *Cards of Identity*. London: Weidenfeld and Nicolson.

Dennstedt, Hermann, and Willibald von Wolffsburg. 1855–56. *Preussisches Polizei-Lexikon: Eine alphabetisch geordnete Zusammenstellung aller in das Gebiet der polizeilichen Thätigkeit einschlagenden Gesetze, Verordnungen, Instruktionen u.s.w. Ein praktisches Hülfsbuch für Polizeibeamte und zur allgemeinen Belehrung für Jedermann*. 6 vols. Berlin: Moeser.

Des Forges, Alison. 1995a. "The Ideology of Genocide." *Issue: A Journal of Opinion* 23, no. 2, pp. 44–47.

Des Forges, Alison. 1995b. "Rwanda." In *Playing the Communal Card: Communal Violence and Human Rights*, pp. 1–17. New York: Human Rights Watch.

Des Forges, Alison. 1999. *Leave None to Tell the Story: Genocide in Rwanda*. New York: Human Rights Watch.

Dion, Kenneth L. 1983. "Names, Identity, and Self." *Names* 31, no. 4, December, pp. 245–57.

Dohse, Knuth. 1981. *Ausländische Arbeiter und bürgerlicher Staat: Genese und Funktion von staatlicher Ausländerpolitik und Ausländerrecht. Vom Kaiserreich bis zum Bundesrepublik Deutschland*. Koenigstein (Taunus): Hain.

Dorward, D. C. 1986. "British West Africa and Liberia." In *The Cambridge History of Africa*, vol. 7, "From 1905 to 1940," edited by A. D. Roberts, pp. 399–459. Cambridge: Cambridge University Press.

Dowty, Alan. 1987. *Closed Borders: The Contemporary Assault on Freedom of Movement.* New Haven: Yale University Press.

Doyle, Sir Arthur Conan. 1993 [1903]. "The Adventure of the Norwood Builder." In *The Return of Sherlock Holmes.* Ware: Wordsworth Editions Ltd.

Draper, Elaine Alma. 1997. "Social Issues of Genome Innovation and Intellectual Property." *Risk* 7, Summer.

Dudley, Leonard M. 1991.*The Word and the Sword: How Techniques of Information and Violence Have Shaped Our World.* Cambridge, Massachusetts: Basil Blackwell.

Dummett, Ann, and Andrew Nicol. 1990. *Subjects, Citizens, Aliens and Others: Nationality and Immigration Law.* London: Weidenfeld and Nicolson.

Dupâquier, Jacques, and Michel Dupâquier. 1985. *Histoire de la démographie.* Paris: Librairie Académique Perrin.

Eamon, William. 1994. *Science and the Secrets of Nature: Books of Secrets in Medieval and Early Modern Culture.* Princeton: Princeton University Press.

Eberhardt, Friedrich. 1837. "Das Silhouettiren als Mittel zur Erleichterung der Sicherheitspflege." *Allgemeiner Polizei-Anzeiger* 4, p. 228.

Ehmer, Joseph. 1997. "Worlds of Mobility: Migration Patterns of Viennese Artisans in the Eighteenth Century." In *The Artisan and the European Town, 1500–1900*, edited by Geoffrey Crossick. Aldershot: Scolar.

Eisenstein, Elizabeth. 1993. *The Printing Revolution in Modern Europe.* Cambridge: Cambridge University Press.

Elias, Norbert. 1982 [1939]. *The Civilizing Process*, vol. 2: *Power and Civility.* New York: Pantheon.

Encyclopedia of the Social Sciences. 1932. Edited by E. R. A. Seligman and A. Johnson. New York: Macmillan.

Enste, Franz Rainer. 1983. "Die Namensänderung nach §3 Abs. 1 NÄG unter besonderer Berücksichtigung der sogennanter Stiefkinderfälle." Diss. Rechtswissenschaft, Münster.

Ericson, Richard V., and Kevin Haggerty. 1997. *Policing the Risk Society.* Toronto: University of Toronto Press.

Erler, Adalbert. 1984. "Pass." In *Handwörterbuch zur deutschen Rechtsgeschichte.* Vol. 3, edited by Adalbert Erler et al., pp. 1527–29. Berlin: E. Schmidt.

Esch, Arnold. 1988. "Alltag der Entscheidung: Berns Weg in den Burgunderkrieg." *Berner Zeitschrift für Geschichte und Heimatkunde* 50, pp. 3–64.

Estrella, Kylza, Bill Jordan, and Dita Vogel. 1997. "Leben und Arbeiten ohne regulären Aufenthaltsstatus—ein Vergleich von London und Berlin am Beispiel brasilianischer Migranten und Migrantinnen." In *Zuwanderung und Stadtentwicklung*, edited by Hartmut Häussermann and Ingrid Oswald, pp. 215–31. Leviathan-Sonderband. Opladen: Westdeutscher Verlag.

Evans, Martin, and Ken Lunn, eds. 1997. *War and Memory in the Twentieth Century.* Oxford: Berg.

Evans, Richard J. 1998. *Tales from the German Underworld: Crime and Punishment in the Nineteenth Century.* New Haven: Yale University Press.

Ewald, François, ed. 1989. *Naissance du Code Civil. An VIII–An XII, 1800–1804.* Paris: Flammarion.

Fahnestock, Jeanne. 1981. "Bigamy: The Rise and Fall of a Convention." *Nineteenth-Century Fiction* 36, pp. 47–71.

Fahrmeir, Andreas. 2000. *Citizens and Aliens: Foreigners and the Law in Britain and the German States, 1789–1870.* New York: Berghahn.

Falconer, Thomas. 1862. *On Surnames and the Rules of Law Affecting Their Change.* London: Charles W. Reynell.

Falkenberg, Carl. 1818. *Versuch einer Darstellung der verschiedenen Classen von Räubern, Dieben und Diebeshehlern, mit besonderer Hinsicht auf die vorzüglichsten Mittel sich ihrer zu bemächtigen, ihre Verbrechen zu entdecken und zu verhüten. Ein Handbuch für Polizeibeamte, Criminalisten und Gensd'armen.* Vol. 2. Berlin: Duncker und Humblot.

Faron, Olivier. 1997. *La ville des destins croisés. Recherches sur la société milanaise du XIXe siècle (1811–1860).* Rome: École française de Rome.

Faulds, Henry. 1912. *Dactylography or the Study of Finger-Prints.* Halifax: Milner and Co.

Favreau-Lilie, Marie Luise. 1994. "Civis peregrinus." *Archiv für Kulturgeschichte* 76, pp. 321–50.

Fehér, Ferenc, et al. 1983. *Dictatorship over Needs.* Oxford: Basil Blackwell.

Ferrell, J. 1996. *Crimes of Style: Urban Graffiti and the Politics of Criminality.* Boston: Northeastern University Press.

Fichte, Johann Gottlieb. 1796. *Grundlage des Naturrechts nach Prinzipien der Wissenschaftslehre.* Jena/Leipzig: Ernst Gabler. (*The Science of Rights.* Translated by A. E. Kroeger. 1889. London: Trubner and Co.)

Fink, August. 1963. *Die Schwarzschen Trachtenbücher.* Berlin: Verlag für Kunstwissenschaft.

Fischer, Thomas. 1980. *Städtische Armut und Armenfürsorge im 15. und 16. Jahrhundert.* Göttingen: Vandenhoek und Ruprecht.

Fitzgerald, Keith. 1996. *The Face of the Nation: Immigration, The State, and the National Identity.* Stanford: Stanford University Press.

Fitzpatrick, Sheila. 1995. *Stalin's Peasants: Resistance and Survival in the Russian Village after Collectivization.* New York: Oxford University Press.

Flaherty, David H. 1979. *Privacy and Government Data Banks: An International Perspective.* London: Mansell.

Flores, Andrés I. c. 1975. *Casos famosos de la crónica policial argentina.* Buenos Aires: Orión.

Fontana, Leone. 1846. *Regolatore amministrativo teorico pratico ad uso degli impiegati.* Vol. 2. Milan: Civelli.

Forbes, Thomas Rogers. 1985. *Surgeons at the Bailey.* New Haven/London: Yale University Press.

Förster, Ernst. 1887. *Aus der Jugendzeit.* Berlin/Stuttgart.

Foucault, Michel. 1977. *Discipline and Punish: The Birth of the Prison.* New York: Vintage. (1979. *Discipline and Punish: The Birth of the Prison.* London: Peregrine Books.)

Foucault, Michel. 1982. "Afterword." In *Michel Foucault: Beyond Structuralism and Hermeneutics*, edited by Hubert L. Dreyfus and Paul Rabinow, pp. 208–26. Chicago: University of Chicago Press.

Foucault, Michel. 1991. "Governmentality." In *The Foucault Effect: Studies in Governmentality*, edited by Graham Burchell, et al., pp. 87–104. Chicago: University of Chicago Press.

Fox-Davies, Arthur Charles, and Phillip William Poole Carlyon-Britten. 1906. *A Treatise on the Law Concerning Names and Changes of Name*. London: Elliott Stock.

Fraenkel, Beatrice. 1992. *La signature: Génèse d'un signe*. Paris: Gallimard.

Frängsmyr, Tore, J. L. Heilbron, and Robin E. Rider, eds. 1990. *The Quantifying Spirit in the Eighteenth Century*. Berkeley: University of California Press.

Franzoni, Carlo. "Rimembranze d'infinite cose e la collezione rinascimentale di antichità." *Memorie dell'antico nell'arte italiana* 1, pp. 321–22.

Frede, Carlo di. 1982. " 'Più simile a mostro che a uomo': La brutezza e l'incultura di Carlo VIII nella rappresentazione degli italiani del Rinascimento." *Bibliothèque d'Humanisme et Renaissance* 44, pp. 545–85.

Freedman, Paul, and Gabrielle Spiegel. 1998. "Medievalisms Old and New: The Rediscovery of Alterity in North American Studies." *American Historical Review* 103, pp. 667–704.

Freeman, Gary. 1994. "Can Liberal States Control Unwanted Migration?" *Annals of the American Academy of Political and Social Sciences* 534, pp. 17–30.

Freeze, Gregory. 1986. "The *Soslovie* (Estate) Paradigm and Russian Social History." *American Historical Review* 91, no. 1, February, pp. 11–36.

Funk, Albrecht. 1986. *Polizei und Rechtsstaat: Die Entwicklung des staatlichen Gewaltmonopols in Preussen, 1848–1914*. Frankfurt am Main: Campus.

Fussell, Paul. 1975. *The Great War and Modern Memory*. New York: Oxford University Press.

Gache, Samuel. 1886. "Congreso penitenciario: Antropología criminal." *Revista de Jurídica* 3, pp. 1028–36.

Gadebusch Bondio, Mariacarla. 1995. *Die Rezeption der kriminalanthropologischen Theorien von Cesare Lombroso in Deutschland von 1880–1914*. Husum: Matthiesen.

Gage, Deanne N. 1997. "Body Language." *Computerworld Canada* 13, p. 25.

Gagliardi, Ernst. 1919. *Der Anteil der Schweizer an den italienischen Kriegen 1494–1515*. Vol. 1, pp. 409–59. Zürich: Schulthess.

Galton, Francis. 1888. "Personal Identification and Description." *Nature*, June 21, pp. 173–77, 201–2.

Galton, Francis. 1890. "Criminal Anthropology." *Nature*, May 22, pp. 75–76.

Galton, Francis. 1908. *Memories of My Life*. London: Methuen.

Gandy, Oscar H. 1993. *The Panoptic Sort: A Political Economy of Personal Information*. Boulder, Colorado: Westview.

Garcelon, Marc. 1997a. "The Estate of Change: The Specialist Rebellion and the Democratic Movement in Moscow, 1989–1991." *Theory and Society* 26, no. 1, pp. 39–85.

Garcelon, Marc. 1997b. "The Shadow of the Leviathan: Public and Private in Communist and Post-Communist Society." In *Public and Private in Thought and Practice: Reflections on a Grand Dichotomy*, edited by Jeff Weintraub and Krishan Kumar, pp. 303–32. Chicago: University of Chicago Press.

Garson, J. G. 1905. "How to Read Finger Prints." *The Daily Express*, July 20, p. 7.

Gebhardt, Helmut. 1992. *Die Grazer Polizei 1786–1850: Ein Beitrag zur Geschichte des österreichischen Sicherheitswesens im aufgeklärten Absolutismus und im Vormärz*. Graz: Leykam.

George, W. L. 1919. "National Registration: Why It Should Be Maintained." *Sunday Times*, April 6.

Geremek, Bronislaw. 1980. *Truands et misérables dans l'Europe moderne*. Paris: Gallimard.

Gerth, Hans H., and C. Wright Mills, eds. 1946. *From Max Weber: Essays in Sociology*. New York: Oxford University Press.

Geselle, Andrea. 2000. "Bewegung und ihre Kontrolle in Lombardo-Venetien." In *Grenze und Staat: Passwesen, Staatsbürgerschaft, Heimatrecht und Fremdengesetzgebung in der österreichischen Monarchie, 1750–1867*, edited by Waltraud Heindl and Edith Saurer, pp. 347–515. Vienna: Böhlau Verlag.

Getrevi, Paolo. 1991. *Le scritture del volto: Fisiognomica e modelli culturali dal medioevo ad oggi*. Milan: Electa.

Giddens, Anthony. 1987. *A Contemporary Critique of Historical Materialism*, vol. 2: *The Nation-State and Violence*. Berkeley/Los Angeles: University of California Press.

Giddens, Anthony. 1990. *The Consequences of Modernity*. Cambridge: Polity.

Giddens, Anthony. 1991. *Modernity and Self-Identity: Self and Society in the Late Modern Age*. Stanford: Stanford University Press.

Gierke, Otto. 1895. *Deutsches Privatrecht*, vol. 1: *Allgemeiner Teil und Personenrecht*. Leipzig: Duncker and Humblot.

Gill, Peter, Alec Jeffreys, and David Werrett. 1985. "Forensic Application of DNA 'Fingerprints'." *Nature*, December, pp. 577–79.

Gillis, John. 1985. *For Better, For Worse: British Marriages, 1600 to the Present*. Oxford: Oxford University Press.

Ginzburg, Carlo. 1980a. "Signes, traces, pistes: racines d'un paradigme de l'indice." *Le débat* 6, pp. 3–44.

Ginzburg, Carlo. 1980b. "Morelli, Freud and Sherlock Holmes: Clues and Scientific Method." *History Workshop Journal* 9, Spring, pp. 5–36.

Ginzburg, Carlo. 1988. "Spurensicherung. Der Jäger entziffert die Fährte, Sherlock Holmes nimmt die Lupe, Freud liest Morelli - die Wissenschaft auf der Suche nach sich selbst." In *Spurensicherungen: Über verborgene Geschichte, Kunst und soziales Gedächtnis*, edited by Carlo Ginzburg, pp. 78–125. München: DTV.

Ginzburg, Carlo. 1990. "Clues: Roots of an Evidential Paradigm." In *Myths, Emblems, Clues*, translated by John and Anne Tedeschi, pp. 96–105. London: Hutchinson.

Glass, David Victor. 1973. *Numbering the People: The Eighteenth-Century Population Controversy and the Development of Census and Vital Statistics in Britain*. Farnborough, Hants.: Saxon House.

Godefroy, Denys, and Lenglet de Fresnoy, M., eds. 1747. *Memoires de Messire Philippe de Commines*, 4 vols., annexe documentaire. London/Paris: Reinet.

Goffman, Erving. 1961. *Asylums: Essays on the Social Situation of the Mental Patient*. New York: Anchor.

Goffman, Erving. 1963. *Stigma: Notes on the Management of Spoiled Identity*. Englewood Cliffs, New Jersey: Prentice-Hall.

Goffman, Erving. 1956. *The Presentation of Self in Everyday Life*. Garden City, New York: Doubleday.

Goldemund, Ingobert, Kurt Ringhofer, and Karl Theuer, eds. 1969. *Das österreichische Staatsbürgerschaftsrecht*. Vienna: Manzsche Verlags- und Universitätsbuchhandlung.

Goody, Jack. 1986. *The Logic of Writing and the Organization of Society*. Cambridge: Cambridge University Press.

Gouldner, Alvin. 1977. "Stalinism: A Study of Internal Colonialism." *Telos* 34, pp. 5–48.

Gow v. Bingham (107 NY Supp 1011).

Grandjonc, Jacques. 1975. "Die deutsche Binnenwanderung in Europa 1830 bis 1848." In *Die frühsozialistischen Bünde in der Geschichte der deutschen Arbeiterbewegung: Vom "Bund der Gerechten" zum "Bund der Kommunisten," 1836–1847. Ein Tagungsbericht*, edited by Otto Büsch and Hans Herzfeld. Berlin: Colloquium.

Gravel, Pierre Bettez. 1968. *Remera: A Community in Eastern Ruanda*. The Hague/Paris: Mouton.

Griesbeck, Michael. 1997. "Asyl für politisch Verfolgte und die Eindämmung des Asylrechtsmissbrauchs." *Aus Politik und Zeitgeschichte* B46/97, November 7.

Groebner, Valentin. 1999. "Inside Out: Dissimulation, Clothes, and the Arts of Accounting in Renaissance Augsburg." *Representations* 66, pp. 52–72.

Groebner, Valentin. 2000. "Accountancies and Arcana: Registering the Gift in Late Medieval Cities." In *Medieval Transformations*, edited by Esther Cohen and Mayke de Jong. Leiden/New York: Brill.

Groebner, Valentin. Forthcoming. *Gefährliche Geschenke: Politische Sprache und das Reden über Korruption am Beginn der Neuzeit*.

Groenendijk, C. A. 1986. "Een nieuwe paspoortwet: tussen bewegingsvrijhied, fraudebestrijding en regelzucht." *Burgerzaken* 527, pp. 294–307.

Gronemeyer, Reimer. 1987. *Zigeuner im Spiegel früher Chroniken und Abhandlungen: Quellen vom 15. bis zum 18. Jahrhundert*. Giessen: Focus.

Grossman, Gregory. 1970. "The Solidary Society: A Philosophical Issue in Communist Economic Reforms." In *Essays in Socialism and Planning in Honor of Carl Landauer*, edited by G. Grossman, pp. 184–211. Englewood Cliffs, New Jersey: Prentice-Hall.

Guazzo, Valentino. 1853. *Enciclopedia degli affari ossia guida universale per la cognizione di qualunque atto, e per lo sviluppo di qualsiasi affare tanto tra privati come avanti qualunque autorità od ufficio*. Vol. 3. Padua.

Guigue, Marie-Claude. 1863. *De l'origine de la signature et de son emploi au moyen age*. Paris: Dumoulin.

Guly, Christopher. 1997. "Digital Security." *Financial Post*, September 6.

Habitual Criminals' Registry, New Scotland Yard. 1909. *Instructions in the Method of Taking Finger Prints, With a Memorandum on the Working of the Finger Print System of Identification.* London: HMSO.

Hacking, Ian. 1990. *The Taming of Chance.* Cambridge: Cambridge University Press.

Hagerman, Randi J., Philip Wilson, Louise W. Staley, Kristen A. Lang, Tammi Fan, Cynthia Uhlhorn, Sabrina Jewell-Smart, Claire Hull, Jodi Drisko, Kerry Flom, and Annette K. Taylor. 1994. "Evaluation of School Children at High Risk for Fragile X Syndrome Utilizing Buccal Cell FMR-1 Testing." *American Journal of Medical Genetics* 51, pp. 474–81.

Hahn, Barbara. 1991. *Unter falschem Namen.* Frankfurt: Suhrkamp.

Hailbronner, Kay, David Martin and Hiroshi Motomura. 1998. "Conclusion: Immigration Admissions and Immigration Controls." In *Immigration Controls: The Search for Workable Policies in Germany and the United States,* edited by Kay Hailbronner, David Martin, and Hiroshi Motomura, pp. 203–24. Providence/Oxford: Berghahn.

Haller, Berchthold, ed. 1902. *Bern in seinen Ratsmanualen 1465–1565.* Bern: Historischer Verein des Kantons Bern.

Halm, Christoph. 1994. *Europäische Reiseberichte des späten Mittelalters: Eine analytische Bibliographie.* Vol. 1. Frankfurt am Main: Peter Lang.

Halsbury, Hardinge Stanley Giffard. 1994. *Halsbury's Laws of England.* 4th ed. London: Butterworths.

Hanania, Elie G., et al. 1995. "Recent Advances in the Application of Gene Therapy to Human Disease." *American Journal of Medicine* 99, pp. 537–52.

Handwörterbuch der Preussischen Verwaltung. 1906. ed. Rudolf von Bitter vol. I. Leipzig: Rossberg.

Haney-Lopez, Ian. 1996. *White by Law: The Legal Construction of Race.* New York: New York University Press.

Hannoversches Polizeiblatt. 1855. Vol. 9.

Hansard. 1852. *Hansard's Parliamentary Debates* (Commons), 3rd ser., vol. 120.

Hansard. 1863. *Hansard's Parliamentary Debates.* (Commons), 3rd ser., vol. 169. Cols. 1573–84.

Haraway, Donna. 1997. *Modest_Witness@Second_Millennium: FemaleMan_Meets_Oncomouse: Feminism and Technoscience.* London/New York: Routledge.

Harris, Roy. 1995. *Signs of Writing.* London: Routledge.

Harst, Gerard van der, and Leo Lucassen. 1998. *Nieuw in Leiden: Plaats en betekenis van vreemdelingen in een Hollandse stad.* Leiden: Primavera Pers.

Härter, Karl. 1993. "Entwicklung und Funktion der Policeygesetzgebung des Heiligen Römischen Reiches Deutscher Nation im 16. Jahrhundert." *Ius Commune* 20, pp. 61–141.

Hartoy, Maurice d'. 1937. *Histoire du passeport français. Depuis l'antiquité jusqu'à nos jours.* Paris: Payot.

Hartwell, Tyler D., Paul D. Steele, Michael T. French, and Nathaniel F. Rodman. 1996. "Prevalence of Drug-testing in the Workplace." *Monthly Labour Review* November, pp. 35–42.

Haste, Cate. 1992. *Rules of Desire: Sex in Britain: World War I to the Present.* London: Pimlico.

Hechter, Michael. 1975. *Internal Colonialism: The Celtic Fringe in British National Development, 1536–1966.* Berkeley/Los Angeles: University of California Press.

Heers, Jacques, ed. 1978. *Itinéraire d'Anselme Adorno en Terre Sainte (1470–71).* Paris: Gallimard.

Heilmann, Eric. 1994. "Die Bertillonage und die 'Stigmata der Entartung.' " *Kriminologisches Journal* 26, pp. 36–46.

Heimann, Heinz-Dieter. 1992. "Brievedregher. Kommunikations- und alltagsgeschichtliche Zugänge zur modernen Postgeschichte und Dienstleistungskultur." In *Kommunikation und Alltag in Spätmittelalter und Früher Neuzeit,* pp. 241–92. Vienna: Österreichische Akademie der Wissenschaften, phil.-hist. Klasse, Sitzungsberichte 569.

Heimann, Heinz-Dieter. 1993. "Zur Visualisierung städtischer Dienstleistungskultur: Das Beispiel der kommunalen Briefboten." In *Visualisierung städtischer Ordnung,* edited by Hermann Maué, pp. 22–36. Nuremberg: Germanisches Nationalmuseum.

Heindl, Robert. 1927. *System und Praxis der Daktyloskopie und der sonstigen technischen Methoden der Kriminalpolizei.* 3rd ed. Berlin: de Gruyter.

Heindl, Waltraud, and Edith Saurer, eds. 2000. *Grenze und Staat: Passwesen, Staatsbürgerschaft, Heimatrecht und Fremdengesetzgebung in der österreichischen Monarchie, 1750–1867.* Vienna: Böhlau Verlag.

Heinroth, Johann Christian August. 1825. *System der psychisch-gerichtlichen Medizin, oder theoretisch-praktische Anweisung zur wissenschaftlichen Erkenntnis und gutachtlichen Darstellung der krankhaften persönlichen Zustände welche vor Gericht in Betracht kommen.* Leipzig: Hartmann.

Heldermann van den Enden, H. T., et al. "Monozygotic Twin Brothers with the Fragile X Syndrome: Different CGG Repeats and Different Mental Capacities." *Journal of Medical Genetics* 36, no. 3, March, pp. 253–57.

Helf, Gavin. 1994. *All the Russias: Center, Core and Periphery in Soviet and Post-Soviet Russia.* Ph.D. diss. University of California, Berkeley.

Hellenthal, Markus. 1995. "Grenzkontrollen als Teil eines nationalen und europäischen Systems zur Kriminalitäts- und Wanderungskontrolle." *Die Polizei* 86, no. 1, pp. 1–24.

Heller, Thomas, Morton Sosna, and David E. Wellbery, eds. 1986. *Reconstructing Individualism: Autonomy, Individuality, and the Self in Western Thought.* Stanford: Stanford University Press.

Hellmich, Nanci. 1995. "Gene Flaw Linked to Obesity." *USA Today,* August 10, p. A1.

Helsinki Watch. 1991. *"Punished Peoples" of the Soviet Union: The Continuing Legacy of Stalin's Deportations.* New York: Human Rights Watch.

Henry, Edward Richard. 1900. "Finger Prints and the Detection of Crime in India." In *Report of the British Association for the Advancement of Science 1899.* Meeting at Dover, September 1899, pp. 869–70. London: John Murray.

Henry, Edward Richard. 1913. *Classification and Uses of Finger Prints.* London: Darling and Son.

Henry, Louis. 1972. "Variations de noms de famille et changements de prénom: Problèmes qui en découlent pour la couplage automatique des données." *Annales de Démographie Historique*, pp. 245–50.

Herbert, Ulrich. 1990. *A History of Foreign Labor in Germany, 1880–1980.* Ann Arbor: University of Michigan Press.

Hermann, Robert. 1862. "Ueber das Recht der Namenführung und der Namensänderung." *Archiv für civilistischen Praxis* 45, pp. 153–69, 314–41.

Hicks, John W. 1998. "The Use and Development of DNA Data Banks in Law Enforcement." In *Stored Tissue Samples: Ethical, Legal and Public Policy Implications*, edited by Robert F. Weir, pp. 305–10. Iowa City: University of Iowa Press.

Higham, John. 1988. *Strangers in the Land: Patterns of American Nativism, 1860–1925.* 2nd ed. New Brunswick, New Jersey: Rutgers University Press.

Hoare, Philip. 1997. *Wilde's Last Stand: Decadence, Conspiracy and the First World War.* London: Duckworth.

Hobsbawm, Eric. 1994. *Age of Extremes: The Short Twentieth Century, 1914–1991.* London: Michael Joseph.

Hochstadt, Steve. 1999. *Mobility and Modernity: Migration in Germany 1820–1989.* Ann Arbor: University of Michigan Press.

Hofmann-Rendtel, Constanze. 1993. "Pilgerzeichen und Sozialprestige." In *Visualisierung städtischer Ordnung*, edited by Hermann Maué, pp. 214–24. Nuremberg: Germanisches Nationalmuseum.

Holzhauer, Heinz. 1973. *Die eigenhändige Unterschrift: Geschichte und Dogmatik des Schriftformerfordernisses im deutschen Recht.* Frankfurt am Main: Athenäum.

Horgan, John. 1993. "Eugenics Revisited." *Scientific American*, June, pp. 122–31.

Horowitz, Donald L. 1985. *Ethnic Groups in Conflict.* Berkeley: University of California Press.

Hubert, Marie-Christine. 1995. "1940–1946, l'internement des Tsiganes en France." *Hommes et Migrations.* 1188–89, pp. 31–38.

Hughes, Steven C. 1994. *Crime, Disorder and the Risorgimento: The Politics of Policing in Bologna.* Cambridge: Cambridge University Press.

Ianovskii, Abel' Efimovich. 1896. "Metricheskie knigi." In *Entsiklopedicheskii slovar*, vol. 37, edited by F. A. Brokgauz and I. A. Efron, pp. 201–4. Leipzig/St. Petersburg: Brokgauz and Efron.

Illgen, Heinrich. 1921. "Die abendländischen Rhazes-Kommentatoren des 14. bis 17. Jahrhunderts." Phil.Diss., Leipzig.

International Association of Chiefs of Police. 1911. *Proceedings*, pp. 158–59.

International Labour Office. 1928. *Migration Laws and Treaties*, vol. 1: *Emigration Laws and Regulations.* Geneva: International Labour Office.

Jackson [Harry]. 1902. *Central Criminal Court Sessions Paper.* 136, 976. London.

Jackson, James H. 1997. *Migration and Urbanization in the Ruhr Valley, 1821–1914.* Atlantic Highlands, New Jersey: Humanities Press.

Jacquart, Danielle. 1994. "La physiognomie à l'époque de Frédéric II: Le traité de Michel Scot." *Micrologus* 2, pp. 19–38.

Jagemann, Ludwig Hugo Franz von. 1838. *Handbuch der gerichtlichen Untersuchungskunde*. Vol. 1. Frankfurt am Main: Kettembeil.

James, Paul. 1996. *Nation Formation: Towards a Theory of Abstract Community*. London/Thousand Oaks/New Delhi: Sage.

Job, F. 1974. "Les Juifs de Lunéville d'après l'inventaire de 1808: état-civil, alphabétisation, professions." *Archives juives* 10, p. 3.

Jordan, Bill, and Dita Vogel. 1997. "Which Policies Influence Migration Decisions?: A Comparative Analysis of Qualitative Interviews in London and Berlin as a Contribution to Economic Reasoning." *ZeS-Arbeitspapier*, November 14. University of Bremen: Center for Social Policy Research.

Joseph, Anne, and Alison Winter. 1996. "Making the Match: Human Traces, Forensic Experts and the Public Imagination." In *Cultural Babbage: Technology, Time and Invention*, edited by F. Spufford and J. Uglow, pp. 193–214. London: Faber and Faber.

Joseph, S. C. 1996. "Policy Refinements for the Armed Forces Repository of Specimen Samples for the Identification of Remains." Washington, D.C.: Department of Defense, Memorandum for the Secretary of the Army.

Jowitt, Ken. 1992. *New World Disorder*. Berkeley/Los Angeles: University of California Press.

Judy. 1891. "Crime and Finger Marks," July 1, p. 3.

Kaluszynski, Martine. 1987. "Alphonse Bertillon et l'anthropometrie." In *Maintien de l'ordre et polices en France et en Europe au XIXe siècle*, edited by Philippe Vigier et al., pp. 269–85. Paris: créaphis.

Kaluszynski, Martine. 1988. "La criminologie en mouvement: Naissance et développement d'une science sociale en France à la fin du XIXème siècle. Autour des *Archives de l'anthropologie criminelle* d'Alexandre Lacassagne." Ph.D. diss., Université Paris VII.

Kaluszynski, Martine. 1999. "Le criminel à la fin du XIXème siècle: Un paradoxe républicain." In *Les exclus en Europe, 1830–1930*, edited by André Gueslin and Dominique Kalifa, pp. 253–66. Paris: Editions de l'Atelier.

Karp, D. 1973. "Hiding in Pornographic Bookstores." *Urban Life and Culture*, January.

Kartschoke, Dieter. 1992. "Über das Erkennen und Wiedererkennen physiognomischer Individualität im Mittelalter." In *Festschrift für Walter Haug und Burkhart Wachinger*, vol. 1, edited by Johannes Janota et al., pp. 1–24. Tübingen: Niemeyer.

Kay, M. A., C. S. Manno, M. V. Ragni, P. J. Larson, L. B. Couto, A. McLelland, B. Glader, A. J. Chew, S. J. Tai, R. W. Herzog, V. Arruda, F. Johnson, C. Scallan, E. Skarsgard, A. W. Flake, and K. A. High. 2000. "Evidence for Gene Transfer and Expression of Factor IX in Haemophilia B Patients Treated with an AAV Vector." *Nature Genetics* 24, no. 3, March, pp. 257–61.

Kern, Stephen. 1983. *The Culture of Time and Space, 1880–1918*. Cambridge, Massachusetts: Harvard University Press.

Khobotov, Anatolii N., and Tamara I. Zheludkova. 1990. *Iz istorii stanovleniia i razvitiia pasportnoi sistemy v SSSR (oktiabr' 1917–1974 gg.)*. Moscow: Akademiia MVD SSSR.

Kirbyson, Geoff. 1996. "The Smart Card Goes to China." *Financial Post* 9, p. 103.

Knaack, Rudolph. 1960. "Die Überwachung der politischen Emigranten in Preussen in der Zeit von 1848 bis 1870." Phil.diss., Berlin (East).

Knight, David. 1981. *Ordering the World: A History of Classifying Man.* London: Burnett Books/André Deutsch.

Kolchin, Peter. 1987. *Unfree Labor: American Slavery and Russian Serfdom.* Cambridge, Massachusetts: Belknap Press of Harvard University Press.

Komlosy, Andrea. 1995. "Ein Land - viele Grenzen. Waren- und Reiseverkehr zwischen den österreichischen und böhmischen Ländern (1740–1918)." In *Kulturen an der Grenze: Waldviertel, Weinviertel, Südböhmen, Südmähren,* edited by Andrea Komlosy, Václav Buzek, and Frantisek Svátek, pp. 59–72. Vienna: Promedia.

Körner, Joseph Leo. 1993. *The Moment of Self-Portraiture in German Renaissance Art.* Chicago: University of Chicago Press.

Koselleck, Reinhard. 1990. *Le futur passé.* Paris: EHESS.

Koss, Stephen. 1981. *The Rise and Fall of the Political Press in Britain.* Vol. 1. London: Hamish Hamilton.

Kotkin, Stephen. 1995. *Magnetic Mountain: Stalinism as a Civilization.* Berkeley: University of California Press.

Kotsonis, Yanni. 1998. "Subject and Citizen: Taxation and Its Meanings in Late Imperial and Early Soviet Russia." Paper presented at the conference on Russia in the First World War, St. Petersburg, May.

Kotulak, Ronald. 1998. "Violence Is Linked to Genetics, Early Abuses That Set Patterns." *Chicago Tribune,* March 29, p. C17.

Kuromiya, Hiroaki. 1988. *Stalin's Industrial Revolution: Politics and Workers, 1928–1932.* Cambridge: Cambridge University Press.

Küther, Carsten. 1987. *Räuber und Gauner in Deutschland: das organisierte Bandenwesen im 18. und frühen 19. Jahrhundert.* 2nd ed. Göttingen: Vandenhoeck und Ruprecht.

Lacassagne, Alexandre. 1887. *Les actes de l'État Civil.* Lyon: A. Storck.

Lambert, R. 1967. "A Victorian National Health Service: State Vaccination." *Historical Journal* 5, pp. 1–18.

The Lancet. 1905. "Identification by Finger Prints," May 13, pp. 1280–81.

Lander, Eric. 1992. "DNA Fingerprinting: Science, Law, and the Ultimate Identifier." In *The Code of Codes: Social Issues in the Human Genome Project,* edited by Daniel J. Kevles and Leroy Hood, pp. 191–210. Cambridge, Massachusetts: Harvard University Press.

Landsman, Stephan. 1998. "One Hundred Years of Rectitude: Medical Witnesses at the Old Bailey, 1717–1817." *Law and History Review* 16, pp. 445–94.

Lapierre, Nicole. 1995. *Changer du nom.* Paris: Stock.

Larson, Erik. 1992. *The Naked Consumer: How Our Private Lives Become Public Commodities.* New York: Henry Holt.

Lassota, Friedrich-Arnold. 1993. *Formen der Armut im späten Mittelalter und am Beginn der Neuzeit.* Köln: Bouvier.

Latane, Bibb, and John Darley. 1970. *The Unresponsive Bystander: Why Doesn't He Help?* New York: Appleton-Century-Crofts.

Laudon, Kenneth. 1986. *The Dossier Society: Value Choices in the Design of National Information Systems.* New York: Columbia University Press.

Lauffer, Otto. 1954. "Der laufende Bote im Nachrichtenwesen der früheren Jahrhunderte." *Beiträge zur deutschen Volks- und Altertumskunde* 1, pp. 19–60.

Le Roux, Hugues. 1889. *Le chemin du crime.* Paris: V. Havard.

Leeuwen, Marco van. 1994. "Logic of Charity: Poor Relief in Preindustrial Europe." *Journal of Interdisciplinary History* 24, no. 4, Spring, pp. 589–613.

Lefebvre-Taillard, Anne. 1990. *Le nom: Droit et histoire.* Paris: PUF.

Leitherer, Friedrich. 1954. "Die Entwicklung des Markenwesens." Diss., Nuremberg.

Lemarchand, René. 1970. *Rwanda and Burundi.* New York: Praeger.

Lemarchand, René. 1994. *Burundi: Ethnocide as Discourse and Practice.* Cambridge: Cambridge University Press.

Lépine, Louis. 1929. *Mes souvenirs.* Paris: Payot.

Leroi-Gourhan, André. 1984. *Hand und Wort: Die Evolution von Technik, Sprache und Kunst.* 2nd ed. Frankfurt am Main: Suhrkamp.

Lévy, E. 1919. *Les transcriptions et les témoins d'état civil.* Paris: Librairie de Droit Usuel.

Lewin, Moshe. 1975. *Russian Peasants and Soviet Power: A Study of Collectivization.* New York: Norton.

Lichem, Arnold. 1935. *Die Kriminalpolizei. Handbuch für den kriminellen Polizeidienst.* 2nd ed. Graz: Leykam.

Liégeois, Jean-Pierre. 1971. *Les tsiganes.* Paris: Le Seuil.

Liégeois, Jean-Pierre. 1977. "Nomades, Tsiganes et pouvoirs publics en France au XXème siècle: du rejet à l'assimilation." *Études Tsiganes* 4, pp. 1–13.

Liégeois, Jean-Pierre. 1980. "Le discours de l'ordre. Pouvoirs publics et minorités culturelles." *Esprit* 5, pp. 17–50.

Liégeois, Jean-Pierre. 1994. *Roma, Tsiganes, Voyageurs.* Strasbourg: Conseil de l'Europe, collection Education.

Lindee, Susan, and Dorothy Nelkin. 1995. *The DNA Mystique.* New York: Freeman.

Lindsey, R. 1985. *The Falcon and the Snowman.* New York: Pocket Books.

Linell, Anthony. 1938. *The Law of Names: Public, Private and Corporate.* London: Butterworth and Co.

Liubarskii, Kronid. 1994. "Pasportnaia sistema i sistema propiski v Rossii." *Rossiiskii biulleten' po pravam cheloveka* 2, pp. 14–26.

Locard, Edmond. 1909. *L'identification des récidivistes.* Paris: A. Maloine.

Locard, Edmond. 1920. *L'enquête criminelle et les méthodes scientifiques.* Paris: Flammarion.

Locré, Jean-Guillaume. 1805–8. *Esprit du Code Napoléon.* 6 vols. Paris: Imprimerie Impériale.

Logan, John R. 1978. "Growth, Politics, and the Stratification of Places." *American Journal of Sociology* 84, no. 2, pp. 404–16.

Lohr, Steve. 1987. "For Crime Detection, 'Genetic Fingerprinting.'" *New York Times*, November 30, p. A9.

Loir, J. N. 1846. "De l'exécution de l'article 55 du Code Civil relatif à la constatation des naissances." *Revue de Droit Français et Etranger* 3.

Lowenthal, Max. 1950. *The Federal Bureau of Investigation*. New York: William Sloane.

Lucassen, Jan, and Leo Lucassen, eds. *Migration, Migration History, History: Old Paradigms and New Perspectives*. Bern/New York: Peter Lang.

Lucassen, Jan, and Rinus Penninx. 1997. *Newcomers: Immigrants and Their Descendants in the Netherlands 1550–1995*. Amsterdam: Het Spinhuis.

Lucassen, Leo. 1990. *En men noemde hen zigeuners: De geschiedenis van Kaldarasch, Ursari, Lowara en Sinti in Nederland (1750–1944)*. The Hague/Amsterdam: SDU and Stichting Beheer IISG.

Lucassen, Leo. 1996a. *Zigeuner: Die Geschichte eines polizeilichen Ordnungbegriffes in Deutschland, 1700–1945*. Weimar: Böhlau.

Lucassen, Leo. 1996b. "Agent of koopman: Theorie en praktijk van de controle op arbeidsmigratie in Nederland, 1918–1980." In *Nieuwe Nederlanders: Vestiging van migranten door de eeuwen heen*, edited by Marjolein 't Hart et al., pp. 151–68. Amsterdam: Stichting Beheer IISG.

Lucassen, Leo. 1997a. "The Invention of the Alien: Immigration Controls in an Emerging Welfare State and the Implementation at the Local Level in the Netherlands (1918–1940)." Paper presented at the 1997 Social Science History Association.

Lucassen, Leo. 1997b. "Eternal Vagrants? State Formation, Migration, and Travelling Groups in Western Europe, 1350–1914." In *Migration, Migration History, History: Old Paradigms and New Perspectives*, edited by Jan Lucassen and Leo Lucassen, pp. 225–52. Bern/New York: Peter Lang.

Lucassen, Leo. 1998. "The Great War and the End of Free Migration in Western Europe and the United States: Explanations and Refutations." In *Regulation of Migration: International Experiences*, edited by Anita Böcker et al., pp. 45–72. Amsterdam: Het Spinhuis.

Lucassen, Leo. 1999. "From National to Local and Back: The Development of Aliens Policies in the Netherlands 1790–1860." Paper presented at the workshop "Migration Controls in 19th century Europe and the US," German Historical Institute (London) and the Center for Research in Immigration, Integration and Citizenship (CEPIC), Paris, June.

Lucassen, Leo, and Gerard van der Harst. 1998. "De vreugde van het tellen: Nut en noodzaak van vreemdelingenregisters voor historisch migratie-onderzoek." *Tijdschrift voor Sociale Geschiedenis* 3, pp. 293–315.

Lucassen, Leo, Wim Willems, and Annemarie Cottaar. 1998. *Gypsies and Other Itinerant Groups: A Socio-historical Approach*. New York: St. Martin's.

Lüdtke, Alf. 1982. *"Gemeinwohl," Polizei und "Festungspraxis": Staatliche Gewaltsamkeit und innere Verwaltung in Preussen, 1815–1850*. Göttingen: Vandenhoeck und Ruprecht.

Lüdtke, Alf. 1993. "'Willkürgewalt des Staates'? Polizeipraxis und administrative Definitionsmacht im vormärzlichen Preussen." In *". . . nur für die Sicherheit da . . ."? Zur Geschichte der Polizei im 19. und 20. Jahrhundert*, edited by Herbert Reinke, pp. 35–55. Frankfurt am Main/New York: Campus Verlag.

Luebke, David Martin, and Sybil Milton. 1994. "Locating the Victim: An Overview of Census-Taking, Tabulation Technology, and Persecution in Nazi Germany." *IEEE Annals of the History of Computing* 16, no. 3, pp. 25–39.

Luke, Dennis E. 1980. *Criminal Record Development*. Godalming: Dennis E. Luke.

Lüpke, Hans von. 1997. "Möglichkeiten und Grenzen der Bekämpfung illegaler Beschäftigung durch Arbeitsmarktkontrolle." In *Illegale Beschäftigung in der Europäischen Union*, edited by Deutscher Gewerkschaftsbund, pp. 26–31. Düsseldorf: Bundesvorstand Migration.

Lyon, David. 1988. *The Information Society: Issues and Illusions*. Cambridge: Polity.

Lyon, David. 1989. "Fragmentation and Cohesion in American Society." In *Disasters, Collective Behavior, and Social Organization*, edited by R. Dynes and K. Tierney. Newark: University of Delaware Press.

Lyon, David. 1990. "Fraudulent Identification and Biography." In *New Directions in the Study of Law and Social Control*, edited by D. Altheide et al. New York: Plenum.

Lyon, David. 1991. "Bentham's Panopticon: From Moral Architecture to Electronic Surveillance." *Queen's Quarterly* 98.

Lyon, David. 1994. *The Electronic Eye: The Rise of Surveillance Society*. Cambridge: Polity/Minneapolis: University of Minnesota Press.

Lyon, David. 1998. "An Ethics for the New Surveillance." *The Information Society* 14, p. 3.

Lyon, David, and E. Zureik, eds. 1996. *Computers, Surveillance and Privacy*. Minneapolis: University of Minnesota Press.

Lyon, R. 1921. *Jugements et ordonnances de rectification d'actes de l'état civil: Examen de quelques difficultés*. Paris: Jouve et Cie.

MacLean, Ian. 1980. *The Renaissance Notion of Woman*. Cambridge: Cambridge University Press.

MacLeod, R. M. 1967. "Law, Medicine and Public Opinion: The Resistance to Compulsory Health Legislation 1870–1907." *Public Law*. Part I, pp. 107–28.

MacStay-Adams, Thomas. 1990. *Bureaucrats and Beggars: French Social Policy in the Age of the Enlightenment*. New York/Oxford: Oxford University Press.

Maczak, Antoni, and Hans Jürgen Teuteberg, eds. 1982. *Reiseberichte als Quellen europäischer Kulturgeschichte*. Wolfenbüttel: Herzog August Bibliothek.

Maddalena, Aldo de. 1974. *Prezzi e mercedi a Milano dal 1701 al 1860*. Milan: Università Bocconi.

Mann, Michael. 1993. *The Sources of Social Power*, vol. 2: *The Rise of Classes and Nation-States, 1760–1914*. New York: Cambridge University Press.

Manning, J. 1863. "Change of Name." *The Athenaeum* 1884, pp. 759–60.

Mannkopff, A. J., ed. 1836. *Ergänzungen und Abänderungen der Preussischen Gesetzbücher*. Vol. 4. Berlin: Naucke.

Marburger, Helga, ed. 1994. *Ost-West-Migration: Lebens- und Arbeitsbedingungen von Migranten aus Osteuropa in den neuen Bundesländern und Berlin*. Frankfurt am Main: Verlag für interkulturelle Kommunikation.

Marks, Shula. 1985a. "Southern Africa, 1867–1886." In *The Cambridge History of Africa*, vol. 6: "From 1870 to 1905," edited by Roland Oliver and G. N. Sanderson, pp. 359–421. Cambridge: Cambridge University Press.

Marks, Shula. 1985b. "Southern and Central Africa, 1886–1910." In *The Cambridge History of Africa*, vol. 6: "From 1870 to 1905," edited by Roland Oliver and G. N. Sanderson, pp. 422–92. Cambridge: Cambridge University Press.

Marrus, Michael. 1985. *The Unwanted: European Refugees in the Twentieth Century*. New York/Oxford: Oxford University Press.

Marshall, Eliot. 1998. "DNA Studies Challenge Meaning of Race." *Science*, October 23, pp. 654–55.

Marshall, Tyler. 1987. "New Techniques Lead to Charges in British Rape-Slaying; Genetic Fingerprints Snare a Suspect." *Los Angeles Times*, September 22, sec. 1, p. 6.

Martin, David A. 1998. "The Obstacles to Effective Internal Enforcement of the Immigration Laws in the United States." In *Immigration Controls: The Search for Workable Policies in Germany and the United States*, edited by Kay Hailbronner, David Martin, and Hiroshi Motomura, pp. 1–44. Providence/Oxford: Berghahn.

Martin, Henri-Jean. 1994. *The History and Power of Writing*. Chicago: University of Chicago Press.

Martin, John. 1997. "Inventing Sincerity, Refashioning Prudence: The Discovery of the Individual in Renaissance Europe." *American Historical Review* 102, pp. 1309–42.

Martin, Philip L. 1998. *Germany: Reluctant Land of Immigration*. German Issues 21. American Institute for Contemporary German Studies, Johns Hopkins University.

Marx, Gary. 1988. *Undercover: Police Surveillance in America*. Berkeley: University of California Press.

Marx, Gary. 1989. "Now the Techno-Snoopers Want to Get into Our Genes." *Los Angeles Times*, September 15, p. 7.

Marx, Gary. 1990. "Fraudulent Identification and Biography." In *New Directions in the Study of Law and Social Control*, edited by D. Altheide. New York: Plenum.

Marx, Gary. 1994. "New Telecommunication Technologies Require New Manners." *Telecommunications Policy* 18, pp. 538–52.

Marx, Gary. 1997a. "Social Control Across Borders." In *Crime and Law Enforcement in the Global Village*, edited by W. McDonald. Cincinnati: Anderson.

Marx, Gary. 1997b. "The Declining Significance of Traditional Borders (and the Appearance of New Borders) in an Age of High Technology." In *Intelligent Environments*, edited by P. Droege. Amsterdam: Elsevier Science.

Marx, Gary. 1998. "An Ethics for the New Surveillance." *The Information Society* 14, p. 3.

Matthews, Mervyn. 1993. *The Passport Society: Controlling Movement in Russia and the USSR*. Boulder/San Francisco/Oxford: Westview.

Mazohl-Wallnig, Brigitte. 1981. "Governo centrale e amministrazioni locali. Il Lombardo-Veneto, 1848–1859." In *Austria e provincie italiane 1815–1918: Potere centrale e amministrazioni locali*, edited by Franco Valsecchi and Adam Wandruszka. Bologna: Il Mulino.

McCracken, John. 1986. "British Central Africa." In *The Cambridge History of Africa*, vol. 7: "From 1905 to 1940," edited by A. D. Roberts, pp. 602–48. Cambridge: Cambridge University Press.

McDonald, William F. 1997. "Illegal Immigration: Crime, Ramifications, and Control: The American Experience." In *Crime and Enforcement in the Global Village*, edited by William F. McDonald, pp. 65–86. Cincinnati: Anderson.

McEwen, Jean, and Phillip Reilly. 1994. "A Review of State Legislation on DNA Forensic Data Banking." *American Journal of Human Genetics* 54, pp. 941–58.

McEwen, Jean E. 1998. "Storing Genes to Solve Crimes: Legal, Ethical and Public Policy Implications." In *Stored Tissue Samples: Ethical, Legal and Public Policy Implications*, edited by Robert F. Weir, pp. 311–28. Iowa City: University of Iowa Press.

Mead, Helen, ed. 1995. *Change of Name*. London: Sweet and Maxwell.

Meier, Thomas Dominik, and Wolf Wolfensberger. 1988. "Carl Durheims Fahndungsfotografien von schweizerischen Heimatlosen und Nicht-Sesshaften." In *Wider das Leugnen und Verstellen. Carl Durheims Fahndungsfotografien von Heimatlosen 1852/53*, edited by Martin Gasser, Thomas Dominik Meier, and Rolf Wolfensberger, pp. 9–23. Winterthur: Offizin.

Mellins, Claude Ann, et al. 1996. "Children's Methods of Coping with Stress: A Twin Study of Genetic and Environmental Influences." *Journal of Child Psychology and Psychiatry* 37, no. 6, pp. 721–30.

Mellor, Philip, and Chris Shilling. 1997. *Reforming the Body: Religion, Community, and Modernity*. London: Sage.

Mergen, Josef. 1973. *Die Auswanderungen aus den ehemals preussischen Teilen des Saarlands im 19. Jahrhundert*, vol. 1: *Voraussetzungen und Grundmerkmale*. Saarbrücken: Institut für Landeskunde im Saarland.

Meriggi, Marco. 1987. *Storia d'Italia*, vol. 18: no. 2, *Il Regno Lombardo-Veneto*. Turin: Utet.

Mersier, E. 1892. *Traité théorique et pratique des actes d'état civil*. Paris: Marescq.

Merz, John F., and Pamela Sankar. 1998. "DNA Banking: An Empirical Study of a Proposed Consent Form." In *Stored Tissue Samples: Ethical, Legal and Public Policy Implications*, edited by Robert F. Weir, pp. 198–225. Iowa City: University of Iowa Press.

Metropolitan Police. Convict Supervision Office, New Scotland Yard. 1904. *Memorandum on the Working of the Finger Print System of Identification 1901–1904*. London: HMSO.

Mineham, Maureen. 1998. "The Growing Debate Over Genetic Testing." *HRM Magazine*, April.

Moch, Leslie Page. 1992. *Moving Europeans: Migration in Western Europe since 1650*. Bloomington: Indiana University Press.

Moenssens, Andre A. 1971. *Fingerprint Techniques*. Philadelphia: Chilton.

Moffit, Terrie, Avshalom Caspi, Paul Fawcett, Gary Brammer, Michael Raleigh, Arthur Yuweiler, and Paul Silva. 1997. "Whole Blood Serotonin and Family Background Relate to Male Violence." In *Biosocial Bases of Violence*, edited by Adrian Raine and Patricia Brennan, pp. 231–49. New York: Plenum.

Moos, Peter von. 1994. "Gefahren des Mittelalterbegriffs." In *Modernes Mittelalter*, edited by Joachim Heinzle, pp. 33–63. Frankfurt am Main: Insel.

Morgenthaler, Hans. 1919. "Kulturgeschichtliche Notizen aus den solothurnischen Seckelmeisterrechnungen des 15. Jahrhunderts." In *Anzeiger für schweizerische Altertumskunde*, N.F. 21.

[Murray, John]. 1843. *A Hand-Book for Travellers on the Continent: Being a Guide through Holland, Belgium, Prussia and Northern Germany* [...]. 4th ed. London: Murray.

[Murray, John]. 1850. *A Hand-Book for Travellers on the Continent: Being a Guide through Holland, Belgium, Prussia and Northern Germany* [...]. 7th ed. London: Murray.

[Murray, John]. 1854. *A Hand-Book for Travellers on the Continent: Being a Guide through Holland, Belgium, Prussia and Northern Germany* [...]. 10th ed. London: Murray.

[Murray, John]. 1867. *A Hand-Book for Travellers on the Continent: Being a Guide through Holland, Belgium, Prussia and Northern Germany and Along the Rhine, from Holland to Switzerland.* 16th ed. London: Murray.

National Academy of Sciences. 1995. *Private Lives and Public Policies: Confidentiality and Access to Information in a Free Society.* Washington, D.C.: National Academy of Sciences Report.

National Genome Project Research Institute. 1998. "Genetic Information and the Workplace." *<www.nhgri.nih.gov:80/HGP/Reports/genetics_workplace.html>* p. 3.

Nederlandsche Staatscourant (NSC).

Nekrich, Alexander M. 1978. *The Punished Peoples: The Deportation and Fate of Soviet Minorities at the End of the Second World War.* New York: Norton.

Newbury, Catharine. 1988. *The Cohesion of Oppression: Clientship and Ethnicity in Rwanda, 1860–1960.* New York: Columbia University Press.

Newbury, David. 1998. "Understanding Genocide." *African Studies Review* 41, no. 1, April, pp. 73–97.

New Scientist (London). 1998. "Unusual Suspects," May 23, p. 18.

New York Times. 1998. "FBI is Set to Open National Databases for Criminals' DNA: The Hope is That the DNA System Will Help Police Catch Repeat Offenders Earlier or Before They Commit Serious Crimes," October 12, p. 10A.

New York Times: Sunday Magazine. 1988. "DNA Detectives: Genetic 'Fingerprinting' May Herald a Revolution in Law Enforcement," December 11, pp. 71–73, 88–89, 104.

Nicklis, Hans-Werner. 1992. "Rechtsgeschichte und Kulturgeschichte: Zur Vor- und Frühgeschichte des Steckbriefs." *Mediävistik* 5, pp. 21–53.

Nissenbaum, H. 1997. "Toward an Approach to Privacy in Public: Challenges of Information Technology." *Ethics and Behavior* 7, p. 3.

Nitschke, Peter. 1990. *Verbrechensbekämpfung und Verwaltung. Die Entstehung der Polizei in der Grafschaft Lippe, 1700–1814.* Müenster/New York: Waxmann.

Nock, Steven. 1993. *The Costs of Privacy: Surveillance and Reputation in America.* New York: Aldine de Gruyter.

Noiriel, Gérard. 1991a. *La tyrannie du national: Le droit d'asile en Europe 1793–1993*. Paris: Calman-Lévy.

Noiriel, Gérard. 1991b. *Réfugies et sans-papiers: La République face au droit d'asile XIXᵉ–XXᵉ siècle*. Paris: Hachette.

Noiriel, Gérard. 1996. *The French Melting Pot: Immigration, Citizenship, and National Identity*. Translated by Geoffroy de Laforcade. Minneapolis: University of Minnesota Press.

Noiriel, Gérard. 1998. "Surveiller les déplacements ou identifier les personnes? Contributions à l'histoire du passeport en France de la Iʳᵉ à la IIIᵉ république." *Genèses: Sciences sociales et histoire* 30, March, pp. 77–100.

Nordman, Daniel. 1987. "Sauf-conduits et passeports, en France, à la Renaissance." In *Voyager à la Renaissance*, edited by Jean Ceard and Jean-Claude Margolin, pp. 145–58. Paris: Seuil.

Nordman, Daniel. 1988. *Frontière, État et Territoire: La construction de l'espace français, XVIᵉ-début du XIXᵉ siècle*. Paris: Gallimard.

Norris, Clive, et al. 1996. "Algorithmic Surveillance: The Future of Automated Visual Surveillance." In *Surveillance, Closed Circuit Television, and Social Control*, edited by Clive Norris, Jade Moran, and Gary Armstrong. Aldershot/Singapore/Sydney: Ashgate.

Nove, Alec. 1982. *An Economic History of the U.S.S.R.* Rev. ed. New York: Penguin.

Nussbaum, Felicity. 1989. *The Autobiographical Subject: Gender and Ideology in Eighteenth-Century England*. Baltimore: Johns Hopkins University Press.

Oexle, Otto Gerhard. 1992. "Das Mittelalter und das Unbehagen an der Moderne." In *Spannungen und Widersprüche: Gedenkschrift für Frantisek Graus*, edited by Frantisek Graus and Susanna Burghartz. Sigmaringen: J. Thorbecke.

Ogris, Werner. 1975. "Die Rechtsentwicklung in Cisleithanien 1848–1918." In *Die Habsburgermonarchie 1848–1918*, vol. II: *Verwaltung und Rechtswesen*, edited by Adam Wandruszka and Peter Urbanitsch, pp. 538–662. Vienna: Verlag der österreichischen Akademie der Wissenschaften.

"O iazyke prepodovaniia Zakona Bozhiia inoslavnykh ispovedanii, 27 oktiabria 1912." 1913. *Vestnik Orenburgskogo Uchebnogo Okruga* no. 1, offits. otdel 17–18.

Olivera, Carlos. 1900. "Psicología del derecho penal." *Revista Jurídica* 18, pp. 353–69.

Ortalli, Gherardo. 1979. *"Pingatur in palatio": La pittura infamante nei secoli XIII–XVI*. Rome: Jouvence.

Outhwaite, R. B., ed. 1981. *Marriage and Society: Studies in the Social History of Marriage*. London: Europa.

Page, D. L., and W. D. Dupont. 1998. "Benign Breast Diseases and Premalignant Breast Disease." *Archives of Pathology and Laboratory Medicine* 122, pp. 1048–50.

Palmer, R. R., and Joel Colton. 1978. *A History of the Modern World*. 5th ed. New York: Knopf.

Pankoke, Eckard. 1970. *Sociale Bewegung - Sociale Frage - Sociale Politik. Grundfragen der deutschen Socialwissenschaft im 19. Jahrhundert*. Stuttgart: E. Klett.

Patriarca, Silvana. 1996. *Numbers and Nationhood: Writing Statistics in Nineteenth-Century Italy*. Cambridge: Cambridge University Press.

Paxton, Robert. 1975. *Europe in the Twentieth Century*. New York: Harcourt Brace Jovanovich.

Pearsall, Kathy. 1998. "This Technology Is Eye-catching." *Computing Canada* 24, p. 2.

Pearson, Karl. 1930. *The Life, Letters and Labours of Francis Galton*. Cambridge: Cambridge University Press.

Perrot, Michelle. 1970. "Délinquance et système pénitentiaire en France au XIXème siècle." *Annales ESC* 1.

Peschanski, Denis. 1994. *Les Tsiganes en France 1939–1946: Contrôle et exclusion*. Paris: Editions CNRS.

Petit, Jacques-Guy. 1990. *Ces peines obscures. La prison pénale en France 1780–1875*. Paris: Fayard.

Pfeiffer, G[eorg] W[ilhelm]. 1828. *Actenmässige Nachrichten über das Gaunerunwesen an Rhein und Main und in den an diesen Gegenden grenzenden Ländern*. Frankfurt am Main: Sauerländer.

Pfister, Ludwig Aloys. 1812. *Aktenmässige Geschichte der Räuberbanden an den beiden Ufern des Mains, im Spessart und im Odenwalde*. Heidelberg: Braun.

Pfister, Ludwig Aloys. 1820. *Merkwürdige Criminalfälle mit besonderer Rücksicht auf die Untersuchungsführung*. Vol. 5. Frankfurt am Main: Hermannsche Buchhandlung.

Phéline, Christian. 1985. *L'image accusatrice*. Paris: Les Cahiers de la Photographie.

Phillimore, W. P. W. 1905. *The Law and Practice of Change of Name*. London: Phillimore and Co.

Pick, Daniel. 1996. *Faces of Degeneration: A European Disorder, c.1848–c.1918*. New York: Cambridge University Press.

Pipes, Richard. 1992 [1974]. *Russia under the Old Regime*. 2nd ed. New York: Collier Books.

Planitz, E. von der. 1841. "Ueber die Annahme veränderter Familien-Namen und deren Genehmigung und Bestätigung aus dem Gesichtspunkte des öffentlichen Rechts." *Zeitschrift für Rechtspflege und Verwaltung, zunächst für das Königreich Sachsen*. N.F. vol. 1, pp. 348–55.

Plant, Sadie. 1995. "The Future Looms: Weaving Women and Cybernetics." In *Cyberspace/Cyberbodies/Cyberpunk: Culture of Technological Embodiment*, edited by Mike Featherstone and Roger Burrows. London/Thousand Oaks/New Delhi: Sage.

Plender, Richard. 1988. *International Migration Law*. 2nd rev. ed. Dordrecht: Martinus Nijhoff.

Polnoe Sobranie Zakonov Rossüskoi Imperii, series 1–3.

Poovey, Mary. 1998. *A History of the Modern Fact: Problems of Knowledge in the Sciences of Wealth and Society*. Chicago: University of Chicago Press.

Porter, Dorothy, and Roy Porter. 1988. "The Politics of Prevention: Anti-vaccinationism and Public Health in Nineteenth-Century England." *Medical History* 32, pp. 231–52.

Porter, Theodore. 1986. *The Rise of Statistical Thinking 1820–1900*. Princeton: Princeton University Press.

Powell, Johanna. 1997. "Eye-dentification." *The Financial Post*, September 27, pp. E1, E11.

Preobrazhensky, Evgenii. 1987 [1924]. "Peasantry and the Political Economy of the Early Stages of Industrialization." In *Peasants and Peasant Societies: Selected Readings*, edited by Teodor Shanin, pp. 405–10. New York: Basil Blackwell.

Price, Robert M., and Carl G. Rosberg, eds. 1980. *The Apartheid Regime: Political Power and Racial Domination*. Berkeley: Institute of International Studies, University of California.

Process Action Team. 1996. *Final Report of the Process Action Team for a Consolidated Military Genetics/DNA Program*. Falls Church, Virginia: U.S. Army.

Proudhon, Pierre-Joseph. 1923–24. "Idée générale de la révolution au XIXe siècle." *Oeuvres complètes*, vol. 3, edited by C. Bouglé and H. Moysset. Paris: Marcel Rivière.

Prunier, Gérard. 1995. *The Rwanda Crisis: History of a Genocide*. New York: Columbia University Press.

Pseudo-Aristotle. 1982. *The Secret of Secrets: Sources and Influence*, edited by W. F. Ryan and Charles B. Schmitt. London: Warburg Institute.

Queller, Donald. 1967. *The Office of the Ambassador in the Middle Ages*. Princeton: Princeton University Press.

Quesada, Ernesto. 1901. *Comprobación de la reincidencia. Proyecto de ley presentado al señor ministro de justicia é instrucción pública, doctor don Osvaldo Magnasco*. Buenos Aires: Coni.

Rademacher. 1837. "Zur Theorie der besonderen Kennzeichen; nebst einem Vorschlage zu deren vollständigeren Benutzung in der Polizey-Praxis." *Allgemeiner Polizei-Anzeiger* 4, pp. 237–40, 242–44.

Rademacher. 1837. "Das Portraitiren als Polizeymassregel." *Allgemeiner Polizei-Anzeiger* 4, pp. 7–8.

Raffestin, Claude. 1992. "L'immagine della frontiera." *Volontà* 4, pp. 43–63.

Ramdohr, Landesrichter. 1899. "Das Recht zum Gebrauch eines Namens nach den Vorschriften des Bürgerlichen Gesetzbuches." *Beiträge zur Erläuterung des Deutschen Rechts* 43, pp. 1–80.

Rauer, K. F. 1844. *Die preussische Pass-Polizei-Verwaltung: Systematisch dargestellt*. Nordhausen: B. G. H. Schmidt.

Read, Donald. 1979. *England 1868–1914: The Age of Urban Democracy*. New York: Longman.

Reed, Christopher. 1998. "Lack of Fingerprints Puts Man Under Thumb of Bureaucracy." *The Globe and Mail* (Toronto), April 23.

Regan, Priscilla. 1995. *Legislating Privacy: Technology, Social Values, and Public Policy*. Chapel Hill: University of North Carolina Press.

Regener, Susanne. 1992. "Verbrecherbilder: Fotoporträts der Polizei und Physiognomisierung des Kriminellen." *Ethnologia Europeae* 22, pp. 67–85.

Report of the British Association for the Advancement of Science 1899. 1900. Meeting at Dover, September 1899, London: John Murray.

Revista de Policía. 1897. "La oficina antropométrica." Vol. 1, no. 6, August 15. Buenos Aires.

Revista de Policía. 1900. "Oficina antropométrica, alcaída y archivos criminales." Vol. 4, no. 81, October 1, pp. 131–33; vol. 4, no. 82, October 16, pp. 149–51. Buenos Aires.

Reyna Almandos, Luis. 1909. *Dactiloscopia argentina. Su historia é influencia en la legislación.* La Plata: J. Sesé.

Reyna Almandos, Luis. 1925. Interview with, by Federico Quevedo Hijosa. "La cuestión dactiloscópica. Necesidad impostergable de reparar una injusticia. ¿Se pretende negar a Vucetich o despojarle de su invento?" *La Argentina 2.*

Reyna Almandos, Luis. 1936. "The Personal Number and the National Book of Personality." *Biblioteca de la Revista de Identificación y Ciencias Penales,* no. 22. La Plata: Impresiones Oficiales.

Reyntjens, Filip. 1994. *L'Afrique des Grands Lacs en crise: Rwanda, Burundi, 1988–1994.* Paris: Karthala.

Ridley, Jasper. 1970. *Lord Palmerston.* London: Panther.

Roberti, Melchiore. 1946. *Milano capitale napoleonica: La formazione di uno stato moderno 1796–1814.* Vol. 1. Milan: Fondazione Treccani.

Roberts, Andrew. 1986. "East Africa." In *The Cambridge History of Africa,* vol. 7: "From 1905 to 1940," edited by A. D. Roberts, pp. 649–701. Cambridge: Cambridge University Press.

Robson, Roy R. 1995. *Old Believers in Modern Russia.* DeKalb: Northern Illinois University Press.

Rodríguez, Adolfo Enrique. c. 1981. *Cuatrocientos años de policía en Buenos Aires.* Buenos Aires: Editorial Policial-Federal Policía.

Rodríguez, Sislán. 1942. "Vucetich y la Dactiloscopia (sintesis enumerativa de las principales fechas)." *Revista de Policía de la Provincia de Buenos Aires* 1, no. 10, pp. 9–19.

Rogers, Colin. 1995. *The Surname Detective: Investigating Surname Distribution in England and Wales, 1086–Present Day.* Manchester: Manchester University Press.

Rogers, Lois. 1996. "Mass Screening for 'Delinquency' Gene Planned." *Sunday Times* (London), June 9.

Rogovin, L. M., comp. 1913. *Ustav o pasportakh. (Svod zakonov vol. 14, izd. 1903, i po prod. 1906, 1908, 1909, and 1910).* St. Petersburg: I. I. Zubkov.

Romay, Francisco Luis. 1975. *Historia de la Policía Federal Argentina,* vol. 6: 1880–1916. Buenos Aires: Editorial Policial.

Rönne, Ludwig von, and Heinrich Simon. 1840. *Das Polizeiwesen des Preussischen Staates. Eine systematisch geordnete Sammlung aller auf dasselbe Bezug habenden gesetzlichen Bestimmungen, insbesondere der in der Gesetzessammlung für die Preussischen Staaten und in den von Kamptzschen Annalen für die innere Staatsverwaltung enthaltenen Verordnungen und Rescripte, in ihrem organischen Zusammenhange mit der früheren Gesetzgebung.* Vol. 1. Breslau: Aderholz.

Rondonneau, Louis. 1810–11. *Corps du droit français, civil, commercial et criminel: Contenant les codes Napoléon.* Paris: Garnery.

Roscher, Gustav. 1912. *Grossstadtpolizei. Ein praktisches Handbuch der deutschen Polizei*. Hamburg: Meissner.

Rosenkranz, Albert. 1927. *Der Bundschuh*. Heidelberg: C. Winter.

Ross, Ijeoma. 1997. "IDs at Fingertip, Harris Predicts." *The Globe and Mail* (Toronto), May 14.

Rule, J. 1973. *Private Lives, Public Surveillance*. London: Allen Lane.

Rule, James, Douglas McAdam, Linda Stearns, and David Uglow. 1983. "Documentary Identification and Mass Surveillance in the United States." *Social Problems* 31, no. 2, pp. 222–34.

Ryzhkov, N. 1915. "Nachal'nyia shkoly OUO po perepisi 18 ianvaria 1911." *Vestnik Orenburgskogo Uchebnogo Okruga*, no. 3, ped. otdel 192–207.

"S formoi vedomosti k otchetu inspektorov narodnykh uchilishch po osmotru imi nachal'nykh shkol." 1912. *Vestnik Orenburgskogo Uchebnogo Okruga*, nos. 7–8, offits. otdel 513–515.

Sachs, Susan. 1999. "Sharpton and A.C.L.U. Assail Pataki's DNA Plan." *New York Times*, January 10, p. B21.

Sachsse, Christoph, and Florian Tennstedt, eds. 1980. *Geschichte der Armenfürsorge in Deutschland: Vom Spätmittelalter bis zum ersten Weltkrieg*. Stuttgart/Berlin: Klett.

Sagnac, P. 1898. *Le législation civile de la Révolution française (1789–1804)*. Paris: Hachette.

Salveton, Henri. 1887. *Le nom en droit roman et en droit français*. Lyon: Imprimerie nouvelle.

Sammlung von Gesetzen, Verordnungen, Ausschreiben und sonstigen allgemeinen Verfügungen für die kurhessischen Staaten. 1836. Kassel: Lukhardt.

Samuel, Raphael, ed. 1989. *Patriotism: The Making and Unmaking of British National Identity*. London: Routledge.

Sanders, Edith R. 1969. "The Hamitic Hypothesis: Its Origin and Functions in Time Perspective." *Journal of African History* 10, no. 4, pp. 521–32.

Sankar, Pamela. 1992. "State Power and Record-Keeping: The History of Individualized Surveillance in the United States, 1790–1935." Ph.D. diss., University of Pennsylvania.

Sankar, Pamela. 1997. "Topics for Our Times: The Proliferation and Risks of Government DNA Databases." *American Journal of Public Health* 87, pp. 336–37.

Schäfer, Hermann. 1982. "Italienische Gastarbeiter im deutschen Kaiserreich." *Zeitschrift für Unternehmensgeschichte* 27.

Schaffer, Simon. 1988. "Astronomers Mark Time: Discipline and the Personal Equation." *Science in Context* 2, pp. 115–45.

Schaffer, Simon. 1995. "Accurate Measurement Is an English Science." In *The Values of Precision*, edited by M. Norton Wise, pp. 135–72. Princeton: Princeton University Press.

Schapiro, Leonard. 1977. *The Origin of the Communist Autocracy: Political Opposition in the Soviet State, First Phase, 1917–1922*. Cambridge, Massachusetts: Harvard University Press.

Schaufelberger, Walter. 1952. *Der Alte Schweizer und sein Krieg*. Zürich: Verlag NZZ.

Scheffler, Thomas. 1997. "Der administrative Blick: Über den Gebrauch des Passes in der Ausländerbehörde." In *Die Befremdung der eigenen Kultur: Zur ethnographischen Herausforderung soziologischer Empirie*, edited by Stefan Hirschhauer and Klaus Anman, pp. 168–97. Frankfurt am Main: Suhrkamp.

Schildt, Gerhard. 1986. *Tagelöhner, Gesellen, Arbeiter: Sozialgeschichte der vorindustriellen und industriellen Arbeiter in Braunschweig 1830–1880*. Stuttgart: Klett-Cotta.

Schmauss, Johann, and Heinrich Senckenberg, eds. 1747. *Neue und vollständigere Sammlung der Reichs-Abschiede*. Frankfurt am Main: Ernst August Koch.

Schnapper, Bernard. 1991. "La récidive, une obsession créatrice au XIXème siècle." In *Voies nouvelles en histoire de la justice, la famille, la répression pénale (XVI–XXèmes siècles)*. Paris: PUF.

School and Society. 1937. "Fingerprints of Children in Schools." 45, pp. 368–69.

Schubert, Ernst. 1983. *Arme Leute, Bettler und Gauner im Franken des 18. Jahrhunderts*. Neustadt/Aisch: Degener.

Schubert, Ernst. 1995. *Fahrendes Volk im Mittelalter*. Bielefeld: Verlag für Regionalgeschichte.

Schulman, J. D., S. H. Black, A. Handyside, and W. E. Nance. 1996. "Preimplantation Genetic Testing for Huntington Disease and Certain Other Dominantly Inherited Disorders." *Clinical Genetics* 49, pp. 57–58.

Schwartz, Hillel. 1996. *The Culture of the Copy: Striking Likenesses, Unreasonable Facsimiles*. New York: Zone.

Schwartz, Robert M. 1988. *Policing the Poor in Eighteenth-century France*. Chapel Hill/London: University of North Carolina Press.

Schwarz, Solomon M. 1952. *Labor in the Soviet Union*. New York: Praeger.

Schwencken, Karl Philipp Theodor. 1822. *Aktenmässige Nachrichten von dem Gauner- und Vagabunden-Gesindel, sowie von einzelnen professionirten Dieben, in den Ländern zwischen dem Rhein und der Elbe, nebst genauer Beschreibung ihrer Person*. Cassel: Hampesche Buchdruckerei.

Scott, James. 1985. *Weapons of the Weak: Everyday Forms of Peasant Resistance*. New Haven: Yale University Press.

Scott, James. 1990. *Domination and the Arts of Resistance: Hidden Transcripts*. New Haven: Yale University Press.

Scott, James. 1998. *Seeing Like a State: How Certain Schemes to Improve the Human Condition Have Failed*. New Haven: Yale University Press.

Sée, Adrien. 1907. *Le passeport en France*. Thèse pour le doctorat, Chartres.

Seligman, Edwin R. A., and Alvin Johnson, eds. 1932. *Encyclopaedia of the Social Sciences*. Vol. 7. New York: Macmillan.

Seutter, Konstanze. 1996. *Eigennamen und Recht*. Tübingen: Niemeyer.

Severin, Klaus. 1997. "Illegale Einreise und internationale Schleuserkriminalität. Hintergründe, Beispiele, Massnahmen." *Aus Politik und Zeitgeschichte* B46/97, November 7.

Sharlett, Robert. 1977. "Stalinism and Legal Culture." In *Stalinism: Essays in Historical Interpretation*, edited by Robert C. Tucker, pp. 155–79. New York/London: W. W. Norton.

Shelley, Louise I. 1996. *Policing Soviet Society: The Evolution of State Control*. New York: Routledge.

Sicherer, Hermann von. 1890. "Namensgebung." In *Wörterbuch des Deutschen Verwaltungsrechts*. Vol. 2, edited by K. von Stengel, pp. 158–61. Freiburg im Breisgau: J. C. B. Mohr.

Sieber, Dominik, and Lorenz Heiligensetzer, eds. 1999. *Die Lebensbeschreibung des Augustin Günzer*. Zürich: Chronos.

Sieber-Lehmann, Claudius. 1995. *Spätmittelalterlicher Nationalismus*. Göttingen: Vandenhoek und Ruprecht.

Siegelbaum, Lewis H. 1998. " 'Dear Comrade, You Ask What We Need': Socialist Paternalism and Soviet Rural 'Notables' in the Mid-1930s." *Slavic Review* 57, no. 1, pp. 107–32.

Siemann, Wolfram. 1985. *"Deutschlands Ruhe, Sicherheit und Ordnung": Die Anfänge der politischen Polizei 1806–1866*. Tübingen: Niemeyer.

Simmel, G. 1964. *The Sociology of Georg Simmel*. Edited by K. Wolff. New York: Free Press.

Skran, Claudena M. 1995. *Refugees in Inter-war Europe: The Emergence of a Regime*. Oxford/New York: Clarendon.

Skuse, D. H., R. S. James, D. V. Bishop, B. Coppin, P. Dalton, G. Aamodt-Leeper, M. Bacarese-Hamilton, C. Creswell, R. McGurk, and P. A. Jacobs. 1997. "Evidence from Turner's Syndrome of an Imprinted X-Linked Locus Affecting Cognitive Function." *Nature*, June 12, pp. 705–8.

Slezkine, Yuri. 1994. "The USSR as a Communal Apartment, or How a Socialist State Promoted Ethnic Particularism." *Slavic Review* 53, no. 2, pp. 414–52.

Smith, Jean Edward. 1996. *John Marshall, Definer of a Nation*. New York: H. Holt.

Smith, Roger. 1981. *Trial by Medicine*. Edinburgh: Edinburgh University Press.

Smith, Stephen Anthony. 1983. *Red Petrograd: Revolution in the Factories 1917–1918*. Cambridge: Cambridge University Press.

Smith, S. L. 1998. "Gene Testing and Work: Not a Good Fit." *Occupational Hazards* 60, p. 7.

Snowden, Lynne L. 1998. "Employer Sanctions: The European Enforcement Experience." In *Regulation of Migration: International Experiences*, edited by Anita Böcker et al., pp. 159–73. Amsterdam: Het Spinhuis.

Société des Nations. 1938. *Régime des passeports*. Geneva.

Solari, Benjamin T. 1902. "La defensa de la raza por la castración de los degenerados: Las ideas profilácticas de Zuccarelli." *Archivos de Psiquiatría: Criminología, Medicina Legal y Psiquiatría* 1, pp. 385–91.

Spencer, Elaine Glovka. 1992. *Police and the Social Order in German Cities: The Düsseldorf District, 1848–1914*. Dekalb: Northern Illinois University Press.

Stadler, Ulrich. 1996. "Der gedoppelte Blick und die Ambivalenz des Bildes in Lavaters *Physiognomischen Fragmenten zur Beförderung der Menschenkenntniss und Menschenliebe*." In *Der exzentrische Blick. Gespräch über Physiognomik*, edited by Claudia Schmölders, pp. 77–92. Berlin: Akademie.

Stagl, Justin. 1995. *A History of Curiosity: The Theory of Travel 1500–1800*. Australia: Harwood Academic Publishers.

Staney, S. F., A. O. M. Wilkie, M. C. Hirst, R. Charlton, M. McKinley, J. Pointon, Z. Christodoulou, S. M. Huson, and K. E. Davies. 1995. "DNA Testing for

Fragile X Syndrome in Schools for Learning Difficulties." *Archives of Diseases in Childhood* 72, pp. 33–37.

Stanislawski, Michael. 1983. *Tsar Nicholas I and the Jews: The Transformation of Jewish Society in Russia, 1825–1855*. Philadelphia: Jewish Publication Society of America.

Staples, William. 1997. *The Culture of Surveillance*. New York: St. Martin's.

Starikov, Evgenii. 1990. "Novye elementy sotsial'noi struktury." *Kommunist* 5, pp. 30–41.

Stärkle, Joseph Anton. 1921. *Tagebuch und Reisememoiren von Joseph Anton Stärkle Gerbergeselle aus Abtwil bei St. Gallen 1852–1854*. Rapperswil: Bauer.

Statutory Rules and Orders and Statutory Instruments Revised to December 31, 1948. 1950. Vol. 2. London: HMSO.

Stearns, Peter, 1974. *The Revolutions of 1848*. London: Weidenfeld and Nicolson.

Steinfeld, Robert J. 1991. *The Invention of Free Labor: The Employment Relation in English and American Law and Culture, 1350–1870*. Chapel Hill/London: University of North Carolina Press.

Steinmetz, George. 1993. *Regulating the Social: The Welfare State and Local Politics in Imperial Germany*. Princeton: Princeton University Press.

Steinwedel, Charles. 1999. "Invisible Threads of Empire: State, Religion and Ethnicity in Tsarist Bashkiria, 1773–1917." Ph.D. diss., Columbia University.

Steinwedel, Charles. 2000. "To Make a Difference: The Category of Ethnicity in Late Imperial Russian Politics, 1861–1917." In *Russian Modernity: Politics, Practices, Knowledge*, edited by Yanni Kotsonis and David Hoffman. London: Macmillan.

Stigler, Stephen M. 1986. *The History of Statistics: The Measurement of Uncertainty Before 1900*. Cambridge, Massachusetts: Belknap.

Stratton, Alfred, and Albert Ernest Stratton. 1905. *Central Criminal Court Sessions Paper*. 142, 978. London.

Streit, Christian. 1996. "Entwicklung, Bedeutung und Rechtsgrundlagen des Ausländerzentralregisters." *Bewährungshilfe* 3, pp. 229–39.

Strikwerda, Carl. 1997. "Reinterpreting the History of European Integration: Business, Labor, and Social Citizenship in Twentieth-Century Europe." In *European Integration in Social and Historical Perspective: 1850 to the Present*, edited by Jytte Klausen and Louise A. Tilly. New York: Rowman and Littlefield.

The Sunday (Straits) Times (Singapore). 1999. "Genomics," September 12, pp. 42–43.

Suny, Ronald Grigor. 1993. *The Revenge of the Past: Nationalism, Revolution, and the Collapse of the Soviet Union*. Stanford: Stanford University Press.

Surtees, Lawrence. 1996. "Spy Tech Set to Thwart Card Fraud." *The Globe and Mail* (Toronto), June 12, p. B4.

Svod zakonov Rossiiskoi imperii, poveleniem Gosudaria Imperatora Nikolaia Pervogo 1857. 1857. Vol. 14. St. P: Tip.: Vtorogo Otdeleniia Sobstvennoi Ego Imperatorskogo Velichestva Kantseliarii.

Szeftel, Marc. 1976. *The Russian Constitution of April 23, 1906: Political Institutions of the Duma Monarchy*. Brussels: Les Éditions de la Librairie Encyclopédique.

Tagg, John. 1987. "Power and Photography—A Means of Surveillance: The Photograph as Evidence in Law." In *Culture, Ideology and Social Process: A Reader*, edited by Tony Benett et al., pp. 285–307. London: Batsford.

Tate, William E. 1969. *The Parish Chest: A Study of the Records of Parochial Administration in England*. Cambridge: Cambridge University Press.

Taussig, Michael. 1993. *Mimesis and Alterity: A Particular History of the Senses*. New York/London: Routledge.

Taylor, Charles. 1989. *Sources of the Self: The Making of Modern Identity*. Cambridge, Massachusetts: Harvard University Press.

Tenfelde, Klaus. 1977. *Sozialgeschichte der Bergarbeiterschaft an der Ruhr im 19. Jahrhundert*. Bonn: Verlag Neue Gesellschaft.

Tessier, Georges. 1962. *Diplomatique royale française*. Paris: A. et J. Picard.

Thompson, Leonard. 1990. *A History of South Africa*. New Haven: Yale University Press.

Thorwald, Jurgen. 1965. *The Century of the Detective*. New York: Harcourt, Brace.

Tilly, Charles, 1990. *Coercion, Capital, and European States, AD 990–1990*. Oxford: Blackwell.

Tilly, Charles, 1993. *European Revolutions, 1492–1992*. Oxford (U.K.)/Cambridge, Massachusetts: Blackwell.

Tilly, Charles, Louise Tilly, and Richard Tilly. 1975. *The Rebellious Century, 1830–1930*. Cambridge, Massachusetts: Harvard University Press.

The Times. 1902. "Central Criminal Court," September 15, p. 12.

The Times. 1905. "The Deptford Murder Trial," May 6, p. 19.

The Times. 1905. "The Deptford Murder Trial," May 8, p. 4.

Tocqueville, Alexis de. 1955. *The Old Regime and the French Revolution*. Translated by Stuart Gilbert. New York: Anchor.

Torpey, John. 1997. "Revolutions and Freedom of Movement: An Analysis of Passport Controls in the French, Russian, and Chinese Revolutions." *Theory and Society* 26, no. 4, pp. 837–68.

Torpey, John. 1998a. "Le controle des passeports et la liberté de circulation. Le cas de l'Allemagne au XIXᵉ siècle." *Genèses* 30 (Mars), pp. 53–76.

Torpey, John. 1998b. "Coming and Going: On the State Monopolization of the Legitimate 'Means of Movement.' " *Sociological Theory* 16, no. 3, pp. 239–59.

Torpey, John. 2000. *The Invention of the Passport: Surveillance, Citizenship and the State*. Cambridge: Cambridge University Press.

Tort, Patrick. 1989. *La raison classificatoire: Quinze études*. Paris: Aubier.

Traven, B. 1926. *Das Totenschiff: Die Geschichte eines amerikanischen Seemans*. Berlin: Buchmeister Verlag. [Translated B. Traven, *The Death Ship: The Story of an American Sailor*. 2nd ed. Brooklyn, New York: Lawrence Hill (1991).]

Troup Committee. 1894. *Identification of Habitual Criminals*. London: HMSO.

Tucco-Chala, Pierre, and Nicolo Pinzuti. 1972. "Le voyage de Pierre Barbate à Jerusalem en 1480." *Annuaire-Bulletin de la Société de l'Histoire de France* 3.

Twain, Mark. 1986. *Pudd'nhead Wilson and Those Extraordinary Twins*. London: Penguin Books Ltd.

Ufimskaia zemskaia gazeta. 1906.

Ufimskie gubernskie vedomosti. 1912.

United Nations. 1998. *International Migration Policies.* New York: United Nations.

U.S. Commission on Immigration Reform. 1997. *Becoming an American: Immigration and Immigrant Policy.* Washington, D.C.: U.S. Government Printing Office.

U.S. Congress, House. 1917. Committee on Immigration and Naturalization. "Registration of Aliens." 64th Cong., 2nd. Sess., February 28.

U.S. Congress, House. 1932. Committee on Naval Affairs. "To Direct the Secretary of the Navy to have Taken Fingerprints of Applicants for Enlistment in the United States Navy and Marine Corps." Bill 9145, April 4.

U.S. Congress, House. 1995. Committee on Crime of the Committee on the Judiciary, *Hearings on H.R. 1241, H.R. 1533, H.R. 1552, H.R. 2359, H.R. 2360.*

U.S. Congress, House. Committee on Appropriations, *Hearings on Department of Justice Appropriations Bill,* Annual.

U.S. Department of Labor, Bureau of Immigration. 1919. *Annual Report of the Commissioner General of Immigration to the Secretary of Labor.* Washington, D.C.: U.S. Government Printing Office.

U.S. Department of Labor. 1934. Immigration and Naturalization Service, "American Consular Procedure and Technical Advisers in Immigration Work," Lecture No. 9, April 2, 1934 by Thomas J. Murphy, Supervisor, Immigration and Naturalization Service.

U.S. v. Kelly (55 F. (2d) 67).

U.S. Public Interest Research Group. 1996. *Theft of Identity: The Consumer X-Files.* (August).

U.S. War Department, 1906. "General Order #68." April 7. General Correspondence-Bureau of Navigation-RG 24, file 5397–1.

Usmanov, Khamza F. 1981. *Razvitie kapitalizma v sel'skom khoziaistve Bashkirii v poreformennyi period.* Moscow: Nauka.

Usteri, Emil. 1975. *Marignano.* Zürich: Orell Füssli.

Uvin, Peter. 1997. "Prejudice, Crisis, and Genocide in Rwanda." *African Studies Review* 40, no. 2, September, pp. 91–115.

Vail, Leroy, ed. 1989. *The Creation of Tribalism in Southern Africa.* Berkeley: University of California Press.

Vallotton, Pierre. 1923. *Le passeport.* Lausanne: Université de Lausanne.

Vaux de Foletier, François. 1981. *Les bohémiens en France au XIXème siècle.* Paris: Jean-Claude Lattès.

Vincent, David. 1998. *The Culture of Secrecy: Britain, 1832–1998.* Oxford: Oxford University Press.

Virilio, Paul. 1991. *The Lost Dimension.* New York: Semiotext(e).

Virnoche, M. 1997. "When a Stranger Calls: Strange-Making Technologies and the Transformation of the Stranger." Paper delivered at Pacific Sociological Association Meetings.

Vogel, Dita. 1998a. "Migrationskontrolle in Deutschland - Systematisierung, Deskription, Thesen." Universität Bremen, Zentrum für Sozialpolitik, Arbeitspapier 10.

Vogel, Dita, 1998b. "Migration Control in Germany and the United States." Unpublished manuscript, Universität Bremen, Zentrum für Sozialpolitik.

Volkov, N., comp. 1910. *Zakony o politsii*. Moscow: I. K. Golubev.

Vsepoddanneishii raport ego Imperatorskomu Velichestvu Ufimskogo Gubernatora Bogdanovuicha. 1899. Rossiiskii Gosudarstvennyi Istoricheskii Arkhiv, Chital'nyi zal.

Vucetich, Juan. 1924. Interview, *El Argentino*, September 1.

Vucetich, Juan. 1929. *Proyecto de ley de registro general de identificación*. La Plata: Impresiones Oficiales.

Wade, Nicholas. 1997. "How Cells Unwind Tangled Skein of Life." *New York Times*, October 21, p. F1.

Wade, Nicholas. 1998. "FBI Set to Open Its DNA Database for Fighting Crime." *New York Times*, October 12, p. A1.

Wagner, David. 1987. "The New Temperance Movement and Social Control at the Workplace." *Contemporary Drug Problems*, Winter.

Walker, Mack. 1971. *German Home Towns: Community, State, and General Estate 1648–1871*. Ithaca/London: Cornell University Press.

Warnke, Martin. 1993. *Cranachs Luther: Entwürfe für ein Image*. Frankfurt am Main: Fischer.

Wcislo, Francis W. 1990. *Reforming Rural Russia: State, Local Society, and National Politics, 1855–1914*. Princeton: Princeton University Press.

Weber, Eugen. 1976. *Peasants into Frenchmen: The Modernization of Rural France 1870–1916*. Stanford: Stanford University Press.

Weber, Max. 1971. *Économie et société*. Paris: Plon.

Weber, Max. 1978. *Economy and Society: An Outline of Interpretive Sociology*. 2 vols., translated and edited by G. Roth and C. Wittich. Berkeley/Los Angeles: University of California Press.

Wecker, Gabriele. 1995. "Das Bundesamt für die Anerkennung ausländischer Flüchtlinge: Aufgaben und Entwicklung im Spiegel der Asylgesetzgebung." In *Einwanderung und Asyl: Eine Dokumentation sozial- und rechtswissenschaftlicher Literatur und Forschung*, edited by Bundesamt für die Anerkennung ausländischer Flüchtlinge/Informationszentrum Sozialwissenschaften, pp. 41–60. Bonn: Eigendruck.

Weedn, Victor. 1995. "Identification of War Dead." Talk given at National Academy of Sciences, Genetic Information and Privacy, June 9–10.

Wehler, Hans-Ulrich. 1987. *Deutsche Gesellschaftsgeschichte, 1815–1845/49*. Vol. 2. Munich: C. H. Beck.

Wehler, Hans-Ulrich. 1995. *Deutsche Gesellschaftsgeschichte, 1849–1914*. Vol. 3. Munich: C. H. Beck.

Weingart, Albert. 1904. *Kriminaltaktik: Ein Handbuch für das Untersuchen von Verbrechen*. Berlin: Langenscheidt.

Wennmohs, Franz Andreas. 1823. *Ueber Gauner und über das zweckmässigste, vielmehr einzige Mittel zur Vertilgung dieses Uebels*, vol 1: *Schilderung des Gauners nach seiner Menge und Schädlichkeit, in seinem Betriebe, nach seinem Aeussern und als Inquisiten*. Güstrow: Ebert.

Werner, George S. 1981. "Traveling Journeymen in Metternichian South Germany." *Proceedings of the American Philosophical Society* 125, pp. 190–219.

Wiarda, Tileman Dothias. 1800. *Ueber deutsche Vornamen und Geschlechtsnamen.* Berlin/Stettin: Friedrich Nicolai.

Wieacker, Franz. 1995. *A History of Private Law in Europe.* Oxford: Clarendon.

Wieczynski, Joseph L., ed. 1978. *The Modern Encyclopedia of Russian and Soviet History.* Gulf Breeze, Florida: Academic International Press.

Wiener, Martin J. 1990. *Reconstructing the Criminal: Culture, Law, and Policy in England, 1830–1914.* Cambridge: Cambridge University Press.

Wilcock, Michael. 1975. *I Saw Heaven Opened.* Leicester: Inter-Varsity.

Wilke, Carsten. 1994. *Jüdisch-christliches Doppelleben im Barock: Zur Biographie des Kaufmanns und Dichters Antonio Enrique Gomez.* Bern/Frankfurt am Main: Peter Lang.

Wilson, Stephen. 1998. *The Means of Naming: A Social and Cultural History of Personal Naming in Western Europe.* London: UCL Press.

Wilton, George. 1938. *Fingerprints: History, Law, and Romance.* London: William Hodge.

Wilton, George. 1951. *Fingerprints: Scotland Yard and Henry Faulds.* Edinburgh: W. Green and Son.

Winseck, Dwayne. 1998. *Reconvergence: The Political Economy of Communications in Canada.* Cresskill, New Jersey: Hampton.

Winter, J. M. 1996. "British National Identity and the First World War." In *The Boundaries of the State in Modern Britain*, edited by S. J. D. Green and R. C. Whiting, pp. 261–77. Cambridge: Cambridge University Press.

Wirsing, Bernd. 1991. "Die Geschichte der Gendarmeriekorps und deren Vorläuferorganisationen in Baden, Württemberg und Bayern 1750–1850." Phil.diss., Constance.

Wise, M. Norton, ed. 1995. *The Values of Precision.* Princeton: Princeton University Press.

Witte, Sergei Iu. 1912. *Po povodu natsionalizma: Natsional'naia Ekonomiia i Fridrikh List*, 2nd ed. St. Petersburg: Brokgauz-Efron.

Wolf, Gerhard. Forthcoming. *The Holy Face.*

Wurms, Friedrich. 1970. "Studien zu den lateinischen und deutschen Prosafassungen des Secretum Secretorum." Phil.diss., Hamburg.

Young, Crawford. 1976. *The Politics of Cultural Pluralism.* Madison: University of Wisconsin Press.

Yvernès. 1883. "La récidive." *Revue Pénitentiaire* 7, pp. 315–28.

Zaleski, Eugene. 1980. *Stalinist Planning for Economic Growth.* Chapel Hill: University of North Carolina Press.

Zaslavsky, Victor. 1982. *The Neo-Stalinist State: Class, Ethnicity, and Consensus in Soviet Society.* Armonk, New York: M. E. Sharpe.

Zeller, Rosemarie. 1994. "Keine besonderen Kennzeichen. Anmerkungen zur Poetik des physischen Porträts." In *Physiognomie und Pathognomie: Zur literarischen Darstellung von Individualität*, edited by Wolfram Groddeck and Ulrich Stadler, pp. 373–86. Berlin: de Gruyter.

Zhurnaly Komiteta Ministrov po ispolneniiu ukaza 12 dekabria 1904 g. 1905. St. Petersburg: Izdatel'stvo Kantseliarii Komiteta Ministrov.

Zimmermann, Gustav. 1845–49. *Die Deutsche Polizei im neunzehnten Jahrhundert.* 3 vols. Hannover: Schlüter.

Zimmermann, Gustav. 1852. *Wesen, Geschichte, Literatur, characteristische Thätigkeiten und Organisation der modernen Polizei. Ein Leitfaden für Polizisten und Juristen.* Hannover: Schlüter.

Zironda, Giovanni. 1906. "Passaporto." *Digesto Italiano: Enciclopedia metodica e alfabetica di legislazione, dottrina e giurisprudenza.* Vol. 18, pp. 725–29. Turin: Utet.

Zolberg, Aristide. 1990. "'Reforming the Back Door: The Immigration Reform and Control Act of 1986 in Historical Perspective." In *Immigration Reconsidered: History, Sociology, and Politics,* edited by V. Yans-McLaughlin, pp. 315–39. New York/Oxford: Oxford University Press.

Zolberg, Aristide, Astri Suhrke, and Sergio Aguayo. 1989. *Escape from Violence: Conflict and the Refugee Crisis in the Developing World.* New York: Oxford University Press.

Zolberg, Aristide. 1997. "The Great Wall Against China: Responses to the First Immigration Crisis, 1885–1925." In *Migration, Migration History, History. Old Paradigms and New Perspectives,* edited by Jan Lucassen and Leo Lucassen. New York: Peter Lang.

Zolberg, Aristide. 1999. "Matters of State: Theorizing Immigration Policy." In *The Handbook of International Migration: The American Experience,* edited by Charles Hirschman, John DeWind, and Phil Kasinitz. New York: Russell Sage.

Zonabend, Françoise. 1977. "Pourquoi nommer? Les noms de personnes dans un village français: Minot-en-Chatillonnais." *L'identité: Séminaire interdisciplinaire dirigé par Claude Lévi-Strauss.* pp. 257–59. Paris: Grasset.

Notes on Contributors

Jon Agar is lecturer in the history of technology at the Centre for History of Science, Technology and Medicine (CHSTM) at the University of Manchester, United Kingdom. He has published on science and technology in the Cold War, and his comparative study of British bureaucracy, information, and technology since the nineteenth century is being published as *The Government Machine* (MIT Press, forthcoming). He is now working on a cultural history of noise.

Peter Becker is professor of Central European history at the European University Institute in Florence, Italy. He is a historian of eighteenth-, nineteenth- and early-twentieth-century Europe with a particular interest in the history of the German Empire and the Habsburg Monarchy. His main research is in the history of local and state authority, social control, and sexuality as well as in the cultural history of criminology and forensic methods. He is currently working on a cultural history of public administration, focusing on the development of a bureaucratic style in the eighteenth and nineteenth centuries. His publications include *Leben und Lieben in einem kalten Land. Sexualität zwischen Ökonomie und Demographie. Das Beispiel St. Lambrecht, Steiermark 1600–1850* (Frankfurt am Main, 1990); *Vom 'gefallenen' zum 'verhinderten' Menschen und minderwertige Individuen. Zur Geschichte der Kriminologie des 19. Jahrhunderts als Diskurs und Praxis* (Göttingen, 2001); together with William Clark (eds.), *Little Tools of Knowledge* (Ann Arbor, 2001).

Jane Caplan is Marjorie Walter Goodhart Professor of European History at Bryn Mawr College, Pennsylvania. Her publications include *Government Without Administration: State and Civil Service in Weimar and Nazi Germany* (Oxford, 1988), and several essay collections, including *Nazism, Fascism and the Working Class: Essays by Tim Mason* (Cambridge, 1995), *Reevaluating the Third Reich*, co-edited with Thomas Childers (New York, 1993), and *Written on the Body: The Tattoo in European and American History* (Princeton University Press/Reaktion Books, 2000). She is an editor of *History Workshop Journal*, and an advisory editor of *German History* and *Feminist Studies*. Her current work is on the conceptual and practical mechanisms by which personal identity was transferred to paper documents in nineteenth-century Europe.

Andreas Fahrmeir is currently a fellow of the German Historical Institute London, where he is working on a history of the "financial" and "civic" City of London in the eighteenth and nineteenth centuries. His publications include *Citizens and Aliens: Foreigners and the Law in Britain and the German States 1789 to 1870* (New York, 2000); ed., with Sabine Freitag, *Mord und andere Kleinigkeiten: Ungewöhnliche Kriminalfälle aus sechs Jahrhunderten* (Munich, 2001), and articles on the development of migration policy, nationalism, and historiography.

Marc Garcelon is currently assistant professor of sociology and anthropology at Middlebury College, Vermont. He has published several articles on the collapse of the Soviet Union, and is completing a manuscript on social movements and political capitalism in postcommunist Russia.

Andrea Geselle is a Ph.D. student in history at the University of Vienna in Austria, and teaches at the University of Siena, Italy. She has worked on the history of women's movements in Europe, and in 1995–98 was responsible for the Italian sector of the research project "Grenzen und Grenzüberschreitungen. Die Bedeutung der Grenze für die staatliche und soziale Entwicklung des Habsburgerreiches von der Mitte des 18. bis zur Mitte des 19. Jahrhunderts," organized by the Österreichisches Ost- und Südosteuropa-Institut in Vienna. Her publications include "Bewegung und Kontrolle in Lombardo-Venetien," in *Grenze und Staat. Passwesen, Staatsbürgerschaft, Heimatrecht und Fremdengesetzgebung in der Österreichischen Monarchie (1750–1867)*, ed. Waltraud Heindl and Edith Saurer (Vienna/Cologne/Weimar: Böhlau, 2000).

Valentin Groebner is a lecturer in the Department of History, University of Basel. He has worked on late medieval and early modern European social and cultural history. His publications include *Ökonomie ohne Haus. Zum Wirtschaften der Armen in Nürnberg am Ende des Mittelalters* (1993) and *Dangerous Liquids: Gift-Giving and Corruption in Renaissance Germany and Switzerland* (forthcoming). He has co-edited with Gadi Algazi and Bernhard Jussen a volume of essays, *Negotiating the Gift in the Middle Ages*, and is co-editor of the journal *Historische Anthropologie*. He is currently writing a book on the practices of identification and the history of identity papers in Renaissance Europe.

Anne M. Joseph has an M.Phil. in the History and Philosophy of Science from Cambridge University and a J.D. from Yale Law School. She is finishing her Ph.D. in Political Economy and Government at Harvard University. She has co-authored an essay with Alison Winter on DNA identification, "Making the Match: Human Traces, Forensic Experts and the Public Imagination," in *Cultural Babbage*, ed. Francis Spufford and Jenny Uglow (London: Faber and Faber, 1996).

Martine Kaluszynski is a researcher at the CNRS/CERAT, Institut d'Études Politiques in Grenoble. She is interested in the sociohistorical construction of the republican state in France, and is currently working on the development of penal policy and of law under the Third Republic. Her publications include essays in *Autrement* and *Genèses*, and chapters in several collective volumes, including *Entre l'ordre et la liberté: la détention provisoire* (Paris: L'Harmattan, 1992), *Ordre moral et délinquance* (Editions universitaires de Dijon, 1993), and *Histoire de la criminologie française* (Paris: L'Harmattan, 1994). She is co-editer (with Sophie Wahnich) of the collection *L'État contre la politique? Les expressions historiques de l'étatisation* (Paris: L'Harmattan, 1998).

Timothy Longman is assistant professor of political science and Africana studies at Vassar College. He also serves as a consultant to Human Rights Watch. He has published numerous articles, book chapters, and human rights reports on

Rwanda, Burundi, and Congo. He recently completed a manuscript, "Commanded by the Devil: Christianity and Genocide in Rwanda," which explores the role of Christian churches in Rwanda's 1994 genocide.

Leo Lucassen is associate professor in the History Department of the University of Amsterdam, where he directs a research program on the "Settlement process of immigrants in the Netherlands 1860–1960" (*www.hum.uva.nl/pion-imm/*). He has published extensively on the stigmatization of gypsies, the long-term development of alien policies in Western Europe, and immigration. His main publications include *"Zigeuner." Die Geschichte eines polizeilichen Ordnungsbegriffes in Deutschland (1700–1945)* (Cologne/Vienna, 1996); *Migration, Migration History, History: Old Paradigms and New Perspectives* (New York, 1997) (co-edited with Jan Lucassen); *Gypsies and Other Itinerant Groups: A Socio-Historical Approach* (London/New York: Macmillan/St. Martin's, 1998) (together with Annemarie Cottaar and Wim Willems).

David Lyon is professor of sociology at Queen's University in Kingston, Ontario, Canada. His work focuses mainly on major questions of social transformation, with particular respect to new technologies. His books include *The Information Society: Issues and Illusions* (Cambridge: Polity/Blackwell, 1988), *The Electronic Eye: The Rise of Surveillance Society* (Polity/Blackwell, 1994), *Postmodernity* (Open University Press/Minnesota University Press, 1994, 1999), and *Surveillance Society: Monitoring Everyday Life* (Open University Press/Taylor and Francis, 2001). He has held visiting positions at the universities of Leeds, Auckland, Tokyo, Monash University and the École des Hautes Études en Sciences Sociales, Paris, and is currently director of an international research project on "Surveillance, Risk Management and Social Ordering in Global Information Societies," funded by the Social Sciences and Humanities Research Council of Canada.

Gary T. Marx is emeritus professor of sociology at M.I.T. His interest in issues of identity and deception was sparked by Ph.D. study with Professor Erving Goffman at the University of California at Berkeley. His main publications include *Undercover: Police Surveillance in America*, *Protest and Prejudice*, and *Undercover: Police Surveillance in Comparative Perspective* (co-editor), as well as widely reprinted and translated articles on race relations, social movements, and social control, some of which can be found on his web page *<http://web.mit.edu/gtmarx/www/garyhome.html>*.

Gérard Noiriel has been director of studies and of the doctoral program in social sciences at the École des Hautes Études en Sciences Sociales (Paris) since 1994. He is co-founder of the review *Genèses. Sciences Sociales et Histoire*, and co-editor of the series "Socio-Histoires" for Éditions Belin in Paris. His current research is on the historical role of the law in the construction of individual and collective identities. Recent publications include *Immigrés et sans papiers. La République face au droit d'asile* (Paris: Hachette, 1998) and *Les Origines républicaines de Vichy* (Paris: Hachette, 1999). Translations of his work in English include *Workers in French Society in the 19th and 20th Centuries* (Oxford: Berg, 1990), *Immigrants in Two Democracies: French and American Experi-*

ence, edited by D. L. Horowitz and G. Noiriel (New York: New York University Press, 1992), and *The French Melting Pot: Immigration, Citizenship and National Identity* (Minneapolis: University of Minnesota Press, 1995).

Kristin Ruggiero is associate professor of history and director of the Center for Latin American and Caribbean Studies at the University of Wisconsin-Milwaukee. She has published *And Here the World Ends: The Life of an Argentine Village* (Stanford: Stanford University Press, 1988), chapters in *Reconstructing Criminality in Latin America*, ed. C. Aguirre and R. Buffington, and *Law, Crime, and Punishment in Latin American History*, ed. G. Joseph, C. Aguirre, and R. Salvatore, and recently completed a book-length manuscript entitled "In Hostage to the Body: Medicine, Law, and Society in Argentina, 1850–1920." She is also a contributor to a multivolume history of Argentine-U.S. relations, edited by A. Cisneros and C. Escude. Research for her current work has been supported by grants from the National Endowment for the Humanities and the National Science Foundation.

Pamela Sankar, Ph.D., is an assistant professor of bioethics at the Center for Bioethics at the University of Pennsylvania. She is also a senior fellow of the University of Pennsylvania's Leonard Davis Institute of Health Economics. Her degrees are in history of ideas, anthropology, and communications. Her research interests include ethical and cultural implications of genetic and genomic research, research ethics, and the history of personal identification technologies. She is currently completing a book, *Regulating Criminal Identity: From Log Books to DNA-Typing* (Columbia University Press). She has recently begun a new project funded by the National Human Genome Research Institute at the National Institutes of Health concerning the social and historical relationships among genetics, genetic stigma, and national identity.

Charles Steinwedel is assistant professor of history at Northeastern Illinois University in Chicago. He is the author of "The 1905 Revolution in Ufa: Mass Politics, Elections and Nationality" (*The Russian Review*, October 2000), and "To Make a Difference: The Category of Ethnicity in Late Imperial Russian Politics" in David Hoffman and Yanni Kotsonis, eds., *Russian Modernity: Politics, Knowledge, Practices* (Macmillan, 2000). He is currently completing a manuscript on estate, religion, and nationality in the Russian Empire.

John Torpey teaches sociology and European studies at the University of British Columbia in Vancouver. He is author of *The Invention of the Passport: Surveillance, Citizenship, and the State* (Cambridge University Press, 2000) and *Intellectuals, Socialism, and Dissent: The East German Opposition and its Legacy* (University of Minnesota Press, 1995). He edits a series on "Politics, History, and Social Change" for Temple University Press. His current research examines the worldwide spread of demands for reparations for historical injustices.

Dita Vogel has been researcher at the Centre for Social Policy Research at the University of Bremen since 1989, specializing in migration and migration policy. Since 1998, she has taught German-Dutch comparative courses at the University of Oldenburg, and participates in the University's Institut für Bildung und Kommunikation in Migrationsprozessen (Institute for Education and Communication in Migratory Processes). Her main interest is comparative international research on illegal migration and migration control policies. A project on migration control in Germany and the United States, funded by the German Marshall Fund, laid the foundations for her contribution in this volume. She is presently part of a European research team investigating migration control in the labor market in Germany, the United Kingdom, Italy, and Greece.

Index

Abercrombie, Nicholas, 294
address location/reachability identification, 313
Adorno, Anselme, 20
"Adventure of the Norwood Builder, The" (Doyle), 164
Agar, John, 8, 101
Alexander I (Russia), 69
Alexander II (Russia), 72, 77
Algerian names, 58–59
Allgemeine Polizei-Anzeiger, 155
Almandos, Reyna, 192, 194–95, 196
Anchel, Robert, 37
Andrieu, Louis, 126
anonymity: cyberspace community, 324; new forms of identifications as form of, 325; public policy debates over appropriate uses of, 325; rationales for, 316–19
Anson, G. A., 180
anthropometry: Argentine cultural resistance to, 185–88; Argentine debate over fingerprinting vs., 188–92; Bertillon's system of, 125–28, 185; compromised success of, 128–29; criminal identification using, 123, 125, 128–29, 134–38, 167–74, 275; declining use of, 170–71; French Nomad Law (1912) application of, 134–37; as French solution to growing recidivism, 125; government policy context of, 123; recommended by Troup Committee (1893–94), 167–70; replaced by fingerprinting, 128, 171–74, 275–76; W.W. II application of, 137–38
Arbeiterlegitimationskarte (worker's German identification card), 250
Argentina: anthropometry used in Farbos-Tremblié case in, 185–88; creation of universal fingerprinting model in, 192–96; debate over fingerprinting vs. anthropometry in, 188–92; identity card introduced (1905) in, 192–94; "personal number" proposal in, 195; Register of Identification of Immigrants (1912) in, 192

Aufenthaltskarten (special identity), 224
Austrian passport (1859), 227*i*
Avé-Lallement, Friedrich Christian Benedict, 228

badges (*Abzeichen*), 21–22
Baptists (Russia), 71–72
Barbate, Pierre, 20
Barthes, Roland, 52
Barthou, Louis, 130–31
Batavian Republic, 239
Beck, Ulrich, 251, 306
Beers, Randall, 284
begger badges (16th century), 21–22
Belgian Ruanda-Urundi identity cards (19th century), 352–54
Belper Committee (Great Britain), 166–67, 170, 171–72, 174–75
Belper, Lord Henry, 171
Bennett, Colin, 295–96
Bentham, Jeremy, 51, 64–65, 118, 310
Berkshire, Frank, 267–68
Berlin criminal album, 159
Bertelsmann, Werner, 256
Bertillon, Alphonse, 123, 125–27, 128, 145, 146*t*-47*t*, 148–49, 150, 168, 189, *See also* anthropometry
Big Lebowski, The (movie), 325
bigamy, 115–17
Billing, Noel Pemberton, 105, 106
Bingham, Gow v. (U.S.), 277
biometric surveillance methods, 300–304
"Biometrics: Chipping Away Your Rights" (Robertson TV segment), 309
"BioMouse," 293
birth registers: British National Register (NR) system of, 104–6; French, 32–46, 56–59; influence of church on naming in, 55n.19
"Blue Dress" DNA-typing (Lewinsky-Clinton case), 288
body surveillance: biometric technologies providing data from, 291–93; in different sectors, 299–304; face-recognition technologies used for, 301; genomics/ge-